STRATEGIC MANAGEMENT
FROM CONCEPT TO IMPLEMENTATION

L. J. BOURGEOIS, III

UNIVERSITY OF VIRGINIA
DARDEN GRADUATE SCHOOL OF BUSINESS

STRATEGIC MANAGEMENT
FROM CONCEPT TO IMPLEMENTATION

L. J. BOURGEOIS, III

UNIVERSITY OF VIRGINIA
DARDEN GRADUATE SCHOOL OF BUSINESS

The Dryden Press
Harcourt Brace College Publishers

Fort Worth   Philadelphia   San Diego   New York   Orlando   Austin   San Antonio
Toronto   Montreal   London   Sydney   Tokyo

Acquisitions Editor	Ruth Rominger
Developmental Editor	Traci Keller
Project Editor	Kathryn Stewart
Production Manager	Jessica Wyatt
Product Manager	Lisé Johnson
Art Director	Lora Knox
Art & Literary Rights Editor	Annette Coolidge
Electronic Publishing Coordinator	Ellie Moore
Copy Editor	Karen Carriere
Proofreader	Timothy Westmoreland
Critical Reader	Kay Kaylor
Text Type	10/12 Palatino
Cover and Text Design	Lora Knox

Address for Editorial Correspondence
The Dryden Press, 301 Commerce Street, Suite 3700, Fort Worth, TX 76102

Address for Orders
The Dryden Press, 6277 Sea Harbor Drive, Orlando, FL 32887

1-800-782-4479, or 1-800-433-0001 (in Florida)

ISBN: 0-03-055789-5
Library of Congress Catalog Card Number: 95-69998

Printed in the United States of America

5 6 7 8 9 0 1 2 3 4   0 6 7   9 8 7 6 5 4 3 2 1

The Dryden Press
Harcourt Brace College Publishers

To Charles E. Summer, Jr., teacher, mentor, and friend.

THE DRYDEN PRESS SERIES IN MANAGEMENT

Dessler
Managing Organizations in an Era of Change

Foegen
Business Plan Guidebook
Revised Edition

Gatewood and Feild
Human Resource Selection
Third Edition

Gold
Exploring Organizational Behavior: Readings, Cases, Experiences

Greenhaus and Callanan
Career Management
Second Edition

Harris and DeSimone
Human Resource Development

Higgins and Vincze
Strategic Management: Text and Cases
Fifth Edition

Hills, Bergmann, and Scarpello
Compensation Decision Making
Second Edition

Hodgetts
Modern Human Relations at Work
Sixth Edition

Hodgetts and Kroeck
Personnel and Human Resource Management

Hodgetts and Kuratko
Effective Small Business Management
Fifth Edition

Holley and Jennings
The Labor Relations Process
Fifth Edition

Jauch and Coltrin
The Managerial Experience: Cases and Exercises
Sixth Edition

Kindler and Ginsburg
Strategic and Interpersonal Skill Building

Kirkpatrick and Lewis
Effective Supervision: Preparing for the 21st Century

Kuehl and Lambing
Small Business: Planning and Management
Third Edition

Kuratko and Hodgetts
Entrepreneurship: A Contemporary Approach
Third Edition

Kuratko and Welsch
Entrepreneurial Strategy: Text and Cases

Lengnick-Hall, Cynthia, and Hartman
Experiencing Quality

Lewis
Io Enterprises Simulation

Long and Arnold
The Power of Environmental Partnerships

McMullen and Long
Developing New Ventures: The Entrepreneurial Option

Matsuura
International Business: A New Era

Montanari, Morgan, and Bracker
Strategic Management: A Choice Approach

Morgan
Managing for Success

Northcraft and Neale
Organizational Behavior: A Management Challenge
Second Edition

Penderghast
Entrepreneurial Simulation Program

Ryan, Eckert, and Ray
Small Business: An Entrepreneur's Plan
Fourth Edition

Sandburg
Career Design Software

Vecchio
Organizational Behavior
Third Edition

Walton
Corporate Encounters: Law, Ethics, and the Business Environment

Zikmund
Business Research Methods
Fourth Edition

THE HARCOURT BRACE COLLEGE OUTLINE SERIES

Pentico
Management Science

Pierson
Introduction to Business Information Systems

Sigband
Business Communication

PREFACE

This textbook is the result of twenty years of teaching strategy to under-graduates, MBA students, and executives, as well as applying some of the concepts and frameworks in consulting to business firms. My experience is that students and practitioners alike appreciate theory when it is directly applicable to business problems, embrace frameworks that enlighten strategic thinking, and engage enthusiastically in active learning when presented with "live" business cases.

This textbook is practical in its treatment of theories and concepts, straightforward in its presentation of frameworks for students to use, and, as important, biased toward field-based cases written with direct input from company executives and their colleagues. (Twenty-three of the thirty-four cases in the text are "live," or field-based cases. All of the "follow-on" cases [available with the instructor's manual] also are field-based.) To further enhance the aliveness of these cases, several of them are accompanied by videos of the company and its chief executive or another senior executive.

Overview of Text

The concepts and cases are organized in a fairly traditional—and, to instructors, familiar—way. We start with *Foundations*, Part I, where we introduce a basic model of strategy and the role of the strategist and general manager. We proceed to *Business Strategy: Gaining and Sustaining Competitive Advantage* in Part II, where we treat strategic analyses of single-business firms. Here, we engage in issues of the integration of functions (marketing, operations, finance, human resources, etc.), competition, industry structure, industry evolution, sources and sustainability of competitive advantage, entrepreneurship, and strategic thinking. Part II concludes with three appendices that outline fundamental analytical frameworks for students to use with each case.

Part III, *Corporate Strategy: Managing Multiple-Business Firms*, introduces portfolio-planning and value-based-planning models, and illustrates how they may be applied to companies (cases) with varying degrees of relatedness across their multiple businesses. Part IV, *Corporate Strategy: Diversification and Synergy*, deals with the management of diversification into related businesses—the so-called search for synergy—as well as the management of the internal corporate venturing process.

Part V, *Leading Strategic Change*, covers the topics of corporate culture, organizational capability as a source of competitive advantage, leading change, and managing the strategic process. This case set is the largest in the book, reflecting my view that strategy implementation and strategic change are the most difficult part of strategic management to either learn or practice. The cases in this section are all "live," and most of them contain supplemental, follow-on, cases that allow students to engage vicariously in the strategic change process over time and through the sequence of events.

Conceptual Foundations

Although the organization of the book is fairly traditional, the treatment of concepts and frameworks differs from standard strategy texts. As stated earlier, the emphasis is on practical application, and as such, the text does not dwell on research findings or abstract discourses. Unlike traditional strategy texts, much of the conceptual foundation presented is rooted in practice. For example, Part I makes the distinction between *strategic thinking* and *strategic planning*. While many companies engage in some form of the latter, the activity is usually performed by a small group within the upper levels of management. Over the past five years, however, more and more companies regard strategic *thinking* as a skill that they would like all employees in the firm to possess. Everyone in the organization can contribute to strategy, although not all will make the major strategy decisions.

To further reinforce the emphasis on practical application, the frameworks presented for business-strategy analysis in Part II and for corporate-strategy analysis in Part III were developed in business practice. All the frameworks have been tested either by the author, various colleagues, or consulting firms in strategy development efforts with companies.

Most important to the users of this book, perhaps, is that all of the concepts and frameworks have been tested in the classroom, as have all of the case studies contained in the book.

Conclusion

The development and execution of strategy is not only an important activity, it is also an adventure. I hope that the users of this text—undergraduates, MBA students, and executives—will benefit from the intellectual adventure presented in this book, as well as find that its practical application enhances their ability to not only think strategically, but as a consequence, helps them guide their firms to superior levels of economic performance.

TO THE STUDENT:
A GUIDE TO ANALYZING BUSINESS CASES[1]

Why We Use the Case Method

The case method is one of the most effective means of management education. It is widely used in schools of business throughout the world, and this use is predicated upon the belief that tackling real business problems—which can be messy, complex, yet very interesting—is the best way to develop practitioners.

Unlike other pedagogical techniques, many of which make you the recipient of large amounts of information but do not require its use, the case method requires you to be an active participant in the closest thing to the real situation. It is a way of gaining a great deal of experience without spending a lot of time. It is also a way to learn a great deal about how certain businesses operate, and how managers manage. There are few programmable, textbook solutions to the kinds of problems faced by real general managers. When a problem does become programmable, the general manager can give it to someone else to solve on a repeated basis using the guidelines he or she has established. Thus the case situations that you will face require the use of analytical tools, as well as the application of your personal judgment.

Sources of Cases

With the exception of the Alaskan Gold Mine case, all the cases in this book are about real companies. (You may recognize several of the names of the companies and some of them may be new to you.) Although the cases share real company situations as their source, they were developed in different ways. Some of the companies approached a business professor and requested that a case be written about that company. In other situations, the professor sought out a company based on his or her knowledge of an interesting or difficult situation faced by this company. Often, the company agreed to allow a case to be written; however, some of the cases were written solely from public sources. This type of case is perhaps the most difficult to write because of the lack of primary data sources.

In those situations where a company agreed to have a case written, the company had to *release* the case, meaning that they had the final approval of

---

[1]Adapted from a note prepared by Associate Professor Dan R. E. Thomas, Stanford Business School.

the content of a given case. (Public source cases do not need a release.) The company and the case writer are thus protected from any possibility of releasing data which might be competitively or personally sensitive. Given the requirement for release, it is amazing the amount of information that companies will allow to be placed in a case. Many companies do this because of their belief in the effectiveness of the case method. Some companies, due to the sensitivity of the situation being described, request that their company names, and sometimes their industries, be disguised. This is true for the OSIM Corporation case for example, the Peninsular Insurance case, and the Big Sky, Inc. case.

Preparing the Case

When you prepare for class, it is recommended that you plan on reading the case at least three times. The first reading should be a quick scan of the text in the case. It should give you a feeling for what the case is about and the types of data that are contained in the case. For example, you will want to differentiate between *facts* and *opinions*. In every industry there is a certain amount of conventional wisdom that may or may not reflect the truth. You should read more closely and for more depth of meaning during your second reading. Many students like to underline or highlight important points in their cases that they know will be needed later. Your goal during a second reading should be to attempt to understand the business and the situation. You should ask yourself questions such as: Why has this company survived? How does this business work? and What are the economics of this business?

On your second reading you should also carefully examine the exhibits in the case. The case writer has put the exhibits there because they contain information that will be useful in analyzing the situation. Ask yourself what that information might be as you study each exhibit. You will often find you need to apply some analytical techniques (for example, ratio analysis, growth rate analysis, and the like) to the exhibit in order to benefit from the information in the raw data. Note that a good calculator is useful.

By your third reading, you should have a good idea of the fundamentals of the case and you should seek to understand the *specific* situation. You will need to get at the root causes of problems and gather data from the case that will enable you to make specific action recommendations. Before the third reading you may want to review the questions in the homework assignment, often times applying a concept or framework from the text. It is during and after the third reading that you should be able to prepare your outlined answers of the assignment questions.

There is only one secret to good case discussion, and that is thorough preparation on the part of the participants.

Class Discussions

Typically, in each class one or several students are asked to lead off the discussion. If you have studied the case and are prepared to answer the assignment questions, you should have no difficulty with this lead off assignment. An effective lead off can do a great deal to enhance a class discussion. It sets a tone for the class that allows that class to probe more deeply into the issues of the case.

After the individual lead off presentation, the discussion will be opened to the remainder of the group. It is during this time that you will have an opportunity to present and develop your ideas about the way the situation should be handled. It will be important for you to relate your ideas to the case situation and to the ideas of others as they are presented in the class.

The instructor's role in the class discussion is to help you, through intensive questioning, to formulate and develop your own ideas. This use of the "Socratic Method" has proven to be an effective way to develop thinking capability in individuals. The instructor's primary role is to manage the class process and to ensure the class achieves an understanding of the case situation. There is no single correct solution to any of these problems. (Although there may be some wrong ones.) The discussion allows the class to explore and debate the cases and problems and gives students practice in defending their points of view with facts, analyses, and interpretations.

The Use of Extra or Post-Case Data

You are encouraged to deal with the case as it is presented, putting yourself in the position of the general manager involved in the situation and looking at the situation through his or her eyes. Part of the unique job of being a general manager is that many of your problems are dilemmas, and there is no way to come out a winner on all counts. Although additional data might be interesting or useful, the "Monday Morning Quarterback" syndrome is not necessarily an effective way to learn about strategic management.

Some case method purists argue that a class should never be told the actual outcome of a case. Each person should leave the classroom situation with his or her plan for solving the problem, and none should be falsely legitimized. The actual outcome of a situation may not reflect what is, or is not, a good solution, and its success or failure is not an indication of the value of your approach. It is, however, interesting and occasionally useful to know what actually occurred. Therefore, in some cases, you will be told the outcome and its effect on the company involved.

Package

For the Instructor. An indispensible instructor's manual written by the author and Anurag Sharma of the University of Massachusetts provides extensive and detailed teaching notes for the cases as well as loose-leaf follow up cases for twelve of the text cases. A video series from the author's collection of classroom visits by executives will enhance the exposition of the case material. The CD-ROM that is available for sale to students will be useful to the instructor who wishes to use it as a lecture presentation tool. A compilation of essay test questions will be available on disk.

For the Student. Dryden has developed an annotated, interactive CD-ROM version of the concepts and cases available for sale to students. Features include background information on many of the cases, including videos, annual report data, abstracts from current periodicals and access to an on line business database.

The Dryden Press will provide complimentary supplements or supplement packages to those adopters qualified under our adoption policy. Please contact your sales representative to learn how you may qualify. If as an adopter or potential user you receive supplements you do not need, please return them to your sales representative or send them to:

Attn: Returns Department
Troy Warehouse
465 South Lincoln Drive
Troy, MO 63379

Darden Cases

For multiple copies of Darden School Foundation cases please contact Ann Morris, Director, Darden Educational Materials Services at University of Virginia, P.O. Box 6550, Charlottesville, VA 22906-6550, Voice (804) 924-3009, Fax (804) 924-4859. Internet Address: Darden School Home Page, Darden Educational Materials, Case Abstracts, HTTP:\\WWW.DARDEN.VIRGINIA.EDU

A complete listing of Darden Cases and their reference numbers may be found in the Credits List starting on page 975 of this textbook.

ACKNOWLEDGMENTS

I am indebted to many people for the development of the ideas and cases contained in this book.

My intellectual debt is to the late Charles E. Summer, Jr., who provided my first guide through the strategic thinking process. As an educator, mentor, and role model, he was unparalleled. Many of the ideas I now take for my own (given the frequent and almost unconscious use with which I employ them) came from my brief but powerful work with Dan Thomas when we overlapped at the Stanford Business School. I owe much of my development of a practical orientation to teaching strategy to my colleague, classmate, and friend, David Jemison. I am grateful to my student and colleague, Anurag Sharma, for his help in developing several of the cases in this book, plus most the instructor's material. His cheerful and enthusiastic contributions were invaluable. My thanks to Carl Zeithamal for persuading me to undertake this project.

I would like to thank several of my colleagues at Darden, some from whom I learned to refine my teaching of strategy (Pete Borden and Bill Harper) and leadership and change (Alec Horniman and Jim Clawson), and several who contributed cases to this volume. My thanks to Lynn Isabella (Astral Records and Grupo Bacardi de Mexico); Les Grayson (Note on Scenario Planning); John Colley (Bacova Guild); Elltott Weiss (Southwest Airlines); Jeanne Liedtka (Copeland/Bain and Disney: The Arrival of Eisner and Wells); John Rosenblum (Copeland/Bain); Alec Horniman (Big Sky and Public Communications Department at New York Telephone); Bob Landel (Public Communications Department at New York Telephone); and Jim Clawson (Stewart-Glapat and Jackie Woods). Thanks also go to former Darden colleagues Bill Fulmer (Walt Disney Productions, Marriott, and Dollar General [A]) and Paul McKinnon (Bennett Association), and to colleagues from other universities who contributed cases: Jeff Barach (Alaskan Gold Mine) and Idalene Kesner (National Gypsum). Thanks to Warren Arbogast and Cal Tate for their support and help in developing the videos that accompany this book. And without Ginny Fisher, my patient assistant for many years, this project would never have reached completion.

I extend my thanks to the many strategic management professors who wrote reviews, answered surveys, and otherwise submitted ideas for making this book the most useful it can be.

Susan Stites-Doe
State University of New York—Brockport

Amit Shah
Frostburg State University

Larry Stimpert
Michigan State University

Terence P. Curran
Siena College

Carmen Santana
New Mexico State University

Kim Stewart
University of Denver

Charles Yauger
Arkansas State University

Janet Spirer
Marymount University

Jeryl L. Nelson
Wayne State College

John M. Champion
University of Florida

Lowell Busenitz
University of Houston

Michael Bernhart
University of Puget Sound

Stanley Zionts
State University of New York—Buffalo

Richard H. Fabris
Jersey City State College

Ercan G. Nasif
University of Texas at Pan American

Tom Brush
Purdue University

Donald R. McCarty
University of Pittsburgh at Johnstown

Tommy Cates
University of Tennessee—Martin

David Basanko
Northwestern University

John Stanbury
Indiana University—Kokomo

Gaber A. Abou El Enein
Makato State University

Jay Barney
Ohio State University

Irene Duhaime
Memphis State University

Steven Floyd
University of Massachusetts—Amherst

Stefanie Lenway
University of Minnesota

Rhonda Reger
Arizona State University

James Thomas
Pennsylvania State University

Ari Ginsberg
New York University

Sal Kakalis
California State University—Long Beach

Cynthia A. Lengnick-Hall
Wichita State University

Steven Markell
University of Houston—Clear Lake

Haskill McClellan
Boston College

Peter Davis
Memphis State University

My gratitude also goes to the professionals at The Dryden Press, for their unflagging enthusiasm and constant encouragement: Ruth Rominger, senior acquisitions editor; Traci Keller, developmental editor; Lisé Johnson, executive product manager; Kathryn Stewart, project editor; Jessica Wyatt, production manager; Ellie Moore, electronic publishing coordinator; Annette Coolidge, art and literary rights editor; and Lora Knox, art director.

L. J. Bourgeois
Charlottesville
November 1995

ABOUT THE AUTHOR

L. J. ("Jay") Bourgeois received his Ph.D. from the University of Washington in 1978, where he wrote an A. T. Kearney Award-winning dissertation about strategic decision making in firms facing volatile environments. Prior to his doctoral work, he was employed as a financial analyst in the corporate planning department of Castle & Cooke Foods, and held several assignments in the firm's Latin American operations.

Professor Bourgeois has taught at the University of Washington, the University of Pittsburgh, McGill University and Stanford Business School, and has been teaching strategy and leadership at the University of Virginia Darden Graduate School of Business since 1986. He has published over two dozen articles and chapters in various management journals and books. He has served on the review boards of the *Academy of Management Journal* and *Strategic Management Journal,* was associate editor of *Management Science,* and was Chair of the Business Policy and Strategy Division of the Academy of Management in 1989–1990.

Professor Bourgeois teaches in several executive programs, including TEP, Darden's senior executive program, and provides consulting for a variety of North and South American, European, Asian, and Australian corporations. He lives with his wife, Maggie, and their three children in Charlottesville, Virginia, where he plays jazz guitar and bikes long distances for relaxation.

CONTENTS

Part III   Corporate Strategy: Managing Multiple-Business Firms   391

Part IV   Corporate Strategy: Diversification and Synergy   601

PART I

FOUNDATIONS

STRATEGIC THINKING

When a roomful of executives is asked, Is it fair to say that your business is getting more competitive? a resounding Yes! from each one echoes in response. This happens regardless of industry or service sector, the size of the executive's organization, whether it is domestic or global, or even whether it is from the public or private sector.

All organizations face competition—for resources, people, cash, or customers. Likewise, all organizations face uncertain environments, because both product and technology life cycles are shortening relentlessly. Never has it been more important for businesses and their leaders to position their organizations strategically for competing successfully in the future. This requires that managers thoroughly understand the dynamics of their industries, the trends in their external environments, and the basic economics of their firms. They also must think creatively enough to craft strategies that make their companies unique and inspire their organizations to perform to ever increasing standards. Finally, they must balance the multiple activities of the various functions in their organizations and galvanize them toward unified action. To accomplish all these activities simultaneously requires that managers engage in *strategic thinking* and *strategic management*.

Strategic management encompasses the activities of senior-level executives in their attempts to influence the overall direction of their corporations. This textbook covers many of the approaches that help executives increase that influence by developing successful business and corporate strategies.

Strategic thinking, on the other hand, can occur at all levels of the organization—from brand managers to production supervisors, from sales executives to financial planners and analysts. Strategic thinking at these levels involves understanding the role of one's firm in the marketplace and how one's individual function contributes to that role. Just as a guitar player or drummer needs to know the bandleader's intent with a piece of music in order to provide masterful support to the whole, every individual in a corporation can provide better customer service, better information back to the home office, and make better personnel decisions if she or he has a good understanding of both the company's strategy and some basic strategic management principles. This textbook provides concepts and tools to aspiring managers who wish to add value to their companies by making strategically sound decisions, whatever their functions or responsibilities may be.

THE EVOLUTION OF STRATEGIC THINKING

Strategic thinking evolved from the different approaches that companies utilize to plan their business activities. Prior to the 1920s, few firms did any of what today might be called "long-term planning." Most businesses were run more or less entrepreneurially, and business decisions were relatively short term in focus. Manufacturing produced products, sales sold them, and accounting counted the money. Many businesses were driven by a focus on survival.

With the advent of the modern corporation, such as General Motors and DuPont in the 1920s, larger and more far-flung enterprises needed mechanisms to plan and allocate resources. **Financial planning** provided senior managers with a sophisticated set of tools with which to plan annual production, expenses, and capital investments. The methods typically involved translating sales forecasts into production schedules, estimating the costs associated with the planned volume, and deriving profit forecasts. Once capital appropriations, research, development, advertising, and administrative overhead were taken into account, projecting cash flows available for dividends was a simple and straightforward matter.

This approach, however, was based on a fundamental assumption that sales projections could be made. In a stable world, this assumption held. Sales forecasters had only to extrapolate from the past. But when times changed—the economy slowed, markets got saturated, or other events affected demand—the limitations of this method became obvious. Also, this approach tended to treat departments within the business as separate functions (sales forecast ➔ manufacturing costs ➔ financial results) and tended to have a one-year horizon. As a consequence, changes occurring over several years, such as shifting consumer preferences or market saturation, would go unnoticed. Finally, the driver of business behavior under financial planning systems tended to have short-term goals, which were often oriented toward meeting the budget for the year.

To deal with longer-horizon changes, **forecast-based planning** was developed in the 1950s and 1960s. Here, the rigor of analyses jumped dramatically, as planners began using such tools and concepts as product life cycles, discounted cash flows and net present value analyses, and statistically valid market research of consumer preferences and buying behavior. Because the level of sophistication and time required by these tools was significantly greater than called for previously, managers needed assistance from a new breed of technical experts—strategic planners, business school graduates, and consulting firms. Business schools grew at unprecedented rates in the 1960s and 1970s, and the consulting profession boomed as new strategic planning firms, such as the Boston Consulting Group and Bain & Company, were founded and flourished.

The behavior driver under forecast-based planning was to predict the future and to plan strategies that would adapt the firm to that future. In other words, it was reactive. At the same time, staff planners and consultants found that many of their strategic recommendations were not getting implemented. This occurred for two reasons. One reason was that often the analyses and recommendations were performed by people who were not responsible for executing the strategy. Without the ownership that comes with participation, many line executives either rejected plans or, at best, were lukewarm in their compliance. The second reason was that plans that were based on analyzing consumer trends and product acceptance often failed to take *competitor* behavior into account. The **strategic management** approach was developed in response to these limitations.

Strategic *management*, in contrast to strategic *planning*, is the function of line executives—the people on the firing line who deal with the real world of customers, machines, products, and people. The philosophy is simple: the people closest to the action are in the best position to know what is going on in the business, what works, what trends are developing, and what competitors are doing. In other words, those who must execute must be involved in developing strategy.

A second part of the philosophy is also simple: it is not sufficient to look forward (at potential consumer demand for a new product, for example). Managers must also look to the right and to the left—at what competitors are doing. In other words, competitive analysis becomes a key feature in strategic thinking.

The dilemma, however, is twofold: (1) Usually, line managers do not have the time to do strategic analyses. As you will see in the Astral Records case, a general manager's life is cluttered with a multitude of conflicting demands on his or her time. So, managers must either take time out—such as at a planning retreat, for example—or they must learn so much about strategy and competition that they are thinking strategically on the job. (2) Even if managers create the time for strategic planning, they often lack the tools. Their training

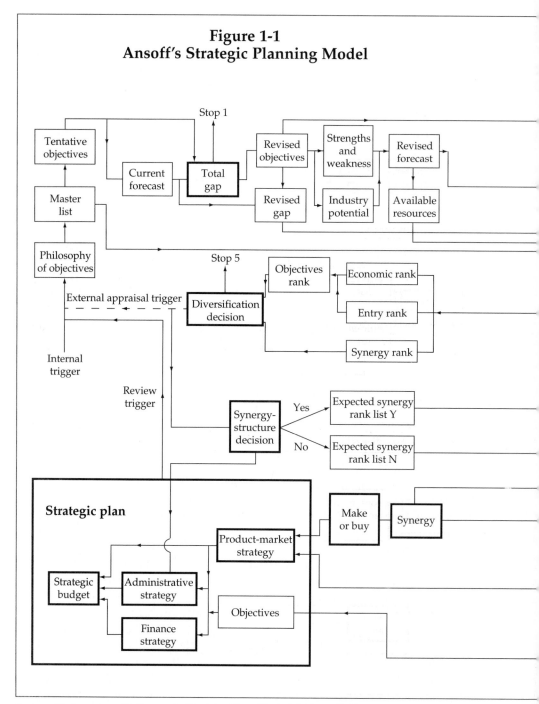

Figure 1-1
Ansoff's Strategic Planning Model

Source: H. Igor Ansoff, *Corporate Strategy*, New York, McGraw-Hill, 1985, pp. 202–205.

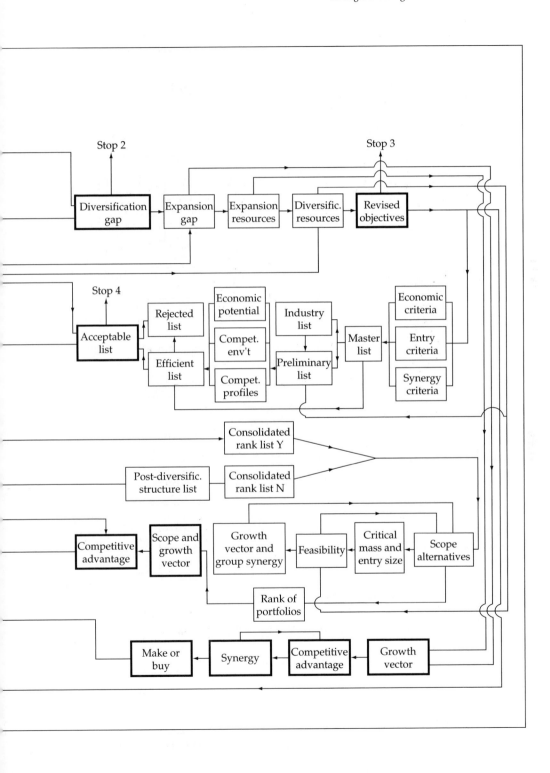

Stop 2

Stop 3

Diversification gap

Expansion gap

Expansion resources

Diversific. resources

Revised objectives

Stop 4

Acceptable list

Rejected list

Economic potential

Industry list

Economic criteria

Compet. env't

Master list

Entry criteria

Efficient list

Preliminary list

Compet. profiles

Synergy criteria

Consolidated rank list Y

Post-diversific. structure list

Consolidated rank list N

Competitive advantage

Scope and growth vector

Growth vector and group synergy

Feasibility

Critical mass and entry size

Scope alternatives

Rank of portfolios

Make or buy

Synergy

Competitive advantage

Growth vector

may have been thorough in the *functional* areas of marketing, accounting, engineering, or human resources, but it may have been insufficient in *strategic* concepts, frameworks, and tools. As stated earlier, the purpose of this book is to provide these tools.

In a firm equipped with strategic management tools and strategic thinking managers and executives, the behavior driver shifts from a mentality of survival, meeting the budget, or merely forecasting the future, to one of *creating* the future by shaping one's industry and markets rather than reacting to them.

A firm that is truly thinking strategically can be identified in a number of ways. First, its executives know and understand what the firm's mission and strategy are. Second, they know their core competencies and capabilities as an organization. Third, they can identify their competitors and predict their reactions to the firm's strategic moves. Fourth, they have developed a culture that supports their strategy. Finally, they are constantly developing new capabilities for renewing their strategies and for competing successfully in the future.

BECOMING A STRATEGIC THINKER

So, how do managers and their companies develop strategic thinking? Must they go through the stages listed above, one at a time? Fortunately, no. It is essential that managers know how to do financial planning, market research, and other fundamental business analyses. But they need not wait to master these before progressing to strategic management and thinking.

ELEMENTS OF STRATEGIC THINKING

Strategic *planning* has a fairly well-established history. The first book on strategy was written in 1965 by Igor Ansoff, an executive at Lockheed Aerospace. Titled *Corporate Strategy*, it presented an extraordinarily logical, step-by-step set of concepts and approaches to making diversification decisions. His complete model for strategic planning, presented toward end of his book, is shown in Figure 1-1.

When presented with this model as a how-to-do-strategy template, most practicing managers run for cover. The thoroughness of the model forces the analyst to think through the logic and economics of the business. But this thoroughness comes at the price of appearing overwhelming to busy line executives.

Strategic thinking is a lot less complicated than the diagram in Figure 1-1 implies. Various approaches to strategic analysis are available, and although the details differ they all have fundamental components in common.

All strategic planning approaches attempt to find an optimal match between the resources and capabilities available within the firm (**S**trengths and **W**eaknesses) and the external market conditions and environmental trends (**O**pportunities and **T**hreats). This match or coalignment (often called a **SWOT** analysis) results in a strategy, whose efficacy translates into some level of corporate performance. The basic dimensions of this fairly straightforward approach are illustrated in the basic strategy model shown in Figure 1-2.

A key feature in the basic strategy model is the reciprocal influence of all of the variables. For example, in the late 1960s a major science-based consulting firm, Sigma Consultants, observed that (1) the level of expenditures on health care in the United States was accelerating, a trend likely to continue, and (2) the firm had several competent professionals on its staff who had carried out health care related assignments such as designing hospitals and evaluating medical group acquisitions. By responding to the market opportunity and articulating a health care strategy or consulting practice, Sigma would define a new domain (as the arrow drawn from strategy to environment in Figure 1-2 illustrates) based on existing internal capabilities (see the arrow drawn from internal organization to strategy). Having chosen the new domain, the firm would now have to respond to the dictates of the marketplace (arrow from environment to strategy) by, for example, designing products and services that were in demand or adapting to whatever governmental regulation might be relevant. To implement the new strategy, Sigma might reorganize its staff so that all professionals working on health care related assignments were grouped together (arrow from strategy to internal organization). Over time, this group might increase its proficiency by sharing experience, knowledge, and the like. The degree of success would be manifested in some level of performance (arrow from strategy to performance), and, in turn, the performance level would serve as feedback, indicating that further adaptations of strategy might be in order (arrow from performance to strategy).

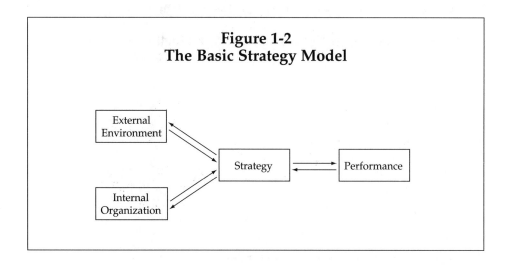

Figure 1-2
The Basic Strategy Model

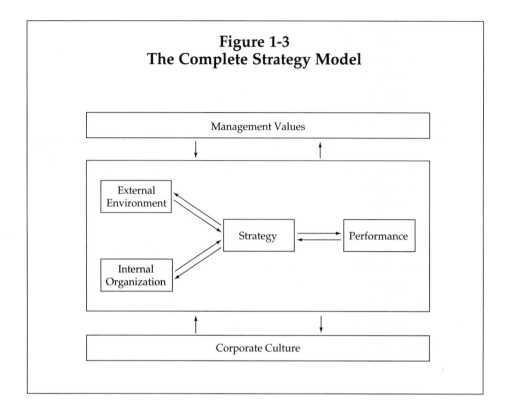

Figure 1-3
The Complete Strategy Model

In essence, then, the model represents a system of interacting parts. But the picture painted thus far is not complete. A "perfect" strategy may be found that violates managers' predispositions. Conversely, management's values may suggest strategies that are not optimal in an economic sense. For example, President Jay Monroe of the Tensor Corporation refused to change his very "functional" high-intensity Tensor lamps when new competitors started introducing style variations. As a result, his company lost 60 percent of the market, which it probably could have retained had Monroe's values been more economic than aesthetic. In formulating any economic strategy, management must also bring its noneconomic values into the picture.

In our Sigma Consultants example, there was strong support for the health care venture among senior management and some of the professional staff. That is, the venture fit the values of top management. However, Sigma was originally organized on the model of a research lab, in which professionals were unimpeded by bureaucratic hierarchy and were free to choose their projects. Assignment to projects was by invitation, and, assuming the invited person was billing sufficient time to avoid the pressure to join projects indiscriminately, he or she could turn these projects down. The health care strategy, in contrast, suggested an organizational unit in which consultants would be expected to dedicate themselves to one major type of activity. This ran smack against the prevailing culture. The strategy was abandoned.

Therefore the basic model shown in Figure 1-2, although it is a very "rational" model of strategy, needs to be amplified to consider the implementability of strategy. Management needs to include the "soft" sides of strategy, political feasibility, and organizational acceptability. Thus, a complete model would include explicit consideration of managerial values and prevailing corporate culture, as shown in Figure 1-3.

The model outlined in Figure 1-3 suggests a sequence of activities in the strategic management process. These activities constitute the fundamental components of strategic management:

- Environmental trends analysis and scenario building
- Industry and competitive analysis
- Identification of past and current strategy
- Strategy evaluation
- Identification of competitive advantages
- Strategic choice
- Cultural analysis
- Strategic change

Throughout the course of this book and its cases, it should be noted that consideration of some of these elements will be different as we progress from single business to multibusiness (diversified) firms while others will remain constant and be relevant to all levels of strategy.

The book is organized to introduce the strategic thinking elements in sequence. Part I examines the foundations of strategic thinking. Part II defines strategy, and lays out methods of external analysis (such as trends, scenario building, and industry analysis) and strategy analysis for single businesses (such as strategy identification, evaluation, and sources of competitive advantage). Part III introduces methods of analyzing strategy in multibusiness firms (corporate strategy). Part IV extends the concepts of Part III into a discussion of diversification strategies. Part V analyzes organizational capabilities and corporate culture and explores issues of strategic leadership and change.

ʼREFERENCESʼ

Andrews, Kenneth R. *The Concept of Corporate Strategy.* 3d ed. Homewood, IL: Irwin, 1987.

Ansoff, H. Igor. *Corporate Strategy.* New York: McGraw-Hill, 1965.

Gilmore, Frank F. "Formulating Strategy in Smaller Companies." *Harvard Business Review* 49, no. 3 May–June, 1971.

Gluck, Frederick W., S. P. Kaufman, and A. S. Walleck. "Strategic Management for Competitive Advantage." *Harvard Business Review* 58, no. 4 July–August, 1980.

Ohmae, Kenichi. *The Mind of the Strategist.* New York: McGraw-Hill, 1992.

Schendel, Dan E., and K. J. Halten. "Business Policy or Strategic Management: A Broader View for an Emerging Discipline." *Academy of Management Proceedings.* 1972, pp. 99–102.

THE ALASKAN GOLD MINE

You have taken a three-month option on a possible gold mine in Alaska. It took you two months of dangerous journey to get there. After two weeks of exploration (and recuperation), you have got your health back except for your injured left hand, which sometimes can suddenly become quite weak. In the last 24 hours, you have finally discovered gold in what appears to be good quantity. You have exactly two weeks to get to the claims office. If you arrive late and attempt to secure the property with the owners knowing you have visited it, they will probably hold an auction, at which you, given your limited resources, could easily be outbid. Here are your alternatives:

1. Wait three to four weeks until the weather warms up and enjoy a safe trip home.

2. Go over the mountains. This is dangerous. It is sometimes impassable. It is quick, however (seven to ten days), if you can make it without harm. If you encounter storms or are injured before you reach the top, you will probably have to turn back. In either case, you may perish, because the longest part of the journey is on the way over the top.

3. Go through the valley passes. This is less dangerous and is usually passable. It is slow and tiring, however. You can probably make it in two to three weeks.

The weather is only moderately favorable; a mountain storm may be brewing. You will know within 48 hours if the storm is coming and will know whether the mountain is passable (if the storm comes) about one day later.

4. Wait two to four days, take #2 if the weather permits; if not, take #3. (There is no advantage to waiting if you prefer #3 anyway, and waiting to take #1 = #1.)

What do you do? (Circle your answer.)   #1 #2 #3 #4

Authored by Jeffrey Barach, Graduate School of Business, Tulane University, New Orleans, Louisiana, 1977. Reprinted by permission. Revisions by Professor L. J. Bourgeois made with permission. Copyright © 1992 by the Darden Graduate Business School Foundation, Charlottesville, VA.

ASTRAL RECORDS, LTD., NORTH AMERICA

The date was August 24, 1993, and Sarah Conner felt overwhelmed and more than a little disoriented. Only two days ago, she had rushed from her office at Bendini, Lambert & Locke (BLL), a well-known venture-capital firm, to board the company jet for Knoxville, Tennessee, where she would assume operating control of Astral Records, Ltd., North America (Astral N.A.). One week earlier, Astral N.A.'s president and chief executive officer, Sir Maxwell S. Hammer, had been killed in a tragic hunting accident. As the owner of 60 percent of the company, BLL had felt an immediate need to protect its investment. Accordingly, BLL's managing director, T.J. Lambert, had asked Conner to run the company while the firm planned its next moves. He had assured her that she would be in Pigeon Forge, Tennessee, for at least a year.

Conner was the obvious choice. After graduating from Wellesley College in 1982 with a degree in classical music, she had gone to work for Galaxy Records, first in marketing and later in production. In 1987 she was admitted to the Darden Graduate School of Business Administration, where she was president of the Entrepreneurs Club, a Shermet scholar, and, upon graduation, a recipient of the Faculty Award for academic excellence. Hoping to combine her love of music with her business acumen, she joined BLL as assistant manager of the entertainment portfolio. That BLL was acquiring new music-industry companies made it the perfect and first choice among her several job offers.

Conner had progressed quickly during her four years at BLL. Nevertheless, she was rather surprised at how quickly she had been asked to assume operating control of one of the fastest growing compact-disc (CD) manufacturers in the world. In two weeks she was scheduled to meet with BLL's principals. They wanted a status report, a set of recommendations, and an action plan for the next year. She knew that a number of important issues were likely to need attention in the wake of Sir Maxwell's death.

THE CD INDUSTRY

In principle, CD technology was an evolutionary refinement of records and tapes. Under the old technology, music and voice were converted into electronic

This case was prepared by Lynn A. Isabella, Associate Professor of Business Administration, and Ted Forbes. Copyright © 1993 by the University of Virginia Darden School Foundation, Charlottesville, VA. All rights reserved. Revised August 1994.

impulses that were then embedded in a medium such as vinyl or magnetic tape. These impulses were then decoded and amplified to reproduce the original music. CDs, however, represented a huge technological leap forward. Sound was converted into digital code that could then be decoded by a laser to reproduce exactly the original digital information.

CDs were produced in two steps. First, a "master" was made. An extremely flat, glass master disc received an adhesive and a thin (0.12 micron) layer of light-sensitive photoresist on one side. The photoresist was then exposed to a 100-milliwatt laser beam that applied the sequence of coded digits in real time to the photoresist. After an alkaline bath removed unwanted resist, a pattern of micropits was left. A nickel impression, known as the "father," was made from the glass master. The positive "mothers" that were produced from the negative father were used to make the stampers of the polycarbonate substrate.

Because the photoresist was damaged when it was developed, the exposed glass master could normally be put to use only once. Four or five nickel mothers were usually made from a single father. Another four or five stampers could be sputtered in metal from each mother, for a total of up to 25 stampers from the single master disc. The master could thus become the source of up to 10,000 discs per stamper, or 250,000 CDs.

In the second step, a mold received polycarbonate resin that was stamped to make the hard, transparent CD wafer. A vaporized metal layer, usually aluminum, was applied in a vacuum chamber as the surface that reflected the laser beam for player reading. Then came another hard, protective resin layer, the printed label, automatic inspection, and packaging.

CDs were first mass-produced in 1980. Since then, CD technology had seen mostly refinements rather than breakthroughs. For example, in 1989 CD-production cycle times were 13 seconds; now those times were less than 7 seconds, and leading-edge technology produced CDs in less than 5 seconds. The machinery was more efficient and less expensive than the old equipment, with the cost of a new small plant in the range of $8–$10 million.

Although industry dynamics had stabilized in recent years, predicting volume and designing appropriate capacity were as much art as science. "Correct capacity, either annually or monthly, is like an Indiana spring. It's only two or three days a year. You're either over or under capacity. If we weren't talking about being over capacity, we'd be talking about a shortage; it's never correct very long," stated Robert McGee, executive director of ComDisc, a trade association.

Quality had improved dramatically over the past ten years. In most plants, quality control was completely automated. The implementation of statistical process controls had a tremendous impact. In 1986 industry reject rates were approximately 12 percent. By 1993 rates were as low as 1.5 percent. "The discs coming off the machines today are simply better quality. Because of our knowledge and machine consistency, inspection is made easy," said Billie Holliday, director of quality for Celestial Records.

As the technology matured, producers discovered that cover art was increasingly important in selling CDs. Many CD replicators now had 5-color capacity. Most CD producers used silk-screen printing, and the large operations used offset printing. Over the years, packaging was standardized around the "jewel box," a hard, plastic case used to hold both the CD and accompanying liner notes. Efforts to move toward "environmentally friendly" packaging had not succeeded.

Wholesale prices for finished product averaged $1.30. Packaging costs were approximately 23 cents per disc and the finished disc itself cost approximately 90 cents. Industry analysts asserted that price competition among disc replicators had come down to pennies and half pennies, as opposed to differences of 15–25 cents in the late 1980s. "When the business is soft and you establish a price, it's very difficult to establish a higher price once business picks up. The gross margins on CDs have eroded tremendously over the past five years. I don't see any more maneuvering left on the price," said Eleanor Rigby, record-industry analyst with Sergeant and Pepper Investments.

Record labels contracted with manufacturing facilities to produce the finished product. The labels then sold, either directly or through a distributor, to the retail outlets. Sales from label/distributor to retail outlets were on a consignment basis. Continued Rigby,

> Although quantity discounts are available, most labels are placing smaller orders and then reordering on a more frequent basis to keep inventory at manageable levels. There are only so many returns a label can take and still turn a profit, so we're seeing labels be a bit more cautious about their opening orders and then coming back for more in a shorter turnaround period than before.

Recent advances in laser technology had opened up the market in both the computer and video arenas. Because the technologies were essentially the same, audio CD manufacturers could easily produce CD-ROM discs for computers or laser discs for video. Sam Cooke, vice president of marketing and sales, Galaxy Records, asserted,

> Quality of the CD in the industry is fairly standard now. A disc we stamp is the same quality as any of the other major houses. What might set a company apart, though, is what we do on the terms of fulfillment services, packaging and design, and drop shipping. Customer service has definitely become the buzzword among replicators for the '90s.

COMPANY HISTORY

Astral Records was founded by Count Francisco Smirnov, a Franco-Russian nobleman, in 1967 in Wollaston-on-Heath, England. Smirnov was a professional musician who had a vision of building a new kind of record company. Appalled by the quality of records at that time, Smirnov set out to construct a studio whose sole purpose would be to produce classical-music record masters of a quality greater than that of any other company in the world. The count had been disappointed to learn that the long-playing records made from his masters were little better in sound quality than most others on the market. Undaunted, he decided to move into manufacturing.

Smirnov's vision was of a utopian musical village, where classical musicians and company directors would reside in luxury and elegance. The count wanted nothing to impede the creative process: "Beautiful music can only happen in beautiful surroundings. If society continues to ignore the high arts, then society will be led into a barbarian condition."

In 1975 Astral purchased a 50-room Georgian mansion on 187 acres near the top of the Cynwyr valley not far from Wales. Each step in the production process would be carried out on site. The ballroom was turned into one of the most elegant recording studios in the industry. The count and five of the seven managing directors continued to live the vision, residing in the exquisitely furnished headquarters and taking all their meals together. Key business decisions were often made casually over lunch and dinner. Recording musicians were invited to live on the grounds for as long as they needed to complete their projects.

Astral Records might well have continued to operate in this idyllic setting, but for a major technological breakthrough. The count was captivated by the emerging compact-disc technology. He immediately saw the medium's potential for producing virtually flawless recordings. The combination of pure digital sound and laser technology became the count's obsession, even though he would be going up against the industry giants.

Instead of simply licensing CD technology from the giants, the count and his researchers decided to develop their own process. In eight months they developed production capabilities that not only saved them millions in royalty fees, but also won them a Queen's Award for technological achievement. Astral Records was the first company in the United Kingdom to produce CDs, two years ahead of its major competitors. By the mid-1980s, more than 50 record labels were using Astral's facilities to record, produce, and manufacture CDs. Astral's own labels constituted a mere 10 percent of the company's sales.

Astral's bold, yet whimsical, business decisions had been wildly successful. In 1980 Astral Records, Ltd., U.K., employed 27 people and grossed 600,000 pounds. By 1992 the company had 500 employees and turned a pre-tax profit of £2.7 million on sales of £20 million.

ASTRAL RECORDS, LTD., NORTH AMERICA

In 1986 the count entered into negotiations with Bendini, Lambert & Locke to secure capital for a planned expansion into the U.S. market. The market for

CDs was booming and the plant in England was struggling to keep pace with demand. One night Smirnov had a vision of the new facility: it would be nestled amongst mountains and streams surrounded by lush pastures. In 1987, in exchange for 60 percent ownership of the U.S. operation, BLL financed the construction of a $14 million plant on 265 acres in Pigeon Forge, Tennessee. The count chose Sir Maxwell S. Hammer, an English aristocrat and hunting partner, to run the U.S. operation. "I shall endeavor to carry the mission of Astral Records to the States," Sir Maxwell stated.

Astral Records, Ltd., N.A., was predominately a manufacturing facility, capable of pressing 100,000 CDs per day. Ninety percent of its business was producing CDs for a variety of other record labels. Diverging from the Astral, U.K., core business and classical tradition, Sir Maxwell had begun to explore recording and producing CDs beyond Astral's classical catalog, which contained 300 titles. Sir Maxwell's wide-ranging interests ran from classical to blues to rock and roll to new age to rap. Having seen the phenomenal sales of many of the artists whose CDs Astral manufactured under contract, Sir Maxwell entered into negotiations with a variety of country, world-music, and new-age artists to bring them under Astral's own labels.

Under Sir Maxwell's leadership, Astral Records quickly became known as the premier CD manufacturer in the United States. Astral's stringent quality-control standards were far higher than those set by its competitors. Within the industry, an Astral CD was widely believed to be playable without error on any CD player. "It's quality. I think if we lost that, then the company would be truly adrift. Music and all the arts are extremely fragile creations and it's quite simple to lose that very thing after which you are chasing," said Mr. Kite, Astral's celebrated music director.

Sir Maxwell built a reputation as an innovator in the industry. Astral invented multisonic recording, a method of capturing reverberated sounds from the rear of the orchestra. Astral also pioneered the use of new packaging systems that used recycled paper. The company's current research focused on creating the ability to compress feature-length motion pictures onto a standard 5-inch disc. In his last interview before his death, Sir Maxwell stated, "People no longer want to just hear music; they want to see it. Video is the future."

He had also embarked on a path of expansion in order to increase capacity in a growing market. In 1991 the company completed a $3-million capital project that increased capacity by 40 percent. Production lines were expanded from five to eight, and two new mastering systems were added. Astral represented the latest in CD-manufacturing systems.

Sir Maxwell ran the U.S. operation as though it were his own colonial outpost. "Sir Max," as his employees called him, affectionately referred to his top managers as "toppers." He quickly established a reputation as a demanding taskmaster, and he insisted on being involved in every aspect of the business.

He oversaw every major decision. Not surprisingly, the managers and employees at Astral were feeling adrift in the wake of Sir Maxwell's death.

SARAH CONNER TAKES CHARGE

At 8:00 A.M., Sarah Conner sat in the walnut-paneled conference room overlooking the Great Smokey Mountains. Sir Maxwell's office was elegant, but Conner did not feel comfortable in it yet. In front of her was an assortment of memos, phone messages, faxes, and other correspondence that had accumulated, mostly over the past week (see the exhibits that follow). Conner believed she needed to deal with all of these papers and also begin preparing the report for the upcoming meeting with the partners from BLL. The next couple of weeks promised to be interesting.

ASTRAL RECORDS, Ltd.   *North America*   *Pigeon Forge, TN*   Tel. (615) 356-9889

TO: All Astral Toppers

FROM: Sir Maxwell S. Hammer

DATE: August 18, 1993

SUBJECT: Staff Meeting

Please join me for high tea in the boardroom on August 24th at 3:00 P.M.

ASTRAL RECORDS, Ltd.   *North America*   *Pigeon Forge, TN*   Tel. (615) 356-9889

August 24, 1993

Sarah—
    Welcome to Astral. We are all glad to have you with us.
    I've gone ahead and told our toppers that you would want to meet them at 3 p.m. as was scheduled. It was so shocking about Sü Max!
    I'm sure you'd appreciate some advice from an "old pro." (I've been Sü Max's right-hand man since the beginning.) Sü Max commanded respect and you should do the same. Make quick decisions. The E.P.A. can wait, for example, but that conflict in production needs your attention. I won't put too much stock in O'Reilly or Sandy either. I'll stop by around 2 p.m. to brief you on what Sü Max would have wanted.

Wallace Alexander

Wallace Alexander
Assistant to the President

To __Ms. Conner__

Date __8/23__   Time __10:03__   ☒ AM
                                 ☐ PM

WHILE YOU WERE OUT

M __Prof. Calhoun__
of __Univ. of Tennessee__

Phone (____)_____

Area Code   Number   Extension

TELEPHONED	✓	PLEASE CALL	✓
CALLED TO SEE YOU		WILL CALL AGAIN	
WANTS TO SEE YOU		URGENT	
	RETURNED YOUR CALL		

Message __Confirming student visits tomorrow @ 10am. Final Count—50 MBA students for tour & mgmt. briefings. Look forward to continuing relationship with Astral.__

Operator

| ASTRAL RECORDS, Ltd. | *Wollaston-on-Heath* | *England* | Tel. 098-765-54 |

August 22

Dearest Sarah,

Alas, I wish the circumstances surrounding your arrival were more joyous. Sir Max was a dear friend and a valued associate.

The directors and I would like to formally welcome you into the company. We will hold a Fox Hunt here at the compound on September 7. The Hunt will be in your honor. Please plan to arrive on the fifth, and stay through the tenth.

We eagerly anticipate your arrival!

Count Francisco Smirnov
P.O.R., R.E.G., R.D.G.

| ASTRAL RECORDS, Ltd. | *North America* | *Pigeon Forge, TN* | Tel. (615) 356-9889 |

August 20, 1993

TO: Bart O'Reilly   FROM: Roberta Prospect
         Vice President, Operations   District Sales Manager
         Astral NA

CC: Sir Maxwell S. Hammer

FAX: 804-555-1234   FAX: 212-458-0000

URGENT ACTION REQUEST!!!!!!!

Purchasing personnel from Republic Music Distributors, Inc., are on their way to see us once again, and we need your help. Can you meet with me on Wednesday, August 25, to help us figure a way out of the current order backlog—particularly since Republic is my largest customer. Currently, we have a production run that is out-of-spec on color and electrical properties, but Republic is still willing to take it. Our plant manager is balking at shipping anything out-of-spec.

The new equipment still has problems. The plant manager and the staff have been working around the clock, it seems, to get the utilization promised by the equipment manufacturers. They have made great progress in stabilizing the production processes, particularly in view of the new technology in the NCC-1701A equipment, but there are still problems.

My issue at the moment is the plant's unwillingness to be a bit flexible in what it ships out to Republic. Here is the latest incident. This afternoon, I called our shipping department to verify that the Republic order would be

(continued on next page)

2

picked up by Smith's Transfer. We had promised a ship date of Tuesday of this week, and I have been reassuring Republic's purchasing agent all week that this shipment would be made by the week's end.

When I found out the products were being scrapped, I really hit the ceiling. I felt like this action would be the last straw with Republic. We will lose all credibility if we don't get product to them by next Thursday. There is no way to meet their needs if we start a new production run. I was able to get the current run placed on hold by the Q.A. manager. The plant manager promises a new run from NCC-1701A by next Friday afternoon. Even if this run goes perfect, and we airship, the product will arrive too late for Republic to meet its customer ship date.

I proposed to the plant manager and quality assurance manager that the plant work overtime on Monday and Tuesday, sorting the products on electrical properties conformance. The purchasing people at Republic said they would be willing to accept "sorted-product." Moreover for this *one order*, they would allow off-specification occurrences for the color schemes on the various outside graphics. (We will have to process all of the 8,000 units through the certifier to sort "good/bad" on electrical properties. There are nine critical electrical performance attributes that must meet specifications.) Then the color consistency must be checked visually by our people. This visual check is a manual process and will take a lot of labor, particularly since the visual check requires a tricky disassembly step to remove the protective shield covering the minted surface.

So, I can get the purchasing people at Republic off my back with this one-time stop gap sort, and yet the plant manager refuses to schedule the overtime. He says that my proposal and the plant's TQM initiative don't go hand-in-hand. Their TQM activities have been underway for eight months, so I don't see how the actions would impact his TQM implementation. We need to be more customer focused at Astral.

Please call me later today and give me some help on this one. Thanks.

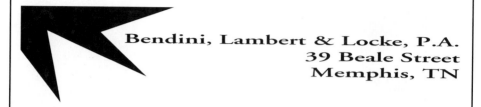

Bendini, Lambert & Locke, P.A.
39 Beale Street
Memphis, TN

FACSIMILE TRANSMISSION

TO: Sarah Conner   FROM: T.J. Lambert
      Astral Records, NA   Partner, BLL

DATE: August 24, 1993

MESSAGE:

Sarah. . . . Welcome to Astral. Hope your flight on the Lear was enjoyable. Just wanted to once again let you know that we are expecting great things from you. This Astral Records affair has cost us a great deal more money than we had anticipated. Arthur and I know that you will work your magic on Astral in short order. Let's get this company straightened out.

As we set up before you left, Arthur, Helen and I will be coming to Astral on September 7th to meet with you. Please arrange appropriate accommodations for us. You know what we like.

By the way, we have been unable to locate the financial model you built for the TechnoWiz deal. As I recall, this was an extremely complex spreadsheet. Celia, your former secretary, left unexpectedly last Friday and no one can find her files. Can you build it for us again by the end of this week as we hope to complete this deal immediately?

Look forward to seeing you in two weeks. Best of luck.

"WE COVER THE WORLD WITH CHEMICALS"

POLYCARBONATE SUBSTRATE INC.
R.D. #3
BOX 4788
KENNER, LOUISIANA

TO: Sir Maxwell S. Hammer

FROM: J. Cash
           Manager, Accounts Receivable

DATE: August 9, 1993

SUBJECT: Overdue Account

This is to notify you that Astral Records, North America, is more than 90 days overdue in its payment to us. You currently owe us $27,914.22.

If payment is not received by August 26, 1993, we will not deliver the next shipment of resins. Thank you for your prompt attention to this matter.

To **Ms. Conner**

Date **8/23** Time **1:43** ☐ AM ☒ PM

WHILE YOU WERE OUT

M **Bea Walters**

of **Billboard Magazine**

Phone (____)_____

| Area Code | Number | Extension |

TELEPHONED		PLEASE CALL	✓
CALLED TO SEE YOU		WILL CALL AGAIN	
WANTS TO SEE YOU		URGENT	
RETURNED YOUR CALL			

Message

Would like interview ASAP regarding management transition.

Operator

ASTRAL RECORDS, Ltd.   *North America*   *Pigeon Forge, TN*   Tel. (615) 356-9889

TO: Sir Max

CC: Bart O'Reilly
        Vice President, Manufacturing

CC: Safety Committee

FROM: Mr. and Mrs. Richard Clark
        Shipping Department

DATE: August 16, 1993

As you may know, the September 1993 Safety Day plans are almost finished. We had a chance to see the last working document that was prepared by the Plant Safety Committee. We are really upset and want to see you ASAP. Can we schedule ourselves into one of your "open doors" later this week?

For the fourth year in a row, there will be a Safety Day exhibition on Home Safety. We applaud Home Safety as one of the key themes. However, this year's focus on "Construction of a Deer Stand: Safety and Safe Hunting" is offensive to many of us. First, it is a fact that 38% of our plant employees are female, and they have no interest in hunting, particularly shooting deer from a stand placed off the ground in trees somewhere on the company's property. Certainly, you understand this point personally. Second, we think it is time to step up to the environmental issues and get our employees involved with recycling (newspapers, aluminum cans, plastic bottles, glass). Can't you order the Safety Committee to drop the "Deer Stand Construction" exhibition? After all, we think productivity/absenteeism and quality suffer at the opening of deer season every year. It is time, we think, to de-emphasize hunting and get people to stay focused on what they are paid to do.

ASTRAL RECORDS, Ltd.   *North America*   *Pigeon Forge, TN*   **Tel. (615) 356-9889**

TO: Sir Max

CC: G. Scott Herron
           Vice President, Marketing and Sales

FROM: Larry Taylor
           Account Manager

DATE: August 13, 1993

SUBJECT: Unauthorized Return of Merchandise

Harris' Sound Machine, the largest chain of retail music stores in New York City, has informed me they intend to return 1,252 CDs with the title, "Buddy Holly's Greatest Hits," and are asking for a full refund. They claim the CDs arrived damaged. The one they sent me looks like it was cut with a knife used to open the shipping cartons. Since this is a slow seller, I am somewhat doubtful about how the CDs were damaged. Please let me know what to do.

YURBANK

"SERVING PIGEON FORGE'S FAMILIES AND BUSINESSES SINCE 1929"
2300 MAIN STREET
PIGEON FORGE, TN

TO: Sir Maxwell S. Hammer

FROM: C. Hewitt Farmington
         Senior Relationship Manager
         YurBank

DATE: July 1, 1993

SUBJECT: Renewal of Revolving Credit Agreement

Sir Max, this is to remind you that your revolver with the bank is due for review and renewal at the end of this month. As it currently stands, the bank is committed to lend you up to $500,000 at LIBOR + 1% with a 0.5% fee on the unused portion of the commitment. In light of the growth of last year's sales and your expectation of future growth, I recommend that we increase the commitment to $600,000. I do not expect the pricing structure to change before the end of this month.

Our understanding is that the line is used for seasonal working capital needs and as such your company will be out of the bank loan for at least 45 days during the next 12 months. Part of the purpose of the review is to see if the financial condition of the company has changed substantially since last year. Historically, your peak loan needs have occurred from September through December. My back-of-the-envelope calculations show that increasing the revolver will not violate the debt-to-equity covenant of the term loan unless equity is unexpectedly low prior to or during your peak seasonal need.

Is the early part of next week too early for your people to get the financials prepared so we can discuss things? I'll check back with you in a day or so to confirm.

To **Astral Records**

Date **8/23** Time **8:00** ☒ AM ☐ PM

WHILE YOU WERE OUT

M **Tony Witherspoon**

of **Environmental Protection**

Phone (_____) **Agency**

Area Code		Number		Extension

TELEPHONED	✓	PLEASE CALL	
CALLED TO SEE YOU		WILL CALL AGAIN	✓
WANTS TO SEE YOU	✓	URGENT	✓
	RETURNED YOUR CALL		

Message

Fish kill in local river downstream of plant. E.P.A. requests full site inspection Wed a.m., Aug. 25.

Operator

ASTRAL RECORDS, Ltd.   *North America*   *Pigeon Forge, TN*   Tel. (615) 356-9889

TO: Sir Max

CC: G. Scott Herron
        Vice President, Marketing and Sales

FROM: John Henry
        Account Manager
        Mississippi See Dee

DATE: August 10, 1993

SUBJECT: Contract Negotiation 1994/1995

Mississippi See Dee's has a fast-growing collection of Delta Blues. (They own the rights to much of John Lee Hooker's, Jimmy Reed's, and Lightnin' Hopkins' titles.)

Larry Johnson, their purchasing agent, says he is willing to increase our share of their business from 15% to 20% if we can guarantee two-week delivery of titles and reduce prices by 5%. I think this is a great opportunity to increase sales.

ASTRAL RECORDS, Ltd.   *North America*   *Pigeon Forge, TN*   **Tel. (615) 356-9889**

TO: Richard & Emma Clark

CC: Sir Max
      Bart O'Reilly, Vice President, Manufacturing

FROM: Maggie May

DATE: August 17, 1993

Will you two get off it! Who do you think you are suggesting that women don't enjoy hunting? I'll have you know I've been hunting since I was six when my daddy let me load his gun. I won't miss deer season and, believe me, these safety reminders are important. Not all women want to join your sewing circle, Emma. So stop writing memos to the VP and accusing us of not doing our work. If you are writing memos, how can you two be doing your own jobs!

To **Astral**

Date **8/24** Time **10:06** ☒ AM ☐ PM

WHILE YOU WERE OUT

M **Tony Witherspoon**

of **E. P. A.**

Phone (_____)_____
  Area Code   Number   Extension

TELEPHONED	✓	PLEASE CALL	
CALLED TO SEE YOU		WILL CALL AGAIN	
WANTS TO SEE YOU		URGENT	
	RETURNED YOUR CALL		

Message **Suggests Astral legal counsel be present during tomorrow's inspection.**

_____
                    Operator

ASTRAL RECORDS, Ltd.	*North America*	*Pigeon Forge, TN*	Tel. (615) 356-9889

TO: Sir Max

CC: Bart O'Reilly, Vice President, Manufacturing
             G. Scott Herron, Vice President, Marketing and Sales

FROM: Phil Kreutzman
             Purchasing

DATE: August 11, 1993

SUBJECT: Proposal for New Plastic Packaging Material

As you know, our packaging costs are substantial. I have a new plastic supplier who can cut our total COGS by 20%. Eventually, costs might be even lower.

The advantage of this company's new formula is that it is *completely* biodegradable in 10 years. The disadvantage is that the package will no longer be serviceable after 3–5 years of normal usage. Should we pursue this project?

ASTRAL RECORDS, Ltd.   *North America*   *Pigeon Forge, TN*   Tel. (615) 356-9889

TO: Sir Maxwell S. Hammer

FROM: Richard Cory
        Treasurer

DATE: July 3, 1993

SUBJECT: Approval of New Packaging Equipment

Below is a summary of the analysis we have been conducting on some new packaging equipment. Based on a discounted cash flow analysis, we estimate that the $1MM investment will increase firm value by $200,000. If we order by the end of this month, we should have the equipment installed and running in time for the increase in production that always occurs around October. The supplier will accept installment payments of $400,000, $300,000, and $300,000 over the next three months as payment. Since we are currently out of the bank, we could use the revolver line to make the $400,000 initial payment.

I hope the numbers on the attached sheet help show the merits of the new system. Frankly, Sir Max, it is rare that such a good opportunity comes around. The sooner we start using it, the better.

(continued on next page)

2

Cash Flow Analysis
New Packaging Equipment

Initial investment:	$1.0MM
Projected annual savings:[a]	$160M
Corporate tax rate:	34%
Economic/depreciable life:	7 years

Cash flow summary ($000):

Year →	0	1	2	3	4	5	6	7
Investment	(1000)							
After-tax savings		106	106	106	106	106	106	106
+ Depreciation		143	143	143	143	143	143	143
Total after-tax cash flows	(1000)	248	248	248	248	248	248	248

Net present value = $209,000
Internal rate of return = 16.1%
Payback = 4 years

_____

[a]After depreciation, before taxes.

◉YURBANK

"SERVING PIGEON FORGE'S FAMILIES AND BUSINESSES SINCE 1929"
2300 MAIN STREET
PIGEON FORGE, TN

TO: Sir Maxwell S. Hammer

FROM: C. Hewitt Farmington
Senior Relationship Manager
YurBank

DATE: August 10, 1993

SUBJECT: Renewal of Revolving Credit Agreement

Things have changed. The credit review committee has put your company on its credit watch list because of our increasing exposure and the growth-induced strain on your balance sheet. They do not want to renew the revolver unless you can give us some sort of indication of how you are going to manage the growth of the firm going forward. Frankly, there is a general concern that your company is growing beyond its financial capabilities and that we might find ourselves with a bad term loan and very little usable collateral.

I spent the better part of an hour arguing with the credit committee, and I can tell you that these people are serious. This is all part of the tightened credit standards that were instituted following the S&L crisis. The only way I can see us doing business in the future is for you to strengthen the balance sheet with an equity infusion. The investment banking folks here would be very interested in helping you take the company public. I think you should consider it. The equity markets are very strong these days, and you may not be able to get a better price in the near future if this bull market turns bearish.

Sorry to catch you with this news with such little notice, but there was nothing I could do. I will meet anytime you are available. Obviously, time is of the essence.

ASTRAL RECORDS, Ltd.   *North America*   *Pigeon Forge, TN*   **Tel. (615) 356-9889**

TO: Sir Maxwell S. Hammer

FROM: Abby McDeere
          Chief Legal Counsel

DATE: July 17, 1993

SUBJECT: Lawsuit against Astral

Please be advised that MasterVision Associates of Burbank, California, has filed suit in the Los Angeles Superior Court against us. They are a worldwide optical disc licensor. They charge that some of our CD manufacturing equipment infringes on their patents. They are seeking unspecified "substantial damages" and note that there is still litigation pending from 1988 when they accused us of two other optical disc patent violations.

The resolution of these charges is uncertain. I will keep you advised.

ASTRAL RECORDS, Ltd.   *North America*   *Pigeon Forge, TN*   Tel. (615) 356-9889

TO: Sir Max

FROM: Sandy Bien-Fait
           Human Resource Manager

DATE: August 16, 1993

SUBJECT: Hiring

Sir Max —

We can't afford to lose any more time addressing the issue of hiring. The increase in production has strained the existing shift personnel. And, as I mentioned last week at our weekly tea, the surrounding area just doesn't have the numbers of workers we need. Either we have to pay more or get them from somewhere else. I need authorization to hire 20 shift workers immediately.

Also, Sir Max, I think it is time to eliminate playing a musical instrument as a hiring criteria. We have simply run out of musicians in the community.

ASTRAL RECORDS, Ltd.   *North America*   *Pigeon Forge, TN*   **Tel. (615) 356-9889**

TO: Sir Max

FROM: Margaret Lee
           Public Relations

CC: Bart O'Reilly
           Vice President, Operations

DATE: March 7, 1993

SUBJECT: CD Rot

There have been an increasing number of articles in the trade press describing a phenomenon known as "CD rot." If the CD rot stories are true, certain CDs may begin to self-destruct within 8–10 years because the ink used for labelling begins to eat into the protective lacquer coating. This in turn can oxidize the aluminum layer resulting in an unplayable CD.

Although we have not yet had any inquiries or returns due to "CD rot," we should nevertheless be prepared to respond to this possible crisis.

ASTRAL RECORDS, Ltd.   *North America*   *Pigeon Forge, TN*   **Tel. (615) 356-9889**

TO: Sir Max

FROM: Carl Christie, Ph.D.
           Research and Development

DATE: August 16, 1993

SUBJECT: Project FutureVision

We are at the breakthrough stage on Project FutureVision. Compression technologies are progressing at an acceptable rate, and we anticipate being able to place full-length motion pictures with Dolby Surround Sound tracks on a 5-inch disc within the next 6 months.

I don't need to tell you about the commercial possibilities. However, the lab is feeling the pinch financially right now. My people have estimated that we need another $3.5 million within the next month in order to complete our work. Since you have been so generous in the past, I know that we all can count on your continued support.

ASTRAL RECORDS, Ltd.   *North America*   *Pigeon Forge, TN*   **Tel. (615) 356-9889**

TO: Sir Maxwell S. Hammer

FROM: Abby McDeere
           Chief Legal Counsel

DATE: August 10, 1993

SUBJECT: Lawsuit against Astral

On August 7th, I met with Richard Milhous, Chief Legal Counsel for Master-Vision. After protracted discussion and negotiation, they have offered a settlement for all litigation pending against us.

They have offered to settle for either a one-time cash payment of $5 million or a 4-cent-per-disc royalty over the next 10 years of production.

We must respond by the 24th of August. Please advise me of your decision.

ASTRAL RECORDS, Ltd.   *North America*   *Pigeon Forge, TN*   Tel. (615) 356-9889

TO: Sir Max

FROM: Bruce Park-Asbury
           Shift Supervisor

CC: Sandy Bien-Fait
           Human Resource Manager

DATE: August 17, 1993

SUBJECT: Employee Reprimand

This is the third time that I have had to reprimand Sonny Barger for being insubordinate. I am at my wits end with him and don't know what to do.

On February 7, Barger refused to clean up his work area, and I gave him a formal reprimand. On March 23, Barger was found taking an unauthorized cigarette break and was again reprimanded. On August 16, Barger left his station 15 minutes before quitting time to run to his car to turn on the air conditioning. I suppose so it would be cool when he got out. I wrote him up for this incident. He told me to watch out, he was going to get me and "the whole damn company."

I honestly believe that Barger is trying to undermine my authority as shift supervisor. If something doesn't change, I may have to leave Astral.

CROSBY, SELLS, CASH AND YOUNG

CERTIFIED PUBLIC ACCOUNTANTS   KNOXVILLE, TN

TO: Sarah Conner

FROM: Janet Young

SUBJECT: Audit Planning Meeting

DATE: August 23, 1993

I wanted to make sure that you were aware of the planning meeting to discuss our audit of Astral's financial statements for the fiscal year ended December 31, 1993, that is scheduled for 10:00 A.M. on Friday, September 10th. We hope to begin our preliminary audit work on Monday, September 27th.

Please be advised that we intend to continue our discussion about Astral's contingent environmental liabilities. We told Sir Max last year that the 1993 financial statements would likely contain at least footnote disclosure of environmental issues and, perhaps, even reflect actual environmental liabilities. Please be prepared to bring us up to date on all environmental matters.

Also, we just heard about the "CD rot" problem. This could have a material effect on Astral's financial statements. We are anxious to learn more about it from your production personnel. Finally, we will need current information about actual and pending litigation. What is happening regarding the MasterVision case?

I look forward to meeting you. If you need to reschedule our meeting, that's OK, but we don't have a lot of flexibility. Please let me know ASAP.

ASTRAL RECORDS, Ltd.   *North America*   *Pigeon Forge, TN*   Tel. (615) 356-9889

TO: Sir Max

FROM: Ed Heath
          Foreman, Waste Disposal Unit

SUBJECT: Equipment Maintenance

DATE: August 13, 1993

The PCB filtration actuators are breaking down regularly these days. We really need to replace these units. I know replacements are very expensive, but this stuff is really toxic and these units are almost to the end of their serviceable life. It won't take much to cause a major problem. In fact, just yesterday, one of our technicians knocked the master valve loose and it took us almost three hours to clean up the spill.

I've talked with the finance people a number of times about getting replacements, but I can't seem to get an answer. We need to move on this soon.

August 17, 1993

Sir Maxwell S. Hammer
President and CEO
Astral Records, N.A.
Pigeon Forge, TN

Sir Max:

DECEMBER is thrilled that Astral Records is interested in placing them under contract. Plans are well underway for the signing party and free concert in Pigeon Forge on the 26th.

I know this will be the beginning of a successful relationship. Attached is our sketch for the cover art of our first CD.

Regards,

Matthew D. Booth

Matthew D. Booth
Business Manager, DECEMBER

Attachments: 1

DECEMBER

For the World is Hollow and I Have Touched the Sky

DECEMBER is
Kevin Albers—Keyboards
Matt Booth—Bass Guitar
Michael King—Vocals
Bryce Smith—Drums

Lighting Techs:
George Ackert, Steven Harper

Road Crew:
Kevin Asherfeld, Dave Erickson

Recorded at: SRS Austin TX

Engineered by: Ben Blank

Send all correspondence to:

DECEMBER
P.O. Box 49188
Austin, TX 78765
(512) 472-8943

Thanks to:
Steven, George, Kevin, Dave, Jim,
Sharron, Tim, Matt, Jeanette W., Mark
P., and Liberty Lunch. Grace Wall,
Derek "Matt kicked me out of the
band" Brownlee. Jan Long, Mark A.,
Dave H., and especially Jill Isreal, and
Lisa McBride.

Back-up vocals on
Darkest Cave by:
Jill Isreal

Lyrics to *A Letter to Vernon Lee*
Inspired by the play *Madame X*
by Anne Ciccolella

ASTRAL RECORDS, Ltd.   *North America*   *Pigeon Forge, TN*   **Tel. (615) 356-9889**

Sir Max,

   You should know that
Roberta Prospect was seen leaving
Arnold Smither's house yesterday
morning at <u>6 a.m.</u>! Smither is the
purchasing manager at Republic Records.
Aren't they one of our biggest customers?
I think this is just <u>scandalous</u>.

                    Your faithful employee
         (Sorry, but I can't sign my name.)

ASTRAL RECORDS, Ltd.   *North America*   *Pigeon Forge, TN*   **Tel. (615) 356-9889**

TO: Sarah Conner

FROM: Richard Cory
          Treasurer

DATE: August 24, 1993

SUBJECT: Capital Structure Summary

In response to your request, I am summarizing Astral's current financial structure below. Note that the line of credit and 5-year term loan are with YurBank and that the 15-year subordinated debt is a loan obtained at a favorable rate from BLL in 1987. As you can see, we have just about reached our debt limit. We probably should discuss this at your convenience. However, the sooner the better.

CAPITAL STRUCTURE ($ MILLIONS)

Line of credit	0.5
Term loan	3.0
Subordinated debt	10.0
Equity	6.5
Total	20.0

PART II

BUSINESS STRATEGY: GAINING AND SUSTAINING COMPETITIVE ADVANTAGE

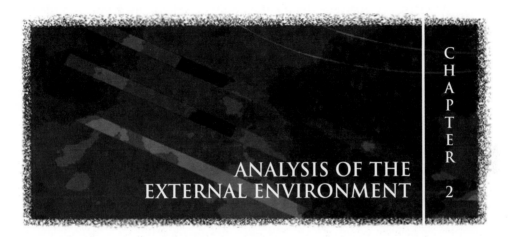

ANALYSIS OF THE
EXTERNAL ENVIRONMENT

CHAPTER 2

Strategy is essentially the act of placing strategic bets on the future of the enterprise. Making these bets requires that managers make predictions or, at minimum, sense where an industry is headed. This is not always easy. The manager often takes cues from his or her immediate surroundings and sources of information to get a feel for the direction of changes in the industry. But even experienced industry observers can draw conflicting conclusions from the same data.

As an example, consider the microcomputer industry in its early years. The early 1980s were exciting in Silicon Valley, when hundreds of start-ups were created and several ordinary people became millionaires in a very short period of time. Steven Jobs, founder of Apple Computers, was one such phenomenon who inspired young "computer nerds" and engineers to reach for success and wealth through new ventures. Although the United States went into a recession in 1983 and 1984, the computer business continued to grow, seemingly untouched by the problems of the economy at large. Then, in a form of aftershock, the microcomputer business and Silicon Valley were hit with their own recession in early 1985. Because the industry was new, valid statistics were unavailable, so predicting a recovery from the slump was problematic at best. Businesses wondering whether to make capital investments for growth or, conversely, to lay off personnel were in a quandary. If they expanded and the slump continued, they would go bankrupt. If they contracted just as recovery came, they would lose their key resources—technical staff and software gurus—to competition and would likewise lose position.

One way for industry participants to get a sense of how the industry might be moving was to gather information at the huge industry trade show, Comdex (Computer Dealers Exposition), held annually in Las Vegas. All the key players would be together and could share perceptions and nonproprietary information.

Two industry analysts—both journalists—did attend the show, and they drew their conclusions from the same data sources: the level of show attendance and a speech by John Young, then-president of Hewlett-Packard. They published their conclusions in the *Wall Street Journal* and the *San Francisco Chronicle* on the same day—November 21, 1985. Their reports are reproduced in Figures 2-1 and 2-2. When inspecting such reports, readers should ask themselves, What data did they use to draw their conclusions? and Why did they draw the conclusions they did?

If the conflicting interpretations of these two industry observers are at all typical, they leave the strategist with a dilemma: What information sources should be trusted? Whose judgment should be relied on? How should the strategist go about painting his or her own picture of environmental trends and industry dynamics? The following three sections on trend forecasting, scenario building, and industry and competitor analysis will help answer these questions.

ENVIRONMENTAL ANALYSIS AND FORECAST

We are not fit to lead an army on the march unless we are familiar with the face of the country—its mountains and forests, its pitfalls.

He who exercises no forethought but makes light of his opponents is sure to be captured by them.

Hence the saying: If you know the enemy and know yourself, you need not fear the result of a hundred battles. If you know yourself but not the enemy, for every victory gained you will also suffer a defeat. If you know neither the enemy nor yourself, you will succumb in every battle.

Sun Tzu, On the Art of War (c. 300 B.C.)

Much recent writing on business strategy has incorporated military metaphors likening economic competition to battle. As in the waging of war, it is the relative irreversibility and long-time commitment implied in strategic decisions that make environmental analysis so crucial to effective strategy making. But the definition of strategy merely as a "match" or coalignment (see Chapter 1) is limited in that it is static. Environments, of course, change; they are discontinuous and often complex, volatile, or even hostile. This means that for the coalignment to remain effective, it must also change. As a result, strategy making is an ongoing managerial process, one that has been likened to shooting at a moving target. The strategist must not only continually reassess the organization's trajectory (as set by prior strategies), but he or

Figure 2-1
Wall Street Journal **Analysis**

Thursday, November 21, 1985   The Wall Street Journal

Computer Vendors, Dealers Voice Fears About Industry Slump at Big Trade Fair

By Randall Smith

Staff Reporter of *The Wall Street Journal*

LAS VEGAS, Nev.—The nation's largest computer trade show opened here with both vendors and dealers expressing concern about how they plan to cope with the industry's continuing downturn.

In a keynote address at the Computer Dealers Exposition, known as Comdex, John Young, president of Hewlett-Packard Co., Palo Alto, Calif., said industry participants face "a struggle for survival," reflecting "what a disappointing and difficult year it has been for just about everybody."

Even John Roach, chairman and president of Fort Worth, Texas-based Tandy Corp., which just introduced a new computer, said he doesn't see anything to indicate that the period of "consolidation among manufacturers and even more dramatically among retailers" is ending.

Mr. Young said the personal-computer industry, the focus of the show, too often has been characterized by products introduced but never delivered and by too many "unmet expectations, Chapter 11s (bankruptcy-law filings) and layoffs, fallings-out, recriminations and lawsuits. And we wonder why customers lack confidence." With potential users increasingly questioning the value of computer purchases, Mr. Young urged vendors and dealers to find better uses for the machines while practicing more self-discipline and cultivating better, longer-term relationships with customers.

Partly reflecting the industry slowdown, the number of exhibitors at Comdex dropped to 1,200 this year, down 200 from the fall 1984 show, although the amount of rented exhibit space hasn't changed. The headline of the show's official newspaper, proclaiming "Industry Rebirth Starts Today," amused some attendees: "I saw that yesterday and chuckled," said Bruce Cummings, vice president for marketing at distributor Softsel Computer Products Inc., based in Inglewood, Calif.

she must also keep an eye on the constantly moving target through persistent scanning, surveillance, and regular and accurate forecasts.

Components of the External Environment

The environment can usefully be thought of as consisting of two parts that overlap. These are termed the *general environment* and the *task environment,*

Figure 2-2
San Francisco Chronicle **Analysis**

Thursday, November 21, 1985   San Francisco Chronicle

Buoyant Mood at Show

PC Executives Confident

By John Eckhouse
Chronicle Correspondent

Las Vegas

The personal computer industry is alive, well, optimistic and currently living in Las Vegas.

A mood of renewed enthusiasm seems prevalent among the thousands of industry executives attending the huge Comdex trade show here. They predict a strong comeback from the sales slump of the past year.

"Our industry has only paused; it will regain its momentum," said John Young, chief executive of Palo Alto-based Hewlett-Packard Co., in a keynote address yesterday.

Although he acknowledged that 1985 has been a "disappointing and difficult year for just about everybody," Young told an audience of more than 1,000 people that pessimism is not warranted.

Edward Gelb, group marketing manager for Panasonic, echoed his view.

"The industry is not dying, it's growing," he said. "It's just going through a period of readjustment after many people overextended themselves expecting industry sales growth to continue at 40 percent or 50 percent a year."

Reflecting personal computer manufacturers' confidence in the future, Comdex sold all 1.4 million square feet of booth space. Although the 1,250 exhibitors number about 100 fewer than last year, the reason is that many signed up for larger booths and forced out companies on the bottom of the priority list.

---

and effective strategy making by coalignment with the environment requires the analysis of both.

The *general environment* includes those elements that affect all organizations in a particular culture. In any one country it will include the political setting and governmental institutions, the cultural setting and social trends, the state of the economy and financial markets and institutions, the law, taxation, and the state of scientific and technological development. Companies operating globally, or those facing foreign competition, must contend with several general environments.

The *task environment*, on the other hand, consists of those elements directly affected by, and impinging upon, the organization in question. It includes such things as the basic structure of the industry—the number and size of firms, the degree of interaction and interdependence among them, and the nature of the cost structure within the industry. Of vital concern are the nature, type, and characteristics of the markets—actual or potential—to which the organization provides goods or services. These, in turn, will dictate the nature of demand (which may, in some cases, be subjected to sophisticated forecasting techniques).

The major components of the environment are listed in Table 2-1.

Table 2-1
Major Components of the Environment

I. General Environment
   A. Macroeconomics
   B. Demographics
   C. Sociocultural system
   D. Political-legal system
   E. Technology

II. Task Environment
   A. Customers and markets
      1. Distributors
      2. End users
   B. Competitors
      1. Competitors for markets
      2. Competitors for resources
   C. Suppliers
      1. Suppliers of physical resources
      2. Suppliers of human resources
      3. Suppliers of capital
   D. Regulatory groups
      1. Government
      2. Union
      3. Special-interest groups
   E. Technology
      1. Rate of development
      2. Potential substitutes for your product or service
      3. Stage of product or industry life cycle

The Analysis

For the task environment, a detailed industry and competitor analysis should be undertaken in order to assess the profit potential of the industry as well as likely competitor behavior in the near term (see Chapter 4).

But for industry analysis to have a context, a broader perspective is required. Numerous techniques are used to assess the environment, such as market research, econometric modeling, or speculations about the future based on trends in news articles (the method described in John Naisbitt's *Megatrends*). The environmental scanning method suggested here, developed by Professor David Jemison while at Stanford, yields much the same results as many sophisticated techniques, but it does so much more efficiently. As its starting point, the approach assumes that the top management team of a firm is constantly interacting with various constituents of its environment. Because each member of management tends to interact with constituents relevant to his or her function—financial managers see bankers, marketing managers see customers, production people see suppliers—the team as a whole continually scans most of the task environment. Thus, the top management team collectively should have a good appreciation of environmental trends. The key task, then, is to collect management's shared perceptions into a consolidated environmental analysis.

The analysis involves three steps: individual analysis, small-group discussion, and team consensus negotiation.

Each individual should go through the following thought process. Think of a major event in the past ten to twenty years or so such as the Watergate scandal of 1973. Now examine the developments since then—in terms of your company, your country, the world. Consider the fundamental changes that have occurred. Few predicted the world oil shock, simultaneous inflation and recession, test-tube babies, or the equivalent of a 1970 mainframe computer reduced to a quarter-inch chip. No one probably could predict all of these developments, but reasonable thought and analysis would allow an individual to discern some trends in his or her external environment.

Next consider the general environment in which your firm operates and, thinking ahead ten to twenty years, try to (1) identify the major environmental trends that will affect the firm's ability to survive and prosper, (2) estimate the anticipated date of the trend's impact on your industry and firm, (3) cite evidence to support your contention that this is indeed an important trend, and (4) rank the trends in descending order of importance. Here you might consider such questions as these: Are there recent political or social developments that will affect the industry or the firm? What economic conditions are present or are likely to develop that will affect the firm? What technological innovations or improvements are possible or probable that might affect our raw materials, production processes, products, or customers? How will these affect the way in which we or our competitors do business?

The next step is for each manager to share his or her perceptions with three or four other managers and for the group to arrive at some consensus regarding what the five most significant trends are for the company.

Finally, compare the group summaries. Frequently at this stage, you will find that several groups have identified different aspects of a common theme (for example, the changing demographics of the post–baby boom marketplace has implications both for selling services and for finding management talent). These themes form the basis for a consensus forecast.

The usefulness and efficiency of this method can be illustrated by the experience of a major law firm (call it Delta & Delta). Most observers recognize the increasing competitive nature of the legal profession and the major forces for change. Delta & Delta was initiating strategic management procedures at the same time that one of the professional organizations to which most lawyers belong established a future issues committee to identify and explore some of the major issues that would be confronting the profession. Consisting of senior partners from major firms and a leading academic in the field, the committee struggled for more than a year with the need for environmental scanning. During this time, the committee engaged the services of a variety of consultants—facilitators, futurologists, John Naisbitt's group, USC's Center for Future Research. The results of their 13-month effort was a list of ten major issues.

Delta & Delta, on the other hand, assembled its 13 top people with a facilitator for four hours and, using the method described here, produced a forecast of five key trends that mirrored the top five issues identified by the future issues committee. These included the increasing computerization of legal practice, the tendency of major clients to expand in-house counsel and rely less on the law firms, the reduced prestige of the profession in the eyes of laypeople, and increasing tax practice competition from CPA firms. These trends had major implications for the strategic management of law partnerships in the next decade.

The key to environmental forecasting is that most management teams have most of the information resources needed for good strategic thinking within their own ranks. The major task in strategic planning is to organize this information in a way that facilitates strategic decisions. One way to organize the environmental trends information is to create scenarios. As the following note on scenario planning indicates, scenarios are more accurate planning tools than those that rely on single-point estimates such as economists' forecasts of GNP growth, interest rates, or inflation. The reason is that point estimates focus on the *unknowable* (e.g., the exact level of inflation next year), whereas scenarios focus on the *inevitable*. As an example of forecasting the inevitable, consider the story told by Pierre Wack, former scenario-builder at Royal Dutch Shell: One can know in March how many homes will have to be evacuated in June from the banks of the River Ganges by measuring the rainfall in the mountains in February. X amount of inches of rain in February translates inevitably into Y feet of flooding at the mouth of the river in June.

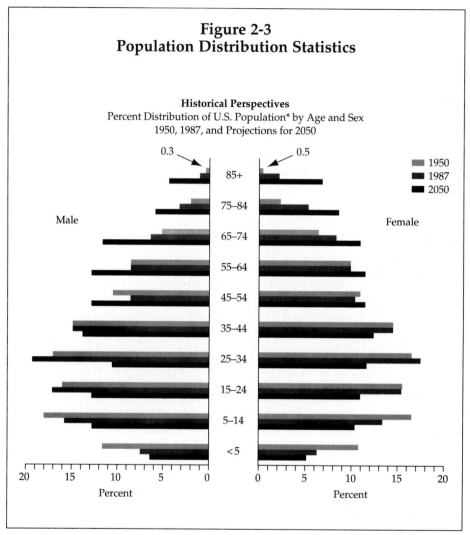

Figure 2-3
Population Distribution Statistics

Historical Perspectives
Percent Distribution of U.S. Population* by Age and Sex
1950, 1987, and Projections for 2050

*Including Armed Forces Overseas.
Source: Bureau of the Census, Current Population Reports.

Another inevitability, albeit less precise, is the level of population at a point in time several years out. Demographics translate births, deaths, in-migration and out-migration into population diagrams such as the one shown in Figure 2-3. These are derived from birthrate charts such as the one shown in Figure 2-4.

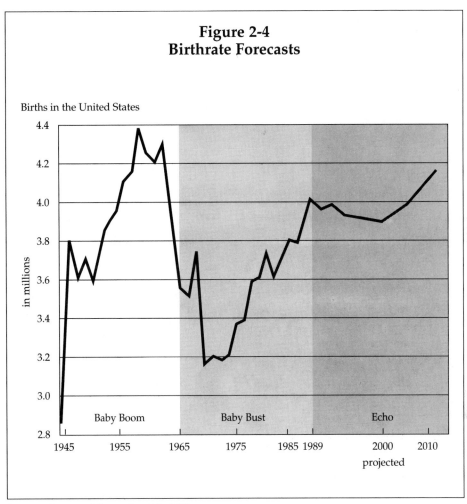

Figure 2-4
Birthrate Forecasts

Births in the United States

Baby Boom   Baby Bust   Echo

1945   1955   1965   1975   1985 1989   2000   2010

projected

Source: *Fortune*, November 29, 1993.

˒SUGGESTED READINGS˒

Aguilar, Francis J. *Scanning the Business Environment*. New York: Macmillan, 1967.

Bourgeois, L.J. "Strategy and Environment: A Conceptual Integration." *Academy of Management Review* 5 (January 1980): 25–49.

Celente, Gerald (with Tom Milton). *Trend Tracking*. New York: Warner Books, 1991.

Naisbitt, John. *Megatrends: Ten New Directions Transforming Our Lives*. New York: Warner Books, 1982.

Schwartz, P. *The Art of the Long View*. New York: Doubleday, 1991.

C
H
A
P
T
E
R

SCENARIO PLANNING | 3

With the environmental trends forecast as background, one can proceed to construct a scenario for the company being studied. The method is outlined in the following section.

NOTE ON SCENARIO PLANNING: AN ABRIDGED VERSION[1]

One of the major long-range planning tools developed and used during the past three decades is scenario planning. Scenarios were developed as alternatives to single-line and range forecasts, because those techniques often proved to be ineffective and inaccurate tools for developing strategic plans, especially during times of economic turbulence. Forecasts present specific, predictive answers to the question of what will happen in the future when all relevant variables have been taken into account. Scenarios, on the other hand, present several plausible but contrasting futures, which force managers to

---

[1]This note was prepared by John B. Bristow under the supervision of Professor Leslie E. Grayson and Charles R. Kennedy, Jr. The note is taken in large part from books by Grayson, *Who and How in Planning for Large Companies* (London: Macmillan, and New York: St. Martin's Press, 1987) and by Kennedy, *Political Risk Management* (New York: Quorum Books, 1987). Copyright © 1990 by the Darden Graduate Business School Foundation, Charlottesville, VA.

consider a range of economic and business possibilities when they are developing strategies. Because they have considered several plausible outcomes, managers will be prepared for the unexpected events of a turbulent economic environment.

Single-line forecasts are appropriate only for a stable world. A forecast is an authoritative statement; it places responsibility on its preparer and excuses the manager who accepts it from any fault or blame when errors in the predictions occur. The world, however, has never been as stable as people think. As managers became more and more aware of the uncertainties not addressed in forecasts, an alternative method of analyzing the future, a method that would address those uncertainties, developed. The result, scenario planning, is a systematic way of analyzing macroeconomic, sociopolitical, and technological changes that could occur in the "task environment," that is, factors external to the firm that affect its business. Scenarios are designed to deal with highly complex and uncertain issues. They also provide the basis for strategic contingency planning.

These trends and developments in planning approaches were summarized by Juach and Glueck (1988), as follows:

> "First-generation planning" means that the firm chooses the most probable appraisal and diagnosis of the future environment and of its own strengths and weaknesses. From this, it evolves the best strategy for a match of the environment and the firm—a single plan for the most likely future. Today's approach is called "strategic planning" or, more frequently, "strategic management." Strategic management focuses on "second-generation planning"; that is, analysis of the business and the preparation of several scenarios for the future. Contingency strategies are then prepared for each of these likely future scenarios.

Given the complexity and uncertainty of today's business environment, the mastery of sophisticated scenario-development techniques in the corporate decision-making process is crucial. Only through such techniques can a manager effectively plan and adopt a strategy that will allow the firm to compete successfully.

History of Business Scenario Planning

One of the first firms to develop a scenario-planning system was Royal Dutch Shell in the late 1960s and early 1970s. Shell's planners learned to distinguish between *predetermined events* and *uncertainties*. Predetermined events are those that have already occurred (or almost certainly will occur) but whose consequences have not yet unfolded. The planners realized that identifying predetermined events is fundamental to scenario planning. However, although there are always elements of the future that are predetermined, seldom are they enough to permit an accurate forecast. By listening to planners' analyses of various scenarios in store for the global business environment, including uncertainties, Shell's management was prepared for the eventuality—if not the timing—of the first oil crisis. Again in 1981, when other oil companies stockpiled reserves in the aftermath of the outbreak of the Iran-Iraq war, Shell sold off its excess reserves before the glut of oil became a reality and prices collapsed.

Comprehensive work on scenario development was also conducted by Hawken, Ogilvy, and Schwartz for SRI International in the late 1970s. In this case also, scenarios were not used as predictive tools; instead, the aim was to project alternative futures so as to make intelligent and responsible choices possible. The SRI study introduced the idea of trends that "drive" or determine alternative scenarios: their "drivers" were values, climate, the economy, energy, and food. Drivers are the elements, or building blocks, whose changes affect the outcome of a scenario. These pioneers laid the groundwork for scenario planning in the 1980s.

In the face of increased uncertainty, scenario planning has become more and more popular. Recent surveys suggest that around a quarter of major U.S. corporations use formal scenario techniques in strategic planning. While by no means universally accepted, planning on the basis of scenarios is expected to become even more important and widespread among corporations in the future.

Scenario Formulation

Techniques of scenario development vary from firm to firm depending on the sophistication of the company and the complexity of the environment. Many of the techniques employed share certain traits, however. A proposed generic approach to scenario development, based in part on the SRI work and in part on further work performed by Conoco, involves six discrete steps:

1. Select the company's business-specific interests.
2. Select key drivers.
3. Project the driver outcomes.
4. Combine drivers into scenarios.
5. Strategically assess the scenarios.
6. Adjust corporate strategy and plans to respond to possible scenarios.

The first step, selection of a firm's business-specific interests, involves identifying the key issues that affect the firm. These issues may be long term or short term in perspective, and they may be country specific or global in nature. These business-specific interests are, in effect, the issues that most concern the future of the firm and are, therefore, the issues executives see as the most relevant. For oil companies, these key issues involve the availability and price of oil. For large U.S. manufacturers, the key issue may concern the market demand for imported products. For international banks, the issue might be prospects for the international debt crisis. In each case, executives in the respective industries are attempting to formulate strategic plans for their companies based on their judgment regarding these key business interests. Of course, if scenarios are being developed with public-policy issues in mind, the planner should identify what specific government concerns are of interest.

The second step, selecting key drivers, requires much thought and a thorough understanding of the present situation. Drivers to be selected are the key environmental elements that affect the business or government interests. They are akin to independent variables that influence the dependent variables, which are the key interests in question. By their very role in the process, drivers largely dictate the scope and direction of subsequent analysis. A driver must meet two important conditions: it must have a direct and significant impact on business or government interests, and it must exert a strong degree of autonomous force on those interests. To assure these two conditions, the scenario developer must understand the past and present relationships of the various elements affecting the situation. Examples of drivers for an international bank concerned with the debt crisis would be Organization for Economic Development (OECD) growth rates, world oil prices, and real interest rates. For an oil company concerned with the world price of oil (note that a business interest for one group can easily be a driver for another group), key drivers might be physical ability of producers to produce and, again, OECD growth rates.

The third step, the projection of driver outcomes, is based on detailed analyses and common sense. Each driver should have two or three possible outcomes. The key consideration here is to ensure reasonableness in considering the outcomes of uncertain and predetermined events—the events that have occurred but whose effect may not yet be apparent. An example of such an event for a U.S. manufacturer might be a recent devaluation of a major exporter's currency: while domestic U.S. manufacturers have not yet been affected, they know with some certainty that this devaluation will affect their task environment and therefore must be considered.

In projecting outcomes of certain drivers, it is wise to state explicitly the assumptions made in developing the outcome, no matter how trivial they may seem. Assumptions can be as straightforward as assuming that a prime competitor will remain in the business or as uncertain as new technological advances. For example, a manufacturer might have growth in real gross national product (GNP) for the United States as one driver. Possible outcomes might be relatively rapid growth, a relatively slower but stable growth rate, and even a negative real growth rate. While an infinite number of outcomes are, of course, possible, it is best to limit the analysis to two or three contrasting outcomes. Otherwise, the process becomes unmanageable.

Combining the driver outcomes into scenarios, the fourth step, is an outgrowth or natural combination of projecting driver outcomes. This combination is not so much a discrete step as a convenient point for checking that driver outcomes provide a diverse enough range of possible futures. The key to combining outcomes is the test of reasonableness and internal consistency. For example, if one has two drivers, such as world oil prices and global GNP growth rates, a reasonable combination is to project that oil prices will rise in the midst of a strong and long-term economic expansion. The skill with which the scenario developer combines the various driver outcomes will determine the ultimate usefulness of the resulting scenarios.

At this point, the scenario-development exercise is essentially complete. The utility of scenarios also often breaks down at this point in many companies. After much analysis and research, many scenario-planning groups simply hand management a written summary of their work that lists several (or sometimes many) possible scenarios for the future. Management takes the "planning document" and contemplates the bewildering task of using this crystal ball to determine the future course of the company. Faced with this prospect, most managers simply discard the scenario information and rely on the same forecasting techniques they have long used.

Therefore, this is the stage at which scenario developers can add the most value to the planning process. It is through the strategic assessment of the scenarios (the fifth step), which entails projecting consequences of each scenario for the business-specific interests, that planners can assist the manager to the greatest extent. The planners' familiarity with the assumptions, the predetermined events, and the driver outcomes bestow on them a special expertise that can greatly aid top executives. By making clear the relative probability of the different scenarios and the means that the firm has at hand to affect the development of different scenarios, the planners can make the sixth and final step in the process much easier.

Scenarios and Competitive Strategy

The last step in the scenario-development process falls, as we have noted, primarily within the purview of the top corporate managers. Theirs is the responsibility and concern for formulating or adjusting corporate strategy and operating plans in response to the information presented in the alternative scenarios. Optimally, one strategy can be found that is best for all possible scenarios. Often, however, different strategies will be optimal according to which scenario develops. In such cases, top management can formulate strategies that maximize gain for most scenarios while minimizing risk. An alternative approach is to choose a strategy that gambles on the development of a certain scenario; such an approach is especially appropriate if a single scenario totally dominates the possibilities or if the benefits of guessing right far outweigh the costs of guessing wrong.

In short, the most difficult part of the scenario process is the translation of a set of scenarios into sound competitive strategy. Merely developing the set is not enough: the effort is wasted if the information the scenarios provide is not incorporated into the firm's strategy. Difficulties at this stage are related to the characteristics or behavior of the scenario developers, the executives, and the uncertainties examined.

Scenario developers, even if they have had past operational experiences, are often, by the very nature of their planning assignments, remote from day-to-day business problems. To be successful, however, the planners must be thoroughly familiar with the firm and the industry. A group of planners should represent as many disciplines and, in the case of multinational companies, as many nationalities as reasonably possible. The team must remain relatively small, however, to avoid bureaucratization.

Executives, in complete distinction from the planners, are often immersed in day-to-day problems. To spend time thinking about multiple futures and possible problems is difficult when one is confronted daily with problems needing immediate solutions. Faced with a choice, most executives continue solving problems as they encounter them without much thought to strategic issues. To overcome this constraint, planners must do some basic marketing. They need to ensure that their "clients"—the executives—get the information they need from the scenarios. Planners must also be sure to state the assumptions they have used, so executives can easily determine the basis on which the scenarios were built.

The final problem concerns the ability of management to handle uncertainty. Executives, like most people, want to know the future and the consequences of their actions. Many executives perceive scenarios not as giving them a range of choices but as offering them risks of error. The solution to this problem lies in the education of managers—making them more aware of the uncertainties and dependencies of their business. If planners present the assumptions and the drivers clearly, managers can easily see the sensitivity of the business interests to changes in the discrete elements. This understanding of the risks present will focus managers on the various options available to maximize their returns.

Translating scenarios into strategy can be accomplished in a number of ways. In any method, however, some selectivity is needed. A strategy built around one scenario is risky, but a strategy designed to ensure success under all scenarios, if possible at all, is usually expensive.

Porter (1985) has identified five basic approaches to dealing with strategy selection:

1. Bet on the most probable scenario.
2. Bet on the "best" scenario.
3. Hedge.

4. Preserve flexibility.

5. Influence outcomes.

Betting on the most probable scenario is the most common technique. To use it successfully, the firm must keep in mind the severity of the results if the scenario does not occur, the fit between the resources of the firm and the strategy required by the scenario, and the difficulty in modifying the strategy mid-course. In option 2, the "best" scenario, the firm designs a strategy for the scenario that gives the firm the most sustainable long-run competitive advantage—the highest upside potential. For this strategy to be successful, the scenario chosen must come to pass. In hedging, the chosen strategy should produce *satisfactory* results under all likely scenarios. Resulting gains may be suboptimal, but minimization of losses results in a large reduction in risk. Flexibility preservation is, in effect, a delaying tactic: the firm postpones significant commitments of resources that would lock it into a particular strategy. This strategy is primarily reactive; its cost may be the loss of strategic position to those firms that commit to a strategy earlier. It does reduce risk and waste, however, by delaying the commitment of resources. Constant monitoring of "trigger" elements is necessary to minimize the drawbacks of this approach. The final approach, one of influencing which scenario will come to pass, is the only truly proactive approach. The firm tries to use its resources, in lobbying, for example, to increase the probability that a particular scenario will occur.

The approaches listed here are by no means mutually exclusive. Prudent managers might choose to pursue several simultaneously or in sequence. A firm may be able to set policies in one area while preserving flexibility in another area. When deciding on which approach to follow, executives must keep in mind the probability of the scenarios occurring, the company's resources and competitive advantages, and likely competitor behavior in response to each option.

ˑSUGGESTED READINGSˑ

Grayson, Leslie E. *Who and How in Planning for Large Companies: Generalization from the Experiences of Oil Companies.* London: Macmillan, and New York: St. Martin's Press, 1987. See particularly Chapter 2.

Hawken, Paul, James Ogilvy, and Peter Schwartz. *Seven Tomorrows.* New York: Bantam Books, 1982.

Jauch, Lawrence R., and William F. Glueck. *Strategic Management and Business Policy.* 3d ed. New York: McGraw-Hill, 1988.

Kennedy, Charles R., Jr. *Political Risk Management.* New York: Quorum Books, 1987. See particularly Chapter 6.

Porter, Michael E. *Competitive Advantage: Creating and Sustaining Superior Performance.* New York: The Free Press, 1985. See particularly Chapter 13, "Industry Scenarios and Competitive Strategy under Uncertainty."

Schoemaker, Paul J. H. "How to Link Strategic Vision to Core Capabilities." *Sloan Management Review*, Fall 1992, pp. 67–81.

Schoemaker, Paul J. H. "Scenario Planning: A Tool for Strategic Thinking." *Sloan Management Review*, Winter 1995, pp. 25–40.

Wack, Pierre. "Scenarios: Uncharted Waters Ahead." *Harvard Business Review,* September–October 1985, pp. 72–89.

Wack, Pierre, "Scenarios: Shooting the Rapids." *Harvard Business Review*, November–December 1985, pp. 139–150.

INDUSTRY AND COMPETITOR ANALYSIS

The manager who confines external analysis to environmental trends forecasts and scenario building will soon confront a key limitation: the threats and opportunities brought on by general environmental trends are usually beyond the influence of the organization. In other words, a firm's response to the forecast or scenario is exactly that—a response. This puts strategy in the role of being reactive.

INDUSTRY ANALYSIS

An important development in strategic thinking was the 1978 publication of Michael Porter's "How Competitive Forces Shape Strategy" (reprinted in Exhibit 4-1 on page 82). Porter's approach to industry analysis took well-established concepts from industrial organization economics and made them accessible to business executives. This is important for two reasons. First, the approach presents managers with a framework and analytical tools that allow a disciplined economic analysis of their business environment. Second, it emphasizes a firm's immediate task environment by focusing on factors managers can influence. This is probably the most important, because now managers can conceive of strategy as shaping the firm's environment, rather than just reacting to it.

As you read Porter's article and use the concepts to analyze the cases in this section, keep in mind the following background on the industrial organization (IO) economics underlying the framework.

First, IO was conceived of and applied at the *industry level*—that is, aggregations of firms producing the same category of products (e.g., machine tools or furniture). It was useful for explaining and predicting how industry *structure* (number of firms in the industry, barriers to entry) and industry *conduct* (output, prices, inventory) would affect industry *performance* (profitability). The framework helped public policy makers decide, for example, if a particular merger would reduce the competitiveness of an industry (and thereby hurt consumers). Although useful at the public policy level in describing the behavior of entire *industries*, IO was not particularly well suited to analysis and action at the *individual firm* level. Porter's framework made the analysis of an industry accessible and useful to individual firms in making strategy decisions.

The second thing to keep in mind as you read the article is that the framework is based essentially on two questions: (1) Why are some industries inherently more profitable than others? and (2) Why are some firms within an industry more profitable than their peers?

The basis for these two questions is simple. We know that every economy consists of a variety of industries and that some are consistently more profitable than others. Therefore, the first question basically has to do with an **industry's attractiveness.** Porter's five-forces model helps explain why an industry is inherently profitable. The answer is critical if one is contemplating investing in a particular industry. It is even more critical if one plans to compete in that industry.

If we array these industries on a profitability line, as in Figure 4-1, we know that in any given year some industries, such as industry A, will outperform others, such as industry B. Why?

We also know, however, that points A and B are industry averages and that performance of firms *within* each industry are distributed around these averages. The distribution within each industry might look as in Figure 4-2.

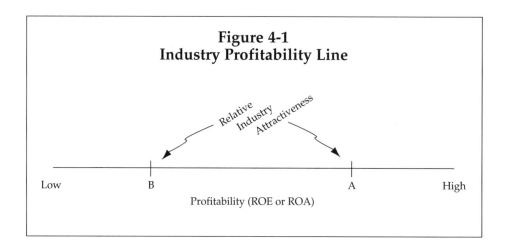

Figure 4-1
Industry Profitability Line

Relative Industry Attractiveness

Low   B   A   High

Profitability (ROE or ROA)

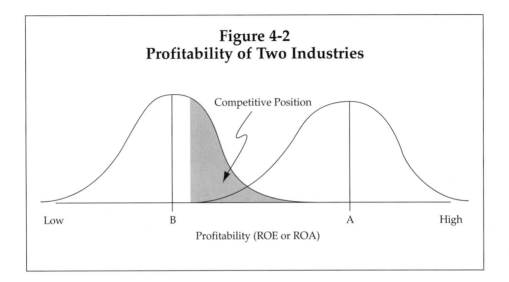

Figure 4-2
Profitability of Two Industries

Competitive Position

Low   B   A   High

Profitability (ROE or ROA)

The illustration suggests that some businesses in industry B, the so-called dog industry, actually outperform some in the so-called star industry, industry A (see the shaded area).

Thus, the article's second essential question concerns competition *within* industries, leading a manager to ask, "Given that I am in a particular industry, how can I **position my firm** such that I outperform my rivals?" Or, to use the economists' technical term, "How do I achieve *supernormal rents*?"

The issues of **industry attractiveness** and **competitive position** are critical because they will determine the value that a firm will create and the economic returns it will yield to investors.

To illustrate these ideas in concrete terms, Table 4-1 shows a rank ordering of 26 manufacturing industries by sales, and Table 4-2 shows the ranking by return on equity (ROE). (Both of these lists were computed from the 1991 *Fortune* 500 survey. The recession year, 1991, was chosen because industry performance differences are magnified.) Why does the pharmaceutical industry rank at the top of the list from year to year, while the apparel industry always ranks around the middle? Why have airlines (not shown) been in the cellar for the past several years?

If we look more closely at two of these industries, such as pharmaceuticals (average ROE of 23.1 percent) and metals (negative 17.2 percent), we can see the distribution of profits in Figures 4-3 and 4-4 (pp. 78, 79), respectively.

If we now superimpose the two graphs on the same scale, as shown in Figure 4-5 (p. 80), we see the phenomenon discussed earlier—namely, that a number of metals companies outperform as many as half of the pharmaceuticals. In other words, competitive position within an industry is more important to economic performance than is choice of industry.

Table 4-1
1991 Total Sales by Industry
($millions)*

Petroleum	$412,165
Motor vehicles and parts	273,541
Food	195,494
Electronics, electric equipment	188,302
Chemicals	162,140
Computer, office equipment	140,052
Aerospace	137,773
Forest products	100,195
Industrial and farm equipment	85,121
Scientific and photograph equipment	83,208
Pharmaceuticals	80,637
Beverages	56,581
Metals	56,367
Soaps and cosmetics	52,462
Publishing, printing	35,472
Metal products	33,347
Mining, crude oil products	31,094
Tobacco	30,835
Building materials	27,236
Rubber and plastic products	20,828
Apparel	18,205
Textiles	16,022
Furniture	14,169
Transportation equipment	6,754
Toys, sporting goods	3,791
Jewelry, silverware	860
TOTAL	$2,262,651

*Computed from *Fortune* 500 rankings, April 1991.

Table 4-2
1991 Industry ROEs

Pharmaceuticals	23.1%
Jewelry, silverware	22.0
Food	20.3
Soaps and cosmetics	16.1
Scientific and photograph equipment	15.9
Tobacco	15.8
Chemicals	15.2
Beverages	12.9
Metal products	12.0
Publishing, printing	10.6
Mining, crude oil products	10.6
Toys, sporting goods	9.0
Apparel	7.8
Petroleum	7.0
Rubber and plastic products	5.9
Forest products	5.9
Transportation equipment	4.0
Electronics, electric equipment	3.5
Textiles	3.0
Aerospace	2.6
Industrial and farm equipment	−4.8
Motor vehicles and parts	−6.0
Building materials	−10.2
Metals	−17.2
Computer, office equipment	−37.0
Furniture	−58.6

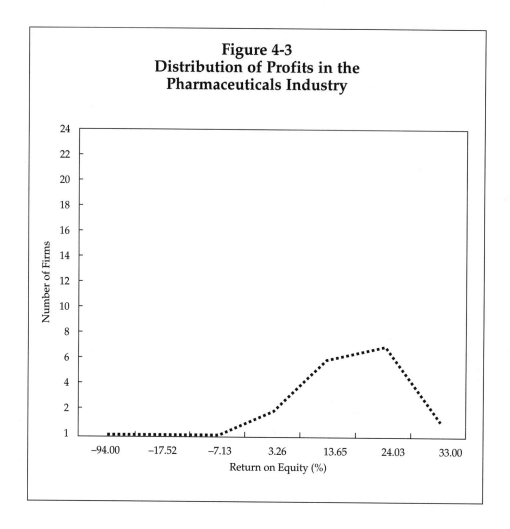

Figure 4-3
Distribution of Profits in the
Pharmaceuticals Industry

COMPETITOR ANALYSIS

One of the most critical faculties of a strategic thinker is the ability to understand and evaluate a competitor's capabilities and to anticipate how that competitor will react to one's own strategic initiatives. Studies of firms in the early years of the microcomputer industry found that one of the key characteristics that distinguished high fliers from failures was the ability to *know one's competition* like the back of one's hand.

Knowledge of competitors has become so important to strategists that they have even formed an organization specifically dedicated to the art and

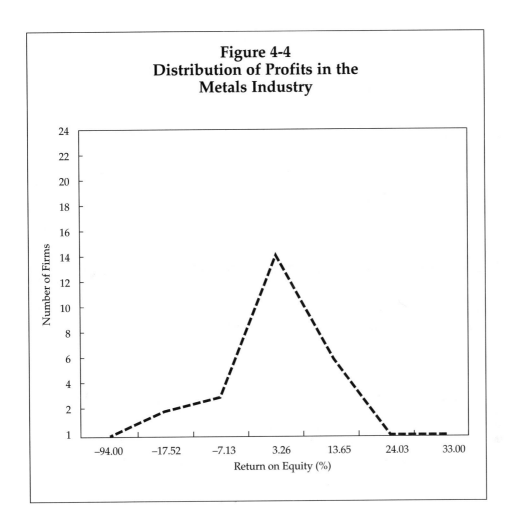

Figure 4-4
Distribution of Profits in the
Metals Industry

science of collecting and processing **competitor intelligence**, the Society of Competitor Intelligence Professionals.

Why is the study of competitors so important? The primary reason is that industries are dynamic—they are shaped by the strategies that firms pursue. Competition is an interactive process in which firms jockey for the best position within the five forces (see Exhibit 4-1, Porter Article, p. 82). Knowledge of the perceptions, intentions, and behaviors of other firms in the industry, therefore, becomes crucial.

The process of competitor analysis is to evaluate (1) the nature and success of the strategies each competitor might pursue, (2) competitors' likely responses

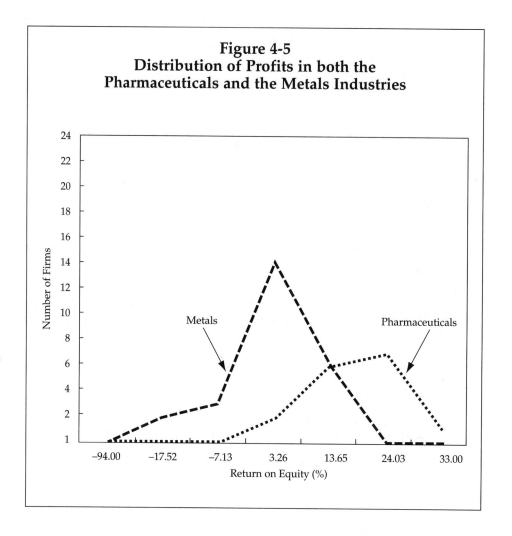

Figure 4-5
Distribution of Profits in both the
Pharmaceuticals and the Metals Industries

to the moves the strategist's firm might make, and (3) each competitor's likely reaction to the trends and scenarios in the industry that could occur.[1]

While much has been written on how to conduct competitor intelligence, a simple method of arranging the information is presented in Table 4-3. Once the questions in Table 4-3 have been answered, a manager should be able to profile a competitor and gauge its likely strategic behaviors and reactions with some degree of proficiency. (A set of summary questions for industry and competitor analysis is given in Appendix 1 at the end of Part II.)

---

[1]Geoff Lewis, Andre Markel, and Graham Hubbard, *Australian Strategic Management,* Sydney: Prentice-Hall, 1993.

Table 4-3
Assessing Your Competition:
Questions about Your Competitor(s)

In order to gauge what your competitors' reactions could be to any of your strategy options, you need to answer the following questions:

1. Identify the major players in your market (including yourselves). Do they fall into related groups?

2. How big and important is your market to each player—revenues, profit contribution, investment, strategic?

3. What is the strength of each player's commitment to this market? Is it financial or strategic?

4. What is each player's marketing objective for this market(s) in the short, medium, and long term?

5. Do each of the competitors really have a vision, or are they short termers (one to two years)?

6. How does each competitor make its investment decisions?

7. What are your competitors' key target market segments? Who are their key customers? What volume and dollars do these customers represent?

8. What are the key factors for success and their key defensible advantage?

9. What is their product strategy? How many products exist in each player's range, and how many are sold in your market?

10. What is their pricing policy and strategy? What do the competitors use as incentives (e.g., discounts)?

11. Will any of the players engage in a price war? Why? For how long? To what extent? What is their capacity to sustain one?

12. What is each player's distribution strategy? Do they sell directly to all their customers?

13. How does each competitor view **us?**

Exhibit 4-1
Porter Article

How Competitive Forces Shape Strategy

Michael E. Porter

The essence of strategy formulation is coping with competition. Yet it is easy to view competition too narrowly and too pessimistically. While one sometimes hears executives complaining to the contrary, intense competition in an industry is neither coincidence nor bad luck.

Moreover, in the fight for market share, competition is not manifested only in the other players. Rather, competition in an industry is rooted in its underlying economics, and competitive forces exist that go well beyond the established combatants in a particular industry. Customers, suppliers, potential entrants, and substitute products are all competitors that may be more or less prominent or active depending on the industry.

The state of competition in an industry depends on five basic forces, which are diagrammed in the Exhibit on page 87. The collective strength of these forces determines the ultimate profit potential of an industry. It ranges from *intense* in industries like tires, metal cans, and steel, where no company earns spectacular returns on investment, to *mild* in industries like oil field services and equipment, soft drinks, and toiletries, where there is room for quite high returns.

In the economists' "perfectly competitive" industry, jockeying for position is unbridled and entry to the industry very easy. This kind of industry structure, of course, offers the worst prospect for long-run profitability. The weaker the forces collectively, however, the greater the opportunity for superior performance.

Whatever their collective strength, the corporate strategist's goal is to find a position in the industry where his or her company can best defend itself against these forces or can influence them in its favor. The collective strength of the forces may be painfully apparent to all the antagonists; but to cope with them, the strategist must delve below the surface and analyze the sources of each. For example, what makes the industry vulnerable to entry? What determines the bargaining power of suppliers?

Knowledge of these underlying sources of competitive pressure provides the groundwork for a strategic agenda of action. They highlight the critical strengths and weaknesses of the company, animate the positioning of the company in its industry, clarify the areas where strategic changes may yield the greatest payoff, and highlight the places where industry trends promise to hold the greatest significance as either opportunities or threats. Understanding these sources also proves to be of help in considering areas for diversification.

CONTENDING FORCES

The strongest competitive force or forces determine the profitability of an industry and so are of greatest importance in strategy formulation. For example, even a company with a strong position in an industry unthreatened by potential entrants will earn low returns if it faces a superior or a lower-cost substitute product—as the leading manufacturers of vacuum tubes and coffee percolators have learned to their sorrow. In such a situation, coping with the substitute product becomes the number one strategic priority.

Different forces take on prominence, of course, in shaping competition in each industry. In the ocean-going tanker industry the key force is probably the buyers (the major oil companies), while in tires it is powerful OEM buyers coupled with tough competitors. In the steel industry the key forces are foreign competitors and substitute materials.

Every industry has an underlying structure, or a set of fundamental economic and technical characteristics, that gives rise to these competitive forces. The strategist, wanting to position his company to cope best with its industry environment or to influence that environment in the company's favor, must learn what makes the environment tick.

This view of competition pertains equally to industries dealing in services and to those selling products. To avoid monotony in this article, I refer to both products and services as "products." The same general principles apply to all types of business.

A few characteristics are critical to the strength of each competitive force. I shall discuss them in this section.

THREAT OF ENTRY

New entrants to an industry bring new capacity, the desire to gain market share, and often substantial resources. Companies diversifying through acquisition into the industry from other markets often leverage their resources to cause a shake-up, as Philip Morris did with Miller beer.

The seriousness of the threat of entry depends on the barriers present and on the reaction from existing competitors that the entrant can expect. If barriers to entry are high and a newcomer can expect sharp retaliation from the entrenched competitors, obviously he will not pose a serious threat of entering.

There are six major sources of barriers to entry:

1. *Economies of scale*—These economies deter entry by forcing the aspirant either to come in on a large scale or to accept a cost disadvantage. Scale economies in production, research, marketing, and service are probably the key barriers to entry in the mainframe computer industry, as Xerox and GE sadly discovered. Economies of scale can also act as hurdles in distribution, utilization of the sales force, financing, and nearly any other part of a business.

2. *Product differentiation*—Brand identification creates a barrier by forcing entrants to spend heavily to overcome customer loyalty. Advertising, customer service, being first in the industry, and

product differences are among the factors fostering brand identification. It is perhaps the most important entry barrier in soft drinks, over-the-counter drugs, cosmetics, investment banking, and public accounting. To create high fences around their businesses, brewers couple brand identification with economies of scale in production, distribution, and marketing.

3. *Capital requirements*—The need to invest large financial resources in order to compete creates a barrier to entry, particularly if the capital is required for unrecoverable expenditures in up-front advertising or R&D. Capital is necessary not only for fixed facilities but also for customer credit, inventories, and absorbing start-up losses. While major corporations have the financial resources to invade almost any industry, the huge capital requirements in certain fields, such as computer manufacturing and mineral extraction, limit the pool of likely entrants.

4. *Cost disadvantages independent of size*—Entrenched companies may have cost advantages not available to potential rivals, no matter what their size and attainable economies of scale. These advantages can stem from the effects of the learning curve (and of its first cousin, the experience curve), proprietary technology, access to the best raw materials sources, assets purchased at preinflation prices, government subsidies, or favorable locations. Sometimes cost advantages are legally enforceable, as they are through patents.

5. *Access to distribution channels*—The new boy on the block must, of course, secure distribution of his product or service. A new food product, for example, must displace others from the supermarket shelf via price breaks, promotions, intense selling efforts, or some other means. The more limited the wholesale or retail channels are and the more that existing competitors have these tied up, obviously the tougher that entry into the industry will be. Sometimes this barrier is so high that, to surmount it, a new contestant must create its own distribution channels, as Timex did in the watch industry in the 1950s.

6. *Government policy*—The government can limit or even foreclose entry to industries with such controls as license requirements and limits on access to raw materials. Regulated industries like trucking, liquor retailing, and freight forwarding are noticeable examples; more subtle government restrictions operate in fields like ski-area development and coal mining. The government also can play a major indirect role by affecting entry barriers through controls such as air and water pollution standards and safety regulations.

The potential rival's expectations about the reaction of existing competitors also will influence its decision on whether to enter. The company is likely to have second thoughts if incumbents have previously lashed out at new entrants or if:

• The incumbents possess substantial resources to fight back, including excess cash and unused borrowing power, productive capacity, or clout with distribution channels and customers.

• The incumbents seem likely to cut prices because of a desire to keep market shares or because of industry-wide excess capacity.

• Industry growth is slow, affecting its ability to absorb the new arrival and probably causing the financial performance of all the parties involved to decline.

Changing Conditions

From a strategic standpoint there are two important additional points to note about the threat of entry.

First, it changes, of course, as these conditions change. The expiration of Polaroid's basic patents on instant photography, for instance, greatly reduced its absolute cost entry barrier built by proprietary technology. It is not surprising that Kodak plunged into the market. Product differentiation in printing has all but disappeared. Conversely, in the auto industry economies of scale increased enormously with post–World War II automation and vertical integration—virtually stopping successful new entry.

Second, strategic decisions involving a large segment of an industry can have a major impact on the conditions determining the threat of entry. For example, the actions of many U.S. wine producers in the 1960s to step up product introductions, raise advertising levels, and expand distribution nationally surely strengthened the entry roadblocks by raising economies of scale and making access to distribution channels more difficult. Similarly, decisions by members of the recreational vehicle industry to vertically integrate in order to lower costs have greatly increased the economies of scale and raised the capital cost barriers.

POWERFUL SUPPLIERS AND BUYERS

Suppliers can exert bargaining power on participants in an industry by raising prices or reducing the quality of purchased goods and services. Powerful suppliers can thereby squeeze profitability out of an industry unable to recover cost increases in its own prices. By raising their prices, soft-drink concentrate producers have contributed to the erosion of profitability of bottling companies because the bottlers, facing intense competition from powdered mixes, fruit drinks, and other beverages, have limited freedom to raise *their* prices accordingly. Customers likewise can force down prices, demand higher quality or more service, and play competitors off against each other—all at the expense of industry profits.

The power of each important supplier or buyer group depends on a number of characteristics of its market situation and on the relative importance of its sales or purchases to the industry compared with its overall business.

A *supplier* group is powerful if:

• It is dominated by a few companies and is more concentrated than the industry it sells to.

• Its product is unique or at least differentiated, or if it has built up switching costs. Switching costs are fixed costs buyers face in changing suppliers. These arise because, among other things, a buyer's product specifications tie it to particular suppliers, it has invested heavily in specialized ancillary equipment or in learning how to operate a supplier's equipment (as in computer software), or its production lines are connected to the supplier's manufacturing facilities (as in some manufacture of beverage containers).

• It is not obliged to contend with other products for sale to the industry. For instance, the competition between the steel companies and the aluminum companies to sell to the can industry checks the power of each supplier.

• It poses a credible threat of integrating forward into the industry's business. This provides a check against the industry's ability to improve the terms on which it purchases.

• The industry is not an important customer of the supplier group. If the industry *is* an important customer, suppliers' fortunes will be closely tied to the industry, and they will want to protect the industry through reasonable pricing and assistance in activities like R&D and lobbying.

A *buyer* group is powerful if:

• It is concentrated or purchases in large volumes. Large-volume buyers are particularly potent forces if heavy fixed costs characterize the industry—as they do in metal containers, corn refining, and bulk chemicals, for example—which raise the stakes to keep capacity filled.

• The products it purchases from the industry are standard or undifferentiated. The buyers, sure that they can always find alternative suppliers, may play one company against another, as they do in aluminum extrusion.

• The products it purchases from the industry form a component of its product and represent a significant fraction of its cost. The buyers are likely to shop for a favorable price and purchase selectively. Where the product sold by the industry in question is a small fraction of buyers' costs, buyers are usually much less price sensitive.

• It earns low profits, which create great incentive to lower its purchasing costs. Highly profitable buyers, however, are generally less price sensitive (that is, of course, if the item does not represent a large fraction of their costs).

• The industry's product is unimportant to the quality of the buyers' products or services. Where the quality of the buyers' products is very much affected by the industry's product, buyers are generally less price sensitive. Industries in which this situation obtains include oil field equipment, where a malfunction can lead to large losses, and enclosures for electronic medical and test instruments, where the quality of the enclosure can influence the user's impression about the quality of the equipment inside.

• The industry's product does not save the buyer money. Where the industry's product or service can pay for itself many times over, the buyer is rarely price sensitive; rather, he is interested in quality. This is true in services like investment banking and public accounting, where errors in judgment can be costly and embarrassing, and in businesses like the logging of oil wells, where an accurate survey can save thousands of dollars in drilling costs.

• The buyers pose a credible threat of integrating backward to make the industry's product. The Big Three auto producers and major buyers of cars have often used the threat of self-manufacture as a bargaining lever. But sometimes an industry engenders a threat to buyers that its members may integrate forward.

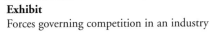

Exhibit
Forces governing competition in an industry

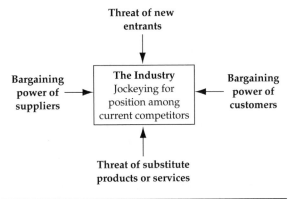

Most of these sources of buyer power can be attributed to consumers as a group as well as to industrial and commercial buyers; only a modification of the frame of reference is necessary. Consumers tend to be more price sensitive if they are purchasing products that are undifferentiated, expensive relative to their incomes, and of a sort where quality is not particularly important.

The buying power of retailers is determined by the same rules, with one important addition. Retailers can gain significant bargaining power over manufacturers when they can influence consumers' purchasing decisions, as they do in audio components, jewelry, appliances, sporting goods, and other goods.

Strategic Action

A company's choice of suppliers to buy from or buyer groups to sell to should be viewed as a crucial strategic decision. A company can improve its strategic posture by finding suppliers or buyers who possess the least power to influence it adversely.

Most common is the situation of a company being able to choose whom it will sell to—in other words, buyer selection. Rarely do all the buyer groups a company sells to enjoy equal power. Even if a company sells to a single industry, segments usually exist within that industry that exercise less power (and that are therefore less price sensitive) than others. For example, the replacement market for most products is less price sensitive than the overall market.

As a rule, a company can sell to powerful buyers and still come away with above-average profitability only if it is a low-cost producer in its industry or if its product enjoys some unusual, if not unique, features. In supplying large customers with electric motors, Emerson Electric earns high returns because its low cost position permits the company to meet or undercut competitors' prices.

If the company lacks a low cost position or a unique product, selling to everyone is self-defeating because the more sales it achieves, the more vulnerable it becomes. The company may have to muster the courage to turn away business and sell only to less potent customers.

Buyer selection has been a key to the success of National Can and Crown Cork & Seal. They focus on the segments of the can industry where they can create product differentiation, minimize the threat of backward integration, and otherwise mitigate the awesome power of their customers. Of course, some industries do not enjoy the luxury of selecting "good" buyers.

As the factors creating supplier and buyer power change with time or as a result of a company's strategic decisions, naturally the power of these groups rises or declines. In the ready-to-wear clothing industry, as the buyers (department stores and clothing stores) have become more concentrated and control has passed to large chains, the industry has come under increasing pressure and suffered falling margins. The industry has been unable to differentiate its product or engender switching costs that lock in its buyers enough to neutralize these trends.

SUBSTITUTE PRODUCTS

By placing a ceiling on prices it can charge, substitute products or services limit the potential of an industry. Unless it can upgrade the quality of the product or differentiate it somehow (as via marketing), the industry will suffer in earnings and possibly in growth.

Manifestly, the more attractive the price-performance trade-off offered by substitute products, the firmer the lid placed on the industry's profit poten-

tial. Sugar producers confronted with the large-scale commercialization of high-fructose corn syrup, a sugar substitute, are learning this lesson today.

Substitutes not only limit profits in normal times; they also reduce the bonanza an industry can reap in boom times. In 1978 the producers of fiberglass insulation enjoyed unprecedented demand as a result of high energy costs and severe winter weather. But the industry's ability to raise prices was tempered by the plethora of insulation substitutes, including cellulose, rock wool, and styrofoam. These substitutes are bound to become an even stronger force once the current round of plant additions by fiberglass insulation producers has boosted capacity enough to meet demand (and then some).

Substitute products that deserve the most attention strategically are those that (a) are subject to trends improving their price-performance trade-off with the industry's product, or (b) are produced by industries earning high profits. Substitutes often come rapidly into play if some development increases competition in their industries and causes price reduction or performance improvement.

JOCKEYING FOR POSITION

Rivalry among existing competitors takes the familiar form of jockeying for position—using tactics like price competition, product introduction, and advertising slugfests. Intense rivalry is related to the presence of a number of factors:

• Competitors are numerous or are roughly equal in size and power. In many U.S. industries in recent years foreign contenders, of course, have become part of the competitive picture.

• Industry growth is slow, precipitating fights for market share that involve expansion-minded members.

• The product or service lacks differentiation or switching costs, which lock in buyers and protect one combatant from raids on its customers by another.

• Fixed costs are high or the product is perishable, creating strong temptation to cut prices. Many basic materials businesses, like paper and aluminum, suffer from this problem when demand slackens.

• Capacity is normally augmented in large increments. Such additions, as in the chlorine and vinyl chloride businesses, disrupt the industry's supply-demand balance and often lead to periods of overcapacity and price cutting.

• Exit barriers are high. Exit barriers, like very specialized assets or management's loyalty to a particular business, keep companies competing even though they may be earning low or even negative returns on investment. Excess capacity remains functioning, and the profitability of the healthy competitors suffers as the sick ones hang on.[1] If the entire industry suffers from overcapacity, it may seek government help—particularly if foreign competition is present.

• The rivals are diverse in strategies, origins, and "personalities." They have different ideas about how to compete and continually run head-on into each other in the process.

As an industry matures, its growth rate changes, resulting in declining profits and (often) a shakeout. In the booming recreational vehicle industry of the early 1970s, nearly every producer did well; but slow growth since then has eliminated the high returns, except for the strongest members, not to mention many of the weaker companies. The same profit story has been played out in industry after industry—snowmobiles, aerosol packaging, and sports equipment are just a few examples.

An acquisition can introduce a very different personality to an industry, as has been the case with Black & Decker's takeover of McCullough, the producer of chain saws. Technological innovation can boost the level of fixed costs in the production process, as it did in the shift from batch to continuous-line photo finishing in the 1960s.

While a company must live with many of these factors—because they are built into industry economics—it may have some latitude for improving matters through strategic shifts. For example, it may try to raise buyers' switching costs or increase product differentiation. A focus on selling efforts in the fastest-growing segments of the industry or on market areas with the lowest fixed costs can reduce the impact of industry rivalry. If it is feasible, a company can try to avoid confrontation with competitors having high exit barriers and can thus sidestep involvement in bitter price cutting.

---

[1] For a more complete discussion of exit barriers and their implications for strategy, see my article, "Please Note Location of Nearest Exit," *California Management Review*, Winter 1976, p. 21.

FORMULATION OF STRATEGY

Once the corporate strategist has assessed the forces affecting competition in his industry and their underlying causes, he can identify his company's strengths and weaknesses. The crucial strengths and weaknesses from a strategic standpoint are the company's posture vis-à-vis the underlying causes of each force. Where does it stand against substitutes? Against the sources of entry barriers?

Then the strategist can devise a plan of action that may include (1) positioning the company so that its capabilities provide the best defense against the competitive force; and/or (2) influencing the balance of the forces through strategic moves, thereby improving the company's position; and/or (3) anticipating shifts in the factors underlying the forces and responding to them, with the hope of exploiting change by choosing a strategy appropriate for the new competitive balance before opponents recognize it. I shall consider each strategic approach in turn.

POSITIONING THE COMPANY

The first approach takes the structure of the industry as given and matches the company's strengths and weaknesses to it. Strategy can be viewed as building defenses against the competitive forces or as finding positions in the industry where the forces are weakest.

Knowledge of the company's capabilities and of the causes of the competitive forces will highlight the areas where the company should confront competition and where the company should avoid it. If the company is a low-cost producer, it may choose to confront powerful buyers while it takes care to sell them only products not vulnerable to competition from substitutes.

The success of Dr Pepper in the soft drink industry illustrates the coupling of realistic knowledge of corporate strengths with sound industry analysis to yield a superior strategy. Coca-Cola and Pepsi-Cola dominate Dr Pepper's industry, where many small concentrate producers compete for a piece of the action. Dr Pepper chose a strategy of avoiding the largest-selling drink segment, maintaining a narrow flavor line, forgoing the development of a captive bottler network, and marketing heavily. The company positioned itself so as to be least vulnerable to its competitive forces while it exploited its small size.

In the $11.5 billion soft drink industry, barriers to entry in the form of brand identification, large-scale marketing, and access to a bottler network are enormous. Rather than accept the formidable costs and scale economies in having its own bottler network—that is, following the lead of the Big Two and of Seven-Up—Dr Pepper took advantage of the different flavor of its drink to "piggyback" on Coke and Pepsi bottlers who wanted a full line to sell to customers. Dr Pepper coped with the power of these buyers through extraordinary service and other efforts to distinguish its treatment of them from that of Coke and Pepsi.

Many small companies in the soft drink business offer cola drinks that thrust them into head-to-head competition against the majors. Dr Pepper, however, maximized product differentiation by maintaining a narrow line of beverages built around an unusual flavor.

Finally, Dr Pepper met Coke and Pepsi with an advertising onslaught emphasizing the alleged uniqueness of its single flavor. This campaign built strong brand identification and great customer loyalty. Helping its efforts was the fact that Dr Pepper's formula involved lower raw materials cost, which gave the company an absolute cost advantage over its major competitors.

There are no economies of scale in soft drink concentrate production, so Dr Pepper could prosper despite its small share of the business (6%). Thus Dr Pepper confronted competition in marketing but avoided it in product line and in distribution. This artful positioning combined with good implementation has led to an enviable record in earnings and in the stock market.

INFLUENCING THE BALANCE

When dealing with the forces that drive industry competition, a company can devise a strategy that takes the offensive. This posture is designed to do more than merely cope with the forces themselves; it is meant to alter their causes.

Innovations in marketing can raise brand identification or otherwise differentiate the product. Capital investments in large-scale facilities or vertical integration affect entry barriers. The balance of forces is partly a result of external factors and partly in the company's control.

EXPLOITING INDUSTRY CHANGE

Industry evolution is important strategically because evolution, of course, brings with it changes in the sources of competition I have identified. In the familiar product life-cycle pattern, for example, growth rates change, product differentiation is said to decline as the business becomes more mature, and the companies tend to integrate vertically.

These trends are not so important in themselves; what is critical is whether they affect the sources of competition. Consider vertical integration. In the maturing minicomputer industry, extensive vertical integration, both in manufacturing and in software development, is taking place. This very significant trend is greatly raising economies of scale as well as the amount of capital necessary to compete in the industry. This in turn is raising barriers to entry and may drive some smaller competitors out of the industry once growth levels off.

Obviously, the trends carrying the highest priority from a strategic standpoint are those that affect the most important sources of competition in the industry and those that elevate new causes to the forefront. In contract aerosol packaging, for example, the trend toward less product differentiation is now dominant. It has increased buyers' power, lowered the barriers to entry, and intensified competition.

The framework for analyzing competition that I have described can also be used to predict the eventual profitability of an industry. In long-range planning the task is to examine each competitive force, forecast the magnitude of each underlying cause, and then construct a composite picture of the likely profit potential of the industry.

The outcome of such an exercise may differ a great deal from the existing industry structure. Today, for example, the solar heating business is populated by dozens and perhaps hundreds of companies, none with a major market position. Entry is easy, and competitors are battling to establish solar heating as a superior substitute for conventional methods.

The potential of this industry will depend largely on the shape of future barriers to entry, the improvement of the industry's position relative to substitutes, the ultimate intensity of competition, and the power captured by buyers and suppliers. These characteristics will in turn be influenced by such factors as the establishment of brand identities, significant economies of scale or experience curves in equipment manufacture wrought by technological change, the ultimate capital costs to compete, and the extent of overhead in production facilities.

The framework for analyzing industry competition has direct benefits in setting diversification strategy. It provides a road map for answering the extremely difficult question inherent in diversification decisions: "What is the potential of this business?" Combining the framework with judgment in its application, a company may be able to spot an industry with a good future before this good future is reflected in the prices of acquisition candidates.

MULTIFACETED RIVALRY

Corporate managers have directed a great deal of attention to defining their businesses as a crucial step in strategy formulation. Theodore Levitt, in his classic 1960 article in HBR, argued strongly for avoiding the myopia of narrow, product-oriented industry definition.[2] Numerous other authorities have also stressed the need to look beyond product to function in defining a business, beyond national boundaries to potential international competition, and beyond the ranks of one's competitors today to those that may become competitors tomorrow. As a result of these urgings, the proper definition of a company's industry or industries has become an endlessly debated subject.

One motive behind this debate is the desire to exploit new markets. Another, perhaps more important motive is the fear of overlooking latent sources of competition that someday may threaten the industry. Many managers concentrate so single-mindedly on their direct antagonists in the fight for market share that they fail to realize that they are also competing with their customers and their suppliers for bargaining power. Meanwhile, they also neglect to keep a wary eye out for new entrants to the contest or fail to recognize the subtle threat of substitute products.

The key to growth—even survival—is to stake out a position that is less vulnerable to attack from head-to-

---

[2]Theodore Levitt, "Marketing Myopia," reprinted as an HBR Classic, September–October 1975, p. 26.

head opponents, whether established or new, and less vulnerable to erosion from the direction of buyers, suppliers, and substitute goods. Establishing such a position can take many forms—solidifying relationships with favorable customers, differentiating the product either substantively or psychologically through marketing, integrating forward or backward, establishing technological leadership.

ANALYSIS OF
BUSINESS STRATEGY

C
H
A
P
T
E
R

5

Once the external analysis is complete, the strategist's attention can turn directly to the analysis of the company's strategy. In this chapter we will define strategy, explain how to identify a business strategy, and then discuss how to evaluate one.

DEFINITION OF STRATEGY

Ask 20 managers to define strategy and you will hear 20 definitions. Most of these, however, will share some key elements, such as:

- A plan for the future
- Setting a goal and the steps to reach it
- A method of facing competition
- A mission
- A path
- A set of integrated decisions
- A battle plan

What these definitions have in common is an orientation toward the future, a sense of deliberate action, and, to some extent, a notion of competitive rivalry. They correspond fairly well with the dictionary definition, which gives the origin of the word as the Greek *strategos,* or "the art of the general."

Figure 5-1
Intended and Realized Strategy

Intended Strategy ⟶ Realized Strategy

These definitions are all appropriate. However, they depict a particular aspect of strategy—that which is thought out in advance, preplanned, or otherwise deliberate or intentional. We might call this **intended strategy**. (One thing that will become clear as we discuss strategy is that the full meaning of the concept expands depending on the adjective we place in front of it.) Between the time intended strategy is formulated and some point in the future, say two or three years, activities to execute the strategy take place, and the company ends up with what Henry Mintzberg calls **realized strategy**[1] (see Figure 5-1).

When asked what percent of intended strategy is realized, executives will give estimates ranging from 10 to 30 percent. When asked, Why not 100 percent?, they usually respond with comments like these:

- Conditions changed.
- Customers didn't respond the way we had hoped.
- The (foreign) government changed the rules.
- We didn't have the resources in place in order to execute.
- The organization resisted change.
- The skills needed to execute were not developed in time.
- The plan came from a consultant, and we were not 100-percent committed.
- We really didn't think the strategy through clearly enough.

As a consequence, a proportion of intended strategy falls by the wayside and is essentially **unrealized** (Figure 5-2).

Additional comments from executives, however, are not stories of failure to implement, but rather stories of seizing opportunities:

- A competitor dropped out of the market, and we jumped into the void.

---

[1]Henry Mintzberg, "Patterns of Strategy Formation," *Management Science* May 24, 1978, pp. 934–948.

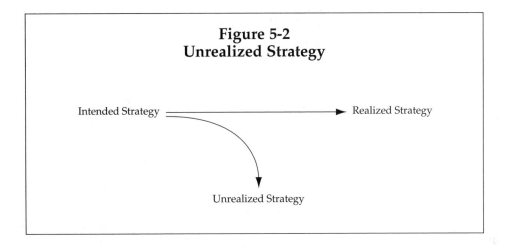

Figure 5-2
Unrealized Strategy

- We changed our product specs to respond to a customer request, and a whole new market (not in the original plan) opened up.
- A field salesperson received an inquiry from an unanticipated source, and we shifted our customer base accordingly.
- We made some lucky mistakes.

Or, as one executive put it:

- We just drifted. We really didn't have an (intended) strategy.

Comments like these suggest that much of strategy occurs by trial and error. In other words, strategy happens. To use Mintzberg's terms, strategy *emerges* from the daily activities of the company, with the consequence that **emergent strategy** becomes part of realized strategy (Figure 5-3).

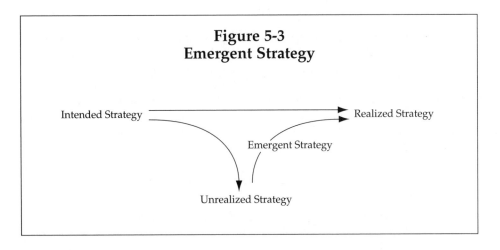

Figure 5-3
Emergent Strategy

The dynamics just described lead to a somewhat different definition of strategy:

Strategy is a pattern in a stream of decisions.

This definition has two advantages: One, it is based on action, not just intentions. Therefore, it makes strategy observable and tangible. (This also means a company can study its competitors' strategies without having to access secret documents.) Second, it defines strategy in a way that does not depend on a firm having gone through a formal planning and documentation process. Many firms do not have strategic plans, per se. But they do have realized strategies: they have been targeting customers, making investments, deciding on prices, designing products and services—all of which position the firm in its industry. As we will see in the following section, a key step in strategy analysis is to identify the decisions that make up this pattern.

LEVELS OF STRATEGY

Strategy is also a hierarchical concept—it takes place at three different levels: corporate, business, and functional. These levels correspond with the activities of managers in different parts of the organization.

- **Corporate strategy** is the set of explicit or implicit decision rules that determines what business(es) a firm will be in and not be in, and how it will allocate resources among them.
- **Business strategy** is how a firm develops and sustains a competitive advantage within an industry.
- **Functional strategy** is the set of decisions made in marketing, operations, finance, research and development, and human resources that supports the business strategy.

Corporate Strategy. *Corporate strategy,* typically located at headquarters, determines which industries the firm will compete in and which ones it will exit. For example, Sears chose to enter the insurance business when it acquired Allstate, and Coca-Cola chose to exit the movie business when it divested Columbia Pictures. Notice how this set of decisions corresponds with the first of Porter's two questions, that is, why is one industry more attractive than another (and, by implication, in which industry should we invest)?

Corporate strategy also has to do with how the corporation allocates both financial and human resources among its various businesses. Thus, given a collection of businesses, which ones should generate cash to fund the growth prospects of another; and which executives, scientists, and so forth should we assign to run which businesses? (The analytical techniques for corporate strategy will be introduced in Part III.)

Business Strategy.   *Business strategy*, typically located at the business unit or division level, determines how a company will compete within a given industry. In other words, given the corporate strategy decision to enter an industry, how does the firm gain and sustain a competitive advantage? Notice how this set of decisions corresponds with the second of Porter's two questions, that is, how does the firm position itself such that it outperforms its rivals? Business strategy decisions are usually the responsibility of the division general manager in diversified firms or the chief executive in single business corporations. Also, as depicted in the Astral Records case, it involves coordinating a number of decisions in the functional areas.

Functional Strategy.   *Functional strategies* are typically the responsibility of the heads (often vice presidents) of the various functions within a product division or business unit. So, while the marketing people make pricing, product, promotion, and distribution decisions (the "four Ps" of the marketing mix), operations people are making decisions about facilities, capacity, inventories, and work flow; financial people are managing debt, receivables, equity issues, and the like; research people are determining the balance between basic and applied research; and human resources executives are deciding on recruitment, pay, and promotion policies.

The challenge, as we shall see, is to weave all these decisions into a coherent whole in a way that creates competitive advantage. But in order to do the weaving, one must first understand the details of the unit's business strategy.

BUSINESS STRATEGY ANALYSIS

To many managers, and most strategic planners, the idea of thinking about and influencing the futures of their firms is an exciting one. Most managers are eager to set corporate goals and then to start formulating strategies that will help achieve those goals. However, two fundamental problems are inherent in approaching the strategic management task this way. First, most businesses are ongoing concerns and have set in motion certain activities that are a reflection of decisions made in the past. To think about the future without a thorough understanding of what is actually taking place may lead managers to formulate strategies that are either unrealistic or impossible to implement. Second, managers sometimes are tempted to engage in a strategic redirection of their firms without a thorough understanding of the *healthy* parts of their existing strategy. This tendency to throw the baby out with the bathwater can be thwarted only by making sure that management thoroughly understands the basis and the results of its present strategy.

All firms have a realized strategy, whether or not management has made that strategy explicit in advance. As we have seen, a firm's actual strategy can be quite different from what management thinks it is or from what it originally was intended to be. The process of delineating the realized strategy is called **strategy identification.**

This section will describe how to identify a business strategy. After this identification process is complete, then a manager can assess the quality of that strategy in order to ascertain which aspects of strategy might be candidates for change and which are certain candidates for retention. (Note that a perfectly acceptable outcome is for management to conclude that no changes are necessary. This process then results in validating an already sound strategy.)

IDENTIFYING YOUR FIRM'S BUSINESS STRATEGY

Strategy identification at the business level is a straightforward process. In essence, a business strategy is built on a set of functional strategies, representing the competitive weapons that a company employs to compete in a given industry. The way to identify a business strategy is simply to first go through each of the functional areas and identify what pattern of decisions have been made in each, as follows.

Marketing Strategy. *What* products or services are being sold by the corporations, to *whom* are these being sold, and *where* (in what geographic areas) are they being sold? *How* does the company's price compare with that of the rest of the industry? Is the company a price leader, or does it tend to match the prices set by others? What are the company's promotion and distribution strategies? Each of these questions should be pursued in detail. For example, the Sigma Consulting Company described in Chapter 1 had a marketing strategy of selling any set of problem-solving skills to any client, at any time, at any place. Its pricing strategy was to charge out their consultants' time at a multiple of four times the individual's hourly salary rate. In contrast with Sigma Consultants, most strategy consulting firms price their services at a multiple closer to five times the consultant's hourly salary rate. Therefore, Sigma would be considered a standard-rate pricer, whereas some of the specialized strategy consultants would be considered premium-rate consulting firms. Whether it is beneficial for a firm to be premium-priced is not an issue under consideration yet. What is important is that, in order to evaluate the quality of one's strategy, it is first necessary to recognize what, precisely, the strategy is and how it compares with the strategies of other firms in similar circumstances.

Operations Strategy. Here, management should consider the question of how it transforms inputs into outputs for the marketplace. For example, what kinds of facilities does the company use? Are they concentrated in one location, or are they dispersed over a broader area? What is the company's capacity strategy—does it build capacity in anticipation of demand, or does it wait until there is a backlog of orders before adding capacity? For example, Sigma Consultants always hired new professionals in anticipation of increased volume. In contrast, Delta & Delta would staff its tax practice with paralegal part-timers during the peak tax season and maintain a leaner staff during the rest of the year.

Is the firm's product or service made to order, or are inventories expanded to serve demand as it occurs? What is the company's strategy with respect to vertical integration? Does it source most materials in-house by integrating backward, or does it subcontract much of its production? For example, prior to its introduction of the SX-70 instant camera, the Polaroid Corporation managed with a low investment in plant and equipment by subcontracting most of its component manufacturing. In contrast, the Kodak Company was fully integrated; at one point it even owned a stockyard to provide the raw materials for some of its chemicals. What Kodak gained in bringing operating margins in-house, Polaroid gained in flexibility and the ability to change products quickly.

Financial Strategy. Although many firms are fairly explicit about the marketing and production strategies that they follow, some of these same firms are vague when it comes to articulating their financial strategies. Usually, this is because a firm just starting its operations pays attention to cash flow and meeting the payroll, but fails to pay close attention to its balance sheet. The identification of the financial strategy can help to assess how the firm is managing its financial resources.

Here, the company should identify its capital structure, how it uses its cash flow (does it pay dividends?), its strategy toward investment in plant and equipment (owning versus leasing), and how it attempts to enhance its stock price.

Research-and-Development Strategy. Firms vary considerably in the extent to which they include research and development as a salient component of their business strategies. For example, the average percentage of sales spent on research is approximately 10 percent in high-technology companies, whereas it might be as low as 0.6 percent in such basic industries as steel and cement. Nevertheless, each of these companies does have a strategy with respect to its activities that might generate new products or a new means of manufacturing its products.

The company should determine whether its research focus is primarily basic or applied. For example, the Polaroid Company was dedicated to the "perfection of photography," which implied a heavy allocation of its research budget to basic research in optics. In contrast, a company such as Crown Cork and Seal, which manufactures steel and aluminum cans, engaged only in a limited amount of applied research and was positioned as a "fast second" in implementing new developments. Crown Cork and Seal's management has felt that, as one of the smaller firms in the industry (in 1978 it was number four in sales and held 8.3 percent market share), it could leave the technological innovation to others.

Human Resources Strategy. The types of people hired to operate a company is not only a reflection of the other functional strategies (for example, all manufacturing done in-house implies more production and maintenance people on the payroll), but they also determine what kinds of *future* strategies can be pursued. Why? Because the human assets represent the capability set of the firm. (The notion of capabilities as a source of competitive advantage will be covered in Part V).

The relevant questions for human resources strategy are: How do we hire, train, evaluate, compensate, and promote (or discharge) people? For example, Procter & Gamble's famed brand management system—a competitive advantage—is fueled by a stringent recruiting procedure followed by rigorous training, evaluation, and promotion in a way that standardizes (some say, homogenizes) a high-performance cadre of marketing executives. Other questions include: How do human resource procedures differ for executives and for rank and file employees? How does the firm socialize new members? How does the firm communicate its strategy to employees?

A summary of these strategy identification questions is given in Appendix 2 following this chapter.

With the identification process completed, the manager should generate a statement of the firm's business definition. That is, How would you define your business in terms of product-market scope and overall economic mission? In an attempt to get to the core of the business, the manager should attempt to answer this question in as few sentences as possible. Examples of business definitions for a variety of firms are given in Table 5-1.

Having identified the components of the business strategy, the manager now has the raw material with which to evaluate the quality of that strategy.

EVALUATING YOUR FIRM'S BUSINESS STRATEGY

Disciplining oneself to go through the strategy evaluation process is important because only after gaining a thorough understanding of the strategy's quality can one know what elements of strategy should be changed and, equally important, *which elements of strategy are sound and should not be altered.* In addition, the evaluation process itself will suggest strategic alternatives.

The complexity of a corporation defies its being evaluated in any single dimension. As any security analyst knows, the quality of a company's stock must be judged on more than the historical performance of the firm; equally important are the firm's plan for the future, the quality of its internal resources, and its management.

Similarly, the strategy of a corporation is best evaluated by examining it through a variety of lenses. Each lens will give a different perspective and, possibly, different answers. It is only through the combined perspective that comes from looking at past results, future plans, and the riskiness inherent in

Table 5-1
Examples of Business Definition Statements

Crown Cork and Seal Company

The Company's business is the manufacture and sale of metal cans, crowns, aluminum and plastic closures and the building of filling, packaging and handling machinery. These products are manufactured in sixty-six (66) plants within the United States and seventy (70) plants outside the United States and are sold through our own sales organization to the food, citrus, brewing, soft drink, oil, paint, toiletry, drug, antifreeze, chemical and pet food industries. (Source: 1991 Annual Report)

Penn Mutual Insurance

Penn Mutual's Individual Insurance Line manufactures, markets, sells and continuously adapts profitable, superior, financially guaranteed products to businesses and high wealth individuals, while continuing to provide service and product opportunities for existing and similar policyholders.

We sell these products through agents and other distribution channels and back them with continuously improving service and support.

Bic Pen Corp.

Bic manufactures and distributes low-priced disposable pens, cigarette lighters, and safety razors. All of its products employ high-volume, precision plastic-injection technology and are distributed through mass retail outlets such as drugstore chains.

Boston Symphony Orchestra

The BS0 presents traditional programs of high-quality classical, symphony music to a select, wealthy, and well-educated segment of the public; it finances such programs by high priced subscriptions and large contributions from patrons. Related components of this strategy are a well-educated, loosely structured administration, a prestigious board of trustees, and a high-quality subsidized music school.

a firm's strategy that a strategist can assess the overall quality of the firm's strategic thrust.

Evaluation of Past Results

Peter Drucker has written that to survive and prosper, firms must both "do things right" (be efficient) and "do the right things " (be effective).[2] Evaluating the past results of a firm reveals whether the firm has been doing things right by giving a reading on the quality of the firm's past decisions. Looking at the past enables management to be objective about accomplishments and to be precise (because evaluating the past will illuminate whether specific targets have been met).

To evaluate past performance, we can look at the extent to which the company has attained certain objectives and how well the company has performed in relation to other firms.

In evaluating performance against objectives, the strategist must take a variety of objectives into consideration. The strategist could simply look at management's objectives and see if these have been met. However, a more rigorous evaluation would look at how well management is meeting the objectives of the corporation's other stakeholders. It is important to realize that not only are the objectives of management sometimes different from those of various other stakeholders, but also, even the objectives of the various stakeholders can conflict. For example, employees might have a different stake in the business than, say, stockholders or suppliers. Employees might value quality of working life and leisure time, which might reduce the efficiency of the firm, while stockholders might be seeking increased dividends and suppliers might want invoices paid rapidly. In a world of limited resources, satisfying all these demands on the firm's liquidity is clearly a delicate balancing act.

Evaluating performance against objectives is relatively straightforward: one must simply answer the questions, What are the company's major articulated goals? and, How has the business been performing with respect to these goals? The answers to these questions should generate a list of goals and a list of actual results to which management should attach some score (say, from 0 to 10) that reflects the degree to which that objective has been reached. An example of this has been given in Table 5-2, part A, which shows the self-evaluation made by the Delta & Delta law firm.

Stakeholder analysis, originated by General Electric and developed by Ed Freeman of the University of Virginia, is straightforward. In evaluating performance against stakeholders' objectives, management should ask the following questions: Who are our major stakeholders? What are their stakes with respect to our business? How well is our strategy meeting these stakes? Some of the stakeholders that might be considered and some of their possible stakes are as follows:

---

[2]Peter F. Drucker, *The Effective Executive*, New York: Harper & Row, 1966, pp. 1–2.

Stakeholder	Stake
Stockholders	Dividends, capital appreciation, safety of investment
Customers	Quality of products, variety, reasonable price, reliability, availability, delivery
Employees	Quality of working life, steady employment, decent wages, safety
Management	Career progress, compensation, excitement
Creditors	Timely payment
Suppliers	Timely payment, steady quantity contracts
Community	Clean air, employment, tax base
Government	Same as community (presumably)

Table 5-2, part B, gives an example of how Delta & Delta evaluated its strategy with respect to its stakeholders' objectives.

The second major way of evaluating performance gauges how well the company has done compared with its direct competitors. In the past, analysts tended to compare a company with its competition by means of a single criterion—financial performance. More recently, research in strategic performance has indicated that other criteria, such as market position and technological performance, are equally important. The key consideration is, at what stage in an industry's evolution is each criterion most appropriate? In the early stages, many companies attempt to develop their product design to satisfy customer needs and (they hope) set the industry standard. At this stage, technological criteria should dominate the consideration of how well the strategy is performing. In fact, it is quite possible that the overzealous application of financial criteria at this stage will prove to be the death knell for struggling new ventures or new projects.

At the middle stages of an industry's evolution, a company should attempt to grow big enough to establish economies of scale and, subsequently, lower product costs. These lower costs will be important as the industry matures and a shakeout takes place, because those companies that can compete with lower prices are more likely to survive than those that are still having difficulty keeping their cost structures in line. After some of the technological questions have been worked out in an industry, competing products start to become very similar and brands begin to compete on price. This shift has become evident, for example, in the personal computer industry, where a large number of firms were competing in 1982, each using different operating systems and hardware. By the end of 1983, however, two or three operating systems became standard, and three companies—Apple, IBM, and Commodore—emerged as the industry leaders, while such prominent firms as Texas Instruments and Osborne dropped out when the price competition became more intense and permanent than they could handle. Further shakeout resulted in only two standards by 1986: Apple's Macintosh operating system and Microsoft's IBM-compatible DOS. So, at the middle stages of industry evolution, criteria such as market share, market penetration, and price leadership become important.

Table 5-2
Evaluation of Delta & Delta Strategy

A.   What are your company's major articulated goals? (List them.) How has your business been performing with respect to these goals?

GOAL	RESULTS	SCORE
1. 430,000 billed hours	447,000 hours	10
2. 85% realization rate	83.2%	5
3. 14% net income	15%	10
4. Name recognition	Definitely improved	7
	Summary Evaluation:	⑧

B.   Who are your major stakeholders? (List them.) What are their stakes with respect to your business? How well is your strategy meeting these stakes?

STAKEHOLDER	STAKES	RESULTS/SCORE
Clients	Service satisfaction	8
	Price satisfaction	6
Partners	Compensation	9
	Personal and professional satisfaction	8
	Reputation	6
	Variety of work	4
Employees	Compensation	8
	Development/career/upward mobility	7
	QWL	2
Families	Visibility, presence at home (i.e., reasonable work week)	3
	Separate "career" from family	2
Profession	Quality standards	10
	Summary Evaluation:	⑥½

C. Who are your major competitors and potential (growing) competitors? How well is your firm performing compared to your competitors in terms of the criteria listed?

COMPETITOR	D&D RELATIVE FINANCIAL PERFORMANCE	D&D MARKET POSITION	D&D TECHNOLOGICAL PERFORMANCE	
			PEOPLE	PRODUCTS
1. Law firm AB	Lower	Losing position to AB	=	−
2. Big NYC firms	Same	Losing position	=	−
3. 4 to 5 locals	Better	Gaining	=	+
4. Other locals	Superior	Clobbering	+	+
Summary:	So-so to OK B	Not so good C−	A	C
Overall:				(B/B−)

D. How does your strategy "fit" with the major trends and discontinuities projected for your environment (refer to environmental analysis exercise)?

TREND	DATE OF IMPACT	HOW DOES STRATEGY MATCH OR MISMATCH?
1. Increasing computerization	1993	Have portable micros and new mainframe (score = 7)
2. Expanding in–house counsel	1990	Poorly (5)
3. Increased tax practice competition from CPAs	1993	Badly (3)
Summary Evaluation:		(5)

(continued on next page)

(continued)

E. How well do your company's internal resources or capabilities support your strategy? Do the following areas represent strengths or weaknesses with respect to your strategic posture?

Resource Area	Strengths (S) or Weaknesses (W) (Why?)	"Fit" with Strategy

1. Financial	W — Constraint on R&D investment
	W — Less able to subsidize
	    a. Discounts for new client acquisition
	    b. Overhead (unassigned people)
	    c. Hiring new specialists
		Low

2. Human	S — Strong "care factor" but less loyalty
	S — Some people willing to do less
	    sophisticated work
	W — No excess or slack; capacity constraint
	W — Unwillingness to engage in PD
	    (marketing)
		Medium

3. Technological	S — Tax knowledge S — Strong background in banking and automotive industries	High

4. Managerial	W — Lots of worker bees; "sole
	    proprietors"; not a "team"
	W — No entrepreneurial skills (e.g., don't
	    read *Inc.* magazine for leads)
		Low

5. Other
  a. Client base
 	
  b. Reputation
	
	S — Some prominent firms in area
	W — Most clients are too small
	Neither S nor W (has improved to
	    "average")
		
		Medium

It is not until the final, or mature, stages of an industry's evolution that the more traditional financial criteria become important. At this stage, most products have become fairly standardized and manufacturing technologies have stabilized. Market positions have, by and large, been established, and the surviving firms compete more along marketing or service dimensions than along technological breakthroughs and product development. At this point it makes sense to evaluate a strategy in terms of return on investment, stock price, return and sales, and other profitability measures. A summary of the relationship between industry stage and evaluation criteria is given in Table 5-3.

A straightforward way for management to evaluate its strategy against those of competitors is to address the following questions: Who are our major competitors and potential competitors? How is our firm performing compared with the others in terms of financial performance, market position, and technological performance? By listing a company's competitors and comparing the company along each of the three dimensions, management will produce a picture of how well the firm has been performing against its competition. An example of Delta & Delta's evaluation of its performance compared to relative competitors is given in Table 5-2, part C.

By evaluating the company's past performance, management will have judged the extent to which a company has been "doing things right," to use Drucker's term. But a look at the past is not sufficient. A firm must also make an assessment of how well the strategy will perform in the future. In this case, we want to look at what Drucker has termed "doing the right things." To

---

Table 5-3
Industry Stage and Strategy
Evaluation Criteria

INDUSTRY STAGE	CRITERIA
I. Embryonic	Technology leadership → establish product viability; set the industry standard or at least brand reputation
II. Growth	Market share → experience curve economies; establish cost position for the shakeout associated with the next stage
III. Maturity	Profitability measures → return on investment, etc.; firms are competing on price, marketing and service, rather than on technology, product features, or product development
IV. Decline	Cash flow → cost control

make this assessment, we examine the consistency of the strategy along a variety of dimensions.

Tests of Consistency

As we have seen, strategy is a multifaceted set of activities that a company performs at any given time. In order to assess the degree to which these activities are helping to move the company in a healthy and appropriate direction, two tests of consistency must be applied: tests of external consistency, or how well the strategy matches the environment, and tests of internal consistency, or how well the pieces of the strategy are mutually reinforcing. One way to think of the tests of internal and external consistency is to refer back to Figure 1-2 (Chapter 1, page 9), where performance was portrayed as the outcome of the firm's "fit" achieved between the firm's strategy, environment, and internal resources.

External Consistency. **External consistency** is the degree to which the strategy fits the environmental trends that have been identified during the forecasting phase of the strategic management process (see the upper part of Figure 1-2). In essence, one must ask the following questions: How does our strategy "fit" with the major environmental trends we have projected? How does the strategy fit with the changing values of the various stakeholders? (See Table 5-2, part D, for the Delta & Delta example.) When Procter & Gamble assessed the demographic trends indicating a lower birth rate in the United States, it concluded, logically enough, that a continued reliance on the baby market for its Pampers brand disposable diapers was inconsistent with the prevailing trends. However, if we were to apply the test of consistency to Procter & Gamble's present strategy of marketing Pampers (renamed "Depends") to incontinent patients, particularly in rest homes, we would conclude that there is a significant logic to entering a market (basically, people age 65 and over) that is expected to grow over the foreseeable future. Similarly, when Sigma Consultants made the assessment that the consulting industry was becoming segmented and that the health care market was emerging as a significant segment, the test of external consistency would have indicated that the present strategy of undifferentiated marketing to all possible client bases was inconsistent with those prevailing trends.

The second test of external consistency involves assessing how the strategy stacks up against the five forces identified in the industry analysis. Is the strategy positioned to take advantage of increased or decreased demand in various buyer segments? Has the firm built switching costs into its buyers' relationships with the firm or its products? For example, once an organization standardizes on a particular word processor across the personal computers in its offices, it is nearly impossible to convince it to switch to an alternative—at minimum, the cost of retraining employees would be too high. Similarly, how has the strategy dealt with supplier power, threat of entry, or threat of substitutes? Has it built enough differentiation against its competitors (see the next section) to maintain a distinctive and protected position in the industry?

Internal Consistency. **Internal consistency** refers to the fit between the strategy and the competencies and resources available within the firm, as well as the fit among the functional strategies themselves. At the business level, it is this latter fit among the functional strategies that underlies the concept of synergy.

In order to test the consistency of the strategy with competencies and resources, management should conduct a resource audit. A **resource audit** can be conducted at two levels—global and specific. At the global level, it is important for management to identify its firm's *core competence;* that is, what factor or set of factors distinguishes the firm from its primary competitors and makes its products or services attractive to customers? For example, does the firm have a unique relationship with suppliers (say, proximity), the ability to deliver on time, or new product development capabilities? Every firm, no matter how seemingly homogeneous its industry, has *some* characteristic that has allowed it to survive in the marketplace. For example, Delta & Delta delivered close partner-client contact to its medium-size business clients. This contrasted with the typical big law-firm practice, where a partner made the initial sale to a large client but most of the ensuing client contact was carried out by midlevel managers. Delta & Delta's core competence was its ability to foster strong personal ties with its clients, resulting in a level of client loyalty unusual in the industry. The importance of articulating a company's core competence is that it forms the foundation for achieving a competitive advantage within an industry and for evaluating the potential for synergies with other businesses in a corporation's portfolio.

At the specific level, management should identify the firm's strengths and weaknesses in at least six areas: financial, human, physical, technological, managerial, and market position. A *financial* analysis is probably the easiest to conduct because the tools are well developed and the measures are relatively objective. In addition, standards of comparison exist for each industry; a firm can assess its relative liquidity, for example, as compared with the average and top and bottom quartiles of its industry, using such publications as Robert Morris Associates and Dun & Bradstreet.

Although most managers believe people to be their company's most important asset, *human* resources are probably the most difficult to assess. Embodied in human resources are the more tangible aspects of investments made in people, such as recruiting, training programs, and experience. But management must also assess the more intangible aspects of human resources, such as loyalty and commitment, creativity, and willingness to cooperate or to adopt new technologies or work methods.

In contrast, *physical* resources are the most tangible aspects of a corporation's assets. One can examine plant and equipment, buildings, and other facilities to determine their condition and adequacy for the volume and nature of activity taking place. Equally important are such factors as the location and adaptability of physical facilities to more than one kind of production.

In assessing *technological* resources, management must ask whether the technology embodied in the acquisition, production, and delivery of the product or service is state of the art and therefore vulnerable to bugs; standard for the industry and therefore tried and tested; or relatively old and therefore perhaps approaching obsolescence. Another dimension to examine is the source of new technology and its application within the firm. That is, are technological changes driven by customer requests, indicating managerial adaptivity to the marketplace, or are they driven by creative forces within the firm? Conversely, a firm's technology can be a reflection of a commitment to the past, but to be "behind the times" technologically may be a real weakness. Finally, the firm should assess the degree of flexibility embodied in its technology. For example, the steel industry has been saddled with assets that are dedicated to the production of steel and are not adaptable to other uses. By contrast, some electronics companies have a job-shop orientation, so they can adapt their technology to new products.

When assessing *managerial* resources, it is essential to cast an unbiased eye on such factors as the skills, level of experience, and company loyalty among management. For example, many new high-technology companies are strong on the engineering side but deficient in marketing. Both Apple and Atari recognized this deficiency, and, as a reflection, each hired CEOs with consumer product and marketing backgrounds in 1983. Similarly, both IBM and Kodak went outside for CEOs in 1993.

In addition to the resource areas mentioned, a company may want to evaluate such intangible resources as market position, brand identification, or patent position.

The resource audit should allow management to answer the following questions: How well do the company's resources or capabilities support management's strategy? Do they represent strengths or weaknesses with respect to the company's strategic posture? Here one should list the resources (financial, human, etc.), identify whether and why each resource is a strength or a weakness, and determine whether this resource represents a fit with that company's strategy. An example of Delta & Delta's evaluation of consistency between the business strategy and internal resources is given in Table 5-2, part E.

To look at the fit of the functional strategies with each other, management should return to the strategy identification procedure and ask, To what extent do the various functional strategies reinforce each other, or detract from each other? For example, the CALMA Corporation, a CAD/CAM manufacturing subsidiary of the General Electric Company, was spending upward of $20 million a year on R&D for new software. Marketable new products, however, originated not in the lab but through sales engineers' interactions with client user groups. Meanwhile, the R&D budget was increasing annually. Unfortunately, this example of marketing and R&D strategies out of synchronization is not unique. As a company increases in complexity, it is not unusual for the various components of the business—its functional departments—to start working at cross purposes. This sometimes results from rewarding different functional managers for different types of behavior. For example, salespeople rewarded according to the volume of sales they generate might strive for sales by making promises to clients that the production department cannot fulfill. Conversely, a production department that is geared toward making standardized products might not be responsive to the custom design promises salespeople made to customers.

Some companies rate high on tests of both internal and external consistency, and these high ratings generally translate into high performance evaluations as well. For example, the Crown Cork and Seal Company thrived financially in what was essentially a commodity industry by managing all of the components of its strategy with precision. By exiting from market segments where decreasing metal can usage was the trend, as in motor oil, and concentrating primarily in the areas where growth was expected (soft drinks and beer), Crown Cork and Seal positioned itself exclusively in the growth part of the market.

Clearly, however, shifting target markets is not enough, because the big competitors are free to do the same thing. This is where the internal and external tests of consistency come into play. Traditionally, the only way to differentiate a company in a commodity industry is by price. Crown Cork and Seal, however, differentiated itself from its competition by maintaining excess capacity so that it could meet surges in customer demand, thereby alleviating customers' inventory needs. In addition, the company was alone in providing technical help on customers' production problems, thereby becoming a problem solver as well as a can provider. Because it was dealing in such "hard-to-hold" products as carbonated beverages and aerosols, the problems of packaging these products were considerable. By providing flexibility in delivery as well as technical advice to clients in the growth segment of the can consuming market, Crown Cork and Seal was able to charge a premium price and avoid the price competition game. The company also followed a "fast second" R&D strategy, in which it would quickly adopt new technological innovations, after allowing other firms to make the initial investment. This made for lower R&D expenditures and, therefore, lower overhead. While Crown Cork and Seal's competitors were using the cash generated by their business to expand into unrelated diversification, Crown Cork and Seal repurchased stock, resulting in steadily increasing earnings-per-share figures.

Note that the marketing strategy of fast delivery and flexibility was consistent with the production strategy of holding excess capacity to meet surges in demand; the technical service component of the marketing strategy was consistent with the fast-adoption R&D strategy; and the premium price marketing strategy was consistent with the financial strategy of generating sufficient margin to provide the cash for repurchasing stock shares. All of these strategies had a high degree of internal consistency, and all were consistent with the trends in the environment and the structure of the industry. As a result, Crown Cork and Seal regularly ranked at the top of the industry in financial returns to investors, as well as growth. This company is an example of how (when strategy is uniformly consistent) a firm can become a well-oiled machine that gathers momentum and builds competitive strength. Crown Cork and Seal's position as the leading performer in the metal can industry has been unassailed for the last 36 years, an enviable record for any strategic manager.

Evaluation of Strategy Flexibility and Risk

Having addressed the question of how well a company's strategy fits with the external trends of the environment and industry and how well the internal parts of the strategy fit with and reinforce each other, a company should ask where its strategy has the most flexibility or inflexibility and how this translates into a risk profile. For example, a strategy that relies on heavy capital investment and assets that are dedicated to a particular type of product may find itself in a position where it cannot exit from an industry or market if conditions should so warrant. Such has been the case for the American steel industry; the closing of steel mills in many northeastern industrial areas is an indication of this difficulty. In contrast, a company such as Crown Cork and Seal found that it could take its old technology for manufacturing tin-plated steel cans and export them to new markets in less developed countries while investing at the same time in the newer aluminum can technology in the United States. Crown Cork and Seal is betting that the market and technological development overseas will lag behind that of the United States and that whenever domestic conditions warrant, the company will have the flexibility of a "technological rollout" to the overseas locations.

In assessing the flexibility of its strategy, a company should question the degree of risk its strategy presents. Traditionally, most such discussions have considered whether or not a company is facing financial risk—risk of bankruptcy, illiquidity, or, from the stockholders' standpoint, earnings fluctuations. But this is just one dimension of risk. Other elements that a firm should consider are the degrees to which it is facing business, competitive, and managerial risks.

Business Risk. *Business risk* refers to the degree to which the company lacks the capability to manufacture and sell a product to present or new markets. It also includes the question of whether there is sufficient customer demand for the product under consideration.

When evaluating a proposed strategy, business risk should also be assessed in terms of the strategy's downside potential and the possible impact of a failing strategy on the firm as a whole. The important dimensions are the strategy's consequentiality, pervasiveness, and revocability. *Consequentiality* refers to the potential negative impact of failure—for example, what percentage of the corporate funds are committed, or how might results affect corporate reputation? IBM's initial introduction of the personal computer (PC) was a relatively small financial commitment, but its failure to hold market share certainly damaged Big Blue's corporate image. By contrast, General Motors' decision to form a separate company to introduce the Saturn had enormous financial consequences because of the huge investment required. *Pervasiveness* refers to how much of the firm becomes involved in the strategy. IBM, by relegating the PC effort to a separate organizational unit in Florida, kept pervasiveness low—an initial failure would be isolated from the firm's core activities. *Revocability* reflects the firm's ability to back out if the market for a new business fails to develop as planned. Polaroid's entry into the SX-70 market was virtually irreversible, given its large investment in specialized plant and equipment. In contrast, IBM sourced most of its PC components externally and entered the business primarily as an assembler—in the early days, any single component of the PC hardware strategy was revocable. In sum, one could conclude that the IBM PC entry strategy had relatively low business risk: IBM had the technical skills, the market was there, and consequentiality, pervasiveness, and irreversibility were all relatively low. IBM's primary risk was to its reputation. Once PCs dominated the computer business, however, the equation changed dramatically. Consequentiality and pervasiveness went up, and revocability was limited.

Competitive Risk. *Competitive risk* refers to whether the present competition will retaliate against any moves being made or contemplated by the company and, equally important, the likely intensity of this retaliation. For example, when Kodak entered the instant camera market, it had severely underestimated the extent to which Polaroid would retaliate by introducing a barrage of new products at lower prices. Kodak found itself caught in a losing price war, which depressed corporate earnings for a two-year period. The assessment of competitive risk is where strategic planning frequently is deficient. Most companies not only underestimate the extent to which present competitors will retaliate against their contemplated strategic moves, but they also underestimate the extent to which new entrants from unanticipated corners might crop up.

Managerial Risk. *Managerial risk* has two components. First, one must consider whether management has the skills, capability, and longevity to execute a particular strategy. For example, although Crown Cork and Seal constantly achieved increased earnings per share, its stock price did not show a healthy price/earnings ratio. The primary reason was the age of John Connolly, the company's president. As of 1989, Connolly, at 84 years of age, was still running the firm, and it was not yet clear that he had groomed a successor. It was probably this last factor that heightened analysts' perceptions of managerial risk for the company, and it consequently dampened enthusiasm for Crown Cork and Seal as a long-term investment.

The second aspect of managerial risk relates to management's enthusiasm for a particular strategy, given the values of the top management team. Sometimes an "ideal" strategy can be worked out on paper but, for whatever reason, does not conform to the true predilections of top management and will not be carried out with as much energy as might otherwise be the case. (Chapter 10 addresses this aspect of strategy implementation.)

Having analyzed the quality of a company's strategy, both by looking at past performance against a variety of criteria and applying various tests of consistency, it is evident that no one technique of strategy evaluation is sufficient because each approach might yield a different result. For example, a strategy that may have been successful in the past may be ill-equipped to provide healthy returns in the future for any number of reasons. It may be out of sync with the trends in the environment, management may be approaching retirement age without having groomed successors, or the plant may be aging. The approaches presented here provide several lenses through which to evaluate a strategy. Management must take all of these evaluations into consideration when making a summary evaluation of the quality of the current strategy. A useful way of summarizing and synthesizing all of these evaluations is to generate a new statement of the firm's distinctive competence and competitive advantage. Having gone through the above analytical steps, management is often able to generate a rich statement of the firm's business definition and its strengths and weaknesses. After completing the strategy evaluation described in this section, Delta & Delta generated the strategy evaluation summary shown in Table 5-4. Notice how the statement encompasses consideration for fit with the external environment, as well as internal resources, and lends some insight into areas that Delta & Delta might wish to address in charting any new strategy.

A summary of this strategy evaluation framework is given in Appendix 3.

SOURCES OF COMPETITIVE ADVANTAGE

Some elements of the concept of competitive advantage have already been introduced in the resource audit, evaluations of flexibility and risk, and the strategy evaluation summary. This section will introduce some additional concepts of competitive advantage.

A firm's relative financial performance in its industry is determined by its competitive advantage. There are two elements of competitive advantage: *source* and *scope*. **Sources** include **cost leadership** (lower relative total costs) and **differentiation** (unique benefits that attract a price premium). Note that the first source is *cost* leadership, not necessarily *price* leadership. Price is a management decision. Cost is a position attained through both numerous decisions (e.g., capacity expansion for economies of scale) and results compared to competitors.

Table 5-4
Delta & Delta Strategy Evaluation Summary

Delta & Delta is a profitable firm, but a susceptible one: the loss of one or two key clients could put it in the red. Because of compensation bonus criteria that reward billed time, it often backs off from investing in practice development (marketing). There are talented, marketing-oriented people at all levels who get along, but who are not really "Delta & Delta loyal," although there is a high level of open communication. The company's "run-lean" philosophy has been a problem and could continue to be one.

It is a tax-oriented office, with above-average skills in the banking, automotive, and manufacturing industries. Client base includes some plums, but not enough to be an asset in getting more. Delta & Delta's reputation has improved; however, the company is still sole-proprietor-oriented with few entrepreneurial skills.

Scope refers to where the competitive advantage is applied: **across-the-board** implies competing across a broad range of products or market segments (such as Sigma's "we will sell anything to anybody, anywhere"); **focus** means competing in only a particular segment or with a narrow product line. For example, Crown Cork and Seal sold primarily two-piece, tin-plated steel cans (product focus) to the beer and soft-drink markets (market focus).

These two elements of competitive advantage form a matrix, as shown in Figure 5-4.

In presenting the framework from which Figure 5-4 is adapted, Porter suggests that a firm can pursue only one of the two sources of competitive advantage. Attempts to try both risks getting "stuck in the middle." His logic is that differentiation is costly, and that cost leadership requires foregoing the operating costs associated with differentiation (e.g., product bells and whistles, added service, more variety of and shorter production runs, and increased advertising to create difference in the mind of the consumer).

Recent experience, however, indicates that both may be necessary. Such is the power of focused factories that deliver variety at low cost. Crown Cork and Seal delivered both low cost through focus (it had almost 50 percent of the industry capacity in two-piece steel cans as well, so it also had experience-curve cost advantages) *and* differentiation through technical service and rapid delivery. Ansell, a division of Pacific Dunlap in Australia, is the world's largest producer of only four latex products: surgical gloves,

Figure 5-4
Source and Scope of Competitive Advantage

	Source	
	Cost Leadership	Differentiation
Across-the-Board		
Focus •Product •Market		

Scope

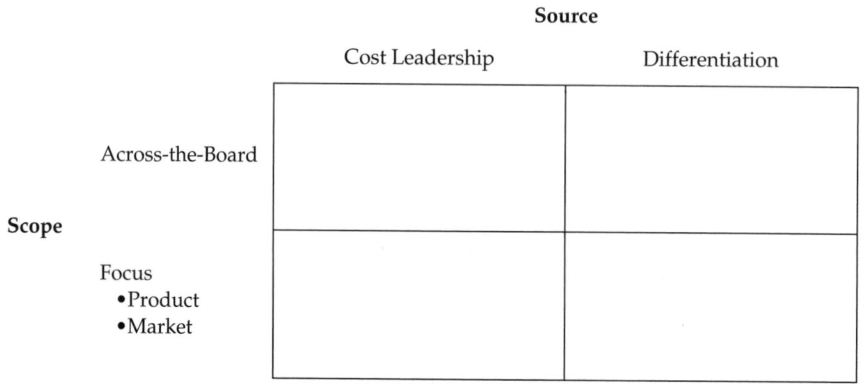

Source: Adapted from Michael Porter, *Competitive Advantage* (New York: The Free Press, 1985), p. 12.

medical inspection gloves, condoms, and kitchen gloves. Size and low-cost latex supply locations (Malaysia and Alabama) give Ansell the low-cost position. It differentiates by inspecting 100 percent of its products (versus statistical sampling, as done by competitors). Being able to offer 100 percent security from leakage in the age of AIDS while pricing below competitors offers an unbeatable competitive advantage.

This discussion examined position-based advantages. Another source, capabilities-based advantages, will be explored more fully in Chapter 10.

˙REFERENCES˙

Ghemawat, Pankaj. "Sustainable Advantage." *Harvard Business Review,* September–October 1986, pp. 53–58.

Montgomery, C.A., and M.E. Porter (eds). *Strategy Seeking and Securing a Competitive Advantage.* Boston: Harvard Business School Press, 1991.

Oster, Sharon M. *Modern Competitive Analysis.* New York: Oxford University Press, 1990.

Porter, Michael E. *Competitive Strategy.* New York: Free Press, 1980.

———. *Competitive Advantage*. New York: Free Press, 1985.

Prahalad, C.K., and Gary Hamel. "The Core Competence of the Corporation." *Harvard Business Review,* May–June 1990, 79–91.

Sun Tzu. *The Art of War*. New York: Delacorte Press, 1983.

Thomas, Dan R.E. *Business Sense*. New York: Free Press, 1993.

Williams, Jeffrey R. 1992. "How Sustainable Is Your Competitive Advantage?" *California Management Review* 34, no. 3 1992, pp. 1–23.

APPENDICES TO PART II

1. Industry and Competitive Analysis
2. Identifying Your Current Business Strategy
3. Evaluating Your Business Strategy

Appendix 1

INDUSTRY AND COMPETITIVE ANALYSIS

This exercise is intended to help management analyze its company's immediate competitive environment. Using the "Questions for Industry and Competitive Analysis" as a guide, the manager should first identify and list the key players or key threats in each of the five forces (competitors, suppliers, potential entrants, potential substitutes, and customers); then, for each force, address the questions that follow in each section.

Once the manager has analyzed the industry, as well as identified and evaluated the company's business strategy, he or she will be ready to address the following five questions:

1. What are the major competitive advantages of each player in the business (including our company)?
2. What will the industry look like in three years? In five years?
3. What are the "rules of the game" in this industry? What are the key success factors?
4. What can we do to change these rules in our favor?
5. How might we carve out an uncontested segment or niche and, in so doing, create a sustainable competitive advantage that would yield supernormal returns?

Questions for Industry and Competitive Analysis

1. Competitors in the Industry
   a. Who are the major competitors (today)? What are their basic characteristics (size, growth, product lines, customer base, geographic coverage, etc.)?
   b. What is their relative position in the industry?
   c. What is the competitive advantage of each? (What "switching costs" have they built?)
   d. How do they compete? What "weapons" or strategies does each use?
   e. What form does competition take—open warfare, polite détente, secrecy, open signaling?
   f. How is product differentiation achieved?
   g. How competitive is the industry? Are any competitors attempting to shape the industry? How?

Source: Adapted from Michael Porter, "How Competitive Forces Shape Strategy," *Harvard Business Review,* March–April, 1979 pp. 137–45. (Reprinted in Chapter 4.)

2. Suppliers
   a. Who are the suppliers, and how large or concentrated are they?
   b. How concentrated is our industry (their buyers) relative to them? That is, how many of us buy what percent of the output?
   c. Can firms in the industry switch suppliers easily?
   d. What percent of their total output is purchased by our industry? How large are the quantities?
   e. How important is their product or service to the quality of ours?
   f. How much of our cost does their product or service represent?
   g. What is the threat of forward integration by each supplier? (Conversely, what is the opportunity for back integration by one or more of us?)
   h. What is their relative bargaining power over us?

3. Potential Entrants
   a. What are the barriers to entry? Are we able to raise them? What factors are tending to lower them?
   b. Who are the potential or imminent new entrants? What are their characteristics (size, number, growth, customer base, etc.)?
   c. What are the entrants' competitive strategies likely to be? How aggressive will they be? How might the new entrants and their strategies reshape the industry?
   d. When will they enter our market(s)?

4. Potential Substitutes
   a. What are the substitutes or alternatives for our product or service?
   b. How big an impact will the substitutes have? (That is, how viable are they as direct replacements for our product or service?)
   c. How quickly will they penetrate?
   d. Which players in the industry will consider substitutes as an opportunity for diversification?

5. Customers
   a. Who are the customers for this industry? How concentrated are they? (Who are the major customers, and what percent of the business do they represent?)
   b. How fast is demand growing overall and in different segments? What is the potential for finding or creating new markets or niches?
   c. What are the switching costs? How high are they?
   d. How price sensitive is each customer segment for each of the industry's services?
   e. How large is the threat of backward integration (i.e., buyers' self-supplying our products or services)?
   f. What is the customer's relative bargaining power?
   g. How are each of the factors listed in *a–f* changing? What will happen in five years?

Appendix 2

IDENTIFYING YOUR CURRENT BUSINESS STRATEGY

This analysis will help management identify the elements of its company's realized business strategy, its functional strategies, its distinctive competencies, and its source of competitive advantage. The questions that will be covered are as follows:

1. What are the primary competitive weapons employed in each of the business's functional strategies?

   a. Marketing
   b. Operations
   c. Technology
   d. Human Resources
   e. Finance

2. What is the company's business definition?

In order to fully assess your business strategy, you should respond to the questions in the Checklist for Functional Strategies section. The information you generate will be used later to evaluate your current strategy (see Appendix 3) and serve as a foundation for developing future strategy.

Source: Adapted from an approach developed by Dan R. E. Thomas, president of Focus, the strategy process consulting firm, in Palo Alto, California.

Checklist for Functional Strategies

Marketing Strategy

A. Product/Market
   1. What products or services do we offer and in what proportion?
   2. What are their characteristics (e.g., custom versus commodity)?
   3. What markets are they offered to?
   4. What customer needs do they fit or fulfill?
   5. How are these markets segmented?

B. Pricing
   1. Is our price higher, lower, or equal to the competition?
   2. Is our price value based or cost based?
   3. Is our business unit a price leader or a price follower?

C. Promotion
   1. How are our products or services promoted (what media/methods)?
   2. What attributes are promoted?
   3. Where are our products or services promoted?
   4. What is the magnitude of our promotion effort?
   5. Is the promotion "push" (incentives to dealers and salespeople to recommend our product) or "pull" (incentives to customers to request our products)?

D. Distribution
   1. What type of distribution technology do we employ?
   2. What channels do we use?
   3. Are the channels independent or owned?

E. Sales
1. What kind of sales force do we use (e.g., technical)?
2. How is our sales force compensated?

Operations Strategy

A. Facilities
1. What types of facilities do we use and how many?
2. What size(s) are they, and where are they located?

B. Capacity
1. How much excess capacity do we have? Why?
2. How flexible is our capacity? That is, how fast can it be expanded, contracted, or changed to alternative uses?

C. Integration
1. How vertically integrated is our operation?
2. How much work do we subcontract, either to other areas within the company or independent of the company?

D. Technology
1. Is our technology state of the art? Why or why not?

E. Infrastructure
1. How is our production scheduled?
2. How is product or service quality managed?

Technology (R&D) Strategy

A. Product Research
   1. What research are we doing?
   2. How does our organization keep abreast of new developments in the industry?

B. Product Innovation
   1. How does our company discover and develop new products?
   2. How much of our resources do we devote to this task?
   3. What kind of organizational arrangements do we use?

C. Process Innovation
   1. How does our company develop new processes for making and delivering products or services?
   2. How much of our resources do we devote to this task?

D. Leader/Follower
   1. Does our company tend to lead or to follow in developing new products, services, or processes?
   2. What is the nature of the lead or lag? (e.g., are we *the* innovator—fast to market with an acquired innovation—or are we a fast second, or even a late entry)?

Human Resources Strategy

A. Workforce Strategy
1. What kind of workforce do we employ? What skills do we seek, and what skills do we develop in house?
2. What do we pay our employees, relative to the market or to the competition?
3. How do we evaluate performance? What incentives do we use?

B. Managerial/Executive Strategy
1. What kind of people do we employ? What are their skills, background, and education?
2. How do we recruit our people? How do we select them?
3. How are new people socialized into our organization?
4. How are new managers trained? How about experienced managers? Senior executives? What and how much training do we offer internally? Externally (outside courses or seminars)?
5. How much time do our managers remain in position before being transferred?
6. How are our managers appraised? Recognized? Rewarded? How does our appraisal system treat assessment of performance and coaching for development—separately (different sessions) or combined? How often do we undertake these activities?
7. How are our executives compensated? What combination of pay and performance incentives do we use? How do our incentives compare to peer institutions?
8. How is career planning carried out in our organization? Is it systematic (done by the company), or do individuals do it for themselves?
9. What is our promotion policy (e.g., from within, time in grade)?
10. How is our business organized, and how are the pieces evaluated?

Financial Strategy

A. Capital Structure
   1. What is our level of debt and equity?
   2. What is the composition of our working capital (cash, inventories, receivables)?
   3. What is the specific composition of our assets?

B. Cash Flow
   1. What is our dividend policy?
   2. Where do we invest the cash flows from the business (dividends, buy back stock, reinvest in P&E or R&D)?

C. Investment
   1. How do we finance our physical assets (e.g., lease, own)?
   2. What are our criteria for approving investments?

D. Stock Price Management
   1. How do we give information to the market (e.g., quality, nature, and timing of information)?
   2. How is our company positioned relative to the market (e.g., diversified, conglomerate, high tech)?

Complete This Summary Identification for Your Company

1. Based on the preceding strategy identification (checklist), summarize the primary functional strategies employed in each of the following areas.

   a. *Marketing Strategy* (products, markets, price, promotion, distribution)
   b. *Operations Strategy* (facilities, capacity, integration, technology, infrastructure)
   c. *Technology (R&D) Strategy* (product or process, leader or follower)
   d. *Human Resources Strategy* (work force, executive)
   e. *Financial Strategy* (capital structure, cash flows, investment, stock price)

2. What is our business definition? That is, how would we define our business in terms of product or market scope and overall economic mission? (Try condensing this statement into one or two sentences.)

Appendix 3

EVALUATING YOUR BUSINESS STRATEGY

This exercise will help management to assess how "good" its strategy is—its areas of strengths and weaknesses—and to determine the company's relative competitive advantage. By completing this exercise, the manager can explore potential areas of strategic change in the business and begin generating strategy alternatives.

The exercise will provide the following analyses:

A. Performance Tests

How does your business strategy measure up against
1. Management's objectives for the business?
2. Stakeholders' objectives?
3. The performance of competitors in the industry?

B. Consistency Tests

Based on your industry and competitor analysis (Appendix 1) and strategy identification (Appendix 2),

1. How does the strategy fit with the economics of the industry?
2. How does the strategy fit with internal requirements and resources?
3. How does the strategy fit with tests of internal consistency (synergy)?
4. How does the strategy fit with tests of flexibility and risk?

C. Sources of Competitive Advantage

1. What are your competitive advantages and disadvantages?
2. What are your competitors' advantages and disadvantages?
3. What are your competitive advantages in five years?
4. What are your preliminary strategic alternatives?

Complete the Following Tests for Your Company

A. Performance Tests
1. What are our company's major articulated goals? (List them.) How has our company been performing with respect to these?

GOAL	RESULTS	SCORE (0–10)
a.		
b.		
c.		
d.		
e.		

2. Who are our major stakeholders? (List them.) What are their stakes with respect to our business? How well is our strategy meeting these stakes?

STAKEHOLDER	STAKES	RESULTS/SCORE
a.		
b.		
c.		
d.		
e.		

135

3. Who are our major competitors and potential (growing) competitors? How well are we performing compared to them in terms of the criteria listed?

Competitor	Financial Performance	Market Position	Technological Performance
a.			
b.			
c.			
d.			
e.			

B. Consistency Tests
1. How consistent is our strategy with the economic structure of our industry (refer to Appendix 1)?

	Expected Situation in Five Years	Strategy Consistency or Inconsistency
a. Buyer power and trends in demand for products or service		
b. Substitutes or alternatives		
c. Likely entrants		
d. Competitors and competitive positions		
e. Supplier power		

2. How well do our internal resources or capabilities support or detract from our strategy? What are our strengths and weaknesses within each of the following areas, and how do they fit with our strategy?

Resource Area	Strengths and Weaknesses (Why?)	Fit with Strategy
a. Human		
b. Physical		
c. Technological		
d. Managerial		
e. Reputation		
f. Other		

Based on the above, generate what would be a preliminary statement of our business unit's core capabilities.

3. Test of Internal Consistency
Refer back to the strategy identification exercise (Appendix 2). How well do our functional strategies fit with and reinforce each other? Where are the internal inconsistencies and lack of synergies within our business?

4. Where is our strategy most flexible? Most inflexible?

137

C. Sources of Competitive Advantage

1. What are our company's competitive advantages and disadvantages?
   a. Economic position (e.g., location, market share, cost structure, image, technology)
      1. Advantages
      2. Disadvantages
   b. Human capabilities (e.g., teamwork, morale, culture, skills set, experience)
      1. Advantages
      2. Disadvantages

2. List each competitor (or grouping of similar competitors) along with the major advantages and disadvantages of each.

3. What will our basis for competitive advantage be in three years? How will we develop these? (This will become part of your strategy implementation plan.)

4. What are some of the major strategic alternatives that presented themselves as a result of these analyses? For example, do the results of these analyses suggest that we should stay the course, grow aggressively, take share from targeted competitors, focus on a particular market or customer group, focus with particular products, go up-market, add features or services, cut costs, streamline the business, shrink the business, exit the business, or something else?

THE BACOVA GUILD, LTD.

INTRODUCTION

Ben Johns, president of The Bacova Guild, Ltd., picked up the phone to get an update from his partner Pat Haynes, who was attending the August 1991 National Hardware Show in Chicago, Illinois.

"Well, Rubbermaid went ahead with it," Haynes said. "Their poly mailbox is being highlighted in the New Product Exposition. It looks like a one-piece mold, but it is really unattractive. What's more is they're asking two times the going rate, listing at an average of $14.99!"

"The problem," Johns reflected, "is that with a name like Rubbermaid you might be able to get away with it."

"I don't know," Haynes responded. "Rubbermaid has a lot of overhead, and it is accustomed to very high margins. And word with retailers is that they're being extremely heavy handed saying 'You *will* buy our boxes or else.' Retailers are upset."

Johns pointed out, "Like it or not, Rubbermaid has quite a bit of leverage with those retailers. It also has a great reputation among consumers.

"The good news is Rubbermaid's entry could be a big plus for the industry. It will bring some credence to the market while putting an upward pressure on prices," Johns continued.

"Regardless, this development really puts some pressure on us for speeding up our strategic planning process. We'll wrap up here late Thursday night. Let's sit down first thing Friday morning," Haynes suggested.

As he hung up, Johns couldn't help but wonder what this latest development meant for this small manufacturer located near Hot Springs, Virginia. Since peaking in 1987, Bacova's sales had declined steadily. (See Exhibits 1 and 2.) While the numbers for the first half of 1991 looked promising, Bacova was having an increasingly difficult time handling competition from larger and more powerful companies. Management's response at this crucial turning

This case was prepared by Eileen Filliben, Darden MBA/J.D. 1994, under the supervision of John L. Colley, Jr., Almand R. Coleman Professor of Business Administration. Copyright © 1992 by the Darden Graduate School Foundation, Charlottesville, VA.

Exhibit 1
The Bacova Guild, Ltd.
Audited Financial Data
($1000s)

	1981	1982	1983	1984	1985	1986	1987	1988	1989	1990
Sales	776.3	1,116.1	1,681.2	2,420.7	3,808.2	9,559.8	19,090.4	15,766.7	14,380.5	13,371.1
Cost of goods sold	506.7	711.8	983.6	1,403.9	2,097.4	5,660.6	11,946.6	10,525.9	10,239.8	9,537.7
Gross margin	269.6	404.3	697.6	1,016.8	1,710.8	3,939.2	7,143.8	5,240.8	4,140.7	3,833.4
SG&A	259.4	308.5	520.6	774.5	1,242.8	2,229.7	3,649.8	3,623.1	4,228.0	3,486.3
Interest expense	32.8	34.6	32.1	30.4	89.1	129.4	224.7	287.3	304.1	338.6
Finance charges	0.0	0.0	(2.5)	(5.8)	(8.3)	(3.5)	(17.1)	9.5	(16.7)	(13.6)
Other income and expenses	(11.7)	(15.3)	(4.7)	(21.8)	(35.8)	(7.0)	(23.7)	(76.4)	(72.8)	(17.5)
Net pretax earnings	(10.9)	76.5	152.1	239.5	423.0	1,590.6	3,310.1	1,397.3	(301.9)	39.6
Taxes	0.0	11.9	54.1	89.3	180.5	782.8	1,489.0	531.0	0.0	0.0
Net earnings	(10.9)	64.6	98.0	150.2	242.5	807.8	1,821.1	866.3	(301.9)	39.6
COGS/Sales	65.3%	63.8%	58.5%	58.0%	55.1%	59.0%	62.6%	66.8%	71.2%	71.3%
Gross margin	34.7%	36.2%	41.5%	42.0%	44.9%	41.0%	37.4%	32.2%	28.8%	28.7%
SG&A/Sales	33.4%	27.6%	31.0%	32.0%	32.6%	23.2%	19.1%	23.0%	29.4%	26.1%
Net margin	-1.4%	5.8%	5.8%	6.2%	6.4%	8.4%	9.5%	5.5%	-2.1%	0.3%

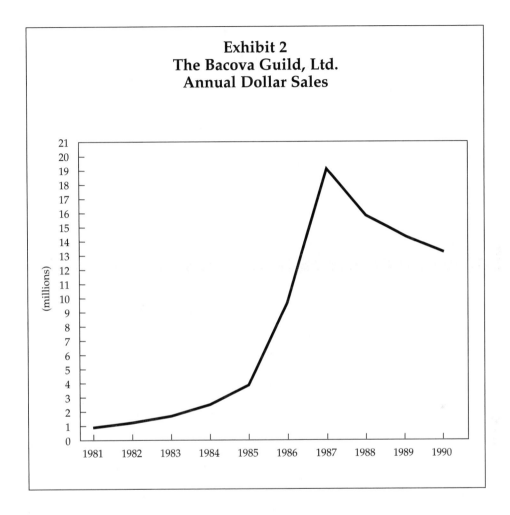

Exhibit 2
The Bacova Guild, Ltd.
Annual Dollar Sales

point would determine if Bacova would reach the partners' goal of having a $25 to $30 million business by 1997.

THE EARLY YEARS

Malcolm Hirsh, an industrialist from Peapack, New Jersey, purchased the entire "company town" of Bacova, Virginia, in 1965. The name came from BAth COunty, VirginiA. After purchasing the town, Hirsh founded The Bacova Guild, Ltd. He joined forces with Grace Gilmore, a commercially successful artist who had a love for painting birds and wildlife. Several years earlier, while living in New Bern, North Carolina, Grace and her husband William perfected the process of silk screening on transparent paper and laminating it in fiberglass. This new technology allowed Grace Gilmore's beautiful wildlife paintings to be preserved and even shaped to be used as inlays for various product applications. The company began producing a variety of laminated fiberglass gift items with Gilmore's designs, including outdoor thermometers, place mats, outdoor cast iron furniture with decorative table tops, and the original Bacova mailbox, which remains the classic Bacova Guild item.

To maintain Bacova's elite appeal, Hirsh kept distribution limited. The company sold its products, primarily the mailboxes (which could be personalized with the name and address of the purchaser), to specialty gift shops and direct mail companies such as Abercrombie & Fitch, Orvis, and L.L. Bean (roughly 600 accounts).

NEW OWNERS, NEW PRODUCTS, NEW MARKETS

In 1981, Hirsh sold the business to two young entrepreneurs. Patrick R. Haynes, Jr., a tennis pro at the nearby Homestead Resort, and Benjamin I. Johns, Jr., a former tennis pro at the Homestead, teamed up and bought Bacova, which had 25 employees, one small building, and 600 customers. In 1980, the business lost $40,000 on sales of $550,000.

The new owners believed the business had to grow to become profitable. Its product line consisted of three rural mailboxes, an ice bucket, an outdoor thermometer, two porch boxes, a picnic basket called the Kool Basket, and a wood tray. The new owners began an aggressive program of expansion with regard to products they sold and markets they served. They took the wildlife designs, the screen printing, and the fiberglass lamination process that had worked with the mailboxes and began to market a wider variety of products, such as ice buckets, window thermometers, card tables, television trays, and bird feeders. All of these products, along with the mailboxes, were purchased from outside manufacturers and then decorated with a laminated Bacova design. The company tried to expand its customer list by aggressively participating in more gift trade shows and producing a full-color wholesale catalog. These efforts quickly showed results as the firm was profitable in 1982.

In 1983, Bacova created a new line of products by printing its traditional designs on indoor/outdoor mats, thus beginning Bacova's diversification into the textile industry. These doormats could be personalized in the same manner as the mailboxes, and they were very successful with gift shops and mail order companies. These mats, 20" by 30", wholesaled for $11.25 ($13.75 if personalized) and retailed for $22.50. In addition to earning $98,016 on sales of $1.7 million in 1983, the company also realized an important lesson: its real strength was in its screen printing expertise and capacity.

The doormats that Bacova developed appealed to mass merchandisers in addition to the specialty gift shops. One large discount chain approached the manufacturer and requested a similar mat at a lower price point. In 1985, a turning point for the company, a smaller (18" by 27"), less expensive version of the Bacova doormat was introduced to the discount chain for $6.25 whole-sale, $13.50 retail, and sales soared. Then came a request for a mat to meet a $9.99 price point. Johns and Haynes hesitated at first because they had built the business to nearly $4 million in sales and were afraid to tamper with suc-cess. The company was able to market a rug that would retail at $9.99 with a switch from acrylic to nylon and a change in the printing process to one where the image went to a sheet of paper and then from the paper to the carpet.

Initially some retailers complained about the new rugs' tacky, "velvet Elvis" look. Fortunately, innovations in dryer technology allowed a switch to polypropylene material, which gave the rugs the sophisticated silk-screen look that was Bacova's trademark. In 1986, the revolutionary AccentMat was introduced, wholesaling at $3.80 and easily meeting the $9.99 price point. AccentMats soon became the leading seller among Bacova products.

This success inspired a similar strategy with the mailboxes. By 1986, Bacova had developed a process for silk screening its traditional images on the reverse side of a flexible piece of polycarbonate that could be fitted over a standard rural mailbox. The new mailbox was called AccentBox, and it sold for about half the price of the Classic Bacova Mailbox because the cover was riveted on, not hand-laminated. This less expensive version of the mailbox was very popular with the retailers. The company's sales leapt to $9.6 million in 1986 and $19 million in 1987. The success of these two product lines demonstrated to Bacova manage-ment the potential of marketing to mass merchandisers.

THE 1987 PEAK

During the mid-1980s, Bacova constantly expanded its workforce and facil-ities. It built an addition onto the original facility, added a new manufactur-ing/screen-printing facility, and leased a building in an industrial park in the next town. It also made arrangements with a carpet manufacturer in Georgia. Bacova would typically source the manufactured product from the outside, cre-ate a series of designs, screen print the designs, and market the product through its growing network of manufacturers' representatives. Bacova could introduce a new product in this manner at such a low cost that it generally did not bother to do any preliminary market testing.

By the end of 1987, sales had grown to $19 million and profits were $1.8 million. The company was selling hardware products including mailboxes, covers, and accessories, and textile products including a wide variety of mats and rugs. Textiles had a record year in 1987, particularly the AccentMats, which accounted for approximately $8 million in sales. Each product line included some higher-priced items that were sold to the specialty gift shops and mail-order companies. Sales and profits declined each year after 1987 as the economy worsened and Bacova continued to face price competition from other manufacturers. In 1990, Bacova earned only $39,539 on sales of $13.4 million. (Exhibits 1 and 2 present financial data for the years 1981–1990.)

COMPETITION

Mailbox sales were divided into the following categories: steel (70 percent), plastic (20 percent), and wood (10 percent). Bacova was sourcing its standard metal mailboxes from the Solar Group in Taylorsville, Michigan. Another primary manufacturer sold nearly 90 percent of all plain steel mailboxes directly to the same mass merchandisers that Bacova was targeting. Bacova's success in creating the decorative mailbox market had attracted the attention of its mailbox supplier. By the end of 1987, the top competitors became aware of the market Bacova had created, and retailers began to ask these competitors why they did not provide a decorative box.

Sales of mailboxes declined rapidly as competition increased. When Steel City entered the market in 1988 with its answer to the AccentBoxes, Bacova was forced to cut its wholesale price from $13.50 to between $7.00 and $7.50. The growing textile division was partially offsetting the lost mailbox sales, but the outlook for Bacova was not optimistic. Management knew that unless it found a way to differentiate itself and compete by creating and filling a profitable niche, the AccentBox was destined to be priced out of the market.

The Solar Group, Bacova's supplier, approached Johns and Haynes to see if it could buy Bacova panels. Johns and Haynes knew their panels were the highest quality and most appealing on the market and thought that by selling them to the Solar Group they would forfeit their advantage in the marketplace. This option did not appear to have any long-term potential. After the Solar Group had improved its own processes for making panels, it would no longer need Bacova. As a result of this conflict of interests, Bacova began to source its mailboxes from Fulton, which served hardware distributorships and which therefore was not a competitor in Bacova's distribution channels.

MARKETING AND SALES

Bacova had a vice president of sales and three regional sales managers who oversaw the activities of approximately 25 independent manufacturers' representative organizations, including about 130 reps. These salespeople sold Bacova's products through a variety of retail outlets. Retailers were moving to eliminate as many vendors as possible; being able to offer one-stop shopping was a real advantage.

The problem with working with mass merchandisers, reported Tim Lindhjem, regional sales manager, was that they can "kill a category within two years because of the downward pressure on prices." He believed hardware stores held the key to Bacova's success.

THE POSTMASTER SYSTEM

In 1988, Bacova decided to try to differentiate itself by creating a total mailbox system, designed to take the mailbox product a step further, to incorporate

---

Exhibit 3
Bacova Guild
PostMaster Development Costs

Original mailbox mold (Taiwan)	$133,158
Second mailbox mold (U.S.)	244,430
Post system mold	127,000
Design consultant	276,252
Total	$780,840

---

plastics to create a wider range of products and prices, and to satisfy consumer demand for easier installation. The process of buying a mailbox and a post, setting the post in the ground, and figuring out a way to attach the box to the post usually became an all-day affair. The total system proposed by Bacova was called PostMaster and included a molded polypropylene mailbox (the Poly-Box), a PVC cross-mount or top-mount post kit that could be installed with no digging or concrete, a universal mounting plate that would hold any standard rural mailbox, a newspaper tube, and a Bacova design on a sheet of polycarbonate that snapped in place over the mailbox. These products would be sold separately, and the covers could be personalized and snapped on or off the Poly-Box so they could be changed for different holidays or special occasions. Bacova sold a variety of interchangeable covers including collegiate and National Football League designs. The PostMaster system could also be used with a standard metal mailbox such as the AccentBox or the Classic Bacova Mailbox.

After deciding to go with this PostMaster System, Bacova made arrangements to have the Poly-Box molds manufactured in Taiwan from its own designs. This was Bacova's first experience with trying to design something and having someone else manufacture it. The molds turned out to be poorly designed and low in quality. The company scrapped everything that had been done in Taiwan and hired a product-development consulting firm to help design the box and the packaging and engineer the system more efficiently. Those costs are broken down in Exhibit 3. The development of the PostMaster System represented nearly an $800,000 investment.

Bacova introduced the plastic PostMaster boxes, the post kits, and the other accessories in the beginning of 1990. These boxes were well received by the marketplace, although they cannibalized sales of the AccentBoxes (see Exhibits 4 and 5). Plastic boxes were definitely thought to be the wave of the future. They had none of the denting, rusting, or rotting characteristics of the metal boxes, cost less to make, and wholesaled for more.

**Exhibit 4
The Bacova Guild, Ltd.
Historical Mailbox Sales**

	1987	1988	1989	1990	1991 Est.
ACCENTBOXES					
Total sales	$2,612,686	$3,615,756	$2,751,523	$631,007	$455,600
Quantity sold	193,195	278,813	247,076	59,159	38,512
Average price	$13.52	$12.97	$11.14	$10.67	$11.83
POSTMASTER BOXES					
Total sales	0	0	$675,601	$1,397,576	$1,880,200
Quantity sold	0	0	92,229	178,832	338,775
Average price	0	0	$7.33	$7.82	$5.55

It had been a major decision for Johns and his partner to undertake the investment in the PostMaster System. They had created a successful product, but it appeared that they had not been able to distance themselves adequately from their larger competitors. Johns wondered if the PostMaster System had been a worthwhile venture. The company evaluated projects using a 15-percent hurdle rate. The U.S. molds could be depreciated straight line over ten years. Had this been a sound decision on a net present value basis? What other qualitative benefits did the PostMaster System provide?

LOOKING FORWARD

Both Johns and Haynes believed their company to be at a turning point. Within the next five years, they would like to see Bacova reach $25 to $30 million in sales with 30 percent gross margins. They knew that things would have to change, though, in order for them to meet their goal.

In assessing which way to go, Johns turned to several trusted industry allies for suggestions. Feedback from the market showed that Bacova was highly respected and known to have superior creativity and design. Its quality, service, and delivery were regarded as above average.

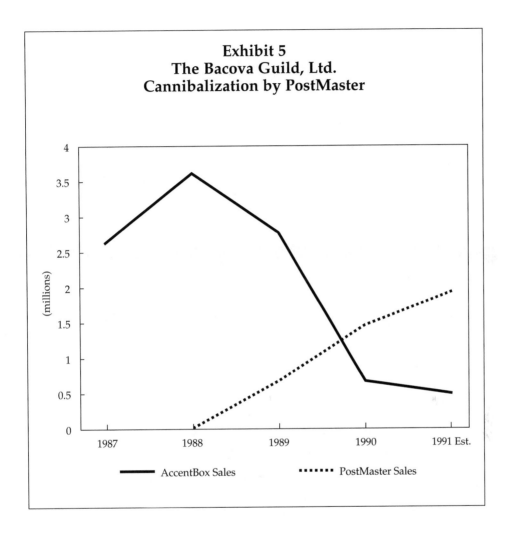

Exhibit 5
The Bacova Guild, Ltd.
Cannibalization by PostMaster

Still, several suggestions were made:

1. Focus on high-quality, crafted products.
2. Go after mom-and-pop retailers who are very loyal and who are willing to pay more for innovation and service.
3. Reduce the amount of paperwork manufacturers' reps need to do.
4. Provide better supporting material for new product introductions.
5. Either support or withdraw products like the veggie markers, driveway markers, and single numbers, which are always shown at shows but which have no supporting materials.

Exhibit 6
Cedar Works, Inc.
1990 Income Statement

Sales	$3,968,693
COGS	2,935,894
Gross margin	1,032,799
Expenses	651,675
Operating income	381,124
Other expenses	88,920
Net income before taxes	292,204
Taxes	101,774
Net income	$ 190,430

---

6. Redesign the conference booth to be more inviting. Make it larger. Highlight new products.

7. Expand the mailbox line so that Bacova can walk into a retailer and offer to supply the entire mailbox department.

8. Add a larger box size in black.

9. Develop more case-cut packaging that goes from truck to floor with little effort.

While these suggestions were all worthwhile, Johns knew the company needed a "big picture" adjustment, one that would have to come from senior management. How the company reacted to the "accelerated rate of change in the marketplace" would dictate its future.

Johns reflected on the lessons he had gleaned from Michael Porter's *Competitive Strategy*, a book he had just read. In this analysis, Porter discussed the two main strategies a company may take in order to gain a competitive advantage in the marketplace. The first involved cost and keeping it as low as possible. The second focused on differentiation, or the ability to add features that separated a product from the rest of the pack.

The key to success for any company was to recognize which single or combination strategy it intended, or was best-suited to employ, and then to make sure that all elements of its marketing, pricing, and distribution were consistent with this strategy.

Clearly, Bacova started out as a specialty gift supplier, charging premium prices. Then, when Johns and Haynes took over and wanted to expand the business, they used upgrades in technology to introduce products such as AccentMats and AccentBoxes that were differentiated and yet low cost. They expanded into mass distribution to keep up with demand and initially earned handsome returns. Unfortunately, given the economics of the business, competitors soon copied Bacova's designs. The company was forced to compete on price and was suffering the low profits of a commodity business. Was Bacova best suited to compete in this arena? If not, where should it compete and how?

Still there were problems with Bacova's current structure as Charlie Bowers, vice president of sales and marketing, pointed out:

> Bacova is a niche business. It has to be more. Right now the textile and hardware businesses are so diverse that it has been very difficult to focus strategically. . . . If we do focus, textiles would be the way to go. They are higher margin and more closely tied to Bacova's strength in printing designs.

One manufacturers' rep felt it would be a mistake to divest its mailbox business: "There are synergies between the two, and Bacova would lose some significance to retailers if it were just a textiles firm."

CEDAR WORKS ACQUISITION

A second option came with Bacova's opportunity to purchase Cedar Works, a small manufacturer of top-of-the-line cedar mailboxes. Charles Bower commented on the prospect:

> Strategically, it would be good to go wood. It broadens the product line and typically commands higher margins. Steel City and Solar have both gotten into the cedar business and have hurt Cedar Works considerably. In fact, Cedar Works lost its Home Depot, Lowes, and Hechinger accounts to these larger competitors. It still retains Wal-Mart, though, which would be a great customer to have.
>
> Cedar Works has the best wood boxes in the business but needs lower costs. Bacova might be able to help. The problem is we can't afford to pay a lot. Even if we could, it comes down to buying a client list. And the main noteworthy client with Cedar Works is Wal-Mart.

Johns had very little financial information on Cedar Works since they were only in preliminary discussions. He knew sales for fiscal year ending June 30, 1990, were about $4 million, with net profit of $190,000. (See Exhibit 6 for a 1990 income statement.) Johns expected 6-percent growth per year. Word in the industry was that Cedar Works might go for as high as $4 million. After ten years, industry experts thought the business might be worth as much as $5.88 million. Would this acquisition make sense for Bacova? How much could Johns and Haynes offer to pay for Cedar Works?

A third option was for the company to focus on its competitive advantage and get back to being a supplier of premium products. Bacova was the undisputed design leader and the favored supplier among gift accounts and upscale hardware stores. Should the company rethink its marketing and distribution to get back to premium craftsmanship at a higher price?

Johns knew his management team would be returning from the Chicago Hardware Show on Friday. He wanted to have thought through the options by then and be prepared to present them with his plan.

CROWN CORK AND SEAL COMPANY, INC.

In 1977, Crown Cork and Seal Company was the fourth-largest producer of metal cans and crowns in the United States.[1] Under John Connelly, chairman and CEO, Crown had raised itself up from near bankruptcy in 1957. After 20 years of consistent growth, the company had emerged as a major force in both the domestic and international metal container markets (see Exhibit 1).

During those 20 years, Crown Cork and Seal had concentrated its manufacturing efforts on tin-plated cans for holding beer, soft drinks, and aerosol products. By 1977, however, the ozone controversy and the trend toward legislative regulation of nonreturnable containers was threatening Crown's domestic business. Was it time for a change in Crown's formula for success or merely time for a reaffirmation of Connelly's basic strategic choices?

To explore these questions, this case looks at the metal container industry, Crown's strategy and position within that industry, and the nature of the problems facing the company during mid-1977.

THE METAL CONTAINER INDUSTRY IN 1977

The metal container industry included 100 firms and a vast number of product lines. This section describes the product segments in which Crown competed, examines the industry's competitive structure, and looks at three industrywide trends: (1) increasing self-manufacture, (2) new material introductions, and (3) the effect of the "packaging revolution" on the competitive atmosphere.

The Products

Metal containers made up almost a third of all packaging products used in the United States in 1976. Metal containers included traditional steel and

Copyright © 1977 by the President and Fellows of Harvard College. Harvard Business School case 378-024. This case was prepared by Karen D. Gordon, John P. Reed and Richard Hammermesh as the basis for class discussion rather than to illustrate either effective or ineffective handling of an administrative situation. Reprinted by permission of the Harvard Business School.

[1]Crowns are flanged bottle caps, originally made with an insert of natural cork—hence the name Crown Cork and Seal.

Exhibit 1
Crown Cork and Seal Company, Inc.
Financial Statement, 1956–1976
($ thousands except where indicated otherwise)

	1976	1975	1974	1973	1972	1971	1966	1961	1956
Net sales	$909,937	$825,007	$766,158	$571,762	$488,880	$448,446	$279,830	$176,992	$115,098
Cost of products sold									
(excluding depreciation)	757,866	683,691	628,865	459,183	387,768	350,867	217,236	139,071	95,803
Selling and administrative expense	31,910	30,102	28,649	23,409	20,883	21,090	18,355	15,311	13,506
% of net sales	3.5%	3.6%	3.7%	4.1%	4.3%	4.7%	6.6%	8.7%	11.7%
Interest expense	3,885	7,374	6,973	4,407	4,222	5,121	4,551	1,252	1,150
Depreciation expense	26,486	25,402	25,525	20,930	18,654	16,981	9,381	4,627	2,577
Taxes on income	43,500	34,925	33,298	26,725	24,900	24,560	12,680	7,625	105
Net income	$ 46,183	$ 41,611	$ 39,663	$ 34,288	$ 31,193	$ 28,474	$ 16,749	$ 6,653	$ 277
% of net sales	5.1%	5.0%	5.2%	6.0%	6.4%	6.3%	6.0%	3.8%	.2%
Earnings per common share	$ 2.84	$ 2.43	$ 2.20	$ 1.81	$ 1.58	$ 1.41	$ .80	$ .28	$ (.01)
Plant and equipment									
Expenditures	$ 21,568	$ 47,047	$ 52,517	$ 40,392	$ 28,261	$ 33,099	$ 32,729	$ 11,819	$ 1,931
Accumulated investment	398,377	401,657	371,297	335,047	316,266	313,214	223,153	107,258	65,196
Accumulated depreciation	149,306	143,406	129,924	116,191	105,377	101,314	68,359	45,004	31,167
Current asset/liability ratio	1.8	1.6	1.4	1.6	1.7	1.6	1.5	2.7	3.2
Long-term debt	$ 25,886	$ 29,679	$ 34,413	$ 37,922	$ 31,234	$ 41,680	$ 57,890	$ 17,654	$ 21,400
Short-term debt	2,984	30,419	45,043	28,504	17,221	31,381	44,784	5,190	6,500
Shareholders' investment	316,684	292,681	262,650	243,916	230,366	211,847	110,841	77,540	50,299
Number of									
Preferred shares	0	0	0	0	0	0	79,370	139,540	275,000
Common shares, average	16,235,040	17,137,030	18,000,792	18,894,105	19,726,799	20,211,810	20,606,835	21,594,720	24,155,800

Source: Crown Cork and Seal Company, Inc., 1976 Annual Report, pp. 4–5.

aluminum cans, foil containers, and metal drums and pails of all shapes and sizes. Of these, metal cans were the largest segment, reaching a value of $7.1 billion in 1976. Cans were being used in more than three-fourths of all metal-container shipments.

Cans were composed of two basic raw materials: aluminum and tin-plated steel. Originally, they were formed by rolling a sheet of metal, soldering it, cutting it to the right size, and attaching two ends, thereby forming a three-piece, seamed can. In the late 1960s, a new process introduced by the aluminum industry made possible a two-piece can. The new can was formed by pushing a flat blank of metal into a deep cup, which eliminated the need for a separate bottom. The product makers adopted the term "drawn and ironed" from the molding procedure.

The aluminum companies that developed the process, Alcoa and Reynolds, had done so with the intention of turning the process over to can manufacturers and subsequently increasing raw-material sales. However, when the manufacturers were reluctant to incur the large costs involved in line changeovers, the two aluminum companies began building their own two-piece lines and competing directly in the end market.

The new can had advantages in weight, labor, and materials costs and was recommended by the Food and Drug Administration, which was worried about lead from soldered three-piece cans migrating into the can's contents. Tin-plated can producers soon acknowledged the new process as the wave of the future. They quickly began to explore the possibilities for drawing and ironing steel sheets. By 1972 the technique was perfected, and investment dollars had begun to pour into line changeovers and new equipment purchases. Exhibit 2 illustrates the rapid switch to the two-piece can in the beverage industry. In the beer segment alone, almost half of the total cans used in 1974 were made by the new process.

Growth

Between 1967 and 1976 the number of metal cans shipped from the manufacturers grew at an average of 3.4 percent annually. As shown in Table A, the greatest gains were in the beverage segment, while shipments of motor oil, paints, and other general packaging cans actually declined. A 6 percent decline in total shipments in 1975 turned around as the economy picked up in all areas except basic food cans. For the future, soft drink and beer cans were expected to continue to be the growth leaders.

Industry Structure

In 1977 the U.S. metal can industry was dominated by four major manufacturers. Two giants, American Can and the Continental Can Division of the Continental Group, together made up 35 percent of all domestic production.

Exhibit 2
Beverage Can Shipments
(billion cans)

	1972	1973	CHANGE 1972–1973	1974	CHANGE 1973–1974
SOFT DRINK CANS					
Total	15,596	17,552	+12.5%	17,980	+2.4%
Three-piece	14,217	15,779	+11.0%	15,589	−1.2%
% of total	91.2	89.9		86.7	
Two-piece	1,379	1,773	+28.6%	2,391	+34.9%
% of total	8.8	10.1		13.3	
BEER CANS					
Total	21,801	24,131	+10.7%	26,077	+8.1%
Three-piece	14,746	14,363	−2.6%	13,237	−7.8%
% of total	67.6	59.5		50.8	
Two-piece	7,055	9,768	+38.5%	12,840	+31.4%
% of total	32.4	40.5		49.2	

Source: *Metal Cans Shipments Report 1974*, Can Manufacturers Institute, p. 6.

National Can and Crown Cork and Seal were also major forces with market shares of 8.7 percent and 8.3 percent, respectively (see Exhibit 3).

Equipment. A typical three-piece can line cost $750,000 to $1 million. In addition, expensive seaming, end-making, and finishing equipment were required. Since each finishing line could handle the output of three or four can-forming lines, the minimum efficient plant required at least $3.5 million in basic equipment. Most plants had twelve to fifteen lines for the increased flexibility of handling more than one type of can at once. However, any more than fifteen lines became unwieldy because of the need for duplication of setup crews, maintenance, and supervision.

The new two-piece can lines were even more expensive. Equipment for the line itself cost approximately $8.5 million, and the investment in peripheral equipment raised the per-line cost to $10 million to $15 million. Unlike

Table A
Metal Can Shipments 1967–1976
(000 base boxes)

	1967	1972	1973	1974	1975	1976
TOTAL METAL CANS	133,980	168,868	180,482	188,383	177,063	179,449
BY PRODUCT						
Food cans	67,283	64,773	68,770	73,104	68,127	64,984
Beverage cans	42,117	75,916	84,617	89,435	85,877	90,084
Soft drinks	14,580	31,660	35,631	36,499	33,284	39,488
Beer	27,537	44,256	48,986	52,936	52,593	50,596
Pet foods	5,797	6,694	7,121	7,083	6,057	6,121
General packaging cans	18,783	21,485	19,974	18,761	17,002	18,391
Motor oil	n/a	3,095	2,756	2,533	n/a	n/a
Paints	n/a	6,086	5,562	5,202	n/a	n/a
Aerosols	n/a	5,877	6,103	5,765	4,808	5,097
All other	n/a	6,427	5,553	5,261	n/a	n/a

Note: A base box contains 31,360 square inches.
Source: Standard and Poor's Industry Survey, *Containers, Basic Analysis*, March 24, 1977, p. C123; *Metal Can Shipments Report 1974*, p. 6.

three-piece lines, minimum efficient plant size was one line, and installations ranged from one line to five lines.

Conversion to these two-piece lines virtually eliminated the market for new three-piece lines. No firms were installing new three-piece lines, and the major manufacturers were selling complete, fully operational three-piece lines "as is" for $175,000 to $200,000. Many firms were shipping their old lines overseas to their foreign operations where growth potential was great. There were few entrenched firms, and canning technology was not well known or understood.

Pricing. The can industry was very competitive. The need for high capacity utilization and the desire to avoid costly line changeovers made long runs of standard items the most desirable business. As a result, most companies offered volume discounts to encourage large orders. From 1968 to 1975, industrywide profit

Exhibit 3
Comparison of 1976 Performance
of Major Metal Can Manufacturers
($ millions)

	CONTINENTAL GROUP	AMERICAN CAN	NATIONAL CAN	CROWN CORK AND SEAL
TOTAL COMPANY PERFORMANCE				
Sales	$3,458	$3,143	$917	$910
Net income	$118.3	$100.9	$20.7	$46.2
Sales growth, 1967–1976	147%	107%	317%	202%
Profit growth, 1967–1976	51%	33%	160%	145%
Return on equity, five-year average	10.3%	7.1%	11.9%	15.8%
Debt ratio	34%	35%	46%	23%
METAL CAN SEGMENTS (DOMESTIC)				
Sales	$1,307.8	$1,177.6	$616.0	$575.0
Pretax income	$73.0	$64.9	$36.4	$49.0
as a % of sales	5.6%	5.4%	5.0%	8.5%
Market share	18.4%	16.6%	8.7%	8.3%
Number of can plants	70	48	41	26
INTERNATIONAL (SALES OF ALL PRODUCTS)				
Sales	$1,147.2	$475.1	n/a	$343.0
Net income (before taxes)	$63.4	$41.5	small loss	$39.4

Source: *Wall Street Transcript*, November 3, 1975, pp. 41, 864, and company 10-K reports.

margins declined 44 percent, reflecting sluggish sales and increased price competition. This trend hurt the small company, which was less able to spread its fixed costs. Raising prices above industry-set norms, however, was dangerous. Continental tried this in the fall of 1963 with the announcement of a 2 percent price hike. Other manufacturers refused to follow its lead, and by mid-1964 Continental was back to industry price levels with a considerably reduced market share.

Distribution. Because of the product's bulk and weight, transportation was a major factor in a can maker's cost structure. (One estimate put transportation at 7.6 percent of the price of a metal can, with raw materials playing the largest part at 64 percent and labor following at 14.4 percent.) A manufacturer's choice of lighter raw materials and plant location could have a large impact on total costs. Most estimates put the radius of economical distribution for a plant at between 150 and 300 miles.

Suppliers and Customers

At one time the big U.S. steel companies were the sole suppliers of metallic raw material used by the metal container industry. Can companies, in turn, were the fourth-largest consumers of steel products. During the 1960s and 1970s, aluminum—and to a lesser extent, fiber-foil and plastic—suppliers increasingly entered traditional tinplate markets.

On the customer side, over 80 percent of the metal can output was purchased by the major food and beer companies. Since the can constituted about 45 percent of the total costs of beverage companies, most had at least two sources of supply. Poor service and uncompetitive prices could be punished by cuts in order size. Because can plants were often set up to supply a particular customer, the loss of a large order from that customer could greatly cut into manufacturing efficiency and company profits. As one can executive caught in the margin squeeze commented, "Sometimes I think the only way out of this is to sell out to U.S. Steel or to buy General Foods."[2]

INDUSTRY TRENDS

Three major trends had plagued the metal container manufacturers since the early 1960s: (1) the continuing threat of self-manufacture; (2) the increasing acceptance of other materials such as aluminum, fiber-foil, or plastic for standard tinplate packaging needs; and (3) the "packaging revolution" leading to new uses and thus new characteristics for containers.

Self-Manufacture

In the years 1971 to 1977, there had been a growing trend toward self-manufacture by large can customers, particularly of the low-technology standard items. As shown in Table B, the proportion of "captive" production increased from 18.2 percent to 25.8 percent between 1970 and 1976. These

---

[2]"Crown Cork and Seal Company and the Metal Container Industry," HBS Case Services No. 6-373-077, Harvard Business School.

Table B
Metal Can Production by Market (%)

	1970	1971	1972	1973	1974	1975	1976
For sale	81.8	80.9	80.8	78.2	76.7	73.7	74.2
For own use	18.2	19.1	19.2	21.8	23.3	26.3	25.8

increases seemed to come from companies gradually adding their own lines at specific canning locations rather than from full-scale changeovers. However, the temptation for major can users such as food and beer producers to begin making their own cans was high. As a result of such backward integration, Campbell Soup Company had actually become one of the largest producers of cans in the United States. The introduction of the two-piece can was expected to dampen the trend toward self-manufacture, since the end users did not possess the technical skills to develop their own two-piece lines.

New Packaging Materials

Aluminum. The greatest threat to the traditional, tin-plated can was the growing popularity of the new, lighter-weight aluminum can. The major producers of this can were the large aluminum companies, led by Reynolds Metals and Aluminum Company of America (Alcoa). Some traditional tin-plated can producers, such as Continental and American, also produced a small proportion of aluminum cans.

From 1970 to 1976 aluminum usage for cans increased, moving up from 11.6 percent to 27.5 percent of the total metal can market. It was expected to reach a 29-percent share in 1977 (see Table C). In absolute numbers, steel use remained fairly level while aluminum use tripled in those years (see Figure A). Most of the inroads were made in the beer and soft drink markets, where aluminum held 65-percent and 31-percent shares respectively in 1976. Additional gains were expected, as aluminum was known to reduce the problems of flavoring, a major concern of both the brewing and soft drink industries.

Aluminum had several other important advantages over tinplate. First, its lighter weight could help reduce transportation costs. In addition, aluminum was easier to lithograph, producing a better reproduction at a lower cost. Finally, aluminum was favored over steel as a recycling material, because the

Table C
Metal Can Production by Material (%)

	1970	1971	1972	1973	1974	1975	1976
Steel	88.4	86.9	82.6	81.4	79.0	74.7	72.5
Aluminum	11.6	13.1	17.4	18.6	21.0	25.3	27.5

Figure A
Metal Can Shipments
(million base boxes)

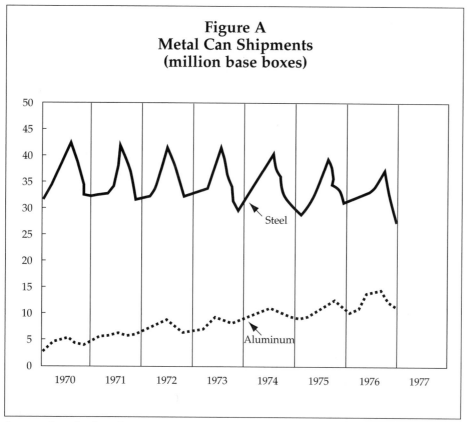

Source: Standard and Poor's Industry Survey, *Containers, Basic Analysis*, March 24, 1977, p. C123.

lighter aluminum could be transported to recycling sites more easily, and recycled aluminum was far more valuable.

Aluminum's major disadvantage was its initial cost. In 1976 the stock to manufacture 1,000 12-ounce beverage cans cost $17.13 using steel and $20.81 using aluminum. Moreover, "in early 1977, steel producers raised the price of tinplate by only 4.8 percent, in contrast to an increase for aluminum can stock of about 9.7 percent. [They did this] in an effort to enhance the competitiveness of steel vis-à-vis aluminum."[3] Some industry observers also expected the gap to widen as the auto companies increased their usage of aluminum and thus drove up aluminum prices. The two-piece tin-plated cans were also considerably stronger than their aluminum counterparts.

Other Materials. Two other raw materials threatened tinplate as the primary product in making containers: the new paper-and-metal composite called fiber-foil and the growing varieties of plastics. Fiber-foil cans were jointly developed by the R. C. Can Company and Anaconda Aluminum in 1962 for the motor oil market. They caught on immediately, and by 1977 this composite material was the primary factor in the frozen-juice-concentrate container market as well. Plastics represented the fastest growing sector of the packaging industry and the principal force in packaging change. The plastic bottle offered an enticing variety of advantages over glass bottles, including weight savings, resistance to breakage, design versatility, and thus lower shelf-space requirements. While can makers felt little initial effects from the introduction of plastics, they too could suffer if plastic bottles began to replace the cans being used as packaging for carbonated soft drinks.

The Packaging Revolution

Not only was the traditional package being reshaped and its materials reformulated, but by the 1970s containers also served a new purpose. Starting in the late 1950s the package itself became increasingly important in the marketing of the product it contained. The container was an advertising vehicle, and its features were expected to contribute to total product sales. This had serious implications for the metal can industry. Although the tin can was functional, aluminum was easier to lithograph, and plastic enabled more versatile shapes and designs. Pressure for continuing innovation to enhance marketing meant that companies had to make greater R&D expenditures in order to explore new materials, different shapes, more convenient tops, and other imaginative ideas with potential consumer appeal.

Increasingly, metal can companies would have to contend with the research and marketing strengths of such giant integrated companies as Du Pont, Dow Chemical, Weyerhaeuser, Reynolds, and Alcoa. In response to the integration of packaging by these major material suppliers, some metal can manufacturers began to invest in their own basic research. In 1963, American

---

[3]Standard and Poor's Industry Survey, *Containers, Basic Analysis,* March 24, 1977, p. C123.

announced the start of construction on a research center where investigations in such areas as solid-state physics and electrochemistry might reveal potential sources of new products.[4]

THE COMPETITION

By the late 1960s all three of Crown Cork and Seal's major competitors had diversified into areas outside the metal container industry. However, in 1977 all three still remained major producers of metal cans (see Exhibit 3).

Continental Group

Because of the extent of its diversification, Continental changed its name in 1976, making Continental Can only one division of the large conglomerate. Although only 38 percent of the total company's sales were in cans, it still held the dominant market share (18.4 percent) of the U.S. metal can market. The remainder of Continental's domestic sales were in forest products (20 percent) and other plastic and paper packaging materials (9 percent).

In 1969 Continental began focusing its investment spending on foreign and diversified operations. In 1972, the company took a $120-million after-tax extraordinary loss to cover the closing, realignment, and modernization of its domestic can-making facilities over a three-year period. Of the $120-million loss, close to 70 percent resulted from fixed-asset disposals, pension fund obligations, and severance pay. By 1976 almost one-third of the company's revenues came from its overseas operations, which covered 133 foreign countries. Domestic investment went primarily to paper products and the plastic bottle lines. Very little was allocated for the changeover to new two-piece cans.

American Can

American also reduced its dependence on domestic can manufacture and, even more than Continental, emphasized unrelated product diversification. American competed in the entire packaging area—metal and composite containers, paper, plastic, and laminated products. In 1972, American "decided to shut down, consolidate, or sell operations that had either become obsolete or marginal [which] resulted in an after-tax extraordinary loss of $106 million."[5]

By 1976, 20 percent of the company's sales came from consumer products such as household tissues, Dixie paper cups, and Butterick dress patterns. American's large chemical subsidiary brought in 15 percent of sales and

---

[4]"Crown Cork and Seal Company and the Metal Container Industry," HBS Cases Services No. 9-373-477, p. 14. Harvard Business School.
[5]Crown Cork and Seal Company Annual Report, 1972, p. 3.

another 15 percent came from international sales. Return on sales for the domestic container segment of American's business had remained stable at about 5 percent for the last five years. For this period American's average return on equity (7.1 percent) was the lowest of the four major can manufacturers, a result of relatively poor performance in its diversified areas (see Exhibit 3).

National Can

National's attempt to join the trend toward diversification achieved somewhat mixed results. Until 1967 National was almost solely a can producer. After that, through acquisitions the company moved into glass containers, food canning, pet foods, bottle closures, and plastic containers. However, instead of generating future growth opportunities, the expansion into food products proved a drag on company earnings. Pet foods and vegetable canning fared poorly in the 1974–1975 recession years, and the grocery division as a whole suffered a loss in 1976. As a result, National began a stronger overseas program to boost its earnings and investment.

Crown Cork and Seal

While its three major competitors turned to diversification, Crown Cork and Seal continued to manufacture primarily metal cans and closures. In 1976 the company derived almost 65 percent of its sales from tin-plated cans; crowns accounted for 29 percent of total sales and 35 percent of profits. The remaining sales were in bottling and canning machinery. In fact, Crown was one of the largest manufacturers of filling equipment in the world. Foreign sales—of crowns primarily—accounted for an increasingly large percentage of total sales (Exhibit 4). In 1976, Crown's return on sales was almost twice that of its three larger competitors. Over the previous ten years Crown's sales growth was second only to National Can, and Crown was first in profit growth. The following sections describe Crown's history and strategy.

CROWN CORK AND SEAL COMPANY

Company History

In August 1891 a foreman in a Baltimore machine shop hit upon an idea for a better bottle cap—a round piece of tin-coated steel with a flanged edge and an insert of natural cork. This crown-cork top became the main product of a highly successful small venture, the Crown Cork and Seal Company. When the patents ran out, however, competition became severe. The faltering Crown Cork was bought out in 1927 by a competitor, Charles McManus, who then shook the company back to life, bursting upon the "starchy" firm, as one

Exhibit 4
Estimated Breakdown of Crown Cork
and Seal's Sales and Pretax Income

	($ MILLIONS)			(PERCENTAGES)		
	1974	1975	1976[a]	1974	1975	1976[a]
A. SALES						
Domestic						
Cans						
Beer	180	209	232	23.5	24.7	24.6
Soft drinks	120	128	140	15.7	15.2	14.8
Food	55	65	70	7.2	7.7	7.4
Other (mainly aerosols)	100	91	101	13.0	10.7	10.7
Total cans	455	493	543	59.4	58.3	57.5
Crowns	25	29	32	3.3	3.4	3.4
Machinery	20	24	27	2.6	2.8	2.8
Total domestic	500	546	602	65.3	64.5	63.7
International						
Cans	46	57	73	6.0	6.7	7.7
Crowns	200	220	242	26.1	30.0	25.6
Machinery	20	24	28	2.6	2.8	3.0
Total international	266	301	343	34.7	35.5	36.3
Total, Domestic and International	766	847	945	100.0	100.0	100.0
B. PRETAX INCOME						
Domestic						
Cans	41.0	43.0	46.0	53.9	52.2	50.9
Crowns	2.0	2.0	3.0	2.6	2.4	3.3
Machinery	1.5	2.0	2.0	2.0	2.4	2.2
Total domestic	44.5	47.0	51.0	58.5	57.0	56.4
International						
Cans	4.0	6.0	8.0	5.3	7.3	8.9
Crowns	25.6	26.4	28.4	33.6	32.1	31.4
Machinery	2.0	3.0	3.0	2.6	3.6	3.3
Total international	31.6	35.4	39.4	41.5	43.0	43.6
Total, Domestic and International	76.1	82.4	90.4	100.0	100.0	100.0

(continued on next page)

[a]1976 figures are estimated and thus do not match actual numbers on other exhibits.
Source: *Wall Street Transcript*, November 3, 1975, pp. 41, 865.

	(PERCENTAGES)		
	1974	1975	1976[a]
C. PRETAX MARGINS			
<u>Domestic</u>			
Cans	9.0	8.7	8.5
Crowns	8.0	6.9	9.4
Machinery	<u>7.5</u>	<u>8.3</u>	<u>7.4</u>
Total domestic	8.9	8.6	8.5
<u>International</u>			
Cans	8.6	12.5	11.0
Crowns	13.0	12.3	11.6
Machinery	<u>10.0</u>	<u>12.5</u>	<u>10.7</u>
Total international	11.9	11.8	11.5
Total, Domestic and International	9.9	9.7	9.6

(continued)

old timer recalled, "like a heathen in the temple." *Fortune*, in 1962, described the turnaround:

> Under the hunch-playing, paternalistic McManus touch, Crown prospered in the thirties, selling better than half the U.S. and world supply of bottle caps. Even in bleak 1935 the company earned better than 13% on sales of $14 million.
>
> Then overconfidence led to McManus' first big mistake. He extended Crown's realm into canmaking. Reasoning soundly that the beer can would catch on, he bought a small Philadelphia can company. But reasoning poorly, he plunged into building one of the world's largest can plants on Philadelphia's Erie Avenue. It grew to a million square feet and ran as many as fifty-two lines simultaneously. A nightmare of inefficiency, the plant suffered deepened losses because of the McManus mania for volume. He lured customers by assuming their debts to suppliers and sometimes even cutting prices below costs. The Philadelphia blunder was to haunt Crown for many years.[6]

With all his projects and passion for leadership, McManus had no time or concern for building an organization that could run without him.

---

[6]"The Unoriginal Ideas That Rebuilt Crown Cork," *Fortune*, October 1962, pp. 118–64.

Neither of his two sons, Charles Jr. and Walter, was suited to command a one-man company, although both had been installed in vice presidents' offices. Crown's board was composed of company officers, some of whom were relatives of the boss. The combination of benevolent despotism and nepotism had prevented the rise of promising men in the middle ranks. When McManus died in 1946, the chairmanship and presidency passed to his private secretary, a lawyer named John J. Nagle.

In a fashion peculiar to Baltimore's family-dominated commerce, the inbred company acquired the settled air of a bank, only too willing to forget it lived by banging out bottle caps. In the muted, elegant offices on Eastern Avenue, relatives and hangers-on assumed that the remote machines would perpetually grind out handsome profits and dividends. In the postwar rush of business, the assumption seemed valid. The family left well enough alone, except to improve upon the late paternalist's largess. As a starter, Nagle's salary was raised from $35,000 to $100,000.

Officers arrived and departed in a fleet of chauffeured limousines. Some found novel ways to fill their days. A brother-in-law of the late McManus fell into the habit of making a day-long tour of the junior executives' offices, appearing at each doorway, whistling softly, and wordlessly moving on. After hours, the corporate good life continued. More than 400 dining and country club memberships were spread through the upper echelons. A would-be visitor to the St. Louis plant recalls being met at the airport, whisked to a country club for drinks, lunch, cocktails, and dinner, and then being returned to the airport with apologies and promises of a look at the plant "next time."[7]

Up to the early 1950s, Crown ran on a combination of McManus momentum and the last vestiges of pride of increasingly demoralized middle managers, who were both powerless to decide and unable to force decisions from above.

Dividends were maintained at the expense of investment in new plant; what investment there was, was mostly uninspired. From a lordly 50% in 1940, Crown's share of U.S. bottle cap sales [in the early 1950s] slipped to under 33%. In 1952 the chaotic can division had such substantial losses that the company was finally moved to act. The board omitted a quarterly dividend. That brought the widow McManus, alarmed, to the president's office. President Nagle counseled her to be patient and leave matters to him.[8]

Matters soon grew worse. A disastrous attempt at expansion into plastics followed a ludicrous diversification into metal bird cages. Then in 1954 a reorganization, billed to solve all problems, was begun. The plan was modeled after Continental's decentralized line and staff. The additional personnel and expense were staggering, and Crown's margins continued to dip. One observer

---

[7]Ibid.
[8]Ibid.

noted, "The new suit of clothes, cut for a giant, hung on Crown like an outsized shroud." The end seemed near.

John Connelly Arrives

John Connelly was the son of a Philadelphia blacksmith who, after working his way up as a container salesman, formed his own company to produce paper boxes. His interest in Crown began when he was rebuffed by the post-McManus management, which "refused to take a chance" on a small supplier like Connelly. *Fortune* described Connelly's takeover:

> By 1955, when Crown's distress had become evident to Connelly, he asked a Wall Street friend, Robert Drummond, what he thought could be done with the company. "I wrote him a three-page letter," Drummond recalls, "and John telephoned to say he'd thrown it into the wastebasket, which I doubted. He said, 'If you can't put it into one sentence you don't understand the situation.'" Drummond tried again and boiled it down to this formula: "If you can get sales to $150 million and earn 4% net after taxes and all charges, meanwhile reducing the common to one million shares, you'll earn $6 a share and the stock will be worth $90."[9]

That was good enough for Connelly. He began buying stock and in November 1956 was asked to be an outside director—a desperate move for the ailing company.

> The stranger found the parlor stuffy. "Those first few meetings," says Connelly, "were like something out of *Executive Suite*. I'd ask a question. There would be dead silence. I'd make a motion to discuss something. Nobody would second it, and the motion would die." It dawned on Connelly that the insiders knew even less about Crown than he did.
>
> He toured the plants—something no major executive had done in years. At one plant a foreman was his guide. His rich bass graced the company glee club, and he insisted on singing as they walked. Connelly finally told him to shut up and sit down. The warning system silenced, Connelly went on alone and found workers playing cards and sleeping. Some were building a bar for an executive.
>
> At another plant he sat in on a meeting of a dozen managers and executives, ostensibly called to discuss the problem posed by customers' complaints about poor quality and delivery. The fault, it seemed, lay with the customers themselves—how unreasonable they were to dispute Crown's traditional tolerance of a "fair" number of defective crowns in every shipment; how carping they were to complain about delays arising from production foul-ups, union troubles, flat tires, and other acts of God. Connelly kept silent until a pause signaled the consensus, then he confessed himself utterly amazed. He hadn't quite known what to make of Crown, he said, but now he knew it was some-

---

[9]Ibid.

thing truly unique in his business life—a company where the customer was always wrong. "This attitude," he told the startled executives, "is the worst thing I've ever seen. No one here seems to realize this company is in business to make money."[10]

The Crisis

In April 1957, Crown Cork and Seal was on the verge of bankruptcy. The 1956 loss was $241,000 after preferred dividends, and 1957's promised to be worse. Bankers Trust Company had called from New York to announce the withdrawal of their $2.5 million line of credit. It seemed that all that was left was to write the company's obituary when John Connelly took over the presidency. His rescue plan was simple—as he called it, "just common sense."

Connelly's first move was to pare down the organization. Paternalism ended in a blizzard of pink slips. The headquarters staff was cut from 160 to 80. Included in the departures were 11 vice presidents. The company returned to a simple functional organization, and in 20 months Crown had eliminated 1,647 jobs or 24 percent of the payroll. As part of the company's reorganization, Connelly discarded divisional accounting practices; at the same time he eliminated the divisional line and staff concept. Except for one accountant maintained at each plant location, all accounting and cost control was performed at the corporate level; the corporate accounting staff occupied one-half the space used by the headquarters group. In addition, the central research and development facility was disbanded.

The second step was to make each plant manager totally responsible for plant profitability, including any allocated costs. (All company overhead, estimated at 5 percent of sales, was allocated to the plant level.) Previously, plant managers had been responsible only for controllable expenses at the plant level. Under the new system, the plant manager was responsible even for the profits on each product manufactured in the plant. Although the plant manager's compensation was not tied directly to profit performance, one senior executive pointed out that the manager was "certainly rewarded on the basis of that figure."

The next step was to slow production to a halt and liquidate $7 million in inventory. By mid-July Crown paid off the banks. Planning for the future, Connelly developed control systems. He introduced sales forecasting, dovetailed with new production and inventory controls. This move took control away from the plant managers, who were no longer able to avoid layoffs by dumping excess products into inventory.

By the end of 1957 Crown had, in one observer's words, "climbed out of the coffin and was sprinting." Between 1956 and 1961 sales increased from

---

[10]Ibid.

$115 million to $176 million, and profits soared. After 1961 the company showed a 15.45 percent increase in sales and 14 percent in profits on the average every year. However, Connelly was not satisfied simply with short-term reorganizations of the existing company. By 1960, Crown Cork and Seal had adopted a strategy that it would follow for at least the next 15 years.

CROWN'S STRATEGY

Products and Markets

Recognizing Crown's position as a smaller producer in an industry dominated by giants, Connelly sought to develop a product line built around Crown's traditional strengths in metal forming and fabrication.[11] He chose to return to the area he knew best—tin-plated cans and crowns—and to concentrate on specialized uses and international markets.

A dramatic illustration of Connelly's commitment to this strategy occurred in the early 1960s. In 1960 Crown held over 50 percent of the market for motor oil cans. In 1962 R. C. Can and Anaconda Aluminum jointly developed fiber-foil cans for motor oil, which were approximately 20 percent lighter and 15 percent cheaper than the metal cans then in use. Crown's management decided not to continue to compete in this market and soon lost its entire market share.

In the early 1960s Connelly singled out two specific applications in the domestic market: beverage cans and the growing aerosol market. These applications were called "hard to hold," because the cans required special characteristics either to contain the product under pressure or to avoid affecting taste. The cans had to be filled in high-speed lines. In the mid-1960s, growth in demand for soft drink and beer cans was more than triple that for traditional food cans.

Crown had an early advantage in aerosols. In 1938 McManus had tooled up for a strong-walled, seamless beer can, which was rejected by brewers as too expensive. In 1946 it was dusted off and equipped with a valve to make the industry's first aerosol container. However, little emphasis was put on the line until Connelly spotted high growth potential in the mid-1960s.

In addition to the specialized product line, Connelly's strategy was based on two geographic thrusts: expand to national distribution in the United States and invest heavily abroad. The domestic expansion was linked to Crown's manufacturing reorganization; plants were spread out across the country to reduce transportation costs and to be nearer customers. Crown was unusual in that it set up no plants to service a single customer. Instead, Crown concentrated on providing products for a number of customers near their

---

[11]In 1956 Crown's sales were $115 million compared with $772 million for American and $1 billion for Continental.

plants. Also, Crown developed its lines totally for the production of tin-plated cans, not for aluminum. In international markets Crown invested heavily in undeveloped nations, first with crowns and then with cans as packaged foods became more widely accepted.

Manufacturing

When Connelly took over in 1957, Crown had perhaps the most out-moded and inefficient production facilities in the industry. In the post-McManus regime, dividends had taken precedence over new investment, and old machinery combined with the cumbersome Philadelphia plant had given Crown very high production and transportation costs. Soon after he gained control, Connelly took drastic action, closing down the Philadelphia facility and investing heavily in new and geographically dispersed plants. From 1958 to 1963, the company spent almost $82 million on relocation and new facilities. By 1976, Crown had 26 domestic plant locations versus 9 in 1955. The plants were small (usually under 10 lines versus 50 in the old Philadelphia complex) and were located close to the customer rather than the raw material source.

Crown emphasized flexibility and quick response to customer needs. One officer claimed that the key to the can industry was "the fact that nobody stores cans" and when customers need them, "they want them in a hurry and on time. . . . Fast answers get customers."[12] To deal with rush orders and special requests, Crown made a heavy investment in additional lines, which were maintained in set-up condition.

Marketing/Service

Crown's sales force, although smaller than American's or Continental's, kept close ties with customers and emphasized Crown's ability to provide technical assistance and specific problem solving at the customer's plant. This was backed by quick manufacturing responses and Connelly's policy that, from the top down, the customer was always right. As *Fortune* described it:

> At Crown, all customers' gripes go to John Connelly, who is still the company's best salesman. A visitor recalls being in his office when a complaint came through from the manager of a Florida citrus-packing plant. Connelly assured him the problem would be taken care of immediately, then casually remarked that he planned to be in Florida the next day. Would the plant manager join him for dinner? He would indeed. As Crown's president put the telephone

---

[12]"Crown Cork and Seal Company and the Metal Container Industry," HBS Case Services No. S373477, p. 28 Harvard Business School.

down, his visitor said that he hadn't realized Connelly was planning to go to Florida. "Neither did I," confessed Connelly, "until I began talking."[13]

Research and Development

Crown's R&D focused on enhancing the existing product line. According to Connelly, "We are not truly pioneers. Our philosophy is not to spend a great deal of money for basic research. However, we do have tremendous skills in die forming and metal fabrication, and we can move to adapt to the customer's needs faster than anyone else in the industry."[14] Research teams worked closely with the sales force, often on specific customer requests. For example, a study of the most efficient plant layout for a food packer or the redesign of a dust cap for the aerosol packager were not unusual projects.

Crown tried to stay away from basic research and "all the frills of an R&D section of high-class, ivory-towered scientists." Explained John Luviano, the company's new president:

> There is a tremendous asset inherent in being second, especially in the face of the ever-changing state of flux you find in this industry. You try to let others take the risks and make the mistakes as the big discoveries often flop initially due to something unforeseen in the original analysis. But somebody else, learning from the innovator's heartaches, prospers by the refinement.[15]

This sequence was precisely what happened with the two-piece drawn and ironed can. The original concept was developed in the aluminum industry by Reynolds and Alcoa in the late 1960s. Realizing the can's potential, Crown, in connection with a major steel producer, refined the concept for use with tinplate. Because of Crown's small-plant manufacturing structure and Connelly's willingness to move fast, Crown was able to beat its competitors into two-piece can production. Almost $120 million in new equipment was invested from 1972 through 1975, and by 1976 Crown had 22 two-piece lines in production—far more than any competitor.[16]

Crown was also credited with some important innovations. The company initiated the use of plastic as a substitute for cork as a crown liner, and in 1962 it introduced the first beverage-filling machine that could handle both bottles and cans.

---

[13]"The Unoriginal Ideas," p. 164.

[14]"Crown Cork and Seal Company and the Metal Container Industry," HBS Case Services No. S373477, p. 30 Harvard Business School.

[15]Ibid., p. 29. Luviano became president in 1976, while Connelly remained chairman and chief operating officer.

[16]In 1976, there were 47 two-piece tinplate and 130 two-piece aluminum lines in the United States.

Financing the Company

After Connelly took over, he used the first receipts from the inventory liquidation to get out from under the short-term bank obligations. He then steadily reduced the debt-equity ratio, from 42 percent in 1956 to 18.2 percent in 1976. In 1970 the last of the preferred stock was bought back, eliminating preferred dividends as a cash drain. From 1970 on, the emphasis was on repurchasing the common stock (see Exhibit 1). Each year Connelly set ambitious earnings goals, and most years he achieved them, reaching $2.84 per share in 1976. That year marked a critical time for Connelly's financial ambitions. As he said in the 1976 annual report:

> A long time ago we made a prediction that some day our sales would exceed $1 billion and profits of $60.00 per share. Since then the stock has been split 20-for-1 so this means $3.00 per share. These two goals are still our ambition and will remain until both have been accomplished. I am sure that one, and I hope both, will be attained this year [1977].

International Expansion

Another aspect of Crown's efforts was its continuing emphasis on international growth, particularly in developing nations (Figure B). With sales of $343 million and 60 foreign plant locations, Crown was, by 1977, the largest producer of metal cans and crowns overseas. In the early 1960s, when Crown began to expand internationally, the strategy was unique. In many cases the company received ten-year tax shelters as initial investment incentives. At that time Connelly commented:

> Right now we are premature but this has been necessary in order for Crown to become established in these areas. . . . If we can get 20% to 40% of all new geographic areas we enter, we have a great growth potential in contrast to American and Continental. . . . In 20 years I hope whoever is running this company will look back and comment on the vision of an early decision to introduce canmaking in underdeveloped countries.[17]

John Connelly's Contribution to Success

Many claimed that John Connelly himself was the driving force behind Crown's dramatic turnaround and that it was his ambition and determination that kept the company on the road to success. Connelly has been described as a strong-willed individual whose energetic leadership convinced and inspired his organization to meet his goals.

---

[17]"Crown Cork and Seal Company and the Metal Container Industry," HBS Case Services No. S373477, p. 33 Harvard Business School.

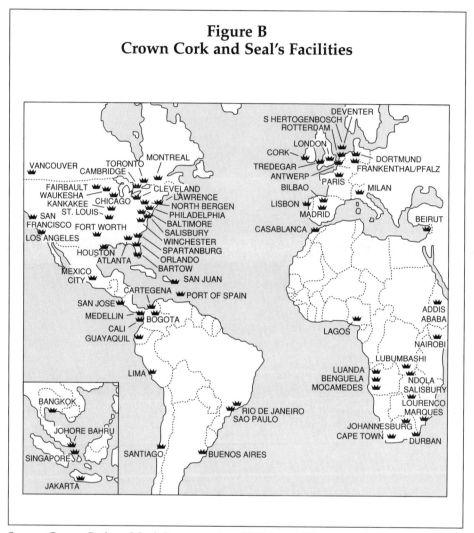

Figure B
Crown Cork and Seal's Facilities

Source: Crown Cork and Seal Company, Inc., 1972 Annual Report.

Yet Connelly was no easy man to please. He demanded from his employees the same dedication and energy that he himself threw into his work. As one observer wrote in 1962:

At fifty-seven Connelly is a trim, dark-haired doer. The seven-day, eighty-hour weeks of the frenetic early days are only slightly reduced now. The Saturday morning meeting is standard operating procedure. Crown's executives travel and confer only at night and on weekends. William D. Wallace, vice president for operations, travels 100,000 miles a year, often in the company plane. But Connelly sets the pace. An associate recalls driving to his home in the predawn blackness to pick him up for a flight to a distant plant. The Connelly house was dark, but he spotted a figure sitting on the curb under a street light, engrossed in a loose-leaf book. Connelly's greeting, as he jumped into the car: "I want to talk to you about last month's variances."[18]

In 1977, at age 72, Connelly still firmly held the reins of his company.[19] "He'll never retire. He'll die with his boots on," noted one company official.[20] Despite comments such as these, Connelly had raised John Luviano—age 54 and a 25-year veteran at Crown—to the presidency of the company.

OUTLOOK FOR THE FUTURE

In 1977, observers of Crown Cork and Seal had a favorite question: How long can this spectacular performance last? Until then, Crown's sales and profit growth had continued despite recession, devaluation, and stiff competition from the giants of the industry. However, in 1977 the ozone scare and the potential legislation on nonreturnable containers threatened the company's beverage and aerosol business.

The Ozone Controversy

In 1973 two University of California chemists advanced the initial theory that fluorocarbons—gases used in refrigerators, air conditioners, and as a propellant in aerosols—were damaging the earth's ozone shield. (Ozone forms an atmospheric layer that prevents much of the sun's ultraviolet radiation from reaching the earth's surface.) Their theory was that the fluorocarbons floated up into the stratosphere where they broke up, releasing chlorine atoms. These atoms then reacted with the ozone molecules, causing their destruction. The problem was compounded because after the reaction the chlorine atom was free to attack other ozone molecules, causing accelerated breakup of the ozone layer. Proponents of the theory asserted that "fluorocarbons have already depleted ozone by 1 percent and will eventually deplete it by 7 percent to 13 percent, perhaps within 50 to 80 years, if the use of fluorocarbons continues at recent levels."[21]

Proponents of the theory argued that there was real danger in allowing the destruction of the ozone shield. As this shield was depleted and more

---

[18]"The Unoriginal Ideas," p. 163.
[19]Connelly reportedly owned or controlled about 18 percent of Crown's outstanding common stock.
[20]*Financial World*, November 26, 1975, p. 12.
[21]*Wall Street Journal*, December 3, 1975, p. 27.

radiation passed through, they predicted, the number of cases of skin cancer would rise alarmingly. Dr. Sherwood Rowland, one of the original proponents of the theory, explained:

> If aerosol use were to grow at 10% annually (half the growth rate of the 1960s), stratospheric ozone content would fall by 10% by 1994. Scientists figure this would mean a 20% increase in ultraviolet radiation reaching the earth and cause by itself at least 60,000 new cases of skin cancer annually in the United States, roughly a 20% increase.[22]

They also cited the possibility of crop damage, genetic mutation, and climatic change.

Although many studies were in progress, by the end of 1976 the theory had not yet been conclusively proven. There were still some major questions about the types and amounts of reactions that would take place in the stratosphere. Nonetheless, most tests supported the basic thesis that fluorocarbons were in some way damaging the ozone layer.

After the ozone theory was publicized, the reaction against aerosols was severe. Aerosols provided about 60 percent of the fluorocarbons released into the air annually. In 1974 aerosol production declined almost 7 percent in reaction to the recession and the fluorocarbon problem. Only 2.6 billion aerosol containers were used, down from 2.9 billion in 1973. Action began immediately—on the scientific front to test the ozone theory and on the legislative front to restrict the use of fluorocarbons.

Soon a bitter battle broke out between industry spokespeople and those advocating an immediate ban. One industry spokesperson, who requested anonymity, said, "All the scientific theories against fluorocarbons are just that—theories, not facts. What we need is more research before there are any more bans or badmouthing. We don't want another false scare."[23] A member of the Natural Resource Defense Council looked harshly upon the aerosol industry's position. "It's like Watergate," he said. "They want to see a smoking gun. We'll have to wait 25 years for that, and by then irreparable damage will have been done."[24]

Despite industry protests and with the support of some additional studies, state legislators began to introduce antifluorocarbon bills. Georgia led the way in June 1975 by passing a bill banning fluorocarbon aerosols effective March 1, 1977. Successful industry lobbying kept other actions to a minimum until May 1977, when federal agencies proposed a nationwide ban. Calling fluorocarbons an "unacceptable risk to individual health and to the earth's

---

[22]Ibid.

[23]*New York Times,* June 22, 1975, p. F3.

[24]Ibid.

atmosphere," the commissioner of the Food and Drug Administration outlined a three-step phaseout of fluorocarbon manufacture and use.[25] The first step in the ban would be a halt to all manufacture of chlorofluorocarbon propellants for nonessential uses. This ban would take effect October 15, 1978. In the second step, on December 15, 1978, all companies would have to stop using existing supplies of the chemicals in making nonessential aerosol products. The third step would be a halt to all interstate shipment of nonessential products containing the propellant gases. This part of the ban would go into effect April 15, 1979.[26]

The Future for Aerosols. Opinions differed widely as to the extent of the problems the ozone issue would cause the industry. By 1977, the latest estimates were that the fluorocarbon ban would cost container manufacturers more than $132 million in lost sales from 1977 to 1980. This was much less than most of the original estimates due to the success of efforts in the previous two years in finding fluorocarbon substitutes. Most of the solutions involved finding substitute propellants or changing the aerosol valve.

A propellant is the pressurized gas used to hold the suspended molecules of aerosol products as they are sprayed out. Until the early 1970s the most common propellant material was fluorocarbon, which was used in about half of the aerosol cans sold. By 1977 the possibility of substituting hydrocarbons was being explored for many applications. However, although they were less expensive, hydrocarbons were known to be more flammable and thus more dangerous to mix with the many personal-care products that include alcohol as an ingredient. Other proposed alternatives included using carbon dioxide or special pressurized cans that did not release propellants at all.

In May 1977 the new Aquasol valve looked to be one of the most promising ways of eliminating fluorocarbons. Developed by Robert Abplanalp, the inventor of the original aerosol valve, the Aquasol used a dual-duct system (rather than the traditional one-duct) that kept the product separate from the propellant. Abplanalp claimed that fillers could get twice as much product into a can with the new valve because the product did not have to be mixed with the propellant. Also, hydrocarbons could be used more safely for many applications.

Industry Recovery. By 1977 recovery in the aerosol market had already begun, with shipments for 1976 up 6 percent. It seemed likely that this trend would continue because of the strong appeal aerosols had for the consumer. In a 1974 study over 59 percent of the population had heard of the ozone problem, yet about 25 percent said they would be "very disturbed to do without" aerosol products. Industry optimism was moderated, however, by the growing popularity of pump sprays and other nonaerosol products, and by the tendency of

---

[25]*New York Times*, May 12, 1977, p.1.
[26]Ibid.

the consumer not to differentiate between fluorocarbons and aerosols using other propellants.

Regulating Nonreturnable Containers

Crown's future was also threatened by moves to legislate restrictions on the use of nonreturnable containers. By 1976 Oregon, Vermont, and South Dakota already regulated the use of disposable containers. Laws requiring mandatory deposits for most beverage containers were approved in November 1976 by voter referendums in Maine and Michigan, while they were turned down by narrow margins in Massachusetts and Colorado. The existing laws required a 5-cent deposit on all bottles and cans, refundable when the empties were brought back for recycling or reuse. Nationally, the Environmental Protection Agency banned throwaways from federal property—parks, federal buildings, and military posts—starting in October 1977.

The main problem was litter. Although it was estimated that only 1 percent of the American population were litterers, the extent of the damage was staggering. Unfortunately, disposable cans contributed significantly to the problem. While containers made up only 8 percent of the solid waste in the United States, they made up 54 percent to 70 percent of highway litter by volume. A second issue was the potential savings of raw materials and energy that could be obtained from reusing containers.

Economic Impact. Part of the controversy involved the potential economic impact of legislative bans on nonreturnables. Industry sources agreed that the laws would bring an increase in beer and soft drink prices and eliminate thousands of jobs. The environmentalists countered that consumers paid 30 percent to 40 percent more for beverages in throwaway containers. "Any increased cost due to retooling would be offset by savings in the use of returnable bottles or recycled cans," claimed a spokesperson for the Michigan United Conservation Clubs. He added that "any jobs lost in the canning or bottling industries would be offset by additional jobs in transportation and handling."[27]

Prospects for the Future. Despite a powerful industry lobby, the fight against nonreturnables gained momentum. In July 1977 legislation was being considered by the Congressional Committee on Energy and Natural Resources to require deposits on throwaways nationwide. Although the Senate had once rejected a ban on pull tops, some states, including Massachusetts, had passed such bills effective in 1978. Returnable bottles, which could be used by more than one manufacturer, were being encouraged under the new laws, but it seemed

---

[27]*New York Times*, October 30, 1976, p. F1.

unlikely that cans would be totally banned. Instead, various schemes for deposits and recycling were emphasized. Proposals were made that metal cans be collected, crushed, melted, and reused to make new cans. Under the new system it was uncertain who would pay the extra transportation costs and whether lower raw material prices to the can maker would result. Unfortunately for tin-plate users like Crown, the new system favored aluminum cans because of the higher value of the reclaimed metal and the recycling network that already existed for aluminum products.

CROWN'S FUTURE GROWTH

Crown's usual optimistic forecasts continued into 1977. The 1976 Annual Report all but ignored the aerosol and bottle bill issues. The strategy stayed the same: no major basic R&D efforts, but quick attention to meeting customer needs and leadership in new applications that involved the traditional metal can. Thus, despite current problems in its markets, some industry observers saw no reason why the company's good record wouldn't continue:

> Even with Connelly's eventual retirement, his Number 2 man seems certain to keep Crown on its upward profits growth trend. While others—like National Can—have ventured into uncharted and at times unprofitable waters, Crown has prospered by doing what it knows best. Under that strategy, prosperity is likely to continue reigning for Crown.[28]

---

[28]*Financial World*, November 26, 1975, p. 12.

SOUTHWEST AIRLINES

It was March 1992, and Herb Kelleher, Southwest Airline's chief executive officer, was laughingly describing the way in which he was about to settle a dispute with Stevens Aviation over the right to use the ad slogan "Just Plain Smart," which Stevens maintained it had developed first. Kurt Herwald, chairman of Stevens Aviation, and Kelleher had decided they would settle things the "old-fashioned way" in a best-of-three arm-wrestling match in the Dallas Sportatorium.

This unusual method of negotiation was entirely in keeping with Herb Kelleher's "disarming" style, which, for some observers, was the principal reason for Southwest's 19 straight profitable years. Many in the industry, however, pointed to a variety of other factors that ensured the Dallas-based airline would continue to maintain its top record of achievement. The bottom line for Southwest Airlines was that it provided high value for low cost and consistently delivered what it promised.

HISTORY

Southwest Airlines was founded in 1967 by Rollin King, a former investment counselor who had been operating a small air-taxi service in Texas. The impetus behind King's organization of Southwest Airlines was his perception of a growing unmet need for improved intercity air service within Texas.

In the late 1960s, Houston, Dallas, San Antonio, and Fort Worth were among the fastest growing cities in the United States. Although each had its own airport, a huge new airport, the Dallas/Fort Worth Regional Airport, was then under construction that would serve both Dallas and Fort Worth. These four cities were primarily served by two Texas-based carriers, Braniff International Airways and Texas International Airlines (TI). For the most part, service to these cities by Braniff and TI consisted of "legs" of interstate flights; in other words, a Braniff flight might stop at Dallas on its way from New York to San Antonio.

This case was prepared by Charlotte Thompson under the supervision of Professor Elliot N. Weiss. Copyright © 1993 by the University of Virginia Darden School Foundation, Charlottesville, VA.

In his talks with consumers prior to embarking on the Southwest venture, King was struck by the amount of dissatisfaction with the current service and discovered that the market was bigger than many realized. Together with his lawyer Herb Kelleher, King was able to raise enough capital to incorporate the airline. On February 20, 1968, Kelleher obtained the Certificate of Public Convenience and Necessity from the Texas Aeronautics Commission, which granted Southwest Airlines the right to provide intrastate air service between Dallas/Fort Worth, Houston, and San Antonio. Southwest's competitors reacted immediately by asking the Texas courts to enjoin issuance of the certificate, maintaining that service was already provided on the proposed routes and that the market was not large enough to support another carrier. The ensuing litigation kept the company's lawyers occupied for several years.

In 1970, King brought Lamar Muse aboard as president, director, and treasurer. An independent financial consultant and former president of Universal Airlines, Muse had become attracted to Southwest after reading about its legal battles and realizing that the market for this kind of carrier was growing: "There was so much interline traffic that most of the seats were occupied by those people. While Braniff had hourly service, there really weren't many seats available for local passengers." Muse also commented that both Braniff and TI, in part because their local service was merely a leg of interstate flights, were rarely on time, and people thus tended to fly only when they absolutely had to.

On June 18, 1971, amid a heavy advertising campaign to promote the new airline and restraining orders issued by judges after complaints by its competitors, Southwest launched 6 round-trip flights between Dallas's Love Field and San Antonio and 12 round-trip flights between Dallas and Houston. The takeoff proved to be less than auspicious. In its first 11 months of operation, Southwest lost $3.7 million. Some days saw the airline carrying a total of only 150 passengers on its 18 round-trip flights. Nevertheless, Muse persevered with his ideas by offering unbelievable prices, gimmicks, and creative advertising.

In Texas, 1972 became the year of the fare war. To compete with Southwest, competitors slashed fares and began offering more in terms of service, for example, free beer, hot and cold towels, one-dollar drinks on routes Southwest flew, and more frequent service. When Braniff decided to offer a half-price fare, Muse countered with a giveaway: free bottles of premium liquor to passengers who paid full fare; passengers who did not want the liquor would pay half fare. Because corporations were used to paying full fare, business travelers became the happy recipients of premium liquor. During the promotion, Southwest became not only the largest distributor in Texas of Chivas, Crown Royal, and Smirnoff, but also the winner in the fare war. After 1972, Southwest consistently made a profit (see Exhibit 1).

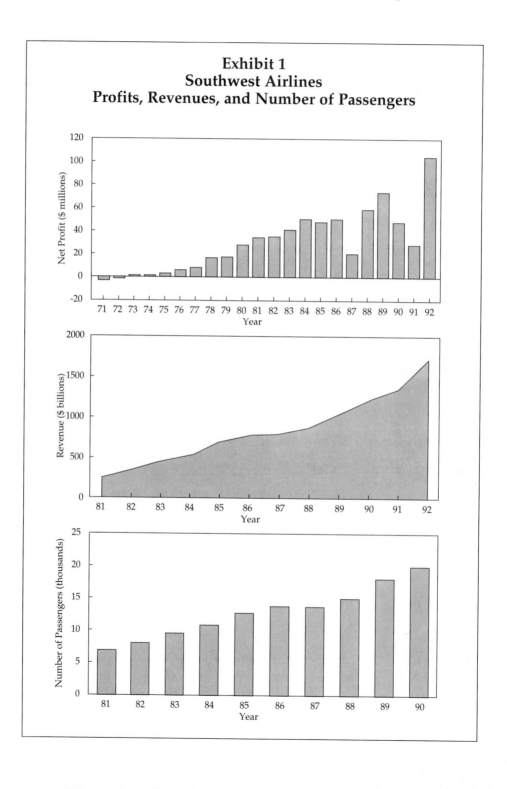

Exhibit 1
Southwest Airlines
Profits, Revenues, and Number of Passengers

HERB KELLEHER

In March 1977, Lamar Muse resigned as president and chief executive officer of Southwest Airlines, and Herb Kelleher was named to replace him. Kelleher, a student of philosophy and literature who later graduated at the top of his law-school class at New York University, was wedded to the Southwest cause from the very beginning. Kelleher did not merely believe in Southwest's mission; in some ways, the initial legal battles with Southwest's competitors enraged him to the point where he knew he had to win. Kelleher likened Southwest's struggles with its competitors to the trench warfare of World War II, and he was determined that Southwest would eventually be able to engage the enemy on its terms, not theirs.

Early on, Kelleher established a reputation for doing the unusual. At company functions he would appear as Elvis Presley or Roy Orbison and perform "Jailhouse Rock" or "Pretty Woman." One Halloween night he showed up at Southwest's hangar in drag, as Corporal Klinger from *M*A*S*H*, to thank mechanics for working overtime. Although Kelleher's behavior was somewhat unconventional for a chief executive officer, his efforts paid off. His colleagues credited much of Southwest's "magic" to him. "Herb has a nice, light perspective on life," stated Jim Wimberly, head of Southwest's ground operations. "We both like Wild Turkey, and we smoke a little too much."

Known for his extreme tenacity and limitless energy, Kelleher slept only four hours a night, read two or three books a week, and chain-smoked. Gary Barron, Southwest's chief operations officer, called Kelleher "the smartest, quickest lawyer—not to mention the best judge of people" he had ever seen.[1] Kelleher was widely credited with much of the airline's success for promoting and maintaining both a culture that favored people and a coherent business strategy that was consistently successful yet deceptively simple. "People always want high-quality service at a lower price, provided by people who enjoy what they do," he maintained.[2] The results of Kelleher's efforts: Southwest's overall costs were the lowest of any major carrier, yet its workers were among the best paid.

OPERATIONS

Start-Up

Initial operations for Southwest Airlines began under extreme pressure and tight deadlines. Additional capital for start-up expenses had to be raised, personnel had to be hired and trained, and a multitude of marketing problems

---

[1]*Inc.*, January 1992, p. 67.
[2]Ibid., p. 66.

had to be resolved. Most important, Muse and King had to make key decisions on the number and type of aircraft to be used. Many weeks of high-pressure negotiations with representatives of several airplane manufacturers resulted in the purchase of three Boeing 737-200 aircraft. This decision proved to be a crucial one for Southwest, not only because the airline would continue to use the same type of aircraft for many years, but also because the planes required fewer crew members than the aircraft used by Southwest's competitors.

Scheduling

Initial decisions regarding scheduling were constrained by the fact that Southwest only had three airplanes. After studying flight times and on-the-ground (turnaround) times, Muse and King concluded that they could offer flights at 75-minute intervals using two planes between Dallas and Houston (the most important route) and at 150-minute intervals (2.5 hours) between Dallas and San Antonio using one plane, which amounted to 12 round-trips per day between Dallas and Houston and 6 round-trips per day between Dallas and San Antonio. Because of low weekend demand, Muse and King decided to fly less frequently on Saturdays and Sundays.

In spite of all their well-laid plans, however, scheduling proved to be a problem. In the first two weeks, the airline reported an average of 13.1 passengers per flight on the Dallas–Houston route and 12.9 passengers on the Dallas–San Antonio route. Because of the lack of planes, management concluded that Southwest was unable to compete effectively and thus set about improving its schedule frequencies. The delivery of the fourth plane in late September helped immensely; but perhaps more important than the arrival of the fourth plane was the company's ability to deliver a turnaround time of ten minutes. Proving its ability to turn a constraint into a competitive advantage, Southwest was able to initiate hourly service between Dallas and Houston and flights every two hours between Dallas and San Antonio by orchestrating maintenance and servicing to the point that no plane stayed on the ground more than ten minutes. This development proved to be a real innovation in the industry; the company became known for its "quick turns."

Strategy and Service

From the beginning, Southwest management's idea was to offer no-frills, low-cost flights to and from secondary airports, and the airline clung tenaciously to this initial strategy. Management's focus was the "short-haul, point-to-point" strategy, which advocated short flights (average flight time of 55 minutes) to uncrowded airports for quick turnarounds. This adherence to a short-haul strategy enabled Southwest to distinguish itself from its competitors, many of whom failed. Several airlines started out in the short-haul business, only to become tempted by the more glamorous routes. "Suddenly they were competing with big people who knew what they were doing," stated Gary Barron. "They got their brains beat out. Southwest will take Lubbock to Little Rock any old time." As Salomon Brothers analyst Julius Maldutis pointed out, "They stay out of the major vegetable patches with big elephants."[3]

Most of Southwest's competitors used a "hub-and-spoke" system in which big planes fly to major airports (hubs) and then link up with smaller airports (spokes). Southwest developed no recognizable hub, preferring instead to maintain a "spiderweb" system in which one strand at a time is spun.[4] Kelleher's reason for implementing this strategy was that a hub-and-spoke network tied up too many valuable assets at too few pressure points, whereas a spiderweb system would allow maximum flexibility to disperse assets and reduce stress in the system.

Southwest's "no-frills" policy included no baggage transfers, no meals, no assigned seats, and reusable boarding cards. When a passenger decided to fly Southwest, he or she would show up at the airport at the designated time, get a ticket at the counter printed out by a machine (at the time, the competition was issuing handwritten tickets), take a reusable boarding card, and board the plane to sit wherever he or she preferred. On board, the passenger could enjoy a drink or two and some peanuts, but nothing more. The reason behind the no-frills policy was that there were other things to offer customers that gave better value: frequent, reliable, on-time flights and very low prices. For Southwest, quality was not a filet mignon dinner with a fine wine; it was on-time flights and no lost baggage.

Southwest's management also made a decision not to subscribe to expensive computerized reservation systems that would link them with travel agencies, opting instead to market the airline through other means. Although initially the airline hired a small sales force that promoted Southwest among travel agents and corporate accounts (companies whose personnel flew Southwest on a regular basis), Southwest used travel agents relatively infrequently because of the small margins it made on ticket sales.

One way the airline was able to keep its costs down was through contracting for such things as major maintenance, data processing, and legal services. Southwest also contracted for about two-thirds of its monthly jet-fuel supply and purchased the rest on the spot market.

Southwest's policy with regard to costs and service paid off: its average number of flights per plane per day was 10.5, whereas the industry average was 4.5; its planes were in the air 11 hours a day (industry average, 8 hours a day), which was an especially significant statistic in that its flights were the shortest of any airline. Given that short flights made for higher fuel costs and a greater number of landing fees than did long flights, Southwest could be especially proud of its cost of 6.5 cents per available seat-mile, the lowest in

---

[3]*Financial World*, May 28, 1991, p. 19.
[4]*Inc.*, January 1992, p. 66.

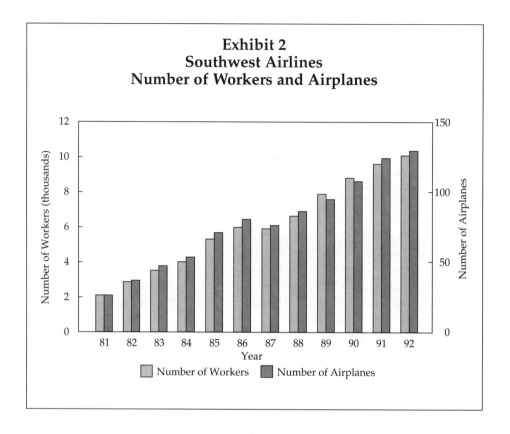

Exhibit 2
Southwest Airlines
Number of Workers and Airplanes

the industry. Southwest's secret was that it made extremely good use of its most expensive asset: its planes (see Exhibit 2).

NEW MARKETS

Part of Southwest's strategy was to investigate potential markets carefully. As flamboyant as Kelleher often portrayed himself, he admitted to being a very cautious businessman. In 1991, 34 cities formally requested that Southwest operate from their airports. Southwest chose only one, Sacramento, and it did so only after USAir left. As Gary Barron put it, "We search out markets that are overpriced and underserved."[5] Small cities and small airports meant that Southwest could get its planes in and out quickly.

Once Southwest decided to enter a market, however, it did so with full force. The airline offered so many flights that customers merely had to show

[5]*Inc.*, January 1992, p. 68.

up at the airport and take the next cheap flight out. This part of the strategy not only enabled the airline to spread its fixed costs over many seats, but also served a marketing function in that Southwest could really "make a statement" in a new airport.

After years of patient watchfulness and careful consideration, Southwest decided to enter the California market. In 1983, it began offering flights on the San Diego–San Francisco route but did not expand service until 1989. The California intrastate market was ideal for Southwest: it combined short-haul, high-frequency routes with good weather and a populace appreciative of Southwest's "unconventional behavior." The airline employed a relatively simple strategy of offering service in the mainly suburban areas outside Los Angeles and San Francisco at prices as low as $19 and no higher than $64 for a one-way flight.

Not surprisingly, Southwest's expansion into California led to a series of fare wars as the major airlines tried to keep Southwest from stealing customers. The intensely competitive market in California saw some losers: USAir and American were forced out of the California intrastate market almost entirely. As airline analyst Harold Shenton noted, "Most of the big airlines are trying to protect long-haul revenue, so they're not dependent on local traffic and they're weakening in the markets outside Los Angeles and San Francisco."[6]

Southwest undercut its California competitors and emerged victorious in the fare battles. The airline continued to use such tactics as offering free tickets in a "Fly One Way, Get One Way Free" campaign and a $59 unrestricted one-way fare for all intrastate California flights as part of the airline's "California State Fare" promotion. Southwest's California campaign was so successful that Southwest saved its California fliers more than $40 million in 1991.

MARKETING

Positioning

Southwest decided from the beginning that it would differentiate itself from its competitors by creating a "fun" image. In contrast to Texas International, which was perceived as dull, and Braniff, which was seen as conservative, Southwest's personality and theme were focused on the concept of "love"; flight attendants wore brightly colored hot pants, and inflight drinks and peanuts were known as "Love Potions" and "Love Bites."

As Southwest began working with the Bloom Agency, a large regional advertising agency, to create its public image, it concurrently came up with a model for the type of person it wanted to hire: the "entire personality description model," which was used as a guide in the recruiting process. Adjectives

---

[6]Ibid., p. 70.

such as "young and vital," "exciting," and "dynamic" were sprinkled through-out the personality-model statement.

Herb Kelleher's fun-loving personality served to reinforce Southwest's lively image among its employees and encouraged them to pass it on to pas-sengers. Employees took to donning holiday costumes such as rabbit garb for Easter, and every holiday became an excuse for inflight parties with balloons and cake.

In 1986, the airline introduced the concept of "Fun Fares," which ranged in price from $19 to $85 for a one-way ticket. A new summer uniform for flight attendants was used to promote the fares: surfer shorts, knit shirts, and tennis shoes.

Under an agreement signed with Sea World of Texas in 1988, Southwest launched "Shamu One," its flying killer whale in the form of a 737-300 air-plane. The painted plane became so popular throughout Texas that Southwest painted two more to resemble Sea World's most popular attraction.

Pricing

Pricing decisions were a particularly important part of Southwest's over-all strategy. Muse and King spent a great deal of time discussing the pricing issue with executives of Pacific Southwest Airlines, which had revolutionized commuter air travel in California through a combined strategy of low fares and aggressive promotion. At the time, Braniff and TI fares from Dallas to Houston were $27 and from Dallas to San Antonio, $28. Muse and King looked carefully at preoperating expenditures, operating costs, and market potential and finally decided on an initial fare of $20 for both routes. To oper-ate at a break-even capacity, Southwest would require an average of 39 pas-sengers per trip, a number the two executives considered reasonable given that the airline would have an initial price advantage over its competition. Before the break-even figure of 39 passengers per flight could be reached, however, they expected an initial period of deficit operations, a development they were willing to accept to get the airline off the ground. Clearly, the mar-keting campaign would be crucial to their future decisions on pricing.

Southwest was only five months old when Muse decided to try some-thing revolutionary in the airline industry. Because the crew had been flying an empty plane from Houston to Dallas at the end of each week for weekend servicing, Muse came up with the idea of offering a fare of $10 for this last flight of the week. Within a period of two weeks, the plane was flying from Houston to Dallas with a full passenger load.

The success of the two-tier pricing system did not escape Muse, who soon decided to cut fares on the last flight of *each day* in all directions, which meant that any passenger flying Southwest after 7:00 P.M. on any day of the week would need a mere $10 to climb aboard. A few months later he was able to raise both prices (regular and "night"), but he continued the two-tier pricing system because of its ability to attract passengers.

Pricing was a key part of Southwest's strategy, and the company was leery of fare increases. From 1972 to 1978, Southwest did not have a single fare increase. "We base our pricing on profit rather than market share," contended Southwest Vice President for Finance Gary C. Kelly.[7]

Southwest's rock-bottom prices won both admiration and scorn from competitors, many of whom immediately dropped their prices when Southwest entered their markets. Many were also resentful: one American Airlines executive commented, "Value isn't quality; it's getting what you pay for."[8] Some competitors accused Southwest of "airline-seat dumping," although the airline made money on its routes from day one.

Promotion

Southwest defined its target market not as the passengers flying with other airlines, but as the people who were using other modes of transportation. As Southwest's director of sales and marketing stated, "We're not competing with other carriers. We want to pull people out of backyards and automobiles, and get them off the bus."

Southwest's promotions were aimed primarily at regular business commuters, who constituted 89 percent of Southwest's traffic. Accordingly, the airline used a heavy advertising campaign and a small sales force targeted specifically at the business traveler. Initially, the airline was striving for name recognition, but its marketing efforts quickly expanded to create an image via mass communications. With a first-year advertising budget of $700,000, this strategy was implemented in a number of ways, including teaser ads announcing incredibly low fares and a follow-up phone number, and the Sweetheart Club, in which secretaries received one "sweetheart stamp" for each Southwest reservation they made for their bosses. For every 15 stamps, the secretary would receive one free ride on Southwest.

Building a Reputation

Although at first many observers believed Southwest's "fun" image and no-frills flights would be the last choice for business travelers and cause the airline to take an immediate nosedive into bankruptcy, the skeptics soon stopped laughing. Initially unprofitable, Southwest ended 1973 in the black and celebrated its millionth passenger early in 1974. As the airline continued

---

[7]*AW*, March 5, 1990, p. 36.
[8]*Time*, March 2, 1992, p. 15.

Exhibit 3
Airline Revenues, Profits, and Passenger-Miles for 1991

AIRLINE	REVENUE ($ MILLIONS)	PROFIT ($ MILLIONS)	PASSENGER-MILES (BILLIONS)
Alaska Air Group	1,116	10.3	5.4
America West	1,420	−222.0	3.0
American	12,993	−240.0	82.3
Continental	5,551	−305.7	41.4
Delta[a]	9,171	−324.4	62.1
Northwest	7,534	−3.1	53.2
Southwest	1,324	26.9	11.3
Trans World	3,688	34.6	28.0
UAL	11,748	−331.9	82.3
U.S. Air Group	6,533	−305.3	34.1

[a]Fiscal year ended June 30, 1991.
Source: "Unfriendly Skies," *Fortune,* November 2, 1992, p. 92.

to expand its routes to cities such as Corpus Christi, Austin, El Paso, Oklahoma City, New Orleans, and Albuquerque, its management continued to maintain its reputation as the feisty underdog that was consistently able to offer low prices and superior, reliable service. (See Exhibit 3 for a comparison of 1991 revenues, profits, and passenger-miles for the major U.S. airlines.)

In 1988, the U.S. Department of Transportation rated Southwest as having the best on-time performance, the lowest number of lost-baggage complaints, and the lowest number of customer complaints among all domestic airlines (see Exhibit 4). Southwest was particularly proud that it was the first airline to "win" all three categories since the department began tracking airline performance. Southwest then proceeded to win the "Triple Crown" the following four years.

PERSONNEL

The company's philosophy toward recruitment and its employees remained consistent throughout its history: Southwest looked for people who were energetic and who wanted to work hard and have fun at the same time.

Exhibit 4
Performance of Major U.S. Air Carriers for 1992

AIRLINE	ON-TIME PERFORMANCE[a] (RANK)	BAGGAGE PROBLEMS[b] (RANK)	CONSUMER COMPLAINTS[c] (RANK)
Alaska Air Group	84.6 (4)	6.04 (7)	0.48 (2)
America West	88.9 (2)	4.42 (2)	1.50 (9)
American	82.1 (6)	4.73 (3)	1.40 (8)
Continental	79.0 (10)	6.13 (10)	1.17 (7)
Delta	79.1 (9)	5.71 (6)	0.58 (3)
Northwest	86.1 (3)	5.49 (5)	0.74 (4)
Southwest	92.1 (1)	3.72 (1)	0.24 (1)
Trans World	82.1 (5)	6.06 (8)	2.82 (10)
UAL	81.3 (7)	5.30 (4)	1.05 (6)
U.S. Air Group	79.6 (8)	6.10 (9)	0.85 (5)
Average	**82.3**	**5.36**	**1.03**

[a]Percentage of flights operating within 15 minutes of their scheduled times.
[b]Reported baggage problems per 1,000 passengers.
[c]Complaints per 100,000 passengers.
Source: U.S. Department of Transportation's *Air Travel Consumer Reports*.

Kelleher maintained that the most important step was choosing the right people, because "if the employees aren't satisfied, they won't provide the product we need."[9]

This philosophy proved effective. Although Southwest's work force was more than 90 percent unionized, the employees owned 11 percent of the company. The average employee age was 34 years, one of the industry's lowest, yet the annual average employee pay ($42,000) was among the industry's highest. Although the airline industry was notorious for contentious labor-management relations, Southwest's employees enjoyed sunny relations with management. One reason for the smooth sailing was that employees had a stake in the company's success. Another reason was that Southwest managed to make employees feel as if they were part of an extended family, even if it was a $1.2-billion family.

[9]*AW*, March 5, 1990, p. 36.

Southwest management did not try to hide the fact that the main reason for the airline's success was the commitment of its employees. The quick turnaround time was a perfect example. As Gary Barron stated:

> Our employees bust their butts out there. Ground crews of six (12 is the industry average) perform 40 or 50 tasks during the 15 minutes that the plane is on the ground. [Jim] Wimberly [head of ground operations] likens those 15 minutes to a ballet, in which everything must be perfectly executed, and if it isn't, the employees have to be flexible enough to adjust. Because of employee commitment, Southwest has consistently kept to its 15-minute "turn" (planes of major airlines spend usually an hour at the gate) and is consequently on time.

Another example of employee loyalty was the automatic ticket machines at Southwest counters that took credit cards and dispensed tickets in just 20 seconds. These efficient machines were built by Southwest employees in their off-hours. Stated Andy Donelson, station manager at Dallas's Love Field, "The machine was thought up by a bunch of guys in a bar one night in Denver."[10]

Annual turnover was 7 percent, the industry's lowest. In 1990, 62,000 people applied for jobs at Southwest. Only 1,400 were hired.

CORPORATE CULTURE

Southwest's culture was perhaps best experienced by strolling down the hallway of the company's Dallas headquarters, where 20 years of Southwest Airlines history could be witnessed through mannequins attired in the various uniforms of Southwest personnel and hundreds of photos of employees. Each year the company hosted a banquet at which outstanding employees were recognized, much in the manner of the Emmy Awards. Kelleher could be seen at these functions mingling with employees from all levels of the company, calling them by name, laughing uproariously with them, and hugging and kissing them.

Even customers were brought into the family circle. Each month Southwest invited its frequent fliers to company headquarters to interview prospective employees, the logic being that the company wanted to hire people who matched customers in personality. The 5,000 letters a month Southwest received from its customers were all answered by the staff; Kelleher himself usually read around 200 letters a week.

Kelleher's role in the formation of Southwest's familial culture was crucial. Jim Wimberly stated that Kelleher had "a knack of really being with you,

---

[10]*Inc.*, January 1992, p. 70.

even if you're one person in a crowd of 1,000."[11] Kelleher firmly believed that employees who were committed to a mission would be more productive than uncommitted employees, and he spent a lot of his time fostering this attitude: "Southwest has its customers, the passengers; and I have my customers, the airline's employees. If the passengers aren't satisfied, they won't fly with us. If the employees aren't satisfied, they won't provide the product we need."

Once a quarter, Kelleher would join his employees to load baggage, serve drinks at 30,000 feet, or hand out boarding passes. Every Friday he wore brightly colored shirts and shorts, regardless of the business to be conducted that day.

Kelleher seemed to have found a formula that worked. During 1990, rising fuel costs caused Southwest to suffer a fourth-quarter loss of $4,581,000. Employees voluntarily created a "Fuel from the Heart" program in which they incurred payroll deductions to purchase fuel for the airplanes. Kelleher was so moved that he dedicated his opening letter to them in the company's 1990 annual report.

As bright as Southwest's history had been, there had also been a few dark clouds. Perhaps the darkest cloud was Southwest's purchase of Muse Air in June 1985. Kelleher changed the airline's name to TranStar, and it operated profitably for two years, until the larger Continental Airlines began an "impossible fare war" by moving into Houston's Hobby Airport. TranStar, with only 18 operating planes, proved to be no match for Continental with its fleet of 618 planes and considerable financial resources. In 1987, Kelleher was forced to liquidate TranStar's assets and report a loss in the first quarter of that year.

Although many observers were quick to praise the airline, some analysts were not as enthusiastic about Southwest's future. The industry itself has always been a risky one, and the prospects of endless competition, unpredictable fuel prices, and fickle customers gave financial analysts reason to advise caution when investing in Southwest. The TranStar case was a good example of how quickly success could turn sour in such a high-risk industry, and how even bright, savvy managers could make disastrous mistakes. Analysts also pointed out that large airlines had the deep pockets necessary to subsidize some of the more important routes if they deemed them important, whereas Southwest did not have much of a cushion.

CONCLUSION

The Southwest success story served as a model for others in the airline business, but none were able to match the airline's stellar record. Southwest's

---

[11]Ibid., p. 67.

strategy of high value and low cost had worked for 20 years; what would the future hold? Kelleher's goal for the airline was simple: increase the number of seats by 15 percent each year and keep costs down. He feared the complacency suffered by many airlines when things appear to be going well. "Our job is to never lose focus on keeping our costs low and to never suffer an excess of hubris so we take on too much debt," he commented. "When you think you've got it all figured out, then you're probably already heading downhill."[12]

---

[12]Ibid., p. 72.

JIFFY LUBE INTERNATIONAL, INC.

In November 1988, Jiffy Lube's chief executive officer, Jim Hindman, was pondering the future of his company from his offices at the company's Baltimore, Maryland, world headquarters. Less than ten years ago, he had purchased this tiny franchise chain of retail fast-oil-change centers and turned it into the internationally recognized industry leader. In fact, the industry had literally grown simultaneously with his company. Jiffy Lube International (JLI) now boasted about 1,000, mostly franchised, centers and reported more than $250 million in systemwide revenues (including those of its franchisees) during the fiscal year ended March 31, 1988.

Despite its phenomenal growth and the fact that JLI now had about three times as many centers as its closest competitor, the company was under considerable pressure from the financial community and the press. The price of JLI's common stock was at its lowest point ever, and the business press had been increasingly negative in its assessment of JLI's financial condition. Moreover, a Washington-area TV station (located next door to JLI's headquarters) had recently broadcast a damaging news segment that suggested that consumers were taking considerable risks by having their cars serviced at local Jiffy Lube centers; and a Philadelphia TV station was planning a five-part segment there soon.

During the last several months, Hindman and his senior management team had formulated a new strategy to take Jiffy Lube through its next phase of development. The emphasis was to shift from growth to consolidation. Because the elements of this new strategy had not yet been widely communicated outside the company, Hindman thought now would be a useful time to consider where the company was going in light of where it had been.

THE JIFFY LUBE SERVICE CONCEPT

Jiffy Lube emphasized preventive automotive maintenance rather than repair. At its drive-up centers, it offered a complete fluid-maintenance service for all types of automobiles, vans, and light-duty trucks. Customers

This case was prepared by Kathi Breen, Darden MBA 1988, under the supervision of John L. Colley, Jr., Almand R. Coleman Professor of Business Administration, and L. J. Bourgeois III, associate professor of business administration. Copyright © 1989 by the University of Virginia Darden School Foundation, Charlottesville, VA. All rights reserved.

needed no appointment, and most centers were open between 8 A.M. and 7 P.M., Monday through Saturday. The standard 14-point service was advertised to take only ten minutes. For an all-inclusive price averaging about $22, the "J-Team" would:

- change the oil (with a well-known brand, usually Pennzoil)
- replace the oil filter
- lubricate the chassis
- check and top off all other fluids:
  —transmission fluid
  —brake fluid
  —power steering fluid
  —differential fluid
  —windshield washer fluid
  —battery fluid
- inflate the tires to proper pressure
- examine the air filter (for excessive dirt)
- vacuum the interior of the vehicle
- examine the windshield wiper blades
- clean the windows (or wash the car, where available)

For an extra charge, Jiffy Lube provided ancillary services and products, including flushing and filling the radiator, gear-box service, recharging air-conditioner freon, changing automatic transmission fluid and filter, and installing new air filters, breather elements, windshield wiper blades, and radiator coolant. These add-on services increased the average ticket by about $6.

The typical Jiffy Lube center looked distinctly different from a gas station. It was clean (with no grease spots or dirty tools lying about) and efficiently designed, and it had a comfortable waiting room for customers. Exhibit 1 shows the layout of a Jiffy Lube center with two service bays, each capable of accommodating two cars simultaneously (some centers had three bays and/or a car-wash facility). Cars were driven into one of the bays, entering from the back and exiting to the front. This drive-through design significantly increased the center's capacity as compared with a traditional service station's drive-in/back-out design. Also, JLI centers had a bi-level layout: the floor had an open pit through to the basement over which the car was positioned for servicing. This setup allowed one "lube tech" working below the car to drain the oil and check the chassis and transmission lubrication while two others worked simultaneously at floor level replacing the oil filter, adding new oil (from pull-down hoses), vacuuming the interior, etc.

Exhibit 1
Jiffy Lube International, Inc.
Design of a Typical Jiffy Lube Center

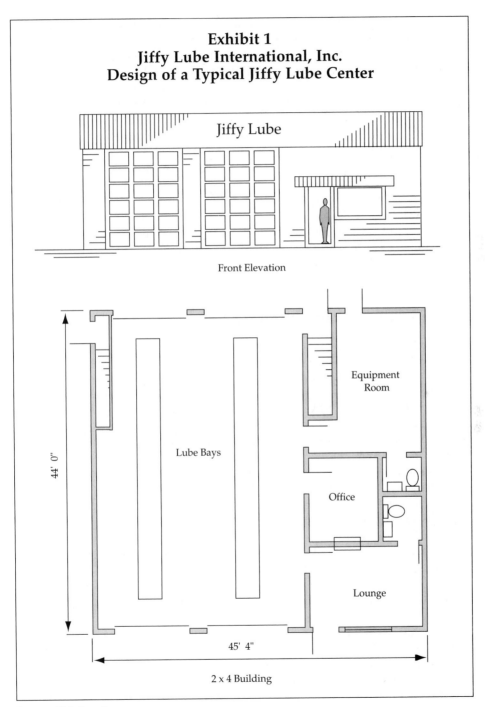

Front Elevation

Lube Bays

Equipment Room

Office

Lounge

44' 0"

45' 4"

2 x 4 Building

Source: JLI drawing.

While the car was being serviced, customers could relax in the waiting room with free coffee and an assortment of magazines or watch the lube techs work through the window. When servicing was complete, the lead technician gave the customer a personal explanation of the exact services performed, at which time the technician could point out any problems and offer ancillary services that could be done on the spot. To encourage repeat business, Jiffy Lube either left a card in the car (noting the mileage at which the next service should be done) and/or mailed a reminder to the customer's home at the appropriate time.

Jiffy Lube's service objectives were modeled after those used by McDonald's: quality, service, cleanliness, and value. To those four, Hindman added another for JLI: convenience. As he often said, "We're selling convenience, not oil." JLI attempted to provide consistent quality across its nationwide system, but visits by this case writer to two centers suggested that service quality varied considerably and that the standard service sometimes took longer than ten minutes.

THE QUICK-LUBE INDUSTRY

The quick-lube (also known as fast-oil-change) industry was one segment of the automotive aftermarket, which included muffler shops (e.g., Midas), Aamco transmission specialists, and Goodyear tire/brake centers. Like them, quick-lube centers specialized in one service to focus their message to consumers and achieve operational efficiencies.

The growth of automotive specialty repair/maintenance firms had resulted largely from a steep decline in the number of full-service gas stations over the last 15 years. The oil price shocks of the 1970s drove many gas stations out of business, and most of the remainder dropped repair services to become gas-only outlets. According to information obtained by JLI, there were 226,000 service stations in the United States in 1972, 90 percent of them full-service outlets. By 1986, there were about 110,000 service stations, less than 30 percent full-service.

Despite the decline in the number of service stations, there were more automobiles on the road than ever before, and people were keeping them longer. The number of autos and light-duty trucks grew from 102 million in 1972 to 160 million by 1986, and their average age increased from 5.7 to 7.2 years. The increase in two-income families had also led people to spend money to save time and hassle in getting their cars serviced.

Car owners had several options for obtaining regular fluid-maintenance service. Auto dealers and independent repair shops were available but required that the car be left for a day while this minor work was squeezed in between larger jobs. A local full-service gas station normally charged a lower price than Jiffy Lube for a basic oil change (averaging $12–$15), but the service required an appointment and took longer (about 45 minutes), because the car had to be raised and lowered twice on the lift. Finally, a car owner could change his or her own oil, which was messy and took time from other activities.

In late 1988, the United States contained over 3,500 quick-lube centers. The exact number of operators was difficult to determine, because quick-lube service was being provided not only in centers such as JLI's, but sometimes in dedicated bays at gas stations and other auto service shops. About 5 percent of all oil changes were performed by quick-lube centers, up from about 2 percent in 1982. The quick-lube industry was expected to grow rapidly over the next several years, with potential market share as high as 35 to 40 percent of the U.S. oil-change market. Longer new-car warranties offered by U.S. auto manufacturers, which required evidence of regular service, might also contribute to growth. Moreover, there was thought to be a large unfilled market of consumers who did not change their oil as often as they should.

JIM HINDMAN

Hindman was the prime motivator in the JLI organization. Jiffy Lube's culture had been shaped by his personal code of ethics, which he communicated often and consistently. In "Ain't It Great!," a bound collection of his personal philosophy as delivered in letters to franchisees and in speeches to training classes, he said, "With the wrong attitude you can do everything right and fail, but with the right attitude you can do everything wrong and still succeed." For Hindman, the right attitude was "we're here to help . . . do what's right and reasonable, even when no one is looking . . . fairness to the customer . . . and always work harder than the next guy."

Hindman's background illustrates his self-reliance and drive to achieve. He described himself in a Jiffy Lube public relations release as having been "a strong-willed kid and a street fighter. You'd have to kill me to whip me." He spent part of his childhood in a boys' home, caring for himself and two younger brothers. He put himself through college and graduate school, spent nine years as a hospital administrator, later formed a partnership that built and operated 32 nursing homes, and bought several other businesses. By 1970, at age 35, he was a millionaire.

As he became successful in business, Hindman began to devote time to his college sport, football. In 1977, he became head football coach at Western Maryland College, working without salary and helping to finance the team by buying equipment and funding scholarships. During his four years as head coach, Hindman turned a losing team into a winning one with an overall record of 21-7-8. He said in a JLI publication:

> I believe firmly in the importance of the old-fashioned American work ethic
> and the team spirit. This was the philosophy that helped our football team

achieve success, and the disciplines that it takes to be a success in football are the same ones it takes to be successful in business.

THE BIRTH OF JLI

When a Western Maryland College student complained about the lack of opportunities for young people to make a million dollars today, Hindman was so incensed that he bet the student he (Hindman) could do it again. He later explained that JLI "was born as a personal challenge to the negativism that runs rampant through much of our society. And the growth, success, and health of the chain proves that opportunity is alive and well today."

In mid-1979, Hindman's partnership purchased the trademark, logo, and franchise agreements of a nine-outlet fast-oil-change company in Salt Lake City named Jiffy Lube. He renamed it Jiffy Lube International, Inc., envisioning that JLI would expand to national and even international prominence.

Initially, Hindman both developed company-owned centers and sold franchises, many to his friends and associates. In 1982, however, he decided JLI didn't have the resources to be in both types of business, because a large network of company centers required a large corporate staff to manage it. That year, JLI sold all its stores to franchisees and focused on selling individual new franchises. When Hindman purchased JLI in 1979, his major objective was to reach 100 centers, considered a critical "level of respectability" for a franchiser. It took Jiffy Lube five years to reach that goal.

GROWTH STRATEGIES

After reaching 100 stores in fiscal 1984, Hindman set a new goal of 1,000 centers by the end of fiscal (March 31) 1989. His strategy was to preempt significant competition before it could get started, and achieve a wide enough scale to support a national advertising effort. (National advertising was considered critical to maximizing daily car counts and establishing Jiffy Lube as the industry leader.) So, the 1,000-store goal became JLI's overriding strategic objective, and it affected almost every action the company took through the end of fiscal 1988.

To accelerate growth, in 1984, JLI began selling area-development rights, which granted an investor the exclusive right to develop and operate Jiffy Lube centers within a particular Area of Dominant Influence (ADI), an advertising term of the Arbitron Rating Service that referred to population centers. The area developer paid a negotiated, nonrefundable fee up front that varied by the potential number of centers to be built, the demographics of the area, and the difficulty of development there. The area developer's continuing right to exclusivity depended on opening a specified number of centers within each year of its five-year contract; in practice, JLI usually granted extensions. The rights to virtually all of the top 30 ADIs had been sold by the end of fiscal 1987.

The area-development program spurred fast growth in the number of franchised Jiffy Lube centers, and area-development fees became an important source of revenue for JLI. JLI discovered that area developers were investors rather than operators, however, who relished "doing deals" over managing their stores and ensuring proper customer service. Hindman believed that this characteristic was a prime reason for the lack of franchisee profitability in some areas, and this problem was to be explicitly addressed in his new strategy.

JLI had also grown by acquiring smaller chains and converting independents to the Jiffy Lube system. In its acquisitions, price had been less a concern than store location and competitive position, because Hindman believed that quick-lube shops would only become more valuable as the industry grew. Most stores JLI acquired were later sold to franchisees, and some acquisitions were made directly by franchisees but financed by JLI. The company also added centers by convincing independent quick-lube operators to become JLI franchisees. Jiffy Lube converted 26 such independents during fiscal 1986, 75 in fiscal 1987, and 83 in fiscal 1988. To encourage these conversions, JLI had sometimes waived initial franchise fees, offered reduced royalty rates for a year or two, and/or provided funds to enable the physical conversion of the centers. JLI rarely built new company-owned centers.

Jiffy Lube's strategy for organizing this growth was to concentrate its centers in the largest (metropolitan) ADIs in order to reach national advertising scale quickly. Furthermore, JLI built "clusters" of centers within each ADI, rather than individual stores in outlying areas, to enhance consumer awareness of both the quick-lube concept and of Jiffy Lube. JLI wanted its name to be the first thing that came to mind when consumers thought about getting an oil change. Clustering was also thought to preempt local competition, and it clearly offered economies of scale in local advertising, distribution of product to the centers, and store management. The distribution of Jiffy Lube centers across the country in June 1988 appears in Exhibit 2.

During this high-growth period from 1984 through early 1988, JLI had pursued several goals simultaneously: expanding to 1,000 centers as quickly as possible, increasing daily car counts across the system, and improving the quality of Jiffy Lube service to the consumer. As the summary operating data in Exhibit 3 show, the results were impressive. By November 1988, JLI had more than 1,000 stores, systemwide revenues increased from $28 million in 1984 to $252 million in 1988, and the average daily car count rose from 35.9 in fiscal 1984 to 43.1 in fiscal 1988. The break-even car count (systemwide) was about 35 cars per day, but some centers regularly serviced over 100 a day.

From the beginning, Hindman had dreamed of expanding overseas, which he did in 1988. By March 31, JLI had opened 9 stores in Canada, 5 in Europe, and 1 in Australia and had another 33 under development abroad. JLI's international strategy was to find local companies to assume a master license, which entitled them to receive initial franchise fees and a share of the royalties of operating centers. In effect, the master licenser was a subfranchisor, investing its

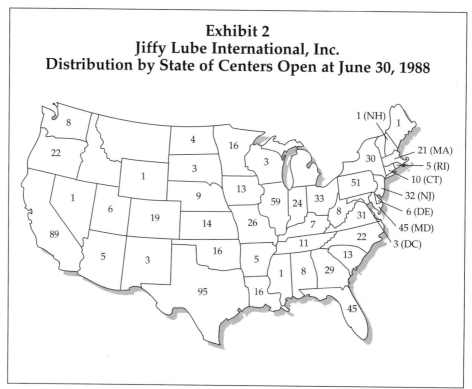

**Exhibit 2
Jiffy Lube International, Inc.
Distribution by State of Centers Open at June 30, 1988**

Source: JLI Map.

own time and money to develop the area. JLI provided support in training, standards, and operating methods and received lower royalties than in the United States because of its reduced role. Elf France, a division of Elf Aquitaine (France's largest oil company), had obtained a direct license for most of Western Europe, and JLI had established an office in Paris to manage its international expansion effort.

MANAGING GROWTH

The Role of JLI Corporate Headquarters

As a franchiser, JLI's most significant responsibilities were assisting its franchisees in developing and operating their centers, maintaining systemwide operating standards, and managing the national marketing effort.

Exhibit 3
Jiffy Lube International, Inc.
Summary Operating Data

FISCAL YEAR ENDING MARCH 31

	1988	1987	1986	1985	1984
NUMBER CENTERS OPEN					
Co-owned	71	29	14	21	1
Franchised	737	532	334	187	119
International	15	—	—	—	—
Total	823	561	348	208	120
NUMBER STATES WITH JL CENTERS	44	39	33	28	23
System sales	$252,082	$151,590	$91,201	$48,750	$27,762
Average ticket price/ vehicle served	$27.63	$27.78	$27.01	$26.24	$24.86
Average no. of vehicles/day	43.1	42.2	41.8	44.0	35.9
Effective royalty rate	5.2%	5.3%	4.6%	4.6%	4.8%

APRIL 30

JLI CORP. EMPLOYEES:	1988	1987	1986
Senior management	16	15	14
Management and professional	77	69	24
Field operations	55	40	25
Clerical	128	81	51
Company-owned centers	855	351	146
Total	1,131	556	260

Source: JLI stock offering prospecti (1986 and 1987) and March 31, 1988, 10-K report to the Securities and Exchange Commission (SEC).

Jiffy Lube provided *development assistance* by helping franchisees select sites, manage construction of the centers, and locate financing. All sites had to be approved by JLI, which generally used the criteria listed in Exhibit 4. The

Exhibit 4
Jiffy Lube International, Inc.
Preferred Site Parameters for Center Locations

The following preferred site parameters are used in the selection of free-standing sites and shopping center pad locations.

LOCATION

- Corner: most desirable
- Inside: preferably with left-hand turn
- Near shopping center and major food stores
- Near other successful services and fast-food restaurants
- Good visibility from both directions

PROPERTY SIZE

- Range: 10,000–15,000 square feet
- A smaller size may be acceptable, depending upon other characteristics of the site
- With common ingress and egress, as little as 4,000 square feet can be utilized

STANDARD BUILDING SIZE

Building	Size	Square feet
2 × 4	46' × 48'	2,208
1 × 3	34' × 61'	2,074
3 × 6	46' × 61'	2,806

ZONING

- Local zoning that will allow a fast lube center or that can be rezoned

TRAFFIC

- 20,000 plus cars per day
- Two-way, undivided traffic
- Traffic speed of 35 mph or less

(continued on next page)

Source: JLI pamphlet for prospective landlords.

(continued)

AREA

- Population of 60,000 within a 3-mile ring
- Median income of $21,000

TERMS

- Lease
- Purchase
- Build-to-suit

PRICE

- The prevailing price per square foot or front foot in the market area

company also supplied franchisees with standard center designs and operating procedures and trained new franchisees and store managers.

To provide *operating assistance*, JLI maintained a field force of district managers (DMs). There were 20 DMs in the field to service 753 franchised centers in fiscal 1988; by the end of fiscal 1989, JLI projected it would have 34 DMs to service 970 franchisees. The functions of the field force included training and supervising new center managers and lube techs, communicating JLI's operating standards and merchandising techniques, and troubleshooting operational problems. Apart from the field force, JLI headquarters staff provided training for center personnel, as well as help in organizing regional advertising co-ops and fleet-maintenance programs.

In 1983, JLI acquired Heritage Merchandising to achieve economies of scale through centralized purchasing of nonoil products. As a wholly owned subsidiary, Heritage supplied both franchisees and company-owned centers with 90 percent of their oil filters and air filters as well as other operating supplies and equipment. From its national network of eight public warehouses, Heritage could reach almost all centers within 48 hours. Heritage also distributed various products to outside customers.

If a franchisee had financial or operational problems, JLI might elect to assist in several ways: arranging additional financing, facilitating a transfer of the license agreement to a new franchisee, extending payment terms on accounts and notes due to JLI, or, as a last resort, repurchasing the franchise rights. In such circumstances, JLI had repurchased franchise rights to 16 centers in fiscal 1987 and 41 centers in fiscal 1988. Historically, JLI had been quite successful in buying back financially distressed centers, turning them around, remarketing them to new franchisees, and recovering at least its acquisition cost.

Maintaining Standards. The relationship between JLI and its franchisees was like a partnership, because the company did not enjoy direct authority over franchises. Under its franchise agreements, JLI could, however, inspect franchise centers at any time to ensure that employees were using approved products and following Jiffy Lube procedures. The company used both field personnel and "mystery shoppers" (who posed as customers and reported back to headquarters) to monitor franchise operations. If a franchisee failed to operate a center according to JLI's standards, the company had the right to revoke the franchise rights and obtain control of the center. This step had been taken for the first time only recently; in its quest for growth, JLI had not always enforced strict adherence to its operating policies.

In mid-1986, JLI made a substantial effort to encourage improved service quality throughout the system. To focus its efforts, the company introduced the "Zero Defects Program" around which to rally franchisees and store managers through working toward the stated goal of 100 percent defect-free performance for every customer. To convey this new attitude to customers, a plaque containing the Jiffy Lube Pledge of Quality was displayed prominently in every store; it encouraged customers to contact JLI headquarters directly if dissatisfied with their service. JLI also developed a computerized tracking system to follow and analyze defects when they did occur.

To help support this renewed focus on quality, JLI significantly expanded its training programs. Previously, the company had offered only a two-week program for franchisees and store managers at headquarters; at this time, it introduced standard training consisting of videotapes and workbooks to "certify" lube techs at the individual center sites.

JLI also expanded its field force, recruiting people who were particularly suited to lead franchisees in the quality-improvement effort. The field force, which in fiscal 1987 consisted of only nine DMs covering 545 franchised centers, was given responsibility for performing the newly introduced operational audits; under this system, DMs formally measured centers on 150 attributes of service. Finally, JLI established a customer service department to follow up on every complaint received at headquarters. During 1988, the number of complaints averaged about 100 a month; the most common was that the customer didn't get the full 14 points of service.

Marketing. Jiffy Lube was the only quick-lube chain with a national advertising effort. Each center contributed 3 percent of gross revenues to a National Ad Fund, which was used to produce commercials, buy media time, and create signs and other materials for systemwide promotions. The fund's expenditures had grown dramatically, from $510,000 in fiscal 1985 to $8.1 million in fiscal 1988. The fund's emphasis had been on TV commercials featuring well-known

TV personalities (Dick Van Patten and family, Sally Struthers, Sherman Helmsley) with the theme: "We treat you like family." Over and above its contribution to the National Ad Fund, each franchisee was required to spend 5 percent of gross sales on local and regional advertising, often through co-ops arranged by JLI.

JLI's Senior Management

Several times over the years, Hindman had hired an outside executive to add skills to the organization and manage JLI's operations; in each instance, however, he was unable to feel comfortable relinquishing control. The most recent such executive was J. Richard Breen, hired in April 1986 as president and chief operating officer. Before coming to JLI, Breen had been president of Tenneco Automotive International (which owned Speedy Muffler King and several other automotive aftermarket businesses); also, he was a former executive vice president of Fram International (which manufactured and sold oil filters). Breen's largest contribution had been developing and spearheading the corporate effort to improve franchise service quality. He resigned on September 1, 1987, to become a franchisee. (In fact, several former executives had become franchisees.)

JLI's present senior management consisted of

- **W. James Hindman,** age 53, chairman, president, and CEO. He owned about 22 percent of JLI's outstanding common stock and was said to control another 8 percent through relatives and associates.

- **Edward F. Kelley, III,** age 35, executive vice president and chief financial officer. Kelley had been an assistant coach to Hindman at Western Maryland College and was one of JLI's six founding stockholders. He was responsible for finance, accounting, headquarters administration, and the Heritage Merchandising subsidiary. He also coordinated the remarketing of company-owned stores. His prior positions included vice president of operations and senior vice president of the Eastern Region.

- **Nicholas A. Greville,** age 44, executive vice president. He had joined JLI in 1985 and was responsible for operations (including both franchise and company-owned stores) and marketing. His offices were located at the JLI Western Region headquarters in California. Greville had formerly been with Midas Mufflers for 11 years in various sales and management positions.

- **Neal F. O'Shea,** age 58, senior vice president. O'Shea was responsible for all international operations and development. An officer of JLI since 1980, he was formerly vice president of franchise development.

- **Eleanor C. Harding,** age 38, vice president and treasurer. She had joined JLI in 1986 after three years as a manager of corporate finance at

Black & Decker. Before that, she had been a vice president of Loyola Federal Savings & Loan.

FINANCING GROWTH

Development of Centers

In 1988, developing a new Jiffy Lube center from the ground up cost about a half million dollars, as shown in Exhibit 5. Franchisees had always been responsible for financing the development of their own stores, but to spur growth of the system, JLI assisted wherever possible. Sometimes the company helped franchisees negotiate "build-to-suit" leases, especially in the early years. It also helped franchisees find construction loans (sometimes providing them itself) and helped arrange permanent financing of real estate and construction expenditures from mortgage lenders with which it had developed

---

Exhibit 5
Costs to Develop a New Jiffy Lube Center in 1988

	ESTIMATED RANGE	
	LOW	HIGH
TYPE OF EXPENDITURE		
Purchase real estate	$100,000	$350,000
Site improvements/construction	225,000	250,000
Start-up operating costs:		
License fee	15,000	35,000
Equipment/fixtures	38,000	78,000[a]
Initial inventory	17,500	17,500
Working capital/prepaid expense	35,900	43,400
First month's rent	4,000	5,000
Total start-up cost	110,400	178,900
Total to develop center	$435,400	$778,900

[a]Includes $40,000 for car wash facility.
Source: JLI March 31, 1988, 10-K report to the SEC.

relationships. With respect to real estate, JLI had come to prefer owning or leasing center sites and buildings itself and subleasing them to franchisees, which was thought to provide better control over the use of these properties. It also allowed JLI to profit on the spread between its mortgage/lease cost and rental revenue. A significant proportion of franchise sites were now subleased from the company, as shown in Exhibit 6. Another way JLI helped its franchisees develop centers was by providing acquisition financing for the purchase of competing stores in their territories. Finally, JLI had often provided loan and lease guarantees of franchisee debt to third parties.

JLI Corporate Financing History

JLI's need for capital was driven by its decision to help finance the growth in centers, which it considered vital. During the early years, JLI had literally lived from hand to mouth, stretching payments and patching together loans from unlikely sources. In 1981, Pennzoil had provided a crucial $1 million when it bought preferred stock with warrants (which Hindman later repurchased) for 30 percent of JLI. In 1985, its major source of mortgage loans (Old Court Savings & Loan) was closed by federal regulators, which precipitated a crisis in funding completion of several centers then under construction. Until as late as 1986, Hindman himself often lent the company large sums of money, and he sometimes waived his salary.

In December 1985, JLI privately placed a $10.5 million loan (with warrants) with Bridge Capital Investors, a well-known New York investment company. This mezzanine financing introduced Jiffy Lube to Wall Street and lent the company an aura of legitimacy to help prepare it for going public. Seven months later, in July 1986, JLI had its initial public offering of common stock on the NASDAQ, which netted the company $28 million and introduced both the quick-lube concept and Jiffy Lube to the investing public. The offering price was $15 per share, but investor interest pushed the price to $21 later that day; it later settled in at about $17.[1] In March of 1987, the stock price peaked at $49, when it was split 2-for-1. During the next quarter, the stock hit an all-time high of $25¼ (adjusted for the split) but had dropped by the time JLI completed its second offering in June 1987. At an offering price of about $15 per share (adjusted), the company raised $34 million. Since that offering, the stock had declined steadily, and it currently traded around $6–$7 per share.

JLI Operating Performance

As shown in the financial statements in Exhibit 7, JLI's corporate revenues were derived from four general areas. Revenues from *operations* represented

---

[1]"Striking It Rich," *Warfield's Magazine*, Baltimore, October 1986.

**Exhibit 6
Jiffy Lube International, Inc.
Ownership of Center Locations during Fiscal Years 1986–1988**

FYE 3/31/86

	OPERATED BY		
	COMPANY	FRANCHISEE	TOTAL
SITES			
Owned by company	3	33	36
Leased by company[a]	11	54	65
Owned/leased by franchisees	0	247	247
	14	334	348

FYE 3/31/87

	OPERATED BY		
	COMPANY	FRANCHISEE	TOTAL
SITES			
Owned by company	8	49	57
Leased by company[a]	21	113	134
Owned/leased by franchisees	0	370	370
	29	532	561

FYE 3/31/88

	OPERATED BY		
	COMPANY	FRANCHISEE	TOTAL
SITES			
Owned by company	14	84	98
Leased by company[a]	57	220	277
Owned/leased by franchisees	0	448	448
	71	752	823

[a]Includes sites where company owns buildings and improvements.
Source: JLI stock offering prospecti (1986 and 1987) and March 31, 1988, 10-K report to the Securities and Exchange Commission (SEC).

Exhibit 7
JLI Financial Statements for Fiscal 1986–1988
and Interim September 30, 1988

INCOME STATEMENT

	6 mos. 9/30/88	1988	1987	1986
REVENUES				
Sales—company stores	$12,556	$18,974	$ 8,079	$ 7,825
Initial franchise fees	1,631	4,706	3,327	2,490
Area development fees	46	5,719	4,481	2,150
Franchise royalties	8,518	12,133	7,551	3,847
Heritage Merchandising	14,657	21,490	13,505	8,792
Rental income	10,216	14,048	6,495	4,288
Other operating revenue	639	1,132	732	59
Total revenue	$48,263	$78,202	$44,170	$29,451
EXPENSES				
Company stores	$15,168	$18,739	$ 7,331	$ 6,548
CGS—products	11,727	16,993	11,217	7,492
Rental properties	7,534	10,397	5,259	4,065
S, G, & A	13,574	21,447	13,029	9,281
Prov. bad debt	1,260	1,391	681	271
Total expenses	$49,263	$68,967	$37,517	$27,657
OPERATING INCOME	(1,000)	9,235	6,653	1,794
OTHER INCOME/(EXPENSES)				
Other income	$ 2,741	$ 4,947	$ 1,940	$ 824
Interest expense	(2,604)	(2,138)	(1,362)	(1,197)
Minor int. in loss	0	(132)	(213)	41
Total other	137	2,677	365	(332)
Income before tax	(863)	11,912	7,018	1,462
Income tax expense	(448)	5,003	3,333	720
Income before extra items	(415)	6,909	3,685	742
Extraordinary items				
NOL carryforwards				470
Debt extinguished			(219)	
Total after-tax	0	0	(219)	470
Net income	(415)	6,909	3,466	1,212

(continued on next page)

(continued)

BALANCE SHEET

	Interim 9/30/88	1988	1987	1986
ASSETS				
Cash and S-T investment	2,146	3,497	1,277	2,474
Accounts and fees receivable	23,919	19,753	7,584	6,771
Notes receivable	13,318	11,844	4,682	1,811
less allowance	(2,551)	(2,054)	(935)	(299)
Net receivables	34,686	29,543	11,331	8,283
Inventory	4,973	4,932	1,217	752
RE held for resale	0	0	0	2,719
Other current assets	3,339	1,742	1,130	258
Total current assets	45,144	39,714	14,955	14,486
Accounts and fees receivable	1,135	1,185	933	783
Stores held for resale	11,376	4,644	2,663	0
Notes receivable	25,715	22,668	9,616	3,181
Inv./Adv.—affiliates	3,875	2,138	2,217	237
FA leased to franchisees				
Construction advances	5,460	15,860	8,592	0
Land	22,066	16,654	8,966	3,613
Buildings and equipment—gross	17,338	9,840	9,807	9,299
Financing leases	77,136	61,624	26,658	7,694
Construction-in-progress	14,171	14,617	4,298	0
Gross	136,171	118,595	58,321	20,606
Less accumulated depreciation	N/A	(1,222)	(938)	(885)
Net	136,171	117,373	57,383	19,721
Net property and equipment	21,246	15,329	1,885	4,271
Intangible assets (net)	13,032	14,783	9,104	6,227
Other assets	7,281	7,929	3,687	1,787
Total assets	264,975	225,763	102,443	50,693

(continued on next page)

(continued)

	9/30/88	1988	1987	1986
LIABILITIES				
Accounts payable/accruals	11,755	10,045	6,926	3,905
Income tax payable	0	125	2,241	0
Notes payable	0	0	1,981	2,403
Construction advance—				
real estate held for resale	0	0	0	2,331
CMLTD	10,589	17,561	1,047	1,355
Total current liabilities	22,344	27,731	12,195	9,994
Long-term debt	91,927	74,911	21,797	9,971
Substantial debentures	19,309	4,299	4,887	9,736
Capital leases	48,456	36,130	18,969	9,586
Def. tax/other liabilities	1,126	1,805	1,054	504
Def. franchise fees	1,306	1,500	872	4,131
Total long-term liabilities	162,124	118,645	47,579	33,928
Total liabilities	184,468	146,376	59,774	43,922
Minority interest	0	0	3,173	10
Common stock	381	380	294	180
PIC-Paid-in-Capital	77,513	75,979	39,479	10,222
Retained earnings	6,217	6,632	(277)	(3,467)
Less due for				
common stock	0	0	0	(175)
Less treasury stock	(3,604)	(3,604)	0	0
Total equity	80,507	79,387	39,496	6,760
Total liabilities + equity	264,975	225,763	102,443	50,692

Source: JLI Annual Reports and September 30, 1988, 10-Q report to the SEC.

sales of the company-owned centers. *Franchising* revenues included area-development and master license fees, initial franchise fees, and royalties. Initial franchise fees were earned when a new center was opened and varied according to each franchise agreement. JLI's average initial franchise fee had been rising; it was $20,900 during the two-year period including fiscal 1987 and 1988, up from $17,300 during fiscal 1985–1986. Royalties, earned monthly, were usually 5 percent of each franchise's gross revenues during a store's first year of operation and 6 percent thereafter. Revenues from *distribution* represented sales of supplies and equipment by Heritage Merchandising to franchisees and outside customers. *Real estate* revenue was rental income JLI earned by subleasing properties to franchisees. Over the years, JLI had recorded significant revenue from *other sources*, including gains on the sale of real estate and company-owned centers and interest on short-term investments and notes receivable from franchisees.

During the past several years, nonrecurring revenues (such as area-development fees, initial franchise fees, and gains on the sale of real property) had contributed a significant portion of total revenues. However, these revenues were expected to decline in relative importance as growth slowed. Rental income would become more significant, because JLI had bought many properties during the past two to three years; lease rates on new centers were typically low in the early years and rose as the centers matured. Also, area-development revenues had been dramatically reduced by a recent order of the Securities and Exchange Commission requiring JLI (and all franchisors) to recognize area-development fees over the term of a contract rather than in current income, as previously done.

The largest drain on JLI earnings was from company-owned centers held for resale. Exhibit 8 shows data on the growth and operations of company-owned centers over the last few years. JLI intended to keep some stores in order to remain knowledgeable about center operations and to test new methods. Over the last two years, however, it had purchased a substantial number of distressed centers to turn around and remarket. At the end of fiscal 1988, JLI classified 34 of its 71 centers as held for resale. During fiscal 1988, operating losses on such centers totaled $950,000.

During the second quarter of fiscal 1989, losses from centers held for resale caused Jiffy Lube to post its first quarterly net loss since going public. For the six months, JLI reported a loss of $415,000 on revenues of $48.3 million. During the same period a year earlier, revenues had been 39 percent lower, but net income was $3.3 million. Systemwide sales for the first six months of fiscal 1989 were $172.8 million, up 50 percent over the previous year. During those months, JLI had acquired 70 centers intended for resale.

JLI Financial Condition

JLI's assets consisted primarily of accounts and notes receivable from franchisees, and real property (most of which was leased/subleased to franchisees). Accounts receivable encompassed all amounts currently due from franchisees, including initial franchise fees on a quarterly payment plan, royalties, rents, and Heritage receivables. A small portion was area-development fees. Accounts receivable were usually personally guaranteed by franchisees. Notes receivable

Exhibit 8
Jiffy Lube International
Data on Company-Owned Centers

	INTERIM 9/30/88	3/31/88	3/31/87	3/31/86
# COMPANY-OWNED CENTERS AT END OF PERIOD				
To keep	25	37	8	14
Held for resale	81[a]	34	21	0[b]
Total	106	71	29	14
CHANGES IN # CENTERS DURING THE PERIOD				
Acquisitions	34	88	61	1
# Centers built by company	21	9	0	0
# Centers sold/leased	(20)	(55)	(45)	(8)
# Centers closed	0	0	(1)	0
Net change in centers	35	42	15	(7)
CENTERS HELD FOR RESALE ($000)				
Assets (year end)	$11,376	$4,644	$2,663	N/A
Results of openings				
Sales	6,783	6,664	2,951	N/A
Operating expenses	9,650	7,614	3,282	N/A
Operating loss	(2,867)	(950)	(331)	N/A
Gain—sale of centers	($17)	$1,242	$1,000	$317

[a]Twenty-eight of these centers were located in Houston, Texas.
[b]Before fiscal year 1987, JLI did not classify centers as held for resale.
Source: JLI stock offering prospecti (1986 and 1987), March 31, 1988, 10-K and September 30, 1988, 10-Q reports to the SEC.

represented amounts due from franchisees under long-term arrangements with scheduled payments. Of the total, 50 percent represented financing of franchisees' acquisitions; 30 percent, working-capital financing for stores in the early stages of growth; 10 percent, term payments of area-development fees; and 10 percent, miscellaneous. Notes receivable were always personally guaranteed and were usually collateralized by a pledge of center assets.

Fixed assets consisted mostly of land and buildings, except for the equipment in company-owned centers (center equipment had historically been financed for individual franchisees by Pennzoil). Fixed assets leased to franchisees at fiscal year end 1988 were about $117 million, of which $85 million represented land and buildings owned by JLI; the remainder was mostly leased property that was subleased to franchisees. Separately, assets of centers held for resale totaled about $4.7 million.

Jiffy Lube had assumed considerable debt in its acquisition of real estate and operating centers. At the end of fiscal 1988, total long-term debt and capital leases of $129 million balanced equity of $79 million. To reduce the impact of future real estate acquisitions on its balance sheet, JLI had formed the Jiffy Lube Insured Income Limited Partnership (JLIILP), which raised $40 million in a public sale of units in early 1988. This vehicle would not only allow JLI to keep future assets and liabilities off its balance sheet, it would also generate property-management income for the company. In an innovative twist, the rents payable by franchisees were 80 percent insured (for the first seven years) by United Guaranty Commercial Insurance Company of Iowa.

Another significant off-balance-sheet issue was the high level of JLI's contingent liabilities. During its growth period, the company had often guaranteed loans and leases for franchisees who acquired or leased center sites and related equipment. The properties were pledged as collateral for these guarantees. Such guarantees totaled $58.2 million in fiscal 1988, up from $24.7 million in 1987 and $1.5 million in 1986.

THE PENNZOIL STRATEGIC ALLIANCE

In March 1988, JLI signed a 20-year Strategic Alliance Agreement with Pennzoil Products Company, which, with 21 percent of U.S. motor oil sales, was the leading motor oil company in the United States. The agreement continued the close relationship the two companies had developed over the years. Pennzoil promised to discontinue financing new independent quick-lube operators and to assist JLI in converting as many of its 750 qualifying independents as possible to the Jiffy Lube system. Pennzoil also committed to make equipment loans to all new franchisees approved by JLI, which formalized the financing of individual franchise equipment it had provided for years. Moreover, Pennzoil agreed to contribute $.20 for each gallon of motor oil purchased by the Jiffy Lube system to JLI's National Ad Fund; this contribution would equal about $4 million in fiscal 1989. Finally, Pennzoil agreed to pay JLI an "administrative fee" of $.05 per gallon sold through the JLI system and to release individual franchisees from any obligations to purchase Pennzoil oil and air filters under existing motor oil supply arrangements.

For its part under the Strategic Alliance, JLI agreed to pay Pennzoil 25 percent of the royalties it would collect from Pennzoil independents who converted. (These independents would pay no initial franchise fee.) JLI also committed to designate Pennzoil as the Jiffy Lube system's "oil of choice," use its best efforts to persuade all JLI franchisees to use it (over 80 percent of the system already did), and feature Pennzoil in its national ads. Finally, JLI promised to place the Pennzoil logo on its own private brand of oil filters and pay Pennzoil $.04 per filter sold.

The conversion of Pennzoil independents was progressing slower than planned. JLI had hoped to convert 350 operators during fiscal 1989 but had converted only 100 by November 1988. The company changed the projection to about 100 a year for the next two to three years. JLI believed, however, that Pennzoil's contribution to its National Ad Fund was more important than the conversion of independents.

QUICK-LUBE COMPETITION

Jiffy Lube was the market leader in both sales and number of centers, as the list of major competitors in Exhibit 9 shows. Like Jiffy Lube, most of the large national chains were affiliated with one of the top motor oil marketers. Minit Lube, the second largest chain (about 300 stores), was owned by Quaker State, which had about 17 percent motor oil market share. Minit Lube was the only major chain with a strategy of growing through company-owned stores instead of franchises. The third largest chain was Instant Oil, at about 178 stores; it was owned by Ashland Oil, whose Valvoline motor oil had about 13 percent market share. Instant Oil had been attempting to grow through acquisition of smaller chains and construction of company-owned stores. It recently announced an intention to concentrate on franchising, however, with a goal of 1,500 franchised centers by 1995.[2] The fourth-largest quick-lube chain, Grease Monkey, had about 120 stores and was independent of any oil company. Its stores were virtually all franchised and were located mostly in the western states in a shotgun pattern, often near Jiffy Lube centers.

Smaller, local and regional quick-lube chains abounded, some with fewer than ten stores. New independents seemed to be springing up all the time. These competitors often attempted to steal Jiffy Lube's customers by advertising 15-, 16-, or up to 21-point services, claiming to take nine minutes instead of Jiffy Lube's ten, and circulating discount coupons.

---

[2]"Ashland's Valvoline Plans to Franchise Quick-Lube Outlets, Stepping Up Rivalry," *Wall Street Journal*, October 24, 1988.

Exhibit 9
Information on Quick-Lube Industry

The industry's only aftermarket weekly…48 Mondays…$85/year

AUTOMOTIVE WEEK

Automotive Week Publishing Co.	Car Care Mall News
P.O. Box 3495	Car Care Mall Seminars
Wayne, NJ 07470-3495	Car Care Mall Directory
210/694-7792 FAX 201/694-2817	Toll-Free and FAX Directory
Circulation/Subscriptions: 201/694-6078	Autoparts and Service Market Data
CHUCK LAVERTY, *Editor and Publisher*	Mailing Lists/Direct Mail/Surveys

IISN 0889-3948

APRIL 4, 1988   VOLUME XIV, NUMBER 13

Good morning, here's the week's news:

A telephone survey by Automotive Week (on March 30th) shows that **the Top Twelve quick lube chains in North America will boost their facility count by an impressive 67% by the end of 1989, and a further 54% by the end of 1990**…See table below…A major new entry into the U.S. market by 1989 will be the **Mr. Lube** unit of **Exxon,** which recently acquired control the the Edmonton/Canada-based firm (now 50 centers) through its Imperial Oil affiliate…The firm projects about **500 U.S. quick lubes** by the Mid-Nineties, and 140 in the Canadian market…Similar rapid-growth patterns are projected for the smaller independents like Speedee Oil Change (Metarie, LA), which currently has 32 operating, but expects more than 10-fold growth to 365 in the next 21 months…

…The independents are also reaching out to many new markets from their historic base of operations, e.g., **Econo Lube 'N Tune** (Newport Beach, CA) will this year open in **Seattle, Georgia,** the **Mid-Atlantic States** and **Massachusetts, Texas, New Mexico,** and **Colorado**…

Company/Base	Current 3/1988	Projected 12/1989	Projected 12/1990
1. Jiffy Lube Int'l/Baltimore, MD	779	1250	1550
2. Quaker State-Minit Lube/Salt Lake City, UT	290	490	735
3. Rapid Oil-Valvoline/Minneapolis, MN	127	275	400
4. Grease Monkey/Denver, CO	116	240	330
5. Econo Lube N Tune/Newport Beach, CA	101	200	250
6. Autospa/Great Neck, NY	88	N/A	N/A
7. McQuik's Oil/Muncie, IN	64	100	130
8. 60 Minute Tune (+Lube)/Seattle, WA	51	N/A	N/A
9. Mr Lube-Exxon/Houston, TX	50	134	640
10. Laser Lube/Mount Laurel, NJ	39	189	400
11. Oil Express/Hinsdale, IL	34	74	115
12. Speedee Oil Change–Tune Up/Metarie, LA	32	365	597
TOTALS:	1771	2952	4550
PERCENT GAIN:		+66.7	+54.0%

Source: Automotive Week, from company-supplied data. (C) Automotive Week, 1988.

…**Speedee Oil** is extending into many Eastern markets, including **New England,** and the Atlanta Region…**60 Minute Tune,** which also performs fast-lube service, disclosed earlier that it is entering **Southern California,** Texas, and other markets East of the Rockies from its Bellevue, WA, base of operations…

…The fast-lube market—which accounts for **less than 15% of the total oil and lube business**—is highly fragmented…In addition to our chart, we believe there are as many as 100 chains with five to 25 centers, and another 1,500 performing dedicated quick-lube operations (i.e., offering general lube services without appointment and within 30–45 minutes…Some major oil chains have erected "quick lube" signage at their gas pumps, but most often the claim isn't delivered: "Next-day" or "Drop Off Your Car" schedules are commonplace.) **More on this market inside.**

FINGERHUT SUED BY INDEPENDENT SALES REP AGENCIES…SEE TOP OF PAGE FOUR.

Source: *Automotive Week,* reprinted by telephone permission.

RECENT NEGATIVE PUBLICITY

Service Quality

In the recent Washington TV broadcast, a two-part news report on quality problems at local Jiffy Lube centers, the reporter elicited on-camera horror stories from consumers. In one, Jiffy Lube had drained a car's old oil but hadn't replaced it with new oil. Later, the engine seized and had to be replaced at a cost of $3,500. JLI responded to these allegations by explaining that, out of the thousands of cars serviced daily, very few had such problems; furthermore, the company had promptly paid for those that did occur. The reporter conceded that area consumer protection agencies had received few complaints against Jiffy Lube but pointed out that the centers hired unskilled labor, training them with a series of videotapes and workbooks. "After all, Jiffy Lube says, lube technicians don't have to be mechanics."[3]

The company had been recently notified of the Philadelphia TV station's planned five-part news segment on Jiffy Lube on "The Consumer's Friend" portion of its show. In early 1987, the former area developer there had agreed to discontinue what the Pennsylvania attorney general charged were deceitful sales practices.[4] Employees had been selling unnecessary transmission and differential fluid changes by showing customers a sample of their cars' "dirty" fluid compared with one of new, "clean" fluid; in fact, automobile performance was not affected by the color of these fluids. Since then, JLI had instructed all its centers to stop showing such "comparisons" to customers and had repurchased this area from the developer.

Financial Condition

In August 1988, the *Wall Street Journal* titled its "Heard on the Street" column "Jiffy Lube Raises Some Eyebrows with Loans to Its Franchisees for Their Up-Front Expenses." The article reported that the stock, then trading at about 9½, had "plummeted nearly 50 percent from its 52-week high of 18¼," and that the outstanding short position was 2.4 million shares (about 16 percent of all outstanding stock). The writer asserted that investor concern over financial interdependence between JLI and its franchisees had caused the decline. He cited one case of a troubled franchisee, Lone Star Lubrication, which owned 67 centers in Texas and Oklahoma. Lone Star had lost $4.2 million during fiscal 1988 and owed a total of $9.5 million in long-term debt (two-

---

[3]"Jiffy Lube Auto Shops Accused of Inefficient Services," Eyewitness News, WUSA Television, Washington, D.C., October 17–18, 1988 (from a transcript provided by Radio-TV Monitoring Service, Inc.).

[4]"Quick-Grease Artists: Fast-Lube Shops Slip into Area Market," *Washington Post*, April 27, 1987.

thirds of it to JLI). Lone Star had projected it would turn profitable in fiscal 1990, however, assuming growth to 85 centers and an increase in its average car counts from 27 to 49 per day.

JLI responded in the article by noting that most of its loans and leases to franchisees were secured by real estate in prime locations and explained that it had financed the franchisees in order to build its 1,000-store nationwide network quickly to win market share before competitors did.[5]

JIFFY LUBE'S NEW STRATEGY

The planned shift in strategic emphasis from growth to consolidation focused on improving the quality of service at Jiffy Lube centers and increasing individual franchisee profitability. Financially, JLI would step back from direct financing of franchisees and attempt to facilitate third-party financing. JLI planned also to cut $3 million in annual sales and general and administrative expenses to help offset current losses.

To increase franchisees' profitability, Hindman set a goal of 65 cars per day systemwide. The company had analyzed historical center data, which showed that systemwide car counts increased with the age of a center, but the Jiffy Lube system was still young: in May 1988, 72 percent of centers were under three years old, 58 percent were less than two years old, and 32 percent were less than a year old. Exhibit 10 shows a graph of the trend in Jiffy Lube center car counts over the past four years. Exhibit 11 shows that, during fiscal 1988, every age category experienced higher daily car counts than during fiscal 1987. JLI's growth was built on the premise that car counts would continue to increase over time.

Resizing Program

In analyzing franchisee performance, JLI found that small operators (those with fewer than ten stores) clearly outperformed those who controlled larger areas. The cost advantages of clustering were outweighed by the dilution of management attention. JLI's new strategy was to carve up the ownership of large areas and encourage more individual owner/operators. Under its new Expansion Qualification Policy, the company would no longer approve new sites under area-development agreements if a franchisee's existing sites were not performing well, or if the developer lacked sufficient start-up capital. The company also planned to encourage large operators to reduce their debt to JLI by selling assets (i.e., stores). Since the company had to approve any new franchisee, it would participate in the remarketing effort. In fact, to facilitate the

[5]*Wall Street Journal*, August 29, 1988.

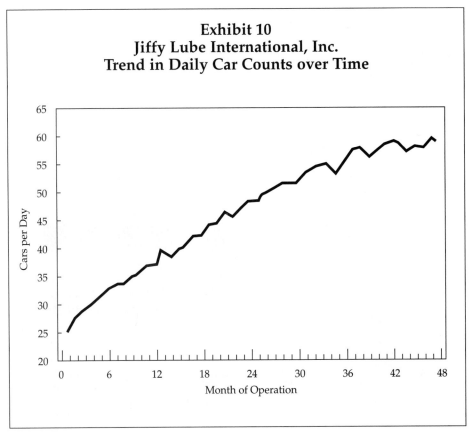

**Exhibit 10
Jiffy Lube International, Inc.
Trend in Daily Car Counts over Time**

Source: JLI internal analysis.

resizing program, JLI would probably be forced to repurchase the rights to some stores in the interim before selling them to new franchisees.

Other Operational Plans

JLI planned to make a major effort to recertify all lube techs at Jiffy Lube centers. With the relatively high employee turnover typical of a mostly teenaged work force, the company had found it difficult to maintain its earlier certification program. Jiffy Lube also intended to commission a time-and-motion study to reexamine car-servicing procedures (unchanged since the early days of the chain) and to test the ten-minute claim. JLI would continue to expand its field force and reduce the number of centers per DM in an effort to enforce its operating standards more diligently than in the past.

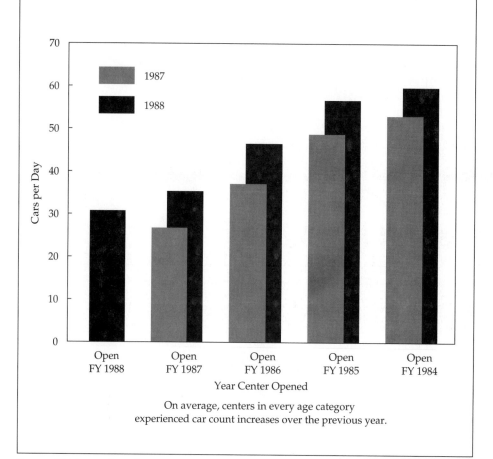

Exhibit 11
Jiffy Lube International, Inc.
Comparison of Daily Car Counts by Age Category
Fiscal Year 1987 versus 1988

On average, centers in every age category
experienced car count increases over the previous year.

Source: JLI internal analysis.

Financial Restructuring Program

JLI had recently announced a seven-step program to reduce its financial leverage. Parts of the plan were already underway. The first element involved restructuring JLI's existing liabilities, replacing some short-term debt with long-term debt. JLI had recently placed $15 million of convertible subordinated debentures with Pennzoil and, separately, $54 million of senior notes maturing over three to ten years with a group of insurance companies.

The second element of the financial restructuring was selling assets. The company planned to sell and lease back its new $10-million headquarters building, purchased in April 1988. JLI also hoped to sell $15 million to $20 million of other real estate (store sites to franchisees) and some of the $30 million of notes receivable. The company had recently received a commitment from Sanwa Business Credit to purchase $5 million of these notes at a minimal discount.

Third, JLI planned to control further increases in debt by initiating an aggressive accounts-receivable collection effort and restricting financing of franchisees. Such loans would be limited to 50 percent financing to facilitate the purchase of company-owned centers and working-capital financing for new centers through its SBIC subsidiary. (SBIC loans were consolidated on JLI's balance sheet but were government guaranteed without recourse to the company; $2.7 million of such loans had been made so far in fiscal 1989.) JLI believed it could attract about 100 new franchisees a year without providing significant start-up financing.

The fourth element of the program was to limit loan and lease guarantees and initiate a tracking system to control outstanding contingent liabilities. Fifth, JLI planned to centralize cash management and capital budgeting to improve expenditure planning. Sixth, JLI would rely more heavily on off-balance-sheet financing, like the JLIILP created the previous spring, to fund the purchase of new center sites. Finally, the company would seek to become more effective at helping franchisees find independent sources of financing. JLI had recently hired a manager who had experience in this area with another franchisor.

QUESTIONS TO CONSIDER

Hindman wondered whether the new strategy had addressed the most important issues facing his company and whether the plan would satisfy the concerns of the financial community. How would he manage the franchisees differently now? What was the impact of the large number of company-owned centers?

Would the new plans help JLI maintain its market position? Hindman was convinced that the JLI service concept, if properly implemented, worked in all parts of the country. Thus, he believed that both his earlier growth strategy and the national advertising effort were justified. Jiffy Lube was by far the largest chain in the quick-lube industry; could the company sustain competitive advantage and improve profitability for both itself and the franchisees?

THE MICROCOMPUTER INDUSTRY IN 1987

The first magic moment occurred about ten years ago, when computers became smaller than humans and able to live in normal, messy office environments. The second came about five years ago, when the price of the average American passenger car passed that of a genuinely usable business computer.

Fortune, February 3, 1986

BACKGROUND

Palo Alto, 1976. As the bearded, blue-jeaned members of The California Home Brew Club gathered around to inspect Steve Wozniak's new circuit board, little did the young computer nerds realize that several of them were destined to become multimillionaires by their mid-20s. Sitting on the overstuffed sofa in their garage meeting room amongst a jungle of circuit boards, wires, silicon chips, keyboards, small TV screens, and open boxes of components wired together, the group's excitement was focused on a small box that was to revolutionize the world's conception of computing—the Apple I.

The microcomputer has come a long way from a hobbyists' machine in 1976. By 1987, annual microcomputer shipments exceeded $20 billion and represented about 30 percent of worldwide computer dollar shipments by U.S.-based vendors—up from about 7 percent in 1980.

The first true micro, the Altair, was a crude machine capable of communicating with the user in machine language only. Developed in 1975 by Ed Roberts of MITS, an Albuquerque, NM, company, the Altair was sold to hobbyists through *Popular Electronics* magazine as a "to-assemble" kit. The unexpected market acceptance of this machine, combined with technological advances in the semiconductor industry, stimulated the entrepreneurial spirit of other business people and engineers. Venture capitalists funded companies

This note was prepared by Anurag Sharma, Darden MBA 1988, and revised by Jaideep Wadhwa, Darden M.B.A. 1989, and Jeffrey Cohen, Darden M.B.A. 1990, under the supervision of Associate Professor L. J. Bourgeois. Copyright © 1988 by the Darden Graduate Business School Sponsors, Charlottesville, VA.

whose typical working environments were characterized by information trading, shirt-sleeve management, flashes of idealism, and a lack of detailed planning. Semiconductor manufacturers and electronics distributors were also entering this promising, but as yet fledgling, industry. Commodore was the first established company with extensive distribution channels for electronics products to enter the market in 1976 by acquiring MOS Technology, a successful manufacturer of a low-cost hobbyist computer.

The first significant growth period was sparked by the introduction of the Apple II in May 1977. The $1,295 machine had two innovative features: the operating system was built into the machine, and the technical specifications were made public. These advances enabled third-party participation in the development of new programs and applications, which, in turn, attracted end users who relied on already written software. The first spreadsheet program (Visicalc) enabled Apple to gain wide acceptance and build credibility for microcomputers.

The microcomputer industry continued gaining visibility as the start-ups grew and established firms such as Texas Instruments became involved. Tandy Corporation introduced its low-end business computer, the TRS-80, in its Radio Shack stores in August 1977. By 1981 nearly 150 companies were making microcomputers, and the battle for leadership was being fought between Apple and Tandy. Then, in August of that year, IBM announced its first generation of microcomputers and called them personal computers (PCs). Packaged with 64K of memory (sufficient to run Visicalc), the basic PC was offered at $2,235.

IBM's entry was expected to have a significant impact for various reasons:

- IBM held a 70 percent share of mainframes sold to *Fortune* 1000 companies. IBM's dominant position in mainframes legitimized micros for serious business use.

- IBM adopted an "open" architecture for its microcomputers. This move was an invitation for third parties to develop software and compatible hardware for its machines and resulted in the emergence of an industry standard. Third-party involvement also led to faster product innovation and price cutting, which further expanded the market.

- IBM had the financial muscle to take a substantial position in the microcomputer market.

IBM soon dominated the microcomputer business, but its open architecture and the increasing software available for its machines tempted others to imitate the IBM PC. This situation, coupled with the inability of the giant to meet the sudden surge in demand for its computers, led to the emergence of a new breed of machines, IBM "clones." Clones were copies of existing IBM machines capable of running almost all the PC software, sometimes at a faster speed. Within a

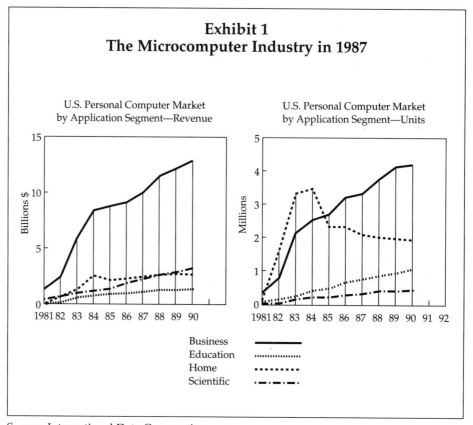

Exhibit 1
The Microcomputer Industry in 1987

U.S. Personal Computer Market
by Application Segment—Revenue

U.S. Personal Computer Market
by Application Segment—Units

Business
Education
Home
Scientific

Source: International Data Corporation.

year, about 300 companies were battling for a piece of the rapidly expanding U.S. market, the majority of which was shared by IBM and IBM clones.

Between 1981 and 1984, sales of personal computers grew 65 percent per year. The end users' growing familiarity with the machine and sharp price declines resulting from intense competition rapidly drew in new customers. The PC was now accepted by productivity-conscious buyers in business and education.

The 1985 economic slowdown substantially decreased capital spending, and PC industry growth dropped to 15 percent, which led to lower microcomputer prices. Thinning margins led to the first industry shakeout as some of the 300 vendors failed.

The result was a complete restructuring of the industry. IBM, with over 40 percent market share, was a clear winner, followed by Apple, Tandy, and Compaq, which were far behind (see Exhibits 1, 2, and 3). Within the dealer network, power was consolidated among a few large retailers. While dealers and vendors were forced to cut costs to bolster shrinking profit margins, their customers demanded even more service and sales support.

After two years of sluggish growth following the general recession in 1985, the personal computer industry began to expand again. Total shipments through the end of 1986 were as follows:

Total Personal Computer Unit Shipments	
1977	24,000
1979	333,000
1980	455,000
1981	819,000
1983	6,500,000
1986	9,737,000

By 1987, the general industry attitude was optimistic as all major vendors showed impressive sales growth in the first quarter. Rod Canion, president and CEO of Compaq, said, "Earlier in the year, we would have predicted growth of about 20 percent this year, which isn't a bad number. Now, we are looking at the 25 percent to 30 percent range."

MARKET ENTRY

To enter the PC business, a company had to make three interdependent strategic decisions: machine design, degree of vertical integration (manufacturing infrastructure), and target market.

PC Design

(See Case Appendix 1 for a description of machine components.) In designing the hardware configuration, or "box," a manufacturer had to decide between building it around standard, off-the-shelf, readily available components (as in the original IBM PC and Apple II) or designing its own proprietary technology (as in the original Apple/Macintosh and Tandy machines). In the former case, referred to as "open" architecture, the manufacturer made the technical specifications public so the user could modify or expand the machine's capabilities by adding circuit boards manufactured by third parties. By contrast, a "closed" architecture prevented users from making any changes in the original machine and, in effect, discouraged third-party participation. Once a potential manufacturer of microcomputers decided the hardware configuration of its machine, it was more or less strategically locked into a specific market.

The next critical choices were of the microprocessor and operating system, which formed the backbone of the machine. The two decisions were technically

Exhibit 2
The Microcomputer Industry in 1987
The Leading PC Vendors and Market Shares

LEADING MICROCOMPUTER MANUFACTURERS IN TERMS OF UNITS, 1983[a]

	% of market
IBM	19%
Apple	15
Tandy	11
Commodore	10

OFFICE PERSONAL COMPUTER MARKET SHARES[b]

	1982	1983
IBM	18.3%	26.0%
Apple	20.0	21.0
Tandy	15.4	13.4
Hewlett-Packard	5.4	6.5

MARKET SHARES (%) BY SEGMENT IN 1986[c]

	Business	Home	Education
IBM	34%	16%	17%
Apple	10	21	58
Tandy	9	11	17
Compaq	7	—	—
AT&T	5	—	—
Others[1]	35	52	8

(continued on next page)

[1]The home market was led by Commodore International with a 23-percent share; Atari had 6 percent.
[a]*San Francisco Chronicle,* October 18, 1983, p. 49.
[b]*Future Computing,* July 1983, as cited in "Note on the Microcomputer Industry," Thomas & Company, Palo Alto, CA 94303.
[c]Various public data.

(continued)

MARKET SHARE OF PC SALES IN THE UNITED STATES
(percentage of dollars)[d]

	1985	1986
IBM	40.5%	29.5%
Apple	10.3	7.3
Compaq	5.2	7.0
Zenith	2.4	4.2
Tandy	4.6	3.4
Commodore	3.8	1.9
Others, mainly clones	33.2	46.7

1986 SHIPMENTS TO U.S. BUSINESS AND PROFESSIONAL MARKETS[e]

VENDOR	VALUE (MILLIONS)	% CHANGE FROM 1985	UNITS (THOUSANDS)	% CHANGE FROM 1985	MARKET SHARE (IN UNITS) 1985	1986
IBM	$3,360	−5%	1,075	−7%	43.0	34.0
Compaq	789	+6	205	0	7.6	6.5
Apple	626	+63	310	+59	7.2	9.8
Zenith	581	+48	110	+34	3.0	3.5
AT&T	340	−6	170	−5	6.7	5.4
Tandy	302	+114	270	+42	7.0	8.6
Unisys	300	−9	63	+192	—	2.0
H-P	279	−11	60	−14	2.6	2.0
Wang	271	−5	68	−4	2.6	2.0
Leading Edge	232	+252	133	+291	1.3	4.2
Other (mainly clones)	2,071	−11	686	+40	18.2	22.0
Total	$9,150	+40%	3,150	+17%		

[d]*EDP Weekly,* March 23, 1987, p. 10.
[e]International Data Corporation.

interdependent, so they were made almost simultaneously. (See Case Appendix 2 for a description of microprocessors and operating systems.) Standard microprocessors were available from established semiconductor companies like Intel

Exhibit 3
Market Shares of Personal Computers in 1985 and 1986

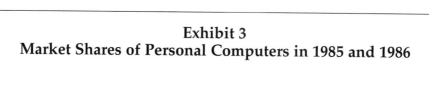

1985 Market Shares—Personal Computers
(U.S. Vendors' Shares of Worldwide Installed Base)

Value

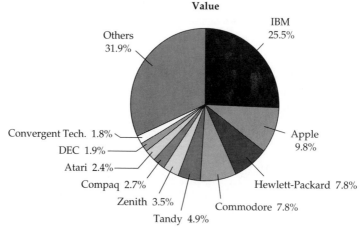

Total: $55.1 Billion

Units

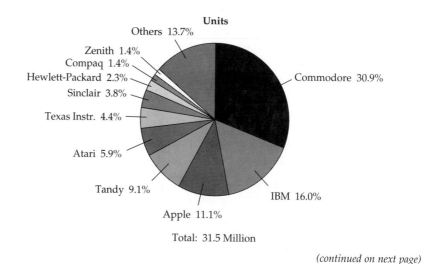

Total: 31.5 Million

(continued on next page)

Sources: *U.S. Industrial Outlook,* 1987 and 1988 and International Data Corporation.

(continued)

1986 Market Shares—Personal Computers
(U.S. Vendors' Shares of Worldwide Installed Base)

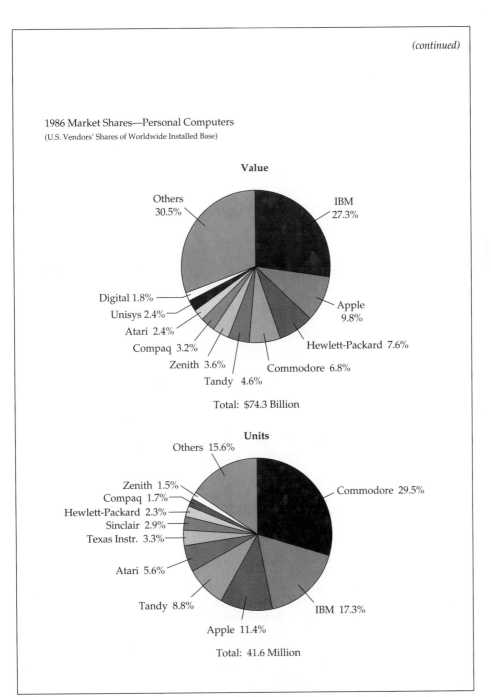

Value

Others 30.5%

IBM 27.3%

Digital 1.8%
Unisys 2.4%
Atari 2.4%
Compaq 3.2%
Zenith 3.6%
Tandy 4.6%

Apple 9.8%

Hewlett-Packard 7.6%

Commodore 6.8%

Total: $74.3 Billion

Units

Others 15.6%

Zenith 1.5%
Compaq 1.7%
Hewlett-Packard 2.3%
Sinclair 2.9%
Texas Instr. 3.3%

Atari 5.6%

Tandy 8.8%

Apple 11.4%

Commodore 29.5%

IBM 17.3%

Total: 41.6 Million

Sources: *U.S. Industrial Outlook,* 1987 and 1988 and International Data Corporation.

and Motorola, although the PC company could get custom-designed chips made at extra cost (rarely done). An operating system was developed around the chip hardware to exploit the chip's capabilities. This step was done by the PC company or by third parties that specialized in software development. For example, MS-DOS was developed by Microsoft for Intel's 8088 microprocessor and the PCs built around that chip. On the other hand, Apple used Motorola's 6502 microprocessor for its first machine and developed the Apple-DOS operating system itself.

After the basic PC design was decided, the potential PC-maker had to decide what components to build in house and which to source outside. This decision was influenced by the company's financial and technical resources. Most small companies assembled computers with sourced components. Big companies (IBM, for example) did a good deal of design and manufacturing in house, although they too relied on third parties to supply parts like microprocessors, disk drives, and power supplies.

When IBM first entered the microcomputer market in August 1981, no industry standards existed for operating systems, microprocessors, or memory capacity. Within two years, however, IBM machines with MS-DOS became the industry standard. Most start-ups adopted the IBM standard to take advantage of already written software. By 1984, established companies like Olivetti and Tandy switched from their proprietary systems to the new industry standard. Apple and AT&T, however, maintained their proprietary systems and built a library of software for their own systems. The following became the two paths to PC design:

	IBM PC	Macintosh
Architecture	Open	Closed
Operating system	MS-DOS	The Finder
Microprocessor	Intel 8086	Motorola 68000
Vertical integration	Low	High
Industry standard	Yes	No

Manufacturing Infrastructure

The PC industry became concentrated in United States geographic areas that offered easy access to technology, labor, and capital. The main advantages of these "company clusters" is best illustrated by Silicon Valley, where companies had easy access to talent through their proximity to Stanford and Berkeley, universities that were particularly strong in engineering and had policies promoting close industry-university collaboration. Moreover, because engineering and computer science were highly applied fields, the professors and students were easily drawn into entrepreneurial activities, which further strengthened the lab-field link.

Because a PC required many diverse engineered products such as chips, disk drives, power supplies, video terminals, and keyboards, even the large manufacturers depended on specialized vendors for some of their components. Consequently, many suppliers formed in and around Silicon Valley, providing a necessary infrastructure for start-up companies. By the late 1980s, multiple sources existed for all materials and services a PC manufacturer might require. This allowed many firms to enter the PC business primarily as component assemblers.

Throughout the 1980s, most component suppliers were abundant with the exception of microprocessors. Manufacturers that could maintain a special relationship with semiconductor suppliers such as Intel had a distinct competitive advantage. However, in late 1987, Intel announced its plans to integrate forward and manufacture its own IBM PC/AT (286 chip) clones.

Target Market Segments

Microcomputer vendors could target one or more of the four broad consumer segments: home, scientific, education, and business.

Home. The microcomputer pioneers had envisioned a PC in every U.S. household, but this dream had yet to be realized. PC vendors competing in this market found themselves selling near-commodity items. Consequently, price competition was intense and profit margins were low. Moreover, success in this segment required a large commitment to advertising. Software developed mainly for home computers included games, word processing, filing management, budgeting, educational packages, and language programming.

Scientific and Engineering. The complex graphics and mathematical computations required by these users necessitated powerful microprocessors and large memory banks. While small, this segment offered high margins on high-performance machines. Uses included computer-aided design (CAD), engineering (CAE), and manufacturing (CAM). Specialized software for these uses usually came from third-party software developers.

Education. Low-end, "affordable" machines were the norm. Like the home market, schools and universities held less potential than business buyers; industry analysts expected education demand to be only about 500,000 units in 1987. Nevertheless, the education segment was targeted by some firms because of its role as a training ground for future computer users. The primary application in this segment was programming, although instruction programs were rapidly gaining in popularity.

Business. Until 1981, when IBM decided to make and market microcomputers, businesses viewed the PC as a hobbyists' toy that would not fit in an office environment either physically or functionally. Since IBM's entry, this segment had grown rapidly, and by the late 1980s it represented the largest market.

Because the business segment was so large, industry players had broken it down into subsegments. One common subcategorization was based on the size of the business: large (*Fortune* 1000), medium, and small businesses. While each segment had various product support needs, all segments were interested in five features: price, performance (speed and memory size), compatibility (with existing software), connectivity (networking), and adherence to industry standards (to facilitate hardware and software add-ons).

While technology drove the PC business in the early 1980s, by the end of the 1980s it had become a low barrier to entry because most vendors had the engineering capability to keep up with changes. Moreover, advances in microelectronics—the primary force behind the growth of the industry—were easily available to PC vendors, who were the biggest customers of the semiconductor companies. In addition, cloning had become a well-developed art. In 1986 some 350 companies worldwide were making clones, software, or added hardware options for personal computers. Their combined revenue was $6 billion, 33 percent more than IBM's PC business. In fact, technological developments had *lowered* entry barriers by virtually eliminating R&D costs (especially for low-end clones), reducing new product time to market, lowering parts costs, and simplifying manual assembly. The major barrier to entry had become marketing costs: typical dealer margins for hardware were 30 percent to 40 percent.

COMPETITIVE WEAPONS

The principal competitive factors in this industry varied by target market. However, firms aiming to gain a foothold in the more lucrative markets competed on the basis of their strength in a number of areas.

Marketing and distribution capabilities were the most important factor in the personal-computer industry in the late 1980s. The battleground had gradually shifted to the retailers, and the successful manufacturers had used well-defined channels of distribution as an effective barrier to entry for newcomers.

Some of the common channels taken by the manufacturers were as follows:

- **Retailer.** Retailers could be divided into two broad categories: at the low end were those who simply sold machines; at the high end were those who also provided service and support; some even consulted.

- **Direct sales force.** This type of selling was normally aimed at large-volume corporate accounts. Because of the heavy fixed expenses associated with supporting a sales force, however, few manufacturers could afford this form of selling.

- **Original equipment manufacturer (OEM).** This channel was used by companies that excelled in hardware engineering but lacked marketing capability. The OEMs integrated and packaged available hardware (from different manufacturers) to create and install customized systems to user specifications.
- **Value-added reseller (VAR).** VARs simply bought machines from the manufacturers, added software and/or modified the hardware, and sold packaged solutions to "vertical markets" such as law, medicine, and dentistry practices. When a VAR made changes to a product, those changes were recognized by the original manufacturer, and the warranty held. Some VARs even provided services such as training, consulting, and maintenance.
- **Mail order.** The original channel for computer hackers and early adopters, this channel made a late entry in the mainstream markets but soon found followers among those who did not want to pay the retailer's margin and were satisfied with telephone solutions to their computer-related problems.

Within channels, manufacturers used service and support as a major differentiating factor. In the microcomputer industry, as in other high-tech industries, these intangible factors were important because the design flaws, bugs, and limitations of a product became apparent months after the purchase. Moreover, since the machines were a substantial investment, ease of use and maintenance facilitated by post-sale service and support could be a competitive advantage in some segments, especially the scientific and business sectors of the market.

Because there was such a diverse range of personal computers available in the market, the confused buyer tended to take shelter in the security provided by a tested name. In cases where the person making the decision was not the ultimate user (as normally happened in centralized purchasing functions of large corporations), the purchaser was reluctant to purchase untested clones from suppliers that might not be around to honor their warranties. (This aspect was especially important because a large number of smaller PC firms had gone bankrupt in the 1984–1986 period.) In fact, there was a saying in the industry, "No one ever got fired for buying IBM."

However, while marketing, post-sale service, and corporate reputation were significant selling factors, the bottom line was still product quality and reliability. End users still wanted the best technology available and assurance that a machine had the capabilities they wanted. Thus vendors had to keep pace with technological trends and provide optimum price/performance characteristics.

Companies often took recourse in lawsuits to protect their technologies and their markets. While technology was not a major barrier to entry in the microcomputer industry, technological breakthroughs in design and functionality of a system did offer competitive advantage to a firm and were zealously guarded through patents, copyrights, and trademarks. In fact, industry observers believed that the major obstacle to copying was not technical but legal.

The effectiveness of the legal weapon can be exemplified by the experience of Franklin Computer Corporation. Franklin's first computer in March 1982 mimicked what was then the best-selling personal computer, Apple II. Apple promptly sued, engaging Franklin in a 19-month court battle. The matter was settled out of court, with Franklin agreeing to pay Apple $2.5 million and promising not to copy any Apple software. The fight with Apple created a heavy burden for Franklin and became an important factor in its decision to file for bankruptcy in June 1984.

Copying a feature in the PC industry was commonly done by reverse engineering, a process in which the duplicator studied the function of the desired feature and achieved it by working backwards. That is, functionality was copied; design did not have be the same.

MICROCOMPUTER INDUSTRY IN 1987

By 1987 the microcomputer hardware industry was highly concentrated, with five vendors sharing about 50 percent of the total PC market (see Exhibit 2). Dominance in the marketplace by IBM, Apple, Compaq, and Tandy was an effective barrier to entry for potential newcomers. Small companies did find niches and prospered with limited applications for their products, but limited access to distribution channels made it difficult for a new company to be as successful.

The established vendors had the advantage of scale economies in production, research, marketing, and service. Furthermore, most of these companies were somewhat vertically integrated: making custom chips for internal use (IBM) or having their own sales outlets (Tandy). Labor-force and management experience did not pose an entry problem because of widespread job-hopping in this industry.

Manufacturers sometimes lost control of pricing in the retail channels. If low sales turnover caused break-even problems, retailers would unload PCs below established market prices. Historically, the industry had experienced 15-percent to 20-percent price erosion each year, and price slashing was gradually becoming a norm in the high-end market too.

In 1987, personal computers could be divided into three categories: those based on the Intel family of microprocessors accounted for about 65 percent of the U.S. market, those designed around Motorola 68000 chips made up about 14 percent of the machines, and the remaining 21 percent were made using a variety of other microprocessors.[1] According to an estimate by International Data Corporation, a market research firm, the U.S. market for

[1]Source: *U.S. Industrial Outlook*, 1988.

microcomputers grew by 6 percent in 1986 and by 13 percent to $16 billion in 1987. Imports, mainly from the Far East, constituted over half the total 1987 revenue figures.

Business and professional users purchased about half (3.3 million) of the microcomputers sold in the United States in 1987, accounting for over 60 percent of the value of all sales. By contrast, sales to the home-user market declined 10 percent to 2 million units, while dollar value increased 9 percent to $2.4 billion. The scientific and educational markets remained strong in 1987, with unit sales increases of 15 percent and 11 percent, respectively.

The highlight of the year was the April 2 announcement by IBM of a new line of higher performance personal computers, the PS/2, based on Intel's new 80386 chip. Technical innovations included 3.5-inch disk drives, a new bus structure (called the "microchannel"), and graphics and user-interface enhancements. Design features and patent protection made reverse engineering of this machine difficult, but industry sources expected clones to be available in 1988.

One interpretation of this move was that IBM was directing its efforts at large corporate accounts to ward off the DEC (minis) and Apple (micros) attacks and was leaving the low-end market open to others. Another interpretation was that this move would eventually set a new standard in the industry and would make the existing products obsolete: that IBM wanted to teach clone-makers a lesson because they had been chipping away at its market share. The reactions of competitors varied: some companies, like Tandy, immediately cut prices; others, like Compaq, believing that the old standard had a huge installed base and would coexist with the new standard, stuck to their guns.

Another significant development in the microcomputer industry was the beginning of shipments of the latest generation of systems based on the Intel 80386 microprocessor. The 80386 was a full 32-bit processor that could address up to 16 megabytes of memory and had the potential to operate in multi-user and multitask modes. The Operating System/2 being developed by Microsoft to take full advantage of the capabilities of Intel 80286 and 80386 microprocessors was to be released in 1988. However, a broad enough range of software programs to justify use of the new operating system was expected to take time to develop. Meantime, software suppliers would probably continue to develop products for the existing installed base of operating systems (primarily MS-DOS).

Software development was becoming an increasingly important factor in the long-term strategies of the microcomputer firms because of price erosion in hardware markets and the fact that software availability helped sell equipment. Three software companies—Microsoft, Ashton-Tate, and Lotus—still dominated the industry, generating more than 50 percent of the revenues of the top 100 independent vendors. Most of the independent suppliers were small, with less than $1 million in sales, and they usually catered to specialized markets. This industry grew 24 percent in 1986 and 23 percent in 1987. U.S. sales of software were expected to grow 30 percent to $5 billion in 1988 and at an average annual rate of 27 percent through 1992. Applications were predicted to continue to lag behind hardware innovations because of the complexity of software, the extensive time required for development, and the shortage of skilled programmers.

The U.S. microcomputer industry was expected to grow at an average annual rate of 6 percent from 1988 onward, reaching $23 billion in 1992. The business/professional sector was expected to account for more than 60 percent of this value.

The technological trends in the microcomputer sector included increasingly more powerful, application-specific chips; sophisticated networking; low-cost, lighter, and more powerful laptop computers; new user-friendly graphics interfaces; erasable optical disks; and software taking advantage of increasingly powerful microprocessors. The question facing manufacturers at the end of the decade was, "How do we obtain a sustainable competitive advantage in such a rapidly changing industry?"

CASE APPENDIX 1

ELEMENTS OF A MICROCOMPUTER

As a device, the personal computer was an assembly of several key components. Since the components represented widely differing technologies, manufacturers often relied on third-party specialists.

Microprocessor (one). Etched on a thin slice of silicon, this was the "brain" of the system and determined the degree of sophistication the machine was capable of attaining. For example, the first IBM PC in 1981 used Intel's 8088 chip, which was considered to be primitive compared with the 1987 Intel 80386.

The suppliers of microprocessors were mainly U.S. companies. Intel had the largest presence in the microcomputer market because of use in IBM machines. It competed with Motorola and National Semiconductor. The most well-known PC company that used Motorola's 68000 series chips was Apple.

Microprocessor technology, while not a big barrier to potential newcomers in the PC industry, was a driving force in this business. Hence, to assure an uninterrupted supply of logic chips, many vendors established long-term, "co-destiny" relationships with semiconductor companies (the IBM-Intel marriage was a case in point). Moreover, when a new, more powerful chip was developed, it represented a potential competitive advantage to the company that had early access to it.

Memory Chips (many). These constituted the "internal" memory of computers and were also silicon based. Unlike microprocessors, memory chips did not have logic circuits of their own and were used only to store data while the machine was on. There had been rapid developments in this area, and by mid-1987, chips that could store 1 megabyte (one million characters) of data were available. Only a few months earlier, the maximum amount of data that could be stored on a single chip was 256 kilobytes.

Each computer had a bank of memory chips that added up to the total internal memory designed for the machine. The more powerful a computer, the larger the internal memory needed to exploit the machine's potential. The memory chip was a commodity item produced in large quantities. This area was dominated by Japanese companies.

Circuit Boards (many). All the silicon chips were mounted on printed circuit boards (PCBs) that, as the name implies, had the circuit already etched on their surfaces. Large companies normally designed and manufactured their own PCBs, but for small companies, sourcing this part from outside was sometimes more economical.

Disk Drives (one/many). These were sophisticated electromechanical devices that facilitated transfer of data to secondary storage media like floppies and hard disks. Normally, microcomputer firms sourced disk drives from specialized manufacturers. Two of the well-known American vendors for disk drives were Seagate Technology and Tandon.

Peripherals. These commonly included the terminal, keyboard, and printer. These units were not always made by the computer manufacturer, as other firms specialized in these areas and could easily supply peripheral devices compatible with the main machines.

The standard manufacturing costs of a PC (in 1985) are shown in Table A.

Table A
Standard Manufacturing Costs of a PC in 1985

In April 1985, the standard cost components per machine of an Intel 80186-based microcomputer for a small, rapidly growing company were as follows:

CENTRAL PROCESSING UNIT AND DISK DRIVES

Material[a]	$1,776.55
Component direct labor	27.02
Component fixed overhead	165.34
Component outside processing	146.50
Assembly direct labor	3.28
Assembly fixed overhead	19.82
Total	$2,138.51

VIDEO DISPLAY UNIT AND KEYBOARD

Material	$ 184.96
Component direct labor	6.10
Component fixed overhead	36.85
Component outside processing	13.50
Assembly direct labor	0.51
Assembly fixed overhead	3.10
Total	$ 245.02
Total Cost per Unit:	$2,383.53

---

[a]The material cost included a 10 MB hard disk ($435) and the Intel 80168 ($42).
Source: Proprietary documents of a small PC manufacturer.

CASE APPENDIX 2

MICROPROCESSORS AND OPERATING SYSTEMS

THE 6502 BASIC SYSTEMS

Microsoft's BASIC interpreter and Mostec's 6502 were the two inventions that created the market for products based on the 8-bit microprocessor in 1977. Apple Computer's first commercial machine, the Apple II, was based on the 6502. Other firms with similar products were Tandy, Commodore, and Atari.

Typical Configuration

> MOS Technology's 8-bit 6502 microprocessor
> 16K RAM main storage
> ROM-based proprietary operating system, often combined with BASIC
>   language
> TV screen monitor
> Audio cassette tape as off-line storage
> Single printed circuit board

THE Z80 CP/M SYSTEMS

Digital Research's CP/M operating system, introduced in 1976, was designed around Zilog's 8-bit microprocessor. The other microprocessor in this class was the Intel 8080. A major innovation in these systems was the S100 bus, which allowed systems to be configured from a variety of vendors' products. This market was dominated by Cromemco, North Star, and Tandy.

Typical Configuration

> Zilog's Z80A 8-bit chip (which had some 16-bit internals)
> CP/M-80 operating system
> 64K RAM
> S100 bus, with separate boards for each subsystem
> Separate video display unit
> Centronics or Epson dot matrix printer
> Floppy disk drive

8088 MS-DOS SYSTEMS

This market came into existence with the introduction of the IBM PC in August 1981. This was the first "16-bit" microprocessor-based personal computer, and in a short time became an industry standard. Other micro-processors in this class included Intel 8086, 80186, and 80286.

Typical Configuration

Intel 8088, 8086, or 80286 microprocessor
MS-DOS (Microsoft Disk Operating System)
256KB RAM expandable to over 1MB
1MB Winchester drive
Ethernet (for networking)
Multi-user capability (4 to 16 users)

EVOLUTION OF MICROPROCESSORS

Chip	Size	Introduction	Application
Intel 4004	4-bit	Late 1960s	Automation of gas pumps
Intel 8080	8-bit	By 1974	Microcomputers
Intel 8088	8/16-bit	Late 1970s	Microcomputers
Intel 80286	16-bit	1980	Microcomputers
Intel 80386	32-bit	1987	Microcomputers

The instruction set of the 8080 is now an industry standard, appearing first in the Z80s and later in the 16-bit chips, such as the Intel 8086, 80186, full 16-bit 80286, and full 32-bit 80386.

Typical Processing Speeds

8-bit	8080	Under 100,000 instructions per second
16-bit	80286	Over 500,000 instructions per second
32-bit	80386	1 to 10 million instructions per second

All the leading personal computers up until mid-1982 used 8-bit micro-computers. The most widely used microprocessor was Zilog's Z80, mainly because the operating system CP/M, which had established an acceptable industry standard, was structured around it.

Radio Shack's first computer product was TRS-80, introduced in August 1977. It was based on the Zilog Z-80 microprocessor.

The M6800, Motorola's 16-bit microprocessor, first appeared in personal computers in 1979.

<u>Worldwide PC Unit Shipments (by Chip Technology) in 1986</u>

IBM originals (Intel)	21.7%
IBM compatibles (Intel)	23.3
Motorola 68000 family	7.5
Others	47.5

APPLE, COMPAQ, IBM, AND TANDY IN 1988

This case summarizes the strategies of Apple, Tandy, IBM, and Compaq—four companies that dominated the personal computer industry in 1988. The story of Dell Computer, an IBM clone-maker, has been included to illustrate niche play in an industry in which the top three players have captured about 40 percent of the market.

APPLE

When Steve Wozniak and Steve Jobs started their little business venture in the now-legendary two-car garage in 1976, they were taking a lead in what was to become a billion-dollar industry within five years. The total microcomputer market in the United States had since grown to more than $20 billion by 1986, and Apple, with 7-percent market share, was one of the leading players.

The company was incorporated on January 3, 1977, to design, manufacture, and market personal computers for use in business, education, and the home. It remained a private corporation until December 1980, when it made an initial public offering of 4.6 million shares of common stock. Since then its stock has been actively traded on the American Stock Exchange, and in June 1987, Apple became the first company in its category to offer dividends to shareholders.

In the late 1980s, the company had two major product lines: the Apple II family of computers (Apple IIe, Apple IIc, and Apple IIgs), targeted primarily at the education and home markets, and the Macintosh family (Mac 128k, Mac 512k, Mac Plus, Mac 512k enhanced, Mac SE, and Mac II), directed at business users. (PC-model information for the firms described in this case is given in Exhibit 1.) In addition, Apple manufactured accessory products such as printers, monitors, and modems for these product lines. In 1987 Apple floated a software subsidiary of its own (Claris) in recognition of software's growing importance in this industry.

The events leading up to the positions outlined in this case are described in a companion case, "The Microcomputer Industry in 1987" (UVA-BP 288). This case was prepared by Anurag Sharma, Darden MBA 1988, under the supervision of Associate Professor L. J. Bourgeois III. Copyright © 1988 by the Darden Graduate Business School Sponsors, Charlottesville, VA. WP4672L

Exhibit 1
Hardware Roundup—Personal Computers, Fall 1987

APPLE COMPUTER, INC.

Model	MICRO CHIP	INTERNAL MEMORY	DISK STORAGE	STANDARD PRICE
Macintosh II	68020	1–8MB	800K	$3,769
Macintosh SE	68000	1–4MB	800K–20M	$2,898
Macintosh Plus	68000	1–4MB	800K	$2,199
Macintosh Enhanced	68000	512K	400K–800K	$1,699

IBM CORPORATION

Model				
PS/2 Model 80	80386	1–16MB	44–628MB	$6,995–13,995
PS/2 Model 60	80286	1–15MB	1.4–70MB	$5,295–6,295
PS/2 Model 50	80286	1–7MB	1.4–20MB	$3,595
PS/2 Model 30	8086	640K	720K–20MB	$1,695–2,295
PC AT 339	80286	512K–15MB	1.2–30MB	$4,595

COMPAQ COMPUTER CORPORATION

Model				
DeskPro 386	80386	1–10MB	1.2–40MB	$6,499–7,299
DeskPro 286	80286	256K	1.2–2MB	$2,999–3,999
DeskPro	8086	256K–640K	720K	$1,699
Portable III	80286	640K–6.6MB	1.2MB	$3,999
Portable II	80286	720K	2MB	$2,999
Portable	8088	256K–640K	720K	$2,199

TANDY CORPORATION

Model				
Tandy 4000	80386	1–16MB	1.44MB	$2,599
Tandy 3000HL	80286	512K–1MB	360K–40MB	$1,699
Tandy 1000SX	8088	384K–640K	360K–20MB	$999
Tandy 1000EX	8088	256K–640K	360K	$599

(continued on next page)

Adapted from: "Hardware Round up, the Final Chapter: Personal Computers," *Computerworld*, October 5, 1987, p. S15.

(continued)

PC'S LIMITED

Model	MICRO CHIP	INTERNAL MEMORY	DISK STORAGE	STANDARD PRICE
386-16	80386	1–16MB	40–150MB	$4,499
286-12	80286	1–16MB	40–70MB	$2,699
286-8	80286	1–16MB	20–40MB	$1,799
Turbo	8088-2	640K	20–40MB	$ 799

Apple's early customers were hobbyists already familiar with computers. These computer "hackers" bought the machines and wanted to write their own programs, but the founders of Apple recognized that wider sales would be blocked if adequate software were not available. The computer had to reach far beyond the hobbyists to the uninitiated to attain the status of a mass market: competition in this infant industry was limited, but the challenge was to convince people to use personal computers. Hence, the first product, the Apple II, was introduced with extensive documentation to make it user friendly, and, at the same time, its technical specifications were made public—making it "open" architecture. This second step was unprecedented in the computer industry but extremely successful for Apple: new programs and applications that poured in from every imaginable source substantially increased the utility of Apple machines.

Good product alone, however, could not have taken Apple to the heights it eventually attained. Steve Jobs (chairman) and Mike Markulla (president) decided that gaining market recognition quickly was critical if they were to dominate the business. They used $600,000 in venture-capital equity funds, not for product development but for promotion, giving Apple an image (in 1977) of a $100 million company at a time when it had just 12 employees. This image-building continued through 1986, with the company spending $158 million on marketing.

While Apple dominated the education market from its inception in 1977 (about 60-percent share in 1986), it faced resistance from corporate buyers because of its unorthodox personality and the dominating presence of IBM in that segment. The two products aimed at business, Lisa and Apple III, failed to generate sufficient market share and were withdrawn from the market after a short life. Then, in 1984, a renegade group of engineers led by Steve Jobs brought out the first of the Macintosh family of products— Macintosh 128k and Macintosh 512k. Jobs had envisioned desktop publishing as a market for Macintosh all along and was careful to incorporate an easy user interface and some legendary graphics gymnastics in these new machines. These features highlighted the productivity of the Macintosh and helped engender a loyal following in the nontechnical pockets of business computing. Apple was finally able to gain a foothold in the corporate world and by 1986 had about 10-percent share of the business and professional markets.

The company kept pace with the fast developments in the personal computer market by coming out with enhanced versions of its products to make them appeal to broader markets. The first Macs had a closed architecture, which prevented widespread third-party support and limited market acceptance. In January 1986, Macintosh Plus was introduced with an open architecture to rectify that error. Apple IIgs, introduced in September 1986, had improved graphics and was developed to consolidate Apple's dominant position in the education market. Then in March 1987 even more powerful machines—Macintosh SE and Macintosh II—were brought into the market to strengthen Apple's position in a (now more amenable) corporate world. (See Exhibit 2 for a chronology of Apple product introductions.)

The surge in Macintosh sales attracted a large number of third-party software and hardware add-on vendors who were looking for positions outside the quickly saturating and highly competitive IBM-compatible market. A key feature of the Macintosh strategy was Apple's insistence that software developers writing for Mac adhere to Apple's strict set of data formatting and command guidelines. This standard resulted in tight intercompatibility of third-party software, which enabled users to exchange files across a spectrum of Macintosh applications. The enforced uniformity increased Apple's attractiveness to potential users.

After cutting off mail-order sales in 1981, Apple kept tight control of its distribution channels. The Mac was distributed almost entirely through Apple's network of authorized dealers, and the sales force was used only to help pair up dealers with large corporate accounts. The more complex products like Macintosh SE and Macintosh II were restricted to the most sophisticated outlets to ensure superior service and support to end users. In 1986 the U.S. dealer organization was trimmed by 25 percent, while the field sales force was kept intact.

Apple cultivated an unusually strong relationship with Businessland, Inc., the San Jose, California, chain that was a major conduit for both Apple and IBM products to large corporations. The single overriding issue for Apple was to make sure that dealers could market its machines effectively.

As the target market shifted from education and home to business and professional, the promotion strategy also changed. Apple spent more on

Exhibit 2
Apple—Chronology of New Products

MODEL	DEBUT	PRICE	COMMENTS
Apple II	June 1977	$1,295	8-bit Mos 6502
Apple II Plus	June 1979	$1,195	
Apple III	September 1980	$3,495	Discontinued 4/84
Apple IIe	January 1983	$1,395	
Lisa	January 1983	$9,995	Lisa was renamed Mac XL in January 1985 and later discontinued in April 1985.
Apple III Plus	December 1983	$2,995	
Macintosh 128k	January 1984	$2,495	
Apple IIc Portable	April 1984	$1,295	
Macintosh 512k	September 1984	$3,195	
Macintosh 512e			
Macintosh Plus	January 1986	$2,599	
Apple IIgs	September 1986	$ 999	
Macintosh SE	March 1987	$2,898	
Macintosh II	March 1987	$4,799	
Macintosh IIx		$5,269	
Macintosh SE/30		$4,499	
Macintosh IIcx		$4,669	

Note: The Macintosh Plus and the SE are based on Motorola 68000s, a 7.83 megahertz chip. The II, IIx, SE/30, and the IIcx are based on the later version 68020 and 68030, which run at 15.667 megahertz.

Source: Apple Computer Company as quoted in the *Wall Street Journal* and by Apple dealers.

focused sales and marketing programs and proportionately less in advertising and merchandising. (A five-year summary of financial data for Apple appears in Exhibit 3.)

The Apple II family for the U.S. market was manufactured in Carlton, Texas; Apple's facility in Cork, Ireland, produced these products for the European market. The Macintosh line was manufactured in one of the most highly automated manufacturing facilities in the nation in Fremont, California. Peripherals for both lines were developed and manufactured in a facility in Garden Grove, California. In addition, Apple maintained a facility in Singapore

Exhibit 3
Apple Computer, Inc., Financials

FISCAL YEAR ENDING SEPTEMBER 30

	1984	1985	1986	1987	1988
INCOME STATEMENT		(in millions of dollars)			
Operating revenues	1,516	1,918	1,902	2,661	4,071
Gross profit	637	800	1,010	1,365	2,080
Profit before taxes	109	120	310	410	656
Net income	59	61	154	217	400
BALANCE SHEET					
Cash and investments	115	337	576	565	546
Inventory	265	167	109	226	461
Current assets	688	822	1,041	1,307	1,783
PP&E (net)	76	90	107	130	207
Total assets	789	936	1,160	1,478	2,082
Current liabilities	255	295	329	479	827
Total liabilities	324	385	466	641	1,079
Common equity	209	235	227	264	226
Net worth	465	551	694	837	1,003

Source: Apple Computer Company 1988 Annual Report.

for the production of logic boards used in Apple computers. In early 1984, Apple formed a joint venture with Mexican investors called Apple de Mexico to manufacture and market the Apple IIe in Mexico and other Latin American countries.

CEO John Sculley, the intense ex-president of Pepsi recruited to Apple by Steve Jobs in 1983, engineered the board's dismissal of the mercurial Jobs in 1985. Analysts' predictions of Apple revenues of $3.8 billion for 1988 were greeted by Sculley's pronouncement that "the next revenue milestone for Apple isn't $5 billion, but $10 billion. We hope to be there in the early 1990s."[1]

---

[1]*Fortune*, August 1, 1988, p. 48.

INTERNATIONAL BUSINESS MACHINES

On taking over as chief operating officer of IBM Corporation in 1981, John Opel completed the implementation of an innovative, low-risk restructuring to allow the company to enter emerging high-technology markets. One step was to form Independent Business Units (IBUs) for ongoing businesses that could manage their own finances, manufacturing, and marketing; the second step was to put fledgling businesses into Special Business Units (SBUs), which depended on the "father" to handle one or more of their operations. The SBU created in July 1980 to develop the PC business was called Entry Systems and had the goal of developing a competitive and easy-to-use machine within a year.

In the process of entering the microcomputer market in August 1981, IBM broke away from both industry and company traditions. To get to market quickly, the company decided against developing its own system software, and instead commissioned Microsoft to write a version of its MS-DOS program for the PC. This move spurred the growth of application programs written for the IBM machines, as anyone could license the Microsoft program, and helped MS-DOS become a *de facto* industry standard by 1983.

A second major strategic move by IBM was to make its PC from off-the-shelf components rather than to develop all the major hardware inputs in-house. This step, along with the decision to make public the design specifications of its product, further enabled third-party participation. As a result, software applications and hardware add-ons flooded the market, enabling IBM and IBM-compatible machines to dominate the PC market within three years.

These strategic decisions and the fact that IBM dominated the mainframe computer industry with a favorable brand image in the corporate world (which was emerging as the largest and fastest-growing buyer segment) helped "Big Blue" climb to the top of the micro market. In 1983 IBM had a 36-percent market share, compared with Apple's 25 percent. By 1986 IBM had shipped more than 3 million PCs, PC XTs, and ATs—the vast majority in the United States to *Fortune* 2000 users, who formed the backbone of IBM's large-systems market. In 1986 about 20 percent of the company's revenues came from its PC operations. (See Exhibit 4 for financial data.)

However, while the use of widely available parts and an open design that let independent companies make software, accessories, and even full computers enabled IBM PCs to become an industrywide standard and displaced Apple from market leadership, these very decisions came back to haunt IBM. The phenomenal, and unexpected, success of the IBM PC, and subsequently of the IBM PC/AT (based on the 80286 chip), created a demand that IBM was unable to fill and led to the rise of clones—computers more-or-less compatible with IBM products. The best known of the clone makers, Compaq Computer Corporation, capitalized on its license for IBM's proprietary basic input/output system (BIOS), its sound financing, and very effective marketing to establish itself as a credible alternative source. Other early clone makers, such as

Exhibit 4
IBM Corporation Financials

FISCAL YEAR ENDING DECEMBER 31

INCOME STATEMENT	1984	1985	1986	1987	1988
		(in millions of dollars)			
Operating revenues	45,937	50,056	52,160	55,256	59,681
Gross profit	27,081	28,953	29,007	30,134	34,033
Profit before taxes	11,623	11,619	8,407	8,630	9,033
Net income	6,582	6,555	4,789	5,258	5,806
BALANCE SHEET					
Cash and investments	600	896	755	782	1,072
Inventory	6,598	8,579	8,039	8,659	9,565
Current assets	20,375	26,070	27,749	34,369	35,343
PP&E (net)	Na	19,680	21,268	22,967	23,426
Total assets	42,808	52,634	57,814	70,029	73,037
Current liabilities	9,640	11,433	12,743	15,939	17,387
Total liabilities	16,319	20,644	23,440	31,766	33,528
Common equity	5,998	6,267	6,321	6,417	6,442
Net worth	26,489	31,990	34,374	38,263	39,509

Source: IBM 1988 Annual Report.

(now defunct) Eagle Computer, were sued by IBM for BIOS infringement and lacked the strength to reach a viable size. Still others survived IBM's hostility to clones but had to be satisfied with less than 100-percent software compatibility in their products. These shortcomings in performance, however, were later more-or-less overcome, and some clones provided advantages over their IBM counterparts.

A second wave of clones that came from Japan had limited success. NEC Corporation, the personal computer market leader in Japan, withdrew a machine that was software-compatible with the PC/XT and redirected its efforts to the high end of the PC/AT market. Seiko's Epson America, Inc., subsidiary was the most visible Japanese supplier in the U.S. market, with a line of mid-priced PC clones based on some proprietary technology and BIOS.

In 1986 low-cost products from Korean and Taiwanese manufacturers invaded the market. Leading Edge from Korea was probably the most visible among these machines. Unlike their Japanese competitors, which sold through wholly owned subsidiaries, these suppliers sold through private-labeling distributors and manufacturers' representatives. The same year also saw the beginning of serious efforts by overseas suppliers to penetrate the mass-merchandising channel.

By 1986 some 350 companies worldwide were making clones, software, or added hardware options for IBM PCs. A significant change that occurred in the IBM PC and compatible market that year was the acceptance of clones in professional and small-business markets. As one consequence of this development, IBM's share of the "IBM-compatible" market dropped substantially. Infocorp, a market researcher, predicted that it would fall to 38 percent in 1987 from 53 percent in 1985 and 40 percent in 1986.

In response to such early signs of market maturity as product proliferation and ferocious competition, IBM started moving away from the overcrowded, low-end, open-architecture segment. In April 1987, Big Blue announced its new microcomputer series PS/2 for the high end of the market. The PS/2 series employed a new "Micro Channel" architecture (MCA), which IBM promoted by touting unspecified advantages in the future. Some analysts felt IBM was making a mistake by "thinking it can sell PCs the same way it sold mainframes—with promised benefits in the future."[2]

IBM's introduction of the PS/2 line created uncertainty in the market. Buyers were undecided about buying the PS/2, as not all models supported MCA (see Exhibit 5 for chronology of IBM product introductions). One year after the PS/2 introduction, only 40 percent of all PS/2s shipped were equipped to run the new OS/2 operating system coming from Microsoft. Despite the PS/2 "clone buster" line, IBM was once again facing lower-priced knockoffs by the end of 1988 (see Exhibit 6).

COMPAQ

When the curtain rose on Compaq in 1982, the founders—Rod Canion, James M. Harris, and William H. Murto—had no idea of the brilliant success their business venture would become (see Exhibit 7). The three founders were executives with Texas Instruments in Houston when IBM announced its first personal computer in April 1981. They quickly recognized the significance of Big Blue's debut in the business market with an open architecture machine. They realized that any competitive product would need to be IBM-compatible, as it was unlikely that the majority of software writers would create packages for an unknown computer.

---

[2]*Computerworld* supplement, November 14, 1988.

Exhibit 5
IBM—Chronology of New Products

MODEL	DEBUT	PRICE	COMMENTS
IBM PC[a]	August 1981	$2,235	16-bit Intel 8088
IBM PC XT	March 1983	$4,995	Intel 8086
3270 PC[b]	October 1983	$5,585	
IBM PC XT 370[b]	October 1983	$8,995	
IBM PC jr.[c]	November 1983	$ 700	64K discontinued 3/85
IBM Portable	February 1984		Discontinued after three months
IBM PC AT[d]	August 1984	$5,795	
IBM RT PC	January 1986		RISC-based work station
PC Convertible	April 1986		Similar to Compaq machine
IBM PC XT 286	August 1986		
PS/2 Model 30[e]	April 1987	$1,695	Intel 8086
PS/2 Model 50[f]	April 1987	$3,595	Intel 286, Micro Channel
PS/2 Model 60	April 1987	$5,295	Intel 286, Micro Channel
PS/2 Model 80	July 1987	$6,996	Intel 386, Micro Channel
PS/2 Model 25	September 1987	$1,350	Intel 8086
PS/2 Model 50Z	June 1988	$3,995	Intel 286, Micro Channel
PS/2 Model 70	June 1988	$5,997	Intel 286, Micro Channel
PS/2 Model 30 286[g]	August 1988	$1,995	Intel 286

[a]The original PC had 64K memory, which was sufficient to run the then popular spreadsheet, Visicalc. It was the first to have a 16-bit microprocessor.
[b]These two workstations were designed to allow desktop access to the power and software of the IBM 370 mainframe.
[c]Basic price was $699. An enhanced version with 128K and one disk drive sold for $1,300.
[d]The IBM PC AT, based on Intel's 80286 microprocessor, was six times faster than the PC and sold for just over two times the price.
[e]Data for PS/2 machines represent most basic configuration.
[f]The model 50 was discontinued in April 1989.
[g]Compatible with original PC AT. Did not use Micro Channel architecture.

The prototype for Compaq's first product (a "portable" 26-pound IBM-compatible PC with a small screen and a carrying handle) was shown at the 1982 National Computer Conference in Houston and began selling in mid-1983. It was an immediate success, with sales topping $111 million in the first

Exhibit 6
Price Comparison of IBM and IBM Clones

	INTEL MICROPROCESSOR		
	8086/8088	80286	80386
"NO-NAME" CLONES			
Whole Earth Electronics	$849	$1,449	$2,995
Tussey Computer Products	$939	$1,399	$2,499
Micro Smart	$1,000	$1,500	$2,700
CompuAdd	$1,165	$1,640	$2,583
NAME BRANDS			
Tandy	$1,628	$3,099	$4,199
Compaq (at 47 St. Photo)	NA	$2,850	$4,350
IBM PS/2 (at Bulldog Computer Products)	$2,089	$3,514	$4,644

Source: Adapted from "Clone Computer Business Is Booming: Low Prices Help IBM Knockoffs Win New Fans," by William M. Bulkeley, p. 86 *Wall Street Journal*, October 7, 1988.

year. In the second year, in spite of a competitive portable from IBM, sales tripled to $329 million. By 1985 the original portable was outselling IBM's by nearly 10 to 1; sales rose to $504 million—marking the fastest climb ever to the *Fortune* 500 list. The big gains for the company came in the fastest growing segment, business computers, where it had about 7 percent share in 1987.

Many analysts in 1987 considered Compaq to be the shooting star of the computer industry. Unlike other start-up companies in this industry, however, Compaq was managed from the beginning as if it were a major corporation. All senior executives had had direct management experience in their areas of responsibility in other high-technology firms. One of their most important decisions—a stumbling block for many other start-ups—was to cultivate a loyal and dependable retail network. In fact, a lack of resources to establish its own sales force and an unwillingness to depend on "third-party" resellers turned out to be a blessing in disguise for the company. Compaq explicitly eschewed com-

Exhibit 7
Compaq Computer Corporation Financials

FISCAL YEAR ENDING DECEMBER 31

	1984	1985	1986	1987	1988
INCOME STATEMENT		(in millions of dollars)			
Operating revenues	329	503	625	1,224	2,065
Gross profit	97	178	265	507	832
Profit before taxes	16	44	77	228	367
Net income	13	27	43	136	255
BALANCE SHEET					
Cash and investments	28	77	57	132	281
Inventory	85	76	81	276	387
Current assets	189	240	260	681	1,115
PP&E (net)	39	67	102	192	429
Total assets	231	312	378	901	1,590
Current liabilities	122	99	119	343	480
Total liabilities	122	175	194	501	775
Common equity		Less than $1 million			
Net worth	109	137	183	400	815

Source: Compaq, Computer Corporation. 1988 Annual Report.

peting with its dealers by selling direct. In 1987 Compaq sold its computers to about 3,000 full-service computer specialty dealers worldwide for resale to end users. The products studiously avoided high-tech glitz and competed in the marketplace on the basis of IBM-compatibility and performance.

Depth in management and engineering played an important role in the company's success. It competed with IBM and other clone makers on the basis of performance measures such as clock speed and disk access time and product features such as portability. According to a Compaq executive, "This company is definitely market driven. Gadgets and technology take a back seat to what users want."[3] Compaq would add features to its machines based on end-user

---

[3]*Industry Week*, April 14, 1986.

surveys. For example, it provided an integrated tape backup to the hard disk, which helped Compaq machines gain acceptability with pharmacists.

Making IBM-compatible machines was not without risk, however. One market analysis said, "Sticking to full compatibility with IBM's machines could be compared to putting your head up an elephant's backside. When the elephant turns, you get your head snapped off."[4]

In April 1987, the elephant turned: IBM introduced the PS/2 line, which threatened to make the existing industry standards obsolete. But Compaq still had its head intact. Net income in the second quarter of 1987 jumped more than three times, to $30.7 million from $9.6 million the previous year. Revenues for the quarter grew 82 percent, to $267.5 million from $147.1 million. Compaq also kept a tight reign on manufacturing, using sophisticated techniques like "Just in Time" for better inventory control and quick turnaround times. The company custom designed its own chips in the same new $14-million office complex where its executives worked. Moreover, Compaq emphasized cost reduction and six-month product-development cycles—about the best in the industry. This allowed a quick response to IBM's PS/2 line (see Exhibit 6).

TANDY CORPORATION

As one of the pioneers of the microcomputer industry, Tandy rode the boom in PC business from the late 1970s through 1980 with its own proprietary product line. The industry slowdown of 1984 and 1985 was a source of concern to the company, however, because the computer business then accounted for about one-third of total revenues. After growth rates of 82 percent in 1980, 77 percent in 1981, 64 percent in 1982, and 33 percent in 1983, Tandy's PC sales grew only 4 percent in 1984 and actually declined 8 percent in 1985 before rebounding 12 percent in 1986. (Financial data are in Exhibit 8.) Recognizing the need to redefine its position in the personal computer market, Tandy had introduced its first IBM-compatible "industry standard" products in June 1984. The decision to enter the clone market on the basis of its strong distribution (Radio Shack stores) enabled Tandy to recover its market-share losses, and the retailer became once again one of the leaders in this business. Revenues from MS-DOS (IBM compatible) products rose from just 3.2 percent of microcomputer sales in 1984 to 41.3 percent in 1986 and 52.6 percent in 1987. The share of proprietary computers in Tandy total microcomputer sales, on the other hand, declined from 52.3 percent in 1984 to 17.6 percent in 1986 and 10.1 percent in 1987.

Competition to Tandy's low-end computer products came mainly from Leading Edge of South Korea, Epson of Japan, AT&T models made in Italy,

---

[4]*Forbes,* January 14, 1985.

Exhibit 8
Tandy Corporation Financials

	FISCAL YEAR ENDING JUNE 30				
	1984	1985	1986	1987	1988
INCOME STATEMENT		(in millions of dollars)			
Operating revenues	2,775	2,841	3,036	3,452	3,974
Gross profit	1,591	1,550	1,565	1,752	1,923
Number of stores	9,018	9,117	7,385	7,031	7,046
Profit before taxes	535	351	387	459	515
Net income	282	189	198	242	316
BALANCE SHEET					
Cash and investments	155	90	274	78	188
Inventory	911	1,197	980	1,128	1,288
Current assets	1,229	1,457	1,419	1,445	1,986
PP&E (net)	289	311	302	337	367
Total assets	1,652	1,923	2,078	1,965	2,530
Current liabilities	275	375	512	303	649
Total liabilities	664	859	772	585	927
Common equity	96	96	96	96	96
Net worth	989	1,064	1,307	1,380	1,603

Source: Tandy Corporation 1988 Annual Report.

and Atari computers made in Taiwan. To survive against these formidable price competitors, Tandy had two broad options:

- Lever the strong purchasing and distribution network to match price cuts;
- Move away from the inexpensive clone business and toward more sophisticated, high-end machines.

Tandy did both. Years of experience as a retailer had enabled the company to attain high operational efficiency through automation, rigid quality control, and lean inventories, making it a very low-cost producer. Moreover, Tandy's high degree of integration combined manufacturing with an impressive captive marketing and distribution system, which permitted the capture of a portion of the available profit from several phases of the manufacturing-distribution-retail chain.

The constantly declining computer prices in the industry further enhanced the value of Tandy's proprietary distribution system. As the popularity of microcomputers rose, an increasing number of unsophisticated purchasers demanding convenience and service as an important part of the package came into the market. Tandy's 430 Radio Shack Computer Centers and 730 computer departments within Radio Shack stores gave consumers a shopping-mall convenience. (This compared to 3,270 rival computer stores, 1,675 of which sold IBMs.)

By staying in the low end of the market, however, Tandy felt it was not fully exploiting the infrastructure it had so carefully developed over the years. With its low-cost operations and large number of retail outlets (which were potential service centers), the company decided that it could make inroads in the high-margin segment of the industry. So in November 1985, Tandy introduced the (Intel 80286-based) 3000 series targeted at small businesses and work-at-home executives. Then in July 1986, it unveiled enhanced versions of the 3000, the HL (faster), and the HD (hard disk) in an effort to distance itself from inexpensive clones and to attract serious business users. While Tandy had been fairly successful in selling its machines to small and medium-sized businesses, success with large corporations had eluded the retailer—in part, because of image.

Traditionally, Tandy's strategy as a retailer had been to make or purchase goods cheaply, place them in their large number of outlets across the country, and advertise heavily to build traffic in stores. This traffic, with the aid of good merchandising, led to constantly increasing sales. Selling computers to large corporations, however, required not only a high-quality product and excellent after-sales service and support, but also a well trained, outbound sales force that could conduct itself professionally with purchasing executives or systems engineers. Radio Shack had never felt the need to develop such a sales force.

Tandy's marketing problem was the flip side of IBM's. When IBM entered the PC market in 1981, it had to overcome the perception by smaller businesses and individuals that IBM sold only to large corporations (IBM's Charlie Chaplin commercials were an attempt to break down this barrier). In contrast, Radio Shack had an image as a place where one makes smaller non-high-tech purchases, and corporate buyers had a hard time justifying computer purchases from this source.

Tandy tried to counter this perception with extensive television advertising to position itself as a serious vendor. In addition, remodeling the Radio

Shack stores (into "Technology Stores") and a new dress code for the (new) outbound sales force attempted to lure the corporate buyer.

Regardless of whether sales were made through conventional Radio Shack stores, Radio Shack Computer Centers, or the company's growing outbound sales force (about 1,200), the entire marketing thrust was supported by the extensive warehousing, distribution, and servicing network that evolved over many decades. Moreover, the company had exceptional management retention. In an industry where executive turnover rates of 20 percent annually were not uncommon, Tandy's top 23 executives averaged 22 years' tenure with Tandy (as of September 1988). The least experienced were one person with 11 years, two with 14 years, and two more with 16 years.

DELL COMPUTER

In 1984, just when the PC market seemed to be saturated with the makers of IBM-compatible machines and most computer-industry pundits were talking about a shakedown, Michael Dell, a 19-year-old dropout from the University of Texas, founded PC's Limited (later named Dell Computers). The first-year sales from the shop in an Austin storefront were $6 million. In 1985 the company began building its own IBM PC clones, and revenues jumped to $34 million. The sales turnover in the third year of operations was close to $70 million.

The story of Dell's success followed the execution of a simple concept: direct business sales (buyers phoned in their orders in response to magazine ads). The strategy was not new, but no one had put it together so successfully before. Compaq, for instance, had broken out of the pack by selling powerful PC clones to experienced computer users. PC's Limited also decided to make powerful clones but sold them directly to end users instead of going through conventional retail outlets. The company saved the dealer's margin and could offer machines at very competitive prices. For example, its first computer, Turbo PC, a direct substitute for the IBM PC/XT, sold at $795—less than half the price of IBM machines.

Selling to large corporations, supposedly solid IBM believers, was no easy job, however. Typical questions that PC's Limited had to answer successfully were "Who are you?" and "How long will you be around?" The company was assisted by excellent product reviews in the trade press, and the help of an effective service/support setup allowed Dell to make a breakthrough: major corporations such as Price Waterhouse and Martin Marietta bought thousands of machines from his company.

Unlike other PC clones, which were mainly assemblies of Asian imports, PC's Limited designed and manufactured its computers domestically. The main strength of the company lay in its handling of orders, delivery, and the post-sale service and support it offered to its clients. The firm handled about

2,500 calls daily that provided direct access to customers. This "direct relationship marketing" not only helped the company understand the needs of the market but also allowed customization of orders and close control of inventory.

PC's Limited's approach was a relatively new phenomenon in the computer industry, and it was extremely efficient. Except for the brand image that it had developed, however, the company had not established much in the way of an entry barrier for its niche.

MICROCOMPUTER INDUSTRY: 1989 ADDENDUM

A quick microcomputer-industry survey was conducted by a market researcher to provide the following information update. Market shares and other industry information available from different research firms often conflicted. For example, in July 1987 the *Wall Street Journal* reported the following estimates of IBM's market share from three different research firms: IMS America Ltd. estimated that IBM's market share had tumbled from 56 to 44 percent. Infocorp believed the drop in market share was much smaller—a 1-percent drop to 23 percent. Dataquest, however, claimed IBM's market share had increased 1 percent to 31 percent.

The information resulting from the survey (mainly summaries of and excerpts from articles) is arranged here by topic: channels of distribution, microchannel and the "gang of nine," market shares and forecasts, new segments, industry dynamics, and the four players (Apple, Compaq, IBM, and Tandy).

CHANNELS OF DISTRIBUTION

A survey of 1,400 U.S. companies having personal computer (PC) sites and more than 500 employees provided evidence of diverse buying habits. Of those who had made purchases in the preceding 90 days, 36 percent had used retailers. Another 25 percent had bought from manufacturers, and 22 percent had gone to distributors. (*Datamation*, August 15, 1989)

Another survey indicated that 44.6 percent of *Fortune* 500 companies preferred buying microcomputers from retailers. Some 28 percent sourced directly from vendors, 2.8 percent by mail order, and 16.9 percent from value-added resellers (VARs). Of the smaller companies (non-*Fortune* 500), 43 percent preferred buying mainly from the manufacturer, 30.7 percent from retailers, and 13.2 percent from VARs. (*Computerworld*, May 9, 1989)

This addendum was prepared by Jaideep Wadhwa, Darden MBA 1989, under the supervision of L. J. Bourgeois. Copyright © 1989 by the University of Virginia Darden School Foundation, Charlottesville, VA. All rights reserved. It was prepared to accompany "The Microcomputer Industry in 1987" (UVA-BP-0288) and "Apple, Compaq, IBM, and Tandy in 1988" (UVA-BP-0289).

Despite user preference for retail channels, Compaq dropped Businessland, Inc., as a distributor. Businessland had accounted for 7 percent of Compaq's 1988 sales, but Compaq disapproved of the chain pushing IBM's Microchannel Architecture PCs. Retailers said IBM had begun to move more and more products through their channel. IBM made market development funds available to stores for advertising and sales training programs. (*Datamation*, August 15, 1989)

Complex networked systems that linked hardware and software from different vendors and the growing number of microcomputers within large companies were factors fueling demand for strong pre- and post-sale service and support—hence, the growing importance of dealers, especially small regional dealers. (*High-Technology Marketing*, June 1989)

After four years of intense competition, during which the clone makers grabbed 30 percent market share, by 1989 IBM, Compaq, and Apple had made a comeback, using distribution channels to their advantage. In some ways, they had locked up the distribution channels; customers were expected to have difficulty even finding clones in retail outlets. None of the second-tier manufacturers were considered likely to become 15-percent-share players. Companies like Dell with unique distribution channels, however, were considered more competitively positioned. (*Business Week*, December 12, 1988)

MICROCHANNEL ARCHITECTURE AND THE GANG OF NINE

IBM's Chairman John Akers commented that, with the benefit of hindsight, he wished IBM had brought out the next generation of computers sooner. (*Wall Street Journal*, March 23, 1988)

Despite the publicity buildup, as late as mid-1988 only three of the core PS/2 models introduced supported Microchannel Architecture (MCA). One year after the PS/2 introduction, 60 percent of all PS/2s shipped could not run the OS/2 operating system software. (*Computerworld*, March 1988)

The high percentage of the cheaper, non-MCA PCs sold also affected IBM's revenues. Eventually, IBM revived its AT in the PS/2 model 30286, which does not use MCA. (*IEEE Spectrum*, January 1989)

On September 13, 1988, Compaq, AST Research, Epson America, Hewlett-Packard (HP), NEC, Olivetti, Tandy, Wyse, and Zenith banded together to promote the Extended Industry Standard Architecture (EISA) to rival IBM's MCA. The "gang of nine" was not without industry clout. According to some estimates, the group was outselling IBM PCs by a ratio of 1.5 to 1. International Data Corporation claimed that clones in 1988 had 76 percent of the IBM PC-compatible market. (*Wall Street Journal*, September 13, 1988)

EISA was designed to allow users to employ new technologies, input/output devices, and multitasking and networking without being forced to use equipment incompatible with existing systems. It supported a wide range of newer microprocessors and operating systems, and a 32-bit bus was provided to meet the requirements of future peripherals while supporting the 8- and 16-bit buses that already existed. Important advantages included a faster bus transfer rate, larger memory capabilities, and a larger option card area. MCA offered advantages in bus timing, efficient board operation, and standardization with larger systems. (*Computer Technology Review*, November 1988) According to IBM specifications, MCA enabled a 400-percent increase versus the AT bus. (*Data Communications*, March 1989)

IBM planned to extend the MCA to mainframe and minicomputers, which would provide standardization beneficial in program development. (*Computer Decisions*, April 1989)

IBM and the EISA group each attacked the technical shortcomings and market bunglings of the other. According to Intel's Rich Bader, the differences between the two systems were subtle, and the real argument between the IBM and EISA groups involved product positioning. The EISA bus did not exist, however, except in the form of diagrams and promises from several manufacturers of IBM compatibles. (*Computerworld*, February 6, 1989)

According to an International Technology Group report, behind the MCA-versus-EISA posturing lay IBM's maneuvering to redirect the (business) PC market into clustered work stations working with a host—specifically, an IBM mainframe. (*Computer Technology Review*, December, 1988)

Although only Tandy had shipped PS/2 clones, other vendors had spent a lot of time copying the Microchannel Architecture, in case it were to gain widespread acceptance. (*Computerworld*, October 12, 1988)

The PS/2 line was highly "manufacturable," which led to great economies for IBM in building the computers. PS/2s would also be cheaper to repair than comparable products. (*Today's Office*, April 1988)

MARKET SHARES AND FORECASTS

The 80386-based personal computer accounted for 16.7 percent of all PCs shipped in the United States in 1988; 52 percent were based on the 80286 chip. IBM's share was expected to fall from 26.2 percent in 1987 to 23.6 percent in 1988. Lower than expected demand for the MCA-based PS/2 series was one of the reasons for the expected decline.

By 1988 the education market in the United States had stagnated, and the computer vendors were working to bolster their sales in the market represented by kindergarten through grade 12. The companies hoped to make sales while planting the seeds of brand loyalty. In 1987 Apple had 59 percent of the educational market, Tandy 16 percent, and IBM 11 percent. With a few exceptions, clone makers did not have a large share of this market. (*Computerworld*, June 6, 1988)

A *Datamation* survey indicated that shipments of PCs would fall 5 percent in 1989. The decline was attributed in part to the lack of new software to take advantage of the more advanced PCs. (The MCA-versus-EISA debate might also have contributed to the slowdown, as buyers could have been waiting for the emergence of a new industry standard.) (November 15, 1988)

Interest in IBM's PS/2 was strong in 1988; a survey that year by *Datamation* indicated a significant increase in the number of respondents planning to standardize on the PS/2. However, 50.3 percent had scheduled their replacements for some time after 1989. The PS/2 had to compete against a generation of installed PCs, and a new generation of applications software had yet to be developed. (July 1, 1988)

Dataquest estimated that more than 30 million PCs were introduced during the boom years and were now (mid-1988) aging. An estimated $4.8 million would be spent in 1991 on maintenance and repair. The upgrade market was also growing; recent survey respondents indicated that 30 percent planned to upgrade their systems. (*Today's Office*, August 1988)

NEW SEGMENTS

International Data Corporation estimated that nearly 1 million portables would be shipped in 1988. Dataquest estimated that the market for laptops would grow to $3.2 billion by 1990. (*Datamation*, November 15, 1988)

Nearly one million PC-based publishing systems were in use by late 1988, and industry shipments were expected to be 648,000 units by 1992. (*Business Week*, November 28, 1988)

INDUSTRY DYNAMICS

By introducing the SYP302, an AT-compatible computer for the original equipment manufacturer (OEM) market, Intel initiated a full-fledged move into the OEM business. According to Intel's vice president Les Vadesz, Intel decided to move into the PS/AT arena because it planned to become more aggressive now that it understood the needs of the industry. Intel's experience in board manufacturing was another reason the firm believed it could offer OEMs competitively priced products. (*Mini-Micro Systems*, May 1988)

Although unit sales growth for PCs declined steadily after 1981, the market was not considered to be saturated. According to some estimates, only 20 percent of the potential market had been served. To reach the remaining 80 percent, the industry had to move away from an emphasis on technology and to focus instead on industry-specific solutions. (*Marketing News*, June 6, 1988)

In 1988 IBM decided to take an aggressive attitude toward patent protection. Back royalty payments were sought by IBM from PC clone makers. When introducing the PS/2 line, IBM made it clear that it did not want to see a flood of PS/2 clones. Royalty rates for future patent licenses were increased to about 5 percent (from about 1 percent on the PC product line). The greatest obstacle to entering the PS/2 clone market, therefore, was likely to be legal rather than technical. (*Datamation*, August 1, 1988)

Prices for computer memory chips more than doubled in 1988. In September, Apple joined Hewlett-Packard, Sun, and Digital in raising its prices because of the "rising cost of parts," especially DRAMs. The price of the Macintosh II increased 29 percent, and that of the SE 30, 14 percent. (*Wall Street Journal*, September 13, 1988)

Six Japanese companies selling computers under their own names managed to garner only 8 percent of the PC market in 1987. The only areas in which the Japanese made any significant inroads was the laptop market. The Japanese were very successful, however, in selling components such as memory chips and monitors.

According to Dataquest, Intel's chips accounted for 20 percent of the total worldwide microprocessor business; and because competitors produced most older Intel designs under "second-source" agreements, Intel estimated that fully 70 percent of all PCs relied on its technology. (*Business Week*, September 26, 1988)

In a *Datamation* survey of buyers considering switching vendors, respondents most often (36.4 percent) cited lack of software and support as reasons for changing vendors. Other pet peeves included price (32.5 percent), sales/service organization (29.6 percent), and proprietary operating system (25.4 percent). Other, though less significant, factors were new-product introductions, systems reliability, and networking. (November 15, 1988)

Increasing user demands for "solutions" and interconnectivity forced vendors to form strategic alliances. Sun and AT&T were in 1988 jointly developing a version of UNIX. Digital Equipment Corporation (DEC) teamed up with Tandy, Compaq, and Apple on three individual projects. (*Computerworld*, December 26, 1988) These alliances were considered to contain potential synergies. For instance, Apple's Macintosh computers were installed at more than one-third of the 12,000 DEC sites. In addition to ensuring connectivity between their products, the joint effort would give Apple greater corporate visibility and would help DEC overcome its weakness in desktop applications. (*Mini-Micro Systems*, March 1988)

THE FOUR PLAYERS

Apple

Apple's revenues totaled $4.434 billion in 1988, an increase of 45.8 percent over the year before. North America was the largest market, accounting for 66 percent of total sales. European operations contributed 21 percent, while sales in Asia accounted for 12 percent. Net income leaped nearly 50 percent over

1987, to $419.3 million. During 1988 Apple reorganized twice. In April the company organized into three marketing/sales groups by breaking out Asia, Europe, and the United States. In August the company split Apple into four operating divisions: Apple Products, Apple USA, Apple Europe, and Apple Pacific. (*Datamation*, June 15, 1989)

Apple's proprietary technology designs had thwarted low-priced copies, allowing the company to obtain profit margins in excess of 50 percent. (*Fortune*, November 9, 1988)

After a disastrous attempt to enter the business market with the Mac, Apple opted to enter the business market through the back door by marketing desktop publishing to individual departments in large corporations. Dataquest estimated desktop publishing helped sell 60,000 Mac's in 1986 and would boost Mac sales by 568,000 in 1991. In 1988, 45 percent of Apple's revenues and over one-half of its profits came from the business sector. Apple estimated it had 7 percent of the corporate market in 1987 and hoped to increase that to 15 to 20 percent by 1990. (Apple was stressing peripherals strength for its computer line and introduced a new series of compact-disk read-only memory drives and laser printers to maintain an edge in desktop publishing.) (*Fortune*, November 9, 1988)

The company continued to work with DEC; it was announced that DEC field staff would service Macs. Apple also unveiled VAR agreements with Texas Instruments and Tandem. (*Datamation*, June 15, 1989)

Apple's greatest challenge could lie in improving its ability to push products through its channels. Apple customers had been known to complain that dealers didn't have the latest models and couldn't offer enough technical support. Apple had begun having its salespeople work closely with retailers in servicing corporate accounts. In addition, Apple recruited sales managers with past successes in selling to corporate customers. (*Fortune*, November 9, 1988)

A report in the *Financial Times* noted that some analysts believed Apple might not be able to maintain its market position. The analysts cited the following reasons: (1) concerns that the famed visual interface of the Macintosh might not be patentable (a lawsuit pending against HP and Microsoft was likely to determine the issue); (2) no plans for new-product introductions until late 1989; (3) lack of a new central processing unit, around which the next generation of machines could be designed; and (4) Apple's absence from the laptop area. (May 1988)

Compaq

Compaq's sales were $2.056 billion in 1988. Sales in North America accounted for 61 percent of total sales; Europe, 35 percent; and Asia/Pacific, 4 percent. During 1988 the company released its long-awaited laptop. Compaq and DEC also announced a technology-exchange program to ensure connectivity of their products. (*Datamation*, June 15, 1989)

Compaq grew into a $1 billion company in five years by developing relations with the network of dealers, suppliers, and software houses that had grown around IBM. Compaq took a unique approach to dealers, refusing to compete by selling directly. Dealers responded by giving Compaq's computers a lot of shelf space. The company also had close connections with its component makers. The support of non-IBM companies enabled Compaq to launch a new family of IBM-compatible computers even before IBM itself. (*Economist*, March 19, 1988)

IBM

Micros contributed $7.15 billion to IBM's $55 billion revenues in 1988. (*Datamation*, June 15, 1989)

Hoping to become more responsive to customers and spur innovation, IBM shifted broad responsibility from corporate headquarters to six product and marketing groups. (*Wall Street Journal*, February 1988) The company was split into six lines of businesses, each with decentralized decision making and product responsibility. The sales force was also reorganized, and sales force compensation was to be determined by revenues per account rather than number of computers sold. (*Datamation*, June 15, 1989)

In response to joint ventures among its competitors, IBM created a complex web of alliances, including partnerships or technology-sharing agreements with old rivals such as DEC, Siemens, and Steve Jobs. IBM was paying millions to Jobs for access to the user-friendly interface from this new company's (NeXT, Inc.) product. (*Datamation*, June 15, 1989)

Tandy

Tandy's 1988 data-processing revenues were $1.729 billion, of which 69 percent were attributed to micros, 23 percent to peripherals, and 8 percent to software. Some 90 percent of its revenues were from North American operations and 5 percent each from Europe and the rest of the world. Tandy began to sell its products outside its Radio Shack retail outlets. The company sold 410,000 PCs in 1988 and was hoping to sell 100,000 PCs outside Radio Shacks in 1989. A recent acquisition, Grid Systems, was given the responsibility for marketing all PC products to large businesses. Several of Tandy's high-end computers were to be sold under the Grid label to avoid the home-computer perception of Radio Shack. The company also signed an agreement to have DEC and Matsushita Electric Industrial Company sell a new line of PCs under their own labels and started selling some of its cheaper models through the Wal-Mart chain. (Tandy was also the only company to have shipped PS/2 clones, although it could also support the rival architecture by virtue of its membership in the EISA consortium.) (*Datamation*, June 15, 1989)

MICROCOMPUTERS IN 1991:
THE NOTEBOOK WAR

By the summer of 1991, microcomputer-industry profits were down, and layoffs—once a rarity in the industry—were spreading. Apple announced a 10-percent reduction of its work force, IBM set in motion plans to cut back 14,000 workers, and Toshiba laid off 250 people in the first quarter of 1991.[1] As sales growth in desktop computers decreased in 1990 and 1991, computer companies prepared to bring lighter, faster, and more powerful portable computers to consumers. New products vying for a piece of the fastest growing segment in the computer industry seemed to appear every month, and the portable-computer market went through a rapid evolution.

By mid-1991, five distinct segments had emerged in the portable market: (1) luggables weighing 13 pounds or more that had full screens, standard keyboards, and many of the other features of desktop machines; (2) laptops weighing between 7 and 13 pounds; (3) notebooks weighing between 5 and 7 pounds, about 8½" x 11" x 2", that could fit in a briefcase and had smaller screens and keyboards than desktop models; (4) pen-based computers similar in size to notebooks but without keyboards; and (5) pocket computers that weighed approximately a pound.

Gone were the days when a user wanting a portable computer had to settle for an unwieldy suitcase that required an electrical outlet or for a lighter, battery-powered unit with distorted screen displays, slow processors, or other limitations not found in desktop counterparts. The product of the new day was the third category, notebook computers, which packed the same punch of a desktop, and the major industry rivals drew up their battle lines to insure they would not miss the next round of innovations.

Apple, IBM, Compaq, Tandy, Dell, Toshiba, and NEC scrambled into battle position, while many new entrants joined the fray, pumping out inexpensive notebook clones at an amazing rate.

This case was written by Christine Lotze under the supervision of Professor L. J. Bourgeois. Copyright © 1991 by the Darden Graduate Business School Foundation, Charlottesville, VA. Revised February 1995.

[1]The layoff figures for Toshiba are found in "It's a Shakier Perch for Toshiba's Laptops," *Business Week*, August 5, 1991. The figures for IBM and Apple are from "How Much More Can PC Makers Toss Overboard?" *Business Week*, June 10, 1991.

COMPETITOR POSITIONS

Apple

Apple's recognition of the significance of the portable market was evident as early as its 1990 annual report:

> Miniaturization and mobility are even more important in the fast growing laptop and portable segments of the industry, where we intend to be a major competitor in the future.

Apple had disappointed its users, however, with its 16-pound Mac Portable in September of 1989. The machine was too heavy and never sold well, despite price cuts. Outbound, a firm in Boulder, Colorado, had jumped in to fill the void Apple left and provided stiff competition. While Outbound's machine was too heavy to classify as a notebook, it was a considerable improvement over the Apple offering in the eyes of many retailers.[2]

No new Macintosh products in the notebook arena hit the market in early 1991. In March of that year, John Sculley, chief executive officer of Apple, assured the industry, "We missed the laptop market. We're not going to miss the notebook market."[3] Apple announced that it would come out with a new line of computers in September 1991. According to one source, several prototypes were "floating around." This approach was consistent with Apple's usual strategy, which Bob Loutham, chief operating officer of Outbound, described as follows: "[Apple] travels around the country and tries out different models to see which is liked the best."[4]

IBM

After leaving the laptop market in 1989 with a miserable failure, IBM reentered the market in March of 1991. Rumors abounded that IBM had not drawn profits from its personal-computer (PC) lines in past years, but the company was struggling to enter the battle in the important notebook market. The speculation was widespread that IBM's product was too little and too late. According to William Bluestein, an analyst for Forrester research,

> IBM is three years late with this product, so the question is whether the train is too far out of the station. If IBM expects to succeed they'll have to make up for lost ground.[5]

---

[2]"Outdistancing Apple Laptops Keeps Outbound Inc. Hopping," (Denver) *Colorado Business Journal*, March 6, 1991.

[3]"Apple Computer's John Sculley Discloses Plans for New Portables," *Wall Street Journal*, March 19, 1991.

[4]"Outdistancing Apple Laptops."

[5]This and next two quotes are from "Big Blue Takes Aim at Toshiba, Compaq," *Advertising Age*, March 25, 1991.

Nevertheless, although some competitors believed that many people had "learned to live without IBM," the company's marketing strength was not to be underestimated. Indeed, IBM planned to use its marketing skill to carve out a position for its notebook machine. The strategy would be to focus on the machine's power. IBM's notebook was not in any way significantly superior to other major contenders, but it was a solid machine featuring a keyboard well-liked by reviewers.

The sheer size of IBM and its past experience prompted the following response from industry pundit and senior analyst at Infocorp, Peter Tiege: "Being IBM they don't have to be first and they frequently are not first, and that does not seem to matter." The market was moving away from IBM's mainstay, the main-frame computer, however, and with the internal cultural upheaval at the company, whether or not notebooks would usher in a new era of success for IBM remained to be seen.

Compaq

Compaq might well be credited with starting the notebook rage. Its LTE386 brought desktop power to notebook computing and gained the interest of many who were previously critical of the limited power in notebooks. Based on Intel's 80386 microprocessor, the LTE386 was widely recognized when introduced as having the "most impressive array of features" of any notebook on the market.[6] (See Appendix 1 for a discussion of the various computer microprocessors.) Its features, in combination with Compaq's ability to distribute the computer in volume, put the LTE386 in a position of competitive advantage, and it garnered 20 percent of the notebook market.[7] (Another estimate of worldwide market shares in notebooks put Compaq at 37 percent.) This market share made Compaq number one in the notebook market in the United States and second only to Toshiba worldwide.[8]

While many U.S. firms used partnerships with Japanese companies to design and develop their products, Compaq had abandoned this approach after the LTE286, on which it had worked with Citizen Watch Co.[9] Compaq's approach to developing computers was to take the best parts and technology from any available source. Its competitive advantage lay in the speed with which it put new, powerful, and innovative products on the market a step ahead of the competition.[10]

---

[6]"The Race to Market," *Financial World*, March 19, 1991.
[7]"Big Blue Takes Aim."
[8]"Compaq Rolls with the Punches," *New York Times*, May 25, 1991.
[9]"The Race to Market."
[10]"The Skin Deep Issue," *Dallas Morning News*, December 17, 1990.

Despite this speed, Compaq was feeling the crunch in the market. It cut prices in April—by 31 percent on the LTE386s/Model 60[11]—and some analysts were beginning to wonder whether Compaq would be able to keep up the pace or whether the company was "losing their direction."[12]

Tandy

Along with Zenith and Toshiba, Tandy was one of the early entrants who cornered the laptop market in 1988, but despite its solid early performance in laptops, computers in general were not Tandy's greatest strength. Therefore, in order to upgrade its "computer image," Tandy acquired Grid Systems in 1989. Grid manufactured sophisticated laptops and peripherals and propelled Tandy to the innovation forefront with a combination of improved image and the development of hard disks that were interchangeable.[13]

At a time when most major computer producers had moved operations overseas, most of Tandy's products, including all its desktop computers, were made in the United States. Tandy even manufactured a notebook computer, marketed under the Panasonic brand name, for Matsushita Electrical Industrial.[14]

One of Tandy's competitive advantages had been its support of its own distribution network, but the shift in distribution away from computer stores was being felt strongly by its retail arm, Radio Shack. Tandy announced the closing of approximately 200 computer stores in 1990. At the same time, part of its plan was to open 6 test stores—Computer City Superstores—that would "cut out the middle men" and attract the business sector, which had previously shunned Tandy products because of image, as well as general consumers. These stores were to carry rivals' computer brands for the first time.[15]

Despite the store closings, in 1991 Tandy was doing well relative to other computer manufacturers and consumer-electronics retailers. In the words of Tandy's chairman, John Roach, "Even in a bad year we've done well." Tandy had a 6.2 percent net return on sales, while IBM had only a 6.0 percent return, and Circuit City stood at 3.6 percent.[16]

---

[11]"Notebook Prices Decline," *Computer Reseller News*, May 20, 1991.

[12]"The Skin Deep Issue."

[13]Information in this and next paragraph is from "We're Still Here," *Forbes*, November 26, 1990.

[14]"U.S. Company to Make Japanese Computer," *Office Equipment and Products*, June 1991.

[15]"Tandy to Finally Snare Corporate America," *Infoworld*, July 8, 1991.

[16]"We're Still Here."

Dell

Dell entered the notebook computer market in February 1991. In addition to having prices that were well below the average, Dell planned to offer its customers a unique service plan. The price of the computer would include on-site service, with next-day system replacement for a year. If necessary, on-site technicians would also transfer data to the replacement unit. Dell planned to replace the system using a third-party vendor and to refurbish the broken machine at Dell and then make it part of a swap option.[17] Peter Tiege seemed optimistic about Dell's entry into the notebook market:

> These are good products for the company because portable computers lend themselves more to mail-distribution. Notebooks are take-it-out, plug-it-in type products; not a lot of set up is needed.[18]

Toshiba[19]

Toshiba was an early entrant in the laptop market and quickly came to dominate it. Its share of the U.S. portable-computer market was reported to be more than 23 percent. (A more conservative estimate gave the company 21 percent of the laptop market.) While Toshiba's product line over the previous two years was key in establishing its strong position, the company was now lagging behind in bringing innovative products to the market. Price cuts of 19 percent to 33 percent in May 1991—which were reported to be a move to "capitalize on economies of scale not available to newer smaller manufacturers"— had been interpreted as a defensive strategy to save market share in the face of stiff competition. In addition, the layoff of 250 employees indicated that Toshiba could no longer rest on its laurels.

Toshiba's current product line was perceived to be outmoded. It had little to offer in the way of notebooks, and many machines were too heavy, or, equipped only with Intel 286 chips (see Appendix 1), too slow to compete. The 286 and 386 machines were latecomers to the market and were greatly over-priced when introduced. Furthermore, Toshiba seemed to have missed the switch to notebooks in the portable market and was left with a huge inventory of obsolete products.

Despite the company's difficulties, however, many believed that Toshiba's early market dominance and leadership in color LCD and nickel hydride battery technology could make it a formidable opponent in a tough battle.

---

[17]"Dell Computer Offers Service for Notebook Computers," *Service News*, April 1991.
[18]"Dell Joins Notebook Arena," *Computer Reseller News*, February 18, 1991.
[19]Information in this section is from "Toshiba Unit's Computer Line Get Price Cuts," *Wall Street Journal*, May 3, 1991; and "It's a Shakier Perch for Toshiba's Laptops," *Business Week*, August 5, 1991.

NEC[20]

Toshiba may have overwhelmed opponents early in laptops, but Japanese rival NEC was successful at both laptops and desktops. In late 1989, NEC, hoping to use the company's broad line and extensive retail network to its advantage, had merged its desktop and laptop units in the United States. The merger into NECT (NEC Technologies) was not going as smoothly as expected, however, and synergies from combining marketing departments were not appearing. While NEC produced the UltraLite, the first notebook, it, like Toshiba, was lagging behind more innovative companies such as Compaq and AST Computer Company (a clone maker).

With only 9 percent of the U.S. portable market, NEC was far behind Toshiba and would need to improve its product line and distribution to catch up with such tough competitors as Compaq and Dell. Another area needing work was marketing, but the shift in product development for the U.S. market from Japan to the U.S. headquarters was expected to aid marketing efforts by helping the company produce a product more in tune with American needs and desires than in the past.

MARKET GROWTH

The growth in demand for portable computers was unexpectedly brisk. Infocorp analyst Tiege said about the notebook computer, "I don't think anyone really anticipated the enormous reception these are getting or how many firms were willing to get into it."[21] While most analysts agreed in predicting that portable computers would be the fastest growing market, with notebooks representing the fastest growing segment of that market, estimates for laptop sales varied a great deal. The Gartner Group's estimate is given in Table 1. New Desktop Strategies Advisory Service provided another set of figures (see Table 2).[22]

Dataquest, Inc., cited the number of portable units sold in the United States in 1990 to be 1.6 million and projected that number to rise to 9 million by 1994.[23] International Data Corporation predicted that notebook shipments would increase from 610,000 at the end of 1991 to approximately 912,000 in 1992 but expected much slower growth for heavier laptops, from 579,000 to 597,000 from 1991 to 1992.[24] IDC forecasted that shipments of

---

[20]Information in this section is from "NEC in the US," *Business Week*, August 5, 1991.
[21]"Local Manufacturers Reaping Rewards from Popularity of Notebook Computers," *Boulder Daily Camera*, January 29, 1991.
[22]"Big Blue Takes Aim."
[23]"PC Portables Join the Executive Ranks," *Datamation*, March 1, 1991.
[24]"Portables and Laptops," *Computerworld*, June 24, 1991.

Table 1
Gartner Group Laptop Sales Estimates

U.S. MARKET
SALES (IN UNITS)

	1989	1990	1994
Laptop	967,000	1,100,000	1,900,000
Notebook	69,000	311,000	3,900,000
Hand-held	34,000	159,000	3,200,000

Table 2
New Desktop Strategies Advisory Service
Laptop Sales Estimates

U.S. MARKET
SALES (IN MILLIONS OF DOLLARS)

	1990	1991
Transportables	$ 200	$ 90
Laptops	4,500	10,900
Notebooks	800	4,700

80386SX-based notebooks in the United States would reach 233,000 by the end of 1991 and would continue to increase to more than 3,500,000 units by 1995.[25]

PRODUCT DESIGN

While machines based on the 386 chip seemed to be setting the standard, a market still existed for the 286 machines, because price remained a significant factor in purchasing a notebook. To some extent, price also determined

---

[25]"Phillips, Goldstar, and Panasonic Enter Crowded Notebook Market," *Computer Retail Week*, May 13, 1991.

important facets of the notebook's construction. Thus, the machines on the market competed on the basis of keyboard design, battery life and size, weight, speed, and screen readability. (See Appendix 2 for a discussion of these components.)

In addition, when considering replacing a desktop with a notebook, a purchaser had to examine (1) connectivity—could the notebook be connected to the user's office computing environment, usually a LAN? (2) color—did the computer connect easily to an external color monitor (Toshiba and NEC offered products with color portability, but the machines were expensive)? (3) mouse—did the unit have an external port to which a mouse could be connected? Table 3 presents a typical user's guide to purchasing a notebook.[26]

Notebook computers seemed to be redefining computer image and style. Designers in the past had scoffed at the unattractive almond boxes that dominated desk space, but notebooks were coming out in new, attractive colors and sleekly styled cases. Tiege considered purchasing a laptop to be different from other computer buys: "This is more of an emotional purchase than other sorts of computers." Laptops, like fountain pens, had apparently become a status symbol. The image of these new computers had many industry players hoping that the notebook would be able to reach buyers who had been reluctant to buy computers in the past, because the new machines appeared less intimidating to technophobes.

PROBLEMS

Although notebooks had come a long way, they still had limitations. Because of the size of a notebook, the screen and keyboard would inevitably be smaller than was desirable for lengthy periods of use. Also, the great expense of color screens would leave users of color-intensive graphic programs dissatisfied. Finally, some reports noted that miniaturization and transportability resulted in other problems. Because components were crammed into small spaces in lightweight hulls, the construction, particularly the casing, had cracked in some models, and the screens had malfunctioned.[27]

TRENDS

An article in the *Washington Post* describing some of the ways in which computers were changing jobs noted that, while the advent of computers had for long promised a great deal of change, the true effect was just beginning to

---

[26]Adapted from Steven Lin's list in "The Notebook Computer as a Desktop Alternative," *The Office*, February 1991.
[27]"Notebooks Crack Under Stress," *Infoworld*, July 8, 1991.

Table 3
Features to Look for When Buying
a Notebook Computer

Dimension and weight	8 ½" × 11"; 2" thick or less; 7 lbs. or lighter.
Processor	A 386SX at 20 MHz; 80286 was cheaper but suffered in performance (see Appendix 1). Memory should be a minimum of 1MB.
Display	Standard VGA 640 × 400 black-and-white LCD. It should also be able to hook up to external monitor.
Battery and charger	Three hours or more. Check to see if it is possible to charge battery and use computer at the same time.
Disk storage	Minimum 20MB hard storage drive. The drive storage should spin down to preserve battery power if not accessed for a preset time level.
Serial and parallel ports	At least one of each. A bidirectional port allowed for LAN hookup.
Pointing device	A mouse was the most popular, but some had special keys.
Other features	Internal modem, fax, and voice-mail capabilities were useful.

be realized.[28] One Dataquest analyst, Bill Lempesis, believed that "the real gains will happen in the 90s." After the purchase of a notebook computer, a life-insurance salesperson could bring the machine to the client's home, type in the client's answers, and produce a fully customized plan on the spot. Meter readers were using portable computers to log in meter figures, thus eliminating computer cards. Accountants could do their work on site instead of lugging back reams of data to a base office or trying to use a client's equipment to run scenarios or complex analyses. A CD-ROM disk for storing

---

[28]"Small Wonder," *Washington Post*, April 8, 1990.

Table 4
Forecasted PC Shipments by Channel

	1991	1992
Dealer	61.2%	54.0%
VAR	14.2	15.7
Direct	7.1	7.1
Mail order	5.5	6.4
Consumer electronics	4.9	7.7
Mass merchant	4.2	4.9
Superstore	1.0	4.0
Other	1.0	0.2

accounting references was also available. Field sales personnel for pharmaceutical companies were being assisted in their pitches to customers by portable computers that hooked up to overhead projectors to display product information in the form of graphs and information sheets during presentations. Other salespeople were able to log in orders on their computers and send them to main offices almost immediately by transferring the information over a phone line to a warehouse. Portable computers were even being used as communication devices between combat units in the field. Police had computers hooked up in their squad cars and were finding them useful for a wide range of procedures, including registration/stolen-car checks and accident reports. The many uses for portable (particularly, lightweight) notebooks seemed to be transforming jobs across America. (Appendix 3 contains a March 1991 *Business Week* article giving further information on the emerging laptop market.) David Zing, an analyst at International Data Corporation, said, "Notebooks are the VCRs of the computer market. Eventually every truck driver is going to have a notebook, every postman will have one."[29]

As the summer of 1991 came to a close, two developments surfaced. First, distribution seemed to be shifting away from traditional dealers as superstores and mail-order firms offered inexpensive PCs to increasingly knowledgeable customers. International Data Corporation predicted that the share of PCs sold by dealers would plummet from 1990's 62.1 percent to 49.1 percent in 1993. IDC's forecast of shipments by channel is shown in Table 4.[30]

---

[29]"Phillips, Goldstar, and Panasonic."
[30]"PC Price Wars Keep Growing Sharper," *PC World*, September 1991.

Exhibit 1
Comparison Chart: Notebook Portables

MAKE/MODEL	PROCESSOR: SPEED	RAM: STD.; MAX.	HARD DISKS: CAPACITY	FLOPPY DISKS: CAPACITY	PAR. PORTS, SER. PORTS
COMPAQ					
LTE Model 20	80C86: 9.54MHz	640K; 1 MB	1:20MB	1:1.44MB	1,1
LTE/286 Model 20	80C286: 12MHz	640K; 2.6MB	1:20MB	1:1.44MB	1,1
LTE/286 Model 40	80C286: 12MHz	640K; 2.6MB	1:40MB	1:1.44MB	1,1
LTE/386s/20 Model 30	80C386: 20MHz	2MB; 10MB	1:30MB	1:1.44MB	1,1
LTE/386s/20 Model 60	80C386: 20MHz	2MB; 10MB	1:60MB	1:1.44MB	1,1
DELL					
System 212N	80C286: 8/12MHz	1MB; 5MB	1:40MB	1:1.44MB	1,1

— = Information not available at press time. All prices are U.S. suggested list.
Source: *Laptop* Magazine, Summer 1991.

DISPLAY	POWER REQUIRED	SOFTWARE INCLUDED	OTHER FEATURES	DIMENSIONS (H×W×D) (IN.); WEIGHT (LB.)	PRICE
Backlit CGA	110/240 VAC	Power conservation utility, disk cache	Supports LIM4.0, soft zippered case	1.9×11×8.5; 6.2	$1,749
Backlit CGA LCD	110/240 VAC	Power conservation utility, disk cache	Supports LIM 4.0, slipcase	1.9×11×8.5; 6.2	$1,949
Backlit CGA LCD	110/240 VAC	Power conservation utility, disk cache	Supports LIM4.0, soft zippered case	1.9×11×8.5; 6.2	$2,249
Backlit CGA LCD	AC adapter, battery	—	4K cache	2.2×11×8.5; 7.5	$4,399
Backlit CGA LCD	AC adapter, battery	—	4K cache	2.2×11×8.5; 7.5	$4,799
Edgelit VGA LCD	Recharg. NiCad battery, AC adapter	None	LIM 4.0 support, 85-key keyboard; optional external tape backup; on-site service with next-day system replacement; built-in tutorial at first boot-up	2×8.5×11; 6.4	$2,699

(continued on next page)

MAKE/MODEL	PROCESSOR: SPEED	RAM: STD.; MAX.	HARD DISKS: CAPACITY	FLOPPY DISKS: CAPACITY	PAR. PORTS, SER. PORTS
System 320N	80C286: 8/20MHz	1MB; 5MB	1:60MB	1:1.44MB	1,1

TOSHIBA

T1000	80C88: 4.77MHz	512K; 1.28MB	—	1:1.44MB	1,1
T1000SE	80C86: 9.5MHz	1MB; 3MB	—	1:1.44MB	1,1
T1000XE	80C86: 9.5MHz	1MB; 3MB	1:20MB	opt. 360K/ 1.44MB	1,1
T1200XE	80C286: 12/6MHz	1MB; 5MB	1:20MB	1:1.44MB	1,1

(continued)

Display	Power Required	Software Included	Other Features	Dimensions (H×W×D) (IN.); Weight (LB.)	Price
Edgelit VGA LCD	Recharg. NiCad battery, AC adapter	None	LIM 4.0 support, 85-key keyboard; opt. external tape backup; on-site service w/ next day system replacement; built-in tutorial at first boot-up	2×8.5×11; 6.4	$3,699
CGA LCD	Recharg. NiCad battery, AC adapter	Borland SideKick, disk cache utility	Opt. 768K memory card; thorough user documentation	2.05×12.2× 11; 6.4	$799
CGA LCD	Recharg. battery pack, 100– 240 VAC	MS-DOS, PCwik Power Pak	AutoResume (battery-backed system memory); thorough user documentation	1.8×12.2×10; 5.9	$999
Sidelit CGA LCD	Removab./ recharg. NiCad battery	MS-DOS, LapLink, PCwik Power Pak	AutoResume (battery-backed system memory); thorough user documentation; power management	1.8×12.2×10; 6.2	$1,399
VGA LCD	Removab./ recharg. NiCad battery, AC adapter	MS-DOS 4.01, PCwik Power Pak	AutoResume (battery-backed system memory); thorough user documentation	2×12.2×11; 7.2	$2,299

(continued on next page)

MAKE/MODEL	PROCESSOR: SPEED	RAM: STD.; MAX.	HARD DISKS: CAPACITY	FLOPPY DISKS: CAPACITY	PAR. PORTS, SER. PORTS
T2000	80C286: 12MHz	1MB; 9MB	1:40MB	1:1.44MB	1,1
T2000SX	80386SX: 16MHz	1MB; 8MB	1:40MB	1:1.44MB	1,1
T2000SXE	80386SX: 20MHz	2MB; 8MB	1:40MB	1:1.44MB	1,1
IBM					
PS/2 L40SX	80386SX: 20MHz	2MB; 18MB	1:60MB	1:1.44MB	1,1
NEC TECHNOLOGIES					
UltraLite 286F	80C286: 12MHz	1MB; 5MB	1:20MB	1:1.44MB	1,1
UltraLite SX20	80386SX: 20MHz	2MB; 10MB	1:40/ 60MB	1:1.44MB	1,1

(continued)

Display	Power Required	Software Included	Other Features	Dimensions (H×W×D) (in.); Weight (lb.)	Price
VGA LCD	Recharg. NiCad battery, AC adapter	MS-DOS 4.01	Power management, 86-key keyboard, external VGA monitor port; thorough user documentation	1.9×12.2× 10; 6.9	$3,149
VGA LCD	Recharg. battery, AC adapter	MS-DOS 4.01	Power management, dual function VGA monitor port; thorough user documentation	1.9×12.2× 10; 6.9	$3,749
VGA LCD	Recharg. battery, AC adapter	MS-DOS 4.01	Power management, external VGA monitor port; thorough user documentation	1.9×12.2× 10; 6.9	$4,199
VGA LCD	Recharg. battery pack,100– 240 VAC	—	84-key keyboard with audible click, power management, external numeric keypad included	2.1×12.8× 10.7; 7.7	$2,895 (20MB) $3,295 (40MB)
Mono. backlit LCD	Battery, AC adapter	MS-DOS 4.01	External floppy disk drive port, memory, expansion slot, 78-key keyboard	2×11.5×8.5; 6.8	$2,999
Sidelit mono. VGA LCD	Battery, AC adapter	MS-DOS 4.01, Windows 3.0	Password protection, power management	2.4×11.5× 8.6; 7.5	$4,899 (40MB) $5,399 (60MB)

The second development was a flurry of notebook entries by several dozen clone makers, as well as Toshiba (three 6.9-pound notebooks in July) and NEC (an upgrade to its original UltraLite). These products joined the existing offerings brought by Dell in February, IBM in March (the PS/2 L40SX), and Compaq and Tandy in the previous year. (For a product feature and price listing, see Exhibit 1.)

Meanwhile, Apple and IBM announced a strategic alliance in which Apple would join its software expertise with IBM's hardware advantages. Apple said it would develop a Macintosh notebook based on the Motorola 68000 chip but would eventually move to IBM-designed RISC (reduced instruction set computing) chips in its new products. Ultimately, Apple said it would go beyond the Macintosh to a new operating system, known as Pink, that would be developed with IBM. Pink would be able to run on a range of microprocessors and on large and small computers.[31]

CASE APPENDIX 1

MICROPROCESSORS (CHIPS) FOR NOTEBOOK COMPUTERS

As with other personal computers, notebooks were built around a central processing unit, or chip. The type of chip (for example, Intel or Motorola, or 286 versus 386) determined the computer's performance characteristics (operating speed, for instance). While Macintosh-compatible systems used Motorola-based chips, the vast majority of the portable market and all notebooks were based on Intel, or Intel-compatible, chips.

New developments in chip-making technology had defined the 80386SX chip as the new market standard. This chip was a lower-cost version of the 80386 introduced in 1986. The 386SX could be obtained with clock speeds of 16MHz and 20MHz. The forerunner, a 386 chip with 16MHz, was called the 386DX. With its 32-bit external data path, it provided faster processing power than the SX, which could only process 16 bits in a single pass. Both 386s were equal internally; they could manipulate 32 bits.[32]

The latest development was Intel's low-cost 486SX. While some speculated that it might redefine the standard, opinion at this time was divided on whether or not the chip offered sufficient advantages over older chips to capture the market. The 486SX appeared to be Intel's effort to ward off chip-maker Advanced Micro Device's AM386/40MHz threat. Intel's 486DX ran at

---

[31]"A Quirky Loner Goes Mainstream," *New York Times,* July 14, 1991, p. F1.
[32]"Portables and Desktops: 386SX Sets the Standard," *The Office,* June 1991.

25 or 33MHz and had an internal floating point unit (internal math coprocessor). The 486SX was a 486DX with the floating point unit disabled, a setup to keep cost down. The math coprocessor could be purchased separately for $799. The 486 was supposed to be two to three times faster than a 33MHz 386 if an operating system with 32 bits were used. The true benefits of the 486, however, could be realized only with the new Microsoft Windows and OS/2 software. The 486 did not seem to provide as great an improvement as the 386 did over the 286 chip.[33]

Prices for the various microprocessors in 1991 were as follows:

	First Quarter	Second Quarter
Intel 486DX/23	$860	$667
Intel 486DX/25	$671	$588
AMD AM386/40	N/A	$297
Intel 486SX/20	N/A	$258
Intel 386DX/33	$214	$208

One reviewer noted that tests were as yet inconclusive as to whether or not the AM386 outperformed the 486SX. An advantage of the 486SX was a lower clock speed, which saved on other components.[34] Other reviewers were not quite so negative. The July edition of *PC World* reported preliminary tests indicating that 20MHz 486SX systems performed significantly better than 33MHz 386 systems and cost less.[35]

Worldwide shipments of Intel CPUs were as follows:[36]

CPU	1990	1991	1992
16MHz 386SX	4,245,000	3,990,000	2,400,000
20MHz 386SX	479,000	2,531,000	3,600,000
25MHz 386DX	1,414,000	2,383,000	2,800,000
33MHz 386DX	312,000	885,000	2,100,000
20MHz 486SX	0	230,000	1,100,000
25MHz 486DX	281,000	469,000	446,000
33MHz 486DX	65,000	546,000	1,200,000

While the SX chips were being used in notebooks, Intel also produced the 386SL (20MHz), which was "expressly designed for the emerging notebook market." Intel claimed that this chip was about 20 percent faster than the

---

[33]Information and prices are from "486SX: Upgrade Now and Upgrade Later," *PC Magazine*, June 11, 1991.
[34]"Low Cost 486SX Remaps PC Midrange," *PC World*, July 1991.
[35]"486SX Systems: More Bang Less Bucks," *PC World*, July 1991.
[36]"Low Cost 486SX Remaps PC Midrange."

386SX and a complete AT could be built on a 4" × 6" board.[37] The SL was also expected to improve battery life.[38] Initially, these chips were not widely used because of the many bugs they contained, but one report suggested that the chips would be debugged shortly. With the improved, bug-free 386SX chips available, notebooks containing 386SL chips would be considered outdated.

CASE APPENDIX 2

COMPONENTS OF THE NOTEBOOK COMPUTER

Keyboard[39]

While several configurations for the placement of keys existed, the standard was 84 keys with the numeric keys embedded in the alphanumeric keys. Often one was able to purchase an external numeric keypad that plugged into an expansion slot. The Control, Shift, and Alternate keys were their standard size and in their usual position. Keys that were used less often were commonly somewhat smaller than usual and in other locations. While 11" were required for a standard keyboard, some models squeezed the keyboard into a smaller space. In order for the keyboard to have the proper feel, it had to have a certain thickness. A standard keyboard had a thickness of 0.15", but half of that was acceptable if the keyboard was set up to provide good tactile feedback. Almost all notebook computers had membrane keyboards to cut down on the thickness. These keyboards had rubber grommets with carbon contacts that, when depressed, completed a circuit with a polyester sheet that had conductive material implanted in it.

Screens

The screen had to show the true shape of text and graphics; to do so, it had to have a 1-to-1 aspect ratio—not compressed to allow for a shorter screen. A size of 11" to 12" wide with an 11" diagonal, and a panel ¼" to ⅛" thick, was sufficient for the display circuitry. LCDs were the most popular type of display panels in use in notebook computers in 1991. While all LCDs had the same basic technology, low-end notebooks had supertwist LCDs, and more expensive models had dual supertwist displays. These LCDs had contrast ratios of

---

[37]"A Laptop on a Chip . . . Almost," *BYTE*, December 1990.
[38]"Laptops That Use 386SL Chip Could Reshape Market," *Computer Reseller News*, April 8, 1991.
[39]This and next two sections are based on "Notebook PC's Set the Portable Standard," *BYTE IBM Special Edition*, Fall 1990.

4-to-1 and 14-to-1, respectively. Both types tended to require a great deal of power for operation, but the dual supertwist display, with its two panels and its added backlighting, required comparatively more. A few notebooks, notably the Macintosh, used active-matrix LCD panels that had a contrast ratio of 100-to-1, but they required a tremendous number of transistors, and a single failure made the whole display inoperative.

Batteries

Batteries represented a large part of the notebook's weight. Of the many types of batteries, two made the best choice in 1991. Most of the computers used nickel cadmium batteries, because lead/acid batteries provided too little power for their weight. The nickel cadmium batteries provided a power source with a very constant output even when much of its energy had been used. Nickel cadmium batteries did have memory problems when recharged before they were completely empty; they ceased to be able to store their original amount of power. Another type of battery that had recently been developed was the nickel hydride battery. It could provide twice the power of an equivalent-sized nickel cadmium battery and did not have the recharging problems, but it was more costly to produce.

Pointing Devices[40]

The standard pointing device, the mouse, was impractical for a machine that was to be used on the go and in cramped places, so various substitutes for the mouse had been developed:

- *Trackball.* The first machine to have one of these devices was the Mac Portable. Unfortunately, it required a great deal of space because it was comfortable for users only when the ball was heavy enough to provide the proper momentum and large enough to be rolled around the palm. It was also not as effective as a mouse.

- *Touchpad.* Resistive-membrane pads were built into the computer, above the keyboard, and allowed fingers to be used as pointers. While the pad did not add a lot of weight, it took up a lot of space and could be difficult and uncomfortable to use.

- *Touchscreen.* Surface acoustic-wave technology drove this device, which allowed one's finger to be the cursor. This option demanded extra power, added significant weight, had poor resolution, was slow, and could be uncomfortable to use.

---

[40]This section based on "Laptop Technologies: Touch and Feel Interfaces," *BYTE,* February 1990.

- *Isopoint.* This device consisted of a small sliding cylinder. Moving the cursor from side to side was accomplished by moving the cylinder back and forth with one's thumb. Spinning the cylinder moved the cursor up and down. The isopoint might not provide sufficient tactile feedback for the user to feel entirely at ease with it, especially when drawing.

- *Home Row Joystick.* A tiny joystick was hidden beneath the *J* key; it could rock on its base. It became functional when the *J* was pressed in combination with the Control, Caps Lock, or Other key. When the joystick was activated, *S, D,* and *F* became "mouse buttons." This option was relatively inexpensive, but it did not allow one to move about the screen with great speed.

CASE APPENDIX 3

LAPTOPS TAKE OFF

The Machines Are Tiny, The Potential Is Huge— But the Market Is Already Crowded

Perhaps you've heard it on a late-night cross-country flight. Or on a commuter train. Or maybe in the waiting room at your doctor's office. At any time of day or night, and just about anywhere, you can trace that click-click-clicking—to an executive, a salesperson, or a student hunched over the keyboard of a tiny laptop computer.

Lately, that clicking has been getting a lot louder. From classrooms to courtrooms, laptops are becoming part of the American routine. Already, these remarkable little machines are posting the fastest growth rates of any type of computer in the world. And by the second half of the decade, some market-watchers predict, they will account for more than half of all personal computers sold.

That click-click-clicking is music to the ears of a PC industry whose mainstay desktop machines have run into a sales slump. "The growth of laptops is going to be the dominant trend in the PC business for the next four to five years," says Albert A. Eisenstat, Apple Computer Inc.'s executive vice president for business development. Shipments of desktop PCs to U.S. businesses, according to Cambridge (Mass.) market researcher

Forrester Research Inc., peaked last year at 6 million units and will shrink to 4.9 million machines by 1993. By then, however, laptop sales will more than triple and account for 35% of all PCs sold in the U.S., up from 19% now.

LEGAL EAGLES

That has computer companies from Apple to IBM to DEC scrambling to get their share of the market. All three—and dozens of other suppliers—are rushing out new models this year to grab a slice of what is already a $7.5 billion market. They will be competing against such well-entrenched laptop leaders as Toshiba, NEC, Tandy, Zenith Data, and Compaq. And despite rapid growth, there are already signs of overcrowding, including price-slashing and a shortage of key parts.

But the move to laptops is anything but a fad. Laptops are so sophisticated now that they can actually substitute for desktop PCs. Workers who spend a lot of time on the road use laptops to give them all the electronic assistance that desktops supply back in the office. And in many instances, laptops are making it possible to work in whole new ways. Take Snow Christensen & Martineau, a

Source: Deidre A. Depke et al., "Laptops Take Off," *Business Week*, March 18, 1991, pp. 18–24.

law firm based in Salt Lake City. These days, its 55 lawyers bring their laptops right into the courtroom. "That sometimes surprises the attorney on the other side," notes Partner Paul J. Graf. It also gives Snow Christensen litigators an invaluable edge: They can tap into a case-precedent data base on their laptops or call up a copy of a witness's deposition to check for discrepancies in oral testimony.

The laptop boom is also changing the computer industry itself. As they take over more of the market, the new machines are altering not only how PCs are used, but also how they are designed, built, and sold. Laptops—especially the new "notebook" models, small enough to fit in a briefcase and weighing eight pounds and less—are far more, well, personal than desktops. For customers, laptops are becoming personal accessories, and something of a status symbol. For computer makers, accustomed to selling bits, bytes, and megahertz, the challenge will be to appeal to consumers on a visceral level: "This is more of an emotional purchase than other sorts of computers," says Peter Teige, an analyst at Infocorp, a Santa Clara (Calif.) researcher.

Laptops are already setting new patterns in computer distribution. By next year, just 30% of all laptops sold in the U.S. will move through computer dealers, says John Dunkle, president of researcher WorkGroup Technologies Inc. These outlets still sell 80% of desktop PCs. But laptops are being sold where consumers buy: through mass-merchandise chains, consumer electronics stores, and mail order.

Because they're more consumer-oriented, laptops are expected to expand the market, perhaps finally reaching the die-hard technophobes who for a decade have resisted laptops. A new variety of laptops, so-called tablet computers, promises to make computers more accessible than ever by "reading" handwriting entered on the screen with an electronic pen. That should make computers usable by the millions of workers and consumers who have never used a conventional PC. Already, such computers are being tested with traffic cops, delivery people, and utility company meter-readers. "The pen computer has the potential for a marketplace bigger than the existing PC market," insists Kathy Veith, the IBM vice president in charge of its pen-based tablet systems.

LIGHTER AND BRIGHTER

So far, the roar of the laptop revolution has produced only a pounding headache at IBM and Apple, America's No. 1 and No. 2 PC makers. In the 1980s, both companies struggled in vain to develop competitive home-grown laptops. IBM's PC Convertible, introduced in 1986, was quickly overtaken by laptops that were smaller, lighter, brighter, and cheaper. Apple's 16-pound Macintosh Portable, introduced in September, 1989, has never sold well, despite two big price cuts. In 1991, both companies are desperately trying to get back into laptops before the market passes them by. "We're not going to miss the boat on this," promises Apple's Eisenstat.

IBM is equally determined. "The market expansion is real, and the opportunity is huge," says Winnie Briney, IBM's personal systems marketing director. To make sure that Big Blue's 1991 laptop isn't a reprise of the Convertible failure, IBM marketing troops criss-crossed America for a year, asking dealers and big customers for input on various laptop mock-ups. "I think I've seen eight versions of the thing," says an executive at a top computer store chain. Those who have been privy to the parade of IBM prototypes report steady improvements. One version, originally due out last October, was scrapped because it used the passé Intel Corp. 80286 microprocessor, not Intel's newer 80386SX. Another improvement, a "stepped" keyboard, was ordered up after customers objected to flat keyboards, says Briney.

HARD LESSON

But IBM's new love affair with consumer research won't help if it can't get its product-development bureaucracy moving faster. Big Blue learned the hard way with the Convertible that the rapid evolution of portable computer technology is unforgiving. By the time the Convertible went into production

LAPTOP MILESTONES

1982
April — Grid announces one of the first successful laptops, a 10-pound battery-powered computer.

1984
May — HP follows with 9-pound machine, but without a floppy disk drive. It has limited appeal.

1986
February — Zenith wins contract to supply 15,000 laptop computers to the Internal Revenue Service. The deal was expected to go to IBM.

April — IBM announces a 12-pound, $1,995 PC Convertible. The machine replaces Big Blue's first portable, a 30-pound "luggable."

November — Toshiba announces the first popular laptop PC clone, the 10-pound, battery-powered T1100. NEC follows with the MultiSpeed.

1988
October — Compaq announces 14-pound SLT laptop, its first battery-powered portable. NEC announces the UltraLite, the first notebook computer. It weighs only 4.4 pounds and fits inside a briefcase.

1989 — U.S. unit sales of laptops reach 570,000.

1990 — Sales hit 32,000 units.

in 1986, its screen was already a generation behind. If anything, the pace has quickened since then.

To keep up, IBM and other U. S. computer makers are learning how to cooperate more closely with Japanese suppliers—even while they compete with them. Indeed, the biggest change wrought by laptops will be a significant expansion of Japan's role in the international computer market. Japanese electronics giants, most notably Toshiba Corp., already control about half the market for finished laptops. And Japanese electronics makers dominate crucial laptop technologies: liquid-crystal-display (LCD) screens, floppy-disk drives, and memory chips.

Relying on Japanese suppliers for key components is nothing new: For most of the PC era, U.S. computer makers have shopped in Japan for memory chips and other essential parts. What is new is that to make laptops, U.S. suppliers must also rely on Japanese expertise in design and manufacturing. Shrinking PCs down to notebook size is impossible without the miniaturization techniques that Japan's electronics giants mastered in calculators, camcorders, and watches.

So, instead of just buying chips and components, U.S.-based manufacturers are creating partnerships with Japanese companies that help design entire laptop systems and then manufacture big chunks of the finished products. "You can't shop around for components in this market; you have to have strategic alliances," says Enrico Pesatori, the newly appointed president and chief executive of Zenith Data Systems Corp. One of his first tasks is

to strengthen ZDS' relations with its Asian suppliers. "You don't fight with them, you work with them," says Pesatori.

That's why IBM has teamed up with Toshiba to catch the next wave in laptop screens: color. Their joint venture will build color LCDs for both companies, starting this spring. "Alliances are the way to do business," says Robert L. Carberry, IBM's assistant general manager for personal systems.

COMEBACK?

IBM's competitors apparently agree. Industry sources say that Apple is negotiating a deal for Japan's Sony Corp. to manufacture a laptop. American Telephone & Telegraph Co. has teamed up with Matsushita Electric Industrial Co. to build its upcoming Safari notebook. Texas Instruments Inc. is plotting a comeback in the PC business by selling laptops designed with a Japanese partner.

Even Compaq Computer Corp., which became an overnight sensation in notebook PCs in 1989, did so largely by teaming up with Japan's Citizen Watch Co. Although the basic design of Compaq's LTE laptop came out of its Houston headquarters, it took a collaboration with Citizen's engineers to squeeze the machine's components into an 8½-by-11-inch package. Citizen subassemblies make up so much of the finished machines that one market researcher counts all LTEs as Japanese imports.

The results of such Japanese-American alliances can be impressive. Today's notebook PCs are a vast improvement over the first battery-powered portables that showed up in the 1980s. As pioneers such as Tandy Corp.'s Grid Systems Corp. subsidiary learned, those machines were so big and expensive that their appeal was limited mainly to jobs such as automating the routines of auditors and other traveling professionals. For the average PC purchaser, buying a laptop then meant paying a 50%-to-100% premium over the price of a desktop—then settling for poor screen quality, no hard-disk storage, and in many cases, insufficient internal memory to run popular programs.

Now, laptops do just about everything their desktop counterparts do. Many use the same Intel 80386SX chips found in the best-selling desktops. Their tiny hard-disk drives can store as many as 60 million characters of information. And they have the internal memory and graphics to run Microsoft Corp.'s Windows 3.0 graphics software. So impressed is AT&T with the current crop that it isn't waiting for its own computer division to start cranking out notebook PCs in April. Instead, it has ordered 2,500 machines from Toshiba, Grid, and AST Research.

AT&T is in a hurry to launch a bold experiment that it hopes will make salespeople in its Business Network Sales Div. more productive: Within the next year or so, thousands of them will be kicked out of their offices, to spend nearly all their work time on the road. "We would have done this sooner, but we couldn't do it with the technology that was available," says Roger D. Dalrymple, manager of information technology. "But all of a sudden, the technology came together."

The new laptop technology played a big role in Operation Desert Storm. Tens of thousands of the machines were used in logistics to track supplies, coordinate troop movements, and figure out how to feed the allied soldiers. Some laptops were used to plan Harrier jet missions, and others were scheduled to go along with troops to the front lines if the land war had continued.

Back at home, laptops are making it possible for American managers and executives to be more responsive. "In the 1970s and 1980s, you could say, 'Let me have your card, and I'll get back to you,'" says J. Bowmar Rodgers, executive vice president at Poqet Computer Corp., a maker of tiny, one-pound "palmtop" PCs. In the '90s, customers want the price quotes or the insurance-premium estimates from a laptop on the spot, he says. Tomorrow's executives are being groomed for the laptop age: When exam time rolls around at Harvard business school now, the traditional blue books are gone. Instead, the school's 1,500 MBA candidates take their tests on laptops, handing in a floppy disk at the end of the exam.

PRICE BREAKS

Even though the U.S. market has always been the first to embrace other types of computers, laptops seem to be an international phenomenon from the start. In Japan, laptops now account for 43% of all PCs sold. By 1993, the figure is expected to grow to 61%. And European buyers are hopping on the laptop bandwagon, too. This year, one in eight PCs sold in Europe will be a laptop.

By 1995, that figure will be one in three, market researchers say. Italy's Olivetti made its biggest product splash in years when it announced on Feb. 28 that it would build its new line of lap-tops at a factory in Nuremberg. Analysts say Olivetti will also build machines for Digital Equipment Corp. to sell in the U.S., starting in April.

The laptop lifestyle is spreading faster and faster as prices for the machines drop. These days, laptop versions of the older IBM PC/XT and PC/AT sell for around $1,000, only slightly more than comparable desktop machines. And the newest notebooks, based on the Intel 80386SX, may not command a premium for long. When Compaq brought out its LTE 386s last October, its price started at $6,499 — 59% more than Compaq charged for a comparable desktop. Three months later, AST Research Inc., a PC clone-maker based in Irvine, Calif., trotted out its own 80386-based notebook machine for $2,995, almost exactly what it charges for a similarly equipped desktop. Since then, other clonemakers have brought out comparable notebook PCs in the $3,000-to-$4,000 range.

Such prices make laptops truly competitive with conventional PCs, widening the market beyond folks who need a mobile computer. Richard V. Miller, vice president for PC product marketing at NEC's American subsidiary, NEC Technologies Inc., says that most of the growth in laptops now will come from customers who are buying them as desktop replacements. William T. O'Shea, vice president for systems marketing and development at AT&T, says

that up to 40% of today's desktop owners will switch to laptops. The result, says NEC's Miller, is that "the number of people who opt for a laptop is going to explode."

If the boom continues at the current, overheated rate, there's danger of a shakeout. With dozens of new competitors crowding into the market, "there are too many people trying to compete for the same dollars," complains Albert J. Agbay, president of Leading Edge Products Inc., the U.S. computer subsidiary of Korea's Daewoo Telecom Co. Leading Edge itself plans to add five aggressively priced machines to its one-model laptop line this year.

THE PAYOFF

But price alone won't guarantee success. An overcrowded market means that suppliers who can keep a constant flow of state-of-the-art laptops coming are the most likely survivors. And that is where Japan's huge investment in electronics manufacturing technology really pays off. Take LCD screens. They were invented in the U.S., but it was Japanese electronics companies that spent the past 20 years learning how to manufacture them, starting with digital watches. These days, the crisp, page-size LCD screens used in notebook PCs are as tricky to produce as semiconductors and require huge investments in manufacturing equipment. Sharp Corp. alone has committed more than $650 million to LCD R&D and production over the next three years, and Toshiba plans to spend $625 million on LCDs within the next four years. Toshiba expects a payoff in color LCD screens later this year, and by 1995, monochrome displays with twice the clarity of current LCDs.

In the U.S., there is virtually no competition for such Japanese manufacturing might. Only a handful of tiny U.S. companies are even working on LCD technology, and they have little chance of ever catching up with Japanese pricing or quality. But despite the commanding lead of Japan's LCD makers, the Commerce Dept. recently substantiated charges by U.S. screenmakers that Japanese manufacturers are selling LCDs in the U.S. at artificially low prices. Commerce will decide in April whether or not to level punitive duties on LCD imports. Even if they do, however, a U.S. LCD industry is unlikely to spring up: Japan's screenmakers are expected to respond to higher duties by shifting some LCD work to the U.S. Sharp has already announced plans to do final assembly of LCDs in Seattle.

FOLDING BOARDS

Screens are only Japan's most visible advantage in laptops. Japanese electronics companies are also pushing hard in technologies such as application-specific integrated circuits (ASICs), which save space by combining the functions of many components on one chip. They are pioneering new chip-mounting technologies, such as tape-automated bonding, a method of gluing chips directly onto the board instead of using solder. And they are working on flexible circuit boards, which can actually be folded up to fit in small spaces.

In the 1990s, Japanese suppliers are also intent on mastering the technologies that have thus far eluded them,

such as miniature hard-disk drives. Toshiba and Victor Co. of Japan (JVC), for example, are racing to perfect drives with 1.8-inch platters that will nearly double the capacity of today's most compact drives.

But it is in laptop manufacturing that the Japanese have their greatest edge over Western PC makers—thanks to their experience in making Walkmans, camcorders, and other portable consumer-electronics items. Those products made the Japanese experts in production engineering. Now, with decades of knowhow, companies such as Toshiba are able to refine the automated manufacturing and assembly process constantly—so that they can keep cranking out high quality products in large volume for less money. "When it's all said and done, what makes or breaks you is how reliably and how cost-effectively you can assemble these laptops," says Pallab Chatterjee, director of Texas Instruments' Semiconductor Process & Design Center in Dallas.

The consumer-electronics experience has also taught Japanese laptop makers how to update their product lines continuously with new models that incorporate the latest technologies. "Computer cycles are short, but nothing compared to the Walkman," notes Susumu Shinbori, general manager in Sony's Supermicro Systems Group. Toshiba, for instance, came up with 12 distinct laptop models in 1990. Zenith, which ships more laptops than any other Western supplier, offers just four basic models.

AMERICAN KNOWHOW

Still, the Japanese don't have all the marbles. U.S. laptop makers continue to

LAPTOPS, 1993-STYLE

- **Upcoming Technology**
- **What It Does**
- **Where It's Coming From**

COLOR LCD SCREENS
- Will improve graphics quality
- Toshiba, Sharp, Hosiden

CHIP SETS
- More highly integrated sets will make notebooks smaller, more efficient
- Intel, Chips & Technologies, VSLI Technology, Western Digital

1.8-INCH HARD-DISK DRIVES
- These 100 MB drives will offer almost twice the storage of today's units but will be 39% smaller
- Conner, Toshiba, JVC

NICKEL-HYDRIDE BATTERIES
- These power sources will have 50% more life
- Hitachi Maxell, Sanyo, Matsushita

FLASH MEMORY CARDS
- Used in place of a hard-disk drive, they will reduce power consumption and cut weight
- Intel, NMB Semi, NEC

FLEXIBLE CIRCUIT BOARDS
- Combined with tape-automated bonding techniques, boards will be more reliable and take up less space
- Sony, Compaq, Toshiba

DATA: COMPANY REPORTS, BW

shop at home for some of the most important laptop technology. Conner Peripherals Inc., for example, remains by far the leader in making miniature hard-disk drives for notebook PCs. The fast-growing Silicon Valley company "has outstanding skill in making small, low-power, high-capacity drives," acknowledges Kiyoshi Hayamizu, director of the application technology department at NEC's PC sales promotion division. Moreover, Intel remains the only source of key microprocessor chips. And laptop makers around the world still turn to a handful of U.S. companies—Cirrus Logic, Chips & Technologies, Western Digital—for vital "logic" chips.

In one area—marketing—U.S. PC makers remain years ahead. Apple, IBM, and others have spent a decade building up a huge base of customers and the distribution channels to reach it. "The issue is not where the parts come from," says Howard Elias, Tandy's vice president for computer merchandising. "The real issue is the value-added, what the marketing company produces." Tandy's value-added is a network of 7,000 Radio Shack stores that blanket the U.S. Personal-computer market leaders Apple and IBM also have thousands of dealers and millions of customers, all primed for their laptop offerings.

IBM's biggest edge, as always, is its decades-old relationship with the leading corporations around the globe. And its new notebook PC, which dealers say will be introduced by April, is clearly pitched at that audience. Big Blue intends to focus its marketing message on reliability, service, and the ability to link the new laptops into corporate information networks. PC clonemakers and Japan's electronics giants already manufacture laptops that are lighter and less expensive than IBM's seven-pound, $5,995 notebook. But they can't begin to match IBM's marketing and customer-support apparatus.

When IBM's laptop customers hit the road this summer, they'll be able to call an 800 number for help, and they can drop in at any of IBM's network of 1,900 U.S. computer dealers for service. To speed things up, IBM plans to use a nationwide depot system to rush replacement parts to dealers. That could be an important advantage, since notebooks take a lot of jostling and are prone to breakdowns. Computer repair shops say that laptop parts—particularly for Japanese brands—are sometimes hard to come by.

WIN-WIN

Can marketing clout continue to overcome Japan's manufacturing might?

Until laptops, there seemed to be no contest. Throughout the 1980s, Japanese electronics giants were surprisingly ineffectual in turning their advantages in desktop computer components into success in the U.S. desktop market. "I have been in this business for eight years, and for all eight years people have been predicting that the Japanese would own this business," says Peter J. Rogers, an analyst at investment bank Robertson, Stephens & Co. "It hasn't happened."

Some experts still think it never will. Market researchers point out that even Japanese companies that lead in laptops haven't had much success in the larger desktop market. Toshiba, for instance, has nearly 20% of the U.S. laptop market. But it supplies just 2% of desktop PCs in the U.S., according to International Data Corp. NEC has 10% in laptops and only 2.4% of desktops.

Still, if laptops do become the best-selling type of computer, the Japanese can't lose. If they simply hold on to what they have now in laptops, they'll wind up with half of the biggest PC market. Even if they don't, they'll still control the key laptop technologies. Either way, Japanese electronics makers seem destined to dominate in the laptop era.

FALLS RIVER CENTER, INC.

Betsy Dalgliesh watched her new Macintosh as the screen saver sent a spray of rainbow-hued fireworks across the screen. As she looked at her computer, she wondered if this would be just what she and Rick Haupt, cofounder of Falls River, needed to get organized. Until now a jumbled mess of paperwork thrown in old shoe boxes represented the filing system for Falls River.

Somehow Dalgliesh wasn't convinced that this new computer, the Quicken software package, and a few sessions with their accountant would be enough to carry their growing experiential learning company to the next stage. Just being "people people and not businesspeople" had been enough to turn Haupt and Dalgliesh's belief in experiential learning into a profitable business; but the strains and pains of growth were all too evident. Falls River was at a turning point. If they wanted to expand in a growing market, Dalgliesh knew it would take more than just a computer. But then again, it wasn't clear that fast growth was what they wanted.

INDUSTRY BACKGROUND

The first outdoor education program was developed during World War II by Kurt Hahn, an expatriate German educator, to train young British sailors in marine and survival skills. He called this program "outward bound" because this was the expression sailors used when they were going out to sea.[1]

Outward Bound USA was chartered in 1961 and ran the first U.S. wilderness program in Colorado in 1962. By 1993, Outward Bound conducted more than 600 courses a year for such diverse groups as inner-city children and cancer patients.

Few of these programs were designed for the corporate world. To fill this need, many new programs sprung up, and corporate adventure training expanded rapidly so that by 1992 more than 100 training organizations provided corporate adventure or experiential learning.[2] These programs ranged

---

This case was written by Christine Lotze, Darden 1992, and Jamie Berger, Darden 1992, under the supervision of Professor L. J. Bourgeois. Copyright © 1994 by the University of Virginia Darden School Foundation, Charlottesville, VA. All rights reserved.

[1]Richard Wagner, et al., "Outdoor Training: Revolution or Fad?" *Training and Development Journal,* March 1991.
[2]Richard Broderick, "Learning the Ropes," *Training,* October 1988.

in size from a one-person operation to big programs like Pecos River, which required several hundred employees to run a 1,000-person program in a day. People involved in experiential learning program organizations formed a grass-roots association, the Association for Experiential Education, based in Boulder, Colorado, to provide a psychological as well as physical meeting place for practitioners. The association sponsored annual conferences and addressed issues associated with very diverse areas of hands-on learning, including, for example, apprenticeship.

Adventure or experiential learning programs focused on building leadership and teamwork skills, and generally fell into two main categories: wilderness and "outdoor-centered" programs. The programs could last from a few hours to several weeks, as in the case of some wilderness programs. The wilderness programs involved outdoor living and vigorous activities such as mountain climbing or white-water rafting. Outdoor-centered programs consisted of "high ropes" activities, which took place at elevations high above the ground, and "low ropes," which involved either team problem solving or individual initiative. Wilderness programs and high ropes were more expensive, with wilderness programs averaging $2,800 per participant. Low ropes averaged $300 per participant.[3] Another estimate of the cost of low ropes per participant was from $100 to $300 per person per day with $600 to $1,200 being the range for high ropes.[4]

One study found the proportion of wilderness and outdoor centered program to be 23 percent and 77 percent respectively. Of outdoor-centered program participants, 70 percent were top executives or middle-level managers, 20 percent were sales representatives or supervisors, and 10 percent were other nonmanagers. The wilderness training programs focused on developing leadership and decision-making skills, while the outdoor centered programs focused on team building, self-esteem, leadership, problem solving, decision making, and a sense of corporate ownership.[5] One study estimated that 13.8 percent of companies used outdoor education training. Pecos River, the largest of the outdoor education training centers with 400 full-time employees, had a gross income of approximately $20 million in 1991.[6]

Despite debate over the programs' effectiveness with regard to the transfer of the course learning to actual business situations, the experiential learning programs were expected to continue to grow in number. Bob Carr, president of the Association for Experienced Based Training, estimated that, in 1990, more than $227 million, or one-half of one percent of the total spending of corporate America on training, was spent on experiential-based training. He predicted "that figure will increase significantly in the next five years."[7]

---

[3]Wagner, "Outdoor Training."
[4]Brad Lee Thompson, "Training in the Great Outdoors," *Training,* May 1991.
[5]Wagner, "Outdoor Training."
[6]Thompson, "Training in the Great Outdoors."
[7]Thompson, "Training in the Great Outdoors."

HISTORY OF FALLS RIVER

Betsy Dalgliesh and Rick Haupt came to Falls River with a wide range of experiences relating to experiential learning. Dalgliesh received an undergraduate degree in education and pursued graduate work in social psychology, educational foundations, and counseling and experiential education. Her initial contact with experiential learning, during her early 20s, was with a wilderness program that worked with schools in northern Georgia. Later, with Outward Bound in their professional development programs, she gained much grounding in the field. Dalgliesh also at one point joined the Santa Fe Mountain Center in New Mexico—a wilderness program for adjudicated youth. Here she became interested in building a business and developed a fund-raising program that continues to be successful for this organization. In 1984 Dalgliesh became involved in professional development with a consulting group in New Hampshire. Dalgliesh had also found that her work with children in summer camp for the previous 21 years complemented these experiences. (See Exhibit 1 for a biographical sketch.)

Since his experience as a Peace Corps Volunteer (PCV) in South America, Rick Haupt had been a licensed professional counselor. He became interested in experiential learning after doing Outward Bound work in the Peace Corps, and in 1986 he continued his work with Outward Bound as an instructor. Haupt and Dalgliesh met at Outward Bound and were later reconnected through mutual friends in Charlottesville, Virginia, in 1987. Dalgliesh was doing experiential learning work, and Haupt thought she might be interested in his idea of building a ropes course on his land. They met every week for a year, and Dalgliesh, who was traveling a great deal for a Harcourt Brace Jovanovich leadership program in Florida, realized she could do the same work in Charlottesville. They decided ropes training had real potential in the area, and building the course would be a great way for Haupt to utilize his 80-acre wooded land in Afton, Virginia, and to spend more time outdoors. (Exhibit 2 contains a biographical sketch on Haupt.)

While neither were particularly interested in running their own business—experiential or otherwise—they agreed that doing so could be fun, creative, and meet their common individual goals. Dalgliesh, in talking with teachers and administrators in the surrounding school system, thought that there was a demand for a program that encouraged and developed teamwork.

In 1988, each provided one-half of the $20,000 initial investment to found the Falls River Center, Inc. Their vision for the business was to stay flexible and to customize their programs to meet individual needs. They felt that Falls River should be a place away from the workplace where people were encouraged to grow both professionally and spiritually. "We believe that when people participate in their own learning it can be very powerful," explained Dalgliesh. "Falls River's method is to develop a process where the group can analyze its own problems and challenges and then learn how to overcome them."

Exhibit 1
Betsy Dalgliesh
Biographical Sketch

Betsy Dalgliesh has been committed to creating positive learning experiences for a variety of populations for almost 20 years. After receiving a B.A. from Hollins College, she trained at Dartmouth College's Outward Bound Leadership Program and with Wolfcreek Wilderness School in Georgia. She worked as an environmental educator, outdoor instructor, and camp director, emphasizing the connections between personal growth and the natural environment.

Subsequent work with North Carolina Outward Bound's Professional Development Program established her belief that business and community groups can greatly benefit from opportunities to experience challenge, self- and team reliance, and adventure. As president and co-owner of Falls River Center in Charlottesville, she designs and conducts action-learning programs that utilize outdoor activities to stimulate leadership and develop effective interpersonal skills. She is the 1994 recipient of the Association for Experiential Education's Practitioner of the Year Award.

One particular interest is in program development. She has designed outdoor programs for youth leaders, families in crisis, teachers, and managers. At Santa Fe Mountain Center, she developed a fund-raising program to support wilderness experiences as adjunct therapy for at-risk youth. She also participated on the coordinating team that initiated a national leadership conference for minority youth.

As an affiliate consultant with Action Learning Associates and Peak Performance of Colorado Springs, Colorado; Hollander, Kerrick Cappy and Associates of Peterborough, New Hampshire; Blue Ridge Consultants of Sugar Grove, North Carolina; TeamCraft of Austin, Texas; and North Carolina Outward Bound School, she has worked in leadership and team development programs for Federal Express, Frito-Lay, Hoescht-Celanese, GE, Anheuser-Busch, Trammel Crow, Dana Corporation, Ciba-Geigy, Dial Page, and Carolina Power & Light.

Dalgliesh lives in Albemarle County near the Blue Ridge Mountains of Virginia, where she enjoys hiking, mountain biking, canoeing, and cross-country skiing with her husband and their dog. Another passion is adventure travel. She speaks Italian and has a working knowledge of French and Spanish.

Exhibit 2
Rick Haupt
Biographical Sketch

Vice president and co-owner of Falls River Center, Inc., Rick Haupt draws much of his experience from his time spent as an Outward Bound instructor and at Project Adventure corporate training programs where experiential learning was combined with ropes course activities. Since 1988 he has been intensely involved with Falls River in its leadership, team development, and corporate training programs.

Haupt attended Ohio State University for undergraduate studies where he also played halfback under football coach Woody Hayes and was on the 1961 national championship team. He did his graduate studies in psychiatry at The Johns Hopkins School of Medicine and graduated in 1977.

In 1964 Haupt served for two years as a Peace Corps Volunteer in the Central American Republic of Panama. He has traveled extensively in Central and South America, Puerto Rico, and the Caribbean, and throughout Europe. He is fluent in Spanish.

Since 1980 Haupt has been in private practice as a psychotherapist doing individual, family, and couples counseling. More and more he has combined the issues of trust, communication styles, and teamwork on the ropes course as a therapeutic tool for families and couples.

Born in a small farming community in the Midwest, Haupt has lived on the East Coast since 1970. He currently lives in rural Virginia with his wife and three daughters.

His hobbies include jogging, biking, tennis, rock climbing, whitewater canoeing, scuba diving, canyon hiking, and family wilderness outings.

The company's overriding goal was quite simple—to have fun. The founders planned on actively running the programs and working directly with the groups, as well as customizing and planning the programs, and taking care of the more arcane side of the business.

The course was designed for one-day, task-oriented sessions, rather than the long programs offered by Outward Bound and others. (See Exhibit 3 for Falls River mission statement.) Outward Bound was brought in to build the

Exhibit 3
Falls River Center
Mission Statement

Our mission is to provide the highest quality action-oriented training programs to intact work teams and the community at large with a goal of professional and personal revitalization.

We accomplish this by developing a safe physical and emotional environment for our participants and providing the highest level of safety and ethical standards in the experiential education field. We respect individual differences, encourage sound environment practices, and value our role of service to the community.

Falls River Center is open to all people regardless of race, gender, age, sexual orientation, or physical abilities.

Statement of Ethical Practices

Falls River Center is committed to providing the highest level of quality in programming, staff, and business operations. Our staff agrees to demonstrate and develop the concepts of compromise, cooperation, empathy, acceptance, and compassion, both in facilitation of programs and in the operation of the corporation. We demonstrate respect for others' rights, styles, and standards. We will, to the best of our ability, maintain the highest level of emotional and physical safety.

course and to train Haupt and Dalgliesh and eight new facilitators on course techniques and safety procedures. The facilitators were part-time employees with varying degrees of knowledge in experiential training, but most had a background in counseling and group dynamics. By the spring of 1988 the Falls River complex was opened with an initial rush of business from public schools and hospitals in the area.

Two of the facilitators, Peggy Amacker and Scott Ziemer, had been part of Falls River from the start. Amacker, a native of Charlottesville, studied communications and business at North Carolina State University and subsequently worked in administration for two years in an outdoor education program in New Hampshire/Peterborough at Boston University's 860-acre Sergeant Camp. She then joined an international program in Seattle that involved dialog training for children living in conflict areas. Amacker specialized in the Middle East and trained Palestinian and Jewish children in dialog training to run programs for their peers in their home countries. Amacker found out about Falls River through an ad in a local paper that called for people with ropes course experience to come and "test" a new course. After signing on, Amacker served as both a trainer and administrator, providing bookkeeping and logistical support.

Ziemer, an armed services dependent, moved frequently during his childhood. After receiving a B.A. in social science from Hiram college in Hiram, Ohio, he worked as a carpenter and eventually co-owned a construction business. Later, he directed the ropes course and counseling services at a drug and alcohol treatment center for children. After hearing about Falls River from an acquaintance of Haupt and Dalgliesh, in 1989 Ziemer came to Charlottesville working part time in carpentry; as a tree surgeon; as a builder, designer, and maintainer of equipment and grounds; and as a facilitator at Falls River.

MARKETING

Initially, there were no marketing efforts at Falls River because Dalgliesh knew the Charlottesville schools were interested in participating in experiential learning programs and Haupt had several therapeutic groups that were interested. They recognized a growing demand for the type of programs they planned to offer and were encouraged by local hospitals and schools to open Falls River.

Haupt and Dalgliesh were encouraged by friends to pursue target marketing immediately, but they planned to "get really good" before they expanded their marketing endeavors. This objective, combined with having enough clients (30 program-days per year) to keep them in business for quite a while, allowed Haupt and Dalgliesh to avoid marketing aggressively. In their second year of operation, the Albermarle County school system was their biggest client; however, with the recession and budget cuts in late 1990, business was much harder to generate.

It was informal word of mouth, or personal marketing, that brought the contract that marked a turning point for Falls River. At a Charlottesville Christmas party in December of 1989, Dalgliesh talked about Falls River and its objectives with a man who had expressed considerable interest in the programs. "Would you be able to run 240 people through your program?" he asked. The person at the cocktail party, John Rosenblum, dean of the Darden Graduate School of Business at the University of Virginia, was very interested in incorporating the Falls River program into the second-year MBA leadership course, which would push the course along the "new wave" in management education.

While they had never dealt with groups that large, Dalgliesh realized that becoming associated with a business school with a national reputation could be tremendous for the long-term growth of Falls River, not to mention the revenue involved. Afterward, several Darden faculty members came to tour Falls River. In the spring of 1989, it was agreed that in October the 240 second-year MBAs would come to Falls River in groups of 60 per day, over four days. This initial contract resulted in several annual contracts with the Darden School: three years of the second-year MBA program, three years of Darden's flagship senior executive program ("TEP"), and six to eight clients from TEP-participant mailings, as well as an additional annual Darden executive program with the Bacardi Corporation. The contacts from the TEP and executive programs opened new avenues for business.

With the Darden contracts in place, Haupt and Dalgliesh began formal marketing efforts. Marketing decisions were difficult since Haupt, Dalgliesh, Ziemer, and Amacker had no formal marketing experience. This lack of knowledge coupled with their lack of a defined target group made their marketing efforts even more perplexing. All four knew they must bring in other business to be able to drop their less profitable groups. Knowing that corporate groups tended to be less price sensitive than other groups, they wanted to pursue these groups so they might also be able to provide their services to other nonprofit groups that could not afford to pay the full rate.

While word of mouth was their most successful form of advertising to date, they also ran a series of ads in the two local papers, *The Daily Progress* and *The Observer*, and in a local business journal. They sent out an extensive mailing to local business leaders, school systems, many groups at the University of Virginia, and others who had expressed interest. (See Exhibit 4 for Falls River brochure.) Unfortunately, they were not able to gauge the success of the ads. Haupt and Dalgliesh thought the mailing had a 0-percent return, while Amacker felt that the budget cuts announced at UVA (University of Virginia) the week of the mailing thwarted the effort.

Amacker found that in eliminating groups that were not cost-effective, Falls River began to get a reputation for being "expensive and not giving breaks." This, she said, was rather unfortunate since "many groups that might not even consider them would have found their rate within their price range."

Prices at Falls River were determined on a case-by-case basis. As of 1990 they had defined three price categories:

- Students up to high-school level
- Professional and community groups
- Organizational rate/corporate

Falls River did not make any profits on the student rates; it only hoped to cover its costs. Profit came from corporate programs with rates ranging from $125 to $250 per person, which was still below the average charge of $300 per person for similar programs. For a group of 100 to 300 persons, $150 per person was considered a good rate in the industry. Falls River had bid on jobs and had been selected even though it was the high bidder. Dalgliesh believed this was a result of the personal attention Falls River afforded its clients. Students were offered a one-half day rate averaging $30 to $40 per person and $50 to

Exhibit 4
Falls River Center Promotional Brochure

Falls River Center

Falls River is an adventure-based training center that offers dynamic opportunities for personal growth through safe, challenging activities.

Programs offered by Falls River can be used to achieve the following outcomes:

- Improve individual and group planning, decision-making, and problem-solving processes.
- Enhance self-esteem and self confidence.
- Learn to manage stress and to function effectively in difficult situations.
- Develop team cohesion and team effectiveness.

A series of rope bridges, nets, cables and platforms offer a stimulating challenge at the High Ropes Course, which is nestled in a beautiful hardwood forest overlooking the Mechums River. This powerful learning tool fosters self-confidence and problem-solving ability.

"The ride on the "Zip Line" is a real experience in letting go of control and trusting something outside yourself...the course is very good for building group cohesion and cooperative spirit. Going through this course is a wonderful life experience."
Peter Sheras, Director of Clinical Psychology, University of Virginia

Managers of large and small corporations, administrators of schools and hospitals, educators from all levels, and helping professionals from social agencies participate in programs offered by Falls River. Students from area schools and churches have benefited from their experiences as well.

Falls River Center, Inc. is an Institutional Member of The Association for Experiential Education and The Virginia Association for Outdoor Adventure Education.

Photos by Phillip Beaurline.
Cover photo and photo of Low Ropes Course by Cynthia DeCanio.

"The challenge offered at Falls River give educators, who often work in isolation, the opportunity to see how their cooperative efforts can exceed individual efforts in reaching goals."
Pamela Moran,
Staff Development Coordinator,
Albemarle County Public Schools

Following each exercise, time is reserved to debrief and explore how your group chose to work together, and how well your actions worked. You are encouraged to support each other with feedback and to share your observations. This often creates a forum for drawing analogies to the work environment.

The program demonstrates how a group of individuals can increase its resources and meet significant challenges when its members choose to work cooperatively as a team.

Underlying all is the sense of camaraderie gained by working together and enjoying each other in a beautiful outdoor setting.

Your classroom is in the fresh air and natural beauty of Albemarle County, only twenty-five minutes south of Charlottesville and the University of Virginia.

Each adventure seminar is custom-tailored to meet the needs of your group. Programs are designed with your input to create positive change in your personal and professional life.

*"Not a day goes by that I don't associate back to the Ropes Course and use the strength I gained to get through tough times. By showing me how I can face fear the Course has allowed me to take new risks.
If I can do the Ropes Course, then I can do anything!"*
Elaine Connors, Owner
Charlottesville restaurant

Many Falls River programs take place at the Low Ropes Challenge Course, which consists of courses built of ropes and cable no higher than five feet from the ground. Here you will embark on a carefully crafted series of interactive tasks designed to build trust and increase your ability to be an effective member of a problem-solving team. Each event presents a different challenge in which you must discover the resources within your team and work cooperatively to achieve your goal.

Staff

You will be instructed by highly trained professional facilitators knowledgeable in the safe, effective management of outdoor learning activities.

Your experience is tailored to fit your physical condition and the capabilities of your fellow participants. Every individual has exercised choice and you are encouraged to determine your personal limits.

Falls River Center, Inc. was founded in 1989 and is owned and operated by Rick Haupt and Betsy Caldwell Dalgliesh.

Rick is a licensed professional counselor in private practice for the past twelve years. In 1986 he became an Outward Bound instructor. He has a passion for creating a place in the wilderness in which people can grow and work together. He was a Peace Corps volunteer in South America and has travelled extensively in South America and in Europe. He is associated with Project Adventure in their Adventure Based Counseling Program.

Betsy is an experiential education consultant with twenty years of experience in leadership and team development programs. She instructs for North Carolina Outward Bound's Professional Development Program, The Santa Fe Mountain Center, and Action Learning Associates, as well as a number of other highly esteemed training programs. She has served on the Boards of the Virginia Council for Outdoor Adventure Education and the Association for Experiential Education.

For further information,
Please call
(804) 971-8599

$60 for elementary or middle-school students. Other companies, such as Pecos River, charged far more than Falls River's $125–$250 range for a day. Pecos River might charge $1,000 per participant for a similar program and pay its facilitators less than half of what Falls River did. The cost of a Falls River program could also include a consulting fee, depending on the work done for a company. For example, if considerable work was required prior to the program, an additional consulting fee ranging from $100 to $1,500 per day might be charged. Dalgliesh felt very strongly about telling corporations that their fee rates allowed Falls River to offer programs to deserving groups not able to afford the standard pricing.

Dalgliesh and Haupt also wanted to educate potential consumers about Falls River's unique services. Falls River offered client group programs and "open" programs. Client groups usually involved intact work groups or companies in transition and required a needs assessment. For a needs assessment, Falls River would gather information from a contact person and/or as many people in the company as it could and ascertain the client's current state, desired state, and how the program could facilitate transition to the desired state.

Open programs allowed couples or individuals to engage in the Falls River experience. Dalgliesh found these "messier to run" since participants had vastly different agendas and goals for the program, and these were usually determined at the program rather than being carefully planned in advance. The number of client-days of open programs was low compared to client group program days; with approximately 600 client-days per year, about 50 client-days were open programs. At the 600 client-days per year level (equivalent to 30–35 actual days per year), Falls River could be considered a small operation. Most of the other experiential learning companies had more than 1,000 client-days per year.

Falls River differed radically from other experiential learning firms in that, because of Falls River's relatively small size, it had the flexibility to offer its clients personalized programs. As mentioned above, a Falls River staff person would perform a needs assessment—discussing in detail with the client the areas of concern and getting a feel for the company culture and the context in which the participants worked. The Falls River staff would incorporate this information into the program development and then after completing the program the staff would follow up with the company and the participants. (See Exhibit 5 for a sample custom program.)

Falls River's unique customized service required each facilitator to be able to take a group through a range of learning experiences (e.g., "the spider web," "the wall," or "Jacob's Ladder"), follow its development, and constantly make adjustments as the group's journey progressed. Comparable firms offered "off the shelf" programs, such as the ones offered by Pecos River, with instructors who were very narrowly specialized and tended to perform only one type of activity (e.g., "the wall") with every group. In these types of programs, a client group might be facilitated by a separate specialist in each of the activities.

Exhibit 5
Falls River Center Action Learning Session
for CAE Electronics
Tentative Program Design (10/28/92)

GOALS

Identify strategies and behaviors that help the team to "win." Develop ways to take these winning strategies back to the workplace. Have fun with each other in an outdoor setting away from work.

PRECEDING AFTERNOON

Meet with participants for introductory briefing. Framing the day, goals articulated, what to wear/bring. Medical release forms.

PROGRAM DAY

9:00 A.M.   All group opening.
            Warm ups.
            Communication barriers.

9:30   Divide into six teams for Action Learning sequence.

            Group Juggle—Team members toss "products" to their customers, focusing on pleasing the customer (good passes) and zero defects (no dropped balls), while remaining in touch with the Big Picture (what the rest of the team is doing).

            Issues: *What is a mistake?*
                        Who owns the mistakes?
                        How was customer satisfaction created?
                        Importance of keeping the big picture in mind.
                        How is this activity like the workplace?

            Speedball—Task is changed; time focus is added.

            Issues: *What were the breakthroughs in solving this problem?*
                        Were everyone's ideas heard?
                        What does it take for an idea to get put into action?

            Mission Possible—Group is paired: one is area supervisors, the other is front line worker; supervisors are given the task that blindfolded workers are to perform. Supervisors can

(continued on next page)

(continued)

communicate, give vision, guide worker, but only workers may handle the tools to complete the task (delivering a product—represented by a bucket—into a new marketplace given time and other constraints).

Issues: *Importance of clearly articulating a vision.*
                Communicating a task to someone who cannot see what the problem is.
                Teaming to get jobs done.
                What learnings can we take with us from this?

Traffic Jam—Half the group changes places with the other half with certain constraints around their movement patterns.

Issues: *How does our "social architecture" affect our ability to resolve problems?*
                What causes frustration level to rise?
                How can we resolve this as effectively as possible?

Quality Web—Group must plan and execute the passing of each individual through a "web," where each opening may only be used once. Group determines the standards by which it wants to adhere.

Issues: *Planning versus execution.*
                Who assumed leadership?
                Did leadership change, and why?
                What are the operating norms?
                Which of these do you like, and which would you like to change?

Blindfold Squares—While all are blindfolded, group is given the challenge of creating a certain pattern with lengths of rope, within a time constraint.

Issues: *How do we approach a challenge that none of us can see?*
                What were examples of effective leadership?
                What got in the way?
                What are our learnings?

Corporate Islands—Entire group stands on small island, which represents "current reality." Island ten feet away represents its "desired state." The group has "resources," human, financial, and technical (represented by three boards).

(continued on next page)

(continued)

The challenge is for the group to reach its desired state, using its resources, without touching the ground.

Issues: *Was everyone able to see the problem?*
   Was the vision clear?
   What are other challenges in our current reality?

The Wall—Entire group attempts to get over a 14-foot wall, utilizing only each other as resources. (May or may not use this.)

The above are suggested activities. (Each team will do a subset.) Options remain flexible as we further refine needs and objectives and depending on how the day itself progresses.

12:00–12:45 P.M.	Catered lunch at Big Top in Meadow.
11:15–4:00	Choice of two: Jacob's Ladder, Zip Line, Leap of Faith, along with other initiatives if they choose.
3:15–3:45	Small group debriefs (some may have to happen during your assigned flex time).
4:00	All groups meet at Zig Zag clearing for final wrap-up.
4:15	Participants leave, staff debrief.

HUMAN RESOURCES

The Falls River Center had no full-time employees. The first eight facilitators were trained during the first year of operations for programs with school teachers, administrators, students, and therapeutic groups. Haupt and Dalgliesh required each of these facilitators to have a counseling background since the skills necessary to be a competent facilitator—particularly in touchy situations—had a lengthy development process. Of these facilitators, only Ziemer and Amacker worked on more than a per-program contract basis. They became intimately involved in the course improvement, administrative tasks, and marketing of Falls River.

In the first year Haupt and Dalgliesh found themselves doing most of the work themselves. Amacker developed a self-managing system for the paperwork submitted by the facilitators and wrote a safety manual for the course. Neither Haupt nor Dalgliesh had any business or finance background, but Haupt kept the books until 1991 when he turned the finances over to Dalgliesh.

Haupt and Dalgliesh complemented each other well as the leaders of the organization. Dalgliesh was constantly focused on the emotional needs of her employees, tried to keep the energy level high, and provided an organizational framework while Haupt always had time to listen, provided stability, and paid attention to the small details that created a special touch. Haupt's calm consistency balanced Dalgliesh's high-gear state just before programs were about to take off. Dalgliesh's good organizational skills helped keep Haupt's "laid-back" nonlinear style from digressing into chaos.

Their differences were well illustrated in their descriptions of an awful day. Haupt's idea of an awful day was one where he would have to "shoot from the hip" and was not grounded. This was not an issue for Dalgliesh because she always spent considerable time planning ahead. For Dalgliesh an awful day was "having to manage the office and be 15 different people" to meet everyone's needs. However, they did share a commitment to delivering "high-quality, totally safe, and the best possible programs in the field."

As the business grew several strains appeared. Dalgliesh's and Haupt's philosophy was always that "most important is having fun." As administrative tasks began to take them away from the programs, both felt that they could not take on more than their current work load. Haupt found himself "overwhelmed" and faced a low point as the tensions of balancing a healthy family life, his therapeutic practice, and Falls River seemed to be pulling him in too many directions. They both found themselves strapped, particularly with large programs such as the 240-person program for Darden. Furthermore, these large programs required that they bring in additional facilitators beyond the original group, usually from outside of Charlottesville. At first, they found it difficult to find enough qualified persons. After the first few programs, however, word of mouth gave Falls River a reputation for being a great place to work. The special attention and expense they put into preparing the facilitators and making their stay comfortable paid off; soon they began receiving requests from people who wanted to work in the next program.

In addition to the increased staff, the program methodology was changed, particularly with regard to the large corporate groups. Having more than 60 participants required a new level of planning, as did groups approaching 60 on high-ropes courses, because the staff had to be at least doubled. New ropes stations had to be built. They now had enough sites to accommodate 120 comfortably on low ropes. For corporate groups the large staff required more sophisticated management techniques and formal training on Falls River's rules and safety procedures. Tying the exercises and the learning to the participants' workplace was essential and required additional training for the facilitators.

FINANCES

Haupt and Dalgliesh started the company as 50/50 shareholders. They each invested $10,000 to create this subchapter S business. When asked if the business was profitable, Dalgliesh replied: "No, not yet. We haven't made back our initial investment, although we did each receive $7,000 last year."

With their lack of formal business skills, they found "learning the language of business difficult." As the business grew, they began to realize that their simplified accounting procedure was no longer adequate. They had been keeping all of their receipts and contracts in paper boxes and logging transactions in a book. Haupt and Dalgliesh found the language of the "business world" very perplexing. Terms such as "equity" and "fair market value" were difficult to comprehend. Trying to make sense of tax laws and legal terms was even worse.

One of Dalgliesh's learning challenges was doing a payroll. She had "never done a payroll before," much less one for 28 employees. The increase in employees reclassified Falls River and generated new concerns with insurance and taxes. She also found herself learning rudimentary accounting (see Exhibit 6 for sample book page and accountant's review) to keep track of the cash flow. She found "doing the books" very complicated and time-consuming and ran into the typical cash-flow problems of a growing small business. In June of 1991 she found herself facing a rather unexpectedly large insurance and tax bill without the money to pay for it. She realized how important it was to plan ahead and to build in cushions when large increases in the payroll required larger amounts of cash.

Although Dalgliesh kept the books, they decided to turn the books over to the accountant every quarter. Yet, even with the accountant, Haupt and Dalgliesh were barely able to distinguish a balance sheet from an income statement, referring to them as "those things we get from the accountant."

As a result of their lack of business expertise, they faced a surprising disappointment after the excitement of the success of their first 240-person Darden program. While the business school had been their largest revenue program, they realized that Falls River had barely broken even after expenses. Haupt and Dalgliesh understood that they would have to develop a better understanding of the company's cost structure before they quoted a price to the school again.

When it came to new equipment, Amacker asserted that Falls River was the best place she had ever worked. In most places Amacker found it "a battle to get new equipment." Haupt and Dalgliesh "were very willing to put more money into equipment despite a tight money supply." When an instructor mentioned a new helmet that would be a great safety improvement for the high ropes, he found ten of them out at the course the next week.

If money were not so tight, Amacker was certain they could do better marketing by improving their brochure and video. While Haupt and Dalgliesh were more than willing to spend money on equipment, they were apprehensive about buying office equipment such as a computer. However,

Exhibit 6
Falls River Center
Ratio Analyses
December 31, 1991
(See Accountant's Compilation Report)

Introduction

The following graphic ratio analyses are calculated from the accounting data provided. They are meant to serve only as an aid to understanding your business. They are useful in charting the progress of a business over time, as well as comparing the business to industry averages. (The different ratios will differ greatly across industries.) As such, ratios are important and useful tools. However, they must be interpreted with care and discretion.

Only some of the ratios are discussed below. Others, such as "Net sales" or "Gross profit margin on sales," should be obvious. If you are uncertain what these other ratios mean, please feel free to ask.

Ratio

This popular ratio measures the ability to pay current liabilities (due within one year) from cash and other assets that can be quickly converted to cash ("current assets"). A current ratio of 2.0 (2:1) is generally accepted as a healthy relationship between current assets and current liabilities. It is calculated by dividing current assets by current liabilities.

Debt-to-Equity Ratio

This ratio compares the firm's debt financing with the amount of owner/stockholder financing. It is commonly used by banks and other long-term creditors, who prefer a low debt-to-equity ratio because it implies less risk for the creditors. It is calculated by dividing total liabilities by total equity.

Employee Costs to Sales

This valuable ratio compares the cost of employees to the dollar amount of sales generated. It is useful to look at it over time and determine the trends. It is calculated by dividing the total of salaries, payroll taxes, and employee benefits by net sales.

(continued on next page)

(continued)

BALANCE SHEET

	1991	1992
ASSETS		
Current Assets		
Cash in bank	$12,689.37	$14,451.32
Money market account	.00	5,168.11
Accounts receivable—return checks	.00	273.00
Total current assets	12,689.37	$19,892.43
Property and Equipment		
Equipment and furniture	21,995.00	27,123.90
Accumulated depreciation	(11,038.07)	(14,930.90)
Total property and equipment	10,956.93	12,193.00
Other Assets		
Organization costs	1,655.00	1,655.00
Accumulated amortization	(801.00)	(1,131.98)
Total other assets	854.00	523.02
Total assets	$24,500.30	$32,608.45
LIABILITIES		
Current Liabilities		
Employee withholdings payable	$ 1,469.99	$ 204.83
Payroll taxes payable	1,223.75	292.43
Loan payable shareholder—current	11,238.00	.00
Total current liabilities	$13,931.74	$ 497.26
Long-term liabilities	.00	.00
Total long-term liabilities	.00	.00
Total liabilities	$13,931.74	$ 497.26
OWNER'S EQUITY		
Common stock	$ 1,000.00	$ 1,000.00
Retained earnings	3,578.00	31,122.66
AAA distributions— Betsy Dalgliesh	(10,777.05)	(24,658.05)
AAA distributions—Rick Haupt	(10,777.05)	(24,658.05)
Net profit/loss	$27,544.66	$49,304.63
Total owner's equity	$10,568.56	$32,111.19
Total liabilities and equity	$24,500.30	$32,608.45

(continued on next page)

(continued)

INCOME STATEMENT

	1991	Ratio	1992	Ratio
REVENUE				
Program income	$84,488.25	100.00	$117,792.40	100.00
Interest income	.00	.00	168.11	.14
Total revenue	$84,488.25	100.00	$117,960.51	100.00
OPERATING EXPENSES				
Advertising	$ 1,908.53	2.26	$ 1,467.38	1.24
Amortization	331.00	.39	330.98	.28
Bank charges	.00	.00	21.31	.02
Contract labor	1,100.50	1.30	320.00	.27
Depreciation	3,853.07	4.56	3,892.83	3.30
Donations	25.00	.03	.00	.00
Dues and subscriptions	170.00	.20	203.97	.17
Entertainment/meals—programs	1,163.64	1.38	506.06	.43
Entertainment/meals—other	606.60	.72	672.77	.57
Equipment rental	1,641.20	1.94	1,178.68	1.00
Insurance	2,731.00	3.23	3,081.00	2.61
Legal and accounting	825.00	.98	1,675.00	1.42
Licenses and permits	168.65	.20	277.96	.24
Miscellaneous expenses	208.03	.25	200.00	.17
Office supplies and expense	1,457.90	1.73	1,862.99	1.58
Penalties	140.50	.17	199.32	.17
Postage and delivery	.00	.00	208.70	.18
Program expenses	.00	.00	1,110.66	.94
Reference materials	50.00	.06	40.70	.03
Rent	4,000.00	4.73	3,250.00	2.76
Repairs and maintenance	1,275.03	1.51	727.55	.62
Subcontractor fees	1,750.00	2.07	14,700.00	12.46
Supplies	914.80	1.08	2,421.99	2.05
Taxes—payroll	2,990.56	3.54	2,739.67	2.32
Taxes—other	212.85	.25	140.61	.12
Telephone	53.89	.06	3.56	.00
Training and development	2,168.26	2.57	273.00	.23
Travel	1,202.06	1.42	1,877.69	1.59
Wages	24,195.52	28.64	13,284.50	11.26
Wages—officers	1,800.00	2.13	11,987.00	10.16
Total operating expenses	$56,943.59	67.40	68,655.88	58.20
Net income/loss	$27,544.66	32.60	$ 49,304.63	32.60

(continued on next page)

(continued)

STATEMENT OF RETAINED EARNINGS

	1991	1992
Retained earnings	$3,578.00	$ 9,568.56
Net income	27,544.66	49,304.63
Dividends declared	.00	.00
Adjustments to retained earnings		
AAA distribution—Betsy Dalgliesh	(10,777.05)	(13,881.00)
AAA distribution—Rick Haupt	(10,777.05)	(13,881.00)
Total adjustments	(21,554.10)	(27,762.00)
Total retained earnings	$9,568.56	$31,111.19

STATEMENT OF CASH FLOWS

	1991	1992
Cash Flow from Operating Activities		
Net income/loss	$27,544.66	$27,648.70
Depreciation	3,853.07	1,921.19
Net receivables	.00	(203.00)
Inventory	.00	.00
Prepaid expenses	.00	.00
Accounts payable	.00	.00
Notes payable	.00	(11,238.00)
Taxes payable		
Federal withholding	506.00	(376.59)
FICA withholding	835.99	(309.92)
Virginia withholding	128.00	(148.94)
Payroll taxes payable	1,223.75	(441.96)
Interest payable	.00	.00
Leases payable	.00	.00
Other current liabilities	.00	.00
Total cash flow from operating activities	$34,091.47	$16,851.48

(continued on next page)

(continued)

	1991	1992
Cash Flow from Investing Activities		
Property, plant, and equipment		
Equipment and furniture	(800.00)	473.00
Intangible assets		
Accumulated amortization	331.00	165.50
Other assets	.00	.00
Total cash flow from investing activities	(469.00)	638.50
Cash Flow from Financing Activities		
Long-term debt	.00	.00
Common stock	.00	.00
Additional paid-in capital—common	.00	.00
Retained earnings		
AAA distribution—Betsy Dagliesh	(10,777.05)	(3,881.00)
AAA distribution—Rick Haupt	(10,777.05)	(3,881.00)
Total cash flow from financing activities	(21,554.10)	(7,762.00)
Net increase/decrease in cash	$12,068.37	$ 9,727.98
Beginning cash balance	621.00	9,891.45
Net increase/decrease in cash	12,068.37	9,727.98
Ending cash balance	$12,689.37	$19,619.43

(continued on next page)

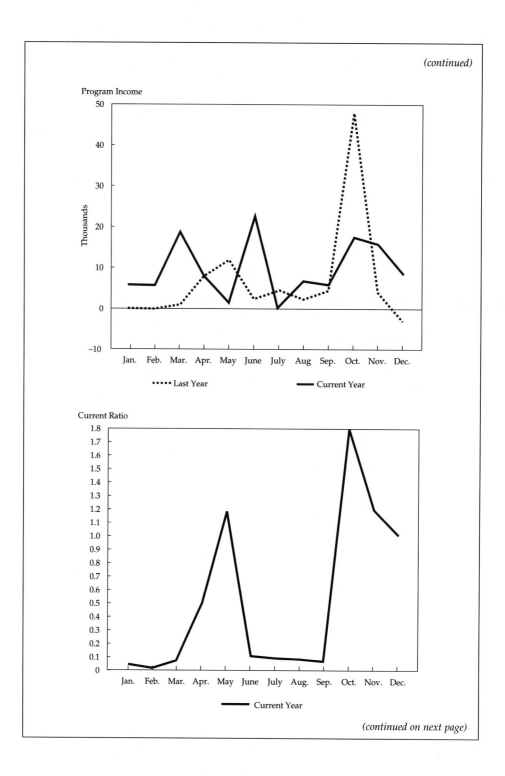

(continued)

(continued on next page)

(continued)

Net Profit Margin on Sales

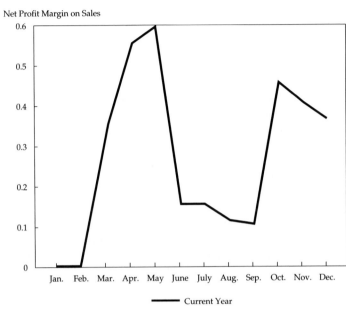

Debt-to-Equity Ratio

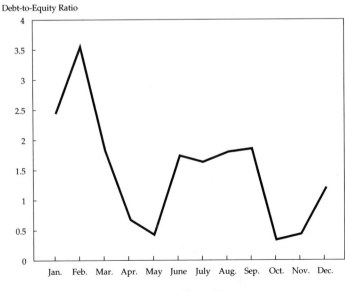

Amacker convinced them that a "computer was as worthwhile as new equipment for the course," and in late 1991 Falls River purchased a Macintosh LC, which now held a prominent position in the office.

THE FUTURE

The work with Darden had become an excellent source of business for Falls River. Darden had run its second-year leadership class through the course for the second year in a row, and the continued positive feedback boded well for a third year. In addition, the school's executive education programs' participants were also being introduced to Falls River programs, generating excellent word-of-mouth publicity in the business world, which resulted in their latest and largest program, the Bacardi Annual Sales Convention.

The program would be the first not run at the Falls River facility but at the convention site in Scottsdale, Arizona. At the convention 156 people would be run through a "series of moderately physical and cognitive 'challenges,'" designed to focus on the "values" that Bacardi wanted its sales and marketing organization to internalize (e.g., quality, productivity, long-term vision).

Since Falls River's work was with only one of the five companies under the Bacardi corporate umbrella, a successful program could translate into invaluable word of mouth within this corporation as well as the business community at large.

Falls River's payroll had jumped from 8 to more than 30; and Dalgliesh and Haupt, who had averaged 8–10 hours per week, now estimated that the company took up 20–24 hours per week. Clearly, it would require an even greater time commitment if it were to grow any further. Overall, the growth potential and business outlook was very good for the partners of a company whose founding goal was to "have fun."

As Dalgliesh considered how much time and effort growing the business would require, she wondered what she and Haupt—who was already having trouble balancing Falls River, his private practice, and time with his family—should do. Dalgliesh was very sensitive to the fact that programs being at Falls River had an impact on the Haupt family; there were possibly other sites, but Falls River was such a beautiful location. Besides, Dalgliesh's passion was not in building ropes courses; it was not her energy that would build another course. Her passion was in the process that happened there and that could happen anywhere. Dalgliesh knew that they "could do really well if they had ten more programs a year," yet it was not her goal to double the business. The idea of doubling the profits, however, did have a certain appeal. She knew it would be to their advantage to increase their business and understood that Haupt had larger financial ambitions than she did. They both wanted to see the company "run easier and better."

If they grew, would she spend even more time on administrative tasks instead of the part she loved: working with and creating the programs? Could they keep people like Amacker and Ziemer, who had become integral to their business, without the security of a full-time position? Dalgliesh knew Ziemer really wanted to work full time, and Amacker was ready and willing also. She began to think about what it would take to bring in the extra ten programs needed to do really well. They had flopped at marketing before, but how else could they bring in new business? What would the ten programs allow them to do? Perhaps Amacker could take over the office work as a full-time employee. Perhaps, she mused, they should just concentrate on continually improving their existing quality programs and forget about growth.

CASE

GEORGIA DIGITAL REPRODUCTION, INC.

On Wednesday, August 10, 1988, Richard Taylor, GDR's third president, heard that the Bank of Maryland would not extend a working-capital loan to his company, Georgia Digital Reproduction, Inc. (GDR). That was bad news. During June, GDR had taken down the last $100,000 of a shareholders' $250,000 note. GDR's only remaining funds were $46,512 in cash and a $130,000 bank line of credit backed by shareholder letters of credit. Clearly GDR could not qualify for more bank financing. Taylor was well aware of GDR's financial position (summarized in Exhibit 1) and that he needed to decide on a new strategy for his Norcross, Georgia, company. Was conserving cash while searching for more equity financing what GDR needed, or was that just part of a major overhaul?

GDR BACKGROUND

Georgia Digital Reproduction was an electronic design and marketing company with 13 employees that subcontracted all its manufacturing. In pursuit of its corporate mission and company objectives (see Exhibit 2), GDR had developed two electronic product lines: (1) a group of digital recorders, electronic devices that recorded and stored audio messages in chip memory for repeated playback, and (2) a series of Travelers' Information Stations (TIS), short-range AM transmitters that broadcast messages repeated by an accompanying digital recorder.

Digital recorders were configured as units to feed recorded announcements to loudspeakers in tour and airport shuttle busses (suggested list price, $5,000–$18,000), as bugle systems for playing bugle calls over the public address systems at military bases ($6,500–$20,150), and as message dispensers in amusement/theme parks, museums, and public parks ($270–$410 for single-channel record and playback units and $2,500–$16,050 for multi-channel record and playback units). Each stored message required its own channel; so, for example, a bugle system for storing and playing "Taps," "Reveille," "To the Colors," and "Mess Call" required four channels and had

This case was prepared by Ambrose S. Kalmbach, Darden 1989, under the supervision of Associate Professor L. J. Bourgeois III and Assistant Professor Andrea Larson. Copyright © 1989 by the Darden Graduate Business School Sponsors, Charlottesville, VA.

Exhibit 1
Georgia Digital Reproduction, Inc.
Financial Statement

	1984	1985	1986	1987	1988 Jan	Feb	March	April	May	June	July	1988 YTD
REVENUES												
Trade products	147,465	149,002	43,598	347,765	24,822	37,245	100,086	81,787	6,721	122,124	32,568	405,335
Other services	0	0	0	0	0	300	421	9,652	0	250	500	11,123
Total revenue	147,465	149,002	43,598	347,765	24,822	37,545	100,507	91,439	6,721	122,374	33,068	416,458
Cost of Sales				Note 1								
Trade products	91,687	94,858	39,968	167,710	11,424	18,254	58,922	52,745	3,921	33,125	16,102	194,493
Other services	0	0	0	0	0	200	1,621	4,585	250	473	198	7,327
Total cost of sales	91,687	94,858	39,968	167,710	11,424	18,454	60,543	57,330	4,171	33,598	16,300	201,820
Gross Margin	55,778	54,143	3,630	180,055	13,398	19,091	39,964	34,109	2,550	88,776	16,768	214,638
OPERATING EXPENSES												
Staff, staff related	0	0	166,296	347,762	61,094	44,373	47,209	46,244	49,079	50,156	50,818	348,905
General & admin.	60,187	89,759	47,172	186,810	42,776	58,232	13,367	8,361	17,400	18,679	21,678	169,035
Sales & marketing	19,451	93,062	76,956	101,647	1,701	5,103	14,421	6,195	8,267	2,940	2,201	40,965
Total oper. exp.	79,637	182,821	290,424	636,219	105,571	107,708	74,997	60,800	74,746	71,775	74,697	558,905
Other Inc./(Exp.)	(8,255)	52,998	(1,860)	(41,473)	1,829	1,431	(5,243)	(6,237)	(5,629)	(8,924)	(8,812)	(42,533)
Pretax Income/(Loss)	(32,114)	(75,680)	(288,654)	(497,637)	(90,344)	(87,186)	(40,276)	(32,928)	(77,825)	8,077	(66,741)	(386,800)
	Note 2		Audited				Unaudited					

Note 1: Composition of 1987 Operating Expenses is estimated, however the total is audited.

Note 2: Unaudited estimates derived from CPA reviewed data (not GAAP certified) for GDR and its predecessor company. Predecessor's data has been shifted from a July 31 fiscal year to GDR's December 31 fiscal year via calendar proration.

(continued on next page)

	1984	1985	1986	1987	1988						
					Jan	Feb	March	April	May	June	July
ASSETS											
Current Assets											
Cash & equivalents	577	15,088	1,914	267,468	149,761	24,445	2,249	7,825	11,451	8,226	6,512
Accounts receivable											
Trade	22,883	7,907	6,345	29,670	35,639	52,987	148,515	195,002	133,238	234,342	168,293
Shareholder	(44,138)	48,629	0	0	253,000	253,000	203,000	150,000	100,000	0	0
Inventory	68,379	39,986	6,865	63,730	45,504	44,697	32,432	23,212	39,389	47,836	119,370
Prepaid expenses	0	0	2,663	5,692	4,218	4,218	4,218	4,639	16,389	4,859	13,445
Total cur. assets	47,701	111,610	17,787	366,560	488,122	379,347	390,414	380,678	300,467	295,263	307,620
Equip., furn., fixts.	4,730	8,441	19,134	20,583	20,483	20,815	22,573	21,573	21,573	28,643	34,496
Less accum. depr.	(718)	(2,160)	(1,151)	(5,126)	(1,941)	(1,971)	(1,977)	(2,007)	(2,287)	(2,287)	(2,587)
	4,012	6,281	17,983	15,457	18,542	18,844	20,596	19,566	19,286	26,356	31,909
Other Assets											
Org. cost net amort.	341	250	11,907	9,944	54,413	53,266	52,119	50,972	49,822	45,222	40,622
Patents	0	0	9,489	10,464	9,489	9,489	9,489	9,489	9,893	9,893	9,894
Total assets	52,054	118,141	57,166	402,425	570,566	490,946	472,618	460,705	379,468	376,734	390,045
	Note 3		Audited					Unaudited			

(continued on next page)

Note 3: Unaudited estimates derived from CPA reviewed data (not GAAP certified) for GDR and its predecessor company. Predecessor's data has been shifted from a July 31 fiscal year to GDR's December 31 fiscal year via calendar proration.

(continued)

	1984	1985	1986	1987	1988 Jan	Feb	March	April	May	June	July
LIABS. & CAPITAL DEFICIENCY											
Current Liabilities											
AP & accr. exp.	56,116	100,087	162,449	241,789	197,721	174,584	193,392	196,813	206,342	198,478	250,152
Notes payable—cur.	36,875	24,367	26,250	176,374	90,000	90,000	90,000	90,000	87,500	85,000	84,028
Cur. capital leases	0	0	4,352	5,420	5,874	5,874	5,874	5,874	5,875	5,875	5,875
Outstg. line of credit	0	0	0	0	0	0	35,000	50,000	40,000	40,000	70,000
Deferred revenue	0	0	0	999	999	1,700	0	0	0	0	0
Total cur. liabs.	92,991	124,454	193,051	424,582	294,594	272,158	324,266	342,687	339,717	329,353	410,055
Long-term bank debt	0	0	70,000	438,386	0	0	0	0	0	0	0
Capital leases	0	0	11,005	5,608	5,412	5,412	4,984	4,548	4,107	3,659	3,010
Total liabilities	92,991	124,454	274,056	868,576	300,006	277,570	329,250	347,235	343,824	333,012	413,065
STOCKHOLDERS' EQUITY											
Series A Convert., Voting PS	0	0	4,091	8,426	8,158	8,158	8,427	8,427	8,427	8,427	8,427
Addit. PIC PS	0	0	325,909	475,963	474,474	474,474	474,474	474,474	474,474	474,474	474,474
Addit. PIC PS optns.	0	0	0	93,987	0	0	0	0	0	0	0
CS $.10 par	800	100	5,000	5,000	5,000	5,000	5,000	5,928	5,928	5,928	5,928
Addit. PIC CS	0	0	5,490	5,490	5,490	5,490	5,490	7,593	7,593	7,593	7,593
Subordinated debt	0	0	0	0	850,000	850,000	850,000	850,000	850,000	850,000	850,000
Deficit accumulated	(41,737)	(5,009)	(557,380)	(1,055,017)	(1,072,560)	(1,159,746)	(1,200,022)	(1,232,950)	(1,310,775)	(1,302,698)	(1,369,439)
Total equity	(40,937)	(4,909)	(216,890)	(466,151)	270,562	183,376	143,369	113,472	35,647	43,724	(23,017)
Total liabs. & equity	52,054	119,545	57,166	402,425	570,568	460,946	472,619	460,707	379,471	376,736	390,048
	Note 4		Audited					Unaudited			

Note 4: Unaudited estimates derived from CPA reviewed data (not GAAP certified) for GDR and its predecessor company. Predecessor's data has been shifted from a July 31 fiscal year to GDR's December 31 fiscal year via calendar proration.

323

Exhibit 2
Georgia Digital Reproduction, Inc.
Corporate Mission Statement

Georgia Digital Reproduction, Inc., designs and markets record/playback digital equipment and related services for communications applications using innovative technologies resulting in flexible, cost-effective, energy-efficient products.

COMPANY OBJECTIVES

---

1. Build a long-term profitable company.
2. Work in a positive, growth-oriented environment.
3. Manage for and expect superior performance by everyone.
4. Exploit and maintain leadership in record/playback digital equipment technology applications.
5. Attain a reputation for commitment to quality of product and all business affairs.
6. Remain diversified in customers and vendors.
7. Sell products requiring installation and service through dealers/distributors except government agencies and corporate accounts.
8. Price products and services at standard (suggested retail) lists with standard discounts recognizing value in use and not commodity.

Source: GDR company records.

---

a higher selling price than a two-channel system with only "Taps" and "Reveille" capability. Prices varied also with the mechanical enclosure.

The most common application for TIS units was transmitting weather, parking, or other information on AM 530 or 1610 to motorists' radios along highways, in state and national parks, entering airports, and around university campuses. Roadside signs informed motorists of the radio-based service. These units had suggested list prices between $8,300 and $12,050 (see Exhibit 3).

Most of GDR's sales were direct from the home office; a growing volume, however, was coming through George Sherman, the Western Region sales manager in GDR's California office. Additionally, Stephen Naegle, GDR's

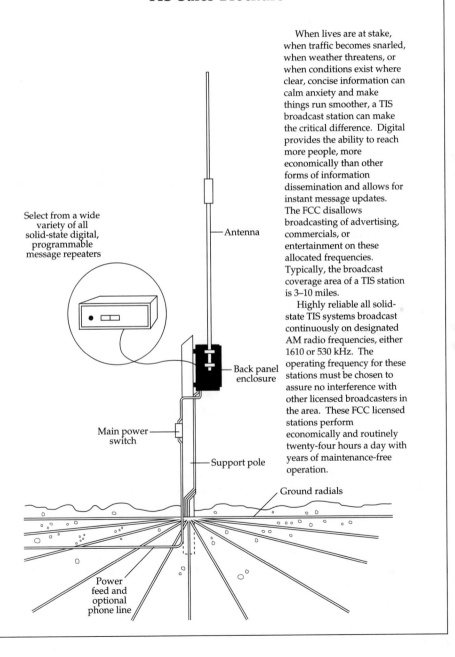

Exhibit 3
Georgia Digital Reproduction, Inc.
TIS Sales Brochure

When lives are at stake, when traffic becomes snarled, when weather threatens, or when conditions exist where clear, concise information can calm anxiety and make things run smoother, a TIS broadcast station can make the critical difference. Digital provides the ability to reach more people, more economically than other forms of information dissemination and allows for instant message updates. The FCC disallows broadcasting of advertising, commercials, or entertainment on these allocated frequencies. Typically, the broadcast coverage area of a TIS station is 3–10 miles.

Highly reliable all solid-state TIS systems broadcast continuously on designated AM radio frequencies, either 1610 or 530 kHz. The operating frequency for these stations must be chosen to assure no interference with other licensed broadcasters in the area. These FCC licensed stations perform economically and routinely twenty-four hours a day with years of maintenance-free operation.

Select from a wide variety of all solid-state digital, programmable message repeaters

Antenna

Back panel enclosure

Main power switch

Support pole

Ground radials

Power feed and optional phone line

director of national sales, was dedicated to building a dealer and distributor network. GDR had set minimum stocking and purchasing requirements for its distributors and dealers to maintain. Just recently it had received orders from two possible candidates—EBI of Florida, a trade-show booth and exhibit distributor, and Lyons Communications of California—and it had made a promising contact with American Communications, Inc. (ACI).

THE FAMILY BUSINESS

GDR's predecessor company had been founded in 1982 by Arthur Butler, now GDR's vice president of research and development. Arthur had been involved in audio electronics for more than 40 years and was experienced in radar, black-and-white and color TV, AM and FM broadcasting, computer peripherals, and telephone equipment. He anticipated a demand for TIS units in 1982 shortly after the Federal Communications Commission (FCC) authorized two AM radio channels to be used as TIS channels for transmission of voice information, but not music, to travelers in a three to five mile radius. These channels could be licensed only to government agencies. Butler designed the TIS units for this emerging market.

This new company, consisting of Butler, his daughter Barbara Gibson, and her husband Phillip, designed the first 10-watt AM TIS unit and started selling it. Butler did the design and engineering work, Barbara handled marketing and sales activities, and Phillip flew all over the country installing the units.

In most early applications, TIS transmitters got their signals from continuous-play cassette players manufactured by other companies. The nonstop wear caused frequent cassette failures and necessitated expensive maintenance and repair trips. Many units were in remote locations. In late 1982, Butler responded by designing a digital recorder/player using 64K dynamic RAM (random access memory) chips. GDR was incorporated as a sister company in early 1983 to handle the redesigned digital recorder/player product line. It also was operated by Butler and his team. A digital recorder sales brochure is shown in Exhibit 4.

Butler spent most of 1983 designing a console for the National Oceanic & Atmospheric Administration (NOAA). This unit could play weather reports to eight incoming phone calls simultaneously. NOAA had promised to buy four but took delivery of only one console. No other applications of this product were developed.

Late in 1984, GDR greatly improved the digital recorders by incorporating 64K static RAMS (SRAMs). With the addition of a small lithium battery, SRAMs retained the recorded messages through power outages. Various SRAM-based products were sold to national and state parks, the U.S. Department of Transportation, the U.S. Army Corps of Engineers, and several national and international airports. Most products had unique features to meet individual customers' needs. Although revenues doubled every year—

Exhibit 4
Georgia Digital Reproduction, Inc.
Digital Recorder Sales Brochure

DR410 and DR420
W2
Models Are Complete Solid-State Recorder/Players in Compact Aluminum Housings

Change messages yourself. Here is compact flexibility that puts audio where you need it. Featuring a rugged, all-aluminum housing and simple controls, the W2 fits almost anywhere and can be ordered with memory of a few seconds to over ten minutes.

The DR-W2 features:
- Multiple message stacking
- User programming without specialized equipment
- Adjustable sampling frequency from 2.5 kHz to 10 kHz
- High-quality sound reproduction
- Memory protection for power outages and storage
- Economical design with attractive pricing
- Unsurpassed power efficiencies at 12 VDC

The DR-W2 comes complete with an 8-ohm stand-alone speaker and a UL listed 110 VDC power converter. Functions include a start switch, audio-in plug, record/play mode switch, power jack, and wiring position bus for speaker and remote start. An ultrasonic sensing kit is available as an option to automatically activate the unit by detecting motion in the sensor range.

DR410 and DR420
OEM
Products Easily Conform to New or Retrofit Environments

Assembled board-level products are available on all DR410 and DR420 components to incorporate with or add on to existing products.

All board-level products have been tested and carefully packaged for easy handling and safe storage. Board-to-board connectors and simple cabling are included to make a complete player/recorder.

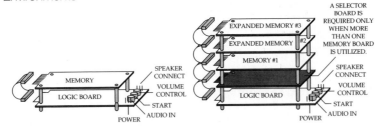

1983, $42,000; 1984, $94,000; and 1985, $178,500 (fiscal year ending on July 31)—the company continued to run a deficit.

THE FIRST ADMINISTRATION

Venture Capital

Realizing that they lacked the resources for a major marketing effort, Butler and Phillip and Barbara Gibson decided to find outside capital. Barbara Gibson spent the last few months of 1985 writing a business plan for presentation at the 1985 Georgia Venture Fair. Their talking Kellogg's Corn Flakes box was the major attraction, and they initiated discussions with Southeast Venture Partners, a prominent venture-capital firm in Atlanta. In early 1986, Southeast agreed to invest $330,000 in June 1986, followed by $100,000 at the beginning of 1987, for partial ownership of GDR, provided that Butler consolidate all operations into GDR, assume the vice presidency of R&D, and recruit a new president.

GDR Staffs Up

During 1986, GDR hired five key employees. Sean Knox accepted the presidency after 14 years in the furniture industry. He had successfully started one company and turned around four others. Stephen Naegle was hired as vice president of sales and marketing. He had 10 years in the banking industry and 4 years marketing and selling corporate communication programs. The vice president of manufacturing position was filled by Vernon Simms, a long-time friend of Butler's who had 20 years' experience with ITT Telecom, CTI Data, NCR, and Control Data. Margaret Guthrie came on board as controller and chief financial officer. She was a CPA with 5 years in public accounting, 2 years as general accounting supervisor for a CAD/CAM workstation manufacturer, and 2 years as corporate accounting manager for a musical instrument manufacturer. Finally, John Bailey became TIS national sales manager.

Because of the restructuring, GDR finished fiscal 1986 with revenues of $80,000 ($23,000 for the last five months of calendar 1986 as the company shifted its fiscal year to the calendar year). GDR's resulting organization is shown in Exhibit 5.

The Big Account Targets

Under Sean Knox's leadership, GDR targeted high-potential accounts. Knox and Stephen Naegle made cold calls themselves; however, these efforts required considerable travel, which depleted much of GDR's cash. As these

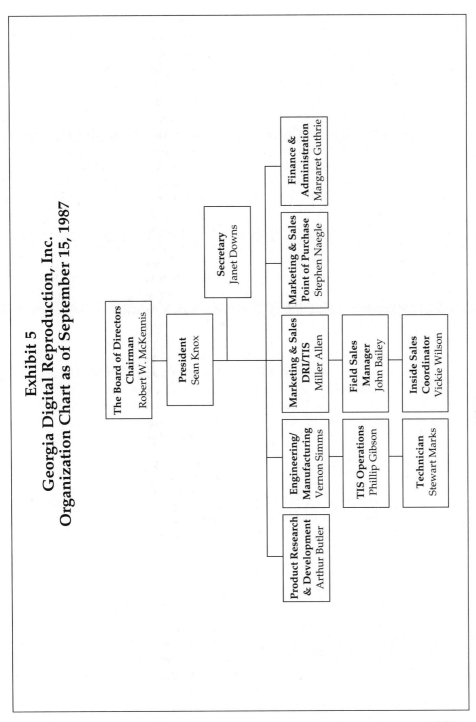

**Exhibit 5
Georgia Digital Reproduction, Inc.
Organization Chart as of September 15, 1987**

The Board of Directors
Chairman
Robert W. McKennis

President
Sean Knox

Secretary
Janet Downs

Product Research
& Development
Arthur Butler

Engineering/
Manufacturing
Vernon Simms

Marketing & Sales
DRI/TIS
Miller Allen

Marketing & Sales
Point of Purchase
Stephen Naegle

Finance &
Administration
Margaret Guthrie

TIS Operations
Phillip Gibson

Field Sales
Manager
John Bailey

Technician
Stewart Marks

Inside Sales
Coordinator
Vickie Wilson

excursions continued, Sean Knox's management style was increasingly seen by many as autocratic. He held few meetings to discuss plans or results.

As part of this effort, GDR first pursued the point-of-purchase (POP) advertising boom. POP advertising was already a $9 billion market, of which $25 million was electronic, and experts expected the electronic segment to expand to $200 million by 1990. The POP revolution was accelerating; consumers were apparently making more of their buying decisions in stores.

GDR approached several large consumer-goods companies to demonstrate its digital recording and playback technology as an enhancement to retail displays. GDR's appeal was that audio inducements similar to the talking Kellogg's Corn Flakes box could spur sales. After much effort, GDR presented the idea to Coca Cola's southeast regional sales manager, whose only response was a letter to the district sales managers suggesting that they share the idea with their advertising agencies. Anheuser-Busch had a similar reaction. No sales resulted.

Fortunately, other marketing efforts expanded the company's base of sales, and during the first half of 1987, GDR sold digital recorders to many new customers. These included Anchorage National Park, The Tennessee Valley Authority, Fort Bragg (U.S. Army), King's Dominion, Sea World of Florida, The Raleigh-Durham Airport, and a number of state transportation departments. Although sales grew rapidly, expenses ballooned.

To bolster its marketing effort, GDR split the marketing and sales department in mid-1987 by making Stephen Naegle vice president of POP and hiring Miller Allen to be vice president of GDR/TIS. Allen had nine years of experience with three advertising and marketing companies in New York City and eight years as an independent communications and marketing consultant. Vickie Wilson was also hired as the marketing manager. She was responsible for proposal and quotation coordination, customer order entry and expediting, distribution of general sales and product literature, product price lists, and discount schedules. The increased salary expense was supported by an additional $100,000 from Southeast and by a $200,000 line of credit with Georgia Republic Bank backed by letters of credit from GDR's shareholders.

A New Business Plan

The third quarter of 1987 introduced a shift in GDR's marketing strategy. Instead of approaching the POP market directly, GDR opted to develop alliances with other firms active in the field. In July GDR signed a contract with Intermark, a leader in state-of-the-art POP marketing systems, selling all rights to GDR's technology for both domestic and international marketing to Intermark for $60,000. Sean Knox (president) negotiated the entire contract, and neither of the sales vice presidents, Miller Allen and Stephen Naegle, were consulted about the contract, nor had either of them seen the agreement.

The Intermark alliance affected only one of the six market segments that GDR had described in its revised business plan dated October 1, 1987.

The second segment cited in the business plan was Short Range Broadcasting (SRB). If a TIS unit transmitted at .1W instead of 10W, it could cover about a ¼-mile radius; thus, it would not need licensing from the FCC and could use voice, music, or commercials. One application would be a "talking house" for the real-estate market. An independent source had estimated the market to be 190,000 realty offices with 20 active listings, on average, yielding a $760-million market.

The third segment was the elevator and fire alarm industry. Although little market data were available, the applications were numerous. Several recently built hotels had talking elevators. Busch Gardens in Tampa, Florida, had already bought several digital recorders for fire alarms and voice evacuation directions.

The fourth segment was the transportation industry. This segment included 16,319 airports worldwide, bus stations, train stations, shuttle buses, tramways, and other mass transit. For example, in an airport, TIS transmitters could direct automobiles as they entered parking lots, and digital recorders could announce public information on the shuttle busses. These airport applications could easily reach $15 million. GDR saw great promise in this market segment, because through one of its major customers, the New York/New Jersey Port Authority, the company had made direct contact with Hudson General Management Corp., one of the largest firms in the United States managing transportation facilities.

The fifth market segment, government entities, was the prime target for TIS units. The Army Corps of Engineers operated 600 lakes and dams and hundreds of waterway projects, each a possible TIS installation. Additionally, the 197 domestic military bases were prime candidates for new multichannel digital recorders to replace the old cassette bugle systems. There were also more than 1,000 national and state parks that could need TIS units, and each of the 380 U.S. Weather Service offices could use $9 million to $11 million in consoles like the one sold in 1984. Also considered in this segment were the 105 nuclear power plants in the United States, the 220 foreign operating plants, and the 176 plants under construction worldwide, in which digital recorders could be installed to expedite evacuations.

The final market segment was replacement of the installed base of cassette players manufactured by other companies. The national parks had at least 10,000 of these older units, but GDR had not explored this segment extensively.

Progress and Disappointment

By the end of 1987, sales had expanded to $347,765 through shipments to customers like the University of North Carolina for the U.S. Olympic Festival.

This festival introduced Richard Taylor to GDR. He had spent 14 years coordinating the safety and transportation aspects of special events such as the 1987 Olympic Festival. When the festival ended in September 1987, Taylor began work for GDR.

The sales growth in 1987 enabled the company to assume $750,000 in debt toward the end of the year, but new problems arose. Personality clashes caused the resignation of Sean Knox, Vernon Simms (vice president, manufacturing), John Bailey (national sales manager), and Barbara Gibson (founder Arthur Butler's daughter) in November and December of 1987. After conducting a search for a new president, GDR's board of directors promoted Richard Taylor to the position.

The business plan Taylor inherited had been designed for $1 million in equity, but in reality was funded with $750,000 of debt. Not only did Taylor face $250,000 less in capital than planned and accrued liabilities from Knox's excursions, but GDR was also saddled with the interest expense and the cash drain of the debt.

THE SECOND ADMINISTRATION

Product-Line Expansion

Taylor's attention turned toward expanding GDR's product line. Early in 1988 Arthur Butler and Carol Campbell, a young electrical engineer, designed, prototyped, and built 19 multichannel digital recording units. Products in this new DR460 family used 256K SRAM memory chips and could store and play up to 16 different 45-second messages. All 19 units were shipped to the New York/New Jersey Port Authority for installation in buses. Although Campbell was pleased with the successful effort, she was troubled because time had not allowed adequate lab testing of the new design. Exhibit 6 shows a brochure for this product.

Next, Arthur Butler interfaced an electronic timer to a DR460 unit and created a replacement for worn-out cassette bugle systems at military bases. He also designed a dial-up interface for the TIS transmitters. Now, instead of being delivered physically to the TIS location, new messages could be phoned to the TIS unit. This enhancement gave GDR the broad line of products shown in Exhibit 7.

The Competitive Situation

The electronic basis of GDR's products gave them several inherent advantages over mechanical cassette systems. The digital recorders were more power efficient, more reliable, and virtually maintenance free with no degradation of sound quality, because no parts or tapes wore out. Users of digital recorders did not have to store, duplicate, or replace tapes; moreover, the wait

Exhibit 6
Georgia Digital Reproduction, Inc.
Multichannel Sales Brochure

Multi-Channel Message Dispatch System
MODEL DR-464

The efficient way to solve transportation information problems

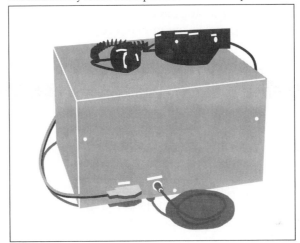

Features:
- All solid-state.
- No tapes to break, replace, or clean.
- Fool-proof operator console.
- Multiple language capability.
- User reprogrammable.
- No anticipated maintenance or service, ever!
- One-year warranty on parts and labor.
- Battery supported memory.
- Crisp, clear sound reproduction.
- No rewinding.
- Compact size.

For use on
- Busses
- Trains/subway cars
- Trams
- Excursion boarts/ferries
- People movers
- Monorails

This truly outstanding messaging system is the only all solid-state recorder/player specifically designed for on-vehicle use. Busses, trains, trams, and people movers now have a compact energy efficient way to communicate with passengers thanks to our digital audio technology.

Permanent messages or on-site reprogramming allows the user flexibility never before available for mass transit vehicles. Messages may be loaded by microphone, cassette player, or through our optional, special high-speed digital loader.

The Model DR-464 may be ordered with any number of channels, to a maximum of 16, and has the capacity to store up to 11 minutes per channel of accumulated message time. Each channel is selectable by dialing the channel number on the remote driver console and the message is activated with a simple push of the start button.

All solid-state technology is your assurance of high performance, reliability, and years of maintenance free operation. The Model DR-464 has been carefully designed to withstand shock and vibration and all electronic components are housed in an all-aluminum and weather-resistant case. Nothing on the market today can compare in size, audio quality, and overall performance.

(continued on next page)

(continued)

Multi-Channel Message Dispatch System
Model DR-462

TECHNICAL SPECIFICATIONS

Audio:

Input: In record, –5 dbm @ 600 Ohm unbalanced

Output: low impedance for speakers, 10-watt audio power

Operation environment: –30°C to 75°C

Power requirements: 1.5 watts plus audio power to 10 watts 12 VDC nominal

Dimensions: Electronic cabinet: 17⅜" × 10⅜" × 16"

Console: 6.5" × 1.9" × 6.5"

Memory: Type: 256K Static RAM (CMOS)

Capacity per board: 8 memory chips per board

Number of boards (memory): max. of 16 bds. per channel and 16 channels per system

Battery to support memory: 3VDC Lithium Battery

Board size: Logic Board: 13⅜" × 2⅛"

Memory Board: 13" × 3" × ½"

---

for cassette tapes to rewind was eliminated, because GDR's electronic products instantaneously reset to the message's beginning for replay.

The company's products were built from commercially available components, but GDR was the only company combining these particular technologies. The 12-volt power requirement allowed installation of GDR products in transportation vehicles; a small battery let the SRAMs retain their data when the ignition was off.

Few cost-competitive products existed in either GDR's TIS or digital recorder markets, but several companies sold substitute products that met the various customer needs GDR was attempting to meet. Three companies— Vari-Tech, McKenzie Laboratories, and 360 Systems—offered alternatives to cassette players. Thirteen other companies manufactured products for related applications and could be drawn into GDR's market if the potential continued to materialize.

GDR faced stiff competition in one arena: TIS sales to government agencies such as national parks. Government sales were almost always by sealed

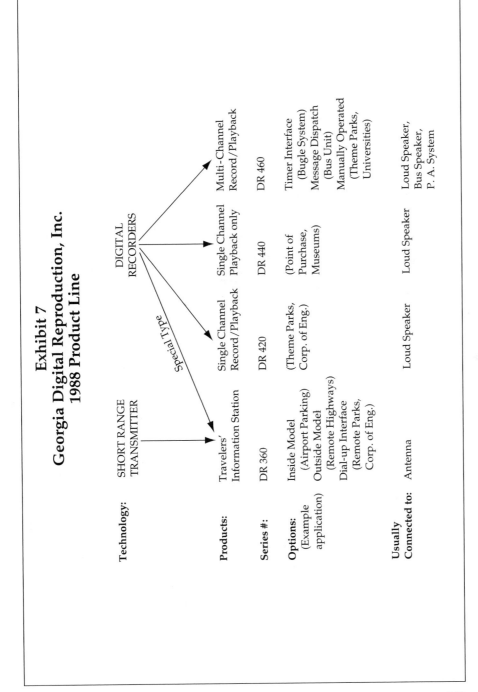

Exhibit 7
Georgia Digital Reproduction, Inc.
1988 Product Line

	SHORT RANGE TRANSMITTER	DIGITAL RECORDERS		
Technology:				
		Special Type		
Products:	Travelers' Information Station	Single Channel Record/Playback	Single Channel Playback only	Multi-Channel Record/Playback
Series #:	DR 360	DR 420	DR 440	DR 460
Options: (Example application)	Inside Model (Airport Parking) Outside Model (Remote Highways) Dial-up Interface (Remote Parks, Corp. of Eng.)	(Theme Parks, Corp. of Eng.)	(Point of Purchase, Museums)	Timer Interface (Bugle System) Message Dispatch (Bus Unit) Manually Operated (Theme Parks, Universities)
Usually Connected to:	Antenna	Loud Speaker	Loud Speaker	Loud Speaker, Bus Speaker, P. A. System

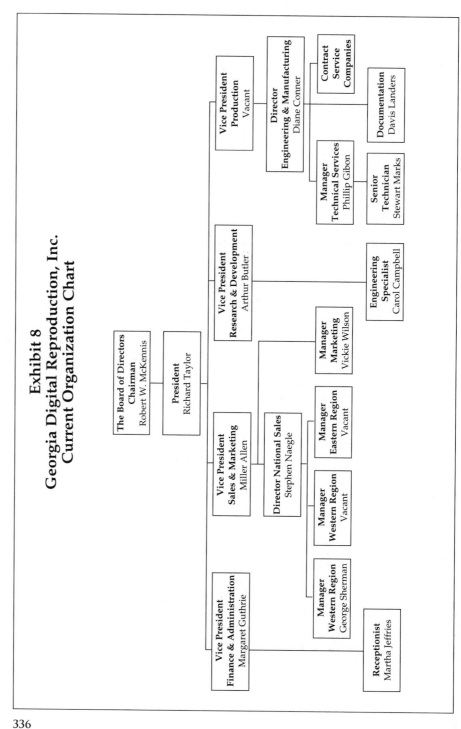

Exhibit 8
Georgia Digital Reproduction, Inc.
Current Organization Chart

The Board of Directors
Chairman
Robert W. McKennis

President
Richard Taylor

Vice President
Finance & Administration
Margaret Guthrie

Vice President
Sales & Marketing
Miller Allen

Vice President
Research & Development
Arthur Butler

Vice President
Production
Vacant

Manager
Western Region
George Sherman

Receptionist
Martha Jeffries

Director National Sales
Stephen Naegle

Manager
Western Region
Vacant

Manager
Eastern Region
Vacant

Manager
Marketing
Vickie Wilson

Engineering
Specialist
Carol Campbell

Director
Engineering & Manufacturing
Diane Conner

Manager
Technical Services
Phillip Gibon

Contract
Service
Companies

Documentation
Davis Landers

Senior
Technician
Stewart Marks

bids and were awarded on price after a three- to six-month wait. ISS, a one-man distributorship in Michigan, competed strictly on price, 30 percent of GDR's price. A recent GDR study concluded that only $24,000 worth of the $300,000 of product put out to bid in 1988 was actually awarded. Although ISS got all of the bids, the dollar value was relatively low.

To address ISS's aggressive approach, Richard Taylor had sent a letter suggesting that ISS become a GDR distributor. Taylor was disappointed by ISS's reply, which cited poor ethics by GDR prior to Taylor's arrival, when GDR had distributed ISS literature copied on GDR letterhead. Sean Knox had halted the counterfeited literature distribution only after ISS's legal counsel sent a letter. Taylor responded with a letter explaining GDR's personnel changes, but he received no response.

Events during the Summer of 1988

As he contemplated GDR's strategic needs in August 1988, Taylor thought back to the past summer. GDR's cumulative loss for the year through July 31 was $386,800 and growing because sales were significantly below forecast. The October 1, 1987, business plan had forecasted $461,000 year-to-date sales with Intermark. In reality, Intermark sales had been less than $5,000. Taylor's summer communications with Intermark had been futile, so he did not know why Intermark had placed no significant orders. Excluding expected Intermark revenues, GDR sales were down only 3 percent from the forecast.

One bright spot during the summer was the hiring of Diane Conner, with more than ten years' experience in inventory control, as director of engineering and manufacturing. (See Exhibit 8 for latest organization chart.) Within three months with GDR, she had devised a part-numbering system, organized all GDR's inventory, started qualified-vendors lists, and was working toward incorporating the part-numbering scheme into engineering. (GDR had some bills of material, but they weren't integrated into the inventory system, nor were part numbers on any schematics.) She was also responsible for planning and coordinating GDR's production subcontractor, Electronic Circuits, Inc. (ECI). This responsibility required visits to ECI and the writing and distribution of a weekly report.

During the summer, GDR had sent letters similar to Exhibit 9 to the commanders of 25 U.S. Army bases. Four responded with orders for bugle systems, DR460s. When the purchasing officer at one fort requested that the unit include battery backup, GDR's sales representative saw nothing unusual and shipped the order with the standard battery backup that enabled the message memory to be maintained through power outages. In reality, the fort wanted the clock/calendar chip battery backed up to maintain time and date through power failures also. That request required a top-priority design change by Butler.

Exhibit 9
Georgia Digital Reproduction, Inc.
Example of Direct-Mail Letter to Army Base

Georgia Digital Reproduction, Inc.
2110-15 Technology Dr.
Norcross, GA 30092

August 18, 1987

Captain David Jenkins
Base Commander
Northside Army Ammunition Plant
P. O. Box 3258
Northside, CA 95637

Reference: Solid State Bugle Calls

Dear Captain Jenkins:

I'd like to introduce you to a concept that is revolutionizing the way the U.S. Army wakes up each morning. Georgia Digital Reproduction, Inc., Model 460 Multi-Channel Digital Recorder/Player automatically plays bugle calls at predetermined times, day after day, year after year—it even calculates for leap year!

All solid-state technology means no maintainance and no repair. Standard audio connections make our player directly suitable to match with existing public address or amplifier systems. Low power requirements allow for convenient auxiliary battery back-up during any power outages.

You may select only the bugle calls you use most or an entire set of all the official U.S. Army calls.

For more information on how you can get your base up on time, please call (404) 834-1733.

Regards,

Vickie Wilson
Vickie Wilson
Inside Sales Coordinator

MA/vw

There were other sales-order problems. Once Stephen Naegle quoted a DR460 based on 64K SRAMs, but GDR had upgraded to 256K SRAMs six months previously. Another problem occurred when an order of DR460s was taken on July 12 for Anaheim, California. The city wanted the units with dial-up control; GDR promised shipment by July 30, but the dial-up control circuitry had not yet been designed for the DR460. This caused another panic design effort by Butler.

To Carol Campbell, Butler's engineering specialist, every unit being sold seemed to be a "custom sales job." Even when the salespeople talked to Butler in advance about a possible order, the problems persisted. Campbell explained the situation as "Arthur says yes to whatever sales says, but sales doesn't ask or say what they should, because they don't know what to ask or say." In a separate conversation, Miller Allen said, "Maybe we just need a better list of questions to ask our customers." Campbell saw it differently: "Sales thinks they know the product; all they really know is what it used to be."

In another incident, a TIS order for the U.S. Army Corp of Engineers had been quoted, and the Corps was very pleased with the price. As Phillip Gibon (manager of technical services) assembled the order, however, he realized the quote included only the enclosure, the transmitter, and a filter board. The power supply, the audio processor board, and the back panel had all been omitted. In the rush to correct the order by the January 1 shipping date, the wrong frequency option was shipped.

GDR's problems were not restricted to booking and shipping orders. GDR had sold four bugle systems, but difficulties with three of them required Campbell's help at the army bases. No major technical issues had to be resolved; the army personnel simply could not program the timer that triggered the bugle calls because GDR had shipped the bugle systems with no documentation. The expense of Campbell's trips had not been included in the prices quoted.

The technical side of GDR also had problems. Butler had incorporated several design changes without considering the cost and scheduling impact. Since most communication with ECI, the manufacturing subcontractor, was verbal, GDR had little documentation of these changes or of overall product design. As the situation worsened, Taylor requested that ECI be paid only for those items on official GDR purchase orders issued by Diane Conner, which improved her control over the manufacturing process.

GDR'S CURRENT SITUATION

After reviewing the development of Georgia Digital, Taylor began to think through the company's current operations and strategy.

Product Design and Manufacturing

Arthur Butler did the initial design and breadboarding (a quick method of physically verifying a paper design). The verified design was then given to Dixie Circuits in Marietta, Georgia, for circuit-board layout and prototype building. After Butler tested and approved the prototypes, the design was given to ECI for manufacture.

ECI operated in a store front in Roswell, Georgia, and all product was built by hand. Most of the company's employees were experienced electronics assemblers and worked at ECI as a second job in the evenings. ECI had been in business for three years and had six customers; GDR and General Electric made up most of the company's business. ECI bought most of the parts used to assemble GDR products.

Marketing

In July 1988, GDR had hired a recent college graduate to test-market a .1W FM transmitter/tape player manufactured by a third party for "talking house" applications. The long-term goal would be to penetrate the real estate market and then upgrade the customers to digital recorders. If the effort was successful, GDR would act as a distributor. The unit would sell for about $350.

For TIS sales, Taylor thought from his experience with universities, a direct mailing to large universities would be an effective addition to government sales. By the end of this month, August 1988, Marketing Manager Vickie Wilson would send out letters to 50 universities in California and Texas. September's mailing would promote bugle systems to Air Force bases, and October's would target more universities.

Other efforts to develop distribution of GDR products were not progressing. The opportunity with ACI of Detroit to coordinate alarm and safety equipment had bogged down this week. The national sales manager of ACI had visited GDR and informed the company that ACI was still interested but needed more time. The information was disappointing, because Naegle and Allen had just spent a week in Chicago at a kickoff meeting for ACI dealers. Fortunately, ACI had given GDR approval to work directly with ACI's six largest dealers.

A new market opportunity had recently arisen in discussions with one of the nation's largest aircraft manufacturers. The Federal Aviation Administration's recent announcement requiring installation of cockpit voice recorders (CVRs) in all existing and newly manufactured commuter aircraft had prompted this company to approach GDR. Both companies thought a viable digital solid-state CVR (DSSCVR) could be developed, and the aircraft company had sent GDR a letter of understanding describing possible DSSCVR products and initial specifications. The letter stated, "Physical size is an important consideration." Taylor thought that GDR could have a prototype by the end of January 1989.

Stephen Naegle, the national sales director, estimated that the commuter aircraft market for DSSCVRs could be 10,000 units worth $20 million and that the commercial aircraft market was four times larger. The pilots' preflight checklist and the stewardesses' well-known monologues could also be done by a digital recorder.

Naegle had also contacted the Naval Air Command concerning DSSCVRs and was progressing on a proposal. According to the usual schedule for such projects, GDR would deliver the first prototypes to the Navy in mid-1991. Naegle's thoughts on the project were, "You can never have it too small. . . . I can't see any down side . . . and technologically I think we're pretty much there."

Employees

Taylor's thoughts shifted from GDR's marketing efforts to the strengths and weaknesses of the staff (see Exhibit 8 for current organization). Recently he had discussed with Marketing Manager Vickie Wilson the need to stay focused on the tasks delegated to her. She had been letting several priorities slide and had been repeatedly making small but important errors. Some of the difficulty with Wilson was attributable to her boss Miller Allen's management style.

Although Allen delegated well, he often failed to check on progress. His previous experience as a consultant helped him develop good sales literature and nurture relationships with customers, but it had not required extensive supervisory effort. He was also able to set up deals, but he could not consistently close them.

Both Allen and Stephen Naegle would often close customers sales by offering discounts. Not only could this upset current and future dealers and distributors, it also lowered GDR's margins. Taylor wanted to price GDR's products by value to the customer, not cost multiples and discounts.

Naegle had slightly different characteristics from Allen. He managed his subordinates better and was also adept at "managing" superiors. He was a good, responsive team player. He built customer relationships well and could close almost any sale to an interested buyer, but he lacked experience in closing tough sales and in negotiating. Unfortunately, he also aggravated the technical staff by making design suggestions.

GDR had a very talented R&D engineer in Arthur Butler, but because GDR had no manager of production, Butler was overly involved in manufacturing coordination. Administration was not Butler's forte, and he candidly didn't want that responsibility. Moreover, Butler was not concerned with career development; he wanted to work with what he loved—product design and development. Instead, he had to coordinate manufacturing situations, which did not fit his background. He preferred that Carol Campbell attend the recently instituted weekly staff meetings as the R&D/engineering representative. Taylor viewed this situation not as a shortcoming in Butler's abilities but as a problem in company staffing.

Campbell's attendance at staff meetings had two disadvantages. She often needed to discuss technical situations with Butler before replying to questions, and she became defensive in discussions concerning product design problems. Although Campbell was an eager contributor, she was fairly new to the company and did not have the technical base that would substitute for Butler's.

Phillip Gibson, the manager of technical services, was a contrast to Campbell. As one of the original three founders, Gibson had grown with GDR. He was an excellent broadcast engineer and was critical to the support of the TIS product line, which he knew better than anyone else.

Recently much of the administrative work had been handled by Diane Conner in engineering and manufacturing. Although Conner had done a superb job organizing GDR's inventory and establishing a part-numbering system, Taylor had been disappointed with her supervisory capabilities. She was a superb doer but was overwhelmed by the management of three subordinates and GDR's contract relationships.

When Taylor had succeeded Sean Knox as president of Georgia Digital, he realized that everyone was doing everyone else's job. Taylor's priority was to focus each employee on his or her own talents, skills, job, and responsibilities.

FUTURE COURSE

Taylor knew that the cash crunch at Georgia Digital was very real. Margaret Guthrie had done almost everything possible to ease it. She had negotiated with ECI to stretch the $80,000 due ECI on August 31 to $10,000 due every two weeks. She was discussing factoring GDR's receivables, which would provide an additional rolling line of credit for 90 percent of everything under 90 days, capped at $200,000. Despite Guthrie's efforts, however, both she and Taylor were concerned that, unless GDR's cash position improved, the company might have difficulty making future payrolls. Taylor knew that any major changes would need approval of GDR's board of directors.

GDR under Richard Taylor had a very open atmosphere, and people freely expressed their opinions. He decided to seek clues to a strategy for GDR in some of the points his staff had made.

- Diane Conner (engineering and manufacturing) was surprised at the lack of manufacturing experience in the company.

- Margaret Guthrie (finance) felt that the toughest thing to handle was changing priorities coming from several people.

- Phillip Gibon (technical services) stated, "Marketing doesn't know enough to sell the products or even write up an order. None of them have electronic backgrounds."

- Carol Campbell (electrical engineering) noted, "At one point in time, sales was selling stuffed printed circuit boards, and all of a sudden we had a system."

- Conner's summation was, "The circuitry's all done. Our packaging needs to be improved. Documentation needs to be done. Basically the back end is unfinished."

- Stephen Naegle (director of national sales) seemed unsure: "I really haven't had a problem with missed orders. . . . It's helter skelter back there."

- Campbell said, "Marketing is constantly asking us to make up this and that. I don't know what they are doing with all those sample units. Maybe they are leaving them with customers."

- Guthrie felt GDR needed to be poised for a big manufacturing hit.

- Naegle explained the custom-order tendency: "We always did it that way; any sale is seductive."

- Campbell warned, "We need to be aware of sending prototypes to customers. Boards with jumpers [wires added to correct design errors] are not reliable."

- Naegle also expressed a word of warning: "We know some needs; needs are not markets."

- Guthrie thought, "We need to build to inventory, but we can't take the inventory-obsolescence risk unless the market and application solidifies."

- Naegle acknowledged that "developing a distributor/dealer network is labor intensive and tough."

- Campbell showed her foresight: "What's going to happen when Arthur Butler leaves?"

- Naegle expressed his slant: "I'm on the road trying to book that one big piece of business."

- Miller Allen (vice president of sales and marketing) stated the challenge as "selling new products to new environs for new customers."

INTERNATIONAL COLOUR
ENVELOPE ADVISORS A/S

Never prostitute yourself for the sake of business.
Never do something if you do not believe in it.

Gorm Kristiansen, 1992

Gorm Kristiansen sat at his desk looking out of the window at the summer rain. He was contemplating the future of the company he had worked so hard to build. The financial situation of International Colour Envelope Advisors A/S (ICEA) was tight: ICEA was growing too quickly; he was unable to buy the machinery necessary to fill all of the orders that ICEA could possibly generate; and getting loans in Denmark was very difficult because the economy was not healthy and many small businesses had failed. If Kristiansen could not get the working capital he needed, he might have to consider making a public offering of ICEA stock—an option he would rather not have to think about right now. Kristiansen preferred to retain his 100-percent control of ICEA.

Coupled with the financial dilemma was the problem that growth had caused in the company's culture. The culture that was appropriate for a small living room–based enterprise might not be appropriate for the growth opportunities ICEA now faced. The business had started out with 3 people but had grown to 72. What sorts of changes would have to be made for ICEA to remain successful? Could the informality of the ICEA workplace be maintained?

COMPANY HISTORY

Kristiansen had started out as a partner in a small company in Pandrup, Denmark, that sold printed business forms. In the course of day-to-day business, he had met several individuals who were involved in the photo-processing industry. Kristiansen had learned that this industry was particularly lucrative and had decided to look for ways to enter into it. He and his partners had decided to buy photo wallets and film mailers from an Austrian

---

This case was prepared by Maria Holcomb, Darden MBA 1993, under the supervision of L. J. Bourgeois. Copyright © 1994 by the University of Virginia Darden School Foundation, Charlottesville, VA. All rights reserved.

company, then sell them to photo processors. By 1979, the photo side of Kristiansen's business accounted for 60 percent of the company's turnover and 80 percent of its profits. Kristiansen was the only one of the partners taking care of the photo business, so he wanted to split the company up and take on the photo business himself. Nevertheless, he owned only 12½ percent of the company's shares. He stated that "my partners ended up kicking me out of the business entirely."

Kristiansen had to start all over again and build a business from scratch. In 1980, Kristiansen decided to start his own company to target the photo-wallet and film-mailer market. He named it International Colour Envelope Advisors (ICEA). Kristiansen worked out of his home as an agent once again, buying mailers and photo wallets from the same Austrian company he had dealt with before. He had two persons working with him: one worked in the living room, another in the children's room; meetings were held in the kitchen. Soon no space was left unclaimed in the house.

ICEA began by selling to Scandinavian photo processors. At the time, it competed with six to eight suppliers, including Kristiansen's old partners. Two years into his business, Kristiansen had become successful enough to dominate the Scandinavian wallet-and-mailer market, which caused his former partners to exit the business, along with many smaller suppliers of these products. Kristiansen credited his highly targeted strategy for this success. Photo mailers and wallets were not the other companies' essential business, so they had not felt overly threatened by Kristiansen's presence there and had been willing to let him dominate this small segment of the market. Kristiansen's success, however, did lead to a backlash from his Austrian supplier, Paka. Paka not only sold supplies to agents like Kristiansen but also had direct customers within the photo-processing business. Suddenly, Paka found itself in a predicament: Kristiansen was able to buy product from Paka and sell it to his customers at a much higher price than Paka was selling to its direct customers. (Kristiansen attributed his ability to command higher prices to the excellent relationships he built with his customers.) Kristiansen was earning so much money that Paka raised its price level to him. This increase put pressure on Kristiansen's margins, which meant that Kristiansen had to create an alternative to keep Paka from increasing its prices further. In 1982, Kristiansen decided to begin producing the mailers and wallets himself.

"I just wanted to have a small amount of production to keep them [Paka] quiet. This was a strategic move on my part," recalled Kristiansen. "I got a partner who would take care of the production management, and I handled the sales. I brought in another person as the company's accountant to handle all of the financial details."

Kristiansen applied for a government loan to pay for his first machinery. The loan was granted and production began. Once production began, however, Kristiansen discovered that, in order to make a profit, he would have to run high-scale production, which meant that he no longer needed to buy from Paka at all. Suddenly, Paka retaliated by beginning to push its products heavily in the Scandinavian market. In response, ICEA attacked Paka's other European markets. ICEA would soon become a dominant force in the marketplace.

THE PHOTO MARKET IN EUROPE

The European photo market was characterized by the demand created by consumers' need for developed film, which led to laboratories' and dealers' need for processing products, including photo mailers and envelopes. Photo mailers were the special envelopes used to send exposed rolls of film from the photo dealer to the processing lab. Photo envelopes were the colorful envelopes used to return the processed photographs to the consumer. In this business, prosperity depended a great deal on consumers' desire to take pictures.

In Europe, the principal markets for photo supplies were experiencing a rise in demand for pictures, measured in terms of exposed film, of 2 percent to 5 percent a year. Because the proliferation of dealers and labs in Europe offered consumers more choice, consumers were beginning to demand better service and quality from photographic suppliers. Dealers and processors had to find ways to differentiate themselves so they could stay in business, and they put emphasis on the quality of the finished product, price, quick development, safe delivery, and personal service.

The advent of new technologies such as CDs, videos, and computers was not expected to impact the market for paper prints to any great extent. Because of this expectation, large photo producers such as Kodak were spending millions of dollars to build factories that produced regular films for exposure. Suppliers to the photo market, however, needed to be aware that new technologies existed that might come into play in the future.

Within the photo-processing industry, an increasing number of mergers and acquisitions of photo labs were taking place, resulting in large chains of photo laboratories across Europe. Many of the acquisitions were done by multinational photo producers (e.g., Kodak and Fuji) that wanted to control the total photo experience. These companies wanted to have a hand in everything from the production of film to the processing of exposed film.

In order to grow their businesses, labs and dealers were concentrating to a greater degree than before on customer segmentation, offering services based on the individual needs of different customer groups. For example, households that used a great deal of film would be given one set of coupons or promotions to reinforce usage, while individuals who took very few pictures would be given another set of coupons to encourage them to try the product. These activities led to an increased need for database technologies within labs and dealerships to help keep up with sales activities and distribution. Photo labs were also entering the direct-mail market so they could bypass photo dealers altogether.

At the same time, the photolab suppliers were developing in two different directions. They were either concentrating on price competition or developing products and services of high quality or distinction that would help labs improve their service and quality images.

PHOTO-WALLET AND MAILER SUPPLIERS

The three main suppliers of photo envelopes and mailers in Europe at this time were ICEA, Kieser, and Paka-Seetal (see Exhibit 1 for the competitors' European market shares). Kieser was a German company that was able to run its production operations efficiently, so it was able to sell at very low prices. The quality of Kieser's products, while good, was not considered to be as high as that of either ICEA or Paka-Seetal. Kieser sold its products through a direct sales force, as well as through agents who represented many suppliers of photo products.

Paka-Seetal, an Austrian company, was a high-quality, low-cost producer. Although it was considered to be a good service provider to its customers, the company was not able to help customers design new or different products. If the specific product that a customer needed was not available in the current catalog, the customer had to compromise. Paka-Seetal sold by means of a direct sales force, as well as through agents. Paka-Seetal, like Kieser, sold other products to other industries; the company did not specialize in the photographic industry.

Exhibit 1
European Market Shares for
Print-Wallet, Workbag, and Mailer Markets, 1991

	PRINT WALLETS	WORKBAGS	MAILERS
Paka-Seetal	45%	20%	25%
Kieser	0	44	35
ICEA	21	1	25
Others	34%	35%	15%

The third competitor was ICEA, a small Danish company that focused on the photo market. ICEA produced photo mailers and wallets and helped dealers and labs develop databases for keeping up with their customers. ICEA had also entered into the photo mail-order market. ICEA was known for its high-quality products and its customer service. If a photo lab or dealer wanted a particular product, ICEA salespeople would do whatever was necessary to get that product produced. ICEA priced its products at a slight premium, but customers believed the price was justified by the specialization and the service. ICEA sold exclusively through a direct sales force.

Originally, suppliers had had to use different sales approaches with photo labs and dealers in each of the European countries. Even if a lab was part of a chain, its needs were distinct because of the variations in language and marketing among European countries. The situation had begun to change, however. As companies like Kodak began to create large networks of labs throughout Europe, and with the advent of the European Common Market, large multi-country contracts were beginning to come into play. It was very important for suppliers to have the service, price, quality, and capacity necessary to fulfill these contracts. This trend also meant that suppliers were beginning to depend on fewer customers for their sales. The loss of a single large customer could be devastating.

ICEA

ICEA was involved in the design and production of photo wallets and mailers. ICEA also helped customers develop databases that enabled labs and dealers to keep track of who their customers were and when and how customers were being served. The data could then be used to formulate marketing plans. In addition, ICEA had entered into the photo-developing mail-order arena by helping mail-order companies handle their customers. ICEA had a computerized system that inserted information and mail-order forms into envelopes, labeled the envelopes, and sent out the mailings for mail-order houses. If a mail-order processor had 300,000 customers on file, ICEA would do the total mailing for the mail-order house. ICEA could also personalize each packet for each customer and insert different information into different customers' mailings.

ICEA stressed quality and service in all that it did. The salespeople worked closely with each customer to help develop the product best fitted to the customer's needs. ICEA handled everything from the design to the production of the wallets and mailers. Kristiansen's basic principle for his company was to sell an idea first, then sell the product. For this reason, ICEA organized its five-person sales force by customer rather than by country. In this way, no overlap occurred, because one salesperson could see to all of a customer's needs. The travel expenses within this system were very high because a customer might have locations in several different countries, but ICEA believed that handling sales this way gave better service and increased quality.

All salespeople had assistants, called order administrators, for planning orders and making quotations. Order administrators planned all production in and out of house, planned deliveries, and drew up contracts. These assistants went out into the field with the salespeople twice a year so the customers could get to know them. ICEA always wanted its customers to be able to reach a familiar person.

The hiring of new office staff could be a problem, because ICEA dealt with a very specialized industry; it took one to two years for ICEA to train a fully functional employee. ICEA tried to hire either product specialists or language specialists. Hiring a person who was both was difficult. A language specialist was better than a product specialist because ICEA dealt with customers in many different countries. Training consisted of six months of education in production to learn about the products. Then, six months were spent in the sales department with a salesperson. Finally, after assisting another order administrator for six months, the trainee was ready to be on his or her own.

COMPANY CULTURE

Although ICEA had grown from a small entrepreneurial company that employed 2 people to one that employed 72, its underlying culture had not changed a great deal. Indeed, maintaining the entrepreneurial feel of the company had been of prime importance to all involved. One of ICEA's employees summarized the atmosphere in this way: "This is a very laid-back place. You have your job. You have to do it. You know that. And it is informal. In many companies, the management is up on a pedestal and everyone else is somewhere below. It is not like that at ICEA. Everyone is very accessible." Unfortunately, the lack of an evolving culture was beginning to present problems to the management and the staff of the company. (See Exhibit 2 for ICEA's organization chart.)

ICEA was considered by its sales and administrative people to be a very dynamic place to work. When employees were asked to describe the atmosphere at ICEA, the two words they used most frequently were "flexibility" and "engagement." The nature of the business and ICEA's desire to accommodate its customers meant that the employees had to be flexible in their day-to-day activities. Adaptability was very important because one never knew what might occur on a given day; the staff had to be ready for changes in customers' needs right up to the moment that printing occurred. People at ICEA had to be willing to work with these changes to get things done on time. Consequently, people were very involved with their work. Everyone still believed that the work they did had a major impact on the success of the company.

The work force of ICEA was divided into two very different and separate groups: administration and production.

The front-office staff (administration and sales) were willing to do whatever it took to make the company succeed. They were amenable to coming in

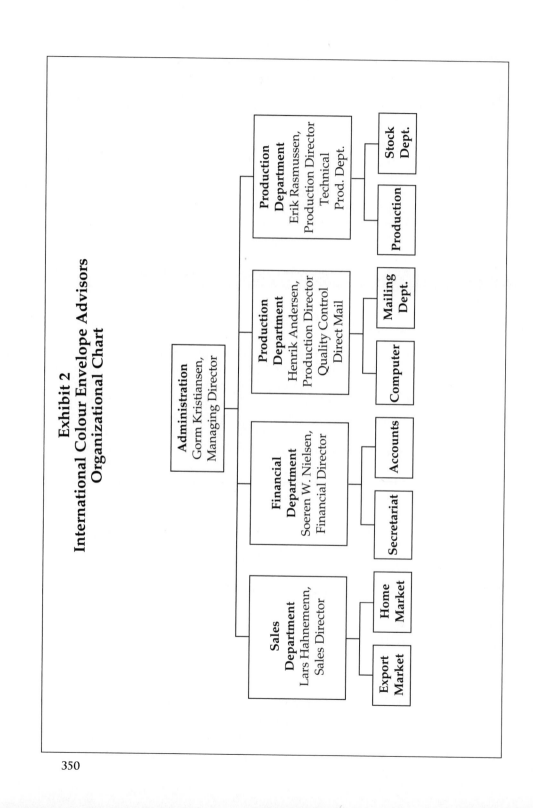

Exhibit 2
International Colour Envelope Advisors
Organizational Chart

early and staying late—anything to make sure that their tasks were accomplished. These jobs were definitely not 9 to 5. Everyone in the sales and marketing departments felt as if ICEA were one big family.

The employees in production, however, did not necessarily feel the same way. Although the employees of the production department were very loyal to the company, they sometimes felt forgotten by management in the front office. Because three shifts were always running, management was not always aware of the great job that someone on the third shift might have done. Because production ran 24 hours a day, the technical staff were not together all of the time. In addition, because two-thirds of the staff were not around during normal working hours, they were not necessarily aware of what was happening in the front office. Thus, the production staff did not feel like a family in the same way that the administrative staff did.

It was very hard for people to describe, but a separation seemed to exist between the sales department and the production department. As one sales employee stated, "The people in production think differently than do the people in sales, and this difference has sometimes led to friction."

Furthermore, the production employees had gone on strike six months earlier. At first, it had simply been a work slowdown, but a three-day strike eventually occurred. The entire process of negotiations had taken about two months. Although the strike was mostly about monetary issues, the nonmonetary issues still lingered. After the strike, people had to get over a lot of bad feelings. A loss of trust had occurred between management and the production staff.

OTHER STRUCTURAL PROBLEMS

The informality of ICEA's culture was leading to problems as the company grew. There was no formal written policy that outlined company structure, responsibilities, decision-making processes, and so forth. In 1990, the employees had together written a document called *ICEA Thoughts*, which was intended to outline the company's strategy until 1995 (see Exhibit 3). This document talked about the past, laid out a mission statement, and looked to the future. Unfortunately, after this document was typed up and circulated, it seemed to fade from sight. It was put away in a file cabinet and forgotten. Many of the newer employees who had started at the company after 1990 did not even know of its existence. Some of the older employees had only vague memories of what the document actually said.

One difficulty arose because of all the extra work people were asked to do; employees stated that they sometimes felt as though they were not appreciated for all of their hard work.

Henrik Andersen, production director, acknowledged this problem:

I think that we sometimes forget to take care of people's time. A major project comes up and you think that a certain individual would be best to handle that project. Then it is given over to that person regardless of how busy he or she

Exhibit 3
Excerpts from *ICEA Thoughts*

TOWARD YEAR 1995

ICEA has now lived through, and—strange as it may sound—survived its first hard years after a "difficult delivery." But, we made it, thanks to an unconquerable will, an incredible performance, and a good solidarity, and lately we have glimpsed improved results in our accounts.

We are now in midstream. Shall we lean back in our chairs and enjoy that we did succeed after all, or shall we try to create an even healthier and more competitive company which is able to deal with the challenges of the future?

In ICEA, we have decided to do the latter. The future has a lot of challenges to offer ICEA, and already now, we have to prepare ourselves to take up these challenges. The competition is hard and will be even harder. And winning is what we like best.

If ICEA is to obtain results on a long view in the term of an increased income and competitive improvements, it is important that we "set out" properly. Therefore, we present the targets and the lines for our work until the year 1995. The year 1995 is close enough to be realistic, and yet so far away that we can adapt ourselves to it.

The most important element is our customers, and it must not be forgotten that ICEA's most important task is not to "sell," but to fulfill the customers' needs for products and services. This is a long view, the only way to make an income and to grow. In most cases, the customers can choose between several suppliers. We are, on the contrary, in our capacity as a supplier, dependent on our customers.

ICEA's future depends on the contribution made by each of us—also you—in common to fulfill the customers' needs. The customer orientation must be intensified, and both the sales staff and the production staff are to cooperate on making the product-and-service package as attractive as possible to the customer. We also have to improve our internal efficiency considerably through a more formalized control and through information about the activities in ICEA.

It is time to start now!

(continued on next page)

(continued)

WE HAVE A MISSION

ICEA will, on its own and in cooperation with partners, develop, produce, and sell solutions to fulfill the photo laboratories' needs in connection with their servicing of the final photo user.

ICEA's product concept is built up with the photo laboratory in the center strongly attached to its three basic needs:

- Marketing
- Production control
- Distribution

ICEA's product-and-service package is directed to fulfillment of the individual customer's special needs for "tailor-made" solutions—partial as well as total solutions.

In this way, ICEA will contribute to the biggest possible dividend on the activities of the company to the shareholders and to good jobs for the employees, with development and career possibilities for each individual employee.

GOOD FOR GOOD PEOPLE . . . THIS IS ICEA

In ICEA, the employees are the most important resource, because ICEA is completely dependent on human beings and human relations.

The quality of ICEA's employees in production as well as sales and administration is of vital importance to the success of the company.

Our contact to our customers is of the utmost importance . . . as *all our activities start here*. In ICEA all employees are—at any time—representing the company.

We believe that success is made through a positive and active performance by each individual employee, no matter what his position in the organization. The employees have a joint responsibility.

We like to be busy—and we like to set high targets and to reach them.

AND IT IS STILL OUR CUSTOMERS WHO ARE PAYING OUR SALARIES

A good employee is trying to solve problems and is not only focusing on questions of guilt or pointing out problems.

(continued on next page)

(continued)

We like employees who are prepared to and capable of working in an environment requiring the key factors of professional competence, efficiency, cooperation, joint responsibility, and flexibility.

We will improve the qualifications of employees through training and increased information, which will make their jobs meaningful and make them understand ICEA's growth and direction of development.

ICEA will offer good employees permanent and lasting working conditions with salaries according to the work performed and modern welfare arrangements.

GOOD QUALITY . . . THIS IS ICEA

Good quality = more satisfied customers = higher profitability. Therefore, ICEA's main task is to create products and services with which the customers will be satisfied. In the long run, this is the only way to make income and to grow.

There is only one reason for charging a good price for a product or a service: the quality is good according to the customers' judgments.

We believe that the employees whose work is of good quality can be proud of their company and satisfied with their work.

If ICEA is to function as a single unit qualitywise, it is necessary that all employees show a positive attitude toward quality.

A good quality of products and services, which will meet the requirements of our customers, is not made by the production staff alone. There are many conditions and activities in ICEA which influence the quality of products and services.

It is important for ICEA that all conditions that influence the quality—both the construction quality of products and processes and the production quality and the marketing quality of sales and services—are systematized.

The way we do our jobs, and the cooperation which can be established across the various functions to make sure that the customers get the right production and service quality, are all factors which influence quality and quality control.

One of the most essential messages we will bear in mind in our efforts to make good quality in all functions is

Do it right each time!

(continued on next page)

(continued)

This message clearly expresses the basics—it is better and more inexpensive to do things right the first time.

ICEA'S IMAGE

We want to establish at any time by means of our first-class products and customer service that

ICEA is an active, creative company oriented toward the photo laboratories—that we are the only company which is professionally fulfilling the photo laboratories' requirements for marketing, production control, and distribution.

ICEA is the only right choice for the good photo-lab customer and for good employees.

There is no reason to hide that we are on the right road, that we are very good at our work and have success. This attracts good customers and creates new successes.

WHAT ABOUT THE CULTURE?

The ICEA spirit is, however, not only a question of strategy, good sales, income, and cost control.

The inner value—which is so difficult to measure—the way we behave toward each other every day is also of vital importance.

We have a good place of work which is to be made even better. What active part do you want to play in this process?

may be. Even if a person is very busy, he will not say no. This leads to some frustration on the part of the employees.

Another problem was the lack of a formalized communication system. Although ICEA did have an open-door policy that encouraged people to discuss their ideas, if someone was not in the office at the time a particular subject was discussed, he or she might never be informed about the outcome of that discussion. The problem of information exchange among sales, administration, and production was becoming especially acute. For many years, ICEA had not been particularly effective in telling its production employees what was going on in the sales department: memos were posted, but they were not always read. Production staff became frustrated because they never really understood why the salespeople were constantly making changes. Production believed that it would make more sense to do large runs of standardized products rather than small quantities of many different products. There also seemed to be a lack of communication between sales and production people regarding the degree of quality necessary for shippable products.

Some believed that management needed to do a better job of instilling in the technical staff a true understanding of how necessary quality was and what ICEA's quality standards were. Because ICEA promoted its products' quality, it was very important for everyone in the company to realize that attention to detail was critical. This lack of communication about quality was demonstrated in an incident where one million envelopes came out spotted. Production had let these envelopes run through the printers even though the envelopes would not be acceptable to a customer. It was a huge waste, and nothing was done about it until it was too late. When asked about the incident, Kristiansen said, "I do not know if the production employees could not fix the problem so they let the envelopes continue through the system, or if they simply did not care that the problem existed."

Some efforts were being made to address the communication problems between management and production. More meetings were held with production employees to keep them informed, work groups had been formed, and time and money were being spent on training. Newsletters were placed in each employee's pay envelope. Several sales managers indicated that they believed it would be a good idea to take production employees out on sales calls or to trade shows so they could get firsthand knowledge of how ICEA tried to meet its customers' demands.

Even though the employees recognized that some changes in the company's culture and structure were necessary for the continued strength of the business, most were resistant to change. They seemed to fear that the introduction of more structure into ICEA would ruin the company. Everyone wanted to maintain the flexibility that the flat organizational structure permitted. Most people equated more structure and enhanced communication systems with extra paperwork and an impersonal workplace.

DECISION-MAKING PROCESS AT ICEA

Some employees believed that teamwork was an important aspect of decision making within the company. Others pointed out that, even though decisions might be discussed, Kristiansen ultimately made most of the decisions for the company. Lars Hahnemann, sales director, stated, "Apart from price setting and sales contracts with customers, Gorm is making almost all of the decisions, big and small." Klaus Pinsker, sales manager, elaborated further:

If we could get into an organization where we would be free of frustrating, impulsive decisions from Gorm, things would run more smoothly. He has ideas on many levels that do not belong to his kind of job. For example, at the beginning of this week he decided that everyone should have a clean desk, and he wanted everyone to straighten his desk. But there is only a limited area of space, and I have a reason for having certain things on my desk. These are ideas outside of Gorm's level of dealing, things which should not belong to his job function.

Another sales manager related another example of Kristiansen's involvement in all decisions of the company:

Last spring, a fuss developed in the company canteen's kitchen about how to organize the dishes. Gorm involved himself 100 percent in deciding how the dirty plates should be stacked. It was completely crazy . . . the staff in the kitchen was completely furious. This kind of discussion should not involve the general manager of the company. It should have been resolved by the canteen manager. If general management is involved in this type of problem, the employees start to wonder why he has so much time for this. Doesn't he have more important things that he should be attending to?

No one was saying that Kristiansen should not be making decisions for his company. The general consensus, however, was that he needed to place limits on his involvement with some of the more mundane decisions—decisions that could be handled quite competently by others in the organization.

In the early years, when ICEA was small, it was possible and necessary for Kristiansen to have a hand in all aspects of running the business. He knew all of the customers. He knew what was needed to make his company perform well. As the company grew, however, Kristiansen had been unable to let go of some of his decision-making power. Several members of the executive board believed that Kristiansen realized he could no longer make every decision for every aspect of day-to-day life within ICEA. Unfortunately, Kristiansen had not been able to relinquish this authority.

Flemming Larson, a salesperson, summed up the situation this way:

Gorm does have to learn something. He has to learn how to go from the role he was in before, where he oversaw all aspects of the company. He has to become the general manager of the company and not the manager of the kitchen, etc. But before he can step out of the old role, the general directors of the company must be ready. If Gorm is always there to pick them up whenever they fall down, then they will never learn to keep themselves from falling. This is not just a requirement for Gorm. Everyone in this organization has to do things differently. We will have to go through turbulence. First-line

management needs more responsibility, and Gorm needs to back off somewhat. He should take a chance not to get himself involved. If something goes
wrong, he should leave it be and let others learn how to pick up after themselves.

GORM KRISTIANSEN

Gorm Kristiansen was a dynamic man. While attending The Executive
Program (TEP) at the Darden Graduate School of Business Administration
during the summer of 1992, he was described by one program manager as
looking exactly like a Viking should look. She said, "He is tall and broad
shouldered with blond hair and a scruff of a beard." Several people in the
ICEA organization said that he had more ideas than was humanly possible to
act on.

During his summer at TEP, one story that circulated about Kristiansen
involved his relationship with his local airport. Apparently, Kristiansen was
always running late and in danger of missing his plane. To avert disaster, he
would simply call the airport to let them know he would not be on time.
The people at the airport knew him well and would hold the plane for him.
This story typifies the self-confidence that Kristiansen was able to project.
(He was usually the last one in at TEP classes as well. Upon his late arrival,
his fellow TEPers would greet him in unison with a hearty "Gorm!")

Kristiansen began ICEA from the ground up. He saw the possibility of
creating a market niche in the photo-wallet-and-mailer market, and he decided to take advantage of that niche. Kristiansen was not averse to taking
risks. Rather, the only thing that frustrated him was seeing an opportunity
and being unable to seize it.

The employees of his company all admired him because of his abilities.
They liked the fact that Kristiansen was accessible to them. They enjoyed
being able to see and interact with him on a daily basis. According to Larson,
"Gorm is really the picture of the entrepreneurial personality. His personality comes straight out of the book. He is the theoretical picture of the great
innovator. He has a lot of ideas and energy. That is why we are one of the
major companies in this business. We are of importance to the market."

When asked why the company had no formal policy or marketing plan,
Kristiansen stated that he did not make a big plan because he was afraid that, if
he came in with a big plan and was unable to fulfill it, he would jeopardize his
position with his employees. He said, "I have no end goal for this company. I
want things to be done better every day." Kristiansen characterized ICEA as a
rolling ball. He had a feeling about where the company was going, but things
moved so quickly in the industry that, if he locked the company into a definite
strategy or investment plan for a certain number of years, he believed that he
could lose out on something else that would be more important. He added:

It is not a question of changing the strategy of the company. It is a question of constantly working with it. We must constantly evaluate it, constantly modify it. This does not mean that you change everything. We must modify our plans as necessary. We must be determined. We must make decisions whenever they need to be made. We must not allow things to change by coincidence.

When employees were asked what would happen when Kristiansen retired or left the company, most responded that he would be irreplaceable. The company would lose some of its dynamics. Henrik Andersen, production director, summed it up best: "Gorm knows every machine and wants to be a part of everything. If we hired a professional general manager, it would mean more paperwork and less flexibility."

FINANCIAL DIFFICULTIES

One of the major problems facing ICEA was a lack of capital. The company had simply grown too fast to meet its monetary needs. The problem weighed heavily on the minds of everyone there.

ICEA was able to generate more orders than it could possibly fill. In addition, large customers like Kodak were demanding higher quality than ever before. New printing machines were needed to make enough high-quality products to meet demand. Hahnemann stated that extra capacity was desperately needed. ICEA was fighting hard to maintain deliveries on time. Normally, ICEA was able to deliver on time, but during peak seasons timely delivery was quite difficult. Nevertheless, because ICEA's sales were based on service, timely delivery was extremely important. ICEA's financial director, Soeren Nielsen, believed that a new printing line could add 12 percent to 40 percent more to the company's bottom line because it would give ICEA the capacity to increase its sales.

Securing financing for expansion, however, was a very large problem. ICEA was currently carrying 37 million Danish kroner (DKK) in short-term debt. The building and machinery were financed through long-term bank loans, while everything else was financed through short-term credit. The amount of interest ICEA had to pay on this debt was dragging the company down. Short-term interest rates were at 15 percent; long-term rates were 9 percent. ICEA wanted, at the very least, to consolidate DKK 10 million of the short-term debt into a long-term loan. Nielsen believed that converting the short-term debt into a long-term loan would give the company more flexibility; ICEA would be able to budget better for the future, and it would feel more secure.

ICEA had several strikes against it whenever it presented its case to the banks. One problem was that the economy in Denmark had been in recession, and many small businesses had failed. Danish banks had lost so much money that they were becoming extremely careful about lending to small businesses.

A second difficulty was that the company had very specialized machinery that the banks did not want to accept as collateral. The buildings that housed ICEA were located in an area of the country that decreased their worth. Had the buildings been nearer to Copenhagen, they probably would have been worth an additional DKK 2 million.

A third problem was the company's financial condition (see Exhibits 4, 5, and 6 for financial statements). ICEA's total equity capital to assets was very low when compared with the amount of debt it was carrying. In addition, ICEA had suffered a loss in 1990 owing to difficulties with a new machine, renovation of old machines, and the loss of a subsupplier at the last moment for the production of print wallets for a major customer. In order not to lose this large customer, ICEA had produced the wallets itself, causing unplanned, heavy extra charges. This loss severely weakened ICEA's financial position, leading most banks to think twice before considering a loan.

If a loan was unavailable, the only way ICEA could get the money it needed for new machinery was to generate it internally. Nielsen stated, however, that internal funds generation would be very difficult because the printers were already running at 120-percent capacity, working 24 hours a day, seven days a week. Because the machines had to be run overtime, ICEA incurred overtime costs. Overtime at ICEA, as stipulated in the union contract, was 2.5 times regular pay. A printing technician at ICEA made the equivalent of US $30/hour on regular time and US $75/hour overtime. Nielsen stated, "If we got money for new machinery, we could save all of that overtime pay, and we could have enough money to pay all of the interest on the new loan."

Nielsen believed that ICEA had a 50-50 chance to get the bank loan it needed. Thus, Kristiansen saw himself as being in a deadlocked situation:

> I could attack the market heavily right now because there is high demand for our products, but I cannot do so with our current presses. I want to keep the majority of my company's shares. If I were to sell 50 percent of ICEA's shares, then I could solve the money problem. But, if I sold 50 percent, the buyer could demand first rights over the other 50 percent of the shares, which I would still hold. I would give up a bit of control. It would be a sacrificial move to do this.

CONCLUSION

ICEA was at a turning point. The confusion over where the company's culture should go, in combination with financial difficulties, put pressure on Kristiansen and his managers. Decisions would have to be made as to the best course for the company to follow so it could continue its success.

Exhibit 4
International Colour Envelope Advisors
Income Statement and Balance Sheet 1989–1992
(in thousands of Danish kroner, DKK 5 = US$1)

	1989	1990	1991	1992
INCOME STATEMENT				
Net turnover	73,206	76,669	75,897	86,752
Variable costs	−46,457	−50,876	−46,283	−51,452
Contribution margin	26,749	25,793	29,614	35,300
Overhead costs	18,099	20,762	20,280	18,325
Return before interest and depreciation	8,650	5,031	9,334	16,975
Depreciation	3,313	4,023	4,273	5,504
Return before interest	5,337	1,008	5,061	11,471
Interest expenses	2,854	3,700	2,975	2,340
Return before extraordinary items	2,483	−2,692	2,086	9,131
Extraordinary items	0	+99	+116	−4,349
Pretax return	2,483	−2,593	2,202	4,782

BALANCE SHEET	1989	1990	1991	1992
Equity capital	4,007	2,031	3,563	15,388
Equity capital including responsible loan capital	8,455	6,407	8,021	15,388
Total balance-sheet amount	46,666	54,193	57,434	44,983
Rate of return	11.4%	1.9%	8.8%	25.0%
Profit ratio	7.3%	1.3%	6.8%	13.2%
Contribution margin ratio	36.5%	33.6%	39.0%	40.7%
Capacity ratio	1.48	1.24	1.46	1.93
Index turnover	100	105	104	119
Index overhead costs	100	115	112	101

Note: The key figures have been calculated on the basis of the return before extraordinary items.

Exhibit 5
International Colour Envelope Advisors
Profit-and-Loss Account
January 1, 1992, to June 30, 1992
(in thousands of Danish kroner)

	REALIZED 1/1/92 TO 6/30/92	BUDGET 1/1/92 TO 6/30/92	REALIZED 1/1/91 TO 6/30/91
Turnover	41,482	39,503	40,373
Variable costs			
Wages	4,950	3,792	4,392
COGS	20,611	20,537	21,074
Total	25,561	24,329	25,466
Contribution margin	15,921	15,174	14,907
Overhead costs			
Sales	2,134	2,277	2,153
Production	4,720	4,410	5,445
Administration	3,241	2,724	3,019
Other (income)	(270)	(248)	(344)
Total overhead	9,285	9,163	10,273
Return before depreciation	6,096	6,011	4,634
Depreciation	2,201	2,590	2,211
Return before interest	3,895	3,421	2,423
Interest	1,390	1,419	1,458
Bad debts	00	100	0
Return before extraordinary items	2,505	1,902	965
Extraordinary income	1,520	00	79
Pretax return	4,025	1,902	1,044

Exhibit 6
International Colour Envelope Advisors
Balance Sheet as of June 30, 1992
(in thousands of Danish kroner; DKK 5 = US$1)

	REALIZED 6/30/92	REALIZED 1/1/92
ASSETS		
Intangible fixed assets		
Goodwill	200	400
Deposit—rent	143	143
Depreciation	(100)	(100)
Total intangible fixed assets	243	443
Tangible fixed assets		
Building	7,402	7,385
Technical plants	17,822	15,617
Machines, fixtures, fittings	2,369	1,782
Computer equipment	1,043	816
Automobiles	288	584
Prepayments	1,832	2,517
Depreciation	2,101	0
Total tangible fixed assets	28,655	28,701
Financial fixed assets		
Sparekassen Nordjylland, account held as collateral	4,970	6,900
Shares—FRS + Sparekassen	22	22
Total financial fixed assets	4,992	6,992
Total fixed assets	33,890	35,966
Goods in stock		
Raw materials	3,756	3,090
Finished articles + merchandise	2,441	2,381
WIP	445	880
Total stocks	6,632	6,351
Credits		
Trade debtors	17,901	11,083
Provision for loss	(80)	(146)
Sundry loans	101	18
Accruals	2,204	146

(continued on next page)

Source: ICEA, July 15, 1992. All numbers are as presented in the original report.

(continued)

	REALIZED 6/30/92	REALIZED 1/1/92
Loan MK	243	247
Total credits	20,369	11,348
Liquid reserves	221	856
Total net current assets	27,222	18,555
Total Assets	61,112	54,521
LIABILITIES		
Equity capital		
Share capital	3,000	3,000
Reserves	00	00
Carried forward to next year	563	563
Return of the period	4,025	00
Total equity capital	7,588	3,563
Contingent taxation		
Set-aside for contingent taxation	669	669
Liable loan capital		
Long-term debt		
RRF Danmark (credit assoc.)	2,244	2,264
Industriend Realkr. Pond (credit assoc.)	1,433	1,449
Finansiaeringsinst. (credit assoc.)	2,728	3,288
Rongerieget DR Hypotekb. (credit assoc.)	3,450	3,450
Advance payment (regional development grant)	1,520	3,450
Installment payments (1992)	(466)	00
Total long-term debt	10,909	13,901
Short-term debt		
Short-term share of long-term debt	466	0
Bank debt	16,259	18,111
Trade creditors and costs due	13,571	12,176
Current accounts with ICEA		
Ruvertering I/S	127	148
Other short-term debt	3,302	1,590
V.A.T., etc., due	3,763	(95)
Total short-term debt	37,488	31,930
Total debt	48,397	45,831
Total Debt Plus Equity	61,112	54,521

COPELAND CORPORATION/BAIN & COMPANY: THE SCROLL INVESTMENT DECISION[1]

In late January 1989, Joanna Engelke and David Bechhofer of Bain & Company were preparing for the initial meeting of the Copeland engagement team. Engelke and Bechhofer had circulated a memo outlining their thoughts (Exhibit 1), together with excerpts from an investment research paper on Emerson Electric, Copeland's parent company (Exhibit 2) and overheads used during a Copeland management presentation to Emerson's board of directors in May 1988 (Exhibit 3). Timing was critical because the Bain team hoped to have recommendations for Copeland's management by May 1, 1989, concerning a capital appropriations request for a major addition to Scroll's compressor capacity.

Interviews with Ed Purvis, Copeland's senior marketing manager for the air conditioning department, and Howard Lance, Copeland's president of sales and marketing, were scheduled for the following week.

This case was prepared by Jeanne M. Liedtka, Associate Professor of Business Administration, and John W. Rosenblum, Tayloe Murphy Professor of Business Administration. Copyright © 1995 by the University of Virginia Darden School Foundation, Charlottesville, VA. All rights reserved.

[1]This case is to be used in conjunction with the Darden Video Module "Copeland/Bain."

Exhibit 1

To: Mike D'Amato
        Vern Altman
From: David Bechhofer
        Joanna Engelke
Date: January 23, 1989
Subject: Overview of Copeland Corporation

The following is a summary of the information that we have learned about Copeland. I hope that it will be valuable as background for the discussions this Thursday in Sidney, Ohio.

HISTORY

Copeland Refrigeration Corporation was founded in Michigan in 1933. The name was changed to Copeland Corporation in 1972 and incorporated in Delaware. The name change signified the growing importance of the air conditioning market in the company's sales mix. In 1981, the company was taken private by Henry Hillman for $215mm. Hillman had been the lead shareholder with 36 percent of the stock prior to the leveraged buyout. He combined the company with Pameco (Pam eee' co), a refrigeration and air-conditioning parts distributor, and formed Cop-Pam Holdings.

In 1986, Emerson purchased the company for $541mm. The logic to the acquisition was that it gave Emerson a full line in the refrigeration and air-conditioning parts business and fit well with the electric-motor division. Before the acquisition was complete, Copeland signed an exclusive distribution agreement with Pameco for aftermarket parts.

While all the annual data is not available, Copeland has grown from $200mm in sales ($12mm profit) in 1976 to $575mm in sales ($31mm profit) in 1986.

TECHNOLOGY

(With apologies to the mechanical engineers in the room)
Copeland's sales are dominated by the compressor business, with more than 90 percent of revenue coming from sales of new compressors,

(continued on next page)

(continued)

rebuilt compressors, and compressor parts. Historically, the two main technologies have been hermetic and semihermetic compressors. Hermetic (.25–22 hp) compressors are completely sealed and difficult-to-repair units that are oriented toward the residential air-conditioning market. Semihermetic (.25–80 hp) compressors are repairable and rebuild-able, larger, more expensive, and oriented toward the refrigeration and commercial air-conditioning markets.

The company has also developed and built condensing units that combine a compressor and an electric motor in one package.

The current "hot" product is the compliant Scroll compressor. While most compressors use a plunging action to compress the relevant gases, the Scroll compressor uses a spiral squeezing action. The value gained is that it is smaller, more efficient, and has fewer moving parts (lower cost) than older technologies. It is currently being targeted for the residential air-conditioning OEM (Original Equipment Manufacturer) market.

The buzzword in the business these days is "variable speed." The ability to combine compressors with variable-speed motors creates a system that is inherently more efficient. Consequently, those companies that can integrate these products should have an advantage. Although Emerson has both motor and compressor divisions, we believe that some competitors may be farther along in this technology.

MARKETS (CUSTOMERS)

The compressors are sold in three definably different markets (or market segments): refrigeration, commercial air conditioning, and residential air conditioning. The refrigeration market includes products such as super-market display cases and walk-in refrigerators and freezers. Copeland has built a strong position in both the OEM business and the aftermarket. There is a large market for rebuilt compressors and for compressor service. (When the display cabinet dies, prompt service turnaround is critical.)

The other end of the spectrum for Copeland is the residential air-conditioning market, where cost and efficiency are critical. Copeland seems to be competitive in the market as well, particularly with its new products.

Overall, the refrigeration and air-conditioning markets appear to be flat for the next five plus years, driven at least partially by the cyclicality of the housing market.

(continued on next page)

(continued)

Less than 10 percent of Copeland's sales come from outside the United States, which is both a competitive risk and a marketing opportunity. We would hypothesize that there are no clear technological barriers to penetrating the world markets.

MANUFACTURING (COST)

All of the Copeland product lines are produced in focused manufacturing facilities. The decision was made in the late 1970s and early 1980s to focus those facilities by product and end market rather than technology or process. It appears that Copeland is a relative model of manufacturing efficiency, and at least part of its competitive advantage comes from its cost position.

The company is backward integrated into stampings (Shelby Manufacturing Company in Sidney) as well as some other key parts. In 1986, Copeland had more than 20 plants, and it is unclear how many acquisitions, divestitures, and closings the company has undergone since then.

COMPETITORS

If one defined the relevant marketplace as those domestic companies that only manufactured compressors, then the top competitor would be Tecumseh, with slightly lower market share than Copeland. Bristol would be a distant third. Tecumseh appears to be more mass-market oriented, aiming for high-volume, lower-price business. (Tecumseh followed this same strategy very successfully against Briggs and Stratton in the small-engine market capturing customers such as Sears in the lawn-mower market.) In air conditioning there are at least some manufacturers (Carrier and Trane) that have backward integrated into compressors. It is unclear what the relative economics are in this case.

There are also clearly some overseas manufacturers, including a number of Japanese companies. One article described Whirlpool's shifting $50mm of Emerson hermetic motor sales to a foreign supplier who could provide both motors and compressors in 1985.

Our hypothesis would be that there are some major risks from both offshore and vertically integrating companies that may begin to have an impact on the compressor market with the decline in end-market growth.

Exhibit 2
Excerpts from Goldman Sachs Investment Research Paper on Emerson Electric Company
(March 26, 1987)

Despite more than $11 million in amortization per year resulting from its acquisition, Copeland's operating income should be relatively flat in fiscal 1987 and increase more than 10 percent in fiscal 1988. However, with 2-percent to 3-percent projected gains in residential air-conditioning shipments and a slowdown in commercial construction, two important Copeland end markets, revenues should be stable. Still, we view the acquisition of Copeland, the leading manufacturer of air-conditioning and refrigeration compressors, as an excellent move.

Copeland has rather consistently maintained 10-percent operating margins, which compare quite favorably with competitors such as Tecumseh. From 1980 to 1985, sales compounded at 8 percent; in calendar 1986, they rose 12 percent to $578. Approximately 23 percent of its sales are outside the United States. Copeland's three main markets are residential air conditioning, commercial air conditioning, and commercial refrigeration. The residential air-conditioning and commercial-refrigeration sectors are extremely attractive given the large replacement markets. Copeland is the dominant company in these two markets.

In refrigeration, a malfunctioning compressor can result in substantial losses at a supermarket from spoilage. The implicit cost of a new compressor becomes almost immaterial. What is required is an efficient service/wholesaling network, and Copeland has the largest. According to industry sources, approximately 40 percent to 50 percent of the air-conditioning and refrigeration-compressor market is tied to replacements. *In sum, Copeland's strengths are its quality products, strong market shares, service franchise, and an orientation away from commodity-oriented import markets.* However, it was also the company's technology that ultimately attracted Emerson.

Copeland plans to introduce a new compressor in fiscal 1987 called the Scroll. Compared with existing technologies characterized by reciprocating and rotary compressors, the Scroll has several advantages. It is more efficient as it is almost constantly "pushing out" small amounts of coolant compared with larger and less-frequent discharges by the others.

(continued on next page)

(continued)

The Scroll also has fewer moving parts, which makes it smaller and easier to produce at a lower cost. The technology behind the Scroll dates back to 1903; however, computerized design and manufacturing have finally allowed it to be produced economically and perform as expected. Hitachi is the other major producer of Scroll compressors, but Copeland's weighs less and takes up less space. Scroll technology fits in extremely well with Emerson's work on variable-speed motors. The combined technologies offer significant energy savings as the Scroll is highly efficient at various speeds. The Scroll compressor will initially be targeted at the residential air-conditioning market.

Copeland Focused on High-Volume, Value-Oriented Markets

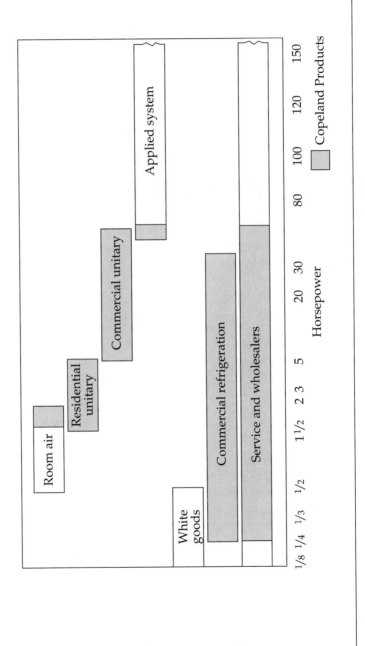

1992 Federal Regulation Will Change
Market Distribution of Efficiencies

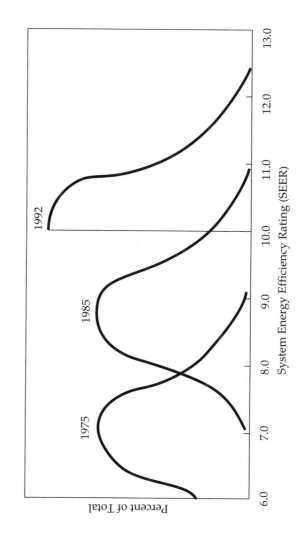

Exhibit 3C

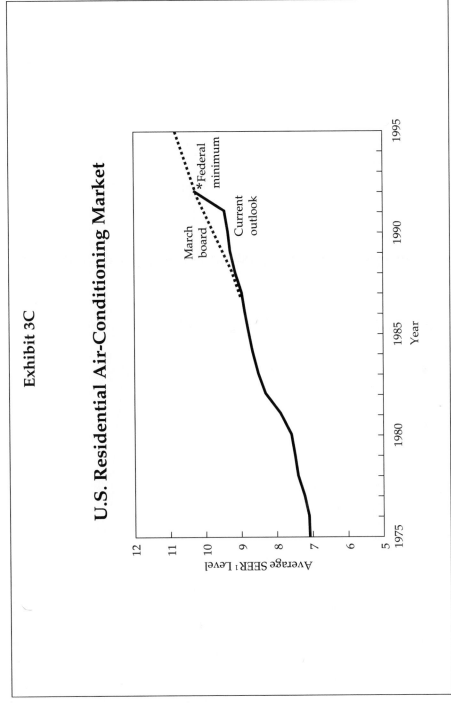

U.S. Residential Air-Conditioning Market

[1]System Energy Efficiency Rating.

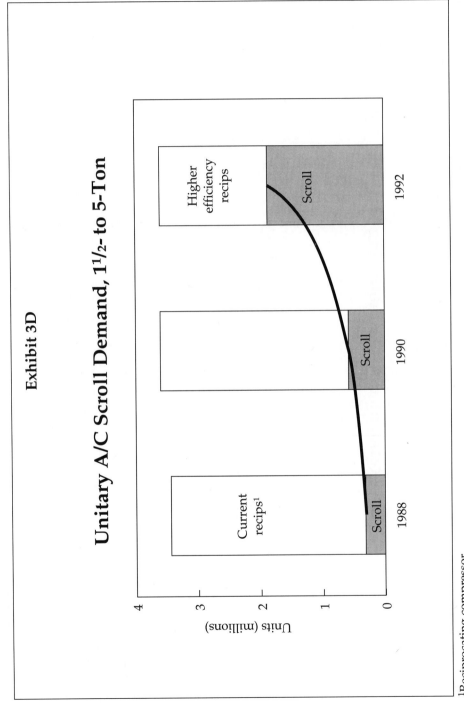

Exhibit 3D

Unitary A/C Scroll Demand, 1½- to 5-Ton

[1]Reciprocating compressor.

Scroll Market Summary

- Scroll is focused on the largest market segment.

- It serves 80% of the U.S. air-conditioning market.

- System efficiency levels continue to improve.

- Scroll offers best cost solution to OEMs.

Exhibit 3F

Eight Major Manufacturers Control 87% of the Residential Market

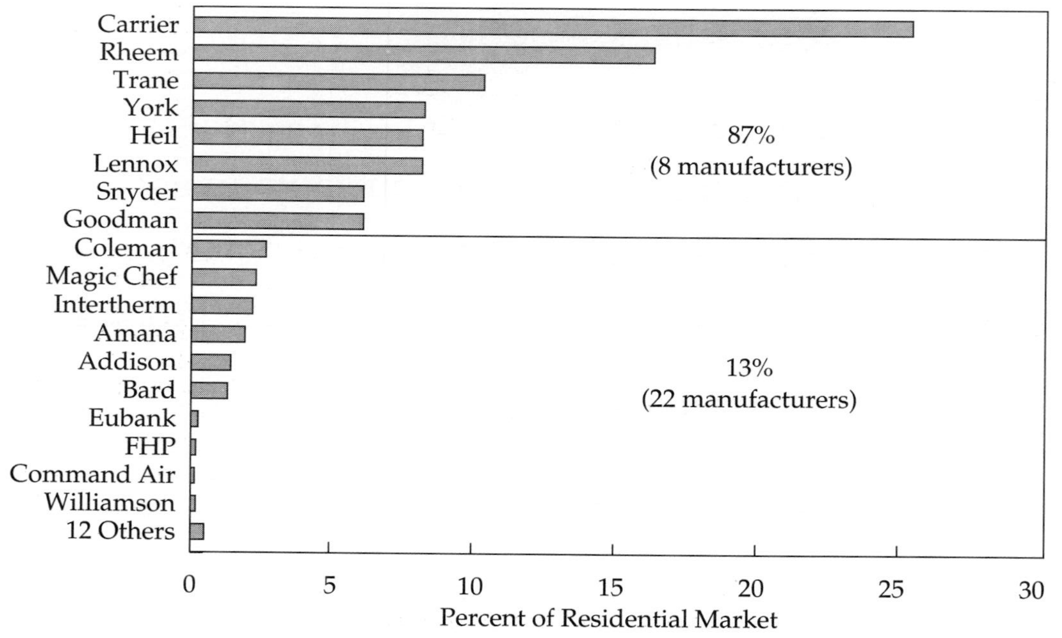

Exhibit 3G

Share Shift Occurring among Major Residential Manufacturers

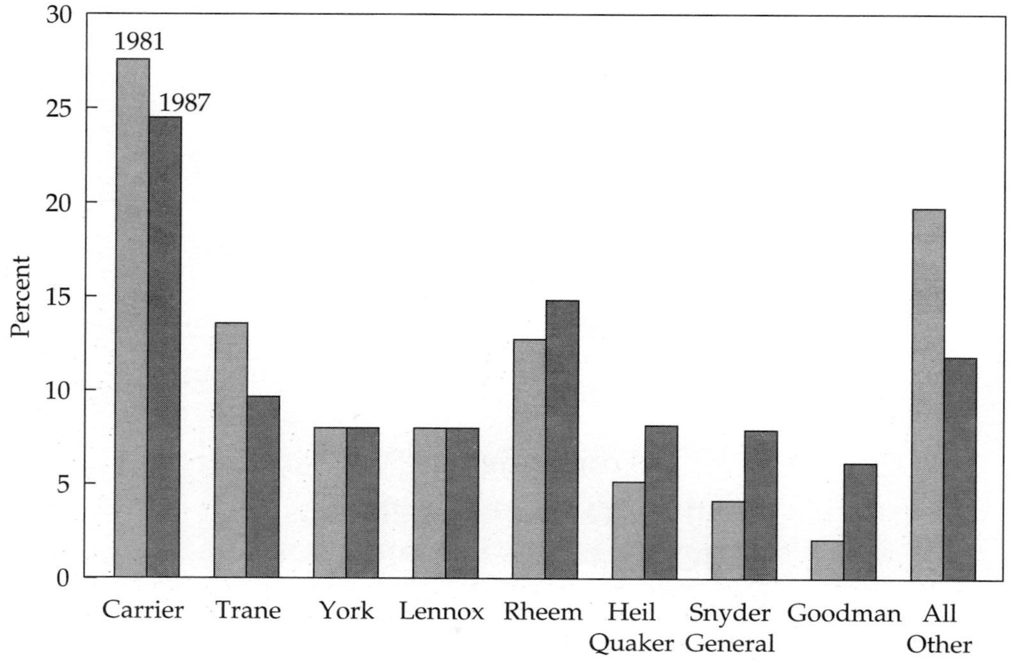

Exhibit 3H

Scroll Reduces Cost for OEMs
System Design Options
Heat Pump

With Recip

With Scroll

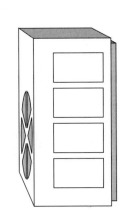

Cost Savings:
- Coil
- Cabinet
- Components

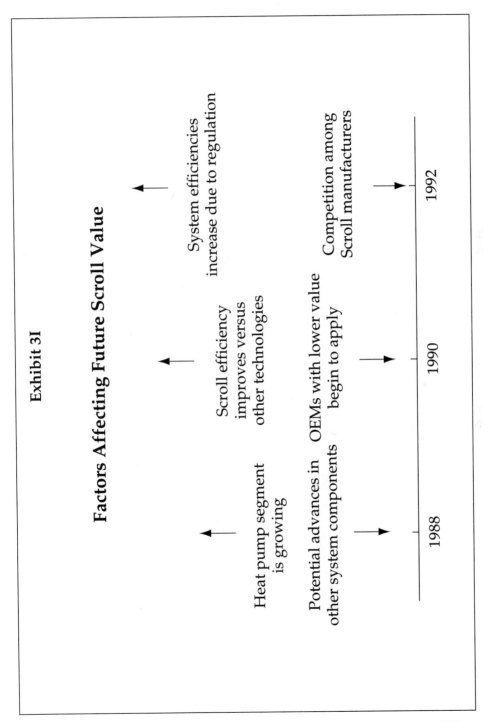

Exhibit 3I

Factors Affecting Future Scroll Value

System efficiencies increase due to regulation

Scroll efficiency improves versus other technologies

Heat pump segment is growing

Potential advances in other system components

OEMs with lower value begin to apply

Competition among Scroll manufacturers

1988

1990

1992

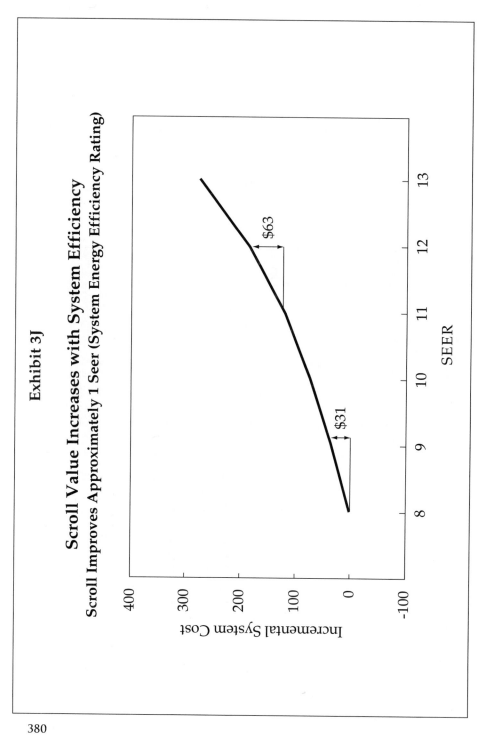

Exhibit 3J

Scroll Value Increases with System Efficiency

Scroll Improves Approximately 1 Seer (System Energy Efficiency Rating)

Scroll Value Is Higher in Heat Pumps

Heat Pump

- Larger coils
- Handle more refrigerant
  -suction accumulators
  -start kits
  -crankcase heaters
- Scroll simplifies design task

Air Conditioning

- Smaller coils
- Less refrigerant
  -crankcase heater only

Scroll Value

	Heat Pump	Air Conditioner
Coil	$18	$11
Cabinet	7	4
Components:		
suction accumulator	10	—
crankcase heater	3	3
	$38	$18

Exhibit 3L

Japan Produces More Compressors Than Any Other Nation

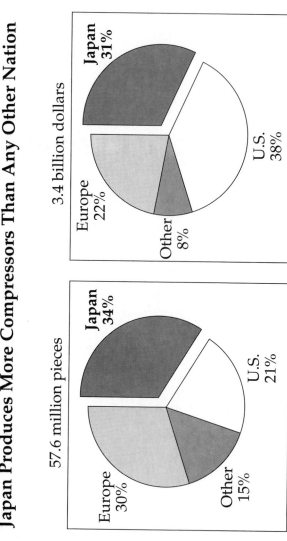

57.6 million pieces

3.4 billion dollars

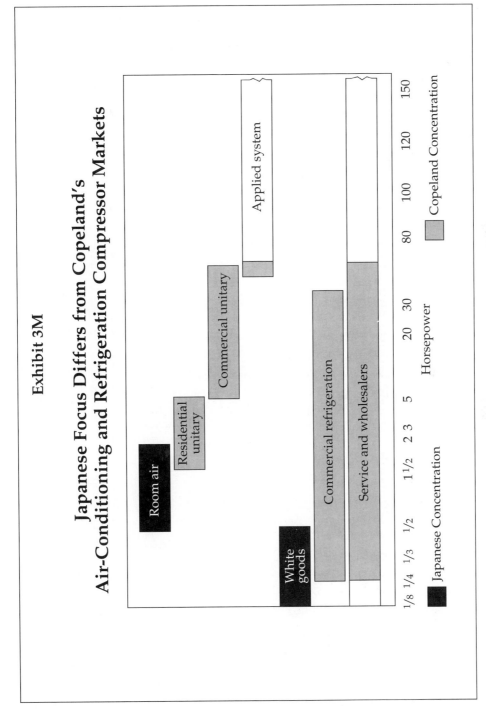

Exhibit 3M

Japanese Focus Differs from Copeland's Air-Conditioning and Refrigeration Compressor Markets

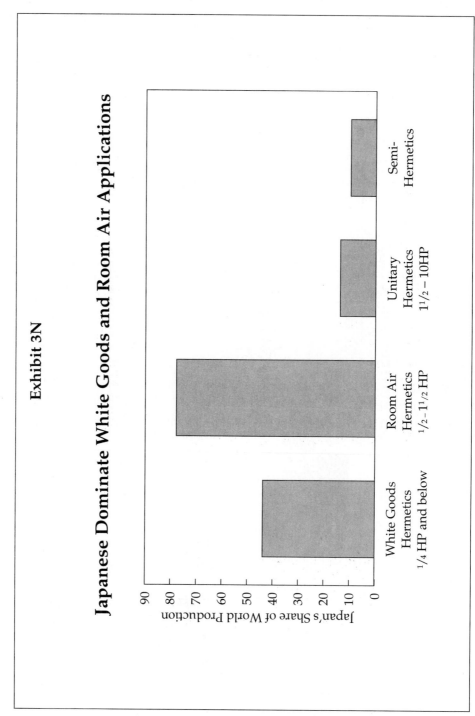

Exhibit 3N

Japanese Dominate White Goods and Room Air Applications

Japanese Scroll Demand
1988 versus 1992

	ACTUAL 1988	FORECAST 1992
Demand		
• Hitachi	110	140
• Melco	20	220
• MHI	20	130
• Matsushita	20	100
• Daikin	—	230
• Toshiba	—	120
• Sanyo	—	60
Total demand	**170**	**1,000**
Capacity (total)	250	1,500
Excess capacity	80	500
Exports	10	300–400

Exhibit 3P

Summary

- The Japanese are major competitors in the world compressor industry.

- Japan has succeeded in markets not targeted by Copeland.

- In the future, the Japanese will place more emphasis on compressors greater than 2 horsepower.

- Several Japanese A/C OEMs will develop Scroll production capabilities.

- By 1992, the Japanese could have 400,000 units available for export.

- Technology and cost advantages protect Copeland from Japanese competition in the short term.

- In the long run, Copeland must prepare to be a significant player in Japan.

Copeland Competitive Position Forecast for 1992

	Copeland Scroll	Best Japanese Scroll
E.E.R. (CHEER)*	19.5	18.0
Cumulative Production volume	3.0M	1.0–1.5M
Production capacity	5x M	x M

*CHEER is the rating standard used by the company to rate compressor performance. Higher compressor efficiency at CHEER equates to lower system operating cost.

Scroll Marketing Strategy Summary

- Target Scroll to highest value segments

- Target recips to lowest value segments

- Minimize penetration of Scroll competitors

- Increases total market share

- Opportunity for strategic alliance with Carrier or Trane to further increase share

- Flexibility is augmented with CR6* capacity

*Higher efficiency reciprocating compressor

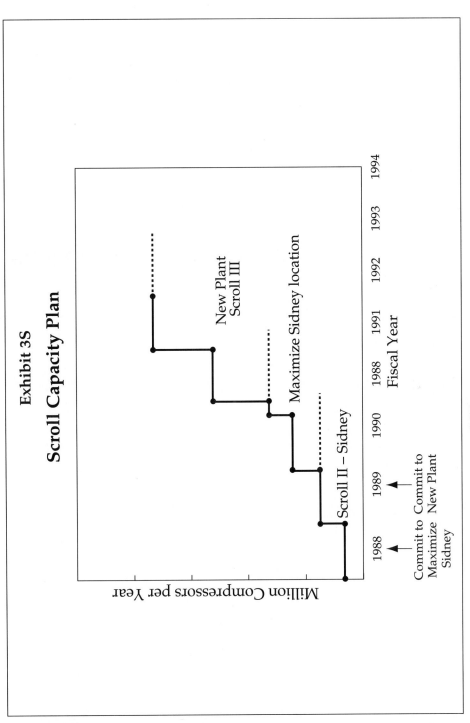

Exhibit 3S

Scroll Capacity Plan

PART

III

CORPORATE STRATEGY:
MANAGING MULTIPLE-
BUSINESS FIRMS

CORPORATE STRATEGY

There are four key aspects of corporate strategy. The first has to do with the *strategic management of the current set of businesses in the company's portfolio* and the allocation of resources among them. The second related aspect is the *creation of shareholder value* through corporate strategy. These first two aspects—portfolio techniques and value-based planning—will be covered in this part (Chapters 6, 7, and 8). The third aspect has to do with the *realization of synergies across businesses* and the identification and management of direct linkages between businesses. The fourth aspect is the *strategy of diversification*, whether through acquisition or internal development. The third and fourth aspects will be covered in Part IV, Chapter 9.

DIFFERENCES BETWEEN CORPORATE AND BUSINESS STRATEGIES

For a company that has not diversified beyond its core business, corporate and business strategies are inseparable. For example, the Bacardi Corporation has been in the rum business since its founding, and, with the exception of a local beer in one small market, it manufactured no other spirits besides rum. Bacardi's corporate strategy was to be in the "light spirits" business. Its business strategy focused on becoming the number-one-selling spirits brand in the world. It manufactured no vodka, scotch, or bourbon (keeping its *focus* on a *differentiated*, premium rum). Its corporate strategy was simply to locate its production facilities in a few strategic locations (close to sugar cane or close to markets) and to allocate its rum distillate and marketing talent to the most promising markets around the world. In this setting, notice how corporate and business strategies intermingle.

In 1993, however, Bacardi acquired Martini and Rossi, the Italian vermouth maker who had more than 100 brands and products in almost as many markets. Now Bacardi had a portfolio of liqueurs, scotches, cordials, and wines, as well as a hotel and a foods distribution business. The attention of senior management turned from the selling of rum to rationalizing a very diverse portfolio of products, brands, and operating companies (corporate strategy). Meanwhile operating management around the world focused on the specifics of competing in their various markets and businesses (business strategy).

The Bacardi-Martini example highlights some of the differences between corporate and business strategic management. As further illustration, listen to the different words used in conversation by managers engaged in each. At corporate headquarters of a diversified firm, you might hear executives speaking of major acquisitions in the works that are (or are not) synergistic with current business, how this might affect EPS and the tax picture, and what the cash-flow implications are. Finally, they might discuss whether or not the proposed acquisition will help move them more solidly into the "energy business" or "technology business." These corporate strategy discussions tend to be somewhat abstract in nature.

Now, at the division level you might hear discussions about working more closely with supplier X, meeting customer Y at a particular trade show, or planning a negotiating strategy for the next labor contract. This discussion might be coupled with speculation about how particular competitors are going to be handling the same issues. These are business strategy discussions. Note how they reflect a world of tangible events, people, and things, whereas the corporate-level discussion dealt with more abstract concepts.

The classic argument that the railroads might have prospered in the wake of the growth of our highway system if they had defined their business as "transportation" rather than "railroads" was simply a suggestion to think of one's business in more abstract (corporate) terms. Saying that your business is "transportation" does not tell you how to compete; that is, it does not define your business strategy—it merely helps to define your scope of activities. Although recognizing a business's scope is important to survival in a changing world, it is clearly not enough. All three—corporate, business, and functional—are necessary strategic management activities.

CORPORATE STRATEGY IDENTIFICATION

When firms expand into a variety of businesses, they frequently transfer successes in the initial business to the subsequent businesses. For example, when Bic Pen Corporation expanded beyond ballpoint pen production into disposable cigarette lighters, it used the same plastic-injection molding technology and similar distribution channels to sell what was essentially another mass-marketed, disposable consumer item. The additional learning required to design and produce this new product was relatively low, given that the same technology was employed in the factory: plastic was injected into a mold to form a casing, into which dispensable liquid was poured, and metal parts were attached to dispense the fluid.

When firms adopt similar business strategies in different lines of business, they have adopted what we might term a *generic* business strategy across all their businesses. Hewlett-Packard and Texas Instruments are two firms that compete in various segments of the electronics industry, that employ generic strategies in many of their product lines, and whose generic strategies are quite distinct (see Table 6-1).

Using generic strategies to build a corporation from a variety of businesses implies the cloning of an original strategy onto new businesses. This, of course, is only one means of extending the boundaries of the corporation into new domains. To the extent that a corporation expands by building upon a core business and the set of skills embodied in that business, we can say that it is realizing synergies across its businesses.

At the other extreme are pure conglomerates, which are built through the acquisition of unrelated business. It was not unusual during the 1960s and the early 1980s for corporations to build conglomerates based on the theory that the acquisition of unrelated businesses in countercyclical industries would smooth out the cash flows for the whole corporation. This led to the development of a variety of portfolio planning techniques for managing corporate strategy by such firms as the Boston Consulting Group and McKinsey and Company. These techniques typically plotted the variety of businesses on a two-dimensional grid, with market position or market share on one dimension and industry growth or attractiveness on the other. The theory was that high-market-share businesses were likely to be lower-cost manufacturers than smaller-share businesses, simply as a result of volume or scale economies, which allowed those businesses to realize higher profit margins and greater cash throw-off per dollar of sales. With a portfolio of businesses, the cash throw-off from the better-positioned firms could be used to fund the growth of more promising—perhaps smaller-market-share—businesses in the portfolio. Essentially, these portfolio techniques were cash management methods for diversified corporations. The details of this approach are outlined in the next chapter, "Note on Portfolio Techniques for Corporate Strategic Planning."

Table 6-1
Examples of Generic Business Strategies

	HEWLETT-PACKARD	TEXAS INSTRUMENTS
MARKETING STRATEGY	Industrial and some consumer markets	Consumer and industrial markets
	High-tech, custom products	High-volume, low-cost standard products
	Premium price, lag experience curve	Low price, push experience curve
	Promote quality/ reliability/service	Promote availability/ price
PRODUCTION STRATEGY	Small plants	Large plants for large volume
	Small-batch/job-shop technology	Mass-production technology with automation and robotics
	Build capacity with demand	Build capacity ahead of demand
FINANCIAL STRATEGY	Self-funding ("pay as you go") within divisions	Allocate cash among divisions according to need
	Make profits early on through high margins	Fund ahead of experience curve
R&D STRATEGY	First to market with new products	Improve existing products in proven markets
	Primarily product R&D	Both product and process R&D
	Features and quality driven	Cost driven
	Design for product performance	Design for cost reduction

NOTE ON PORTFOLIO TECHNIQUES FOR CORPORATE STRATEGIC PLANNING

PORTFOLIO PLANNING: THE ORIGINS

Research on Experience Curves and Market Share

Portfolio planning originated from two independent, though simultaneous, streams of applied research in industry, one stream conducted by the Boston Consulting Group (BCG) and the other by the General Electric Company.

BCG research in the late 1960s focused on discerning the origins of cost advantages experienced by certain industries. The research uncovered the *experience curve* effect—the fact that unit costs in an industry tend to decline steadily with accumulated volume.[1] At the individual business level, this cost decline could translate into a cost advantage—and therefore a competitive advantage—for the firm with the greatest accumulated volume, or "experience." To simplify its estimation of competitor cost structure, BCG suggested the use of *market share* as a surrogate for accumulated experience. In other words, the firm with the largest market share in a particular market is most

This note was prepared by Professor L. J. Bourgeois, III. Copyright © 1988 by the Darden Graduate Business School Foundation, Charlottesville, VA.

[1]For a concise explanation of the experience curve concept and its implications for strategy, see "Note on the Use of Experience Curves in Competitive Decision Making," HBS Case Services No. 175-174.

likely to enjoy the lowest cost position. The greater the difference in market share between the leader and the next-largest firm (termed *relative market share*), the greater the flexibility the leader has in competition. For example, at any given industry price, the cost leader has larger margins and can therefore spend more on research and development, advertising, or plant expansion. Alternately, the share (and cost) leader has greater flexibility in price competition, because a price war will inflict greater damage on the higher-cost producers in the market.

At the same time, the General Electric Company(GE) initiated an internal research project to discover why some of their 160 businesses seemed to outperform others. In the attempt to uncover the "economic success factors" underlying businesses in differing circumstances, GE constructed a database, which included information on 87 different variables such as product quality, capital intensity, advertising expenditures, relative market share, cash flow, and return on investment (ROI). A statistical analysis (multiple regression) indicated that the strongest predictor of ROI was market share. The desire to corroborate as well as share these findings led GE to establish the independent Strategic Planning Institute (SPI) jointly with the Harvard Business School. The SPI's database is now known as the PIMS ("Profit Impact of Market Strategies") project and contains data from more than 2,000 individual businesses over several years.[2]

The coincidence of both BCG's and GE's research results supported the conclusion that market share is a valid strategic objective and laid the foundation for the portfolio planning models that each firm was to later develop independently.

The Impetus to Portfolio Planning

The main impetus to portfolio planning models was the wave of diversification that took place in the 1960s, which led companies into new, often unrelated, businesses. As diversity increased, so did the strains on managements' cognitive capacities; that is, it became increasingly difficult for executives at the top of diversified firms to understand all of the competitive situations and economics of each business in which they participated. In addition, the rapid growth characteristic of the 1950s and 1960s frequently led to severe cash needs, which often outstripped the companies' abilities to fund these needs internally. With most businesses in the corporation requesting capital funds simultaneously, financial resources became increasingly scarce. In addition, as inflation accelerated during the 1970s, capital markets became less and less

---

[2]For a description of the PIMS project and its conclusions, see Sidney Schoeffler, R. D. Buzzell, and D. F. Heany, "Impact of Strategic Planning on Profit Performance," *HBR*, March–April 1974, pp. 137–45, and R. D. Buzzell, B. T. Gale, and R. G. M. Sultan, "Market Share—A Key to Profitability," *HBR*, January–February 1975, pp. 97–106.

attractive sources for funds. These conditions led executives to seek a method for internal resource allocation. Finally, the diversification trend was accompanied by a trend toward decentralized management, which led business-level managements to behave more autonomously and to make strategic resource allocation decisions independently of each other. As a result, cash-starved growth businesses were constrained from pursuing opportunities that would have been deemed attractive from a total corporation perspective, and cash-rich mature businesses were funding their own conservative projects internally. The combination of this independent behavior with the increased cognitive strains associated with diversity, *plus* the difficulty in rational resource allocation, caused central headquarters management to sense a loss of control. Portfolio planning was perceived as a means of regaining control of the diverse businesses in the corporation.

The Birth of Portfolio Planning

The market share/cost advantage relationship discovered by BCG and PIMS indicated that a viable strategic objective was to grow market share. Growth of any sort, however, requires cash infusions. Participation in high-growth markets amplifies this resource drain, causing a dilemma for those who wish to pursue share-gaining strategies in growth markets. BCG and GE both, however, recognized that the end of the experience curve tended to coincide with industry maturity. That is, as more volume was accumulated, fewer cost-reduction benefits were accrued—the end of the experience curve, like the end of a product life cycle, tended to flatten. Businesses at maturity (low-growth industries) tended to require less cash. In fact, dominant firms—those with the most experience (or the greatest share)—tended to throw off significant amounts of cash because of the reduced need to reinvest in the business.

It became evident that a diversified firm might contain businesses at several stages of industry maturity with differing relative positions of dominance. If they are arrayed on a grid, one could indicate pictorially where each particular business was located relative to the two dimensions of industry growth and competitive position. This array could demonstrate in a compact way the number and location of cash consumers and cash providers.

At this point, the approaches of the different firms began to diverge. BCG, given its orientation toward the scientific and the quantifiable, pursued its theory of portfolio management as a science. GE, with the collaboration of McKinsey, created an approach that relied more on managerial judgment and "art." Arthur D. Little (ADL), attempting to combine "science" and "art," developed its own process of portfolio planning. The next section will elaborate the differences among these approaches, including the additional set of techniques developed by the Arthur D. Little consulting firm.

PORTFOLIO PLANNING: THE DIFFERENT APPROACHES

The Basic Concept

The basic idea behind portfolio planning is shared by all the approaches and is rather straightforward. The steps go something like this:

1. For planning purposes, identify separate business units that correspond to the markets or industries that the company serves. Most approaches refer to these as strategic business units, or SBUs. Many, but not all, approaches take the existing divisional arrangement as a first approximation to SBUs.

2. Classify the SBUs on a two-dimensional portfolio grid that indicates competitive position versus market potential. The change of position from the past year to the present is usually plotted to indicate changing competitive position and resource allocations.

3. Assign to each SBU a *strategic mission* within the portfolio: grow (consume cash), maintain position (usually through self-funding), harvest (throw off cash), or divest (in order for cash to be reinvested in one of the growth SBUs or to fund an acquisition). In general, these strategic missions coincide with the positions of the businesses on the grid:

   • Growth—Nondominant (e.g., not the number-one share), but promising businesses in high-growth industries.

   • Maintain—Dominant businesses in growth industries.

   • Harvest—Dominant businesses in mature industries.

   • Divest—Weak businesses in mature industries.

   (For reference, BCG has termed the businesses falling into these four categories the familiar Question Mark, Star, Cash Cow, and Dog, respectively.)

4. Having assigned a strategic mission to each SBU, resources can now be allocated within the firm accordingly.

The result of the approach is to balance sales growth with the financial resources of the firm.

BCG AND THE GROWTH/SHARE MATRIX

The Value of Market Share

As indicated above, the BCG approach is grounded in the company's experience curve research. The strategic implication of the experience curve effect is that a company should always seek a dominant market position if it intends to invest in a business. The less the company's market share resembles a dominant position, the less valuable it is for the company to be in that business. The best strategy for a business that does not have a dominant position is to seek dominance, perhaps in a limited segment, or to get out. Once a business has achieved dominance, the basic strategy should be to maintain that position.

The Importance of Growth

A business's market growth determines both its opportunity and its risk. When a business is in a fast-growth market, assets must be added at least at the market growth rate over the long term for the business to remain viable. Thus, a 20-percent-growth business requires that assets also grow at least at 20 percent. Growth businesses demand large cash input. Slow-growth businesses are the opposite: very slow market growth requires comparatively small cash input to maintain position.

Market growth has competitive implications. If the growth rate is high, market shares can change dramatically in a short period of time. A 20-percent-growth market roughly doubles annual volume in four years. Thus, a company that starts from a zero base and takes all the growth while its competition maintains its annual volume would command 50 percent of the market in only four years. In contrast, a 3-percent-growth market takes 24 years to double annual volume. The only way a new entrant could achieve a significant market position in such a low-growth business in a reasonable period of time would be to force competition to close down current production capacity. Even when this is possible, it is very expensive. Thus, *fast* growth means market shares can be changed at low cost over short periods of time. This presents an opportunity to the low-share competitor and a risk to the dominant company. *Slow* market growth means market-share relationships are very stable and expensive to change.

The Growth/Share Matrix[3]

The value of market share and the importance of growth can be combined to help explain a company's portfolio of businesses, as Figure 7-1 illustrates.

---

[3]This and the following section outline the bare bones of the theory behind the growth/share matrix. For a more complete treatment, see "Note on the Boston Consulting Group Concept of Competitive Analysis and Corporate Strategy," HBS Case Services No. 175-175. (The note was produced by the Harvard Business School and is endorsed by BCG as an accurate presentation of its approach.) In addition, see "Drawing Product Portfolio Charts," UVA-M-0187, which explains the technical details behind BCG's graphics.

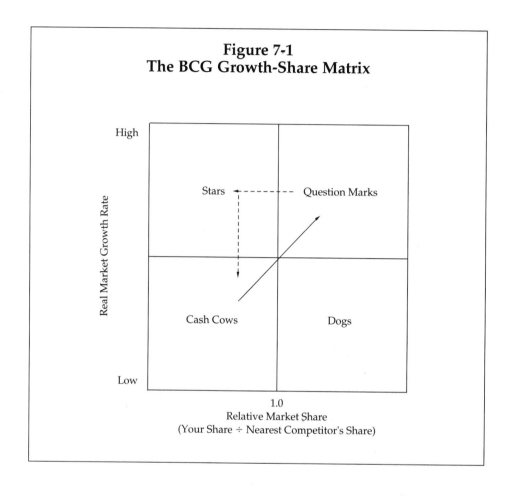

Figure 7-1
The BCG Growth-Share Matrix

Businesses with high market shares and high market growth are characterized as "stars." Their high shares indicate high profitability and potentially high cash generation. High growth means that cash must be continually put back into these businesses to maintain their dominant position. These businesses generate cash and require cash, leaving them in about a zero net-cash-flow position. The proper strategy maintains or improves market dominance.

Businesses with a high market shares and low market growth are characterized as "cash cows." Their high shares indicate high reported profits and cash-generation capability. Their low growth means that little cash is required for new assets to maintain market position. The proper strategy for a cash cow is to maintain dominance and produce cash flow for other corporate purposes.

Businesses with low market growth and low market shares are characterized as "dogs." The low share indicates low profits and little cash-generation capability. Although the low growth indicates that little cash is required to stay in the business, there is also little opportunity to alter the market-share relationships. Unless reinvestment is held to a minimum, these businesses can become "cash traps," using up more cash than they generate with no real hope of improved profitability.

The last category is the "question mark" business with high market growth and low market share. Here the reported profits and cash throw-off are low due to the market-share situation as well as the inherent lack of efficiency in fast-growth situations. On the other hand, the cash demands are high. Either the company should invest massively to gain market dominance while the high market growth provides the opportunity to alter market-share relationships (moving it to a star business, as shown by the dotted arrow in Figure 7-1), or it should get out. Any other path leads to a large cash investment merely to build a future dog as the market matures.

Balancing the Portfolio

Even when the businesses inside a company are unrelated in any manufacturing or marketing sense, they are always related by the needs of the company to balance its cash resources. The cash generated by the businesses must equal the cash used. Otherwise the company will build up cash reserves or go bankrupt. A company can achieve the ideal cash balance by having its star businesses largely fund their own growth and by having the cash throw-off of the cash cows fund the cash requirements of the question-mark businesses (the solid arrow in Figure 7-1). In this way, the company has both high reported profits (from its cash cows and stars) and good growth (from its stars and question marks).

Rarely do the characteristics of the businesses result in such an ideal cash balance, however. Usually a business has either too many growth opportunities (question marks) or too much cash-generation capability. Often the real chance of achieving dominance is so slim that the cash investment in the opportunities available would be largely wasted. In these cases, the company also has excess cash, although it can unwittingly get itself in a cash bind.

The major task of corporate management is balancing the cash flows among the portfolio of businesses to achieve the corporate goals of profits and growth. This is the essential resource allocation problem. The strategy for balancing cash flows must be devised with a long time horizon; it must focus on entire businesses rather than projects; and it must be designed to achieve a dominant market position in all the businesses in which the company participates.

Philosophy behind the BCG Approach

The BCG approach is to gather large amounts of quantitative data about the economic issues involved in marketing and manufacturing a client's products. This usually includes market size and historical and projected growth, industry and competitor cost structures, and the client's cost structure. This phase essentially involves detailed cost accounting to determine the profitability and cash flows associated with each SBU and each product line within each SBU.

These economic analyses are usually conducted by teams of extraordinarily bright MBAs from prestige schools, and the analysis is usually performed away from the client's premises. The result is an economic model intended to guide the client's decisions about growth, acquisition, divestment, and financial resource allocations. The model is usually presented to the client as a final presentation—frequently an oral report backed up with useful visual aids and summarized in a written document.

BCG rarely behaves informally with its clients. Its conclusions are usually revealed at the end of a project, often with the salutary effect of surprising complacent executives. BCG's distinctive competence lies in its ability to take an economic overview of the client's industry, to focus impressive brain power on voluminous data, to relate the firm to its competition, and to recommend a choice among strategic alternatives.

Limitations

One of the shortcomings of the BCG approach is that it can lead managers to treat each business unit as if it were totally independent of any other unit. That is, recommendations to grow a particular question mark or to divest a particular dog frequently fail to take into account the fact that the two businesses might be closely related and have a strong dependence on each other. For example, the two businesses might share manufacturing facilities, raw material sources, or a distribution channel or sales force. To reduce the activity in one business might result in increased costs for the sister business, given that a lower overall volume would be realized in the shared resource.

A second shortcoming is that, as an acquisition guide, the BCG approach can delude managers into believing that they can buy their way into above-average growth by acquiring stars or potential stars. There is a logical fallacy in this belief: (1) by definition, only one firm can be to the left of the 1.0 line—only the largest market-share holder will be there—and (2) few industries have a growth rate in excess of 10 percent (or even 5 percent—most GNPs grow at less than a 4 percent annual rate). Therefore—again, by definition—most firms in industrialized countries would fall in the lower right-hand quadrant; that is, they would be classified as dogs. It is next to impossible for a firm to acquire its way into a growth portfolio. (A firm can, of course, acquire second- or third-best players and manage them into reasonably good positions, as ITT did with Avis or Phillip Morris did with Miller Beer.)

A third shortcoming is motivational and stems from the labels given to nonstar SBUs. Few managers are excited about the prospect of being classified as managers of dog businesses.

Finally, BCG has not traditionally been known for giving top management direct assistance in implementing a new strategic direction. The firm is typically not prepared by disposition or skill to help line executives fight it out in the trenches when power is redistributed during the change process. In addition, due to the motivational problems associated with derogatory labeling, plus the fact that the analysis is conducted by outsiders and not line managers, implementation is often impeded by significant resistance from line personnel.

MCKINSEY AND THE MULTIFACTOR MATRIX

McKinsey & Company developed its approach to portfolio planning as part of its involvement in helping General Electric install the SBU planning system in 1970. Its collaboration was initiated in part because GE was uncomfortable with the way BCG's growth/share matrix depends on only two variables (market growth rate and relative market share). The discomfort was due, in part, to the sense that executives were being encouraged to make major financial decisions on the basis of two numerical calculations. What if market shares are misspecified? What if market growth rates are misforecasted? The BCG approach seemed to leave no room for judgmental inputs by the decision makers themselves. The project stemming from this discomfort led to McKinsey's development of the market attractiveness versus business strength matrix.

Multifactor Assessment[4]

The McKinsey approach makes two judgments: (1) How attractive is the market? and (2) How strong is the current position of a particular business in that market? In one sense, these judgments are similar to the BCG product portfolio—growth is part of market attractiveness and relative share is a component of business strength. The major difference is that the McKinsey approach suggests *several* factors that should be analyzed before judging market attractiveness and business strength. The standard set of factors considered usually include the following:

Industry Attractiveness	Business Strength
Market size	Size
Market growth	SBU growth
Market diversity	Market share
Competitive structure	Competitive position:
Cyclicality	• Product quality
Inflation sensitivity	• Technological leadership

---

[4]This and the following section were adapted from "Note on the Market Attractiveness-Business Strengths Matrix," UVA-M-0180.

<u>Industry Attractiveness</u>   <u>Business Strength</u>
International competition   • Marketing leadership
Role of technology   • Relative cost position
Legal environment   People
Industry profitability   Profitability
Labor environment   Image

Whether these particular factors or others are used in any analysis will depend on the specific market and business being studied.

Business Screen

The second step is to match a strategy to a business according to the combination of its competitive strength and market attractiveness. These strategies are usually displayed on a nine-cell matrix as in Figure 7-2.

Thus, strong businesses in attractive industries (top left cells) receive investment, weak businesses in unattractive industries (bottom right cells) are divested, and businesses along the diagonal are managed for earnings.

In practice, managers who use the matrix have found it more helpful to think of six generic strategy options:

1. *Invest to Hold.* This strategy seeks to prevent a business's position from eroding and to maintain its current position. This might include, for example, the decision to lower prices and improve distribution and service in an attempt to hold unit share.

2. *Invest to Penetrate.* This strategy is expansive; it seeks to strengthen the current business position by, for example, launching an advertising and promotional blitz and broadening the product line in order to build market share.

3. *Invest to Rebuild.* This strategy seeks to restore the strength of a business that has been weakened by managers "milking" the business for profit. It is essentially a share recovery strategy.

4. *Selective Investment.* This strategy is expansive in selected market niches where the benefits from gaining share are estimated to be higher than the costs, and it is contracting in niches where costs exceed benefits.

5. *Harvest.* Harvesting is a strategy that deliberately allows share to fall so that short-run income and cash rise. This might include cutting back on advertising, reducing equipment maintenance, discontinuing discounts, and so forth.

6. *Divestment.* Divestment means trying to sell the business to somebody else. Any investment made under this option would be minimal and solely to make the business more attractive for sale.

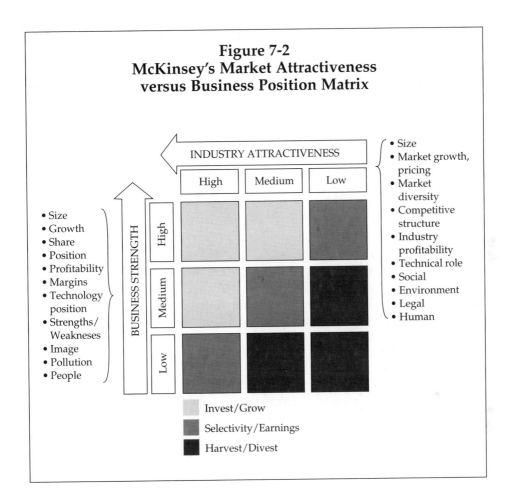

Figure 7-2
McKinsey's Market Attractiveness
versus Business Position Matrix

Invest/Grow

Selectivity/Earnings

Harvest/Divest

Philosophy behind the McKinsey Approach

Although McKinsey uses concepts similar to BCG's, it tends to give greater emphasis to a participative approach in working with clients. Whereas BCG assumes that the consultants can work alone to research and gather all the necessary data, McKinsey has a project team work on the client's premises to collect data. In addition, the project team will usually include management personnel from the client company. Whereas BCG's approach assumes that their job is to do high-quality research aimed at finding an answer to the client's strategic problem, McKinsey assumes that the strategist is just as important as the strategy; that is, McKinsey focuses on changing top management's behavior.

In the opinion of the author, a major influence on McKinsey's philosophy is its heritage as a general management consulting firm. Because of its experience in conducting organizational studies for clients, the firm is probably more sensitive than BCG to the political and motivational aspects of implementing strategy. As a result, McKinsey's approach is more akin to a partnership with the client (or, more precisely, the client's chief executive).

In sum, the contrast between the BCG and McKinsey philosophies may be summarized as follows:

- **BCG:** "The overwhelming weight of a good rational argument will convince the client."
- **McKinsey:** "An effective working relationship between client and consultant leads to good strategy planning and implementation."

Limitations

The multifactor approach has a few limitations. First, the factors are unweighed, yet common sense suggests that not all factors are equally important in assessing market attractiveness or business strength. For example, in assessing industry attractiveness, should market size receive the same weight as market growth?

The fact that the previous question might be answered differently by two different executives in the same firm leads to the second limitation: the approach is ultimately subjective. A real issue that arises is, whose business judgment should carry more weight when executives disagree?

A third limitation is that the relationships between the factors have not been established (in the sense, for example, that the PIMS relationships have been). Which factors are positive and which are negative? For example, some businesses benefit from inflation, whereas others do not.

In short, the matrix contains a multifactor model that has not been specified and calibrated. To be very critical, it could be said that the approach is nothing more than a shopping list of factors that ought to be checked off in a strategic analysis. On the other hand, one could argue that the shortcomings listed above are in fact strengths, because they force the analyst to think through the behavior of each factor in the specific situation under review. Thus, one could argue, this approach can prevent oversimplification of complex situations and the naive application of strategic principles.

ARTHUR D. LITTLE'S SBU SYSTEM[5]

ADL built its strategic planning system around the concepts of market segmentation, the product life cycle, and competitive position. Segmentation

---

[5]Most of this section, pages 408 to 415, quotes heavily from "Becton Dickinson and Company" (A_1), UVA-M-0247.

suggests that a company should be divided into strategic business units (SBUs) according to the industry segments in which they compete. ADL extended the product life-cycle concept to encompass the evolution of a whole industry and its market, with the argument that a view broader than that of a single product is required to formulate a strategy for an SBU. Similar to McKinsey, the concept of competitive position covers more than market share alone.

Arthur D. Little has incorporated these extended concepts into a system for managing diversified corporations that involves five sequential tasks:

1. Definition of SBUs
2. Classification of SBUs
3. Strategy development
4. Establishing priorities within the portfolio
5. Achieving objectives

Tasks 1 through 3 belong to the divisions, or, once they have been identified, to the SBUs. Task 4 belongs exclusively to corporate executives. Task 5 belongs to both corporate and division executives—corporate executives must establish incentive, measurement, and control systems; the division must implement strategy and achieve objectives.

Profiling

Tasks 1 through 3, on which the ADL system focuses, are accomplished in two-day profiling sessions held for each division and attended by the division president, all first-line functional managers, and usually several managers below the first line. Rank is dismissed as much as possible, and the profiling session is conducted by a knowledgeable outsider. According to Ray Gilmartin, a former ADL consultant,

> The purpose of the profiling session is to gather the information that exists in an SBU and organize it so that it is useful for formulating strategies. The SBU's managers, rather than a consultant's industry expert, are the data source; and the managers are the master strategists, not the consultant. Profiling is really a sort of anti-consulting. It recognizes that nobody knows more about a business than the people who run it.[6]

The first part of a profiling session is given over to building a database, which the session leader usually writes down on presentation sheets spread around the meeting room. In a sense, the session is much like a business-strategy case analysis (like the ones in Part II of this book), but the case study

---

[6]Becton Dickinson and Company(A_1), UVA-M-0247, p. 5.

is of the division itself. Vital statistics on the division's business and data about competitors, customers, and so on are collected in order to conduct industry analysis and to identify business strategy. Once the database is established, the profiling group moves in turn to each of the three tasks: defining SBUs, classifying them, and developing broad strategies for each.

Task 1: Defining SBUs

A strategic business unit is usually defined as "a natural business comprised of a group of products which serve common markets, contend with the same competitors, and are linked together so that strategies cannot be formulated for any of the products without impact on the others."[7]

To distinguish among a division's businesses and to define the SBUs within the division, the profiling group uses a set of clues provided by ADL. For example, how do price, quality, or style changes in one of the unit's products affect other products and product lines within and outside the unit? What distinct set of customers does the unit sell to? What distinct sets of competitors does it have? Although none of the clues is conclusive by itself, generally the examination of customers and competitors tends to be the most important factors in defining an SBU. The acid test—if a division's SBUs are hard to delineate—is whether a portion of the business can be divested or liquidated without altering the division's competitive situation. If it can, that portion is a distinct SBU.

Task 2: Classifying SBUs

Using a matrix with axes similar to McKinsey's, the next step is to classify each SBU and position it on a 24-cell grid of industry maturity versus competitive position. Although the axes are similar, their substance differs from McKinsey's:

Maturity is assessed at the level of the industry or market being served by the SBU. An industry's maturity is determined by the maturity of the function or need fulfilled by the set of products serving that need. Indicators of maturity include the industry's growth rate over time, the age of products in the SBU's industry, industry potential, the behavior of product lines within the industry, the number of competitors and the distribution of their market shares, ease of entry, customer loyalty, and the role of technology. For example:

- **Embryonic industries** usually experience rapid sales growth, frequent changes in technology, and fragmented, shifting market shares. The cash deployment to these businesses is often high relative to sales, because investment is made in market development, facilities, and

---

[7]Becton Dickinson and Company (A$_1$), UVA-M-0247, p. 6.

technology. Businesses in embryonic industries are generally not profitable, but investment is usually warranted in anticipation of gaining position in a developing market.

- **Growth industries** are generally characterized by a rapid expansion of sales as the market develops. Customers, shares, and technology are better known than in the embryonic stage, and entry into the industry can be more difficult. Businesses in growth industries generally produce low to good earnings and are capital borrowers.

- **In mature industries,** the competitors, technology, and customers are all known, and market shares show little volatility. The growth rate of these industries is usually about equal to the GNP. Businesses in mature industries tend to provide cash for the corporation through high earnings.

- **Aging industries** are characterized by falling demand for the product and limited growth potential. The number of competitors is shrinking, and survivors gain market share through attrition. Product lines have little variety. Little, if any, investment is made in research and development or plant and equipment, even though the aging business typically generates extremely high earnings.

Competitive position is a qualitative assessment of an SBU's standing in its market relative to its competitors. To assign a ranking of competitive position, the profilers study a wide range of factors: market share over time, relative breadth of product line, degree of customer concentration, technological strength compared to competitors, value of brand name or corporate name in the market, strength in the channels of distribution, degree of integration, quality of production facilities and nearness to capacity, and cost of production compared to competitors.

The rankings of competitive position range from dominant to nonviable:

- *Dominant.* Controls behavior or strategies of other competitors. Can choose from widest range of strategic options, independent of competitors' actions.

- *Strong.* Able to take independent stance or action without endangering long-term position. Can generally maintain long-term position in the face of competitors' actions.

- *Favorable.* Has strengths that are exploitable with certain strategies if industry conditions are favorable. Has more than average ability to improve position. If in a niche, holds a commanding position relatively secure from attack.

- *Tenable.* Has sufficient potential or strengths to warrant continuation in business. May maintain position with tacit consent of dominant company or the industry in general, but is unlikely to improve position significantly. If in a niche, is profitable, but clearly vulnerable to competitors' actions.

- **Weak.** Has currently unsatisfactory performance, but has strengths that may lead to improvement. Has many characteristics of a better position, but suffers from past mistakes or current weaknesses. Inherently a short-term position; must change (up or out).

- **Nonviable.** Has currently unsatisfactory performance and few, if any, strengths that may lead to improvement (may take years to die).

In this ranking system, a leading competitor truly dominates its industry. An industry can have only one company with a leading position, and not every industry has a company with that strong a position. Note that this is a major difference from the BCG assumption that there is only *one* viable position in an industry—that of number-one market share. In ADL's scheme, a variety of viable positions are possible that do not necessarily dominate the market.

Task 3: Developing Strategy

The third task of the profiling group is to develop broad strategies for the SBUs. The profiling group is responsible for identifying what ADL calls "natural" strategies for its SBUs, strategies based on economic logic. Natural strategies are appropriate to the maturity of the SBU's industry and the competitive strength of the SBU.

To aid in the development of strategies, ADL employs a competitive position/industry maturity matrix and divides the cells into three zones: green, yellow, and red (see Figure 7-3).

Those SBUs falling into green (G) cells can be expected to have a fairly wide range of successful strategies to choose from. SBUs in the red (R) zone will generally have few to choose from, or none; in most cases their choices would be to withdraw to a market niche or to leave the market. SBUs in the yellow (Y) caution zone might have an adequate range of options for the present, but unless they strengthen their competitive position, the natural maturation of their industries will carry them into the red (R) zone, restrict their options, and probably dampen their financial performance in the later phases of the industry's life.

According to the theory followed by ADL, the financial characteristics of an industry can be expected to follow a predictable pattern. *Sales* should grow during the embryonic and growth stages, peak during the mature stage, and decline thereafter. The industry should begin to show *profits* late in the embryonic stage or early in the growth stage. *Cash flow* should be negative through the embryonic stage and most of the growth stage, and become positive late in the growth stage.

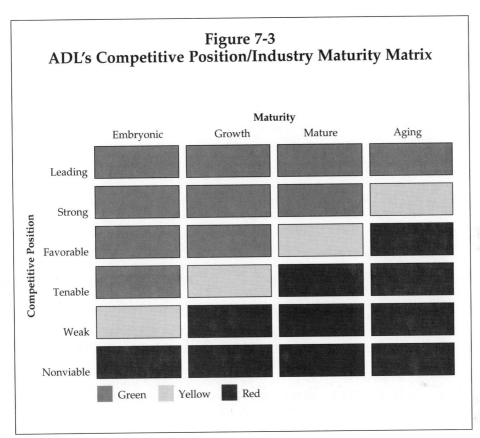

Figure 7-3
ADL's Competitive Position/Industry Maturity Matrix

Source: Arthur D. Little, Inc.

This normal pattern of financial characteristics, in conjunction with the varying degrees of strategic flexibility belonging to different positions in the matrix, suggests that certain generic strategies are appropriate to certain positions in the matrix and inappropriate to others. Backward integration, for example, could be expected to have a higher value in the mature phase than in earlier or later phases, and a higher value for stronger than for weaker competitors. As they select strategies for their SBUs, profiling groups work from a menu of 25 generic strategies, such as backward integration, distribution rationalization, and excess capacity. These strategies are then debated as to their appropriateness for the specific business being studied.

The 25 generic strategies of the ADL system can be used for three broad kinds of strategic moves: to build, to maintain, and to retrench. These, in turn, have variations that result in seven strategic thrusts: two maintenance roles, three building roles, and two retrenching roles.

1. ***Build Aggressively.*** Appropriate for moving up in competitive rank early in the industry's life or for increasing competitive distance for an SBU that already has a leading position.

2. ***Build Gradually.*** Strategic actions to continue the momentum of an aggressive move.

3. ***Build Selectively.*** Actions to establish a strong position in a subsector of the industry or to exploit the weaknesses of a particular competitor.

4. ***Maintain Aggressively.*** Aggressive action to maintain competitive distance or to resist attacks by competitors on an SBU with a leading or strong position.

5. ***Maintain Selectively.*** Actions to increase short-term profitability at the expense of market position.

6. ***Prove Viability.***

7. ***Divest or Liquidate.***

Tasks 4 and 5: Establishing Priorities within the Portfolio and Achieving Objectives

These tasks can only begin after the corporation has been divided into SBUs, all the SBUs have been profiled, and the appropriate strategic role has been assigned to each. ADL does not prescribe or specify a particular method for undertaking these tasks. At this stage, the consultant will work with corporate-level management to think through various alternatives and a plan for implementation.

The Philosophy behind the ADL Approach

ADL's philosophy can be summarized by the firm's four axioms of strategic planning:

1. Planning is a process based on data.

2. Strategic business units can be identified within a corporation.

3. Strategy is more condition driven than ambition driven.

4. There is a finite set of available strategies from which a business chooses those it will pursue.

What these axioms mean, in essence, is that although there are some basic economic realities to strategic management, and even though critical decisions should be based on hard data, the *process* of arriving at those decisions is as critical as the decisions themselves. By relying on line and staff executives of the SBUs to both provide the data *and* make the strategic decisions, the probability of successful implementation is enhanced considerably.

In sum, the contrast between the ADL philosophy and those of BCG and McKinsey may be as follows: in contrast to the data-gathering and analysis role assumed to be the consultant's job, ADL believes that a high percentage of the data needed to do strategic planning is available *within* the client organization, and that a participative group process will lead to the best strategy analysis and most likely implementation.

Limitations

The primary limitation of the ADL approach is that it is sometimes seen as being deterministic. That is, the assumption that "strategy is *condition driven*" and not ambition driven seems to suppose that good strategy is not driven by passion or emotion and that strategies can be reduced to 25 alternatives that should "fit" certain conditions as defined by industry maturity. Although ADL's approach is clearly not as severe as BCG's deterministic approach to strategy, some observers have wondered how the role of creativity might better be brought into the strategic management process.

SUMMARY CONTRAST OF THE THREE APPROACHES[8]

Following is a contrast of the three consulting firm approaches based on the dimensions of (1) how they work with a client, (2) the basic features of the approaches, and (3) what they deliver to their clients ("deliverables," in consulting industry parlance).

How Each Firm Works with the Client

BCG. Treats the development of business strategy as a problem that can be researched, mainly by examining economic, financial, and marketing data. These data are sorted and understood by using a number of business strategy concepts (experience curves, growth share matrices, sustainable growth formulas, and so forth).

McKinsey. Uses concepts similar to BCG, but gives greater emphasis to a participative approach in working with its clients.

---

[8]Adapted from John R. White, "Notes on Competitive Approaches to Strategy Consulting," a presentation made at Arthur D. Little Strategic Planning Workshop, September 1981.

ADL. Assumes that much of the knowledge and skill a firm needs to pre-pare its business strategy is held by the company's mid- and upper-level man-agers. The job of the consulting firm is to help identify these managers and then train them in the techniques needed to do strategic planning. The con-sultants will often manage the actual meeting to facilitate the surfacing of information and the making of decisions.

The Basic Features of Each Approach

BCG
- Team of BCG consultants acting as outside researchers
- Data from client and industry sources
- Extensive use of BCG's concepts to alter the client's perspective

McKinsey
- Team of McKinsey consultants frequently on site
- Data from client and industry sources
- Use of strategic concepts similar to BCG's, but often uses organization studies to complement the economic analysis aspects of strategic planning

ADL
- Profiling group processes facilitated by ADL consultants
- Analysis based largely on data provided by the client
- Analysis intended to give the client's managers a new, common lan-guage to apply to strategic decisions

What Each Firm Delivers

BCG. A presentation highlighting an answer to a strategic problem and the method BCG used to find it. A top-down approach that treats the corpo-ration as a holding company.

McKinsey. A report with an answer, plus the development of a close rela-tionship between the senior McKinsey consultant and the client chief execu-tive. This relationship becomes the medium for the CEO's attempts at behav-ior changes that will make him or her a better strategist. A top-down approach that contains some line executive involvement in data gathering.

ADL. A division-centered process that develops strategic thinking among line managers.

VALUE-BASED PLANNING

One shortcoming of the traditional portfolio techniques was that they did not take into consideration the inherent risks associated with different businesses and their industries. A number of consulting firms, such as Marakon and Strategic Planning Associates (SPA), applied modern portfolio theory to strategic planning and developed what has become known as **valued-based planning.**

Probably the leading proponent of value-based planning is Professor Alfred Rappaport of Northwestern University. His article, "Selecting Strategies That Create Shareholder Value," is reprinted on the following pages.

Selecting Strategies That Create Shareholder Value

Alfred Rappaport

In today's fast-changing, often bewildering business environment, formal systems for strategic planning have become one of top management's principal tools for evaluating and coping with uncertainty. Corporate board members are also showing increasing interest in ensuring that the company has adequate strategies and that these are tested against actual results. While the organizational dynamics and the sophistication of the strategic planning process vary widely among companies, the process almost invariably culminates in projected (commonly five-year) financial statements.

This accounting format enables top managers and the board to review and approve strategic plans in the same terms that the company reports its performance to shareholders and the financial community. Under current practice the projected financial statements, particularly projected earnings per share performance, commonly serve as the basis for judging the attractiveness of the strategic or long-term corporate plan.

The conventional accounting-oriented approach for evaluating the strategic plan does not, however, provide reliable answers to such basic questions as:

- Will the corporate plan create value for shareholders? If so, how much?
- Which business units are creating value and which are not?
- How would alternative strategic plans affect shareholder value?

My chief objective here is to provide top management and board members with a theoretically sound, practical approach for assessing the contributions of strategic business unit (SBU) plans and overall corporate strategic plans toward creating economic value for shareholders.

LIMITATIONS OF EPS

A principal objective of corporate strategic planning is to create value for shareholders. By focusing systematically on strategic decision making, such planning helps management allocate corporate resources to their most productive and profitable use. It is commonly assumed that if the strategic plan provides for "satisfactory" growth in EPS, then the market value of the company's shares will increase as the plan materializes, thus creating value for shareholders. Unfortunately, EPS growth does not necessarily lead to an increase in the market value of the stock. This phenomenon can be observed empirically and explained on theoretical grounds as well.

Of the Standard & Poor's 400 industrial companies, 172 achieved compounded EPS growth rates of 15% or better during 1974–1979. In 27, or 16%,

Author's note: I wish to thank Carl M. Noble, Jr., and Robert C. Statius Muller for their many helpful suggestions.

of these companies stockholders realized *negative* rates of return from dividends plus capital losses. For 60, or 35%, of the 172 companies, stockholders' returns were inadequate to compensate them just for inflation. The returns provided no compensation for risk. *Exhibit I* gives a more complete set of statistics. Additional evidence of the uncertain relationship between EPS growth and returns to shareholders is offered by the 1980 *Fortune* "500" survey of the largest industrial corporations. Forty-eight, or almost 10%, of the companies achieved positive EPS

Exhibit I

EPS growth rates versus rates of return to shareholders for
Standard & Poor's 400 industrial companies

	1976–1979	1975–1979‡	1974–1979
Companies with Annual EPS Growth of 10% or Greater*			
Total	259(100%)	268(100%)	232(100%)
Negative rates of return to shareholders	32(12%)	7(3%)	39(17%)
Rates of return inadequate to compensate shareholders for inflation†	65(25%)	36(13%)	89(38%)
Companies with Annual EPS Growth of 15% or Greater*			
Total	191(100%)	205(100%)	172(100%)
Negative rates of return to shareholders	14(7%)	2(1%)	27(16%)
Rates of return inadequate to compensate shareholders for inflation†	33(17%)	20(10%)	60(35%)

Note: EPS growth and rate-of-return calculations prepared by CompuServe, Inc., using Standard & Poor's Compustat data base.
*Restated primary EPS excluding extraordinary items and discontinued operations.
†The annual growth rates in the consumer price index for 1976–1979, 1975–1979, and 1974–1979 are 7.7%, 7.6%, and 8%, respectively.
‡The small number of companies with negative rates of return to shareholders for this period is due to low level of market at the end of 1974. Standard & Poor's stock index at the close of 1974 was 76.47 and, in subsequent years, 100.88, 119.46, 104.71, 107.21, and 121.02.

growth rates, while their stockholders realized negative rates of return for the 1969–1979 period. Thirteen of these companies had EPS growth rates in excess of 10% during this period.

EPS and related accounting ratios, such as return on investment and return on equity, have shortcomings as financial standards by which to evaluate corporate strategy for the following six reasons:

1. Alternative and equally acceptable determinations are possible for the EPS figure. Prominent examples are the differences that arise from LIFO and FIFO approaches to computing cost of sales and various methods of computing depreciation.

2. Earnings figures do not reflect differences in risk among strategies and SBUs. Risk is conditioned both by the nature of the business investment and by the relative proportions of debt and equity used to finance investments.

3. Earnings do not take into account the working capital and fixed investment needed for anticipated sales growth.

4. While projected earnings, of course, incorporate estimates of future revenues and expenses, they ignore potential changes in a company's cost of capital both because of inflation and because of shifting business and financial risk.

5. The EPS approach to strategy ignores dividend policy. If the objective were to maximize EPS, one could argue that the company should never pay any dividends as long as it expected to achieve a positive return on new investment. But we know that if the company invested shareholders' funds at below the minimum acceptable market rate, the value of the company would be bound to decrease.

6. The EPS approach does not specify a time preference rate for the EPS stream, i.e., it does not establish the value of a dollar of EPS this year compared with a year from now, two years from now, etc.

SHAREHOLDER VALUE APPROACH

The economic value of any investment is simply the anticipated cash flow discounted by the cost of capital. An essential feature of the discounted cash flow technique, of course, is that it takes into account that a dollar of cash received today is worth more than a dollar received a year from now, because today's dollar can be invested to earn a return during the intervening time.

While many companies employ the shareholder value approach using DCF analysis in capital budgeting, they use it more often at the project level than at the corporate strategy level. Thus, we sometimes see a situation where capital projects regularly exceed the minimum acceptable rate of return, while the business unit itself is a "problem" and creates little or no value for shareholders. The DCF criterion can be applied not only to internal investments such as additions to existing capacity but also is useful in analysis of opportunities for external growth such as corporate mergers and acquisitions.

Companies can usefully extend this approach from piecemeal applications to the entire strategic plan. An SBU is commonly defined as the smallest organizational unit for which integrated strategic planning, related to a distinct product that serves a well-defined market, is feasible. A strategy for an SBU may then be seen as a collection of product/market-related investments and the company itself may be characterized as a portfolio of these investment-requiring strategies. By estimating the future cash flows associated with each strategy, a company can assess the economic value to shareholders of alternative strategies at the business unit and corporate levels.

Steps in Analysis

The analysis for a shareholder value approach to strategic planning involves the following sequential steps:

- Estimation for each business unit and the corporation of the minimum pre-tax operating return on incremental sales needed to create value for share-holders.

- Comparison of minimum acceptable rates of return on incremental sales with rates realized during the past five years and initial projections for the next year and the five-year plan.

- Estimation of the contribution to shareholder value of alternative strategies at the business unit and corporate levels.

- Evaluation of the corporate plan to determine whether the projected growth is financially feasible in light of anticipated return on sales, invest-ment requirements per dollar of sales, target capital structure, and dividend policy.

- A financial self-evaluation at the business unit and corporate levels.

(Before proceeding to the case illustration in the next section, the reader may wish to refer to the *Appendix* to examine the basis for estimating the minimum pretax operating return on incremental sales needed to increase shareholder value, as well as the calculation of the absolute shareholder value contributed by various strategies.)

CASE OF ECONOVAL

Econoval, a diversified manufacturing company, divides its operations into three lines of business—semiconductors, energy, and automotive parts (see *Exhibit II*).

Before beginning their detailed analysis, Econoval managers must choose appropriate time horizons for calculating the value contributed by each business unit's strategy. The product life cycle stages of the various units will ordinarily determine this choice. If we were to measure value creation for all businesses arbitrarily in a common time horizon, say 5 years, then embryonic businesses with large capital requirements in early years and large payoffs in later years would be

---

Exhibit II
Strategic overview of Econoval's lines of business

Business unit	Product life cycle stage	Strategy	Risk	Current year's sales in $ millions
Semi-conductors	Embryonic	Invest aggressively to achieve dominant market position	High	$50
Energy	Expanding	Invest to improve market position	Medium	75
Automotive parts	Mature	Maintain market position	Low	125

---

viewed as poor prospects even if they were expected to yield exceptional value over the life cycle. Therefore, in this case, I have extended the projections for the semiconductor unit to 10 years and have limited projections for the energy and auto parts units to 5 years in the company's long-term financial plan.

Step 1—*Estimation of minimum return on incremental sales needed to create value for shareholders.*

The basis for calculating the minimum acceptable return on incremental sales appears as Equation (4) in the *Appendix*. For each business unit, four parameters need to be estimated: capital expenditures per dollar of sales increase, cash required for working capital per dollar of sales increase, the income tax rate, and the weighted average cost of capital. *Exhibit III* summarizes the results.

Before proceeding, I should comment on how to estimate these variables. To estimate the recent values for capital investment required per dollar of sales increase, one simply takes the sum of all capital expenditures less depreciation over the preceding 5 or 10 years and divides this amount by the sales increase during the period. Note that if a business continues to replace existing facilities in kind, and the prices of these facilities remain constant, then the numerator (i.e., capital expenditures less depreciation) approximates the cost of real growth in productive capacity.

However, the costs for capital expenditures usually rise each year owing to inflationary forces and regulatory requirements such as environmental control. These cost increases may be partially offset by advances in technology. Thus the numerator reflects not only the cost of real growth but price changes in facilities as well as the impact of product mix changes, regulation, and technological improvements. Whether the historical value of this variable is a reasonable basis for the projection period depends significantly on how quickly and to what extent the company can offset increased fixed capital costs by higher future selling prices, given the competitive structure of the industry.

Exhibit III

Minimum pretax operating return on incremental sales based on initial planning projections

Business unit	Investment requirements per dollar of sales increase		Cost of capital	Minimum return on incremental sales
	Capital expenditures	Working capital		
Semiconductors	.40	.20	.15	.145
Energy	.20	.20	.14	.091
Automotive parts	.15	.20	.13	.075

The increase in required working capital should reflect the cash flow consequences of changes in (1) minimum required cash balance, (2) accounts receivable, (3) inventory, and (4) accounts payable and accruals.

The appropriate rate for discounting the company's cash flow stream is the weighted average of the costs of debt and equity capital. For example, suppose a company's aftertax cost of debt is 6% and its estimated cost of equity 16%. Further, it plans to raise capital in the following proportion—20% by way of debt and 80% by equity. It computes the average cost of capital at 14% as follows:

	Weight	Cost	Weighted cost
Debt	.20	.06	.012
Equity	.80	.16	.128
Average cost of capital			.140

Is the company's cost of capital the appropriate rate for discounting the cash flow projections of individual business units? The use of a single discount rate for all parts of the company is valid only in the unlikely event that they are identically risky.

Executives who use a single discount rate companywide are likely to have a consistent bias in favor of funding higher-risk business at the expense of less risky businesses. To provide a consistent framework for dealing with different investment risks and thereby increasing shareholder value, management should allocate funds to business units on a risk-adjusted return basis.

The process of estimating a business unit's cost of capital inevitably involves a substantial degree of executive judgment. Unlike the company as a whole, ordinarily the business unit has no posted market price that would enable the analyst to estimate systematic or market-related risk. Moreover, it is often difficult to assign future financing (debt and equity) weights to individual business units.

One approach to estimating a business unit's cost of equity is to identify publicly traded stocks in the same line of buisness that might be expected to have about the same degree of systematic or market risk as the business unit. After establishing the cost of equity and cost of debt, the analyst can calculate a weighted-average cost of capital for the business unit in the same fashion as for the company.

The cost of equity or minimum return expected by investors is the risk-free rate (including the expected long-term rate of inflation) as reflected in current yields available in long-term government bonds plus a premium for accepting equity risk. The overall market risk premium for the last 40 years has averaged 5.7%.[1] The risk premium for an individual security can be estimated as the product of the market risk premium and the individual security's systematic risk, or beta coefficient.[2]

Following is the estimate for Econoval's semiconductor unit's cost of equity:

Risk-free rate + average beta coefficient for selected similarly financed semiconductor companies
× market risk premium for equity investments = cost of equity

$$9.25\% + 1.5\ (5.7\%) = \underline{17.8\%}$$

Assuming an aftertax cost of debt of 6.5% and financing proportions of 25% debt and 75% equity, the semiconductor unit's risk-adjusted cost of capital is estimated to be 15%. Risk-adjusted rates for the energy and auto parts units are 14% and 13%, respectively.

Step 2—*Comparison of minimum acceptable rates of return on incremenatal sales with recently realized rates and initial planning projections.*

Having developed some preliminary estimates of minimum return on incremental sales, Econoval now wishes to compare those rates with past and initially projected rates for each business unit's planning period. This comparison *(Exhibit IV)* provides both a reasonable check on the projections and insights into the potential of the various business units for creating shareholder value.

From *Exhibit IV,* we can determine that the semiconductor unit is projecting substantial improvement over historical margins on the basis of a continuing product mix shift toward higher-margin proprietary items and substantial R&D expenditures to maintain competitiveness in the learning curve race.

---

[1]Roger G. Ibbotson and Rex A. Sinquefield, "Stocks, Bonds, Bills and Inflation: Updates," *Financial Analysts Journal,* July–August 1979, p. 40.
[2]For a method of predicting beta, see Barr Rosenberg and James Guy, "Prediction of Beta from Investment Fundamentals," *Financial Analysts Journal,* May–June 1976, p. 60, and July–August 1976, p. 62.

Exhibit IV

Econoval's rates of return on incremental sales

Business unit	Historical		Minimum acceptable	Initial forecast
	Last year	Past five years		
Semiconductors	.115	.110	.145	.155
Energy	.100	.120	.091	.110
Automotive parts	.070	.080	.075	.080

Exhibit V

Semiconductor unit's planning projections for various scenarios

	Year									
	1	2	3	4	5	6	7	8	9	10
Conservative										
Sales growth rate	.25	.25	.20	.20	.18	.18	.18	.18	.18	.18
EBIT/sales	.115	.12	.125	.13	.135	.135	.135	.135	.135	.135
Working capital per dollar of sales increase	.20	.20	.20	.20	.20	.20	.20	.20	.20	.20
Capital expenditures per dollar of sales increase	.42	.42	.42	.40	.40	.35	.35	.35	.35	.35
Cash income tax rate	.41	.41	.41	.41	.41	.41	.41	.41	.41	.41
Most Likely										
Sales growth rate	.30	.28	.25	.22	.20	.20	.20	.20	.20	.20
EBIT/sales	.12	.125	.13	.135	.14	.145	.15	.15	.15	.145
Working capital per dollar of sales increase	.20	.20	.20	.20	.20	.20	.20	.20	.20	.20
Capital expenditures per dollar of sales increase	.45	.45	.44	.42	.42	.40	.38	.38	.35	.35
Cash income tax rate	.40	.40	.40	.40	.40	.40	.40	.40	.40	.40
Optimistic										
Sales growth rate	.32	.30	.30	.25	.25	.25	.25	.25	.25	.25
EBIT/sales	.125	.13	.14	.145	.15	.15	.15	.15	.15	.15
Working capital per dollar of sales increase	.18	.18	.18	.18	.18	.18	.18	.18	.18	.18
Capital expenditures per dollar of sales increase	.40	.38	.38	.36	.36	.35	.35	.35	.35	.35
Cash income tax rate	.39	.39	.39	.39	.39	.39	.39	.39	.39	.39

If the planned margins materialize, the semiconductor unit will contribute to shareholder value. At this initial stage, the company is concerned with the reasonableness of the projections and the small distance between projected and minimum acceptable margins. The energy unit is projecting a rate of return on incremental sales in line with its recent experience, and this 11% rate is comfortably over the 9.1% minimum acceptable rate.

The problem business unit is the automotive parts division. Margins have been eroding steadily, and the projected five-year margin is just above the acceptable minimum. Econoval managers are thus committed to investigating a full range of strategic alternatives for the automotive unit.

Step 3—*Estimation of shareholder value contribution for alternative strategies at the business unit and corporate levels.*

Once the company has developed and analyzed its initial planning projections, SBU managers and the corporate planning group can prepare more detailed analyses for evaluating alternative planning scenarios. *Exhibit V* shows the semiconductor unit's planning parameters for conservative, most likely, and optimistic scenarios.

The worst case or conservative scenario assumes significant market penetration by Japanese producers via major technological advances coupled with aggressive price cutting. The most likely scenario assumes the semiconductor group's continued dominance in the metal-oxide-semiconductor (MOS) market, substantial R&D expenditures to enable the semiconductor group to maintain its competitiveness in the learning curve race, and gradual Japanese technological parity, which will place pressure on sales margins. The optimistic scenario projects more rapid industry growth and great success in the unit's effort to carve out high margin proprietary niches.

Exhibit VI presents the shareholder value contribution for each of these three scenarios and for a range of discount rates.

Econoval expects the semiconductor unit's 10-year plan for the most likely scenario to contribute $10.60 million to shareholder value. The range of shareholder values from conservative to optimistic scenarios is from $4.87 million to $29.93 million for the estimated cost of capital or discount rate of 15%.

An assessment of the likelihood of each scenario will provide further insight into the relative riskiness of business unit investment strategies. For example, if all three scenarios are equally likely, the situation would be riskier than if the most likely scenario is 60% probable and the other two are each 20% probable.

Econoval performed similar analyses for the energy and automotive parts units. *Exhibit VII* summarizes the results for most likely scenarios. To ensure consistency in comparing or consolidating scenarios of various business units, it is important that the corporate planning group establish that such scenarios share

Exhibit VI

Semiconductor unit's shareholder value contribution for different scenarios and discount rates (in $ millions)

Scenario	Discount rate				
	.140	.145	.150	.155	.160
Conservative	$ 9.30	$ 6.96	$ 4.87	$ 2.99	$ 1.30
Most likely	16.92	13.59	10.60	7.91	5.48
Optimistic	39.64	34.53	29.93	25.79	22.05

Exhibit VII

Shareholder value, sales growth, and earnings growth rates by business unit for most likely scenarios

Business unit	Years in plan	Shareholder value increase			Growth rates	
		$ millions	Per discounted $ of sales increase	Per discounted $ of investment	Sales	Earnings
Semiconductors	10	10.60	.077	.128	22.4%	26.1%
Energy	5	8.79	.175	.438	15	17.7
Automotive parts	5	3.57	.068	.194	10	11.9
Consolidated		22.96				

common assumptions about critical environmental factors such as inflation and energy prices.

On closer inspection, we see that the analysis in *Exhibit VII* provides support for management's concern about the automotive unit's performance. While the unit now accounts for 50% of Econoval's sales, the company expects it to contribute only $3.57 million, or about 15% of the total increase in shareholder value.

On the basis of traditional criteria such as sales and earnings growth rates, the semiconductor unit clearly emerges as the star performer. However, its high investment requirements and risk vis-à-vis its sales margins combine to limit its value-creating potential. Despite the fact that the semiconductor unit's sales and earnings growth rates are substantially greater than those of the energy unit, the semiconductor unit is expected to contribute only marginally more shareholder value in 10 years than the energy unit in 5 years.

The shareholder value increase per discounted dollar of investment provides management with important information about where it is realizing the greatest benefits per dollar of investment. Indeed, this *value* return on investment (VROI), rather than the traditional accounting ROI, enables management to rank various business units on the basis of a substantive economic criterion.

The numerator of the VROI is simply the shareholder value increase of a strategy and the denominator, the present cost or investment. When the VROI ratio is equal to zero, the strategy yields exactly the risk-adjusted cost of capital, and when VROI is positive, the strategy yields a rate greater than its cost of capital. Note that the semiconductor unit ranks last, even behind the auto parts unit, in this all-important performance measure.

Ranking units on the basis of VROI can be particularly helpful to corporate headquarters in capital-rationing situations where the various parts of the business are competing for scarce funds. In the final analysis, however, corporate resources should be allocated to units so as to maximize the shareholder value of the company's total product-market portfolio.

Step 4—*Evaluation of the financial feasibility of the strategic plan.*

Once the company has established a preliminary plan, it should test its financial feasibility and whether it is fundable. This involves integrating the company's planned investment growth strategies with its dividend and financing policies. A particularly effective starting point is to estimate the company's maximum affordable dividend payout rate and its sensitivity to varying assumptions underlying the strategic plan.

To illustrate, Econoval calculates the maximum dividend payout for the first year of the five-year plan. On a consolidated basis, Econoval projects sales growth of 15.5%, earnings before interest and taxes (EBIT) to sales of 9.56%, an investment of $.481 per dollar of incremental sales, a cash income tax rate of 42.2%, and a current and target debt-to-equity ratio of 45.2% and 44.3%, respectively. Econoval can pay out no more than 6.3% of its net income as dividends. At the 6.3% payout rate, the earnings retained, plus added debt capacity, are just equal to the investment dollars required to support the 15.5% growth in sales from $250 million to $288.75 million.

It is easy to demonstrate this result. At $.481 per dollar of incremental sales, investment requirements (net of depreciation) on the projected $38.75 million sales increase will total $18.63 million. This amount will be financed as follows:

Aftertax earnings on sales of $288.75 million	$13.34 million
Less 6.3% dividend payout	.84
Earnings retained, i.e., increase in equity	12.50
Added debt capacity	5.08
Increase in deferred taxes	1.05
	$18.63 million

The maximum affordable dividend payout rate table *(Exhibit VIII)* shows how sensitive this rate is to changes in growth, profitability, investment intensity, and financial leverage. Note, for example, that if sales growth is increased from 15.5% to 16.5%, the maximum affordable dividend payout rate decreases from 6.3% to 1.1%, while a 1% increase in EBIT/sales raises the maximum affordable rate from 6.3% to 16.6%.

Exhibit IX presents Econoval's strategic funds statement for its five-year planning period. The cash required for investment in working capital and fixed capital exceeds the cash sources from operations in each year. This difference is reflected in the "net cash required" line. Another source of funds is, of course, debt financing.

The increase in debt capacity is established by reference to the target debt-to-equity ratios of Econoval's three principal businesses. Adding the increase in debt capacity to the net cash required provides the maximum affordable dividend, which, as seen earlier, is $.84 million or 6.3% in the first year and rises annually to 22.3% in the fifth year.

In *Exhibit X,* strategic funds statements for each of Econoval's main lines of business provide improved insights into product portfolio balancing opportuni-

Exhibit VIII

Maximum dividend payout rate analysis

Sales growth		Investment requirements per dollar of sales increase								
		.431			.481			.531		
		Debt/equity			Debt/equity			Debt/equity		
		.393	.443	.493	.393	.443	.493	.393	.443	.493
.145										
EBIT/sales	.086	−9.6%	10.1%	28.5%	−20.8%	−0.7%	18.1%	−31.9%	−11.5%	7.6%
	.096	3.8	21.2	37.4	−6.1	11.7	28.2	−15.9	2.2	19.0
	.106	14.4	29.9	44.4	5.6	21.4	36.2	−3.2	12.9	28.0
.155										
EBIT/sales	.086	−15.1	4.7	23.1	−26.9	−6.7	12.1	−38.7	−18.1	1.1
	.096	−1.0	16.4	32.6	−11.4	6.3	22.9	−21.9	−3.7	13.2
	.106	10.1	25.7	40.2	0.7	16.6	31.5	−8.6	7.6	22.8
.165										
EBIT/sales	.086	−20.4	−0.6	17.8	−32.8	−12.6	6.2	−45.3	−24.7	−5.4
	.096	−5.7	11.7	28.0	−16.7	1.1	17.7	−27.7	−9.5	7.5
	.106	5.8	21.4	36.0	−4.0	11.9	26.8	−13.8	2.4	17.6

Book tax rate = .460, cash tax rate = .422
Current debt/equity = .452
Current equity = $53.550 million

ties. The semiconductor group places a substantial burden on corporate funds. Over the next five years it will require more than $26 million of cash while the energy and auto parts units will throw off about $7 million in cash. Even after taking into account the estimated debt capacity contribution of semiconductors, corporate headquarters will still have to transfer $11 million to the unit.

After some further analysis, Econoval managers concluded that the strategic plan was financially feasible. The analysis did, however, raise two concerns. First, Econoval had a low affordable dividend payout rate and was vulnerable to sales margins lower than those projected. Of immediate concern was that the current year's dividend is larger than next year's projected affordable dividend.

Also, the strategic funds statement underscored the risk associated with the semiconductor group's aggressive competitive positioning and the related high level of investment requirements. This group's large cash requirements, coupled with its modest VROI, prompted Econoval managers to launch a study of alternative product portfolio strategies.

Exhibit IX

Econoval strategic funds statement for five-year planning period (in $ millions)

| | Year | | | | | |
	1	2	3	4	5	Total
Net income	13.34	15.74	18.54	21.75	25.44	94.81
Depreciation	3.84	4.74	5.82	7.03	8.32	29.74
Increase in deferred taxes	1.05	1.29	1.56	1.88	2.23	8.02
Sources of Funds	**18.23**	**21.77**	**25.92**	**30.66**	**35.99**	**132.57**
Capital expenditures	14.71	17.58	20.22	22.55	25.66	100.72
Increase in working capital	7.76	8.97	10.16	11.33	12.66	50.88
Uses of Funds	**22.47**	**26.55**	**30.38**	**33.88**	**38.32**	**151.60**
Net cash provided (required)	(4.24)	(4.78)	(4.46)	(3.22)	(2.33)	(19.03)
Increase in debt capacity	5.08	5.89	6.60	7.20	8.02	32.79
Maximum Affordable Dividend	**0.84**	**1.11**	**2.14**	**3.98**	**5.69**	**13.76**
Maximum affordable dividend payout rate	6.3%	7.1 %	11.5%	18.3%	22.3%	14.5%

Step 5—*A financial self-evaluation at the business unit and corporate levels.*

Increasingly, companies are adding financial self-evaluation to their strategic financial planning process.[3] A financial evaluation poses two fundamental questions: How much are the company and each of its major lines of business worth? How much would each of several plausible scenarios involving various combinations of future environments and management strategies affect the value of the company and its business units?

The following types of companies would especially benefit from conducting a financial evaluation:

[3]For a more detailed description of how to conduct a corporate financial self-evaluation, see my article, "Do You Know the Value of Your Company?" *Mergers & Acquisitions,* Spring 1979.

Exhibit X

Strategic funds statement for five-year planning period by business units (in $ millions)

	Semiconductors	Energy	Automotive parts	Consolidated
Net income	$34.53	$30.92	$29.36	$ 94.81
Depreciation	17.95	6.07	5.72	29.74
Increase in deferred income taxes	4.21	2.55	1.26	8.02
	56.69	**39.54**	**36.34**	**132.57**
Capital expenditures	62.31	21.24	17.17	100.72
Increase in working capital	20.45	15.17	15.26	50.88
	82.76	**36.41**	**32.43**	**151.60**
Net cash provided (required)	(26.07)	3.13	3.91	(19.03)
Increase in debt capacity	15.05	9.26	8.48	32.79
Maximum affordable dividend	**($11.02)**	**$12.39**	**$12.39**	**$ 13.76**

- Companies that wish to sell and need to establish a minimum acceptable selling price for their shares.
- Companies that are potential takeover targets.
- Companies considering selective divestments.
- Companies evaluating the attractiveness of repurchasing their own shares.
- Private companies wanting to establish the proper price at which to go public.
- Acquisition-minded companies wanting to assess the advantages of a cash versus a stock offer.

The present equity or shareholder value of any business unit, or the entire company, is the sum of the estimated shareholder value contribution from its strategic plan and the current cash flow level discounted at the risk-adjusted cost of capital less the market value of outstanding debt. *Exhibit XI* summarizes these values for Econoval and its three major business units. For example, the semiconductor unit's current cash flow perpetuity level is $2.97 million, which, when discounted at its risk-adjusted rate of 15%, produces a value of $19.8 million. Subtracting the $5 million of debt outstanding provides the $14.8 million pre-strategy equity value. To obtain the total equity or shareholder value of $25.40

Exhibit XI

Business unit and corporate financial evaluation summary—for most likely scenario
(in $ millions)

	Semiconductors	Energy	Automotive parts	Consolidated
Risk-adjusted pre-strategy equity value	$14.80	$20.93	$25.10	$60.83
Shareholder value contribution from strategic plan (see *Exhibit VII*)	10.60	8.79	3.57	22.96
Total equity value	**$25.40**	**$29.72**	**$28.67**	**$83.79**
Percent of total equity value	30.3%	35.5%	34.2%	
Econoval equity value at corporate cost of capital of 14%				$87.57

million for the semiconductor unit, simply add the $10.60 million value contributed by the strategic plan.

The sum of the three business unit values is $83.79 million. Combining the cash flows of the individual businesses and discounting them at the 14% risk-adjusted corporate cost of capital yields a value of $87.57 million. In this case, the difference between the value of the whole and the sum of the parts is minor. However, this may not always be true.

Aggregating the values of the company's business units is consistent with the assumption that the riskiness of each unit must be considered separately. If, however, the company's entry into unrelated businesses reduces the overall variability of its cash flows, then the lower expected probability of bankruptcy can decrease its cost of debt and increase its debt capacity.

What happens to the company's overall cost of capital naturally depends on any changes in the cost of equity capital as well as on the cost of debt. Analysis of the impact of business units on the total risk of the company is at best extremely difficult and subjective.

A more attractive alternative is to (1) assume risk independence in establishing cost of capital for business units and (2) interpret the difference between the value of the company and the aggregate value of its individual businesses as a broad approximation of the benefits or costs associated with the company's product portfolio balancing activities.

Econoval's corporate financial evaluation gave management not only an improved understanding of the relative contribution to shareholder value coming from each business but also the basis for structuring the purchase of an acquisition currently being negotiated. Econoval's market value was then about 25% less than its own estimate of value. Because the cash and exchange-of-shares price demanded by the selling shareholders was not materially different, Econoval management decided to offer cash rather than what it believed to be its undervalued shares.

MEETING THE FIDUCIARY DUTY

A fundamental fiduciary responsibility of corporate managers and boards of directors is to create economic value for their shareholders. Despite increasing sophistication in strategic planning applications, companies almost invariably evaluate the final product, the strategic plan, in terms of earnings per share or other accounting ratios such as return on investment or return on equity.

Surprisingly, the conventional accounting-oriented approach persists despite compelling theoretical and empirical evidence of the failings of accounting numbers as a reliable index for estimating changes in economic value. How should the board member of a company that has reported a decade of 15% annual EPS growth and no increase in its stock price respond when asked to approve yet another five-year business plan with projected EPS growth of 15%? The shareholder value approach to strategic planning would enable the board to recognize that despite impressive earnings growth projections, the company's increasing cost of capital, rising investment requirements per dollar of sales, and lower margins on sales are clear signs of value erosion.

A number of major companies are now using the shareholder value approach to strategic planning. The method requires virtually no data not already developed under current financial planning systems; moreover, an interactive computer program such as the "strategy valuator" (used in preparing the numerical illustrations) can help implement all of the steps I have outlined. Use of this approach should improve companies' prospects of creating value for their shareholders and thereby contribute to the long-run interests of the companies and of the economy.

APPENDIX:
CALCULATION OF VALUE CONTRIBUTED BY STRATEGY

The present value of a business is defined simply as the anticipated aftertax operating cash flows discounted by the weighted average cost of capital. The present value of the equity claims or shareholder value is then the value of the company (or business unit) less the market value of currently outstanding debt. The value of equity for a business that expects no further real sales growth and also expects annual cost increases to be offset by selling price increases in given by the following formula:

$$E_t \quad \frac{p(1 - T)S}{k} - D_t \qquad (1)$$

where:

E_t value of the equity at time t

p earnings before interest and taxes divided by sales

T income tax rate

S Sales

k weighted average cost of capital

D_t market value of debt outstanding at time t

The change in shareholder value (ΔE) for a given level of sales increase (ΔS) is then:

$$\Delta E_t \quad \frac{P_t(1 - T)\Delta S_t}{k} - \frac{(f_t + w_t)\Delta S_t}{(1 + k)} \qquad (2)$$

where:

p' $\Delta EBIT/\Delta$ sales, i.e., incremental operating margin on incremental sales

f capital expenditures minus depreciation per dollar of sales increase

w cash required for net working capital per dollar of sales increase

The change in equity or shareholder value is the difference between the after-tax operating cash flow perpetuity and the required investment outlay for fixed and working capital. Since all cash flows are assumed to occur at the end of the period, the outlays for working capital and fixed assets are discounted by $(1 + k)$ to obtain the present value. There is neither an increase nor a decrease in shareholder value for a specified sales increase whenever the value of the inflows and outflows is identical. Specifically, when

$$\frac{p_t'(1 - T)}{k} = \frac{(f_t + w_t)}{(1 + k)} \qquad (3)$$

From Equation (3) the break-even operating return on sales or the minimum pretax operating return on incremental sales (p'_{min}) needed to create value for shareholders is derived as:

$$p_{min}' = \frac{(f + w)k}{(1 - T)(1+k)} \qquad (4)$$

The shareholder value contributed by any strategy can be estimated by taking the capitalized value of the difference between the projected and the minimum acceptable operating return on incremental sales. More specifically, the change in shareholder value for time t is given by the following equation, which assumes book and cash income tax rates are identical. If they are not, another term must be added.

$$\Delta E_t = \frac{(p_t' - p_{t\,min}')(1 - T_t)\Delta S_t}{k(1 + k)^{t-1}} \qquad (5)$$

Minimum acceptable returns on incremental sales for a range of investment requirements per dollar of sales and costs of capital are presented below.

*Minimum pretax operating return on incremental sales to create value for shareholders**

Cost of capital	Investment requirement per dollar of incremental sales						
	.20	.30	.40	.50	.60	.70	.80
.12	.040	.059	.079	.099	.119	.139	.159
.14	.045	.068	.091	.114	.136	.159	.182
.16	.051	.077	.102	.128	.153	.179	.204
.18	.056	.085	.113	.141	.169	.198	.226
.20	.062	.093	.123	.154	.185	.216	.247

*Assumed income tax rate, 46%.

To illustrate, consider a business with sales of $50 million for its most recent year and the following assumptions for its five-year plan: sales growth rate = 15%; pretax operating margins on incremental sales = 13.5% for the first two years and 14.5% for the remaining three years; book and cash tax rate = 46%; working capital per dollar of sales = .20; capital expenditures per dollar of sales = .35; and cost of capital = 14%. Applying equation (4) for the minimum return on incremental sales (p'_{min}), we obtain 12.5%. A summary of the shareholder value contributed by the five-year plan is presented below.

	Sharehoolder value contributed by five-year plan (in $ millions)					
	Years					
	1	**2**	**3**	**4**	**5**	**Total**
Sales	$57.50	$66.12	$76.04	$87.45	$100.57	$387.68
Sales increase	7.50	8.62	9.92	11.41	13.12	50.57
Projected return on incremental sales minus minimum return	.01	.01	.02	.02	.02	
Shareholder present value increase*	$.29	$.29	$.59	$.59	$.60	$2.36

*Computed by using equation (5).

Note: The present value of the five-year plan is $2.36 million.

DISNEY PRODUCTIONS: THE WALT YEARS

> I just want to leave you with this thought that it's just been sort of a dress rehearsal . . . so if any of you start resting on your laurels, I mean, just forget it, because . . . we are just getting started.
>
> Walt Disney, quoted in *The Disney Management Style*

Almost 50 years after the company's founding, manicured lawns and ethereal quiet conveyed a campuslike atmosphere at Walt Disney Productions (WDP) in Burbank, California. Executives still arrived at work wearing Mickey Mouse polo shirts, animators still played the volleyball games Walt Disney encouraged on a studio lawn, Disney's favorite chili remained on the menu, and everyone still went by first names; but behind the facade was a very different company from the one Walt Disney left behind.

In early 1984, Raymond L. Watson, the new chairman of Walt Disney Productions, and Ronald Miller, the president, were faced with serious problems. Earnings had been sliding; for the company's fiscal six months ending March 31, although revenues had increased to $648.3 million, income declined 34 percent to $31.3 million. In the second quarter, the company's stock price, after reaching $84 the previous year—still a far cry from the heady days of the 1970s when it sold at 80 times earnings—had dropped to $51. In some brokerage houses, the stock had been downgraded from a "buy" to a "hold." To make matters worse, many prominent business and news publications were reporting the possibility of a takeover.

COMPANY HISTORY

Melville Bell Grosvenor, former editor of *National Geographic*, said in a 1966 edition,

> When future historians sit down to choose a Hall of Fame for our time, there will be trouble over the name of Walt Disney. Some judges will list him as an

This case was revised by Jeanne M. Liedtka, Associate Professor of Business Administration. The original case was written by William E. Fulmer and Robert M. Fulmer. In addition to the publications mentioned in this case, a selected bibliography is given in the teaching note. Copyright © 1993 by the University of Virginia Darden School Foundation, Charlottesville, VA.

artist; others will call him an educator. Still others may insist that Disney belongs with the inventors, and some will argue that he was a naturalist. Each, in my view, will have a point, for Walt Disney is all these things. But on one question the historians are bound to agree: Walter Elias Disney was a genius who brought laughter and knowledge to the world in a distinctive American way.

Animation

Walt Disney lived the American dream. Born in Chicago in 1901 and raised in rural Missouri, by the age of 10, he rose every morning at 3 A.M. to deliver newspapers in the suburbs of Kansas City. At home, he drew pictures of animals, only to have his father tear them up. Later, while working as a cartoonist for the *Kansas City Tribune*, he used some of his free time to make a few short movies that combined live characters and animation. In 1923 he moved to Hollywood with $40 and a head full of ideas.

In the fall of 1927, Disney traveled to New York with his wife Lillian (called Lilly) to negotiate a new contract for an animated series called *Oswald the Rabbit*. The distributor stole the series and hired Disney animators away. It was a doleful trip back; Disney needed a whole staff of animators, and he also needed a new character—fast.

The idea for Mickey Mouse was born on that return train trip. "I've got it," Walt told Lilly. "I'll do a series about a mouse. I'm going to call him Mortimer Mouse." Lilly liked the idea but thought "Mortimer" sounded "too dignified for a mouse." Walt responded, "All right, we'll call him Mickey Mouse. Mickey has a good friendly sound."

In Hollywood, Walt, his brother Roy, and chief animator Ub Iwerks began work on Mickey Mouse. That first Mickey cartoon, *Plane Crazy*, was a bit of nonsense inspired by the Lindbergh flight. When Disney took the movie to New York, film distributors were not interested. Nor were they interested in a second Mickey film, produced while Disney was traveling.

About this time, sound was being introduced in films. So Disney and Iwerks rigged a homemade radio with a microphone, put up a white sheet as a screen, and with two helpers, stood at the mike behind it with noisemakers, a xylophone, and a harmonica played by Wilfred Jackson, a newly employed animator. For six hours, Roy projected a short bit of animation from *Steamboat Willie*, the third Mickey film. The "sound crew" watched the image and whanged away. The result was ragged, but Disney was convinced that sound was for cartoons.

He hurried to New York with the film to complete the *Steamboat Willie* sound track. During the process, he had to wire Roy for more money. To raise it, Roy sold, among other things, one of Walt's proudest possessions, his Moon Cabriolet, an automobile with red and green running lights. The additional capital, however, enabled Disney to add sound to the first two "mouse films."

Suddenly the talking mouse was the darling of distributors. Now they came to Disney, asking him what he wanted to do and what they could do to help him. They got only part of the answer they were hoping for. He did plan to go on making Mickey Mouse cartoons, but he did not want to sell the film outright. Remembering his earlier experiences, he insisted on retaining complete control of his product. He signed Pat Powers as exclusive distributor for the Mickey Mouse cartoons on a one-year contract with no guaranteed option for renewal.

By the time Disney left New York in 1929, he had a package of four Mickey Mouse films ready for release: *Plane Crazy, Gallopin' Gaucho, The Opry House,* and *Steamboat Willie.* The reception when these films went into national distribution was so positive that he decided to attempt an animated short without Mickey or Minnie. He created *The Skeleton Dance,* the first of the Silly Symphonies.

The Skeleton Dance had no story and no characters. It was set in a graveyard in the smallest hours of the night, when the skeletons emerged from their graves and vaults, danced together for a few minutes, and then, with the coming of dawn, climbed back into their resting places. One distributor told Disney it was simply too gruesome, and Pat Powers told him to stick to mice.

Disney was beginning to suspect that his deal with Pat Powers was not working out, however. Powers would send them occasional checks for $3,000 to $4,000 from New York, which were enough to keep them going but not nearly what the Disneys believed they should be receiving for their widely acclaimed series. Walt and Roy were unable to get a full financial report on distribution revenues, and Powers, they discovered, had a somewhat shady business reputation. An even more disturbing rumor suggested that Powers was trying to make off with Ub Iwerks.

Roy and Walt casually mentioned to Powers that they needed additional cash. To indicate his goodwill, and in hopes of a tighter contract, Powers wrote a check for $5,000. Disney stalled him until the check cleared, then broke off contract negotiations. The Disneys made no attempt to retain the immensely talented Iwerks who, with Powers' backing, set up a new shop to produce a series called *Flip the Frog.* Flip did not catch on, because Iwerks lacked the one talent Disney had in abundance—that of story editor. Within a few years, Iwerks was back at work for Disney, on a strictly businesslike basis. Witnesses reported that, when passing Iwerks on the lot, Disney carefully looked the other way or, at best, spoke to him in monosyllables. Iwerks' technical genius was of enormous value to Disney, but his moment of disloyalty was never forgotten.

Disney continued to work with the Silly Symphonies because of their diversity and challenge. Because they were free of the script demands of Mickey and his gang, the Symphonies allowed more freedom to experiment with new concepts and techniques.

His next project involved Technicolor's new three-color process for film. Although a Silly Symphony called *Flowers and Trees* was already fully photographed in black and white, he decided to remake it in color. It was a gamble, because Technicolor was extraordinarily expensive, but the color version of this Silly Symphony caused a revolution in the animated-cartoon industry. In 1932 it became the first cartoon to win an Oscar.

Donald Duck made his first sputtering appearance in 1934. *The Wise Little Hen* made Donald an immediate hit. He went on to surpass Mickey as the star of the Disney stable. According to Disney,

> We're restricted with the mouse. He's become a little idol. The duck can blow his top and commit mayhem, but if I do anything like that with the mouse, I get letters from all over the world. "Mickey wouldn't act like that," they say.

As the pictures were cranked out, the art of animation progressed. Characters were given more dimension and perspective than the first, flat figures, but Disney was never satisfied with the status quo. "I knew locomotion was the key," he once said. "We had to learn to draw motion. We had to learn the way a graceful girl walks, how her dress moves, what happens when a mouse starts or stops running." Disney set up an elaborate school for his artists. "It was costly, but I had to have them ready for things we would eventually do." Even during financial difficulties, Disney maintained his commitment to the studio's extraordinary art school, where classic art and the old masters were studied.

His next dream was to make *Snow White and the Seven Dwarfs*, as the world's first feature-length cartoon. When word of this project got around Hollywood, many movie people said Disney was making his biggest mistake.

While his artists were training, Disney had technicians working on a new kind of camera he planned to use for *Snow White*. He was no longer satisfied with just round figures; now he wanted the illusion of depth in the scenes. To achieve it, he developed the radically different "multiplane" camera—and won an Academy Award for it. In photographing animated films, three separate drawings were usually involved, each done on a sheet of transparent celluloid. One showed the foreground, one the animated figures, and the last the background. Before the multiplane camera, the three celluloids were simply stacked together and the camera shot through them all, giving a flat image. With the multiplane, more than three celluloids could be used, and they could be placed in different planes, sometimes as much as three feet apart. The camera could focus in and out among these planes to give an effect of depth and motion.

Snow White cost $1.5 million. When the bankers became nervous about the costs, Disney reluctantly showed their representative the unfinished product to try to retain their confidence. He reported,

We needed a quarter of a million dollars to finish the picture, so you can guess how I felt. He sat there and didn't say a word. Finally, the picture was over and he walked to his car, with me following him like a puppy dog. Then he said, "Well, so long. You'll make a lot of money on that picture." So we got the money.

Snow White and the Seven Dwarfs went on to make cinema history and brought many honors to Disney. In 1938, Yale gave him an honorary master of arts. The same year brought honors from Harvard and the University of Southern California.

The immediate manifestations of this euphoria were the studio at Burbank (which cost $3,800,000) and the animated films *Pinocchio* ($2,500,000), *Bambi* ($1,700,000), and *Fantasia* ($2,300,000). The Disneys were soon heavily in debt. According to Roy Disney, "Success is hard to take."

Walt's intensity in pursuit of quality reached into every aspect of the studio, and his animators were known for their talent as artists in the truest sense of the word. The great English political cartoonist, David Low, said of Disney,

I do not know whether he draws a line himself. I hear that at his studios he employs hundreds of artists to do the work. But I assume that his is the direction, the constant aiming for improvement in the new expression, the tackling of its problems in an ascending scale and seemingly with aspirations over and above mere commercial success. It is the direction of a real artist. It makes Disney, not as a craftsman but as an artist who uses his brains, the most significant figure in graphic art since Leonardo.

The making of *Fantasia* was a perfect example of the Disney style: innovation and the "constant aiming for improvement." *Fantasia*, released in 1940, started out to be a kind of super Silly Symphony for Mickey Mouse, with Leopold Stokowski directing a full orchestra in "The Sorcerer's Apprentice." Disney built it into much more, a brilliant combination of animation and fine music—from Beethoven's "Pastoral Symphony" to Stravinsky's "Rite of Spring." *Fantasia* introduced stereophonic sound 15 years before it was generally used in motion pictures.

Fantasia was released at a time when Disney was losing much of his freedom to experiment. The company's heavy debts and the war in Europe, which knocked out the lucrative foreign market, had forced him to go public. In 1940 Walt Disney Productions issued 155,000 shares of 6 percent convertible preferred stock at $25 a share, raising $3,500,000. Walt and Roy received employment contracts with the company, but they were never again to run the firm with the same freedom and creativity as before. *Fantasia*, the high point of Disney's experimentalism, had to be released in an abbreviated version. "The bankers panicked," said Disney. "*Fantasia* was never made to go out in regular release. I was asked to help cut it. I turned my back. Someone else cut it." It failed at the box office.

In the summer of 1941, the studio was hit by a jurisdictional strike, an event that so dismayed Walt Disney that he wept. With one catastrophe after another, the Disney stock slumped to $3 a share. According to Roy, "More than once I would have given up, had it not been for Walt's ornery faith that we would eventually succeed."

The crisis in the company was overshadowed over the next four years by war. The wartime public showed little interest in animated films. People wanted live action. Just before Pearl Harbor, Disney converted to war work, and soon about 94 percent of his efforts involved making training and propaganda films. There was little profit, but this war work helped reduce the company's bank loans to $500,000.

While Disney prints brought in some money and helped ease the company's debt problems, wartime production simply postponed the firm's other problems. "We had to start all over again," Walt said. The old free-wheeling, free-spending days were over. Roy commented, "When you go public it changes your life. Where you were free to do things, you are bound by a lot of conventions—bound to other owners."

True-Life Adventure Films

The nature films had begun with the animated *Bambi*, but after the war, Disney began looking for new kinds of films to make. He decided that "to get closer to nature we had to train our artists in animal locomotion and anatomy." He introduced live animals into the studio, deer and rabbits and skunks:

> But they were not good. They were just pets. So we sent the artists out to zoos, and all we got were animals in captivity. Finally I sent out some naturalist-cameramen to photograph the animals in their natural environment. We captured a lot of interesting things and I said, "Gee, if we really give these boys a chance, we might get something unique!"

Disney sent Alfred Milotte and his wife Elma to Alaska. They sent back miles of film. In reviewing it, Disney stumbled on one of the great stories of nature: the saga of the fur seals coming up from the sea to crowded island beaches in the Pribilofs to mate and calve. The film was *Seal Island*, which won an Oscar as 1948's best two-reel subject.

For another film, Disney kept cameraman-naturalist Milotte in the wild for more than a year, photographing the beaver's life habits. Out of Milotte's footage came an Oscar for *In Beaver Valley*. Other Oscar-winning films in the True Life Adventure series were *Nature's Half-Acre, Water Birds, The Alaskan Eskimo, The Living Desert, Bear Country, The Vanishing Prairie,* and *White Wilderness*. Between 1950 and 1960, more than a dozen films were produced in this series.

The True Life Adventures were sometimes criticized for being subjective and emotional. Because the producers anticipated the audience's tendency to identify with the animals on an emotional level, animal behavior was interpreted in human terms. The films were designed for the enjoyment of a mass audience—what Disney called the "big family."

Live-Action Films

Live-action feature-length films were a greater challenge than nature filming: "I had to grow with them," Disney said. "I couldn't make a live-action feature until I had experience." This came after the war as a result of money the company had impounded abroad. Disney went to England to use some of those funds and decided to experiment there with live action. "I struggled with it. I kept playing around. I couldn't decide what kind of live action I should do, what would please that big family." The format finally crystallized in the early 1950s with *Treasure Island, The Story of Robin Hood and His Merry Men, The Sword and the Rose*, and *Rob Roy, The Highland Rogue*. They were immensely popular films with the public, and Disney knew he could succeed with live action.

Meanwhile, he was working on another animated feature. It took him over two years to make it, but he hit the jackpot with it. *Cinderella* grossed more than $4 million domestically, and WDP, which had been in the red for two years, was solvent again.

The company's position was further strengthened in the 1950s by a rising tide of affluent youngsters and by further diversification, this time into ventures other than motion pictures. Roy Disney established a profitable film-distribution subsidiary in 1953, the Buena Vista project, which gave the company control of its film releases and reduced distribution costs from 30 percent of gross rentals to an estimated 15 percent.

Television

The motion picture industry had no clear notion of how to cope with television in the mid-1950s. Most studios were fearful. Roy Disney commented, "When the industry was cussing television and trying to ignore it, Walt moved in and worked with it and made it work for him."

Disney's strategy was simple enough. With the opening of Disneyland in the works, he started *The Wonderful World of Disney* in 1954. The series ran for two decades on NBC-TV. He also developed the *Mickey Mouse Club* television show. Television made a modest profit for Disney, but, more importantly, it provided free advertising for Disneyland, Disney motion pictures, and Disney himself. The TV productions went into the company's film library and were wholly owned by WDP.

Disney's ability to relate to his audiences was exemplified by the process of choosing kids for the *Mickey Mouse Club* show. Disney told producer Bill Walsh, "Don't get me those kids with the tightly curled hairdos—tap dancers—get me children who look like they're having fun. Then later we can teach them to tap dance or sing or whatever." He suggested going to ordinary schools and watching kids at recess, because "pretty soon there would be one we would watch—whether he was doing anything or not—because that would be the one we'd be interested in. And that would be the kid we'd want for the show." They used the technique and found Annette and Darlene and Cubby and the bunch—and they all became popular.

Along with launching *The Wonderful World of Disney* in 1954, the studio also released *20,000 Leagues Under the Sea*, the most ambitious live-action picture in company history. It was a big-budget movie using major Hollywood stars (Kirk Douglas, James Mason, Paul Lukas, and Peter Lorre) and spectacular special effects. The film combined fantasy and adventure with an excellent script and direction; it won two Oscars. It was followed by *Swiss Family Robinson, The Shaggy Dog, The Absent-Minded Professor, Son of Flubber, Pollyanna,* and *The Parent Trap*. In 1964 *Mary Poppins* became one of the greatest hits in the history of the industry and captured five Academy Awards.

The studio was now enjoying success with a wide variety of live-action productions and animation. The outlook for Disney was bright, partly because of the decision to move into television rather than hoping it would not interfere with the movie business. Most other major studios experienced a sharp decline in their fortunes.

Disneyland

Walt Disney had been thinking about Disneyland for 15 or 20 years before it became a physical reality. The idea of sinking millions of dollars into an amusement park, even Disney's kind of amusement park, seemed so preposterous that he did not mention it to anyone for a long time. He just quietly began planning. "I had all my drawing things laid out at home, and I'd work on plans for the park, as a hobby, at night."

He borrowed $100,000 against his life insurance policy to finance the planning of Disneyland. To find a proper site for it, Disney called in the Stanford Research Institute, which recommended three locations as alternatives. Disney picked Anaheim because it had five inches less rain a year than the San Gabriel or San Fernando Valley sites. It also happened to be in the population center of southern California and only 26 miles from Los Angeles. Disney purchased 244 acres of land, mostly orange groves, with his own money. To finance Disneyland, he brought in three investors: WDP, the American Broadcasting Company (ABC), and Western Printing and Lithographing Co. [1]

---

[1]Disneyland in 1989 was owned solely by Walt Disney Productions, which began buying out the other investors in 1957. For example, Disney bought out ABC's interest for $7.5 million and took over the food services as soon as the leases could be terminated.

Disney wanted a park that adults could enjoy (adult guests outnumbered children three and a half to one). According to Dick Nunis, the boss of outdoor recreation, Disney believed, "Everyone's a kid at heart—all you have to do is let him find a way to be one." Disney people were also quick to point out the educational aspects of theme parks, but Disney had said, "I'd rather entertain and hope people learn than teach and hope they are entertained." He always maintained his audience was "honest adults."

In the park, Disney was a stickler for quality, authenticity, and attention to detail. There were 700 varieties of plants from all over the world. (It took 30 gardeners to care for them.) The trash bins cost $150 each to paint and were designed to be highly visible without clashing with their surroundings. Audio-Animatronic figures were so lifelike that they often invoked arguments as to whether they were real. An air jet was put in front of every porthole in the submarine, because fewer people suffered from claustrophobia if they had moving air and something to see.

The Matterhorn was $1/100$ the height of the real one. It contained 500 tons of structural steel, and almost no two pieces were the same length, size, or weight. Disney designers studied hundreds of pictures of the rugged peak to create as close a copy as they could. Roy Disney opposed building the Matterhorn, because of the $7 million cost, but when Roy was away on a trip to Europe, Walt called an executive meeting. "We're going to build the Matterhorn and when Roy gets back from Europe, let him figure out how to pay for it." Walt had once commented, "The folks who win financially are the ones who don't worry about money."

Disneyland characters and entertainers underwent several days of training before meeting the public. They were to be neat, friendly, and courteous. No stone was to be left unturned to ensure people an enjoyable and hassle-free escape from the troubles of everyday life.

At the opening in July 1955, Disney said, "Disneyland will never be completed. It will grow as long as there is imagination left in the world."

Mineral King Project

"The fun is in always building something," Disney said. "After it's built, you play with it a little and then you're through. You see, we never do the same thing twice around here. We're always opening up new doors."

The next new door came out of Walt's personal interest in skiing. The Forest Service asked for bids to develop the Mineral King area into a year-round recreational area. An Alpine-like area, with its peaks rising as high as 12,400 feet in the Sequoia National Forest, Mineral King is about halfway between Los Angeles and San Francisco.

The most ambitious of the six bids submitted was by WDP. Disney's successful bid called for the construction of permanent housing with 2,400 beds plus temporary summer units with 4,800 beds; a 2,600-car parking area, and an Alpine Village from which cars would be excluded. Ski lifts would be designed to handle 15,000 to 20,000 skiers on the slopes at one time. A 25-mile road, part of it through the Sequoia National Park and over some of the most rugged terrain in the Sierra Nevada Mountains, was planned.

Disney's plan, and particularly the road, was opposed by the Sierra Club, a national organization of conservationists with considerable strength in California. Disney, surprised at the strength and tenacity of the Sierra Club, was ultimately forced to abandon the Mineral King project.

Walt Disney World

In October 1965 (approximately the same time as the Mineral King project was announced), Disney announced "the biggest thing we have ever tackled." The project (eventually, Walt Disney World and EPCOT) involved building two cities, one called "Yesterday" and one called "Tomorrow," in central Florida. These cities would include an airport, hotels, motels, convention facilities, industrial exhibits by U.S. corporations, shopping centers, camping grounds and facilities, curio and gift shops, service stations, golf, swimming, boating, a game refuge, power generators, and possibly even a movie studio. The project required seven years of planning and $600 million to build.

WDP firmly resolved to avoid repeating the principal business error made in the development of Disneyland: allowing hundreds of motels and other businesses to spring up around the periphery of the park. Calling them "honky-tonks," Disney believed they detracted from the park's image. Also, hotels in the vicinity of the park were grossing $300 million a year at a time when Disneyland grossed only $65 million. E. Cardon "Card" Walker, then executive vice president of WDP, said, "We were determined that if we ever did it again, we would buy enough land to control the complete environment."

In the early 1960s, the company's real estate agents purchased 27,443 acres in about 18 months at an average cost of just under $200 an acre under the company names of Tomahawk and Compass East. In October 1965, an announcement was made that the entire tract was owned by subsidiaries of Walt Disney.

Perhaps Disney's biggest coup in the project was the enabling legislation won from the state of Florida. It gave the company the powers of a county. It could establish its own building code and zoning regulations, form its own improvement district, and finance improvement with municipal bonds. It established two municipalities, Reedy Creek and Bay Lake, in which top Disney people were councilors. The company also got Florida to ban the use by others of any Disney characters in a business name anywhere in the state, and no business could advertise itself as being so many miles from Disney World.

Disney also worked out an impressive agreement with 17 building trade unions that contained no-strike, no-lockout clauses and provisions for handling grievances, including binding arbitration. When it became clear that the

Florida management could not attract the number of attractive, personable young people it needed, the company decided to hire 1,200 students to rotate in 300 jobs. By working with colleges, they were able to hire 300 students each quarter in jobs related to their majors. Some colleges even gave credit for the experience. Although few inside opportunities to advance beyond entry-level positions existed, Disney created an outplacement program that brought employees who did not want to remain in park-related jobs together with corporations who did business in the park.

Work on the landscaping began three years before the park was built. The Jungle Cruise had to have real African flora, and Liberty Square had to have a 32-ton Liberty Oak. In all, 55,000 trees and shrubs were brought in from all over the world—not for planting but for testing.

Culture at the Theme Parks

The "service-through-people" theme at the Disney parks started with a special language. There was no such thing as a worker at Disney. The employees out front were "cast members," and the personnel department was "casting." Whenever someone worked with the public, he or she was "on stage." Red Pope (a long-time Disney observer and writer) noted this phenomenon when two of his children, aged 16 and 18, were hired by Disney World to take tickets. For this seemingly mundane job, four eight-hour days of instruction were required before they were allowed to go "on stage." They learned about Guests—not lowercase *c* customers, but uppercase *G* Guests.

When Pope asked his children why it had taken four days to learn how to take tickets, they replied,

> What happens if someone wants to know where the restrooms are, when the parade starts, what bus to take to get back to the campgrounds? We need to know the answers and where to get the answers quickly. After all, Dad, we're on stage and help produce the Show for our Guests. Our job every minute is to help Guests enjoy the party.[2]

People were brought into the Disney culture early. All of the parks had a grooming and behavior code. Men had to have their hair cut above their ears and collars and be clean-shaven. Women had to be "natural" and not wear large earrings, eye shadow, or noticeable makeup. Employees were to be pleasant and helpful at all times and not eat, drink, smoke, curse, or chew gum while working with the public. Everyone had to attend Disney University and pass "Traditions I" before going to specialized training. According to Red Pope,

---

[2]The comments by Red Pope are reported in Thomas J. Peters and Robert H. Waterman, Jr., *In Search of Excellence* (New York: Harper & Row, 1982), pp. 167–68.

Traditions I is an all-day experience where the new hire gets a constant offering of Disney philosophy and operating methodology. No one is exempt from the course, from VP to entry-level part-timers. Disney expects the new CM (cast member) to know something about the company, its history and success, its management style before he actually goes to work. Every person is shown how each division relates to other divisions—Operations, Resorts, Food and Beverage, Marketing, Finance, Merchandising, Entertainment, etc. and how each division "relates to the show." In other words, "Here's how all of us work together to make things happen. Here's your part in the big picture."

Employees were well indoctrinated with the eleven characteristics of "The Disney Management Style": (1) we're a friendly, informal organization, (2) we work as a team, (3) it's all "our responsibility," (4) we're a Disney Democracy, (5) we communicate openly, (6) we make mistakes, because we're human, (7) we have a sense of humor, (8) we're creative people, (9) we're curious people, (10) we're businesspeople, and (11) we're not only dreamers, but doers.

The systems support for people on stage was also impressive. For example, hundreds of phones were hidden in the bushes as hot lines to a central question-answering service. The amount of effort put into the daily cleanup amazed even the most calloused outside observers.

Intense management involvement in the parks was highlighted at Disney by an annual week-long program called "cross-utilization." As Pope described it, this program entailed Disney executives leaving their desks and their usual business garb to "don a theme costume and head for the action." For a full week, the boss would sell tickets, popcorn, dishes of ice cream, or hot dogs, load and unload rides, park cars, drive the monorail or the trains, and take on any of the 100 on-stage jobs that made the entertainment parks come alive.

TRANSITIONS

In the midst of all this activity of the mid-1960s, Walt Disney was diagnosed as having cancer. According to Roy Disney, "I heard him refer to this cruel blow only once. 'Whatever it is I've got,' he told me, 'don't get it.'"

Having resigned all official positions in the company as early as 1960, Walt now was encouraging others to take on more responsibility. He claimed that his "greatest accomplishment was that I built an organization of people that enable me to do the things I wanted to do all my life." He had given his seven top producers an opportunity to share financially in the success or failure of their projects. He hoped that one of them would emerge as a clear successor. None had.

He was asked in 1963, "What happens when there is no more Walt Disney?"

Every day I'm throwing more responsibility to other men. Every day I'm trying to organize them more strongly. But I'll probably outlive them all. I'm 61.
I've got everything I started out with except my tonsils, and that's above
average. I plan to be around for a while.

He died on December 15, 1966, two weeks after his 65th birthday.

Walt Disney's death left a creative void at Disney. Because he was such a
catalyst for ideas, talented men and women had been willing to work for him.
"When Walt was alive, he was the leader because he was a creative cyclone,"
said Roy.

Red Pope commented:

How Disney looks upon people, internally and externally, handles them,
communicates with them, rewards them, is in my view the basic foundation upon which five decades of success stand. I have come to observe
closely and with reverence the theory and practice of selling satisfaction
and serving millions of people on a daily basis successfully. It is what
Disney does best.

   He was a genius, but a moody genius. If he liked an idea, he was lavish
in his praise, but if he disliked an idea, he could be abrupt, curt, and bitingly
critical. He had no patience with anyone who would settle for second best. As
a result, Disney people sometimes worked with butterflies in their stomachs
trying to come up with "what Walt wants."

Roy Disney, at age 74, tried to replace his brother's distinctive brand of
creative leadership with management by committee. Working with Roy to
carry on were William H. Anderson, production vice president; Donn B.
Tatum, assistant to the president; Card Walker, marketing vice president; and
Ronald W. Miller, Walt's son-in-law and a board member. Roy explained,

I know a committee form is a lousy form in this business, but it's the best
we've got until someone in the younger crowd shows he's got the stature to
take over the leadership. If the chips are down, I've got the decisions. My way
is to compromise, and I admit that that isn't a sound basis. But, I think I would
do even more damage trying to make creative decisions the way Walt did.

Walt left a legacy of products. Five brand-new movies were all but in the
can. Disneyland had just undergone an expansion, and Disney World was
well along in the planning stages. Just weeks before his death, he first
sketched EPCOT on a napkin and described it in a film as a model city, "a
working community with employment for all." According to Roy,

We've never before had this much product on hand. Walt died at the pinna-
cle of his producing career in every way. The big thing that is bugging
American industry is planning ahead. We've got the most beautiful ten-year
plan we could ask for.

As CEO, Roy Disney supervised the completion of Florida's Walt Disney World, which opened in October 1971, and later that year, he died at the age of 78.

Now the leadership passed to Card Walker. Walker, who had joined the company in 1938 as a mail clerk, possessed an encyclopedic knowledge of the business that had made him invaluable to the Disneys. He was very close to their families, a good friend, and an enthusiastic supporter. He tried to continue the Walt Disney spirit. He once remarked, "Walt's in this room. He'll always be in this room. We know what he would think is right or wrong, and that's good enough for us."

EPCOT

The immediate success of Walt Disney World spurred the decision in the mid-1970s to proceed with the Experimental Prototype Community of Tomorrow, EPCOT. Walt's original model-city concept, however, with a dome controlling the climate of the central city and office buildings that would be orbited by residences, schools, and green space, was too ambitious for even the most loyal Walt Disney followers. Disney management abandoned it as too expensive to keep technologically up to date and too difficult to control. Furthermore, the idea for 20,000 people to live and work in the community was scrapped. Instead, EPCOT evolved into two theme parks: Future World, to showcase past and future technologies and the expression of human imagination, and World Showcase, which simulated the cultures of nine nations (more to be added later) in a sort of permanent world's fair. It was a $1.2-billion project, and more than its predecessors, Disneyland and Disney World, EPCOT was aimed primarily at grown-ups.

As with all Disney endeavors, the logistics strained the imagination. Some 54 million tons of earth were moved; 16,000 tons of steel were used; and 500,000 board feet of lumber went into construction of the sets alone. Around the 40-acre man-made lagoon, 70 acres of sod were laid, 12,500 trees and 10,000 shrubs planted. More than 1.5 million feet of film were shot in 30 different countries and edited for more than four hours of shows. An entire 3-D camera and projection system was invented for the 360-degree wraparound show in the Imagination pavilion.

Money from corporate tie-ins was crucial to Disney's ability to finance EPCOT, by generating more than one-third of the total cost. Large corporations paid up to $25 million each for the privilege of affixing their names to individual pavilions.

Just before EPCOT opened in the fall of 1982, Disney officials were surprised when Disney World characters voted 45 to 41 to be represented by the Teamsters. Although Disney had defeated earlier efforts by characters to join the stagehands' union, management accepted Teamster representation quietly. The Teamsters became the 17th union at Disney World and EPCOT.

(Disneyland had 28 unions.) According to *Forbes,* "There had already been enough bad publicity from employees—evading the Disney ban on talking to the press—complaining anonymously to reporters about hot and dirty costumes, abusive child customers and low wages." (The wage base for Disney World employees, many of whom were food-and-beverage or sanitation workers, in 1983 was $4.60 to $6.00 per hour, resulting in a payroll of $4 million per week.)

Tokyo

In April 1983, after two years of construction involving 3,000 workers, the biggest Disneyland of them all at that time opened on 202 acres of landfill in Tokyo Bay. Oriental Land Company, the Japanese real-estate company that built and owned the park, had begun reclaiming the land almost 20 years earlier. For this desolate mudflat land, it paid $70 per 3.3 square meters. By 1984 those 3.3-square-meter parcels were worth more than $2,000 each. With 300 acres still undeveloped, Oriental Lands stood to clear $740 million on resale, more than enough to cover the $673 million borrowed from Japanese banks to build this Disneyland.

Walt Disney Productions had started talks with Oriental Land in 1974, but a final agreement was not reached until 1979. Disney had zero cash investments in the project and, therefore, risked only its name. For the use of the name and the Disney know-how, Disney received 10 percent of the entrance gross and 5 percent on all food and souvenirs sold in the park. WDP retained "theme supervision" for the life of the project, which meant everything had to be done "Walt's way." Except for signs, which had Japanese subtitles under larger English words, there was little that was distinctly Japanese about the park. Only 2 of the park's 27 restaurants sold Japanese food, and they served only sushi and bento, basically an oriental box lunch. A weatherproof skylight covered the entire World Bazaar complex (Main Street USA). Sheltered queue areas, walkways, and enclosed patios were also provided. Most of the electronic show and ride designs represented the latest in Disney technology and were more advanced than similar attractions at U.S. Disneyland and Disney World.

One-third of Japan's population lived within 90 minutes of the site, and first-year attendance was projected to be 10 million visitors, but the project was not without problems and risks. The weather was the most obvious difficulty. Tokyo averages 58.52 inches of rain and 108 rainy days every year. It snows every winter in Tokyo, and the park lies squarely in the path of the famous Pacific typhoons. This double threat obliged Disneyland's gardeners to provide gas heating for the park's 300,000 newly planted trees, and to tie every one down with four solid guy wires. Furthermore, Japanese children put in six, and sometimes seven, days per week at school, with only a week of vacation in May and two more in August.

Management Changes

Card Walker stepped down as chairman of WDP in May 1983 at the age of 68. He was succeeded by real-estate developer Raymond L. Watson, a long-time Disney board member. President of California's Irvine Company for 4 of his 17 years there, Watson was credited with much of the planning for the development of 60,000 acres that included the entire city of Irvine and sections of five adjacent cities.

The 57-year-old Watson was described as an "analytical planner with a conservative management track record" who was unlikely to tamper with the Disney heritage or "The Disney Way of Leadership" (Exhibit 1). According to Watson, "You don't come to a tradition-minded company and say, 'I'm going to change everything.' The employees would run you out of town."

Also in 1983 Ronald W. Miller, the 50-year-old one-time tight end for the Los Angeles Rams, was named president. Miller had joined the Disney studios three years after marrying Walt's eldest daughter in 1954. (They were separated in 1983.)

At least since the 1970s, company observers had voiced concern for the future of Walt Disney Productions. Some wondered whether the company had the creativity needed to capture new markets. Many of the "new" plans were leftover ideas of Walt Disney's. Top managers suggested that, if their plans seemed to fit a strategy of attracting older audiences, that was merely a coincidence. "What we are doing is intuitively based on a hell of a lot of experience," explained Card Walker. "More important than planning and research is the combination of experience we get from a lot of segments of the company." According to a former senior executive with Disney, "The company is creatively burned out. All those guys [top management] are so square you can't roll them downhill." A research analyst described current management as being "very businesslike and competent, but . . . squelching creativity." (For a list of the company's management team, see Exhibit 2.)

A REVIEW OF OPERATIONS

Movie Division

The crisis facing Disney was most visible in the film division. In 1979 it had accounted for 20 percent of pretax earnings. In 1982 films lost $33 million. Part of the problem was demographics. Disney films had always appealed to a young (under 14) audience. That group comprised 14.7 percent of the population in 1950, 18.2 percent in 1960, 15 percent in 1970, and 13.6 percent in 1980.

The traditional Disney audience had indeed shrunk, but as Card Walker saw it, the problem ran even deeper: "Young adults today want a more sophisticated point of view, with more sex and violence. We don't ever want to go that far." Ron Miller, who served as executive producer throughout the decade of the

Exhibit 1
The Disney Way of Leadership

Another element of our management style is our strong belief in our people-oriented approach to leadership.

A Disney Leader Gets Results Through People

Simplified, this means that a Disney Leader is a people specialist. He does not get results by doing his own thing ... he works with other people and helps them put on a good show. It is a known fact that leadership is a science and can be learned like any other skill, but you have to work at it every day. There are some key skills important to the Disney Way of Leadership.

Human Relations Skills

Good Human Relations is a basic cornerstone of the Disney people philosophy. The success of our organization depends on the way we deal with people, and it begins with the way we deal with our employees.

Our ability to work positively with people lies in continually putting to practice some key points.

- Set the example ... it starts with you.
- Encourage a positive attitude.

- Get to know your employees ... treat them as individuals.
- Be with your team ... provide encouragement and attention.
- Use empathy ... look at the other person's point of view.
- Have respect for others.
- Be objective ... be firm, fair, and consistent.
- Give recognition for a job well done.
- Maintain your sense of humor.
- All problems are not the same ... treat each individually.
- If an employee has a problem ... help solve it.
- If a promise is made ... keep it.
- See that your employees have good working conditions.

Communications Skills

One of the most valuable and important skills of the Disney leader is his ability to effectively communicate. All of the positive human relations techniques available today are virtually useless without effective communication.

Since communication means getting ideas across and finding out what other people have to say, we

(continued on next page)

Source: *The Disney Management Style,* Walt Disney Productions (1977), pp. 32–34.

(continued)

stress the following points in the Disney Way of Leadership.

- Communicate clearly . . . get your message across.
- Let your employees know how they're doing.
- Encourage upward and downward communications.
- Listen to what employees have to say.
- Keep an open door and an open mind.
- Tell employees how they fit in . . . explain the big picture.
- Let your employees feel like they belong.
- Communication should be direct, open, and honest.

Training Skills

Training is the method of developing the basic skills to create an efficient work group, and is the responsibility of every Disney leader.

An efficient operation can never come about as the result of a "happy accident." Each employee must have a clear-cut idea of what they are expected to accomplish and how to achieve it with the greatest proficiency.

Some key training points to remember:

- Be sure your employees receive the proper training which they need for doing their job.
- Provide for your employees' future growth and development.
- Give employees a chance to learn and participate.
- Encourage new ideas and creative contributions.

Other Leadership Skills

In addition to the aforementioned skills, the Disney Leader also needs to be aware of and skillful in areas of planning, organizing, directing, and controlling his/her team's efforts.

Planning is really just looking ahead. Once objectives are understood, the means necessary to achieve them are presented in plans. Organizing is the process of putting all the resources together to carry out the plan. Directing involves the process of carrying out the plan using all the resources gathered. Controlling measures performance in relation to expected standards of performance.

The Disney Way of leadership stresses arranging work into a logical and workable manner to insure its successful completion. Keep in mind these helpful points.

(continued on next page)

(continued)

- A plan of action is the best control to make sure we get there.
- Don't over-structure a plan . . . stay flexible.
- Set clearly defined priorities and completion schedules.
- Be realistic with target dates . . . but set them.
- Don't assume . . . follow-up on assignments and requests.
- Organize around jobs and people.
- Find the right person for the job.

- Issue effective and understandable instructions and directions.
- Establish effective controls to get things done in a timely manner and by priority.

In summary, the Disney Way of Leadership actually integrates all of these skills, applies them as appropriate at the point of action. For it is only through daily application and practice that we "fine tune" the essential skills of effective leadership.

1970s, described the situation in personal terms. "We were not reaching that broad audience. I saw it with my own children. The moment they turned about 14 or 15, I would run a Disney film at home and they'd look and say, 'Oh God, not that corn again.'" Miller had been frustrated by being unable to bid for scripts like *Kramer vs. Kramer* and *Raiders of the Lost Ark* because of the Disney image.

The reluctance of freelance Hollywood talent to adapt to Disney's narrow range and stingy compensation deals had often kept Miller's instincts from bearing fruit. According to a former Disney executive, "Card [Walker] would listen but not hear. Ron would listen but not act." Reportedly, Miller had eagerly pursued Michael Eisner, president of Paramount Pictures (*Raiders of the Lost Ark, Saturday Night Fever, Flashdance, Terms of Endearment*, and three *Star Trek* movies) for the Disney studios, but *Business Week* reported,

> Industry experts assume that Eisner would have wanted more control than Disney was prepared to give. Says a key executive at a rival studio: "Disney's movie division is relatively small. Even though they are beefing up production, they will release only about seven films a year. The majors each release more than 15. The movies are a small part of Disney's total business. Any heavy-weight would want some control of the theme-park operations. That would upset too many long-time Disneyites." And he adds: "People still doubt that Disney wants to—and can—change its image."

Exhibit 2
Walt Disney Productions
Management Team

BOARD OF DIRECTORS

Caroline Leonetti Ahmanson*†
Businesswoman, civic leader, and philan-thropist

William H. Anderson
Independent producer

Robert H. B. Baldwin†§
Chairman—Advisory Board, Morgan Stanley, Inc. (investment bankers)

Roy E. Disney*
Chairman of the Board, Shamrock Holdings, Inc. (radio and television broadcasting)

Philip M. Hawley†§
President and Chief Executive Officer, Carter Hawley Hale Stores, Inc. (retail merchandising)

Ignacio E. Lozano, Jr.*†
Publisher, LA OPINION (newspaper publishing)

Ronald W. Miller‡
President and Chief Executive Officer

Richard T. Morrow
Vice President—General Counsel

Richard A. Nunis
Executive Vice President—Walt Disney World/Disneyland

Donn B. Tatum‡§
Chairman of the Finance Committee

E. Cardon Walker‡
Chairman of the Executive Committee

Raymond L. Watson‡
Chairman of the Board

Samuel L. Williams
Senior Partner, Hufstedler, Miller, Carlson & Beardsley (law firm)

CORPORATE OFFICERS

Ronald W. Miller
President and Chief Executive Officer

Raymond L. Watson
Chairman of the Board

E. Cardon Walker
Chairman of the Executive Committee

Michael L. Bagnall
Executive Vice President—Finance

Carl G. Bongirno
Executive Vice President—Administration

Barton K. Boyd
Executive Vice President—Consumer Products and Merchandising

Ronald J. Cayo
Executive Vice President—Business Affairs and Legal

James P. Jimirro
Executive Vice President—Telecommunications

Jack B. Lindquist
Executive Vice President—Marketing

Richard A. Nunis
Executive Vice President—Walt Disney World/Disneyland

Martin A. Sklar
Executive Vice President—WED Creative Development

John J. Cornwell
Vice President—Management Information Systems

Jose M. Deetjen
Vice President—Tax Administration and Counsel

(continued on next page)

*Member of Audit Review Committee.
†Member of Compensation Committee.
‡Member of Executive Committee.
§Member of Finance Committee.
Source: 1983 annual report.

(continued)

Dennis M. Despie
Vice President—
Entertainment

Robert W. Gibeaut
Vice President—Studio
Operations

Luther R. Marr
Vice President—
Corporate and
Stockholder Affairs

Richard T. Morrow
Vice President—General
Counsel

Howard M. Roland
Vice President—
Construction Contract
Administration and
Purchasing

Doris A. Smith
Vice President and
Secretary

Frank P. Stanek
Vice President—
Corporate Planning

Donald A. Escen
Treasurer

Bruce F. Johnson
Controller

Leland L. Kirk
Assistant Secretary-
Treasurer

Neal E. McClure
Assistant Secretary

Alvin L. Shelbourn
Assistant Treasurer

Donald E. Tucker
Assistant Treasurer

Douglas E. Houck
Assistant Controller

Joe E. Stevens
Assistant Controller

**Corporate Management
Committee**
Ronald W. Miller,
Chairman; Michael L.
Bagnall, Richard L.
Berger, Carl G. Bongirno,
Barton K. Boyd, Ronald J.
Cayo, James P. Jimirro,
Jack B. Lindquist, Richard
A. Nunis, Martin A. Sklar

Principal Domestic
Divisions (*) and
Subsidiaries with Chief
Operating Executives

**Buena Vista
Distribution Co., Inc.**
Charles E. Good,
President

**Buena Vista
International, Inc.**
Harold P. Archinal,
President

**Canasa Trading
Corporation**
Harold P. Archinal,
President

The Disney Channel
James P. Jimirro,
President

Disneyland*
Richard A. Nunis,
President

Disneyland, Inc.
Richard A. Nunis,
President

**Lake Buena Vista
Communities, Inc.**
Richard A. Nunis,
President

MAPO*
Carl G. Bongirno,
President

**Reedy Creek Utilities
Co., Inc.**
Ronald J. Cayo,
President

**United National
Operating Co.***
Barton K. Boyd,
President

Vista Advertising*
Jack B. Lindquist,
President

**Vista Insurance
Services, Inc.**
Philip N. Smith,
President

**Vista-United
Telecommunications**
(a Florida Partnership)
James Tyler, General
Manager

**Walt Disney
Educational Media
Company***
James P. Jimirro,
President

**Walt Disney Music
Company**
Gary Krisel, President

Walt Disney Pictures
Richard L. Berger,
President

(continued on next page)

(continued)

Walt Disney Telecommunications and Non-Theatrical Company
James P. Jimirro, President

Walt Disney Television*
William Brademan, President

Walt Disney Travel Co., Inc.
Jack B. Lindquist, President

Walt Disney World Co.
Richard A. Nunis, President

WED Enterprises*
Carl G. Bongirno, President
Martin A. Sklar, Executive Vice President

WED Transportation Systems, Inc.
Richard A. Nunis, Chairman and President

Wonderland Music Company, Inc.
Gary Krisel, President

FOREIGN SUBSIDIARIES WITH PRINCIPAL MARKETING EXECUTIVES

BELGIUM
Walt Disney Productions (Benelux) S.A.
Andre Vanneste

CANADA
Walt Disney Music of Canada Limited
James K. Rayburn

DENMARK
Walt Disney Productions A/S Danmark
Gunnar Mansson

FRANCE
Walt Disney Productions (France) S.A.
Armand Bigle, Richard Dassonville, Dominique Bigle

GERMANY
Walt Disney Productions (Germany) GmbH
Horst Kobhschek

ITALY
Creazioni Walt Disney S.p.A.I.
Antonio Bertini

JAPAN
Walt Disney Enterprises of Japan Ltd.
Matsuo Yokoyama
Walt Disney Productions Japan Ltd.
Yosaku Seki, Mamoru Morita, James B. Cora

PORTUGAL
Walt Disney Portuguesa Criacoes Artisticas Lda.
Laszlo Hubay Cebrian

SPAIN
Walt Disney Iberica, S.A.
Enrique Stuyck

UNITED KINGDOM
Walt Disney Productions Limited
Dino Troni, Monty Mendelson, Terry Byrne, Keith Bales

In recent years, there had been a talent drain, some of which was the result of the retirement of long-time animators. Don Bluth, a talented animator who produced the well-received film *The Secret of NIMH*, walked out of Disney in 1979 with 2 colleagues. They were soon followed by 14 more. As Bluth repeatedly told the press, his goal was to return to the "classic" Disney techniques of *Snow White* and *Pinocchio*.

Recent write-offs in the movie division included

Something Wicked This Way Comes	$21.0 million
Night Crossing	10.5 million

The Watcher in the Woods	6.8 million
Midnight Madness	4.5 million
Condorman	$20.5 million

Not all of the movies in recent years had been losers. *The Rescuers*, an animated film, surpassed 1964's *Mary Poppins* in revenues. This fact escaped the attention of most Disney observers, however, because a large portion of the gross came from West Germany, where the movie was the biggest hit of all time. *The Fox and the Hound* cost $12 million to produce and earned $50 million. *The Black Hole* was disappointing but was expected to break even.

The Disney film library was another important company asset. Valued at $60 million and with annual amortization costs of approximately $66 million, it was estimated by some to be worth $400 million to $600 million. The library contained 650 titles ranging from classics such as *Mary Poppins* and *Snow White* to lesser films such as *The Shaggy D.A.* and *The Bootniks*. In 1983 *Snow White* was rereleased and brought in $20 million.

In 1981 Thomas Wilhite, who had been the company's publicity director, was given responsibility for all film production. Wilhite, then 27 and the company's youngest vice president, represented youth and a fresh approach. He was a film buff but had never produced a picture. Wilhite's first film, *Tron*, did not do well (a $10.4-million write-off) despite enormous advance publicity. Wilhite's next venture was *Tex*, a $5-million production about a teenager growing up in Oklahoma. It was favorably reviewed but drew small audiences.

In March 1983, Richard Berger, senior vice president for Worldwide Productions at 20th Century Fox, was made president of a new Disney subsidiary, Walt Disney Pictures. Eight months later, Wilhite quit, claiming "the film company is big enough for only one head of production." According to *Variety*,

> With unusual candor for a departing exec, Wilhite said that "Richard Berger and I didn't see things the same way. We disagreed on the viability of *Splash*, which he'd turned down at Fox. He never fulfilled his promise to bring staff salaries and titles up to industry standards. Everyone who came from the outside got the good salaries, but not those already here. I think my exit has been inevitable, one way or the other, for some time."

Consumer Products

The consumer products division was responsible for collecting royalties on the Disney name and characters. Every item that carried the name of Disney or any of its characters generated revenue—everything from Mickey Mouse ears, books, watches, and T-shirts to Tokyo dolls with Mickey wearing a kimono. On divisional assets of $37 million and revenues of $111 million, consumer products earned income of $57 million in 1983. In 1979 its pretax earnings were nearly a 200 percent return on assets. Some analysts had valued the consumer products division at $350 million.

Cable Television: The Disney Channel

TV revenues had declined from $44.4 million in 1982 to $27.9 million in 1983. The company that had produced *The Wonderful World of Disney* and *The Mickey Mouse Club* for network television no longer had any hit shows on the air.

To counter the decline, the Disney Channel was formed in April 1983, with an initial programming investment of $45 million. Offering a 16-hour-a-day schedule, seven days a week, the Disney Channel, six months later, had more than 532,000 basic subscriber homes and had signed agreements with 1,123 cable systems offering the service to 9.9 million homes in all 50 states. By March 31, 1984, the number of subscribers was 916,000. This record established the Disney Channel as the fastest growing and most successful new pay-television service in history and put it on target toward its projected breakeven of 2 million subscribers by the end of 1985.

Subscribers paid between $7 and $11 a month for Disney's family-oriented programming. The foundation for this service was the Disney library of feature films, cartoons, true-life adventures, educational shorts, and television shows. The Channel also acquired exclusive pay-television rights to 12 classic Charlie Chaplin features and purchased films such as *Can Can* and *Guys and Dolls* from other studios. In addition, Disney announced that 25 production crews were working on 658 shows (all half-hour and four-hour series) in Los Angeles, Orlando, and a dozen other sites throughout the United States.

If objectives were met, pay-TV services could generate profit margins of 25 percent. According to Jim Jimirro, president of Walt Disney Telecommunications, "The number of viewers who are interested in family entertainment has been very underestimated. There is every evidence that those people will reach vigorously for our type of product." More than 80 percent of the subscribers gave the channel high marks, and 21 percent of those surveyed never before had subscribed to any pay service (20 percent of the subscribers did not have children under the age of 13). Still, Jimirro admitted in 1984, "We have not yet reached our projected penetration levels." Only 7 percent of the homes that could get the channel were taking it. He had anticipated 15 percent.

In the first quarter of 1984, the Disney channel lost $11 million. The projected loss was cut from $15 million to $9 million in the second quarter by producing and acquiring less programming, cutting marketing expenditures, and amortizing some programming costs more slowly.

Some cable operations complained that management was too rigid in its marketing strategies. One reported, "They don't know the cable business, and they don't listen. We wanted to give the channel away free for two weeks to create a viewing habit among children so the parents would buy. But it was a tough struggle to finally convince Disney to do it."

Another complaint came from the National Coalition on Television Violence. After monitoring the channel for two weeks in 1984, the organization reported an average of 9 violent acts an hour on real-life programming and 18 an hour on cartoons, nearly as high as on the three networks. The Coalition described the level of violence as "quite troubling," and its chairman, a University of Illinois psychiatrist, claimed the violence could be harmful to children.

Theme Parks

In early 1984, concern also was being expressed about Disney's theme parks. Attendance had been virtually flat for the past decade. Disney World and Disneyland generated 87 percent of total 1983 income. EPCOT attendance rose in 1983 but fell 8 percent in the quarter ending December 31, 1983. Early 1984 attendance was off 19 percent. According to an analyst with Wertheim & Co., "The 19-percent drop was a big disappointment. It raises a real question about whether EPCOT Center has the growth potential the investors expected."

Some of the attendance drop could be attributed to the harsh eastern winter, but Disney World's decline was greater than neighboring attractions such as Cyprus Gardens and Sea World. According to Watson, "We think we may be losing the young marrieds, for example, because we are not marketing the resort and recreational aspects of the park."

According to one entertainment analyst, "The increment to the theme park's operating earnings from Disney's $1.2-billion investment probably did not exceed $80 million before taxes. After charging itself taxes, Disney is left with about $45 million. That represents less than a 4-percent return on EPCOT. If Disney had invested in Treasury bills, it could have done better." In 1983 depreciation on the amusement parks was $88 million. Total revenues were approximately $1 billion.

Attendance at California's Disneyland rose 10 percent in the first and second quarter of 1984 because of Disney's $45-million investment in rebuilding Fantasyland. Response to Tokyo Disneyland had been strong, with 1983 royalties estimated to be $10 million to $20 million.

Because of the Tokyo experience, top management was considering the desirability of building a Disneyland in Latin America or Europe. Another project being debated was a series of mini-Disney entertainment parks throughout the United States. If such projects were undertaken, some Disney executives thought the parks should be in urban centers; others championed suburban sites near popular shopping malls. Other executives feared such parks would cheapen the Disney name. According to Watson, "The idea has been around for years. I've told Ron [Miller, president] we should either decide on it or stop talking about it." Another option was to buy other amusement parks and add Disney's distinctive touch. Theme parks in North Carolina, Virginia, Texas, and Ohio recently had sold for just under two times revenue.

Real Estate

Outsiders expected Ray Watson to bring his expertise to Disney's real-estate holdings, including approximately 40 underdeveloped acres at the California Disneyland site. In Orlando, Disney owned 28,000 acres—a tract twice the size of Manhattan. According to Watson, "If we've used up more than 3,000 acres of that I'm surprised." There had been talk about more hotels and Disney ventures such as shopping centers, residential housing, or industrial parks. Although some of the Florida property would be hard to develop, analysts estimated that its value would range from $1,000 to $1 million an acre. In addition to its central-Florida land, the company also owned about 40

Exhibit 3
Walt Disney Productions
Revenue by Major Groups (000)

	1983	1982	1981	1980	1979
ENTERTAINMENT AND RECREATION					
Walt Disney World					
Admissions and rides	$ 278,320	$153,504	$139,326	$130,144	$121,276
Merchandise sales	172,324	121,410	121,465	116,187	101,856
Food sales	178,791	121,329	114,951	106,404	95,203
Lodging	98,105	81,427	70,110	61,731	54,043
Disneyland					
Admissions and rides	102,619	98,273	92,065	87,066	75,758
Merchandise sales	72,300	76,684	79,146	72,140	60,235
Food sales	45,699	44,481	44,920	41,703	35,865
Participant Fees					
Walt Disney Travel Co., Tokyo Disneyland royalties and other	83,044	28,502	29,828	28,005	26,843
Total revenues	$1,031,202	$725,601	$691,811	$643,380	$571,079
Theme Park Attendance					
Walt Disney World	22,712	12,560	13,221	13,783	13,792
Disneyland	9,980	10,421	11,343	11,522	10,760
Total	32,692	22,981	24,564	25,305	24,552

Source: 1983 Annual Report.

acres of undeveloped Florida coastal property. Disney's total Florida land holdings were estimated to be worth $300 million to $700 million.

CONCLUSION

By February 1984, the personal shareholdings of Roy E. Disney (Walt's nephew) had dropped from $96 million in 1983 to $54 million because of the declining value of Disney stock. As Watson and Miller examined the latest financial reports for the company (Exhibits 3–7), they wondered what could be done to restore the value of the assets that the Disney brothers had built.

	1983	1982	1981	1980	1979
MOTION PICTURES					
Theatrical					
Domestic	**$ 38,635**	$ 55,408	$ 54,624	$ 63,350	$ 49,594
Foreign	**43,825**	64,525	76,279	78,314	57,288
Television					
Worldwide	**27,992**	44,420	43,672	19,736	27,903
Home video and non-theatrical Worldwide	**55,006**	37,749	22,231	10,565	9,273
Total revenues	**$165,458**	$202,102	$196,806	$171,965	$144,058
CONSUMER PRODUCTS AND OTHER					
Character merchandising	**$ 45,429**	$ 35,912	$ 30,555	$ 29,631	$ 24,787
Publications	**20,006**	20,821	24,658	22,284	18,985
Records and music publishing	**30,666**	26,884	27,358	23,432	16,129
Educational media	**10,259**	15,468	21,148	21,908	19,967
Other	**4,327**	3,453	12,704	1,905	1,768
Total revenues	**$110,697**	$102,538	$116,423	$ 99,160	$ 81,636

Exhibit 4
Walt Disney Productions
Consolidated Statements of Income (000)

	FOR THE YEAR ENDED SEPTEMBER 30		
	1983	1982	1981
REVENUES			
Entertainment and recreation	$1,031,202	$ 725,610	$ 691,811
Motion pictures	165,458	202,102	196,806
Consumer products and other	110,697	102,538	116,423
Total revenues	1,307,357	1,030,250	1,005,040
COSTS AND EXPENSES OF OPERATIONS			
Entertainment and recreation	834,324	592,965	562,337
Motion pictures	198,843	182,463	162,180
Consumer products and other	53,815	54,706	65,859
Total costs and expenses of operations	1,086,982	830,134	790,376
OPERATING INCOME (LOSS) BEFORE CORPORATE EXPENSES			
Entertainment and recreation	196,878	132,645	129,474
Motion pictures	(33,385)	19,639	34,626
Consumer products and other	56,882	47,832	50,564
Total operating income before corporate expenses	220,375	200,116	214,664
CORPORATE EXPENSES (INCOME)			
General and administrative	35,554	30,957	26,216
Design projects abandoned	7,295	5,147	4,598
Interest expense (income), net	14,066	(14,781)	(33,130)
Total corporate expenses (income)	56,915	21,323	(2,316)
Income before taxes on income	163,460	178,793	216,980
Taxes on income	70,300	78,700	95,500
Net income	$ 93,160	$ 100,093	$ 121,480
Earnings per share	$2.70	$3.01	$3.72

Source: 1983 Annual Report.

Exhibit 5
Walt Disney Productions
Consolidated Balance Sheets (000)

	FOR THE YEAR ENDED SEPTEMBER 30	
	1983	1982
ASSETS		
Current assets:		
Cash	$ 18,055	$ 13,652
Accounts receivable, net of allowances	102,847	78,968
Income taxes refundable	70,000	41,000
Inventories	77,945	66,717
Film production costs	44,412	43,850
Prepaid expenses	19,843	18,152
Total current assets	333,102	262,339
Film production costs—noncurrent	82,598	64,217
Property, plant, and equipment, at cost:		
Entertainment attractions, buildings, and equipment	2,251,297	1,916,617
Less: Accumulated depreciation	(504,365)	(419,944)
	1,746,932	1,496,673
Construction and design projects in progress		
EPCOT Center	70,331	120,585
Other	37,859	39,601
Land	16,687	16,379
	1,871,809	1,673,238
Other assets	93,686	103,022
	$2,381,195	$2,102,816
LIABILITIES AND STOCKHOLDERS' EQUITY		
Current liabilities:		
Accounts payable, payroll, and other accrued liabilities	$187,641	$ 210,753
Taxes on income	50,557	26,560
Total current liabilities	238,198	237,313
Long-term borrowings, including commercial paper of $118,200 and $200,000	346,325	315,000
Other long-term liabilities and noncurrent advances	110,874	94,739
Deferred taxes on income and investment credits	285,270	180,980
Commitments and contingencies		

(continued on next page)

Source: 1983 Annual Report.

(continued)

	1983	1982
Stockholders' equity:		
Preferred shares, no par		
Authorized—5,000,000 shares, none issued		
Common shares, no par		
Authorized—75,000,000 shares		
Issued and outstanding—34,509,171		
and 33,351,482 shares	**661,934**	588,250
Retained earnings	**738,594**	686,534
	1,400,528	1,274,784
	$2,381,195	$2,102,816

Exhibit 6
Walt Disney Productions
Consolidated Statements of Changes
in Financial Position (000)

	FOR THE YEAR ENDED SEPTEMBER 30		
	1983	1982	1981
Cash provided by operations before taxes on income (see below)	$308,369	$309,431	$316,949
Taxes paid (received) on income, net	(28,987)	34,649	106,144
Cash provided by operations	337,356	274,782	210,805
Cash dividends	41,100	39,742	32,406
	296,256	235,040	178,399
Investing activities:			
EPCOT Center, net of related payables	250,196	566,428	285,651
Other property, plant, and equipment	83,542	47,988	47,756
Film production and programming costs	83,750	52,295	55,454
Rights to the Walt Disney name	(3,640)	40,000	
EPCOT Center and The Disney Channel pre-opening and start-up costs	18,253	19,170	1,907
Long-term notes receivable and other	11,406	26,881	4,023
	443,507	752,762	394,791
	(147,251)	(517,722)	(216,392)
Financing activities:			
Long-term borrowings	137,500	205,000	110,000
Reduction of long-term borrowings	(99,925)		
Common-stock offering	70,883		
Common stock issued (returned) to acquire rights to the Walt Disney name and certain equipment	(3,640)	46,200	
Participation fees, net of related receivables	11,169	23,867	24,745
Collection of long-term notes receivable and other	35,667	2,030	7,646
	151,654	277,097	142,391
Increase (decrease) in cash and short-term investments	4,403	(240,625)	(74,001)
Cash and short-term investments, beginning of year	13,652	254,277	328,278
Cash and short-term investments, end of year	$ 18,055	$ 13,652	$254,277

(continued on next page)

Source: 1983 Annual Report.

(continued)

	1983	1982	1981

The difference between income before taxes on income as shown on the "Consolidated Statements of Income" and cash provided by operations before taxes on income is explained as follows:

	1983	1982	1981
Income before taxes on income	$163,460	$178,793	$216,980
Charges to income not requiring cash outlays:			
Depreciation	90,184	41,917	38,886
Amortization of film production and programming costs	65,575	64,868	55,222
Other	15,526	9,950	9,449
Changes in:			
Accounts receivable	(25,863)	1,077	(18,591)
Inventories	(11,228)	(6,944)	(5,125)
Prepaid expenses	(1,691)	(2,754)	(3,960)
Accounts payable, payroll, and other accrued liabilities	12,406	22,524	24,088
	144,909	130,638	99,969
Cash provided by operations before taxes on income	$308,369	$309,431	$316,949

Exhibit 7
Walt Disney Productions
Selected Financial Data (000)

	1983	1982	1981	1980	1979
STATEMENTS OF INCOME					
Revenues	$1,307,357	$1,030,250	$1,005,040	$914,505	$796,773
Operating income before corporate expenses	220,375	200,116	214,664	231,300	205,695
Corporate expenses	42,849	36,104	30,814	25,424	20,220
Interest expense (income), net	14,066	(14,781)	(33,130)	(42,110)	(28,413)
Taxes on income	70,300	78,700	95,500	112,800	100,000
Net income	93,160	100,093	121,480	135,186	113,788
BALANCE SHEETS					
Current assets	333,102	262,339	457,829	506,202	484,141
Property, plant, and equipment, net of depreciation	1,871,809	1,673,238	1,069,369	762,546	648,447
Total assets	2,381,195	2,102,816	1,610,009	1,347,407	1,196,424
Current liabilities	238,198	237,313	181,573	145,291	119,768
Long-term obligations, including commercial paper of $118,200 (1983) and $200,000 (1982)	457,199	409,739	171,886	30,429	18,616
Total liabilities and deferred credits	980,667	828,032	442,891	272,609	235,362
Total net assets (stockholders' equity)	1,400,528	1,274,784	1,167,118	1,074,798	961,062
STATEMENTS OF CHANGES IN FINANCIAL POSITION					
Cash provided by operations	337,356	274,782	210,805	204,682	182,857
Cash dividends	41,100	39,742	32,406	23,280	15,496
Investment in property, plant, and equipment	333,738	614,416	333,407	149,674	56,629
Investment in film production and programming	83,750	52,295	55,454	68,409	44,436
PER SHARE					
Net income (earnings)	2.70	3.01	3.72	4.16	3.51
Cash dividends	1.20	1.20	1.00	.72	.48
Stockholders' equity	$40.58	$38.22	$35.99	$33.22	$29.76

(continued on next page)

Source: 1983 Annual Report.

	1983	1982	1981	1980	1979
Average number of common and common-equivalent shares outstanding during the year	34,481	33,225	32,629	32,513	32,426
OTHER					
Stockholders at close of year	60,000	61,000	60,000	62,000	65,000
Employees at close of year	30,000	28,000	25,000	24,000	21,000

(continued)

CALMA COMPANY (A; CONDENSED) AND THE CAD/CAM INDUSTRY

"You're quite right, Art," said Bob Benders, president of Calma, to his manager of R&D, Art Collmeyer. "Except for reaffirming our competitive strength in ICs (integrated circuits), it's not clear to me what business strategy the McKinsey people are recommending. Considering all the data and management time we have provided, it appears that they have hedged on making specific recommendations. You and I will have to sit down with Ron Hill [head of marketing] and Lem Bishop [finance] and hammer out our basic strategy for ourselves."

It was December 1979, and Calma Corporation had just received McKinsey's final presentation after six months of intensive study and analysis. Having achieved a significant market position in the young and fast-growing CAD/CAM (computer-aided design and computer-aided manufacturing) industry, Calma executives recognized the need to take stock of their current situation and formulate a coherent strategy to guide subsequent activity. Their sales growth from $6.9 million to $42.9 million in four years (see Exhibits 1 and 2) placed Calma on the threshold of even more explosive growth. Benders wished to position his organization to handle this growth in vigorous but orderly fashion.

COMPANY BACKGROUND

"Calma" was a combination of the names "Calvin" and "Irma," the couple who, in the early 1960s, founded the company in Santa Clara, California, to serve as sales representatives for several newly formed computer graphics components manufacturers.

In 1964, Ron Cone, a client from California Computer Products (Calcomp), sold his founder's stock in Calcomp and purchased Calma. Calma incorporated later that year. As a sideline, Cone began to manufacture digitizers (machines that convert a drawing into machine-readable form) in Calma's back room. Cone gave Bob Benders, then an engineer with Lockheed, a night

This case is a condensation of "Note on Computer Graphics" and "CAD/CAM (S-BP-22DN) and CALMA Company (A)" (S-BP-214A), both written by Christine Blouke, Research Associate, Stanford Graduate School of Business, and L. J. Bourgeois III, Associate Professor of Business Administration, The Colgate Darden Graduate School of Business Administration. Copyright © 1990 by the University of Virginia Darden School Foundation, Charlottesville, VA.

Exhibit 1
Calma Company
Statement of Income 1971–1978

	Following U.T.I. Purchase Twelve Months Ending December 31	Twelve Months Ending December 31	Twelve Months Ending August 31						
	1979	1978	1977	1976	1975	1974	1973	1972	1971
NET SALES AND SERVICE REVENUES	$42,797,602	$27,160,051	$14,278,552	$9,484,164	$6,919,332	$6,146,236	$3,461,912	$1,586,339	$670,215
COSTS AND EXPENSES									
Cost of sales and service revenues	25,184,616	16,058,001	7,989,661	5,235,188	3,773,395	3,715,763	1,997,681	854,332	552,059
Research and development	3,698,410	2,419,039	1,430,367	1,057,548	866,365	524,436	320,662	151,542	124,119
Selling	7,874,392	5,393,815	2,102,508	1,391,221	991,925	791,915	448,903	238,957	173,499
General and administrative	1,175,514	1,017,897	520,946	404,411	446,401	335,820	186,566	88,593	51,689
Interest, net	1,740,588	709,608	125,078	129,309	108,335	110,841	64,501	60,804	61,894
Total Costs and Expenses	39,673,520	25,598,370	12,168,560	8,217,677	6,186,421	5,478,775	3,018,313	1,394,228	963,260
PROFIT FROM OPERATIONS* (1978, 1979)	4,864,670	2,271,289							

(continued on next page)

*Net of interest expense.
Source: Company records.

(continued)

FOLLOWING U.T.I. PURCHASE

	TWELVE MONTHS ENDING DECEMBER 31		TWELVE MONTHS ENDING AUGUST 31						
	1979	1978	1977	1976	1975	1974	1973	1972	1971
INCOME BEFORE PROVISION FOR INCOME TAXES	3,124,082	1,561,681	2,109,992	1,266,487	732,911	667,461	443,599	192,111	(293,045)
PROVISION FOR INCOME TAXES	1,279,000	356,309	880,000	519,300	335,000	255,000	223,000	105,000	
INCOME (LOSS) BEFORE EXTRA-ORDINARY ITEM (1971–1974)						412,461	220,599	87,111	(293,045)
EXTRAORDINARY ITEM—Reduction of federal income taxes arising from carryforward of prior years' operating losses						150,000	191,000	92,000	
NET INCOME	1,845,082	$1,204,778	$1,229,992	$ 747,187	$397,911	$562,461	$411,599	$179,111	($293,045)

(continued on next page)

(continued)

	FOLLOWING U.T.I. PURCHASE TWELVE MONTHS ENDING DECEMBER 31			TWELVE MONTHS ENDING AUGUST 31					
	1979	1978	1977	1976	1975	1974	1973	1972	1971
EARNINGS PER SHARE (1971–1977)									
Income before extraordinary item			$1.88	$1.22	$.66	$.70	$.38	$.18	$(.64)
Extraordinary item						.26	.32	.18	
Net income per share	——	——	$1.88	$1.22	$.66	$.96	$.70	$.36	$(.64)

474

Exhibit 2
Calma Company
Balance Sheet 1971–1979

	TWELVE MONTHS ENDING DECEMBER 31			TWELVE MONTHS ENDING AUGUST 31					
	1979	1978	1977	1976	1975	1974	1973	1972	1971
ASSETS									
Current Assets:									
Cash	$ 976,649	$ 1,052,218	$ 19,144	$ 16,491	$ 6,854	$ 6,830	$ 1,511	$ 9,142	$ 2,160
Receivables, less allowance for doubtful accounts	11,908,769	10,412,117	6,000,238	4,612,847	2,668,684	1,982,341	1,283,143	498,224	332,631
Income taxes refundable	—	—	—	11,717	73,500	—	—	—	—
Inventories	15,541,102	10,647,684	3,347,010	1,996,896	1,225,457	1,185,500	751,340	275,323	254,659
Prepaid expenses	334,245	248,049	143,722	90,981	49,115	32,035	29,326	32,545	22,640
Total current assets	28,760,765	22,360,068	9,510,114	6,728,932	4,023,610	3,206,706	2,065,320	815,234	602,090
ADVANCES TO SUBSIDIARIES	158,786	—	—	—	—	—	—	—	—
LONG-TERM RECEIVABLES									
Equipment contracts, due after one year	—	—	183,070	77,894	178,249	29,841	53,676	47,575	—

Source: Company records.

(continued)

| | Twelve Months Ending December 31 | | Twelve Months Ending August 31 | | | | | | |
	1979	1978	1977	1976	1975	1974	1973	1972	1971
Other	—	—	47,700	38,500	40,500	—	—	—	—
			230,770	116,394	218,749				
EQUIPMENT, IMPROVEMENTS, AND LEASES									
Communication, computer equipment and other property	6,649,964	4,580,463							
Production equipment	—	—	341,116	276,113	78,017	77,072	70,225	62,748	48,128
Automotive equipment	—	—	11,788	11,788	11,788	14,448	12,423	15,084	10,032
Equipment leased to customers	—	—	150,037	160,702	122,834	53,647	24,058	24,058	25,446
Office furniture and equipment	688,060	251,781	79,012	58,187	39,517	36,840	28,257	20,174	19,663
Leasehold improvements	670,394	503,750	194,201	175,851	140,442	127,041	86,229	74,972	74,167
Demonstration system under capital lease	—	—	117,576		—	—	—	—	—
	8,008,418	5,335,994	893,730	682,641	392,598	309,048	221,192	197,036	177,436

(continued on next page)

(continued)

| | Twelve Months Ending December 31 | | | Twelve Months Ending August 31 | | | | | |
	1979	1978	1977	1976	1975	1974	1973	1972	1971
Less-Accumulated depreciation and amortization	(1,810,732)	(841,985)	376,266	254,135	191,621	148,208	111,371	91,873	81,205
	6,197,686	4,494,009	517,464	428,506	200,977	160,840	109,821	106,163	96,231
Total assets	$35,117,237	$26,854,077	$10,258,348	$7,273,832	$4,443,336	$3,397,387	$2,228,817	$967,972	$698,321
LIABILITIES									
Current Liabilities:									
Borrowings under bank line of credit/debt	$5,000,000	$8,500,000	$ —	$1,653,151	$937,360	$607,324	$624,011	$233,107	$140,000
Current portion of installment note payable to bank	527,624	455,150	466,300	290,625	—	50,000	—	—	—
Current portion of note payable to majority shareholder	—	—	—	62,264	62,264	71,175	72,345	35,000	651,100

(continued on next page)

(continued)

	Twelve Months Ending December 31		Twelve Months Ending August 31						
	1979	1978	1977	1976	1975	1974	1973	1972	1971
Accounts payable	2,017,975	3,625,496	1,704,528	1,131,159	797,785	904,580	611,871	268,837	136,318
Accrued expenses									
Payroll and commissions	678,858	530,673	423,746	260,491	129,150	131,634	104,105	31,460	14,804
Other	2,260,691	737,959	265,898	197,134	256,758	176,761	38,647	—	91,043
Federal and state income taxes									
Currently payable	2,798,846	1,115,903	618,649	22,300	—	80,774	20,000	13,000	—
Deferred	—	—	1,103,906	861,232	408,091	—	—	—	—
Advance from UCS 1978, 1979	4,665,587	1,040,858	—	—	—	—	—	—	—
Total current liabilities	17,949,581	16,006,039	4,619,027	4,478,356	2,591,408	2,002,248	1,470,979	610,674	1,033,265
Long-Term Liabilities	1,144,425	1,669,889	2,140,157	481,168	237,460	256,592	201,912	213,131	—

(continued on next page)

	Twelve Months Ending December 31		Twelve Months Ending August 31						
	1979	1978	1977	1976	1975	1974	1973	1972	1971
Shareholders' Equity:									
After purchase by UTI									
Shareholders' Equity	$10,216,213	$ 5,216,213							
Accumulated Earnings	3,961,936	3,961,936							
Current Year Earnings—1978	1,845,082								
1971–1977:									
Common stock, no par value									
Authorized—800,000 shares									
Outstanding—at $.50 per share	—	—	312,633	304,134	298,173	280,667	280,587	280,507	230,507
Additional paid-in capital	—	—	814,544	775,528	769,080	688,576	688,496	688,416	438,416
Retained earnings	—	—	2,317,987	1,234,646	547,215	149,304	(413,157)	(824,756)	(1,003,867)
	16,023,231	9,188,149	3,499,164	2,314,308	1,614,468	1,118,547	555,926	144,167	(334,944)
TOTAL LIABILITIES	$34,117,237	$26,854,077	$10,258,348	$7,273,832	$4,443,336	$3,397,387	$2,228,817	$967,972	$698,321

(continued)

job designing digitizers. (Benders, born in Latvia in 1936, had moved to Michigan from Germany in 1950, taken his BSEE from the University of Michigan in 1962, and, after a brief stint at Boeing Digital Systems, moved to Lockheed in 1965.) In 1968, Cone offered Benders the job of chief engineer and asked him to develop a new, more marketable product to take Calma out of the hardware business and into complete graphic systems. As Benders, Calma's current president, explained it,

> The offer appealed to me. It was a chance to get out of engineering and into management, and interactive graphics systems looked like they could offer us a good opportunity. The cost of computers was coming down. Tektronics had just introduced a memory tube display that drew pictures on a screen, and memory disk drives were coming down in price.
>
> We analyzed the semiconductor industry—integrated circuit microchips were already getting too crowded for manual design methods—and after calculating our costs we figured we could build a single-terminal graphics system for about $50,000 and sell it for around $100,000. So we put together a system and began writing software to make it interactive. Well, we underestimated everything—costs, time to produce the software, you name it. Early in 1970, Cone got out. The recession was on and our banker called our loan. Cone said to me, "I've had enough of this #@?! You can take this company if you want, but I can't give you any money; otherwise, I'll fold it." So I took it. I was lucky enough to find a banker who was an adventurer. He loaned me $100,000, and then we landed a government contract to develop a mapping system. The contract had progress payments, which funded our integrated circuit CAD development, too.

In 1970, Calma made the shift from hardware to complete system (hardware plus software) development and entered the interactive graphics market. As Benders recalled,

> In late 1970 I approached Intel. They had one of our digitizers, were interested in automating, and there was nothing else on the market. We made a $150,000 deal with the specs and purchase order number written on half a sheet of paper. Calma shipped them our first system in 1971 and it worked. Then Motorola bought a system. It was famine to feast. We've been making money every since.

Organizational Development

During the first few years, Calma had a part-time financial manager, but by 1972 Benders decided Calma's growth required full-time attention in that department. Lem Bishop, 36 (at the time), was hired in May 1972. Bishop had been controller and financial officer for a subsidiary of GTE; he came to Calma from the controller's job at a subsidiary of Pacific Lumber. (Bishop had a BA in political science and an MBA from the University of Santa Clara.)

By 1974, Calma's employment had doubled. Benders began to look for a professional manager to head the research and development department. He hired Art Collmeyer, 33, who had been manager of CAD System Development at Xerox. Collmeyer had a Ph.D. in microelectronics and was a skilled line manager. He was well received as head of R&D, an area within Calma (and the computer industry as a whole) that had a unique culture, often attracting "brilliant eccentrics"—a difficult group to manage, at best. Collmeyer was able to impose discipline on this group while still maintaining the group's creative productivity.

"Art is the first to arrive and the last to leave here," commented one of his employees, who credited Collmeyer with building a strong team spirit among his staff. "He makes us work like dogs and enjoy it." Of his own style, Collmeyer observed:

> I try to hire the best people, give them responsibility and accountability—the large picture of what they are part of—and I try to get their personal commitment to the job and to Calma's and my own goals. Line management is a people-intensive job. I don't tell my people what to do or how to do it; I just tell them what results to get. And I give them plenty of chances to make mistakes. One mistake is OK. The second time, I'll get all over 'em. The third time the same mistake is made, I'll can them.
>
> I avoid creating staff functions; all my line managers are asked to do their own staff work. Good line managers want to know what their jobs are. Staff guys only want to know what *I* want them to do.

By 1976, Benders had begun to worry about marketing. "I saw that we were good hot-shot development types and could peddle what we designed, but we had no real marketing knowledge to help guide design. We usually worked on the guess that the 'product was right.'" In 1977, Benders organized Calma's first marketing department and "went through two or three marketing bosses" with unsatisfactory results. Following this rapid succession of "technical people without a real understanding of the difference between marketing and sales," in May of 1978 Benders hired Ron Hill from Tektronix. With a Ph.D. in engineering, an MBA, and marketing experience, Hill brought needed expertise to Calma's marketing effort. Originally installed as vice president of corporate planning, and after a six-month experience as head of field engineering in Europe, Hill was named senior vice president for marketing in April 1979.

Within the marketing group, the sales department was organized by geographic region and sold the full array of products and applications to all markets and customers. The marketing department, on the other hand, specialized according to application (for example, microelectronic applications such as printed circuits and integrated circuits or mechanical applications such as automotive design). In addition, the field engineering group, which provided after-sales service to customers, was brought under the marketing umbrella. (See Exhibit 3 for the December 1979 organization chart.)

Decision-Making Style

Bob Benders summarized the early years:

> We were just building and selling and hoping the product was right. Although in 1976 I realized that we really needed a separate marketing department, that's been a painful process. We still have not made a successful change from being a research and development-driven company to becoming a market-driven company. However, we have remained good at guessing what the market needs.

By the end of 1979, Calma's executive team had developed an identifiable style. According to one executive, "Calma has a strong top management; it's not very participative, it's all top down. All the important decisions are made by three or four people."

While this perception was seen by several managers as a positive aspect of leadership, it was not uniformly shared. Another manager said that "like all CAD companies, Calma's decision making is fairly flaky; we all run by the seat of the pants."

While Calma had an annual operating plan and budgeting system, performance reviews and budget reviews were fairly informal.

Several guiding decision-making and ideological principles were articulated by top management:

> If you have a good market position, you protect it. If you see a reasonable market, go after it. But we will not go into a market unless we can be among the top three competitors within three or four years.
>
> —Bob Benders

> Bob has some very strong philosophies that guide him. For example, the superior competence of our technical people, the need for excellence—these are basic requirements for success. Also, he believes competitors will turn over every stone when competing with us.
>
> —Lem Bishop

> In the high-tech business, the superior product will win—assuming you do the other things reasonably well.
>
> —Bob Benders

> This business depends heavily on our R&D gurus for product innovation and competitive dominance. The problem is that a lot of these people don't want

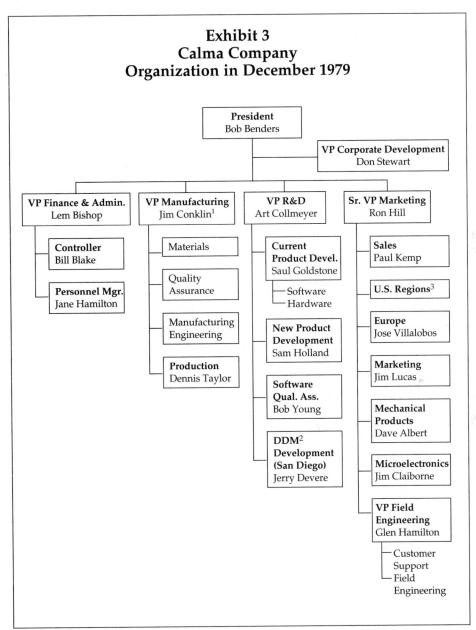

**Exhibit 3
Calma Company
Organization in December 1979**

[1]Left December 1979 to join Evans & Sutherland (E&S) in Salt Lake City.
[2]DDM stands for design, drafting, and manufacturing applications.
[3]Regions included West, Central, and East.

to grow up. What they need is healthy doses of discipline without spoiling their enthusiasm.

—Art Collmeyer

Most people think marketing has to do with determining future directions and future products. But that just isn't something you do every month. The *real* marketing problem is getting the product to market—training the sales people, documenting the product for customer use, and providing after-sale support.

—Ron Hill

Product Development

The basic appeal of Calma's CAD system was the increase in the efficiency of human input required to perform certain high-level design tasks. For example, the design and debugging of a particular integrated circuit (IC) might take an engineer as long as six months to do manually, whereas the CAD system reduced this to approximately five weeks.

Calma's first product, named CHIPS, was created to design ICs. It made Calma the market leader in IC CAD systems, a position it had maintained through 1979. Systems for printed circuit board (PCB) design, called CARDS, were first introduced in 1974; in this market segment Calma had strong competition from several other CAD vendors. Graphic Display System I (GDS I) provided the core software and basis for both the CHIPS and CARDS products.

Calma had acquired, in 1975, a small San Diego-based graphics development company, which specialized in CAD for mechanical applications. Under the direction of Jerry Devere, Calma's third product, DDM (design, drafting, and manufacturing), had been developed there. Dave Albert, a Ph.D. in physics who had specialized in high-speed computing, had also come to Calma through its acquisition of the San Diego group. Albert was put in charge of marketing for the DDM system. (See Exhibit 4 for product descriptions.)

Calma also sold mapping systems. In 1976 Calma held a significant share of this market. However, by 1977 its initial product was experiencing database problems, as customers demanded more sophisticated software. Calma chose to withdraw from the mapping market to concentrate on circuit design and to develop mechanical (such as automotive) design software, which forecasts indicated would be the CAD application to experience the fastest growth.

Calma's geographic location was a key factor in its success. Located in the heart of Silicon Valley, a high-tech industry area, Calma was surrounded by most of the nation's largest users and manufacturers of integrated circuits. "Close geography eliminated the necessity of a marketing department," according to one employee.

Exhibit 4
Calma Company
Product Descriptions

Calma's products all contained some common hardware features. These could include a minicomputer, a digitizer, electronic tablets, digitizing pens, disk and magnetic tape storage, alphanumeric and graphics terminals, plotters, and printers. The products themselves were differentiated primarily by the software described below.

CHIPS (CAD for ICs): $364,500 (Applicon's price was $326,500)

CHIPS was used by the IC (integrated circuit) industry to design and produce IC artwork, or masks, necessary to manufacture ICs. The core of CHIPS was the 16-bit GDS I (Graphics Display Software), although the state-of-the-art 32-bit GDS II (Graphics Display System) software was currently under development.

The engineer either designed from scratch at the interactive terminal or prepared a sketch to be input into the system by an operator. The graphics terminal displayed the drawing, at up to 1,000 times actual size. It could show different segments and layers of the device in different colors and at different magnifications; and it could display one or many layers of the IC simultaneously. The software gave indications of errors, performed design rule verifications, and stored all the information about the IC. When desired, the IC artwork could be output as a drawing or onto a magnetic tape. The magnetic tape could then be used as input for the IC manufacturing process.

CARDS (CAD for PCBs): $706,300 (CV's price was $491,900)

CARDS was used for designing printed circuit boards (PCB). PCBs were composed of many ICs. CARDS provided automation for all aspects of PCB development from schematic creation until final documentation and artwork to prepare the PCB for production. Like CHIPS, CARDS used the GDS I and would later use GDS II software. CARDS' higher price value was due to the requirement for two CPUs.

The designer prepared a drawing, which was input to the computer. CARDS then displayed the drawing on the screen, showing different connections and different layers in different colors. The CARDS system

(continued on next page)

(continued)

determined connections for the ICs, allowed easy design modification and artwork generation, conducted design review checks, and indicated errors. It also provided parts lists and assembly drawings and generated a drawing or magnetic tape as the final output.

DDM (CAD for Design, Drafting, and Manufacture): $458,850
(CV's price was $456,700)

DDM was a three-dimensional system used primarily by mechanical engineers for computer-aided design, drafting, and manufacture. Examples of products for which DDM was used included automobile frames, airplanes, and household appliances.

DDM enabled a designer to explore several solutions to a design problem, perform engineering analyses, check clearances of moving parts, and produce engineering drawings and documentation. As with the other products, the designer worked with the graphics terminal, which displayed the drawing in two or three dimensions and could show six different perspectives of it.

CADEC (CAD for the Architect-Engineer-Contractor Industry): (Price N/A)

CADEC was used by architects, engineers, and contractors (the A-E-C industry) for project management, design, drafting, and documentation needs. The uses for CADEC included creating architectural drawings of buildings and parts of a building, performing structural and frame analyses, doing pipe stress and simulation calculations, and keeping track of all associated data. CADEC included capabilities for two- and three-dimensional design, support calculations, and project management. Output could be in the form of a drawing and/or hard-copy support documentation.

In the early years client needs were communicated directly to Calma's R&D staff, who then developed the requested software. All integrated circuit designers could utilize the same software to produce ICs; but Calma developed the most efficient graphics design system on the market and soon dominated the IC market. As a result, Calma was the industry price leader.

Considering itself the Cadillac of the industry, Calma did not compete in the market for systems selling below $250,000.

As Calma began to diversify its product line to include printed circuits and mechanical design applications, momentum slowed. The diversity of users presented a real dilemma as each new graphics customer requested different applications software and system capabilities.

Market diversification had its costs. Calma's dominance in the IC market was challenged by Applicon's aggressive entry in 1978. "Calma was squashed," according to one executive. "Applicon's entry caused a lot of instability in our sales force. We had to refocus and get back in control. To do so, we had to neglect the other markets."

By 1979, Calma was back in control in ICs but was "hanging by our fingernails" in the mapping, architecture, and mechanical design markets. "We were now David to Computervision's Goliath in the mechanical applications markets."

Calma, like its other graphics systems competitors, sold "on futures." Many sales were made upon the salesperson's promise that desired applications would be made available within 6 to 18 months with a percentage of purchase price withheld until delivery. Since Calma was operating on the leading edge of graphics technology, customers were willing to purchase less-sophisticated systems because there were no better alternatives available. Customers occasionally were frustrated when promised developments could not be delivered on schedule; however, the problem was industrywide.

Operations

Calma manufactured a very small percentage of the components of its graphics systems. Most of the hardware was purchased "off-the-shelf" from original equipment manufacturers (OEMs). Calma designed the cabinets, and Calma's software was added to make the pieces of the graphics system work together. Once the system was assembled, diagnostic software was used to assure the equipment was properly connected and integrated (i.e., that the terminal could communicate with the disk memory, the plotter, and the cpu, etc.).

During a quality-control check, the equipment was externally examined for such things as paint chips, properly connected cables and wires, and so forth. Calma's graphics software was then added, and an "expert" trial user from customer support performed a software audit, using the system as its purchaser would use it. The equipment was then delivered to the customer. Representatives from field engineering set up the equipment, performed a quality check, and retested the equipment with diagnostic software. A customer support person then performed a final software check, demonstrated the system for the customer, and occasionally stayed for a short period to train the customer staff to use the system.

Acquisition by UTI

In September 1978, Calma was purchased by United Telecommunications, Inc., for $17 million. UTI had previously engaged McKinsey and Company, the management consulting firm, to assist several of its subsidiaries in strategic planning. It was suggested that McKinsey examine both Calma and United Computing Systems (UTI's computer services subsidiary to which Calma was now reporting) to assist both companies in evaluating their strategies and competitive strengths and weaknesses and to assess their relative positions in the corporate portfolio.

MANAGEMENT CONSULTANT'S REPORT

In its report on phase I of its study, begun in June 1979, the McKinsey team identified and examined major sources of information about the industry and the company. Orientation interviews with Calma's upper and middle management had been performed. A four-part internal analysis had been made to examine Calma's financial, marketing/sales/service, research and development, and manufacturing processes and procedures. Calma's primary customers had been interviewed, a literature search had been performed, and a competitive analysis had been conducted.

In November 1979, McKinsey made a presentation of its phase I findings at a Calma senior management meeting. The three-part presentation first described the evolution of the industry; second, it outlined Calma's competitive position and internal skills; and third, it described the strategic issues facing Calma.

The following pages contain the highlights of McKinsey's presentation, supplemented in places by other available industry information.

THE CAD/CAM INDUSTRY

Automated computer graphics technology originated in the mid-1950s as a result of military research done at MIT and research for General Motors. During the 1960s, following the rapid development of computer hardware capabilities and sophistication, "view only" graphic data input and output became possible.

By 1970, graphic systems suppliers had entered the market. Hardware costs had dropped dramatically following technological advances that led to development of minicomputers and microprocessors. The graphics systems suppliers, operating on the leading edge of technology, developed increasingly sophisticated software, which allowed graphic data manipulation in two and three dimensions.

Increasingly advanced software capabilities and breakthroughs in distributed systems were anticipated for the 1980s. This would lead to additional product innovations by turnkey systems suppliers, like Calma, who had been historically most effective in matching software with improving hardware price performance trends.

McKinsey's presentation identified computer graphics—CAD/CAM—as a high-growth, rapidly evolving industry characterized by the following:

1. Product innovation, which first created and still drove the systems segment of the industry

2. A favorable set of demand and buying characteristics, which would generate increasing sales and service requirements

3. Moderate competitive pressures forecast to remain constant over the next few years

As illustrated in Table A, the CAD/CAM industry could be divided into four segments: specialized hardware, stand-alone software, remote services, and turnkey systems, which was Calma's major emphasis.

Specialized hardware, components for interactive graphics systems, were manufactured by more than 70 companies, many of which had vertically integrated to sell complete graphics systems rather than single components.

Stand-alone software, which worked for a variety of graphics equipment configurations, was available from several suppliers. Some were independent; others had formal cooperative agreements with turnkey systems suppliers or hardware manufacturers.

Table A
Structure of the CAD/CAM Industry, 1979

MAJOR PRODUCT SEGMENTS	SHARE OF TOTAL MARKET	PROJECTED GROWTH RATES (1978–1983)
Specialized hardware	58%	21%
Stand-alone software	3	26
Remote computing services	5	22
Turnkey systems	34	45
	100%	31% (average)

Remote computing services sold all types of data-processing services and applications; a few had begun to offer CAD services. The user bought time, not equipment.

Turnkey systems suppliers sold complete packages for graphics applications, including hardware, software, equipment servicing, and training.

The worldwide CAD/CAM market at the end of 1978 was $510 million, and the consensus of several industry observers polled by McKinsey indicated that the 1983 CAD/CAM market would reach $1,985 million.

By 1978, all of the leading competitors in the four basic CAD/CAM segments had developed strength in a single segment only. While a few companies had begun movement across segment lines, the majority of 1978 sales, as well as new product introductions, were concentrated in the segment where each competitor was strongest.

Nature of Competition within the Industry

McKinsey indicated that a dramatic increase in competition would be inevitable in the long term, given the nature of the rapidly evolving systems segment. But between 1978–1980, competitive pressures were not expected to increase significantly:

- Existing competitors in each of the four computer graphics segments (specialized hardware, stand-alone software, remote services, and turnkey systems) historically tended to concentrate in their proprietary area, choosing not to enter other related segments.

- Even within the (turnkey) systems segment, competitors were apt to focus on special application niches.

- While a variety of new entrant competitors either have tentatively entered the systems business or could have very easily, there appeared to be little evidence of any significant competitive pressures from this area.

However, industry observers agreed that the potential markets for interactive computer graphics and CAD/CAM were bound to attract the large computer firms:

> "Any company still privately held, run by its founders, and using raster scan technology is probably being considered to be bought," said Marty Duhms, an independent consultant and former vice president of marketing for Lexidata Corp. [1]
>
> IBM, which for some years has been offering a Lockheed-developed CAD/CAM system that runs on IBM computers, is highly interested in factory

---

[1] "CAD/CAM Continues to Fuel Graphic Terminal Growth . . . ," *Electronic News*, February 23, 1981, p. 37.

automation as an expanding market. Both Sperry Univac and Honeywell also have plans to offer big CAD/CAM computer systems that will go beyond the smaller versions offered by Computervision, Applicon and other independent vendors. The mainframe makers feel that advanced solid modeling in particular will demand huge number crunching capability.[2]

Minicomputer manufacturers, including Hewlett-Packard, Digital Equipment, Control Data, and Prime Computer, were likely entrants— expected to enhance their CAD/CAM software packages, if not actually progressing to full turnkey services.

Large companies like General Electric and Westinghouse, who were among CAD/CAM's largest users, had made big internal investments in their own systems development and might choose to market their systems.

The turnkey vendors were expected to hold their own in the short term, primarily because of their software libraries.

> "Computervision's base of software would be as easy to re-create as it would be to create a baby in one month using nine women," says Phillippe Villers, a founder of Computervision who has left the company.[3]

There was no standardization within the CAD/CAM industry—a part designed on one system could not be built on another. Support was growing among private and government users for a common standard called IGES— Interactive Graphics Exchange Specification. Within the industry, support of standardization was mixed. As Jim Lucas, a spokesperson for Calma, observed in *Barrons*, "It's like disarmament—everybody wants to do it at the same time. The person who does IGES first will give his competitor an advantage."

Pressure for standardization was intensifying among CAD/CAM's major users, who often had incompatible systems for several vendors in house. Once IGES was adopted, it would lead to hot competition among turnkey vendors and from small start-up ventures run by entrepreneurs who had learned the business at established graphics firms.

Marketing and Sales[4]

The turnkey CAD/CAM system vendors did their marketing directly in the United States, although there was still a fairly heavy dependence on distributors to reach the international market.

---

[2]"A New Industrial Revolution Is on the Way," Gene Bylinsky, *Fortune,* October 5, 1981, p. 144.
[3]"Selling the Workhorse," *Barron's,* December 22, 1980, p. 6.
[4]The source for this section is L.F. Rothschild, Unterbridge, Towbin industry study, as quoted in "Note on Interactive Computer Graphics and CAD/CAM" (S-BP-220N).

The sale of a system was a highly sophisticated process involving high-level management and substantial communication between the vendor and the prospective client. Competition was intense. In more than half the sales consummated, customers evaluated the systems of at least two vendors, often on their own premises, in addition to the elaborate demonstration facilities on the vendor's premises. It took about 6 months to close the average sale (versus more than 24 months only a couple of years previously). Interestingly enough, each vendor enjoyed a high proportion of repeat business.

Among other things, a typical system sale requires the following:

1. Integration of the system with several departments that frequently become a part of the total buy decision
2. The tailoring of a system's configuration and applications programs to fit a customer's needs
3. The training of potential users
4. Economic justification

The key buying factors involved in a sale were (in decreasing order of importance):

- *Software:* breadth of software applications and software problem-solving capability
- *System performance:* response time, picture and drawing quality, and ability to expand system features, such as additional storage and remote terminals
- *User-machine interface:* ease of interface between user and machine (i.e., ease of learning the particular system's command language and menus) and, not unimportantly, the human engineering features incorporated in the work station
- *Field service:* fast response time and low systems downtime
- *Product support:* software maintenance and advancement, responsiveness to user's needs
- *Vendor reputation*
- *Size and activity of user's group*
- *Price*
- *Delivery*

While most of the above are self-explanatory, the reference to *user group* deserves further elaboration. To a degree, this was a participative industry. A large user base was attractive to a potential customer since it put pressure on the supplier to provide solid service support. Users were organized into a variety of different groups to share information, which allowed them to expand applications, utilization, and efficiency of their CAD/CAM systems.

Customer Support[5]

A substantial level of customer support was required of the vendors. Above and beyond the purchase of a system, each customer contracted annually for field service and systems support at a fee that approximated the vendor's cost of the support service. This included software maintenance in the form of upgrades or improvements to operating system software and applications packages. The vendors typically promised eight-hour field service, which was made possible by the modular nature of the systems, allowing replacement rather than actual repair in the field.

Education and training was critical in a first system installation. Training courses were typically conducted for two weeks at the vendor's facilities on the customer's system. After installation, two additional weeks of training were provided.

Manufacturing[6]

Operations of all the systems producers consisted mainly of assembly, quality control, inspection, and testing. Metal fabrication and painting were generally done on the premises. Some hardware components—primarily displays, plotters, and digitizers—were being produced in house by several turnkey system vendors, a trend that seemed to be growing as each vendor attempted to capture more margin and to differentiate its product offering.

The optimum level of vertical integration was a controversial strategic issue in the industry. The argument against vertical integration was that outside suppliers could better keep pace with advancing hardware technology and thus offer the best and, in the long run, the cheapest products, since they were dedicating more development spending to their particular areas. Thus, the turnkey vendors could direct more of their dollars toward critical areas such as software development and not duplicate what was already available in competitive markets. The argument for a high degree of vertical integration was based on two premises: (1) through in-house manufacturing operations, a turnkey supplier was able to boost gross margins and overall profitability, thereby improving its ability to finance a fast-growing business; (2) a product both designed and manufactured in house could be specially tailored for CAD/CAM applications, thereby possibly giving a systems supplier improved performance and systems throughout.

Computervision reflected an example of the latter philosophy. CVN had the highest degree of vertical integration in the group, manufacturing most of the major components in its system, including its own 16-bit minicomputer and

---

[5]Ibid.
[6]Ibid.

raster display station. Applicon, another company moving more of its hardware requirements in house, manufactured its own digitizers, plotters, raster-scan graphic displays, and a specialized 32-bit I/O controller. Auto-trol, which had always made its own digitizers and plotters, recently began assembling its own graphic work station, incorporating a Tektronic storage/refresh display. As each turnkey supplier increased in size, selective components would be increasingly manufactured in house rather than purchased. However, industry observers thought that in contrast to Computervision, very few of these companies would go so far as to manufacture their own minicomputers.

Forecast for the Future

It was difficult to predict the nature and probability of technological breakthroughs that would impact the industry. McKinsey speculated,

> Given the move to distributed data processing, the trends in hardware/software costs, and the revolution in microelectronics, new breakthroughs are likely to be applications-oriented, intelligent terminals. They will likely come from hardware or systems suppliers migrating to firmware capability.

Market Forecast for Turnkey Systems Segment

In 1978 three end-use industries accounted for 80 percent of the turnkey systems market: aerospace, 30 percent; automotive, 25 percent; and electronics, 25 percent. The remainder was divided among mechanical, construction, civil engineering, and other industries. Turnkey systems sales were $165 million worldwide in 1978 and were forecast to reach $1.1 billion by 1983, an average growth rate of 45 percent per year. Table B shows market segments by end-use industry and by systems application. (See Exhibit 5 for consensus forecasts of the systems market.)

Believing that the future would bring robust growth and limited cyclicality, McKinsey asserted that systems suppliers had a unique opportunity to develop "selling partnerships" with their customers, given the customers' reliance on them for expert advice. Sales and service were also considered of great importance to customers, whereby vendors could gain credibility and differentiate themselves.

Assessment of the Competition

Within the turnkey systems segment, six competitors accounted for 90 percent of the total market. McKinsey believed that Calma's competitors were improving their competitive position through "a combination of aggressive strategic actions and development of internal skills." Table C profiles the six

Table B
Systems Market Segmentation
(1978 Sales = $165 million)

END-USE INDUSTRY		SYSTEMS APPLICATIONS	
Aerospace	30%	Mechanical	39%
Automotive	25	Integrated circuits	16
Electronics	25	Civil/structural	15
Mechanical	10	Printed circuits	13
Construction	5	Mapping	9
Civil engineering	2	Other	8
Other	3		100% = $165M
	100% = $165M		

turnkey systems competitors, and Exhibit 6 (p. 498) presents an overview of their product-market strategies. Turnkey suppliers had historically focused on one application area and were just beginning to move into additional related areas in 1979.

Assessing Calma's Position in the Industry

Since Calma was growing slowly in the mechanical applications segment, McKinsey predicted that the company's total market share would drop to 14 percent by 1979.

Calma was judged to have products with superior capabilities in its major lines: integrated circuits (CHIPS), printed circuits (CARDS), and DDM (an interactive system for design, drafting, and manufacture). McKinsey cautioned that "while the systems generally provide good price/value, this may deteriorate unless capabilities continue to be enhanced and/or prices maintained at competitive levels." Exhibit 7 (p. 500) is McKinsey's assessment of Calma's competitive position and projected market share. Exhibit 8 (p. 501) shows McKinsey's comparison of Calma's relative performance on several financial indicators.

Calma had grown quickly and profitably (see Exhibits 1 and 2). Sales were concentrated in one basic product line, Calma's GDS I, the software base for both CHIPS and CARDS, and with a relatively small group of key customers.

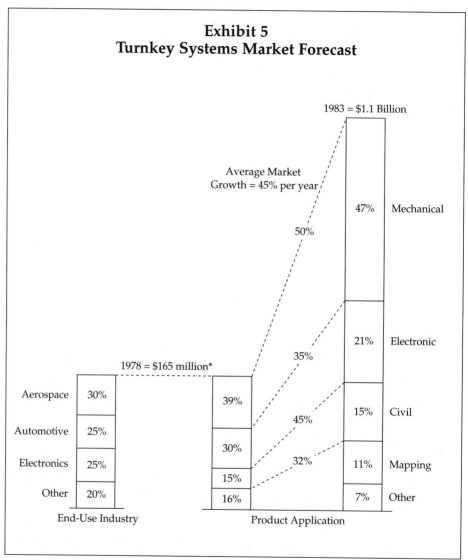

Exhibit 5
Turnkey Systems Market Forecast

1983 = $1.1 Billion

Average Market
Growth = 45% per year

50%

47%   Mechanical

35%

21%   Electronic

1978 = $165 million*

| Aerospace | 30% | | 39% | | 45% | 15% | Civil |

Aerospace 30%

Automotive 25%

Electronics 25%

Other 20%

39%

30%

15%

16%

45%

32%

15%   Civil

11%   Mapping

7%   Other

End-Use Industry   Product Application

*U.S. sales = $124 million; Europe = $30 million; Japan = $11 million.
Source: McKinsey report. Data compiled from research by Arthur D. Little, Inc., Merrill Lynch and others.

Calma was attempting to extend its success in electronics to other application areas; four new product introductions were planned for 1980. They were also working on a second-generation software package, called GDS II, which would greatly expand chip design capabilities.

Historically Calma had made product commitments based on futures. Introductions timed for 1976–1978 had not gone as smoothly as anticipated,

Table C
Leading Turnkey System Competitors

COMPANY	1978 SALES ($ MILLIONS)	%MARKET SHARE (1978)	PROJECTED AVERAGE ANNUAL SALES GROWTH (1976–1979)	MAJOR APPLICATION
Computervision	$ 48.4	29%	76%	Mechanical
Calma	27.2	16	58	Integrated circuit
Applicon	22.0	13	62	Integrated circuit
Auto-trol	21.9	13	68	Structural
M & S	20.1	12	50	Mapping
Gerber	9.0			
	$148.6			

resulting in some internal pressures, as well as some customer discontent. For instance, in customer contacts between 1976 and 1978, Calma had targeted high-resolution VMD (Vector Memory Display) on GDS I by 1979. In the fall of 1979, only low-resolution VMD was anticipated, for introduction in March 1980. Calma had also been forced to abandon a proposed matrix plotter controller for Versatec, geared originally for several GDS I customers, and had moved the completion date of a structural package sold in October 1978 from June 1979 to January 1980.

McKinsey's interviews with Calma's customers indicated that mismanaged expectations appeared to be the major source of customer discontent. Typical of comments made to McKinsey interviewers was "Calma has the most advanced integrated circuit product available. But they made unrealistic commitments to us, and the GDS II startup has been fraught with problems."

To handle a projected average annual growth rate of 26.4 percent, Calma had been aggressively expanding its work force. As a result, in 1979, the average tenure was only 1.6 years, and 37 percent of the employees had been hired within the previous 12 months. The service department had the least number of new employees (30 percent), while administration had 50 percent. The influx of personnel had occurred at all levels—from senior management to the production floor—and it explained in part some of the operating problems identified by McKinsey:

Exhibit 6
Overview of Competitor Strategies

COMPANY	APPARENT STRATEGY AND POSITION
APPLICON	• Mix is comparable to Calma. • Establish product leadership in IC and build distribution. • Shift emphasis in mechanical to low-end product, stressing role in "factory of the future." • Develop industry-oriented packages for specific CAD/CAM market segments. • Market share vulnerable but bluechip installed base generates repeat sales.
AUTO-TROL	• Dominate civil/structural applications by emphasizing price performance of 2-D product and building distribution. • Enter mechanical by introducing 3-D product. • IBM style marketing, customer support. • All customers are on service contracts. • Basic product is unsophisticated but functional.

Source: McKinsey & Company analysis.

Marketing: New department, performing sales support function, conducting little market research.

Service: Lacks total service concept; responsible for activities beyond department's control.

Production: Few cost reduction efforts; poor procurement and MRP (Material Requirements Planning) with a new production planning program in the works.

Within Calma's sales force, 36 percent of 1979 sales revenue had been generated by its top four U.S. sales representatives; 25 percent of sales revenue had come from the 12 other U.S. reps, 24 percent from Calma's Japanese agent, and 15 percent from the European reps. Seventeen of Calma's 23 sales reps had been hired since 1978.

COMPUTERVISION	• Dominate mechanical by offering good product and emphasizing sales/service (strong marketing and sales organization).
	• Enter new segments (e.g., IC) with similar approach.
	• Aggressively fight competitors with deep, selective discounts and future capability promises.
	• Vertical integration and high volume reduce costs.
	• Productivity services consultants enhance customer support strength.
	• Marketing effort organized around product capability/applications lines, not toward specific market segments.
GERBER	•Dominate 2-D mechanical with sophisticated product and leverage established sales force.
	•Enter PCB segment with new product.
M&S	•Dominate mapping through product leadership.
	•Enter closely related segments (e.g., civil/structural) with similar approach.

In the fall of 1979 there were seven openings for sales representatives. According to McKinsey,

> This low staffing level and/or apparent lack of management interest accounts for the absence of badly needed controls. Staffing plans are done informally and nonroutinely. No formal prospect identification or account planning tools appear to be used. Methods for preparing proposals, negotiating corporate agreements, and requesting discounts are only beginning to be rationalized. Building Calma's sales force appears to be an improvement opportunity with significant short-term benefit.

Calma's competitors appeared to be aggressively building their sales forces (see Table D).

Exhibit 7
Mckinsey's Assessment of Calma's Competitive Position

| Market Segment | Sources of Competitive Advantage | | | | | Market Share | |
	Product	Price	Selling	Service	Overall	1978	1979 est.
IC	Outstanding	Average/ Weak	Weak	Average	Outstanding/ Average	41%	43%
PC	Outstanding	Weak	Weak	Average	Average/ Weak	29%	12%
Mechanical	Outstanding/ Average	Average	Weak	Average	Average	10%	15%
Civil/ Structure	Average	Weak	Weak	Average	Average/ Weak	6%	7%
Mapping	Average	Average	Weak	Weak	Average/ Weak	8%	3%
Overall	Outstanding/ Average	Average/ Weak	Weak	Average	Average	Total 16%	Total 14%

Source: McKinsey research.

Marketing

McKinsey identified Calma's marketing function as an area of slow development needing examination. The marketing department had recently been formed and its management turnover had been high. Its initial responsibility had been more toward sales support than marketing, and its product managers had limited end-use industry experience. Little market research had been conducted.

McKinsey's Profile of Organizational Capability

Calma's struggles were determined to be primarily product related. The company had been a highly innovative product developer. Within Calma, "winners" came from the research and development department, which was the largest single professional functional department.

Exhibit 8

FINANCIAL PERFORMANCE (1978)	INDUSTRY	CALMA
Return on capital (EBIT/capital)	21.6%	10.0%
Operating margin (EBIT/sales)	11.7%	8.4%
Asset turnover (Sales/assets)	1.53×	1.01×
EXPENSE RATIOS (1978)		
SGA expense/sales	27.2%	23.6%
R&D expense/sales	10.5%	8.9%
Gross margin	48.0%	40.9%

Source: Company records.

Table D

COMPANY	SIZE OF SALES FORCE	SALES OFFICES	DEMO CENTERS	1979 PRODUCTION LEVEL FORECAST (SALES ÷ SALES FORCE SIZE)
Calma	23	15	8	$1.7
Applicon	28	24	9	$1.5
Computervision	39	23	12	$2.4

New product development had been driven by R&D rather than by marketing, which McKinsey believed had led to a lack of customer and market orientation. Calma was organized around functions rather than markets, and the marketing department had been organized around existing products. The top management team had no prior exposure to market-driven organization.

As a result, McKinsey noted, sales and service capabilities were inconsistent. Sales and service plans were informal, management systems embryonic, and internal communications poor. There was no specialization within the sales force around products and markets (the force was organized by region), and the focus had traditionally been on selling a system, not on developing an account.

McKinsey felt Calma's cost control and asset management systems were weak; the CEO was the only person with true profit responsibility. Production planning and control systems had just been developed, and product line profitability figures were difficult to develop.

McKinsey suggested that Calma needed a more effective compensation system to reward long-term performance and improve turnover rates. Calma had not instituted a recruiting and management development function or a "Calma culture" to build loyalty. As a result, team spirit was judged to be lacking. At best, the culture at Calma was typical of young high-technology firms: "If we have a good product, everything else will follow."

McKinsey Identifies Leadership Requirements

McKinsey identified two issues to be given top priority. First was to upgrade the effectiveness of sales and service efforts. Next, McKinsey recommended that Calma determine how to focus near-term product planning and development activities to other marketing efforts. Controlling R&D programs and supplementing R&D resources was recommended.

Determining alternatives and resource requirements for each market segment was also considered. Critical issues were to be addressed:

1. How much additional effort is needed to secure Calma's leadership position in integrated circuits?
2. How to participate, if at all, in the printed circuit segment?
3. How to develop a meaningful position in mechanical?
4. How to participate, if at all, in other emerging segments?

Longer term business strategy issues were also considered in McKinsey's presentation, particularly how product leadership could be maintained. Major issues presented for discussion included (1) how to sustain a leadership position in the core business, (2) how to determine an appropriate sustainable level of vertical integration, and (3) how to develop a leadership role in the evolution of the office and factory of the future.

At the conclusion of the November 1979 presentation, McKinsey outlined the steps it would take during phase II of its investigation to develop strategic alternatives for Calma. Those alternatives were to be prepared by the McKinsey task force for presentation at the December 1979 senior management meeting.

Study of Strategic Alternatives

On December 4, 1979, the McKinsey task force met with Calma's senior management team. McKinsey had prepared a discussion draft of Calma's strategic alternatives by product-market segment. For each of five markets (integrated circuits, printed circuits, mechanical, architecture/engineering, and mapping), McKinsey had analyzed Calma's situation, its strategic position, and its strategic alternatives.

The discussion draft prepared by McKinsey follows as Case Appendix I.

CONCLUSION

Following McKinsey's presentation, Bob Benders met with Lem Bishop, Art Collmeyer, and Ron Hill. The four men did not agree totally with McKinsey's perspective of the company or the issues presented, and they had some misgivings about the value of the consultants' presentations. Benders had also begun to question McKinsey's objectivity, believing that McKinsey's conclusions were being dictated by what corporate headquarters might wish to hear. Nevertheless, it was clear that unless they moved quickly, some key opportunities might be lost.

CASE APPENDIX 1

OUTLINE OF CALMA'S STRATEGIC ALTERNATIVES BY PRODUCT-MARKET SEGMENT

This document contains summaries of Calma's strategic opportunities organized by segment. The segments covered and contents of each summary are as follows:

Segments	Contents
Integrated Circuit (IC)	Situation Analysis and Strategic Position
Printed Circuit (PC)	
Mechanical	
Architectural/Engineering/Construction (AEC)	
Mapping	

These documents were prepared on the basis of conversations with product managers, as well as the inputs from customers and other analysis performed by the task force.

It is important to recognize that these summaries are only a first cut. They are to be used for discussion purposes, and it is expected that they will go through many iterations culminating in a more formalized product management process.

SITUATION ANALYSIS
SEGMENT: IC
(INTEGRATED CIRCUITS)

CALMA POSITION

_____

Volume/Share
- 1978: $10.9M (41.2%)
- 1979:   15.0   (42.1%)
- 1980:   16.5   (34.3%)
- 1983:   22.0   (18.5%)

Customers

Past	Current	Opportunity	
Natl. Semi (13)	IBM (2)	TI	RCA
Intel (8)	Hitachi (4)	H-P	AMD
Motorola (20)	Toshiba (5)	DEC	Zilog
Plessey (12)		NEC	Mostek
( ) = Systems sold			

Product Parity
- Major strengths are edit features, analytic capabilities, manufacturing interfaces, and overall reliability
- Product weaknesses are relatively slow display speed and lack of data management capability

Selling and Service Capability
- Core group of account executives (AEs) and salespeople exist particularly on West Coast
- Hardware field service capability exists in major geographic locations only

MARKET ATTRACTIVENESS

_____

Size and Growth
- 1978: $ 26.4M   Projected growth 35%/year
- 1979:   35.6   Volume figures represent only the available market
- 1980:   48.1   There is purportedly a market of equal size
- 1983:   118.8   satisfied by in-house initiatives.

Demand Patterns
- Fundamental sources of demand very favorable
  - Design constraints for VLSI
  - Proliferating use of all ICs (Δ = 30%/year)
  - Increasing number of designers/fabricators
- Lingering concern about cyclicality

Customers/Concentrations

- Large captives (e.g., IBM)
- Small captives (e.g., Atari)
- Standard component (e.g., Intel)
- Custom component (e.g., AMI)
- Service bureau (e.g., Design Only)
- User (i.e., Design Only)

Buying Patterns

- Customers tend to standardize on a CAD vendor—this has important implications for early penetration
- Trend toward CAD committees who are increasingly influential in purchase decisions
- Design systems usually assigned to major project teams.
- First-time and less sophisticated customers generally more price sensitive

COMPETITIVE SITUATION

Competition/Share (1979 approximate)

Calma	42%
Applicon	33
GCA/Mann	15
Computervision	5
Others	8

Strategies

Applicon—Dominate segment by establishing product superiority (through Intel initiative) and building national account selling program

GCA/Mann—Establish meaningful position in CAD by introducing suitable product and leveraging contacts/expertise in IC fabrication

Computervision—Opportunistically sell low-end IC machine. If development efforts succeed, introduce new IC CAD system

Strengths and Weaknesses

Applicon—Good referenceable customer base; ongoing product development effort; new initiatives in sales and marketing

- Unproven product; poor service record

GCA/Mann—Unknown

Computervision—Excellent sales and marketing

- Obsolete product; small customer base

CURRENT STRATEGY

Product: CHIPS

- High-end graphic product on par or superior to competition
- Current product development efforts directed at analytic capability (i.e., DRC*) and new terminal (i.e., VMD†), yet little attention being directed at data management

Cost

- Probably the high-cost producer. While customers are relatively price insensitive, it causes margin problems
- Recent cost reduction efforts successful, but no logical action plan exists

Selling

- Selling activities are largely reactive and focus on only responding to established customers
- Little initiative in this segment demonstrated in Midwestern or Eastern regions

Service

- Hardware service is adequate
- Software service is dependent on R&D
- Training activities are only in initial stages, and little attention paid to account management

Summary

- Stated objectives are to dominate business, yet a realistic goal is only to hold share
- Strategy hinges on maintaining product leadership and depending on customers to pull it through
- Efforts to reduce cost, and particularly to improve sales and service capability, lack substantial management attention and resource commitment

---

*DRC: Design Rule Check.
†VMD: Vector Memory Display.

SITUATION ANALYSIS
SEGMENT: PC
(PRINTED CIRCUITS)

CALMA POSITION

Volume/Share/Profitability
• Market share declining sharply

	1978	1979E	1980E
Dollars	$6,000	$5,000	$5,000
SOM	20%	12%	9%

• Gross margin below average due to discounting
• Selling cost level unclear

Customers
• Significant installed base, directed toward large accounts with high-end product needs
• Reputation and image varies widely with current and potential customers
• Core customers are Burroughs (7), Hughes (7), Intel (7), ITT (8), and NCR (10)

Product Parity
• Above par high-end product now; but only par by 1981
• No product at low end and middle range
• Product development efforts behind and vulnerable to more slippage

Selling and Service Capability
• Little proactive selling; heavy repeat business
• Product and application selling skills in field minimal, e.g., few experienced AEs
• Very limited sales coverage; hardware service capabililty and training marginally adequate

MARKET ATTRACTIVENESS

Size and Growth
• Overall segment $30M in 1978; overall growth at 35% although Calma's core market may slip to 20% by 1983
• Geographic breakdown; United States, 60%; Europe, 30%; Japan, 10%

Demand Patterns
- Concurrency trends unclear
- Strong overall demand by all subsegments, little cyclicality
- Several emerging subsegments demanding low-end products
- Slow overall product mix shift

Customer/Concentrations

Subsegment	% of Market	Concentration
Computer peripherals	40%	High
PC/mechanical	25	Very high
(Auto, Aero, etc.)		
Industrial controls	20	Very low
Consumer electronics	15	Very high

Buying Patterns
- "First system purchase" penetration at 40–50% for U.S. buying centers but only 10%–20% internationally
- Repeat buying patterns unclear but U.S.-based accounts probably committed to entrenched vendors

COMPETITIVE SITUATION

Competition/Share/Trend
- Computervision, 35%, slowly declining
- Calma, 20%, rapidly declining
- Applicon, 25%, slowly declining
- Gerber, 5%–7%, increasing rapidly at low end
- S-C, 5%, increasing rapidly at high end
- Redac and 30 others, 3%–5%, fringe competitors

Strategies
- Computervision; maintain slow, steady product enhancements but use sales, service, low COGS, and installed base to slowly grow share; major focus on large, long-term customers
- Gerber and S-C entering low and high end, respectively
- Applicon; unclear, appears vulnerable

Strengths and Weaknesses
- Computervision; market coverage, mechanical reputation are major strength. Marginal product line is only weakness
- Applicon; installed base and image/weak sales and product; software niche
- Others; software niche

CURRENT STRATEGY

Product: CARDS

- Current efforts to improve high-end capability (e.g., design automation features) focused on rewriting software package

Cost

- Clearly high-cost competitor with significant margin problems except for large, high-end buyers
- Product enhancements listed above will eliminate dual CPU requirement

Selling

- Sales effort largely focused on repeat, established customers
- No apparent sales program in Japan
- Little sales support for high-end product line

Service

- Training aids inadequate and training process too complex, suggesting need for an improved applications software package
- Field service capabilities unknown

Summary

- Overall objective unclear; holding share may be difficult
- Product development and sales effort lacks focus

STRATEGIC POSITION
SEGMENT: MECHANICAL

CALMA POSITION

Volume/Share/Profitability
- Early market share increases have reached a plateau

	1977	1979	1980	1983
Dollars	$7,000	$16,000	$18,000	$28,000
SOM	10%	15%	12%	5%

- Gross margin and operating margin below par to start up operating costs

Customers
- Established customer base fragmented but with some important niches in key segments
- Marketplace image limited
- Current and potential core customers unclear
- Strongest position in Japan

Product Parity
- Superior high-end product, but requiring significant customer application software development
- Expensive mid-range systems and no low-end systems
- Product family and next-generation development program unfocused

Selling and Service Capability
- Selling largely reacting to many customer inquiries, lowering productivity
- Application and technical selling skills weak; no industry specialization
- Unable to provide demos to current prospects requesting them

MARKET ATTRACTIVENESS

Size and Growth
- Overall market largest and fastest growing ($105M/40%)
  - Subsegments still unclear; probably tend towards buying pattern clusters
  - Japan and Europe markets independent, but lag United States

Demand Patterns
- Customer sophistication low
- Major amount of latent demand

Customers/Concentrations
- Dominated by a few large customers with many, fragmented buying centers (i.e., automotive and aerospace make up 50 percent of today's market)
- Flagship customers are key influencers
- 70 percent of customers require full capability, i.e., layout, design, drafting, and manufacturing interface; 25 percent require PC/DDM product
- Slower rate-of-change in product requirements than in IC

Buying Patterns
- Large repeat-buy accounts standardizing on installed vendors
- First-time buyers follow complex, performance-oriented evaluation process
- Large accounts standardizing via CAD/CAM efforts

COMPETITIVE SITUATION

Competition/Share
- Computervision increasing rapidly, holding key accounts and penetrating first-buy customers using broad sales coverage and substantial discounting when needed
- Second-tier competitor shares stable in key niches, e.g., Applicon in auto
- Minor inroads by new competitors

Strategies

Computervision—Future strategy a continuation of past; product strategy unclear

Applicon—Plans to devote major market resource to the mechanical market in the next five years. However, no outward signs, i.e., new product or sales effort, indicate this

Strengths and Weaknesses

Applicon—Entrenched base and joint customer development linkage is major strength/high-end product flexibility for new applications major weakness

Gerber and new competitors—unclear

CURRENT STRATEGY

Product: DDM

- Superior product performance, but needs final packaging
- Next generation of enhancements include improved FEM, NC, and dimensioning capabilities plus surface package
- Introduce Scorpio low-end product (?)

Cost

- Cost reduction efforts unfocused
- Competitive costs, particularly Computervision's, lower than Calma's

Selling

- Largely reactive due to people shortage
- Still developing basic skills, which lowers productivity
- Account focus unclear

Service

- Limited experience, but major customers would clearly buy a more aggressive hardware and software service package

Summary

- Ambitious goal to displace Applicon as number two largely unfocused
- Product leadership only source of clear competitive advantage

STRATEGIC POSITION
SEGMENT: AEC

CALMA POSITION

Volume/Share
- 1978: $1.5M   (6.1%)   Cumulative sales:
- 1979:   3.0   (8.4%)   10 systems
- 1980:   4.5   (8.7%)   Projected growth:
- 1983:   25.0   (15.2%)   75%/year

Customers

Past	Current	Opportunity
Procter & Gamble	Elin-Union	BC Hydro
Ontario Hydro	Stone & Webster	Boeing
Royal Graphics	Japan Gas	AECs
		("50 good prospects")

Product Parity
- Calma has the most advanced product spec, yet it is incomplete. Key features include 3-D database, which facilitates analysis and dimensioning. Key weaknesses include speed and user interfaces, plus currently high price
- Competitors are successfully selling 2-D schematic systems with complete AEC work packages at a low price. They have been promising a 3-D capability

Selling and Service Capability
- Very little sales force effort has been dedicated to CADEC
- No track record to evaluate service

MARKET ATTRACTIVENESS

Size and Growth
- 1978: $24.7M   Projected growth = 45%/year
- 1979:   35.8   Potential market = 1,000 users
- 1980:   51.9
- 1985:   165

Demand Patterns
- Major sources of demand are energy crisis; technological breakthroughs in low-cost terminals; cumulative effects of product acceptance; and lack of enough engineers
- CAD systems are usually purchased for specific projects involving large structures

Customers/Concentrations
- Independent AEC firms (e.g., Sargeant & Lundy, Gibbs & Hill, Bechtel, Brown & Root)/ Top 30 = 30% and Top 400 = 80%
- Commercial accounts (e.g., Procter & Gamble)/ Top 500 = 80%
- Government

Product Needs

Basic Needs	Disciplines
• Schematics	• Process (e.g., P&ID, Flow)
• Dimension drawings	• Electrical
• Analysis/reports	• Piping (e.g., Isometrice)
	• Structural steel (e.g., Flaming)
	• Structural concrete
	• Civil (e.g., roads)
	• Architectural (e.g., layouts)

- CAD systems have historically only been able to do schematics (2-D). In mid-1970s, they were linked with report generators (e.g., bill of materials). More recently, the capability to do dimension drawings has been added, and 3-D databases created to allow stress analyses, etc.

Buying
- KBF (key buying factors) are quite variable. However, minimum product requirements are schematics for process and electrical disciplines, and selling is increasingly important as competition intensifies
- An "easier" sale than mechanical
- Customers regarded as buying very conservative and price sensitive

COMPETITIVE SITUATION

Competition/Share (1979 approximate)

Auto-Trol	33%
M&S	27%
Computervision	20%
Applicon	9%
Calma	8%
Others	3%

<u>Strategies</u>

Auto-Trol—Dominate segment by leveraging establishing customer base and introducing new product

M&S—Dominate segment by rolling out superior product with agressive pricing

Computervision—Establish meaningful position by pushing product through sales effort

<u>Strengths and Weaknesses</u>

Auto-Trol—Adequate product; good position with AEC firms; excellent selling effort

—Inability to complete new product; potential risk of losing focus

M&S—Superior product (3-D software, DEC hardware); good applications knowledge, improving position with AEC firms
—Modest selling skills

Computervision—Excellent sales and marketing; adequate product
—Product does not receive a lot of sales-force attention

CURRENT STRATEGY

Product: CADEC

- High-end product with specifications superior to competition
- Product development efforts dedicated to completing ten work packages

Cost

- Probably the high-cost producer. This reduces available market and flexibility considerably because it is perhaps the most price-sensitive segment
- Pricing is based on DDM product—prices are 20-percent higher than two key competitors

Selling

- Product training and documentation has been provided to sales force by marketing
- Problems of small sales force complicated by the fact that opportunities in DDM and IC are perceived as more significant, resulting in essentially no attention being given to product

Service

- Efforts in service are similar to other product lines with the exception that documentation is more complete

Summary

- Stated objective is to increase share, yet current approach is likely to result in no change or decrease
- While lack of complete product is part of problem, the more serious shortcomings lie in poor understanding of customer needs/buying patterns and total lack of sales-force attention

SITUATION ANALYSIS
SEGMENT: MAPPING

CALMA/NIS POSITION

Volume/Share
- 30 CGI systems sold through 1977
- 1979:   3 systems
- 1980:   6 systems   (Projections based on
- 1981:   13 systems   Corporate Business Plan)

Customers

Past	Current	Opportunities
Brooklyn Natural Gas	West Coast	ConEd
San Diego Gas & Electric	Engineering Firm	ARCO
Washington Gas & Light		PG&E
Columbus & Southern		UTI
Union Gas		

Product Parity
- Product is six years old. Product strengths include good input capability, yet it lacks a report writer
- Product development efforts significantly behind competitors
- Product requirements include intelligent terminal and color display
- Calma's R&D is directed at other areas

Selling and Service Capability
- Corporate headquarters has only two sales representatives
- Service capability is inadequate to handle current accounts
- No prospecting done; answer RFPs that hit the street

MARKET ATTRACTIVENESS

Size and Growth
- 1979: $23M
- 1980:   41
- 1983:   125

- Market is generally regarded to be very latent (e.g., 1979 potential = $130M). Incremental growth is dependent on investment in marketing

Demand Patterns
- Two distinct sources of demand: (1) automating the mapping of uncharted geology (e.g., energy companies); and (2) converting hard copy maps to automated database (e.g., utilities)
- The underlying needs vary as well: (1) new maps = speed and flexibility; and (2) old maps = cost

Customers/Concentrations	Buying Center Concentration
Utilities	High
Petroleum company	Low
Natural resource company	Low
Federal and state government	Medium
Service bureaus	Low

Product Needs

Service
- Data collection and conversion (65%)
- Software consulting (20%)

Product
- Turnkey systems (5%) (i.e., digitize and edit)
- Data storage (10%)

( ) = Percent of overall market

Buying Patterns
- Utilities are slow and conservative
- Government is slow and cumbersome
- Overall, buying centers and patterns are quite complex, and not well understood

COMPETITIVE SITUATION

Competition/Share (1979 approximate)	
M&S	55%
Synercom	15
Applicon	14
Computervision	11
Others	5

<u>Strategies</u>

M&S—Sell consulting service with turnkey systems; develop product for federal government, then sell in commercial market

Synercom—Target municipalities and utilities

IBM—Introduced Geo-Facilities Graphic Support Package (IGSS)

<u>Strengths and Weaknesses</u>

M&S—Understand the product/market and have good related development skills

—No competitor offers full-service capability, i.e., data collection, conversion, and turnkey system

<u>Summary</u>

This strategy is doomed for failure because Calma's R&D resources are being allocated elsewhere, and headquarters group has limited market knowledge and inadequate resources.

AMER GROUP, LTD. (A)

FEBRUARY 1986

A few hours earlier, Leif Ekstrom, 43, had phoned the headhunter who had placed him in his present position just two years ago, this time to tell him that he had decided to accept the offer to be president and chief operating officer of Amer Group, a dynamic and growing diversified corporation. In the quiet and relaxed confinement of his sauna, Leif now took time to reflect on his decision. As he felt the sweat begin to bead on his skin, he poured a little water from the bucket onto the heated rocks to add a bit of moisture to the dry heat. As he watched the steam rise, the warm sensation and sweet smell of pine relaxed him. He took a deep breath, and wondered how, as an outsider, he would be able to provide leadership and add value to the firm he would be heading as of April l.

Leif Ekstrom was at the time executive vice president of a forest products company in the midst of restructuring. The uncertainties presented by these changes, coupled with structural threats in the forest industry, gave him just enough reason to consider the Amer opportunity. In his mind, the consumer-oriented businesses at Amer Group had fascinating possibilities in terms of growth potential and international expansion, and, in spite of his strong financial background, he had always enjoyed the marketing aspects of business. He thought Amer Group had not been an outstanding company until the mid-1970s, but since Heikki O. Salonen had become president, it had undergone many transitions to become a highly successful and respected organization in the Finnish business community. Much of the company's success was a result of the corporate and divisional strategies that had been well defined in the last few years. Ekstrom liked the excitement of a changing organization, and he saw management freedom and the flexible decision-making policy at Amer Group as attractive challenges for his professional growth.

Amer Group was a multibusiness company, among the 30 largest in Finland, with corporate headquarters in Helsinki. The company was involved in motor vehicles, tobacco, communications, paper wholesaling, textiles and

This case was written by Ann Yungmeyer under the supervision of Associate Professor L. J. Bourgeois III. Copyright © 1988 by the Darden Graduate Business School Foundation, Charlottesville, VA. Revised February 1993.

clothing, sporting goods, metals, and plastics. Its major international brand names included Toyota, Citroen, Suzuki, Marlboro, Belmont, Marimekko, Seiko, Casio, and After Eight. Amer had sales in North America, Europe, Scandinavia, Japan, and the Soviet Union.

Heikki Salonen had steered the company as president since 1972, and now, at 53 years of age, was taking the title of chairman and chief executive officer. Salonen stated that Amer's board members, investors, and outside analysts thought the company was "too much in one man's hands." He himself agreed with comments that, although his single-handed leadership of the firm had been effective, it was no longer healthy for the future of the company. Amer's rapid growth, recent acquisitions, and the subsequent need to strengthen top management made some organizational changes necessary.

As COO, Ekstrom would be assuming the primary day-to-day leadership role in the firm. He felt confident in his abilities to handle the challenge ahead. "As foreign as these businesses are to me," he thought to himself, "it is not necessary to know the technical aspects of these products; rather, it is more important to know their roles and have vision about how to develop them in the marketplace."

FINNISH HISTORY AND CULTURE

Historians believe the Finns migrated north from near Hungary around 2,000 years ago, pushing the indigenous Lapps into more northern regions. Finland was incorporated into Sweden in the 12th century, in 1809 was conquered by Alexander I, and remained an autonomous grand duchy of the Russian Empire until 1917. Shortly after the Bolshevik Revolution, Finland declared independence. In 1918 it experienced a civil war that had colored domestic policies to the present. Finland fought the Soviet Union twice during World War II and was left with huge reparation debts. In 1948 an agreement was signed with the Soviet Union under which Finland was obligated to defend its own territory in the case of an armed attack against the Soviet Union via Finland.

Finland's active neutrality was reflected in its basic goal since 1944: to stay out of Great Power conflicts while building mutual confidence with the Soviet Union. Finland was culturally, politically, and socially Western, but the Finns realized they had to live in peace with their eastern neighbor.

Finland had a dynamic industrial economy as a result of technology and significant capital investment over the last two decades. Because industry expansion occurred later in Finland than in other industrialized countries, fixed assets, on the average, were modern and suited for volume production. In the early 1980s, the economic growth rate was among the highest in Europe. Exports amounted to roughly one-third of gross national product (GNP). Wood processing, metals manufacture, shipbuilding, foodstuff, and textiles were the main industries. Finland was self-sufficient in meat, dairy, grains, timber, and most minerals, while fruits, vegetables, nonwood raw materials, and energy were mainly imported.

The Finns held their history and nationalism, as well as traditions, in high regard. Important themes throughout their literature were humanity's unity with nature and an appreciation for the common people, the Finnish folk. The underlying appreciation for simplicity could be seen in artistic creations such as jewelry, textiles, glass, and furniture designs.

The most well-known feature of the Finnish way of life was the sauna. Most Finns took saunas at least once a week for cleansing and relaxation. Many corporate office buildings contained saunas for use at the end of the workday. Many Finns had a rustic cottage in the country where they went on weekends to enjoy peaceful relaxation and a sauna heated by natural wood fire. As one Finn put it, "This is our way to get back to nature and close to our traditions."

The Finns were very precise and punctual—in business, clean, neat, and orderly. Plans were usually well prepared and laid out, and good communication was stressed. They paid much attention to detail, even to the point of how they folded the napkins for coffee in a conference room. In short, Finns embodied Scandinavian values of simplicity, precision, tradition, pragmatism, and love of nature.

BACKGROUND ON AMER GROUP

Amer Group was founded in 1950 as a tobacco company by members of four major Finnish associations: the Engineering Society in Finland, the Association of Graduates of the Schools of Economics and Business Administration, the Student Union of the Helsinki School of Economics and Business Administration, and the Land and Water Technology Foundation. They had worked together successfully in fund-raising projects, and their aim was "to create a business from which the profits would be used to fund commercial and technical university education and research."[1] Industrial machinery was difficult to find after World War II, but they had an opportunity to purchase machinery for manufacturing cigarettes from a small liquidated company, and the association members saw a great future in new American-blend cigarettes, introduced to Europe by American soldiers during the war. They had an idea for a product that would later become the "Boston" brand. Thus the idea, product, and future plans led to development of the company and its original name, Amer-Tupakka.

In 1986 the four founding organizations still had representatives on the company's advisory board and remained principal shareholders. Amer Group

---

[1]Company public relations brochure.

(the company name that followed) had been listed on the Helsinki Stock Exchange since 1977 and on the London Stock Exchange since 1984, and by 1986 it had 16,330 shareholders, some of whom were foreign institutional investors.

Diversification from the tobacco industry began with a peat moss and shipping business; in the early 1970s, the company acquired a publishing and printing business. Later in the decade, it established a flower growing business, formed a division to import and market high-quality branded products such as watches and confectionery and made acquisitions in the ice hockey equipment and paper wholesaling business. Amer Group continued expansion in the 1980s to auto imports, plastics and metals manufacture, textiles, and ready-to-wear clothing.

When Heikki Salonen arrived in 1972, the tobacco business was still small, and the peat moss and shipping companies were losing money. He immediately began to stabilize the businesses, turning around or divesting loss-making operations. In 1973 he reorganized by trimming representation on the board of directors and establishing the actual Amer Group as a holding company for the various independent business concerns. His vision for the company at that point was only "to diversify into areas where Amer Group could use proven strengths and well-developed skills." This process of strategy definition led to Amer Group's mission, "To market high-quality branded products." He reflected, "Many mistakes were made during this process of giving the company direction, but we managed to improve our overall result every year."

The four founding organizations could not provide the capital to finance further growth, so in 1977 when Salonen saw the company was in good financial condition, he decided to offer stock on the Helsinki Exchange. Shortly thereafter, Amer Group's independent companies were consolidated into a single corporate entity in order to improve its image to shareholders as well as for tax benefits. Although each division continued to operate more or less independently, in effect, Amer Group's central management was strengthened. Internationalization began with the acquisition of two hockey equipment businesses in North America. By 1984 Amer managers had been successful at balancing paying dividends with retaining enough earnings to finance growth and decided to list on the London Exchange. Management believed that foreign financing would improve Amer's investment alternatives and give the company higher visibility in the financial markets.

By this point, Amer had acquired or established nearly 30 businesses and made several divestments along the way. The company was gaining a reputation for being very fast paced. One veteran at Amer Group explained the active spirit: "It is the American influence; American firms tend to move fast, and our key management people in Amer Group have had training in the U.S. We have also learned quite a bit through our cooperative agreement with Philip Morris." Heikki Salonen summed it up: "Innovative, active spirit, even aggressiveness, have been and will be characteristic of our operations."

Amer had deliberately sought to invest in areas where marketing was the key factor and where management experience and understanding of markets could contribute to success. The mid-1980s' strategy was to find market vacuums that could be penetrated with the company's existing marketing expertise and to market, worldwide, products of superior quality. Amer Group concentrated in areas that were not particularly sensitive to economic fluctuations and did not require heavy investment in industrial fixed assets. Guiding principles for operations were high yield on capital employed, profitability, growth, and the safeguarding of operations. Amer Group's policy was to hold part of its capital in investment properties, with the aim of ensuring some stability in the long-term development of Amer Group's business.[2]

Heikki Salonen described Amer Group's philosophy:

> Our specialty is marketing know-how. It is the same for each division—to know how to plan and control the sales organization. It is a sophisticated yet very precise methodology. Each division develops its own specialized marketing and distribution skill and formulates its own strategy in terms of market share, positioning, and competitive factors. The aim is to establish or maintain a leading position in the domestic market while paving the way for international expansion. In a country the size of Finland, internationalization is a must for sustained market growth.

Salonen took pride in trying to recruit the best managers and encouraging them to come forward with new ideas. At the same time, he emphasized planning and tight financial control, as well as a certain conservatism. "I encourage my managers to reach for the stars while keeping their feet firmly on the ground" (which, he said, sounds better in Finnish). "We need creativity while taking reasonable risks. Small problems mean we are trying. If you have no loss-making operations, the shareholders will say you are not trying all possibilities enough."

Group Structure

Amer Group was organized into seven autonomous divisions (see Exhibit 1), plus the three headquarters departments of corporate planning, finance, and communications and public relations. All the divisions were part of the parent company, with the exception of Korpivaara (autos) and Marimekko (textiles), which had remained separate legal entities.

Finland was experiencing a strong trend toward decentralized management in the mid-1980s, and Amer Group was among those beginning to restructure their organizations. Objectives of the reorganization were to enhance the autonomy and efficiency of the operating divisions and to simplify Group management. Discussions about how to achieve these goals were taking place during the time the decision was made to hire a chief operating officer.

Major investment decisions and finance were Amer Group's principal centralized activities. Division presidents were consulting Salonen, however,

---

[2]Summary taken from Amer Group planning documents and annual reports.

Exhibit 1
Amer Group Structure
Group Headquarters

Board of Directors
President
Finance and Administration
Corporate Planning
Communications and Public Relations

DIVISIONS

TOBACCO DIVISION

    Amer-Tupakka
    Amer-Brokers confectionary

COMMUNICATIONS DIVISION

    Weilin+Goos publishing and printing
    Finnreklama Oy printing
    Kiviranta advertising services
    Salomo Karvinen Oy direct marketing company
    AmerInstitute, Amersoft education services

PAPER MERCHANTING AND CONVERTING DIVISION,
AMERPAP SPORTS GOODS DIVISION

    Amer Sport International, Inc., Canada, USA
    Koho, Finland, Europe

MARKETING UNITS DIVISION

    Golden Leaf consumer durables
    Kukkameri cut flowers
    Fionia Plant Export ApS, Denmark

KORPIVAARA

    Toyota Group
    Auto-Bon Citroyen, Suzuki
    Kone-Diesel service and accessories
    Metals

(continued on next page)

Source: 1984–1985 Annual Report.

(continued)

Konemuovi plastics
Trading furniture exports
Moottorialan Luotto financing

MARIMEKKO

Decembre Oy
Marimekko, Inc., USA
Marimekko GmbH, Fed. Rep. of Germany

whenever other types of decisions were necessary. Communication between the divisions and headquarters theoretically took place through the finance department. Management reporting was sketchy, however, and problems were not dealt with through normal organizational channels but in a "management by happening" manner (i.e., fires were put out as necessary). One corporate executive commented, "The administration was built around people and personalities, not structure."

Corporate planning conducted business development and personnel activities. Business development activities included procedural handling of acquisitions and divestitures, research of future business opportunities for Amer Group in areas outside the existing business divisions, as well as research support to the divisions for closely related businesses. The personnel department planned and coordinated in-house training and development programs in the areas of management and financial reporting for all of Amer Group. In addition to the training objective, these sessions provided an opportunity for division managers to come together to meet and have discussions in an educational environment.

Financial Structure

Amer Group's strong financial position was evident in net operating cash flow, which improved from negative 2 million FIM (Finn marks) in 1980 to positive 168 million FIM in 1984–1985.[3] Debt to equity came down from 1.1 in 1981 to .8 in 1984 and was at 1.0 after large acquisitions in 1984–1985. From 1981 to 1985, net sales grew at a 42-percent compound annual growth rate,

---

[3]*Trade with Finland*, Helsinki School of Economics, 1986.

profit before tax at 23 percent, and earnings per share at 13 percent. (See Exhibits 2 and 3 for financial statement highlights.)

Amer had 7.2 million shares outstanding and a total of 16,330 shareholders. Two types of shares were issued. All 1.5 million "K" shares were owned by the founder organizations of the company. Each "K" share had the right of ten votes, and every ten "A" shares had the right of one vote. "A" shares had been quoted on the Helsinki Stock Exchange since 1977 and on the London exchange since May 1984. "A" shares took precedence over "K" shares in receiving dividends and were always entitled to a dividend at least equal to that of "K" shares. New share issues were primarily for the purpose of financing acquisitions. For example, Amer Group acquired the majority holdings in Korpivaara and Marimekko in part with the issue of "A" shares.

The founding organizations owned more than 40 percent of total outstanding shares, representing 97 percent of the votes. In addition to all "K" shares, the founding organizations owned 28 percent (1.6 million) of the "A" shares.

The price of Amer Group shares had risen annually by an average of 30 percent during 1976–1985. During the same period, the prices on the Helsinki exchange rose an average of 11 percent a year. The corresponding rate of inflation was around 8 percent a year.

AMER GROUP'S BUSINESSES

A corporate document summarizing Amer's businesses is provided as Exhibit 4 (p. 533). Division performance figures are given in Exhibit 5 (p. 536).

Tobacco Division

Amer-Tupakka was Finland's leading distributor of tobacco products. It manufactured and sold primarily American-blend cigarettes such as Marlboro, Belmont, and L&M. The company's philosophy was to be "first on the market," and in 1955, Amer-Tupakka introduced the first filter-tipped cigarette in Finland, the "Boston Filter." In the opinion of Martti Santala, tobacco division president from 1972, "The success of this product was the real economic base of the company. We had gained 20-percent market share by the late 50s, and big volume with one product is very economical." A license agreement with Philip Morris Companies, Inc., began in 1961, which involved cooperation in product development, marketing, and manufacture, and in the procurement of raw tobacco. In Finland, Marlboro had the highest market share of any country in the world. Amer Group held a 59-percent share in the total Finnish cigarette market, with Philip Morris products accounting for roughly 90 percent of sales.

Amer's chief competitors were Rettig, a Finnish company that held a license agreement with R. J. Reynolds, and British American Tobacco, a foreign-owned company. In 1970 Amer was the smallest tobacco company in Finland,

Exhibit 2
Amer Group, Ltd.
Five-Year Financial Summary
(figures in FIM millions [mmk])

CONSOLIDATED STATEMENT OF INCOME[1]	1981	1982	1983	1984	1985
Gross sales	1,522	1,780	2,023	2,277	4,299
Net sales[2]	611	680	768	875	2,483
Foreign sales	138	87	109	155	246
Wages, salaries, and social expenses[3]	144	153	160	192	315
Operating profit before depreciation	100	93	101	121	297
Depreciation (statutory and IAS)[4]	18	22	22	26	168
Net interest expense	30	30	26	20	95
Profit before taxes and appropriations	57	49	60	81	132
Taxes	6	10	6	2	3
Net profit	4	9	9	16	32
CONSOLIDATED BALANCE SHEET					
Financial assets[5]	383	460	463	622	903
Inventory and finished goods	180	207	198	220	606
Fixed assets	228	230	266	295	955
Total assets	791	897	927	1,137	2,464
Current liabilities	362	382	368	407	1,035
Long-term liabilities	170	198	215	254	511
Untaxed reserves	157	195	200	252	652
Shareholders' funds	102	121	144	224	265
Total liabilities and equity	791	896	927	1,137	2,463

(continued on next page)

[1]The figures for 1985, 1984, and 1983 are for the 12 months to August 31; figures for 1982 to 1981 are for the calendar year. Consolidated statements include Finnish and foreign subsidiaries in which the parent company owns more than 50-percent voting rights. These statements were prepared in accordance with Finnish Accounting Standards. Because of differences with IAS standards in account classification, it is not possible to calculate ratios with the information given. Selected ratios are provided under Key Information.

[2]Net sales reflect adjustment to gross for excise duty, sales taxes, commissions, royalties, internal sales, and other adjustments.

[3]Social expenditures include statutory, contractual, and voluntary.

[4]The statutory portion of depreciation is charged as an appropriation.

[5]Financial assets include cash, A/R, advances, prepaid expenses, and other.

Source: 1984–1985 Annual Report.

(continued)

KEY INFORMATION	1981	1982	1983	1984	1985
Capital expenditures (mmk)	37	28	54	64	504
Return on capital employed	22%	17%	17%	18%	16%
Return on shareholders funds	37%	22%	19%	24%	18%
Debt-to-equity ratio	1.1	.9	1	.8	1
Dividend per share (mk)	1.3	1.8	2	2.7	3.4
Earnings per share (mk)	11.3	9.8	10.4	13.7	18.7
P/E ratio	2.2	5.1	7.6	8.6	5.2
Price of restricted "A" share (mk)	25	50	78.7	118	98
Average personnel	1,997	1,984	2,016	2,041	2,983

but in 1974, after two strategic pricing moves to match prices with the competitive Rettig brand, Amer's market share jumped from 27 to 42 percent. Ever since, Amer had continued to gain on competitors.

A tobacco law passed in 1977 banned all cigarette advertising in Finland. Amer responded by increasing its sales force and, because of its already established high-market-share position, was not hurt by this legislation. "Big brands and brand groups advertise themselves," commented one tobacco executive. "In theory, the ban helps international brands, which continue to benefit from outside promotions, and it prevents competitors from successfully launching new products." Amer's cigarette prices increased whenever the government imposed a higher consumer sales tax, with no effect on the consumption level.

The total Finnish cigarette market had shown an increase of 8 percent since 1980, with a leveling off in 1984 and a slight decrease in 1985. Consumption was expected to remain the same in spite of a 5-percent price increase in January 1985. The trend toward quitting smoking had thus far not affected Amer's sales. Jukka Ant-Wuorinen, vice president of marketing, speculated that young smokers were replacing the "quitters," who tended to be over age 40.

The division also manufactured and sold Clan pipe tobacco and Rizla cigarette tobacco on a small scale, as well as filter cigars and cigarette filters for export.

Amer-Brokers was a small subsidiary unit that marketed confectionery and Kodak products under agreements with its principals. Products ranged

Exhibit 3
Amer Group, Ltd.
Financial Statements in Accordance with
International Accounting Standards (IAS)

Accounting principles in Finland differ in a number of ways from those in other countries. Financial statements of Finnish companies are significantly influenced by tax law, with the result that taxable profit can be reduced by appropriations to "untaxed reserves" and depreciation allowances. Because financial statements prepared according to Finnish standards may be unfamiliar to overseas readers, supplementary financial statements prepared in accordance with IAS are included here.

CONSOLIDATED STATEMENT OF INCOME SUMMARY	1984	1985
Gross sales	2,277	4,299
Net sales	875	2,483
Profit before tax and extraordinary items	88	132
Tax	(3)	(3)
Extraordinary items	—	17
Net profit	85	146
Transfer to/from untaxed reserves	(48)	(17)
	37	129

CONSOLIDATED BALANCE SHEET SUMMARY

	1984	1985
Current assets:		
Cash	122	112
Stock and work in progress	232	626
A/R and prepaid expenses	451	722
Total current assets	805	1,460
Fixed assets	247	745
Investments	44	56
Deposits	41	57
Goodwill	11	9
Total assets	1,148	2,327

(continued on next page)

Source: 1985 Annual Report.

(continued)

	1984	1985
Current liabilities:		
A/P and accrued liabilities	275	651
Current portion of long-term loan	45	78
Short-term loans	108	332
Total current liabilities	428	1,061
Long-term loans	232	485
Share capital	124	145
Share premium	73	183
Untaxed reserves	210	243
Retained earnings	81	207
Minority interest	0	3
Total liabilities and equity	1,148	2,327

SOURCE AND APPLICATION OF FUNDS

Sources:

	1984	1985
Profit before tax and extraordinary items	88	132
Adjustment for depreciation	22	68
Sales of fixed assets	6	84
Issue of shares	72	131
Other increase in shareholder funds	0	33
Increase in long-term loans	64	331
	252	779

Application:

	1984	1985
Purchase of fixed assets	63	631
Purchase of investments	1	12
Repayment of long-term loans	47	45
Dividends paid	11	17
Taxes paid	3	3
Deposits	6	16
Other applications	1	0
Increase in working capital	120	55
	252	779

Exhibit 4
Amer Group Divisional Structure

Division	Division Segments/ Activities	Segment Companies/ Activities	Products	Trademarks/ Brand Names	Market Served
Tobacco	Amer-Tupakka	—	Tobacco products	Philip Morris Co.: "Marlboro," "Belmont", "L&M," "Multifilter" Others: "Clan," "Barres"	Consumer
	Amer-Brokers	—	Confectionary	Rountree Mackintosh pk: "After Eight," "Toffo,""Big Cat," Other:"Kit Kat"	Consumer
			Photographic products	Kodak	Consumer
Communi-cations	Weilin+Goos	—	Textbooks, encyclopedias	Otava	Educational institutions in Finland and other Western European countries
	Finnreklama Kivranta, Kuva Oy	—	Books Lithography	Finnereklama Kivranta, Kuva Oy	Soviet Union Advertising agencies
	Amer Institute	— —	Training pro-grams for sales management		Educational
	Amersoft	—	Microcomputer software	Amersoft	Consumer, business
	Salomo Karvinen Oy	—	Multivolume reference books, domestic appliances	Salomo Karvinen Oy	Consumer
Paper merchanting and converting	Amerpap	Paper merchanting	Special purpose papers for printing, art, commercial use	A. Ahlstrom Oy, Kymi Stromberg Oy, C.A. Serlachius Oy, United Paper Mills, and Others	Commercial, industrial, art

(continued on next page)

Source: Company documents.

(continued)

Division	Division Segments/ Activities	Segment Companies/ Activities	Products	Trademarks/ Brand Names	Market Served
		Paper Converting	Postal wrappers, packaging materials, envelopes	—	Postal
		Other	Franking machines, mail handling machines, printing ink	Hasler	Postal, art
Sporting goods	Amer Sport International, Inc.	—	Hockey equipment	"Koho," "Canadien"	North American Sporting goods
	Koho	—	Hockey equipment	"Koho"	European and North American sporting goods
Marketing units	Golden Leaf	—	Watches, clocks, calculators, pens, cigarette papers	"Seiko," "Pulsar," "Lorus," "Casio," "Montblanc," "Zebra," "Rizla"	Consumer market in Western Europe
	Kukkameri	—	Flowers	—	Consumer market in Western Europe
	Fionia Plant Export ApS	—	Danish potted plants	—	Consumer market in Western Europe
Korpivaara	Vehicle business	Toyota Group, Auto-Bon	Cars, vans, trucks for sale and lease, spare parts	Toyota, Citroen, Suzuki	Consumer Purchasers, dealers
		Trade school	Training for automotive salesmanship	—	Automotive dealerships
		Kone-Diesel	Automotive accessories	Kone-Diesel	Consumer purchasers

(continued on next page)

(continued)

DIVISION	DIVISION SEGMENTS/ ACTIVITIES	SEGMENT COMPANIES/ ACTIVITIES	PRODUCTS	TRADEMARKS/ BRAND NAMES	MARKET SERVED
	Metal business	Hydor	Air and oil compressors	Hydor	Industrial customers
		Pemamek	Welding positioners, workpiece handlers	Pemamek	Industrial customers including metal fabricators
		Skavenir	Mechanical handling equipment	Skavenir	Industrial customers
	Plastics business	Konemuovi	Plastic sheets, ski boxes, partition walls, floor covers for vans, boats	Konemuovi	Automotive accessory purchasers, sporting goods purchasers, industrial customers
	Moottorialan Luotto	—	Financing of automotive purchasing and leasing	—	Automobile purchasers
Marimekko	—	—	Clothing, interior decoration, retail store operation	"Marimekko"	Consumer

from After Eight, Toffo, and KitKat chocolates, Swedish desserts and berry puddings to films and cameras sold in stores dealing in perishable goods. The unit planned to expand the sales organization to cover the entire country and to develop the product range by entering new cooperative agreements.

The tobacco division accounted for 13 percent of Amer Group's total net sales. Division net sales had been steadily increasing over the previous four years, and profit history had been rated "good." (See Table 1, p. 538, for an explanation of profit-rating terms.)

The tobacco division contributed a high percentage of profit to Amer Group in proportion to sales volume. Whether Amer-Tupakka would be classified as a "cash cow" was disputed, because Amer Group was still

Exhibit 5
Amer Group, Ltd.
Five-Year Period Division Highlights
(sales in FIM million)

Sales of the profit centers within each division are shown separately if products or markets are dissimilar.

	1981	1982	1983	1984	1985
TOBACCO					
Sales:					
Amer Brokers	—	—	—	7.2	11.5
Amer Tupakka	208.9	209.8	250.0	301.7	326.9
Division *total* sales	208.9	209.8	250.0	308.9	338.4
Share of Amer Group sales	34%	30%	32%	35%	13%
Personnel	357	338	335	355	352
Profit rating[a]	Good	Good	Good	Good	Good
COMMUNICATIONS					
Sales:					
Weilin+Goos	133.8	143.9	143.0	151.2	197.9
Advertising services	21.0	21.5	19.2	13.7	17.0
Finnreklama	—	—	—	—	34.6
Less internal sales	—	—	—	—	7.3
Division *total* sales	154.8	165.4	162.2	164.9	242.3
Share of Amer Group sales	25%	24%	21%	19%	9%
Personnel	696	675	637	641	828
Profit rating[a]	Good	Good	Good	Good	Good
PAPER					
Division *total* sales	101.5	148.4	167.4	180.7	199.5
Share of Amer Group sales	16%	21%	21%	20%	8%
Personnel	244	254	249	237	230
Profit rating[a]	Good	Good	Good	Good	Satis.
SPORTING GOODS					
Sales:					
Koho (Finland)	35.3	35.5	37.1	40.9	40.5
AmerSport International	44.6	51.1	60.7	70.6	69.8
AmerSport USA	15.2	16.9	25.6	43.4	38.0
Less internal sales	11.6	17.2	15.2	10.9	8.7
Division *total* sales	83.6	86.4	108.1	144.0	139.6

(continued on next page)

[a]Explanation of profit rating is given in Table 1.

(continued)

	1981	1982	1983	1984	1985
Share of Amer Group sales	14%	13%	14%	16%	5%
Personnel	471	375	646	542	433
Profit rating[a]	Fair	Loss	Loss	Fair	Loss
MARKETING UNITS					
Sales:					
Golden Leaf	8.1	32.3	37.1	42.0	39.3
Flowers and plants	22.2	24.6	26.8	34.4	44.1
Other	18.8	24.3	28.7	12.4	—
Division *total*	69.1	81.2	92.6	88.8	83.4
Share of Amer Group sales	11%	12%	12%	10%	3%
Personnel	118	123	131	101	107
Profit rating[a]	Fair	Fair	Fair	Good	Loss
KORPIVAARA					
Sales:					
Vehicles				1,149.1	1,389.7
Metals				45.7	51.1
Plastics				24.7	30.1
Other operations				12.2	41.0
Less internal sales					30.0
Division *total* sales				1,231.7	1,481.9
Share of Amer Group sales					57%
Personnel				745	816
Profit rating[a,b]				—	Good
MARIMEKKO					
Division *total* sales				109.2	102.1
Share of Amer Group sales					4%
Personnel				434	397
Profit rating[a,b]				—	Loss

[b]Marimekko and Korpivaara were acquired in 1984; profit rating is not applicable.

investing in the business, market share was still gaining, and profits continued to increase.

Amer-Tupakka had increased its market share by an average of two percentage points each year since 1981 and expected to hold its current 59-percent

---

Table 1
Amer Group Profitability Definitions

"Fair"—operating profit before depreciation is sufficient to cover the costs of the central administration, interest expense, taxes, and depreciation.

"Satisfactory"—operating profit before depreciation, in addition to the above, covers dividends, depreciation based on current cost, and the need for additional working capital caused by inflation.

"Good"—operating profit before depreciation, in addition to the above, is sufficient to cover the need for an increase in Amer Group's shareholders' funds.

"Loss making"—the criteria for fair profitability are not met.

Source: Annual Reports.

share over the next year. Pipe- and cigarette-tobacco market share remained about the same at 4 percent.

The Amer corporate culture had changed as the company grew and more acquisitions were made. The family spirit of the 1970s eroded as each division cultivated its own, but the tobacco division continued to have the closest relationship "in spirit" with Amer Group because of strong ties to the company origins. Amer-Tupakka was located on the same premises as the Group headquarters. According to one tobacco executive, "As the climate gets 'colder' in the cigarette business, and if tobacco companies' social image becomes more negative, Amer-Tupakka employees are likely to associate themselves more closely with Amer Group than the tobacco operation."

Communications Division

Amer Group's communications division consisted of several units involved in graphics and education. The primary unit was Weilin+Goos, the third-largest publisher in Finland, acquired by Amer in 1970. Weilin+Goos specialized in publishing and printing textbooks and encyclopedias, multivolume books, and general literature, as well as diaries and calendars. For nearly 100 years, the company had held monopoly rights to publishing all almanacs and calendars in Finland, but in 1985, Weilin+Goos lost these rights to a competitor. Because this loss of a core business was to take effect in 1988, the division was in the process of redefining its strategies.

Another unit, Finnreklama, specialized in the printing of high-quality art books and other printed materials for the Soviet Union. Another business unit of the division, Kiviranta, was a leading service company in advertising copy materials. It produced copy material for newspaper and magazine advertisements and printed advertising. Other profit centers, added to the communications division in 1983–1984, included a direct marketing company of multivolume reference books, the Time/System time-management product, and domestic appliances.

In line with the electronic publishing trend, the division had entered the software business with the establishment of Amersoft, which produced and marketed Finnish-language software for home and business use. In the area of education, the division had established the Amer Institute to produce and market training programs for sales personnel and for PC-user training. The Amer Institute was the first training establishment in Europe to be authorized by Lotus Development Corporation of the United States.

The graphics industry in Finland was characterized mostly by small firms engaged in publishing, printing, binding, and photo and text processing. The ten largest companies controlled a major share of the market. The biggest customers were the government (which included schools), mass media, and industrial and wholesale organizations.

In book publishing and printing, Weilin+Goos had two main competitors, both of which specialized more in novels and general literature. Weiling+Goos held roughly a 20-percent market share in primary-school textbooks and a smaller share in the secondary-school and adult-education segments.

Printed advertising had increased significantly over the previous five years. As a proportion of GNP in 1983, total advertising expenditure in Finland was the fifth highest in the world.[4]

The printing industry was still quite labor intensive, although in the last decade major investments had been made in high-capacity machines capable of computerized phototypesetting and offset printing. Wages and salaries were the largest cost item, but raw-material costs (notably paper) were also sizable. Because printing technology was advancing rapidly, the industry had to reinvest an average of 10 percent of its annual turnover.

The Finnish graphic arts industry was largely based on the domestic market; exports accounted for only about 5 percent of total production in 1985. Industry exports had grown steadily over the previous few years, however, and prospects for increasing exports were quite good as a result of technological advances and added capacity. One drawback in international markets was price competition, but the strengths of Finland's leading printing exporters included state-of-the-art machinery, reliability, expertise, and good transport connections.

---

[4]*Graphic Arts in Finland,* industry publication, 1985.

The communications division had been in a growing and experimental phase, becoming very diversified within its own widespread industry. Weilin+Goos accounted for 82 percent of division revenues in 1985, and its profits had been "good," whereas the other units reported either "losses" or "satisfactory" results for the year.

Top management was unclear about the division's future direction. Division managers had established that internationalization of markets was one opportunity for growth, but they had not defined their objectives in terms of products and services. The printing business would obviously change with the loss of monopoly rights on calendar printing, and the publishing business needed to move away from its arts and culture orientation toward a stronger profit orientation.

The communications division represented 9 percent of Amer Group's net sales. Seppo Saario, the president of the division, was a seasoned executive who had been in the company for many years and, as an executive vice-president of Amer Group, worked closely with Heikki Salonen.

Paper Merchanting and Converting Division

Amer Group established its paper merchanting (wholesaling) and converting (manufacturing) division in 1979 by acquiring the largest paper wholesaler in Finland. Operating under the name Amerpap, the division held a domestic market share of more than 40 percent . Distributed products included coated and uncoated fine papers, high-quality art papers, self-adhesive papers and vinyls, carbonless copying papers, and office, household, and packaging papers. The converting unit produced envelopes and other packaging materials and sold related products such as mail-handling equipment and printing ink. Some 67 percent of division sales were from papers for printing, 14 percent from office and other paper products, and 19 percent from converted products.

Amerpap's major buyers included commercial printers and manufacturers of office supplies, art supplies, and commercial paper products. Amer's paper suppliers were generally large mills that manufactured only a few grades and, in general, did not stock ready-made products. The end customers that used printing paper, however, generally wanted smaller units, used several grades of paper, and required rapid deliveries. Thus the challenge for wholesalers was to buy paper in large quantities and deliver it rapidly in smaller, individual orders. Printing papers were supplied primarily by four large domestic suppliers supplemented by some special, imported art papers and self-adhesive materials. Amerpap had sole agency rights with its foreign suppliers and had relations with domestic suppliers, both of which were important factors to success.

In Finland's wholesale paper business, total consumption of printing papers grew by 3 percent in 1985 and was expected to continue at that rate. The consumption of high-quality art printing papers continued to grow faster than the overall market, whereas growth in the consumption of office papers, which had been rapid in previous years, leveled off during the year. For the third year in a row, prices of both printing and office papers had risen more slowly than inflation, partly because of intense price competition within the industry. In an industry where margins were already thin, profitability had lowered for most paper wholesalers. In the case of Amer, gross margin had remained steady as a result of rationalization of production.

There were five or six large competitors in printing-paper wholesaling. There was little product differentiation in the assortment offered to wholesalers, price competitiveness was characteristic, and barriers to entry were low. The situation was somewhat different in the office stationery trade, but competition was equally sharp.

Olli Laiho, president of the paper division, believed, "Service to the customer is a principal factor to success in this business." Amerpap's state-of-the-art computerized control system enabled it to keep track of product availability, offer quick delivery, and handle complaints and problems efficiently. To stay competitive, the sales force used techniques such as calling on customers' customers to influence graphic-design paper specification.

In the paper-converting market, total consumption of mail wrappers (envelopes and letter bags) had grown over the previous few years at about 3 percent annually because of growth in direct marketing and catalog selling. The circle of clients in this market was quite large, with small individual deliveries. Investment in fixed assets was light when compared with other areas in paper manufacturing.

The division's share of Amer Group net sales was 8 percent in 1985, and the profit report for the year was "satisfactory." The management team at Amerpap was fairly new, and the company had recently moved to a modern warehouse facility with large-volume capacity. Laiho had been in the company for six years and had run the operation independently; Salonen's interaction with the business had been minimal.

Sporting Goods Division

Amer Group's sporting goods division manufactured and sold ice hockey sticks and equipment under the Koho and Canadien trademarks, as well as motocross equipment. The division began with exports from a factory in Finland and developed an international sales network and overseas manufacturing, with several operations in Finland, another factory and management office in Quebec, and a sales and distribution company in New York. "It was a rough start with the North American operations, but we saw a great future in the leisure industry as free time was increasing," said Salonen. There were problems with Koho competing against its fellow product, Canadien, and with integrating the business. After the appointment of a new president and a reorganization, the business had started to recover, but excess capacity was a lingering problem.

During the 1984–1985 financial period, Amer Group was the largest manufacturer of ice hockey sticks in the world, with a 34 percent market share in Western countries. For ice hockey equipment, Amer Group was the largest manufacturer in Europe and the second largest in North America. Of the division's total sales, about 91 percent were outside Finland.

The market for ice hockey–related products was narrow and, of course, seasonal. Industry profitability was weak on the whole, and business conditions were further aggravated by tough price competition. To combat these difficulties, companies were moving toward increased use of subcontracted manufacture in low-cost labor countries and increasing the marketing of products used in summer sports. Many hockey-stick companies were owned by larger companies that could absorb the profit losses.

The principal market area for ice hockey sticks and equipment was North America, where 1985 sales fell below the level of the previous year. One Amer executive speculated that the hockey market was shrinking as competing leisure sports were gaining, and that would-be hockey players were losing interest because of increasing violence in the game.

Product development in sticks had been aimed at replacing the traditional wood structures with more durable and lighter plastic. Amer's Koho factory was progressing with this trend; 77 percent of its manufactured sticks contained a synthetic blade. Growth in sales of fully synthetic sticks continued, but the long-term effect of greater durability in sticks would lead to a reduction in total volume sold.

Sporting goods represented 5 percent of Amer Group net sales. The profit rating was "poor" for 1985. The division had been unprofitable throughout most of its history, but Amer Group was reluctant to retreat from its first step toward internationalization.

Marketing Units Division

In 1978, Amer's top management decided to consolidate several small profit centers into a separate import/marketing division, specializing in consumer goods. Of three marketing units in the division, the largest was Golden Leaf, which marketed consumer durables such as Seiko watches and clocks, Pulsar watches, Lorus alarm clocks, Casio calculators, and Montblanc and Zebra pens. The consumable product range included Rizla cigarette papers and cigarette machines and Ventti cigarette filters. Watches and clocks were distributed through watchmakers and jewelers, calculators and pens through bookshops and stationers, and consumable goods through nationwide whole-sale chains.

Another business unit sold cut flowers, some of which were cultivated in Finland and the rest imported from various suppliers in the Netherlands, Italy, Spain, West Germany, Thailand, the United States, and Denmark, where Amer had a subsidiary company. In addition to cut flowers, this unit also sold pots, soil, plant nutrients, and flower-arrangement materials. A subsidiary export company, known as Fionia, was located on the isle of Fyn in Denmark and exported plants to continental Europe and Scandinavia.

Because of poorer-than-expected Christmas sales and consequent over-stocking, 1985 sales of watches and clocks fell by 10 percent. Furthermore, consumers were favoring watches in the cheaper price range. Cigarette rolling was on the decline, which led to a 6-percent reduction in the total market for cigarette papers in 1985. Consumption of flowers was trending upwards, however, which was reflected in an 11-percent increase in wholesale pur-chases in 1985; but profitability in that industry was susceptible to energy-price fluctuations and high energy consumption during severe weather.

Marketing units accounted for 3 percent of Amer Group net sales and reported a loss in 1985. The division, primarily a distribution network, did not generate much discussion inside the Amer organization. One Amer executive simply referred to it as a "carousel," because three division presidents had been rotated through the unit over the 1982–1986 period.

Marimekko

Perhaps the best-known Finnish trademark internationally, Marimekko was a designer, manufacturer, and distributor of high-quality interior-decorating tex-tiles, linens, other fabrics, and kitchenware, as well as ready-to-wear clothing and related accessories. The clothing line included cotton dresses, jersey and knitwear, shirts, canvas bags, and accessories, mostly for women. The products were frequently characterized by brightly colored, graphically forceful patterns and geometric designs (see Exhibit 6).

Amer Group acquired a majority holding in Marimekko at the beginning of 1985. Several Amer Group employees viewed the acquisition as "Heikki's baby." (Salonen had been a member of Marimekko's board of directors for several years prior to the acquisition).

Marimekko, once a family business, had been built on dreams, designs, ideology, and individuality. The public had an image of Marimekko as more of a "cultural phenomenon" than a business, yet Marimekko had been exposed to the harsh realities of the business world.

The company was established in the early 1950s, and the first ten years of operation were characterized by a growth and expansion so rapid that it

Exhibit 6
Amer Group, Ltd.
Example of Marimekko Garment

Source: *Phenomenon Marimekko*, Amer Group, Finland, 1986.

gave rise to almost unlimited confidence in the future. Uncontrolled growth led to increasing debts and general costs, and the capital shortage turned into financial crisis by 1968. After a radical retrenchment and restructuring, the company was eventually restored to its health and went public in the mid-1970s.

Marimekko was very much a personal reflection of Armi Ratia, its artistic and creative founder. The culture she bred in the organization was still alive, even several years after her death. Her spirit was reflected in one of her memos to the staff, written in April 1975 (see Exhibit 7).

The strengths on which Marimekko was built were also some of the weak threads in its unraveling. Armi Ratia stated from the beginning, "We would not court the public's favour by making the sort of garments we thought they wanted but by creating a totally new line, designed to our taste." One of the chief designers commented, "It is my job to educate the public's taste." Marimekko had constantly strived to keep its distance from international trends and popular fads. In one sense, this philosophy worked: the company set trends. In other ways, it was detrimental: Marimekko had products that could be easily imitated at far cheaper prices, albeit with a quality difference. In essence, Marimekko had been riding on its established trademark for many years and did not adopt the changes occurring throughout the industry—competitive price and product and low contract labor outside Finland.

Marimekko was a classic example of Finnish design and lifestyle, which was part of the "popular" Scandinavian look. Markets for this theme were well defined, but competitors were not so clearly identified. There were many specialty clothing and interior-design looks and many indirect competitors with varying themes. "It is difficult to formulate a general strategy, because the competitors are different in different markets. Our strategic problem is centered around the difficulty of finding a place in changing markets while maintaining the legendary Marimekko image," commented one executive.

Marimekko owned several retail stores and also marketed through licenses and franchises (7 domestic and 13 overseas licensed manufacturers). A West German subsidiary, Marimekko GmbH, was a distribution agent in Germany and central Europe. Marimekko, Inc., was the U.S. subsidiary responsible for coordinating operations in the United States.

The world clothing industry was undergoing a structural change. Production of clothing was shifting to newly industrialized countries, and several developing countries were launching their industrialization with clothing production. Companies in industrialized countries were increasingly sending part of their production to countries with low-cost labor.

Consumer buying behavior was also changing. The seasonal concept and demand for variety in clothing put pressure on retailers and the industry to update collections frequently and to extend clothing lines. The trend toward constantly changing lines translated to shorter time between

---

Exhibit 7
Armi Ratia's Memo to Marimekko Staff

Marimekko Oy
Helsinki
21 April 1975

In order that we don't have to use our last shirt to sail through the threatening storms of this working life, I seriously suggest that each one of us at Marimekko reads this memo and STARTS ACTING ACCORDINGLY AND TAKES SOME INTELLIGENT MEASURES IN HIS OR HER OWN FIELD.

We are not in any immediate danger. We have time. And this we intend on using to dig our defenses. How is it these military terms creep in? Ha ha.

The matter about which I am talking sounds distressing, but we stand before it together, as a company, as individuals. We, like young upstarts, have been living beyond our means on all fronts; and savings, from money for food to the market in houses, have been scarce and battered by inflation. NOW WE MUST SAVE. The banks have closed their doors. The reserve fund is exhausted. We're running out of means. BUT NOT OUT OF TRICKS. OR FAITH. OR HOPE. WE'LL MANAGE AGAIN, BUT WE'LL HAVE TO PUT EVERYTHING BEHIND IT.

Everybody, try to save in the right way. From paper to electricity. From decorations to beauty. Photos to flowers and cloth to costs. Save time, not thoughts. Draw patterns, learn better the parts of the whole. So we'll survive and nobody will be crowing over our defeat.

With best wishes,
Armi Ratia

Source: *Phenomenon Marimekko*, Amer Group, Finland, 1986.

---

orders and deliveries and emphasis on punctual deliveries. Flexibility in clothing manufacturers' activities was becoming a more important competitive factor.

Because of their inability to be price competitive, Finnish clothing manufacturers had been losing market share in the European markets since 1981. They had not been able to control rising labor costs. Marimekko was no exception, and its clothing had always been perceived as expensive. The clothing industry was characterized by falling operating margins, evidenced by a drop in 1983 to an average of 6 percent, with no improvement in 1984 or 1985.

Marimekko's net sales, which were down 7 percent from the previous period, accounted for 4 percent of Amer Group's consolidated net sales in 1985. The company reported a loss during the financial year. Because of Salonen's representation on its board, and management and financial problems in the company, Marimekko was one of Amer's more closely monitored subsidiaries.

Korpivaara

Amer Group acquired a company larger than itself with the acquisition of Korpivaara, the oldest and largest importer of cars in Finland. Korpivaara, established in 1917, was a family-owned business until 1984, when Amer acquired 88 percent of the company. The company was the exclusive importer in Finland of Toyota, Citroen, and Suzuki cars and vans, as well as Toyota forklift trucks and Lotus sports cars. Vehicles were sold or leased either wholesale or at one of Korpivaara's two retail sales units.

A relaxed management style at Korpivaara had developed from family history and influence on the company. Only in 1976 were profit centers and the first five-year strategies introduced; the company gradually adopted a mixture of "family" and more structured, "hard profit" management.

When the three Korpivaara brothers reached retirement age and decided to sell to Amer, the change of ownership was not easily accepted by those who were part of the strong culture. Korpivaara's management felt pressure from Amer Group in the integration process, in areas such as modification of reporting systems and additional reporting requirements. Friction developed, and some people, "afraid to be swallowed," left the company—including Korpivaara's president. According to one long-standing employee, "The president was unwilling to listen to shareholder voice in a cooperative way." By 1986 the initial friction had subsided, but although Korpivaara executives recognized the value of the image association with Amer Group in commercial and financial markets, they preferred to continue their autonomous operation as a separate legal entity.

Automotive trade was very competitive in Finland because of the relatively small market of 5 million people. Finland's high personal income-tax structure and 50 percent excise and sales tax on automobiles made price elasticity high. Therefore, pricing was the number-one marketing factor. Mikko Ennevaara, Korpivaara's current president, explained, "It is difficult to maintain profit, especially in retail, as margins are thin and volume is the key."

The number of passenger cars and vans registered in Finland had increased over the previous five-year period because of a relaxation of monetary controls (which made credit easier to obtain), a reduction in motor vehicle tax, and a stable price level for cars.

Of Korpivaara's three major auto brands, Toyota was the leading make in passenger cars, vans, leased cars, and company cars and had been the leader in new-car registrations in Finland for several years. Citroen's market share was increasing in Finland, however, with the introduction of new models and favorable exchange rates. Suzuki marketed in the small-car range where price competition was keenest. Korpivaara held a 16.5-percent market share of Finland's total car and van market.

A separate unit of Korpivaara supplemented the auto-distribution lines by operating a countrywide service network and by selling imported car parts and accessories. About half the unit's sales were made through car dealers, with the remainder through car accessory and tire stores. "This service network has become an important competitive advantage for Korpivaara, as has our tire accessory line. We sell tires for all auto makes, and the margins are relatively high," commented Ennevaara.

Korpivaara also had the equivalent of a financing unit, which financed leasing operations for the company, its regional dealers, and customers.

Although roughly 93 percent of Korpivaara's revenues came from the motor-vehicle operations, there were several other profit units within the division, which included metals, plastics, and a trading department. (See Exhibit 5 for a sales breakdown.)

The metals unit (2.8 percent of Korpivaara sales) comprised three leading companies in Finland specializing in the manufacture of compressors, welding equipment, and mechanized materials-handling robots for use in engineering workshops. The Nordic countries and the Soviet Union were important markets.

Executives at Korpivaara questioned whether the metals unit would be able to find real opportunities in the high-tech metals market. The operation was relatively small, making competition against larger companies' R&D difficult. One executive expressed a preference for "only wanting to be in automotive."

The plastics unit (1.6 percent of Korpivaara sales) manufactured plastic sheet for its own finishing operations and for wholesale, mainly in Finland. It also produced vacuum-molded and rotation-molded products such as ski boxes, partition walls, and floor coverings for vans, as well as Terhi brand boats, sold through area dealers.

Korpivaara's trading department (1.0 percent of Korpivaara sales) exported Finnish furniture and Finnish-designed products to Japan.

Total net sales of the Korpivaara division accounted for 57 percent of Amer Group's net sales during the 1985 financial period. The division's sales had been increasing steadily over the previous five years, and profitability overall had been "good."

CORPORATE CULTURE

One of Amer Group's objectives, related to its stated strategy "to market well-established, high-quality, branded products," was "to build corporate managerial power through training and development." If Amer's businesses, although unrelated, were within the same "characteristic framework," then Amer Group would be able to train managers uniformly and interchange them as necessary. For example, when an international acquisition was made, the objective was to be able to draw from a corporate management pool, if necessary, to place a representative at the subsidiary post. The process involved building up a resource bank, sending managers out, and bringing them back. "In order to use this process," one executive noted, "the company must be expanding all the time."

The explicit mission statement had been questioned by several managers at Amer Group, who believed that the statement did not cover the full spectrum of business units and products within the divisions: "Right now the 'high-quality, branded-product' image does not fit for all products—like paper, metals, or plastics." The philosophy that marketing know-how was the Group's competitive specialty was also questioned; one young executive claimed, "Our area of expertise is really in financial control and insight."

These two challenges raised the questions of what the corporate umbrella actually represented and what direction it was taking. One manager answered,

> The Group needs to redefine its mission and stick to its strategy. Are we a holding company or something more? Growth in some of our product areas is very limited. Amer is a holding company today even if it doesn't admit it. It is a legal unit owning a portfolio. We should go more specialized in one direction or state that we are a holding company, but a holding company has no competitive edge.

Historically, divisional management had not been involved in strategy formulation for Amer Group, but some believed that the divisions should participate more actively in this process. The general feeling about corporate culture was summed up by one manager's comment that "there is no umbrella over Amer Group as far as culture; the businesses are so diverse, and each division has its own separate culture." Most thought this situation was proper: the divisions should be encouraged to have their own images. At corporate headquarters, the perception of a common culture was not uniform. One executive stated, "Theoretically, the corporate umbrella prevails through our business mission." But from another, "In principle, people are thinking positively together, but there is no real synergy or concrete direction." As described by another executive, "We have a dynamic image towards hard values; the culture is based on cold facts—profits."

According to one recently hired employee, Amer Group's public image was overall quite strong, especially in commercial and financial markets. Many young business and economics graduates saw Amer as a progressive, efficient, and profitable organization. The hard-line profit orientation was not, however, looked upon favorably by all. For example, when Amer acquired

Marimekko, the press communicated some resentment that Marimekko might lose its refined artistic qualities by being swallowed up. Amer Group's association with the tobacco business also did not convey a popular social image.

Internally, conflicts and tensions had resulted from the organization's fast-paced growth. "No one was really controlling the environment," as one manager put it. The corporate planning and finance departments were "competing" in some areas, and the two groups seemed to have different chemistries. One manager described the situation as "new versus old schools" (young, talented financial juniors versus experienced, more conservative veterans). Kai Luotenon, head of corporate planning, had worked closely with Salonen and was "very much an action man; he initiated and implemented many changes in the Amer Group and hired lots of 'new schoolers.'" One of Amer's division managers believed strongly that, in order to resolve these conflicts within the Group, some changes in personnel were necessary.

CORPORATE LEADERSHIP

Heikki Salonen, wearing a blue-and-green-striped Marimekko shirt, showed his relaxed style as he sat on the couch in his office suite. He had a casual demeanor, yet commanded respect. He seemed to have an open and friendly relationship with his managers, at the same time carrying a certain mystique. Salonen was not visible around the office; he used a separate entrance and was often there at odd hours. Several people in the organization commented on his style: "He has a strong, colorful personality with a lot of charisma in Finnish business circles as well as at Amer Group." "He is a man of vision, a clever, quick decision maker and an action man." "He steers through the person-to-person approach." "He is a dominant leader, with many people reporting directly to him." "He has built an empire and it is hard for him to delegate." "His major hobby is work." Salonen described his own style of management as "more art than science." (See Exhibit 8 for a brief résumé.)

Salonen noted that, when he had decided more tactical management control was needed for Amer Group, he looked within the organization and also contracted with a headhunter. He said of the COO whom he would appoint, "He must be strong but not the same type as I am, to balance things." Necessary qualifications were management and an international business background, strong in economics; Salonen believed the marketing philosophy could be learned. Age was also a factor he considered: "You cannot have everyone retiring at the same time. On the other hand, they cannot be too young—the organization must accept them." It was a careful search process; Salonen believed, "We can make money only by our people."

Because the 1984–1985 acquisitions had more than doubled the size of the company, Amer Group's executives had fully anticipated Salonen's taking on a second person to handle operational issues. According to one manager, three or four insiders were considered or expected themselves to be considered for the position. Another manager commented, "There were two princes [internally]. Heikki took an outsider—typical for him." General speculation was that, from Salonen's point of view, the choice among internal candidates was not obvious, and potential conflicts could be avoided by looking outside the organization. The need for restructuring was not questioned, and the announcement of a COO and new president was apparently well received.

Leif Ekstrom was described as a "professional manager" who would bring strong organizational, financial, and leadership skills to Amer Group. At 43, he was known in Finnish business circles as one of Scandinavia's "rising young stars." (See Exhibit 9, p. 554, for résumé.)

In the process of evaluating the company he would soon be managing, Ekstrom thought that Amer Group was financially sound, but he wondered how long the group of businesses, as currently structured, would continue to meet shareholder objectives. Moreover, not only would he have to work out the corporate-divisional relationship, but also his role vis-à-vis Heikki Salonen. Ekstrom realized the necessity for separate tasks and the practical division of responsibilities between CEO and COO, but he saw the relationship as delicately entwined in terms of vision and leadership of the company. "In your thinking, you must consider things that are not your responsibility; you must work as if you had both roles," he thought to himself. "Now, how will I make my mark, come April 1?"

Exhibit 8

Heikki O. Salonen

Chairman and Chief Executive Officer, Amer Group
Curriculum Vitae (Abbreviated)

Born: May 12th, 1933, Joroinen

Marital Status: Wife Kirsti; children Marju and Jyri

Education: B.Sc. (Econ.) from the Helsinki School of Economics in 1958
                    M.Sc. (Econ.) from the Helsinki School of Economics in
                    1962

Military Rank: Lieutenant

Following Books Published:

The Distribution Channels in the Foreign Trade and the Factors Affecting Their Structure (Helsinki Research Institute for Business Economics, 1962).

The Selection of the Export Organization (Ekonomia—series, 1977).

Previous Occupations:

Finnish Institute of Management
—One of the First Course Administrators   1961–1967

The Finnish Institute of Export
—The First President   1962–1967

Saastamoinen-Yhtyma Oy Teollisuus
—Executive Vice President   1968
—President and Member of the Board   1969–1972

Main Occupation: Amer Group Ltd.
—President and Chief Executive Officer   1972– 1986
—Chairman and Chief Executive Officer   1986–
—Chairman of all Amer Group company boards

(continued on next page)

(continued)

Outside Board Memberships (selected list):

Helsinki Research Institute for Business Economics	(Chairman, 1978–1985)
Finnish Employer's General Group	(1982–)
Confederation of Finnish Industries	(1984–)
Pohjola–yhtiot (Finland's biggest insurance company)	(1983–)
MTV Oy (Finnish commercial TV)	(1975–)
Foundation for Economic Education	(1983–)
The Finnish Heart Association	(1983–)
Helsinki School of Economics	(Advisory Board, 1979–)
Mannerheim League for Child Welfare	(1979–)
Medical Research Foundation	(1978–)
Scout Foundation	(1980–)
World Wildlife Fund Finland (Board of Trustees)	(1980–)
The Finnish Institute of Export	(1976–)
Kansallis Banking Group	(1986–)
Employer's Association of Food Industries	(1985–)

Exhibit 9

Leif Ekstrom

President, Amer Group
Curriculum Vitae

Born:	October 31, 1942, Vantaa
Marital Status:	Wife Heli; children Thomas and Niklas
Education:	B.S. (Econ.) from the Swedish School of Economics and Business Administration in 1966
Military Rank:	Second Lieutenant
Career:	Kone Oy
	Manager, Finance, 1966–1969
	Kone Hissar Ab Sweden
	Manager, Finance, 1969–1972
	Kone Oy Lift Group
	Controller, 1972–1978
	Kone Oy Lift Group
	Director, 1978–1980
	Oy Wilh. Schauman Ab
	Vice President, Finance, 1980–1984
	Rauma-Repola Oy
	Executive Vice President, 1984–1986

Other Commissions:

Karhu-Titan Oy
—Member of the Board

The Association of Finnish Advertizers
—Member of the Board

Midland Montagu Osakepankki
—Member of the Supervisory Board

Hobbies:	Golf, tennis, slalom

ARVIN INDUSTRIES, INC.

To Jim Baker, president and CEO of Arvin Industries, the visit to the Far East had been a means to two useful ends: the inclusion of the entire board and all the division presidents was more than symbolic of Arvin's commitment to globalizing its business, and the November 1985 board meeting in Taiwan had been a good forum to communicate to the division presidents the firm's new emphasis on external acquisitions.

It had been a nice getaway. The smells, the colors, the crowded streets—in fact, the whole way of life—were a world away from the quiet of Columbus, Indiana, where Arvin was headquartered. The Orient seemed strange, and, although far from home, it was good for a change.

Now, on the day before the flight back to the United States, as he rode through downtown Taipei in a rickshaw, Baker reflected on the company's past and thought about how he would actually get his management team to buy into his vision for Arvin.

Arvin had been a conservative company for many, many years. Most division officers had come up through manufacturing and had generally been rewarded for being risk averse. "It was," Baker thought, "like pushing a noodle through a hole. You tell those people that 'cash is available, now do it,' but they have never done it before." So the issue was not simply one of implementing a new strategy. Baker believed a change of the culture of the company was needed. Arvin had to become more aggressive in the use of its plentiful resources.

"Easier said than done," he said to the rickshaw puller.

COMPANY BACKGROUND

In 1920 Richard H. Arvin invented the world's first automobile heater. Recognizing that he had a viable product but no resources to commercialize it, he formed a partnership with Indianapolis Air Pump, producer of hand-operated tire pumps, to gain access to its manufacturing and marketing facility. Within a few years, however, the pump maker bought the inventor's 50-percent share, ending Dick Arvin's association with the company.

This case was written by Anurag Sharma, Darden MBA 1988, and Associate Professor L. J. Bourgeois III. Copyright © 1989 by the Darden Graduate Business School Foundation, Charlottesville, VA. Revised May 1992.

Indianapolis Air Pump changed its name three times over the next 30 years before finally settling on Arvin Industries, Inc., in 1950. In the ensuing 20 years, Arvin solidified its position in the automotive market, entered the advanced electronics field with an acquisition, and established an overseas presence by building plants and offices in the Far East.

The Anderson Era

Gene Anderson joined Arvin in 1947. Born and bred in Indiana, Anderson worked his way up through manufacturing, became a plant manager in 1957, moved up to works manager of the automotive division in 1952, and then became vice president and general manager of that division in 1960. In 1961 Anderson was elected to the board of directors, was named one of the two executive vice presidents in 1968, and took over as the president and CEO in 1969. In December 1975, he was elected chairman of the board.

The most significant events during his tenure were (1) the decision to manufacture catalytic converters in an uncertain regulatory climate, (2) diversification beyond the core automotive business, and (3) changing the organization structure to a divisionalized form in 1973.

Catalytic Converters

In 1973, based on the rumors that Congress might mandate catalytic converters, Arvin took a gamble and invested more than $40 million to manufacture the new product. This move was significant; the previous annual capital investment had averaged about $5 million. Fortunately, the gamble paid off when the converters were mandated for 1975 model vehicles, positioning Arvin solidly into the automotive OEM market.

Diversification

At the beginning of the 1970s, more than 70 percent of the firm's revenues came from its core automotive OEM (original equipment manufacturer) business. This dependence on one business segment resulted in uneven financial performance but was not viewed as a significant threat to the firm until the Arab oil embargo of October 1973. The embargo led to a big slump in auto production, causing a major financial crisis for Arvin.

As a result of this experience, Arvin accelerated its efforts to diversify into businesses that were less cyclical but still offered opportunities that could be exploited with the firm's existing capabilities. Management decided to strengthen the firm's nonautomotive businesses through capital spending, internally developed new products, and acquisitions.

The success of the new corporate strategy was evident in the company's financial results between 1972 and 1977. During that period, revenues doubled, and the contribution of the nonautomotive groups to total operating profits went up from 4 percent to 28 percent.

By 1977 Arvin had become a leading supplier of original equipment to the Big Three in the auto industry and had a small presence in the replacement-parts market. Compact stereo was Arvin's flagship product in consumer electronics, and portable electric heaters gave it a good foothold in consumer housewares. The metals group provided the company with expertise in coating steel and aluminum coils and in sheet-metal stampings and assemblies. The applied technology group manufactured video equipment for adverse environmental conditions and special-purpose automated fabricating and assembly machinery; it also designed and installed security and process-control systems.

Divisionalization

During the course of diversifying, Arvin had begun to outgrow its centralized management structure. A need was felt to break the company into more manageable parts. Loren ("Chick") Evans, president of the North American automotive division, said, "The divisionalized approach to running the company had only really been put in place in about 1973. Those of us who were general managers before '73 really operated the business by running the engineering, the manufacturing, and the sales functions. All of the other support services were centralized. And, as we started growing in this period, we started having a lot of trouble because staff services could not keep pace. The staff would tend to give most attention to whoever made the most noise. So, naturally, the guys who ran the automotive business, the big business, got all the attention. We had to change that."

And changed it was. The staff functions devolved to the divisions so that the operating units could have more autonomy in conducting their businesses. In addition, Arvin continued the tradition of setting up plants of no more than 400 workers. While the new structure gave the impression of decentralization, in practice, most of the decision-making authority remained with the chief executive.

Other Management Concerns

In early 1977, in view of the heightened merger activity during the previous ten years, the board engaged White, Weld & Co. of New York to assess the vulnerability of Arvin to a hostile takeover. In a report to Anderson, the consultants pointed out that the firm's low price-to-earnings (P/E) ratio (five times), strong cash position, high return on equity (ROE), and highly fragmented shareholder base were some of the weaknesses that could lead to a hostile takeover attempt. On the other hand, the report suggested, the outstanding results of 1976, the relatively high financial leverage (44 percent at the end of 1976), the highly concentrated and cyclical nature of Arvin's business, the significant dollar value of its assets, the Indiana antitakeover statute, and the defensive measures in Arvin's corporate bylaws were significant deterrents to any unwelcome bid.

White, Weld urged Anderson to strengthen Arvin's defenses, however. The firm recommended that Arvin set up a defense unit consisting of internal management and outside professionals, strengthen its relationships with existing shareholders, improve earnings per share via an aggressive investment program, and consider creating a new series of preferred stock that, when issued, would give the holders a two-thirds class vote on any consolidation, merger, or sale of significant assets.

Baker, then executive vice president, said, "At that time the kinds of acquisitions that were going on were Harry Grey's [United Technologies'] unfriendly takeover of Otis and Carrier—the kind that seemed to be very logical business combinations. Even though they were unfriendly, they seemed to make a lot of sense. Yet, we did not want to be subject to one of those."

Subsequent to the report, Baker started to build the firm's expertise in takeover defense. The law firm of Wachtel, Lipton, Rosen & Katz was engaged to provide the legal perspective; Hill & Knowlton was engaged for financial public relations; and for investment banking services, White, Weld was retained. Merrill Lynch eventually replaced White, Weld after it acquired them.

The rationale for these moves was explained by Baker: "When the raider strikes, oftentimes it is what they call a Saturday Night Special or a Bear Hug—you have such a short period of time to respond and react and defend yourself that you have to do as many prior preparations as possible to put yourself in some kind of a balance with the guy that has his arms around you."

Late 1970s Operating Performance

In 1978 the business-segment classification was changed from one based on technology and product characteristics to one based on end markets. The new categories were automotive, appliances and hardware, government and utility, and commercial and industrial. The highlight of 1978 was the acquisition of Calspan for its research and development capabilities, which were to solidify Arvin's presence in the important government segment.

The year 1979 was tough for the company. Price competition intensified in the consumer electronics business, and a 60-percent capacity expansion in the coil-coating operation coincided with a decline in demand for automotive pre-coated metal as domestic production of light trucks and cars dropped 11 percent. Sales increased only slightly from $489 million to $493 million in 1979, and earnings dropped from $23.1 million to $20.4 million. Arvin's five largest customers accounted for approximately 70 percent of its total revenues for the year.

The depressed state of the automotive industry and continuing high inflation caused a carryover of pressure on margins into 1980. A 28-percent decrease in the North American production of cars and light trucks contributed to a 13-percent drop in sales to $428.8 million in 1980 and a decline in income to $7.6 million.

Arvin management decided that the automotive industry was experiencing not just the normal cyclical fluctuations but was, in fact, caught in a period of revolutionary economic and market changes. Rising gasoline prices and the poor state of the economy had shifted consumer preference toward smaller, fuel-efficient, imported cars. Foreign manufacturers, notably Japanese firms, had increased their market share from about 16 percent six years earlier to nearly 27 percent in 1980.

To deal with this industry realignment, Arvin recognized that, even as it consolidated its share of business on new models emerging from Detroit, it needed to develop supplier relationships with foreign automakers who established plants in the United States.

In 1981 Arvin put major cost-reduction programs in place as the firm tightened up its operations. Large numbers of people were laid off, and three automotive plants were closed. At the end of the year, each of the six operating divisions showed a profit, and corporate earnings had climbed to $12 million on a 15-percent increase in total sales. Revenues from the five largest customers were 62 percent of the total (see Exhibits 1 to 3 for financials).

Change of Guard

On April 1, 1981, the 12-year reign of Eugene Anderson came to an end as he retired from operations and Executive Vice President James K. Baker stepped up to become president. Baker became CEO of the company on November 1; Anderson retained his position as chairman of the board.

Baker was not the flamboyant personality one would expect to find in the rising star of a *Fortune* 500 company. He was a quiet man who shunned media attention and believed in being effective by putting the pieces together behind the scenes. After getting a bachelor's degree in mathematics and physics from DePauw University in 1953 and serving in the U.S. Army for a few years, he had decided to get an MBA at Harvard in 1956. There his silent nature soon got him in trouble. He was pulled up by the first-year faculty for not participating in the class discussions and was told he might not get through the program. Recalling this experience, he said, "The classes were 90 in size. It was very easy for someone to hide behind the other 89 and not participate, and I was one of those. It was not very long before professors called you and said you had to participate."[1]

Baker's reserved style carried into his professional career at Arvin, which he joined upon graduation. Brooke Tuttle, director of the Columbus Economic Development Board and a close Baker friend, once said, "Jim Baker's perception

---

[1]Bill Koenig, "The Quiet Man," *The Indianapolis Star*, March 15, 1988, p. 1.

Exhibit 1
Arvin Industries, Inc.
Income Statement
(figures in thousands of dollars)

	1984	1983	1982	1981	1980	1979	1978
NET SALES	781,986	600,605	513,905	495,136	428,849	493,211	489,079
COSTS AND EXPENSES							
Costs of goods sold	663,085	508,265	434,890	421,560	363,129	410,562	397,315
Selling, general and administrative	62,624	59,437	58,482	51,406	48,615	45,570	40,383
Interest expense	7,801	7,960	8,356	7,684	7,861	9,075	9,088
Other income—net	(5,212)	(5,738)	(6,335)	(7,699)	(2,198)	(3,960)	(2,824)
	728,298	569,924	495,393	472,951	417,407	461,247	443,962
Earnings before income taxes	53,688	30,681	18,512	22,185	11,442	31,964	45,117
Income taxes	23,461	12,343	7,646	9,761	3,854	11,542	22,051
NET EARNINGS	30,227	18,338	10,866	12,424	7,588	20,422	23,066
Return on sales	3.87%	3.05%	2.11%	2.51%	1.77%	4.14%	4.72%
Return on equity	15.20%	10.01%	6.16%	7.15%	4.40%	12.26%	15.41%
Common shares outstanding	11,352	11,343	10,519	10,280	9,936	9,795	9,668
Primary EPS* ($)	2.59	1.58	0.93	1.09	0.61	1.92	2.24
Cash dividend per common share* ($)	0.75	0.74	0.75	0.75	0.75	0.68	0.66
Book value per share*	$ 17.84	$ 16.05	$ 15.61	$ 15.49	$ 15.30	$ 15.56	$ 14.44
Stock price at year end*	20.30	17.17	13.96	11.36	n/a	n/a	n/a

*Note: All per-share numbers are adjusted for a three-for-two stock split in 1984.

of talking to the public is like Woody Hayes's perception of the forward pass. Three things can happen and two of them are bad."[2]

Success for Baker at Arvin was rapid, however. By 1960 he was general manager of Arvinyl and in 1966 was named a vice president. Two years later, he was named one of two executive vice presidents and elected to the board.

Baker was active in Indiana community affairs. At the time of taking over the leadership of Arvin in 1981, he was the chairman of the Associated Colleges of

[2]Ibid.

Exhibit 2
Arvin Industries, Inc.
Balance Sheet
(figures in thousands of dollars)

	1984	1983	1982	1981	1980	1979	1978
ASSETS							
Current assets:							
Cash and temporary investments	21,031	30,098	26,664	38,296	32,242	32,424	40,380
Accounts receivable—net	87,435	70,817	59,186	51,454	66,726	68,273	64,846
Inventories	81,545	66,570	65,108	64,053	72,021	68,669	80,482
Other current assets	10,337	9,164	9,760	8,693	2,595	2,748	2,608
Total current assets	200,348	176,649	160,718	162,496	173,584	172,114	188,316
Other noncurrent assets	17,860	20,527	20,753	17,702	10,752	10,871	8,889
Property, plant and equipment:							
Land	2,400	2,732	2,635	1,908	2,034	2,162	2,242
Buildings and leasehold improvements	66,997	70,743	68,061	62,037	61,510	59,804	54,905
Machinery and equipment	173,712	153,582	145,494	132,655	130,729	120,645	94,668
Construction in progress	4,871	2,820	1,371	1,270	1,482	3,620	14,642
	247,980	229,877	217,561	197,870	195,755	186,231	166,457
Less: Allowance for depreciation	116,115	103,978	93,585	86,556	77,656	67,839	59,058
	131,865	125,899	123,976	111,314	118,099	118,392	107,399
Special tools, etc.—net	4,382	4,980	4,764	1,890	2,164	1,749	3,444
Total noncurrent assets	136,247	130,879	128,740	113,204	120,263	120,141	110,843
Total assets	354,455	328,055	310,211	293,402	304,599	303,126	308,048
LIABILITIES AND SHAREHOLDERS' EQUITY							
Current liabilities:							
Short-term debt	4,716	6,485	6,646	5,258	5,471	5,262	4,636
Accounts payable	35,294	23,975	17,091	14,176	27,652	20,100	24,795
Accrued expenses	28,135	23,680	19,798	15,865	13,054	14,033	12,463
Income taxes payable	2,667	2,728	2,954	4,672	3,164	2,789	4,934
Total current liabilities	70,812	56,868	46,489	39,971	49,341	42,184	46,828
Noncurrent liabilities:							
Deferred income taxes	11,220	9,052	6,561	5,782	5,085	4,359	3,175
Long-term debt	63,773	73,105	79,949	72,165	78,197	83,684	97,887
Total noncurrent liabilities	74,993	82,157	86,510	77,947	83,282	88,043	101,062
Shareholder's equity:							
Capital stock:							
Preferred shares (no par value)	6,368	7,067	13,280	15,564	19,071	19,579	19,607
Common shares ($2.50 par value)	28,735	18,905	17,531	17,132	16,561	16,324	16,113

(continued on next page)

	1984	1983	1982	1981	1980	1979	1978
						(continued)	
Capital in excess of par value	30,462	38,730	31,447	29,482	26,545	25,861	25,465
Retained earnings	145,779	124,679	115,276	113,306	109,799	111,135	98,973
Cumulative translation adjustments	(572)	(351)	(322)	none	none	none	none
Common shares in treasury (at cost)	(2,122)	none	none	none	none	none	none
Total shareholders' equity	208,650	189,030	177,212	175,484	171,976	172,899	160,158
Total liabilities and shareholders' equity	354,455	328,055	310,211	293,402	304,599	303,126	308,048

Indiana, a trustee of DePauw University, and a director of the Columbus-area chambers of commerce. His business affiliations included directorships at Columbus Bank and Trust Company, Norlin Corporation, and Indiana National Corporation.

ARVIN GAME PLAN FOR THE 1980s

Baker's appointment as chief executive was viewed as a significant break from the past. Chuck Watson, president of Arvinyl division, noted, "Prior to Jim taking the head role in the company, Arvin had been run by the automotive people and by [the] manufacturing people. When Jim took over, he came from a broader background within the company and was probably more oriented towards finance and sales. That he came from the nonautomotive area must be considered a big change within the company."

Baker inherited difficult business conditions. The national economy, which had begun a downward slide almost three years earlier, was still laboring under the burden of unprecedented double-digit interest rates, and the third-quarter recovery in auto sales appeared to have stalled in the fourth.

In his first letter to the shareholders, Baker articulated the need for the firm to take the offensive. He outlined a three-pronged thrust for the 1980s: new products, meaningful presence in the global automotive market, and creative development of new businesses. With regard to new business development, he said, "We intend to acquire product lines that are compatible to our own. We want to find products with a satisfactory market share and high value added. Some of these additions may give us an expanded overseas presence."

One of Baker's first actions in his new role was to make, in his words, "a very hard-nosed assessment of how good we were and how weak we were in

Exhibit 3
Arvin Industries, Inc.
Financial Information by Business Segments

	1984	1983	1982	1981	1980	1979	1978
NET SALES							
Automotive	$408,269	$338,276	$281,178	$281,687	$258,133	$325,613	$340,722
Consumer	225,983	136,397	119,716	97,576	93,896	88,118	87,578
Government	94,512	84,069	77,800	75,400	41,205	44,326	32,910
Industrial	53,222	41,863	35,211	40,473	36,615	35,154	27,869
Total net sales	$781,986	$600,605	$513,905	$495,136	$429,849	$493,211	$489,079
INCOME FROM OPERATIONS							
Automotive	$41,392	$29,869	$17,602	$20,458	$13,844	$30,594	$42,017
Consumer	15,984	5,606	6,599	5,059	7,205	7,059	11,385
Government	4,986	3,245	1,476	2,754	704	1,866	1,281
Industrial	4,014	3,181	2,594	154	(760)	3,197	1,835
Total from operations	$66,376	$41,901	$28,271	$28,425	$20,993	$42,716	$56,518
Less:							
Interest	(7,801)	(7,960)	(8,356)	(7,684)	(7,861)	(9,075)	(9,088)
General corpora- tion expense	(4,887)	(3,260)	(1,403)	1,444	(1,690)	(1,677)	(2,313)
Total EBT	$53,688	$30,681	$18,512	$22,185	$11,442	$31,964	$45,117
IDENTIFIABLE ASSETS							
Automotive	$167,653	$154,645	$152,118	$162,978	$176,722	$185,190	$176,373
Consumer	88,013	78,617	60,455	45,223	43,353	38,933	40,293
Government	20,549	18,474	18,644	20,590	23,189	24,118	16,344
Industrial	30,438	27,465	25,822	27,431	25,991	18,703	13,278
Total assets	$341,255	$319,133	$301,806	$299,000	$303,862	$305,587	$291,905
DEPRECIATION AND AMORTIZATION							
Automotive	$ 9,169	$ 8,816	$ 8,903	$ 9,430	$ 9,185	$10,554	$10,019
Consumer	5,450	4,579	3,243	1,942	1,954	1,524	1,292
Government	949	761	950	803	709	633	606
Industrial	1,487	1,254	976	990	925	652	495
General corporation	13	52	34	33	35	13	7
Total depreciation and amortization	$17,068	$15,462	$14,106	$13,198	$12,808	$13,376	$12,419

(continued on next page)

(continued)

	1984	1983	1982	1981	1980	1979	1978
ADDITIONS TO PROPERTY, PLANT, AND EQUIPMENT							
Automotive	$18,375	$ 8,143	$ 4,460	$ 3,734	$ 8,466	$17,943	$19,105
Consumer	6,670	7,435	24,392	2,035	2,530	2,158	1,823
Government	1,363	1,376	1,002	652	1,045	1,257	4,764
Industrial	1,122	878	2,379	735	1,764	2,336	1,852
General corporation	43	241	5	24	0	0	0
Total capital additions	$27,573	$18,073	$32,238	$ 7,180	$13,805	$23,694	$27,544

certain areas. We used that to build what we called the Arvin Game Plan, and we published it, much to the delight of the financial community. [See Table 1.] We started publishing that in the 1982 annual report and have carried that almost unchanged ever since."

Chuck Watson recalled, "In addition to the outside world, it was the first time that everybody within the company had seen an articulated game plan, or set of objectives. . . . That would be representative of Jim Baker: setting some goals, setting some direction, and telling the world about it.

"One of the things that Jim did was just significant as the dickens. At one point, when the U.S. automotive industry was going down the tube, he made a strong statement that Arvin would be in the automotive OEM business. And that was really significant because many manufacturers were bailing out of the U.S. automotive OEM business, and he made a recommitment to stay."

Realignment at the Top

Once in the driver's seat, Baker decided that the reporting relationships of the senior executives ought to reflect his own management philosophy— that of more autonomy to the divisions. "April to November of 1981," Baker recalled, "I was the president but not CEO. I did some reorganizing and let go four top staff officers: the vice president of strategic planning, the treasurer, the controller, and house counsel. The controller was ready to retire, and I did not think that there was enough time to bring him up to speed with myself. Two of the four were not suitable team players and were not well regarded in the organization."

Table 1
The Arvin "Game Plan" for the 1980s

1. Maintain auto parts as the core business. Manage assets to proper capacity levels.
2. Increase exhaust replacement parts business through new products and acquisition.
3. Establish automotive presence in selected foreign countries.
4. Innovate new features and packaging concepts in home stereo products. Use electronics know-how to expand product lines into telecommunications, CATV, and energy areas.
5. Acquire new electronics product lines.
6. Continue Arvin leadership in portable electric heaters, and develop or acquire related products.
7. Fund aggressive research and product development in all operating divisions.
8. Manage metals group to provide cash for growth.
9. Manage advanced technology group in selected scientific areas, and provide technological support to other Arvin businesses.

Source: 1982 Annual Report.

He then established the office of the president, which comprised three group vice presidents, the chief financial officer, the vice president of public affairs, and the vice president of administrative services. In essence, everybody reporting directly to the president was in this group.

Among the issues that the office of the president resolved were capital expenditures above threshold amounts, labor negotiations, and new product lines. These matters were routine, and the process was not new to the company; but Baker described it as "more regularly scheduled. The intention was to step up the pace. To do more things. To be more action oriented."

In addition, in order to have personal influence on the divisions, Baker created an executive staff, which was the office of the president plus the division presidents. "One of the important changes I made," he recalled, "was in the planning process. I never did feel that planning could be a staff function at the corporate level when you had so many divisions. That had to be done within the divisions and reviewed at the top level—note that I dismissed the vice president of strategic planning.

"One of the key elements in decentralized planning is that they [division executives] have to know what it is that you are looking for in the way of plans, what are the outside limits, how aggressive they should be. If they are too aggressive and it gets slapped down, they have wasted a lot of time in doing their plan. So you have to have a lot of discussion on what you as a CEO feel are the goals of the company in very specific terms, so that they know what their parameters are when they start their planning process." Executive staff meetings were a forum for these discussions.

Signs of Recovery

In 1982 prospects for a modest economic recovery appeared to be good. Short-term interest rates had dropped decisively in the middle of the year, and the accompanying rally in stock and bond prices was reassuring both as a precursor of improved economic performance and as evidence that the dramatic recovery made against inflation was viewed as durable. Arvin's annual sales increased slightly to break the $500-million mark. Net income, however, declined 12.5 percent to $10.9 million, reflecting carryover of the recessionary pressures from previous years.

About 10 percent of total 1982 sales came from new products, and this percentage was expected to increase during the remainder of the decade. Arvin introduced a whole new line of replacement exhaust parts manufactured in the United States for imported cars, whose growing industry segment accounted for a 28-percent market share in 1982. In addition, the firm entered the evaporative cooling business by purchasing the international metal products division from McGraw-Edison Company. The division's line of evaporative cooling products, said Baker, "shares a similar customer base, similar manufacturing processes, and energy-efficient characteristics with Arvin's existing heating and ventilating products." The new acquisition was renamed ArvinAir and formed the seventh operating division of the corporation.

The Jitters of Recession

Reflecting on his first year as the head of Arvin, Baker commented, "The thing that always escapes you, I think, is that the president's job looks much easier from even one chair away than it actually is. You are always surprised with how much responsibility you really feel when you step into that job. You realize that every person and every asset is essentially your responsibility, and the buck stops here. . . .

"I was really shaken up by how difficult it was to operate in that '81–'82 time frame. We closed three plants quickly, while most of the other automotive suppliers waited for many months, and in some cases two or three years, before they adjusted their capacity to the new world of the 1980s.

"The major incentive for division presidents was cash generation—rather than cash being the responsibility of the treasurer. That gave all of us focus during a period of time. I didn't know what else to focus on. I wasn't bold enough to make any major moves. . . . It would have been wonderful to be able to do so, but I was not in the mood to make any major moves in 1981 or

1982. . . . It was a tough time and I was nervous, and I was not very bold, so cash management was the name of the game."

Chic Evans agreed: "It was not a period of growth but one of survival—being sure that we were being very wise."

Results of 1983

By the end of 1983, virtually all economic indicators were strongly positive, and most observers expected recovery to continue through 1985. Private housing starts had bottomed out more than a year earlier and had begun a strong upward surge in the July indicator. Automobile sales, another traditional end-of-recession leading indicator, had not yet given a clear upward signal, but there was considerable optimism based on lower interest rates and gasoline prices.

The year 1983 was good for Arvin. Sales increased 17 percent to cross $600 million, and net income shot up by $7.5 million to $18.3 million. Because of increasing raw-material prices and the inability of the company to pass on higher costs to the customers owing to intensifying competition, the 3-percent after-tax return on sales was far below the goal of 4.5 percent to 5 percent. The cash position, however, was strong at the end of the year, and the debt-to-capital ratio was less than 30 percent for the first time in ten years.

In the same year, Arvin solidified its presence in Brazil by restructuring COFAP, a joint venture to supply automotive parts in the Brazilian market. The expanded operations were to meet the needs of Arvin's two major U.S. OEM customers who were in the process of increasing their investments in Brazil.

Also in 1983, the board of directors gave approval for the formation of a joint venture with Belgium's Bosal International to manufacture tubular products from exotic materials. The new venture, with plants in West Germany, was to combine Arvin's catalytic-converter expertise with Bosal's manufacturing know-how and marketing expertise. This alliance would position Arvin against the day when Europe decided to mandate catalytic converters.

Clarifying his company's position regarding growth, Baker said at the annual shareholders' meeting, "While our long-range strategy is to use acquisitions and joint ventures to strengthen our business relative to competition, our diversification objective does not include assembling a group of businesses with an equal number of cyclical and contra-cyclical units . . . instead, it includes assembling a broad range of first-class customers who will ultimately provide us with the increased sales and profits we need to meet our goals."

Business Upturn

The accelerating economic expansion of 1984 helped Arvin set all-time records (see Exhibit 1). Each business segment expanded significantly, and the automotive proportion of sales declined to 52 percent. With sales as a measure, Arvin advanced from the 408th to the 355th place in the *Fortune* 500 ranking of the largest U.S. industrial corporations. Its ten largest customers accounted for 74 percent of total corporate revenues in 1984. Financially, Arvin was on a strong footing. Debt-to-capital dropped to less than 25 percent, and a healthy cash flow eliminated any need to borrow, despite significant working-capital outgo and capital expenditures to support higher sales.

To management, the year's performance was evidence of the success of its business strategies. While a favorable economic climate did help financial performance, the deliberate actions taken to contain costs, to improve productivity from investment in robotics and computerization, and to increase the flow of internally developed new products were beginning to pay off.

Internally developed new products remained the highest priority for the company. Sales of stainless-steel tubular manifolds (introduced in 1982), telecommunications products, newly designed compact stereo systems, and a larger number of fabricated metal parts for various industrial applications, to name only a few, accounted for more than $100 million of the 1984 sales volume.

In 1984 Arvin also made two additions to its business: the acquisition of AP de Mexico, S.A. de C.V., solidified its position as a supplier to automotive manufacturers and the aftermarket in Mexico, and the acquisition of Franklin Research Center strengthened the advanced research and testing business.

THE ECONOMIC LANDSCAPE, 1980–1985

In addition to strengthening its business portfolio for a more secure future, in light of the merger wave that was gripping the U.S. financial markets during the 1980s, Arvin reinforced its position to ensure organizational independence. The latest merger activity was influenced by deregulation in certain industries, prevalence of divestiture transactions as conglomerates of earlier years rationalized their business portfolios, and an increasing frequency of leveraged buyouts facilitated by the availability of financing. In addition to the reinvigorating economy, other factors that contributed to the merger wave of the 1980s included (1) a changing political climate with the Reagan administration's stated policy of minimizing intervention in the free market; (2) stock-market undervaluation of corporate assets coupled with financial innovations such as junk bonds; (3) the rise of arbitrageurs; and (4) the emergence of some very aggressive, financially astute deal makers.

The junk bond was created by Mike Milken of Drexel Burnham Lambert, Inc., to raise money for fledgling companies that did not have access to the traditional lending institutions. As Milken's idea gained acceptance among large institutional investors, he entered the takeover wars, providing empire builders with easy access to large sums of money. Drexel's power, according to one analyst, had been a "catalyst for a wave of large leveraged buyouts." He said, "Big companies used to worry only about takeover threats from other big companies. But with Drexel doing the financing, anybody long on ideas and short on capital is a threat."

A New Breed of Raiders

Sure enough, a handful of "takeover artists" began creating havoc in American board rooms. T. Boone Pickens was one such person. A sharp critic of senior managers of public corporations and a self-appointed champion of shareholders' rights with uncompromising ideas about how managers ought to run their corporations, Boone Pickens made a fortune buying oil companies for their undervalued assets and restructuring the assets of the acquired corporations. He believed in ownership for those in management positions, because, he claimed, professional managers often adopted a "me first, stockholder second" attitude. He boasted that he had played a large part in restructuring corporate America, which, he claimed, would make the country competitive again.

Carl Icahn was another raider who made managers nervous. He, too, scoffed at management ineptness and projected himself as a savior of stockholders' interests. His modus operandi was also to make hostile bids for companies he thought were undervalued because they were run by people he considered venal or nincompoops. At least some of his millions, however, came by greenmailing target companies.

Icahn's notable assault was on TWA in May 1985, when he was persuaded by the pilots' and machinists' unions to fight Frank Lorenzo of Texas Air, who, in turn, was lined up as a white knight by TWA's management. Lorenzo's higher bid was turned down by the board on August 20, and Icahn obtained a major piece of the airline.

While Pickens had a "mission" to protect the rights of the "little guy," and Icahn made similar altruistic claims, the Belzberg brothers of Canada made no bones about their intentions to make a quick buck. Controversial and wealthy, the Belzbergs were opportunistic acquisitors who regarded their capital as too risky to be invested in anything but the safest tangible assets. To assure a return on their investments, they usually controlled 4 percent to 8 percent of their target's stock before attempting a takeover. According to one report, "'Sam Belzberg' whispered over the phone is enough to send the managers of ... North American companies into wild-eyed panic—and prompt ... arbitrageurs to begin merrily snapping up shares of the next Belzberg victim."[4]

---

[4]Gregory Miller, "What Does Sam Belzberg Really Want?" *Institutional Investor*, June 1986, p. 150.

By 1984 the Belzberg brothers had built a huge conglomerate with interests in financial services, real estate, energy, and manufacturing. Most of their millions came from greenmailing their prey, such as their 1984 raid on Gulf Oil (jointly with Pickens), which earned them more than $50 million. In December of 1984, they threatened to take over Scovill Corporation on Christmas Eve. The investment community was surprised when, instead of greenmailing Scovill, they actually acquired it in January 1985.

"The Porcupine Defense"

In the face of this heightened takeover environment, Arvin decided that even as the company was being managed for survival during the 1981–1982 recession, a select group of company executives and outside consultants should meet occasionally to review Arvin's defenses. By 1985 the company had installed a range of barriers: a fair-price provision was in place to mitigate pressure on shareholders at the time of a tender offer; directors were elected to the board on staggered terms; stock was purchased and put in the savings and pension plans, to be voted by the (presumably friendly) trustees; and a supermajority provision, requiring approval of 80 percent of the board before change in control, was placed in the company charter. These defensive measures had evolved piecemeal over a decade, as the issue of defense was not at the top of management's agenda. However, these did represent the state of the art in takeover defense at the time.

Reacting to criticisms that each of these measures had inherent weaknesses, Fred Meyer, vice president of public affairs, said, "We are using what I call the Porcupine Theory. A porcupine with one quill, anybody can grab. A porcupine with hundreds of quills, however, causes some discomfort when grabbed. So the thing to do is to get them [defenses] all together, and that means that you have more items that a raider must deal with."

ARVIN IN 1985

The prospects for 1985 looked good. Automobile manufacturers were doing well, and the model mix was favorable to Arvin's applications. The industrial segment was experiencing a small increase in the shipment of pre-coated steel for pre-engineered buildings and in research and development activity for private industrial customers. The Department of Defense's increased emphasis in areas like the Strategic Defense Initiative (SDI) secured a favorable market for Calspan. Sales of brand-name products, comprising both automotive aftermarket and nonautomotive consumer businesses, were down, however, as a result of lack of anticipated market growth.

The numbers released for the first nine months of 1985 showed an increase in earnings to $24.7 million from $21.6 million during the corresponding period in 1984. Sales were up $32 million to $603 million over the same nine months.

At the end of 1985, eight operating divisions were serving the four broad market segments. Each operating division is briefly described below, and the division/segment matrix shown in Exhibit 4 gives a bird's-eye view of the various businesses of the corporation.

North American Automotive

North American Automotive was a major supplier of original equipment exhaust systems for Ford, General Motors, and Chrysler; of catalytic converters for Ford and Chrysler; and of fuel filler tubes for General Motors, Volkswagen of America, and American Motors. In addition, through its Aftermarket Products Division, Arvin manufactured mufflers and a full line of exhaust-system replacement parts that were distributed through traditional channels under both the Arvin and Supreme brand names.

The rebound in automotive sales after the 1980–1982 recession enabled Arvin to have strong gains. The annual build rate in the North American auto industry increased 30 percent to 10.3 million units in 1983, and then again 19 percent to 12.25 million in 1984. Arvin's auto business had further success from new applications of its lightweight products, and it continued to gain from the cost-reduction and consolidation programs of the past few years.

Commenting on the direction of his division's business, Chic Evans said, "The heart of our aftermarket problem, besides the fact that we only had 4- or 5-percent market share, was that we never really had a business that stood out [on its own]." So in 1984 he decided to separate the production of replacement exhaust systems from the automotive plants and consolidate the manufacturing and distribution of the aftermarket business in one facility at Princeton, Kentucky.

The prospects for 1985 looked good. Segment sales were growing even faster than in the previous two years. A major factor was the rapid acceptance of the stainless-steel tubular manifold, whose growth in sales was expected to remain high for at least another year. In addition, a favorable industry model mix was helping an increase in market penetration for exhaust-system parts and decorative stampings of vinyl-on-metal laminate.

Consumer Electronics

Consumer Electronics was a major contract supplier of compact and component stereos to large retail chains and well-known U.S.-based manufacturers such as Radio Shack, Yorkx, and Sears. Arvin relied on low-cost manufacturing in Taiwan, supported by the engineering and distribution capability in the United States.

Exhibit 4
Operating Division and
Business Segment Information

BUSINESS SEGMENTS

	MARKETING AND DISTRIBUTION	Automotive	Consumer Appliances	Government and Utilities	Commercial and Industrial
ARVIN AUTO-MOTIVE	Original equipment parts produced for Ford, General Motors, Chrysler, American Motors Corporation, and Volkswagen of America. Replacement parts marketed by Arvin and Supreme brands and private brand names.	Original equipment mufflers, exhaust and tail pipes; catalytic converters; tubular manifolds; fuel filler tubes; small diameter tubing; replacement exhaust system parts.			
ARVINYL	Fabricated parts and vinyl metal laminates are shipped to customers for a variety of end uses.	Decorative stampings of vinyl metal laminates; diesel engine oil pans and components; press-molded thermoplastics.	Vinyl metal laminate stampings.	Faceplates for telephone equipment; ship interior panels.	Vinyl metal laminate stampings.

ROLL COATER	Coils of steel and aluminum are prepainted and shipped to customers for fabrication into end use products.	Pre-coated coils of steel and aluminum for fabrication into products such as drapery hardware and refrigerator housings.
	Coil steel coated with zinc-rich primer for fabricating into automobile and track body parts.	Pre-coated coils of steel and aluminum for pre-engineered buildings, motor homes, vending machines, and office furniture.
ARVIN *Consumer Housewares*	Distributed nationally to leading retailers. Marketed under the Arvin brand name and private brand names.	Portable electric heaters; fireplace heat exchangers; wind turbine home attic ventilators.
ARVIN *Consumer Electronics*	Distributed to large retail chains and electronics manufacturers for marketing under private brand names.	Compact stereos and component systems; electronic assemblies; cable television converters; satellite receivers.

(continued on next page)

BUSINESS SEGMENTS

	MARKETING AND DISTRIBUTION	Automotive	Consumer Appliances	Government and Utilities	Commercial and Industrial
ARVIN *ArvinAir*	Distributed through wholesale and national retail channels. Marketed under the Arvin brand name and trade names.		Evaporative coolers.		Evaporative coolers.
ARVIN CALSPAN	Contracted by U.S. government and private industry.	Comprehensive restraint testing; research and tire testing services; automotive accident research.		Research, development, and testing services.	Research, development, and testing services.
ARVIN DIAMOND	Contract basis			Security systems for power-generating plants.	Industrial video cameras.

(continued)

By 1980 the home audio industry had begun to show signs of maturing; industry shipments were down, and most manufacturers felt a squeeze in margins because of intensifying competition. Arvin reacted to these trends by emphasizing product innovation and extending its technological base in related areas. It became involved in the manufacture of cable television converters and satellite receivers as original equipment.

In 1985 sales for compact table and rack stereo systems were down from a record high of the previous year, mainly because of soft market conditions and inventory correction in the channels. The outlook for 1986 looked favorable, however, because of an acceptable level of inventory in the pipeline and a variety of new product introductions.

ArvinAir

In August 1985, Arvin announced the consolidation of the consumer housewares division with the ArvinAir division. Portable electric heaters and related products manufactured at Verona, Mississippi, and product engineering located in Columbus were scheduled to be merged into the ArvinAir facility in Phoenix, Arizona, where evaporative coolers were manufactured. The counter-seasonal nature of the markets for these products were expected to favor improved capacity utilization and operating efficiencies.

The consumer markets that this division served valued ready availability of products and competitive pricing. In addition to cutting costs at the manufacturing end, Arvin was meeting the saturated market conditions with a steady introduction of new products. By 1985 the cost-reduction initiatives had begun to pay off, and the new products, helped by expectations of market recovery, had begun to relieve the pressure on margins for the division.

Roll Coater

This capital-intensive, energy-guzzling division was the largest independent U.S. coater of coiled steel and aluminum for the automotive, appliance, construction, and agricultural markets. The key concerns of management included cost reduction, quality assurance, service, and maintenance of plant capacity utilization. New applications for coated metal strips were being developed to broaden the demand for the division's products.

The recession of 1981–1982 constrained demand for coated coils in automobiles and construction, but the division maintained its share in all its major markets with tight cost control and new product introductions. The resurgence of the automotive industry in 1983 boosted sales of coated coils to auto manufacturers. And because Roll Coater had expanded its nonautomotive businesses during the auto industry's four-year slump, the division was poised for growth in all the markets it served. In 1984 a new metal-embossing line was added so that the division could offer embossed designs in pre-painted finishes applied to coils of steel.

Arvinyl

Arvinyl fabricated vinyl-on-metal laminates for a variety of end uses in consumer durables, commercial products, automotive applications, and office furniture. Product development for existing and new markets was a key to sustained leadership. In 1978 a decorative "soft touch" laminate was developed to give automotive stylists greater aesthetic freedom.

Another important product innovation was the development of damped metal, which consisted of a sheet of visco-elastic plastic laminated between two sheets of steel. This material offered opportunities to develop parts such as oil pans and valve covers for major engine manufacturers that would meet federal noise regulations for trucks.

The economic recession of the early 1980s derailed the anticipated growth in two of Arvinyl's major markets, microwave ovens and diesel engines, but the diversity of markets that Arvinyl served prevented its total collapse. Then, after two years of upbeat sales, the industrial slowdown of 1985 reduced the shipments of vinyl laminates and parts for industrial use, particularly formed parts supplied to diesel-engine manufacturers. With a more diversified customer base, however, Arvinyl was better positioned to handle another economic recession.

Advanced Technology Group

The advanced technology group consisted of Arvin/Calspan and Arvin/Diamond, which provided services and products to both private industry and the government. Calspan offered scientific research, development, and testing capabilities through its seven regional technical centers. Diamond manufactured electronic products and systems for heavy industry, broadcast, CATV, and nuclear security markets. In addition, the technology group was a major contributor to the U.S. Department of Transportation's New Car Assessment Program and conducted extensive automotive crash tests.

Government regulation and defense policy were important variables that affected the business of these divisions. Regulations calling for improved communications and monitoring systems in nuclear power plants presented continuing growth opportunities for Arvin/Diamond. Also, the Reagan administration's avowed support of expanded defense investment promised an increased market for Arvin/Calspan's advanced technology services. For instance, by 1985 Calspan had approximately $10 million in contracts supporting the administration's Strategic Defense Initiative (Reagan's so-called Star Wars).

Project-management experience was a significant strength of this group, which helped the company win contracts from government and industry. One example was the three-year, $95.6-million contract to manage the wind-tunnel facilities for the U.S. Air Force at the Arnold Engineering Development Center in Tullahoma, Tennessee.

Calspan's technical skills and resources were enhanced by a joint venture formed in 1983 with The Research Foundation of the State University of New York, Buffalo, to conduct research on lasers, DNA molecules, and turbines. In September 1984, Franklin Research Center, a Philadelphia-based research and testing concern, was purchased for its technical expertise and new markets.

In 1985 Calspan won a five-year contract, valued at approximately $245 million, from the U.S. Air Force to operate aerospace flight-dynamics test facilities. In September of the same year, Calspan and the University of Tennessee arranged a nonprofit joint venture to conduct aerospace research.

The 1986 outlook for business with the government looked favorable, although the full impact of the new Gramm-Rudman-Hollings legislation on R&D funding was yet to be ascertained.

STRATEGY FOR GROWTH

Having successfully combated the economic downturn of 1981–1982, and confident that the healthy upward trend of the business in the last two years was based on the intrinsic strengths of the company, Jim Baker set out to grow Arvin through external acquisitions: "It had appeared that internal product development would neither generate enough growth nor absorb our cash flow. My attitude was: let's do more. We have the resources, and if we don't use them, somebody else will. There is both the positive and also the threat."

Beginning in 1982, the operating divisions were encouraged to compile a working list of companies that were potential acquisitions, even if they were not up for sale. Baker said, "There was a possibility that those companies might come on the market for sale at some time. If we tracked them, we could move quickly. . . . We tried to establish a relationship with them. In some cases, we told the CEO, 'We are entirely friendly, and if you decide to sell, we would like to be first on your list.'" In order to guide the search for acquisition possibilities, Baker issued his "rules for success" for screening options (see Exhibit 5). The list of acquisition possibilities that had been compiled at headquarters is shown in Exhibit 6.

Chic Evans agreed with the new philosophy, "Arvin had always correctly prided itself on finding growth internally—the catalytic converter, tubular manifold—you do better with those things than just going out and finding an acquisition. It was only really in this time frame that it became apparent that (a) we cannot invent everything internally, and (b) we cannot get larger market share in some products just because we might have a little better product or a little better strategy.

Exhibit 5
Arvin "Rules for Success"

The Arvin acquisition strategy is to acquire only those businesses that

- Are in subsegments of the industries where we now excel
- Maintain market leadership positions and low unit costs
- Compete with only "second-tier companies"
- Possess strong product development skills
- Bring products with high volume and steep cost curves
- Maintain a "culture" that is compatible with ours
- Retain good management

"Aftermarket was one of those that there was no way really to grow the business significantly without finding someone who had better distribution. And those were the steps that we started to take."

Ronald Rosin, president of ArvinAir, saw this new emphasis as an encouraging sign: "We, as one division, [were] already in the acquisition mode, [because] in a mature business such as ours, it is easier to grow through acquisitions. Our problem at this time is overcapacity, and we are trying to address that by finding product lines [that] will fill the excess capacity in our plants."

Chuck Watson's (Arvinyl) response was less enthusiastic. He said he did not think there was "a sense of urgency" but certainly encouragement that had not been there before. The stress had always been on developing products from within. "I guess my perception would be that acquisitions are not what we were really focusing on as a company. There have not been many made, and those we have made have not been all that wonderful. Roll Coater would have to be, from a pure profitability standpoint, the best acquisition we have made yet. And that was made in 1966."

James Smith, president of Roll Coater, also had a lukewarm response. "Since 1966," he said, "the production capacity at Roll Coater has been increased sixfold. So, our major emphasis has been on product diversification to maximize capacity utilization. Of course, we understand corporate priorities and are looking outside for acquisitions that fit our business. But, nothing is really coming out of it."

Exhibit 6
Acquisitions Possibilities, August 16, 1985

AUTOMOTIVE

Champion Spark Plug
Midwest Auto Distributors
NA-SA Auto Parts Distributors
Purolator-Stant
Champion Parts Rebuilders
Maremont
Midas
Trico
Moog
Parker-Hannefin
Echlin
Fram
Sealed Power
Dayco
Gates
Douglas & Lomason
Fatauba

ELECTRONICS

Tokheim
Lyall Electric

ARVINAIR

Bairuco
Scovill Divisions (Schrader)
W.P. Johnson

CALSPAN

Flightsafety International
Dynalectron
SPC
SRL
IITRI

OTHER

D & M
Standex International
Harmon-Motive
Mitsubishi Bank

Source: Company documents.

In preparation for a board meeting of August 29, 1985, Baker sent to each member a copy of an article on asset redeployment, with a memo highlighting the point: "It was recently said of Gulf & Western, 'They have to put their cash to work or somebody else will do it for them.' The theme of this board meeting will center on our management of financial resources."

The board agreed with Baker's statement that Arvin could be more aggressive than it had been, not only as a defense but also in a proactive manner. The board was very supportive in its own statements and gave a clear go-ahead to Baker: "Use the balance sheet to incur debt; look for acquisitions. You certainly can make cash acquisitions."

Implementing the decision, however, was not easy. According to Baker, "The way we were brought up at Arvin was available cash was what you brought in from operations. My charge to division presidents was, 'If you have a good deal, don't worry about where the cash comes from.'

"Acquisitions," he said, "are not easy for operating people, in that it is a high-risk action, [and] it takes a lot of time, both before and after the transaction. So, in spite of it being in the thinking, it just was not moving."

Evans said, "From the mid-1960s, when we stopped making acquisitions, to the mid-1980s, there had been few or no acquisitions. So we are not geared to making them."

Acquisition Options

Although the divisions themselves were not aggressively pursuing acquisitions, in November of 1985, Baker was looking closely at two acquisition possibilities: Schrader Automotive, the world's leading manufacturer of tire valves for automobiles and trucks, and Lyall Electric, which specialized in high-quality wire assemblies for the heating, air-conditioning, appliance, and electronics industries. Schrader had originally been brought to Chick Evans's attention earlier that year, but at the suggested price of $60 million, he was uninterested. Arvin's information on these companies is given in Appendices I and II.

The Meeting in Taiwan

To reflect his commitment to an overseas presence, Baker had invited the board and all the division presidents to a visit to the company's Far East operations in November 1985. The scheduled board meeting was held in Taiwan during this visit, and the theme, again, was to use the firm's resources more aggressively to make external acquisitions.

To galvanize his division presidents into action, Baker told them, "you either grow your division by 12 percent a year, or, if you don't, you will be generating cash, and I will use that cash to make acquisitions so that the company will grow by 12 percent a year."

"In addition," he told the case writers, "incentive plans have always reflected corporate goals. Sales growth, in my view, is the key to the future. Our division presidents are so ingrained with profit making that my worry is not profits, but growth. Sales from acquisitions and joint ventures are included in their incentive plans. Sales growth from an expanding economy are given small credit."

Baker's 1985 incentive plan permitted division presidents to earn a bonus of up to 50 percent of base salary, with approximately 25 percent coming from growth in earnings per share, and up to 6 percent each from increases in share price, ROE, returns on sales, and "new sales" growth of more than $40 million. "New sales" included sales above threshold volumes of existing products, sales to new customers (e.g., heaters to Wal-Mart), sales in new countries, sales from new products, and sales from joint ventures and acquisitions completed in 1985.

"Now," thought Baker, "if I can only get them to go for it."

CASE APPENDIX I

LYALL ELECTRIC, INC.

Set up in 1952 by Lyall D. Morrill and Chester E. Dekko to make ready-made wiring assemblies for commercial refrigerators, Lyall Electric grew by expanding into a number of related businesses. By 1984 it was a privately held, multidivision company serving the appliance, automotive, and electronic industries with wire products. It was the most completely vertically integrated wire manufacturer in the United States.

The operations of the company were broken down into three categories: materials, with seven companies; assemblies, with three companies; and machinery and equipment, which comprised three more units. Transcending the entire organization was component sales, a separate group that handled the marketing of all corporate products. The products sold by the components group included wiring harnesses, connectors, service cords, flexible conductor assemblies, control boxes, and special electrical assemblies.

The firm's operating strategy was to keep the manufacturing units small and intimate. Seldom did a plant have more than 50 employees. In addition, almost all the plants were located in small towns, where not only did the employees know each other, but also a typical rural American work ethic prevailed.

The company's annual sales had risen sharply since 1982 and had reached $147 million in 1985. Management expected to maintain a 20-percent-per-year growth rate over the foreseeble future. Profit before taxes in 1985 was $13.658 million, and net profit was $7.658 million.

All the capital stock was owned by the directors and the estate trust of the late Lyall D. Morrill. No individual owned control, but the chairman, Chester Dekko, and secretary, Amy Morrill, the widow of Lyall Morrill, held a majority of the stock. Because Chester Dekko was emotionally tied to the company, any agreement would have to include his active role in running the firm after the merger/acquisition.

Lyall Electric, Inc., Its Consolidated Subsidiaries, and Its Operating Affiliated Companies
Balance Sheet

ASSETS	October 25, 1984
Cash and cash equivalent	$ 3,811
Marketable securities	245
Notes, receivables, and affiliates	400
Accounts receivable	11,351
Inventories	15,881
Prepaid expenses	101
Refundable federal income taxes	529
Total current assets	$32,318
Land	$ 867
Buildings	11,282
Machinery and equipment	20,917
Construction in progress	1,021
Less accumulated depreciation	(13,398)
Net PP&E	$20,689
Other	128
Total assets	$53,135

LIABILITIES AND SHAREHOLDERS' EQUITY	
Short-term debt	$ 3,964
Current portion of LTD	879
Accounts payable	4,843
Accrued expenses	5,714
Federal income taxes payable	312
Customer deposits	96
Total current liabilities	$15,709
Net liability safe-harbor leases	510
Term debt, noncurrent portion	8,502
	24,721
Common stock, paid-in capital, and retained earnings	28,414
Total liabilities and shareholders' equity	$53,135

CASE APPENDIX II

SCHRADER AUTOMOTIVE

A division of Scovill Corporation, Schrader Automotive Group was the world's largest producer of valves for pneumatic tires and inner tubes. It had manufacturing operations in the United States, France, Brazil, Canada, South Africa, Australia, Mexico, and India. From those locations, Schrader served every major valve market except the Far East.

Schrader's market share in each area served was as follows:

Australia/Oceania	38%
Latin America	79
Europe/Africa	39
India/Eastern Asia	47
Mexico/Central America	96
South Africa/Southern Africa	85
USA/Canada	35

Schrader's overall worldwide market share was estimated to be 31 percent in 1984. An opportunity for the firm to grow its business was in the Far East market, which had good potential because many U.S. tube manufacturers had moved off shore, mainly to Korea and Taiwan. Tube production in the United States had dropped 40 percent in the first half of the 1980s. The total worldwide tire valve and accessories market was estimated at $260 million in 1984, with 60 percent going to OEMs and 40 percent to the aftermarket.

OEM customers included tube manufacturers, automobile manufacturers, and manufacturers of industrial products that used pneumatic valves. Aftermarket outlets were tire-equipment specialists, warehouse distributors, and mass merchandisers. Products sold in these two markets included valves for passenger and truck innertubes, passenger and truck snap-in-tubeless valves, clamp-in valves for high performance, valve cores for automotive and industrial applications, caps and extensions, gauges, air chucks, and various other accessories. Products related through manufacturing processes or distribution included tire-repair materials and wheel weights.

The valve business was considered to be in the mature phase and was closely tied to automobile sales and tire-replacement rate. No significant growth was expected. Product innovations were rare, and whatever new products were introduced were basically a manufacturer's attempt to maintain its market position.

New products launched by Schrader in 1985 included (1) a Red Alert valve, which turned red when tire pressure was low, and (2) Visualizer, which equalized dual tires. Both were unsuccessful.

A potential product innovation that had strategic implications was the use of plastics to replace brass in valves. Prototype plastic valves with both brass and plastic cores had been produced in sample quantities, but none had been introduced as of the end of 1985.

In 1984 and 1985, Schrader consolidated its manufacturing operations. The facilities in the United Kingdom, Hong Kong, and Dickson, Tennessee, were closed, and a significant portion of production was shifted to France, Canada, and Brazil.

Because of the nonrecurrent expenses associated with plant closures, profitability had suffered over the last three years. The firm was expected to regain some of its operating margin in 1986, primarily from the gains in the U.S. market. Summary financial statistics for Schrader were as follows (figures in millions):

	1983	1984	1985	1986 Plan
Sales	$74.0	$81.9	$80.3	$82.6
Operating income	3.0	8.0	5.7	8.8
Net income	$ (2.2)	$ 1.6	$ 3.6	$ 3.2

Schrader's sales and assets broke down as follows:

Schrader Automotive, Inc.
Financial Highlights
($ in millions)

	NET SALES			NET INCOME[†]			NET CONTROLLABLE ASSETS		
	1984	1985	1986	1984	1985	1986	1984	1985	1986[*]
United States	34.5	29.7	31.6	(2.1)	.6[‡]	1.4	24.8	21.3	22.9
France	16.0	22.7	23.5	1.0	1.8	1.6	6.5	12.6	10.4
Brazil	11.6	14.1	14.4	1.4	1.2	(.2)	9.5	10.5	12.7
Canada	3.2	3.0	3.2	.2	.3	—	1.8	1.9	2.2
Mexico	5.6	4.7	3.4	.7	.2	.1	3.2	3.0	2.9
Australia	3.5	3.1	3.7	—	(.4)	(.1)	2.6	1.6	1.6
South Africa	3.5	2.4	2.8	.5	.4	.4	1.7	1.5	1.7
Other (closed operations)	4.0	.6	—	(.1)	(.5)	—	1.4	.1	—
Total	81.9	80.3	82.6	1.6	3.6[‡]	3.2	51.5	52.5	54.4

[*]Forecast.
[†]FIFO basis.
[‡]Excludes approximately $1.5 million Dickson closing expenses (pretax).

YAMAHA CORPORATION AND THE ELECTRONIC-MUSICAL-INSTRUMENTS INDUSTRY

> A change to a new type of music is something to beware of as a hazard of all our fortunes. For the modes of music are never disturbed without unsettling of the most fundamental political and social conventions.
>
> –Plato, *The Republic*

As Seisuke Ueshima, the newly appointed chairman and president of the Yamaha Corporation, looked down at the game of Go, he had an uneasy feeling that his stones controlling the center of the game board were vulnerable to being surrounded. Although Ueshima generally found playing Go relaxing, this game reminded him of the competitive position of the Yamaha Corporation.

The Yamaha board of directors expected Ueshima's strategic plan for Yamaha, the faltering giant of the musical-instruments industry, the next morning. The implications of his presentation would quickly be felt throughout the organization and among shareholders and would even be discussed in the gossip columns of the *Nikkei Weekly*.

Seisuke Ueshima, successor to three generations of the dynastic leadership of the Kawakami family, was something of an outsider because he came from Yamaha's sister company, Yamaha Motor Corporation. President Ueshima now had the tasks of improving the company's recent lackluster performance, strengthening morale, preserving Yamaha's positive brand reputation, maintaining the skills and competencies of the company, positioning the company for the impending market changes, and quickly developing the core capabilities needed to build Yamaha's future strategic position.

COMPANY BACKGROUND

In 1993, Yamaha Corporation was the world's largest manufacturer of musical instruments, accounting for almost half of the world's new musical-instrument sales. With a far more diversified product range than any of its competitors in the electronic-keyboard market, Yamaha had pursued a corporate

This case was written by Andrew W. Spreadbury, MBA/J.D. 1994, under the supervision of Professor L. J. Bourgeois. Copyright © 1994 by the University of Virginia Darden School Foundation, Charlottesville, VA. All rights reserved.

strategy of sprawling conglomeration since World War II. While Yamaha's musical- and electronic-instruments businesses boomed during the 1950s–1970s, the profits from these core businesses were used to support other business divisions, such as the company's leisure, living, and sporting-goods divisions, which were financial losers. By 1993, the Yamaha Corporation owned a golf course, operated resort hotels, and produced furniture, kitchen sets, golf carts, computer chips, televisions, videocassette recorders (VCRs), and audio equipment, as well as virtually every type of musical instrument sold. All of these businesses were held loosely under the umbrella of the Nippon Gakki holding company, together with Yamaha Corporation's sister companies, Yamaha Motor Corporation—the world's second-largest motorcycle manufacturer—and the Yamaha Music Foundation, a network of music schools teaching millions of children around the world.

In the musical-instruments business, Yamaha Corporation had pursued a strategy of broader product, technology, and geographical scope than any of its competitors. Unlike any of its rivals, Yamaha produced musical instruments of all kinds—traditional acoustic as well as electric and electronic instruments—with products positioned at almost all price points. Yamaha was so large that it had a significant portion of almost every niche in the musical-instruments industry, and it was the clear leader in most niches. Struggling U.S. rivals accused Yamaha of emphasizing quantity over quality and of selling with advertising rather than with sound, but the strongest quality claims of those competitors was that their products were "every bit as good" as Yamaha's.[1]

Yamaha's broad-scoped business strategy and conglomerating corporate strategy were developed by three generations of the Kawakami family—who had presided over Yamaha since the mid-1930s, when Kaichi Kawakami rescued Yamaha from near bankruptcy—around what former Yamaha president Hiroshi Kawakami, grandson of Kaichi Kawakami, called the "bread-and-butter piano division."[2] Because the Japanese education system required every elementary-school child to learn to play at least one keyboard instrument and one wind instrument, Japan offered Yamaha a mass market for low-priced pianos that Yamaha came to dominate. Yamaha kept prices low by using, whenever possible, assembly-line techniques for its pianos, of which Yamaha produced 238,000 annually.[3]

Yamaha had made every effort however, not to sacrifice quality. The company openly declared its goal of catching up with Steinway, the world-renowned leader in sound quality. It tried to do so by concentrating on its vertical pianos—the pianos used in schools—in order to capture the loyalty of future virtuosi.[4]

---

[1]"Here's How to Beat Japanese Firms: With a Drumstick!" *Kansas City Business Journal*, May 21, 1993, p. 1.
[2]"Yamaha Changes Management Tune," *Nikkei Weekly*, February 1, 1992, p. 9.
[3]"On Yamaha's Assembly Line," *New York Times*, February 22, 1981, p. 8E.

Yamaha used the same lumber to build its pianos that Steinway used. Yamaha carefully followed Steinway's research-and-development efforts and regularly purchased and disassembled Steinway pianos.[5] "We are chasing hard; we want to catch up with Steinway," Yamaha's managers declared in 1981.[6]

From its piano-making experience, Yamaha had developed capabilities in bending and laminating woods (for piano cabinets) and in marketing and distributing pianos. Yamaha subsequently applied these production, marketing, and distribution capabilities to guitars and drums. High production volume to meet local need strengthened Yamaha's skills in producing efficiently at low cost. Yamaha attained its position as world leader in musical-instrument sales by seizing markets for inexpensive beginners' instruments first, then conquering the middle-price range, and finally expanding into the top-of-the-line market.

With this expansion, Yamaha built large financial resources and brand-name recognition. Yamaha's annual income rose to a range of $60 million to $100 million by the early 1990s, and sales passed $4 billion (see Exhibit 1). This strong financial development allowed Yamaha Corporation an advertising budget that exceeded the annual sales of most of its niche competitors. Yamaha's ubiquitous product and price positioning, combined with its large advertising budget, made for extensive consumer recognition and loyalty, especially in Japan, the world's largest market for musical instruments.

Yamaha was also able to capitalize on its financial resources and knowledge of the musical-instruments industry to obtain patent rights to, and build on, its core of electronic-music-synthesis technology, enabling the company to capture its leading position of 30 percent to 35 percent of total market sales in electronic musical instruments. Yamaha built this leading position just as it had built its dominant position in the traditional-musical-instruments markets: beginning with low-price segments and moving up. This growth increased Yamaha's work force to more than 12,000 skilled artisans and electronics experts. Yamaha had grown so large in relation to its many competitors that it had become largely insensitive to their activities.

Following its success in musical instruments, Yamaha began to diversify by making a multitude of sideline products that shared unique materials or manufacturing techniques with its "bread-and-butter" piano business, such as skis, tennis rackets, and furniture.[7] Similarly, from the relatively high-margin electronic-organ business, the company branched into the cutthroat competition of television, VCR, and audio-equipment production.[8] With only manufacturing-related capabilities supporting these businesses, Yamaha Corporation did not

---

[4]David A. Garvin, "Steinway & Sons," Harvard Business School (9-682-025).
[5]Ibid.
[6]"On Yamaha's Assembly Line," *New York Times*, February 22, 1981, p. 8E.
[7]Brenton R. Schlender, "Yamaha: The Perils of Losing Focus," *Fortune*, May 17, 1993, p. 100.
[8]Ibid.

Exhibit 1
Fact Sheet for Yamaha Corporation
Hamamatsu-shi, Shizuoka, Japan 430

Chairman: Hideto Eguchi
Chief executive officer: Seisuke Ueshima, president
Employees: 10,775
Current shares: 194,077,033
Shareholders: 9,964
Major shareholders: Sumitomo Bank, 4.92%; Daiichi Kangyo, 4.92%;
   Sumitomo Life Insurance Co., 4.92%

YAMAHA CORPORATION WORLDWIDE SALES (YEAR ENDING DECEMBER 31, 1991)

Electronic musical instruments (18% of total)	$ 736 million
Pianos (16%)	656
Conventional musical instruments excluding pianos (13%)	536
Home furniture and entertainment systems (13%)	533
Electronic equipment and metals (11%)	451
Other (29%)	1,192
Total sales of all products	$4,104 million

YAMAHA CORPORATION WORLDWIDE SALES BY REGION (1991)

Japan	71%
North America	10
Europe	11
Asia	5
Other	3
Total	100%

YAMAHA CORPORATION WORLDWIDE SALES

1983	$2,680 million	1988	$3,736 million
1984	3,256	1989	3,896
1985	3,408	1990	4,074
1986	3,304	1991	4,104
1987	3,488		

Source: Worldscope, 1994; extrapolations from *Hoover's Handbook of World Business* and assorted periodicals.

fare well with them. As Hiroshi Kawakami explained, top executives well versed in the musical-instruments market were not able to move aggressively on less familiar turf.[9] Yamaha's diversity of operations grew to be cumbersome because independent-minded divisions failed to pool resources and expertise.

Yamaha's earnings from the sale of its pianos and other traditional acoustic instruments had slowly declined from their peak in 1980 because world demand had fallen, stemming partly from the weak Japanese economy and partly from the declining birth rate in Japan and the rest of the developed world. In the United States, demand for pianos had fallen as a result of reduced birth rates, a drop in school and music programs, high interest rates, a decrease in disposable income, and sales-outlet closures.[10] Moreover, margins had narrowed because of price competition from Korean manufacturers. As a result of poor earnings from pianos, Yamaha took funds intended for other divisions to continue feeding the declining piano division.

Too much diversification, a lack of any major articulated goals or focus, and the resulting lackluster performance in all but the electronic-musical-instruments (EMI) businesses had produced a decline in employee morale and a loss of trust in the Kawakami dynasty that had guided the company for three generations. To the union, Hiroshi Kawakami appeared to be more interested in sports cars, skiing vacations, and concerts than in improving Yamaha's performance. In February 1992, the union joined with management to bring about a leadership coup, demanding that Hiroshi Kawakami resign as president and forcing him to relinquish his seat on the board in March 1993. (Kawakami was left—like his father, the president before him—with about 1 percent of Yamaha Corporation's stock.)

This dramatic move filled Yamaha Corporation and Japanese newspapers with tales of intrigue. It was a highly unusual display of Japanese labor-union power. Surveys taken in 1993 of Yamaha's union workers found that most would not recommend working at Yamaha to family or friends and that most would start working at another company if they could choose to start again—an unusually negative finding for a Japanese company.

THE DEVELOPMENT OF ELECTRONIC MUSIC

Technology helped make music a popular, mass-marketed product. Starting with nineteenth-century developments of various forms of player

---

[9]"Yamaha Changes Management Tune," *Nikkei Weekly*, February 1, 1992, p. 9.
[10]"A Study on the Conditions of Competition between Imported and Domestically Produced Pianos," Report to the Subcommittee on Trade, Committee on Ways and Means, U.S. House of Representatives, on Investigation No. 332-159 under Section 332(b) of the Tariff Act of 1930, pp. 35–36.

pianos, manufacturers provided reproductions of great musical performances to listeners who lacked access to the performers. In 1896, American inventor Thaddeus Cahill patented the first electric musical instrument, which generated sound with rotating electromechanical tone wheels.[11] In the 1920s and 1930s, several composers expressed dissatisfaction with conventional instrumental resources. The technological developments of the era provided amplifiers and speakers to change sonority.[12] In the late 1920s, optical-track recording, which converted electrical impulses from a microphone into photographic images on film that could then be read to another microphone for playback by an optical reader, was developed for sound film.[13] Around the same time, developments with electromagnets brought the ability to induce and sustain vibrations in piano strings.[14] By the 1930s electric pianos had been developed that replaced traditional-acoustic-piano soundboards with electrostatic pickups for amplification.[15]

The phonograph and the radio broadened popular access to, and interest in, music. With the U.S. postwar baby boom came a boom in interest in popular youth-oriented music such as rhythm and blues, rockabilly, rock 'n' roll, and heavy metal, as well as family-oriented varieties such as themes to popular films. In the United States, the largest and most influential market for recorded music since World War II, interest in music was driven by radio. As a result of local radio stations' delivering listeners to advertisers that wanted a specific, predictable audience, music styles and groups of consumers interested in those styles were highly segmented.[16] The increase in the number of radio stations and the market-targeting abilities of advertisers brought a more diverse range of musical styles.

At the same time recorded music was flourishing, play-it-yourself music was burgeoning. Although the total market for recorded music grew larger than that for play-it-yourself music, by 1993 more was spent each year in the United States on sheet music, music software, and instruments ($3.5 billion) than people under age 25 spent on records, cassettes, compact discs, and music videos ($3.2 billion).[17] The proliferation of high-quality stereo equip-

---

[11]Richard Dobson, *A Dictionary of Electronic and Computer Music Technology* (New York: Oxford University Press, 1992), p. 150.

[12]*The New Grove Dictionary of Music and Musicians* (London: MacMillan Press Ltd., 1980), vol. 6, p. 107.

[13]*The New Grove Dictionary of American Music* (London: MacMillan Press Ltd., 1986), vol. 2, p. 30.

[14]Dobson, *Dictionary of Electronic and Computer Music Technology*, p. 124.

[15]*The New Grove Dictionary of American Music*, vol. 2, p. 29.

[16]"A Survey of the Music Business," *The Economist*, December 21, 1991, p. 12.

[17]Ibid, p. 18.

ment, which, in turn, exposed listeners to the nuances of sound, increased consumer demand for high-quality sound from musical instruments.[18]

In the 1950s, musician-inventors such as Robert Moog and Donald Buchla developed synthesizers, which allowed all sound properties—pitch, envelope, amplitude, timbre, reverberation, modulation, and so forth—to be controlled by variations in voltage. Such instruments offered a great variety of sounds, far surpassing the scope of any mechanical instrument.[19]

MIDI

During the 1970s, the development of synthesizers paralleled that of the computer: the hardware was usually a pianolike keyboard and computer chips containing the synthesizer sounds and sound-controlling capabilities; the software was the operating system allowing the manipulation and storing of sounds and sound sequences. The storing of sound sequences in digital form was labeled "sequencing," a process similar, in principle, to storing analog sounds on a tape recorder. A sequencer, in contrast to a tape recorder, permitted the manipulation of individual digital signals, allowing, for example, the correction of errors with a single keystroke. It was, essentially, akin to a word processor. As with early computers, each manufacturer developed proprietary operating systems, thus making different keyboards (and the music sequences stored in them) incompatible with each other.

In the early 1980s, the invention and standardization of the electronic-musical-synthesis technology called MIDI introduced a great advance in music-making potential. MIDI (musical instrument digital interface) established a set of specifications that provided an efficient means of digitally conveying real-time musical-performance information such as which sounds should be generated, which notes should be played, and how loud notes should be.[20] More important, MIDI was a universal digital interface that enabled instruments such as synthesizers, drum machines, sound samplers, and sequencers from any manufacturer to communicate with each other by standardized conversion of analog sound waves into digital signals and back again.[21] MIDI allowed for easy music editing and the ability to change the playback speeds and pitch or key of the sounds independently.[22] Since its

---

[18]"A Study on the Conditions of Competition between Imported and Domestically Produced Pianos," p. 36.

[19]*The New Grove Dictionary of Music and Musicians*, vol. 6, p. 108.

[20]"Crystal Semiconductor Demonstrates Family of New CD-Quality Wave-Table Synthesizer Chips," *Business Wire*, June 28, 1993.

[21]Dobson, *Dictionary of Electronic and Computer Music Technology*, 1992, p. 102.

[22]"Crystal Semiconductor."

introduction, MIDI was applied to an increasingly diverse range of instruments and computer equipment.[23] It seemed to spark consumers' creativity, enabling a broad range of musical applications. The predicted trend of consumer demand was for products offering users an increased potential for expression and customization.

THE ELECTRONIC-MUSICAL-INSTRUMENTS (EMI) INDUSTRY

The EMI market exploded from virtually ground zero in 1983 to almost $3 billion in sales worldwide in 1993. Roughly three-fourths of this market was for electronic keyboards. Although sales faltered during the 1990–1992 world recession, the general trend seemed to be up. Demand was historically linked to significant bursts of new-product technology, with demand subsiding in years in which product improvements were little more than cosmetic.

The EMI industry commanded margins roughly 10 percent to 12 percent higher than those in other consumer-electronic industries, primarily because it had built product differentiation with features that consumers wanted but found difficult to compare and value monetarily, such as musical "expressivity" and "voicing" (the recorded and copied sound of acoustic instruments).[24] Patents and talented design engineers gave the leading manufacturers the ability to predict what the competitors' next products would be like while keeping their own products different, which was the key to success in keyboard differentiation. Continual cost reductions also helped. Firms able to diversify by offering products in many price ranges tended to be the most profitable, as were the firms that scored a big hit with a very popular product.

The EMI industry was particularly influenced by Yamaha Corporation, which held and fiercely defended the rights to most of the patents essential to MIDI. Although competitors developed other technologies and purchased rights to or copied Yamaha's technologies, Yamaha's basic technological advantages, combined with its vast production, marketing, and distribution capabilities, made Yamaha's products the biggest sellers in the industry (see Exhibit 2). Yamaha's patents had long been the key to its success in the industry, and Yamaha defended them vigorously with ongoing patent-infringement litigation.

Popular products such as Yamaha's DX-7 and Clavinova organ were huge hits, and sales of electronic musical instruments and related MIDI products had grown to be about one-third of Yamaha's profits, making electronic musical instruments Yamaha's most successful business. Although some early,

[23]Dobson, *Dictionary of Electronic and Computer Music Technology*, p. 106.
[24]"Mass Merchants, Dealers Singing Profitable Tune from Keyboard Sales; Electronic Musical Keyboards," *Weekly Home Furnishings Newspaper*, © 1991.

Exhibit 2
Leading Manufacturers in the
Electronic-Musical-Instruments Industry

Ultrapro Market	Pro/Home Market	Home Market
Retail Value $10,000	Market Share and Position	Retail Value $300

10%	Yamaha 30%–35%	30%
	Roland 20%	
	Korg 20%	
10%	Peavy 15%	
	Casio 5%	50%

End Users

Stars who record mass-marketed popular music	Musicians, studios, bands, schools, churches, and amateur home players	Tinkerers and children

Products

Not portable	MIDI interface, CD-ROM, compatible with computer systems—portable, all self-contained	Portable keyboards

leading competitors like Moog Music and ARP had been forced out of the market, Yamaha had managed to keep a 30 to 35-percent share. Yamaha had built broad-based digital- and computer-technology capabilities, making it the leading producer of computer sound cards, the producer of the world's fastest 16-kilobyte SRAM chips, and the producer of 0.4 percent of the world's computer chips. As a result of these efforts, 78 percent of the consumers who owned one or more electronic keyboards owned one or more Yamahas—a level of brand penetration more than twice as high as that of any other competitor.[25]

---

[25]1991 *Keyboard* magazine survey.

Yamaha's Major Competitors

The world's second-largest manufacturer of musical instruments in 1993 was the Kawai Musical Instruments Manufacturing Company (see Exhibit 3). Kawai sold pianos, electronic pianos, electronic organs, electronic musical instruments, formed-metal products, computers, software, and music lessons.[26]

The Young Chang Musical Instrument Company was the world's largest manufacturer of traditional acoustic pianos in 1993 (see Exhibit 3). Known for making high-quality pianos costing 20 percent less than comparable U.S. and Japanese models, the Korean firm had received training from Yamaha under a contractual agreement from 1967 to 1976.[27]

In 1993, Yamaha's most powerful competitors in the electronic-musical-instruments industry were primarily Japanese. Roland, with slightly more than 20 percent of the market, had almost as wide a range of MIDI instruments as Yamaha. It had a staff of capable musicians who gave Roland's electronic instruments what was probably the best voicing in the industry. Roland intended to expand into the amateur market, although its products were perceived as too expensive for most amateurs.

Korg had almost as much market share as Roland, and also had the advantage of exceptional voicing talent. Once owned by Yamaha, Korg was known for its workstation keyboards, sophisticated sound effects, drum machines, and sequencers. All Korg parts were custom-made. The company appeared to be planning a strong emphasis on software-synthesis machines that would be entirely programmable by the user.

Peavey, the one leading U.S. manufacturer, had a 15-percent share of the EMI market. It had strong relationships with U.S. dealers and offered the largest dealer margins. Peavey required its dealers to attend classes at Peavey University so they would understand and push Peavey products. In return, Peavey gave its dealers larger-than-average margins. The company did not allow the sale of its instruments via mail order. Peavey had a few strong products, including a sample playback box and a pianolike weighted keyboard (based on technology licensed from Yamaha). Peavey was suspected to be in trouble, however, because it had a poor image among professionals and was limited in software-based synthesis.

Smaller manufacturers included Akai, Ensoniq, and EMU. Akai produced mostly expensive products for professionals. Ensoniq, whose products appealed primarily to American rap musicians, was strong in cost cutting and software innovation, but its products had quality problems; its samplers had relatively low fidelity, its playback hardware was considered outdated and inefficient, and

---

[26]COMLINE Corporate Directory, COMLINE International Company, 1993.
[27]"Tacoma Strikes Right Chord for Korean Piano Maker," *Puget Sound Business Journal*, April 3, 1993.

Exhibit 3
Yamaha's Competitors

KAWAI MUSICAL INSTRUMENTS MANUFACTURING CO., LTD.
HAMAMATSU-SHI, SHIZUOKA-KEN 430, JAPAN

	Revenue
1988	¥ 85,628 million
1989	90,515
1990	96,603
1991	101,440

Chief executive officer: Hirotaka Kawai, president
Incorporation: 1951
Employees: 3,570
Capital: 3,600 million yen

YOUNG CHANG MUSICAL INSTRUMENT CO., LTD.
SEO-KU, INCHON, SOUTH KOREA

	Revenue
1989	US$55,787,000
1990	55,817,000
1991	54,929,000

Chairman: Jae-sup Kim
President: Sang-eun Nam
Employees: 4,597
Shareholders: 887
Major shareholder: Jae-sup Kim, 17.2%
Business: Of 1991 revenues, upright pianos accounted for 78%; grand
   pianos, 10%; digital pianos, 3%; other, 9%.

ROLAND CORPORATION
SUMINOE-KU, OSAKA 559, JAPAN

	Revenue		
1988	¥30,000 million	1991	35,119
1989	31,818	1992	33,464
1990	33,803		

(continued on next page)

Source: COMLINE Corporate Directory, COMLINE International Corporation, 1992;
Teikoku Databank American, Inc., 1993; Worldscope, 1993.

(continued)

Chief executive officer: Ikutara Kakehashi, president
Incorporation: 1972
Employees: 695
Capital: 7,641.6 million yen

KORG, INC.
SUGINAMI-KU, TOKYO 168, JAPAN

	Revenue	Profits	Dividends
1992	¥14,177	¥18,560	50%
1993	12,883	11,044	284

Chief executive officer: Seiki Kato
Incorporation: 1964
Employees: 381
Shareholders: 4,848,000

CASIO COMPUTER CO., LTD.
SHINJUKU-KU, TOKYO 163, JAPAN

	Revenue
1991	¥304,826 million
1992	335,228
1993	383,423

it cut corners on digital and analog hardware. EMU, based in California, focused on the professional market, had a polished image and a good marketing department, and was lowering its prices.

Casio, the Japanese consumer-electronics manufacturer, was the leader at the low end. Whenever consumers perceived innovation stagnation among the higher-end producers, Casio could be expected to increase its market share.

The threat of new entrants appeared low. Brand equity among leaders seemed high, entering the distribution chain was difficult, and substantial musical and engineering expertise and creativity—though not necessarily money—were required to develop products. Barriers to entry were raised as technology grew increasingly sophisticated. New players were entering the field of MIDI-based digitally recorded music, but there seemed to be little chance of their becoming manufacturers of synthesizer musical instruments. Only Matsushita, which had expressed interest in the EMI market, had the name and resources to do so successfully.

In 1993, the competition among suppliers to the EMI industry was high. Components used in making electronic keyboards were either commodities such as standard computer chips and plastics that were produced by many different suppliers and purchased for many different uses, or they were custom-made by the EMI manufacturers themselves. The largest EMI manufacturers were backward integrated.

Musical-instruments dealers were the direct buyers of electronic musical instruments. Although dealers could not force manufacturers to modify their products in order to carry them, they could threaten to drop product lines entirely. The applications of MIDI technology appeared to have reached a plateau, the marginal benefits of innovation were minor, and the products were becoming increasingly commoditylike. The likelihood of dealers increasing their strength through consolidation seemed small, however, because dealers were a diverse group. No single customer represented a significant portion of sales.

The same was true of consumers. Despite the diversity of musical tastes and desired product application, consumers could be placed in three categories (see Exhibit 2). The ultraprofessionals bought systems ranging from $10,000 to $250,000. Local professionals and high-end amateur consumers were interested in instruments priced from $300 to $10,000. The children's and tinkerers' market was for products priced below $300.

There seemed to be few identifiable market niches that had not been served. Consumer demand appeared to be relatively flat because the market had been saturated with MIDI products. Consumers who already owned MIDI products had little incentive to buy additional ones because they found that sound differences among products appeared to be minor. Although buyers were not overly price sensitive when paying for brand-new capability, they demanded lower prices for products without new capability.

OUTLOOK FOR THE FUTURE

In the past five years, the gap between prices of high- and low-end MIDI instruments had narrowed. Consumer demand for production of high-quality sound samples programmed by manufacturers into MIDI instruments had increased. Consumers also wanted more miniaturization and self-containment. Consumers could now use computers to create initial sound signals to be entered into the memory of MIDI instruments. Products had grown more complicated and offered more features than before. Manufacturers offered improved customer services such as speedy delivery and 800-number information. Producers had also tried to increase purchases with cosmetic differentiation, niche marketing with size and number of features, shortened product-life cycles to create the appearance of innovation, price imaging, and celebrity associations. The industry goal had traditionally been to "get an orchestra into a small box," but all advances to date had brought the industry no closer to attaining that goal.

Market conditions were changing. With the market saturated with the aging MIDI technology and products becoming increasingly commoditylike, prices and profit margins were dropping. Profit margins were also reduced because of falling consumer interest from a lack of significant product advances in recent years and the recent global economic downturn. Consumer desire for musical instruments that were simple and easy to understand put extra downward pressure on prices of higher-end models.

At the same time, the electronic-music industry was at the beginning of a new wave of technology. Engineers at Stanford University had developed computer hardware and software that modeled the physical vibrations of piano wires and the flow of air blown through wind instruments. Experts at Yamaha and its competitors believed this technology promised musical quality far superior to that of the MIDI-based synthetic musical instruments then available to consumers. The developers of this technology had promised to sell the rights to many manufacturers in the EMI industry rather than to Yamaha only. Some of Yamaha's executives believed this action would allow Yamaha's competitors to catch up with Yamaha in the EMI market. If the physical-modeling technology were licensed widely, they feared, the stable market positions of the leading manufacturers might be entirely upset.

The other major technological development in the electronic-music industry was the computer sound card, a computer chip or board of chips that generated audio output. Sound cards improved the capabilities of electronic musical instruments, added complex sound and voice simulation to video games, and turned personal computers into multimedia centers. The world market for sound cards was expected to grow from $112 million in 1992 to $436 million in 1996.[28] The market for sound cards in computers and a variety of home entertainment centers would be accompanied by a need for software to control the musical hardware. Because the manufacturers of home multimedia centers would be more likely than consumers to choose the brand of sound-card hardware and software to be used, strategic alliances were expected to be formed between electronic-musical-equipment companies and video-game and computer-multimedia-center manufacturers.

---

[28]1992 study by Dataquest, Inc., a market-research firm.

Yamaha at a Crossroads

Although Ueshima was experienced in managing international industrial operations, Yamaha Corporation's business seemed very different from the business of Yamaha Motor. He wondered what physical modeling and sound cards might mean to Yamaha in the future. He also wondered whether future consumer demand for simple, user-friendly instruments would increase. He had heard that music production was moving from a few big studios to many small studios tailored to individual artists. He had also heard that price pressure seemed likely to continue downward at all levels as a result of general advances in the computer industry. Consumer demand for sound-synthesizing technology might shift from the keyboard to other forms, such as the increasingly popular MIDI saxophone, guitar, bass, and drums.

Advances in other industries of which Ueshima had little knowledge also threatened to make an impact on Yamaha's market. For example, some experimenters had turned the "data-gloves" used in virtual-reality-simulation games into prototype "hyperinstruments," which converted the movements of a musician mimicking the playing of an instrument—for example, a violin—into music.[29] Consumers had always sought new sounds, increased expressivity, and "better-feeling" instruments. Some in the industry also feared that the popularity of well-known stars' "unplugged" (acoustic instrument) recordings would cause consumers to lose interest in electronic musical instruments entirely.

Ueshima studied the Go board and tried to determine where his opponents' next moves would be and how he could position himself to remain on the offensive. He had the same task in managing Yamaha.

---

[29]"A Survey of the Music Business," *Economist*, December 21, 1991, pp. 16–17.

PART IV

CORPORATE STRATEGY: DIVERSIFICATION AND SYNERGY

DIVERSIFICATION
AND SYNERGY

C
H
A
P
T
E
R

9

The portfolio and shareholder value approaches discussed in Part III are excellent tools for sense making when the number of business units in a firm grows very large—thereby reducing cognitive overload at senior management levels—and they are excellent cash management tools when resources are insufficient to cover all opportunities and strategic requirements at the business unit level. In essence, they treat corporate strategy as an exercise in balancing an existing portfolio of businesses. What they do not do, however, is tell the strategist how to locate and exploit synergies among existing businesses, how to find appropriate new businesses, or how to generate new strategies that expand the scope of the firm.

Two frameworks can help the strategist analyze how to expand the boundaries of the firm in a way that maximizes the potential for transference of skills, or synergy, among the businesses. These are Ansoff's **growth vector matrix** and Thomas's **direct and indirect linkages** approaches.

THE GROWTH VECTOR MATRIX

Igor Ansoff outlined a simple, yet elegant, approach to generating options for diversification. (These options also are useful for generating strategic alternatives at the business strategy level.) He proposed a growth vector matrix, also known as the **product/market matrix.**

On the top of the matrix, one arrays both current and potential (new) markets. Along the side, one arrays current and new products (see Figure 9-1).

Figure 9-1
Growth Vector Matrix

Markets

	Current	New
Current	1	2
New	3	4

Products

Source: Adapted from Igor Ansoff, *Corporate Strategy* (New York: McGraw-Hill, 1965), p. 109.

The four cells present four strategic alternatives for expansion. If a business is attempting to grow within its current product/market arena (cell 1), it will then pursue a strategy of **market penetration.** This strategy is easiest to pursue in the introduction and growth stages of an industry, as all competitors can grow together and the perceived level of rivalry is low. At the mature and decline stages, however, continued growth comes through taking a share from competitors. This can be costly, and, as the portfolio approaches pointed out, short term in focus.

A second strategy is to grow by finding new customers or markets for the firm's current products (cell 2). This is a strategy of **market development,** and it can be pursued in a variety of ways. For example, a firm can franchise its operations and grow geographically, as Jiffy Lube and McDonald's have done. Or, it can find new uses for its products. When the baby boom ended, Procter & Gamble stood to lose significant profits from its Pampers disposable diaper business. The solution was to reconstitute and rename its product as Depends and sell into the hospital and rest-home markets (for incontinent patients), where the new demographic growth is concentrated. Similarly, Arm and Hammer employed a marketing executive whose responsibility was to discover and promote alternative uses for the company's baking soda (refrigerator deodorant, toothpaste, stain remover, bee sting application, and so on). Business schools offering executive MBA (EMBA) programs for working managers at night or on weekends offer another example of taking a current product, suitably modified, to a new market. Finally, most multinational corporations initiated their international expansion through exports to (new) markets in other countries.

A third strategy is to grow through **product development** (cell 3), by selling additional products to current customers. Examples include salads at Pizza Hut, software and laser printers from Apple Computer, tax planning and management consulting from auditing firms, and amplifiers from Fender guitar company. Whereas market development requires marketing and selling skills, product development requires technical and research and development skills. (An alternative approach to new products for current customers is to use licensing agreements with other firms to provide their products under one's brand, such as IBM's Canon-produced printers. This requires strategic alliance skills.)

The fourth strategy, new products to new markets (cell 4), involves the greatest risk. Ansoff calls this an **unrelated diversification** strategy. Dan Thomas calls it the "suicide square" because of the risks associated with moving simultaneously into unfamiliar markets, products, and, possibly, technologies. These risks are amplified if the unfamiliarity causes management to divert its attention from the core business in order to learn the new business. They are further compounded if a fundamental change takes place in the core business while management is distracted by the new one.

The four strategies are summarized in Figure 9-2.

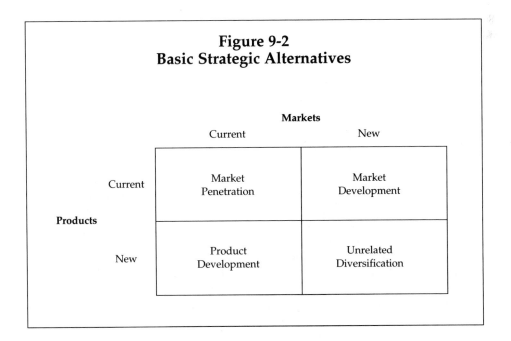

Figure 9-2
Basic Strategic Alternatives

		Markets	
		Current	New
Products	Current	Market Penetration	Market Development
	New	Product Development	Unrelated Diversification

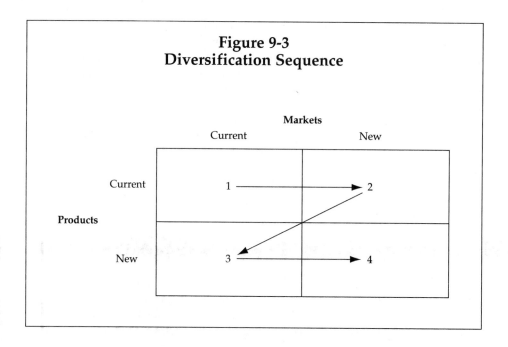

Figure 9-3
Diversification Sequence

Most companies progress through these strategies in sequence, as illustrated by the diversification sequence "Z" in Figure 9-3.

DIRECT AND INDIRECT LINKAGES

A shortcoming of both the portfolio and value-based planning techniques presented in Part III was that they treated each business unit as if it were totally independent of every other unit. That is, recommendations to grow a particular business or to divest another frequently failed to take into account the fact that two businesses might be closely related and have a strong dependence on each other. For example, the two businesses might share manufacturing facilities, raw material sources, or a distribution channel or sales force. To reduce the activity in one business might result in increased costs for the sister business, given that a lower overall volume would be realized in the shared resource. In addition, some academic research completed in the mid-1970s indicated that corporations consisting of closely related businesses performed better economically than corporations composed of unrelated businesses. This led to the development of some concepts concerning the degree to which businesses in the corporation are linked to each other, forming a basis for synergies. Specifically, the works of Professor Richard Rumelt and later that of Dan R. E. Thomas, founder of Focus (a strategy-process consulting firm) introduced one of the more modern theories of corporate strategic management. That theory relies on the concept of direct and indirect linkages.

Direct linkages exist to the extent that businesses share a common resource, knowledge, or experience base that is specific to markets, technologies, or product characteristics. **Indirect linkages** are those with *no* specific market, technology, or product relationships. For example, for GE to state "We will be number one or number two in any business in which we operate" is to declare that an *indirect* linkage is the basis for corporate strategy. The research evidence indicates that companies characterized primarily by *direct* linkages among their businesses tend to secure a higher degree of economic return. There are three kinds of direct linkages: market, technology, and product linkages.

Market Linkages

A market linkage exists when a company uses its current customer base to sell new products. One example is the expansion of Sears, Roebuck and Co. into such areas as insurance (Allstate) and income tax services (H&R Block). Once consumers are under the Sears roof to purchase merchandise, Sears personnel can presumably sell them these and other services. Restaurants in hotels and movie theater concession stands are other examples.

Another type of direct market linkage is exploited when a company uses the same distribution channel to distribute different products. For example, McDonald's hamburger outlets were sitting vacant during the early-morning hours, so the company introduced breakfast foods: same distribution channel, new products. Similarly, Bic exploited synergies in distributing disposable cigarette lighters and safety razors through the same outlets that it had developed to sell its highly successful disposable ballpoint pens.

A third type of direct market linkage is the use of brand identification to develop and market totally unrelated products. A vivid example in recent times is the broad line of products tied to the immensely popular *Star Wars* films: toys, clothing, comic books, and so on. The success of the Head metal tennis racquet can be directly attributed to the successful, high-quality brand image gained by the original Head skis. Similarly, Porsche sunglasses and polo shirts capitalize on the Porsche image.

Technology Linkages

A second kind of direct linkage occurs through technology. A company experiences direct technology linkages when it uses the same operations technology to manufacture a variety of products or render a variety of services. For example, General Motors manufactures not only automobiles but also trucks and locomotives. The Bic Pen Corporation applied the same plastic-injection molding technology to the manufacture of a variety of products—the same skills, assembly processes, and raw materials were used for each of its disposable pen, cigarette lighter, and safety razor product lines.

Another type of technology linkage occurs when corporations find that they can sell by-products to an external market. For example, the chemicals that were originally a waste by-product of the petroleum refining process formed the foundation for today's petrochemical industry. Exxon Chemicals is a major player in this market and represents a technology linkage to the original Standard Oil Company, which refined gasoline and kerosene products.

Product Linkages

A product linkage occurs as a company extends its product line to new markets. This happens, for example, when the company provides the same products or services to buyers in new geographic locations, as do most franchises and many multinational corporations. Another product linkage occurs when a vertically integrated company experiences excess capacity at different points backward or forward along the product flow chain and can market these products or services externally. For example, General Motors can market its Delco radio products independently of its automobile dealerships. The United Fruit Company, which extrudes plastic bags for use in packaging bananas in Central America, fills excess capacity by supplying local bakeries with printed bread bags.

Why is it important to understand direct linkages in a company? For one, it is a convenient way of identifying the company's corporate strategy and isolating which parts of the corporation are closely, or loosely, related to the rest of the corporation. Second, it can provide clues to high-potential expansion opportunities.

A useful way of conducting a linkage analysis is to diagram the direct linkages within a company. For example, Figure 9-4 illustrates the direct linkages among Bic Pen Corporation's businesses. Where our analysis shows that direct linkages exist between any two businesses, we draw a line. Next to the line we draw a T, P, or M wherever there is a technology, product, or market linkage, respectively. As illustrated in the diagram, the ballpoint pen, felt-tip pen, disposable cigarette lighter, and disposable safety razor businesses all have very solid, direct linkages between them. In contrast, the disposable pantyhose business was one in which there was no shared sales force or distribution channel (the pantyhose were sold in supermarkets, whereas most Bic pens were sold in drugstores), the production technology was different— textiles versus injection-molded plastic—and the function of the product was totally unlike that of the previous products. Correspondingly, our diagram shows no direct linkages between this business and the others. Not surprisingly, Bic's attempted entry into the pantyhose business failed.

Figure 9-4
Direct and Indirect Linkages: Bic Pen Corporation

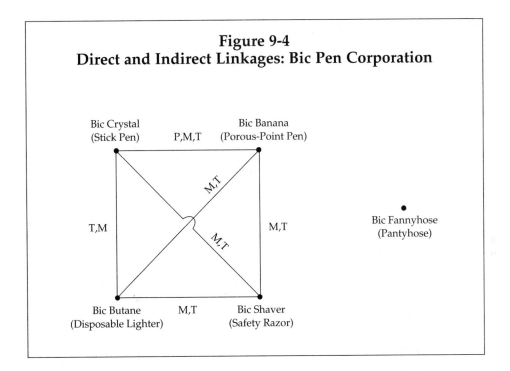

The Bic example is one of a relatively simple and uncomplicated corporation. Linkage analysis becomes particularly useful when a company consists of a variety of businesses and grows to a level of considerable complexity. For example, consider the Indo Jaya Corporation in Southeast Asia. Indo Jaya is a large producer of instant noodles in one of the fastest-growing regions of the world. The corporation was built by an aggressive entrepreneur who started a variety of companies in different lines of business (see Table 9-1). Although some of these businesses were originally set up to complement the manufacture of noodles—for example, the plastics packaging firm provided retail packaging for the noodles—many of the businesses, such as the motorcycle dealership, were started as a means of investing the cash flow from the original business. When the entrepreneur wanted to make greater sense out of the collection of businesses he had assembled and to build an integrated corporation, he applied a linkage analysis. At first glance, his business seemed to be a rather jumbled collection, as diagramed in Figure 9-5. After going through the logic of linkage analysis, however, the picture of his corporation was clarified and resulted in the diagram shown in Figure 9-6. Notice how Figure 9-6 "cleans up" the depiction of the relationships among the different parts of the Indo Jaya businesses. As a result of this analysis, the firm's executives gained a clearer understanding of their corporation and could then make critical

Table 9-1
Indo Jaya Corporation

DISTRIBUTION COMPANY
(IMPORT/EXPORT)
Noodles
Beer
Confectionery
Printing inks
Office supplies

INSTANT NOODLES
MANUFACTURE

WOOD PRODUCTS
MANUFACTURE
Toothpicks
Pencils
Rulers and yardsticks

PRINTING AND
PACKAGING CO.
Offset printing
Flexible packaging

PLASTIC PRODUCTS
MANUFACTURING
Fishing line
Fishing net
Polyester
Polyethylene sheets
Polyethylene bags

IJ MUSICAL AND
DISTRIBUTION
Pianos
Band instruments
Guitars
Amplifiers and electrical

MOTORCYCLES
Yamaha distributorship
Motorcycle parts and service

TRADING COMPANY
Cooking oil
Spices and condiments
Toiletries

strategic decisions about which parts of the business should be emphasized and which might be candidates for divestiture. (The musical distribution business was eventually divested through a leveraged buyout to the division general manager.)

Figure 9-5
Indo Jaya's Jumble of Businesses

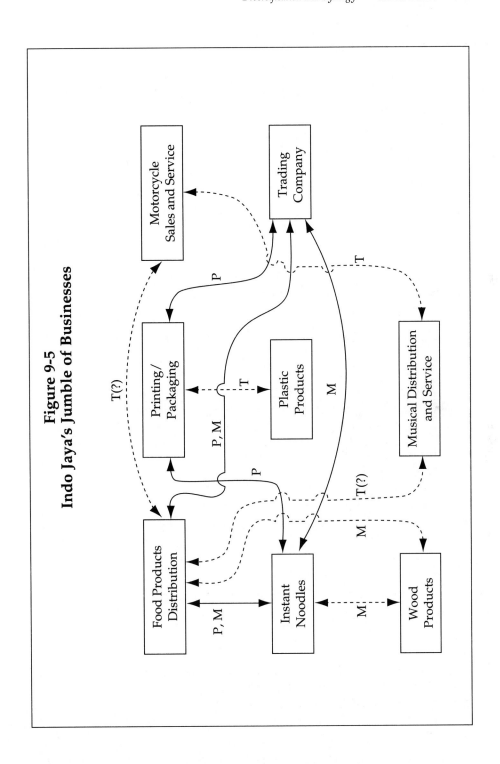

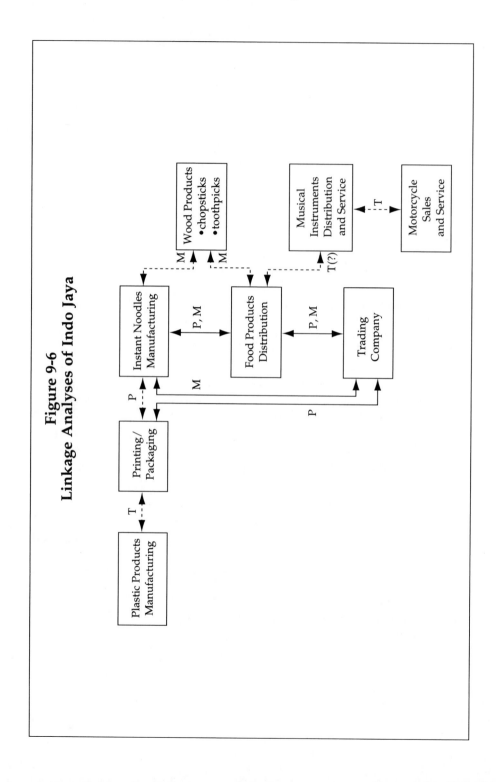

Figure 9-6
Linkage Analyses of Indo Jaya

MACGREGOR GOLF COMPANY

HELSINKI, SEPTEMBER 1986

As they invited their American guests into the sauna at corporate head-quarters, Leif Ekstrom, president of Amer Group, Heikki O. Salonen, chairman, and Kai Luotenon, head of corporate planning and development, wondered what price and terms they would have to offer to get MacGregor Golf Company.

At the same time, fatigued from their round of golf immediately following their arrival at Helsinki airport from Albany, Georgia, George Nichols, president of MacGregor, Nick Sarge, chief operating officer, and George Chane, representing Jack Nicklaus, owner, looked forward to heat-induced relaxation, a warm shower, and sleep.

As the unaccustomed whiff of heat hit him, Chane thought of Jack Nicklaus's lifelong association with MacGregor Golf, wondering if Jack could ever really part with it. Nichols leaned back and shut his eyes: "Ahh, this heat feels wonderful!" After working hard to turn the business around, he now dreamed of finally having enough cash to grow MacGregor to its full potential.

"Well, gentlemen, shall we begin?" said Salonen softly.

AMER GROUP, SPRING 1986

Ekstrom, new president and chief operating officer of Amer Group, had studied much about Amer Group's businesses prior to his official appointment in April, so when Salonen decided to sell off the poorly performing ice hockey business, Ekstrom was in agreement. During and after the ice hockey spinoff, however, they considered other opportunities in the sports and leisure industries; in spite of the ice hockey failure, sporting goods seemed to fit Amer's strategy. Although segments of the sporting goods industry were highly competitive, especially since the entry of many Far East companies,

This case was written by Ann Yungmeyer under the supervision of Professor L. J. Bourgeois III. Copyright © 1988 by the University of Virginia Darden School Foundation, Charlottesville, VA. All rights reserved.

and profits were generally not high, the general feeling among Amer's executives was that Amer, over the years, had learned many lessons about the industry and had created a strong image in commercial and financial markets. Interest in sports, leisure time, and sales of sports casual wear, which had been termed "an exploding fashion" by Ekstrom, were growing.

Salonen focused right away on the golf business and, to a lesser extent, tennis: "Tennis is the more competitive of the two segments, and the established brand names in tennis are very strong. Golf is a rapidly growing sport, more than 10 percent a year, especially in Europe and Japan." In comparing golf with ice hockey, he noted, "It is not so much a seasonal sport, except in Scandinavia. Golf markets are broader, and it can be a family sport, to include women, children, and retirees. You can play golf for 60 or 70 years of your life." As to the business, he continued, "Margins are higher, and golf companies are making money. Golf is a sport [that], at present, does not fluctuate with the economy, [because] golfers seem to be in good financial health."

Because Amer Group's business-development team was continuously researching many possibilities for growth, it was not unusual to have 20 projects going on at the same time. In addition, because Amer Group was well known for sporting goods among foreign investment bankers, at any given time there were literally "hundreds of choices" for acquisitions, as one Amer executive phrased it. In May 1986, one of Amer Group's U.S. institutional investors called and asked if Amer would be interested in contacting Jack Nicklaus, owner of MacGregor Golf Company, about a possible buyout. Amer's development team immediately began researching the golf business, MacGregor, and its competitors. Outside consultants were contracted to conduct two separate research studies of industry and competitive factors.

THE GOLF EQUIPMENT INDUSTRY

Historically, the number of golfers had correlated closely with the number of golf facilities. In the United States, golf had two explosions: one in the 1920s and one that began in the 1950s with a crescendo in the 1960s (see Exhibit 1). The number of golfers in the United States was projected to grow to between 18.5 million and 23.5 million by 1990. In the year 2000, the number of golfers would be 20 million to 41.5 million. (The lower numbers assumed the same historical percentage of players by age category. Higher numbers assumed a 5 percent additional increase in participation, which is 50 percent of the growth that golf experienced during the 1960s boom era.) The National Golf Foundation was projecting that by the year 1990, the average golfer would play 25 rounds per year. By the year 2000, the average number of rounds played was projected to be 29 per golfer.

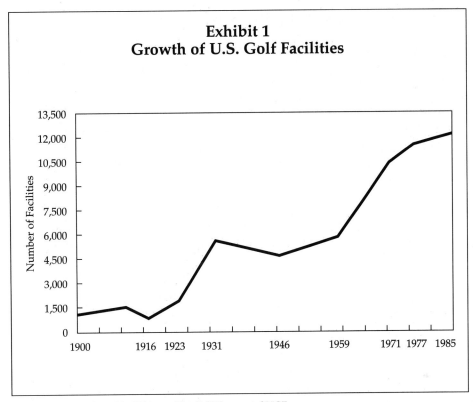

Exhibit 1
Growth of U.S. Golf Facilities

Source: G. Cornish and R. Whitten, *The Golf Course and NGF.*

Competitors selling to golfers in the United States could be divided into two segments: playing equipment and golf balls. In the equipment segment, MacGregor, Wilson, Ping, Spalding, and Hogan were the main competitors; while in the ball segment, Titleist and Spalding controlled the market. Internationally, the golf market was very fragmented, with MacGregor, Mizuno, Wilson, Dunlop-Slazinger, and Spalding serving roughly 25 percent of the market, and the remaining 75 percent being served by other companies.

THE PIMS STUDY

As part of its research on MacGregor's position in June 1986, Amer Group engaged a PIMS program analysis, a consulting approach based on the 1960 General Electric project that studied the profit impact of market strategies

(PIMS).[1] Amer Group made the results of the PIMS study available to MacGregor as well.

PIMS evaluated MacGregor in terms of its four business units: U.S. clubs and bags, international clubs and bags, soft goods, and golf balls. Among its conclusions were that MacGregor's 8-percent market-share position in golf clubs and bags was fifth behind Wilson (20-percent share), Ping (11 percent), Spalding, and Hogan (10 percent each). Internationally, its share was 6 percent, whereas no other company held more than 5 percent of the non-U.S. market. MacGregor's U.S. positions in golf balls (1-percent share) and soft goods (4 percent) were relatively minor.

MacGregor's 1986 total sales of $37.2 million and investment of $18.5 million were distributed as follows:

	Sales	Investment
U.S. clubs and bags	72%	67%
International clubs and bags	10	18
Soft goods	11	6
Golf balls	7	9

The company's actual return on investment compared with PAR ROI (see footnote 1) by segment for 1986 was as follows:

	Actual ROI	PAR ROI
U.S. clubs and bags	28%	14%
International clubs and bags	−7	6
Soft goods	35	16
Golf balls	−38	2

---

[1]The PIMS approach used a detailed multiple regression analysis of the profit experiences for many businesses. The processed data were expected to answer, based on the experiences of other businesses operating under similar conditions, the following: (1) what profit rate is normal for a given business, (2) if the business continues on its current track, what will its future operating results be, (3) what strategic changes in the business have promise of improving these results, and (4) how will profitability or cash flow change given a specific future strategy? The basic idea behind PIMS was to provide top managers with insight and information on expected profit performance of different kinds of businesses under different competitive conditions. Among the factors investigated and analyzed were market share, total marketing expenditures, product quality, R&D expenditures, and investment intensity. Thirty-five factors accounted for more than 80 percent of the variation in profit in the 600 business units analyzed in the PIMS database. Reports generated from the PIMS analysis included the PAR report, which specified the return on investment (ROI) that was normal (or par) for similar businesses. It also identified the major strengths and weaknesses of the particular business that accounted for the variation in PAR ROI when compared with all businesses in the PIMS database.

For the total operation, historical and projected ROI and PAR ROI were estimated to be as follows:

| | Historical | | | Projected | | | |
	1983	1984	1985	1986	1987	1988	1989
PAR ROI	17%	28	11	12	14	17	21
Actual/Planned ROI	21	−1	8	17	22	25	28

A financial forecast by PIMS is given in Exhibit 2. In general, PIMS concluded that MacGregor had a potential overall ROI of at least 15 percent if relative product quality were improved, investment intensity were reduced (by, say, reducing inventory), and capacity utilization increased.

MacGregor seemed to fit the Amer product image—high-quality, brand-recognized goods. MacGregor's products fell in line with Amer's strategy of obtaining a trademark and using brand development. It was an established company in an industry that offered growth opportunities, especially in international markets. Yet Amer Group had identified certain risks concerning the golf business and MacGregor specifically. According to Salonen, one concern was MacGregor's dependence on subcontractors in the Far East, where 80 percent of sporting goods were (at least partially) manufactured. One group of suppliers was supplying all of the major competitors with golf shafts and heads. A second area of concern was MacGregor's very dramatic history: it was a 90-year-old company that had been nearly bankrupt several times. A closer look at the company's history and management seemed wise.

HISTORY OF MACGREGOR GOLF COMPANY

In 1874 a Scotsman named John MacGregor bought an interest in the Crawford Brothers shoe-last manufacturing operation founded in Dayton, Ohio. He introduced his partners to golf just as the United States was beginning to take to the game. Near the turn of the century, one year after A. G. Spalding Company became the first American company to sell its own clubs, MacGregor began making golf clubs with the same persimmon wood used in shoe lasts. In 1920 the shoe-last company was sold, and golf equipment became MacGregor's main business.

Following the Great Depression years in the 1930s, business suffered and the ailing MacGregor was sold to another sporting goods firm, P. Goldsmith Sons. Over the next few years, a revived MacGregor set most of the industry standards for quality and innovation. At the time, an established practice was for golf professionals (pros) to be under contract to specific equipment companies, but MacGregor saw a connection missing between club makers, the pros, and the best players. In order to bridge this void, MacGregor created customized clubs for pros and attracted stars such as Toney Penna, Ben

Exhibit 2
PIMS Projections (1986–1989) of MacGregor
Financial Performance
($ millions)

	1983	1984	1985	1986	1987	1988	1989
INCOME STATEMENT							
Sales	49,9	52,3	34,0	37,2	43,3	47,0	50,5
Purchases	23,8	28,6	15,8	19,1	23,5	24,9	26,4
Value added	26,1	23,6	18,2	18,1	19,8	22,1	24,2
Manufacturing and distribution	10,9	11,2	8,9	8,3	8,1	9,1	10,2
Depreciation	0,1	0,3	0,4	0,5	0,5	0,5	0,5
Gross margin	15,1	12,1	8,9	9,3	11,3	12,5	13,5
Marketing	8,2	9,6	5,7	4,5	5,3	5,4	5,7
R&D	0,5	0,5	0,5	0,4	0,4	0,4	0,4
G & A	1,8	2,2	1,3	1,3	1,5	1,7	1,8
PBIT	4,6	−0,2	1,4	3,0	4,0	5,0	5,6
ROS (%)	9,2	−0,3	4,1	8,1	9,3	10,6	11,0
ROI (%)	21,0	−0,9	8,1	16,5	22,2	25,5	27,2
BALANCE SHEET							
Receivables	12,9	14,8	11,3	11,7	11,8	13,5	14,5
Inventories	16,8	15,6	8,6	8,3	8,9	8,3	8,3
Current liabilities	8,6	8,7	6,2	5,1	5,5	5,9	6,1
Working capital	21,0	21,8	13,7	14,9	15,3	15,9	16,8
GBV[a] of plant and equipment	0,8	2,0	2,6	2,7	2,9	3,6	4,1
Accumulated depreciation	0,1	0,2	0,7	0,8	1,1	1,7	2,1
NBV[b] of plant and equipment	0,7	1,8	2,1	1,9	1,8	1,9	2,0
Other assets	0,2	1,6	1,4	1,6	1,0	1,6	1,7
Investment	21,9	25,2	17,1	18,5	18,1	19,4	20,5

[a]Gross book value.
[b]Net book value.
Source: PIMS report to Amer, June 1986.

Hogan, and Louise Suggs to the "MacGregor family" advisory staff. In addition to the technical expertise they brought to the company, these staff players also enhanced the firm's reputation and image.

The winning records and popularity of MacGregor's touring staff players contributed an important measure to the company's postwar success. Between 1937 and 1959, MacGregor's staff won 8 U.S. Open titles, 11 Masters, and 10 PGA championships—adding up to about 37 percent of all major championships during that period. In addition, impartial counts taken at tournaments during the postwar years consistently revealed that more than 50 percent of the fields in PGA events used MacGregor woods and irons.

Even as MacGregor was enhancing its image by contracting professional golfers, it continued to acknowledge and cultivate young talent. Players using MacGregor clubs captured British or U.S. amateur titles 12 times between 1946 and 1961.

Selling Strategy

MacGregor focused on selling high-end equipment. Because retailers were generally more price sensitive than quality conscious, MacGregor chose to distribute its premium equipment through the pro shops, which were more concerned with product attributes. "Don't just sell the most; sell the best," was the philosophy. Approximately 75 percent of company sales were made through pro shops, and 25 percent through retailers. As a result, MacGregor built a commanding position in the professional golf market, with about 40-percent share during the 1940s and 1950s. The company entered the apparel and accessories segment also, selling sportswear and shoes during World War II.

While tour staff players helped promote MacGregor equipment, sales came from the efforts of golf-club shop professionals. To make the pro policy work, MacGregor management needed direct salespeople who could gain the respect of golf professionals. Personal relationships were a key to success in such a business environment, so the company assembled a team of salespeople who understood golf and were themselves outstanding players. In addition, a common industry practice was to grant extended payment terms (up to five months, prior to the spring season). MacGregor often financed small pro shops until they made a sale. The result was that receivables represented up to 40 percent of total assets.

The Ball Controversy

Although MacGregor manufactured its own clubs, it subcontracted the production of a complete line of pro and dealer golf balls to the Worthington Ball Company of Elyria, Ohio. The pro ball "Tourney" sold well, and pros such as Ben Hogan, Demaret, and Nelson had used it regularly in all the major tournaments.

Following World War II, MacGregor decided to produce its own golf balls. The first run of balls was a disaster, however, because of MacGregor's lack of expertise in ball manufacturing and quality control. Every player who tried them decided to keep away from the "new" Tourney balls. This negative perception about the Tourney stuck in the minds of the golfing community, and the ball never recovered. "In golf," said an expert, "a ball becomes an old familiar friend. And even if it slices now and then, or betrays [a golfer] at the lips of cups, the player will not change to another brand unless there is a very severe circumstance." Even the firm's own contracted professionals resisted changing over to the Tourney. Tour players were required to play with the company ball, but most of them switched to other balls surreptitiously.

Changes in materials and production methods eventually rectified the ball problem. By 1953 MacGregor executives believed the new ball ranked at least equal with any other brand, but perceptions were hard to change. Players still refused to use the company ball. Management then tried to force the issue by passing a "play the Tourney, or else!" edict, an action that produced a lot of ill will. Ben Hogan was the first to leave as a result of this controversy, and he was soon followed by other professionals who would not use the MacGregor ball. Hogan founded a competing golf-equipment company shortly after. The exodus of top professionals tarnished the company's image and seemed to symbolize the decline of MacGregor Golf Company in a new, more competitive industry.

Change of Ownership

In 1958, after a few years of poor financial performance, MacGregor was sold to Brunswick-Balke-Collender Co. of Chicago for roughly $5 million. Brunswick, a respected company in the sporting goods industry, had significant presence in the bowling-equipment business.

Brunswick's management style deviated significantly from that of the former MacGregor leaders. Ted Bensinger, president of Brunswick, used sophisticated accounting methods and the most modern and efficient ways to increase production. The studied, impersonal culture of the new parent company began to replace the easygoing, family-style atmosphere at MacGregor. "To some of the older MacGregor workers, it was as if all of a sudden this big corporation waltzed in and changed MacGregor," said Nick Sarge, chief operating officer at MacGregor. "The core group of individuals now working for Brunswick were making more money and had better benefits than ever before, but they weren't as happy."

Bensinger had an ambition to make Brunswick the country's largest sporting goods conglomerate within five years. Naturally, MacGregor could not therefore keep serving just the pro market; extension into the retail market was imperative if it was to meet its goal of becoming *the* largest golf company owned by *the* largest sporting goods firm. Because the retail market demanded volume, not painstaking concern for the perfection of each club, in 1960 Brunswick expanded the golf division by adding a low-cost facility in Albany, Georgia, to service the retail golf equipment segment. The Ohio facility continued to produce the custom pro clubs.

MacGregor executives did not favor this redirection, which meant competing head-on with Wilson, a company that had dominated the retail market for 30 years. The market's reception was equally unenthusiatic: MacGregor posted a loss of $4 million in 1964. The company's share of the retail market remained at a low 3 percent, although it still commanded 30 percent of the pro market.

If there was a saving grace for MacGregor during the 1960s, it was the company's continued ability to recognize top golfing talent. Arnold Palmer began his career playing MacGregor clubs, as did Gene Littler. The best catch, made in the late 1950s, was a big kid with a crew cut whom the media called "Ohio Fats." His name was Jack Nicklaus.

The Nicklaus name began paying dividends for MacGregor early. In the first five years after signing his contract, the company used the Jack Nicklaus name exclusively on dealer-line equipment, and the name had significant impact in the retail arena as well.

Troubled financial times continued, however, throughout the 1960s and 1970s. In response, management closed the Ohio facility and consolidated all manufacturing in Albany, where the production of both custom and retail clubs was comingled. The new location had its problems, however. "The basic problem with the Albany plant was that retail clubs did not require the same care [that] pro-line clubs did," Sarge recalled. "A consulting firm recommended that we construct a wall to separate the manufacturing of custom and retail clubs. You couldn't craft pro clubs next to retail and not expect the quality of pro clubs to suffer."

In 1979 the Wickes Company purchased the MacGregor Golf division from Brunswick, while Equilink purchased all nongolf MacGregor sporting goods. Wickes provided temporary relief by pumping much needed capital into the Albany factory but soon came into its own financial problems. In 1982, several weeks before declaring bankruptcy, Wickes looked for a buyer for MacGregor.

Jack Nicklaus, who had played with MacGregor clubs since he was 11 years old, had by 1982 been associated with the firm for more than 20 years through equipment contracts and his advisory role in golf-club design. Already the owner of a company called Golden Bear, Nicklaus decided he now wanted a stake in MacGregor.

A New Phase Begins

In 1982, leveraging the assets of MacGregor Golf, Golden Bear borrowed money from banks to acquire 80 percent of MacGregor stock, and Clark

Johnson, senior vice president at Wickes, bought the rest. By January 1984, the original debt of $14.5 million had grown to $30 million, and the losses continued. Nicklaus thus sought the advice of George Chane, a friend and well-known "no-nonsense" consultant and trouble shooter, to identify problems at MacGregor.

On the advice of Chane, Nicklaus bought out Clark Johnson's 20-percent share of the company and began looking for a new president. "Our bank showed up with the attorneys wanting the keys to the front door and to liquidate the company," recalled one MacGregor executive. "George Chane requested several weeks to prepare a plan and began a massive program to streamline the company." He cut overhead by moving corporate offices from Atlanta to Albany. He implemented a hard asset-management program by reducing inventory through price reductions and by collecting receivables, and one "Black Friday" he reduced the work force by one-third. "Chane did what he could on one end—cutting expenses and getting overhead down—but now it was time to turn to selling our way out."

In July 1984, Nicklaus hired George Nichols as the new president. Nichols had been president of Johnston and Murphy Shoe Company for ten years and, before joining MacGregor, was the president of the Bostonian Shoe Division of Clarke's of England, a company where Nicklaus had held a royalty contract for several years.

A study done by a consulting firm about this time identified the strengths and weaknesses of MacGregor. Brand recognition, credibility of Jack Nicklaus and his reputation in the market, inventory management, and expense control were the strong areas in the company. On the other hand, MacGregor needed to regain its reputation as an "innovator," consolidate its marketing and planning skills, revive the lackluster sales organization, and strengthen the distribution channels. Financial position, too, was weak, as net worth was negative, and working capital needs were being met by asset-based loans from Union Bank of California, which had attached severely restrictive covenants.

Nichols thus came into a bleak situation at MacGregor. "Morale was extremely low. Executives were working 12-hour days, seven days a week, trying to keep the company afloat," recalled John Baldwin, vice president of marketing and sales, who had been with MacGregor since the early Brunswick days. Earl Saxman, director of marketing, who came on board about the same time as George Nichols as a "hired gun," commented that he would never have taken the job if he had known how bad a shape MacGregor was in at the time: "There was no capital; the bank kept us in business and really did yeoman's work for us."

Besides financial woes, MacGregor also had product problems. As Nichols explained, "We were seen as a classic company [that] made traditional clubs; we were not regarded as innovators. We had a polarized product line which was big in the low-end and small in the high-end, with nothing in the middle range—at the price points where customers were willing to buy.

MacGregor had relied on a manufacturing mentality, but in the highly competitive modern golf industry, a successful company needed a marketing mentality."

Over the next two years, Nichols implemented a strategic plan whose objective was to get the company profitable and attract an infusion of badly needed capital. He withdrew the company from the golf-ball business, where it had no meaningful market share. He then reorganized the sales function to cut the number of territory sales representatives and regional managers, and he improved the compensation plan.

The product line was segmented by price point and the development of "game improvement" clubs. MacGregor was moving away from its heritage of traditional woods and forged irons to the popular metal woods and a new casting process for irons. Several old-model clubs were dropped, and new designs were introduced—most notably, wedges and putters. The company adopted a "good, better, best" strategy with price/value, proven quality, and innovation being the respective key selling points. Other product lines such as golf bags, rain gear, and gloves were extended, a shirt and sweater line was introduced, and MacGregor entered the golf-shoe market.

Meanwhile, after a difficult period of tournament defeats, Jack Nicklaus began putting with the new Response ZT, which MacGregor had introduced at the 1986 PGA show in January. When the Masters rolled around at Augusta, Georgia, in April 1986, Nicklaus achieved his comeback victory. The morning after this victory, MacGregor received 5,000 orders for the Response ZT. MacGregor then increased its advertising budget from $300,000 to $1,000,000 and changed the message to both consumers and the trade to emphasize the following three points: (1) MacGregor makes products to help you play a better game and to enjoy the game; (2) the greatest player in the history of the game, Jack Nicklaus, is directly involved in the design, quality assurance, and performance of our products; and (3) MacGregor sets the quality standards for the golf industry.

The Nichols Management Style

George Nichols was described by his associates at MacGregor as "dictatorial, opinionated, and very demanding." Said one executive, "We had some loud meetings; he stepped forward and really ran the show. He was a taskmaster. George quickly identified weak links and weeded out several people."

Nichols' plan for MacGregor required improved communication throughout all levels of the management organization: "The plan specified that everyone in the organization must know what the company is trying to do and why; everyone must feel that [they are] accountable for results; everyone must truly believe that their contribution is meaningful; and everyone must be informed." The process of achieving those objectives included a weekly meeting of the key executives in each operative area—sales and marketing, administration, engineering, and manufacturing. The meetings examined business on the basis of the happenings of the previous week that would require greater coordination among the different functional areas, and they also served as an important communication device across the management layers.

The changes implemented by Nichols began to pay off in his first year. In 1984, MacGregor made a small operating profit but was still unable to service its debt. The loan was renegotiated at a more favorable interest rate. In the second year, the company made a small pretax profit, but it was insufficient for both debt service and funding additional growth. Nichols reflected, "Things were looking up because we now knew the company *could* produce a profit."

The recovery was given a boost by breakthroughs in new product development. Jack Nicklaus's success with the Response ZT putter in the 1986 Masters and Chi Chi Rodriguez's endorsement of CG 1800 woods and irons in the same year spurred the sales of MacGregor clubs. With these two successes, MacGregor reestablished its presence in the premium market segment. Confident that the business could be run profitably, Nichols laid out optimistic plans to grow and consolidate the firm's position in the industry. "Now that we had our act together," he affirmed, "we wanted to flex a little muscle." For that purpose, he estimated MacGregor had an immediate cash need of $10 million.

The high debt from the 1982 leveraged buyout ruled out borrowing from financial institutions, so the only option was an equity infusion. Nichols and Nicklaus considered taking the company public or forming a partnership with an individual or a group of investors, but neither option seemed feasible because Nicklaus wanted to retain majority interest to be able to run the company the way he wanted.

In March of 1986, in a telephone conversation with an old friend from his shoe business days, George Nichols was referred to a venture capitalist in Minneapolis. Although the venture capitalist turned out not to be interested in MacGregor, he knew a banker in Finland, who then introduced MacGregor to Amer Group.

A MERGER POSSIBILITY

In May 1986, following an initial meeting with Kai Luotenon of Amer Group, George Nichols met with Jack Nicklaus's executive committee to ascertain the interests and needs of the the three stakeholders in a merger: MacGregor, Jack Nicklaus (represented by Golden Bear), and Amer Group. The perspectives of the three players as they evaluated the option are briefly discussed in the following sections.

(The concerns of MacGregor and Golden Bear are presented in more detail in a companion case, MacGregor Golf Company (B-1): MacGregor [UVA-BP-0293], and those of Amer in MacGregor Golf Company (B-2): Amer [UVA-BP-0294].)

MacGregor

The real needs of MacGregor were clear: the company needed cash to pursue future opportunities, and it could not borrow any more. As an aid to Nichols's analysis, he prepared a financial forecast to 1990 for presentation to the Amer executives (see Exhibit 3).

Exhibit 3
Financial Data Summary: MacGregor Golf
(1984–1986 actual; projected to 1990)
($000s)

	1984[a]	1985[b,c]	1986[c]	1987	1988	1989	1990
Net sales	52,583	34,292	38,615	44,641	48,754	52,212	55,320
Operating profit	−387	1,182	2,654	4,500	5,406	5,876	6,415
%	−0.7	3.4	6.9	10.1	11.1	11.3	11.6
Pretax profit	−4,543	−1,890	237	2,281	3,766	4,303	5,093
%	−8.6	−5.5	0.6	5.1	7.7	8.2	9.2
Net income	−5,206	−1,932	237	1,859	2,459	2,810	3,326
%	−9.9	−5.6	0.6	4.2	5.0	5.4	6.0
Average bank debt	23,576	18,681	19,035	15,667	12,967	11,461	9,756
Average net assets[c]	26,023	17,242	18,927	20,115	21,954	23,175	24,472
Ending equity	−3,228	−658	261	8,052	10,511	13,324	16,625
Average RONA %	−20.0	−11.2	1.3	8.9	11.2	12.1	13.6
Average ROI %	n/a	n/a	n/a	33.9	27.4	24.0	22.6
Asset turnover	1.49	1.45	1.59	1.69	1.77	1.79	1.81

Notes to Amer Management:
These pro forma financial data incorporate the fiscal year 1987 revised budget presented to the Union Bank on September 16, 1986, with the following additional assumptions:
  1. Equity infusion of $5 million in November 1986
  2. Royalty accrual of $1,009,000 reclassified to equity
  3. Nicklaus royalty of $400,000 paid to Nicklaus semi-annually

Footnotes to Summary:
[a]Fiscal 1984 includes the results of operations for Japan for the entire year, while fiscal 1985 includes the results of operations for Japan for five months. Japan is now accounted for by the equity method of accounting.
[b]Fiscal 1985 net loss of $1,932 does not reflect a gain on sale of Japan of $4,273.
[c]Depreciation (not shown) = $346,000 in 1985; $339,000 in 1986.

Golden Bear

For Jack Nicklaus, the thought of selling MacGregor was an emotional issue. He had played with MacGregor clubs since childhood and had always wanted to "control the tools of my trade." He took a great deal of pride in having his peers praise his equipment on tour. He did not want to sell the business, but he knew he had no other choice. A key concern for Nicklaus was being able to liquidate the $4.5 million of MacGregor-related liabilities he had accumulated, as well as recouping the $1,009,000 in accrued royalties from MacGregor.

Amer Group

Having gone through the analyses of the golf industry and of MacGregor, Heikki Salonen wanted to get to know MacGregor's management; so he invited them to Helsinki in July for plant visits, golf, saunas, Russian dinners, and conversation. Following a full day of informal discussions, he began to feel confidence in MacGregor's management and optimism about the future outlook for the company.

THE DEAL: SEPTEMBER 1986

George Nichols knew how to answer the question that Amer Group was asking, "What do you want for your company?" but as he and the Golden Bear executives traveled to Finland for the preliminary negotiations, he was anticipating a complicated twist to the proceedings because the three parties had different interests. He knew he would be in a tough "middle position of the triangle," serving as both conduit and peacemaker. His challenge would be to "stay true to 'x' amount of cash infusion" for MacGregor.

HEWLETT-PACKARD (CONDENSED)

For John Young, the 53-year-old president of Hewlett-Packard (HP), 1986 was shaping up as the worst year in recent history. Not only were profits declining, but with the electronics industry slumping and with HP now using fewer internally manufactured components in its products, HP was overstaffed by 1,500 to 2,000 people. Furthermore, HP had "bet the store" on a radical technology to stay in the computer business. By mid-1986 it was clear that what some were calling the "biggest gamble" in the company's 47-year history had encountered new delays. Dave Packard, age 73, and Bill Hewlett, age 72, controlled 30 percent of the company's stock but would soon be playing a much smaller role in the company than in the past. The future course for HP was largely in Young's hands.

COMPANY BACKGROUND

In 1939 Bill Hewlett and Dave Packard, both Stanford graduates, set up shop in a one-car garage. Their first product was a new type of audio oscillator used to test sound equipment; Walt Disney Studios ordered eight of them to improve the sound in the movie *Fantasia*. HP's products for the first 20 years were primarily electronic test and measurement instruments for engineers and scientists. Since then HP had added computers, peripherals, calculators, medical electronic equipment, instrumentation for chemical analysis, and solid-state components.

The HP Way

During the company's early years, the founders developed a number of management concepts that evolved into a set of corporate objectives and a business style known as "the HP Way." First put into writing in 1957, these objectives remained the fundamental, active guiding forces at HP. The HP

This case, a condensation of UVA-BP-268, was prepared by Professor L. J. Bourgeois III. The original case was prepared by Professor William E. Fulmer. Copyright © 1989 by The University of Virginia Darden School Foundation, Charlottesville, VA. All rights reserved. Revised January 1994.

Way was reflected directly in a statement of company objectives distributed throughout the organization (see Exhibit 1). According to Dave Packard,

> Early in the history of the company, while thinking about how a company like this should be managed, I kept getting back to one concept: If we could simply get everybody to agree on what our objectives were and to understand what we were trying to do, then we could turn everybody loose and they would move along in a common direction.

In addressing a training class for company managers, Packard had observed,

> I think we've done a really remarkably good job to maintain this so-called "HP Spirit" as the company has grown larger. . . . Let's work on that because it is just one of the real strengths. It's the key to productivity and to leadership and continuing progress and success in our company.

One HP manager noted that the subtlety of the system made it difficult to describe:

> It is basically a faith in people to use their discretion and to be sure along the way to make some mistakes as well as to make some contributions in a way that, over time, generally will continue to take the company in the direction it wants to go—consistent with its basic underlying set of objectives. These objectives continue to drive us, they really do.

According to a vice president,

> There is something useful in not being too precise—a value to fuzziness. No one can really define the HP Way. If it weren't fuzzy, it would be a rule! This way leaves room for judgment. Without that, there wouldn't be room for the constant micro-reconciliations needed in a changing world. This is designed as an adaptive company.

Another vice president said,

> There's not a lot of flexibility in the way you use the process. The process has got a very good track record, and people don't like you to mess with it. Also, if individuals start to mess with the process, then I think the company breaks down pretty quickly.

New employees were not always enthusiastic. According to a relatively new MBA, "It can also feel intrusive. It can feel presumptuous, and it's much, much more demanding than any other company that I've ever been affiliated with. . . . You just have to do the right thing." Another relatively new employee described his adjustment to it:

> We hear about the "HP Way" almost ad nauseam. It's sort of "truth, justice, and the HP Way." I went through a real struggle with the concept. Initially exposed to it, I thought: Boy! There's an awful lot that makes sense. But I guess I came to the point where I said this is over-indoctrination . . . some of

Exhibit 1
Excerpts from HP's Statement of Corporate Objectives

The achievements of an organization are the result of the combined efforts of each individual in the organization working toward common objectives. These objectives should be clearly understood by everyone in the organization and should reflect the organization's basic character and personality.

Objectives

1. PROFIT: To achieve sufficient profit to finance our company growth and to provide the resources we need to achieve our other corporate objectives.

   . . . It is the one absolutely essential measure of our corporate performance over the long term. . . .

   . . . Our long-standing policy has been to reinvest most of our profits and to depend on this . . . to finance our growth. This can be achieved if our return on net worth is roughly equal to our sales growth rate.

   . . . Profits vary from year to year . . . our needs for capital also vary, and we depend on short-term bank loans to meet those needs. . . . However, loans are costly and must be repaid; thus, our objective is to rely on reinvested profits as our main source of capital.

   Meeting our profit objective requires that . . . every product . . . is considered a good value . . . , yet is priced to include an adequate profit.

2. CUSTOMERS: To provide products and services of the greatest possible value to our customers, thereby gaining and holding their respect and loyalty.

   . . . products that fill real needs and provide lasting value. . . .

3. FIELDS OF INTEREST: To enter new fields only when the ideas we have, together with our technical, manufacturing, and marketing skills, assure that we can make a needed and profitable contribution to the field.

   . . . The key to HP's prospective involvement in new fields is *contribution*. This means providing customers with something new and needed, not just another brand of something they can already buy.

4. GROWTH: To let our growth be limited only by our profits and our ability to develop and produce technical products that satisfy real customer needs.

(continued on next page)

(continued)

5. OUR PEOPLE: To help HP people share in the company's success, which they make possible; to provide job security based on their performance; to recognize their individual achievements; and to help them gain a sense of satisfaction and accomplishment from their work.

   . . . Relationships within the company depend upon a spirit of cooperation among individuals and groups, and an attitude of trust and understanding on the part of managers toward their people. These relationships will be good only if employees have faith in the motives and integrity of their peers, supervisors, and the company itself.

   . . . Job security is an important HP objective . . . the company has achieved a steady growth in employment by consistently developing good new products, and by avoiding the type of contract business that requires hiring many people, then terminating them when the contract expires. . . .

6. MANAGEMENT: To foster initiative and creativity by allowing the individual great freedom of action in attaining well-defined objectives.

   . . . insofar as possible, each individual at each level in the organization should make his or her own plans to achieve company objectives and goals. After receiving supervisory approval, each individual should be given a wide degree of freedom to work within the limitations imposed by these plans, and by our general corporate policies. . . .

7. CITIZENSHIP: To honor our obligations to society by being an economic, intellectual, and social asset to each nation and each community in which we operate.

   . . . to make sure that each of these communities is better for our presence.

Source: "Human Resources at Hewlett-Packard," pp. 28–29.

it must be baloney. I've come not quite full circle, but part way back to the realization that, gee, there is an awful lot that is distinctive, an awful lot that is good in the HP Way, an awful lot that as an employee I feel grateful for.

Telling company stories was part of The HP Way: Naming Bill's and Dave's first instrument the "200A" so that people would not know that they were just starting out; Dave's smashing of an instrument in a lab because it was poorly designed and unreliable; and the avoidance of layoffs in 1970 by having all employees take a 10-percent pay cut and work nine out of ten days (the "nine-day fortnight," in HP lore).

As the organization grew and word-of-mouth storytelling became more difficult, executive seminars and courses for supervisors were increased. Materials were presented to all HP employees, approximately 30 employees at a time, as a four half-day course called "Working at HP." The first part dealt with the history of HP and the HP Way, and the remaining sessions provided comprehensive coverage of personnel policies, performance evaluations, salary administration, and personal development. The program was considered most effective if attended after about six months of employment at HP.

Hiring Policies

HP tended to hire people straight out of college and steep them in the corporate tradition. According to a division manager,

> There are a lot of different types of people who have been successful in the company. There is no prescription for background. There probably *is* a prescription for style. If you look at the makeup of the Executive Committee or the Operations Council, there are very definitely some different personalities and different styles. But the similarities are probably greater than the differences when it comes to style. Each one of these people has strong belief in individual freedom. We can accept widely different backgrounds but don't accept divergent style.

Turnover (5 to 10 percent in 1983) was low by industry standards, and, even after leaving, many employees remained loyal. HP also had shown a willingness to rehire people who had left to try other fields or to start their own companies.

People were rarely hired directly as managers. As Packard explained,

> Now there are some who say that a person is a good manager who has mastered managerial technique; he can manage anything. Well, maybe he can. But I hold very strongly that he can manage it a hell of a lot better if he really knows the territory.

Structural Devices and Work Systems

At HP a division was an integrated, self-sustaining organization with a lot of independence. The objective was to create a working atmosphere that encouraged solving problems as close as possible to the level where they occurred.

HP worked to keep the product divisions relatively small (about 1,000 people) and well defined. In 1980 HP had 40 divisions and 10 groups, by 1982 more than 45 divisions and 12 groups (Exhibit 2). According to a general manager in 1982,

> New divisions tend to emerge when a particular product line becomes large enough to support its continued growth out of the profit it generates. Also, new divisions tend to emerge when a single division gets so large that the people involved start to lose their identification with the product line.

The product divisions were considered HP's tactical business units, each responsible for its own R&D, manufacturing, marketing, finance, and personnel management. All sales organizations reported to the group level (e.g., the Computer Group), however, and were separate from the product divisions. Divisions were kept small to allow considerable individual freedom while maintaining a focused business purpose.

Each of the six major product groups in 1982 had developed a selling strategy that was highly individualized for its particular market, yet according to the vice president of marketing,

> Many of our customers, especially the major accounts, need products and service from two, three, or more product lines. So there has to be a lot of interaction [among] the salespeople in servicing these customers. They have to work together as a team, using common sense as to who should lead the team.

Each division was measured along two dimensions: (1) financial results of the actual manufacturing of products in the division and (2) the total worldwide activity in the division's product lines, wherever they were manufactured. (Divisions could produce other divisions' products to improve service and reduce transportation costs around the world.) Reporting of worldwide results was accomplished by adjustments to the divisional profit-and-loss statement. Intracompany sales discounts (structured to minimize customs and tariffs) were reversed so the selling division would consider domestic and international customers evenly. Because of the many "incestuous" products, which divisions bought from each other, incorporated into more complex assemblies, and then sold as combined products, each division was allowed credit for only the value it added (which was negotiated among the divisions). In addition, a "license fee" was paid by divisions manufacturing products designed by other divisions. A division could thus be both receiving fees for products it had designed that were made by other divisions and also paying fees to other divisions for products of others it was making. These fees were percentages of sales revenues negotiated among the divisions.

The adjusted worldwide profit-and-loss statement was the basis for allocation of each division's R&D funds (usually 9 percent of sales). This policy rewarded the innovative divisions with additional funds for further innovation and acted as an indirect form of asset allocation. Plants started purely as desirable manufacturing activities could attain full divisional status only by

Exhibit 2
Hewlett-Packard Corporate Organization, November 1982

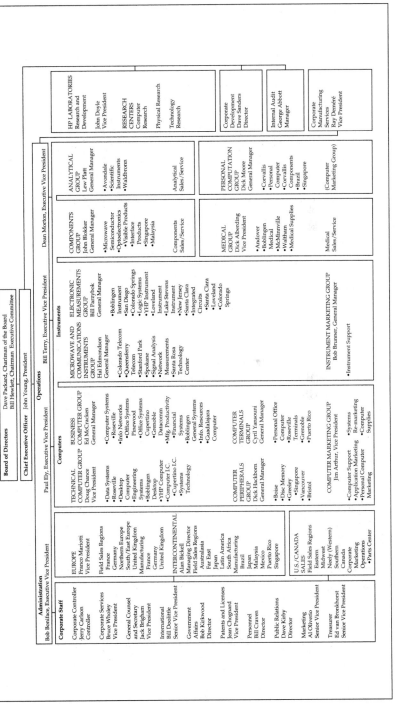

somehow creating a new product. Then it would be allocated R&D funds— the key to growth.

Balance sheets were produced only at the group level. HP felt that below that level the large allocations necessary for such items as corporate overhead, the sales force, and marketing assets created too much distortion to make the statements useful.

Capital allocations were negotiated during the yearly budgeting process. Although divisions were expected to be self-financing over any period of time, for start-ups or major expansions in any one year, a division might be allowed to spend more capital than it could provide for itself. Most capital-rationing negotiations were resolved within the group.

A corollary to the division and group focus was the moderate size and influence of the corporate staff. The special "cross-boundary" types of projects that were often undertaken by corporate staffs in other companies were at HP given to *ad hoc* task forces drawn from many parts of the company. According to Bill Hewlett,

> Our strength lies in the fact that our divisions have real freedom of choice in their operations, yet we have learned to talk across these divisional and group boundaries. This has enabled us to share our problems and strengths, thereby building a much stronger company.

HP used a large number of task forces and committees. Task forces were temporary assignments with a specified deadline. The task force would typically consist of five to ten people, often from different functions and levels within HP and including the people most affected by the particular project. Committees, or councils, were ongoing teams concerned with issues affecting either a single part of the company or the whole organization.

Packard described the cooperation as follows:

> One of the things that we have tried to achieve and I think we have achieved is this concept of teamwork. That's one of the reasons we don't have special awards for a division for something that it does particularly well. The only way this company is going to run successfully is if we can insure that there is a maximum flow of information and cooperation between all the elements of it.
>
> . . . I've often expressed this in terms that everyone in the company is equally important. It's just as important that the person who is responsible for sweeping the floor does a good job as it is if Bill and I do a good job.

Communications

Most places throughout HP had no doors to individual offices. Top executives, including the president, had offices within large administrative areas that were divided by freestanding, low partitions. An open-door policy was stressed. According to an HP group vice president,

Employees have every bit as much access to John Young as I do. They don't see him as frequently, because they don't have as many reasons to talk to him. But the door is as open to them as it is to me.

Common coffee breaks had become practically a ritual at HP, with the company providing coffee and croissants to all employees every morning and afternoon. There were periodic "beer busts" and picnics for the whole plant, often at recreational facilities owned by the company. Management meetings and retirement and division parties often included spoofs written by employees, and managers normally cooked and helped serve other employees at division picnics. Frequent plant meetings were held to discuss the latest company and plant news. A loudspeaker system allowed the announcement of company operating results and discussions of topics of general interest.

Managers at all levels were encouraged to spend a part of each day wandering through the organization, often without specific purpose other than to see what was going on and to build new channels of communication. This practice was called "management by wandering around" (MBWA). According to the HP employee magazine,

> There had to be a way of describing the extra step that HP managers needed to take in order to make the HP open-door policy truly effective. It was not enough to sit and wait for people to come through the door with their problems and ideas—they probably wouldn't in many cases. The managers had better get off their chairs and go out and get in touch with people. In that way people would know the managers were accessible whenever they had something important to communicate.
>
> Straightforward as it sounds, there are quite a few subtleties and requirements that go with MBWA. For one thing, it is not always easy for managers to do—so some of them do it reluctantly or infrequently. And its purpose is not always apparent to people—especially new HP people—at the receiving end of visits, so they may view it suspiciously and respond uneasily.

Promotion and Reward Systems

People at HP referred to the "career maze" to describe the cross-functional, cross-divisional, and lateral moves that often occurred. According to one employee, "If you're doing an excellent job within the HP context, that means you're affecting and involved with a lot of other people in a lot of functional areas. And as openings come up, there are going to be people aware of your skills. " A manager noted, "In my first eight years, I guess I had about seven or eight different jobs and four different functions. A couple of them were lateral moves." According to a group manager, another advantage of HP's frequent use of task forces was that "it also gives a lot of visibility to people."

All employees were salaried, and all aspects of salary administration were open. Each employee saw his or her wage curve and the one on the level above. Performance appraisal and salary administration made use of wage curves, where various levels were set to be competitive with relevant labor markets. Individual pay was set by a combination of relevant experience and "sustained performance," with the emphasis on performance. Within each wage curve, normal distribution was expected to result in 10 percent exceptional performers, 40 percent very good, 40 percent good, and 10 percent acceptable or new in the range. Unacceptable performance resulted in counseling, repositioning, or firing. Because sustained performance was emphasized, dramatic changes in performance were rare. Those whose performance declined were given small or no increases.

A bonus plan was initiated in 1940, and all employees were included in it, as well as being eligible for stock options. When an HP employee married, he or she was recognized by the gift of a silver bowl, and the birth of an employee's first child was recognized with a blanket.

In 1973 flexible hours were introduced for all HP employees. According to an HP group vice president, "People making PC boards here don't punch time clocks, and they haven't for over the 15 years I've been here. They do have flexible hours. They got them as soon as I did."

The HP Way of Doing Business

Just as the internal management of HP was dictated by the HP Way, an "HP Way of Doing Business" provided guidelines for running the company. First, HP maintained a pay-as-you-go attitude. The absence of long-term borrowing helped maintain a stable financial environment during depressed business periods. Packard noted the importance of this policy:

> In some industries, particularly those [that] require large capital investments, the pay-as-you-go approach is not feasible. There is also a school of thought in management that capital needs should be attained by leveraging equity financing with large amounts of debt. This school of thought says you can make your profits go further if you do this. Whatever the arguments, it is not Hewlett-Packard Company policy to lever our profits with long-term debt. We want every manager to know this and to act accordingly. . . . I see no possible circumstance that would justify a change.

According to a vice president,

> Our feeling is there is enough risk in the technology—we have all we can handle there. This philosophy provides great discipline all the way down. If you want to innovate, you must bootstrap. It is one of the most powerful, least understood influences that pervade the company.

A second major element of the HP Way of Doing Business was that any market expansion or leadership was based on new products. A dominant emphasis at HP had been for R&D to create products that would compete by new technical contributions rather than through marketing or other competitive devices. HP products were thoroughly designed, tested, and specified before being brought to market. HP's approach traditionally was to design its products first and worry about how much they were going to cost later. HP management had always placed great emphasis on product development programs, which they considered a fundamental strength of the company. An indication of the importance of this effort was the fact that more than half of 1982 orders came from products introduced during the prior three years.

HP avoided doing contract work and instead designed general-purpose devices suitable for a broad range of customers. All commercial customers bought from one catalog that listed almost all the products HP made. Only exterior modifications such as special colors or extra protection for environmental extremes were made. The basic designs or purposes of the instruments were not modified. These rules were the same for government purchases.

A focus on technical contributions and profit rather than volume had led HP to conclude that trying to gain market share with a low introductory price was not appropriate for the company. Dave Packard believed that "market share is not an objective, but a reward." He noted,

> It is just as easy to make a profit today as it will be tomorrow. There are, of course, occasions when actions should be taken [that] will jeopardize the short-term profit. These need to be considered very, very carefully because, more often than not, they tend to be rationalizations [that] simply put off what you should be doing today. . . .
>
> If a new product is really as good as we think it is going to be, we'll be able to sell more than we can make in the initial period anyway, and so you are jeopardizing the whole situation with really nothing to gain. . . . You can reduce the price later on, if, in fact, you are able to achieve your lower production costs and keep your costs down.

Another significant element of the HP Way of Doing Business was to stress honesty and integrity in all matters as a guiding principle for HP employees. For example, there was no tolerance for dishonest dealings with vendors or customers, and open and honest communication with employees and stockholders alike was stressed.

JOHN YOUNG[1]

In May 1978, one day before his 65th birthday, Bill Hewlett resigned from his position as chief executive officer of HP. He was appointed chair of the

---

[1]Much of this section is based on Bro Uttal, "Mettle-Test Time for John Young," *Fortune,* April 29, 1985, pp. 242–48.

executive committee and joined David Packard, chairman of the board, in semiretirement, although he remained very active in HP affairs. John Young, who had succeeded Bill Hewlett as president and chief operating officer in November 1977, was named CEO.

Young, an athletic-looking 46-year-old who had capped his electrical engineering degree from Oregon State with an MBA from Stanford University, joined HP in 1958. Ten years before Young was named CEO, some of his peers had already pegged him as the heir apparent. *Fortune* later noted, "The praise strains belief. 'John Young is ideal for Hewlett-Packard, a gift from heaven,' exclaims a retired board member." A close observer said, "I've worked with thousands of leading businessmen, and he's absolutely at the top of the heap." *Fortune* continued with these observations:

> He has been described as a cool, confident, television surgeon. "When I first met him," says a company veteran, "he seemed so smooth and polished that I wanted to take his pulse to see if he was alive." Ernest C. Arbuckle, a former dean of Stanford Business School and a retired Hewlett-Packard director who lives next door to Young, puts it more sympathetically: "It's not easy to get under his skin. He's extremely self-controlled. I've never seen him get angry. But that's also the Hewlett-Packard way. You want to get the best out of people, so you control yourself."

Fortune also asked Young to contrast his management style with those of Hewlett and Packard:

> Young tends as always to be modest. "Bill is a brilliant engineer and Dave is a great businessman," he says. "I stress organization, planning, and the process." Young builds consensus decisions by asking penetrating questions and listening closely to the answers. Robert Minge Brown, a corporate lawyer and former director, describes Young as far and away the best-organized manager who ever made a presentation to the board. Young's memory for details is prodigious: though he crowds more events into his schedule than most people can believe, he keeps the schedule in his head, not in an appointment book.

Fortune used terms like "fierce determination" and "a powerful drive to master new skills" to describe Young:

> He is an accomplished pilot and fly-fisherman. "For him, even relaxation is highly focused," observes Tom McCabe, the tennis pro Young retains to be on the other side of the net whenever Young wants him there. "After he gets through with a lesson, there are puddles of good, honest effort all over the court."
>
> Young uses his superb organizational skills to make plenty of time for his wife, Rosemary (they met in first grade), and their three grown children. "He is getting way up there to being a pretty important guy," says his father. "But he doesn't get excited about it. Everything gets kept track of. He has time for his family, no matter what." Young calls his parents once a week. Several times a year he gathers the clan at his rustic 40-acre spread not far from

Klamath Falls (Oregon). The highlight of these trips: fishing for trout along the six miles of Five Mile Creek.

According to one insider, "His style is to lead people where he wants them to go rather than tell them what to do."[2] One of the areas where Young had led HP was into computers.

HP AND COMPUTERS

HP backed into the computer business in 1966 by introducing a minicomputer intended for controlling HP instruments; in fact, it was called an instrumentation computer. After a weak start with its initial entrance into business computers (1971), HP reintroduced the HP3000 in 1973. According to *Fortune,*

> In early 1973, David Packard threw a fit about the company's fledgling minicomputer business, which in 1972 had made only $100,000 on $100 million in revenues. He dispatched Paul Ely, then general manager of the microwave division, to straighten things out.[3]

By 1975 the HP3000 had firmly established HP as a leading computer manufacturer. In fact, the small, time-sharing HP3000 minicomputer was a primary contributor to the development of "distributed data processing," which expanded computing power beyond the data processing department.

In 1980 John Young launched a recruiting campaign to beef up R&D in the computer area. Longtime R&D head Bernard Oliver had focused HP Labs on physical-science problems instead of the software and design issues crucial to developing new computers. Of 200 HP Labs professionals, only 50 had been working in the computer field. When Oliver retired in 1981, Young appointed Doyle, the company's personnel director, to the post. Doyle recruited a team of 220 computer-oriented professionals and started forming HP's first research partnerships with universities. Young then raised R&D spending from 8.8 percent to more than 10 percent of sales.[4]

Young's prize catch in 1981 was Joel Birnbaum, who for five years had been the head of computer sciences at IBM's Thomas Watson Research Center. He had been at IBM when the pioneering work was done on RISC (reduced instruction-set computing) computers in the 1970s. RISC represented a shift from building more functions into computers to increasing speed by leaving out complex functions. The technology had been the subject of experimentation for ten years when Birnbaum and several former IBM researchers

---

[2]John W. Wilson, Catherine L. Harris, and Gordon Block, "Can Hewlett-Packard Put the Pieces Back Together?" *Business Week,* March 10, 1986, p. 115.

[3]Uttal, "Mettle-Test Time," p. 244.

[4]"Can John Young Redesign Hewlett-Packard?" *Business Week,* December 6, 1982, pp. 74–76.

brought the concepts to HP. Young soon vetoed at least four competing approaches to building high-powered computers. He agreed with Birnbaum that HP should be making simple computers.

In 1981 Young championed a much publicized effort to launch a 32-bit desktop work station for engineers. The basic computer was ready to go in time, but parts of the system that were being developed in other divisions, such as software, held up the launch for nearly a year. Nevertheless, by 1982 HP had succeeded in penetrating the explosive market for small-to-medium-sized (less than $250,000 system price) computers.

By 1982, computer products sales for HP reached $2.2 billion (out of total HP sales of $4.25 billion from a line of more than 5,000 products). Total sales had grown at a compound annual rate of 24.3 percent over the previous ten years, while earnings had increased tenfold. About half of the company's sales were to the United States, with the rest to other parts of the world. There were 40 manufacturing locations spread across the United States and 10 others around the world. In addition, there were more than 240 sales and service locations. More than half the 68,000 worldwide work force had been with HP for less than three years. Also by 1982, 22 of the divisions were directly related to computers, and the portion of total revenues attributable to computer products had increased from 16.8 percent in 1971 to 51 percent in 1982.

This dramatic shift had been especially challenging to HP because of the differences between the instrument and computer businesses. Instruments were essentially stand-alone products, whereas computers required a systems integration. In instruments, HP could rely on its technological superiority to sell customers premium-priced products. Furthermore, instrument customers could be left with the job of tailoring the equipment to their own particular needs because they were usually technical people. Those market segments were well defined, and HP held the leadership position in most product categories. Information processing markets, in contrast, were not clearly defined and were marked by fierce competition. Computer customers demanded increasingly better performing products at lower prices. They often wanted ready-to-use products designed for specific applications.

The systems approach required for designing and selling computers presented a problem for the HP way of doing business. According to Young, his biggest challenge in 1982 was "to orchestrate the divisions and provide a strategic glue and direction for the computer effort, while keeping the work units small." He added, "Having small divisions is not the only way to organize a company, but having organizations that people can run like a small business is highly motivational, especially for professionals. Keeping that spirit of entrepreneurship alive is very important to us."[5]

---

[5]Ibid., p. 74.

Based on 1981 revenues, HP was ranked the seventh largest computer manufacturer in the world. Only HP and DEC (Digital Equipment Corporation) had grown at more than 30 percent a year between 1978 and 1981. A study by an independent market research firm in 1981 indicated that only four computer firms would exceed $5 billion in sales by 1985 and suggested that HP would maintain the fastest growth rate, nearly 30 percent a year, between 1980 and 1985. Having been the pioneer system in the market for interactive business systems for on-line processing, in mid-1983 the HP3000 remained the leader, with 12,000 systems installed worldwide. A 1982 survey of minicomputer users, conducted by Datapro Research Corporation, attested to HP's ability to satisfy its customers. When asked if they would recommend the HP3000, 95 percent of HP3000 users said yes.

HP's ability to manage such rapid growth while maintaining a healthy working environment was acknowledged in a 1982 *Fortune* survey, in which HP was ranked the second most admired U.S. corporation, following IBM. It was recognized as being among the top three companies in each of five areas: ability to attract, develop, and keep talented people (number one ranking); innovativeness; quality of product; management reputation; and investment value.

An example of the innovation that had allowed the continued development of technically outstanding products was the HP9000, introduced in 1982, which had the power of a mainframe in a desktop unit. Some considered it the ultimate personal computer for scientists and engineers. The HP9000 incorporated HP's new integrated-circuit technology, which allowed up to 600,000 transistors to be put onto a single silicon chip.

By the mid-1980s the number of divisions at HP was 50, producing 9,000 products. Autonomy in proliferating divisions had resulted in some overlapping products. Customers complained about products developed in one HP division not being compatible with products from other divisions. The company's position in one of the most critical markets, personal computers, was threatened by a lack of cohesive effort between three geographically separated divisions. Each was individually engaged in the design, manufacture, and marketing of personal computers. According to a division marketing manager,

> With three independent divisions working on personal computers, there was no well-defined strategy. Products overlapped, and distribution channels were not standardized. This internal competition, while providing benefits up to a point, resulted in an inefficient use of the company's resources.

In an effort to coordinate its more than 20 information processing divisions, HP used a computer strategy council composed of that business's top management. The computer strategy council, set up by Young and headed by Executive Vice President Paul Ely, Jr., addressed issues ranging from product introductions to data communications standards.

In addition, HP used an experimental program-management style to provide unified direction on cross-divisional projects, and it improved planning through a number of task forces and committees. Despite some positive outcomes from these efforts, however, some observers were concerned that these coordinating activities might be damaging HP's entrepreneurial spirit.

In 1982 employee turnover and concern for the health of HP's entrepreneurial spirit led Young to commission a survey of 12,000 employees to pinpoint problems. In addition, HP improved its benefit program and launched new efforts to communicate with employees, especially when divisions were split up or moved. He noted, "We're constantly dealing with the trade-offs. We work hard at creating an exciting environment, but in the computer area interdependence is also very important."[6] He also commissioned McKinsey and Company to begin studying HP's marketing abilities.

The 1983 Reorganization

In early 1983 HP announced the most significant restructuring of its computer operation since the company entered the information processing business (Exhibit 3).[7] The organization had two major purposes, as outlined in a letter from Ely to the company's top 150 customers:

1. Unify our development and manufacturing activities in three strategic centers: system processors, personal computers, and networks. This will . . . provide a more cohesive product offering for customers.

2. Combine the marketing of all HP computers into a single organization to improve our effectiveness in interacting with our customers.

The 1983 reorganization began in January with the consolidation of the Personal Computation Group and the Computer Terminals Group. The new group, the Personal Computer Group, would be responsible for developing and manufacturing personal computers, terminals, personal computer

---

[6]Ibid., p. 78.

[7]Several earlier reorganizations had occurred in response to HP's growth into computers. The first major restructuring in 1969 established HP's first group structure. Further growth into several new markets led to a second major regrouping in 1974. The six product categories remained HP's basic lines into the mid-1980s: (1) electronic test and measuring instruments, (2) computers and computer-based systems, (3) calculators, (4) solid-state components, (5) medical electronic products, and (6) electronic instrumentation for chemical analysis. By 1976 HP had decided to refocus its computer strategy by separating technical/industrial systems from business/commercial systems, a strategy that had worked well to position HP as a strong player in both markets. In 1979 the Computer System Group had been reorganized into five groups: (1) Technical Computer, (2) Business Computer, (3) Computer Peripherals, (4) Terminals, and (5) Computer Marketing.

Exhibit 3
Hewlett-Packard Corporate Organization, June 1983

Board of Directors   Dave Packard, Chairman   Bill Hewlett, Vice Chairman

Chief Executive Officer   John Young, President*

Operations

Bill Terry, Executive Vice President	Paul Ely, Executive Vice President	Dean Morton, Executive Vice President**
Instruments	Computers	Medical

Administration
Bob Boniface, Executive Vice President

Corporate Staff

Corporate Controller
Jerry Carlson
Controller

Corporate Services
Bruce Wholey
Vice President

General Counsel
and Secretary
Jack Brigham
Vice President

International
Dick Alberding
Senior Vice President

Government
Affairs
Bob Kirkwood
Director

Public Relations
Dave Kirby
Director

Patents and Licenses
Jean Chognard
Vice President

Personnel
Bill Craven
Director

Marketing
Al Oliverio
Senior Vice President

Treasurer
Ed van Bronkhorst
Senior Vice President

Instruments

EUROPE
Franco Mariotti
Vice President

Field Sales Regions
France
Germany
Northern Europe
South/Eastern Europe
United Kingdom

Manufacturing
France
Germany
United Kingdom

INTERCONTINENTAL
Alan Bickell
Managing Director

Field Sales Regions
Australasia
Far East
Japan
Latin America
South Africa

Manufacturing
Brazil
Canada
Japan
Malaysia
Mexico
Puerto Rico
Singapore

U.S./CANADA SALES
Field Sales Regions
Eastern
Midwest
Neely (Western)
Southern
Canada

Corporate
Marketing
Operations
 •Parts Center

ELECTRONIC MEASUREMENTS GROUP
Bill Parzybok, General Manager
 •Boblingen Instrument
 •San Diego
 •Colorado Springs
 •Logic Systems
 •YHP Instrument
 •Loveland Instrument
 •Lake Stevens Instrument
 •New Jersey
 •Integrated Circuits
 •Santa Clara
 •Loveland
 •Colorado Springs

MICROWAVE AND COMMUNICATIONS INSTRUMENTS GROUP
Dick Anderson, General Manager
 •Colorado Telecom
 •Queensferry Telecom
 •Stanford Park
 •Spokane
 •Signal Analysis
 •Network Measurements
 •Santa Rosa Technology Center

INSTRUMENT MARKETING GROUP
Bob Brunner, General Manager
Sales: N. America/Europe/Intercon.
 •Instrument Support

Computers

COMPUTER PRODUCTS GROUP
Doug Chance
Vice President
 •Data Systems
 •Computer Systems
 •CSY/Roseville
 •Ft. Collins Systems
 •Engineering
  Productivity
 •YHP Computer
 •Computer I.C.
 •Cupertino I.C.
 •Systems
  Technology
 •Corvallis
  Components
 •Boblingen
  Computer Products

PERSONAL COMPUTER GROUP
Cyril Yansouni
General Manager
 •Roseville Terminals
 •Portable Computer
 •Grenoble Personal
  Computer
 •Personal Office
  Computer
 •Vancouver
 •Personal Software
 •Puerto Rico
 •Singapore
 •Brazil

INFORMATION PRODUCTS GROUP
Dick Hackborn
Vice President
 •Boise
 •Disc Memory
 •Greeley
 •Computer
  Peripherals
 •Bristol
 •Roseville
  Networks
 •Information
  Networks
 •Colorado
  Networks
 •Grenoble
  Networks

BUSINESS DEVELOPMENT GROUP
Ed McCracken
General Manager
 •Systems Marketing
  Center
 •Business
  Development Center
 •Business
  Development Europe
 •Information
  Resources
 •Systems
  Re-Marketing
 •Guadalajara Computer
  Manufacturing
 •Application Marketing
 •Office Productivity

COMPUTER MARKETING GROUP
Jim Arthur, Vice President
Sales: N. America/Europe/Intercon.
 •Computer Support
 •Application Marketing
 •Computer Supplies

Medical

MEDICAL GROUP
Ben Holmes, General Manager
 •Andover
 •Boblingen Medical
 •McMinnville
 •Waltham
 •Bedside Terminals
 •Medical Systems
 •Medical Supplies

ANALYTICAL GROUP
Lew Platt, Vice President
 •Avondale
 •Scientific Instruments
 •Waldbronn

COMPONENTS GROUP
John Blokker, General Manager
 •Microwave Semiconductor
 •Optoelectronics
 •Visible Products
 •Interface Products
 •Singapore
 •Malaysia

CORPORATE MANUFACTURING
Hal Edmondson
Vice President

(Research)

HP LABORATORIES
John Doyle
Vice President
Research and
Development

RESEARCH
CENTERS
Computer
Research

Physical Research

Technology
Research

CORPORATE DEVELOPMENT
Dave Sanders
Director

INTERNAL AUDIT
George Abbott
Manager

Corporate & Support Functions
Business Segments
Division
Operation
 * Chairman, Executive Committee
 ** Chairman, Management Council

643

peripherals, and other personal computation products, such as calculators. This change provided for the first time a cohesive overall strategy for HP's personal computer efforts. Decisions about marketing and R&D could now be made at the group level by a single manager. Before the reorganization, the only common manager for the separated divisions had been the company president. According to Young, "Creating the personal computer group was an extremely good way of getting a focus on marketing. It was a way of communicating to everyone that this [i.e., marketing] was okay, that it's okay to eat quiche."

The most undefined of HP's five reorganized computer groups was the Business Development Group (BDG), which was responsible for the strategic marketing and business-development activities for all HP computer products. BDG would generate three-year plans to position HP in three key markets: computer-integrated manufacturing, office automation/personal computers, and commercial data processing. These plans would be developed in conjunction with the divisions involved in the particular market.

Another significant change was the creation of two sales centers, in California and in Germany, under BDG. The sales centers would consolidate into single locations all the sales development activities previously conducted in each individual division. The primary role of sales development was to support and help motivate the sales force. Sales development provided the interface between the product divisions and the sales force. In the past, when sales representatives or HP customers wanted information, they were often forced to deal with several sales groups. With the change, the sales centers would serve as the sole source of information. HP termed it "one-stop shopping."

Opinions as to the benefits of the 1983 reorganization and the need for it were generally favorable. According to a group vice president,

> The top managers of the computer groups [computer strategy council] have been discussing a reorganization of this magnitude for some time. I proposed a structure similar to this one about two years ago to John Young and Paul Ely. Although John and Paul agreed such a change was needed, they felt the organization (i.e., the people) were not ready for such a change.
>
> We could have forced the restructuring earlier. Instead we chose to allow the organization to go through its own osmosis in coming to accept that such changes were needed. We may have waited a couple years, but I believe it would have taken just as long for people to absorb something forced on them, if ever. People are more committed when they come to the conclusion on their own. This osmosis process is much like Japanese consensus management.

A marketing manager commented,

> Until now HP has tried to manage its computer business much like it has run the instruments business—with decentralized divisions selling stand-alone products based on technological superiority. The computer marketing man-

agers, division managers, and group managers all knew HP had to become more marketing-oriented, but the organization structure didn't allow for it.

Another group vice president reflected,

A single entrepreneur has only a few people to communicate his vision to. A large organization must establish and communicate boundaries, set objectives, and let people loose.

There is a big difference between being independent and being entrepreneurial. Independence implies there may not be a cohesive overall fit among the pieces of an organization. Entrepreneurial units, on the other hand, can be managed to fit together if direction is provided. HP's divisions have always had innovation, pride, and openness. The reorganization will get them operating within an overall strategic framework.

The 1983 reorganization was designed to make HP, over the next five years, a worldwide leader in providing integrated information solutions for medium to large companies.

HP believed that, in addition to an outstanding sales/support organization and commitment to R&D, the company had three other competitive advantages to help achieve its goals. First, HP was developing high-volume, low-cost manufacturing capabilities. Many of those state-of-the-art capabilities could be transferred to HP's customers as an added selling point. Second, HP produced nearly $200 million worth of integrated circuits for internal consumption. Second only to IBM, this captive production was several times larger than any other competitor. Last, and probably most important, HP had long provided computer systems for both technical and business applications, both of which would be needed to meet the integrated processing needs of manufacturers. DEC, HP's leading competitor in technical computers, had a limited business computer offering and did not even have a commercial-user sales force. IBM, traditionally a business computer supplier, had substantially less to offer the engineering and scientific markets than did HP.

Spectrum

Although HP enjoyed a reputation for highly reliable machines and consistently ranked first in customer satisfaction, by 1983 customers were showing signs of impatience with the failure to upgrade the HP3000. Some were defecting to other, more powerful machines. According to the *New York Times*, "Numerous projects were started to upgrade the 3000, beginning in 1974, but all were either cancelled or failed." A former HP manager complained, "Divisions were small and not allowed to do big things."[8] The problem was such that Young said, "We had to do something, or we'd sink."

---

[8]Andrew Pollack, "Hewlett Bets the Store on Spectrum," the *New York Times*, November 17, 1985, p. 28.

HP decided to turn the 3000 into a hub for both its own personal computers and those of IBM. The 3000 was to be the ultimate departmental computer—a low-cost machine that could link personal computers and enable people to tap into information in bigger machines all over the country.

In addition, HP began promising an answer to its critics with Spectrum, a new project to unify HP's product line. Based on the relatively untested RISC technology, Spectrum sought to boost a computer's power by simplifying the complexity of its central processor. Young intended to launch the new family of Spectrum computers in the fall of 1985. He set up an 800-person group to develop every basic component of the Spectrum family. Young declared that the results of the Spectrum project would be the technological basis for every type of computer, and some instruments, sold by HP. He hoped to be able to ship significant quantities in 1986.

According to *Business Week,*

> Once Young developed the consensus he wanted to give Spectrum a final go-ahead in February, 1983, he needed someone who could make sure that all the divisions agreed on the details of how the project would proceed. That job fell to Douglas C. Chance, general manager of HP's Information Systems Group. Young saw Chance as a strong strategist who could build a team and develop confidence. This was crucial because many technical decisions had to be made quickly before the machine could be handed over to a development team.
>
> Chance set up a committee of top officers and division managers that met monthly over dinner. As often as not, Chance learned, the issues that worried them most weren't technical. "The real concerns had to do with whether they could trust the others to do what we had all agreed to do," he recalls. Such fears "typically surfaced late at night after several bottles of wine."
>
> Eventually, as Spectrum grew, HP's divisions learned to cooperate under the new umbrella called the Information Technology Group. At its helm was veteran engineer George E. Bodway, a hearty, rumpled man with a knack for administration. "Nothing escapes him," an admirer says. Formed in May, 1984, ITG quickly built a staff of 1,000 and for the first time brought into one group the people who develop such key elements of computers as operating systems, programming languages, and integrated-circuit designs. Some 20 divisions chipped in specialized software, peripheral devices, and other elements of Spectrum, with disagreements arbitrated by Bodway and a series of specialized councils.[9]

Spectrum was to be a powerful business minicomputer representing the first fruits of what was widely regarded as one of the most sweeping product transitions ever undertaken in the electronics industry. It also was the first product to reflect the new centralized approach. Spectrum eventually was to produce a common internal design for all the company's desktop and minicomputer product lines well into the 1990s.

---

[9]Wilson, "Can Hewlett-Packard Put the Pieces Back Together?" p. 116.

According to Dean Morton, executive vice president in 1983, "We made a clear and unequivocal commitment and we expect that it will pay off. We don't have any alternative plans for the next-generation computers."[10]

The 1984 Reorganization[11]

On July 16, 1984, John Young announced a reorganization designed to accelerate the company's move toward a wider market and to compete more effectively with an increasingly aggressive IBM. The new structure (Exhibit 4) regrouped HP's dozens of product divisions under sectors focusing on markets rather than product lines. Two major sectors now would sell computers: one would concentrate on business customers, while the second would market computers and instruments to scientific and manufacturing customers. Young also closed down some computer-aided engineering (CAE) operations, lumping the remaining CAE activities under one executive, and authorized the licensing of software written by outsiders—an act verging on heresy.

A significant element of the reorganization was the shift of two of HP's top executives. Executive Vice President Ely, who had built the company's computer business from $100 million a decade earlier to a $2.4 billion in fiscal 1983, was "shunted aside, to a post where his relationship to the computer business will, by most accounts, be largely advisory. He will take charge of a smaller, more mature sector that includes medical and analytical products and the company's research laboratories."[12] The other move was the elevation of Executive Vice President Morton to the new post of chief operating officer, in line to become CEO. *Business Week* noted,

> The statesmanlike Morton is perceived as more akin in management style to Young and company founders William R. Hewlett and David Packard. Sources close to the company claim that Ely became increasingly difficult to work with during the 10 years that he built computers into HP's largest business. "He has been a disruptive force in the company—lecturing, browbeating, and intimidating people," complains one former executive.

In reacting to the changes, Ely commented that chief operating officer was "not high on my list of most-wanted jobs."

Young and the board had worried since 1978 that customers were demanding complete systems of computers and instruments for solving broad problems, such as factory automation, rather than individual instruments. As the dividing line between computer systems and test and measurement equipment

---

[10]Pollack, "Hewlett Bets the Store."
[11]Most of this section is based on Uttal, "Mettle-Test Time," pp. 242–48, and "Why Hewlett-Packard Overhauled Its Management," *Business Week,* July 30, 1984, pp. 111–12.
[12]Ibid.

Exhibit 4
Hewlett-Packard Corporate Organization, July 1984

Board of Directors Dave Packard, Chairman Bill Hewlett, Vice Chairman

Chief Executive Officer John Young, President
Chief Operating Officer Dean Morton, Executive Vice President

---

INTERNAL AUDIT
George Abbott, Manager

CORPORATE DEVELOPMENT
Tom Uhlman, Director

ADMINISTRATION
Bob Boniface, Executive Vice President

MARKETING AND INTERNATIONAL
Dick Alberding, Executive Vice President

U.S. FIELD OPERATIONS
Jim Arthur
Vice President and Director
Field Sales Regions: Eastern, Midwestern, Neely (Western), Southern

EUROPEAN OPERATIONS
Franco Mariotti
Vice President and Director
Field Sales Regions: France, Germany, Italy, Northern Europe, South/Eastern, United Kingdom
Manufacturing: France, Germany, United Kingdom

INTERCONTINENTAL OPERATIONS
Alan Bickell
Vice President and Director
Field Sales Regions: Australasia, Far East, Japan, Canada, Latin America
Manufacturing: Brazil, Canada, Japan, Korea, Malaysia, Mexico, Puerto Rico, Singapore

MAJOR ACCOUNTS MARKETING
Al Oliverio
Senior Vice President

CORPORATE MARKETING
Art Dauer
Director
Marketing Communications
Marketing Operations
Marketing Information Center
Finance and Remarketing Division
Computer Supplies Operation
Instrument Products Operation
Computer Support Division
Instrument Support Division
Corporate Parts Center

MEASUREMENT, DESIGN AND MANUFACTURING SYSTEMS
Bill Terry, Executive Vice President

MICROWAVE AND COMMUNICATIONS GROUP
Dick Anderson
General Manager
Stanford Park Division
Network Measurements Division
Signal Analysis Division
Spokane Division
Colorado Telecom Division
Queensferry Telecom Division
Microwave Technology Division
Queensferry Microwave Operation

ELECTRONIC INSTRUMENTS GROUP
Ned Barnholt
General Manager
New Jersey Division
Santa Clara Division
Boblingen Instrument Division
YHP Instrument Division
YHP Computer Operation
Integrated Circuits Division
Santa Clara Tech Center
Loveland Tech Center
Colorado Springs Tech Center

DESIGN SYSTEMS GROUP
Bill Parzybok
Vice President and General Manager
Fort Collins Systems Division
Logic Systems Division
Logic Design Operation
Colorado Springs Division
Boblingen Computer Division
Lake Stevens Instrument Division
Boblingen Engineering Operation
Fort Collins Engineering Operation

MANUFACTURING SYSTEMS GROUP
Lew Platt
Vice President and General Manager
Data Systems Division
Advanced Manufacturing Systems Operation
Manufacturing Productivity Division
Loveland Instrument Division
Ponocorm Automation Operation
Manufacturing Test Division
Lyon Manufacturing Systems Operation

INFORMATION SYSTEMS AND NETWORKS
John Doyle, Executive Vice President

INFORMATION SYSTEMS GROUP
Doug Chance
Vice President and General Manager
Computer Systems Division
CSY Roseville Operation
Boblingen General Systems Division
Office Productivity Division
Guadalajara Computer Operation
Administrative Productivity Division
Information Resources Operation
Administrative Productivity Operation
Financial Systems Operation

PERSONAL COMPUTER GROUP
Cyril Yansouni
Vice President and General Manager
Roseville Terminals Division
Portable Computer Division
Handheld Computer & Calculator Operation
Grenoble Personal Computer Division
Personal Office Computer Division
Personal Software Division
Puerto Rico Operation
Singapore Operation
Brazil Operation
Personal Computer Distribution Operation
Personal Computer Group Operation

PERIPHERALS GROUP
Dick Hackborn
Vice President and General Manager
Greeley Division
Computer Peripherals Bristol Division
Disc Memory Division
Boise Division
Vancouver Division
San Diego Division

INFORMATION NETWORKS GROUP
John Doyle (interim)
Colorado Networks Operation
Grenoble Networks Division
Roseville Networks Division
Information Networks Division

INFORMATION TECHNOLOGY GROUP
George Bodway
General Manager
Cupertino IC Division
Fort Collins IC Division
Northwest IC Division
Information Hardware Operation
Information Software Operation

ANALYTICAL, COMPONENTS, MEDICAL, AND TECHNOLOGY
Lew Platt

ANALYTICAL GROUP
Dieter Hoehn
General Manager
Avondale Division
Lab Automation Systems Operation
Scientific Instruments Division
Waldbronn Division

COMPONENTS GROUP
John Blokker
Vice President and General Manager
Microwave Semiconductor Division
Optoelectronics Division
Optical Communication Division
Southeast Asia Operation

MEDICAL GROUP
Ben Holmes
General Manager
Andover Division
Boblingen Medical Division
McMinnville Division
Waltham Division
Medical Supplies Center
Health Care Productivity Operation

HP LABORATORIES
Joel Birnbaum
Vice President and Director
Manufacturing Research Center
Design and Measurement Research Center
Distributed Systems Center
Application Technology Center
Technology Research Center
Bristol Research Center

CORPORATE MANUFACTURING
Hal Edmondson
Vice President and Director

CORPORATE ENGINEERING
Chuck House
Director

CONTROLLER
Bob Wayman
Vice President

TREASURY
George Newman
Treasurer

PERSONNEL
Bill Craven
Director

GENERAL COUNSEL AND SECRETARY
Jack Brigham
Vice President

PATENTS AND LICENSES
Jean Chognard
Vice President

GOVERNMENT AFFAIRS
Bob Kirkwood
Director

PUBLIC RELATIONS
Dave Kirby
Director

Hewlett-Packard is organized to provide its customers around the world with solutions to their increasingly complex measurement and computational needs.

Of the company's four business sectors, three offer a wide range of advanced electronic-based products. The fourth encompasses worldwide sales and marketing activities and integrates HP's diverse product lines. Giving the company common direction and cohesion are shared philosophies, practices and goals as well as technologies.

Within this context, the individual business units—called product divisions—are relatively small and self-sufficient so that decisions can be made at the level of the organization most responsible for putting them into action. Consistent with this approach, it has always been a practice at Hewlett-Packard to give each employee considerable freedom to implement methods and ideas that meet specific local objectives.

Since its founding in 1939, the HP organization has grown to some 50 product divisions. To provide for effective overall management and coordination, the company has aligned these divisions into 12 product groups characterized by product and market focus.

HP's corporate structure is designed to foster small-business flexibility within its many individual operating units while supporting them with the strengths of a larger organization.

The accompanying chart provides a graphic view of the relationship of the various organizational elements. The organization has been structured to allow the groups and their divisions to concentrate on their product-development, manufacturing and marketing activities, while sharing common administrative systems for many of the tasks required of a company doing business worldwide. Normal and functional lines of responsibility and communication are indicated on the chart; however, direct and informal communication across lines and between levels is strongly encouraged.

Here is a closer look at the company's basic organizational units.

PRODUCT DIVISIONS/OPERATIONS
An HP division is a vertically integrated organization that conducts itself much like an independent business. Its fundamental responsibilities are to develop, manufacture and market products that are profitable and which make contributions in the marketplace by virtue of technological or economic advantage.

Each division has its own distinct family of products, for which it has worldwide marketing responsibility. A division also is responsible for its own accounting, personnel activities, quality assurance and support of its products in the field. In addition, it has important social and economic responsibilities in its local community.

Operations are organizational units dedicated to particular tasks, usually in support of a product group or various divisions within a group. They also are generally smaller in size than divisions.

PRODUCT GROUPS
Product groups are composed of divisions and operations having closely related product lines or market focus. Groups are responsible for coordinating the activities of their respective divisions. The management of each group has overall responsibility for the operations and financial performance of its members. Further, each group has worldwide responsibility for its manufacturing and marketing activities.

BUSINESS SECTORS
Reflecting its increased customer orientation and concentration on major markets, the company was realigned in August 1984 into four major sectors.
Measurement, Design and Manufacturing Systems
Information Systems and Networks
Analytical, Components, Medical and Technology
Marketing and International
These sectors provide the focal points for creating the common strategies needed in managing product lines that are increasingly interactive, and for developing overall HP solutions to the complex needs of customers.

By consolidating its worldwide field marketing and international manufacturing, the company is able to apply its unique range of computation and measurement solutions to the business and technical problems of customers around the world. Management staffs of the U.S. and international sales organizations assist the three product sectors in coordinating the sales and service functions.

The executive vice president in charge of each business sector is directly responsible to the chief operating officer for the performance of the sector's product groups.

CORPORATE ADMINISTRATION
The principal responsibility of Corporate Administration is to insure that the corporate staff offices provide the specialized policies, expertise and resources to support the field division and groups adequately on a worldwide basis. The executive vice president in charge of Corporate Administration also reports to the chief operating officer, providing an important upward channel of communication for the corporate staff activities.

CORPORATE RESEARCH AND DEVELOPMENT
HP Laboratories is the corporate research and development organization that provides a central source of technical support for the product-development efforts of HP operating divisions. In these efforts, the divisions make important use of the advanced technologies, materials, components and theoretical analyses researched or developed by HP Labs. Through endeavors in areas of science and technology, the corporate laboratories also help the company develop new areas of business.

CORPORATE MANUFACTURING
Corporate Manufacturing has responsibility for the coordination of manufacturing activities throughout HP, including the following functions: materials planning and procurement, manufacturing support and standards, quality improvement and assurance, manufacturing information systems, regulatory standards, environmental control, employee safety and health, and corporate physical-distribution systems.

CORPORATE ENGINEERING
Corporate Engineering is responsible for coordinating the company's engineering activities, with an emphasis on measures to increase engineering productivity through improved design tools, engineering processes, training and development programs and strategic coordination.

BOARD OF DIRECTORS
The Board of Directors and its chairman have ultimate responsibility for the legal and ethical conduct of the company and its officers. It is the board's duty to protect and advance the interests of the stockholders, to foster a continuing concern for fairness in the company's relations with employees, and to fulfill all requirements of the law with regard to the board's stewardship.

The board counsels management on general business matters and also reviews and evaluates the performance of management. To assist in discharging these responsibilities, the board has formed various committees to oversee the company's activities and programs in such areas as employees' benefits, compensation, financial auditing and investment.

CHIEF EXECUTIVE OFFICER/CHIEF OPERATING OFFICER
The chief executive officer is responsible for the direction and long range performance of the company, subject to the authority of the Board of Directors. Also, the chief executive officer serves as chairman of the Executive Committee. Reporting directly to the CEO are Corporate Development and Internal Audit.

The chief operating officer, who reports directly to the chief executive officer, has responsibility for the day-to-day operating performance of the company. Reporting directly to the chief operating officer are the four operating sectors of the company and Corporate Administration. The chief operating officer serves as chairman of the Management Council.

EXECUTIVE COMMITTEE
The Executive Committee is the company's primary policy-setting body. It reviews broad issues affecting the company and initiates strategies designed to maintain its direction and meet its goals. Members include the chief executive officer (who serves as committee chairman), chief operating officer, and the five executive vice presidents. Meetings are normally scheduled on a weekly basis.

MANAGEMENT COUNCIL
Primary responsibilities of this body are to review and formulate operating policies, and to turn policy decisions into corporate action. The council, chaired by the chief operating officer, also reviews performance expectations as reflected in the forward planning of the business sectors and monitors their operating results.

Council members serve variously on five committees charged with policy-setting responsibility for personnel, operations, marketing, computer architecture and networks and information systems. Each committee is chaired by an executive vice president; in addition, the 22 council members are all group and senior managers of the company.

HEWLETT PACKARD
Corporate Public Relations
3000 Hanover Street, Palo Alto, CA 94304

blurred, different HP salespeople sometimes tried to sell the same customer different equipment for solving his or her problems, with different discounts and other conditions of sale. At one time, a customer might be offered any of 16 types of purchase agreements, depending on which salesperson was pitching.

Although Young insisted that the restructuring was a logical follow-up to the 1983 reorganization, outside observers thought it was a further reaction to the orders HP had been losing to IBM. Young cited the CAE failure as a reason for the reorganization. HP's 9000 series of computer work stations, intended to spearhead the company's drive into the CAE market—whose 30-percent growth rates prompted Young to call it "hotter even than personal computers"—had been announced in late 1982. However, the software needed to do computer-aided design and engineering would not come out until November 1985, and then it would be based heavily on software from two outside companies, one since bought by HP. *Business Week* believed that engineers who bought these kinds of computers to design integrated circuits had all but bypassed the 9000 in favor of products from small start-up companies, such as Calma Corporation. The reason HP was late in CAE was that CAE had fallen between the cracks of the company's two main businesses.

HP also floundered in its 1984 move into consumer markets with the HP 110 portable computer, introduced in May. Apart from the $3,000 price tag, major criticism of the 110 was its lack of the most-wanted software. Some expected it to perform like the first consumer PC, the HP 150, with the touch screen, but it sold better via direct sales to HP's loyal customers than in retail channels.

Even the continued 30-percent growth of the flagship 3000 series of minicomputers resulted largely from sales to the existing customer base. The 3000 series was trailing the growth rate of comparable machines from IBM and DEC.

MOUNTING PROBLEMS

1984 Results

In 1984 HP sales grew at a compound annual rate of 23.3 percent to more than $6 billion, compared with 20.8 percent for the prior seven years, but profit growth had slowed. Whereas between 1978 and 1982, profits grew at an annual rate of better than 25 percent, 1983 and 1984 saw growth of 19.5 percent.

Another area of concern for Young was management turnover. Not only did 38 of 750 managers quit the company in 1984 (nearly twice the number as in 1983), it was also reported that almost every upstart CAE venture now employed HP refugees. In January 1985 HP experienced its first departure of a top executive—Paul Ely, who left to head Convergent Technologies of San Jose, California.

According to *Fortune*,

Ely's achievements are widely acknowledged. . . . By 1983 the workaholic Ely had helped boost sales to $2.4 billion, racking up a compound growth rate of

33 percent and pretax profits of $392 million. Despite recent problems with personal computers, he made computers Hewlett-Packard's biggest business.

But Ely also cut up like a professional bad boy. Former subordinates say he believed that even a wrong decision was better than no decision at all, and that he would shoot from the hip, correcting his errors later. Although he was an inspiring manager, Ely didn't build strong teams, and he went on the warpath against the instruments side of Hewlett-Packard.

Last July, after announcing a new organizational structure, Young named a chief operating officer. "Young made a presentation showing that as second in command, Dean O. Morton would do a better job inside the H-P culture than Ely," recalls Antonie T. Knoppers, a director. "Ely was able but cocky. Within the parameters of H-P's culture, he was just in bounds."[13]

1985 Results

By 1985, HP's share of the minicomputer market had slipped from 7 percent (in 1979) to 6 percent as competitors surpassed the HP3000, which processed 16 bits of information at a time, by offering much faster "superminis" that handled 32 bits. Despite spending more than $50 million between 1983 and 1985 to launch a line of personal computers, HP still had little visible market share, except with its innovative, low-cost printers.

Also, after investing at least $50 million, the company had yet to launch a competitive system into the booming market for CAE. Part of the problem was attributed to the fact that ten highly competitive divisions were responsible for developing different components of CAE systems. Young hoped to demonstrate some CAE systems at the Design Automation Conference in June of 1985, but several new firms had a long head start on HP.

By July 1985 Spectrum was long overdue. Originally the first of the new computers was to be announced before the end of 1985, but the date was postponed. It was now expected to be announced later in the year. HP acknowledged that it was having more difficulty than expected making the new machines capable of running software developed for its older computers. There also were reports that HP was behind in developing chips for the new machine. According to *The New York Times,* "Each time information is revealed, the project seems to be further off and less impressive than it once appeared."[14]

The most positive area for HP was the 3000. By mid-1985 20,000 HP3000s were in use—double the number three years previously—making it the most popular minicomputer after IBM's System/34 and System/36. It also had given HP 4 percent of the business departmental market. Its 23-percent increase in revenues over the previous six months accounted for virtually all of

---

[13]Uttal, "Mettle-Test Time," p. 224.
[14]Pollack, "Hewlett Bets the Store," p. 28.

the company's 10-percent growth in sales (profits had declined by 12 percent). The spearhead of HP's new thrust was Series 37, the latest and smallest of the 3000 family. The size of a two-drawer file cabinet and starting at $20,000 (about half the previous lowest price for a 3000), "Mighty Mouse's" key selling point was its software, which went farther than other makers in tying software applications on the large system to applications on the personal computer. By late 1985 the company had announced Vectra PC, the first HP computer compatible with an IBM model, PC-AT.

To sell its departmental concept, HP developed a two-pronged marketing strategy: it used its own sales force to reach big customers, and it sold to small businesses through third-party companies that wrote software geared to specific market niches and sold complete systems that met specific needs. For the first time, HP was selling to customers with revenues as low as $5 million.

By the end of the fiscal year, it was clear that 1985 would be the first year with an earnings decline since Young had become CEO—by 10 percent to $489 million. (See Exhibits 5–7 for financial statements.) HP's overall revenues grew only a modest 8 percent, to $6.5 billion. (The 3000 line accounted for about a third of 1985 revenues.) That figure had to be compared with double-digit growth rates for most other computer makers. HP's earnings in the same period fell for the first time since 1975, and HP's overall share of the worldwide minicomputer market had slipped to 5 percent from 5.5 percent in 1983. In the $37-billion market for commercial minis, it dropped from a 4.2-percent share in 1983 to 3.9 percent in 1985, while DEC moved from 5 percent to 7 percent. In the $15-billion market for technical minis, HP dropped to 7.8 percent from more than 12 percent five years earlier. DEC was a major reason, but so also were IBM and AT&T. In instrument sales, company revenues had dropped 3 percent over the previous year but provided more than one-third of revenues and regularly earned, before taxes, more than 20 cents on every dollar of sales.

1986 Results

On February 25, 1986, after spending an estimated $200 million, HP unveiled Spectrum. For the past three years, almost the entire company had been working on the project. Its cost in 1986 alone was expected to run in the hundreds of millions of dollars. Actually unveiled were two machines that would double and triple the power of the top model in the 3000 line. The smaller model, the Series 930, which was supposed to perform better than competing $450,000 minicomputers from DEC and IBM for about half the price, would be available by the end of 1986, and the larger Series 950 by the second half of 1987. To minimize risks, HP used well-proven chips instead of the latest available. Although the chips limited the speed of the machines, they were faster than most conventional ones. The company also introduced a 3000 series upgrade that did not use the new RISC technology.

Exhibit 5
Hewlett-Packard
Consolidated Statement of Earnings
(millions)

	OCTOBER 31	
ORDERS	<u>1985</u>	<u>1984</u>
Measurement, design, information, and manufacturing equipment and systems	$2,819	$3,135
Peripherals and network products	1,537	1,440
Service for equipment, systems, and peripherals	1,135	904
Medical electronic equipment and service	458	402
Analytical instrumentation and service	256	238
Electronic components	190	231
	$6,395*	$6,350*
NET REVENUE†		
Measurement, design, information, and manufacturing equipment and systems	$2,929	$2,879
Peripherals and network products	1,560	1,375
Service for equipment, systems, and peripherals	1,125	970
Medical electronic equipment and service	448	377
Analytical instrumentation and service	248	229
Electronic components	195	214
	$6,505	$6,044
Costs and expenses:		
Cost of goods sold	3,166	2,865
Research and development	685	592
Marketing	1,181	1,066
Administrative and general	715	661
	5,747	5,184

(continued on next page)

For the years ended October 31	<u>1985</u>	<u>1984</u>	<u>1983</u>
Domestic orders	$3,662	$3,629	$2,901
International orders	2,733	2,721	2,021
*Total orders.	$6,395	$6,350	$4,922
Equipment	$5,204	$4,934	$3,862
Services	1,301	1,110	848
†Net revenue.	$6,505	$6,044	$4,710

‡Reversal of DISC taxes accrued prior to 1984 due to a change in U.S. tax law.

(continued)

Earnings before taxes	758	860
Provision for taxes	269	313
Reversal of DISC taxes‡	—	(118)
Net earnings	$489	$665
Net earnings per share	$1.91	$2.59
Cash dividends per share	$.22	$.19

The company operates in a single industry segment: the design and manufacture of measurement and computation products and systems. The statement provides supplemental information showing orders and net revenue by groupings of similar products or services. The groupings are as follows:

- Measurement, design, information, and manufacturing equipment and systems: equipment and systems (hardware and software) used for design, manufacturing, office automation, and information processing; general-purpose instruments and computers; and hand-held calculators.
- Peripherals and network products: printers, plotters, magnetic disc and tape drives, terminals, and network products.
- Service for equipment, systems, and peripherals: support and maintenance services, parts and supplies related to design and manufacturing systems, office and information systems, general-purpose instruments and computers, peripherals, and network products.
- Medical electronic equipment and service: products that perform patient monitoring, diagnostic, therapeutic, and data-management functions; application software; support and maintenance services; and hospital supplies.
- Analytical instrumentation and service: gas and liquid chromatographs, mass spectrometers and spectrophotometers used to analyze chemical compounds; support and maintenance services.
- Electronic components: microwave semiconductor and optoelectronic devices that are sold primarily to manufacturers for incorporation into electronic products.

By this time several small, start-up computer companies were offering products with RISC designs, and in January IBM had introduced a RISC-based engineering work station. Spectrum, however, represented by far the industry's biggest gamble on RISC to date. HP claimed that customers would have no difficulty converting software that was used on its current products.

Exhibit 6
Hewlett-Packard Consolidated Balance Sheets (millions)

	OCTOBER 31		
	1985	1984	1983
ASSETS			
Current assets:			
Cash and temporary cash investments	$ 1,020	$ 938	$ 880
Accounts and notes receivable	1,249	1,180	951
Inventories:			
Finished goods	401	373	279
Purchased parts and fabricated assemblies	592	650	469
Other current assets	80	60	53
Total current assets	$3,342	$3,201	$2,632
Property, plant, and equipment:			
Land	$ 230	$ 202	$ 167
Buildings and leasehold improvements	1,653	1,416	1,102
Machinery and equipment	1,400	1,173	888
Total P, P, and E	3,283	2,791	2,157
Accumulated depreciation and amortization	(1,134)	(923)	(726)
Net P, P, and E	2,149	1,868	1,431
Other assets	189	84	98
Total assets	$5,680	$5,153	$4,161
LIABILITIES AND SHAREHOLDERS' EQUITY			
Current liabilities:			
Notes payable	$ 260	$ 217	$ 148
Accounts payable	240	281	203
Employee compensation and benefits	397	398	300
Other accrued liabilities	302	162	103
Accrued taxes on earnings	111	203	112
Other accrued taxes	63	61	54
Total current liabilities	1,376	1,322	920
Long-term debt	102	81	71
Other liabilities	92	93	46
Deferred taxes on earnings	128	112	237
Total liabilities	$1,698	$1,608	$1,274
Shareholders' equity:			
Common stock and capital in excess of $1 par value	780	775	733
Retained earnings	3,202	2,770	2,154
Total shareholders' equity	3,982	3,545	2,887
Total liabilities and shareholders' equity	$5,680	$5,153	$4,161

Exhibit 7
Hewlett-Packard
Consolidated Statement of Changes in Financial Position
(millions)

| | OCTOBER 31 | | |
	1985	1984	1983
Funds provided by operations:			
Net earnings	$489	$665	$432
Expenses not requiring an outlay of funds:			
Depreciation and amortization	299	237	191
Deferred taxes on earnings	97	(81)	105
Other, net	54	47	45
	939	868	773
Funds used by operations:			
Investment in property, plant, and equipment	632	661	466
Increase (decrease) in working capital, excluding			
net cash: Accounts and notes receivable	69	195	178
Inventories	(30)	256	89
Other current assets	20	(9)	(1)
Accounts payable and accrued liabilities	(22)	(179)	(104)
Accrued taxes on earnings	92	(78)	39
Other, net	19	(22)	2
	780	824	669
Nonoperating funds provided (used):			
Employee stock plans:			
Shares issued	156	112	108
Shares purchased	(240)	(142)	—
Dividends to shareholders	(57)	(49)	(40)
Other, net	21	24	32
	(120)	(55)	100
Increase (decrease) in net cash (cash and temp-			
orary cash investments, net of notes payable)	$ 39	$ (11)	$204
Net cash at beginning of year	721	732	528
Net cash at end of year	$760	$721	$732

For the quarter ended April 30 revenue was up 6 percent, but earnings had fallen 2 percent—the fifth such decline in a row. Although Young had been proclaiming that the computer slump had passed its low point and had predicted modest improvement for the year, he now admitted, "The fact is, our U.S. business has been essentially flat for nearly two years. It continues to be a difficult business environment." Nevertheless, in May HP lifted a 5-percent management salary cut it had imposed the previous summer. As a result, overhead grew, so tight hiring controls were maintained.

With a sharper-than-expected decline in European and other non-U.S. orders, net income for the third quarter (ended July 31) now was expected to decline by 13 percent, to $117 million—even lower than expected. Revenue would increase slightly, perhaps to $1.61 billion. This would mean that orders for the nine-month period would be essentially flat, rising 1 percent, with domestic orders declining 2 percent and international orders rising 4 percent.

On top of these developments, it was becoming clear that because of software snags, HP would have to delay shipping the 930 for at least six months, to mid-1987. Since two-thirds of the $100 million of orders for new Spectrum-technology computers were for the 930 machines, HP's 1987 computer sales might be lowered by about $200 million, or roughly half of anticipated revenue from the Spectrum-based product lines. When the news became public the company's stock, which was trading in the mid-$40 range, was likely to drop to its lowest point of the year. *Business Week* had recently raised the question: "Can Hewlett-Packard Put the Pieces Back Together?"

MARRIOTT CORPORATION (A)

Bill Marriott, Jr., president and CEO of the ninth largest hotel chain and the third largest server of food in the United States, was concerned. Although he had led the company through an impressive 12 years of growth, with sales increasing almost nine times, earnings seven times, and return on equity more than doubling, the annual compounded growth rate was only 17.3 percent, which was below the company's 20-percent goal and compared poorly with the 20.5 percent for the previous 15 years. Furthermore, the company's major source of growth, hotels, appeared to be facing a decline in growth rate. According to Fred Malek, executive vice president for Marriott's Hotel Group, "We can't maintain our rate of room growth at 20 percent. We see a compound growth rate of 16 to 17 percent for the next three years, but beyond 1986 the markets will be fully supplied and our growth rate could decline to 10 to 12 percent.

Bill Marriott was "getting heat" from Tom Curren, his senior vice president for planning, to branch out of full-service hotels for the first time. It was clear to Marriott that some change was needed:

> I have seen chains that have adopted a no-growth approach in the hotel business, and I have seen them go out of business. The reason is that a good person, after he's been in the same job for five years . . . starts looking around for something else. And then the whole ball of twine starts to unravel. You lose your senior people . . . then your properties start deteriorating, service starts going, and you start losing money.

Don Washburn, the vice president of hotel planning and the newest member of the Marriott management team, also was concerned. As the "product champion" for a new chain of Marriott budget hotels, he had been assigned by Bill Marriott the task of developing a detailed implementation plan that could generate substantial future growth for the company. It was clear to Washburn that although Bill Marriott was open minded about such a chain, he was still skeptical about execution of the concept and wanted to see the project move faster. Other managers were not just skeptical; they were opposed to the new concept.

This case was prepared by Jim Kennedy, Research Associate, under the supervision of Professor William E. Fulmer. Copyright © 1986 by the University of Virginia Darden School Foundation, Charlottesville, VA. All rights reserved.

COMPANY BACKGROUND

In 1927 John Willard (Bill) Marriott opened a small root beer stand in Washington, D.C. A decade later, after opening his eighth stand, now called Hot Shoppes, he expanded into in-flight catering of the airlines. In the early 1950s he built his first hotel and took his company public. (For more information on J.W. Marriott and the early days of his company, see Exhibit 1.)

The success of the first hotel led J.W. Marriott to construct additional properties, and by 1958 the hotel division had been established, with J. Willard Marriott, Jr. (Bill Jr.), as vice president. According to J.W., "I think we're opportunists in a way. I never had any great dreams about what I was going to do. But what I was doing I wanted to make successful. When I made that successful, I wanted to go on to something else."

In 1960, to the dismay of many traditional Mormons, the Philadelphia Marriott opened with the company's first cocktail lounge. As J.W. explained to the church elders, "If I want to stay in the hotel business, I've got to sell liquor."

By 1964 J.W. Marriott was worried, however. Although he operated 45 Hot Shoppes, four hotels, and the airline catering service, he was experiencing some health problems and the company appeared to be a "runaway horse." For example, in 1964, 17 new eating establishments were opened (three cafeterias, three restaurants, six parkway and turnpike establishments, and five institutional cafeterias); Bill Jr. was building hotel number five (a 500-unit in Atlanta), was about to start construction on another one in New Jersey, was breaking ground in Boston, and had three more on the design boards. In J.W.'s opinion, the company was plunging into debt like a "ne'er-do-well crap shooter" and it was Bill Jr.'s hotels that were responsible.

According to J.W. Marriott, "I told my sons that this is a tough business and that you'd better be a stockbroker or something." Despite his reservations, in late 1964, he decided that the time for change had come. At an announcement ceremony in November, he named Bill Jr. president of the company. Earlier that year, as he had wrestled with the decision, he had written Bill Jr. an outline of his management philosophy (Exhibit 2).

J. WILLARD MARRIOTT, JR.

According to a 1985 *Management Review* article:

When Bill Marriott talks, his attitude is open and warm, his voice young and lively—almost preppy. His vocabulary is speckled with "gosh," "gotta," and "sure betcha." He believes in God, country, and family, and thinks good character is a "must" in a manager. In a one-hour interview he uses the word "fun" six times—and each time the word is used in relation to running his business.[1]

---

[1] S. M. Sullivan, "Money, Talent, and the Devil by the Tail: J. Willard Marriott," *Management Review,* January 1985, p. 19.

Exhibit 1
The Founding of Marriott: Bill Marriott, Sr.

John Willard (Bill) Marriott was born in the Marriott Settlement near Ogden, Utah, on September 17, 1900. The son of a sheep farmer, he was a third-generation Mormon, whose grandfather moved to Utah in 1854 with the second wave of Mormons.

At the age of 19, J.W. Marriott, as encouraged by his church, set out to preach the gospel of Mormonism for two years. His father sold the family car and his mother her gold watch and chain to finance his mission to New England. While there, he received a rude awakening one night when an angry mob chased him and his partner out of town by torchlight and with gunfire. After completing his mission in another state, he returned home by way of Washington, D.C. It was September, and J.W. took special note of how the soda pop vendors were selling cart after cart of soda pop and ice cream in the sweltering heat.

At home he discovered that the postwar depression in livestock prices had forced his father to borrow nearly $50,000 from the Ogden State Bank. J.W. quickly concluded that his life was somewhere else and that his ticket out was education. The fact that he had never finished high school did not deter him; he convinced an administrator at recently established Weber State Junior College in Ogden to enroll him and allow him to make up high school credits and arrange odd jobs to pay tuition. In 1923 J.W. was a member of the first graduating class. The next fall he enrolled at the University of Utah, where he met Alice ("Allie") Sheets. They were engaged in 1926, just before J.W.'s graduation.

After graduation J.W. returned to Weber College to teach English and theology and to help with fund-raising. He became intrigued, however, with a new drink being sold from stands in Salt Lake City—A&W Root Beer. After learning that franchises were available and that some vendors made enough in the summer months to take the rest of the year off, he borrowed $1,500 and invested $1,000 of savings in franchises for Baltimore, Richmond, and Washington, D.C.

In 1927, just prior to Allie's graduation and their wedding, J.W. returned to Washington to open a small root beer stand on 14th Street, N.W. The A&W franchise agreement forbade the sale of any product other than A&W Root Beer, but, realizing that in winter people would lose interest in cold drinks, J.W. successfully sought a change in his franchise agreement so

(continued on next page)

(continued)

that he could sell food. Drawing on her western background, Allie cooked tamales, chili, hot barbecue sandwiches, and hot dogs in their apartment, and J.W. served customers in a nine-stool unit. At the suggestion of a customer, the stand was named the Hot Shoppe—a name "so bad it's good," Allie said.

After the success of the original Hot Shoppe, J.W. opened another on Ninth Street, N.W. Then for the third Hot Shoppe, he looked for a location that would allow plenty of parking for curb service because he had decided to use a new invention—a tray that affixed to an open car window—to introduce the first drive-in restaurant east of the Mississippi River. With an expanded menu that included salads and ham sandwiches flavored with Allie's own sauce, the third Hot Shoppe, opened in 1929, served as a model for others to come. The new sandwiches sold for 15 cents, the tamales and hot dogs for 10 cents, and the drinks for a nickel. By the time the stock market crashed, the Marriotts were selling $1,400 of food and drink each day from the three units.

As the chain grew throughout the 1930s, J.W. and Allie continued to visit every restaurant every day—ordering meals, talking to customers, and even checking the garbage cans. After the fifth unit, J.W. began using central mass production and procurement systems.

In 1937 Hot Shoppe number eight was built near Washington's old Hoover Airport. Not only did people stop, eat in their cars, and watch the planes take off and land, but the manager noticed that travelers on their way to the airport would stop in, buy food to go, and take it on the plane with them (in-flight service at the time was primitive at best). So Hot Shoppes began selling box lunches for airline travelers, along with large thermos bottles of milk and coffee. Soon J.W. convinced Eastern Air Lines to buy Marriott bag lunches for its passengers. As Hot Shoppes expanded geographically, so did the in-flight catering, and soon the company was serving the Newark and Chicago airports.

J.W. opened his first contract cafeteria in 1942 and soon had the navy as a customer.

Hot Shoppe number eight was located between two heavily traveled highways and about a half-mile from National Airport. After successfully resisting pressure from two government agencies to sell the land for an approach to the 14th Street bridge, in 1950 J.W. purchased the adjoining eight acres for $60,000 per acre. The site provided the perfect location for his latest project: a $7-million motor hotel that, in J.W.'s words, would be

(continued on next page)

(continued)

"the logical extension of Hot Shoppes' traditional concern for the American family on wheels."

Considered upscale at the time, the 370-room unit was the largest motor hotel in the world and featured such amenities as soundproofing, drive-in registration, a Hot Shoppe overlooking the swimming pool, an observation deck to view the Washington skyline, TV sets in every room, king-size beds, wall-to-wall carpeting, and baby-sitters on call. Allie picked the red-and-gold room decor, the family hung pictures on the walls, and Bill Jr., just out of the Navy, supervised the final months of construction and the grand opening with daughter Debbie cutting the yellow ribbon.

In the early 1950s, J.W., seeing the growth of other area companies that had gone public, sold 229,880 shares of Hot Shoppes, Inc., to the public (for $10.25 a share) and 18,000 shares to employees (at $7.54 a share). The family retained control of about two-thirds of the company's 704,800 shares.

As a kid, Bill and his younger brother, Dick, frequently accompanied his father on business trips and began working with the company part time as soon as he was old enough to get a permit. During college Bill started most mornings at 4:00 A.M. at the Salt Lake Hot Shoppe with the breakfast chef. He worked the grill, the fountain, the deep fryer, and the salad block.

In college Bill had all of the advantages of an oldest son of a multimillionaire. Nevertheless, the former Eagle Scout dressed plainly, made consistently high grades, and graduated from the University of Utah with top honors from the business school and the Navy ROTC. His only indulgence was the flame-red Jaguar that he sported around campus. According to Bill, "When you are raised in a religious family, you have to be a person of character and good standards to be accepted."

After a stint in the navy, Bill Jr. married his college sweetheart, and he joined the Marriott Corporation in 1956. He spent his first six months in the restaurant division but was soon transferred to public relations. Later that year he began coordinating the final stages of construction of the company's first hotel—The Twin Bridges. By 1958 Bill was running the newly formed hotel division, and one year later he was also named president of Hot Shoppes.

Although the growth was not as fast as he would have liked, within a year Bill had opened three more hotels: "I felt that the company had to grow and that to grow we had to have more hotel units. Hotels are a greater challenge than restaurants. They generate higher profits." Bill financed the growth by debt. "As my father was always saying, he owed $2,000 when he first came to

Exhibit 2
Letter from J. W. Marriott, Sr., to J. W. Marriott, Jr.

January 20, 1964

Dear Bill:

I am mighty proud of you. Years of preparation, work, and study have shown results.

A leader should have character, be an example in all things. This is his greatest influence. In this you are admirable. You have not taken advantage of your position as my son. You remain humble.

You have proved you can manage people and get them to work for you. You have made a profit—your thinker works. You are developing more patience and understanding with people, more maturity.

It is not often that a father has a son who can step into his shoes and wear them on the basis of his own accomplishments and ability. Being the operating manager of a business on which probably 30,000 people depend for a livelihood is a frightening responsibility, but I have the greatest confidence you will build a team that will insure the continued success of a business that has been born through years of toil and devotion by many wonderful people. I have written down a few guideposts—all born out of my experience and ones I wish I could have followed more closely.

Love and best wishes.
Sincerely,
(signed) Dad

Bill's 15 "guideposts":

1. Keep physically fit, mentally and spiritually strong.
2. Guard your habits—bad ones will destroy you.
3. Pray about every difficult problem.
4. Study and follow professional management principles. Apply them logically and practically to your organization.
5. People are No. 1—their development, loyalty, interest, team spirit. Develop managers in every area. This is your prime responsibility.
6. Decisions: Men grow making decisions and assuming responsibility for them.

(continued on next page)

(continued)

    a. Make crystal clear what decisions each manager is responsible for and what decisions you reserve for yourself.

    b. Have all the facts and counsel necessary—then decide and stick to it.

7. Criticism: Don't criticize people but make a fair appraisal of their qualifications with their supervisor only (or someone assigned to do this). Remember, anything you say about someone may (and usually does) get back to them. There are few secrets.

8. See the good in people and try to develop those qualities.

9. Inefficiency: If it cannot be overcome and an employee is obviously incapable of the job, find a job he can do or terminate *now*. Don't wait.

10. Manage your time.

    a. Short conversations—to the point.

    b. Make every minute on the job count.

    c. Work fewer hours—some of us waste half our time.

11. Delegate and hold accountable for results.

12. Details:

    a. Let your staff take care of them.

    b. Save your energy for planning, thinking, working with department heads, promoting new ideas.

    c. Don't do anything someone else can do for you.

13. Ideas and competition:

    a. Ideas keep the business alive.

    b. Know what your competitors are doing and planning.

    c. Encourage all management to think about better ways and give suggestions on anything that will improve business.

    d. Spend time and money on research and development.

14. Don't try to do an employee's job for him—counsel and suggest.

15. Think objectively and keep a sense of humor. Make the business fun for you and others.

Washington in 1927 as a young man; now he owes $20 million, and that, he says, is progress!"

In 1964, at the age of 34, Bill was named executive vice president of the company and later that year was elected president. In 1967 the company's name was changed to Marriott Corporation and one year later was listed on the New York Stock Exchange. In 1972 Bill was officially designated chief executive officer (CEO).

After assuming control of the company, Bill realized that the rapid growth it had been experiencing required management expertise that the company did not have. "I had to terminate between 20 and 30 people. My dad could never have done what I did." Some of those let go were relatives and long-time family friends of his father. He compensated most of them handsomely and allowed many to retire. Friends say that the ordeal made him physically sick. He quickly moved to bring in outside professional management.

In 1975, when earnings per share dipped slightly after years of growth, Bill decided that there were too many unproductive assets and a lack of marketing and finance professionals in the company. He hired new managers who could begin to dispose of unproductive businesses and concentrate on expanding hotels at a faster rate. When the recession of 1979–1980 helped to depress the stock price below $25, management spent $259 million to buy back a third of its stock.

Under Bill Marriott, Jr., the company grew through expansion of the hotel operations and acquisition of restaurant and travel-related businesses:

1965–1970: Big Boy and Roy Rogers franchises and a travel agency (since sold).

1970–1975: Sun-Line cruise ships, Great America theme parks (since sold), and Farrell's ice cream parlors (since sold).

1975–1984: Host International airport restaurants and Gino's fast-food restaurants for conversion to Roy Rogers units.

By 1984 Bill Jr. was president and CEO of the largest private employer in the Washington area (20,000 employees) and one of the largest in the United States. His 1.1 million shares of Marriott stock made him a very rich man, but according to Bill it was not the money that satisfied him: "You get to a point where it's not really that any more. Then most businesspeople, they're in it for the pride of accomplishment and the success in what they do. It's fun to do things and get things done. The key is to keep that going." He also adds, "If you don't generate excitement, you don't generate much."

According to *Business Week,* Bill was a "self-confessed, Type-A, workaholic" who regularly spent 70 to 80 hours a week on the job, about half of it on the road. It is estimated that he traveled 200,000 miles a year on company business, visiting 100 hotels and 25 flight kitchens and eating at company restaurants as often as five times a week. In 1982 he spent 180 days on the road. Bill said he practiced "management by moving around" (Exhibit 3):

> That's not original, but it's what I do. You can check up and appraise how things are really going if you get down on the line. You can get a feel if the people are up or down, if they're being motivated and care. You can see if a place is getting worn. You don't see that if you're sitting behind your desk.

Exhibit 3

"Keeping in Touch," February 27, 1985, *The Wall Street Journal*

WASHINGTON— J. Willard Marriott Jr., the Chief Executive Officer of Marriott Corp., is wandering around the basement of his flagship hotel here. Randomly yanking a dinner plate out of a storage cabinet, he spots a splotch of dried food. "You really ought to soak some of these dishes," he reminds the hotel manager.

. . . .

Often he checks out his hotels at odd hours: midnight in the kitchen, for instance, or 5 A.M. in the laundry room. "When you start trying to anticipate what he'll find, you get better as a manager," says John Dixon, the general manager of the new JW Marriott hotel here.

On a recent visit, Mr. Marriott found plenty. Seconds after entering the atrium-style lobby, his eyes darted left to a pink marble pillar. On a visit to the hotel a few weeks before, Mr. Marriott had noticed an unwaxed strip about half-an-inch wide circling the pillar's base. "I see you cleared up that problem. Looks good," he said approvingly, shaking Mr. Dixon's hand.

A few minutes later, Mr. Marriott was in the kitchen. Looking like a man running for office, he greeted about a dozen employees with firm pumps of the hand, a broad smile and a "Hi, how ya doin'?" He addressed a few of the old-timers by their first names and embraced one.

Then he grimaced as he discovered a batch of hash browns left over from breakfast two hours earlier, a violation of one of the strict written rules that dictate food portions and preparations. "This is a penny business," says Wes Merhige, the general manager of the Santa Clara, California Marriott, "and Bill knows how to keep track of the pennies."

Before his two-hour tour ended, Mr. Marriott peeked in on the front desk, the laundry ("good, no wrinkles"), the loading dock, the exercise spa, storage lockers ("what's hidden in here?") and about half-a-dozen rooms and suites. At the employee cafeteria, he swept through the room, shaking hands with at least 50 startled workers.

In fact, Mr. Marriott is so involved in every detail of his business that he selects the color of the carpeting for hotel lobbies. . . . Mr. Marriott believes his involvement has given the company an advantage. "The edge in this business is people," he says. "I'm trying to communicate that I care and that the role they play in the organization is an extremely vital one."

I have a nice office. It would be a lot more fun to sit in the easy chair in the office and read reports and talk on the telephone every now and then and think up great strategic ideas rather than fly 200,000 miles every year to visit another hotel, or a flight kitchen, or a customer.

I found that the successful managers in our hotels stay out of their offices. They are out inspecting rooms, checking restaurant food and service, pouring coffee at breakfast in the dining room, welcoming our guests when they check in, and bidding them goodbye when they check out. They are walking the property, listening to the guests and the employees, looking for problems to solve and solving them.

According to *The Washingtonian*, when traveling,

Bill asks guests at a hotel what they think, what they like and don't like. He joins a stranger at breakfast to check the service. He asks a flight attendant about the food that's being served—and gets an opinion from the passenger next to him as well.

He's quick to suggest changes. On a visit to the Boston Long Wharf Marriott, he thought the carpet in the lobby looked dirty, and ordered it replaced with a darker color. The Newport Beach Hotel had bought 50 clay pots and filled them with flowers; Bill thought they looked so good he ordered similar planters for all the California Marriotts.[2]

Although he admitted that travel was a strain, he saw it as "part of the culture of doing business today." He rejected the idea of a corporate plane, however, choosing to fly commercial coach most of the time: "Too expensive. It would drive me crazy knowing two guys were sitting around out there with their meters ticking, waiting for me to fly off." He told an anecdote about his father's thriftiness:

I have a lot of great people working for the company, among them a half dozen so-called superstars who report to me, who think we should have a corporate jet. And I remind them that, although we are a $3-billion company and probably the only one in the country that does not have a $3-million jet, we do have 17 beautiful used Rambler automobiles that belong to my father. Anytime they want to use one of those, they are privileged to ask his permission (he probably won't let them do it). You see, he served on the board of American Motors many years ago and was on long enough to get a new car every year at cost. When he went to turn in his current car for a new model, they would never give him the cost back on the car, so we now have 17 used Ramblers in our family.

---

[2]Hope Lampert, "How Did This Quiet, Nice, Religious Man Become One of the Most Successful Businessmen in the Country?" *The Washingtonian*, January 1984, p. 151.

In general Bill believed "Work is good and necessary. That was the attitude around me when I was growing up. My father worked hard. My mother worked hard. I was *expected* to get all As when I was in school or I sure was asked why." (For more information on some of Bill Marriott's other interests, see Exhibit 4).

Another characteristic of Bill Marriott's management style was described by one of his managers:

> He's got to be one of the world's greatest listeners. He conveys to you that you have his full attention. He can handle great diversity. He tolerates spirited diversity of opinion in meetings; he doesn't squelch it. Consequently, most decisions are reached by talking them through. Once there were two schools of thought about an issue. After 30 minutes of debate, no one had changed their opinion and someone remarked, "That's why we have a chief executive."
>
> Bill said, "Oh hell" and made the decision. But that's not the typical way a decision is reached at Marriott. Bill prefers to have a consensus develop from the dialogue.

Another executive commented on his leadership:

> He doesn't run a financial holding company. His leadership can attract strong people to him. He can create a climate where there is healthy disagreement. In the Finance Committee, he says, sometimes he doesn't get a word in edgewise. He's secure enough in his leadership that you don't have people jockeying to be president next year. He provides a stable climate that allows people to use their strengths. He utilizes his counselors very well.

One of his counselors was his father. Although Bill was quick to give his father credit for "getting the company started," "making it work," and "establishing the culture," he once remarked,

> Working for your father is very difficult. You say things to your father that you would never say to your boss, and he says things to you he'd never say to a subordinate.
>
> Whenever there was a major decision, he [his father] would tell me all the things he saw wrong with it—and, believe me, there were plenty. But if I insisted on going ahead he never stopped me, because the decision was mine and I knew I had better make it work. I also knew that if I was going to make it work I had better anticipate the problems before they hit me head on. I had to be sure, as much as possible, that the light at the end of the tunnel was that ray of hope that we all look for when we make decisions, and not the Santa Fe Super Chief.
>
> If I have had any success in business, I think it is because I have had a teacher who was willing to let me make mistakes and then to know that I had to fix them. . . . I guess that is why I try hard not to veto the recommendations of those who work for me.

Exhibit 4
Other Interests of Bill Marriott, Jr.

Bill devoted time to the Boy Scouts, Chamber of Commerce, and Business-Industry Political Action Committee and gave about 15 to 20 hours a week (evenings, Saturdays, and Sundays) as well as 10 percent of his gross income to his church. Not only was his family instrumental in building the Washington Mormon temple, but Bill, a former bishop, was currently president of the Washington "stake," the equivalent of a diocese, and oversaw the spiritual well-being of 35,000 Mormons:

> I don't know how much you know about our church, but it is basically a lay church. We have no paid ministry, and so they put us all to work. They installed me as a bishop about 12 years ago. I was really the parish priest. I had 750 members in my ward: I had a lot of singles, I had Spanish, and I had American families. I had all kinds of diverse people to take care of.
>
> I spent 30 hours a week listening to marital problems, youth problems, father problems, mother problems, parenting problems. And I think it did more to develop me as an executive than any experience I have ever had, because I was put into a position of having to deal with people's lives, people's aspirations and hopes and sorrows and fears.
>
> I preached funerals; I performed marriage ceremonies. I did everything that the parish priest or the parish minister does in other churches. And so I learned firsthand again the . . . importance of being empathetic toward people, taking care of people, learning to listen to people, and learning to help them solve problems. It was a great reinforcement for me in the business world and probably one of the great experiences in my life.
>
> In many of my counseling sessions, I saw that if I listened they solved their own problems. I have definitely learned to listen better and to be more compassionate. When you listen to a woman with kids who is divorcing, you become exposed to people and their problems in their own context, not just how you saw them before. I've learned to deal with people whose lives have not been as fortunate as mine. I've learned to deal with compassion. It's given me understanding.
>
> I think my people feel I am a pretty good listener. I'll listen to what they say, and I'll try to get their input. But I'm still willing to make the decisions.

The Washingtonian article tied together Bill Jr.'s Mormon heritage with his life and philosophy:

(continued on next page)

(continued)

He believes the Mormon doctrine—God lives on a planet and has a wife—and he follows the church's puritanical scriptures: no liquor, tobacco, or caffeine. His verities are God, country, hard work, self-denial, and strength of character. . . .

Bill Jr. says that the Mormon emphasis on family has made him a better executive. In many ways, the Marriott Corporation is an extension of the Marriott family. Bill Jr. says that the Mormon ethic of hard work has become the company's ethic. "We try to instill the Mormon ethic in the employees," explains his brother Dick. "But we don't preach the Mormon doctrine here. We just have a good Christian work ethic."

He's a family man. He tries to get to his youngest son's soccer games every Saturday. He spends his free time with his wife and kids; he never misses Sunday dinner, and the whole Marriott clan gets together for Mother's Day, Father's Day, Christmas, and Easter. He has simple tastes. He lives in a small two-story colonial house in Chevy Chase. He buys his suits off the rack at Joseph Bank. His one passion is speed: During college he drove a Jaguar; later, he zipped around in a Lamborghini; he is now the proud owner of a new Jaguar sedan. He also likes to race powerboats.

During the summer of 1983, although the plan had been discouraged by the Marriott board, Bill raced up the Mississippi River in an effort to set a new record for the 673-mile race:

It was like being in a black closet with sort of a pale light in front of you from the buoys. So at night for about two hours there was a risk. You don't know if you're going to hit a boat; you don't know if you're going to run aground; you don't know if you're going to hit a big log.

Yet, he described it as

more fun than anything I've done in years. I thought as I was driving that boat, "Not only am I doing something I like to do, but I am also trying to achieve something. I'm moving toward a goal. I'm not out for a joy ride in a boat riding around in a circle. I'm headed from Point A to Point B in an attempt to get there faster than anyone else has ever done it before."

In 1984, at the age of 83, as chairman of the board, J.W. Marriott still took an active role in the business, talking to his son almost every day and studying memos and cost reports. He and his wife, also on the board, owned 862,412 and 939,431 shares of Marriott stock, respectively. He once observed,

"People say 'Weren't you ever satisfied?' I've never been satisfied. I see things now that haven't been right all along."

MANAGEMENT PRACTICES

Although Bill Jr. considered his father "one of the pioneers of the chain restaurant systems," he would rather "perfect than pioneer." In reflecting on his approach, he commented, "To make the right decisions, you have to have a thorough understanding of your people, your business, and your products. Lacking that, you make bad decisions." A key to Marriott's success, he believed, was its employees (Exhibit 5)—motivating, teaching, helping, and caring about them. Bill Sr. explained:

> If your managers can treat your people right and be sincerely interested in them, then you'll be successful. We must be interested in people, all people. I believe that the success of our company from the very beginning was simply because we have been interested in our people. When we had only a few restaurants, the people who worked for us were just like members of our own family. If they got sick, we went to see them. If they had trouble, we tried to get them out of trouble, and they, in turn, developed a warmth and a loyalty to us that money couldn't buy. . . . Those who work for us must like us. If they like you and have respect for you, then they will do almost anything for you. They will look after your customers properly, and a spirit of friendliness will pervade your whole organization. And what a wonderful thing that sort of harmony is.

The company was decentralized when it came to recruiting, training, and staffing, with each division, hotel, or restaurant hiring its own employees. College recruiting was coordinated centrally (with Bill Jr. occasionally joining in), but each division recruited for itself at approximately 40 colleges and at seven MBA programs. In this recruiting effort, Bill Jr. wanted recruiters to look for certain qualities—people skills ("Some of the brightest often don't have people skills"), high motivation, and willingness to sacrifice:

> I have been concerned that our business schools around the country are not graduating businessmen. I would go to business colleges and universities and try to talk to and recruit graduates. The ones that I talked to seemed to be anxious to become administrative assistants, strategic planners, financial analysts, treasurers. I asked them, "Do you want to learn to cook? Do you want to work in a kitchen? Do you want to carry suitcases, to check in people at the front desk? Would you like to learn the business?"
>
> And the answer was almost always, "No, why would I do that when I can work on corporate strategy or make big financial transactions?" And I told them that by not wanting to learn the basics of the business, they were not developing a foundation of knowledge and skill that would equip them to move into a senior manager's position, which is what they all

Exhibit 5

Dave Roberts, John Dixon, and Donna Moore:
Three People Who Show Why
Marriott Is a Winner

Dave Roberts started working for Marriott Corporation nine years ago as a grill man at a local Hot Shoppes Jr. He worked part time at a Roy Rogers while he studied at the University of Maryland. Then he decided to become a restaurant manager, so he took a three-week course at Marriott headquarters on how to run a Roy Rogers. He worked as a management assistant for a couple of months, then was named a unit manager. He took charge of a Roy Rogers in Waldorf, Maryland; then he supervised the openings of some of the newly converted Gino's; now he's managing Roy Rogers number D55 on upper Connecticut Avenue. And he's looking up: In three years, he hopes to be a district manager.

He is blond, blue-eyed, and 26. He wears wire-rimmed glasses. He gets to the restaurant at six every morning to supervise the opening. The tables have to be sparkling clean; the salad bar has to be prepped; the beef roasts have to go into the oven at eight o'clock. He stays "till death do us part," sometimes as late as ten at night. He usually works the night shift on Fridays.

On the job, Roberts wanders from station to station making sure that the cooking is up to standard, that the person at the cash register is working efficiently, that the tables are cleaned after each diner leaves. He handles all customer complaints. He's in charge of ordering supplies for the unit and counting the receipts every night. He watches who comes in. There's a regular clientele: elderly residents of the Van Ness community down the street, UDC students, IBM employees from the offices upstairs. And Roberts supervises the three management trainees who are at his store for three weeks to learn how a real Roy Rogers works.

His favorite job is spotting management potential. If Roberts thinks that one of his hourly workers could handle a supervisory job, he suggests that the employee apply for a training course. The employee goes to headquarters for two months to learn some management basics, then comes back to Roberts's shop to learn how to run each of the hourly stations. Next, a management internship, assisting a manager like Roberts. In the past year, Roberts has spotted seven trainees. One left the company when her husband moved out of the area; another couldn't handle the pressure of a management job; five now manage Roy Rogers units.

The long hours don't give Roberts much time to spend with his wife, Maya, an advertising executive at Sentinel Publications. When he can, he

(continued on next page)

(continued)

works at fixing up the couple's new house in Crofton, Maryland. He also plays tennis and rides his bike. Roberts loves his job, and he was tickled a couple of months ago when he met cowpuncher Roy Rogers in person at the opening of a new unit. "He was a lot smaller than I'd imagined," says Roberts. "I thought he was a tough, tall cowboy. He's small and delicate." Roberts wasn't disillusioned, however, and he's never given a thought to leaving the company. "There's never a day the same as the next," he says. "There is always something out of the ordinary. I like that."

John Dixon was no novice when he joined Marriott Corporation three years ago: For eight years, he'd been a general manager at the Hyatt Hotel on Union Square in San Francisco. But Dixon still had to go through the Marriott management training program. He started with a week-long course called "Introduction to Management," which taught him how Marriott Corporation deals with people. Then he went to food school for a week to learn to cook from the company's recipe cards. After that, Dixon spent three months training at the Tysons Corner hotel. The first day he worked on the loading dock, unpacking boxes from delivery trucks. The next day he was in the kitchen, first as a banquet cook, then as a line cook. He worked at the front desk making reservations, checking in guests. He was a housekeeper for a day, learning how to make up a room. The manager at Tysons Corner

gave Dixon written tests on what he was learning. Dixon passed with flying colors.

Finally Dixon was named a "resident" at the Crystal City Marriott. That meant he was responsible for hotel operating areas like housekeeping and the front desk. A year after he joined the company, Dixon was made a general manager at Tysons Corner. He worked there for a year. Then he was tapped to be manager of the new JW Marriott at National Place.

He's a big man with a jaunty mustache. He wears a three-piece suit and a gold pocket watch. He's a bachelor. Mostly, however, he's in the office: eight in the morning till eight at night. And he couldn't be prouder of his job. The new hotel will be a showcase that Bill Marriott says will "represent what the new Marriott hotels stand for."

"It will be a very special hotel," says Dixon. There will be two concierge floors, a floor of luxurious suites overlooking Pennsylvania Avenue, and a presidential floor offering full butler service. Rates start at a steep $98 a night; the largest suites will go for $750.

For the past two years, Dixon has supervised a sales team and has put together a 700-person hotel staff. Once the hotel opens, he'll be the head troubleshooter, and he expects guests to come to his mezzanine office and tell him if the hotel is doing something wrong. He loves his work. He recently took a course in advanced management techniques, and he hopes to move up the management ladder, perhaps opening another larger hotel in

(continued on next page)

(continued)

the next few years. "What I like best about this company is the pace," he says. "It's exciting. It's challenging. This is not a company that has found its place under the sun."

Donna Moore has been running the Marriott hotel gift shops for nine years. When she took the job, the shops weren't managed as a unit. Each one had its own image and did its own purchasing; the quality varied considerably from hotel to hotel—and Bill Marriott wasn't happy about that. Moore's assignment was to make the shops more uniform and more profitable. And she has. The gift shops are now geared to the Marriott business guest—they sell everything from ashtrays to Hathaway shirts to designer stockings to Kachina dolls. Goods are bought at headquarters; quality and service are tightly controlled. The bottom line: Marriott gift shops are about twice as profitable as the top New York department stores.

The secret, says Moore, is hard work. Moore supervises everything: floor plans, hiring, training, merchandising. She spends half her time on the road visiting gift shops, talking to regional managers, examining merchandise. She is always looking for new items, and her friends never stop making suggestions. Often those aren't helpful, but a few work out. A friend in California showed Moore a handmade doll last year; Moore ordered some samples from the maker in North Carolina and liked them so much she asked the woman for 1,200 dolls—three times what the woman can deliver this year. Sometimes, Moore develops her own product ideas. When the JW Marriott opens next month, the gift shop will boast a Gund bear with a custom sweater reading, "JW Bear," a Moore innovation. J. Willard Marriott Sr. got a sample for Christmas. "He's a teddy bear," says Moore.

She is a small woman with red hair and brown eyes. She lives in Annapolis with her husband, a boat maker. Moore has a daughter and a fourteen-month-old granddaughter. She spends her free time sailing: Mexico, the Caribbean. For years she worked at Joseph Magnin, a women's retailer based in San Francisco. She left when Cyril Magnin retired and the company stopped being a family enterprise.

Her next goal at Marriott is to spin off the gift shops as a separate division, run as a retail outfit instead of a hotel unit. She thinks that would be more profitable. "Working for Marriott is fantastically exciting," she says. "This is still a family business. If Mr. Marriott sees something he likes or doesn't like in the shops, I hear about it. There is lots of contact with the people at the top. It is important to have people talk to you on a first-name basis. It's thrilling for me."

wanted to do anyway. They did not realize that, to be truly effective future managers, they had to learn to manage in their own particular sphere in business.

I was also not able to convince them that the truly effective manager succeeded because he had the knowledge and the skill [that] gave him the self-confidence to operate comfortably as the boss. They had thought the operations people would respect and perform for them even if they didn't understand the business.

He also believed effective managers let their people try new things and yet held them accountable:

It is not really the mistake that concerns and upsets me nearly as much as the refusal by someone to try and make it work. For I believe we must try and try and never give up until success is achieved. We must be willing to take some risks. The guy that shot the hole-in-one had to get on the golf course in the first place.

Bill Jr. also believed that it was important to know what prospective employees had "done with their lives" and what their relationships with their spouses and families had been like. He believed, "We are living in a much more righteous and puritanical society than just a few years ago. Much of what has happened in the way of business scandals that have almost ruined companies is making businesspeople much more cognizant of honesty and good character in managers." He also believed that another advantage to the business of good character was honesty in giving opinions: "I don't want a bunch of yes men. Your people are your best resource. If they aren't helpful, why have them? You want people to challenge you. You've got to have good advice."

Another quality Marriott was seeking in recruiting was the ability to get along with all types of people; the company wanted corporate people who were not "too entrepreneurial." As Bill Jr. explained, "We are in the people business, and from waiters to maids to truck drivers, our employees must be able to get along pleasantly with others all day long."

As *The Washingtonian* described Marriott,

It's an egalitarian company, with few perks for executives: no company plane, no limos, no executive dining hall. Top executives lunch at the employee cafeteria; the fancy health club at headquarters is open to all employees for $1 a month—and even Bill Jr.'s brother Richard, vice president in charge of restaurants, has to reserve his racquetball court in advance.

Bill Jr. also insisted on giving people "a fair shake." Consequently, every employee received a formal performance evaluation at least once a year that identified both strengths and areas that needed improvement, including suggested ways for improving. Each division was required to follow certain guidelines in matters of discipline. In particular, except for a few very serious offenses, no one could be fired unless warned in writing three times. Bill Jr. maintained,

It seems like common sense to me. When you abdicate in fairness or responsibilities, the union takes over by default. . . . In a lot of companies there is a very hostile attitude. Let's admit it. There are people who like to fire people. Some managers may not know it, but they have created a fear-oriented attitude. They may call it "productivity-oriented," but if their people are afraid of them and tattle on each other, it's no good.

Although compensation standards were established for the corporation as a whole, with a 28-grade salary structure, each division was able to adjust its compensation levels to remain competitive in its respective markets. Ninety percent of Marriott employees were paid on an hourly basis, and except for 10 percent who had come with acquisitions, none were union members.

Part of the fair shake was a companywide profit-sharing plan, under which the company donated an average of $1.55 for every dollar paid in by an employee. Recently a retired dishwasher had received $104,000 after 17 years with the company, a secretary $149,000 after 20 years, and a top executive $477,000 after 21 years.

Partially as a result of some "bad experiences" in hiring people from outside into line positions, Marriott emphasized internal promotion and training. For example, 30 percent of Marriott's managers were estimated to have started as hourly employees. Furthermore, the company spent $20 million annually on training. *The Washingtonian* article noted:

Perhaps the most important part of the training program is attitude. It's hard to teach an employee to be nice, but Marriott tries with twelve rules, printed in each job manual: (1) Listen to guest complaints. (2) Filter through to the real problem. (3) Develop alternative solutions. (4) Act immediately and visibly. (5) Never promise what you cannot deliver. (6) Defer that which is beyond your authority to control. (7) Look for something (however unimportant) in the guest's remarks with which you can agree. (8) Give the guest your individual attention. (9) Smile and be pleasant. (10) Initiate the conversation. (11) Give your name. (12) Follow up on any guest complaints to insure satisfaction.

New managers and executives at Marriott spent as much as eight months working in the field. Bill Jr. explained that they needed exposure to actual operations:

What happens with MBAs is they come in here and like strategy; they become junior CEOs. That's OK, but they've had a steady dose [of that] for two years. Involvement in the details gives you the basis for planning. If you know your business, you understand what's going on out there, and you can't be led along by strategists or theorists who don't know the real world you operate your business in.

He added,

> Today many people say the image of a Marriott manager is a person who is leaning over to pick up the piece of paper off the lobby floor. Well, I've caught myself picking up pieces of paper off the floor at the Sheraton, the Hyatt, the Hilton, even in airports—and I end up putting them back down where they belong.

Operations at Marriott were strictly controlled. For example, each hotel maid had a list of 66 things to do in cleaning a room: Step number 7—dust the tops of pictures; Step number 37—make sure the Bible and telephone books are in good condition. Bill Jr. asserted, "The more the system works like the army, the better." After all, he said, "We make our profit in small increments, not home runs." In the restaurants, each portion, plate, and presentation was standardized; the cooks, regardless of their authority or training, were forbidden to deviate from the 6,000 carefully tested and approved (in central kitchens) Marriott recipe cards: "Deviation from the standard written specification may not be made without prior approval and written consent of the vice president of food and beverages." In 1981 at an American Bar Association luncheon, the system resulted in 600 burned chickens. Nevertheless, the ABA was trying to book another Marriott hotel for 1986.

Each month top managers received, via computer terminals in every office, the equivalent of a 50-page report on how the company was doing. It included such information as profit margins, revenues, customer counts, and occupancy rates. It was management's goal to develop computerized information networks that linked each restaurant, hotel, and flight kitchen to its respective regional office and divisional center in Washington.

Bill Jr. met frequently with senior executives and kept a loose-leaf notebook that listed everything he had asked anyone to do. He also read letters from 20 random Marriott guests each week. As he said in one of his magazine ads: "I have to make sure we do things right. After all, it's my name over the door."

DIVISIONAL STRUCTURE

In the words of one executive, Marriott was "a loose confederation of businesses" that emphasized "high-quality growth" (Exhibits 6–8). It was divided into three strategic business units: restaurants, contract food services, and lodging. Each was led by an executive vice president.

The restaurant group, headed by Dick Marriott, a Harvard MBA who owned 1.3 million shares of Marriott stock and served on the board, basically consisted of Roy Rogers and Big Boy restaurants. With a menu that included chicken, burgers, roast beef sandwiches, and hot-topped potatoes, Roy Rogers sought to provide high-quality fast food to adults in the Mid-Atlantic and Northeastern states from 388 company-operated and 131 franchised units. Big Boy was a full-service coffee-house restaurant that featured breakfast bars and

Exhibit 6
Marriott Corporation
Financial History, 1975–1985

Years

	1984	1983	1982	1981	1980 (53 weeks)	1975	5-Year Compound Growth Rate	10-Year Compound Growth Rate
SUMMARY OF OPERATIONS[1]								
Sales	3,524,937	2,950,527	2,458,900	1,905,659	1,633,892	775,866	19.8%	17.7%
Earnings before interest and taxes	284,794	240,331	200,345	173,339	150,278	63,160	16.4%	16.5%
Interest cost, net	48,691	55,270	66,666	52,024	46,820	23,017		
Income before income taxes	236,103	185,061	133,679	121,315	103,458	40,143	17.5%	18.9%
United States and foreign income taxes	100,848	76,647	50,224	45,176	40,567	15,995		
Income from continuing operations	135,255	108,414	83,455	76,139	62,891	24,148	16.9%	18.8%
Net income	139,765	115,245	94,342	86,136	72,030	24,148	14.5%	19.2%
Funds provided from continuing operations[2]	322,485	272,655	203,556	160,770	125,790	75,486	22.4%	16.8%
Capital expenditures and acquisitions net of hotel sales	286,289	499,439	483,498	247,999	168,289	132,500	13.2%	6.2%
CAPITALIZATION AND RETURNS								
Total assets	2,904,669	2,501,428	2,062,648	1,454,876	1,214,264	830,975		
Total capital[3]	2,330,683	2,007,507	1,634,504	1,167,458	977,690	739,311		
Shareholders' equity	675,560	628,204	516,005	421,729	311,505	263,730		
Debt and capital lease obligations	1,115,287	1,071,611	889,325	607,743	536,607	405,658		
Percent to total capital	47.9%	53.4%	54.4%	52.1%	54.9%	54.9%		
Return on average shareholders' equity	22.1%	20.0%	20.0%	23.4%	23.8%	9.5%		
Return on average total capital (before interest and taxes)	14.1%	14.4%	14.8%	17.6%	18.0%	9.1%		

PER SHARE AND OTHER DATA

Fully diluted earnings per share:								
Continuing operations	5.01	3.90	3.04	2.83	2.27	.69	24.1%	21.8%
Net income	5.18	4.15	3.44	3.20	2.60	.69	21.6%	22.2%
Cash dividends	.465	.38	.315	.255	.21	—	22.3%	
Shareholders' equity	26.22	23.37	19.43	16.12	12.43	7.68		
Quoted market price at year-end	73.50	71.25	58.50	35.88	31.75	15.46	33.4%	27.4%
Shares outstanding	25,760,968	26,876,344	26,554,692	26,158,762	25,061,265	34,358,503		
Hotel rooms:								
Total	60,873	54,986	49,432	40,419	30,169	16,072	18.3%	15.7%
Company-operated	50,930	45,909	41,126	33,088	23,704	12,987	19.4%	16.1%
Employees	120,100	109,400	109,200	81,800	67,300	47,600	12.8%	10.5%

[1]Operating results have been restated for theme park operations discontinued in 1984. . . .
[2]Funds provided from continuing operations consist of income from continuing operations plus depreciation, deferred taxes, and other items not currently affecting working capital.
[3]Total capital represents total assets less current liabilities.
Source: Annual Report, 1984.

Exhibit 7
Marriott Corporation
Income Statement, 1982–1984
(dollars in thousands, except per share amounts)

SALES	1984	1983	1982
Lodging	1,640,782	1,320,535	$1,091,673
Contract food services	1,111,300	950,617	819,824
Restaurants	772,855	679,375	547,403
Total sales	$3,524,937	$2,950,527	$2,458,900
OPERATING INCOME			
Lodging	$161,245	$139,706	$132,648
Contract food services	90,250	73,300	51,006
Restaurants	76,220	61,634	48,492
Total operating income	327,715	274,640	232,146
Interest expense	(61,638)	(62,786)	(71,760)
Interest income	12,947	7,516	5,094
Corporate expenses	(42,921)	(34,309)	(31,801)
Income before income taxes	135,255	108,414	83,455
Income from discontinued operations	4,510	6,831	10,887
Net income[1]	$139,765	$115,245	$ 94,342
PRIMARY AND FULLY DILUTED EARNINGS PER SHARE			
Continuing operations	$5.01	$3.90	$3.04
Net income	$5.18	$4.15	$3.44

[1]Discretionary cash flow for 1984 = $278 million; 1983 = $246 million; 1982 = $192 million.
Source: Annual Report, 1984.

a greenhouse effect. Marriott held franchise rights for 26 states, where it operated 209 units and was responsible for the franchises of another 636 units.

Contract Food Services, headed by Bob Schultz, the former president and CEO of Barwick Corporation and an executive with both Colt Industries and General Housewares, supplied food for more than 350 airlines, businesses,

Exhibit 8
Marriott Corporation
Balance Sheet, 1983–1984
(dollars in thousands)

ASSETS	1984	1983
Current assets:		
Cash and temporary cash investments	$ 22,656	$ 92,279
Accounts receivables	195,874	151,975
Due from affiliates	46,467	17,655
Inventories, at lower of average		
cost or market	111,722	95,806
Prepaid expenses	53,330	43,655
Total current assets	430,099	401,370
Property and equipment, at cost:		
Land	141,714	171,984
Buildings and improvements	245,367	373,593
Leasehold improvements	658,815	716,461
Furniture and equipment	415,634	475,003
Property under capital leases	77,566	86,539
Construction in progress	668,845	388,025
	2,207,941	2,211,605
Depreciation and amortization	(375,108)	(419,823)
	1,832,833	1,791,782
Other assets:		
Investments in and advances to affiliates	268,177	68,412
Assets held for sale	230,760	81,312
Cost in excess of net assets of		
business acquired	26,742	26,380
Other	116,058	132,172
	641,737	308,276
Total assets	$2,904,669	$2,501,428

(continued on next page)

health care facilities, and educational institutions. This group was divided into four divisions: airline catering, airport operations, food service management, and highway restaurants. Airline catering, or in-flight services, served

LIABILITIES AND SHAREHOLDERS' EQUITY	1984	1983
Current liabilities:		
Short-term loans	$ 7,486	$ 8,895
Accounts payable	252,806	194,499
Accrued wages and benefits	129,452	111,420
Other payables and accrued liabilities	152,654	149,308
Current portion of debt and capital lease obligations	31,588	29,799
Total current liabilities	573,986	493,921
Debt:		
Mortgage notes payable	632,923	491,999
Unsecured notes payable	420,860	509,144
Total debt	1,053,783	1,001,143
Capital lease obligations	61,504	70,468
Other long-term liabilities	99,323	55,175
Deferred income	160,371	4,834
Deferred income taxes	280,142	247,683
Shareholders' equity:		
Common stock, 25.8 and 26.9[1] million shares outstanding, respectively	29,419	29,422
Capital surplus	145,756	140,882
Deferred stock compensation and other	3,141	4,160
Retained earnings	622,283	494,585
Treasury stock, at cost	(125,039)	(40,845)
Total shareholders' equity	$ 675,560	$ 628,204
Total liabilities and shareholders' equity	$2,904,699	$2,501,428

(continued)

[1]Marriott family holdings are approximately 22%.
Source: Annual Report, 1984.

150 airlines from 90 flight kitchens worldwide. Airport operations included terminal vending machines and restaurants. The acquisition of the Host chain in 1982 for $148 million aimed at giving Marriott a greater presence in this area. Marriott estimated that 60 percent of all people who flew in the United States passed through a Marriott/Host terminal facility. Food Service Man-

agement included institutional feeding, especially company cafeterias. Highway restaurants operated Marriott Restaurants on some major turnpikes and thoroughfares.

THE LODGING INDUSTRY AND THE HOTEL GROUP

The daily average number of hotel/motel rooms in the United States had experienced constant growth in recent years. One industry source estimated the numbers to be 2.2 million in 1978, 2.3 million in 1980, and 2.4 million in 1982. During the same period, average room rates increased from the low $30s to approximately $50 in 1982.

Marriott research identified 2,150,000 competitive rooms in the lodging industry, broken down into 80,000 luxury, 620,000 quality, 750,000 moderate, and 700,000 budget rooms. Other analysts identified only the three large segments, while some segmented by price band or price/value, an attempt to measure the amenities provided against the price.

Revenues for most U.S. hotels came from room rentals (60 percent), food sales (24 percent), beverage sales (10 percent), and miscellaneous services (6 percent). The gross profit on a room was often as high as 70 percent, which did not reflect depreciation or debt-service costs. For food the gross profit was 15 percent to 20 percent.

Hotel properties were managed in a variety of ways, but the two most common were management contract and franchise. Under management contract, chains agreed to sell their properties, in whole or in part, and contracted to operate them for the owners. Usually the fee was a percentage of the gross revenues or gross profit. This method had grown increasingly popular in recent years. Hilton Hotels, for example, managed 35 properties under contract in 1983 and received $20.5 million in contract fees; they collected only $23 million in franchise fees from 194 franchised properties.

With franchise arrangements, hotels were neither owned nor operated by the hotel company. Instead, the company received a percentage of revenues in exchange for the use of the company name, advertising support, and reservation system. Most large chains were heavily franchised. For example, in 1983, 1,489 of Holiday Inn's (HI) 1,707 properties and 255,213 of its 310,337 rooms were franchised. Most of those properties were 10 to 20 years old, and approximately 50 percent of HI's 600-plus franchise holders owned 2 or fewer properties. The typical HI franchise agreement required an initial payment of $300 per room plus 4 percent of revenues.

The customer base for domestic hotels could be divided into three groups: pleasure, business, and personal markets. Approximately 180 million Americans took at least one pleasure trip of greater than 100 miles from home each year. They accounted for about 40 percent of all hotel nights sold. Approximately 18 million people took business trips each year and accounted for 45 percent of the hotel rooms sold. In contrast to business travel, which was generally paid by employers, personal travel, such as job hunting, funeral attendance, and so forth, was usually at the traveler's expense; it accounted for the remainder.

In recent years hotel construction had been concentrated at the upper end of the market, primarily because of rapidly escalating construction costs. Two industry rules-of-thumb held that room rates should equal $1 for every $1,000 of construction cost applicable to a given room, and that breakeven was an occupancy rate of 55 to 60 percent. In many markets, owners of commercial-class hotels, which cost about $95,000 a room to build, could not charge sufficiently, while operators of luxury hotels, which cost about $125,000/room, could. Some firms, such as HI's Crowne Plazas and Ramada's Renaissance Hotels, were aggressively pursuing the higher segments with traditional rooms, while other firms, such as Quality Inns and Brock Hotels, had announced plans to enter the all-suite market. Other hotels were diversifying into gaming (gambling casinos). In 1983, Ramada Inns derived 55 percent of revenues and 45 percent of operating profits from gaming operations; HI earned 37 percent and 40 percent, respectively.

There had also been growth in the budget end of the market (Exhibit 9). The companies ranged from the economy segment (Motel 6, Super 8, Econo Lodge, Red Roof, and Scottish Inns) that could be built for $15,000 to $20,000 a room and charged $18 to $29; to "luxury budget" (Days Inns, LaQuinta, and Comfort Inns) at $30,000 to $37,000 to build and $25 to $39 in room rates.

The Marriott Hotel Group, headed by Fred Malek, former Green Beret and Harvard MBA, operated 142 hotels and resorts in almost all of the top U.S. markets plus Mexico, Central America, the Caribbean, Europe, and the Middle East. From 1975 to 1984, the number of Marriott rooms increased from 14,000 to more than 60,000 and by 1990 was expected to reach more than 100,000—a rate faster than any of the other major hotel chains:

| | Number of Rooms | |
Chain	1975	1982
Holiday Inn	240,500	265,585
Best Western	82,841	150,188
Ramada Inns	87,251	86,503
Sheraton	74,500	79,803
Hilton Hotels	59,931	80,473
Friendship Inns	59,000	84,000
Howard Johnson's	57,800	59,360
Days Inns of America	36,992	43,549
Trusthouse Forte (TraveLodge)	29,404	29,000
Quality Inns International	31,975	48,350
Best Value Inns/Superior Motels	14,400	21,300
Motel 6	21,788	33,166
Hyatt Hotels	19,500	36,300
Mariott Hotels	14,953	42,182
Rodeway Inns International	18,855	17,860

Exhibit 9
Top 50 U.S. Economy/Limited-Service
Lodging Chains

Chain Name	Ownership Structure	Number of Properties	Number of Rooms	Average Property Size	Geographic Concentrations[a]	Published Room Rate Ranges: Single
1. Days Inns	Company owned/ Franchised	291	45,410	156	MA, USA, ENC, WSC, UM, LM, P	$23.88–$56.00 X-Person $5
2. Motel 6	Company owned	394	43,881	111	National	$16.95 X-Person $4
3. La Quinta Motor Inns	Company owned/ Franchised	157	19,545	124	SA, ENC, ESC, WNC, WSC, UM LM, P	$29.00–$49.00 X-Person $5
4. Econo Lodges	Franchised	233	17,561	75	National	$21.95–$39.95 X-Person $4
5. Super 8 Motels	Company owned/ Franchised	234	14,967	64	National and Canada	$21.88–$42.88 X-Person $5
6. Hospitality International (Master Host/ Red Carpet/ Scottish Inns)	Franchised	161	13,265	82	MA, USA, SA, ENC, ESC, WSC	$22.00–$34.00 X-Person $5
7. Red Roof Inns	Company owned	123	13,161	107	NE, MA, USA, SA, ENC, ESC, WNC, WSC	$21.95–$26.95 X- Person $5
8. Comfort Inns (a division of Quality Inns)	Franchised	130	11,599	89	NE, USA, SA, ENC, ESC, WNC, WSC, UM, LM, P, CANADA	$21.00–$52.00 X- Person $5
9. Knights Inn	Company owned	60	6,594	110	USA, ENC, SA, MA	$24.00–$32.00 X-Person $5

[a]Geographic Concentrations Legend

Region	States	Region	States
New England (NE)	ME, NH, VT, MA, CT, RI	West North Central (WNC)	IA, KS, MN, MO, NE, ND, SD
Mid Atlantic (MA)	NY, NJ, PA	West South Central (WSC)	AR, LA, OK, TX
Upper South Atlantic (USA)	MD, DE, WV, VA	Upper Mountain (UM)	CO, ID, MT, UT, WY
South Atlantic (SA)	FL, GA, NC, SC	Lower Mountain (LM)	AZ, NV, NM
East North Central (ENC)	IL, IN, OH, MI, WI	Pacific (P)	CA, OR, WA
East South Central (ESC)	AL, KY, MS, TN		

(continued on next page)

Source: *Hotel & Management*, April 1985.

(continued)

Chain Name	Ownership Structure	Number of Properties	Number of Rooms	Average Property Size	Geographic Concentrations	Published Room Rate Ranges: Single
10. Affordable Inns (Regal 8)	Company owned/	50	5,604	112	ENC, ESC, WNC, WSC, UM, IM	$19.88–$23.88 X-Person $5
11. Western 6 Motels	Company owned	54	5,346	99	WSC, UM, LM, P	$24.95–$29.95 X-Person $5
12. Vagabond Inns	Company owned	47	3,841	82	WSC, LM, P	$21.95–$38.95 X-Person $5
13. Imperial 400	Company owned/ Joint venture	67	3,674	55	MA, USA, SA, ENC, WNC, WSC, UM, LM, P	$23.95–$33.95 X-Person $5
14. Drury Inns	Company owned	29	3,456	119	ENC, ESC, WNC, WSC, UM	$28.00–$44.00 X-Person $6
15. Chalet Susse Int'l	Company owned	30	3,025	101	NE, MA, SA, ENC	$23.70–$26.70 X-Person $4
16. L-K Motels/ Penny Pincher Inns	Company owned	54	2,849	53	SA, ENC, ESC	$20.00–$29.00 X-Person $4
17. Sixpence Inns	Company owned	24	2,653	111	NE, ENC, LM, P	$21.00–$24.00 X-Person $5
18. Thrifty Scott Motels	Company owned/ Joint venture	32	2,627	82	WNC, UM	$20.90–$29.90 X-Person $4
19. Exel Inns	Company owned	20	2,345	117	ENC, WNC, WSC	$18.95–$33.95 X-Person $5
20. Shoney's Inns	Company owned/Franchised	19	2,299	121	SA, ESC, WSC	$23.00–$45.00 X- Person $5
21. Budgetel Inns	Company owned/ Joint venture	21	2,184	104	NE, SA, ENC, ESC, WNC, WSC	$21.95–$28.95 X-Person $5
22. Lexington Hotel Suites	Company owned	15	2,173	145	WSC, LM, P	$32.00–$52.00 X-Person $6
23. Family Inns	Franchised	26	2,171	84	SA, ENC, WSC	$21.95–$27.95 X-Person $5
24. Ha'Penny Inns	Company owned	18	2,106	117	P	Not available
25. Turnpike Properties (Cricket Inns)	Company owned	14	1,717	123	SA, MA, ESC, WNC	$24.95–$34.95 X-Person $5

(continued on next page)

(continued)

Chain Name	Ownership Structure	Number of Properties	Number of Rooms	Average Property Size	Geographic Concentrations	Published Room Rate Ranges: Single
26. Passport Inns	Franchised	22	1,630	74	SA, ENC, ESC, WNC, WSC	$24.00–$50.00 X-Person $5
27. Luxury Budget Inns	Company owned	18	1,459	81	MA, USA	$19.95–$29.95 X-Person $4
28. Texian Inns	Company owned	12	1,380	115	WSC	$38.00–$45.00 X-Person $5
29. E-Z 8 Motels	Company owned/ Franchised	17	1,342	79	LM, P	Not available
30. Shilo Inns	Company owned	15	1,315	88	UM, P	Not available
31. Dillon Inns	Company owned	11	1,263	115	ENC, WNC, WSC	$25.95–$39.95 X-Person $5
32. America's Best Inns	Company owned/ Franchised	9	1,104	123	ENC, WNC, ESC	$21.95–$29.95 X-Person $4
33. Skylight Inns	Company owned	9	1,004	112	SA, ENC	$34.95–$39.95 X-Person $5
34. Koala Inns	Company owned	10	973	97	NE, MA	$29.95–$48.00 X-Person $5
35. Mid Continent Inns	Company owned/ Franchised	15	961	64	SA, ENC, ESC, WNC, WSC	Not available
36. Travel Host Motor Inns	Franchised	18	847	47	WNC, UM	$18.95–$22.90 X-Person $5
37. McIntosh Motor Inns	Company owned	7	813	116	MA	$23.95–$29.95 X-Person $5
38. Bargaintel Inns	Company owned	8	812	102	ENC	$24.95–$27.95 X-Person $5
39. Budgeteer Inns	Company owned	6	778	130	ENC	$21.95–$33.95 X-Person $5
40. Stratford House Inns	Company owned/ Franchised	11	770	70	WNC, WSC	$31.00–$42.00 X-Person $5
41. Roadstar Inns	Company owned	9	709	79	ENC, WNC	$23.95–$29.95 X-Person $5
42. Econ-O-Inn	Company owned	8	688	86	WNC	$21.95–$26.95 X-Person $4

(continued on next page)

(continued)

CHAIN NAME	OWNERSHIP STRUCTURE	NUMBER OF PROPERTIES	NUMBER OF ROOMS	AVERAGE PROPERTY SIZE	GEOGRAPHIC CONCENTRATIONS	PUBLISHED ROOM RATE RANGES: SINGLE
43. Prime Rate Models	Company owned	8	677	85	WNC, UM	$21.00–$28.00 X-Person $5
44. Signature Inns	Company owned	6	670	112	ENC	$34.00–$38.00 X-Person $5
45. Pony Soldier Motor Inns	Company	8	669	84	UM, P	Not available
46. Interstate Inns	Company owned/ Franchised	17	600	35	WNC, WSC, UM	$20.00–$25.00 X-Person $4
47. Hampton Inn Hotels (a division of Holiday Inns)	Company owned/ Franchised	4	488	122	SA, ESC, WNC, WSC	$29.95–$36.95 X-Person $5
48. Tapadera Motor Inns	Company owned	7	481	69	UM, P	Not available
49. Tourway Inns	Company owned	5	476	95	SA	Not available
50. Wynfield Inns	Company owned	3	408	136	SA, UM	$32.00–$38.00 X-Person $5

Chain	Number of Rooms	
	1975	1982
Westin Hotels	13,213	14,012
La Quinta Motor Inns	5,762	14,705

By 1985, 80 percent of Marriott's rooms would have been built during the previous decade, 90 percent built or renovated in the previous five years, and 26 percent would be less than two years old. Marriott estimated that 60 percent of its rooms were in the quality group and 20 percent in each of the luxury and moderate groups. The "mix of property types" included downtown locations (32 percent), airports (24 percent), suburban sites (28 percent), and resort areas (16 percent).

Marriott targeted four groups for its hotels: high-income business travelers (40 percent), conventioneers (38 percent), well-to-do pleasure travelers (15 percent), and contract rooms for flight crews (15 percent). Company research showed that those planning meetings used Marriott more often than any other chain.

The average Marriott hotel stressed service over architecture. Each offered a full line of services (restaurants, gift shops, automatic checkout, bellhops, convention and ballroom space, pool and recreation areas) and such features as French milled soap and all-cotton towels. A full-scale hotel usually required one employee for every room and one manager for every ten employees. The average room rate for Marriott's full-scale hotels was $80 to $100 a night, compared to a 1983 lodging industry average of $51.90.

Marriott's hotel occupancy rate usually averaged at least 10 points higher than the industry, which in recent years had ranged from the low 60s to low 70s. In 1981 Marriott's occupancy rate, at 79 percent, was 16 percentage points above the industry average. To assure such high rates, Marriott was constantly changing. Recently the company had developed an automatic check-out system in which the bill was slipped under the door at night, and it was working on an automatic check-in system. Management monitored the complimentary items left in the room to see what was used. When they discovered that bath crystals were not being used, those were replaced with cable television at no additional cost. Some hotels boasted a "concierge floor," where for an extra $10 guests got bigger rooms, complimentary breakfast and bar, and a concierge. In 1982 the company set up 28 model rooms and questioned 1,000 people for two hours each about the layout, color, and furnishings.

When taken as a whole, food and beverage contributed 35 percent of industry sales and 37 percent of Marriott sales. Whereas the industry reported 15 percent of gross income from food, Marriott achieved 50 percent to 60 percent higher profit margins on food services by consolidating purchases from all of its kitchens and putting the giant contracts out to bid once a year.

Since 1980 the company had financed the construction of more than $3 billion of lodging facilities. To combat high interest rates, the company began to sell the hotels as soon as construction was completed, either as equity interest partnerships (usually to large institutions such as Equitable Life Assurance Society) or as limited partnerships. Potomac Hotel Limited Partnership put up $18 million and borrowed $365 million from banks to buy 11 hotels in 1983, and Marriott expected to raise $1 billion from them in 1984. Chesapeake Hotel Limited Partnership owned 9 Marriott hotels. Marriott was the general partner, and all partnerships agreed to hire Marriott under management contract to operate the hotels. The contracts usually were for 75 years and paid Marriott a fee of 3 percent to 8 percent of operating revenues, plus an incentive fee of 20 percent to 30 percent of cumulative operating profits, making the contracts among the most generous in the industry. According to Marriott's chief financial officer, "We don't just broker a deal. We take a position and sell it off." In 1985 Marriott either owned or managed 80 percent of its rooms, making it the largest operator of hotel rooms in the United States.

Marriott's rapid growth had been managed without any apparent loss of ability to build and operate quality hotel facilities. The company's guest ratings increased significantly in 1984 in the areas of check-in and check-out, efficient reservations, meeting facilities, and friendliness of employees. In fact, Marriott led all chains in the latter category and was one of America's two most preferred business hotels. According to Bill Jr., "We receive over a thousand customer comment forms and letters every day . . . , and the most complimentary . . . are those written by guests who are impressed by our people and by some small thing that one of our staff went out of his or her way to do for them." The rooms were also rated particularly high. The company had received more four- and five-star awards than any other U.S. hotel chain.

Bill Jr. took a special interest in the hotels: "It's fun to build hotels; it's fun to make money. Being a playboy or a semi-playboy, that's really not fun. I like the pace. There's something different all the time. It's challenging." He added, "It's dirty work but the opportunities for people with brains are incredible in this industry."

PLANNING THE FUTURE AT MARRIOTT

In 1977 Bill Jr. had hired Tom Curren away from McKinsey & Co. to become the first full-time staff member to focus primarily on strategic issues. After earning his MBA from the Wharton School in 1967, Curren had served a stint in the Navy Supply Corps. and later worked with Compton Advertising and McKinsey. Until 1980 Curren's work was primarily project-oriented planning with a heavy financial emphasis—for example, stock valuations, debt policy, and determining hurdle rates.

In 1980 Curren began working to increase the number of people doing strategic thinking in the organization and began systematically examining new business opportunities for Marriott. According to Bill Jr., "We decided that by 1990 we would have saturated the upscale market that had been our area—we would have a Marriott everywhere that it was important for us to have one. If we wanted to grow, we would have to find another area."

As stage one of early business development, Curren worked with a small task force and a developmental budget and, under a steering committee of two senior executives, began "idea generation" about alternative new businesses. The task force was expected to help answer such questions as, What are our most attractive market segments? On what basis could Marriott build a meaningful competitive advantage? Is there a way to enter the business profitably? Curren wanted the alternatives to meet three objectives: (1) build or maximize shareholder wealth, (2) maintain the values of the company, and (3) allow for Marriott to control its own destiny.

Among the alternatives being considered were the following:

- *All Suites.* Although several companies had launched all-suite hotels, it was not clear if these were a fad or a serious alternative to traditional hotels.

- *Upscale Hotels.* Bill Jr. was known to be interested in architect John Portman's plan to build a 1,877-room, 48-story hotel, with a 1,507-seat theater and some 1,400 lounge and restaurant seats in New York's Times Square—an area one developer called a "cesspool." Bill Jr. had once remarked, "I had a chance to buy . . . [Portman's Hyatt Regency in Atlanta] and if I had, there would be no Hyatt chain today. But I didn't understand the importance of architecture then." Portman wanted to combine the $400-million Times Square project to a $250-million, 1,674-room unit in Atlanta.

- *Time-Sharing Condominiums.* Time-sharing facilities that allowed owners to purchase a condo for certain specified weeks of the year might allow a number of carryovers from Marriott's lodging business that would permit efficiencies in operations.

- *Retirement Communities.* Units for approximately 400 people that offered residential, recreational, and health care facilities might be a good fit with the company's food and lodging strengths.

- *Casinos.* The company had recently purchased the Seaview Resort and Country Club near Atlantic City, New Jersey, that could easily be outfitted for gambling.

- *Funeral Homes.* Not only were there Marriott skills that could be successfully brought to the funeral industry, but the company could provide a useful service and enter a very profitable industry.

- *Downscale Hotels.* The company had had no experience running a limited-service facility, but the move was a possibility. Bill Jr. had at one time expressed an interest in purchasing La Quinta Motor Inns but rejected the idea because of the asking price.

THE CLUBCOURT PROJECT

After considering the options, Curren decided to recommend undertaking an "initial business analysis" of a downscale hotel, code-named Clubcourt. Bill Jr., "whose knowledge of the business is the best in the building," according to Curren, agreed that the idea was worth further exploration.

Curren hired Don Washburn from Booz, Allen & Hamilton to be vice president of hotel planning. Washburn, a Northwestern MBA, had started his career with Inland Steel in 1963 but later joined Quaker Oats in brand management. When the Justice Department sued the large cereal companies for monopolistic behavior, Washburn found himself on the team preparing the analysis for Quaker's defense. Since it appeared that the proceedings would stretch for years, Washburn decided to attend law school in the mornings and work afternoons and nights. Ultimately, he ended up as an attorney on the case. When the government dropped Quaker from the case in 1978, Washburn moved to Booz, Allen & Hamilton and one year later to Marriott.

In describing his decision to join Marriott, Washburn observed,

> The job seemed to fit me. The first part of my work combined the skills of a consultant and a brand manager: Where were the markets? Then I needed to be creative and find a way to fill it; then ramrod the process of creating and introducing the product.
>
> I found the place very cooperative. There was a lot of conventional wisdom built around full-service hotels and some resistance to thinking about new ideas. The company, however, is filled with some of the best people I've known—honest, hard-working, dedicated to quality. I was impressed. With their participation, I was able to make headway.
>
> Because of our high growth, you find very little petty conversation. Everyone is focused on growth. When you have growth goals you have to focus on things that create value. In our meetings we are very candid. You don't have time for maneuvering. The world will move past you. We all like each other. We have a lot of respect for each other. It's very nice.
>
> We like the business and the people we work with. I think we look forward to getting to work. Times like these don't last forever. It's a challenge for a CEO to keep them going. Bill Marriott has kept them going for many years.

Curren and Washburn, as part of their "category assessment," began a thorough research effort, using various analytical models of the lodging market, to determine where a real need existed. They had concluded that there were at least four segments (classified by room rates) below Marriott's current hotels: under $30s, low to mid-$30s, high $30s to low $40s, and mid-$40s to low $50s. They also began breaking down the lodging experience into its smallest parts to determine what constituted "value" for the guest. Through an extensive motivational segmentation research effort that in the first year cost $400,000, they tried to determine a variety of price/value trade-offs and develop a better understanding of industry trends.

As the concept of Clubcourt became better known within the company, the initial response outside the team, especially from the Hotel Group, was less than enthusiastic. When Don tried to recruit people to work on the project, most people had little interest and saw it as high risk. Many wanted to stay with the glamour of the larger hotels. Some managers feared the possibility of cannibalization and, as a result, worried about its prospects. Others argued that a lower-line product was not consistent with Marriott's values. In addition, there were questions of how quality-sensitive the market was and how Holiday Inn would react to a move into its niche. It was estimated that, if Clubcourt cost around $50,000 a room to build and rooms were priced at $50, break-even occupancy might be as high as 75 percent.

Curren and Washburn therefore hit the road, with Washburn personally staying in or inspecting more than 200 moderate-priced hotels to evaluate how the competition did business and determine if there were any geographical differences that should be considered. The road time exposed them to a number of interesting ideas. For example, in Dallas they liked the size and feel of one hotel. In San Diego, they noted several hotels that had a centralized computer system. Washburn described what they discovered:

> First, we analyzed our competition at all levels of the lodging industry. Then we studied the consumer at these levels. By comparing the results of these two studies, we determined which segments were most vulnerable. We found more customers in the mid-price segment dissatisfied with existing supply than any other segment.

They concluded that, although the markets were changing rapidly, the largest group of travelers placed most value on five characteristics: (1) an attractive, comfortable, functional room; (2) a relaxing, secure environment; (3) a simple restaurant with good food; (4) friendly, helpful employees; and (5) all at a good price. In general, Washburn believed that a Marriott mid-price hotel should give people "an 'Ahaaaa!' experience": "When you've done a good job of creating an experience people wanted but didn't expect—people say 'Ahaaa! That is what I've been looking for!'"

When Curren and Washburn presented the five-point proposal at a meeting with Bill Marriott, Jr., the Hotel Group head, and the executive vice president of finance, Marriott was positive about the concept but skeptical about the execution of the idea. What would the physical facilities look like? How would it be managed and staffed? What level of service could be provided? He also expressed a desire to see the project move faster. Before it could be presented to the finance committee, which he chaired, and ultimately to the eight-member board of directors, it was necessary that a "full business concept" be developed.[3] Only if the finance committee approved could the venture start-up phase begin where, under the sponsorship of one of the four

---

[3]The board members were J. W. Marriott, Alice Marriott, Bill Marriott, Dick Marriott, Thomas Piper (Harvard Business School professor), Harry Vincent, Jr. (vice chairman of Booz, Allen & Hamilton), Frederick Deane, Jr. (chair and CEO of Bank of Virginia), and Don Mitchell (director of other corporations).

executive vice presidents, the idea would be test-marketed and, if successful, followed by a national roll-out.

In Curren's opinion, the decision whether to go with Clubcourt would be "80 percent based on superior execution." It was up to Don Washburn to take the lead in developing a detailed implementation plan that would win Bill Marriott's and the board's approval.

PART V

LEADING STRATEGIC CHANGE

CORPORATE CULTURE, VALUES,
AND STRATEGIC CHANGE

Up to this point we have been treating strategy primarily through the lenses of the "basic" model introduced in Chapter 1. Here, we will introduce the culture and values element of the "complete" model (see Figure 1-3, page 10).

THE STRATEGY EQUATION

To place a discussion of culture and values in perspective, we need to review a basic premise running throughout this book. The basic premise is summarized in the following **strategy equation**, which holds that financial performance is a function of both *industry attractiveness* and *competitive advantage or position* (the two dimensions of the McKinsey matrix or the two questions underlying Porter's five-forces framework). The equation, then, reads:

$$FP = f(IA, CA)$$

where

$$
\begin{aligned}
FP &= \text{financial performance} \\
IA &= \text{industry attractiveness} \\
CA &= \text{competitive advantage}
\end{aligned}
$$

A competitive strategist, however, seeks more than average financial returns. He or she seeks above average or *superior* financial returns. In addition, this quest is for the long term, so he or she also seeks *sustained* superior financial performance. We might rewrite the equation as

$$\text{SSFP} = f(\text{IA, CA})$$

where

$$\text{SSFP} = \text{sustained superior financial performance}$$

Let us expand the equation further. *Industry attractiveness,* as we saw in Chapter 2, is a function of industry structure (five forces) and environmental trends. So,

$$\text{IA} = f(\text{IS, E})$$

where

$$\text{IS} = \text{industry structure (five forces)}$$
$$\text{E} = \text{environment trends}$$

Competitive advantage has traditionally been treated by economists as being based on competitive *position.* This would include but is not limited to the following:

- Cost position
- Differentiation
- Advantageous location
- Brand equity
- Reputation
- Patents or proprietary technology
- Market share
- Move order (first mover advantage)
- Size
- Government protection

Note that many, if not all, of these position-based advantages can be imitated or otherwise circumvented by competitors. By investing in the latest manufacturing technology, one firm can "jump the experience curve" of an entrenched competitor and overcome its cost or location advantage. The Japanese steel industry did this to U.S. steel companies in the 1960s and 1970s; and in the 1980s the Koreans, and later the Malaysians, each leapfrogged their predecessors with newer and more efficient technologies, each coming in with a lower cost position than the previous low-cost producer. Research by Professor Pankaj Ghemawat at Harvard indicates that most position-based competitive advantages can be copied, imitated, or overcome within 17 months (on the average).

This reality poses the rather stressful spectre of always having to scramble to stay one or two steps ahead of one's competitors, and even this perpetual striving does not yield permanent advantage. In this view, one can never *sustain* competitive advantage (as both General Motors and IBM have seen) but must be constantly scurrying frantically to find or create that next, and unfortunately, *temporary* source of competitive advantage.

Another view, one brought by organizational sociologists such as Professor Jay Barney and strategists such as C.K. Prahalad and Gary Hamel, states that competitive advantage is not only position based, but is also *capability* based. Capability advantages are based on human interactions, coordination, experience, culture, and even trust. Capability-based advantages include the following:

- Technological skills (Hewlett-Packard)
- Speed (Federal Express)
- Creativity (3M)
- Customer responsiveness (Wal-Mart)
- Agility (Nucor Steel)
- Corporate culture (Intel)

So, to complete our strategy equation,

$$CA = f(P,C)$$

where

$$P = \text{position-based advantages}$$
$$C = \text{capability-based advantages}$$

(These two sources of competitive advantage were treated explicitly in Appendix 3 of Part II as the final section in the strategy evaluation.)

ORGANIZATIONAL CAPABILITIES AS COMPETITIVE ADVANTAGE

Capabilities as a source of competitive advantage is discussed in the following excerpt from *Australian Strategic Management* by Geoff Lewis:[1]

To be a source of sustained competitive advantage, a firm's capabilities must be distinctive. For capabilities to be distinctive, three conditions must be met:[2]

1. *The capabilities must be valuable.* They must actually be the source of competitive advantage in the form of either cost leadership or differentiation; that is, they must enable the firm to do things and behave in ways that lead to higher sales, lower costs, or higher margins (price). While this condition may appear obvious, firms often cling to capabilities that were once, but are no longer, valuable.

[1] Geoff Lewis, Andre Markel, and Graham Hubbard, *Australian Strategic Management*, Sydney: Prentice-Hall, 1993, pp. 28–30.
[2] Jay B. Barney, "Organizational Culture: Can It Be a Source of Sustained Competitive Advantage?" *Academy of Management Review*, vol. II, no. 3 (1986), pp. 656–65.

2. ***The capabilities must be rare.*** For a capability to be a source of competitive advantage it must have attributes and characteristics that are not commonly found in firms. If everybody's got it, it is not worth much.
3. ***The capabilities must be imperfectly imitable.*** Firms without these capabilities must not be readily able (in terms of time and cost) to copy the capabilities of the successful firm.

Strategic capabilities can be categorized as follows:

- **Technological Capabilities**—the know-how implicit within products, processes, physical plant and facilities, and people's skills and experience.
- **Human Capabilities**—the skills, style, attitudes, and behavior of organizational members. Ultimately, all capabilities are embodied in, or exercised through, human skills.
- **Organizational Capabilities**—the structures, systems, and norms of behavior that guide and coordinate the behavior of the members of the organization towards the achievement of task outcomes. A useful way of thinking about these capabilities is provided by the concept "organizational culture"—the organization's shared and learned beliefs and values, and the behaviors and artifacts that reflect and reaffirm those beliefs and values.
- **Managerial and Leadership Capabilities**—the abilities to create, coordinate, and change economic technological, organizational, and human capabilities. Leadership capabilities determine the preference for certain types of action (vision, commitment, and strategies), and the ability to translate these strategies into action.

The last two categories—organizational and management capabilities—are termed "socially complex capabilities."

Sustainable competitive advantage is grounded in the systemic nature of capabilities. That is, [position-based advantages] are by **themselves** usually not sustainable sources of competitive advantage—they are too easy to imitate (although this may be costly). Linked to socially complex capabilities, [position-based advantages and] technological capabilities are much harder to imitate; i.e., they are a source of sustainable competitive advantage. Hence, the two most socially complex capabilities—culture, which is primarily concerned with continuity, and leadership, which is concerned with change—are central concepts of strategy.

The identification of capabilities was outlined in Chapter 5 under the discussion of resource audit. A method of analyzing corporate culture is described in the next section. Leadership and strategic change are the subject of Chapter 11.

ANALYSIS OF CORPORATE CULTURE AND VALUES

Anthropologists have long known that the introduction of any new social change can meet with failure if those recommending or implementing the change ignore the culture of the community in which the change is introduced. Managers, however, often think they should formulate a strategy first and then create the culture and other implementation mechanisms required to implement the strategy. The method introduced here should be used during the strategy analysis process itself in order to allow a firm to assess its own culture and values and analyze the degree to which that culture will facilitate or hinder the achievement of the proposed strategic alternatives. The ultimate outcome of the analysis is the mutual adjustment of both the strategic alternatives under consideration and some of the management-practice and corporate-culture elements needed for strategic health.

Culture is ultimately reflected in actions, and actions embody values. Because neither individual nor organizational values themselves are visible, the method described here focuses on observable behavior. Management values, or ideology, contain a set of assumptions and guidelines that influence how management thinks about the future and how it directs the daily activities of the corporation. Often, they are not explicitly articulated, although some firms, such as Hewlett-Packard, Johnson & Johnson, and Cray Research, have been able to crystallize their values and translate them into a statement of corporate creed. However, many companies publish a so-called corporate creed that reflects an idealized version of what the company should stand for or else state certain platitudes that are not explicit guides to action. For example, many companies make statements about the need to be responsive to the community and to employees while serving the interests of stockholders. These principles are worthy but vague; they do not really serve as guides to action. The procedure described here is designed to reveal the basic ideology of the firm and to state it in operational terms.

The recommended procedure is as follows. First, management should set aside for the moment any existing statement or publication regarding a corporate creed or mission. The procedure's intent is for management to crystallize the corporate ideology and develop a consensus around the bare minimum number of guidelines. In order to do that, top management should produce a list of what it considers to be the "ten commandments" the company uses to guide corporate behavior. They should then assume that immediately upon issuing these commandments, top management will be isolated on a desert island for two years. Top management should feel that, once issued, these guidelines will provide sufficient direction for the firm's decisions, such that all decisions made in their absence will be regarded as acceptable, as long as they satisfy the guidelines.

Now, most managers will find that a list of ten is much too short to encompass what they think is basic to corporate behavior. However, as Ian MacMillan of Wharton states, "If the God of Moses can condense his set of principles to a list of ten, and if the framers of our constitution were satisfied with a bill of ten rights, then any corporate executive should be able to do the same with his or her firm."

Managers often would prefer to state their commandments in a manner that reflects how they wish their company would behave rather than the

Table 10-1
Selected Commandments
of Sigma Consultants

1. The consultant is king; he or she is the firm's key resource and shall be treated as a professional.
2. No bureaucratic hierarchy shall be imposed upon the professional staff.
3. Work on projects is by invitation, not by assignment from above. (Consultants are free to decline invitations, subject to commandment 4.)
4. Time is money. (Staff should stay at least 82 percent billable; i.e., up to 18 percent of chargeable time can be devoted to prospecting, personal development, etc.)
5. We will sell anything to anybody. (We will accept any interesting problem-solving assignment that comes in over the transom, as long as a staff member is willing to spearhead it.)

. . . .

10. Keep work fun as well as profitable.

actual set of values guiding the firm. To provide a reality check on the initial list of ten commandments, it is helpful to list three to five of the most important decisions made by the corporation in the past five years. Then try to determine which of the listed commandments relate to those actual decisions. If any decision cannot be linked to a commandment, perhaps the list of commandments should be amended to better reflect reality.

As an example, Table 10-1 shows some of the selected commandments of Sigma Consultants. Notice that the commandments reflect a combination of value statements, managerial style, and strategy statements. For example, marketing strategy is reflected in the commandment that the company will take any business that comes in over the transom, and an administrative value statement is reflected in the commandment that there should be no hierarchy or bureaucracy.

IMPLEMENTING STRATEGIC CHANGE

Having articulated the company's ideology, the firm is now ready to approach the final stage of strategy analysis. At this point, management will have considered all the important strategic elements and can now begin to pinpoint the areas that need to be changed and the areas that need to be sustained for future strategic advantage. The question often arises, however, of how and where to begin to implement a new strategy. Here is where the ten commandments can be of use.

First, decide which commandments should be preserved as inviolate. These should take into account the industry and competitive environment, the firm's competitive position, and those values that give the firm a competitive advantage. These preserved commandments form the bedrock upon which to build the future. Second, given the environment forecasted for the future, decide which commandments should be changed in order to either correct weaknesses or build new strengths. Then, consider which of these commandments should be attacked first. Note that the minute one commandment is addressed, another might be affected. For example, if Sigma Consultants were to decide to develop a more focused marketing strategy in order to pursue the health care business, then commandment 5 should be amended to state, "We will accept any assignment that comes in, *and* we will target a sales effort in the health care business." In order to do that effectively, Sigma Consultants might have to establish a separate administrative unit to handle just the health care business. Since this would violate the prevailing corporate culture and ideology, it is possible that the only way to implement this kind of strategic change would be to set up a separate administrative unit to handle this line of business. Clearly, this unit would have to be staffed voluntarily by those professionals in the firm who are already predisposed to pursue health care consulting. Perhaps, in the Sigma case, it is only by isolating a separate administrative unit with its own set of strategies and values, or corporate culture, that this kind of strategic thrust can succeed. Such an arrangement is not unusual. For example, when IBM decided to pursue the personal computer business, it set up an entirely separate administrative unit in Boca Raton, Florida, in order to develop the product and pursue its own marketing strategy. In the words of John Carey, the president of IBM at the time, "We had to set up a bureaucratic mechanism to protect the new venture from the bureaucracy."

For selecting a place to start implementing strategic change, a few principles can serve as useful guidelines:

1. *Initiate those changes that require the least amount of change* from prior behaviors or that require only minor adaptations to the current way of operating. For example, a move from a profit-centered, divisional organization to investment centers, where performance evaluation is based on return on assets as well as return on sales, would imply a much less dramatic shift than one from functional departments to divisions. In the case of Sigma Consultants, the move from a loosely structured system to, perhaps, a task force with part-time responsibility for health care would be a smaller step in the direction of a new strategy than would be implied by an entirely new administrative unit.

2. *Choose changes that are the least systemic.* This means that a strategic move that affects a part of the organization is preferable to one that affects the entire organization. For example, many firms have experienced an information system or payroll system disaster when a computerized system is adopted companywide, rather than pilot-testing it in a small segment of the organization.

3. *Institute changes where clearly identifiable champions exist.* In this case, one should attempt to initiate strategic change that has already been proposed by committed managers at lower levels of the organization. In such a situation, energy for implementation has already been invested, and the implementation of the strategy can be concluded far more successfully.

4. *Get some early, visible wins.* It is always beneficial to initiate strategic change in parts of the organization that are best equipped to succeed and that are more likely to be seen by the rest of the corporation.

A successful early win by a visible part of the corporation provides what is known as a demonstration effect. If one division sees another division of the corporation earning above-average profits that are the result of some strategic changes, it is far easier to persuade the remaining divisions to adopt whatever change was tried in the pilot attempt.

A further elaboration of strategy implementation and leadership is given in Chapter 11.

˙SUGGESTED READINGS˙

Collins, David J., and Cynthia A. Montgomery, "Competing on Resources: Strategy in the 1990s," *Harvard Business Review,* July–August 1995, pp. 118–28.

Ghemawat, Prankaj, "Sustainable Advantage," *Harvard Business Review,* September–October 1986, pp. 53–58.

Hamel, Gary, and C. K. Prahalad, "Strategic Intent," *Harvard Business Review,* May–June 1989, pp. 63–76.

Prahalad, C. K., and Gary Hamel, "The Core Competence of the Corporation," *Harvard Business Review,* May–June 1990, pp. 79–91.

STRATEGY IMPLEMENTATION

Most discussions of strategic planning focus on how to formulate strategy. Several tools and techniques are used widely. Management consulting firms offer strategic planning on a commodity basis, and business school programs are adorned with methodologies for choosing the "best" strategy.

By contrast, scant attention has been given to how to implement those strategies. Yet many people have recognized that problems with implementation in many companies have resulted in failed strategies and abandoned planning efforts. This chapter will identify many of these implementation problems and then offer some remedies for them.

Our discussions will provide suggestions that can help managers be more successful in three general areas:

- Developing strategies that can realistically be implemented, given not only the marketplace but also the politics, culture, and competence of the firm

- Putting strategies into action

- Revising strategies continually so as to take advantage of new opportunities and respond to threats

FIVE WAYS COMPANIES IMPLEMENT STRATEGY

In studying the management practices of a variety of companies, David Brodwin (of Arthur D. Little) and the author found that their approaches to strategy implementation can be categorized into one of five basic descriptions.[1] In each one, the chief executive officer plays a somewhat different role and uses distinctive methods for developing and implementing strategies.

The first two descriptions represent traditional approaches to implementation. Here the CEO formulates strategy first and thinks about implementation later.

1. *The Commander Approach.* The CEO concentrates on formulating the strategy, giving little thought to how the plan will be carried out. He or she either develops the strategy alone or supervises a team of planners. Once satisfied that the best strategy is at hand, he or she passes it along to those who are instructed to "make it happen."

2. *The Organizational Control Approach.* Once a plan has been developed, the executive puts it into effect by taking such steps as reorganizing the company structure, changing incentive compensation schemes, or hiring staff.

The next two approaches involve more recent attempts to enhance implementation by broadening the bases of participation in the planning process.

3. *The Collaborative Approach.* Rather than develop the strategy in a vacuum, the CEO enlists the help of senior managers during the planning process to assure that all the key players will back the final plan.

4. *The Cultural Approach.* This is an extension of the collaborative model to involve people at middle and sometimes lower levels of the organization. It seeks to implement strategy by developing a corporate culture throughout the organization.

The final approach takes advantage of line managers' natural inclinations to develop opportunities as they are encountered.

5. *The Crescive Approach.* In this approach, the CEO addresses strategy planning and implementation simultaneously. He or she is not interested in planning alone, or even in leading others through a protracted planning process. Rather, the CEO tries, through statements and actions, to encourage and guide managers into coming forward as champions of sound strategies.

In studying these five approaches we noticed several trends. First, the two traditional methods are gradually being supplanted by the others. Second, companies are focusing increasingly on the organizational issues involved in

---

[1] L. J. Bourgeois and David R. Brodwin, "Strategy Implementation: Five Approaches to an Elusive Phenomenon," *Strategic Management Journal,* vol. 5, July–September 1984, pp. 241–64.

getting a company to adapt to its environment and to pursue new opportunities or respond to outside threats. Finally, the trend is for the CEO to play an increasingly indirect and more subtle role in strategy development.

METHOD 1: THE COMMANDER

The typical scenario depicting the most traditional approach to strategy formulation and implementation is as follows: after the CEO approves the strategic plan, he or she calls the top managers into a conference room, presents the strategy, and tells them to implement it.

The CEO is involved only with formulating the strategy. Assuming that an exhaustive analysis must be completed before any action can be taken, the CEO typically authorizes an extensive study of the firm's competitive opportunities. In general, focusing on the planning at least gives the CEO a sense of direction for the firm, which helps him or her make difficult day-to-day decisions and also reduces uncertainty within the organization.

However, this approach can be implemented successfully only if several conditions are met. First, the CEO must wield a great deal of power to simply command implementation. Otherwise, unless the proposed strategy poses little threat to organizational members, implementation cannot be achieved very easily.

Second, accurate information must be available to the strategist before it becomes obsolete. Because good strategy depends on high-quality information, critical information entering the firm at lower levels must be compiled, digested, and transmitted upward quickly.

Third, the strategists must be insulated from personal biases and political influences that can impinge on the plan. Managers are likely to propose strategies favorable to their own divisions but not necessarily to the corporation as a whole.

One problem is that this approach often splits the firm into "thinkers" and "doers," and those charged with the doing may not feel that they are part of the game. The general manager must dispel any impression that the only acceptable strategies are those that he or she develops with the planning staff, or the CEO may face an extremely unmotivated, uninnovative group of employees.

METHOD 2: ORGANIZATIONAL CONTROL

With this approach, the CEO makes the strategy decisions and then paves the way for implementation by redesigning the organizational structure, personnel assignments, information systems, and compensation scheme.

This method goes beyond the first one by having the CEO consider how to put the plan into action. The CEO basically uses two sets of tools: (1) changing the structure and staffing to focus attention on the firm's new priorities and (2) revising systems for planning, performance measurement, and incentive compensation to help achieve the firm's strategy goals.

The first set of tools—changing the organizational structure and staffing—has been the traditional approach espoused in most business strategy textbooks. Generally, the organizational structure should reflect the diversity of the firm's strategies. For example, if a company's strategy calls for the worldwide coordination of manufacturing in order to capture cost efficiencies, the CEO would implement a *functional* organization for production, while a strategy calling for selling diverse product lines to various markets would demand a *divisional* organization of separate profit centers. (See Appendix 4 following this chapter for an overview of organization design as a means of implementing strategy.)

The second set of tools involves adjusting administrative systems. Various planning, accounting, and control tools, such as those governing capital and operating budgets, can be used to help achieve desired goals. For example, if the firm's strategy calls for investing in certain businesses and harvesting others, or for channeling profits from one national unit to the funding of others, these goals should feature prominently in the capital budgeting procedure so that business-unit managers can effectively plan their resource requests and others can effectively evaluate them.

Performance measures should be designed so that they target meaningful short-term milestones to monitor progress toward strategic goals. The incentive compensation scheme should then be tied into the clear-cut numerical terms of the performance measures. At a minimum, the general manager must ensure that the current compensation plan is not thwarting the achievement of the strategy, such as by rewarding short-term profitability at the expense of long-term growth.

One company that the researchers studied clearly illustrates the problems that can arise when performance measures and administrative systems are inappropriate. A major diversified manufacturer concluded that a steady stream of new products was the most important factor in maintaining the stock price at the desired level, yet the performance measures and management reports imposed on the division heads stressed quarterly profit above all else.

Unlike the first approach, in this method the CEO does not merely command subordinates to put the plan into action. The CEO supervises the implementation and may reveal the strategy gradually, rather than in one bold proclamation.

However, it usually is inadequate for the CEO simply to tack "implementation" onto "strategy." This approach does not deal with the problem of obtaining accurate information nor does it buffer the planner from political pressures. Also, as in the first approach, imposing the strategy downward from the top still causes motivational problems among the "doers" at lower levels.

Another problem can develop when the CEO manipulates the systems and structures of the organization in support of a particular strategy. The general manager may lose important strategic flexibility. Some of these systems, particularly incentive compensation, take a long time to design, install, and become effective. If a dramatic change in the environment suddenly demands a major shift in the strategy, it may be very difficult to change the firm's course, because all the levers controlling the firm have been set firmly in support of the now-obsolete game plan.

In the interest of retaining strategic flexibility in situations where environmental uncertainty is high, it may prove more advisable in the long run to refrain from using some of the tools described here. For example, many high-technology firms, which rely on the rapid development and introduction of a continuous stream of technological innovations, avoid imposing bureaucratic administrative systems that would cripple their ability to create strategic change.

Conclusion

Dependence upon the commander approach has significant limitations. Yet many line managers are all too familiar with this approach to strategy implementation. Strategy implementation is most divorced from strategy formulation under this approach.

But, with a set of powerful implementation tools at his or her disposal, the executive using the organizational control approach can implement more difficult strategies or plans in a wide variety of organizations.

The strategist who uses either of these two traditional approaches eventually confronts a basic dilemma: How do I make realistic strategic decisions based on accurate and unbiased information and then set up an administrative system to put those decisions into action over the long run? Of course, these goals should also be achieved without hurting managers' motivation, stifling creativity, or creating an inflexible bureaucracy. The other three approaches to implementing strategy offer some solutions to these challenging issues.

METHOD 3: THE COLLABORATIVE APPROACH

In contrast to the two earlier approaches, in which the chief executive makes most of the strategic and organizational decisions, the collaborative approach extends strategic decision making to the organization's top management team. The purpose here is to get the top managers to help develop and support a good set of goals and strategies.

In this model, the CEO employs group dynamics and brainstorming techniques to get managers with different points of view to contribute to the strategic process. Research indicates that in effective top management teams the executives will have conflicting goals and perceptions of the external environment, so the CEO will want to extract whatever group wisdom is inherent in these different perspectives.

A typical depiction of this approach should be familiar to readers: with key executives and division managers, the CEO embarks on a week-long planning retreat. At the retreat, each participant presents his or her own ideas of where the firm should head. Extensive discussions follow, until the group reaches a consensus around the firm's long-range mission and near-term strategy. Upon returning to their respective offices, each participant charges ahead in the agreed-upon direction.

By relying on collaboration among top executives, this approach depends on the skillful structuring of group interaction. This can take a variety of forms. For example, the consulting firm of Arthur D. Little engages in a process designed to gain team consensus on which generic strategies fit their particular industry situation. (See "Note on Portfolio Planning Techniques" in Chapter 7 for a full description of ADL's approach.)

Another variant of the collaborative method involves *teaching* analytical tools to the top management team. These variations all involve the managers' participation in contrast to the typical approach used by consulting firms, in which top managers rely on outsiders to provide a final report and recommendations.

A number of corporations now use some type of collaborative method. General Motors formed business teams consisting of managers from different functional areas; the role of the team was simply to bring out different points of view on whatever strategic—usually product-focused—problem was identified.

The CEO of a wholly owned Exxon subsidiary informed us that his job was not to make and implement strategy. Instead, he was responsible for assembling a team of competent managers—most more competent than he in their respective functional fields—which could, jointly, collaborate in the formation of strategies.

The collaborative approach overcomes two key limitations of the previous two methods. By incorporating information from executives who are closer to line operations and by engaging several points of view, it helps provide better information than the CEO alone would have. Also, because participation breeds commitment, this method helps overcome any resistance from top managers—which improves the possibility that the plan will be implemented successfully.

However, what the collaborative approach gains in team commitment may come at the expense of strategic perfection. That is, it results in a compromise that has been negotiated among players with different points of view.

The strategy may not be as dynamic as one CEO's vision, but it will be more politically feasible.

A second criticism of the collaborative approach is that it is not real collective decision making from an organizational standpoint, because the managers—the organizational elite—cannot or will not give up centralized control. In effect, this approach still retains the wall separating thinkers from doers, and it fails to draw upon the resources of personnel throughout the organization.

The fourth approach to strategy implementation can help an organization overcome that shortcoming.

METHOD 4: THE CULTURAL APPROACH

The cultural approach extends the benefits of collective participation into lower levels of the organization in order to get the entire organization committed to the firm's goals and strategies.

In this approach, the CEO sets the game plan and communicates the direction in which the firm should move but then gives individuals the responsibility of determining the details of how to execute the plan.

The implementation tools used in building a strong corporate culture range from such simple notions as publishing a company creed and singing a company song to much more complex techniques. These complex—and usually effective—techniques involve implementing strategy by employing the concept of *third-order control.*

Because implementation involves controlling the behavior of others, we can think of three levels of control. First-order control involves direct supervision. Second-order control involves using rules, procedures, and organizational structure to guide the behavior of others (as in the organizational control approach). Third-order control is a much more subtle—and potentially more powerful—means of influencing behavior through shaping the norms, values, symbols, and beliefs that managers and employees use in making day-to-day decisions.

The key difference between managers using the cultural approach and those simply engaged in "participative management" is that these executives understand that corporate culture should serve as the handmaiden to corporate strategy, rather than proselytizing empowerment and the like for its own sake.

Some of the tools used in the cultural approach involve some readily identifiable personnel practices, such as long-term employment, slow promotion of employees, less-specialized career paths, and consensus decision making. For many managers, the cultural approach leads to a change in their management style because it involves more interaction with subordinates who will be seen as partners.

The cultural approach begins to break down the barriers between thinkers and doers. Examples of the successful application of this model are numerous.

Hewlett-Packard is a much-heralded example of a company where the employees share a strong awareness of the corporate mission. They all know that the "HP Way" encourages product innovation at every level and at every bench. Matsushita starts each day at 8:00 A.M. with 87,000 employees singing the company song and reciting its code of values. Dollar General relied on its strong family culture to avoid bureaucratic systems to guide the behavior of employees in remote store locations.

Once an organizational culture that supports the firm's goals is established, the chief executive's implementation task is 90-percent done. With a cadre of committed managers and workers, the organization more or less carries itself through cycles of innovation in terms of new products and processes at the work bench, followed by assimilation and implementation at the lower levels.

The most visible cost of this system also yields its primary strength: the consensus decision-making and other culture-inculcating activities consume enormous amounts of time. But the payoff can be speedy execution and reduced gamesmanship among managers. At Westinghouse, as William Coates, executive vice president of the corporation construction group, described it, "We spend a lot of time trying to get a consensus, but once you get it, the implementation is instantaneous. We do not have to fight any negative feelings."[2]

Based on our assessment of the nature of the companies generally held up as examples of this approach to strategic management, we have reached some tentative conclusions about the organizational characteristics for which it is best suited. The cultural approach works when power is decentralized, where shared goals exist between the organization and its participants, and where the organization is stable and growing.

The last point may be key: sufficient organization slack (i.e., unused resources) is needed to absorb the cost of installing and maintaining the culture. Consider that some of the example firms—Hewlett-Packard, Microsoft, Matsushita, and Intel—tend to be high-growth firms. As *Fortune* magazine describes Intel's experience, "To lessen the threat of change, Intel promised not to fire any permanent employee whose job was eliminated. The company's phenomenal sales growth helps absorb everyone who wants to stay."[3]

The cultural method has several limitations. For one, it works primarily with informed and intelligent people (note that most of the examples are firms in high-technology industries). Second, it consumes enormous amounts of time to implement. Third, it can foster such a strong sense of organizational identity among employees that it becomes almost a handicap—that is, it can be difficult to bring in outsiders at top levels because the executives will not accept the infusion of alien blood.

---

[2]Jeremy Main, "Westinghouse's Cultural Revolution," *Fortune*, June 15, 1981, pp. 74–93.
[3]Jeremy Main, "How to Battle Your Own Bureaucracy," *Fortune*, June 29, 1981, pp. 54–58.

In addition, companies with excessively strong cultures often suppress deviance, impede attempts to change, and foster homogeneity and inbreeding. The intolerance of deviance can be a problem when innovation is critical to strategic success. But a strong culture will reject inconsistency.

To handle this conformist tendency, companies such as IBM, Xerox, and General Motors have separated their ongoing research units and their new-product development efforts, sometimes placing them in physical locations far enough away to shield them from the corporation's culture.

Homogeneity can stifle creativity, encouraging nonconformists to leave for more accepting pastures and thereby robbing the firm of its innovative talent. The strongest criticism of the cultural approach is its overwhelming indoctrinal air. It smacks of faddism and may really be just another variant of the CEO-centered approaches (i.e., commander and organizational control approaches). As such, it runs the risk of maintaining the wall between thinkers and doers.

Preserving the thinker/doer distinction may be the cultural approach's main appeal. It affords executives an illusion of control. But holding tight the reins of control (a natural tendency in turbulent times) may result in lost opportunities—opportunities encountered by line managers in their day-to-day routines.

How can executives capitalize on their line managers' natural inclinations to want to develop opportunities as they encounter them on the firing line? The answer to this question is contained in the fifth implementation method, the crescive approach.

METHOD 5: THE CRESCIVE APPROACH

Although each of the first four approaches can be effective in certain companies and business environments, none has proven adequate for complex companies in highly diversified or rapidly changing environments. The best way to implement strategy in this challenging situation is by what we have identified as the crescive approach. The name means "growing," indicating that under this method the CEO cultivates or allows strategies to grow from within the company instead of imposing the strategies of top management onto the firm.

Here is a scenario depicting the crescive approach:

> As a general manager, you have just received a proposal to pursue continued development of a new product. You evaluate the report, deflate some overly optimistic figures, and consider the manager's track record. The product offers attractive profit potential and seems to fit the general direction you envision for the firm, so you approve the proposal.

The crescive approach differs from others in several respects. First, instead of strategy being delivered downward by top management or a planning department, it moves upward from the doers (salespeople, engineers, production workers) and lower middle-level managers. Second, "strategy" becomes the sum of all the individual proposals that surface throughout the year. Third, the top management team shapes the employees' premises—that is, their notions of what would constitute strategic projects. Fourth, the chief executive functions more as a judge—evaluating the proposals that reach his or her desk—than as a master planner.

Why Did the Crescive Approach Arise?

At first, the crescive approach may sound too risky. After all, it calls for the chief executive to relinquish a lot of control over the strategy-making process, seemingly leaving to chance the major decisions that determine the long-term competitive strength of the company.

To understand why the crescive approach is sometimes appropriate, one must recognize five constraints that impinge on the chief executive as he or she sets out to develop and implement a strategy.

1. *The Chief Executive Cannot Monitor All Significant Opportunities and Threats.* If the company is highly diversified, it is impossible for senior management to stay abreast of development in all of the firm's different industries. Similarly, if an industry is shifting very quickly (e.g., personal computers), information collected at lower levels often becomes stale before it can be assimilated, summarized, and passed up the ranks. Even in more stable industries, the time required to process information upward through many management levels may mean that decisions are being based on outdated information.

   As a result, in many cases the CEO must abandon the effort to plan centrally. Instead, the chief executive establishes an incentive scheme or "free-market" environment to encourage operating managers to make decisions that will further the long-range interests of the company.

2. *The Power of the Chief Executive Is Limited.* The chief executive typically enjoys substantial power derived from the ability to bestow rewards, allocate resources, and reduce the uncertainty for members of the organization. However, the chief executive is not omnipotent. Employees can always leave the firm, and key managers wield control over information and important client relationships. As a result, the CEO must often compromise on programs he or she wishes to implement.

   Research indicates that new projects led by managers who were coerced into the leadership role fail, regardless of the intrinsic merit of the proposal. In contrast, a second-best strategy championed by a capable and determined advocate may be far more worthwhile than the optimum strategy with only lukewarm support.

3. *Few Executives Have the Freedom to Plan.* Although it is often said that one of the most important jobs of an executive is to engage in

thoughtful planning, research shows that few executives actually set aside time to plan. Most spend the majority of their work days attending to short-range problems.

Thus, any realistic approach to strategic planning must recognize that executives simply do not plan much. They are bombarded constantly by requests from subordinates. So they shape the company's future more through their day-to-day decisions—encouraging some projects and discouraging others—than by sweeping policy statements or written plans. This process has been described as "logical incrementalism" because it is a rational process that proceeds in small steps rather than by long leaps.

4. *Tight Control Systems Hinder the Planning Process.* In formulating strategies, top managers rely heavily on subordinates for up-to-date information, strategic recommendations, and approval of the operating goals. The CEO's dependence on subordinate managers creates a thorny control problem. In essence, if managers know they'll be accountable for plans they formulate or the information they provide, they have an incentive to bias their estimates of their division's performance.

A branch of decision science called "agency theory" suggests how this situation should be handled. First, if the CEO wants them to deliver unbiased estimates, managers cannot be held tightly accountable for the successful implementation of each strategic proposal. Without such accountability, great emphasis is placed on commitment as a force for getting things done.

Second, to assess the true ability and motivation of any subordinate, the CEO must observe the subordinate over a long period of time on a number of different projects. Occasional failures should be expected, tolerated, and not penalized.

One means to promote the ongoing flow of strategic information is to establish a special venture capital fund to take advantage of promising ideas that arise after the strategic and operating plans have been completed. Like the IBM Fellows program or the Texas Instruments Idea program, this approach allows opportunities to be seized and developed by their champions within the company.

5. *Strategies Are Produced by Groups, Not Individuals.* Strategies are rarely created by single individuals. They are usually developed by groups of people, and they incorporate different perspectives on the business. The problem is that groups tend to avoid uncertainty and to smooth over conflicts prematurely.

To reduce the distortions that can result from group decision making, the CEO can concentrate on three tools: first, encouraging an atmosphere that tolerates expression of different opinions; second, using organizational development techniques (such as group dynamics exercises) to reduce individual defensiveness and to increase the receptivity of the group to discrepant data; and third, establishing separate planning groups at the corporate level and the line organization.

How the CEO Can Use the Crescive Approach

As the preceding discussion indicates, the CEO of a large corporation simply cannot be solely responsible for forming and implementing strategy. The crescive approach suggests that the CEO can solicit and guide the involvement of lower-level managers in the planning and implementation process in five ways.

1. By keeping the organization open to new and potentially discrepant information
2. By articulating a general strategy of superordinate goals to guide the firm's growth
3. By carefully shaping the premises by which managers at all levels decide which strategic opportunities to pursue
4. By manipulating systems and structures to encourage bottom-up strategy formulations
5. By approaching day-to-day decisions as part of strategy formulation in the so-called logical incrementalist manner described earlier. [4]

One of the most important and potentially elusive of these methods is the process of shaping managers' decision-making premises. The CEO can shape these premises in at least three ways. First, the CEO can emphasize a particular theme ("We are in the information business") or strategic intent (Komatsu's "encircle Caterpillar") to direct strategic thinking. Second, the planning methodology that the CEO endorses can be communicated to affect the way managers view the business. Third, the organizational structure can indicate the dimensions on which strategies should focus. A firm with a product-divisional structure will probably encourage managers to generate strategies for domination in certain product categories, whereas a firm organized around geographical territories will probably evoke strategies to secure maximum penetration of all products in particular regions.

CONCLUSION

The five approaches to developing and implementing strategy that we've discussed represent a range from which one can choose the techniques most suited to a particular situation. Most managers find that one of these five approaches is predominant in their company, although often one or two of the other approaches may also play a limited role.

---

[4]J. Brian Quinn, *Strategies for Change*, Homewood, IL: Irwin, 1980.

In the few cases where two different approaches played equally strong roles in the same company, an explanation could be found in the history and makeup of the company. For example, one company we studied was active in two distinct industries: its aerospace divisions, based in California, used a crescive strategic management process while its automotive operation, headquartered in the Midwest, used a planning system incorporating elements of both the commander and the control approaches.

Our research suggests that the commander, control, and collaborative approaches can be effective for smaller companies and firms in stable industries while the cultural and crescive alternatives are used by more complex corporations.

To conclude, a summary of the five approaches, the strategic question each addresses, and the CEO's role in each is given in Table 11-1. The method chosen should depend on the size of the company, the degree of diversification, the degree of geographical dispersion, the stability of the business environment, and, finally, the managerial style currently embodied in the company's culture.

Table 11-1
The Five Approaches
to Strategic Management

APPROACH	THE CEO'S STRATEGIC QUESTION	CEO'S ROLE
Commander Approach	"How do I formulate the optimal strategy?"	Master planner
Control Approach	"I have a strategy in mind. Now how do I implement it?"	Organizational architect
Collaborative Approach	"How do I involve top managers in planning so they will be committed to strategies from the start?"	Coordinator
Cultural Approach	"How do I involve the whole organization in implementation?"	Coach
Crescive Approach	"How do I encourage managers to come forward as champions of sound strategies?"	Premise-setter and judge

APPENDIX 4

NOTE ON STRATEGY IMPLEMENTATION THROUGH ORGANIZATIONAL DESIGN

In studying industry structures and competitive dynamics, the basic issue is usually the formulation and choice of a business strategy. The implementation of strategy is usually thought of in terms of securing and allocating resources. Once secured, these physical, human, financial, and informational resources must be managed in some fashion. The primary means for doing so is to divide assets and responsibilities into chunks and then to provide an administrative arrangement for assigning authority over operating decisions for those chunks. This division of assets, responsibilities, and authority is essentially an architectural activity referred to as organization design.

This appendix will summarize a few principles of organizational design, which will be presented in two groups. In the first group, we assume that the strategist has the luxury of starting from scratch and can choose a design to fit his or her previously formulated strategy without regard to how the organization is currently structured or who is currently employed in it (that is, what types of skills and knowledge are available). In the second group, we assume that inexorable forces are at work that more or less predestine industrial organizations to evolve in a particular way.

CHOOSING A STRUCTURE (FROM SCRATCH)

If you were to take an engineering approach to the problem of implementing organizational purpose, you might ask yourself two questions:

1. In order to achieve my organization's strategic objectives, how should I break the total task into specific activities to be performed? That is, what is the most effective division of labor? How can I differentiate the tasks enough to get them accomplished through the single-minded attention of the individuals responsible for performing them?

2. Having decomposed the overall tasks into subtasks that can be performed by groups of individuals (such as departments or divisions), how do I now ensure that the tasks can be reintegrated? That is, what is the most effective integration device for coordinating divided responsibilities?

Note that these two questions focus on how to engineer the *workflow* of the organization: how to transform raw material, energy, financial, and human-effort inputs into products or services for delivery to the external market.

To answer the two questions, three basic alternatives have been developed. These three are pure or ideal types, however, in that they rarely occur exactly as depicted here. Most organizations do exhibit the basic characteristics of one or the other type, however, either individually or in some hybrid or combination.

Exhibit 1 depicts the three organizational types. The characteristics of each and the strategies under which each form is appropriate are listed in Table 1.

THE STAGES MODEL OF STRUCTURAL EVOLUTION

As a result of more than a decade of research at the Harvard Business School, which looked at the strategies and structures of more than 200 of the *Fortune* 500 companies in the United States and more than 300 industrial firms in Western Europe, a stages model of corporate development was created. The stages of corporate development usually correspond to a move from entrepreneurial to integrated (type I in Exhibit 1), to diversified (type II). (So far, there is only a limited trend to type III, the matrix form, among multinationals that are laying a product management over a geographic divisionalized form. Some would argue that type III here is more like an entrepreneurial firm in a dynamic environment.)

The basic assumptions underlying the stages-of-evolution model are as follows:

1. Firms tend to add activities as they grow, either in their traditional fields or in new fields.

2. With the addition of activities, the increasing returns to scale, and the tendency to become increasingly capital intensive, firms experience an increase in the number of subunits or departments, some of which become ever more specialized.

3. The increasing number of specialized subunits results in an increase in the complexity of administrative problems.

4. There appear to be three characteristic stages or forms dealing with these successively more complex problems: entrepreneurial, functional, and divisionalized. (Matrix, or type III in Exhibit 1, would be a fourth form not considered by this stages model.)

5. Over time, a company will pass through these stages in a 1-2-3 sequence, if and when it adds sufficiently to its scope of activities; that is,

   • It will reach a *functional* form as it increases activities in one or a few related fields (through vertical integration).

   • It will reach a *divisionalized* form as it makes major commitments in several fields of activity (through horizontal diversification).

Exhibit 1
Three Types of Organizational Structures

I. Functional Form (Sequential Interdependence)

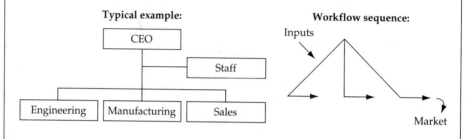

Typical example:

CEO

Staff

Engineering | Manufacturing | Sales

Workflow sequence:

Inputs

Market

II. Divisional Form (Pooled Interdependence)

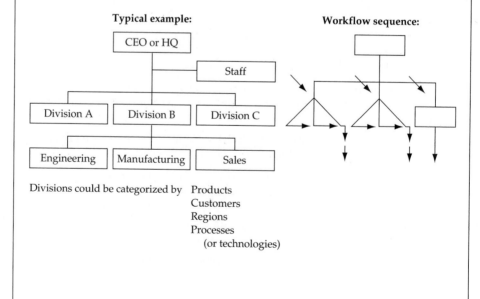

Typical example:

CEO or HQ

Staff

Division A | Division B | Division C

Engineering | Manufacturing | Sales

Workflow sequence:

Divisions could be categorized by   Products
Customers
Regions
Processes
(or technologies)

(continued on next page)

(continued)

III. "Team" or Matrix Form (Reciprocal Interdependence)

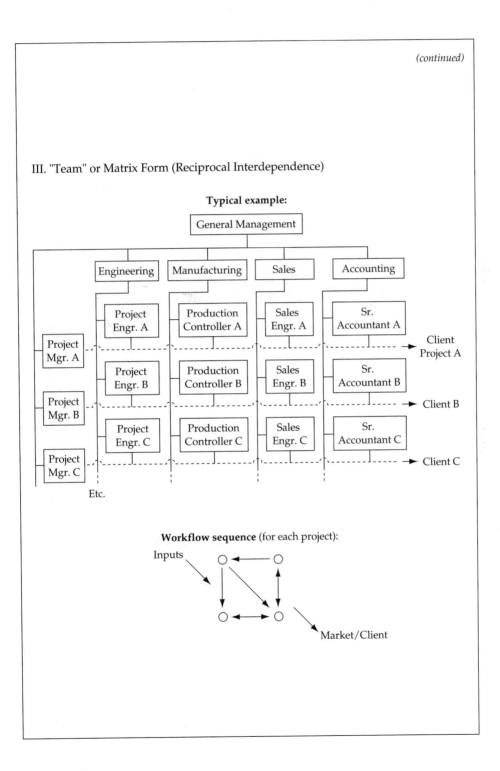

Typical example:

Workflow sequence (for each project):

Table 1
Choosing an Organizational Structure

Type	I. Functional	II. Divisional	III. Team or Project
Workflow Characteristics	Series (pre-engineered)	Parallel (though engineered within each self-contained unit)	Mutual adjustment (within projects); shifting
Differentiation	By functional areas; each attending to different segments of task environment	By product-market; each unit attending to an entire task environment	By client or project: each team crossing various task environments
Integration	Across functions	Across businesses	Across both functions and projects
Most Appropriate When:			
Strategy Is:	Single mission (product or service)	Diversified (multiple products and/or markets)	Constant innovation
Environment Is:	Stable, predictable	Multiple and mixed (some stable, some changing)	Uncertain, volatile
Nature of Work Is:	Programmable, with strong sequential coordination required	No coordination required between units (though draw upon common, usually financial, pool of resources)	Nonprogrammable; problem solving on a case-by-case basis

Strategic Concerns of Top Management	Meeting market needs, efficiency	Portfolio balance of "strategic business units" (SBUs)	Creativity, systems approach, effectiveness
Main Strategic Problem	Market share, cost reduction	Return on investment (ROI)	System delivery
Growth through	Market penetration or vertical integration	Same as I, plus diversification or acquisition	Same as I
Nature of Middle Management	Departmental	General (SBU)	Technical
Face-to-Face Contact of Decision Makers	Occasional, for planning operations	Infrequent, usually only with headquarters	Constant interaction
Accounting and Evaluation Form	Revenue or cost centers	Profit or investment centers	Profit centers or projects
Examples	Steel, food processing, paper, chemicals, football team or relay team, military command: single campaign	Conglomerates, auto firms, chain retailers, fast foods, other diversified, track team, military: multiple fronts	Construction, consulting, aerospace, other high-technology firms, basketball team, military: multiple theatres, services, and allies

6. If there is no increase in the scope of a firm's activities (that is, it stays in related areas), the tendency to increase capital intensity in production and distribution, plus an increasingly sophisticated management information system, will lead to an increasingly integrated (and centralized) form of organization:

   • Leading functional (type I) firms toward more integration.
   • Leading divisional (type II) firms that stay with a given set of activities, toward a more integrated form, perhaps even back to type I.

Thus there are two opposing forces at work:

   • A proliferation of domains or activities causing the 1-2-3 (entrepreneurial-functional-divisional) sequence, versus
   • Increasing efficiency through capital intensity, causing both entrepreneurial and divisionalized firms to revert to the centralized functional control of a type I organization.

˒REFERENCES˒

Articles

Fouraker, L. E., and J. M. Stopford. "Organization Structure and Multinational Strategy." *Administrative Science Quarterly,* vol. 19, 1974, pp. 493–506.

Galbraith, Jay R. "Matrix Organization Designs." *Business Horizons,* vol. 14, 1971, pp. 29–40. (Galbraith is the leading expert on matrix structure.)

Goggins, William. "How the Multi-Dimensional Structure Works at Dow-Corning." *Harvard Business Review,* vol. 52, January–February 1974, pp. 54–65.

Greiner, Larry E. "Evolution and Revolution as Organizations Grow." *Harvard Business Review,* vol. 50, July–August 1972, pp. 37–46.

Scott, Bruce R. "The Industrial State: Old Myths and New Realities." *Harvard Business Review,* March–April 1973, pp. 133–48. (This article presents a stages model similar to Greiner's but in more detail and with a more strategic or economic perspective.)

Books

Chandler, Alfred D. *Strategy and Structure.* Cambridge, MA: M.I.T. Press, 1962. (This is the classic book presenting the structure-follows-strategy argument, based on a historical study of 70 major U.S. enterprises.)

Galbraith, Jay R. *Designing Complex Organizations.* Reading, MA: Addison-Wesley, 1973. (This is the original best-seller on matrix design. The author did most of his research at the Boeing Company in Seattle.)

Mintzberg, Henry. *The Structuring of Organizations.* Englewood Cliffs, NJ: Prentice-Hall, 1979.

DOLLAR GENERAL CORPORATION (A)

You won't go wrong shopping at the Dollar General Store,
Where you can spend much less and take home much more,
Whether rich or poor, we have merchandise just for you,
We have the off brands and the name brands too.

> From the DG poem, "Pride in
> Dollar General," by Diana Schafer,
> Clerk, Williamsburg, Kentucky

In February 1984, Cal Turner, Jr., the 44-year-old president of Dollar General Corporation (DG), had finally been able to reflect on the hectic pace of the past few months. The company had been understaffed even before the 1983 acquisition of 280 Hirsch stores from Interco, Inc. Now, just as the conversion of these stores to DG stores was on schedule, and Cal Jr. was looking forward to returning to business as usual in a few months, Interco was offering to sell DG another chain.

COMPANY BACKGROUND

It's nothing fancy—just a lot of country stores.

Dollar General's roots stretched back to a time long before the first stores were opened. At age 11, with only a third-grade education, J. L. Turner, grandfather to current president Cal Turner, Jr., and father to chairman Cal Sr., had to quit school to help support his widowed mother and three younger children living on a small, mortgaged farm. In his mid-20s, he began running a local general store. Later he bought two stores of his own, only to see them fail, and he then went to work for a grocery and dry-goods wholesaler.

As J. L. traveled the small towns of Tennessee and Kentucky during a time "when everybody's belly was flat up against their backbone," a fellow merchant suggested to him that the depression was forcing near-bankrupt retailers to sell their inventories for next to nothing. So J. L. began taking out short-term bank loans for $2,000 or $3,000 and buying complete inventories from hard-up

---

This case was prepared by Jim Kennedy, Research Associate, under the supervision of Professor William E. Fulmer. Copyright © 1987 by the University of Virginia Darden School Foundation, Charlottesville, VA. All rights reserved. Revised January 1995.

merchants. He would sell the merchandise as quickly as possible and repay the bank, usually within 30 days. Financing was easy because depression-era banks were starved for good loans.

According to Cal Jr., "My grandfather was a keen observer of people and what they needed." On one occasion, J. L. noticed in a cold tobacco barn that tobacco farmers were paid by produce companies once a year by check, not cash. To attract them to his store, Turner had a boy distribute right-hand gloves with a message pinned to them: "If you let us cash your check, we'll give you the left glove free." Cal Jr. also described his grandfather as one "who would buy anything he could turn around for a profit, and he believed in hard work, common sense, and fairness." Cal Sr. added, "My father really was a trader."

A February 2, 1968, article on Cal Turner, Sr., in *The Louisville Courier-Journal* noted that, before he had graduated from Scottsville High School and while he was attending Vanderbilt University, he was already a storekeeper:

> Merchandising is all he ever wanted to do, he admitted. A crack basketball player, he played on the Vanderbilt freshman team before dropping out of college to take a job with a Nashville wholesale firm.

From 1931 to 1936, he worked for the Neely Harwell Company but, in 1936, opened a "bargain store" in Old Hickory, Tennessee. In a short time, he had opened stores in Gainesboro and Manchester, Tennessee. Later that year, he bought a small store in Scottsville and married the cousin of the governor of Tennessee.

Three years later, after he and his father had sold their stores, each put up $5,000 and established J. L. Turner & Son, Wholesalers, based in Scottsville, with Cal Sr. in charge and J. L. acting largely as an adviser. But as Cal Sr. said, "Ten thousand dollars wasn't a lot of money to start a business on, even back then." The venture got off to a slow start, and they had to seek bank loans after 60 days. Nevertheless, both partners went on the road, and in their first year sold $65,000 worth of goods.

Turner & Son was not picky about what it purchased. Although buying primarily soft goods, they once bought a tomato cannery. According to Cal Sr., "[When] the war came along, and it was hard to get all the merchandise you wanted, this canning factory made some money for us."

"We got into retailing," claimed Cal Turner, Jr., "when my Dad got stuck in ladies' panties." After World War II, Cal Sr. found himself trying to sell thousands of dozens of ladies' panties. He had purchased them at $7.50/dozen, but because so much merchandise hit the market after the war, the price dropped to $4.50. Cal Sr. lowered his price and went from retailer to retailer trying to convince them to buy his stock at $4.50 and average the cost in with their more expensive merchandise. The merchants all told him the same thing: they couldn't buy his cheaper stock until they sold the more expensive stock that they previously had bought from him. "I came home and told my father we were going to have to do something to protect ourselves," related Cal Sr. So they decided to go directly to the consumer by opening a retail store in Albany, Kentucky, in May 1946 and buying 50-percent interests in various bargain stores in the area that bought merchandise from Turner & Son.

During the early 1950s, Turner & Son began to expand its retail operations and, by 1955, had 35 self-service dry-goods stores and sales of $2 million. Observing that larger department stores occasionally held dollar-day sales where all items were priced at one dollar or less, Cal Sr. decided that "with low overhead and volume buying, we should be able to have dollar days the year around in smaller towns. That's the way we figured, but, frankly, I was very uncertain about the response when we opened our first dollar store more or less as an experiment at Springfield, Kentucky, in May of 1956." The store sold $8,000 of its $13,800 stock in the first two days. Later a Knoxville store moved $42,000 the first week, a Memphis store sold $1 million during the first ten months, and a Bowling Green store dispensed with half of its stock in the first two days.

The Turners discovered that, as volume increased, more companies became interested in selling merchandise to Turner & Son. According to Cal Sr.:

> When a manufacturer has an item he wants to clean out, we'll buy all he has on hand, if it's quality merchandise, and then try to sell it quickly in our dollar stores.
>
> I remember very well that around that time the color pink in men's clothes was the fashion. Well, pretty soon we ran hundreds and hundreds of dozens of pink corduroy pants for a dollar. People driving through these little towns saw nearly every man on the street was wearing pink pants.

After several stores were operating, Cal Sr. said,

> People were chasing down our Dollar General trucks, trying to find out where they could buy the goods. People came looking for us. This is really how the franchise end of our business started. In the beginning . . . we called them associate stores. They would be called Sam's Dollar Store, or whatever the associate wanted to call it, but they would buy the goods from us.

In 1957, with his father's health declining, Cal Sr., almost single-handedly, was running a company that had sales of more than $5 million from its 14 self-service dry-goods stores (no item more than $10) and 15 Dollar General stores (no item more than $1). During the 1960s, the associate stores were converted to franchise stores in an effort to obtain greater control over the merchandise. According to Cal Sr., the problem was that the associates "would come in and cherry-pick the merchandise, and we never really knew what they did with [it] after they bought it." In return for accepting more centralized control of merchandise allocations and agreeing to use the name "Dollar General" on their stores, associate owners were offered higher discounts on merchandise.

Franchise fees were low, usually $1,000 plus about $25 per month to cover advertising.

Even after prices in the stores rose above one dollar, DG insisted that pricing be in even dollars, which eliminated the need for adding machines at the register. A small card showing tax amounts for each price level was taped onto the cash register. A store manager plus a couple of clerks could run the stores, and because of the small-town locations, rent was reasonable.

By 1966, the company consisted of 255 stores with sales of $25.8 million. At about this time, the company began using television ads to supplement its annual mailing to potential customers. In 1968, with sales of $40.5 million, the company went public with a 300,000-share offering at $16.50 a share. The same year, the company changed its name to Dollar General Corporation. A year later, the chain consisted of 345 stores, and stores with the Dollar General sign accounted for 88 percent of revenues (5 percent of revenues came from a chain of larger stores operating under the Gibson's name and 7 percent from such stores as Turner's, Nationwide, and Valley Salvage).

When DG's stock price rose to more than $50 per share and split two for one, a second public offering was undertaken at $33.50 a share. These funds were used in 1973 to finance the acquisition (by assuming the leases and fixtures) of 70 Silco store sites.

In 1973, the family proved that they were in Scottsville to stay by constructing, with the help of a Scottsville bond issue, a distribution warehouse and office complex. The structure, occupied under a leaseback arrangement and often referred to as "the main warehouse," tied together three freestanding warehouses into a total warehouse about the size of five football fields. They also converted the old office building—a former warehouse—into a fixture factory where all the display tables in Dollar General stores were made.

The recession of 1974 prompted the Turners to purchase approximately 300,000 of DG's 2.3 million outstanding shares for $1.5 million. In addition, DG added to its product mix such health and beauty aids as toothpaste, deodorant, and detergents—all at the lowest possible price. Previously, soft goods accounted for 70 percent of sales; now the level dropped to around 55 percent.

In 1977, Cal Turner, Jr., was named president of a company with 680 stores—418 company owned and 262 franchised—in 22 states. The previous year, sales had reached $109 million, with 80 percent from retail sales and 20 percent from sales to franchisees. Return on sales was 3.9 percent, up from 3.7 percent and 3.1 percent in the prior two years, respectively.

COMPANY HEADQUARTERS: SCOTTSVILLE

Although the place was an unlikely home for a $500-million retailer, Cal Jr. made no apologies for headquartering in Scottsville, Kentucky: "I feel sorry for anybody who doesn't live in Scottsville. The culture of our company largely emanates from Scottsville." Population "4,500 and growing," Scottsville was the county seat of Allen County, deep in southern Kentucky, about an hour north of Nashville and 20 miles from the nearest interstate highway.

A visitor to the town would probably stay in one of the motels in Bowling Green, Kentucky—some 30 miles away. Driving into town, one's first stop would most likely be at one of the town's two traffic lights. Then a left turn, a drive past establishments like the Sonic Drive-In Restaurant and the local Chainsaw World, and the visitor eventually would arrive at the town square.

The square was typical "small town America," with a mixture of old and new buildings, one of which was, of course, a bank. On one corner, attached to an old but well-kept redbrick storefront, was a huge black and yellow Dollar General sign. This store—like most Dollar General outlets—was immune to architectural classification. Dollar General didn't care, however, and neither did their customers, which was the important thing to the company.

Although the building was plain, it wasn't uninviting. Neatly stacked bargain items outside the store spoke of better buys inside. The interior was brightly lit, with merchandise displayed in an orderly fashion—shirts stacked on sturdy wooden tables, jeans hung on racks in the center of the store, and overalls somewhere in-between. Along the walls of the air-conditioned store were long rows of toothpaste, shampoo, laundry bleach, and assorted other "health and beauty aids." Piles of disposable diapers rose nearly to the ceiling. Every few feet, large red signs proclaimed ground-floor prices: jeans for $8; shirts at two for $7, or $5 apiece; men's leather deck shoes for $15. Customers could also buy Dollar General motor oil or Dollar General grape soda by the two-liter bottle. Some 90 percent of the goods were priced less than $10, and nothing was more than $30.

At each table, clothes were stacked smallest to largest, left to right. A browse through the store revealed such labels as Van Heusen and Sedgefield. On hangers, pants were spaced about two finger widths apart to prevent overcrowding. Shoes were in the rear right-hand corner, displayed by size. The "impulse" rack stood by the cash register and contained items like batteries, razor blades, and Goo-Goo Cluster candy bars. Clerks smiled and offered to help. (Every DG customer had to be greeted, and some came in every day to see if new merchandise had arrived.)

About one-half mile west of the square on U.S. Highway 31 was DG's carpentry shop, where the company made most of its own fixtures at a 50-percent cost saving. This building used to be the site of the warehouse and offices of Turner & Son. When the new corporate headquarters opened in 1973, the shop moved here from a converted chicken coop. Inside, 18 workers busily manufactured tables, wall units, checkout counters, auxiliary checkouts, flats, circles for the wooden racks, and end caps for the shoe racks. (Only metal racks and a few specialty containers were purchased.)

The corporate headquarters was located one-half mile past the carpentry shop. A three-story administration building adjoined a huge silver warehouse that connected three smaller warehouses, formerly tobacco barns, by underground passage. Next to the warehouse, on the first level, trailers nestled close by as they were loaded. The three warehouses were on a slight elevation above the main building, which was said to be "down in the holler."

Space was cramped inside the office building—a testament to DG's rapid growth. On the third floor were executive offices and a bullpen where 28 bookkeepers busily fed weekly store results into computer terminals. People chatted and laughed, but all seemed to be working diligently.

CAL TURNER, JR.

After graduating from Vanderbilt University in 1962, with a major in business and economics, and a three-year tour in the navy, Cal Jr. wrestled with whether to go into the ministry or business:

> I decided to do both, by joining Dollar General. I know this is going to sound corny, but I really believe that running this company and practicing the Protestant work ethic are my calling. Dollar General is more to me than a job—it's a mission and a responsibility. There are givers and takers in this world, and I want to make sure I end up on the right side of the fence.

In 1966, he was made executive vice president (at the time there were only two officers: president and secretary/treasurer), and, as noted, he assumed the presidency in 1977.

According to Cal Jr., Dollar General's "people-centeredness and tight-fisted control of overhead" have always been hallmarks of the company, values that traced back to J. L. Turner, whose portrait hung on the wall outside the executive suite.

Cal Jr. saw his job as primarily one of perpetuating the long history of success his family had experienced in retailing:

> The test of anyone under God is stewardship of their God-given resources. The scripture that says "unto him to whom much is given, much is required" is a driving force for me. I don't consider the stock in my name to be mine. You pass it on.

In 1977, in its largest acquisition to date, the company had acquired the bankrupt United Dollar Stores (UDS), an Arkansas-based chain of 89 company-owned and 61 franchised stores (1976 sales of $30 million), as well as 176 Dollar General franchised units operated by Rankin Co. of Columbia, Mississippi.

According to Cal Turner, Jr., the $6-million purchase of UDS was made in part because of potential liquidation values. In the first 11 days of liquidation sales, the company grossed more than $3 million. Moreover, Dollar General acquired the UDS warehouse in Dumas, Arkansas, which provided the company a second warehouse of 350,000 square feet. Obtaining the warehouse made the repurchase of the Rankin franchises particularly attractive. Not only could the warehouse be operated rent-free until 1980, when the company would buy it for $1.4 million, but the Dumas warehouse, because of its location, would be able to serve the Rankin stores more efficiently than had been possible in the past. Management also hoped that the second warehouse would allow the company to achieve its goal of reducing store delivery times from every three and one-half weeks to every two weeks. The acquisition took longer to digest than the Turners had hoped, however—two years—because almost three-fourths of the stores had been unprofitable at the time of purchase.

Dollar General increased its marketing efforts during this period. It had been sending out a full-color, 12-page, direct-mail advertising circular every August; it now sent the circular five times a year to 2.3 million households. The company also expanded its use of television advertising and began using country music star Jim Ed Brown to sing the DG jingle: "Who says a dollar won't buy much anymore? Every day is dollar day at the Dollar General Store."

After the acquisition, Cal Jr. quickly decided that the company was growing too rapidly to permit "seat-of-the-pants" management. He therefore hired several experienced managers to bring some order to the operation, including Ed Burke, manager of operating analysis of National Industries, as vice president of finance, and Bobby Carpenter, marketing officer and assistant general counsel for First American Corporation, as general counsel and vice president of administration, and he promoted his younger brother Steve Turner to executive vice president of merchandise.

Perhaps the biggest change wrought by Cal Jr. was the introduction of formal strategic planning. He had become convinced of the need for it at a management conference in the late 1970s. Dollar General did not even have a budget, so Cal Jr. was unsure what his father's reaction to his decision would be:

> I went straight into my father's office, shut the door, and said, "Dad, we have a decision. Do we start doing this now or wait until you die?" I didn't know if he'd like the idea or not, but he looked at me and said, "Would you tell me what it is?" Then he said, "Not only do I support you, I think it's the only way to go. I can't do it, but I'm behind you."

Soon, Dollar General had a strategic plan and better training for employees—partly because of Cal Jr.'s own ideas and partly because of his willingness to go outside the company for managerial talent when necessary. According to Cal Jr., "I'm a generalist. I've been exposed to the entrepreneurial feel of my

Dad, but I see the trap of it, and the need for systems and structure. Yet I have a strong desire to keep it simple."

RECENT COMPANY HISTORY

During the early 1980s, DG's strategy was gradual growth in existing regions:

Year	Beginning of Year	Stores Opened	Stores Closed	Stores at End of Year
1979	632	88	32	688
1980	688	65	31	722
1981	722	79	40	761
1982	761	98	36	823

Cal Jr. explained that there was plenty of room for geographical expansion doing just what the company had been doing; all of Pennsylvania, for example, had only 21 Dollar General stores.

The recession of that period seemed to work to the company's advantage. When other retailers were struggling, DG was, according to Cal Jr., "grinning like a mule eating briars. Simply put, recession increases demand for our stores. People out there are looking for bargains." Steve Turner believed that recessions created "opportunities to buy" and referred to hundreds of thousands of children's apparel batches purchased at 50-percent off and dress shirts at 10 percent of retail prices.

In 1983, Interco, a St. Louis-based manufacturing and retailing conglomerate, offered to sell its poorly performing P. N. Hirsch chain (annualized 1983 sales of $135 million) to Dollar General. Hirsch consisted of about 280 stores in 11 midwestern and southern states (70 in towns with DG stores), plus a modern but union-represented warehouse. Although the acquisition did not fit with current strategy, and DG had no unions, Cal Jr. had been interested: "We just use a good ol' commonsense approach, [but] we also believe in breaking the rules for the right reason."

He had been concerned about "how you unplug the air conditioner in the warehouse and decertify the union." He was also concerned that the average Hirsch unit, 7,700 square feet, had sales per square foot of only $50, compared with $75 for Dollar General. To learn more about Hirsch's performance, at Hirsch management's suggestion, he had Dollar General employees posing as insurance inspectors visit 90 percent of Hirsch's stores. "That's a great way to observe employees at work when they're not putting on airs," he said. "Who wants to impress an insurance man, for crying out loud?"

"What we really wanted," he explained, "was Interco's Eagle chain down in Florida." Nevertheless, he found the whole Hirsch deal attractive, because it increased the number of stores by 30 percent and the total selling space by

50 percent. "With [Hirsch] . . . we obtained favorable leases in locations . . . that are often better than those of our own stores," he noted. "The purchase represents about three years of normal store growth for us." The acquisition also allowed additional efficiencies from the company's warehouses. Both the Dumas and Scottsville facilities added second shifts, and the Scottsville ware-house was expanded by 100,000 square feet to 430,000 square feet. The company also added 86 new trailers and 17 tractors to its fleet to help service all the new stores.

The purchase price for Hirsch was $50 million, financed with a ten-year, $40-million revolving term loan and internal funds. Cal Jr. estimated that it would take about three years to bring the acquired stores up to DG's level.

Dollar General wasted no time in converting the Hirsch units. By sending large numbers of DG employees and managers to the store locations and working long, hard hours, nearly 100 of the 250 stores were converted from November 1983 to March 1984, and the rest were expected to be opened in time for the back-to-school selling season. The Hirsch acquisition and regular growth resulted in a net gain of 304 stores—338 new stores and 34 closed—for 1983. See Exhibit 1 for locations of DG stores in 1983.

In the wake of the Hirsch acquisition, Dollar General went to 12 major advertising mailings a year; hired Jim Barton, a 26-year veteran and former regional director of retail operations for Ben Franklin Stores, as vice president of retail operations; and added two outside directors, the former president of Kmart and the former president of the American Management Association.

CURRENT OPERATIONS

By the start of 1984, Dollar General had 5,500 employees (3,500 full time), annual sales of $350 million, and 2,200 shareholders (45 percent of the common stock was held by the Turner family). See Exhibit 2 for a ten-year summary of financial operations of the company and Exhibits 3 and 4 for current consolidated income statements and balance sheets, respectively.

The company's stated mission was "to serve, better than anyone else does, our customer's needs for quality, basic merchandise at the lowest everyday price." In Cal Jr.'s words, "We are renegade retailers. We operate in markets other retailers don't want. We occupy buildings other retailers don't want. We buy merchandise other retailers don't want. And we serve customers other retailers don't want." He was proud of such things as a DG television ad that showed a little boy, wearing jeans and a jacket, getting on the school bus. His "whole outfit from the skin out cost $22.52," all from Dollar General. Serving this market was, to Turner, "more than just a business; it's meeting the needs of a huge segment of the population. I have a letter from one lady who says she couldn't send her child to school without Dollar General."

Exhibit 1
Location of Company-Owned Dollar General Stores
(as of December 31, 1983)

● = 0–50
▲ = 51–99
★ = 100 and above

	DOLLAR GENERAL	ACQUIRED		DOLLAR GENERAL	ACQUIRED
Alabama	25	5	Ohio	38	—
Arkansas	54	11	Oklahoma	37	—
Delaware	9	—	Pennsylvania	23	—
Florida	37	—	South Carolina	6	—
Georgia	46	—	Tennessee	102	24
Illinois	10	64	Texas	47	—
Indiana	35	32	Virginia	61	—
Iowa	—	2	West Virginia	53	—
Kansas	8	6	Totals	851	276
Kentucky	102	12			
Louisiana	56	23			
Maryland	26	—	Company-owned Total		1,127
Mississippi	36	28	Franchised total		57
Missouri	33	69	System total		1,184
North Carolina	7	—			

Exhibit 2
Dollar General Corporation
Financial Information, 1974–1984
(dollars in thousands except per-share amounts)

	1974	1975	1976	1977	1978	1979	1980	1981	1982	1983	1984
Net sales	$74,201	$87,844	$109,132	$129,559	$161,694	$177,774	$209,753	$245,453	$290,069	$346,655	$480,514
Net income	2,317	3,261	4,223	4,805	4,881	6,259	5,852	7,208	11,333	15,126	20,598
Net income per share	$.15	$.21	$.27	$.31	$.31	$.40	$.37	$.46	$.73	$.97	$1.32
Cash dividends per share	—	$.01	$.02	$.03	$.04	$.05	$.07	$.11	$.13	$.16	$.20
Weighted-average shares outstanding (000)	15,462	15,744	15,720	15,720	15,721	15,721	15,721	15,699	15,620	15,628	15,654
Return on average assets (%)	6.35	8.12	9.46	8.87	7.32	8.35	7.26	8.29	11.56	11.61	12.55
Return on average equity (%)	9.90	12.88	14.70	14.64	13.15	14.92	12.44	13.87	19.14	21.54	24.16
Total assets	38,455	41,872	47,165	60,863	72,439	77,402	83,905	89,971	106,223	154,299	173,963
Stockholders' equity	23,854	26,777	30,660	34,986	39,233	44,677	49,375	54,580	63,825	76,582	93,916
Long-term obligations	4,260	3,383	2,563	6,938	16,964	15,574	14,428	13,276	12,118	35,720	26,950
Company-owned stores	402	410	418	761	632	688	722	761	823	1,127	1,080
Franchised stores	242	246	262	90	101	59	63	65	60	57	48
Inventory turnover	3.0	3.1	3.2	2.6	3.0	2.9	3.2	3.6	3.5	3.0	3.4

Source: 1984 Annual Report.

Exhibit 3
Dollar General Corporation
Consolidated Statement of Income, 1982–1984
(in thousands except per-share amounts)

	1984	Percent of Net Sales	1983	Percent of Net Sales	1982	Percent of Net Sales
Net sales	$480,514	100.0	$346,655	100.0	$290,069	$100.0
Cost of goods sold	337,029	70.1	244,094	70.4	205,837	71.0
Gross profit	143,485	29.9	102,561	29.6	84,232	29.0
Operating expenses	99,341	20.7	71,077	20.5	60,834	21.0
Operating profit	44,144	9.2	31,484	9.1	23,398	8.0
Interest expense	4,146	.9	1,808	.5	1,665	.5
Income before taxes on income	39,998	8.3	29,676	8.6	21,733	7.5
Provision for taxes on income	19,400	4.0	14,550	4.2	10,400	3.6
Net income	20,598	4.3	$ 15,126	4.4	$ 11,333	3.9
Net income per share	$1.32		$.97		$.73	
Weighted-average number of shares outstanding	15,654		15,628		15,620	

Source: 1984 Annual Report.

Exhibit 4
Dollar General Corporation
Consolidated Balance Sheet, 1983–1984 (in thousands)

ASSETS	1984	1983
Current assets:		
Cash and cash equivalents	$ 4,681	$ 15,863
Merchandise inventories	142,264	113,903
Other current assets	2,530	5,430
Total current assets	149,475	135,196
Property and equipment, at cost:		
Land	93	93
Buildings	5,319	3,834
Furniture and fixtures	24,772	20,767
	30,184	24,694
Less accumulated depreciation	11,675	9,368
	18,509	15,326
Other assets	5,979	3,777
Total assets	$173,963	$154,299
LIABILITIES AND STOCKHOLDERS' EQUITY		
Current liabilities:		
Current portion of long-term obligations	$ 875	$ 5,346
Accounts payable, trade	33,040	18,996
Accrued expenses	9,610	8,001
Income taxes	5,760	7,858
Total current liabilities	49,285	40,219
Long-term obligations	26,950	35,720
Deferred income taxes	3,812	1,778
Total liabilities	$80,047	$77,717
Stockholders' equity:		
Common stock, shares outstanding		
1984—15,651		
1983—15,655	9,226	9,226
Additional paid-in capital	22,250	22,236
Retained earnings	64,760	47,293
	96,236	78,755
Less treasury stock, at cost	2,320	2,173
Total stockholders' equity	93,916	76,582
Total liabilities and stockholders' equity	$173,963	$154,299

At the DG store in Russellville, Kentucky, store manager Melba Brown sold canvas handbags embroidered with ducks for about $2, $5 less than a large department store in nearby Bowling Green. "These kids can carry handbags just like the upper crust," said Brown. "A child who comes from a poor family wants to look like anyone else. That peer pressure they feel is so enormous, especially in a small town." In a similar vein, Cal Jr. related the story of a woman whose son loved Izod shirts. "She buys a pair of Izod socks, removes the alligator, and sews them onto a Dollar General polo shirt."

Jim Barton, vice president of retail operations, emphasized the importance of knowing DG's customers: "We know our niche—the low-to-middle-income family. [Discounters] who have upgraded have left their customers behind. [This leaves us] a bigger base to choose from. We try hard not to upgrade." He pointed out that most of DG's customers were women and cited statistics that showed women spend the vast majority of the household income.

The Stores

Roughly 80 percent of the company's stores were located in towns of less than 25,000 population. The rest were mainly in inner-city urban areas where customers were likely to be blue collar, use public transportation, and live downtown. The average store size was approximately 5,500 square feet—about one-eighth of an acre. The decor was plain: tile floors, pegboard walls, and bright fluorescent lights. According to Cal Jr.,

> In Scottsville, we think ambience is something you ride to the hospital in. It's hard to convince the customer he's getting a bargain if he sees carpeting and a boutique setting. We deliberately avoid frou-frou. Besides, you can cover a lot of sins with some paint and some paneling.

Dollar General didn't buy real estate; they leased it for $1.70 per square foot on the average. The typical store had 29 months remaining on its lease, but some were occupied on a month-to-month basis. The company generally preferred downtown locations that other stores had abandoned long ago in favor of suburban malls (where rents typically were $14 to $35 per square foot). On the other hand, an increasing number of Dollar General stores—currently 50 percent—were located in suburban "strip" malls. (Nationally, such locations rented for $4 to $15 a square foot.) The stores were open six days a week, at least one evening, and, where possible, on Sundays.

About 35 percent of the merchandise for a typical store was ordered at the store manager's discretion from the "want list"—made up from a corporate checklist of merchandise available for sale. The remaining 65 percent came from specials and other merchandise dictated by headquarters. All merchandise was divided into four categories: soft goods such as clothes (47 percent); health and beauty aids (21 percent); hardware such as motor oil (24 percent); and shoes (8 percent).

Pricing was simplified because many of the items had "price points," which meant they would always sell for the same price, or never above a given price (for example, jeans never sold for more than $10). The stores did not accept credit cards, only cash or a personal check, and there was no lay-away program.

Ninety percent of store managers were women. Barton claimed that the key in small towns was "local people," and it just so happened that there were many more women than men to choose from. According to another manager, women "do a better job of minding the store. Men have something in their hormones that makes them want to go out and see what's happening over at the barber shop or post office." A store manager could expect to earn about $12,000 plus a bonus of 10-percent pretax profits, which would typically be a second income for a "working wife" in a small town, according to Barton. Medical benefits were available to the entire family of the store manager; full-time clerks paid $5 to $10 a week for the coverage.

A major task for each manager was to hire a chief clerk and one or two other clerks and train them. Also, at the end of each week, the manager paid each clerk in cash and deposited the remaining money in the bank.

The DG People

Dollar General's 1,080 stores were divided into 15 areas and 84 districts. Gene Cartwright, director of recruiting/training, was charged with the task of developing the district managers (DMs) and store managers (SMs). The entry level for college graduates was usually district manager, although most DM slots were filled by promotion of successful store managers. In general, the company preferred to recruit DMs at small, regional colleges and universities like Western Kentucky in Bowling Green.

In recruiting DMs, Cartwright looked for "commitment to excellence" and the "willingness to work hard"—qualities Cartwright called "want to." Cartwright also looked for a "people orientation." "We're a people business. Our two most important assets are people and merchandise, in that order."

In reflecting on his involvement in recruiting, Cal Jr. observed,

> I want a leader who has our style, but I don't want a clone. When everybody wears the same suit, you don't have a company; you have an army. I want people who have skill and expertise, but my discussion is always of values: What are your goals? How will you reach them? Tell me about your kids, and your dad. Being a manager is being both a teacher and a parent in a different setting.

Linda Nelson was typical of the people DG liked to hire:

> On March 11, 1982, Dollar General had their grand opening in Portageville, Missouri. I worked at Fred's (a discount store) across the street as a sales clerk. At 8:30 A.M. people were lined up in front of the store waiting for the doors to open. We had very little business that day, so at lunch time I went across the street to see what Dollar General had to offer. Once I got inside, I was surprised at the low prices. I liked what I saw. The merchandise and the prices were great.

Four months later, she became a clerk at DG, and, in less than a year, she was promoted to store manager. In her first year as manager, the store recorded sales of $252,883 and profits of $8,546; one year later, sales were $285,564 and profits $19,185. Nelson, like many employees, did most of her shopping at DG, even though employees received no discounts.

Although selection of people was usually by "gut instinct," the company had moved toward such techniques as written profiles designed to measure "intrinsic, extrinsic, and systemic values." Consultants hired by Dollar General to interpret test results had explained that the test showed how honest and hard working a person was and what made him or her tick.

John Berry, a recent addition to the buying staff, had this to say about his impression of DG in a recent newsletter:

> [In comparison with my prior job] Dollar General is much easier to work for . . . there's no politics here. . . . This company is doing nothing but going up, . . . and I think it will continue to go up because everyone is a part of the company. That's why Dollar General does so well, because of the way they treat people; they are a people-oriented company, and when a company is good to you, you will do anything for them.

Jim Barton cited several reasons for his decision to join the company, the main one being the "phenomenal growth" of Dollar General. Having come from a retailer that "was opening new stores, but closing even more of them," Barton had experienced firsthand the atrophy that can accompany stagnation. Barton also noted that Dollar General had been remarkably consistent in executing its strategy of delivering the basics at the lowest price, and he was enthusiastic about both the management team and the participative style of Cal Jr.:

> Dollar General is a company, but it also is a feeling. There is a sense of excitement. The staff works six days a week; it's a work-oriented place. We all have titles, but we don't talk about them. We don't wear our titles—we're on a first-name basis.

TRAINING

Cal Turner, Jr., described the old training system for store managers as follows:

We'd go into a new town, hire some local help, and spend several days open-ing a new store. After the store was stocked, we'd look over the local crew and pick the one who seemed the brightest and most hard working. We'd give him the keys, show him how to fill out a deposit slip, and in a couple of weeks a truck would come to bring some more merchandise.

The results were not always as the company hoped. Some stores were energetically and enthusiastically managed—neat and clean. In another you could find a manager with "a cigarette hanging out of the side of her mouth." The store would be dirty, and customers could be in there 15 minutes before a clerk would even know they were there.

Consequently, the company began training store managers in all the fine points of successfully running a Dollar General store. The training included instruction on ordering, stocking, filling out the operations reports, and deal-ing effectively with customers. The DG wisdom was summarized in the operations manual—a comprehensive loose-leaf notebook that told managers where to display merchandise, how to rotate stock, when to post advertise-ments, how to dress, and always to greet customers—even if only to say hello. Every employee, including clerks, was required to read the manual and agree to work within its provisions. Although each store was different, procedures were standardized as much as possible. Cartwright explained, "We want everybody to be singing out of the same hymn book."

As part of this effort, in 1984 the company began holding one-day regional SM meetings. Small groups of store managers would be exposed to the latest management techniques and given the chance to air their com-plaints and to cavort with fellow employees. In 1985, at least 500 managers would be so trained. Jim Barton attended all of the meetings, and Cal Jr. either opened or closed them. He liked to "dare employees to reach their highest capabilities" by citing the book *I Dare You,* by William Danforth:

> This book is for the daring few who are headed somewhere. It will not be overly popular, because it calls for courage, swift and daring. But in the eyes of you, one of the priceless few, I trust will come a renewal of purpose. You can be a bigger person than you are now.

Several participants had written the company to comment on the usefulness of the meetings.

Training for new DMs involved a six-month program (although only three months were conducted at any one time) that included stocking and dis-playing merchandise and becoming intimately familiar with DG's "way of doing things." Trainees also practiced opening and closing stores at the full-size, "mock" store in Scottsville and spent substantial time in the field gaining hands-on experience with a veteran store manager in a district different from the one they would run.

At a meeting of the American Management Association's President's Association, Cal Jr. had become intrigued with a seminar series that encouraged improved employee communication. Thus, in 1984, the company also began holding a series of seminars entitled "Communicating through Productivity." Employees attended two four-day labs spaced two to three months apart. The first focused on developing management tools such as job descriptions and standards of performance, conducting progress reviews, and creating development plans. The second session focused on communicating one-on-one and emphasized listening skills.

Despite these programs, one part-time clerk, a college student, observed: "I think you would find that most of the people who work for Dollar General feel that the company doesn't push a lot on you about 'our way'."

Information Systems

Operational reporting from the stores filled 75 mailbags each week. These simple forms, prepared by hand by each store manager, essentially totaled the accompanying cash-register tapes into a net sales figure and summarized weekly expenses. After the forms were received in Scottsville, 28 bookkeepers computerized the data. Each bookkeeper was responsible for about 35 to 40 stores. The information was consolidated into operations reports by district, area, and store, returned to the appropriate managers, and sent to Barton (see Exhibit 5). Turnaround was roughly one week.

When Barton received area reports, the first figures he checked were weekly sales, weekly sales versus the budget, and year-to-date sales versus the budget. He also checked salary figures particularly closely if a store was in trouble.

In addition to the standard reports, a "watch list" showing the stores that were performing below expectations was also prepared. Most of the stores on the watch list were new stores that were not as profitable as expected. Stores generally moved into the black within 30 to 60 days, but if the store was still losing money after six to nine months, the company began to reevaluate the decision to be in that market. Although it took four days to open a store, it took only one to close a "sour store." According to Cal Jr., "We're going to close a store that doesn't work. Shucks, that's just simple redeployment of assets."

Barton liked to stick with a store as long as possible: "Quite often the problems are correctable; poor promotion or even a bad attitude on the part of clerks can reduce a store's sales." To check out the situation, Barton used "designated shoppers," who were unknown to store personnel, to report on the attitude displayed to customers.

Barton spent approximately half of each week visiting stores, occasionally accompanied by Cal Sr. After strolling around the store and observing employees at work, Barton would introduce himself to the entire crew. He encouraged employees to air their complaints and was not reluctant to hand out compliments if appropriate. He would discuss matters privately with the

Exhibit 5
Sample Operations Reports

Store Hours: 54

	Week	Year to Date	Store Opened	Lease Expires	Options	Selling Area	Rating
Sales This Year	13,884.68	260,497.69	08/01/74	06/30/86	2/5	4,186	8
Budget	12,686.04	248,364.32					
Sales Last Year	11,114.48	217,596.51					
% Inc./Dec.	24.92	19.72		1 Year Previous	2 Year Previous		
Budget %	9.45	4.89					
			Sales	480,160.01	430,908.76		
Overrings	70.10	2,053.58					
Refunds	65.68	2,195.76	% Cost	12.30	11.78		
Cash Over/Short	2.92	5.02					
Invoices	25,666.42	285,322.66	Profit	18,935.27	24,699.68		
35 Turns	3.39	34 Turns 3.45					

EXPENSES	THIS YEAR				LAST YEAR			
	% to Week Sales	Week	Year to Date	% to Year Sales	% to Year Sales	Year to Date	Week	% to Week Sales
Salaries	3.84	533.75	14,448.40	5.55	5.91	12,851.83	479.90	4.32
Rent		80.77	2,261.56	0.87	1.04	2,261.56	80.77	
Utilities		0.00	3,717.77	1.43	2.34	5,102.52	763.74	
Taxes		61.02	3,060.11	1.17	1.35	2,927.54	56.98	
Insurance		0.00	0.00	0.00	0.00	0.00	0.00	
Advertising		0.00	0.00	0.00	0.19	416.03	0.00	
Depr. & Amort.		25.22	685.24	0.26	0.42	921.87	35.17	
Repairs		0.00	1,541.10	0.59	0.08	167.00	0.00	
Miscellaneous		15.00	528.00	0.20	0.21	446.68	54.43	
Supplies		134.47	1,421.08	0.55	0.59	1,281.85	72.95	
Bad Checks		0.00	18.72−	0.01−	0.02	37.07	0.00	
Freight		0.00	0.00	0.00	0.00	0.00	0.00	
Total	6.12	850.23	27,644.54	10.61	12.14	26,413.95	1,543.94	13.89
Markdowns		0.00	8,992.18	3.45	3.80	8,273.72	80.75	
					TYR Avg. Inv.		LYR Avg. Inv.	
Book Inventory		92-105,000	182,751		154,159	146,662	131,736	

(continued on next page)

Source: Company documents.

store manager and leave it to him or her to inform the crew and implement corrective action. He preferred to give the manager a chance to talk and then cover any negative findings discreetly and positively, in what he called "corrective conversation."

(continued)

District Reports (Pre 1/1/84)

	WEEK	YEAR TO DATE	STORE OPENED	LEASE EXPIRES	OPTIONS	SELLING AREA	RATING
Sales This Year	164,396	4,274,042				91,007	
Budget	170,978	4,186,001					
Sales last year	150,346	3,685,057					
% Inc./Dec.	9.34	15.98					
Budget %	3.85−	2.10					
Overrings	881	43,043					
Refunds	2,038	60,687					
Cash Over/Short	47−	482−					
Invoices	215,118	4,733,476					

	1 Year Previous	2 Year Previous
Sales	8,857,438	7,264,714
% Cost	13.14	14.05
Profit	517,716	351,713

EXPENSES	THIS YEAR				LAST YEAR			
	% TO WEEK SALES	WEEK	YEAR TO DATE	% TO YEAR SALES	% TO YEAR SALES	YEAR TO DATE	WEEK	% TO WEEK SALES
Salaries	6.59	10,832	265,064	6.20	6.35	234,119	8,975	5.97
Rent		3,140	82,200	1.92	2.16	79,634	3,121	
Utilities		2,439	76,961	1.80	2.24	82,498	4,837	
Taxes		1,105	47,549	1.11	1.18	43,657	1,051	
Insurance				0.00	0.04	1,372		
Advertising			328	0.01	0.40	14,804		
Depreciation and Amortation		268	8,006	0.19	0.29	10,710	368	
Repairs		98	9,576	0.22	0.17	6,096	50	
Miscellaneous		880	12,571	0.29	0.34	12,574	925	
Supplies		680	21,780	0.51	0.57	21,056	1,370	
Bad Checks		46−	125−	0.00	0.01	215	36	
Freight				0.00	0.01	218		
Total	11.81	19,416	523,910	12.26	13.76	506,955	20,752	13.80
Markdowns		1,068	134,453	3.15	2.90	106,701	349	
Book Inventory	Min. 1,878,000 Max. 2,179,000		3,688,697			3,074,668		

Barton was quick to point to a six-inch stack of suggestions on his desk as evidence that the company listened to ideas from store personnel. "We're always challenging the store managers for new ideas," he said.

In 1984, Dollar General started a companywide newsletter that contained a column from the president, articles about how to improve store operations, special-interest articles about employees—both senior managers and clerks—and letters from employees or retirees (see excerpt in Exhibit 6).

In addition, the company had recently installed "voice mail," which allowed employees to send telephone-recorded messages to 10,000 voice mailboxes. These messages could relate to new merchandise or any other information needed by employees. "We had to do something about our long-distance bill," said Cartwright. "Voice mail eliminates the small talk and still gets the message across." After his visits to stores, Barton used voice mail to inform district and area managers of his findings.

The Merchandise

According to Cal Jr., "The fun part of this business is haggling. First you haggle on the price. Then you haggle on the terms." He added, "A Turner will buy just about anything if it's at half-price. . . . And my grandfather always said, 'If it's bought right, it's half sold.'" Although there was a staff of eight buyers, headed by Steve Turner, Cal Sr. still enjoyed trading. "He's so smooth on the phone," said Cal Jr., "that you get to liking him so much that before long you're giving him a better deal." Cal Jr. was convinced that many sellers came to Scottsville because of the long-established relationships built by his father. "Salesmen can't buy us lunch," he emphasized. "We buy. We're also very loyal. If you're selling to us, we'll stick with you unless you get out of line."

According to Cal Jr., "Too many people think we just sell junk. We're in the business of giving value to our customers. We cut our teeth in Kentucky and Tennessee towns serving the farmer—a very demanding consumer who has to have something that holds up well." The majority of Dollar General's soft goods were irregulars (IRs) or closeouts (a garment that the manufacturer had overproduced or was discontinuing). An irregular garment, usually 3 percent of a manufacturer's production, was one that for some reason failed to meet the standards of a manufacturer, but one often could not tell the difference between IRs and normal merchandise. For example, as a highly successful ploy to get analysts to come to Dollar General's financial presentations, Cal Jr. used to give away free IR golf shirts to all attendees—just to show how good irregulars could be. Cal Jr. occasionally bought his own clothes at DG. After describing a sports jacket he bought for 30 percent of its original price, Steve Turner commented, "It was a great buy, but we made a bundle." (The average cost for the jackets was approximately 11 percent of the original retail price.)

Twenty manufacturers, under contract to DG, sent in a steady stream of irregulars in almost every clothing category. The company agreed to buy all of the goods a manufacturer wanted to ship, so long as they met Dollar General's standards. (Some manufacturers were shunned by DG because of the low quality of their merchandise.) In return, the prenegotiated prices usually ran 40 to 50 percent less than normal. No single supplier accounted for

Exhibit 6
Portions of a Dollar General Newsletter

DOLLAR GENERAL STORY

Vol. 1, No. 2   For Dollar General Employees and Their Families   Sept./Oct. 1984

Dollar General Pride

The rich agricultural community of Dumas, Arkansas in the southeastern part of that state sets the stage for another chapter in the Dollar General Story. Here, in a region where cotton and rice battle for the title as the number one money-making crop, about 280 good Dollar General folks work hard each day to fill orders and ship merchandise to almost half of our 1100 stores.

The Dumas warehouse operation became a part of Dollar General in October of 1977 when we acquired United Dollar Stores, Inc. It was here that shoe department supervisor T.C. Pickett began his career. In April of 1962 T.C. came to work as a warehouse order puller, and by the next day he had been promoted to a department supervisor. T.C. has also been taking care of the mail at the Dumas warehouse for the last 22 years. In that time,

T.C. Pickett

he has never been tardy or lost a piece of mail.

T.C. is proud to be working for Dollar General. He says the difference between UDS and Dollar General is that "Dollar General is constantly changing; this keeps me more alert to grasp the changes and be more productive with them."

T.C. shows his pride in Dollar General by being our

(continued on next page)

Comments from the President

Since publishing our first newsletter, General Story has insisted that I remember that Dollar General Story is dedicated to all the employees who comprise our family. I think he meant for your president to "keep his mouth shut" for a change, and I'm going to show him I can. So . . . the president's message this time has really been written by our employees!

I appeal to all of you to let General Story hear from you. I promise that he and I (plus others here in Scottsville) will read every letter sent. Here's your chance for store employees to speak to each other and to the warehouse, buying, accounting, and data processing employees. General Story

(continued on next page)

PRIDE, continued

representative in his community. His community activities include: 10 years as alderman, member of the Chamber of Commerce and the Jaycees, and board member of a local Daycare Center and Center for the Handicapped.

In speaking of his work with the Center for the Handicapped T.C. says, "That's one of my prides and joys; I came out of a large family . . . whatever little bit I can give back to society, that's where I get my joy."

At home, T.C. and his wife Geneva take care of their 7-year-old daughter Raven and 1 7-month-old son Kirby.

As if T.C. didn't keep busy with all of this, he also drives a school bus during the school year, and he is an active member of St. Peter's Rock Missionary Baptist Church.

T.C.'s friendship with Sammy Allen, Dumas Warehouse Supervisor, and Willie Lowe, Assistant Warehouse Supervisor, plays a big part in his feelings toward Dollar General. "I'll tell you what, I don't know how I'd work without Sammy . . . and Willie is just great too because we all work right there together all the time," T.C. says; "I've always respected Sammy and Willie and in turn I feel they respect me. I've always felt that you set the tone of how you want people to treat you by the way you do yourself."

If you're ever in Dumas, stop by and let T.C. Pickett tell you about the company and community he is proud to be a part of.

COMMENTS, continued

and I want you to help make this **your newsletter!**

From Virginia Ragsdale, manager of the Blackstone, Va. store, we have received the following poem.

"I accept the challenge to do my best,

And ask for guidance from above to meet the test.

I go to work each morning with an open mind

As the days go by, there's never "two-of-a-kind."

I learn something new, and store it away,

Possibly put to use on another day.

I may sometime falter, or even fall,

With confidence and perseverance,

I'll meet the call.

The objective I strive for is a job well done.

It's not always easy, and often no fun.

But a reward of satisfaction when I know I've won.

Quite often it's like a puzzle with none of the pieces in place.

You take an effortless approach and try to set things straight.

With your mind on the task, and your eye on the goals

It can be most surprising as the picture unfolds.

With your head, heart and hands, always your conscience you heed,

With God on your side— What more do you need?

I will in the future, and as of the past ten years,

Look forward to satisfaction that surpasses any fears."

"Today is the Tomorrow you looked forward to Yesterday."

Virginia has been a part of the Dollar General family since August 12, 1974. She and her husband George live in Blackstone, Va.

A portion of the note I received from Juel Winfrey, one of our retirees, follows.

"I have read with much interest the first issue of the Dollar General Story. I am quite impressed with it and am glad that it is to be a regular publication.

The performance of Dollar General in retail industry makes me proud to have been a small part in the tremendous growth picture the Company has had and the continued growth it is experiencing."

Juel retired on January 31, 1982 as area manager in the "Oklahoma end" of Dollar General. He and his wife Billye are enjoying retirement in McAlester, OK. Receiving his note proves that retirees still follow the Company with interest, and General Story's printing it proves that we still care deeply about our retirees.

Other delightful letters come from Dollar General

(continued on next page)

COMMENTS, continued

retirees Regina Boone and Carrie Freeman. Regina Boone, who retired as a store manager in May of this year after nearly 21 years with us in Springfield, Ky. writes:

"My son Henry Boone gave me a copy of Dollar General Story newsletter. I enjoyed reading it very much; I just had to write and tell you how much I enjoyed being a part of Dollar General for 21 years. It is a great company to work for. I have worked with some wonderful people. George Coley was my supervisor; he hired me in 1963. I have seen many changes. It was a good feeling to be able to help the poor people when we had children's shirts and tops at 2/$1.00 and pants for $1.00 but we have gone forward and got bigger and better, but still the same friendly people from the top on down, we now cater to people in all walks of life. It was hard for me to retire but I had to. My husband's health was bad. He had five major surgeries, and I could not give my all to my work, so my son Henry followed in my footsteps. He sort of grew up with Dollar General. He would help unload trucks and help me any way he could. I prayed for him that the Lord will guide him in his work, as he did me. I still go to the store when I can to see the people and see how things are going. Thanks again for a wonderful job."

Retired store manager Carrie Freeman, who was with us from 1967 until 1976 in Summerville, Ga., writes the following:

"Thank you for sending me a copy of your first newsletter, Dollar General Story. It was good of you to remember me after all these years.

I have pleasant memories of my eleven years with Dollar General. I have missed the excitement of a Dollar General grand opening, the sales and promotions of back-to-school, Easter and Christmas. I have also missed my association with loyal Dollar General customers and the good people for whom I worked.

May you have continued success in the years to come."

Helen Bewley is also retired from Dollar General; Helen worked in our Scottsville warehouse for 3 years after working in a Gibson's store for 8 years before. She writes:

"Received my Dollar General Newsletter. Thanks so very much for still considering me a part of Dollar General.

First, I want to say how proud I am to be part of the Dollar General family. It was really hard work, but I enjoyed it from the day I started to work at Gibson's 'till the day I left Dollar General. I appreciated how kind everyone was to me. . . I never cease to get a thrill each time I hear Jim Ed Brown with the Dollar General Jingle, or when I see a Dollar General truck . . . I never worked at a place where I felt like I did at Dollar General."

A special thanks to Helen as a warehouse spokeslady-

General Story wants to hear from the warehouse also.

Following these comments from retirees, we now hear from the other employment extreme—Toni Gruenefield, manager of the Scott City, Mo. store, has only been a part of Dollar General since November of last year. She was formerly employed as a clerk by the P.N. Hirsch store there and is already feeling a part of the Dollar General Family. She writes:

"I'm writing this to tell you how much I enjoyed the Dollar General Story. I'm proud to be employed by Dollar General and have been made to feel a part of a giant family. As a store manager and a stockholder I watch very carefully the growth of the company. We do our very best to make this a store that anyone can be proud of and one the customer wants to come back to."

I am sorry that space does not permit us to print all of your wonderful responses, but it's nice to know that the Dollar General family is one that likes to keep in touch with each other. Please keep your letters coming!

As you know, Christmas is just around the corner. Please have your children jot me a note telling me what they're asking Santa for Christmas this year. I would also like you to share with me a special Christmas story from your past. If you can send these to me by Nov. 1st, I will include as many responses as I can in our next issue.

Thanks!

—THE GENERAL STORY

more than 6 percent of total purchases. Labels were unimportant, because the company never advertised brand names, even when they were available in the store.

Closeouts provided about one-third of the soft goods sold by Dollar General. For example, DG had recently bought 15,000 dozen pairs of girls knee-high socks for 23 cents a pair and sold them for 75 cents a pair, because the producer had discontinued the pattern and color. Dollar General would not buy closeouts or fashion errors under contract, because it preferred to negotiate each deal separately with manufacturers and brokers.

DG drove a hard bargain. In the words of one salesman who had dealt with the company for a long time:

> My advice for those wanting to sell to Dollar General: If the price isn't lower than low, don't even go! I had 700,000 pairs of panties that had a retail price of $4.50 each and a wholesale cost of $25.08 per dozen. Mr. Turner Sr. offered me $5.50 per dozen, claiming he only charges 75 cents per pair in his stores no matter how good they are! Ultimately, I accepted his offer.
>
> I enjoy sitting in the waiting room and observing first-time salesmen come out of the office. Often their faces are pale. They've just realized that they have been picked clean of everything but the fillings in their teeth, and now they have to go back to New York and explain why they gave the merchandise away.

Dollar General's purchasers strongly believed in "limited price points." According to Cal Turner, Sr.,

> Let's say Sam has a couple of thousand-dozen blouses he wants to close out and sell me for $48 a dozen, and he sold these in his line for $60 a dozen. Well, then we have no choice but to say, "Sam, we are very sorry. You know we would like to help you, and we can take all of the blouses off your hands. But, you know, in our stores with our pricing, we can't get more than $5 for a blouse. So you will have to do a little work on the price."

But fairness was important. According to Cal Jr., "My father and grandfather always preached that you can't deny the seller his profit, that you have to treat him fairly."

If an item would sell, the company was willing to buy whatever was available. "If somebody will let us help set the price, we'll let them help set the quantity," said Cal Sr.

Even though closeouts and IRs made up most of the soft-goods inventory, the company did not hesitate to complete certain irregular lines by buying "the gaps" at full price or by purchasing "fill-ins." Thus a shipment of Rustler jeans IRs with three sizes missing would be rounded out by jeans bought at full price. Fill-ins were one of two things: staple merchandise such as socks or underwear that were often unavailable as closeouts or IRs, or seasonal garments such as winter jackets. While most items of this type were purchased through importers, the company had purchasing agreements with many domestic manufacturers as well.

The company also did not ignore fashion trends and had opened a buying office in New York City in late 1983. "There's no point in buying something unless the consumer wants it," said Cal Jr. "[And] clothing no longer is simply something to cover one's nakedness. Even people living on welfare buy according to fashion."

To buy "health and beauty aids," DG usually waited for manufacturers' price promotions and then bought as much as possible at the promotion price—whether they needed it or not. Also, for instance, if a shampoo maker changed the package or formula, truckloads of the old product could be expected to arrive at the DG warehouses.

Not every purchase was successful. The August 19, 1980, issue of the *Wall Street Journal* reported:

> Steve Turner thought he had pulled off a real coup last Christmas, buying 100,000 silk scarves for 85 cents apiece. "Not much happened," he says, "so I figured . . . people didn't realize what a good buy this was." So, he says, "in a brilliant move," he raised the price to $8.50 from $2.00. The result? "Still nothing," he says. "Now they're selling for $1.00, and I hope I'm getting down to about 50,000. Maybe we tried to sell a Rolls Royce out of a Chevy dealership."

Also, a recent purchase of imported five-quart dutch ovens with aluminum bottoms, which regularly retailed for $49, did not sell well. According to one store manager, "It's a great buy, but our customers don't expect us to carry a . . . pan for $15." The store's best seller was a "flimsy," lightweight aluminum pan costing much less.

The Warehouses

Once the goods were "bought right," they arrived by the truckload at the Dollar General warehouses. Most contract vendors shipped to DG once a month, but if the manufacturer did not deliver, the company would backhaul—meaning that one of the trucks on routine delivery to a store would pick up the manufacturer's merchandise on the way back to Scottsville or Dumas.

When the goods arrived at one of the warehouses, employees (mostly women) would sort the merchandise by size, color, and price point. For example, in Scottsville, clothes would be loaded on one end of more than 20 long conveyor tracks and be sorted or separated as they rolled by. Workers at the end of the conveyor would pack the goods into boxes. Frequently, Dollar General took blouses or shirts and pants bought at various prices, and with different retail price points, and grouped them into coordinates that could be sold together for slightly more than they could be sold separately.

After the merchandise had been sorted, it was carefully stored in one of the warehouses. Warehouse "pickers" (employees who gathered merchandise for store orders) daily fanned through the shelves with copies of each store's order, or "want list." They were assisted by automated baskets that traveled through the warehouse on an overhead conveyor. The baskets were filled and then sent to the loading dock, where the goods were stacked by store in a trailer. Each truck—or trailer—could service three stores on a single trip. The Scottsville warehouse could load about 65 of the company's 250 trailers per day, and each store was serviced every two weeks.

DOLLAR GENERAL'S FUTURE

As Cal Jr. reflected on the future of the company and his role, he thought that the company would have to continue its emphasis on "tight-fisted control" of overhead: "We'll have to continue our opportunistic buying but still satisfy our customer's needs," claimed Turner. And he thought they would have to communicate better, which meant "letting employees know what's expected of who by whom." He added,

> The workplace is the primary instiller of values in a person and can help meet a person's need for self-esteem. Most people spend more time at work than they do with their families, their church, or themselves. All gripes boil down to "I don't understand my mission; what's expected of me?"

Cal Jr. believed that hard work was important "not just because the extra productivity will make more money for the company." He felt that a lot of work and responsibility increased employee commitment: "We'd rather someone have too much to do than not enough." He recognized the inherent difficulties in motivating people and providing a challenging and rewarding work environment, while at the same time being a penny-pincher about expenses. "It's tough," he admitted. "The question is 'How do you be Scrooge and Santa Claus at the same time?'"

He believed that he had brought down considerable hardship on his employees by asking them to convert all 280 Hirsch stores to Dollar Generals in an eight-month period: "People will walk off a cliff for a company, but our people walked through the fire of hell."

Although he thought the stores were a good buy, the company's strategy was to build sales in existing stores, not by acquisition: "There's really too much growth in our existing markets to worry too much about acquisition.

Besides, we don't need the ego trip of being a national retailer." Exhibit 7 gives information on recent industry performance.

Cal Jr. discounted any serious competitive threats to Dollar General: "We're our own worst enemy. In the past, we've had poor training, poor delivery, and an absence of systems. We've executed poorly." He was optimistic that Dollar General "could recognize and correct it's mistakes," however, and still maintain its "unique ability to laugh at itself." Exhibit 8 presents information on DG's three major competitors.

For the future, Cal Jr. thought he personally should

> place a great deal of emphasis on doing those things that are unique to me— planning and people. I'm responsible for determining the direction of the company, articulating it to the constituents, and preserving the culture. As I have to delegate more, I find I hold on to the people-intensive activities—communicating, recruiting, etc. I also need to remember that my name is Turner and get into the warehouse and stores. No one wants to work for a bureaucracy.

Exhibit 7
Industry Data

OPERATING RESULTS OF SELF-SERVICE
DISCOUNT DEPARTMENT STORES (ALL FIRMS)

ITEM	26 Chains 1981–1982	28 Chains 1982–1983	Range for Middle 50%
Gross margin, expense and earnings (percent of sales)			
Gross margin	28.70	28.26	26.67–31.48
Leased department income	.45	.41	.00–.64
Gross income	29.14	28.87	27.06–32.04
Total expense	24.88	24.74	23.64–29.83
Net operating profit	4.26	3.93	1.32–5.03
Other income or deduct	−1.05	−.68	−1.50–.45
Earnings before income taxes	3.21	2.93	1.14–4.58
Federal and state income taxes	1.45	1.28	.31–1.87
Net earnings after taxes	1.76	1.66	.58–2.50

(continued on next page)

Source: Annual Mass Retailing Institute. All data have been revised.

(continued)

DISCOUNT STORE SALES BY CATEGORY

	Volume (bil. $)	Sales per Store (mil. $)	Annual Sales per sq. ft. ($)	Annual Turns	Initial Markup (%)	Gross Margin (%)
Women's apparel	13.3	1,644	164	5.2	46.5	36.0
Men's and boys'	7.4	915	120	3.2	45.1	35.3
Housewares	5.9	729	127	3.4	40.0	31.5
Health and beauty aids	5.2	642	282	4.2	25.4	18.8
Automotive	4.8	593	259	3.2	36.6	28.3
Hardware	4.5	556	173	2.3	41.3	32.9
Sporting goods	3.4	420	168	2.5	38.0	28.2

Source: Standard & Poor's Industry Surveys.

(continued)

DATA STORE PROFILE	1982[a]	1983
Footage	583,911,000	579,400,320
Net gain in footage	7,696,000	−4,510,675
Number of stores	8,282	8,217
Net gain in number of stores	118	−65
General merchandise sales ($)[b]	66,600	73,300
Average sales/foot/year of general merchandise ($)[b]	114.40	126.51
Average sales/store/year ($)[b]	8,041,150	8,920,531
Average store size (sq. ft.)	70,504	70,512

[a]Estimated.
[b]Does not include sales from discount supermarkets.
Source: *Discount Store News.*

Exhibit 8
Competitor Financial Data, 1981–1984

KMART

	1981	1982	1983	1984
Sales (millions)	$16,527	$16,772	$18,598	$21,096
Net income (millions)	220.3	261.8	492.3	499.1
Inventory turnover	5.3	5.1	5.2	4.6
Long-term debt (millions)	2,167.0	2,420.4	2,533.5	2,887.0
Net worth (millions)	2,455.6	2,601.3	2,940.1	3,233.8
Payout ratio	53%	47%	27%	30%
Shares outstanding (millions)	123.98	124.49	125.91	125.02

Kmart was the nation's second-largest retail chain with 2,174 stores in 48 states, the District of Columbia, Puerto Rico, and Canada, plus 15 Builders Square home improvement stores, 898 Walden bookstores, 52 Designer Depot off-price retail outlets, 178 Jupiter and Kresge stores, and 155 cafeterias. Some of the more recent projects had met with mixed results. For example, the off-price chain Designer Depot was losing money, the video pizza parlors were closed after 18 months, and the jury was still out on the company's attempt to open financial centers in 110 of its stores. In addition to acquisitions, Kmart was trying to increase sales from its existing stores by renovating store appearance, adding specialty departments, and upgrading label merchandise—especially apparel. By the end of 1984, 435 stores had received complete renovation to "the Kmart of the 1980s" and were showing 50-percent volume gains. The company planned to have all stores finished by 1986.

WAL-MART

	1981	1982	1983	1984
Sales (millions)	$2,455.0	$3,376.3	$4,666.9	$6,400.9
Net income (millions)	82.8	124.1	196.2	270.8
Inventory turnover	5.0	6.1	6.4	5.8
Long-term debt	258.8	329.1	380.8	491.1
Net worth	331.4	495.0	743.9	990.6
Payout ratio	10%	10%	10%	11%
Shares outstanding (millions)	129.68	134.42	139.92	140.22

(continued on next page)

Sources: *Value Line; Fortune,* May 27, 1985; *Business Week,* October 14, 1985; *Forbes,* January 28, 1985; *Dun's Business Month,* March 1985.

(continued)

Started in 1962, Wal-Mart had opened 800 stores in 20 southeastern and south-central states, most within a 450-mile radius of corporate offices in Bentonville, Arkansas, or one of five other regional warehouses. Most Wal-Mart stores were located in towns of 10,000 to 15,000 people and were comparable in size to Kmart, averaging about 40,000 square feet. Each store had 36 merchandise departments that marketed 60,000 items in both hard- and soft-goods categories, although hard goods made up about 65 percent of the merchandise. Most goods were name brand. The store boasted convenience with plenty of parking, speedy checkout lines, layaway, and credit. All stores were fully computerized with registers that fed information to the company's central computer. Same-store sales growth had averaged 12 to 15 percent in the past few years, and new stores were being opened at a rate of approximately 115 a year. Wal-Mart was expected to continue growing much faster than the projected 2.4-percent rate for department stores and chains. Recently the company had begun upscaling somewhat in order to compete more effectively with Kmart. In addition, it had recently started a wholesale chain, Sam's Wholesale Club.

FAMILY DOLLAR

	1981	1982	1983	1984
Sales (millions)	$181.7	$207.4	$264.4	$340.9
Net income (millions)	9.1	10.7	15.7	23.6
Inventory turnover	4.1	4.0	4.3	4.9
Long-term debt	0	0	0	0
Net worth	46.4	55.0	70.0	91.0
Payout ratio	21%	21%	17%	14%
Shares outstanding (millions)	28.2	28.24	23.53	28.64

This Charlotte, North Carolina, company, started in 1960, operated 889 stores in 20 states. Located primarily in shopping malls in small southeastern towns of fewer than 15,000 people, Family Dollar also had stores in metropolitan areas such as Atlanta, New Orleans, and Pittsburgh. The heaviest concentrations were in North and South Carolina, but Family Dollar had recently spread to Texas, Missouri, Indiana, and New Jersey and hoped to go nationwide with 1,000 stores in 1985. All growth was financed through internal earnings, and Family Dollar carried no long-term debt. It had only closed 22 stores

(continued on next page)

(continued)

over the past 15 years. Most of Family Dollar's growth came from new stores, as same-store sales growth hovered in the 7 to 9 percent range. The stores offered a wide variety of goods, and 95 percent of the prices were less than $17, with the average shopper spending $6 on each trip. The average store was a leased, 6,000- to 8,000-square-foot "cookie cutter" that could be stocked in 12 days. The stores were self-service, and all purchases were in cash. Name-brand merchandise accounted for about 30 percent of the total, with the balance in unlabeled or manufacturer-label products. Irregulars and seconds accounted for less than 4 percent of store merchandise. Sales were divided equally between soft and hard goods, including toys, toothpaste, bleach, and motor oil. Most stores were run by women, who earned $15,000 to $20,000 a year for a workweek that often reached 70 hours. The average store grossed about $500,000 to $550,000 a year, with a few grossing more than $1,000,000. Headquarters, with 12 buyers who worked with more than 1,000 suppliers, forced about 60 percent of the goods on each store, but even items left to the store manager's discretion were carefully limited by management. In addition, headquarters set all prices and markdowns and shipped from a single warehouse. Computerized shelf labels indicated the maximum and minimum that was to be stocked at any one time. Theft, or "shrinkage," was kept at 1.5 percent, comparable with the industry. Inventories were counted at 5 percent of the stores each week, and lie-detector tests were administered annually to every employee.

Cal Jr. also hoped to be able to devote more time to some of his personal interests, like preaching an occasional sermon at the Scottsville Methodist Church, taking a more active role in his church's music program ("A lot of little ol' ladies want me to sing at their funerals."), getting his golf and tennis games back in shape, and maybe even spending some time with his family on the ski slopes.

THE EAGLE PROPOSAL

Such was the situation when, in February 1984, the chief executive officer and the executive vice president of Interco arrived in Scottsville on short notice, ostensibly for a friendly visit and a tour of the facilities. At the conclusion of the visit, however, as the guests took a seat in Cal Turner, Jr.'s, office, the Interco CEO remarked, "We didn't just come for the fun of it. We're ready to sell the Eagle stores."

"When?" asked Cal Jr.

"By the end of the year," was the reply. The asking price was $50 million (including a substantial amount of goodwill). Although the chain was described as "marginally profitable," with estimated sales of $90 million to $100 million, Interco was unwilling to release operating statements on it.

Eagle Family Discount Stores consisted of more than 206 leased stores, of about 6,000 to 8,000 square feet each, in prime locations all over Florida, plus a warehouse near Miami. Some stores were in small towns, but most were in cities of considerable size, such as Miami, Jacksonville, and Tampa–St. Petersburg. Most were also in strip shopping centers, anchored by Winn-Dixie grocery stores and Eckerd drugstores, and had rental rates twice DG's average. Among their major products were sporting, automotive, electrical, and plumbing goods, and swimming pool chemicals and accessories; 40 percent of the stores' sales were cigarettes.

As Cal Jr. considered the pros and cons of the offer, he thought about how nervous his father had been about the recent growth. Cal Sr. felt that the new Hirsch stores needed "tender loving care" and that Dollar General needed to "settle down, sell some merchandise, and let growth take care of itself."

Besides, management was on record with the stockholders as opposing one acquisition on the heels of another and had stressed in the company's recent annual report that the company's primary strategy was to "[build] sales in existing stores." The secondary growth strategy was "to increase the number of stores in operation in an orderly and profitable manner."

Furthermore, the company was already understaffed, with ten vacant DM positions. The Eagle deal would create a need for at least another ten district managers.

The vice president of finance, Ed Burke, repeatedly pointed out to Cal Jr. that the current financial statements (Exhibits 2–4) would take a beating and that few of the Hirsch stores were yet profitable. Inventory turnover and return on assets would be especially affected. Furthermore, previously planned improvements in distribution facilities for 1984 (including a third warehouse) could cost $5 million, and advertising expenses were scheduled to increase by $3.4 million over the 1983 level of $6.8 million. He only half-jokingly pointed out that this acquisition, combined with the Hirsch acquisition, would require Dollar General to acquire more debt than the company had had in sales a few years earlier.

According to Cal Jr., "I was in turmoil. Our people had gone through hell with the Hirsh acquisition. Yet here was the opportunity I had wanted in 1983." He decided to call a meeting of the planning group (the vice presidents of retail operations, finance, and administration, the executive vice president of merchandise, and the general merchandise manager) to discuss the offer. He wanted a consensus on the decision. He also hoped the quote on the wall plaque just outside his office would remain true: "Things work out best for those who make the best of how things work out."

GRUPO BACARDI DE MEXICO, S.A.

The cold, blue eyes of Pepin Bosch stared down from the portrait on the wall of the boardroom. Bosch's gaze fell directly on Isaac Chertorivski, executive president of Bacardi y Cia, and his management team as they concluded their annual review of Grupo Bacardi's successes. It had been a good meeting, for 1991 had been yet another exceptional year. In this boardroom, whose walls were lined with a connoisseur's collection of Mexican art, Chertorivski felt the weight of four generations of management: Don Facundo Bacardi y Maso, who founded the company; Pepin Bosch, who had set the course for Bacardi Mexico 60 years earlier; Ernesto Robles Leon, the patrician dictator whose tenure had been marked by extremes of success and failure; and Juan Grau, the brilliant engineer whose strategy, management philosophy, and personal charisma had led to a rebirth of the operation.

Mexico had been one of the first foreign markets for Cuban-born Bacardi, and the site of many valuable lessons in managing the growth of the line of rum products invented by Don Facundo in 1862. The Mexican corporate headquarters, designed by the prominent Bauhaus architect Ludwig Mies van der Rohe in 1956, was one of Pepin Bosch's many monuments to his global strategy, a strategy that had increased the wealth of the family shareholders and had made BACARDI® rum the number-one-selling spirit in the world.

As he considered the experiences of his predecessors, Chertorivski was faced with the challenges of how to manage success and how to use the new management team structure to meet the opportunities and risks of the future. He warned the team, "We have fought our way to the top, yet we must be wary of complacency and arrogance. Do you know the saying '*Establo de vacas contentas*'?[1] I will never tolerate this."

THE BACARDI HERITAGE

Meeting risks and challenges had always been a part of Bacardi's heritage. How these risks were met became focal points of corporate legends. These legends, passed down through the company, focused on the actions and work of

---

This case was prepared by Ted Forbes under the supervision of Lynn A. Isabella, Associate Professor of Business Administration. Copyright © 1994 by the University of Virginia Darden School Foundation, Charlottesville, VA. All rights reserved.

[1]Spanish for "stable of content cows."

individuals who had become tiles in the mosaic that was Bacardi. They served as illustrations of the spirit and culture that defined Bacardi: a culture held tightly together by the common bonds of friendship and loyalty and a spirit best described by the shared values of Bacardi people: quality, teamwork, creativity, long-term vision, productivity, high energy, and, most of all, family.

From its inception, Bacardi was a family affair. In 1862, Don Facundo Bacardi y Maso developed the secret formula and process that took the rough molasses made from sugar cane and transformed it into a pure, mellow, and dry light rum (Exhibit 1). Word of the quality of Don Facundo's blend spread rapidly, and *ron BACARDI*® won gold medal after gold medal at world expositions; it was even credited with saving the life of the future king of Spain. While Don Facundo supervised the distilling, aging, and blending, his eldest son, Emilio, ran the office, and his two younger sons, Facundo and Jose, worked in the distillery and in sales and promotion.

From the humble beginnings of a small tin-roofed distillery, shared with a colony of fruit bats, BACARDI® rum became one of the world's most powerful brands—and *el murcielago* ("the bat") became its symbol. Currently, the descendants of Don Facundo still ran the company, maintained the culture, and answered each challenge with the same spirit as their ancestors. For almost a century after Don Facundo made his first bottle of rum, Cuba served as the base for a business that seemed to grow without limits. In 1958, because of the imminent danger of nationalization, Bacardi took the brand out of Cuba. Then, in 1960, the Bacardi spirit faced its ultimate challenge: Fidel Castro illegally confiscated the financial and physical assets of Bacardi and Company. There were other assets, however, he was not able to steal: the brand, the people, and their spirit. These assets were the foundation of all of Bacardi. These assets built Grupo Bacardi de Mexico.

THE ERA OF PEPIN BOSCH

The Beginnings of Bacardi Mexico

Pepin Bosch was born in 1898 in Santiago de Cuba, the site of the tin-roofed building that housed the first Bacardi operation. Educated in the United States, Bosch returned to Cuba to work in his family's sugar mills. Bosch quickly worked his way into management and amassed a sizable fortune; nevertheless, the price of sugar collapsed in 1920, and Bosch soon found himself in Havana, working as a bookkeeper with First National City Bank, an American concern managed by a contact he had made in the sugar business. During his summers in Santiago, Bosch had fallen in love with a childhood friend, Enriqueta Schueg Bacardi, granddaughter of Don Facundo Bacardi. In 1922, they were married. In 1931, he began to work for Bacardi.

Hoping to expand internationally, Bacardi opened its first plant outside Cuba in Mexico in 1931. The man sent to open the Mexican operation was Jose

---

Exhibit 1
How Rum Is Made

Rum is a spirit obtained from the distillation of fermented sugarcane products. Originally produced in the West Indies, rum is commonly made in all areas of the world where sugarcane grows. Sugarcane was introduced to the West Indies in the fifteenth century by Spain soon after Christopher Columbus opened up trade routes to the area. Rum was initially known as "kill devil," later referred to as "rumbullion," and eventually became the colloquial "rum." Early rums were known for their rough taste and were commonly cut with water. Most navies considered rum an essential ingredient in the well-being of their fleets. Differences in raw materials, fermentation processes, distillation, and aging methods now account for the wide variety of taste, color, and bouquet.

Rum is most commonly made from molasses, which is fermented through the introduction of yeast cultures. The fermentation takes from 2 to 12 days, depending on the process used; the fermented mixture is known as a "mash." Following fermentation, the mash is distilled; it is heated, and the evaporate is forced through a column, where the alcohol condenses out first. The resulting product is raw rum with a high alcohol content (at least 100 proof). The raw rum is stored in oak barrels, which add color and flavor and which mellow the distillate. After several years, the rum is charcoal filtered and blended to taste.

Various types and grades of rum are produced through combinations of filtering, aging, and blending. The clear, or white, rums are filtered both before and after aging. The darker rums are usually filtered before aging and often filtered after aging. All rums are combinations of different fermentation, distillation, and aging methods. Each of these phases directly influences the quality of the final product, which places a premium on the raw materials and yeasts, as well as the distiller's and blender's arts.

Rum is often consumed with fruit juices, colas, and other mixers, although the older, darker, premium blends are best enjoyed straight up or with tonic water and lime.

Bacardi Fernandez. His business instincts, however, were not the best. When he died in May 1933 of pneumonia, the Mexican operation was in a shambles. Fearing a drain on an otherwise healthy business, Enrique Schueg asked Pepin Bosch to go to Mexico City to close down the operation. When Bosch got to Mexico, however, he sensed not an operation in disarray but a real business opportunity.

Observing that most Mexicans mixed their liquor with Coca-Cola, Bosch launched a marketing campaign linking the two. A bottle of Bacardi and a case of Coke made an instant *fiesta*. To differentiate BACARDI® rum from other liquors, Bosch had the product packaged in the same wicker-covered jugs that were used in Cuba. He increased the advertising budget, broadened distribution channels, and expanded production. Within a year, sales revenues had doubled, and by the end of 1934, all of the corporate debts were retired. Most important, the Mexican operation paid its first dividend to the Bacardi family shareholders.

Mexico was a formative experience for Bosch because it confirmed and solidified the management style he had set for himself. With his cold, blue eyes, soft speech, photographic memory, and clear sense of direction, Bosch could be an intimidating boss. He was always willing to reprimand a subordinate but was uncomfortable offering direct praise for a job well done. Bosch preferred to pass along congratulations indirectly, often telling a coworker how he had been pleased with someone's work, knowing that the word would eventually reach the right person.

The Legacy of Bosch

The Mexican turnaround proved to be the springboard for Bosch's career at Bacardi, a career that not only marked similar successes in other international markets but that also ultimately took him to the very top of the company. Immediately after reviving the Mexican market, Bosch went to Puerto Rico in 1936 to establish a facility to supply the U.S. market. Bosch finally returned to Santiago in 1947, with an unmistakable aura of success surrounding him as he took over as president.

From the top of the organization, Bosch began to leave his imprint on the whole company. Believing he needed to have his eyes and ears in all aspects of the company, he had the headquarters in Santiago gutted and redesigned so that all employees worked at their desks in one large room, Bosch included. A visitor to the facility would see a waiting room with swinging glass doors at the far end; through the glass doors was the single large office, and in the back left corner was Bosch's desk. He could see every employee, and every employee could see him. One executive recounted, "If you wanted to speak with Bosch, you would stand at the front of the room and wave to him. If he had time to meet with you, he would motion you over to his desk."

Bosch directed the careers of all Bacardi employees with a high degree of success. His instinctive approach to personnel decisions, however, sometimes led to mistakes; he often decided on new hires and promotions purely on the basis of people being *simpatico* to him. For example, Bosch selected the vice president of administration for the new plant in Recife, Brazil, based on an acquaintance he made at dinner. Once, the company plane was flying Bosch to Brazil on business. It was a 40-hour flight from Cuba, and the pilot had inadvertently forgotten to notify the Brazilian authorities of his flight plan. When the plane landed in Brazil to refuel, unannounced and unauthorized, Bosch, his wife, the pilot, and the copilot were thrown in jail. A friend of Bosch's, the president of Pan American Airlines in Brazil, helped clear up the misunderstanding, and they were soon on their way again. When they arrived at their destination in Recife, they were met by the district manager for Pan Am, who had set them up in the best suite in town and invited them out to dinner. Over dinner, it became clear to Bosch that he and the district manager saw things alike, and Bosch, who was there to initiate the opening of a new Bacardi distillery in Recife, appointed the man vice president of administration for the new plant. Unfortunately, the choice ultimately proved to be a bad one.

Bosch was a man who found it hard to admit he was wrong. When the sales manager for Brazil proved to be dishonest, lining his savings account with fictional expenses and paying for exotic family trips out of the company's treasury, Bosch obstinately refused to fire him. Despite the fact that all of the other vice presidents confronted Bosch with evidence and pushed for the man's removal, he would not give in. One of Bosch's key executives ultimately resigned over Bosch's handling of this dishonest manager. Three months after the loss of that key executive, Bosch finally let the sales manager go.

Despite his dictatorial mien and obstinate ways, Bosch had a soft side. He was known to pass out pesos to the poor in Santiago; several times he paid for the entire university education of complete strangers. He created harmony among the Bacardi labor force by paying better wages and offering better benefits than any other local company. As one executive commented: "Bosch controlled through an almost mystic process of terror, love, appreciation, and loyalty. You put it all together, and they don't sound right. But it worked."[2]

Bosch left Mexico in 1934, but he continued to run the operation from Cuba until the mid-1950s, when he hired Ernesto Robles Leon. Although Bosch had turned the organization around almost 20 years earlier, the personality and initiative of Robles Leon resulted in phenomenal success. Unfortunately, they also culminated in phenomenal failure that would once again jeopardize the future of Bacardi Mexico.

THE ERA OF ERNESTO ROBLES LEON

Bacardi Mexico Grows

Ernesto Robles Leon was a lawyer, "a tall, eloquent, charming, aristocratic figure with slicked-back hair and a pencil mustache. Like Bosch, he possessed

---

[2]Peter Foster, *Family Spirits: The Bacardi Saga*, Toronto: MacFarlane, Walter & Ross, 1990, p. 66.

the all-important quality of *presencia*."[3] Robles Leon had two crucial talents for the Mexican market: a flair for marketing and an adroit political hand. He took the strategy that Bosch had begun and built BACARDI® rum into the dominant brand in the spirits industry in Mexico. By marketing a tropical image of fun and popularity and by using a very successful and famous radio campaign *(Si hay BACARDI®, hay ambiente)*[4], Robles Leon increased sales every year. He kept prices competitive, while positioning the product as a premium brand. He built and solidified relationships with the Mexican government, which was a crucial component in running a successful business in Mexico.

Robles Leon ran his business as a family affair. At one point, he had four sons on the payroll. His style was decidedly authoritarian; he saw Bacardi as a personal empire. So strong was Robles Leon's need to control that he even fired his own son, Eduardo, in order to maintain his grip on the company.

Bacardi Mexico's Downhill Slide

Ultimately, Robles Leon was affected by his own pride and success. Because his income was based on a percentage of gross sales, he seemed interested only in increasing the number of cases sold, without regard to profitability or income stream. In addition, he enjoyed the trappings of power, most particularly the corporate plane, which he reserved for his own personal use. Robles Leon grew complacent and arrogant, as did many of his managers. The bar in the executive dining room was open from 1:00 P.M. until 6:00 P.M., and most of the managers were there as soon as it opened. Robles Leon reportedly said, "If you are going to sell rum, you have to drink rum."

These attitudes, coupled with strategic shortsightedness, finally brought Bacardi Mexico to the brink of destruction. In 1974, the price of sugarcane molasses tripled, and Robles Leon responded by raising the price of rum. Then, in an effort to boost gross sales, he introduced a line of cheaper rum, PALMAS®, and *aguardiente,* an inexpensive liquor, under the BACARDI® name and trademark. In order to maintain an uninterrupted dividend stream, he reduced advertising expenditures. These actions cheapened the BACARDI® brand image and identity and eroded rum's share of the liquor market.

Moreover, Robles Leon failed to realize the gravity of the market challenges coming from the Mexican brandy producers. The grape growers and the brandy industry successfully lobbied the Mexican government for preferred tax status, which resulted in the brandy industry's obtaining a $60-million operating-income advantage over Bacardi and the rest of the rum

---

[3]Ibid., p. 116.
[4]Spanish for "If there is Bacardi, there is atmosphere."

industry. The grape growers and brandy producers put this advantage to work by advertising heavily. Although marketing studies showed that brandy products were gaining ground, Robles Leon ignored them, refusing to believe that BACARDI® rum could lose share. These highly mixable brandies began to eat away steadily at Bacardi's market share, and, by the mid-1970s, the brandy industry had captured 90 percent of the rum market. The Mexican market, which Bacardi had turned from tequila to rum, had turned into brandy country.

Matters were made worse by a falling out with the Mexican government in the early 1970s that resulted in severe penalties for Bacardi. The government assessed Bacardi for taxes on spirits that the Mexican Treasury declared as sold, but which had actually evaporated during the aging process. The resulting audit led to a charge of $160 million, which exceeded the value of the entire company.

After the death of Robles Leon's wife in the mid-1970s, he became even more interested (aided by the company plane) in traveling and social pursuits than in running the company. As one employee recalled, "When Robles's wife died, there was no one to control him."

While Robles Leon was losing his grip in Mexico, major management changes were unfolding for Bacardi worldwide.

A NEW MANAGEMENT PHILOSOPHY FOR BACARDI

Top Management at Bacardi Changes

In 1976, changes in top management began to signal a new era for Bacardi worldwide. With the resignation of Pepin Bosch, the new top managers of Bacardi, Eddy Neilsen and Manuel Jorge Cutillas, both descendants of Don Facundo, split the responsibilities of overseeing the Bacardi empire. Power, which was once wielded by a single individual, Bosch, was now shared by two executives: Neilsen ran Bacardi Imports (Miami, Florida), where he oversaw the U.S. market, while Cutillas served as chairman and chief executive officer (CEO) of Bacardi Mexico and also headed Bacardi & Co. (Nassau, Bahamas) and Bacardi International Ltd. (Bermuda) as shown in Exhibit 2. Together, they initiated a new style of management for Bacardi.

This new era would have a direct effect on the evolution of Bacardi Mexico. Mexico was Cutillas's first CEO position. He had previously been worldwide director of quality assurance, and a number of family members believed that Cutillas did not have the training for the job. However, as one executive stated, "The result was that he came to Mexico, he listened, he worked, and he began to believe in the country and its people."

In 1977, Eddie Neilsen and Manuel Jorge Cutillas chose Juan Grau to bring the new management philosophy to Mexico. According to Grau:

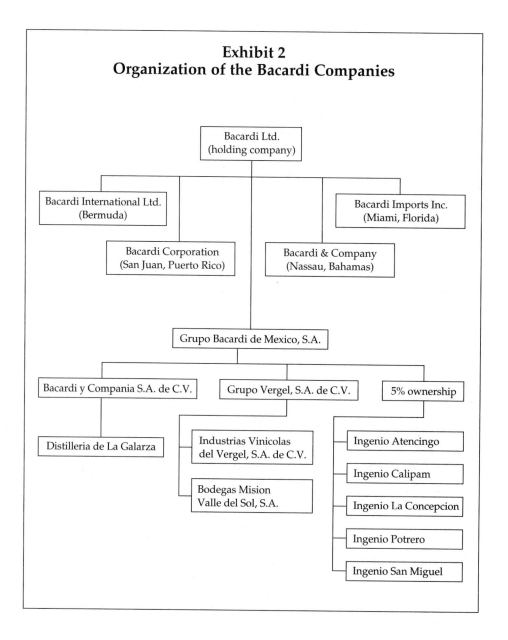

Exhibit 2
Organization of the Bacardi Companies

When I came, Mexico was in big trouble. There was doubt as to whether we could continue the operation. Part of my charge was to make that assessment. Although Robles Leon had done a tremendous job from 1952 to 1960, he had taken it easy after that. He didn't realize what was happening and had not built an organization under him. That was not his style.

THE ERA OF JUAN GRAU

Back to Mexico

Juan Grau has been described as charming, intelligent, conceptual, known for moments of explosive anger, confident in his authority and unafraid to use it—in short, a man with *presencia.* Grau grew up in Santiago de Cuba as childhood friend of Neilsen, Cutillas, and other Bacardi family members. Among his other friends was Fidel Castro. He received a degree in chemical engineering from the Massachusetts Institute of Technology in Cambridge, a prestigious engineering school in the United States. Unbeknownst to Grau, his father had secured him a job at the Bacardi-owned HATUEY® brewery in Havana. Upon graduation, however, he took a job with Procter & Gamble in Havana. He worked there for a year. When his father died in 1950, Grau accepted a position as technical director of the BACARDI® rum distillery in Santiago, a choice that would link his future to BACARDI® rum.

Grau's time at the distillery set the tone for his future experiences:

> We had a wonderful team at that plant. The distillery and the brewery were on the same premises, and Mr. Bosch was the president of both. He brought in a group of young engineers, including his son, George. There was tremendous team cooperation; it was really the best years of your life. It was a family. The guy in charge of the brewery, Joaquin Bacardi, Sr., was also an engineer. I talked with him every day in the brewery. My direct boss was Daniel Bacardi, and I had regular contact with him even though he was at the rum plant. In the afternoon, at 5 o'clock, Mr. Bosch would come to the lab to see what was happening. I was 22 years old and was in direct contact with the top guys in the company. They were your family and your friends. You felt that you belonged, that everyone wanted to help you.

Grau's analytical and engineering skills impressed Pepin Bosch, and in 1954, Bosch sent Grau to Mexico to help design and build a new distillery. The taste of Mexican rum had always been slightly different from the Cuban product. Soil variations in Mexico gave the molasses a different flavor, resulting in a slightly different-tasting rum. Bosch wanted Grau to design and build a new facility to rectify the taste variance as well as to increase capacity to meet sales forecasts. Grau recalled:

> I was sent to Mexico when I was 27 to design the distillery—I went by myself. I hired a couple of draftsmen, and I designed the thing myself. I wasn't too sure of the design, so I went back to Cuba and sat down with two of the engineers and asked for their advice. There was no hierarchy, no boss to clear this with . . . we were informal and very much a team.

Although the plant was completed in 1956, Grau stayed on in Mexico until 1959, operating the pilot plant where Bacardi honed its abilities to produce the same rum taste from different molasses grown in varying climatological conditions around the world. This expertise had become one of the core competencies of Bacardi worldwide. After Mexico, Bosch moved Grau to Puerto Rico to oversee the expansion of the plant in Catano. This plant had become the linchpin in Bosch's strategy for supplying the U.S. market.

In 1960, Bosch planned and executed a strategic move to Brazil and once again chose Grau to build the facility. The site chosen in Recife presented many problems and difficulties, but Grau solved the problems quickly and had the plant up and running in 11 months.

A difference of opinion between Grau and Bosch over the management of the BACARDI® rum plant in Recife was to interrupt Grau's steady rise within the Bacardi organization. In 1963, Grau left Bacardi at the age of 36. A dispute over the firing of a dishonest sales manager was for Grau "the straw that broke the camel's back." Grau resigned and returned to Mexico, intending to go into business on his own. He ran his own business for several years, noting that "This was when I discovered concepts such as cash flow!"

Grau's Management Philosophy Evolves

Grau's time in Mexico away from Bacardi was crucial to his development as a manager, for it taught him two important lessons. The first was cost consciousness:

> Very few people realize that the real reason for being in business is to create wealth. Most people say it is to make profit, but it is in fact to create wealth. And people often don't realize *where* you create wealth; it is in added value and in gross margin. This is when I learned about what I call the *critical resource.* I am a chemist, and the idea came to me from thinking about chemical reactions and their limiting reagents. There is always one resource in a company that is more scarce, and you have to optimize that. For example, when I was at Crane Valves, a U.S. company in Mexico, there were two large lathes making parts for valves and pumps. I realized that we could not make enough of both because we just didn't have the capacity. And then I saw that, per hour, when I was making pumps, I could get four times as much added value out of those two lathes as when I was making valves; I decided I had to choose—I decided that I would convert to being a pump manufacturer even though Crane was better known for making valves. The president of Crane in New York said to me, "But Juan, we are a valve company." I said, "Do you want to make money, or do you want to be a valve company? If you want to make money, we will be a pump company; if you want to be a valve company, buy a page in *Time* magazine; it is much cheaper." The president accepted that, and we took a company that had been losing money for five years and turned it around.

Grau's other seminal lesson came from his exposure to the concept of participative management. After turning Crane's operation around, Grau was looking for new challenges. During the early 1970s, with the Arab oil embargo in place, Mexico was in a boom period. One of Grau's competitors in the pump-and-valve business had bought an oil-field-equipment company and hired Juan Grau to run it.

> I [Grau] did not know anything about this business, and this company had tremendously good managers. They were excellent managers, except each one was concerned with his own function and they did not work together as a team. One was making parts, another was buying parts, another was in charge of quality . . . but each one was doing his own thing. It became a question of changing people or changing the attitudes of people.

One of the executives in the parent corporation of Grau's company introduced Grau to a fellow Cuban, Faustino Sotto, who was also an engineer. Sotto had become fascinated with the field of organizational development. Together, they began to plan the reorganization of the company, a reorganization that was to solidify Grau's participative style. Sotto recalled:

> One of the first things that happened with Mr. Grau took place in a management meeting . . . a meeting with two vice presidents. They decided to make big changes in the company. When they finished, Grau called me up and said, "Now we know what we are going to do." He explained everything to me, and I said, "That's fine, now how are you going to do it?" Juan replied, "Well, I'm going to summon all of the heads of the departments and tell them that this is how it is going to be." I said, "Juan, that is not going to work." He almost jumped out of his chair, saying "What do you mean it won't work? It is fine!" I replied, "Yes, it is fine, but people won't have any commitment, and if you want this to work, you have to involve the people. Let's go and give the people all of the data without making any conclusions and ask them what would be the ideal company." Grau initially rejected the idea, but he finally agreed with me. We had several meetings and then an executive retreat. Much to our surprise, the conclusion of the people was exactly what these three "geniuses" had already concluded. It was really dramatic because it all took place before vacation, and they restructured the company while all of the workers were gone. When they came back, it was a totally different company.

Back to Bacardi

After ten years on his own, Juan Grau could still not ignore the influence Bacardi had on him, and, in 1974, he accepted an offer from Manuel Jorge Cutillas to run the research-and-development laboratories in the new Jacksonville, Florida, facility:

> My heart was always with Bacardi. I choose my friends very carefully; I am very selective. For I have found that friendship is like money, easier made than kept. I believe that from a good enduring friendship comes a trust that

binds forever and brings peace and enjoyment. The main reason I came back
to Bacardi in 1974, to a much lesser position than I was holding, was to work
again with my friends. The link between friendship and success is the climate
for encouragement, for support, for enjoyment that trust creates. In this climate, the attributes of friendship, candor, and deep mutual concern become
the attributes of a successful company.

In 1976, Grau, responding to Manuel Jorge Cutillas's challenge to evaluate the ongoing viability of the Mexican operation, returned to Mexico. Until
Neilsen and Cutillas could convince Robles Leon to retire, Grau's title was
controller, but his responsibilities were more in line with those of chief operating officer. Grau faced daily battles in bringing the company to profitability.
As one employee recalled, "Every day was a fight between Robles Leon and
Juan Grau." Grau himself recalled those early days:

> Before I came to Mexico, my office was used to house the information system.
> When it was converted to an office, Robles Leon told the chief engineer to
> shut off the air conditioning because the room had not been air conditioned
> before the computers were put in. That office is unbearable without air con-
> ditioning, so he had me suffering in there.

When Robles Leon finally retired after six months, Grau assumed the
position of general manager. He had not fully realized, however, what a disastrous state of affairs awaited him. Relations with the Mexican government
were at an all-time low. The workers were restless and talking with the
unions. Some did not know what was happening, some did not care, and
some were taking advantage of the situation. The sales force was demoralized; salespeople were paid on strict commission, and the decrease in sales
volume did not leave them enough money to pay for traveling. As a result,
they were not in the field and, thus, were not selling. Market share had eroded
substantially, and the once premium image of BACARDI® rum was in a shambles. Bacardi Mexico was in a vicious downward spiral.

Bringing Mexico Back to Profitability

Grau's plan was simple in concept, yet complex in execution. The challenge was viewed as simultaneously external and internal: improve the image
of the brand and the morale of the people:

> I went to the records and found out what had happened to sales and gross
> profit, what was the gross profit, product by product, and what each one
> brought to the picture. Then we had a company meeting with everyone,

including the workers. They had been kept in the dark so long that the first thing I had to do was to bring them into reality. Everyone had been talking in the halls, but I decided to bring it all into the open. I told them we were in really tough shape. I told them we had the support of the Bacardi family. I told them that we had this facility, we had the brand, and, most of all, we had them . . . and we had to fight together. I learned a long time ago that the most important thing that I could do was to get that feeling in the people. When you get that fighting spirit, you make ordinary people do extraordinary things.

The overall strategy for Mexico unfolded in distinct stages, which were reflected in the organizational structure (see Exhibit 3). Grau referred to the first stage as "The Turnaround":

Robles Leon did not have an organization. He had everyone reporting directly to him. The gardener could not move a tree without talking to him. I had to build some structure, because there was none. The simplest thing was to go with a functional organization; I decided I needed a financial/administrative vice president, a marketing/sales vice president, and an industrial vice president. For the industrial position, which would be in charge of plant, equipment manufacturing, and unions, I chose Marco Antonio Delgadillo. He had been my partner in the construction business. For the financial position, I chose Ernesto Rodriguez Mellado, who had been chief accountant. For sales and marketing, I promoted Isaac Chertorivski, who had been in charge of advertising and coordinating the sales force.

Decisively and steadily, other changes were made. The compensation system for the sales force was changed so that the company reimbursed travel expenses and provided a base salary plus commission. The product line was pruned, eliminating *aguardiente* altogether and removing the BACARDI® name and trademark from PALMAS. Grau identified advertising as the critical resource and increased the budget; he also launched a new marketing strategy based on *"Carta de Oro . . . el Sabor Premiado."*[5] When this campaign failed, he moved quickly to change the marketing strategy; Grau and Chertorivski fired the ad agency. After an extensive search and selection process, a new ad agency was hired; it launched a market-research project that revealed that BACARDI® Añejo had an unexpectedly strong image. The product line was segmented to reach two distinct target markets. Carta Blanca was aimed at the younger population, with the *Agarra la Jarra*[6] campaign, while Añejo was aimed at the older, more affluent population, with the *Añejo . . . la prueba*[7] campaign. Television advertising was used extensively.

---

[5]"Gold Medal . . . the Premium Flavor."

[6]"Grab the Jug."

[7]"Aged . . . the proof (or test)."

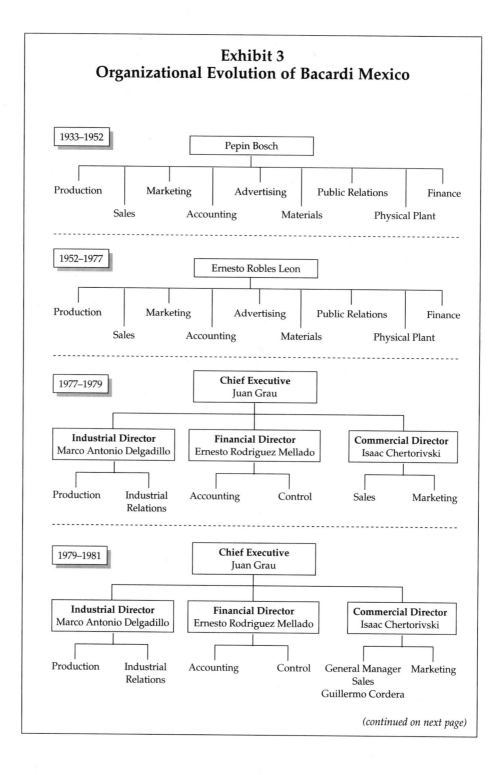

**Exhibit 3
Organizational Evolution of Bacardi Mexico**

1933–1952

Pepin Bosch

- Production
- Sales
- Marketing
- Accounting
- Advertising
- Materials
- Public Relations
- Physical Plant
- Finance

1952–1977

Ernesto Robles Leon

- Production
- Sales
- Marketing
- Accounting
- Advertising
- Materials
- Public Relations
- Physical Plant
- Finance

1977–1979

Chief Executive
Juan Grau

Industrial Director
Marco Antonio Delgadillo
- Production
- Industrial Relations

Financial Director
Ernesto Rodriguez Mellado
- Accounting
- Control

Commercial Director
Isaac Chertorivski
- Sales
- Marketing

1979–1981

Chief Executive
Juan Grau

Industrial Director
Marco Antonio Delgadillo
- Production
- Industrial Relations

Financial Director
Ernesto Rodriguez Mellado
- Accounting
- Control

Commercial Director
Isaac Chertorivski
- General Manager Sales
  Guillermo Cordera
- Marketing

(continued on next page)

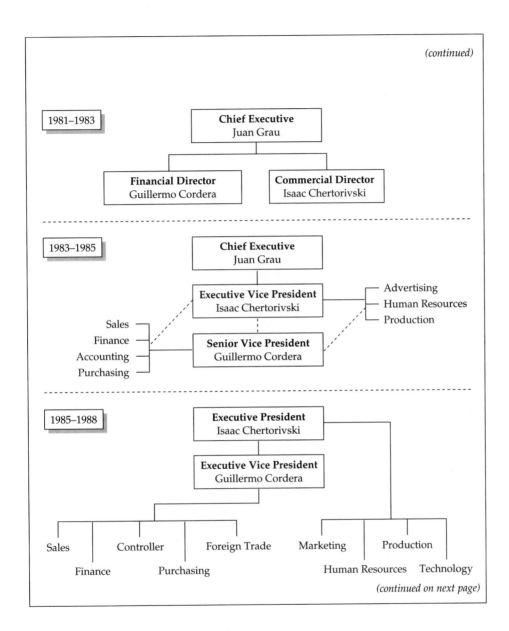

(continued)

1981–1983

Chief Executive
Juan Grau

Financial Director
Guillermo Cordera

Commercial Director
Isaac Chertorivski

1983–1985

Chief Executive
Juan Grau

Executive Vice President
Isaac Chertorivski

Advertising
Human Resources
Production

Sales
Finance
Accounting
Purchasing

Senior Vice President
Guillermo Cordera

1985–1988

Executive President
Isaac Chertorivski

Executive Vice President
Guillermo Cordera

Sales   Controller   Foreign Trade   Marketing   Production

Finance   Purchasing   Human Resources   Technology

(continued on next page)

Grau encouraged the sales force to create wealth rather than to increase sales volume; creating wealth was accomplished by increasing sales of those products that had the highest contribution margins. Because contribution per case varied across the product lines, Grau devised a new measurement system called margin-equivalent cases (MEC). MEC used the margins on *Carta Blanca* as a baseline and awarded sales commissions on the basis of margin

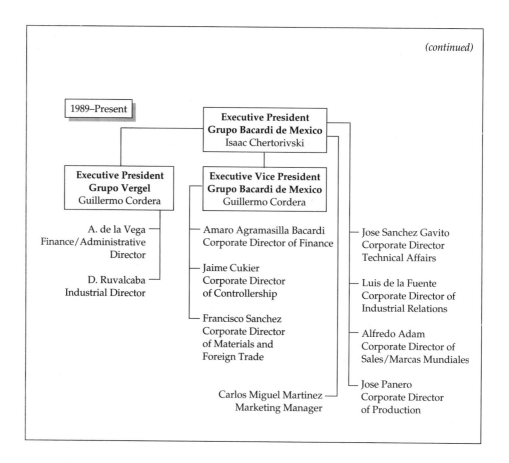

returned by the sale. In order to increase sales of the high-margin products, the sales force had to be persuaded to focus on margin rather than volume. For example, Añejo produced five times the margin of *aguardiente*. In 1977, one-third of Bacardi's 900,000 cases in sales were *aguardiente*. Grau demonstrated to the sales force that the same commissions would be returned by selling only 60,000 cases of Añejo. The concept was simple, but change was not immediate:

> It took years, and it took changing a lot of people. We had 60 salespeople. Sounds simple, but for people who were used to straight commission, it was a difficult transition. Isaac, who was very young at the time, and Guillermo Cordera, who came in later, both took that message very clearly to the people. They did it every time, at every sales convention.

Underpinning all of the changes Grau was implementing, there was a basic operating philosophy. To convey this message, Grau used the *el carrito* model:

The company and each of its employees had to run on four wheels: hard work, enthusiasm, professionalism, and honesty. I didn't mind if the first three of these lost some air—we could blow them back up; but if one wheel, honesty, went down, you were out. And we had quite a few people leaving the company. We lost 10 percent of our sales force to the honesty wheel. People learned very quickly that there was no room for dishonesty.

Grau's initial changes during the turnaround put the company back on course. Sales and profits began to grow, and the precious brand image was improved. Not all of his actions, however, worked out. Delgadillo, the industrial director, proved to be less than adept at managing the unions; he antagonized their leadership and tried to intimidate the workers, and as a result the unions won control of the work force. Grau's initial response was to reduce Delgadillo's areas of responsibility. When that action proved unsatisfactory, Delgadillo was let go. Chertorivski and Ernesto Rodriguez Mellado did not get along well, either. They were constantly fighting over the advertising budget, with Chertorivski wanting to spend and Mellado holding the purse strings tightly. Neither one was willing to concede the middle ground, and, finally, in 1980, Ernesto Rodriquez Mellado gave Grau an ultimatum: either Chertorivski left or he would. Grau fired Rodriguez Mellado and promoted Chertorivski to the position of executive director and chief operating officer (COO) with additional responsibility in human resources, production, acquisitions, and commercial activity.

Synergistic, Three-Headed CEO

With this new management team in place in 1981, Grau began the second phase of his Mexican adventure, what he referred to as the "synergistic, three-headed CEO" (Exhibit 3). Joining Grau at the top were Isaac Chertorivski and Guillermo Cordera:

> We had these two fairly old gentlemen as heads of the sales department. I let the older guy go and brought in a younger one, but he didn't make the grade. Guillermo Cordera had been in Venezuela with American Express; he was a manager there. I knew his family very well. He showed a lot of drive, to go work in Venezuela. He came back to Mexico and wanted to know if there was a job for him.
>
> Isaac and I decided to bring him into sales even though he had no experience in that area. He was 29 when he came to the group. We formed "the triumvirate"; that's what the staff called us. Eventually what we did was crisscross functions. Isaac was in charge of marketing, human resources, and technical/production. Cordera was in charge of sales and finance and responsible for accounting and purchasing. One was strong in advertising and marketing, and the other was strong in systems. Both were very bright. By crisscrossing functions and responsibilities, no one was all sales or all marketing or all production. We were so intertwined that we had to work together.

So well did they work together that their success was later immortalized in a three-branched *candelabro* that each kept in his office. The *candelabro* was given to them by the board of directors of Bacardi Mexico. Each branch was engraved with a name and an element: Fire—Isaac Chertorivski; Water—Guillermo Cordera; and Air—Juan Grau.

Fire—Isaac Chertorivski. Chertorivski was a second-generation Mexican; his grandparents emigrated from the Ukraine. He grew up "with limited resources, but with plenty of love, help, and strength." While still at the university, he opened an advertising agency with friends.

> It was a tremendously great experience. . . . I think it was one of my greatest experiences in the whole world because I learned how to build and grow a business. I learned how to deal with clients, how to run a business, how to build a team, and how a business goes broke!

Chertorivski was also involved in the student movements of the 1960s and later coordinated antigovernment activity at the university. After his own ad agency went broke, Chertorivski became media director for the Leo Burnett advertising agency in Mexico City. At 24, he made his first contact with the Bacardi Company.

> I was working at Leo Burnett, the advertising agency. BACARDI® rum was my account; and I made a relationship with Eduardo Robles Leon, the boss's son. Eduardo invited me to join Bacardi Mexico as their media manager—he said that they needed new blood. I was not at all sure about taking the job; Robles Leon was crazy . . . a dictator, a difficult person with no team. However, they offered me lots of money. I was thinking career management—it would be good to go to the client's side for a while—so I took the job.

Six months into his Bacardi Mexico position, Chertorivski decided to return to Leo Burnett. Three days before Chertorivski's departure, Robles Leon communicated how he felt about Chertorivski's upcoming departure. Chertorivski recalled: "He told me that if I left Bacardi, he would pull the BACARDI® rum account from Leo Burnett. I called the general manager of Burnett, and I told him that if I go with you, you will lose this account. And so I stayed with Bacardi."

It soon became clear to Chertorivski that Robles Leon was running the company into the ground.

> In the mid-seventies, I had developed a relationship with Manuel Jorge Cutillas, who was in charge of worldwide quality. He came to Mexico and once asked me how things were going; I told him the truth. I told him that things were very bad, we were going broke, and that Robles Leon was crazy. I told him I was looking for a new job. He asked me to wait—he said that things would change quickly. I kept looking for another job, but then Manuel Jorge became chairman of the board and brought Juan Grau to Mexico.

Chertorivski continued, his face breaking into a broad smile:

And then I began to train Juan Grau! He trained me to be a manager, and I trained him in marketing! I became Juan's right hand. He was the quarterback, and I was the fullback. He says why don't we do this . . . and I get it done. He is very analytic and has a great strategic mentality; he is the great conceptualizer, the great operator—but I am the great doer. He knows how to put it on paper, and I know how to make it happen.

Four to five months into Grau's tenure in 1977, Chertorivski again almost left Bacardi. As Grau was reorganizing the company, he wanted to put Chertorivski in charge of marketing and hire a sales manager from outside the company.

I [Chertorivski] said, "If you hire someone from outside, I'm going to leave." I was *hungry,* and even though I lacked the experience, I *wanted* this responsibility. Juan sent me away, but a week later he called me back. "I am going to make you commercial director," Grau told me, "with responsibility for both sales and marketing. But if we don't do well, the first head that will fall will be yours, Isaac." And so we shook hands and went to work. We worked together, we traveled together, and we built a good team.

Water—Guillermo Cordera. Cordera came on board in February 1979 as manager of the sales force. Trained as a certified public accountant, Cordera had risen rapidly through the ranks of IBM and American Express to a general manager's position in Venezuela. Guillermo did not like Venezuela, however, and wanted to return to Mexico. Cordera recalled expressing concern to Grau, when offered the position at Bacardi, about his lack of experience in managing a sales force:

Grau's reply was, "Management doesn't make the sales; the salesmen make the sales. What we need is a *system* to manage the salesmen; just think of sales as a system, Guillermo." I took the job because I wanted to return to Mexico, because of the prestige of Bacardi, and because of the great challenge it presented to me. They were in bad financial shape, and I could bring financial knowledge. And I had the utmost respect for Juan Grau . . . he was a very strong man, and this was a chance to work for him.

The changes Cordera made quickly were instrumental to Grau's turnaround plan. He reorganized the structure of the sales force and eliminated redundancies in the territories and tasks. He also demanded that the sales force begin to polish Bacardi's tarnished image:

On a trip to Guadalajara, Grau, Chertorivski, and I visited a store where the BACARDI® rum display was a shambles. Juan asked, "How can we sell with such a bad image?" We launched Operation *Escoba* (broom), which removed old, damaged products from the store shelves and spruced up the shelf displays.

The salesmen were provided with new labels, and every single bottle of BACARDI® rum in Mexico was dusted, polished, and relabeled. Cordera instilled cost consciousness in all the sales force, introducing forms to fill out for product giveaways. Soon the sales force became aware of the cost of their generosity.

> We were operating under the motto, "We have not a single peso to waste, but we have millions to invest." This was not an easy job. The average salesman had 18 years with Bacardi and was 50 years old. I was 28. I worked with a 50-year-old sales manager; people were set in their ways; they thought their way was the only way. It was hard to be accepted by them.

At the 1979 sales convention in Acapulco, MEC was used for the first time in the corporate sales contests. The top three sales teams, measured by MEC, won a trip to Rio de Janeiro. Sales goals were posted on the walls of the factory in "alliterative" steps: 2,222,222 liters sold; 3,333,333 liters sold; 4,444,444 liters sold. The plan began to work, and the target grew ever higher.

Bacardi Mexico established a reputation with its wholesalers as a professional company, tough but fair. Cordera shortened credit terms and offered an extra 1-percent discount to wholesalers who attached a check to their order. Although Bacardi demanded much from its distributors, it gave good discounts to those who followed the plan. Cordera remembered having to revoke the account of one of Bacardi's biggest wholesalers in Guadalajara because of late payments: "We had to send a message to the trade that this was the way it was going to be with Bacardi. If you play it our way, we will take very good care of you, but if you don't. . . . "

Organizational Schizophrenia Creates a Management Team

Grau, Chertorivski, and Cordera each had offices in a corner of the large, rectilinear building that was the headquarters of Bacardi Mexico. While the "holy trinity" made tremendous strides in furthering the profitability of Bacardi Mexico, Grau was aware of the difficulties the arrangement caused other managers:

> Isaac and Guillermo were more or less at the same level. We found two things; there was a big gap between the triumvirate and the managers, and the company was beginning to split into the Isaac group and the Cordera group. So we decided that we had to change that organization. We were very flexible and found it easy to change it in response to how people were behaving and to the maturity of the people. Instead of forcing a structure, we adapted the structure to the people.
>
> We decided that we could not have two people here at the same level. Manuel Jorge Cutillas and I decided to make Isaac executive vice president—this was in 1983–84—second to me, and Cordera, senior VP; then we had a group of functional directors, but they were really vice presidents.

At this point (1983), Mexico had arrived at the third phase, the "management team" (Exhibit 3).

With the turmoil of the late 1970s behind them, Grau and his team began to show significant growth in the Mexican liquor market. The BACARDI® brand had been rehabilitated to the point where a superpremium rum, Solera, was launched successfully. Gains were made in the political arena as well. Bacardi Mexico succeeded in convincing the Mexican government to rescind the favorable excise-tax status it had granted to brandy producers. Bacardi found a level playing field on which to compete with Domecq, Mexico's leading brandy producer.

When Grau took over in 1977, sales were 750,000 cases per year; in 1983, sales hit 2 million cases. With the spotlight of the Mexican business community shining on Grau, he saw a chance to send a message about the role young managers played and the values he had learned earlier in his career.

> We were approached by a prestigious organization called the Association for Sales and Marketing Executives. Every year they chose an "executive of the year." In late 1983, they came to see me and decided that I would be named "Distinguished Executive of the Year for 1984." I was delighted, but I didn't think they could honor me alone. The young men who had worked with me were just as responsible. So I told them that I would not accept unless they honored all three of us. This was important, to show what the team could do. To have three people named as executives of the year was a first in Mexico, and it has not happened again. It was important to send a signal in Mexico that you could work as a team and have very young people. In my speech I said that we were a synergistic executive body, to which each brings our special talents, and, together, we become a very strong executive. Isaac and Guillermo bring youth and enthusiasm, and I bring my international experience.

By 1985, sales in Mexico had reached 3.3 million cases. At that time, Grau was asked to head the U.S. operation, Bacardi Imports. After consulting with Manual Jorge Cutillas and the board of directors, Grau asked Isaac Chertorivski, one of those young executives who had been instrumental in accomplishing the turnaround, to come to his office. "Isaac, I think it's the moment . . . we have decided to appoint you president."

THE ERA OF ISAAC CHERTORIVSKI

Isaac Chertorivski was a large man, six feet tall and very fit. Although his wide face broke rapidly into a smile, there was an underlying intensity to his gaze—and to his opinions. Chertorivski's desk sat at one end of a large suite. To his left was a floor-to-ceiling window that ran the length of the room. At 1:00 P.M. every day in the summer, he looked out to see 500 children in Bacardi hats and T-shirts—sons and daughters of Bacardi workers—waiting for their mothers to take them home from the company-sponsored day camp. On the walls were photographs of Chertorivski with former President Miguel de la Madrid; with current President Carlos Salinas de Gortari; with his wife, son, and daughter; and with Juan Grau. Behind him was a bookcase with more photographs, assorted books and binders, and more than a dozen bottles of BACARDI® rums. At his left side was a table with five telephones and a pair of interesting sculptures. His desk chair was missing the casters on two legs, and he rocked back and forth as he talked. He picked up one of the sculptures.

> As a child, I always knew I wanted to be a leader of something. I studied business administration at the University of Mexico because I wanted to be a leader. I get a lot of satisfaction working in a big position in a big company, and I want to make Bacardi the best company in Mexico. This sculpture . . . every year a survey is made of the top 20 companies in Mexico, and Bacardi has been first in each category for the last eight years in a row—with a 10- to 20-percent lead. This one [sculpture] is for the best human resources company in the country. This other one is for the best marketing company; we also have the award for the best work environment. I am proud of these awards because of the competition from very highly structured companies like Unilever, Procter & Gamble, and Coca-Cola. We are not so structured. We are very free here, totally professional, and unencumbered by rigid structures.

At 44, Isaac Chertorivski was one of the most successful and influential executives in Mexico. In his wallet, Chertorivski carried two business cards, one engraved "Executive Presidente, Grupo Bacardi," the other engraved, "Asesor Del Presidente de la Republica."[8]

Grupo Bacardi de Mexico's expanding sales base helped push worldwide BACARDI® rum sales to new heights in the late 1980s. In 1987, BACARDI® rum sold 20 million cases worldwide, with 25 percent of those sales in Mexico; in 1988, 21 million cases worldwide, with 27 percent in Mexico; and in 1989, 22 million cases worldwide, with 28 percent in Mexico; in 1989, Grupo Bacardi sold 6.1 million cases in Mexico and became the third-largest producer of beverage alcohol in the world. Between 1981 and 1991, sales increased 539 percent. In 1991, sales exceeded 7.7 million cases, and Bacardi held a 90-percent share of the Mexican rum market and 34 percent of the total Mexican spirits market. (See Exhibit 4 for products and Exhibits 5, 6, and 7 for sales and market-share information.)

Chertorivski's Current Management Team

The combination of business success and management camaraderie heavily influenced the organization that Chertorivski built for Grupo Bacardi. The

---

[8]"Advisor to the President of the Republic."

Exhibit 4
Products Manufactured by Grupo Bacardi

RUMS

Bacardi Solera 1873
  A super-premium product positioned at the top of the Bacardi line.

Bacardi Añejo
  A premium product that helped Bacardi Mexico recover its position in the spirits market.

Bacardi Carta de Oro
  An amber rum that is similar to the white rum.

Bacardi Carta Blanca
  This white Bacardi rum sets the standard for the company's products.

Ron Palmas Oscuro
  Less expensive than the Bacardi brand rums, Ron Palmas targets the middle of the rum market.

BACARDI COCKTAILS

Planter's Punch
  A fruit-based Bacardi rum cocktail.

Piña Colada
  A popular cocktail made with Bacardi rum, pineapple juice, and coconut milk.

Mango Colada
  Similar to the Piña Colada, except mango is substituted for pineapple.

Daiquiri
  One of the oldest rum drinks, using lime juice as a base.

Fraesi Colada
  Similar to the Piña Colada, except strawberry is substituted for pineapple.

(continued on next page)

(continued)

BRANDIES

Viejo Vergel
Vergel's premium brandy.

Gran Vergel
Vergel's basic brandy.

WINES

Chateau Avignon
A classic red wine.

Tannhauser
A white table wine.

Cordianne—Vino Tinto
A red-wine cooler.

Cordianne—Vino Blanco
A white-wine cooler.

corporate ethic was built around results, quality, and teamwork. When he gained the presidency in 1985, Chertorivski began to build.

> My first challenge was to build a strong executive team. Everything is a continuing process, and I often talked with Juan during this phase. I began by looking at the team that was in place at that moment, then I considered what kind of team we were going to need.
>
> I had a different idea from other companies. For example, most companies want their financial area under one director; I put two—one in finance and one controller. Why? In finance was Amaro Argamasilla Bacardi, with 20 years in the company. I wanted to reinforce this area so I brought in a man from IBM, Jaime Cukier. He was their corporate controller for all of Mexico, and he had 22 years' experience. This combination gives me a solid "A" team in finance.
>
> In the operations area, we had three people. First was Jose Panero, who had built six Bacardi plants yet never worked for Bacardi; he's a lone wolf, never before worked on a team. I made him VP for production. As VP for technical affairs, I put in Jose Sanchez Gavito; he is in charge of the distillery and

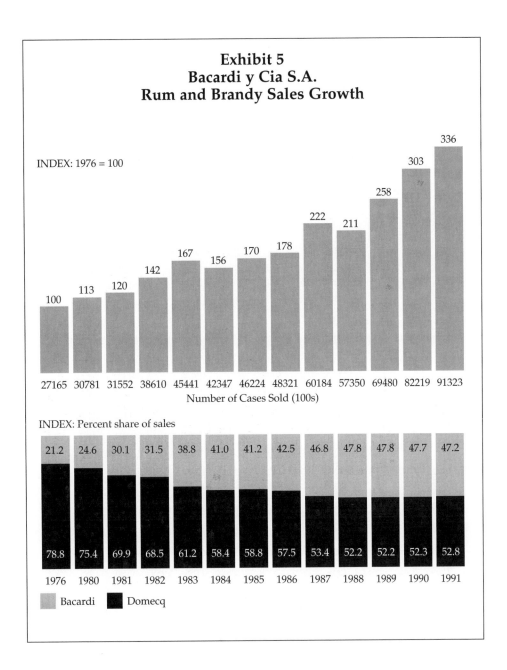

Exhibit 5
Bacardi y Cia S.A.
Rum and Brandy Sales Growth

INDEX: 1976 = 100

100	113	120	142	167	156	170	178	222	211	258	303	336
27165	30781	31552	38610	45441	42347	46224	48321	60184	57350	69480	82219	91323

Number of Cases Sold (100s)

INDEX: Percent share of sales

21.2	24.6	30.1	31.5	38.8	41.0	41.2	42.5	46.8	47.8	47.8	47.7	47.2
78.8	75.4	69.9	68.5	61.2	58.4	58.8	57.5	53.4	52.2	52.2	52.3	52.8
1976	1980	1981	1982	1983	1984	1985	1986	1987	1988	1989	1990	1991

☐ Bacardi ■ Domecq

quality control. And in materials we have a man who has been with us 25 years, who has earned our confidence, Francisco Sanchez. The way this all works is that when one guy is not in Mexico, the other can cover for him. They each get along very well, and they can visit our various plants interchangeably.

Exhibit 6
Bacardi y Cia S.A.
Evolution of Liquor Sales by Category

Total Liquor Sales

INDEX: 1981 = 100

Year	Index	Number of Cases Sold (100s)
	100	92120
	109	100303
	117	107747
	107	98558
	105	96912
	108	98802
	130	119414
	118	108939
	129	118419
	147	135360
	155	142479

Number of Cases Sold (100s)

INDEX: Percent share of sales

Category	1981	1982	1983	1984	1985	1986	1987	1988	1989	1990	1991
	15.4	16.4	19.2	21.3	24.1	25.0	28.7	30.5	32.3	32.8	33.3
	52.6	52.5	49.1	48.0	48.5	46.7	44.0	39.9	41.4	41.1	41.9
	27.8	27.5	28.9	27.8	24.7	25.7	24.8	22.4	19.5	19.2	18.6
	2.2	1.9	1.0	1.0	0.7	0.8	0.6	2.0	2.9	3.3	2.8
	2.2	1.7	1.8	2.0	1.9	1.8	1.9	4.4	3.9	3.7	3.3
	9.4	12.5	16.4	17.0	19.7	20.6	23.6	25.2	28.0	28.9	30.3
	24.0	28.9	26.0	26.1	28.0	27.0	26.9	27.5	30.6	31.8	33.6

▮ Ron   ▮ Brandy   ▮ Tequila   ▮ Whisky[1]   ▮ Vodka[2]   ▮ Bacardi   ▮ Domecq

[1]A partir de 1984 solo whisky nacional, a partir de 1988 whisky nacional y importado.
[2]A partir de 1983 solo Valle de Mexico, a partir de 1988 total Mexico.

Then we have human resources. When Juan Grau named me executive vice president of the company, he put me in charge of HR. I said, "Well, Juan, I need someone I can trust." So I brought in a friend of mine, an old college

Exhibit 7
Bacardi y Compañia, S.A. de C.V.
Ventas por Años Calendario

000' CAJAS DE 9 LTS

	1981	1982	1983	1984	1985	1986	1987	1988	1989	1990	1991	% 91/90
Solera	30	55	77	100	136	158	210	257	430	660	937	42
Añejo	495	677	754	936	979	1074	1185	1562	2037	2656	3179	20
Carta Oro	277	399	526	315	243	234	246	267	210	297	258	(13)
Carta Blanca	629	1045	1895	2223	2031	2389	3246	3519	3395	3993	3332	(17)
	1431	2176	3252	3574	3389	3855	4887	5605	6072	7606	7706	1
Index	100	152	227	250	237	269	342	392	424	532	539	
Palmas	77	86	55	47	45	31	44	43	43	64	109	71
Cocteles	—	—	18	63	62	33	35	89	104	130	109	(16)
Martini & Rossi							17	14	15	18	9	(51)

pal, who had been my political rival. He had many years of HR experience with Kimberly-Clark, Bimbo [a very large Mexican baked-goods company], and Unilever. This is Luis de la Fuente, and he has been with us 12 years now.

Next is sales; today Cordera looks at sales. In marketing, we don't have a VP, but we have three managers. Marketing is my area. It is the key in this type of company. I work with the managers and I see *everything* that goes on in marketing.

This is the group (see Exhibit 8). We are nine people—first-class people, very willing—a great team. We have a special kind of organization that can handle any situation. No one is stuck in one particular area, and this is how we like to work. This team, our average time working with Bacardi is 14 years, and our average work experience is 25 years. All are professionals, and we are all friends. All have worked in other companies, and we all bring a wide variety of experiences.

When asked what he looked for in a team member, Chertorivski replied:

First of all, we like to have friends: honest, loyal builders who work to help the team. These people who are on the team, they have been VPs since August 1985. We try to get people who will be happy with this group, this company, and themselves. We are not like Procter & Gamble. I tell people if they want to change titles, go to P&G, but if they want to enjoy their work and grow personally, Bacardi is the place to be.

And we are a tight team. For example, we once had a general sales manager. One November day he came in and said, "Isaac, I'm going to leave the company in January." Cordera and I talked it over, and we went back to him and said, "You won't be leaving in two months; you'll be leaving in two minutes."

Cordera and Chertorivski

Cordera believed that he and Chertorivski had developed a strong working relationship:

Isaac treats me as his equal. I always consult with him, and he always consults with me. I listen to him; he listens to me. That is part of the success; we are able to talk, to see what is good and what is bad. His expertise is marketing, and I listen to him; my expertise is finance, and he listens to me. I think that is the key.

And we work out our differences well. For example, Isaac was concerned about the sales force, and that is my responsibility. He felt that they were having problems as a result of how we paid them. We pay a lot—five or six months' salary—at a time. Isaac wanted to increase their purchasing power so they would spend more time selling. So he called me in and says, "Let's give them a raise in pesos and an advance against their profit sharing."

I said, "Let me take a look at it." So I got together with the sales managers and came to the conclusion that this was not the real problem. The problem was that 30 percent or more of their salary was commission, and, for some

Exhibit 8
The Bacardi Management Team

JAIME CUKIER
VICE PRESIDENT, CONTROLLERSHIP, GRUPO BACARDI

Birthdate: 15 March 1936
Citizenship: Mexican
Education: B.S., Chemical Engineering, 1960
M.B.A., 1982
Experience: Joined Bacardi in 1986 as director of controllership, Bacardi y Cia. Twenty-two years with IBM de Mexico in sales, planning, and marketing and as general controller. In present position since 1988 (September).

JOSE SANCHEZ GAVITO
VICE PRESIDENT, TECHNICAL AND RUM BLENDING, GRUPO BACARDI

Birthdate: 28 March 1948
Citizenship: Mexican
Education: B.S., Chemical Engineering, 1972
Advanced Management Skills, 1982, 1987
Experience: Joined Bacardi in 1978 as a supervisor of Tequilena, after he was manager, planning and control. In present position since 1989.

LUIS DE LA FUENTE
VICE PRESIDENT, INDUSTRIAL RELATIONS

Birthdate: 8 October 1948
Citizenship: Mexican
Education: B.A., Business Administration, 1971
Advanced Management Skills, 1984
Experience: Joined Bacardi in 1981 as industrial relations manager. In present position since 1988. Ten years' experience in human resources with Kimberly Clark, Grupo Industrial Bimbo, and Unilever.

(continued on next page)

(continued)

JOSE PANERO
VICE PRESIDENT, PRODUCTION

Birthdate: 17 August 1932
Citizenship: Argentine
Education: B.D., Engineering, 1959
             Advanced Management Skills, 1986, 1987
Experience: Originally joined Bacardi in 1964. Rejoined Bacardi in 1972.
             Supervised construction of various Bacardi facilities,
             including Recife, Brazil (with fellow Cuban, Juan Grau);
             Mexico; Martinique; Spain; Venezuela; and Puerto Rico. In
             present position since 1988 (September).

AMARO ARGAMASILLA BACARDI
VICE PRESIDENT, FINANCE

Birthdate: 20 May 1952
Citizenship: Mexican
Education: C.P.A., 1976
             Advanced Management Skills, 1987
Experience: Joined Bacardi as clerk in 1971. Progressed through finance
             department. In present position since 1988 (September). He
             is a member of the board of Bacardi, Ltd.

FRANCISCO SANCHEZ
VICE PRESIDENT, MATERIAL AND FOREIGN TRADE

Birthdate: 9 March 1939
Citizenship: Mexican
Education: C.P.A., 1964
             M.B.A., 1978
Experience: Joined Bacardi in 1971 as accountant and progressed
             through comptroller's office. In previous position since
             1989. Previously with IBM and Pfizer Mexico in financial
             positions.

(continued on next page)

(continued)

ALFREDO ADAM
VICE PRESIDENT, SALES, VERGEL

Birthdate: 25 January 1943
Citizenship: Mexican
Education: B.A., Accounting, 1968
              C.P.A., 1970
Experience: Joined Bacardi in 1990 at current level. Previously worked
              as public accountant; worked in the Mexican government,
              and was dean of accounting and business school of the
              National University of Mexico for eight years.

people, all of their annual sales come at the end of the year. They make very little money during the year, but at the end of the year there is a lot of money.

I suggested to Isaac that we change the whole concept. Let's forget about commissions and keep them on a good steady salary for 12 months; then we can give them a performance bonus every three months. Isaac was totally against it. He said, "A salesman without a commission is not a salesman! I don't want this system."

So we started looking for ways to resolve the issue. We talked a lot. We argued a lot. But we are working together for the company, and we are looking out for the goals of the company. In the end, we created the best possible solution to the problem.

For the seven vice presidents, the team was a major part of their lives. Regular meetings were held every other Monday. Meetings began with lunch in the executive dining room and ran until about 6:00 P.M. A typical agenda would have 10 to 18 items; the agenda for a recent meeting included the following items:

- A review of the semester's (six months) business results
- Sales goals for the next semester
- An analysis of the new company mission statement
- A review of the total-quality plan for the Vergel plant

When asked what it was like to be part of the team, several of the vice presidents compared it to a marriage. One noted: "Sometimes it is good, and sometimes it is not. There is always the potential for conflict, yet we are able to work through that because we share a common bond. Overall, we feel we are very successful, but we often hear that we are in a crisis."

Managing the team was not always easy for Isaac Chertorivski:

> It depends on the day. Some days I hear very clearly and discuss things, but there are other days when I don't. I try to be very participative; I try very hard. My style of leadership is to work in a team, but it is not always easy. Sometimes I am very explosive.

Every January, a three-day meeting of the executive team took place at *La Galarza,* the converted *hacienda* that housed both a distillery and the company retreat facility. The strategy sessions began with discussions among the men of the things that were important to them. "We begin with the human side to reinforce the team. Each man takes a few minutes to talk with his colleagues about how the year has been for him personally, his friends, his family, his ups, his downs, and how he feels about being part of the team." Then, for the next two to three days, the team put in 14- to 16-hour days planning.

When asked if everyone had an equal voice, all the vice presidents laughed, but Chertorivski laughed loudest. "They try to influence me, but none has been successful!" There was also a sharing of expertise: "When we discuss difficult issues, highly conceptual things, we help each other. We don't want to let the team down . . . to be the one who drags the team down. And if we make a mistake, we correct it."

To which Cordera replied, "Depends on how big a mistake it is!"

Each man had a particular point of view that was respected and synthesized. "We have room to grow in this team; we can make our own decisions, and there is no one looking over our shoulder." The company was poised to face its challenges, both personal and strategic.

Guillermo Cordera was currently facing one of the biggest challenges. The acquisition of Grupo Vergel in 1989 gave Bacardi a position in the Mexican brandy market and an opportunity to take on Domecq in its own backyard. VERGEL® brandy ran a distant third to Domecq's Presidente and Don Pedro brands. The acquisition was not easy for Grupo Bacardi. Some found it difficult to accept Bacardi Mexico's entry into the brandy business. As executive president of the Vergel division, Cordera found himself in an unaccustomed position as regards a Bacardi product—being in back of the pack, rather than in front:

> My challenge is to put Vergel on the map. We have volume but no profit. We need to grow Vergel more. We have extra capacity that we need to use, and we have to fight for shelf space. It is tough. I am impatient, impulsive, and ambitious. It is frustrating to move slowly; sometimes it is hard to accept that Bacardi Mexico is a company with stable growth.

Chertorivski faced a different challenge. Flush with the success of sales in Mexico, Chertorivski was concerned that complacency and arrogance were lurking:

> Today I think I need to create a crisis to make my people work more. There are two kinds of crisis, real and fabricated. Perhaps our people are a little complacent. Yesterday when talking with Cordera, I said it is time to create a crisis. How to do this? Tell them that we are not growing, that we must work harder. Be very upset, very gruff, and talk hard. We will hold a lot of analysis sessions to find out what is wrong. And there will be specific examples of what must be corrected. And three or four months later, they have things fixed. And then I will take them out to lunch and tell them how well they have done.

Behind Chertorivski's desk was a credenza, on which a gray phone sat. There was an identical phone in Cordera's office. They were connected to a private line that only Chertorivski and Cordera shared. The two executives were in constant contact. Chertorivski, with his marketing and public-relations skills, supplied the perspective of growth and expansion; Cordera, with his financial and systems background, supplied the long-range financial perspective. According to Grau, "Either one could run the company on his own, but together they are unbeatable."

BIG SKY, INC.: THE MAGASCO PAPER MILL (A)

BIG SKY, INC.

Big Sky was an integrated forest-products company headquartered in the Northwest with operations throughout the United States and Canada. Founded when two well-established lumber companies merged operations, Big Sky was a young organization by industry standards. The company manufactured and distributed paper and paper products, office products, and building products and owned and managed timberland to support its operations. In 1990 Big Sky reported sales of $4.5 billion and earnings of $275 million. Paper and paper products accounted for $2.5 billion in sales and represented 70 percent of the company's operating income and 55 percent of its revenue. Office and building products accounted for the balance.

During the fiscal year 1990, Big Sky invested a company record $750 million in the expansion, modernization, and improvement of its plant and facilities. The majority of these improvements were made at the company's paper-manufacturing facilities. Most of these operations were located in the Pacific Northwest, the Southeast, and the Northeast. Because papermaking required vast amounts of lumber, the majority of Big Sky's paper mills were located in rural timberlands. Big Sky manufactured a broad range of products, including uncoated white papers for printing and general business use, newsprint and uncoated groundwood paper for the manufacture of such products as paperback books, coated paper for magazines and catalogs, containerboard used in the construction of corrugated containers, and market pulp that was sold to other manufacturers.

Paper operations at Big Sky were divided into two primary groups: P-Three and Plain Paper. The P-Three division was responsible for producing three primary paper products: newsprint for publishing, linerboard for packaging, and marketable pulp. The Plain Paper division was responsible for producing all other products, including business forms, envelopes, and carbonless and copier papers.

Prepared by F. B. Brake, Jr., under the supervision of Alexander B. Horniman, Professor of Business Administration. Copyright © 1991 by the University of Virginia Darden School Foundation, Charlottesville, VA. All rights reserved. Revised September 1995.

THE PAPER INDUSTRY

The practice of papermaking dated back to at least the third millennium B.C. when the Egyptians first recorded their activities on pounded papyrus stalks. Although not as ancient as papyrus, the basic process of changing wood chips into pulp and then drying and pressing the pulp into paper sheets had not changed much over the past several hundred years. By 1990, however, papermaking had evolved into a highly capital-intensive and technology-driven industry. As a result of the introduction of modern information systems and computer-aided manufacturing, papermaking was an increasingly efficient and sophisticated process.

Because of the nature of the extensive plant and equipment required to operate a modern paper mill, the cost structure of papermaking was heavily weighted toward fixed costs. In 1990 a single paper machine capable of producing 500 tons of paper a day was estimated to cost in excess of $500 million. The raw-material cost of timber and labor costs—the two primary variable costs—had traditionally received little attention.

Historically, the papermaking industry had close ties to the lumber industry. In fact, many companies such as Big Sky were direct descendants of lumber companies. Because of the paper industry's dependence on timber as a raw material, most paper companies were vertically integrated and owned or were closely affiliated with timber operations in order to reduce their exposure to commodity price fluctuations. Culturally, the paper industry shared the Paul Bunyan mystique of the timber industry. Papermakers, like lumberjacks, were often characterized as "macho" and "tough, rugged individualists." Because of the manual nature of the work, both industries were known for their high incidence of injury. The Occupational Safety and Health Act (OSHA), passed by Congress in the 1960s, cited the forest-products industry, including papermaking activities, along with more celebrated industries such as meat packing, as the focus of OSHA's early efforts to reduce work-related injuries and deaths.

Large organized labor groups such as the United Paper Workers International represented much of the industry's work force. At some mills, workers in different industry trade groups represented workers in various functional areas—the machinists, who were responsible for performing the maintenance function, or the paper-machine operators. Over the years, these groups had negotiated lucrative contracts for their members. In addition to wages that were comparable to those paid in the steel industry, the industry trade representatives had negotiated for a number of concessions that were commonly found in the timber industry. For example, lumber companies and the saw mills they owned typically operated on a 40-hour workweek, closing on weekends and holidays. Because these operations were so labor intensive, this was considered an acceptable practice. Many union representatives at paper mills had successfully negotiated similar "cold shutdowns" at their locations. Because of the high fixed costs associated with running a paper mill, this practice was, however, extremely costly to the paper companies. One mill manager estimated that a cold shutdown for a three-day holiday weekend had cost his mill almost $6 million.

In addition to wage and benefit concessions, the unions had been very successful in negotiating for restrictive work practices that specifically defined individual work practices and job assignments. Restrictive work practices often precluded qualified personnel from performing tasks at different locations within the mill or on different mill machinery, regardless of the employee's ability to perform the job. Management was often unable to deploy its work force efficiently as a result of these work practices. Mill managers regularly compensated for the inflexible nature of their labor agreements by simply hiring additional employees. Many of the restrictive work practices and spiraling wage costs were tolerated by management because the industry had traditionally considered wage costs to be just a fraction of the total manufacturing cost.

Throughout much of the 1970s, demand exceeded supply in the industry, and papermakers were reluctant to close their mills over strikes for wage concessions they knew they would not have to absorb. A company executive addressing an industry gathering explained this logic:

> From the mid-60s to the mid-70s, we found it much easier to simply let union representatives dictate conditions to us without offering much resistance, perhaps believing—or hoping—that things would correct themselves. . . . Often we were fairly certain that many of the conditions demanded—whether they related to work practices or wage and benefit rates—were not in the best interests of our operations or our employees long term, but it was simply easier, less hassle, to acquiesce to union demands and then simply pass on increased costs to the customer. We had a business environment that allowed us to do that.

By the late 1970s, however, the situation had clearly gotten out of control. "We found ourselves in a fight for the very lives of our companies—and the jobs of our employees," said another executive. The industry was facing increasingly stiff competition from foreign manufacturers, particularly from Scandinavia and South America. Most foreign manufacturers had substantially lower labor costs than U.S. papermakers and were receiving assistance from their home governments in the form of subsidies and import restrictions.

Because demand for domestically manufactured paper products had historically exceeded supply, most U.S. manufacturers had traditionally operated at, or near, capacity. Many consumers would accept virtually any product shipped from the mill, so most manufacturers had adopted a manufacturing philosophy based on quantity as opposed to quality. As a direct result of encroaching foreign competition, however, capacity throughout the United States was on the rise. For the first time in recent memory, supply exceeded demand. At the same time, foreign manufacturers were also introducing higher quality products. Consequently, domestic consumers of paper products were increasingly demanding in terms of the quality they expected from U.S. manufacturers. As a result of increased industry capacity and the relatively low rate of annual inflation during the early 1970s, however, manufacturers were unable to pass along cost increases associated with the quality programs they needed to initiate in order to remain competitive. Industry profitability thus declined throughout the late 1970s.

In order to increase efficiency and productivity, in the late 1970s and early 1980s, many companies attempted to introduce new, more relaxed work practices when bargaining with unions. As one industry executive stated, "We needed to be substituting more flexible work practices for antiquated work rules that, over the years, had virtually immobilized many of our operations in a web of inefficiency and lowered productivity." Many industry observers were convinced that fierce foreign competition, increasing customer demands, rising labor costs, and restrictive labor practices would force many mills out of business.

In response to dwindling profits, more and more companies were willing to operate mills during strikes, a practice long avoided by the industry. In some extreme cases, when striking employees refused to return to work, they were replaced. Despite these apparent hardball tactics, most experts agreed that concessions would be required of everyone; something serious had to be done. In response to critics who claimed that the paper companies were just trying to drive out the unions, one industry veteran offered the following response: "None of these tactics were meant to bust the union as some would suggest. Rather, they demonstrated our increased willingness to maintain commitments to our customers and to the communities who depend on the successful operation of our facilities."

THE MAGASCO MILL

The Magasco Mill, a member of Big Sky's Alpine Division, was located in an area commonly known as Texarkana, where the borders of Texas, Arkansas, and Louisiana converge. Because of the proximity of vast pine groves and a temperate climate that accommodated accelerated tree-growing cycles, the area was ideal for papermaking. Opened in the early 1970s, Magasco was one of the first mills actually built by Big Sky. Most of the company's other paper-making operations had been acquired through various mergers and acquisitions. The mill was equipped with the latest technological innovations, including three cutting-edge paper machines capable of producing in excess of 1,500 tons of newsprint and linerboard a day.

When plans for the Magasco Mill were originally announced, Big Sky stated that it intended to introduce state-of-the-art management practices at the new facility. The hope was that the *de novo* effort would enable managers to introduce new work practices free from the influence of established cultures found at facilities purchased by Big Sky. The company hoped Magasco would serve as a model for other company mills as well as the rest of the industry.

While many other new mills in the South were discouraging the formation of unions at their mills, Big Sky actually invited organized labor into the Magasco Mill. They anticipated that this action would foster a cooperative environment and reduce the possibility of future conflicts between labor and management.

None of the approximately 500 skilled laborers, all of whom were represented by the Amalgamated Paperworkers Union (APU), or 150 managers and engineers was required to use a time clock. Management perceived the absence of a time clock, a symbolic gesture, to be a token of the trust between management and labor. The concept of "multicraft" was also introduced to provide flexibility in the maintenance functions. Multicraft required each employee to be skilled in and to perform multiple tasks rather than discretely defined job functions. At the time, these practices were considered revolutionary by industry standards.

Magasco, like most other papermaking operations at the time—with demand exceeding supply—was profitable even in the start-up years. The fact that the mill opened in the middle of a recession had little bearing on its initial performance. Despite early financial success, little headway was made, however, with management's attempt to to institute what some observers considered to be the most progressive work practices in the industry. After five years of Magasco operation, it was clear that, despite a contractual agreement between the APU and management, a functional craft distinction had evolved and the multicraft initiative had failed. Time clocks also appeared, at the APU's request. The union claimed that without time clocks its members were not being equitably compensated for overtime.

As was the case at many other mills, management found complying with labor's demands easier than following through on its own initiatives. Despite hopes for a mutually cooperative work environment, an adversarial relationship between labor and management soon established itself at Magasco. The mill quickly developed a reputation throughout the industry as a labor-relations hotbed. Part of the reason for this reputation stemmed from a much publicized strike at Magasco in the early 1970s.

The primary catalyst for the strike was management's unwillingness to grant further concessions in the area of restrictive work practices. The strike involved so much violence at the mill that a judge issued a permanent restraining order restricting picketing activities from anywhere within sight of the mill gate. As one employee said, "This place had a reputation in the industry as the Alamo. . . . It was a place you were sentenced to." Another employee related an incident in which, when he was introduced to a group of executives from competing mills at an industry gathering, and it was announced that he worked at Magasco, the group erupted in laughter.

In addition to continued labor strife, the Magasco Mill faced a number of other challenges during the late 1970s. As a company, Big Sky, like many other major corporations, had adopted a corporate strategy of diversification during the 1960s. Before long, the company found itself managing operations ranging from South American cattle ranches to Caribbean cruise lines, in addition to its core businesses, the paper operations. Operations at Magasco were largely ignored by the corporate staff throughout this period, as more attention and resources were directed toward the company's other businesses.

As a result of the declining profitability of the paper industry (as well as a number of its diversified holdings), Big Sky experienced dire financial problems in the mid- to late 1970s. In an attempt to save the company from financial ruin, executives at corporate headquarters began to exert significant pressure on individual operating units. As a result, mill managers throughout the company were forced to surrender much of their autonomy.

Not surprisingly, Magasco experienced a tremendous amount of management turnover during this time. Some Magasco veterans claimed that the only constant at the mill was the union representatives who sat down at the bargaining table every three years to negotiate a new contract. As one long-time employee said, "There are a lot of management teams buried in this mill." The high attrition rate in the managerial ranks at the Magasco location was widely acknowledged not to be necessarily attributable to the quality of mill managers. "It was," as one employee said, "as if they were facing insurmountable odds."

Throughout the late 1970s and early 1980s, management attempted to introduce a number of new initiatives and mandates. The APU, however, was extremely reluctant to comply with any of management's change initiatives, because the union had come to understand the short-lived nature of most of management's proposals. Many employees shared the following story: no sooner would a change be initiated at the mill than a Big Sky corporate jet would fly over the plant with a representative from headquarters on board and land at the small municipal airport outside of town. Before the plane took off at the end of the day, the change would be reversed.

The mill's problems during the late 1970s and early 1980s were not solely financial. Despite the presence of safety procedures—warning signs and posters located throughout the facility promoting safe work practices—the mill had a dismal safety record. Two people were killed at Magasco in industrial accidents during one year, and every year a number of others were disabled so badly they could not return to work. As one employee said, "It wasn't a big deal for any number of people to be so severely injured that they never came back to the mill after being hurt on the job." In addition to the tremendous pain and suffering incurred by the injured employee and his or her family, these accidents directly influenced the mill's financial performance. Under state worker's compensation regulations, Big Sky could be required to set aside as much as $300,000 immediately following an accident for future payment to a disabled employee.

"TIMES, THEY ARE A CHANGING"

Jock Duncan joined Big Sky as the director of human resources at Magasco a few months before the mill management was set to negotiate its three-year contract with the APU in the summer of 1983. Duncan came from the chemical industry, where he had nearly two decades of experience in human resources. Initially, he was surprised by the restrictive nature of the work practices in the paper industry. He quickly concluded that relations between management and the union employees at Magasco were adversarial at best. "The work force here at the mill was much more compliant than those in the chemical or petroleum industries at that time," Duncan later recalled.

Duncan was disturbed by the assumptions made by management and labor about the role hourly employees should play in the workplace. He knew these assumptions were the result of years of behavioral observation and reinforcement. As illustrated in Exhibit 1, in a mutual compliance organization such as Magasco, management, based on behavioral observations, assumed employees were antagonistic and apathetic. Systems and work technologies were eventually developed on the basis of these assumptions. This approach often resulted in fragmented work assignments and constant supervision by management. Employees, perceiving management as adversarial and non-trusting because of the work practices instituted, often responded by exhibiting apathetic and antagonistic behavior, thereby reinforcing management's original perception.

Despite Big Sky's original expectations, by the time of Duncan's arrival, the Magasco Mill, along with most of the company's other facilities, was characterized by poor labor relations and hazardous working conditions. The mill

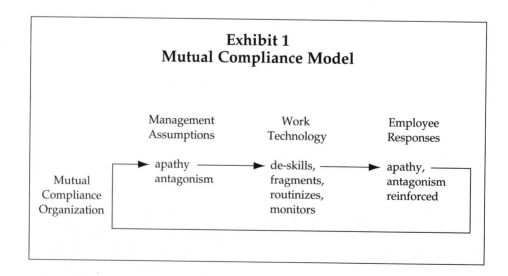

Exhibit 1
Mutual Compliance Model

	Management Assumptions	Work Technology	Employee Responses
Mutual Compliance Organization	apathy antagonism	de-skills, fragments, routinizes, monitors	apathy, antagonism reinforced

was also losing nearly $35 million a year. Magasco's newsprint machines were operating at just over 80-percent capacity, and the linerboard machines were producing at just over 90 percent of total capacity. As a result of increased competition and increasing capacity, the market price of the mill's paper was falling at a rate of 9 percent a year, while its total manufacturing cost per ton was increasing by 9 percent. Duncan and the other senior members of the mill's management team believed that the mill's survival hinged on the successful introduction of significant changes at the upcoming labor negotiations.

The discreet work assignments that had developed over the years as a result of various managements' reluctance to aggravate labor had put a choke hold on the mill's ability to produce paper efficiently and affordably, particularly in the face of foreign competition. Management concluded that more flexible work practices had to be introduced. Although recent labor agreements had clearly defined step-by-step job descriptions and work assignments for the APU members at the mill, Duncan and the other managers proposed new language that would provide management with greater discretion in defining and assigning work. Duncan knew from past negotiations that a change in the wording from one contract to another of this magnitude was serious enough to instigate a walkout.

In order to facilitate the change to a more flexible work environment, management planned to introduce the team concept. This approach represented a radical departure from the mill's traditional work assignments and was reminiscent of the multicraft concept originally introduced at the mill nearly a decade earlier. In the team approach, the mill would be divided into three primary functional areas: the paper machines, the pulp mill, and the wood yard. Whereas each area might have previously had anywhere from 10 to 15 individual jobs, it was proposed that these jobs be divided into three or four clusters or teams consisting of 3 to 4 jobs. Teams of employees would be assigned to a particular cluster, and each employee would be expected to perform every job in the cluster on a rotating basis. This process would broaden the skill base of every employee and provide management with greater flexibility in developing work assignments.

The rationale for introducing the team concept was described in the proposed contract as follows:

> The team concept is designed to improve the efficiency and competitive position of the mill [by] providing for the flexible utilization of production and storeroom personnel. The elements of the Team Concept are considered essential to the survival of the mill.

Mill management was acutely aware of the sensitivity of the proposed changes but believed that a crisis situation had developed and that without tremendous change the mill might go under. As Duncan noted, "We knew we were introducing a tremendous amount of change, but it had to be done."

In an attempt to alleviate some of the anxiety regarding the proposed changes, management assured the APU that no union jobs would be threatened as a result of the introduction of the team concept. In the preamble to the proposed labor agreement, management included the following statement: "No current employee will lose his employment or suffer a reduction in his wage rate due to the implementation of the team concept."

THE WALKOUT

Unfortunately, it came as no surprise when the APU representatives recommended a walkout at the beginning of the talks. "Change requires loss," said Duncan, a key figure in the negotiations, "and the union representatives realized that they were being asked to make sacrifices—sacrifices they felt they could not make." While the union members walked out of the mill, management was determined to keep the mill up and running. For what may have been the first time in industry history, the salaried staff of a paper mill actually took over running the paper machines.

In the weeks leading up to the contract negotiations, Duncan and the other members of the staff had been preparing for the logistical nightmare that would follow in the wake of a walkout. In order to keep the mill operating, Big Sky was prepared to keep the production facilities fully staffed. A camp was set up on the mill property, and salaried employees from throughout the company were ferried on commercial airlines as needed in order to meet the mill's production schedule. One participant likened the experience to a military airlift.

In another break with tradition, management made every effort to keep all employees, including those on strike, as well as the community, abreast of the ongoing negotiation. In the past, Magasco had left it up to the union to keep its members informed. This time, however, management wanted to ensure that everyone knew what was happening. In addition to establishing a hotline that any employee could call to get daily updates, mill management worked closely with the press to keep the community informed. As managers of the largest employer in the surrounding three-county area, Magasco Mill management also met regularly with community and business leaders to keep them up to date on the situation.

About a month into the strike, when little progress was being made and both parties appeared to be deadlocked over the proposed changes in the contract, the federal mediators who had been called in to oversee the negotiations announced that the talks were at an impasse. Management developed a replacement strategy.

In accordance with its contingency plan, mill management began interviewing prospective applicants to replace the striking workers. Because the country was still recovering from a recession, Big Sky had no shortage of qualified applicants from which to choose. Unemployed papermakers drove in from as far away as Ohio and Maine to be processed. Throughout this time, tensions continued to rise as some of the striking employees realized that they might soon be replaced. Acts of violence and harassment, including instances of gunfire, were reported at several of the assessment centers Big Sky had established around Magasco for the processing of applicants. Several of the incidents were captured on videotape. The situation became so charged and received so much attention that the site was visited by the FBI and the Bureau of Alcohol, Tobacco and Firearms.

Despite these incidents, management was determined to keep the mill running and continued to process applicants. Finally, Big Sky announced that it would implement all changes outlined in its proposed labor agreement during the first week of November, two months after the contract had originally been proposed, and any striking employee who wished to return to work at that time would be welcomed; those who didn't would be replaced.

The day before the changes were scheduled to go into effect, the mill was contacted by the office of the governor-elect, who had strong ties to labor and felt a moral obligation to lend his assistance. He asked Big Sky to delay action for 24 hours while he personally attempted to resolve the situation. Big Sky agreed to postpone its initiative but informed the governor-elect that it would agree to no concessions and would institute the changes as outlined in its original proposal regardless of the outcome of his discussions. To the surprise of many observers, the governor-elect was able to reach an accord with the union and informed Big Sky that the striking employees would come back to work with no conditions. They would accept the originally proposed labor agreement, including the contested team concept.

Despite the governor-elect's assurances, when Duncan and the rest of the negotiating team met with the APU representatives to ratify the contract, the APU suddenly demanded a condition. Specifically, the union asked for amnesty for those employees captured on videotape during the conflicts that erupted at the processing centers. The mill manager was furious with the APU's lack of good faith. He was not about to begin bargaining at that point, and he informed the governor-elect that the union representatives had not followed through on his promise. The governor-elect responded with tremendous disappointment and told management to do what it had to do.

During the strike, a phone bank had been established at the mill to inform applicants of Big Sky's decision to hire them as replacements in the event an agreement between Big Sky and the APU could not be reached. As the meeting broke up in downtown Magasco, Duncan prepared to drive out to the mill to initiate the replacement process. When he arrived at the mill and began to gather the team to phone, he was informed that the union representatives had changed their minds and would not request any concessions.

The news hit Duncan like nothing he had ever experienced. Now what would he and the mill manager do? Was it possible to really create a "new

Magasco mill"? Was it possible to transform all the negative energy that had been focused on the strike to building a totally different organization? These questions and what seemed like hundreds of other ideas flooded his mind. What was possible? How should the journey start?

STEWART-GLAPAT CORPORATION

On June 7, 1985, during the nine-hour drive from Charlottesville, Virginia, to Zanesville, Ohio, William Tanner Stewart had lots of time to consider what he would do upon his arrival; on Monday, June 10, he would take over operating control of his family's business, Stewart-Glapat, Inc., a maker of conveyor systems. Tanner had been away from the business for ten years pursuing a career in engineering and business education before deciding to return to the company his father had founded and his brother had run for the seven years since his father's death.

Tanner had a number of concerns as he drove along: although the company had been profitable, competition was stiffening considerably from both domestic and international companies; production efficiency was not nearly what Tanner thought it should be; sales volume was bumping along without the kind of steady growth Tanner believed the company needed to survive in an increasingly competitive environment; the plant seemed dirty to him—always congested and cluttered with stacks of steel stock and subassemblies—and the bathrooms were filthy; the equipment was old and generally worn out; there was a need for new products to augment the company's basic line; and the workers complained of the heat in the summer and the cold in winter and the poor air quality in the plant. He also could not see the kind of management teamwork that he felt was needed. Many of the management processes in the firm seemed to Tanner to be nearly as old and dilapidated as much of the equipment upon which the firm depended. Perhaps the most significant of these was the lack of formal production schedules.

Through the hills of West Virginia, Tanner reflected on the advice of his brother Charlie (currently the chairman and CEO): "Don't try to change too much at once," he had said. "Move into your office next to mine, nose around a bit, and just get to know the situation here. Get to know the people and how we do things now before you start changing things."

It seemed incongruous to Tanner to have made the major career decision to leave the University of Virginia where he had been a tenure-track associate professor of operations, to come "home" to the family business, and not to *do* anything. Not only was he going to have to change his lifestyle and his daily work routine to make this change, he was also going to have to change his name: all of his Zanesville friends, including the people at the plant, knew him as "Bill," but he had gone by "Tanner" while in academe. Changing his name seemed symbolic of the magnitude of the change he was now a part of. Tanner mumbled, "That's not my style. I grab it by the throat. If I don't want to live with it, I get it resolved. Some people say I try to move too fast, but I've got to make a difference, or these people won't have jobs in five years."

Tanner wondered what his dad would have done and, as he did, became a bit sad. He had never been close to his father, but he respected and admired his engineering genius greatly.

C. T. STEWART AND THE FOUNDING OF STEWART-GLAPAT

Charles Thomas Stewart's first job after receiving his degree in mechanical engineering from Massachusetts Institute of Technology was as an industrial engineer for the Heisy Glass Co. in Newark, Ohio. Stewart moonlighted, designing glass equipment on the side, because the company discouraged his experimentation. He invented several pieces of glass-handling equipment, including machinery that made glass goblets, polished glass, and loaded glass cases into trucks. He could not put his name on his inventions because he was employed by Heisy, so he registered the patents under the name Glapat for "glass patent." The first telescoping conveyor Stewart made was not used for loading and unloading trucks but for putting glass ingots into a furnace.

In 1942 Stewart disagreed with the Heisy Company's marketing manager about whether or not to trim the company's product line from 2,000 to 500 items; as a result he was fired. With his father, C. O. Stewart, Charles Stewart (or "C.T." as he was sometimes called) started his own company making glass-handling equipment. Taking the lead from his patents, he named the company Stewart-Glapat, Inc.

Stewart liked to tinker and invent. Tanner mused aloud as he remembered days spent with his father:

> My dad was one of the most brilliant design engineers I ever met. He had great spatial perception, in terms of visual kinematics. He could envision complicated pieces of machinery in his head, and that was a gift. He made the very first airplane loader. They took a telescoping conveyor and put it on a Jeep. I remember as a child out at the local airport here; we went out one night, I rode on the Jeep, and they flew in a TWA DC3, and he had to load it for them. It turned out that nobody wanted it.
>
> He made the very first extendable package conveyor. I can remember as a small child, five or six years old, being out in the older part of the plant and sitting on a telescoping conveyor at night when my dad was running it in and out, playing with me. That is as vivid as if it had just happened.

My dad was an entrepreneur in the sense that he would never run away from an engineering challenge. In fact, as a young college student, I would travel with him during the summer. We would go to various customers. I knew a good bit about our product, since I had worked in our plant when I was younger. We would go out and look at an application. And he would say, "Yeah, we can do that, and here's what it will cost you." The guy would give him an order. I would be sitting in the car, and I would say, "Dad that looks like a damned complicated thing you're going to do. I've never seen us do that." He would say, "Well, we've never done it, but we will figure out a way." And 95 percent of the time he would. And 5 percent of the time, we would end up in a lawsuit.

Dad got involved in opening bags automatically—something nobody had ever successfully done—bags of asbestos and chemicals and other harmful stuff. He built a fully automatic bag opener that never really worked. He kept building and selling them and always got into problems. We built one of these for Romania, but the ship sank on the way to Europe. We got paid in full from the insurance company, and they never ordered another one. We don't build those anymore. If you think about the liability of having workers around an asbestos machine that you claim is dust-proof, you'd have to put a gun to my head to do that. And yet Dad was doing it off the cuff: "No problem! Sure we will do that." He just didn't really envision the risk.

Back in those days, it was a very single-dimensional company, in that Dad made all the big decisions. People just did what he told them to do.

Stewart was a remarkable engineer and inventor; he was not, however, as accustomed to managing the financial side of the business. He was eager to accept engineering challenges even when the financial return was not immediately apparent. One employee who used to travel extensively with him on road trips noted that one customer, who had been a classmate of Stewart's at MIT, had asked him, "How's Charlie's little toy laboratory doing?" The comment seemed to fit Stewart's interest in tinkering in the shop and building new machines. The employee noted:

Charlie [senior] was a genius. He was always thinking about how he could do it better, redesigning a machine he'd seen in his head. He was not a practical man, though, not a business manager. The plant was like his personal lab: he'd want to try something out, we'd build it for him, and then he'd go on to the next idea. On the road, he'd treat you like a king, but in the plant, you worked for him: he'd say little needling things to keep you in line. He was in here seven days a week.

When he passed away of a heart attack in 1978 on a business trip to Germany, Stewart left a company recognized by most to be on the brink of bankruptcy. Employees walking down the street in Zanesville would be asked if their jobs were still intact. Some thought that Stewart's passing would mean a large layoff, even the demise of the company.

CHARLIE JUNIOR

When Stewart died, his eldest son, Charlie Jr., took control of the company. Charlie Jr. had played football in college and was, some said, more interested in sports than the family business. Many were surprised when he joined the business after graduating from Denison University in 1966, but Charlie Jr. began as purchasing agent and in 1971 was elected vice president. When his father died, Charlie Jr. became president. Meanwhile, Tanner was pursuing his engineering doctorate at Ohio State University.

Charlie had little interest in the engineering features of the machines the company built and seldom went out on the shop floor. As a sportsman, his philosophy was what he called the "team concept." He assembled the best people he could find to run sales, design, machine shop and assembly, and finances of the firm and let them do their work. He did periodically review the financial results and would become very animated if the firm was not making money on each project. He refused to bid for or accept any projects that were not profitable, a practice substantially different from his father's.

Charlie coached Little League football in Zanesville. He noted with pride in 1985 that, in the 16 years he had coached, his teams failed to win the league championship only twice. Charlie's office was very different from the rest of the Stewart-Glapat company space, which was austerely functional. Charlie's office looked and felt like the head coach's office of a major college football program—carpeted floor, leather couches and chairs, built-in bookcases filled with trophies, team pictures, autographed footballs, certificates, and other sports memorabilia.

Charlie also sponsored a Division B American Softball Association slow-pitch softball team that won many trophies and even took the national championship in 1984. Because only a few of the players actually worked for Stewart-Glapat and the cost of supporting the team was substantial, it caused some controversy among the family and employees. The old drafting room in the basement under the machine shop was filled with 58 softball trophies, some of them six feet tall.

Under Charlie tutelage, the firm paid off its debts and became quite profitable. Tanner mused aloud about Charlie administration of the company:

> When Dad died and I was gone, something happened to the company that was very important. My brother was not an engineer and was faced with "What do I do? Do I go coach football because that is my education, or do I still try to maintain this company?"
>
> He decided to maintain the company. We were in terrible financial difficulties. Basically, what happened was the company decided to do only what it knew how to do well, which was telescoping conveyors, and tried to beef up the product, to make it a better product, and to learn how to sell it better. Those things paid off. We became a very prominent, profitable small company.

In the years that my brother was in charge, basically, he paid the people very good salaries, [gave] tremendous benefits, kept the key people here, and then muddled through.

According to Dutch Lewis, the sales manager, as long as the bottom line was okay, Charlie Jr. didn't get involved in department policy:

As long as he had competent people heading up each department, he would keep his hands out of those departments. He would be a very close observer of performance levels, but, generally, he was the type of boss, as long as the bottom line was coming out, then that was good enough. He did not get involved in departmental policy. If the bottom line was not what he liked to see, then he would get involved, and we would have our sessions—our management sessions—and discuss policy. And it would be a joint effort. We got along well and worked together well. He did oversee all of our price changes, too.

One manager described Charlie Jr. this way:

Everybody thought that since C.T. died, we'd go under. If he'd *lived*, we'd have gone under! After three weeks, Lewis got rolling, moved us in a different direction. He said, "Let's market this exclusively." And Charlie agreed. Charlie trusted us. He had the personnel around him; he didn't know what we were doing, but he believed we were working for the benefit of the company. He got the work rolling through here. He was like a coach, walking the sidelines, watching, while we did the work. But he is very moody. You don't know what will happen with him. Charlie'd put decisions back on the team, though.

Another employee described Charlie as "more of a businessman. He left all the engineering and design to the departments, and the money kept coming in. If it wouldn't make money, Junior wouldn't touch it."

During this period the management team assembled by Charlie became accustomed to having autonomy in their jobs. Each manager developed his own systems and managerial style.

THE MANAGEMENT TEAM

Charlie Jr.'s team consisted of Dave Redman, plant manager; Dutch Lewis, sales manager; Ronald Bachelor, engineering manager; Jack Rutherford, materials manager; and David Shaeffer, office manager (see Exhibit 1).

Dave Redman, plant manager, joined the company in 1961 when he finished high school and supervised plant operations since 1966. His responsibilities included building the company's products to the specifications of the engineering department; supervising the machine shop, assembly, and paint crews; managing cost reduction; and managing the flow of the work through the factory.

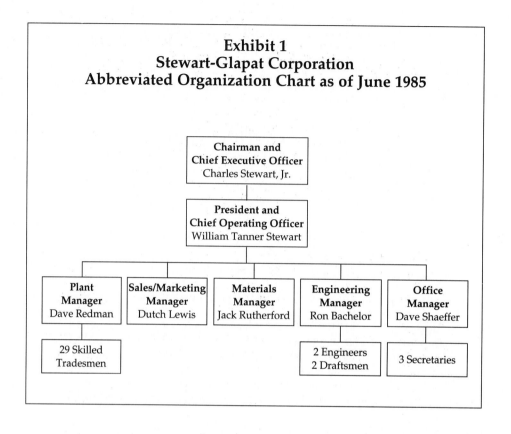

**Exhibit 1
Stewart-Glapat Corporation
Abbreviated Organization Chart as of June 1985**

Dutch Lewis, sales manager, received his J.D. degree at the Ohio State University, where he and Tanner were roommates for a brief period, and then worked in Columbus in real estate. He came to Stewart-Glapat when Tanner invited him to come and manage the company's sales efforts. As the sales manager, Lewis was responsible for identifying and bidding on new business—in essence, managing the revenues of the firm. The bidding process was a key part of the company's success: because most of the machines were custom designs, Lewis had to estimate what the machine would cost to build, often without any company experience on that machine, and then price the bid competitively against the rest of the industry.

Before Lewis joined the company, Stewart-Glapat had had a difficult time selling its products. Lewis joined the company in May 1976 and was trained by Tanner in the basic product and manufacturing knowledge of the firm. When Tanner left three months later to pursue his doctorate, Lewis made several changes in the way the company went to market. He decided to concentrate on civilian contracts, because the company hadn't been successful in getting and maintaining government contracts. He concentrated on pre-engineered, more standardized extendible conveyors that would be cheaper to make and easier to bid. Lewis also was able to have Stewart-Glapat products listed in the material-handling catalogs of Litton and Rexnord, two major industry sales tools.

By 1985, Lewis did not have to travel a lot. He reported,

> I don't have to make cold calls. I would do it if we got some major house accounts, but we don't want to step on the toes of our distributors, reps, and major OEMs. I do proposals, answer phone calls, do contract administration on our work with the government, keep track of what bids are being let out, and participate in marketing policy. I talk to people and keep in touch, and, because of that, I guess we are in on 95 percent of the extendible bids that are let.

Ronald Bachelor, engineering manager, joined the company in 1974 to be responsible for overseeing all engineering activities—such as design specifications, rework, parts design, and drafting. In 1985 Bachelor's team consisted of two senior and two junior designers.

Prior to joining Stewart-Glapat in 1981, Jack Rutherford, materials manager, had been inventory controls and materials manager for Schrader-Bellows, a division of Scovill, for 14 years. Rutherford received a bachelor's degree in economics from Wittenberg University in 1966. His responsibilities included materials procurement and supervising the shipping employees.

David Shaeffer, office manager, received an associate's degree in accounting from Columbus Business University and worked as an accountant and cost controller for several companies (primarily 12 years with United Technologies) before joining the Stewart-Glapat management team in 1982. His responsibilities at Stewart-Glapat included managing the office (with three secretaries); overseeing the billing, collecting, and correspondence of the company; and preparing the financial statements.

And now as part of the team, of course, there was William Tanner Stewart, who with his wife and four children was going back to Ohio to be the president and chief operating officer. The younger Stewart son had been active in the company as vice president of engineering from 1969 (upon his graduation from MIT) until 1976, so many of the managers in the firm had some experience working with him. He earned a Ph.D. at the Ohio State University and became an assistant professor at Purdue University for four years, after which he was an associate professor at The Colgate Darden Graduate School of Business Administration at the University of Virginia for three years.

Although Tanner visited the company infrequently during his work in academe, several of the managers and employees had formed initial impressions of him. One manager described him as "more hands-on, likely to be involved in all departments," while another described him as "radical. He takes everything personally." Another described him as

> moody. He can be very sarcastic when you ask him a question. I don't like it. It's a bunch of BS. He feels like he's too smart for the people around here. It's obnoxious. . . . He's been around college too long. You need that attitude

there, but not in dealing with the people here. There's a difference between asking and telling.

His approach is to go off the deep end. He doesn't think things out rationally. Charlie, on the other hand, wants to work things back and forth until you get an answer. If Bill doesn't get what he wants, he says, "G———t, then let's just send someone else!" He doesn't think things through rationally. If I need to talk to him about a problem, he just says, "Why can't *you* handle that? That's not my job."

Another employee stated:

Bill's more like his Dad, lots of intelligence; smart, but not too practical. He doesn't understand life from a working man's point-of-view; he's never had to live like we do. A lot of guys don't like his overbearing attitude. He comes out with his stopwatch and clipboard and times the cutters to see how long it takes to cut angle iron. They don't like it.

Another employee noted:

Bill doesn't listen well. There's not much communication between the men and him. He has a certain sarcastic manner. He wants it done his way or else. He thinks that if somebody doesn't like it, he can quit. Or if he doesn't like it, we'll fire him.

STEWART-GLAPAT IN 1985

By 1985, Stewart-Glapat had grown in size and volume but remained a small, family-owned business. The number of all employees, including about 10 managers and office staff, had hovered around 25 to 30 during C.T.'s administration. For one brief, 18-month period, C.T. had hired an additional 100 people, but when anticipated business did not materialize, the work force was cut back to its previous level. Under Charlie Jr.'s guidance, the number of employees grew gradually to fluctuate from 33 to 35.

During the period when Charlie was in operating control, the company had focused on relatively few markets: newspaper companies, retail distribution, and units for the U.S. Postal Service. The latter, however, had not proved to be a stable market. At one time, Dutch Lewis secured a contract with another company to market the Stewart-Glapat machines under its own name. The stability and widespread markets served by this company helped revive Stewart-Glapat's financial health to the point that sales began to average $3 million per year while profits substantially exceeded the 4.28 percent of sales average of other firms like Stewart-Glapat.

The building had been extended significantly from when the company opened for business, yet there was sufficient land surrounding the plant to more than double its size. Prior to 1972, the plant had been added onto three times, twice by extending it directly back from the original building (see

Exhibit 2) and once by pushing out sideways from the machine shop. Of that addition, one employee noted, "The worst thing they did was build the new engineering department. We used to get a draft, a breeze across the plant, but that [addition] blocked the big windows, so now we get no breeze. And it's so hot in here in the summer."

Even with floor space of more than 47,000 square feet, Tanner was concerned that the production scheduling and manufacturing flow was not what it should be. Most of the machinery in the plant was original and showing severe signs of wear. Scheduling was done ad hoc. Several jobs would be in the assembly process at any one time. If a job couldn't be completed because of delays in parts or subassemblies, it was simply pulled aside and left standing until the necessary parts were ready. Similarly, jobs had no completion deadlines. When the jobs were done, the machines were shipped. Customers were given a general idea about shipping but seldom firm dates.

Even with plenty of space, there was an irritatingly unkempt appearance of the shop floor; parts, scrap, partially assembled machines, and raw inventory stocks of steel in various shapes and sizes littered the shop floor from the office door to the raw-materials dock at the back. During his visits, Tanner attempted to get employees to clean the plant, but he was met with explanations that it could not be done with the kind of work they were doing.

Overall, though, most employees seemed to like working at Stewart-Glapat. Earl Rupe, the union steward, commented on what it was like:

> Working here is decent money, including the five hours on Saturdays. It's not steady work; they lay off and add on, and the working conditions are fair to poor. It should be cleaner here. The money is better than average, but not the best in town. On July first, they announced a new retirement plan that was negotiated. The plan came out of the International Association of Machinists where they contribute $3 a week if you haven't missed any time that week.

ADJUSTOVEYOR

The Stewart-Glapat Corporation manufactured and sold extendable conveyor belts under the name of Adjustoveyor. (See Exhibit 3 for an example of the company's product brochure.) The company's main product since 1950, extendable conveyor-belt systems were used to load and unload trucks—typically at warehouses or shipping terminals that had to do so dozens of times a day. The name Adjustoveyor came from the ability of the conveyor belt to extend and retract. A typical Adjustoveyor had a simple set of hand controls on the leading edge of the cantilevered boom, so that a single person could unload a semitruck trailer by extending the boom into the truck as he or she worked.

Because most applications of its product line required special features, Stewart-Glapat was essentially a custom job shop. The company made most

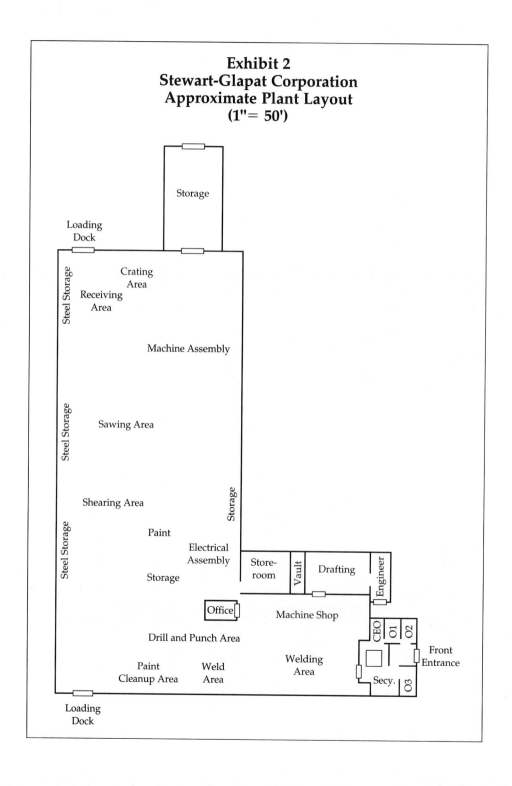

Exhibit 2
Stewart-Glapat Corporation
Approximate Plant Layout
(1"= 50')

Exhibit 3
Sample Stewart–Glapat Product Brochure

ADJUSTOVEYOR offers you a new era in truck loading/unloading productivity

● **Labor savings through productivity improvement** ● **Economic payback of one year or less**
● **Fast turnaround of vehicles** ● **Reductions in product damage**
● **Smooth, continuous product flow** ● **Load rating of 65 lbs. per lineal ft.**

The model 2580T triple boom Adjustoveyor was developed to offer industry improved material handling productivity for loading and unloading the longer over-the-road vehicles which are widely used today. With a seven foot dock leveler and a 48' trailer, a full 55' of cantilevered extension is required to serve the entire vehicle. Previous designs often fell short when confronted with these new requirements. But no longer! The Model 2580T features a 25' closed length, extending to an overall length of 80 feet, thus providing the full 55' of powered cantilevered extension required

Adjustoveyor is shown installed in a large midwestern distribution center where it is used to rapidly strip inbound vehicles of product needed for shipments to catalog sales customers. This unit is self-propelled and serves two dock locations. The unit was designed for around-the-clock duty and for the severe operating conditions often encountered in dock areas. The live load rating of 65 pounds per lineal foot is the highest in the industry and provides that extra margin of safety and reliability for long and continuous service. This customer had used a smaller Adjustoveyor for three years and specified the new larger model for a new system addition due to the increased use of 48' vehicles.

(continued on next page)

Source: Courtesy of Stewart-Glapat Corporation.

(continued)

The unit unloads inbound trailers and connects with a takeaway system which conveys product to a sortation station, prior to placing the goods in inventory. The lifeblood of the total system is the smooth, uninterrupted flow of product from the producers, through the Distribution Center, and on to the final customers. Bottlenecks cannot be tolerated and with a requirement for JUST-IN-TIME inventory management, product cannot sit in a trailer or linger on a dock, while a customer is told the item is out of stock. COMPETITIVENESS IS BUILT ON PERFORMANCE, AND THE ADJUST-OVEYOR HAS ALWAYS BEEN A KEY PLAYER IN OVERALL SYSTEM EFFICIENCY.

Many truckloads have both conveyable products and palletized loads which must be quickly unloaded. To accommodate forklift movement, dock levelers are used to gain access to trailers of differing heights. The typical 7' dock leveler requires that the Adjustoveyor be set back from the door opening, thus reducing the effective reach into the vehicle. The Model 2580T is designed to extend over the dock leveler and still reach the end of a 48' trailer. Since the unit is fully cantilevered, no support in the trailer is necessary.

Write or phone us for full information.

Your employee working on the loading dock controls the flow of your operation. Once material reaches your facility, you cannot afford to impose delays on that needed material. The Model 2580T is designed with the safety and productivity of your employees clearly in mind. All controls are located on the front end of the unit for easy access. A safety bar protects the operator from extensions beyond safe limits. All pinch points are guarded and operator safety is stressed in a videotape provided with each unit. The Adjustoveyor provides the link between your employees on the dock and overall system productivity. Don't saddle your employees with shorter units which hinder their efforts to be fully productive in longer trailers.
ADJUSTOVEYOR IS YOUR BEST LONG-TERM CAPITAL INVESTMENT!

of its own parts to specification from the design group (two senior designers and two apprentice designers) in the company machine shop. Lately, however, the firm had been subcontracting many of the higher volume parts, because the Stewart-Glapat wages could not meet the low costs of the dedicated machine shops.

By 1985 Stewart-Glapat had built the largest extendable, cantilevered conveyor system in the world, a machine with a 36-inch-wide belt that would extend through three steel booms 55 feet into a truck trailer and carry 65 pounds per linear foot of belt. These large machines rested on railroad-like tracks set in a warehouse floor and could roll back and forth to service several doors. The company also built smaller machines.

STRATEGIC PLANNING

As Tanner, becoming more and more "Bill" as he drove down to the flatlands of Ohio, thought about the future of the company, he was convinced that it needed to expand its volume and manage its costs to become the low-cost, volume producer of extendable conveyors in order to bid successfully against the growing tide of competitors. Shipping costs for the large machines were extensive, yet the company had recently lost contracts to overseas producers. This worried Tanner, and he wondered how he might build the volume of the company's plant so that it could pass on the cost savings to customers through the bidding process. One way would be to introduce a new product that would revolutionize the industry. A conveyor that would load and unload pallets automatically would be such a machine, but so far the technical aspects of this project had been insurmountable. Other ways, he thought, would be to increase sales and add a second shift, or to increase the efficiencies of the plant, or both.

The second-shift alternative raised the questions of the local labor market and Stewart-Glapat's reputation in it.

ZANESVILLE, OHIO

The Stewart-Glapat Corporation was located in Zanesville, Ohio, a small town rich in history. It had been formed by Ebenezer Zane in 1797 when he and a group of woodmen cut a path in the wilderness from Wheeling, West Virginia, through Ohio to Maysville, Kentucky. One clearing that they made was called the Zane's Trace, which, in becoming a gateway to the West, formed the nucleus of what later became Zanesville.

In 1985 Zanesville was the county seat of Muskingum County and boasted 150 manufacturing and processing establishments. Some of the principal products produced in Zanesville were agricultural machinery, alloys, batteries, boilers, cement, ceramic products, conveyor systems, corrugated fiber shipping containers, dairy products, egg solids, electrical sheet steel, electronic components, meat products, radiators, tile transformers, pet food, bakery goods, and carpets. Even though Zanesville had a diversity of industry so that employment was not concentrated in any one, it had an unemployment rate of 12.5 percent in 1985, when the Ohio average was 8.9 percent and the national average was 7.2 percent.

Despite these statistics, Tanner wondered if the company could attract the people for a second shift. Stewart-Glapat had a reputation for hiring short term to meet contract needs and then laying off shortly thereafter when the contract expired. In addition, if Tanner could find the business to support a second shift (and he thought he could) and then be able to hire one, he wondered who would supervise it; he felt sure that none of the current managers would be willing to work 3:30 P.M. to midnight. Tanner had reached this conclusion in part because of an earlier effort to institute change at the company.

While still at the University of Virginia, Tanner had succeeded in getting the company to buy two microcomputers. One was assigned to the design department and was attached to a modern, computer-aided-design (CAD) software package and a wide-carriage plotter. The other was assigned to the front office for use in managing accounts receivable, correspondence, billing, and other office functions. Tanner knew by the time he was driving home that neither of these computers was being well utilized and that, in fact, some managers were refusing to try to learn how. The CAD machine had sat idle for the ten months it had been in the design office, and the office machine was ignored by all but one of the other officers and secretaries.

MANAGEMENT TEAMWORK

Remembering that incident brought Tanner's mind to another concern: the ability of the Stewart-Glapat management team to work together. Since they had all been working independently for the past ten years, Tanner was concerned that in many areas of interaction among the various departments, the company was wasting time, energy, and financial resources. Sometimes subcontracted parts were not available when the assemblers were ready; other times designed parts did not fit the machine under assembly. Accounts receivable were building up, and no one seemed to worry much about the increasing competition.

Tanner wanted to build a strong sense of cooperative teamwork, but he was very aware that the managers had been operating as autonomous individuals for a decade. During this time, they had developed a set of common beliefs. Tanner noted that many of these perceived "sacred cows" limited company growth. He had heard many of them repeated in the past few months:

If our costs aren't competitive, we should get out of that market.

You can't find good enough welders. There are only five people in Zanesville who can weld our equipment.

There is a fixed market volume for our product. Whatever it is, it is.

If there is a problem, it must be somebody's fault.

This place has always been messy and always will be because our workers are slobs.

The unit will be shipped when it is done. We cannot predict when that will be.

Computers are a waste!

Put off telling the boss about a problem. He'll just get mad.

Tanner did not believe any of these, but knew that his vision for the company would be tarnished by each and every one of them.

In the middle of these reflections, Tanner realized that he was crossing the Muskingum River in Zanesville. The next exit was his; he was home. As he circled down the ramp into his hometown, he began to lay his plans for the following Monday morning. He also was eager to get out of the car and stretch his legs on his usual daily five-mile run.

THE PUBLIC COMMUNICATIONS DEPARTMENT
AT NEW YORK TELEPHONE

There is no organization in the whole telephone company that is held in higher esteem.

Doug Mello, Group Vice President
Manhattan, August 1992

According to Bob Bellhouse, former general manager of the $300-million public communications department of New York Telephone (PubComm), "A few years ago, the public telephone business in the New York Telephone Company was generally considered to be a backwater, leave-it-alone, laissez-faire operation." Under his leadership, however, the department had been transformed into a model of organizational effectiveness. Furthermore, since his move to the corporate engineering department in October 1991, the team he left behind had continued to chart a course of improvement and success. Donna Torres, who had taken over as general manager when Bellhouse left, said in August 1992:

> There isn't any task or any job that is too difficult for these people. You just give them a problem and they solve it. I guess part of the magic of what happened was not only a lot of good, creative, solid technical innovation but also the building of a team [that] is without peer.

COMPANY BACKGROUND

In 1982, AT&T signed a consent decree with the U.S. Justice Department agreeing to divest its local communications networks by January 1, 1984. The divestiture spawned seven new regional Bell operating companies (RBOCs), which were independent but held joint and equal ownership in Bell

---

This case was written by William F. Allen, Darden M.B.A. 1992, under the supervision of Alexander B. Horniman, Professor of Business Administration, and Robert D. Landel, The Henry E. McWane Professor of Business Administration, Darden School, University of Virginia. Copyright © 1992 by the University of Virginia Darden School Foundation, Charlottesville, VA. All rights reserved.

Communications Research (Bellcore), AT&T's former laboratory research division. NYNEX Corporation, one of the seven new RBOCs, provided local service and access to long-distance carriers in the New York and New England regions. Within its area, independent companies that had not been part of the AT&T system, such as Southern New England Telephone Company (SNET), also continued to operate.

In 1992, NYNEX was organized into 11 principal subsidiaries. New York Telephone Company provided telecommunications services within the state of New York; New England Telephone and Telegraph served New England. Other major groups included NYNEX Science & Technology, NYNEX Worldwide Services, and NYNEX Mobile Communications. For financial reporting purposes, revenue and expenses were grouped into five segments. Exhibit 1 contains segment descriptions and selected segment financial data for the 1989–1991 period.

THE PUBLIC COMMUNICATIONS DEPARTMENT

Prior to the divestiture of AT&T, the pay-telephone business was a "regulated stepchild" of the former Bell System companies, according to John Chichester, a PubComm District Manager. Chichester explained:

> The word *profitability* never came [across] the lips of anyone. That's the way AT&T worked. They just poured money into us as they did the many other units within the Bell System. They took it from their profitable entities and put it into the nonprofitable entities. They would just force-feed you with money. . . . It was something in those days they felt they had to do; they had to provide the public with pay telephones. Most regulatory agencies would have crucified them if they ever attempted to stop [providing pay telephones].

At that time, public telephone stations and booths were placed without regard to any strategic implications or profitability. Key telephone operations were divided among other larger departments, which operated basically without any budget constraints.

PubComm was not formally organized as a unified department until late 1978. According to Staff Manager Susie Satran, "One of the problems in the beginning was getting other groups, even within the telephone company, to recognize our existence and our worth." In particular, technical assistance from other departments was difficult to obtain.

Looking back on that period, Bellhouse said he believed

> Morale suffered because the department had been neglected in terms of the resources provided to it. There had been no formal training curriculum for public telephone operations in almost twenty years. We had to completely reinvent training.

Exhibit 1
NYNEX Financial Data
(in millions)

SEGMENT REVENUES

	1991	1990	1989
Telecommunications	$11,138.1	$11,076.2	$11,029.9
Cellular	324.1	310.4	237.4
Publishing	849.2	850.8	815.6
Financial/Real estate	78.9	83.8	57.0
Other operations	838.4	1,260.9	1,055.5
	$13,228.8	$13,582.1	$13,195.4

SEGMENT OPERATING INCOME

	1991	1990	1989
Telecommunications	$1,978.3	$2,407.0	$1,939.5
Cellular	48.5	60.2	48.2
Publishing	47.4	118.1	115.4
Financial/Real estate	27.0	75.7	50.9
Other operations	(169.3)	(374.0)	(120.9)
	$1,608.4	$2,105.3	$1,756.7

SEGMENT DESCRIPTIONS

Telecommunications
Local telephone service, network access to long-distance services, materials management, technical and support services, Bellcore, product development, and marketing.

Cellular
Wireless telecommunications services and products.

Publishing
White and Yellow Pages, telemarketing products and services.

Financial/Real estate
Financial products and services.

Other operations
Information delivery, software, and consulting services.

Source: 1991 NYNEX Annual Report.

INTRODUCTION OF COMPETITION

In 1985 the Federal Communications Commission (FCC) decided to allow private ownership of public telephone stations. Later that year, the Public Service Commission of New York State passed an enabling act that cleared the way for competition in the public telephone business beginning in 1986. A number of competitors quickly entered the business.

By 1988, these competitors, which serviced customer-owned, coin-operated telephones (COCOTs), had captured roughly 14 percent of the New York public telephone market. In many instances, these companies promised to proprietors higher commissions than New York Telephone. The COCOT vendors also generally enjoyed a cost advantage by employing nonunion labor and using cheaper phone equipment. At the same time, COCOT vendors were experimenting with state-of-the-art technology in a few of their stations and offered many features unavailable at New York Telephone stations.

The COCOT vendors were only forced by regulation to maintain the basic 25-cent local call. Unlike New York Telephone, the COCOT vendors could set their own rates for such classes of phone calls as cross-city and long-distance overtime and operator-handled calls. In addition, the COCOT vendors aggressively pursued new locations, often finding very profitable spots that had been neglected by New York Telephone.

At first, New York Telephone simply continued its past practices. According to Chichester:

> We handled competition in those early stages very poorly. We had the Bell mentality that said "No one can come in and take this over from us. We're too good. We know what we're doing. We're the best."

Bellhouse stated later, "We knew competition was occurring, and we didn't know what to do about it."

Because of the lack of information on revenues and expenses, PubComm had no idea how much it earned or spent. The department focused mainly on repairing and installing phones. The sales effort consisted of sitting back and waiting for the phone to ring with new orders.

The COCOT vendors made significant inroads into the business in the first few years of competition, but New York Telephone then stopped the hemorrhaging. By 1992, it was losing only about 1 percent of market share a year. However, Chichester noted that the COCOT vendors "were here to stay and have made our lives very interesting."

THE BELLHOUSE TASK FORCE

In June 1986, George Barletta, New York Telephone's vice president of customer services, assembled a six-person task force to examine the feasibility of creating a divested, lightly regulated public telephone subsidiary. Bob

Bellhouse was brought in to lead the team, which included three people on loan from other departments and two permanent PubComm assignees.

For more than a year, the team conducted an iterative business case analysis of the public telephone business. The team consistently concluded that the cost of taking the business out on its own was too high and that the public telephone business was too tightly entwined with the New York Telephone network to separate it. In performing the study, however, the team introduced a very powerful notion. Bellhouse stated:

> We discovered how to run that department as a business. In other words, we adopted a mindset that said you don't really have to legally set up a separate subsidiary. You can close your eyes and pretend that you are a separate subsidiary and run it like a business. And that's what we did.

The next two years were spent developing the mindset and tools necessary to compete.

In February 1988, Bellhouse was promoted to general manager of Pub-Comm. At the time, PubComm was losing money, and it was mired in service problems that left New York Telephone highly vulnerable to its competitors. Bellhouse was given three years to make the business profitable and to fix the service problems. Two of the most pressing problems were vandalism and fraud. As Chichester noted, "We happen to have New York City, which is the most difficult place in the country to do business in pay telephones."

TAKING ON THE VANDALS AND THIEVES

> These days, New Yorkers who want to use a pay phone to reach out and touch someone usually end up wanting to punch someone.
>
> Don Broderick
> *New York Post,* April 18, 1990

The temptation posed by millions of dollars worth of quarters sitting on the streets of New York had proved to be irresistible to New York's highly creative criminal element. Chichester estimated that between 150,000 and 200,000 acts of pay-telephone vandalism were committed each year, with roughly 15,000 stations accounting for most of the damage. Thousands of phone stations were blown up beyond recognition. According to Bellhouse,

> The deteriorating service of public telephones wasn't because New York Telephone was not fulfilling its responsibilities. It was largely because there was an organized group of people who were vandalizing the phones to get the money out of them or to keep our phones in poor working condition.

As the crippling combination of vandalism and the service repair crisis threatened the PubComm business, New York Telephone established a campaign to increase awareness of the vandalism problem among city officials, community boards, and law enforcement agencies. The company's efforts were aided by the media, with which NYNEX's department of external affairs enjoyed a very good relationship. In addition, newspaper and television organizations were willing to cover the stories, because the vandalism and fraud made for good copy. Bellhouse noted that the coverage "served our purpose because it enabled us to get the attention of the police department, the judicial system, [and] the courts." Bellhouse also met with local community boards and the district attorney's office to increase the pressure on the courts to hand out stiff, meaningful sentences to phone vandals.

In addition, PubComm redirected its own security unit to catching vandals. Previously, PubComm had relied on the corporate security group, but it was not in a position to deal with public telephone vandalism. The department also engaged a professional security agency to focus on increasing the number of arrests and convictions. The security group used contacts in local precincts to aid its effort. The in-house security group proved very effective, snaring an average of about 90 people per month.

PubComm also used technology to attack the constantly evolving stream of vandalism and fraud engendered by the very creative and adaptive thieves of New York. For example, after the 1987 release of a popular movie that included a scene showing people how to make free calls by grounding the phone with a pin pushed through the transmitter, New York Telephone found itself replacing 190,000 handsets per year at $30 per piece. To solve the problem, Pubcomm developed a stainless-steel cover for the transmitter unit. The thieves responded by breaking the steel cord and inserting a straight pin into the cord to ground the phone. Moreover, the vandals quickly discovered that the pay telephone stored the coins inserted while the pin was in the cable, and, when the pin was removed, all the change was released into the coin-return bucket. The PubComm Department eventually developed a $30 circuit isolator that eliminated the grounding vulnerability.

PubComm tackled the problem of long-distance phone fraud by working directly with its pay-telephone equipment manufacturer. Enterprising thieves were making up to $2,000 a day stealing calling-card numbers and selling time to people who wanted to make international calls. Places such as Grand Central Station and Port Authority bus terminals were ideal for the operation because they were air conditioned, well equipped with phones, and experienced transient traffic. Some people would bring their families to these locations and spend the day making illegal calls to relatives overseas at well below market rates. Other criminals discovered how to dial into the switchboards of large New York City businesses and then get an outside line to make long-distance calls.

PubComm used an electronic device to monitor these locations and gather the data necessary to solve the problems. Armed with the dialing sequences and routines being used by the criminals, PubComm approached the supplier of the electronic phones and requested that the software be changed to block certain dialing sequences. Within 60 days, the company had successfully installed the new software.

COMMITTING TO QUALITY

> Quality is not a program or a buzzword at NYNEX. It is a way of life. It is the key to achieving sustained excellence over time in satisfying customers, share owners, and fellow employees.
>
> William C. Ferguson
> Chairman of the Board and Chief Executive Officer
> NYNEX, March 6, 1991

The executives of New York Telephone's parent believed in the importance of quality. The challenge in 1990 was to spread that belief to all levels of the organization. NYNEX Chairman Ferguson approached this challenge by sending a letter in Spring 1990 to NYNEX managers introducing the Malcolm Baldridge Award as an award worthy of pursuit by the company and its employees. In time, the company began to focus on the components within the Baldridge Award.

The turning point for PubComm came in the fall of 1990 when New York Telephone conducted a "Strategic Quality Planning Seminar" (SQPS). Because of their unique synergies, the public communications and operator services departments were selected for the coordinated pilot run of the seminar. According to Bellhouse, the seminar "gave us an opportunity to get away for a few days and focus in on quality in a way that had not been done before at New York Telephone."

The managers spent a lot of time talking about processes. New York Telephone had traditionally focused on internal results, without recognizing the importance of work and social processes. Managers also learned about quality management tools such as pareto analysis and fishbone diagrams. As Bellhouse observed:

> During the post-SQPS period, our language changed. We were ready for it, and it occurred just at the right time. We started talking among ourselves using the words that you find in a quality pamphlet. It was natural. . . . It didn't feel artificial.

He also noted:

> A crucially important block of time in this seminar was delivered by a consultant to Florida Power & Light. This module was called "Voice of the Customer." We talked about all the different ways that you should be listen-

ing to your customer—ranging from measurements, technical systems, what you read in the newspaper, [to] what your employees can discern—and that became a major change for us. We started asking customers in a different way than we had before.

This new approach led to increases in customer satisfaction. For example, PubComm established a system of calling its proprietary customers and informing them that their phones were fixed. At the same time, these customers were asked if they were satisfied with the repair and the service in general. When the program was first started, the satisfaction rate was only about 70 percent. The customer satisfaction rate in 1992 was more than 97 percent.

Several steps were taken to increase customer satisfaction. Technical training was provided to the technicians. In addition, the dispatch system was improved so that the technicians had more information about the problems when they arrived at the location. Previously, technicians conducted rudimentary tests but often found nothing wrong. Only after subsequent calls from the customer were the problems properly diagnosed. The PubComm department also worked with the purchasing organization to improve or replace substandard phone parts.

Bellhouse considered the focus on training vital to PubComm's quality improvement.

> The Strategic Quality Planning Seminar was so important. We were so enthused about it. We quickly put every management person in the department through that training. We didn't bring in trainers. We trained ourselves. We rolled the training down. So my directors and I conducted the training for the next group, and then they trained their people, so we had a sense of shared understanding throughout the department.

Bellhouse summed up the success story of the quality movement by stating:

> There was no golden relay, no magic bullet, no one thing that fixed it. It was all of those things—managed not from the top but from the middle—and empowerment of those people—just giving them broad goals and a lot of training and coaching.

EMBRACING TECHNOLOGY

> Right now, I believe that New York Telephone is on the leading edge of technology in the pay-telephone industry across the country.

John Chichester
August 1992

In addition to dealing with the vandalism and service problems, Bellhouse had recognized early in his appointment that PubComm needed to decrease costs and position itself to move quickly as new customer requirements arose. PubComm decided that it needed new technology to compete against the product offerings of the COCOT vendors in 1987, but it took three years for New York Telephone to master the technology it envisioned.

Collecting the Right Data

Prior to the Bellhouse era, the public communications department had little useful data to guide its planning and decision making. Chichester recalled:

> We used to manage the business without ever having data. It's not that we didn't want to use data. I don't think we had the systems. We didn't have the people.

PubComm significantly improved its analysis of maintenance data by taking advantage of a corporate system that had been originally intended for marketing analysis and modifying it for a specialized maintenance application. The Strategic Quality Planning Seminar reinforced this notion of managing from data. Chichester noted that "when we started basing our decisions on factual data, it was a big improvement. You can't fix something unless you know what's broken and how bad it's broken."

One of the first requests to Bellhouse by the sales organization was to develop a system to track profitability. After several frustrating false starts with consultants, PubComm developed a successful partnership with the corporate comptroller's office. Together, they developed the coin contribution model to capture revenue, expenses, and profitability along several different dimensions, including by phone station, group, building, and account. The model, an activity-based costing system, focused on cost drivers as a more accurate means of allocating overhead costs.

According to the sales manager, Jay Ruiz, without the coin contribution model, "we could not operate in today's environment." In the past, PubComm had offered standard commission rates to proprietors. The advent of competition, which opened commission rates up for negotiation, added a complexity that could only be tackled with relevant and reliable data. PubComm had to seek stable, long-term sources of revenue and profit. From 1990 to 1992, approximately 2,300 phones were identified as unprofitable, and half of them were taken out of service. The remainder were left operative primarily because of public safety concerns. The New York Telephone Company recognized the value of the coin contribution model by selecting it as a winner in its Technical Excellence Program.

Retrofitting Phones

Technological improvements were also made on the phones themselves. Virtually all of New York Telephone's public telephones were Western Electric 1C/2C electromechanical sets, which were equipped with mechanical coin chutes. These chutes were highly susceptible to both failure and vandalism. New York Telephone could not afford the investment necessary to replace the Western Electric sets entirely with the new technology offered by the COCOT vendors. Unfortunately, no off-the-shelf technology existed to upgrade the New York Telephone pay phones.

To solve this problem, a cross-functional team of managers from New York Telephone and New England Telephone assembled in 1987. This team spent two days designing the current equipment into the public telephone of the future. The team divided technical requirements for transforming the current phones into two categories. The first contained the minimum requirements for improving internal components. Key requirements were a free-fall electronic coin chute, remote self-diagnostics, automatic trouble reporting to a host computer, remote programmability, coin-box accounting to allow collection scheduling, fraud prevention, and receiver amplification.[1] The new phone also had to operate with the standard central office line and without any external power source.

The second category of requirements called for a modular design to allow for the offering of new high-end customer features as the market demanded them. The final design used a bus architecture to allow for this addition of features.

After the meeting, a request for information was sent to 50 vendors, asking them to submit a set of detailed functional and technical specifications to match the team's design. At the time, an industry journal commented, "NYNEX has asked for the impossible." Several vendors responded, however, and Mars Electronics International (MEI), a vending equipment division of M&M/Mars Company, was chosen because of its reputation for quality and experience in developing custom applications.

The retrofit project progressed slowly. The prototypes received in 1988 did not work properly, and, in early 1989, a trial of 200 stations was also unsuccessful. Senior management grew increasingly impatient with the lack of improvement in the "customer trouble report rate," a common telephone service measurement. Bellhouse and his team were under great pressure to cancel or downsize the project, but by the end of 1989, management decided the technology was ready for large-scale deployment. Unfortunately, the deployment came at a very difficult time for New York Telephone.

---

[1]John Bonczek and John Chichester, "New Tricks for Old Telephones," *Telephone Engineer & Management*, July 15, 1992, p. 25.

In August 1989, the International Brotherhood of Electrical Workers and the Communication Workers of America, which represented approximately 35,000 New York Telephone craftspeople, had staged a walkout. The main stumbling block in the negotiations had involved employee contributions to medical benefit plans. The company was gripped by a bitter and divisive four-month strike. Many incidents of violence and vandalism punctuated the growing rift between management and craftspeople. In response to the service crisis that ensued, management personnel worked 12- to 16-hour shifts as they assumed the maintenance and collection responsibilities.

The 1989 strike generated a serious morale problem for the Bellhouse organization. The bitter nature of the strike, combined with the deepening service crisis and long working hours, created a stressful working environment. The logjam was finally broken in December, but management morale sank at the news of concessions. Although NYNEX Chairman William Ferguson maintained that, overall, the company had actually got more than it had sought, some managers believed they had been abandoned by senior management.

Because of the labor strike, the new retrofit technology was installed by inexperienced management people, and the installation of the 10,000 retrofit units exacerbated the service crisis. Chichester noted:

> There was a key word that was missing from our perspective—*patience*. We were attempting to fix a service crisis by deploying this technology quickly as opposed to sitting back and making sure it was right.

When the striking technicians returned to work in December, they were confronted with service problems involving a technology they had never seen. The department immediately conducted a mass training campaign to educate the work force about the new technology. In the wake of the settlement, craftspeople and management held many meetings and conferences to clear the air, resolve differences, and reopen lines of communication. In the summer of 1991, a full year ahead of schedule, the unions and NYNEX negotiated a four-year extension of the labor contract.

By the end of 1991, New York Telephone had installed 23,000 retrofit kits and another 24,000 stand-alone chutes.[2] The breakthrough in limiting vandalism and improving customer service as a result of the deployment was extraordinary. On the retrofitted stations, vandals were no longer able to ground the transmitter leads. The self-diagnostics feature allowed PubComm to solve problems before they were reported. The average collection amount per station increased 18 percent because of improvements in collection scheduling, which resulted in substantial reduction of the collection expenses.

---

[2]A stand-alone chute was a modification of the pay station that, while improving service, did not contain the full complement of features deployed with the retrofit kits.

Key internal signs of the improved quality of customer service included the following:

- Total troubles cleared reduced by 30 percent.
- Number of full coin boxes decreased by 40 percent.[3]
- Number of stations out of service longer than 24 hours dropped by 38 percent.
- False alarm dispatches reduced by 32 percent.[4]

Quality Confidence Agreements

During the retrofit operation, PubComm discovered the importance of holding its suppliers accountable for the quality of equipment shipments. Although the new technology was improving customer service, the failure rate was generating some concern among management. The failure rate for the stand-alone chute reached 40 percent during the first developmental trials. PubComm negotiated a quality confidence agreement with its supplier to help curb the chute quality problem.

The agreement, the first of its kind at NYNEX, required the supplier to replace defective parts and to remit a $75 rebate for each defect above a 4-percent acceptable failure rate. The rebate amount represented an estimate of the total handling costs incurred by PubComm as a result of a defective component. Chichester noted:

> When people at NYNEX first hear about this arrangement, they focus on the money aspect, but the money is only a device, a way to put teeth in the program. We'd prefer that our suppliers not have to pay us anything—that they always would meet our quality goals.[5]

After the quality confidence agreement was signed in July 1991, the failure rate for the stand-alone chute decreased 87 percent and remained close to the acceptable 4-percent rate outlined in the agreement. Future agreements were to focus on cutting the failure rate even further.

Other Technological Innovations

In 1989 PubComm received another Technical Excellence Program citation for its development of a robotic key system. The robot prepared a shackle

---

[3] Phone stations automatically become inoperative when the coin box is full.
[4] Bonczek and Chichester, "New Tricks for Old Telephones," p. 26.
[5] "Supplier to NYNEX: 'We'll Put Our Money Where Our Mouth Is,'" *Impact*, Summer 1992, p. 6.

of keys for each technician based on the collection schedule for the day. The introduction of the robotic system eliminated many labor-intensive positions.

In 1992, the department was testing a new electronic lock system that would allow technicians to carry a small handheld computer device. The necessary codes for opening the locks would be downloaded from the host computer back at the collection center.

PubComm also used technology to change the way the customer pays for service. The first effort was coinless, or "charge-a-call," stations. The number of coinless phones deployed throughout the state had been level at 4,400 for several years. In 1989, however, PubComm replaced 700 coin telephones on the New York City sidewalks with the coinless variety. Bellhouse observed that the coinless phone was

> the first significant shift in our product mix. Up until that point, we had basically said, like the Model T Ford, "you can have any kind of phone you want as long as it's this one." We began an evolution to change the product mix away from coins.

The change-card phones represented the second phase of that evolution. This new type of station accepted only small credit-card-like cards that had been purchased in advance in $5 denominations. PubComm was hoping to deploy 3,000 change-card phones a year. Donna Torres, who estimated that at some point half of all pay phones would be change-card phones, commented:

> This whole business is changing very drastically. Change card is a technology three years ago we thought we'd never do. It's all over Europe and it's all over Japan; everyone has it. We are the first company in the United States to have it. That's something that could change the face of the way public communications looks in the streets of New York over the course of the next five years.

"CATCHBALLING" THE BUSINESS PLAN

> Our Department Business Plan is the sum of the ideas of all of our people. We hoped that a "top down" vision would couple with "bottoms up" practical knowledge and creativity. And that's what happened.
>
> Public Communications Business Unit Plan 1991–95
> September 18, 1991

The 1991 business plan for PubComm was developed through a "catchball" approach. First, Bellhouse and his four district managers discussed the NYNEX vision statement, mission statement, and corporate strategy. Next, the planning team focused on the New York Telephone mission, vision, and values statements contained in Exhibit 2. PubComm then chose to concentrate on four of

Exhibit 2
New York Telephone's Business and Goals

MISSION STATEMENT

New York Telephone will provide quality communication services at prices viewed as reasonable by our customers, with competitive earnings, in a corporate environment that encourages employee excellence and development, making our company, in the eyes of its employees, the greatest company to work for in America.

VISION STATEMENT

New York Telephone is a member of the NYNEX family of companies, a leader in the information industry through the combined efforts and skills of all employees.

- Quality is our hallmark. We profitably market quality products and services and anticipate opportunities to serve our customers better.
- The heart of our business is an information network driven by highly sophisticated technology.
- We are financially strong. Each segment of our business makes a profitable contribution to the competitive earnings essential for our long-term success.
- Individual leadership is manifest throughout our company, inspiring excellence based on mutual trust and respect.
- We have a common commitment to our corporate mission, goals, and objectives, and achieve them through individual and team initiatives which are recognized and rewarded on the basis of performance.
- We rely on open communication and teamwork as our style of management and foster individual growth and opportunity.
- We demand integrity of ourselves in all that we do.
- Through the day-to-day efforts of every employee, we constantly earn our corporate reputation for responsible leadership in the eyes of our customers, our investors, and the communities we serve.

(continued on next page)

(continued)

- We have transitioned into a company that has learned to adapt and flourish in a competitive environment.

VALUES

New York Telephone's values embrace the highest levels of customer satisfaction, quality, integrity, respect for our people, and commitment to communities in which we operate.

New York Telephone's ten corporate strategies: "Employee Communications and Trust," "Meet Customer Requirements," "Manage Down the Costs," and "Make Quality a Strategic Tool." In addition, a fifth corporate strategy, "Improving Earnings Growth," was addressed as a result of implementing the other four strategies.

A planning team next created a mission statement for PubComm to serve as a framework for pursuing the strategies. PubComm dedicated itself to becoming the premier public telephone service in the State of New York. The department had already developed an extensive understanding of what customers required from public telephones. Thus, the 1991 business plan concluded, "simply stated, the public wants convenient, low-cost, clean, simple to use, working phones; and agents want commissions and hassle-free service."

The planning team defined "premier" in terms of the achievement of "future state objectives" congruent with the four corporate strategic goals and the identified customer requirements. These objectives, presented in Exhibit 3, guided the development of detailed action plans to move the department to where it wanted to be.

Once the core strategies and future state objectives were identified, the district managers were allowed considerable flexibility in developing their own business plans. Each district contained different organizational functions. As the planning team observed:

> There are now four separate but interrelated district business plans. Together, they form a mosaic which, as it is completed, will bring us much closer to our objectives.

The district plans were the product of the inputs of every level of management. The district managers built on the ideas of the people closest to their customers. More than 200 individual action plans supported the overall busi-

---

Exhibit 3
Public Communications Department Objectives

MISSION STATEMENT

We pledge to be the premier Public Telephone Company in New York State no matter who enters the field. . . . We're here to stay.

FUTURE STATE OBJECTIVES

When benchmarked against customer requirements and other public telephone operations, New York Telephone Public Communications will:

1. employ at every level and in every position the most professional and valued employees.
2. have the best understanding of customers' needs, anticipate their requirements, and provide solutions [that] exceed their expectations.
3. utilize the best data and analysis to guide our decisions.
4. provide the most reliable station equipment and network.
5. provide the fastest repair service with perfect customer satisfaction.
6. provide the quickest installation service with perfect customer satisfaction.
7. operate with the lowest material costs.
8. benefit from the highest degree of brand recognition and customer/agent satisfaction.
9. ensure that Public Communications employees are the most enthusiastic, valued, and satisfied employees.

---

ness plan. Each plan represented a proposal and commitment from a specific management person. All managers were held accountable for the implementation of those plans, through the performance appraisal process.

OPERATION DESERT STORM

In April 1991, an interruption in Bellhouse's stewardship threatened the momentum of the PubComm organization. Bellhouse, a lieutenant colonel in the U.S. Army Reserve, was summoned to active duty to participate in the protection of Kurdish refugees in northern Iraq following the conclusion of Operation Desert Storm. Chichester stated that, by the time Bellhouse departed, "Things were on the move back into the right direction." Nevertheless, some uncertainty arose over how the department would operate in Bellhouse's absence. He had been able to gain the support and respect of upper management and was able to accomplish many things by virtue of his contacts and power. Rich Chapman, an area operations manager, said, for instance, "I lost a lot. I relied a lot on Bob to use his name to push things, to get things done. I lost my hook."

Speaking for his district organization, Chichester said, "We kind of thought we were going to head downhill." Susie Satran, staff manager, on the other hand, observed that "because [Bellhouse] had structured the organization as such a team, there wasn't any kind of fear that everything was going to fall apart." Chichester added that "Bellhouse had a lot of confidence in us. He stated that many, many times."

Jim Parla, one of the district managers, was chosen to be the acting general manager in Bellhouse's absence. Chichester noted:

> Parla was very open-minded. He listened to the people that did know, that did have the answers. He wasn't one to shove things down our throat. He left us kind of alone. We did what we had to do. We had some fears, but they went away quickly.

In the words of Jay Ruiz, sales manager, "everything moved smoothly" while Bellhouse was gone.

Bellhouse returned in July and was thrown a big welcome-home party by his department. In recognition of their performance in building the team and sustaining the process of continuous improvement, all of the district managers received on-the-spot awards.

REFLECTIONS ON SUCCESS

Bellhouse cited three important approaches that guided his success in turning around the Public Communications business: gathering the right information, exploiting technology, and taking care of his people.

Bellhouse asserted:

> Information that we needed was initially almost nonexistent. The information that we could get had little credibility. So improving the quality of the information and designing that information in a way that it was not a stick—not something that we used to beat up on each other about, but the information was designed and delivered in a way that management at each level got the information that they could use.

Since they knew what the goal was and now they had information and they had been trained how to use information—what kind of steps to take— it worked. It took a long, long time to build the information systems to do that. Some of it was trial and error. Sometimes you thought you had good information and it ended up you didn't, so that was really a struggle.

Bellhouse noted that he had

an intrinsic belief that we could achieve a great deal through an integrated system of technological improvements. There was a school of thought in the company that said, "Don't do that! The way you should manage that department is with labor and leave everything plain and simple. Don't overcomplicate things." I don't believe that is the right answer. So we advanced the state of technology on a whole host of things. And we did this in a way, while it's not complete and it's not perfect, that these technological mechanizations and data improvements were all interconnected. We didn't do a coin contribution model just because we wanted to understand profitability. We did it because it gave you a whole host of activity-based cost information. For example, it gave you a new way of looking at maintenance costs you couldn't see the old way. On the other hand, we chose not to do bar coding—we postponed it— because we didn't understand how it would fit in. We didn't understand how it would connect into all the other things, so we decided we were not ready to deploy that yet.

Bellhouse had recognized that he had a tremendous employee morale problem on his hands:

Morale in the department had suffered greatly over the years. It was poor when I arrived because of isolation, stagnation, and weak leadership at the upper levels of the department. Only two of the top eight managers in the department then were still in their positions in 1991. On the other hand, we promoted a record number of excellent people throughout the department and brought in people with fresh perspectives from the outside.

Morale also suffered because the department had been neglected corporately in terms of the resources provided to it. There had been no formal coin-telephone training curriculum for that business in almost 20 years. We had to completely reinvent training.

We had to find ways to make people feel better about their jobs [and to] feel better about their successes. We had to proclaim success to ourselves as well as to upper management to restore that vitality that is in our department now. We did this by local recognition programs and by successfully competing for corporate excellence awards.

During the difficult times, the New York Telephone Company was extremely critical of the department, threatening to go out of the business or threatening to downsize it to an absolute minimum number of phones that they could get by with in terms of the Public Service Commission. We reported results on a monthly basis, and every month when the numbers weren't right, it was crucifixion time again. And it was hard to maintain the long view. Some of the things we did had a fairly shallow learning curve. You had to achieve a critical mass of technology out in the field in order to gain the benefits.

At the time Bellhouse was orchestrating the turnaround, several anonymous allegations of wrongdoing by members of his department were submitted to the Office of Ethics and Business Conduct. Bellhouse noted how important it was to protect his people:

> There were a lot of investigations going on at that time—really unpleasant stuff. While we were trying to fix the service and improve the department, others were making anonymous accusations that could quite literally destroy people's careers. My philosophy was: I believe in you; I will do everything in my power, to extreme lengths, to protect you—not to protect you because you've done something wrong, but because I know you, and I know you haven't done anything wrong. And what I need you to do, because you are the expert, is to equip me with information so that I can then go and do what I need to do with my supervisors.

REFLECTIONS ON LEADERSHIP

PubComm's district manager, John Chichester, a highly decorated Vietnam veteran, believed that Bellhouse's military background helped him as a leader. Chichester stated, "I think it teaches leadership better than anything in the world."

Commenting on his military background, Bellhouse said:

> Some people misread that. A lot of people think I went to West Point. I did not. I graduated from Hofstra's ROTC[6] program. My military background does have a big part, but in a way that a lot of people don't know, because I don't talk about it very much. When I was a second lieutenant in Germany, I was a platoon leader in an armored cavalry division. I made a lot of really big mistakes; no one got hurt, but I made a lot of mistakes that, when I look back on them now, I feel ashamed. I can put it in perspective. My college education did not equip me for that, so I made mistakes and as a result was transferred out of that unit to a headquarters organization. At headquarters, I did very, very well. I stayed in the Reserve program and have had a great military career. It was a good learning environment, because while I made mistakes there, I was allowed to get past them and grow. I didn't have to carry them with me. Aside from that, I think my military experience keeps my head clear, because it gives me a separate organizational environment in which to participate.

---

[6]Reserve Officers Training Corps.

Summing up his experience at PubComm, Bellhouse stated, "In my career, I have never been as fully engaged as I was when I was there." He believed that he gained much insight into his roles as leader and manager:

> You can learn from everybody around here, but you've got to have that trust; you've got to have that communication. You've got to think of each other as real people, not just an empty suit or "the boss." You've got to feel comfortable with being wrong and letting people tell you when you are wrong.
>
> You've got to have ears, and then you have to respond to what you see, not just react to what the numbers say. One of the nice things about that department is that you get to see your customers all the time. You could see if people were happy with the product or not. You get a different set of eyes. Believe me, when the phones are not working, you see people slamming down handsets.
>
> You've got to have fun at work. You've got to somehow not get bogged down in a defensive behavior of finger pointing. My philosophy is to force ourselves to fully discuss those things and then make a decision and move on. People are not permitted to attack others. It's just not in the acceptable set of behaviors. If you have a good idea—great. If you have a problem—you folks had better talk about that and get it resolved, because that's what is needed to solve the problem.
>
> You've got to have a real clear vision. You have to have this burning passion of the way you want it to be. You have to test everything out against that. It's all got to fit together. It has to be internally consistent. All the pieces have to fit.

THE NATIONAL GYPSUM COMPANY (A):
THE GOLD BOND DIVISION

Peter Browning, the newly appointed president of the Gold Bond division of National Gypsum Company (NGC), faced a difficult situation. The operating performance of Gold Bond had declined in the previous three years and was expected to continue its downward slide in the foreseeable future. Its core gypsum wallboard business, which was closely tied to the housing market, was suffering because of creeping recession and intensifying price competition. At the same time, the $1.1 billion in junk bonds on the balance sheet of the firm's parent were creating pressure to generate steady cash flows to support the demanding principal and interest payments. Browning wanted to make sure that the payment schedule was not a drain on the financial resources that were badly needed to improve his division's long-term competitive viability.

Browning was keenly aware, however, that the strategic and operating repositioning of Gold Bond could not be achieved without substantially altering the company's culture. Since coming to Gold Bond only six months earlier in February 1989, Browning had realized that there was a lack of communication up and down the hierarchy as well as across functional areas. Employees described the company as "autocratic"—a work environment where they had little sense of participation. Additionally, there were layers of bureaucracy that hindered the organization's ability to respond to the structural changes occurring in the gypsum wallboard industry (see Exhibit 1 for organizational chart).

The challenge, in short, was to reconceive the gypsum business and motivate people to embrace the necessary but hard changes that would have to precede the implementation of a new strategy. But, in a 64-year-old tradition-bound organization that had for a long time been a comfortable second in an oligopolistic industry, changing the culture was easier said than done. Browning knew that there were many sacred cows in Gold Bond and any

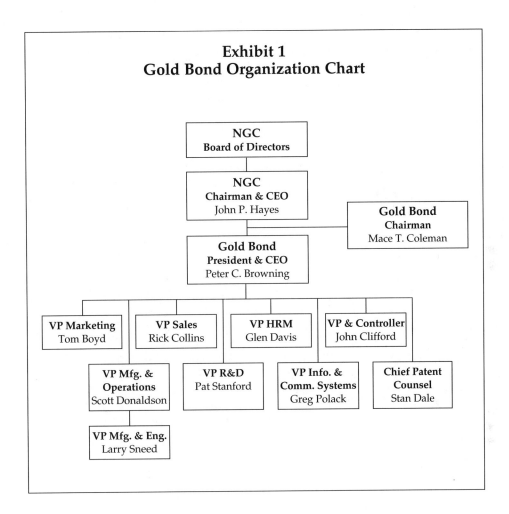

Exhibit 1
Gold Bond Organization Chart

NGC
Board of Directors

NGC
Chairman & CEO
John P. Hayes

Gold Bond
Chairman
Mace T. Coleman

Gold Bond
President & CEO
Peter C. Browning

VP Marketing
Tom Boyd

VP Sales
Rick Collins

VP HRM
Glen Davis

VP & Controller
John Clifford

VP Mfg. &
Operations
Scott Donaldson

VP R&D
Pat Stanford

VP Info. &
Comm. Systems
Greg Polack

Chief Patent
Counsel
Stan Dale

VP Mfg. & Eng.
Larry Sneed

actions that violated the tacit understandings of longtimers were likely to backfire.

Only 48 years old, Browning had a reputation for getting results and was already a veteran at turning around ailing businesses. Still, he understood that the massive changes necessary at Gold Bond would take all the skill and finesse he could muster.

PARENT COMPANY BACKGROUND

Product History

National Gypsum Company was incorporated in Delaware on August 9, 1925. It was based on a new formulation for wallboard that was fortuitously developed by three business associates, Joe Haggarty, Melvin Baker, and Clarence Williams.[1] Although lighter and stronger than anything else then on the market, the product by itself was not enough for business success in an industry already dominated by the two large producers: U.S. Gypsum and Universal Gypsum. Because wallboard was a low-margin, commodity business, merchants were usually not enthusiastic about stocking a new entrant's products for fear of offending their big suppliers and further eroding their own profit margins. NGC overcame its vulnerability to both price competition and distribution bottlenecks by offering its wallboard only through lumberyards and by positioning it as a premium product. Exclusive dealerships, NGC figured, would encourage lumberyards to back the product with sales support, ultimately making it more successful. Moreover, NGC supported its claim of superior quality by including in every shipment of wallboard a "Gold Bond" that offered $5,000 to anyone who could prove that NGC's assertions about its product were untrue. These steps paid off, and by 1927 business was good enough to commission a second plant in Michigan. Gold Bond became the trademark for the company and was later assumed as the name for the division that made the firm's gypsum products.

Threatened by this emerging competitor, and unable to inhibit its advance through competitive measures in the market, the incumbents U.S. Gypsum and Universal Gypsum brought patent infringement lawsuits against NGC. The issue concerned the production process and was controversial, but in the end NGC was found to be the guilty party in both cases. To keep the company from going bankrupt, Baker negotiated with U.S. Gypsum and Universal to allow him to continue using the patented process at the cost of 8 percent of sales—at a time when margins were paper thin anyway. With margins under additional strain because of royalty payments to the big producers, Baker realized that NGC had to continually seek to be the low-cost producer to remain viable for any length of time. To implement this objective, he felt it was necessary to control the supply of raw materials (i.e., vertically integrate the operations), locate plants close to both quarries and markets to minimize transportation costs, and run efficient plants at full capacity. In addition, in anticipation of eventual maturing of the wallboard business, it was considered prudent to diversify into new segments of the wallboard market as well as into nongypsum-based products.

Through the Great Depression and in the decades thereafter, Baker made a number of opportunistic acquisitions inside the gypsum industry. By the 1960s, NGC had become a highly integrated, national operator in the wallboard business, owning quarries, docks, ships, plants, and paper mills. At the same time, the company launched an aggressive acquisitive-diversification program, which continued well into the 1980s. Viewing NGC broadly as being

---

[1]See M. Bockmon, *Turning Points: The National Gypsum Story,* Dallas: Tayor Publishing, 1990, for a description of the early history of National Gypsum Company.

in the "shelter" business, management moved into products such as lime, acoustic and ceramic tile, metal lath, paper, cement, fiberboard, wood insulation, vinyl wall coverings, drapes, shower curtains, aluminum doors and windows, and fine wallpaper.[2] Then, in 1984, NGC entered the business of building "complete shelters" by acquiring The Austin Company, a large design/engineering/construction firm that built everything from factories to office buildings. In spite of extensive diversification, however, gypsum wallboard products remained at NGC's core.

By 1985, NGC was organized into several highly autonomous divisions. Cyclicality in earnings was subdued somewhat by the fact that the three largest divisions served markets with distinctly different business cycles. The flagship Gold Bond Building Products division, for instance, made half its sales to the new-residential market and the rest to commercial and renovation markets. The American Olean Tile division, by contrast, obtained only 15 percent of its revenues from the new-residential market. Finally, the third-largest unit, The Austin Company, was involved primarily in industrial and institutional construction and had a negligible stake in residential housing. Much credit for this diversification to stabilize earnings was attributed to John Hayes, who had risen through the ranks as a salesperson to become CEO in 1983. As an analyst noted, "John Hayes has done very well at trying to diversify the company from being extremely cyclical, and broadening the base of the company by picking up Austin Construction Company. They've taken tile and made it very successful, and I think National Gypsum is a very well managed company. He has good people under him, and he's good at picking good people and getting the best out of them."[3] Another analyst pointed out the aggressive management of the firm's different businesses: "They've streamlined the wallpaper, and they got rid of their ceiling tile which was not competitive. They acquired the office company which is probably going to work out to be a good move . . . they've been doing some things right too."[4]

A Hostile Environment

Not everyone on Wall Street was impressed with management, however. One concerned follower of the construction industry observed, "They're more concerned about making bigger and bigger companies and acquisitions than doing their best to increase shareholder wealth. National Gypsum has made a ridiculous acquisition by buying an engineering and construction firm, the Austin Company. . . . they just get bigger for the sake of getting bigger, and there is no reason for it. . . . They generate enormous amounts of cash and then throw it in the wastebasket by buying silly companies like Masonite

[2]Ibid.
[3]*The Wall Street Transcript*, 1985, p. 78011.
[4]Ibid, p. 78013.

(acquired by U.S. Gypsum) and the Austin company, when they could repurchase their own shares and generate as good if not a better return than making acquisitions."[5]

This comment was reflective of the perception that managers of huge firms squandered shareholder wealth by making ill-fitting acquisitions, and it was often used as a pretext for hostile takeover bids. NGC, in many people's view, had set up itself for such an action. The relatively stable housing cycles of the early 1980s raised expectations about steady future cash flows and were bound to attract suitors.[6] In fact, the view that NGC may have been spread too thin, coupled with the public facts that NGC was highly diversified and had low debt, fueled a rumor that a hostile bid by Canada's Belzberg brothers was imminent.[7]

The threat of takeover, and the desire to retain control of the company, led a management group, headed by Hayes, to make a preemptive bid for NGC in November 1985. The initial offer of $49 per share, or $1.1 billion, was considered to be low by many observers, although some felt it was justified because of the potentially costly liability arising from asbestos-related litigation.[8] Following a handful of shareholder suits and a brief bidding war with Wickes Company, the incumbent management completed a leveraged buyout of NGC in April 1986. Each publicly held share of NGC's common stock was converted into the right to receive $46 in cash and $44 stated face amount of a new issue of 15.5-percent subordinated redeemable discount debentures due 2004. Aside from cash already on the balance sheet, and the discount debentures mentioned above, financing for the merger came from a revolving credit agreement, the sale of $350-million principal amount of 14.5-percent senior subordinated debentures due 2001, and the proceeds from the sale of the capital stock of Aancor.

Technically, the buyout was a merger between NGC and Aancor Holdings. The latter was a shell company incorporated in Delaware specifically for this transaction. All of NGC's issued and outstanding shares were

---

[5]Ibid, p. 78011.

[6]As John Hayes, CEO and chairman of NGC, noted, "In recent years, some fundamental changes have occurred in mortgage financing that promise to reduce the volatility in new-home construction. These changes include the rapid growth of the secondary mortgage market and the introduction of adjustable-rate mortgages. Smoothing out the new-residential construction cycle will keep more consumers, builders and suppliers in the market, thus reducing the economic and social costs of severe housing swings." Source: J. P. Hayes, *National Gypsum Company: The Power of Balance,* New York: The Newcomen Society of the United States, 1985.

[7]*Wall Street Journal,* November 26, 1985, p. 3, and *Business Week,* December 9, 1985, p. 44.

[8]The company, like U.S. Gypsum, was once a major producer of asbestos building products and had been sued in more than 100 cases by schools, hospitals, cities, and other building owners. Plaintiffs were seeking to recover the billions of dollars it cost to remove potentially cancer-causing asbestos from their buildings.

owned by Aancor, and all of the of the outstanding stock of Aancor was held by certain current and former managers of NGC and certain institutional and other investors. More than 50 percent of the shares were held by a corporation with long-term investment ties to NGC. The company, Lafarge Coppee, S.A., was a publicly held French company engaged primarily in the manufacture and distribution of cement and other building materials.

In response to the highly levered capital structure created by this transaction, management began a systematic pruning of the firm by selectively divesting assets and businesses. Within a few months after the merger, the company sold the cement division, Binswanger Glass Company, Binning's Building Products division, the decorative products division, and National Gypsum Energy Company. In 1988, it sold one of its three divisions, the American Olean Tile, to Armstrong World Industries for $330 million. And, in 1989, the company sold a large board mill to Newark-Sierra Corporation. Although these measures helped repay some of the loans, the company continued to he highly leveraged—still holding more than $1.1 billion in junk bonds in 1989.

With the sale of the tile business, the Gold Bond division assumed an even more important role in generating profits for NGC. While Gold Bond and The Austin Company each represented about 50 percent of total revenues, for example, Gold Bond was much larger in terms of assets and contributed nearly four times the operating income of Austin (see Exhibits 2, 3, and 4 for financial information). In fact, because the synergies originally anticipated between Austin and Gold Bond were still elusive, corporate management was beginning to question the rationale for being in the engineering and construction business.

THE GYPSUM INDUSTRY

In 1989, Gold Bond manufactured and supplied gypsum-based products to mass merchandisers, building materials dealers, contractors, distributors, and industrial and agricultural users. The division's principal products included regular and predecorated gypsum wallboard, plaster, and joint treatment products. The division had a network of 18 gypsum plants spread out across the continental United States. Additionally, it owned or leased 8 mines and quarries of gypsum rock, operated 3 paper plants, and owned 3 plants for other related products (see Exhibit 5 for locations of wallboard and paper plants).

As of 1989 Gold Bond had 12 competitors in the gypsum wallboard industry. Most significant among these was its historic rival, U.S. Gypsum (a division of USG), which controlled more than 35 percent of the market compared to Gold Bond's 25-percent market share. Other major producers of wallboard were Georgia-Pacific (12 percent), Domtar (11 percent), and Celotex (7 percent). The remainder was divided among several smaller producers. Gold

Exhibit 2
National Gypsum Company
Income Statement ($mm)

	FOR YEARS ENDING DECEMBER					
	1988	1987	1986	1985	1984	1983
Sales	1,220.88	1,379.79	1,432.28	1,340.01	1,717.51	1,130.87
Cost of goods sold	975.74	973.92	979.72	938.07	1284.73	858.12
Gross profit	245.14	405.87	452.55	401.94	432.78	272.74
Selling administrative	102.41	152.68	147.76	137.13	168.30	133.81
Operating income before depreciation	142.73	253.19	304.80	264.81	264.48	138.93
Depreciation and amortization	73.92	94.53	61.14	42.31	43.21	41.99
Operating profit	68.81	158.66	243.66	222.49	221.27	96.94
Interest expense	163.61	179.17	129.61	16.53	20.36	16.17
Nonoperating income/Expense	6.78	−5.12	−2.11	12.49	−3.46	5.27
Pretax income	−88.01	−25.63	111.93	218.45	196.37	86.05
Total income taxes	−32.19	−3.42	58.58	102.40	89.60	36.70
Income before extraordinary items	−55.82	−22.21	53.35	116.05	106.77	49.35
Extraordinary items	39.16	−0.20	0.00	0.00	0.00	4.45
Discontinued operations	−62.95	0.00	1.99	−28.41	0.00	0.00
Net income	−79.60	−22.41	55.34	87.65	106.77	53.79
Preferred dividends	0.00	0.00	0.00	0.00	0.00	0.00
Available for common	−55.82	−22.21	53.35	116.05	106.77	49.35
Earnings per share (fully diluted excluding extra items and discontinued operations	NA	NA	NA	5.02	6.86	3.01
Earnings per share (fully diluted including extra items and discontinued operations	NA	NA	NA	3.79	6.86	3.29
Dividends per share	0.00	0.00	0.00	1.43	1.71	1.52

Exhibit 3
National Gypsum Company
Balance Sheet ($mm)

	FOR YEARS ENDING DECEMBER					
ASSETS	1988	1987	1986	1985	1984	1983
Cash and equivalents	163.15	22.97	17.06	68.30	41.87	40.75
Net receivables	164.90	181.35	195.15	236.26	218.47	182.64
Inventories	60.09	106.68	112.33	154.82	162.39	159.51
Other current assets	3.20	15.69	15.46	22.42	27.42	13.18
Total current assets	391.34	326.69	340.00	481.81	450.14	396.09
Gross property, plant, and equipment	793.74	1092.78	709.62	905.30	879.56	859.47
Accumulated depreciation	144.53	124.87	40.87	429.31	441.56	455.21
Net property, plant, and equipment	649.22	967.91	668.75	476.00	438.01	404.26
Intangibles	0.00	529.91	505.94	0.00	0.00	0.00
Other assets	569.44	149.52	141.44	93.17	77.44	65.57
Total assets	1,609.99	1,974.04	1,656.13	1,050.97	965.58	865.92
LIABILITIES						
Long-term debt due in one year	2.34	3.66	3.15	7.54	7.18	6.68
Notes payable	0.00	0.00	0.00	0.00	0.00	0.00
Accounts payable	92.96	76.29	71.74	83.01	88.85	49.52
Taxes payable	76.39	3.61	4.63	6.82	9.59	14.35
Accrued expenses	68.33	67.27	74.97	87.86	73.41	48.34
Other current liabilities	31.77	42.50	18.00	0.00	0.00	0.00
Total current liabilities	271.78	193.33	172.49	185.22	179.02	118.89
Long-term debt	1,029.72	1,298.29	1,350.45	119.36	133.59	134.66
Deferred taxes	190.79	271.68	5.38	83.77	73.93	67.20
Other liabilities	40.36	55.47	36.28	68.27	26.58	20.68
Common stock	0.00	0.00	0.00	14.38	9.58	9.18
Capital surplus	90.00	90.00	90.00	221.31	225.12	197.50
Retained earnings	−12.66	65.26	1.52	487.79	430.14	353.58
Less: Treasury stock	0.00	0.00	0.00	129.14	112.38	35.78
Common equity	77.35	155.26	91.52	594.34	552.46	524.48
Total liabilities and equity	1,609.99	1,974.04	1,656.13	1,050.97	965.58	865.92

Exhibit 4
National Gypsum Company
Business Segment Data ($mm)

	FOR YEARS ENDING DECEMBER	
NET REVENUES	1988	1987
Gypsum and related products	$ 570.79	$ 623.52
Engineering and construction services	528.84	444.94
Specialty and other products	126.52	106.71
Less: intersegment sales	(5.30)	(2.70)
	$1,220.85	$1,172.47
OPERATING INCOME (LOSS)		
Gypsum and related products	$ 116.58	$ 167.23
Engineering and construction services	9.58	8.44
Specialty and other products	(20.72)	(5.29)
	$ 105.44	$ 170.38
EXPENSES		
Corporate expenses	$ (24.19)	$ (23.39)
Interest expense	(163.32)	(177.94)
Amortizations of goodwill	(12.44)	(12.40)
Sundry, net	6.49	7.19
Earnings or loss before taxes and extraordinary items	$ (193.46)	$ (206.54)
IDENTIFIABLE ASSETS		
Gypsum and related products	$1,140.78	$1,185.22
Engineering and construction services	182.09	161.53
Specialty and other products	92.17	83.90
Discontinued operations	—	435.06
Corporate expense	194.95	108.32
	$1,609.99	$1,974.03

(continued on next page)

		(continued)

DEPRECIATION, DEPLETION, AND AMORTIZATION	1988	1987
Gypsum and related products	$ 62.02	$ 60.53
Engineering and construction services	3.15	2.85
Specialty and other products	3.41	3.80
Corporate expense	5.66	14.11
	$ 74.24	$ 81.29

ADDITIONS TO PROPERTY, PLANT, AND EQUIPMENT		
Gypsum and related products	$ 17.64	$ 12.14
Engineering and construction services	1.21	1.82
Specialty and other products	5.26	0.97
Discontinued operations	3.46	7.76
Corporate expense	0.33	1.09
	$ 27.90	$ 23.78

Bond and U.S. Gypsum were much better positioned than the rest, however, because only they had a national network of plants as well as captive sources for the gypsum rock and paper. Since rock and paper accounted for up to 40 percent of the total cost of manufacturing gypsum wallboard, these two producers had the lowest manufactured cost positions. Additionally, both companies, by virtue of being around for so long, were better known by architects, building inspectors, wallboard hangers, and others who played an important role in the final sale.

In spite of the dominant position of U.S. Gypsum and Gold Bond, the wallboard business was highly competitive. According to Mark Mann, an executive in sales at Gold Bond,[9]

> What you earn as the big producer is to have the right to last look, and you get some premium—maybe a buck or two per thousand feet of wallboard.

---

[9]Names of all the vice presidents of Gold Bond have been disguised for confidentiality.

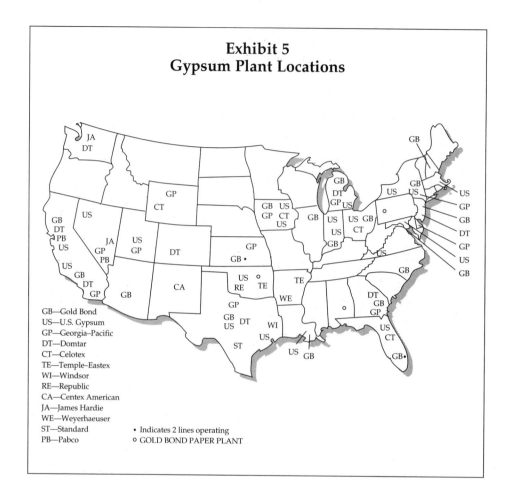

Exhibit 5
Gypsum Plant Locations

GB—Gold Bond
US—U.S. Gypsum
GP—Georgia–Pacific
DT—Domtar
CT—Celotex
TE—Temple-Eastex
WI—Windsor
RE—Republic
CA—Centex American
JA—James Hardie
WE—Weyerhaeuser
ST—Standard
PB—Pabco

• Indicates 2 lines operating
o GOLD BOND PAPER PLANT

Basically, it is price. You try and get price to a certain level in some place, and the guy in some other region will ship a railroad car to your area. If you get the price high enough and a producer in some other part of the country can afford to ship a car to your market and beat your price, he will do it. If he did not get enough business down where he is, he will ship to your area and sell it for less than you and probably still make money. It used to be that you would look at a plant and say "okay, a 350-mile radius is all he can supply." But, today, transportation capability exists to ship the products long distances across the country. And that impacts prices.

In other words, gypsum wallboard was perceived to be a commodity. Interestingly, although the industry was an oligopoly and dominated by two producers, all competitors considered themselves to be price takers. Consequently, they focused much of their attention on driving down costs. In this sense, the nature of the business had not changed since the late 1920s when Melvin Baker realized that vertical integration, easy access to mines and markets, and production efficiency were critical for superior competitive position. (See Exhibit 6 for cost components of wallboard.)

Even though competition was based largely on price, however, it was common for the producers to try to differentiate their products in terms of factors such as actual and perceived quality, product mix, and service. In the area of product quality, for example, wallboard hangers tended to prefer U.S. Gypsum's Sheetrock®. It was perceived to have a smoother surface, better "score and snap" qualities, better bond between paper and plaster, and cleaner edges. Indeed, the fact that the name Sheetrock® had become a generic term, synonymous with wallboard, seemed to give U.S. Gypsum a distinct advantage. In addition to brand-name recognition, sales of wallboard were also influenced to a degree by the quality of the sales force. As Mark Mann noted,

> Gold Bond's salespeople are supposed to spend time in the field getting contractors to use, like, and ask for *our* products. Naturally, if our price is very different, they are not going to buy it. We and U.S. Gypsum have the most salespeople on the road—that helps in terms of following up on complaints,

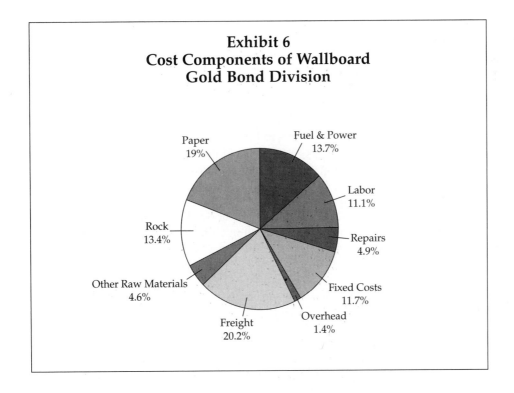

Exhibit 6
Cost Components of Wallboard
Gold Bond Division

Paper 19%
Fuel & Power 13.7%
Labor 11.1%
Repairs 4.9%
Rock 13.4%
Fixed Costs 11.7%
Other Raw Materials 4.6%
Overhead 1.4%
Freight 20.2%

introducing products, and more than anything else, to articulate what is going on with the company.

Over time, the cost reduction efforts by firms in the industry had been successfully implemented by all the majors, enabling them to drive down the marginal cost of wallboard continually. Ironically, by 1989, these measures had also made the gypsum wallboard industry one of the most capital intensive in the U.S. economy. [10] The business, as a result, had become even more volume sensitive than it had ever been in the past. This created a great deal of pressure on producers to maintain high-capacity utilization in their plants. According to one industry analyst, when capacity utilization dropped below 90 percent, prices fell to the cash cost level of the highest-cost plant whose capacity was needed to fill industry demand. When capacity utilization reached above 90 percent, on the other hand, producers began to have pricing power. This power did not last very long, however, because higher margins attracted new capacity, which could be brought on stream within 18 months at a cost of approximately $35 million.

Capacity utilization in the wallboard industry was usually driven by the conditions of supply and demand. On the supply side, excess capacity in the industry put pressure on the producers to drop prices in order to achieve volume sales necessary to cover fixed costs. On the demand side, since wallboard was used mostly in building construction, the fortunes of the industry were closely tied to the overall health of the economy—and particulary the housing market. In a faltering economy, for instance, there was pressure on producers to drop prices to stabilize and/or increase sagging demand. (See Exhibit 7 for Gold Bond's price trends.)

Since the real-estate boom of the mid-1980s, both of these factors turned from bad to worse for firms in the industry. Although the years 1984 to 1986 were of record revenues and earnings, the average annual rate of household formations was down in the 1980s to 1.5 million from an annual average of 1.7 million in the 1970s. Many experts expected the downward trend to continue, predicting annual housing starts to average between 1.2 million and 1.4 million during the 1990s. In the nonresidential sector, too, new construction was expected to remain depressed. Some estimated that there was about 20 percent excess commercial capacity, brought about largely by the expansion of the mid-1980s. The only positive projection seemed to be that expenditures for repair and remodeling, both residential and commercial buildings, would grow in the foreseeable future.

Paradoxically, some of the troubles faced by the wallboard producers were brought about by their own actions. In response to record level earnings

---

[10]In 1989, the net revenues/identifiable assets for the gypsum business of NGC was just more than 50 percent.

Exhibit 7
Gold Bond Building Products Division
Invoice Price—All Wallboard
$/MSF

	1986	1987	1988	1989
January	154.03	133.32	116.39	108.07
February	146.84	128.47	111.83	105.01
March	141.25	125.67	108.83	104.64
April	146.92	127.61	113.73	104.51
May	145.71	128.71	108.82	104.01
June	144.50	122.28	105.60	102.69
July	138.05	116.98	103.65	101.31
August	131.47	116.33	106.61	
September	134.28	117.14	110.96	
October	140.44	120.98	114.13	
November	143.09	123.79	112.38	
December	142.99	121.59	107.89	
Yearly average	142.46	123.57	110.07	
Volume—MMSF	5,111	5,219	5,286	
EBITDA	$286,944	$222,016	$120,186	

in the mid-1980s, the wallboard production capacity was increased by 31 percent, from 18.82 billion board feet in 1982 to 24.60 billion board feet in 1988. In the southwestern United States, where natural gypsum deposits were plentiful, wallboard capacity grew by almost 60 percent. As luck would have it, the additional production capacity, which came on line 18 months after the peak sales year, hit the market just as the general economy began yet another slowdown. Consequently, the new plants began shipping wallboard outside the regions they would typically cover. The average capacity utilization dipped to 85 percent in 1987 and 84 percent in 1988. Not surprisingly, the gypsum product prices declined about 9 percent in 1987 and fell almost another 13 percent in 1988. In 1989, prices were expected to drop another 2 percent.

The competitive environment in the gypsum wallboard industry was intensified by the presence of many small producers who operated one or a few plants on shoestring budgets. It was common for these producers to "mothball" their plants when the prices fell too low, only to come back on stream as soon as prices rose high enough to meet their break-even points. The mothballed plants could be up and running in just a few months. Among the larger producers, Domtar was beginning to articulate increasingly aggressive aspirations. It had rapidly increased capacity during the 1980s and was intent upon becoming a strong second in the foreseeable future. Although Domtar did not have the same degree of vertical integration as U.S. Gypsum and Gold Bond, its ambition for a stronger competitive position was not a pipe dream. Emerging technologies were beginning to make synthetic gypsum and paperless wallboard feasible.

Although those outside the industry were quick to see these conditions as a sign of major structural shifts in the wallboard business, many insiders took a different view. They preferred to believe whatever industry downturn the company was facing was only temporary and a function of the usual sine wave pattern in U.S. housing cycles. According to this view, economic troughs would be followed by economic peaks, and therefore firms should work to position themselves for the inevitable upswing in the market.

At the same time that the industry was experiencing these changes, Jack Hayes (age 68) was nearing retirement. NGC was, therefore, seriously considering candidates to succeed him. Hayes recognized that his successor needed to be a strong leader in order to navigate the company through the troubled times. Although top managers in the company usually rose through the ranks and had typically spent their entire careers looking out from the inside, Hayes saw the need to bring a fresh perspective by going outside NGC. After a brief search, in February 1989 NGC named Peter Browning as the executive vice president of Gold Bond. He was to report to Mace Coleman, the division president. The charge given Browning was to "learn the gypsum business and stabilize Gold Bond's position in the industry." If he was able to accomplish this, it was conceivable that Browning could move up the organization rapidly enough to succeed Hayes as CEO of NGC.

PETER BROWNING

> Every institution, every society down to every company, or, for that matter, each individual product has a finite life, be it years, decades, or centuries. In each instance, longevity is determined by a whole host of factors including the not insignificant influence of plain old good luck. But for me, the single most important determinant of how long an institution, a society, or a company survives and prospers is its ability to revitalize. It is the capacity to respond to the inevitable changes that alter the very reasons for its earlier rise and fortune.

These thoughts articulated by Browning soon after coming to Gold Bond reflected the attitude with which he approached management of organizations. Indeed, Browning had developed and lived by this view of the world since beginning his career as a sales representative with the White Cap division of Continental Can in 1964. By 1979, he had risen through the sales and marketing organization to become the vice president and general manager of Continental's Bondware division, a producer of waxed paper cups. When he took over Bondware, the division was in a state of despair, having lost $25 million between 1975 and 1979. Browning adopted a strategy of "radical surgery," cutting employment in half, eliminating an entire product line, and shutting down four out of six manufacturing sites to turn the business around in five years. His success under such difficult circumstances propelled him in 1984 to what some considered an even more challenging assignment as executive vice president of Continental's White Cap division.

Unlike Bondware, however, when Browning took over White Cap he was taking over Continental's "crown jewel"—a division that held a preeminent position in the bottle closure industry. Even so, industry conditions were changing so rapidly that the division faced rapid deterioration in its position if it did not respond quickly. At the same time, Browning's marching orders from his boss at Continental were "White Cap needs changes, but just don't break it while you are trying to fix it. Continental can't afford to lose White Cap." At his new assignment, Browning inherited a family-style culture, which was rife with tradition, liberal benefits, and paternalistic management. Nevertheless, he was successful here too. Among the actions he took were replacement and transfer of many employees, elimination of several positions mainly by attrition, development and introduction of major presentations for key accounts, and even building new plants utilizing the latest in emerging technologies.

The people who worked with Browning often described him as "high energy," "charming, "enthusiastic," "the best person I have ever worked for." In addition, Sarah James, a former colleague of Browning at both Bondware and White Cap, noted that

> He is probably more down to earth and more people sensitive than the typical CEO. So often people get in that corner office and they sort of forget where they have come from. Peter has always been able to stay connected with the average employees and what their concerns are. He is pretty down to earth and no nonsense in that if someone is violating a basic principle, such as "no territoriality," a lot of people will never confront it. Peter will do it, in a nice way usually, but he will confront it.

A senior manager at Gold Bond observed that what set Browning apart from other managers was his competence on both technical and people dimensions.

> What's so special about Peter is the breadth of his competence. This is a guy who you can talk to about sales issues, marketing issues, finance issues, accounting issues. . . . The man is extremely competent—unlike many CEOs who have expertise in a particular field through which they have come up but do not have a whole lot of insight in what goes on in other areas. In addition, he communicates very well, making every effort to keep people informed. People see him as fair and honest.

Taking Stock

Once at Gold Bond, Browning was quick to recognize that "we operate in a highly competitive, relatively undifferentiated, low value-added business where the same companies produce the same product on the same equipment from the same raw material for the same customer. Therefore, the difference between success and failure will be determined by people. Not just any people but committed people." So, from February through June 1989, Peter Browning set out to learn about the people that made up Gold Bond. During those five months he visited 24 plants and nearly 31 sales offices, attended two conventions, met with some 150 customers, and took extensive notes on what he observed (see Exhibit 8). As he later recalled,

> I got halfway through it and realized that's a lot. I mean that's all I did. I'd show up here once a month at the corporate office in Charlotte and couldn't even find my office. It was one way to keep out of the president's (Mace Coleman) hair. And, it's another way to earn credibility when the customer starts saying, "Hey, yeah, this guy isn't a bad guy." And the employees in the plants start saying, "Yeah, gee, I haven't seen anybody in this plant in five years."
>
> I would go into a plant, for example, and shake everybody's hand on the first shift and try and get the second shift. We would then go into a conference room, and we would do the same thing in the sales office. We would sit around and I would say, "I appreciate you all getting together, and you're probably wondering why I am here. So let me start. My name is Peter Browning, I am 48, married, and have four children," and then I would tell them a little about some of my background and experience. Then I would say, "Now, let me tell you why I am here. Why did they hire me?" I then gave them a little bit of my philosophy, and I asked each person, "If you don't mind, tell me a little bit about yourself." And, we would go around, and people would introduce themselves, and we would talk about how long they had been there. And, then I would say. "Do you have any questions? I am new; I will tell you as much or as little as I know." And, I learned an awful lot about the concerns in peoples' minds. And, I learned that there was a lack of communication and information and a need to know about where the company stood financially and what was really going on. So that helped move me in certain directions on communications. I also talked with customers and traveled with salespeople. I would ask, "How are you; how are things going; what's with the company?" They would respond, "Well we got this 'Avis Syndrome'—we're a comfortable follower." So, again I picked up anecdotal information from customers. It was an osmotic process.
>
> I waited to talk to the office in Charlotte because I thought that would be disruptive for Mace. So I waited until it was announced in July that I'd be taking over as president. I met with 10 to 15 separate groups each comprising about ten people from different departments. There I did the same thing. They would update me on what was going on and answer questions. It was another way to get information. I started something called "Speak to the President," which was a program where employees could fill out forms if they had questions or suggestions for me [see Exhibit 9]. I put the forms in

Exhibit 8
Critical Issues Facing Gold Bond
Notes of Peter Browning

STRATEGIC PLAN AND PLANNING PROCESS

1. No current, well-articulated Gold Bond long-term plan, direction. Organization seems to view tomorrow as yesterday.
2. Planning process has become bureaucratic and involves too many committees.
3. SBU breakdown not good.
4. Process handled by VP HRM.
5. Little or no effort to capitalize on competitors' weaknesses.
6. Strategic plans don't reflect company and product's image.
7. Strategy not based on financial parameters (e.g., returns, cash flows, pricing).
8. Strategies are separate by functional area and division. No consistent, linked strategy tying together all areas.
9. Company's strategy seems to be based on sales orientation rather than satisfying customer needs.

MIS/COST SYSTEM

1. Cost system not competitive and reporting of costs is poor.
2. Reporting systems ineffective, costly, and time-consuming. Systems don't supply timely, useful information. Systems lack direction.
3. Monthly management book.

SALES

1. Limited integration/interaction between marketing and sales.
2. Poorly configured order entry/sales services
3. No analysis of most effective size for sales organization (e.g., sales personnel, district managers, regional managers).
4. No information on how sales personnel spend their time (e.g., selling vinyl? resale? new customer development? existing customers?)
5. No information on how many territories are low volume, low value added. Not clear as to what level of coverage is necessary. No clear market/capacity strategy in various areas (e.g., Northeast, Midwest, West Coast).
6. Sales organization is overwhelmed; everyone wants a piece of their time.

(continued on next page)

(continued)

MARKETING

1. Marketing mostly staffed with salespeople rather than marketing people.
2. Pricing is separated from marketing.
3. Not enough coherent product/market strategies.

MANUFACTURING

1. Need information on the quality of personnel in quarries and mines.
2. Need information as to whether company is optimizing costs at this level.
3. Highly centralized leadership. Are we developing others?
4. Land issues and geology strategy program seems random and opportunistic.
5. Productivity and quality programs seem to be manufacturing only (not total business) and not supported by most of manufacturing.
6. Division often in conflict with rest of organization.

R&D

1. R&D orientation may be outdated or unclear.
2. Division seems isolated from manufacturing and not linked to any overall strategy.

HUMAN RESOURCES

1. Has more of a labor-law focus than HR.
2. Few comprehensive HR systems.
3. Deficient succession planning and manpower development.
4. No organized bonus programs for manufacturing or sales.
5. Conflicts exist between HR department and manufacturing.
6. Problems with leadership that are not openly discussed or understood.
7. No clearly articulated direction, purpose, or labor strategy.

FINANCE

1. Debt reduction plan not well understood or articulated and not connected to forecasts.
2. No clear programs within area (e.g., receivables).

(continued on next page)

(continued)

ENVIRONMENT

1. Highly structured and stylized—too formal and perfunctory (e.g., meetings).
2. Generally good people who like company and want to succeed but need direction.
3. In the past, company has been willing to accept second best rather than number one ("Avis Syndrome").
4. Feeling of alienation at lower levels.
5. Everything by committee.
6. Too many shibboleths/slogans and programs.
7. Poor communication.
8. Dislike and distrust of corporation.
9. Too many politics and internal conflict.
10. Governance by fear and fiat.

every plant, sales office, and facility. It was a way to open things up. It was threatening in the sense that you had a layered organization, and each layer kept the information to itself. And, here was a way to speak directly to the boss. I must have gotten a thousand in the first few months. And, I answered all of those.

What Browning found was an organization that most of the employees described as autocratic and bureaucratic. As one senior manager recalled about the decision-making climate in the organization,

The executive committee meeting was very formal—you came in with your coat on. No one really ever discussed anything that was really a problem. It was very rehearsed—canned speeches, etc. You did not own up to what was going on. We got on by softening things as much as we could, not taking issues, not being embarrassed in the executive committee meeting so that some corporate officer or president would take issue with anyone in front of everybody else. If you wanted to have a last word, it was probably on the way out the door. Every single one of us did business that way. That's the way we managed. You told your subordinates what to do, and, if [they] did not do it, you would get somebody else to do it. There was a perception that everyone was focused on self-gain—not necessarily as an individual but for their areas. There was no other common goal that everyone linked up with.

Exhibit 9

TO THE PRESIDENT

Gold Bond
Building
Products

Tell President Peter Browning about a problem that needs action or a question or concern you have that you would like to have an answer to. State clearly, with facts, so you can be understood. Please do not include items such as working hours, vacations, holidays, or other benefit items. What are your general concerns, questions, and comments in regards to the quality, service, products, and people that make up Gold Bond Building Products?

_____

_____

_____

What solution do you suggest? _____

_____

_____

_____

What form of response would you prefer, if any?

_____ Personal and Confidential memo from the President

_____ Personal and Confidential memo from Human Resources

_____ Your suggestion _____

_____ No response is required

Please mail response to me at:

_____ Home

_____ Work

This information is optional unless a response is requested.

Your Name _____ Date _____

Your Location _____

Home Address _____

City _____ State _____ Zip _____

If the response to your question, comment, or concern is of general information, may we use it in one of the company communication vehicles such as the newsletter or video?

_____ yes _____ no

Browning saw that, as in so many industrial firms, manufacturing and sales had different missions. The only common goal they had was to get enough volume to keep the plants running seven days a week. The plant managers were worried about costs and meeting certain measurements and objectives, while salespeople were off on their own trying to fulfill customers' requirements. According to Mark Mann, an executive in the sales organization,

> The manufacturing and salespeople did not spend a lot of time together. There was no cross-functional activity between plant managers and salespeople. There was this group, and there was that group. The split was all the way up to the top at the vice president level. There was always this adversarial relationship. When the sales organization would talk to manufacturing about the need for special products, new products, or any variation that would affect costs, they would say, "You got yourself a crazy customer; we hope you will work it out." We thought in silos.

The "silo" mentality in Gold Bond was also evident in the relationship between R&D and the rest of the organization. Although the efforts of this function were focused on improving the production processes in order to reduce manufacturing costs, there was little interaction or coordination between development engineers and plant managers. Moreover, product development was highly subdued at Gold Bond because the sales and marketing personnel were rarely, if ever, involved in R&D. Instead, salespeople were often given fully developed products that nobody wanted to buy.

There was little delegation of decision-making authority from Gold Bond's central office in Charlotte to the various sales offices and plants. Marketing, which was distinct from the sales organization, was primarily responsible for pricing decisions, all of which came from Charlotte. Plant managers could make discretionary expenditures of $1,000 or less and had to make formal requests to the central office to make procurements over that limit. The organizational climate was characterized by committees that made decisions about *everything*. This made the decision-making environment highly structured, formal, bureaucratic, and slow. According to one plant manager, decision making at the time could be described as "paralysis by analysis." No one seemed to be able to take a definitive stand when it came to prudently investing the plentiful cash in the core business. Inevitably, politicking was widespread, and, as Browning noted, there were "too many shibboleths and slogans and programs." There was a feeling of alienation at the lower levels as employees felt that they were being managed by fear and fiat. Sixty percent of the division's plants were being unionized, and dealings with labor were seen as being primarily the domain of labor lawyers.

While bureaucracy was rampant, there was also no coherent, well-articulated, long-term direction for Gold Bond. Nor was the debt reduction plan clearly articulated so as to be understood by employees and customers. What little strategic planning was done was handled by a market researcher, who reported to the vice president of human resources. There did not appear to be a clear understanding or strategy for satisfying customers' needs, and the sales force concerned itself mainly with taking orders and pushing the product.

Leading the Charge

Within the first month after becoming president of Gold Bond, Browning turned his attention to two tasks. First, he realized he had to develop and clearly articulate a strategic direction for the immediate future. He also knew he had to set realizable, yet ambitious, operational goals for the division. Based on his notes from the visits to plants and sales offices during the previous six months, Browning had a fairly good understanding of what he wanted Gold Bond to look like in the foreseeable future. Yet, the success of his efforts would be determined at least in part by the manner in which he went about achieving this vision.

Second, Browning knew from his previous experiences that developing a new vision and strategy for organizational turnaround would be only a beginning. The greater challenge would be to quickly and effectively communicate the revised imperatives throughout the organization. He had to set the environment in which such communication would be possible, and, for that, he needed a management team that was compatible with his style of leadership. Changes in the top management team would not be easy, however, because most executives had been with the company for 25 to 30 years, and they felt very good about what they had accomplished. Moreover, they represented continuity with Gold Bond's suppliers and customers.

Partly because of his conviction that an organization was only as good as the people in it, Browning held that the human resource department played a crucial role in bringing about the necessary changes. At the time, however, the HR function was perceived by many to be incapable of responding to the demands of the new leadership. Under Vice President Glenn Davis, 50, the department was regarded as more reactive than proactive. There were few, if any, well-defined training or development programs in place and few consistent company policies or practices. In response to this void at the corporate level, different functional areas developed their own mini-HR departments for handling things like performance evaluation, training, and compensation. The systems that did exist at the departmental level were largely mechanistic in application. Compensation of plant managers and district sales managers, for example, was based *solely* on their meeting quarterly production or sales targets. There was little regard for the quality of effort and things such as teamwork, leadership, or morale-building capabilities. This evaluation criterion was reflected in the more than 100 different salary bands into which employees were classified. In addition, the department was heavily staffed with labor lawyers, who pursued an adversarial relationship with the unions.

Davis had been with the company for five years. Although perceived by his peers and subordinates as a "nice guy," he was considered by others as less than competent, delegating away most or all of his job responsibilities to subordinates. Indeed, in cross-functional meetings he often brought in subordinates to report on his division's activities and to answer questions. In short, people within the company generally did not have much professional respect for Davis and had a low regard for the HR department, tolerating it as a "necessary evil."

The office of the vice president of manufacturing also played a key role in the organization. The affairs of the gypsum rock mines, the 3 paper mills and the 18 wallboard plants, purchasing, distribution, and engineering all came under its purview. This position was held by Scott Donaldson, who had been with Gold Bond for more than 30 years and had risen through the ranks in manufacturing. He was regarded as one of the most competent people around when it came to gypsum manufacturing. He was also perceived to be loyal, hard working, and dedicated to the job. At the same time, he was considered to be very demanding, not hesitating to fire, move, or demote those who "crossed his path." Over the past few years, he had been aggressively pursuing the division's objective of cutting costs. And, like many in the HR area, his attitude toward the unions was highly adversarial.

Perhaps because of his technical competence and demanding style, Donaldson was often characterized as "autocratic" and "top down." He was the one, for example, who insisted on clearing procurements of more than $1,000. His approval was also necessary to let nonplant personnel tour the plants and learn about Gold Bond's products. This was true regardless of whether they were from outside the division (e.g., customers) or from inside Gold Bond. Donaldson's influence was perceived to be so great that his subordinates rarely questioned any of his decisions or actions. On the other hand, Donaldson was known to go to bat for the manufacturing function when its autonomy was felt to be threatened by other areas. Over time, this created a conflictive relationship between manufacturing and functional areas such as human resources, sales, and R&D. His differences with Glenn Davis, for example, were well known in the division. His critics often noted that Donaldson reinforced the "silo" mentality already pervasive at Gold Bond.

Marketing and sales were maintained as two separate departments. Marketing, headed by Vice President Tom Boyd, was responsible primarily for pricing the division's products. Historically, marketing had little or no say in defining the other three *P*'s (product, place, promotion) of the marketing mix. Boyd was often characterized by his peers as a "super salesman with a firm grasp of the numbers." He was perceived as having excellent rapport with customers and people inside his department, although managers in other functional areas seemed to feel that he did not have a strategic or long-term perspective on the business. According to one of his peers in another area, "Tom has a good sense of the here and now, but he finds it difficult to plan for five years out." Having been with Gold Bond for his entire career, Boyd, 63, was extremely loyal to the division and, perhaps, to the old ways of doing things. It was doubtful, therefore, that he would be enthusiastic in his support for any major change efforts, let alone participate in designing them.

Because of its large size and direct role in generating revenues for the division, the sales department seemed more powerful and important than marketing. This department employed more than 250 salespeople and 150 administrative staff and maintained 31 sales offices spread throughout the United States. It was headed by Vice President Rick Collins, 56, who had been with the division for more than 30 years and had also risen through Gold Bond's sales organization. Collins was generally well liked and well regarded both by his peers and subordinates. At the same time, he was perceived as being emotional and was known to act on impulse. Like Boyd, Collins was seen as having a strong "sales" personality. He was a doer rather than a strategic thinker. In addition, he seemed to have trouble making the "hard decisions, particularly those involving people." On the other hand, Collins was considered to have a very good sense of the wallboard business, and he had strong, longstanding relationships with customers. Moreover, he had made many important contributions in developing new markets for Gold Bond's products.

Peter Browning pondered his many observations regarding the state of affairs in the different functions at Gold Bond, and the leadership provided by the various vice presidents in their respective departments. He thought to himself, "There is a great deal of managerial talent and a wealth of knowledge about the gypsum business among the current personnel. These are very proud men, and for good reason. They have maintained a strong second position in the face of fierce competition, and that's quite an accomplishment."

Ironically, it was this past success that concerned Browning the most. Would the culture that produced that success be a barrier to future change? While the external and internal problems that faced NGC were obvious to him, would they be equally obvious to those inside the company who were a product of NGC's history? Indeed Browning wondered how many people inside the company were thinking to themselves, "If it ain't broke, don't fix it. Sure we may be in a slump, but it's temporary. Things aren't as bad as they seem." Many of the organizational processes were dysfunctional, however, and he felt that "a groove had turned into a rut." What had worked so well in the past, in Browning's opinion, was actually impeding the divisions' responsiveness in the emerging new competitive climate. The challenge he faced was to rejuvenate an organization that had begun a slow downward slide—and to do this without demoralizing the managers and the work force. What was more, he had to introduce all this change from the position of relative newcomer to the company and industry. "No easy task," he thought to himself. But, then, that is what made the job so tempting in the first place.

OSIM CORPORATION (A)

On Thursday, June 9, 1983, Tom Stark was walking toward the office of Bob Cedarholm, OSIM's chairman of the board, contemplating the alleged internal "revolt" to overthrow Dave Wright, the president. Stark was wondering what and how much to say to Cedarholm during their impending meeting.

Stark had returned to work at OSIM just three days earlier, following a one-year in-residence Executive Management Program at a prestigious eastern business school. Prior to this time, Stark had earned a Ph.D. in industrial engineering from MIT and had spent nine years at OSIM. Now, at age 37, he was OSIM's first director of strategic planning and had the task of introducing strategic planning to the company. From the first day, however, in addition to the technical task of strategic planning, Stark had also been confronted with this highly charged political situation. It was made even more complicated for Stark because Dave Wright had acted as Stark's mentor during much of Stark's time at OSIM and had sponsored him in the Management Program. The situation had implications for the future of the firm, Stark's relationship with Wright, his career, and his personal ethics.

In his mind, Stark was going over his first days back at OSIM:

I came back to work on June 6, a Monday, and I had a conversation with the president about start-up tasks and priorities. Then on Wednesday, Frank Lewisburg, the marketing director, invited me out to lunch. We spent about two and one-half hours together. During this lunch period, he brought up a number of points rather forcefully. The first one was that there is a conspiracy going on in the company. Frank and other members of the group feel that company goals are not being achieved because of Dave Wright's ineffective leadership, and they are meeting nightly, essentially to discuss how to remove Dave or to make him ineffective so that the company can move ahead on its growth plans. He announced, in essence, that he was lined up with Bob, the chairman of the board; that they had pressured Bob in the past into making some organizational changes (some of which would increase Frank's responsibilities); that the chairman of the board was himself lined up with management at Shilo [OSIM's parent company] in New York; and that there was an impending reorganization, at which time these problems would be taken care of. He predicted the reorganization would take place around the first of August and advised me to state my preferences and alliances now, because when that reorganization took place, things were going to be different. He said if I wanted to be on the right side of things, I'd better get on the chairman's team.

My initial reaction was disbelief. I knew Frank was prone to hyperbole, and I felt maybe this was a combination of that characteristic and two glasses of wine. And then my next reaction was, "Wow, these guys are playing hardball, and they seem to be playing for keeps." This is not a nice, cozy academic problem you can ponder for awhile but something in the middle of the swirl of events. I was sort of resenting this—being placed in such a position so quickly. And damn it, I hardly have my feet on the ground. I don't even know where my office is, and here I am being invited to join a palace revolt.

Then Frank ended up by saying that he would make an appointment for me with the chairman of the board; he would talk to the chairman before I went to see him and would tell him that he had had this conversation with me. Then he told me that I should go in and pledge my allegiance if I knew what was good for me. I agreed to talk to the chairman, because I was already committed to meet with him that week.

HISTORY OF OSIM CORPORATION

OSIM Corporation was a medium-sized consulting firm located in Sunnyvale, California. Founded in the 1930s following the Great Depression, OSIM had prospered and grown slowly but steadily by providing engineering services to local businesses. In the 1950s, OSIM entered the commercial real-estate business to capitalize on the beginning westward population migration. During the 1960s, OSIM's growth accelerated as the economy in Silicon Valley, based on high-technology businesses, boomed. To service the new companies, OSIM instituted financial advisory services and combined business services, which provided small and emerging companies with a wide range of services. Finally, OSIM began providing specialized litigation support in response to existing client demand for such services. By 1982, OSIM had revenues of $75 million, although both revenues and profits had fluctuated in the previous few years as the nature of the consulting business changed (see Exhibit 1).

OSIM Corporation had five basic services areas, with many types of sub-services (see organization chart in Exhibit 2):

- *Engineering.* The engineering services division provided a broad range of services to a wide variety of client organizations, both industrial and governmental. The division's distinctive competence lay in developing and implementing innovative approaches to engineering problems

Exhibit 1
OSIM Corporation
Financial Highlights
($ in millions)

	1982	1981	1980	1979
Revenue	$75.2	$65.9	$60.3	$45.0
Net income	.4	1.8	1.5	1.1
Total assets	46.8	34.9	27.6	24.4
Shareholders' equity	$ 9.1	$ 8.7	$ 6.9	$ 5.4
Number of employees at year-end	1,322	1,230	1,206	1,056

through the use of operations research, process control, network analysis, information processing, and computer system development. OSIM bid almost solely on "one-off" type projects that required sophisticated technical competence and creativity—the staff's "power alleys." Engineering services accounted for approximately 55 percent of OSIM revenues in 1982 and exerted substantial influence on the company as a whole, partly because it was the oldest business within the company and partly because it was the largest.

- *Real Estate.* The real-estate division developed and managed commercial real estate, particularly shopping centers and industrial parks. OSIM entered the real-estate business during the 1950s when commercial and industrial growth began to accelerate throughout Silicon Valley. Having operated in Sunnyvale since the 1930s, OSIM had developed a strong reputation for high-quality work and had accumulated a great deal of knowledge about the local area, which aided the real-estate division immeasurably.

- *Financial.* The financial advisory services division provided financial consulting, investment banking services, and seed capital to local firms. It originated in the 1960s as a follow-on to the engineering and real-estate businesses, since financing was a central element in both. Having the financial services capability in addition to engineering and real-estate expertise allowed OSIM to meet a substantial portion of many organizations' outside consulting-service needs.

- *Combined Business Services.* The CBS division provided a full range of financial and consulting services to small, privately held businesses.

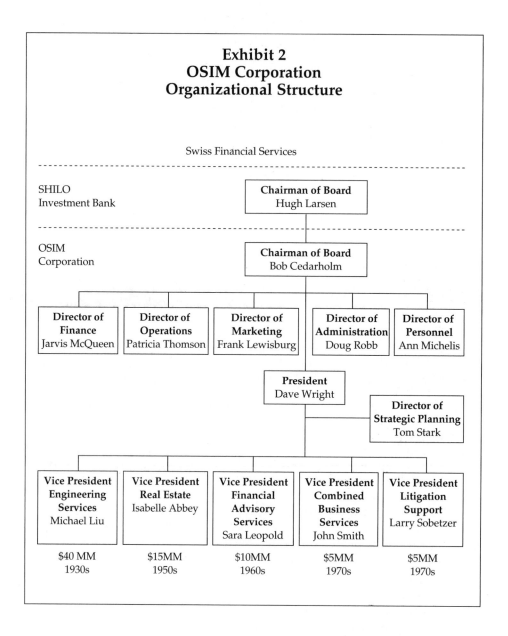

Exhibit 2
OSIM Corporation
Organizational Structure

Swiss Financial Services

SHILO
Investment Bank

Chairman of Board
Hugh Larsen

OSIM
Corporation

Chairman of Board
Bob Cedarholm

Director of Finance Jarvis McQueen	**Director of Operations** Patricia Thomson	**Director of Marketing** Frank Lewisburg	**Director of Administration** Doug Robb	**Director of Personnel** Ann Michelis

President
Dave Wright

Director of Strategic Planning
Tom Stark

Vice President Engineering Services Michael Liu	**Vice President Real Estate** Isabelle Abbey	**Vice President Financial Advisory Services** Sara Leopold	**Vice President Combined Business Services** John Smith	**Vice President Litigation Support** Larry Sobetzer
$40 MM 1930s	$15MM 1950s	$10MM 1960s	$5MM 1970s	$5MM 1970s

Although these companies did not require major investment banks or accounting firms, they did need professional advice across a wide spectrum of their activities. The CBS group employed CPAs, MBAs, financial analysts, and lawyers. OSIM was well positioned to serve the small company market in Silicon Valley because it was so well known and respected in the area. OSIM's strategy was to develop strong relationships with emerging companies, with the idea of providing additional services as the companies expanded. CBS grew rapidly during the 1970s as small companies flourished in the Sunnyvale area.

- *Litigation Support.* OSIM also had consultants who worked solely on providing litigation support to firms needing expert testimony and witnesses. Most of this business arose through San Francisco Bay area law firms that drew on OSIM's expertise and reputation in the engineering area. Client development was particularly haphazard in this group, although litigation support was both OSIM's fastest growing and most profitable (per hour) service area. Because many consulting firms appeared to be ready to enter this business within the next couple of years, a group of people at OSIM wanted to invest in the litigation support division and rationalize client development in order to capitalize on the field's apparent attractiveness.

OSIM's work was project oriented and technical in nature. Each project involved delivering a service, but the services varied greatly among divisions and types of clients. OSIM's revenue was usually generated by one-off types of projects, with little follow-on work.

OSIM's customers could include almost any organization. Business clients ranged from small start-ups to large, established *Fortune* 500 firms. Most industries were represented, including electronics and other high-technology areas, chemicals, construction, defense, and agriculture. OSIM also worked for nonprofit organizations, especially hospitals, and some local governments.

The kind of people OSIM believed would succeed at consulting, and whom OSIM had to hire and retain, were highly skilled, professional, energetic, willing to work long hours, and independent and entrepreneurial on the one hand but able to work as a member of a team on the other. Most of the professional staff were attracted to OSIM because of the intellectual stimulation, financial compensation, and flexibility it offered. Virtually everyone had an advanced degree, either in a technical or engineering specialty or from a business school. Many could have worked independently, but they benefited from OSIM's reputation, from contact with other talented people, and from the financial resources OSIM could apply to support their work. After a few years at OSIM, they could expect to be able to choose their own work.

The culture at OSIM strongly reflected the characteristics of the consulting profession and the types of people attracted to it. It was a loosely coordinated corporation that had had virtually no central planning. The name of the game was "chargeable hours." Projects were bid on the basis of "total revenue" or "hourly billing rate," but, in either case, hours were closely tracked. An hour not billed was an hour's revenues lost forever. Compensation and advancement at OSIM were linked to chargeable hours, although technical competence, ability to generate new business, and ability to get along with people also entered into the picture.

Exhibit 2 shows OSIM's organizational structure. Below the vice presidents, who were heads of divisions, were project managers, senior associates, and junior associates. Background information on the primary protagonists with Stark in this situation is given in the case appendix. The VPs and the project managers were accustomed to choosing the type of work they wanted to do and to structuring it themselves in order to complete it. Not much corporate focus characterized this approach, but the professional staff enjoyed their independence.

HISTORY OF SWISS FINANCIAL SERVICES/SHILO INVESTMENT BANK AND THE ACQUISITION OF OSIM

Shilo Investment Bank, based in New York, was a wholly owned subsidiary of the huge international financial conglomerate, Swiss Financial Services (SFS). SFS owned several dozen companies in just about as many countries, which gave it a strong worldwide presence in the expanding financial services arena. With Switzerland as a base, SFS could provide clients with a broad array of services and make the most of increasing global interdependence and easing regulatory restrictions.

Shilo was SFS's North American investment banking arm. It was one of the dominant U.S. investment banks and provided a full range of financial services. At SFS's request, and consistent with its own objectives, Shilo embarked on a plan of acquisitions during the late 1970s and early 1980s. Shilo intended to secure and bolster its position in the U.S. market, where financial service and consulting competition was fierce, mergers were occurring, and inefficient firms were starting to disappear.

The decision to sell OSIM to Shilo was made in January 1983 and announced in March. Stark was at the Executive Management Program but learned of the decision sometime during February. Although OSIM was a corporation, four people maintained most of the control: Chairman Cedarholm, President Wright, Michael Liu (vice president, engineering services), and Isabelle Abbey (vice president, real estate). These four people benefited financially from the acquisition, while the other vice presidents and the directors of OSIM did not. The result was some bad feelings, particularly from officers who had spent many years at OSIM and felt they had not been adequately compensated for their time and efforts.

Most people within OSIM realized that being part of Shilo—and even more significantly, SFS—would provide OSIM with financial resources to compete effectively in the changing world of consulting and financial services. Some also worried, however, that Shilo and SFS would impose additional structure and control on OSIM, thus detracting from its independence. In addition, some people were contemplating the potentially lucrative move of leveraging the investment made in previous R&D work by selling "solutions" over and over again. Such a step could lead to two groups within

OSIM: those who would design and create solutions to client problems and those who would be charged with merely repeatedly implementing already-developed, cookie-cutter products.

OSIM STRATEGY EVOLUTION TO DATE

OSIM's strategy had evolved over time to include provision of a wide range of services to an ever-wider range of clients. The majority of OSIM's business came from small and middle-sized companies and some government agencies, and the company had developed some specialization in electronics and construction.

In general, OSIM's strategy evolved implicitly rather than through any explicit, centrally planned process. Basically, whatever technical problem, real-estate project, or deal-making opportunity any officer wanted to pursue, he or she could. The expansion of services arose from several factors: (1) OSIM's high level of technical competence, (2) the industry trend toward an increasing overlap of consulting and financial service suppliers, (3) the independent, entrepreneurial characteristics of the staff, and, probably most importantly, (4) the desire on the part of OSIM's staff for intellectual and creative challenge, which was more likely to occur with new types of services, projects, and client industries than with repetitive projects.

OSIM had also been influenced by Dave Wright's management style. As Stark described it,

> The management style of the president could be characterized as decentral-ized management over the years. He's an inspirational-type leader but not at all an operations manager. He had let the organization run—the divisions run—independently and autonomously.

Some of the officers who were upset about the terms of OSIM's acquisi-tion by Shilo were also unhappy with Dave Wright's objectives and style. Again, according to Stark,

> Frank Lewisburg [the marketing director] told me that a good company is one where there's structure and discipline and a style of each person playing his role, a team approach, and so on; whereas this company has really been run on an entrepreneurial basis, very informal communications, lack of deci-sion making, delegation of everything to the divisions, and a resulting pro-tective, highly autonomous behavior on the part of the divisions. Frank found that bothersome, and he didn't think it was going to work in the long run. He felt a company couldn't develop to any size with that, and I think that's absolutely right. He comes from a very-large-company background, so he's very familiar with that culture. He doesn't understand a small-company, entrepreneurial culture and found it very uncomfortable to work with the lack of structure and lack of rules; he just had a general uneasiness about who is he and what role is he playing. The only disagreement that I have with

Frank is that Dave Wright brought the company to where it is today, and it's kind of hard to argue with the fact that it's been very successful. It doesn't mean that we don't have growth problems and challenges from here on out, but let's not ignore the strength of the approach that Dave used. It may have outlived its usefulness, but it did work up to this point.

Strategic planning had been tried on occasion in the past at OSIM, but to no avail. Stark explained,

In our case, planning is viewed as a nuisance task that is separate from management, and there has been no breakthrough on the several attempts that have been made. In fact, the very title or term *strategic planner* has been contaminated.

THE OUTLOOK FOR STRATEGIC PLANNING AND STRATEGIC CHANGE AT OSIM

Stark had to consider several key factors in initiating strategic planning at OSIM. The first was the attitudes toward planning, which varied at different levels of the firm. Stark recalled,

The general attitude that I got from talking to any vice president was, "Oh, you want to know about what we're doing and what kind of business we're in? Ask me anything you want to know, and I'll tell you, but don't bother my people." It's the autonomy and "chargeable hours" business again. There was a definite crust in the organization at the vice president level through which it was difficult to move. Whereas if I talked to managers or senior associates, they were all enthusiastic about planning, talked about what they were doing, saw a critical need for planning in the organization, and were willing to support it. This was generally true, firmwide. There may have been pockets of resistance, but generally there was a lot of energy and enthusiasm at the lower levels.

The second factor was the degree and form of support from top management. Stark explained,

The president, Dave Wright, may be intellectually committed to the process but may not actually give firm backing to the planning sequence as we go through it. The chairman, Bob Cedarholm, will be bottom up and pragmatic. This affects my posture regarding the division heads and other officers: in particular, it defines the level of formal or implicit authority that I have. The view is that, if the chairman and president publicly endorse and support this effort and are willing to make it happen, it makes my job easier and I have more implicit and formal authority. If they are not going to back it up, if they are just going to *talk* strategic planning, then I've got to do much more persuasion, particularly of the division heads and other officers.

I think I designed my own job to a large extent. When I was in the Management Program and learning of the acquisition, I was having discussions with the president about playing some sort of planning role when I got back. We talked extensively about that because, under the acquisition, the planning function was even more important and more complex, especially with the interaction with the other parts of the SFS group. Through a series of discussions at the end of May, we shaped plans for a strategic-planning staff position which I would move into when I came back to OSIM. During that time, I also had one conversation with the chairman of the board. He was very enthusiastic about this role and thought it was very important for OSIM. I guess I contributed most of the initiative in terms of defining it.

A third factor was Stark's own credibility as a planner with OSIM:

On the positive side, I come from the ranks and have had experience with different parts of the company, so I understand their problems. The extent to which I appear to be using this position for my advantage is important, so I am very careful to present the image of putting OSIM first, that planning isn't everything, and that no one should get the idea that this could come out big for me in the short run. That is what I need to be sensitive to, I believe. The planner's own personal style will influence his acceptability also, whether he is directive in nature or more of a facilitator.

Another part is my detachment from previous associations. If they think I'm partial to the engineering services VP, I will lose credibility, and I have to be careful about that. My previous job was manager in the engineering services division, and I reported to the vice president.

Finally, and very important I think, is the credibility of my formal education, and whether or not they believe there is something to that. But I'm not going to explain to them the full scope and extent of what I know, because that always remains a competitive advantage in promoting and implementing strategic planning.

The fourth issue was the integration with Shilo planning:

To the question, "Are OSIM's changes being dictated by New York?" I would say that, in an implicit way, the perception is that if we don't get our act together, New York will get it together for us, and so it's our chance to do it on our own. There's a definite influence, but it's indirect.

One factor in this is the conscious attempt on our part to use to our advantage in planning the fact that nobody knows what Shilo expects from us. So we'd better get our act together before Shilo comes swooping in and lays goals on us, and the way to get our act together is through planning. Nobody can say, "Well, I've talked to those guys; I know what they want, and they are not going to do any planning for five years and forget it." It is the anxiety about what the new owners are going to do to us that can be used to our advantage. The director of operations and I will consciously be using that anxiety as we go through the budgeting cycle and then into the planning cycle with the VPs. You might go to them and say that we need to get our act together; we need to put our plans together. Shilo will probably require that from us, so we better design our own system. Some of that may be true or not, but we can use that as part of the internal selling process on the stick end. Another uncertainty is whether or not our system is compatible with the Shilo planning process. I know that it is, because Shilo doesn't have a planning process, so that's no problem. And another political factor is Shilo's belief in the effectiveness of planning. Particularly, the chairman of the board of Shilo is an ex-planner and believes in it; so we've got his support and it helps.

The fifth issue was OSIM's previous experience with planning, mentioned earlier. Because most people viewed planning as nonsense and didn't believe anything would happen, Stark had to deal with this bias:

> There was the whole set of issues having to do with how to sell this process to the vice presidents and the use of "small wins" early on to overcome their concern about what's going to happen to them when you start planning. Are we going to plan them out of a job? Are we going to cut up their organization and give parts to someone else? And just the cultural inertia against planning and the focus on operations—the general resistance to change.

PERSONAL CHALLENGES AND RISKS

Stark's intellectual challenge involved the technical issues of instituting strategic planning at OSIM. To begin, he organized his thoughts and asked a series of questions:

> How am I going to plan my attack on my firm? Is an incremental strategy right for the organization, or a so-called synoptic strategy? Do we start with a set or statement of corporate goals, or do we start with a business definition? How do we organize people into planning groups in the company, and at what level? Implicit in that question is how to get around the vice presidents—this crust level I was encountering. What portfolio-analysis tools are appropriate for our kind of business? How should competitor analysis be done? How about industry analysis? At what levels do you do portfolio analysis in the organization? How do you organize into business units? Is the current organization appropriate? Are charters well enough defined? And there are other specific issues having to do with the planning relationship between us and Shilo and the planning relation between us and the rest of SFS. Then we get into issues like performance measurement, computer-based support systems for monitoring progress, reporting systems, and so on.

Stark was looking forward to his position at OSIM:

> Coming into the job, it looked like an ideal set-up. I'd been with the company for nine years; I knew the style of business, the customers, the people. I had watched it grow over the years. As part of a network in the company, I had a lot of contacts. I had been working in the technical areas and had a technical background similar to the people in the company. On the other hand, going through the Management Program and seeing how things *might* be done, I could see a lot of payoff in bringing some of the strategic management techniques to this company. Also, the president and the chairman, but particu-

larly the president, were talking strategic management strongly. The acquisition had provided capitalization and the potential for working toward a world-class international consulting and financial services firm. So, it was all very exciting and timely and fortuitous.

However, Stark

saw the problem of dealing with a consulting-type culture and moving that into a planning mode as a significant implementation problem, as well as a significant challenge in the area of how you define businesses, how you think about planning in the consulting and financial services industries, how you might structure a rational planning process. That part was to be a challenge. It was further complicated by the passive management style of the president.

So already there was substantial challenge requiring a good deal of clearheaded thinking. But then things were further complicated by the political intrigue that I walked into in the first week. Here I was, with a formidable technical task, and now I had to deal with politics as well. My reaction was, "Oh, s—t. I thought this was going to be fun. Now it's going to be work."

Then there were the calculations of personal risk:

There was discussion on several levels. One was with the marketing director at lunch my first week back at OSIM. He said, "You know, if we don't get our act together, this place could fail. You and I can't be hired by A. D. Little or others, because we're too old. If we don't make it here. . . . We can sit around five years from now and laugh about this, but now's the time to take action. We all want to get rich" and that kind of thing. And, "You've got a family to support; you'd better think about *them*." Talking later to my wife Janet, I said, "I have to think about you and the kids."

So you know there's self-preservation there. I don't know to what extent that enters in—maybe at an unconscious level. I did not sit down and calculate what the odds are. Another concern is that I'm possibly going to be thrown out on my ass, and therefore I had better go talk to the chairman.

During the lunch with Frank Lewisburg, Stark was startled to learn that Patricia Thompson, director of operations, and Doug Robb, director of administration, were Lewisburg's coconspirators. "My general reaction to this whole thing was disbelief. Like, oh come on, this can't be real."

These thoughts, and the ones described previously, were running through Stark's mind as he headed for his meeting with Bob Cedarholm.

STARK'S MEETING WITH THE CHAIRMAN

Stark went in to see the chairman on Thursday, June 9, the morning after his discussion with Lewisburg. The meeting started out interestingly; Cedarholm closed the door and said, "Well, Tom, how candid do you want to be?"

CASE APPENDIX

HISTORIES OF KEY PLAYERS IN OSIM

- *Hugh Larsen.* Chairman of the board of Shilo Investment Bank, OSIM's parent company. Larsen had extensive consulting and financial analysis experience and had been a strategic planner. As such, he believed in the process of strategic planning and could be expected to encourage and push it at OSIM.

- *Bob Cedarholm.* Chairman of the board of OSIM Corporation. Cedarholm was a financial wheeler-dealer and a "business" type of person. He was beginning to talk strategic management.

- *Dave Wright.* President of OSIM Corporation. Wright held a Ph.D. and was very technically oriented. He had been with OSIM for many years and had risen through the engineering services division. Wright was Tom Stark's mentor.

- *Patricia Thompson.* Director of operations.

- *Doug Robb.* Director of administration.

  Thompson and Robb had been with OSIM Corporation for many years, including the high-growth years of the 1970s. Because of the length of their terms with OSIM, they were unhappy not to have benefited financially from the acquisition. They performed staff functions and were administrative, nontechnical types who were more naturally inclined to work with the chairman than the president.

- *Frank Lewisburg.* Director of marketing. Lewisburg was an administrative, nontechnical, big-company, business-type person. He believed he could lead OSIM to higher growth but felt held back by OSIM's president and the president's unstructured management style.

- *Michael Liu.* Vice president, engineering services. Liu had worked for OSIM for more than 20 years and was a major financial beneficiary of OSIM's acquisition by Shilo. His power in the organization stemmed from his long tenure and his competent control of OSIM's largest division.

- *Isabelle Abbey.* Vice president, real estate. Abbey joined OSIM in the mid-1960s and was responsible for solidifying and expanding OSIM's real-estate division. As a result, she exercised substantial influence within the company and was rewarded financially for her achievements at the time of the acquisition.

PENINSULAR INSURANCE (A)

Patrick Wale stood in the conference room staring in amazement at the chairman, Tan Sri Ibrahim Nassan. Ibrahim Nassan, the titular head of Peninsular Insurance, had just taken charge of Wale's planning meeting with an interruption that Wale saw as an attempt to subvert his authority with his managers. By the looks on their faces, Wale surmised that his managers were just as surprised as he by such an overt power play. With the 1985 Malaysian economy in recession, and company revenues sliding, now was not the time to play politics. As his adrenalin began to flow, Wale was at a loss as to how to regain control of the meeting and, by implication, of his Malaysian insurance organization. As his mind raced, he thought, "All I know is that, whatever I do next, it's going to have to be played by the Malay rules: respect for elders and 'saving face.' The question is whether I can show one without losing the other."

BACKGROUND

Patrick Wale had arrived in Kuala Lumpur ("KL", capital of Malaysia) almost three years previously to oversee the merger of the wholly owned Malaysian subsidiary of New Zealand Insurance Corporation (NZI) with the Malaysian-majority-owned Peninsular Insurance. He should have been finished within the first 12 months. In fact, however, after the first two years, he had barely scratched the surface of a project that was becoming more Byzantine by the week.

Wale considered himself good at adapting and working with other cultures. His work for NZI had taken him to Nigeria, South Africa, India, and, in his last position as branch manager, to Hong Kong, NZI's largest branch in Asia ($8 million in annual sales). (See Exhibit 1 for a profile of Wale and other key executives.)

Wale had felt at home in the freewheeling, business-first culture of Hong Kong. The absence of political barriers allowed him to concentrate on "getting on with business" without the worry of government regulations. But when NZI's then-general manager of international operations called to offer him the

This case was prepared by James M. Berger, Darden MBA 1992, under the supervision of Professor L. J. Bourgeois III. Copyright © 1992 Darden Graduate Business School Foundation, Charlottesville, VA.

Exhibit 1
Peninsular Insurance
Central Characters

PATRICK WALE: AGE 42

After dropping out of high school in New Zealand, 16-year-old Patrick Wale began work in 1961 as an office boy with NZI. He studied in night school for three years to complete the insurance exams and began to move up the corporate hierachy. In 1966, he was offered a position with the overseas staff.

A self-described adventurer, Wale accepted transfers to offices around the world, including Nigeria, India, South Africa, and Hong Kong. Each move improved his position within the corporation and finally led to his present appointment as CEO of the NZI joint venture with a Malaysian partner.

Married in 1969, Wale met his wife in Calcutta, where she was working for the British High Commission. Their two children, a 14-year-old son and a 13-year-old daughter, had been recently sent to boarding schools in England.

NIGEL FISHER: AGE 57

Fisher had been employed by NZ since 1942; he was appointed to a senior position with the home office in 1960 after a series of international transfers. His progress within the company appeared stalled after the 1981 merger produced a surfeit of middle managers, but he was appointed general manager of the international group in 1985 after its previous two years of results fell well below corporate expectations for the Asian operations. Fisher was due to retire in June of 1986.

Fisher was described by a colleague as possessing strong analytical but weak interpersonal skills and having a dour personality.

TAN SRI HAJI IBRAHIM NASSAN: AGE 73

Tan Sri Haji Ibrahim Nassan Bin Haji Ibrahim Siddiq[1] (his full name) had a prominent civil-servant career with the Malaysian government, cul-

(continued on next page)

---

[1]A convention in Malaysian names and titles conveyed social and political rank, lineage, and Muslim pilgrimage: "Datuk" was a title conveyed on men of accomplishment. "Tan Sri" was a higher honor, fewer in number. It was given by the sultan, usually for public servants of high rank. "Tan" was the highest honor possible in Malaysia, short of royalty. "Haji" indicated that the individual had made the pilgrimage to Mecca. "Bin" meant "son of."

(continued)

minating in his role as secretary general of Internal Affairs, responsible for the police, justice, and immigration. Retired at age 55, he was quickly invited to sit on several company boards and had been Peninsular Insurance's chairman since 1967. He was required to retire from all but Peninsular's board at age 70.

Nassan was known as a man who paid strong attention to detail and required a high level of protocol at all times. He was married and had five sons.

position of chief executive officer of the Malaysian joint venture, Wale jumped at the opportunity.

The combination of NZI's $12-million subsidiary with its 49-percent owned, $4-million Peninsular would be double the size of the Hong Kong division in staff and sales. The task was an unusual one, because Wale would actually be wearing two hats: as the head of the NZI subsidiary reporting to the home office in New Zealand and as general manager of Peninsular reporting to the local board. That situation would change, however, when the merger went through and the combined ($16-million) entity would be 74-percent owned by NZI and working under a single management.

NZI, LTD.

New Zealanders pride themselves on their self reliance . . . it's called kiwi ingenuity.[1]

NZI was a diversified financial services company based in Auckland, New Zealand. One of the country's largest companies, NZI was formed in 1981 from the merger of New Zealand Insurance (founded 1859) and South British Insurance Company (founded 1872). The result was a multinational corporation operating in 24 countries through hundreds of offices.

Revenues of the merged company had reached $630 million in 1982, with a reported net income of $28 million. The international divisions of NZI's

---

[1]Annemarie Orange, Darden 1992, native of New Zealand.

General Insurance Group contributed 35 percent of divisional income. (See Exhibit 2 for organization of NZI.) Each of the seven divisions of the company was run as a profit center.

NZI had concentrated its foreign business in the Pacific Rim and Africa and adopted a strategy of growth through local offices in order to gain a balance in both operations and the product mix offered by the company.

NZI had recently been riding a tremendous wave of new business brought about by booming regional economies and an aggressive new corporate style of management that expanded the company's business into previously unconventional areas. NZI had also concentrated on shifting power to

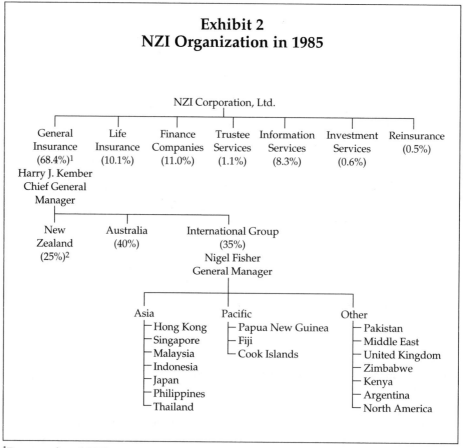

Exhibit 2
NZI Organization in 1985

[1]Percent of total NZI revenues.
[2]Percent of total general insurance revenues.

the local offices in order to encourage growth, and the new strategy called for equally aggressive management by NZI's field managers, who were afforded a large degree of autonomy by the home office. Within the financial services industries of the Pacific and Asia, NZI was considered to be one of the most aggressive in its mix of markets, products, and technologies.

NZI held interests in two key Malaysian operations. NZI Malaysia was a branch network offering the full range of insurance services and accounting for $12 million in revenues. Peninsular Insurance Company, with $4 million in revenues, was 49-percent owned by NZI, with the remainder owned by Malaysian nationals. Peninsular had been formed by NZI in 1967 with the ultimate aim of controlling all its business interests in Malaysia, in line with government policy of local incorporation of foreign branches.

Weak profits in an otherwise growing economy had led to a decision in 1982 to consolidate all Malaysian operations in order to reduce costs and provide for a more coherent strategy. An agreement was reached that Peninsular Insurance would merge with NZI Malaysia in a pooling-of-interests transaction.

MALAYSIA

The Federation of Malaysia was a peninsular country located at the southern tip of Thailand, with two Malaysian states located several hundred miles across the South China Sea on the island of Borneo. Following independence from the United Kingdom in 1957, the federation was established in 1963. Malaysia was a constitutional monarchy whose king (the Yang di Pertuan Agong) was elected for a five-year period by a council of nine ruling sultans from the federated states.

Natural Resources and the Economy

Malaysia had a population of 14 million people, with the capital of Kuala Lumpur housing 938,000. The country held a dominant world position in rubber, palm oil, pepper, tin, and tropical hardwoods; these and other abundant natural resources had given Malaysia one of the highest annual growth rates per capita in the world: growth at 4.5 percent per year since 1965 and per-capita gross national product of more than $1,555 by 1985.

The government had been aggressively pushing the economy toward a manufacturing base since the 1970s. Emphasis was on building the travel and communication infrastructure necessary for industrial growth, and the government maintained a policy of encouraging rapid population growth in order to stimulate domestic demand. The policy appeared to be working: manufacturing began to overtake agriculture as a percentage of gross domestic product and, by the 1980s, was the main source of economic growth. The unemployment rate was 5.6 percent in 1985 and the inflation rate was 3.7 percent.

Political Aspects and the NEP

> It's not a law, its a government policy, and it is really like shadow boxing because you never really know quite where the target is.[2]

Because Malaysia was a multiracial society, friction generated by the different cultures was the most important aspect of Malaysian politics. Political parties were based primarily on racial lines; the United Malays National Organization was the largest but shared power in a broad-based coalition with the Malaysian Chinese Association, the Malaysian Indian Congress, and several other, smaller parties.

After a violent anti-Chinese race riot in 1969, the Malaysian government established the "mitigation of inequity between races" as the overriding goal for the government. As a response to this goal, the New Economic Policy (NEP) was established in 1970 to help the "bumiputra" (Malay for "son of the soil"), which refers to native Malays, who were considered the main beneficiaries of the policies. One way the NEP attempted to reach its goals was through increased spending on education and basic services. Public enterprises such as the Trust Council for Indigenous Peoples were chartered to finance native Malay businesses and to provide advice to prospective Malay businesspeople.

The government had also set a goal of increasing native Malay ownership in the corporate sector to 30 percent by 1990. All other Malays were designated 40-percent corporate ownership, and foreign-owned stakes were to fall to the remaining 30 percent. In addition, foreign-owned companies were required to restructure equity so at least 70 percent was held by Malaysian investors.

According to Wale, at the time of his arrival in 1982 the government was putting extra pressure on foreign firms to "domesticate" their firms and to increase their local share holdings. One way of applying this pressure was to grant very limited term work permits. Government regulations in 1982 required all foreign nationals to apply for a Visitor's Work Visa, usually for 12 months. But when pressure on a company was desired, only 3 or 6 months were given, and the threat was always present that a visa would not be renewed. As Wale described this threat, "I had no idea whether I would be here for the full five years of my assignment or I would be on the plane in a month's time. They were playing the game with all insurance companies here that the best way to make foreign companies take on local partners was to mess around with their work permits."

---

[2]Patrick Wale.

Another important factor in the Malaysian political structure was the presence of the military. In the early years of the federation, in a period known locally as "the emergency," the country was plagued by civil war. Not until the middle 1970s did the threat from the Communist insurgents greatly lessen. The product of the civil war was a virulently anti-Communist government that retained full constitutional control of the professional military force.

THE NZI MALAYSIAN STAFF

> Well it's all very much tied into the Asian face thing, that you don't just say what's on your mind to the guy in case you offend him.[3]

Not long after taking over as general manager of Peninsular, Wale established good working relationships with the management and board. (Wale was appointed to the board in March 1983, as an alternate for Harry Kember, a board member based in New Zealand.) The foremost figure of the company was the local chairman of the board, Tan Sri Ibrahim Nassan, a prominent citizen in Malaysia who had once served as a high-level government official in the Interior Department (see Exhibit 1).

Wale soon realized that the chairman was remote from any real decision making for Peninsular; he served in a mostly ceremonial role. The chairman would show up at board meetings, start the occasion with a brief speech (usually written for him), and then leave management to discuss the mundane operational issues. Wale found the chairman to be a supportive gentleman; he allowed Wale to go about the business of modernizing the company's operation and organizing the mechanics of the merger, and he was particularly helpful in the area of smoothing over potential problems with the government. Immigration had been one of the departments under the chairman's supervision, and he expedited Wale's reapplication for a work permit several times.

The 73-year-old chairman, at 5'7", was quite a contrast with Wale who, at 42, was 6'4" and weighed 250 pounds. Recently, Nassan had been forced to leave most of his other board positions because of the mandatory retirement age written into most public companies' bylaws. Peninsular, as a private company, did not have such a rule. The chairman was thought to be quite well off financially, although Wale had also heard that he had recently been involved in some rather unfortunate investments, probably in the volatile Malaysian stock market.

Since the early, supportive days, Wale had found himself on occasion becoming annoyed by the chairman's tendency to bypass Wale and call the corporate secretary, Goh Lai King, when he wished to check on the business

---

[3]Patrick Wale.

or consult with a manager. King had been with Peninsular for almost 15 years, and the chairman had formed a separate line of communication with him. Wale believed that, as a matter of protocol, the CEO should be the first to be consulted for advice or questions, but he had also recognized how petty it would be to try to cut off this communication. (See Exhibit 3 for Peninsular organization.)

Wale had also quickly formed a close working relationship with the Malaysian operations manager, Tan Peng Soo. Soo was particularly knowledgeable about the daily workings of Peninsular, and Wale relied on his judgment about how best to implement the new training and computerization programs that would bring Peninsular's operations up with the rest of the NZI organization. Because Wale expected to move on when the merger was consummated, he began grooming Tan Peng Soo for the CEO position. Wale understood that Soo's strong business acumen and Malaysian nationality would make him a natural choice to run the merged company.

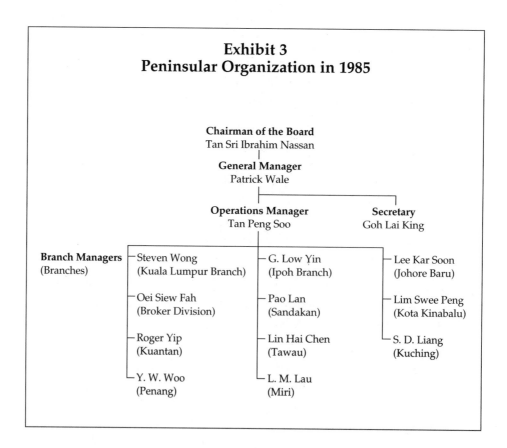

Exhibit 3
Peninsular Organization in 1985

Chairman of the Board
Tan Sri Ibrahim Nassan

General Manager
Patrick Wale

Operations Manager   **Secretary**
Tan Peng Soo   Goh Lai King

Branch Managers
(Branches)

Steven Wong   G. Low Yin   Lee Kar Soon
(Kuala Lumpur Branch) (Ipoh Branch)   (Johore Baru)

Oei Siew Fah   Pao Lan   Lim Swee Peng
(Broker Division)   (Sandakan)   (Kota Kinabalu)

Roger Yip   Lin Hai Chen   S. D. Liang
(Kuantan)   (Tawau)   (Kuching)

Y. W. Woo   L. M. Lau
(Penang)   (Miri)

MEETING WITH THE CHAIRMAN

The question was whether the merger would ever come to fruition. Wale had become increasingly frustrated by the tortuously slow nature of Malaysian business dealings, particularly those with the vast government bureaucracy. Two years had already passed, and almost nothing had been accomplished. He spent most of his time waiting months for written replies from government officials, replies that would have taken days in Hong Kong.

During this first two years in Malaysia, Wale occasionally visited the chairman at his home in a wealthy KL neighborhood to update him on the progress of the merger and discuss how the business was doing in general. Wale had arranged such a meeting to discuss the slow replies of the government and an upcoming board meeting with the visiting directors from New Zealand.

As a courtesy, Wale had always visited the chairman at home, but he was becoming increasingly uncomfortable with the practice. He had noticed that, while they were seated in the chairman's sitting room discussing business, the chairman's wife would be sitting in the adjacent room apparently listening in on their conversation. She would often make an excuse to come in and interrupt and would then linger on during the discussion. The chairman's wife was quite a bit younger than he, probably 15 or 20 years. Wale recognized that she was a strong-willed woman, and perhaps this trait, combined with her ability to make her presence felt and known, was what made Wale uncomfortable.

On this humid July 1984 day, the chairman seemed to have little to offer in regard to the government delays. Wale then asked, "Well, sir, do you have any suggestions on where we may want to host the dinner for our visiting board members? I thought that your club did a superior job on the last occasion."

The chairman leaned forward, "Yes, well, I believe . . ."

"The club? Certainly not the club!" His wife suddenly emerged into the room. "Why don't we try the Rasa Sayang for a change? I think the gentlemen from the home office would much prefer that."

Wale observed the chairman as his wife continued telling them where the meeting should be and what should be on the menu. The chairman was obviously a bit taken aback, and Wale realized that he probably had the same expression on his own face.

Driving back to his office that afternoon, Wale decided to discontinue the practice of going to the chairman's house to talk business. Perhaps he was being silly, but the wife's interference was bothersome.

NIGEL FISHER VISITS

Several months later (February 1985), Wale received a call from Nigel Fisher in the New Zealand office telling him that Fisher would be visiting the

Malaysia office in two weeks. Fisher was the newly appointed general manager in charge of international operations, the third general manager in as many years. Fisher had worked with Wale before, and Wale looked forward to being able to discuss with him the reasons for the merger's slow going. Wale hoped to receive the level of support from the home office necessary to accelerate the merger.

A few days before Fisher's arrival, the chairman called Wale to his office. He requested that Wale arrange for King, the company secretary, to be present at Nassan's meeting with Fisher "just in case there is anything that I would like to put on the record." Wale checked with King later that day to arrange for him to attend the meeting.

The day before the meeting, King approached Wale and asked whether it was really necessary for him to attend. King said, "I am very sorry, but I realized that I have a prior appointment with the Tax Department and think that it oughtn't be broken." Wale readily agreed that the appointment was important and promised that, if necessary, he would take notes. Wale assured King that the chairman would not mind.

"Well, the chairman did bloody well mind," Wale recounted later. Before the meeting with Fisher, Wale went to the chairman's office and asked whether he would like for Wale to sit in and take notes on the meeting. "No, I would prefer this meeting to be one on one," the chairman responded. The meeting lasted almost an hour, and, immediately afterward, the chairman called Wale into his office. "Where was Mr. King?" he asked as Wale took a seat. "I instructed you to have him here to take notes."

"Yes, he came to me yesterday and informed me that he had a previous engagement with the tax office. I told him to carry on with his meeting and that I would take any notes if you wanted. But obviously you . . ."

"This is very upsetting, Patrick. Why did you countermand my specific instructions for the secretary?"

Wale had never heard this kind of tone from the chairman, who was always scrupulously polite. "I must apologize if it seems that way. It was a genuine misunderstanding on my part. I had thought that under the circumstances he should carry on with his meeting and I could take notes."

"The circumstances were that I gave specific orders, and you saw fit to ignore them. If you ever countermand my instructions again, I will call the home office to have you removed from Malaysia."

Wale left the office feeling confused and a bit angry at the chairman's behavior. It was becoming apparent that he would have to start keeping his eyes open to what was a changing situation at Peninsular.

Soon thereafter, Wale asked Fisher about what had transpired during the meeting. Although Wale had never particularly got on with Fisher, finding Fisher's style too aloof for his tastes, he was confident that Fisher was sufficiently loyal to him not to discuss things with a local chairman behind Wale's back. Fisher said, "Oh, we mostly discussed the mechanics of the merger, the pricing of the shares, and that sort of thing. I told Tan Sri Nassan that NZI believes in keeping an arms-length relationship with our foreign offices. Said we would act as corporate advisers and assured him that we wouldn't steam-roll the minority stockholders." When Wale brought up the timing of the merger and his troubles with the bureaucracy, however, he was frustrated by Fisher's lack of support.

"I'm sure you will get things moving along. You're just going to have to stop spending so much time dealing with the politics," Fisher said, smiling weakly.

Wale understood that his point was not getting through. If he had learned one thing from his two and a half years in Malaysia, it was that business *was* politics here.

THE ANNUAL PLANNING MEETING

I guess I was fairly stunned.[4]

In the next six months, the two companies made some real progress toward the merger. Wale met with the corporate attorneys, who calculated that, at the negotiated pricing, NZI should control 76 percent of the new entity, which would afford the company similar representation on the board. The company planned to keep the present four-to-four ratio of NZI representative and local board members, however, to keep up the appearance of a joint venture.

For the moment, Wale was concerned with the annual planning meeting scheduled for the end of September. During the meeting, the managers of each of Peninsular's 12 regional branches would present their individual financial plans and their strategies, staffing, and support needs for the coming year. As Wale described it, "We would put all these into the melting pot at this work-shop and then come back about a month later with a finalized plan on a coun-trywide basis. This was the start of that cycle—asking each territory to stand up for 15 to 20 minutes and give a rundown on their major objectives for the year, their strategies, and where their strengths and weaknesses were. Nor-mally, it would be the practice of two or three of us at the KL office to ask probing questions of the branch manager." The managers were encouraged to try out new ideas and to question each other or Wale about operational prac-tices. Wale saw this open forum as serving two purposes: it encouraged branch managers to think beyond their own office's needs, and it could antic-ipate many of the questions that would come from the home office when bud-get requests were reviewed.

This year, Wale was particularly concerned about the downturn in the Malaysian economy and wanted to keep the next year's costs to a minimum. (Peninsular was projecting a small loss for the year—see Exhibit 4.) As he always did, Wale asked the chairman if he would like to address the meeting

---

[4]Patrick Wale.

Exhibit 4
Peninsular Insurance
Financial History

NEW ZEALAND INSURANCE, LTD.
(NZ $ MILLIONS)

	1982	1983	1984
Revenues	630	752	805
Net income	28	18	49

PENINSULAR INSURANCE
(NZ$MILLIONS)[1]

	1982	1983	1984	1985(e)
Revenues	5.6	4.9	4.8	4.2
Net income	.3	.6	.4	(.04)

[1]Converted at NZ $1.00 = 1.17 Malaysian Ringitt. In 1985, NZ $1.00 = US $0.468.

before morning tea. The chairman agreed and accepted Wale's offer to write a brief speech on the state of the company.

The meeting was held in the board room; the large, adjustable table was that day configured in an open square, at which sat the 12 branch managers, the corporate secretary, the technology manager, Tan (the operations manager), Wale, and the chairman (seated next to each other). The morning started normally enough. The chairman offered his welcome to the branch managers and read Wale's opening statement. After the morning tea, Wale called the meeting to order. To his surprise, the chairman had not slipped out as he normally did but had come back to his seat next to Wale.

During the second presentation by a branch manager, Wale interrupted to question the manager's figures:

Wale: "Mr. Lan, I'm not sure I see the basis for your staffing requirements. What are the growth projections that you are using for your figures?"

Branch Manager: "We are forecasting a 15-percent growth in sales and revenues."

Wale: "From what I have seen of your present operations, I would say that you already have the excess staffing necessary to support even a 15-

percent growth, which is certainly aggressive. From a cost basis, I do not see how you can justify that many more people. Do you suppose . . . "

Chairman: "Hold on, Patrick. It is very easy for you managers in the central office to look at numbers and question them. But this man is dealing with the reality of working in the field and seems to have very good reasons for his staffing numbers. You always expect these poor chaps in the branch to meet the targets, but then they never get the proper support from you. Now they cannot even get the staff they require to do their job correctly."

Wale (after pausing for a moment): "Mr. Chairman, perhaps we should take a look at this situation after the meeting. I'm sure we can discuss this and have it sorted out very quickly."

Chairman: "The issue is certainly an important one. I believe that all of the branch managers would like clarity about the signals they are getting from the central office in Kuala Lumpur. Mr. Lan's projections seem perfectly reasonable, and I know from my long association with Peninsular Insurance that his office is one of the finest in this organization. Mr. Lan, please continue with your excellent presentation. And Patrick, I will be happy to discuss this with yourself and Mr. Soo at the end of these proceedings."

The chairman waved his hand at Lan as a signal for him to continue. The branch manager stammered to a start and quickly moved on to a new topic.

Wale did not hear a word of it. The chairman's outburst had come as a complete shock, and Wale was trying to gather his wits and consider what his next move should be. He scanned the faces around the table as the managers quickly switched their eyes from him and back to the speaker. Soo returned his gaze with a look that was both stunned and quizzical, and Wale knew that they were thinking the same thing: "What is the old bugger up to?"

Wale was not about to stand aside. For the rest of the day, he continued to facilitate the meeting, but there was almost no free exchange of ideas from the managers from that point on. Everyone seemed to be concerned about saying something that might lead to another controversy. Meanwhile, the chairman continued to chime in, making it perfectly clear who he thought was in charge of the proceedings.

Wale wondered what his next move should be. He wondered what the chairman's next move would be. The man did have connections, and the merger was six months, at least, from completion. Having a retired bureaucrat who knew nothing about business attempting to run the show certainly was not going to help things along. And what about the other managers? Wale had never considered questioning their loyalty, but this episode put everything in a new light.

BENNETT ASSOCIATION (A)

In mid-October 1981, as Michael Silva reviewed his management plans for the Bennett Association, he wondered about all he needed to accomplish. Having been CEO for less than two weeks, he felt he needed to make some significant changes in the companies that formed the Bennett Association. He wanted to have a clear picture of his strategy before he began, because he would need to implement the changes as quickly as possible. Despite having worked with the company for six months as a consultant, Silva was unsure whether the actions he was considering would be sufficient to turn the company around. Developing suggestions as a consultant and implementing them as a CEO were two entirely different things.

Part of the problem, he believed, was the very nature of the company he now ran. A group of traditional, family-owned companies, the Bennett Association had developed a strong, conservative, even paternalistic culture, which could make it resist adapting to changing situations. Several members of the Bennett family still worked at the various Bennett companies, including three as presidents of the paint and glass business, the leasing company, and the car rental agency. Perhaps Silva's most important concern was Wallace F. Bennett, for 24 years the U.S. Senator from Utah and current chairman of the Bennett board. Although "the Senator" had pledged his support to Silva, clearly the Senator's primary allegiance was to the company he had guided for 50 years and to the 200 family members for whom it provided a source of income.

The Bennett Association needed change, however. The banks had made that much evident when they demanded that an outside president be brought in to manage it. For the last four years, the Bennett companies had lost money, and this trend was continuing in 1981. Silva's major concern was whether the tradition-bound Bennett family would accept the fundamental changes necessary to save the company.

Another consideration was how many of the changes he should implement before his six-week vacation began on December 1. A three-month delay might result in even larger losses. On the other hand, if he wasn't there to push for the changes, staff resistance could undermine implementation of his strategy.

This case was prepared by Paul D. McKinnon and Elizabeth Bartholomew. Copyright © 1983 by the Darden Graduate Business School Sponsors, Charlottesville, VA. Revised May 1990.

HISTORY OF THE BENNETT ASSOCIATION

The Bennett Association was organized in 1917 as a Massachusetts trust to function as a holding company responsible for the financial interests of the trust beneficiaries—the descendants of John F. Bennett. The descendants received income from the trust according to the number of shares they held, which were similar to stock certificates. The decision-making authority rested with a board of trustees composed of family members. No nonfamily member could own shares.

Bennett's Paint and Glass, originally a grain and feed store known as Sears and Liddle (which dated from 1882), had always been the primary source of the Bennett Association's income. In 1884, John F. Bennett joined the company, and, in 1900, he bought out the owners to save the store from bankruptcy and changed the name to Bennett's.

The company soon became profitable, and it began to manufacture paint in 1904. As profitability continued, the physical plant doubled over the next 20 years. In 1920, John F.'s son, Wallace, a graduate of the University of Utah, joined the growing company. In that year, Bennett's also entered the retail glass business.

Wallace was given increasing responsibility for the store's operations. By the mid-1920s, he was running the entire manufacturing and sales functions. His brother Harold, two years his junior, saw little opportunity for himself in the family business and began a career at ZCMI, a large department-store chain in Utah. Harold, however, retained a seat on the board of directors.

In 1932, a struggle for control of the company after the death of one of John F. Bennett's brothers ended with John F. narrowly retaining control. However, he became increasingly dependent on his son Wallace to make day-to-day decisions. Although John F. Bennett remained president until his death in 1938, Wallace effectively ran the company.

During the next ten years, under Wallace's guidance, the company not only survived the Great Depression but also opened four new branches. During that period, Wallace developed a process that radically changed the paint industry. Until that time, all paint was tinted in the factory, with only 8 to 12 colors available to consumers. Dealers carried large inventories of the few colors in a variety of sizes. Although some experiments had been made with premeasured tubes of tint that could be added to basic white paint by the dealers to create varied colors, the process had met with limited acceptance.

Expanding on this idea, however, Wallace hired an interior decorator who created 3,000 distinct colors of paint by mixing tints. In 1935, Wallace decided to distribute 1,320 colors, launching Colorizer—the nation's first controlled tinting system. With this new system, paint dealers could carry much lower inventories. Using white paint as a base, dealers could add specific amounts of pigment to create a previously unavailable spectrum of colors. In 1949, Bennett organized Colorizer Associates as a group of regional paint manufacturers to promote the system nationally. These companies paid Bennett's royalties in exchange for tints and color cards. In 1981, Bennett's still owned and operated Colorizer Associates, although it represented a small stream of income.

In the late 1930s, Wallace expanded and diversified the association by acquiring a local Ford franchise—Bennett Motor Company—of which he became president.

In 1949, when he became president of the National Association of Manufacturers (NAM) headquartered in New York, Wallace turned the business over to his brother Richard (12 years younger than Wallace), who had worked in the company for some time. In 1950, after his stint as NAM president, Wallace returned to Utah to reassume control of Bennett's. Because Richard was reluctant to step down, Wallace, at the urging of several friends, chose to run for the U.S. Senate. He won and held the seat for four terms. (A more complete biography of Senator Bennett can be found in the Case Appendix on page 908.)

Under Richard's leadership, the Bennett Association continued to grow in profits and revenues. Although the Ford franchise was sold in 1967, the Bennett Association retained two spin-off businesses: Bennett Leasing, which was involved in all types of automotive, truck, and equipment leasing, and a National Car Rental franchise at the Salt Lake City airport. In 1976, an advertising company, Admix, was created to meet the promotional requirements of the Bennett Association and other Salt Lake City businesses.

After Richard's unexpected death in 1976, operating control of the Bennett companies fell to Wallace (Wally) G. Bennett, the Senator's oldest son. Although Richard had been formally president only of Bennett's Paint and Glass, he had exercised strong, if informal, control over the other companies. When Wally assumed control, he focused all his attention on Bennett's Paint and Glass, allowing the other company presidents freedom to manage their own operations. Although they still shared a common board of directors, the companies became increasingly independent, and each maintained control of its own finances. (See Exhibit 1 for a partial family tree.)

Serving with the Senator on the board of directors in 1981 were his brother Harold, by then chairman of the board of ZCMI, nephews Richard K. Winters and Kenneth Smith, and nephew-in-law Donald Penny. Voting power was unequally distributed, with the Senator having three votes; Harold, two; and the others, one each.

Financial Situation

Many internal and external factors contributed to the financial problems that the Bennett companies had faced since 1976. The Arab oil embargo and unprecedented levels of inflation had driven material costs higher and higher. However, to remain competitive, the paint company could not raise prices at a rate that would compensate for these increases. Compounding this problem was the lack of strong, central financial controls. Richard had been familiar

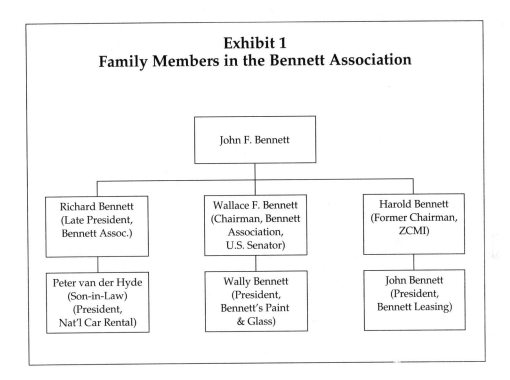

Exhibit 1
Family Members in the Bennett Association

John F. Bennett

Richard Bennett
(Late President,
Bennett Assoc.)

Wallace F. Bennett
(Chairman, Bennett
Association,
U.S. Senator)

Harold Bennett
(Former Chairman,
ZCMI)

Peter van der Hyde
(Son-in-Law)
(President,
Nat'l Car Rental)

Wally Bennett
(President,
Bennett's Paint
& Glass)

John Bennett
(President,
Bennett Leasing)

with the financial needs of the various businesses and had relied on his experience to notice any expenses that appeared out of line. The weakness of this piecemeal control system and lack of centralized budget became painfully apparent, however, when Wally assumed control. He was inexperienced with financial controls and could not convince his managers to institute a companywide budget.

As a result of these and other factors, in 1976 the Bennett Association suffered its first loss in over 50 years, and it continued to lose increasing amounts in successive years. In 1981, the anticipation of a $3.2-million loss on revenues of $28 million precipitated the bank's demand that an outside CEO be hired.

When Michael Silva became president, the Bennett Association included Bennett Leasing, Bennett's Paint and Glass, National Car Rental, and Admix (see Exhibit 2). The first three of these generated the majority of revenues and were each headed by a member of the Bennett family. The four were in different markets, however, and faced different challenges.

Despite the five years of operating losses, the Bennett financial situation was not without its bright spots. The Bennett Association owned more than $12 million in unencumbered assets, including eight acres of prime industrial land in Salt Lake City; various stocks and securities; the buildings and

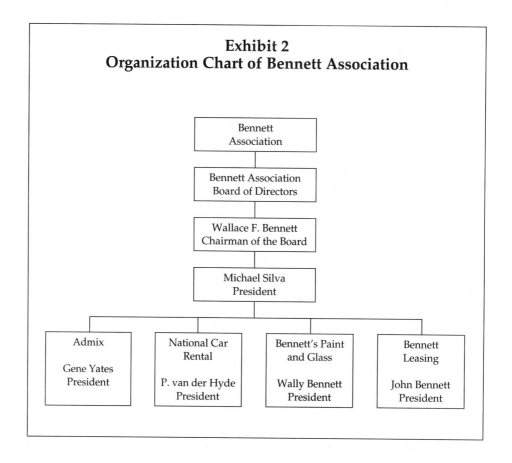

Exhibit 2
Organization Chart of Bennett Association

manufacturing facilities; and stores in Utah, Nevada, and Idaho. In addition, the Bennett name was recognized and respected throughout the region.

THE BENNETT COMPANIES: INDUSTRY AND COMPANY BACKGROUND

Bennett's Paint and Glass

In 1981, the U.S. paint and coatings industry was widely dispersed and included nearly 1,200 producers. Half of all the paints, varnishes, and lacquers sold covered buildings, predominantly houses. The second-largest primary market was automobile and other original equipment manufacturers, which used a third of the coatings produced. The remaining share of the market went to special-purpose coatings, which were high-performance coverings used to prolong equipment life in such industries as petroleum and chemicals.

Forecasts over the next ten years indicated that this segment would be the fastest growing in the coatings industry.

Building-paint sales were seasonal, peaking in the spring and summer, and closely tied to the construction industry. Since 1979, the depressed housing and automobile markets had caused a slump in paint sales (see Exhibit 3, U.S. paint shipments). In addition to the decline in new home construction, the recession had hurt sales in the large repainting market as people put off painting their homes. Recovery in the paint industry lagged that of the construction industry, because coatings are applied toward the end of home building.

Employing a total of 345 people, Bennett's Paint and Glass was the most well known of the Bennett companies and traditionally the most successful. Since the advent of the Colorizer concept in the 1930s, Bennett's had dominated the paint business in Utah and Idaho. Bennett's original store on 23rd South Street was well remembered by Salt Lake City residents even though it had long since changed hands and now housed a dress shop. Although it was a well-established and prominent Salt Lake City business, Bennett's high visibility within the community nevertheless seemed disproportionate to its size.

Exhibit 3
Paint, Varnish, and Lacquer Trade Sales, 1971–1981
(millions of gallons)

YEAR	SALES
1971	431.0
1972	451.5
1973	424.0
1974	474.7
1975	451.5
1976	473.5
1977	486.2
1978	512.3
1979	571.3
1980	529.5
1981	504.9

Sources: U.S. Department of Commerce, Bureau of the Census; *Kline Guide to the Paint Industry*, 1981.

As elsewhere, the paint and coatings market in Utah was fragmented and competitive. Neither Bennett's nor any of its major competitors (Fuller-O'Brien, Howells, Pittsburgh Paint & Glass, and Sears) had much more than a 10-percent share of commercial and consumer sales. Estimates indicated that Bennett's, with more than $1 million in consumer sales, outsold Sears in this area.

The manufacturing, warehousing, distribution, and leasing operations of the paint and glass business were located on an eight-acre parcel of land on 23rd South in Salt Lake City. Topped by the Colorizer trademark, a bold spectrum of colors, Bennett's light-green, nine-story warehouse dwarfed all other buildings in the area and was easily visible from the nearby freeway. Under the same roof were the paint-manufacturing and the glass-tempering operations and one of Bennett's 14 retail outlets.

Representative of all the Bennett's stores, the Salt Lake City outlet carried a complete line of Bennett's paints, along with painting supplies, bathroom and lighting fixtures, and a variety of sample windows. Windows were made to order for both walk-in customers and private contractors. Bennett's also bid on window contracts offered by large, national construction companies, although it had recently had difficulty securing contracts.

Branch and Outlet Sales. Each Bennett retail outlet in Utah, Nevada, and Idaho employed between 10 and 20 people. Dealers reported to an area manager, who then reported to a sales vice president in Salt Lake City. In addition to the Bennett-owned branches, salespeople visited 200 to 300 independent hardware stores that stocked Bennett's paint. Only about 20 percent of these stores generated the majority of all sales made through this channel. Salespeople were assigned to a specific geographical district, received a car and an expense account, and were paid on a commission basis.

Captive dealers purchased paint from Bennett's at cost and then used a 50-percent markup to determine retail price. The dealers either sold the paint to customers at full price or applied a variety of trade discounts. For example, depending on the volume of business, contractors purchased supplies for as little as 10 percent above dealer cost. Each dealer's performance was evaluated by sales volume.

Manufacturing. Bennett's manufactured a whole line of paints, including both latex and oil-based brands. The manufacturing facility included a research department (experimenting with different additives to improve product quality) and a maintenance staff of three full-time and two part-time people who kept the operation running smoothly. Productivity for the facility was 1,969 gallons per person per month in 1981, well below the industry average (see Exhibit 4).

As president, Wally Bennett had added both the huge new warehouse and a modern tempering that gave Bennett's state-of-the-art technology. The ware-

Exhibit 4
Paint Industry Productivity, 1970–1980

YEAR	AVERAGE GALLONS PRODUCED PER PERSON PER MONTH
1970	1,737
1971	1,931
1972	1,946
1973	1,959
1974	2,030
1975	2,154
1976	2,132
1977	2,184
1978	2,144
1979	2,371
1980	2,260

Source: *Kline Guide to the Paint Industry,* 1981.

house on 23rd South measured 80′ × 80′ × 80′. Merchandise was arranged along high corridors serviced by modern forklifts that moved both vertically and horizontally.

Thirty-nine employees working in three shifts staffed the warehouse. The morning shift filled the "will call" orders from the previous day, the afternoon shift stored the morning's paint production, and the night shift filled dealer orders.

Three unions represented workers in the plant: the Glaziers, the Allied Glass Workers, and the Steel Workers. In June 1981, the unions called a strike for a wage increase. For several weeks, management successfully ran the plant, and many felt that Bennett's was on the verge of winning, but the unions compromised on a contract that provided a 5-percent wage increase each year for three years. Although some managers wanted to hold out, Wally Bennett decided to accept the compromise.

Management. Years of profitability had lulled most of Bennett's highly tenured employees into a strong sense of security. Both the managerial and production staffs seemed unresponsive to calls for financial improvement and appeared unaware of the toll the economy was taking on the company's income statement.

A particular problem had been the attitude of Jack Nielson, former executive vice president of Bennett's. Jack Stevens, vice president of finance for the Bennett Association, commented on how Nielson's recent retirement had solved some of the problems:

> Jack was a VP of production, and he had been something of a favored son of Richard. He was quite egotistical and difficult to work with at times. Anyone who opposed him created a lot of problems, since this guy would always lose his temper. Because of that and Wally's style, he seemed to exercise more dominance over Wally than any of the other people. Wally always appeared to be rather cautious with this guy and would listen to him more than anyone else. Unfortunately, this guy didn't always have the best business insights. He was an engineer by trade and had been running the production operation, but he was promoted to executive vice president and began to have a bigger say in the way the rest of the business was run. As a result, it was often very hard to get new ideas into motion.

Jack Stevens had also wanted to get the company to use some form of budgeting:

> I know that budgeting is an excellent tool for management, but to others at Bennett's it is just an irritating accounting system. I provide each cost center with a history of their expenses for the current year, so all they have to do is put in a new number. The whole thing falls on deaf ears. When DeVon Johnson [currently VP of marketing] came on board, he had an interest in it, but he can't implement it. Wally, in fact, came to me one day with a figure that represented the expenses that we would have for the coming year and asked me to calculate the amount of sales we would have to generate to cover those expenses. Jack O'Brien had said that we couldn't cut expenses without adversely affecting our sales function, so that number became our sales target for the year.

Bennett Leasing

The equipment-leasing industry dated from the 1950s, when tax credits and accelerated depreciation incentives for investment enhanced the popularity of equipment leasing. The industry experienced explosive growth in the 1960s, particularly in the transportation area (trucks, autos, airplanes, railroad cars), office and information-processing equipment, and industrial equipment and facilities. In 1981, leasing remained one of the fastest growing industries in the United States with more than 1,800 firms writing agreements for billions of dollars of equipment. Not only the number, but also the value of transactions had increased substantially, facilitated in part by the development of leveraged leasing. (Exhibit 5 describes leasing trends.) Infla-

Exhibit 5
Equipment-Leasing Growth

YEAR	EQUIPMENT COST ADDED (000s)
1979	8,039,000
1980	10,214,400
1981	13,374,700

Sources: American Association of Equipment Lessors; *1982 Survey of Accounting and Business Practices; World Leasing Yearbook,* 1982.

tion, risky business cycles, and high interest rates had forced firms of all sizes to turn to leasing.

Firms leased equipment for a variety of reasons, primarily to take advantage of tax credits and to have more flexible financing. Many small firms leased because they lacked sufficient capital to support debt financing of equipment purchases. Leasing companies could take advantage of certain tax benefits resulting from accelerated depreciation and investment tax credits and pass the benefits on, through reduced rates, to firms that could not. Differences in capital costs to a leasing company and an operating company encouraged leasing. Operating companies also gained more financial flexibility, because leasing extended the length of financing, allowed constant-cost financing, and conserved working capital. Leases could be tailored to the needs of lessees, such as those in seasonal businesses, and because few or no restrictive covenants were required, as with debt financing, firms could conserve existing lines of credit.

In addition to the numerous quantifiable benefits, leasing reduced the risk of equipment obsolescence, particularly important in an era of rapid technological change, and often was simply more convenient than borrow-and-purchase options. The convenience factor was particularly influential in automobile leasing. While automobile purchases were down throughout the country in 1981, the leasing population remained stable and was expected to grow. Projections indicated that, by 1985, more than 40 percent of cars purchased would be lease financed, double the 1981 lease base.

With the growing acceptance of the equipment-leasing concept, there arose increasing demand for specialized leases and fast, low-cost maintenance plans. These trends, along with inflationary pressures, were forcing small leasing companies to tighten and streamline operations in order to compete in this highly competitive marketplace.

The Bennett Leasing Company was a holdover from the Bennett Association's expansion into the automobile industry in the 1930s. Senator Bennett retained his role as president of the franchise throughout his presidency of NAM and his Senate terms. He had turned over operating control, however, to a resident manager. In 1967, when Ford announced that it didn't want absentee franchise owners, Bennett decided to sell. Although it could have resisted Ford's demands, the Bennett Association sold the franchise, retaining car and truck leasing and truck maintenance. These operations, headed by John Bennett, Harold's son, constituted the leasing company when Michael Silva arrived.

Management. Tall, laconic, and thoughtful, John Bennett bore a strong physical resemblance to other members of the family, especially his cousin Wally. John liked to explore thoroughly each business decision made by the company. His analytical style and careful consideration of each issue led many around him to observe that he might have been a good college professor. He enjoyed the people with whom he worked and felt that his organization was strong, stable, and customer oriented.

By 1981, Bennett Leasing had 35 employees and had had as many as 40 at one time. Although it was willing to lease nearly any type of equipment, automotive and truck leases to major fleet customers, small businesses, and individuals provided the bulk of the revenues. In 1981, 1,800 autos and light trucks were under lease.

Like many leasing companies using floating-rate leases, Bennett Leasing lost money between 1979 and 1981 because of sustained high-interest-note levels. Despite the increasing losses, neither the sales staff nor management appeared to be concerned. John Bennett commented:

> When Mike (Silva) took over the business, I realized that several changes needed to be made. I know that Michael is looking at the trucking business because it has lost money for us over the past several years, but I have some misgivings about that. I've been here since 1954, and I've noticed that the trucking business is the least interest-sensitive business that we have.

About half of the leasing company's employees worked in the trucking side of the business. The truck-leasing segment was growing along with the rest of the leasing industry, increasing the number of units in service by 31 percent and revenues by 22 percent in ten years.

At Bennett Leasing, many of the employees were experienced mechanics, involved in the maintenance operation. John added:

> Mike is wondering what to do with the people in our company. He just doesn't know them as well as I do. There are some of them who might be a bit mediocre, but they have some skills and experience that would be very hard to replace. Many of these people are good friends of mine, and some of them have been here longer than I. We probably need some change in the

climate, but you also need stability, experience, and knowledge. We don't want to get rid of expertise.

National Car Rental

The car rental industry began in 1916, but the most rapid growth had occurred since 1960. Although 8 to 12 corporate systems could be considered the leading national firms in the business, as many as 5,000 independent firms and system licensees operated on a local or regional basis. By 1981, 40 million car rental transactions generated more than $3 billion in revenues. The current 19 percent rate of growth (see Exhibit 6) was predicted to continue through 1981 because of the high cost of car ownership, the price of gasoline, and increasing reliance on "fly/drive" forms of business and vacation travel.

The overwhelming majority of rental-car service consumers were business travelers, and between 75 percent and 85 percent of rental car revenues were generated through rentals made at airports. More than 90 percent of car rental fleets were rented to commercial users.

The National Car Rental franchise at the Salt Lake City Airport became part of the Bennett Motor Company in 1959. The franchise had nearly 400 cars, and in a good week all were rented. Closely tied to tourism and business travel, the business was somewhat cyclical. In 1981, the winter snowfall in the Salt Lake City area had not been plentiful, and there was some concern throughout the area about the impact of this situation on the local economy. In addition, after Budget Rent-A-Car started a premium giveaway to increase business in October 1981, the other major rental companies, including National, became involved in a premium war. As a result, National Car Rental Corporation eventually lost $15 million, and the local

Exhibit 6
Car Rental Growth—Selected Years

YEAR	UNITS IN SERVICE	REVENUES (MILLIONS)
1970	319,000	$ 936
1972	341,000	1,048
1978	448,000	2,303
1980	512,000	3,349

Source: American Car Rental Association, 1983.

Bennett-owned franchise dropped from third to fourth in its share of the Salt Lake–area market.

On the other hand, Salt Lake City had been tabbed the second-fastest-growing city of the 1980s in the United States, and Western Airlines had plans to make Salt Lake City its new hub of operations, which would result in expansion of the airport. Many corporations were moving there, which increased the level of business travel. All these developments boded well for the local car rental franchise and the local economy.

Management.   Peter van der Hyde, president of the company, had run the franchise for many years. Born in Holland, he had married one of Richard Bennett's daughters and then came to work for the Bennett Motor Company before it was sold. Van der Hyde worked closely with Richard until the latter's death, and many felt that, if Richard had outlived his brothers, van der Hyde might have been his successor. Tall and tanned, he still spoke with a slight Dutch accent:

> I try to run a tight ship here. I feel a moral obligation to the stockholders, and I think it's paid off. Our profit has gone up every year since I took over in 1976. In this business, it's very easy to lose customers and hard to get them back. I think you need three things to be successful here: good financing, good luck, and common sense.

Van der Hyde operated a lean, efficient business with no intermediate levels of supervision. Although concerned about the company as a whole, van der Hyde was proudest of his own operation. Even when the other Bennett companies were losing money, the National franchise was always in the black. As one observer noted, "That company does nothing but generate cash. The nature of the work is relatively routine, so they can pay low wages, and all transactions are in cash or by credit cards."

Admix

Admix, employing only five people, was the smallest of the Bennett companies. Most of its business was in developing commercials, and the operation stayed small by contracting out much of the work. Before coming to Admix, President Gene Yates had worked for several ad agencies managing large accounts, including Western Airlines and Rockwell International. Under his leadership, Admix had been profitable since its founding—unaffected by the depressed economy. It was not generally known that Bennett owned Admix; the company had deemphasized the relationship so as not to reduce the number of potential clients.

There was little interaction between Admix and the other companies owned by the Bennett Association. Michael Silva noted, "No one has paid much attention to Gene. He was making money before I came, and he seems to be doing okay now."

BENNETT ASSOCIATION:
KEY MANAGEMENT PERSONNEL (SEE EXHIBIT 7)

Wally Bennett: Paint and Glass

The eldest son of the Senator, Wally Bennett, after serving in the military for three and one-half years, had spent his entire career with Bennett's. Like his father, he attended the University of Utah and then held a variety of positions at Bennett's Paint and Glass (most recently, director of personnel) before taking control of the company in 1976. As were many family members, he was active in church and civic affairs.

Wally was tall, with graying hair, and had a patrician air about him. Now in his mid-50s, he was popular around the Salt Lake area; most people who met him found him very agreeable and enjoyed his company. Extremely sensitive to the needs and feelings of others in the business, he would often postpone decisions that might upset his staff until he could

---

Exhibit 7
Key Management Personnel

	POSITION	YEARS WITH COMPANY	APPROXIMATE AGE
John Bennett	President, Bennett Leasing	20+	55
Wallace F. Bennett	Chairman, Bennett Association	50+	82
Wallace G. Bennett	President, Bennett's Paint and Glass	25+	55
DeVon Johnson	Executive Vice President, Bennett's Paint and Glass	1	57
Michael Silva	CEO, Bennett Association	0	30
Jack Stevens	Controller, Bennett's Paint & Glass	5	52
Peter van der Hyde	President, National Car Rental	20+	53

contact all the parties involved. He would gather his staff together to try to resolve many of the problems facing the company through consensus decision making. If the group could not arrive at a decision, he would often put the issue off until a later meeting, where it could be discussed more thoroughly.

He had inherited from his father a strong concern for the welfare of the company's employees, and he always tried to act in a way that reflected that concern. Although he maintained a high regard and respect for his father, Wally tended not to consult him on most business decisions. He relied mostly on his 25 years of experience in the company and the expertise of his staff. Although he could have exercised more control over the other Bennett companies, as did Richard before him, he chose to devote himself almost exclusively to the paint and glass business.

DeVon Johnson: Executive Vice President, Paint and Glass

DeVon Johnson was relatively new to the company. Immaculately and elegantly dressed, he tended to speak rapidly and directly, generating tremendous energy. Before coming to Bennett's, he spent 35 years in the paint business with Fuller-O'Brien, where he rose from stockboy to vice president of the company. Adhering to the management philosophy of "putting in a little more than you expect to get back," Johnson dramatically improved Fuller's sales and profits in each position he had held. He was the youngest branch manager in the history of the company. Eventually, because of the breadth of his sales and operations experience, Fuller began to depend on him to turn around problem areas.

Johnson resigned from Fuller-O'Brien for family reasons and contacted Bennett's about a job shortly thereafter. He was hired as vice president of marketing, and, by September 1981, he replaced Jack Nielson, who retired, as executive vice president of the company.

Johnson had a full slate of objectives for the company. First, he felt it should become more customer oriented, particularly in responding to complaints more quickly. Second, he was concerned about plant productivity. Although fully staffed, the plant's output was below industry average. Third, Johnson wanted to increase Bennett's market share:

> I'd love to run a company ten times this size. I don't like to sit still. I can't wait to get to work in the morning. I know that I'm impatient, but I've never been a flash in the pan. We're still learning here, and some of the people don't know what they can do yet. In the morning, I get here before 7:30, and I work through the day. I usually don't even leave the office for lunch because I bring along a bag lunch that I can eat right here at my desk. I got used to that in other jobs, and I don't want to change now.

Johnson was concerned about the constraints he felt in meeting the challenges facing the company. Because it was a family-owned, traditional business, led by the son of the chairman, implementing major changes would probably mean repeatedly going back to the board.

The lack of concern shown by others in the company about the growing losses also puzzled him. Despite all the problems, he did not believe people were changing their approaches to the problems. Also, although he liked Wally and enjoyed working with him, he wasn't sure whether Wally's deliberate, consensus-oriented style was what Bennett's needed to pull it out of this slide.

The Senator

Senator Wallace F. Bennett was an active board chairman. Known throughout the company and the family as "the Senator," he provided continuity to a company that had had three presidents in five years. His energy, creativity, and leadership skills served him well, not only in running the companies but also in his successful careers as president of NAM and as a U.S. Senator. Throughout his terms in Congress, the Senator had kept his post as chairman of the board and had kept abreast of company activities.

Eighty-two at the time Michael Silva became president, the Senator remained physically and mentally active. His daily routine included long walks (up to six-and-a-half miles) and a full schedule of activities at his office on the second story of the original Bennett's building on First South. He was a prominent and respected figure in the city, involved in civic and church affairs.

The Senator was ordinarily modest about his many accomplishments but exhibited a justifiable pride about Bennett's early years under his presidency:

> We were bold then. We dominated the paint business in Utah. When we developed the Colorizer concept, everyone told us it wouldn't work. But overnight, we revolutionized the paint business.
>
> I feel very close to Mike because we can give each other ideas. I think I have been able to suggest a few things that Mike has agreed with, and I know that he has come up with a lot of ideas on his own that I thought were great. I think we can be a good team.
>
> I wonder about the future of the Bennett Association. Within the company, there has been a real political struggle for power since Richard's death. I think we needed an outsider.

Michael Silva

Michael Silva grew up in Hawaii and attended Brigham Young University (BYU), where he was active in school politics and competed successfully in several intercollegiate and national debate tournaments. Upon graduation, he enrolled in a masters program in organizational behavior at BYU, where his quick, analytical mind and remarkable verbal abilities soon distinguished him. In an argument or discussion, Silva's debating prowess made him an intimidating opponent. Generally, Silva had gotten along well with the faculty and peers but at times appeared impatient and aloof. Although he had completed 95 percent of the degree requirements and had grades well above the class average, several confrontations with faculty members caused him to leave the program shortly before graduation.

Silva was 30 years old when he took over as president of the Bennett Association, but he had a wealth of experience behind him. After leaving BYU, he had been through a series of remarkable job changes, each of which gave him more responsibility. He began as an assistant to the president of Skaggs Foods but, after a year, moved back to Hawaii to take a staff job as a corporate planner at State Savings and Loan, a large Hawaiian operation with assets of $500 million, 16 branches, and more than 300 employees. At the S&L, he worked his way up to a position as assistant to the chairman of the board. After two years with State, he returned to the Intermountain West area as manager of Peat, Marwick, Mitchell's bank consulting unit. While Silva was in this position, Warren Pugh, owner of Cummins Intermountain Diesel Company, asked Silva to come straighten out his banking problems, which were costing the company tens of millions of dollars. He was able to put Cummins on a sound financial footing, but only by laying off 70 percent of the work force. Silva then moved to Arthur Young, Inc., as manager of consulting services for the Salt Lake City office.

Silva began to work with the Bennett Association when it engaged the services of Arthur Young in late February 1981. In June 1981, the banks informed Bennett that, because of continued losses, they were going to call in their loans unless the company would agree to an outside CEO—a first in the history of the Bennett Association. Bennett then asked Arthur Young to help them find someone who could make the company profitable once again.

Several candidates with impressive credentials were interviewed by the Senator and the board. Although each candidate felt that he could improve Bennett's position, they all agreed a complete turnaround would take at least five years. The board members (in particular, the Senator) were not impressed with the applicants. Wallace finally said, "Gentlemen, I don't think we need to go outside and look for people to help us. I think we have the man right here who is best suited for the job."

In August 1981, Silva was offered the job and, after some negotiation, signed a three-year contract as CEO of what would be called Bennett Enterprises, a central management company that would control the various companies owned by the Bennett Association. He would begin his duties as CEO in early October 1981.

Management Style. Silva's office, located in the Bennett Leasing Company building, was pleasantly, if sparsely, decorated. His office and his secretary's office were separated from the leasing operation by a heavy, black, swinging door, referred to as the "Iron Curtain." Relatively small by executive standards, the office had few of the trappings that one might associate with a CEO. He did have a small computer, one of two he owned. A small, framed quotation (from Machiavelli) immediately caught the eye of any visitor:

> There is nothing more difficult to carry out, or more doubtful to success, or more dangerous to handle, than to initiate a new order of things. For the reformer has enemies in all those who profit by the old order, and lukewarm supporters in all those who would support by the new order.

The existence of the Iron Curtain was significant. Silva was explicit about his non-open-door policy. He was protective of his office time and went out of his way to make it difficult for people to find him. He believed that if people knew his time was valuable and he was difficult to find, they were better prepared than otherwise when they did catch him. Besides, he felt his lack of availability often encouraged people to solve problems themselves.

He managed telephone calls with the same spirit. His secretary, Dixie Clark, screened all calls. Only those from his family or the Senator were allowed to come through immediately. For all other calls, he was "out of the office" or "in a meeting." Periodically during the day, Silva would sort through the messages and return the calls that seemed important. By the end of the day, message slips littered his desk.

When he entered the building, he would greet everyone cheerfully, at times almost playfully. He seemed genuinely pleased with those in the company who would banter with him:

> That is something that I encourage. I like the atmosphere of mild sarcasm that we have created here. I encourage people to tease me because I get better information about how people are feeling. It's a type of informal communication.

Schedule. Silva's daily routine as CEO followed one of two patterns. In the first, he arose early and arrived at the office at 5:00 or 6:00 A.M. He wrote, dictated correspondence, and planned until 8:00 or 9:00, when he began to see people and make calls. After lunch he went home to enjoy the rest of the day with his family. In the second pattern, Silva stayed home in the morning and helped prepare the children for school. He then arrived at the office around 10:00 A.M. and worked until lunch. After lunch he would remain at the office until around 3:00, when he went home to be with his family.

In the evenings, his schedule was less variable. He helped with dinner (he was an accomplished cook) and afterward put the children to bed. Often he worked (usually on his own writing) from 10:00 P.M. until 1:00 or 2:00 A.M. He seldom needed more than four or five hours of sleep:

> I have never worked one Saturday or one Sunday in my career. I don't think I have ever worked an eight-hour day. I made a decision when I started to work that my family was always going to come first in my life. This is the first job

that has offered me real flexibility. I found that I could easily become too involved with my work, but I don't want to. I work hard at keeping my family number one. I don't want my work to become my life. I really like the freedom that this job could offer me now. I like both the freedom and the money, but I probably wouldn't give up the freedom for the money. I want time to be with my family. Time, in fact, probably drives everything I do. I'm something of a time fanatic. Everything is driven by my time resource. I won't take on anything that will require any more of my time than I already give.

I don't think that it is any big deal to be a good manager. Most anyone could probably be a reasonable manager. The real question is whether you can do it differently. Can you do it in a way that doesn't eat up your life? Can you have an impact in your job and still maintain a family life?

I think that there are three roles that have to be mastered in management. You need to know strategy, the culture, and the numbers. The problem that you generally find is that few people who are sensitive to issues like culture enjoy working with numbers. You can usually find people who like to do two of those roles, but not all three.

MICHAEL SILVA DISCUSSES THE COMPANY SITUATION

After assuming control of Bennett Association on October 1, 1981, Silva felt that he had a good understanding of how the company operated but was unclear about which problems to attack first, which managers were reliable, and which approach he should take to making changes. He also knew that the six-week vacation he negotiated as a part of his contract was to begin soon, and he was unsure about initiating any major change only to have it sputter and die in his absence. Silva interviewed the key managers from each of the businesses and spent a considerable amount of time with the Senator. He wanted to have as much input as possible before he began to implement a plan.

He talked at length about the situation he faced:

When the company brought in all of the outside applicants for the job, they all took a strictly financial approach and said it would take at least five years to turn the company around. I don't think we have that much time, and I think we can do it in less than that. All of the other people they interviewed for this job said that it was a financial problem. I think the problem is as much cultural as it is financial.

Silva noted that employees at Bennett's seemed to have an unwritten expectation that if they had a job with Bennetts, they would never be laid off. Even during the Great Depression, no one in Bennett's had been let go. Perhaps for this reason, even though the company was having severe financial troubles, there was a noticeable lack of concern among employees and managers about losing their jobs. They had made no special efforts to improve performance or productivity, or even to attract new customers. Some pressure had been put on the sales districts, but with limited response.

Commenting on his goals, Silva stated:

We're going to have a difficult time turning this around. Our biggest businesses are tied directly to the housing and automobile markets, and so we are
going to have a hard time if this recession gets any worse.

We need to stress excellence and making a profit in the long run. It's
important to remember that all the variables that insure a profit in the long
run are human resource variables. I want people to think they are the best. I
will not stand for mediocrity. We should demand the absolute best from our
people, but then pay them accordingly. Many companies try to pay their
people the least amount possible and still keep them. I think that's crazy. I
think you should pay them as much as possible to still make a profit. It
makes a big difference in the way they think about themselves. More than
anything, I think we should be strategy driven. We want to have revenues of
$100 million by 1990.

I want to be a leader here. The difference between a leader and a manager is that a manager manages systems and a leader manages values. We
need to stress new values, those that emphasize performance. I need to have
the confidence of the people here, because when an organization doesn't
sense that their leader can get them through a crisis, they lose their incentive.

One factor Silva worried about particularly was the reaction of members
of the Bennett family to any changes he might make:

Part of my contract states that the board cannot counteract my decisions.
They can cancel my contract at any time, but I don't have to get their approval
for any of my decisions, and they can't counteract what I decide. I don't think
I have time for an educational process each time I make a decision. Decisions
will have to be made in a hurry, and I don't have the time to go back and forth
with the board. I do stay in close contact with the Senator, though. He has
been very helpful so far. I probably see him two times a week, but I talk to
him at least once a day.

I like to define culture as the personality of a company, and so I think there
are two ways to change that personality. The first is by long-term change,
where you gradually work at some of the problem areas in the culture. The
second is trauma, where you massively address the company problems.

Given Bennett's unique history and his goals, Silva was not sure what exactly
he should do.

CASE APPENDIX

SENATOR WALLACE FOSTER BENNETT'S BIOGRAPHICAL SKETCH

The first of five children of John Foster Rosetta (Wallace) Bennett, Wallace Foster Bennett was born November 13, 1898, in Salt Lake City, Utah. Both his parents were of English ancestry and of the Mormon faith. At the time of Wallace's birth, his father, who had crossed the plains in a covered wagon at the age of three, was occupied in establishing the paint and glass concern his son now heads. Bennett has quoted with approval his father's dictum that "no transaction of any sort is good unless both sides profit from it."

Young Bennett attended the Salt Lake City public schools and the church high school known as the Latter-Day Saints University, where he took part in debating and choral singing (he says he has an "ordinary bass voice"). Graduated in 1916, he entered the University of Utah, where he majored in English and won a varsity letter in debating. A member of the university's ROTC, 19-year-old Wallace Bennett was commissioned a second lieutenant of infantry in September 1918 and was assigned to Colorado College as an instructor. His own college education completed and the B.A from Utah having been awarded to him in 1919, Bennett returned to Colorado as principal of a Mormon school, the San Luis State Academy at Manassa. "It was always my understanding," he has stated, "that I would come into the family business, in which I had spent most of my summers during high school and college. I returned to the business June 1, 1920, and have been with it ever since."

Beginning as an office clerk in the family's business, Bennett soon advanced to cashier, then production manager, then sales manager. He became secretary-treasurer by 1929, the year he also assumed the same post in the Jordan Valley Investment Company of Salt Lake City. Three years later Wallace Bennett took over the general management of the Bennett Paint and Glass Company, his father retaining the presidency. In that year, too, Bennett embarked on a one-hour daily broadcast series, called "The Observatory Hour," over station KSL.

During the depression of the 1930s, Bennett recounted, none of his firm's employees was discharged, though this meant cutting wages. At his father's death in 1928, the eldest son became president and general manager, with one brother, Harold, serving as vice president, and the other, Richard, as secretary-treasurer.

In 1939, he and several friends organized the Bennett Motor Company, a Ford dealership, with him as president. During the next eight years, the Bennett Paint and Glass Company went through an expansion phase: in 1949 it had warehouses and seven retail stores to handle its stock of paints, enamels, polishes, cleansers, mirrors, and other "decorator and household specialties." What its president described as the most modern paint manufacturing plant in the West was completed in 1948, two years after he shortened the firm name to "Bennett's." To illustrate his labor-relations program to a NAM audience in 1948, Bennett told them, "The man who sweeps out our retail store calls me Wallace."

While retaining the presidency of the paint and glass company, in 1947 Bennett turned the management over to his brother Richard. Another business association of Wallace Bennett's was with Zion's Savings Bank and Trust Company, of which he was a director and executive committee member. The Utah manufacturer also served on the boards of the Utah Home Fire Insurance Company, the Utah Oil Refining Company, and the Bannock Hotel Corporation. He was a former president of the National Glass Distributors Association, a former vice president of the National Paint, Varnish and Lacquer Association, and a director and former chairman of the public relations committee of the Utah Manufacturers Association. These business interests were to result in his selection as a vice president and director of the National Association of Manufacturers.

In December 1948, Bennett addressed about two thousand of them at a session on labor-management teamwork, declaring: "If we can give these people (employees) satisfaction as well as wages, we can overcome the philosophy of the class struggle. If we do not give them a feeling of partnership and achievement, then forces that would tear us apart will take over. Time is running out." Bennett was elected by the NAM board in December to succeed Morris Sayre as president. One statement Bennett made was: "My selection is a recognition of the growing importance of Western industry and of the importance of small business. This is the first time the presidency of NAM has gone west of Chicago."

At his first press conference, the Utah businessman told reporters that he intended to spend his presidential year traveling throughout the United States, preaching "the partnership of the men who put up the money, and the men who do the work, and the men who tie the whole thing together" and the responsiblity of management to convey this to the workers. He urged NAM not to serve the interests of free industry alone, but of all freedom, because "if any part of freedom falls, the whole thing falls." Bennett said that in his business he accepted the AFL glaziers' closed shop, despite his personal disapproval, because the closed shop was "traditional in the building trades." The new NAM president also stated that his strongest competition came not from larger but from smaller firms, and he recommended that the government deal with inflation by shifting its bonds from the hands of banks into those of private investors.

THE WALT DISNEY COMPANY:
THE ARRIVAL OF EISNER AND WELLS

In the fall of 1984, Walt Disney Productions announced the selection of a new executive team:

Michael D. Eisner was elected Chairman and Chief Executive Officer of Walt Disney Productions in September 1984.

Formerly President and Chief Operating Officer of Paramount Pictures Corporation for eight years, Mr. Eisner was closely involved in that studio's major motion picture successes during his tenure, including *Saturday Night Fever, Grease, Raiders of the Lost Ark, Indiana Jones and the Temple of Doom* and *Terms of Endearment.* He also was instrumental in Paramount's lineup of hit television series, including *Happy Days, Taxi* and *Cheers.* During Mr. Eisner's tenure, Paramount Pictures Corporation enjoyed unprecedented success, achieving six consecutive fiscal year records for revenues and earnings.

Prior to joining Paramount, Mr. Eisner was Senior Vice President, Prime Time Production and Development, for ABC Entertainment. Under his leadership, ABC became the No. 1 prime time network through development of series, limited series and motion picture programming. Earlier, ABC gained network leadership in daytime, early morning and children's programming under Mr. Eisner's direction.

Mr. Eisner began his career in the entertainment industry at CBS Television with the network's programming department.

A native of New York City, Mr. Eisner attended Lawrenceville School and graduated from Denison University of Granville, Ohio.

Frank G. Wells was elected President and Chief Operating Officer of Walt Disney Productions in September 1984.

Previously, Mr. Wells was Vice Chairman of Warner Bros., Inc., the motion picture subsidiary of Warner Communications. During 15 years with Warner Bros., Mr. Wells also served as Vice President-West Coast (1969), President (1973) and as Co-Chief Executive Officer (1977).

Before his association with Warner Bros., Mr. Wells was a partner in the Hollywood Law firm of Gang, Tyre and Brown, practicing in the field of entertainment industry law for 10 years.

A Phi Beta Kappa graduate of Pomona College at Claremont, California, Mr. Wells attended Oxford University as a Rhodes Scholar and later earned an LLB degree from Stanford University.

This case was prepared by Jeanne M. Liedtka, Associate Professor of Business Administration. Copyright © 1993 by the University of Virginia Darden School Foundation, Charlottesville, VA. All rights reserved.

The son of a career U.S. Navy officer, Mr. Wells is a native of Coronado, California. He served two years in the U.S. Army, earning the rank of first lieutenant.

Mr. Wells has had the personal goal of scaling the summits of the highest mountains on each of the seven continents. With the exception of Mt. Everest, from which he was forced to turn back a day away from the top, he achieved his objective during 1983.[1]

Eisner and Wells arrived to find in decline the firm that had captured a unique place in American culture. Profits had fallen for three consecutive years. Theme park attendance was similarly eroding. Disney's market share of box office revenues had dropped to 4 percent, placing it last among the major studios. Furthermore, the takeover battle waged against Saul Steinberg in spring of 1984 had diverted management attention away from repairing the ills in company operations while increasing debt burden dramatically. Although previous CEO Ron Miller had been in the job only 19 months, the Disney board of directors believed that decisive new management was needed from the outside to revitalize the firm. In making its selection, the board hoped that the combination of Eisner's creativity and Wells' business acumen, both legendary in Hollywood, would restore the luster of the firm's unique assets.

In their first annual report, produced two months later, Eisner and Wells addressed their letter to "Our Owners and fellow Disney employees":

> We joined Disney at the culmination of the most difficult period in the company's 61 year history. . . . On September 22, we joined 28,000 other dedicated employees who are eager to build and create value through excellence. As the newest "cast members" of Walt Disney Productions, we are both enthusiastic and respectful in becoming a part of a corporate culture that is unparalleled in American industry. As we approach our task of building Disney excellence around the world, we do so with a sense of pride and humility in following previous management successes in producing animated classic motion pictures, imaginative theme parks and entertainment magic. . . .[2]
>
> Our job, essentially, is to accelerate Disney even further into the mainstream of American entertainment. We will do this by emphasizing creativity in every aspect of the company's business. This challenge requires that we give great latitude, within pre-set financial boundaries, to the resources at hand while at the same time carefully managing Disney's largely untapped measure of assets. . . . The first objective in our new business plan calls for a dedicated effort to improve performance in *every* area. We intend to achieve a greater degree of balance between the various sectors in order to avoid substantial swings in income due to possible adverse effects on a single line of business.
>
> Among our corporate goals is assuring the success of The Disney Channel, returning Disney to an industry leadership role in motion pictures

---

[1] Walt Disney Company press release, September 22, 1984.
[2] Walt Disney Productions Annual Report, 1984, p. 1.

and network television, expanding film distribution in both under-utilized and untapped ancillary markets, accelerating land development, and extending our important Consumer Products business.[3]

Upon his arrival, Eisner settled into Walt's old office, hired his former secretary, and, over a six-month period, fired more than 400 Disney people. The new "Disney team" embarked immediately on an ambitious series of moves in each of the firm's major lines of business.

THE MOVIE BUSINESS

Given the backgrounds of Eisner and Wells, it was no surprise that they focused immediate attention on the live action portion of the movie business. Within a week of their arrival, they had hired Jeffrey Katzenberg, former production chief at Paramount, to head the movie division. Within six months, he had been joined by 30 more former Paramount executives. They set course on a new strategy of film making that "combined Hollywood's creative chutzpah and strict financial self-discipline."[4] Their goal was to make movies having broad audience appeal at below-average costs. To accomplish this, they utilized both performers whose careers had gone into decline (Bette Midler, Richard Dreyfuss, Robin Williams) and television actors (Ted Danson, Tom Selleck) for starring roles. To protect them on the downside, they set up a risk-sharing arrangement with Silver Screen Pictures that pumped new funds into the business and reduced potential loses on flops. Katzenberg, with a reputation for scheduling staff meetings at 10:00 P.M. and expecting seven-day work weeks, quickly geared up production to meet Eisner's stated goal of 10 to 15 live-action features annually.

The new team's commitment to the animation business was equally evident, though more of a surprise to many. Rumors circulated at the time of their arrival that Eisner and Wells would shut down the animation unit. Its animator corps had already fallen from a high of 400 to 200, with the public loss of several prominent talents (Don Bluth and Tim Burton) especially painful. Instead, Roy Disney asked to head the unit himself and called the entire group together in late 1984, and challenged the animators to "show them (Eisner and Wells) that we can contribute." Within six months, Eisner set a goal of producing a new animated film every 18 months, versus the four- to five-year norm at Disney. He launched a new intern program and authorized the purchase of $12 million in computer equipment—a request made more than three years before but rejected by Walker and Miller as too expensive.

---

[3]Ibid, p. 2.
[4]"How Disney Keeps the Magic Going," *Fortune*, December 4, 1989, p. 112.

Equally important, Eisner launched the search for a new animated character worthy of joining the ranks of Mickey and Donald. He thought that he had found one in the person (or animal) of Roger Rabbit and began producing a film of the same name in late 1986. An ambitious combination of live action and animation, it was intended to push the state of the art to new boundaries in the old Disney tradition. Eisner hired Steven Spielberg, veteran of *E.T.* and *An American Tail*, to direct. Spielberg felt that Disney animators were not up to the task. As part of a compromise, a joint animation unit was set up—for every new animator hired, a Disney animator would also be used. When the film opened, *Newsweek* noted:

> In a marriage made in Hollywood heaven, Disney brings marketing savvy and a proud tradition of animation back to the ground-breaking days of Walt Disney himself.[5]

Eisner's search for successful new characters continued with the decision to produce *The Little Mermaid.* Disney's first classic fairytale since *Sleeping Beauty* almost 30 years before, *The Little Mermaid* was meant to be, Roy Disney recalled, "the kind of movie that Walt would have made."[6]

Eisner and Wells also made the decision to release, on a gradual basis, the entire set of Disney classic films, a film archive that analysts had valued at $400 million, for sale to the home market on videocassette. The first offering was *Pinocchio.* This reversed a long-standing policy created by Walt Disney himself, who had been vehemently opposed to the frequent showing of his classics.

TELEVISION

Shortly after their arrival, Eisner and Wells stated publicly that they viewed the Disney Channel's current losses as "excellent long-term investments in a business that represents a cornerstone of our future." Within a month, they had negotiated a ten-year contract with Cablevision Systems of New York, setting a precedent for the type of long-term pacts they hoped to establish with other multiple systems operators. Investment in the Disney Channel continued as new rates were negotiated to increase the channel's attractiveness to cable system operators, and new shows, such as the new Mickey Mouse Club, were added.

The new team also expanded Disney's network exposure, producing a series of weekly shows *(The Golden Girls)* and Saturday morning cartoons. The *Magical World of Disney* was resurrected on Sunday nights, with Eisner acting as host.

---

[5] Michael Reese, "The Making of Roger Rabbit," *Newsweek,* June 27, 1988, p. 54.
[6] "How Disney Keeps the Magic Going," p. 111.

THE THEME PARK DIVISION

Eisner, Wells, and their families spent three days in Orlando, Florida, riding every ride and sampling every restaurant at Disney World in the first two weeks after taking their new jobs. Impressed, they decided that the theme park operation would be left largely untouched. "I couldn't understand *how* a company that was this badly mismanaged at the top could be so fantastic at the middle management level. The executives at the park remembered how Walt had done it," Eisner commented after his visit.[7]

Nevertheless, they felt, the parks were suffering from under-investment and a lack of new attractions. Eisner and Wells committed to doubling park spending, financed via a $5 increase in daily ticket prices (from $18 to $23), implemented gradually over a two-year period. They also authorized the first major marketing campaign in the company's history. By 1985, seven major attractions had been added in Orlando (including the Disney-MGM Theme Park, Typhoon Lagoon, and the Living Seas Pavilion at Epcot), and four each were added at Disneyland in California and Tokyo. Euro-Disneyland was scheduled to open in 1992. They hired renowned architects such as Michael Graves and Robert Stern to design new luxury hotels. Within five years, nearly 3,800 rooms had been added in Orlando.

MERCHANDISING

The new team brought, for the first time, top management support for aggressive marketing. The first Disney retail store opened in March of 1987. Two years later, 50 stores were in operation, with 50 more planned. Disney began partnering with major corporations such as McDonald's and Coca-Cola for joint promotion of products. The *Disney Catalog* was launched in 1985, and the *Childcraft* catalog firm was acquired soon after.

REAL ESTATE

Arvida Corporation was sold for $404 million in 1987.

CONCLUSION

Throughout these changes, Eisner's and Wells's personal styles were a pervasive influence. "Wells knows the details of every budgetary dispute, contract negotiation, legal problem, or personnel issue," *Fortune* noted in profiling Wells as one of the "great second bananas."[8] Eisner was known for

---

[7]Ron Grover, *The Disney Touch*, Homewood, IL: Richard D. Irwin, Inc., 1991.
[8]John Huey, "Secrets of Great Second Bananas," *Fortune*, May 6, 1991.

orchestrating frequent "Gong Shows," in which executives were expected to present new ideas that were then gonged if deemed unappealing. *Fortune* observed:

> Eisner is a CEO who is more hands-on than Mother Teresa. His chief duty at Disney is to lead creatively, to be a thinker, inventor, and cheerleader for new ideas—in founder Walt's own words, to be an Imagineer. Says Eisner: "Every CEO has to spend an enormous amount of time shuffling papers. The question is, how much of your time can you leave free to think about ideas? To me, the pursuit of ideas is the only thing that matters. You can always find capable people to do almost everything else. . . . My problem is not too few ideas; my problem is too many *bad* ideas. . . . When I hear a bad idea coming out of my mouth, I've got to stop before it gets to somebody who's going to spend money."

JACKIE WOODS (A)

Jackie is like the first firecracker lit in a package of firecrackers . . . there is this constant energy, this constant edge. Once she is lit, she lights everything else around her. It becomes contagious, just like a package of firecrackers; one right after the other, they just start to go. Once she has accomplished something, there is this huge explosion around it.

In May 1992, Jackie Woods, vice president of business marketing for Ameritech Services, was walking down the hall in the east wing of the new Ameritech office building in Hoffman Estates, Illinois. Jackie had recently been asked to participate on a task force of 100 senior managers from throughout Ameritech charged with exploring significant strategic issues facing the company, including how the company should be organized to face the next century. The task force also had the responsibility of designing a structure that would allow Ameritech to reduce the layers of supervision for its 70,000-person work force. The duties of the task force were expected to span a period of at least six months. To be included in such a significant task force was a source of deep satisfaction to Jackie and signaled just how favorably she was viewed by Ameritech executives. As Jackie turned a corner, she bumped into Bob Brown, a colleague on the reorganization task force.

"So, Jackie, when are you going to tell the family?"

"Tell them what, Bob?"

"You know, about the committee and the work we're going to be doing this summer. I know that you've planned a vacation to Europe with your family. I'd planned to take what we considered a once-in-a-lifetime trip to Belize this summer, but given the hectic schedule for the task force, I had to go back and cancel it. It wasn't easy. How are you going to break it to the girls?"

Woods smiled and made a pleasant comment before continuing down the hallway. She and her husband, Jack, had been planning a trip to Europe with

---

This case was prepared by Catherine M. Lloyd, Darden MBA 1993, under the supervision of James G. Clawson. Copyright © 1993 by the University of Virginia Darden School Foundation, Charlottesville, VA. All rights reserved. Revised September 1993.

their two daughters. In fact, they had already paid for the trip before Jackie was assigned to the task force. She grimaced as she remembered the earnestness in her daughters' eyes as they anticipated the trip and in Bob's eyes as he expressed his empathy for Jackie's dilemma.

BACKGROUND

The major milestones in Jackie's life are shown in Exhibit 1. Born in 1947 in Cleveland, Ohio, Jackie was the only child of Jack and Gladys Dudek. She first left home to attend Muskingum College in southern Ohio. During the summer between her junior and senior years, she met Jack Woods, a student at the University of Akron. She graduated in 1969 with a double major in communications and psychology, and, within a few months, she and Jack were engaged.

Two months before the big day, however, Jack was drafted into the army and sent to basic training at Fort Polk, Louisiana, interrupting both his new

---

Exhibit 1
Major Milestones for Jackie Woods

Summer 1968	Jackie Dudek meets Jack Woods.
September 1969	Jackie gets job at Ohio Bell.
November 1969	Jack gets drafted.
December 1969	Jack and Jackie get married.
Mid-1978	Jack is transferred to Philadelphia, and Jackie accepts job with Bell of Pennsylvania.
January 1982	Jackie accepts sales job at Ohio Bell.
June 1984	Divestiture puts Jackie in autonomous subsidiary.
January 1989	President tells Jackie that she needs headquarters experience; she accepts CFO position in Chicago (family moves); Jack gets job in procurement at Ameritech.
August 1990	Jackie moves back to marketing.
December 1991	Jack and Jackie plan European trip for family.

career at B.F. Goodrich and the couple's wedding plans. Jack and Jackie were married in December 1969 when he came home on leave. In March 1970, Jack was shipped out to Vietnam, where he spent the next two years.

This turn of events made it necessary for Jackie to look for a job. In September 1969, she started working in the Ohio Bell business office, where she was responsible for customer ordering and billing operations in the Cleveland area:

> All of it started right then [when Jack was drafted]. Would my career ever have played out this way if Uncle Sam hadn't taken Jack away for the first three years of our marriage, or would I have worked a few months and said, "I don't think that the career life is for me?" So when people say to me, "How did you decide to have a career?" I say, "It just happened, at least a little bit, because of the war." If you would have asked me at the time whether I was going to have a 20-year career [and reach this level of success], I would have told you most likely not.

At that time, Jackie noted, many employers required their female workers to submit signed statements declaring that they would not get pregnant within the first two years of their tenure at the company. Noncompliance was grounds for dismissal.

Jack returned from Vietnam in 1971 and went back to work for B.F. Goodrich. Jackie chose to continue working with Ohio Bell, and they continued to live and work in Cleveland. Then, in 1978, B.F. Goodrich told Jack that he would have to move in order to advance his career and assigned him to a petrochemical facility in Philadelphia, Pennsylvania. Because they had lived all their lives in Ohio and now had a six-month-old daughter, Nicole, their decision was very difficult. Nevertheless, they left their families and friends behind as they made the decision together to move to Pennsylvania to pursue Jack's early career goals.

Originally, Jackie thought she would not work after the move:

> I agreed to sacrifice—if that is the appropriate word—my career for my husband's at that point . . . and I did not intend to work. I said, "Well, I've had a nice career here for seven or eight years; I'll tend to my family now and not do this."

Much appeared to be changing in Jack and Jackie's lives. Jackie's relationship with the Bell System seemed to be a source of stability in their lives, however, so when they got to Philadelphia, Jackie decided to pursue a job with the local telephone company:

> I interviewed at Bell of Pennsylvania and decided to go ahead and pursue a career with them just to see how it would work. We moved to Philadelphia, [and I] worked in public relations, public affairs, and then moved to marketing.

Jackie's new job required her to take a step down not only in salary but also in management responsibility. Although such a reversal can be extremely frustrating for anyone, both Jack and Jackie were confident that she would do a good job and move up quickly. Furthermore, the job allowed her some flexibility to spend more time with Nicole.

THE WOODSES RETURN TO CLEVELAND

Four years later, in 1982, Jack was transferred back to B.F. Goodrich's corporate headquarters in Cleveland. With Nicole and now Stephanie, ages four and two, Jack and Jackie gladly headed back to Ohio. Jackie went back to Ohio Bell and found a job in sales. Ironically, she was not given the same level of management responsibility that she had enjoyed before she left the company in 1978. The transfer to sales, however, added another dimension to her professional experience. Reflecting on her move into sales, Jackie noted:

> My recommendation to young people starting in careers—and I would say this to men or women—is to get into highly measurable jobs. Sales is one of those. If you are in a position that is subject to someone's decisions about you and based on pretty subjective criteria, you can sit and wonder what you could have done, would have been, if there hadn't been this personality conflict or this difference in management style. If you get into a highly measurable job, the results speak for you.

Despite the general reality that women in the telephone industry seldom went beyond first-line management, Jackie's work at Ohio Bell was punctuated by a series of promotions. Although her success was driven by her management skills, her career path was certainly influenced by her multicompany experience and geographical moves.

DIVESTITURE TRANSFORMS
AN INDUSTRY AND A CAREER

In June 1982, Federal Judge Greene directed American Telephone and Telegraph (AT&T) to divest itself of its local telephone operations, which comprised 22 operating companies, of which Ohio Bell was one. The reorganization of the Bell system created 7 regional Bell operating companies (often referred to as RBOCs). The 5 Bell companies serving Michigan, Indiana, Illinois, Ohio, and Wisconsin became a part of American Information Technology Corporation (Ameritech). The divestiture also greatly enhanced the importance of the sales and marketing functions in the telephone companies nationwide. Under AT&T's service orientation, sales and marketing had been relatively quiet; they now had major responsibilities for revitalizing and building the new phone companies. The sales departments of the 5 Bell companies in Ameritech were consolidated into a single, unregulated organization, Ameritech Services, that was allowed to operate with little interference from its regulated telephone sibling.

In 1986, Jackie was made president of Ohio Bell Communications, the sales subsidiary of Ohio Bell. In this capacity, she oversaw a wide variety of functions, including finance, human resources, quality, vendor relationships, labor negotiations, sales, and marketing:

> I found that customers that were going to spend a substantial amount of money, whether it be $40,000 or $1,000,000, wanted to see the president. They wanted somebody that would come out and sit there and say, "Your business is important, and I'm going to make sure that this team cares about your business and delivers the service to you that we're committing to in this contract."

FAMILY AFFAIRS

Jackie's aging parents were living with the Woodses at this time. When Jackie's mother went into a nursing home, Jackie found herself balancing visits to day-care schools to see the two girls and to the nursing home to see her mother. This routine continued for eight months until her mother passed away. Jackie's father, Jack, continued to live with them:

> The thing that helped [him], at least according to my dad, was that we had small children who provided a great deal of joy and entertainment. He would frequently say to us that [if it weren't for the girls], living there with my husband and me would be just terribly boring because we came home late at night if we had work to do. We weren't any fun.
>
> We met with the pediatrician [about this time] and had a family conference about the role my father would play. He's a very strong kind of domineering guy, but the role he chose to play was one of unconditional love with the children. He would do no disciplining. He left that up to Jack and me.

Jackie went on to explain the additional support she and Jack received in raising their children and managing the house:

> I have always had someone [who] helped me with the children even if it was picking them up from day care or working in the house, and that directly influenced how well things went. If this person worked well with us and got along well, our family life was much easier.

BACK TO BUSINESS

In 1988, Ed Bell, the president of Ohio Bell, told Jackie that her current position within the company would be the highest she would ever achieve if she chose to stay in Cleveland. He advised her that she needed experience at Ameritech headquarters in Chicago, Illinois. Jackie agreed to think about it, and, within a matter of months, she was offered the job of chief financial officer of Ameritech services division (see Exhibit 2 for Jackie Woods' résumé.) The family was now faced with a decision similar to the one it had encountered when Jack was transferred to Philadelphia. Jack had been doing quite well since his transfer back to Cleveland (see Exhibit 3), and Nicole and Stephanie, now ages 11 and 9, faced the possibility of separation from friends and family. The girls expressed resistance to the move. Jackie had her own misgivings:

> At Ohio Bell Communications I was really running a microcosm of a large company like Ohio Bell. And it was a very successful operation. We enjoyed it. When the time came to leave, it was sad because the company was doing very well, and I very easily could have stayed. In addition, we had a home we loved to live in. My children loved their school and their friends. My husband loved his career; he'd done very well since we had come back from Philadelphia and was moving ahead.

Nevertheless, after considerable discussion with Jack and the girls, they agreed, now, to support Jackie's career. The family moved to Chicago in January 1989. As it turned out, Jack also took a position at Ameritech Services in the information technology department managing the procurement and deployment of computers within the firm.

Jackie's new job increased her responsibility, allowed her to expand her technical and analytical skills, and gave her additional exposure at the corporate offices. She found, however, that she actually disliked the job:

> It was an awful job, I mean a *boring* job. You know, they all wore navy blue suits and were wringing their hands all the time. It was just terrible! And here we were coming out of sales where you did things that mattered, where you got a lot of reinforcement from your customers when you were successful with them! And to go into something where all you heard about was if you did something wrong—and something always went wrong.

WRENCHING CHANGES AT HOME AND OFFICE

Soon after Jackie's arrival in Chicago, Ameritech faced some difficult market conditions and began a series of serious reorganizing efforts that included unprecedented cutbacks in the corporate work force. Many people who had supported Jackie's move to headquarters were no longer with the firm, which caused Jackie some concern:

> We came here, and [shortly thereafter] the company changed its focus and actually fired some of our top management—people who had made commitments to me to bring me here. So, the rug was really pulled out from under us. [They] were redesigning the corporation so the kinds of jobs that I would typically look to as my next move were being done away with.

Exhibit 2
Jackie's Résumé, June 1992

EDUCATION

Northwestern University	Chicago, IL
Executive Education Program	

Muskingum College	Muskingum, OH
Graduated May 1968	
B.A. in Psychology	
B.S. in Communications	

EXPERIENCE

1990–Present	Ameritech Services—Business Markets General Manager and Vice President	Chicago, IL
1989–90	Ameritech Services Vice President of Finance and Administration	Chicago, IL
1986–89	Ohio Bell Communications President and Chief Executive Officer	Cleveland, OH
1982–84	Ohio Bell Communications Vice President of Marketing	Cleveland, OH
1978–82	Bell of Pennsylvania Public Affairs Office Marketing Department	Philadelphia, PA
1970–78	Ohio Bell Communications Public Affairs District Manager Public Relations Manager Business Office Supervisor	Cleveland, OH
Outside Activities	United Way, Muskingum College Alumni Association, Chicago Junior League, Chicago Executive Club, Chicago Easter Seals	

Exhibit 3
Jack's Résumé, June 1992

EDUCATION

University of Akron   Akron, OH
Graduated May 1964
B.S. in Business Administration

EXPERIENCE

1992– Present	Ameritech Services Asset Management Director	Chicago, IL
1990–92	Ameritech Services Supplies Management Director	Chicago, IL
1989–90	Ameritech Services Procurement Director	Chicago, IL
1988–89	B.F. Goodrich Chemical Purchasing Director	Cleveland, OH
1985–87	B.F. Goodrich Procurement and Materials Management Director	Cleveland, OH
1984	B.F. Goodrich Plant Purchasing General Manager	Cleveland, OH
1970-78	B.F. Goodrich Plant Purchasing Regional Manager	Philadelphia, PA
Outside Activities	Shelter, Inc. (Director), American Legion, Computer Dealers/Lessors Association (Customer Advisory Council)	

The increasing competition and speed of technological change forced Ameritech and the other RBOCs to reexamine their basic decision-making processes. Jackie explained that, in the past,

we were an industry that could make decisions on substantial analytical data that was gathered over a period of time. You could go back and reassess that data before you actually had to decide. It was almost no risk to delay the decision versus making an incorrect decision by moving quickly. Well, today, in the competitive marketplace, you can't do that. So, you have to make decisions on minimal amounts of data that you assess maybe once—and on a lot of feeling about your customers.

In August 1991, Jackie moved over to marketing at Ameritech Services (still in Chicago) and was given the responsibility for all of Ameritech's business customers in a five-state region.[1] Her new department, however, was not immune to the substantial reductions in force occurring throughout Ameritech. The layoffs signaled a change in culture at the company:

> If you started with the telephone company and you did a good job, you were recognized, and you were promoted, and, I don't know if I'd say that you had a lifelong career, but you certainly had an extensive career. That isn't how it is today. We're really changing the design of how one succeeds in the business, so I need to go and build [my department's] morale at this point.

As a part of Ameritech's downsizing efforts, all employees were evaluated according to a variety of skills that the company believed to be crucial to its future success. Many individuals were identified as not having the necessary qualities to continue with the company. Jackie commented on the serious changes people were experiencing:

> Now some of those people could retire, so the changes were a pretty easy move for them. Some of them, in their 30s and 40s who couldn't retire, viewed it as a betrayal on the part of the company—changing the way we deal with them, the contract, as they call it. To them, we had literally broken the contract. But instead of deserving a job or believing that it's your right to have the job, we believe you have to earn the job every day. And you earn it through customer service. As a result, we took the bottom tier of people and moved them out of the business. It was a very painful thing to do.
>
> I think the real signal, though, is to people who were on the next tier. We've said to them, "We don't know if we're ever going to have to do this again, but if we do, you're at risk and here's why."

The upheaval caused by the downsizing prompted Ameritech officers to think carefully about how news of the restructuring was communicated to the 70,000-person work force. Jackie commented on the approach:

> [Traditionally,] we let our employees read something in the newspaper or trade journals [about changes] that they should have understood and had explained to them before it appeared in print. Now, sometimes things just

---

[1]Ameritech Services provided planning, development, management, and support for the Ameritech Bell Companies to help achieve common marketing and operational goals.

happen if there wasn't any planning, but there are other things we can do. We're working right now to figure out a decentralized communications process which says that the head of each unit would be able to [communicate the message] the way they want to. But the communication would be coordinated and prepared in documents from a centralized point of view.

What we have found was that if each of us explains why the corporation is downsizing, we each kind of ad-lib why we think that's happening. And then we communicate that to 100 people who each kind of ad-lib to others. The message needs to be very clear. Now, whether I decide to do that over videotapes and you decide to have small group sessions and talk about it will be your decision. These messages require conversation and interactive discussion while others are able to be communicated, maybe, in print. So, what we're trying to balance now is the centralized message and the information around it, but with a decentralized distribution system. That isn't how we've done it to date. We've had one answer for everybody. We're going to send this out in print, it'll be distributed to 70,000 employees, and you'll read about it like everyone else.

As she examined her new job and the changes occurring in her markets, Jackie began to make what others called revolutionary changes for a telephone utility:

One thing I've done here is reach down and create a multilevel reporting structure so that I have some people who would come to my staff meetings who, in our hierarchy, might be several levels below someone else, but they are an expert in their field. Now the people feel honored because they're being recognized for their expertise and the role they're playing and are thrilled to come! What people began to realize was that the reason they were being brought in was that in this meeting we were going to make decisions that required very specific operational information about very specific projects. So, you couldn't have some [who were] representing it who didn't understand the project, or we'd probably make the wrong decision. We invite them to the meetings based on what the subject matter is. So, you get to attend a meeting based on what your role is and what's going to be discussed and your contribution, not because of your approved *right* to attend something because of the job you hold. So, the job doesn't necessarily convey the authority in power as much anymore as the individual and what they are responsible for.

The number of wrenching decisions that were being made and the daily increasing demands of marketing in a broad five-state area with stiffening competition placed an enormous load on Jackie. Because the challenges of reorganizing her department were only partially offset by the excitement of working with corporate customers, Jackie was concerned about her experience at Ameritech Services. She missed the direct responsibilities of the line jobs she had had at Ohio Bell and, frankly, missed her roots and relationships in Ohio (see Exhibits 1 and 2). Further, the changes in management made her wonder if the kind of guidance given by those who had talked about and coordinated her move to Chicago had disappeared. She wondered how long and in what capacity she might stay in Chicago.

With those thoughts in mind, she and her husband began to talk about other options. Should they look for other jobs in other firms back in Cleveland? How long should they wait to see if their decision to follow Jackie's career would prove to be a dead end? How could they tell if the executives at Ameritech were aware of and interested in their situation? (Comments about Jackie by some of her peers and subordinates and some of her own views on various topics are included in Exhibit 4.) As they discussed their thoughts, Jackie and Jack decided early in 1992 to wait another two years to see what would happen. Then, if nothing materialized, they would begin to consider other options:

> Our mind-set was probably [oriented toward] the beginning to middle of 1994. We didn't say, "We're gonna ride this out, and we'll see how it is in two months." I mean, I had invested 20 years at Ameritech! It seemed worth it to invest 15 months more. We had decided that we would ride this out and see— with the feeling that if it did not play out by that point, we would both reassess where we wanted to be.

EUROPEAN VACATION PLANS

Meanwhile, in December 1991, Jackie and Jack had decided to plan a big European family vacation for July 1992. They wanted their children to have the experience of seeing Europe firsthand, something they considered an essential part of the girls' education. In the months following the decision to go, everyone—including Nicole, 14, and Stephanie, 11—spent a considerable amount of time planning all aspects of the trip. They paid for all of the travel and lodging arrangements in advance. Although the package was quite expensive, the Woodses felt good about the itinerary and the experience it would be for the family. Their plans were complicated somewhat by Ameritech's restructuring announcement in May 1992 and by Jackie's subsequent assignment to the reorganization task force. Jackie viewed the assignment with mixed feelings. Although it signaled to her that she was not forgotten, it also conflicted directly with the planned family vacation:

> We had been working with the travel agent since January, and we very specifically picked someone here in town so on Saturday morning you could go up to town, stop at the corner store and get coffee and a doughnut, and go in and sit down and chat with this lady. We laid out maps. The girls went and ate bagels over her desk, and everybody talked about where we were going and had a very vested interest. The girls got to pick places they thought would be interesting. Jack and I contributed. Everybody had read the tour books, and,

Exhibit 4
Comments from and about Jackie Woods

Jackie on Networking

I also find it interesting that men have had a very strong network, so it has been easier [for them] to make decisions based on fact. You could go ask some of your buddies or your boss or the president, "Here's what I see happening; is that how it's going to be?" Women and minorities spent a lot of time guessing because they either didn't have the network or they were afraid to ask. What we're seeing now is that these new networks are being built. There are women's groups; there are minority groups. There is a formal network within their firms so that people can get better information to understand the alternatives.

Jackie on Balancing Work and Family

That is the trade-off. If you are going to say, in a business environment, that you want to have so much more, that these are the jobs that I want to have, then you need to understand what it is going to take to get there. And if that's not what you are willing to do, then you have to take the responsibility for that as well.

A Colleague's Observation of Jackie

Jackie is probably one of the most complete managers that I have encountered throughout my career with Ameritech. She has an incredible amount of energy, an outstanding ability to retain information and absorb detail. She tends to encourage and motivate her staff effectively as well.

Jackie on Being Close to Employees and Customers

What I found was that if you go out and talk to people and spend your time with both your employees and your customers, it becomes easy to understand how to integrate their input into company operations. Employees

(continued on next page)

(continued)

need to know they have your support, and customers need to know the top executives draw what's going on at the front line.

Jackie on Setting Priorities

Even if there are things that are very important to the business, basic tenets that the business is built on, you really need to question them. Let me give you an example: the pricing philosophy of how we price service. Maybe my customer data tell me that [the current way] isn't the way we are going to be able to do that in the future. And my competitive data tell us that we are going to have to change. Well, pricing is something very basic to this business. Changes are going to have millions of dollars of impact. That isn't something I am going to bring up offhandedly in a meeting and expect to have resolved. I am going to evaluate the data, get more facts, and I am going to listen to people's positions on it, and I am going to, as you might say, work the issue. [Anything] that could have immediate impact to our customers is something to fight for. So, having that sense of balance of how big this [issue] is to the corporation and customers is important to determining how quickly we need to act.

Jackie's Colleague on Her Consensus-Building Skills

The Bell Operating Companies [in Ameritech's five-state region] do not want us here. They would prefer to continue to run their own organizations, manage their own budgets, develop their own strategies, and do it in five different ways. So, we go out to the state operating companies and talk to the sales and support vice presidents about our plans, and the minute we walk into the room with the presidents and vice presidents, the guns are loaded. But by the time we leave that meeting, Jackie has really gotten a consensus on every issue that she has gone there with, and everyone feels like they have won at the end of the meeting. It's incredible how she builds the whole win-win situation.

(continued on next page)

(continued)

Jackie on Management Fads

I think that American management has to have a lot of confidence in what they do real well. We sometimes decide that someone else is good at something, and all of a sudden we drop everything we do. We read this book or we heard in this country they do this, so let's drop what we are doing. American management has to develop its own style. Certainly we should utilize things from other cultures, but we should build on a framework of what we really believe in this country and on what we really want to do in managing our businesses. We can't decide quality, for example, is the program for the day! And so now all the CEOs are going to walk out and talk about quality, and all are going to have a quality advisor, and in a few months we are going to decide, well, quality isn't it anymore. I mean, quality has to be in the very basic way that we approach the business and every decision we make.

about June, with everything pretty well paid for and arranged, [Ameritech] said, "Well, maybe you'd better not go."

Bob Brown's comment in the hallway heightened Jackie's concern about the trip. Clearly, that summer would be a very important time in the history of the company. Decisions would be made that could shape the future of Ameritech—and of the Woods family.

NEW ZEALAND DAIRY BOARD

While milk is a raw material, milk is a thousand raw materials.
        John Murray, Company Secretary, New Zealand Dairy Board

Producing commodities keeps you a peasant forever.
        John Parker, Deputy CEO, New Zealand Dairy Board

It was early January 1994, and Warren Larsen reread the Boston Consulting Group's recently released performance audit on the New Zealand Dairy Board (NZDB). The Boston Consulting Group (BCG) conducted its study to fulfill a requirement that NZDB's performance be audited every five years. Larsen, the recently appointed chief executive, was generally pleased with BCG's report, which compared NZDB with a variety of world best practices. However, in some areas NZDB departed significantly from best practice (see Exhibit 1). In addition, increasing global competition, volatility in commodity markets, over-supply of milk products, and foreign government subsidies would make continued performance in the world market a challenge. Larsen also counted shareholder (dairy producer) satisfaction among his chief priorities. The question the new CEO contemplated that January evening was how to crystalize NZDB's strategic direction while ensuring that the concerns of the BCG report and shareholders were addressed.

NZDB HISTORY

In 1993 dairy products accounted for 17 percent of the value of New Zealand's exports, similar to meat (17 percent), and followed by forestry (12 percent), metals/minerals/chemicals (12 percent), horticulture (7 percent), fishing (7 percent), and wool (5 percent). From the early days of the dairy industry in New Zealand, farmers had joined together to form cooperatives to collect, process, and market their members' milk. Traditionally, the members of each cooperative jointly owned the cooperative's assets (processing plants, collection and delivery vehicles, and so forth). The cooperatives retained a share of each year's profits for investment and financial reserves and distributed the remaining profits to the member farmers by way of increments to the basic

The case was prepared by Brad Webb, Darden 1995, under the supervision of Professor L. J. Bourgeois III. Research funding was provided by Ernst & Young, New Zealand. Copyright © 1995 by the University of Virginia Darden School Foundation, Charlottesville, VA. All rights reserved.

Exhibit 1
Boston Consulting Group Report
to New Zealand Dairy Board

Topic	Contrary to Best Practice	Some Significant Departures from Best Practice	In-line with Best Practice with Some Qualifications	In-line with Best Practice
1. Objectives				
2. Policy and Strategy Development				
3. Financial Management and Control				
4. Organizational Structure and Management				
5. Personnel				
6. Finance and Investment				
7. Marketing				
8. Research and Development				
9. Payment System				
10. Quality				
11. Communication				

7 out of 10 and improving

---

milk price. The cooperative's net profits were divided by the total kilograms of milk solids (fat and nonfat components) received during the year to compute a payout per kilogram. Farmers were then paid according to the number of kilograms of milk solids they supplied during the year. Since all farmers in the cooperative received the same dollar payout per kilogram, the only way for an individual farmer to increase his or her payout was to add additional cows or to increase the volume of milk produced per cow. Individual cooperatives competed against each other, and the size of cooperatives was limited by the distance milk was able to be transported in half a day.

During World War II, the United Kingdom paid premium prices for more than 90 percent of New Zealand's dairy produce under a bulk marketing arrangement designed to counter wartime food shortages. This arrangement continued until 1954 when the United Kingdom released New Zealand from its obligation. Even after termination of the formal arrangement, the United Kingdom continued to buy the majority of New Zealand's dairy products, and New Zealand was referred to as "Britain's farm."

The New Zealand Dairy Board was formed as a statutory board under the Dairy Board Act of 1961. Under this act, NZDB was given the power to purchase, market, and control all dairy products manufactured in New Zealand for export. The act resulted in the formation of a single-desk export marketing organization which was required by statute to take all dairy products produced for export in New Zealand. Except for some coordinating activities, NZDB was not involved in the marketing of products within New Zealand, where the individual dairy cooperatives continued to compete freely with one another.

In the years immediately following its formation, NZDB participated in the commodity markets and became exceptionally skilled at exploiting the low-cost advantage of New Zealand's dairy farms. The majority of dairy farms in the United States, Japan, and parts of Europe fed cattle year-round with processed feed, which had to be grown, harvested, stored, and transported to the individual farms. The large amount of labor, equipment, handling, and transport involved resulted in high feed costs, which required higher milk prices to cover the costs of milk production. In contrast, New Zealand's dairy cattle grazed in lush pastures, which minimized the feed cost to the farmer. A comparison of the different costs of production by country is shown in Exhibit 2.

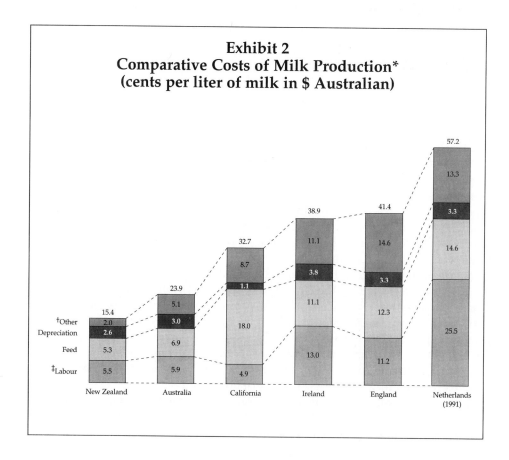

Exhibit 2
Comparative Costs of Milk Production*
(cents per liter of milk in $ Australian)

Although each cooperative contracted with selected farms to supply milk year-round for domestic consumption (also known as "town milk"), the great majority of New Zealand's dairies experienced seasonal production linked to the cycle of grass growth in pastures. The "milk curve" is shown in Exhibit 3. Weather conditions had tremendous influence on the volume of milk produced and caused total annual milk volumes to fluctuate as much as 10 percent.

INDUSTRY OVERVIEW

Production

Virtually every country in the world has had some form of milk production. The export market for dairy products, however, was relatively small when compared to the total volume of milk produced globally. In 1993, only 8 percent, or 36 million tons, of the world's milk production from dairy cows entered export markets, while the other 92 percent was consumed domestically. Of that 36 million tons, only 27 million tons fell into the category of "accessible," or unrestricted, trade, while the remaining 9 million tons was traded bilaterally.

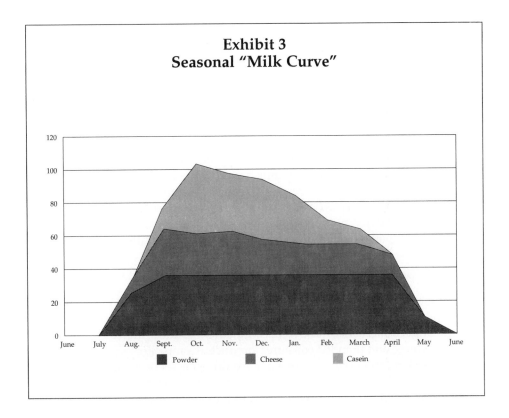

Exhibit 3
Seasonal "Milk Curve"

Powder   Cheese   Casein

Table A
World Milk Production
and Accessible Dairy Product Trade

COUNTRY	1993 MILK PRODUCTION[a]	TOTAL SHARE OF PRODUCTION	EXPORTER'S SHARE OF ACCESSIBLE TRADE
European Union	114.7 MMT	22%	49%
Former Soviet Union	79.0	15%	15
United States	69.0	13%	5
India	60.9	12%	—
Brazil	15.2	3%	—
Poland	11.9	2%	—
New Zealand	5.9	2%	22
Australia	0.4	.09%	8
Others	157.6	30%	6

[a]Total world production of 519 million metric tons (includes dairy cow, sheep, goat, and buffalo milk).

World milk production could be segmented on a national basis. New Zealand produced 2 percent of the world's milk annually but accounted for 17 percent of the world's trade in dairy exports in 1993 (see Table A). New Zealand's relatively small population base consumed only 5 percent of New Zealand's annual milk production, leaving the other 95 percent available for export. Other large producers of milk included the European Community, the United States, India, Australia, and Japan. With the exception of the liquid milk market, unprocessed milk had little value because it spoiled quickly. As a result, most dairy products were exported in processed form in products such as milk powder, cheese, protein concentrate, and butter.

Market Segments

The world trade in dairy products could be separated into four broad product categories. In ascending order of complexity of processing, packaging, and marketing requirements, these were commodity products, ingredients, food service products, and branded consumer products. Competitors in the commodity business were primarily governmental export agencies or national cooperative marketing boards, while buyers tended to be government agricultural agencies who bought commodities in large volumes on a tender-offer basis. Players in the ingredients and food services sectors included national cooperative marketing organizations, government export agencies, and multinational food companies; buyers included large food manufacturing companies, multinational food service companies, and other manufacturing companies, such as pharmaceutical firms. The consumer products area was dominated by multinational food consumer products companies such as Philip Morris and Nestlé, with some limited participation from national export organizations. NZDB competed in all four categories.

Commodity Markets. Of the four primary dairy product segments, commodity markets grew the least and offered the lowest margins. World demand for dairy products was linked to population growth, and prices reflected supply and demand. (See Exhibits 4 and 5 for general production and price trends of skim milk powder and butter on the world markets for 1980 to 1994.) Government subsidies of dairy exports such as the United States' Dairy Export Incentive Program further complicated the smooth functioning of the commodity markets. With the exception of New Zealand, dairy exports from all countries were subsidized to some extent. In 1992, total worldwide dairy product export subsidies totaled US$6.0 billion, as compared to NZDB's total 1992 revenues of US$1.5 billion. Subsidies were greatest in the European Community, Japan, and the United States. In 1982, EEC export subsidies totaled US$2.2 billion and increased to US$4.5 billion in 1992. New Zealand was the only country that could profitably sell its products on the commodity markets at the world minimum prices established in the International Dairy Arrangement, a multicountry organization of dairy exporting nations.

Ingredients and Food Service Markets. Advances in technology and processes vastly expanded the number of dairy products traded internationally. The traded volume of both primary ingredients and specialized food service products increased significantly. Ingredient products included milk proteins such as caseinate, which were used in end products ranging from soft drinks to Cool Whip to pharmaceuticals. Food service products included such items as the cheese used by fast-food franchise operations and confectionery butter used by large food companies. These products were intermediates in the production process and were typically sold in bulk or large quantities to the manufacturer of the end product.

Consumer Markets. Branded consumer products included whole and skim milk powder, ice cream, spreadable butter, specialty cheeses, aerosol whipped cream, and short-shelf-life products such as fresh milk and cultured dairy products. (Exhibit 6 shows the range of products in the consumer segment.) These products were typically distributed via traditional retail distribution channels and required intensive advertising and promotion. Production of consumer dairy products was driven by high value-added processing with an emphasis on smaller quantities than other dairy product categories. Margins in the consumer segment were higher than in the other three segments. The profitability and

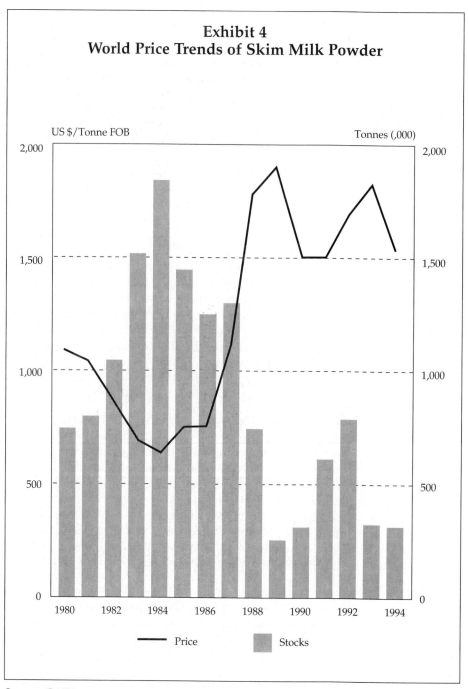

Exhibit 4
World Price Trends of Skim Milk Powder

US $/Tonne FOB

Tonnes (,000)

—— Price   Stocks

Source: GATT.

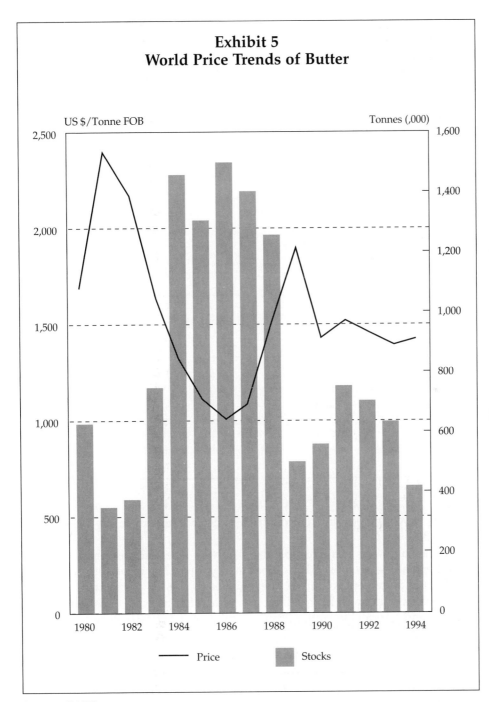

Exhibit 5
World Price Trends of Butter

Source: GATT.

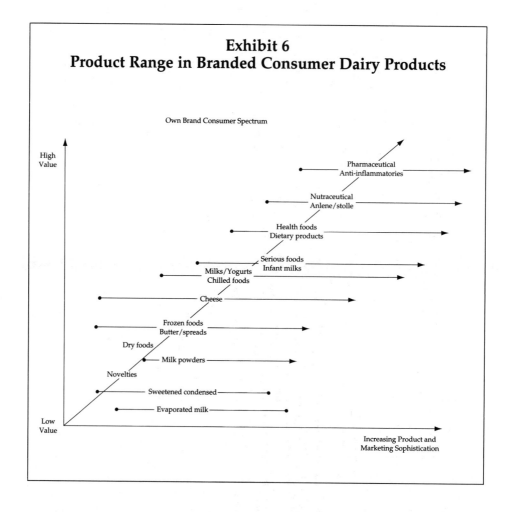

Exhibit 6
Product Range in Branded Consumer Dairy Products

Own Brand Consumer Spectrum

High Value

Pharmaceutical
Anti-inflammatories

Nutraceutical
Anlene/stolle

Health foods
Dietary products

Serious foods
Infant milks

Milks/Yogurts
Chilled foods

Cheese

Frozen foods
Butter/spreads

Dry foods

Milk powders

Novelties

Sweetened condensed

Evaporated milk

Low Value

Increasing Product and
Marketing Sophistication

additional margins captured through a branded consumer strategy are shown in Table B.

The following relationships also apply: a 1-percent net profit on commodity trading equates to US$18 per metric ton, a 5-percent net profit on an industrial ingredient sold in-market equates to US$100 per metric ton, and a 12.5-percent net profit from selling into retail after all costs, including advertising and promotion and return on in-market infrastructure, equates to US$500 per metric ton.

GATT Uruguay Round Results

On December 15, 1993, the GATT (General Agreement on Tariffs and Trade) Uruguay Round was successfully concluded after seven years of nego-

Table B
Analysis of In-Market Profits
and Consumer Milk Powder Prices

			USD per Metric Tonne
Retail Price, Retailers' Costs and Profit	20%	Retail	5,000
Distribution, warehousing selling costs, and profit	15		4,000
Marketing costs and profit	20	Distribution price	3,250
Processing and packing costs and profit	10	Ex-factory	2,600
Freight and insurance	5	CIF price	1,900
Bulk FAS equivalent	30	FAS price	1,800

tiations. The provisions of the agreement provided for significant changes in the world dairy product trade. Both the levels of subsidies and the volumes of products to which subsidies could be applied were reduced significantly. These changes promised to have a significant impact in the EEC countries, which accounted for more than one-half of the world's traded dairy products. Under the new agreement, New Zealand received a 50-percent increase in its butter quota to the United Kingdom (from 52,000 MT to 76,600 MT) as well as improved access into the United States for its cheeses. The increase in the U.K. butter quota was significant for New Zealand, as the United Kingdom paid NZDB a premium price for a product that was becoming increasingly harder to sell due to global oversupply. New Zealand's U.K. butter quota was fixed at the increased level indefinitely. The effects of GATT would also increase the competitiveness of other dairy producers currently being subsidized to varying levels.

Capital Costs

Capital costs in the dairy industry were dependent upon the product sector in which an organization wished to compete and in which portion of the value chain the organization's involvement was focused. Investment requirements ranged from milk processing and recombining facilities to distribution infrastructure to brand building. Producers of commodity products had to be able to separate milk into the desired constituents and produce bulk quantities of relatively unsophisticated finished products such as whole milk powder (WMP), skim milk powder (SMP), butter, and cheese. Significant economies of scale could be realized in the commodities sector.

Given that the ingredients and food service sectors required further processing of the milk constituents, additional investment in both processes and technology was required. What was most crucial in the ingredient and food service sector was an organization's ability to produce consistently high-quality products delivered on time to the required specifications.

The consumer segment required significant investments in packaging, consumer research, distribution infrastructure, and advertising and promotion. Because fresh milk could not be shipped very far without spoiling, traded dairy products were transported in processed form. Shipping could represent a significant portion of a dairy exporting country's cost structure. Chris Kelly, NZDB's director of strategic planning, cited "the tyranny of distance" as being one competitive factor with which NZDB had to regularly contend.

Suppliers

Milk was produced by dairy farmers whose farms varied in scale depending on the price paid for milk in the producing country (see Exhibit 7). Milk could be processed into fresh milk for drinking or manufactured into processed products such as cheese, butter, and ice cream. The proportion of milk used in manufacturing also varied by country (see Exhibit 7). In general, milk was a commodity raw material, and excess production capacity existed globally as a result of dairy subsidies. Dairy farmers generally had little bargaining power with the organizations to whom they sold their milk.

In some countries, including New Zealand and Denmark, dairy farmers were organized into a cooperative structure in which the farmers themselves owned the processing facilities and exerted some influence over the way in which the milk products were manufactured and marketed. Farmers had the ability to change to whom they sold their milk. However, in reality, because of costs of transport of milk to the processing units, only those farmers on the borders between one processor and another could be able to change their processor.

Customers

The profile of dairy product buyers varied by product segment as follows:

- **Commodity.** These buyers were typically government or national-scale agencies who bought primarily on price through tender offers. These purchasers frequently had no loyalty to one seller, provided a compet-

Exhibit 7
International Comparisions
Herd Size[a] and Milk Production[b]

	TOTAL COWS 000 HEAD	AVERAGE HERD SIZE	MILK PRODUCTION[c] 000 TONNES	PERCENT USED IN MANUFACTURING[d]
New Zealand	2,357	169.6	7,873[d]	94.3
Australia	1,628	110.0	7,327[d]	75.7
United States	9,850	48.1	67,717	63.3
Canada	1,270	42.5	7,100	63.5
Japan	2,082	37.8	8,580	—
EEC—Total 12	21,900	19.6	97,799	73.2
Denmark	708	33.0	4,406	—
France	4,685	22.0	22,989	—
United Germany	5,382	17.3	25,610	—
Ireland	1,262	24.6	5,271	—
United Kingdom	2,747	68.2	13,884	—
Netherlands	1,821	40.5	10,504	—
C.L.S. (former USSR)	38,200	—	50,700[e]	—

[a]Latest available figures; all are 1991 figures, apart from New Zealand, Australia, and Japan, which are 1992 figures.
[b]Provisional figures for 1992, based on national statistics.
[c]Sales to factories and dairies (milk available for processing).
[d]1992/1993 season.
[e]State purchases.
Source: New Zealand Dairy Board documents.

ing seller could meet the same minimum quality standards. Sellers who participated in the commodity markets frequently worked through an agency structure and had little or no contact with the government issuing the tender. Buyers in this segment would purchase from as many sources as were necessary to obtain the required volume. Thus there were "world commodity prices" which varied with global supply and demand.

- **Ingredients.** Large regional, national, or multinational companies purchased these products and sought consistent taste, quality, and appearance from dairy products suppliers. In addition, these customers often required extensive technical assistance in tailoring a dairy ingredient to a product-specific application. Long-term partnerships were standard practice in this segment, a practice partially driven by necessity as many dairy ingredients had specific functional properties that were proprietary in nature.

- **Food service.** These buyers were typically large national or regional food manufacturing or retail companies, including fast-food franchise operations like McDonald's and Pizza Hut. Because these companies stressed product consistency across their various outlets, they sought the same consistent quality that ingredients purchasers did, as well as on-time delivery. These customers were typically very loyal and also sought to form long-term, mutual trust relationships with their suppliers.

- **Consumer.** In industrialized Western countries, consumer products were distributed through extensive wholesale and retail structures, where large retail chains were increasing in size and geographic coverage. This phenomenon was less pronounced in developing countries.

The organizational infrastructure requirements needed to successfully compete in each segment were varied. For commodity products, the only requirements were "an agent, a phone, and a fax," according to John Parker, the current deputy chief executive and a 30-year veteran of NZDB. For in-market ingredient sales, marketing, sales, and technical capabilities were required. The food service segment required processing capabilities in addition to those skills needed for ingredient sales, while the consumer segment required distribution and brand marketing capabilities in addition to all the others.

Substitute Products

Two significant challenges to dairy products had arisen recently. The first involved health concerns about the consumption of animal fats, including those contained in dairy products such as cheese, ice cream, and butter. These concerns suggested a link between coronary disease and consumption of high levels of animal fat. The dairy industry responded by actively promoting the health benefits of dairy products, including osteoporosis prevention. The other significant challenge involved vegetable proteins in the ingredients segment. Vegetable proteins, including soy proteins, had many of the same performance characteristics of dairy proteins but were considerably cheaper to produce.

(Depending on how soy proteins were produced, however, there could be hormonal traces which, if digested in large quantities, could harm consumers.)

Competition

Few companies competed across all segments of the dairy product business. However, some companies, like NZDB and MD-Foods of Denmark, had diversified into more than one segment.

Geography also defined competition in the dairy industry. The Irish Dairy Board competed in the European Community markets, and the Australian dairy companies targeted markets in Southeast Asia. When considered solely in terms of dairy products, NZDB competed in more product categories and regions than any of its major competitors.

Nestlé.   Nestlé first entered the dairy products business in 1866 when it began producing condensed milk for the European market. In 1993, this Swiss multinational had total sales of US$39.1 billion, employed more than 209,000 personnel in 489 factories in 69 countries, and sold products in more than 100 countries. Nestlé's principal lines of business included beverages, prepared dishes and cooking aids, chocolate and confectionery, pharmaceuticals, and milk products and dietetics. The milk products and dietetics group generated US$10.85 billion in 1993, or 28 percent of Nestlé's sales. Nestlé's products, which were marketed globally under the umbrella of the Nestlé corporate logo, included sweetened and unsweetened condensed milk, yogurts, fresh cheese, powdered milk, vegetable-fat coffee creamer, infant nutrition formulas, slimming and weight control products, and ice cream.

In 1985, Nestlé acquired Carnation, a major dairy products company in the United States, and established a research center dedicated solely to human nutrition. In 1993, Nestlé further expanded its presence in the global ice cream business as it battled its arch rival, Unilever, for global dominance in this category. Nestlé also acquired Perrier and several milk companies in various locations. Nestlé competed with NZDB in the branded consumer products segment, especially in milk powders.

In Malaysia, Dumex, Dutch Lady, and two other marketers purchased milk powder from NZDB for repackaging and sale. Nestlé was disturbed by their success, but it reflected the tensions that were occurring between NZDB and some of its large business customers. NZDB supplied Nestlé with skim milk powder and anhydrous milk fat for recombining, and in 1993 it sold more than US$360 million of products to Nestlé. Nestlé tolerated NZDB's infringement of their consumer territory because NZDB's product quality and service were unsurpassed.

Kraft-General Foods.   In 1988, Philip Morris acquired Kraft and merged it with General Foods to form a food industry giant. For decades, Kraft had been a significant force in the world cheese market, especially in the processed cheese category. In 1992, Philip Morris had total sales of US$59.13 billion and employed more than 161,000 people. Philip Morris's four principal lines of business included tobacco, beer, real estate and financial services, and food.

Kraft-General Foods served both the North American and international food markets and produced a wide range of food products in addition to cheese, including salad dressings, hot and cold instant beverages, lunch meats, frozen pasta, baked goods, cereals, ice cream, frozen dinners, and barbecue sauces. In the North American market, Kraft also had food service and food ingredients businesses. In 1992, Kraft held a greater than 40-percent share of the North American cheese market. Kraft's overall cheese sales volume increased in the international foods segment, accounting for US$1.48 billion in 1992. The company's research efforts focused on providing consumers with nutritional and healthy products, including reduced-fat and fat-free cheeses. In 1992, Philip Morris was still struggling to realize the synergies that drove the Kraft-General Foods merger. Several manufacturing operations were discontinued, and personnel reductions continued in the Kraft-General Foods division.

Australian Dairy Companies (ADC).   The ADC was an export marketing organization formed by members of the Australian dairy industry to market the excess milk remaining after domestic consumer requirements had been met. Its 1993 revenues were $185 million Australian, and total volume sold was 440,000 tons. On a national level, Australia was the only country that approached New Zealand's ability to produce on a low-cost basis. However, exports of Australian dairy products were subsidized through the assessment of a levy on all dairy farmers. ADC was active in the commodity segments and did not have the same structure or export and manufacturing strategy as NZDB.

Irish Dairy Board (IDB).   The IDB was a national export organization that marketed the export products of the Irish dairy industry. In 1993, IDB's total production was 519,000 tons, and total revenues were 1.214 billion Irish pounds. IDB was primarily involved in commodity trading of bulk products with a significant focus on exports to European Community members. With the results of the GATT Uruguay Round, it was expected that IDB would focus its future efforts on selling more products within the European Community.

MD Foods   MD Foods, a cooperative formed by members of Denmark's dairy industry, controlled 86 percent of Denmark's milk production and produced products for both domestic and export consumption. Products included a wide range of specialty cheeses, whole milk powder, and casein and whey concentrates. Exports were handled by MD Foods-International, an affiliated company capitalized by market investors. MD Foods had a superior reputation for technical excellence in product development. Additionally, MD-Foods had targeted many of the same markets and opportunities as NZDB, including the United States as a market for its casein and whey products. In 1992/1993, MD Foods had sales of US$2.01 billion, of which US$1.2 billion was from exports.

NZDB: 1973 TO 1993

In 1973, the United Kingdom joined the Common Market. Not only were exports to the United Kingdom now governed by restrictive EC trade policies, but the EC also increased subsidies to support its own exports. With the new restrictions on its U.K. market, the Dairy Board was forced to scramble to sell its annual production. It was during this period that NZDB established its worldwide network of traders and agents, all of whom were dedicated to moving as much product at the highest prices on the world's commodity markets. This network of agents and relationships would later prove crucial when NZDB branched out into value-added products in the late 1970s and the early 1980s. NZDB sold nearly all of its annual production on the world's commodity markets, suffering the volume and price swings so common to commodity goods. However, the NZDB staff became skilled at selling commodities and managing their effective market placement, even going so far as to purchase commodities from other nations' dairy marketing organizations for later placement into commodity markets when supply was short (and prices up). To NZDB, subsidized dairy producers from other countries did not seem to care about balancing supply with demand on the world markets. NZDB, however, saw an opportunity and became, in effect, a commodity manager and intermediary for other dairy producers.

After experiencing price swings and accompanying erratic payouts to farmers for several years, NZDB management decided in the late 1970s to vertically integrate the organization in order to capture the greatest returns for New Zealand dairy farmers. It was at this time that the agent network was leveraged. NZDB already had a presence, as described by Deputy CEO John Parker, "in the 80 least desirable countries in the world in which to do business," and these countries, with their underdeveloped or nonexistent dairy product markets, were not attractive to the major food industry giants like Nestlé and Kraft. NZDB saw an opportunity to build on its commodity-selling relationships by seeking out distribution partners through its agent network. Building on NZDB's limited experience in consumer goods from its days as the United Kingdom's primary dairy product supplier, the value-added aspect of NZDB was born.

Over time, NZDB shifted from being a heavily dependent trading body that focused on exports to a single market—the United Kingdom—to becoming a manufacturing and marketing organization offering a diverse range of products to customers and companies around the world. The rationale for changing the market orientation was twofold: to capture a greater percentage of the total market value of each product produced and to increase the stability and security of returns to dairy farmers.

**Table C
Development Profile
for NZDB Offshore Company Network**

INVESTMENT PROGRESSION	MANAGEMENT LABEL	RISK LEVEL
Sales to anyone ↓	Random shots	Very low
Sales to a few ↓	Aimed shots	
Agent appointed ↓	Bombardment	Low
Liaison ↓	Office infiltration	
Joint Venture ↓	Pacification	Moderate
Buy out joint-venture partner ↓	Annexation	
Own company	Conquest	High

NZDB's shift to a marketing organization involved several key strategies, but according to John Parker, this shift was more "evolutionary than revolutionary." However, throughout this process, the emphasis remained focused on leveraging New Zealand's position as the world's low-cost milk producer. The primary strategic change was to minimize sales of commodities by shifting into producing and marketing products in all segments of the value chain. To achieve this end, NZDB invested in and developed a substantial offshore network of agents, joint ventures, and wholly owned subsidiaries. The model for building an offshore network is shown in Table C and was followed by NZDB in nearly all of the countries in which it conducted business. To further emphasize the transition to a customer and marketing-driven organization, the senior managers of NZDB attempted to decentralize the organization and move its applied research closer to customers by opening five regional research and development centers and by managing the organization by region rather than as one global company.

The transition to competing in all four product segments was completed by 1993. Table D shows NZDB 1994 sales by segment and projections for 2004.

Table D
NZDB Business Line Segmentation
1994 and 2004 (Projected)

	1994	2004
Commodities	20.0%	15%
Ingredients	52.5	43
Food Service	5.0	7
Consumer	22.5	35
Total Volume (MTs)[a]	1,000,000	1,4000,000

[a]Tons of *product* (as distinct from the tons of *liquid milk* reported in Table A); that is, minus water.

Sourcing and Exporting

By early 1994, 15 dairy cooperatives existed in New Zealand, and the total investment in the industry exceeded NZ$15 billion. These cooperatives ranged in size from the huge New Zealand Cooperative Dairy Company (NZCDC), which produced nearly 44 percent of New Zealand's milk, to the tiny Kaikoura Dairy Cooperative, which produced only 0.3 percent of New Zealand's milk (see Exhibit 8). These 15 cooperatives represented the 14,000 dairy farmers who owned NZDB. The basic product flow was 8,000,000 tons of milk from 14,000 dairy farmers through 15 cooperative manufacturing dairy companies. These cooperatives produced more than 1 million metric tons of products, which were sold in more than 100 countries by NZDB's 80 offshore companies (see Exhibit 9). Table E on page 95 shows New Zealand's top-ten trading partners for dairy exports. Exhibit 10 shows NZDB's actual and forecasted totals by region for its own brand consumer products business.

Strategy

As defined in its mission statement, NZDB sought "to be the world's premier marketer of dairy products," with the accompanying goal of returning the highest possible payout to New Zealand's dairy farmers. To achieve these aims, NZDB committed itself to focusing solely on dairy products. Consequently, NZDB had no plans to diversify into or acquire nonrelated lines of business. Additionally, NZDB endeavored to sell all products within the year they were produced. Achieving a total sell-off of each year's production was becoming

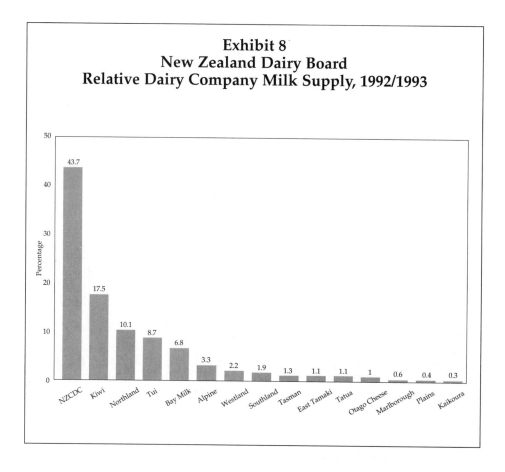

Exhibit 8
New Zealand Dairy Board
Relative Dairy Company Milk Supply, 1992/1993

more difficult for two reasons: (1) herd sizes were increasing and (2) new entrants were converting to dairy farming from other types of pastoral farming due to the financial attractiveness of dairy farming (see Table F). Both of these events further increased the industry's capacity in New Zealand.

Traditionally, New Zealand dairy farmers considered their end customer to be NZDB in Wellington. NZDB provided the farmers with the bulk of their income and dealt with the cooperatives on production and financing issues. However, as NZDB moved offshore, decentralized, and emphasized a market-specific and customer-driven focus, NZDB's senior staff attempted to influence the management teams of cooperatives and, in turn, individual farmers to view its customers as being the offshore companies and specific in-market customers.

Products and Markets

Commodity. In its early stages, NZDB concentrated on the commodity markets, selling large volumes of products such as milk powders, butter, and

Exhibit 9
New Zealand Dairy Board Worldwide

Overseas Companies[a]	Countries Represented
Milk Products Holdings Australia Pty, Ltd.	Australia
Milk Products Holdings Europe, Ltd.	United Kingdom, Germany, Italy, Denmark, Egypt
Milk Products Holdings Latin America, Ltd.	Bermuda, Guatemala, Mexico, Peru, El Salvador, Venezuela, Chile, Jamaica
Milk Products Holdings Middle East EC	Bahrain
Milk Products Holdings North America, Inc.	United States, Canada
Milk Products Holdings South East Asia Pte, Ltd.	Singapore, Bangladesh, Mauritius, China, Hong Kong, Malaysia, South Africa, Taiwan, Sri Lanka, Thailand, Philippines
New Zealand Milk Products Japan, Ltd.	Japan, South Korea
New Zealand Milk Products CIS A.O.	Russia
Milk Products Holdings New Zealand, Ltd.	New Zealand
Finance Companies	New Zealand, Bermuda, Cayman Islands, United Kingdom

[a]Major subsidiaries and associate companies engaged in the marketing, distribution, processing, technology, or financing of the dairy industry and related products listed by country of incorporation.

cheese. After the United Kingdom's admission to the Common Market in 1973, the Dairy Board began to provide commodity products differentiated by extra service and guaranteed quality. Customers in the commodity trade were typically government agencies, and business was conducted through tender

---

**Exhibit 10
New Zealand Dairy Board Sales
by Region, Consumer Products (Tons)**

REGION	1991/1992 ACTUALS	1992/1993 FORECAST	1993/1994 PLANNED
North America	100	100	120
North Asia	200	450	500
Southeast Asia	46,000	60,000	72,000
Central/South America	18,000	25,000	32,000
Africa/Europe	4,000	6,600	32,000
Middle East	9,800	10,500	12,000
Australia	6,500	10,000	12,000
Pacific	3,000	3,500	4,000
United Kingdom	65,000	65,000	65,000
C.I.S.	—	—	5,000
Totals	152,600	181,150	239,620

---

offers in which an agency provided a set of product specifications—quality or nutritional—and sought to purchase a large volume of the product that met those specifications. Milk powder used for human nutrition in United Nations refugee camps is one example of such a product. However, because of the certified quality and higher level of service that NZDB offered to customers, the Dairy Board was really providing *ingredients* at commodity prices.

Ingredients. NZDB's wide variety of ingredient products included, for example, specialty fats for bakeries (used in Korea), rennet casein for imitation cheese (Italy), protein hydrolysates for medical applications (Japan), skim milk and whole milk powders for repackaging (Asia), and whey protein concentrate for use in meat (United States).

The ingredient area led to NZDB's success in the United States. Due to trade restrictions, NZDB was prohibited from bringing in large volumes of traditional ingredient products like milk powder and cheese. However, NZDB was able to bring in "obscure" dairy products like protein hydrolysate and

Table E
New Zealand's Top-Ten Dairy Trading Partners

	1987	1990	1992
Japan	7.3%	10.9%	13.2%
United Kingdom	16.1	13.4	12.6
United States	15.0	12.2	10.3
Mexico	1.6	9.1	5.5
Malaysia	5.1	5.9	6.9
Philippines	4.2	4.2	3.3
Algeria	1.5	3.1	2.5
Taiwan	1.9	2.5	3.4
Australia	1.7	2.7	3.3
Germany	1.6	3.3	2.6

Table F
New Zealand Pastoral Farming Returns by Sector

FARMING SECTOR	RETURN PER STOCK UNIT[a] ($NZ)
Dairy	$103
Deer	$45
Beef	$36
Sheep	$30

[a]Per Stock Unit = per animal.

caseinate, dairy products that had a wide variety of applications ranging from food service to pharmaceuticals. By and large, the subsidized U.S. dairy industry considered casein and whey, which was a by-product of cheese manufacturing, to be waste by-products of dairy production. NZDB approached and worked with numerous companies in the United States and elsewhere to develop specific products tailored to a customer's exact needs. For example, caseinate was used both in button manufacturing and in food manufacturing, where it was used to provide stiffness to Cool Whip. The vast majority of NZDB's ingredient formulations were proprietary. By 1994, NZDB's North American operations had revenues of US$400 million.

Food Service.   In the food service segment, organizations like McDonald's, Pizza Hut, and Taco Bell were NZDB customers. Again, it was the outstanding quality of its products and stellar service reputation that led to NZDB's success here. NZDB targeted this segment as a key future area of focus for its sales force and was pushing its reputation for quality as its key selling point.

Business-to-Business Marketing and Sales.   In its business marketing efforts, NZDB targeted technically sophisticated customers who had very specific applications in mind. As such, the NZDB sales force was well educated and typically had either a bachelor's or master's degree in a relevant discipline such as food science or industrial engineering. The sales force worked with specific large-account customers in an effort to meet current and future needs. In general, potential customers approached NZDB due to the outstanding reputation of its products. Typically, senior executives in Wellington were involved in transactions with key clients like Nestlé or Coca-Cola. The marketing staff was relatively lean for an organization of NZDB's size, and the members of the sales force had the power to make decisions in the field when it would help gain a new customer or satisfy an existing customer. Each sales rep was seen as one member of a customer service team, the other members coming from research and development, production, and finance.

Consumer Sector.   NZDB had succeeded in shifting a significant share of volume from its commodity business into branded consumer products (see Table D). Several success stories resulted from a combination of marketing aggressiveness and research and development persistence and innovation, including Anchor-brand spreadable butter in the United Kingdom, Anlene milk powder in Southeast Asia, and Anchor-brand milk powders in Latin America.

Consumer Marketing and Sales.   NZDB typically leveraged its existing market presence and contacts—agents and joint-venture partners—to establish its consumer business in a given country or region. Often, these relationships provided it with a distribution network, significant knowledge about consumer preferences, and insight into the positioning of competitors. NZDB's control of distribution ensured service and promptness for retailers and greater margins for the Dairy Board. NZDB generally entered consumer markets only where it could become the dominant brand or capture a strong second place. It also established a five-year, break-even profitability horizon by which time all brand investments had been recouped and the brand had achieved the targeted share. Entry into a specific market was generally viewed as a long-term commitment by the Dairy Board.

NZDB did not have an umbrella branding strategy. Instead, the Dairy Board used a variety of brands around the world, which posed challenges as the Board's global presence expanded. The Anchor brand was the most widely used and the most well known. NZDB relied heavily on New Zealand's "clean, green image" to appeal to consumers around the world. Television commercials presented images of cattle grazing on verdant pastures, firmly establishing in the consumer's mind the link between New Zealand's "clean and green" attributes and healthy, nutritious milk. NZDB also highlighted the "all-natural" composition of its products, especially Anlene, a calcium-fortified milk powder sold throughout Southeast Asia as a preventative for osteoporosis. Whereas the supplemental calcium in this milk powder had been recovered during milk processing operations, Anlene was positioned against similar products containing calcium extracted from chalk deposits. Consumers seemed to display a distinct preference for natural calcium.

In Malaysia, NZDB relied on the strength of "a mother's love" to sell milk powder for children. Although competing products touted nutritional and health benefits, NZDB believed that mothers already recognized that milk was good for their children and did not need to be told this. Instead, NZDB relied on a strong emotional appeal to suggest that mothers who really care about their children choose the New Zealand product.

NZDB was also able to leverage its role as an ingredient supplier in a Malaysian advertising campaign in the consumer milk powder category. In Malaysia, many of NZDB's milk powder competitors bought their bulk milk powder from NZDB, then recombined and packaged the milk powder for sale to consumers, competing directly against the Dairy Board's consumer milk powders. However, NZDB calculated that the volume of milk powder it sold in the combined ingredient and consumer product sectors made it the number-one supplier of milk powder in Malaysia, and an entire advertising and promotional campaign was designed around this theme. Although NZDB's product was not actually the leading consumer product, Malaysian consumers were bombarded with the message that New Zealand Dairy Board milk powders were the biggest and best-selling brand in Malaysia, resulting in NZDB's capturing the top spot in the consumer milk powder segment. According to Alistair Betts, group general manager of marketing, NZDB frequently relied on "guerrilla marketing" tactics like this milk powder campaign to capture share in new markets. This behavior sometimes drew criticism from its ingredient customers, Nestlé among them, who found themselves competing with the Dairy Board in the consumer segment while buying from it in the ingredients segment.

In many of its markets, NZDB had to educate consumers about the positive aspects of dairy products. In many Asian countries, including South Korea and Japan, cheese had not been a traditional food. However, the large populations in these countries made them attractive markets, and NZDB had frequently embarked on advertising campaigns that introduced and promoted dairy products. NZDB's overall advertising and promotion expenditures totaled NZ$55 million, $65 million, $83 million, and $102 million in 1991, 1992, 1993, and 1994, respectively.

Operations

Throughout its existence, NZDB's manufacturing philosophy had been threefold: to achieve a product mix that provided the maximum possible financial returns, to sell all products within the year they were produced, and to be a low-cost processor. The primary challenges were that NZDB had no control over the quantity of milk produced in a given year and that NZDB had to purchase all milk products offered for sale by the cooperatives. Given that weather could cause total annual milk volumes to vary by as much as 10 percent, defining the most profitable product mix was also a challenge. Additionally, because milk production was seasonal with a peak in November, dairy company facilities were designed to handle the peak production volumes, which often resulted in significant excess production capacity during the rest of the year.

At the beginning of each season, the product mix group forecasted milk production for the current season and for the next five years. As the season progressed, these forecasts were modified, and any necessary adjustments in the target product mix were made. Production of the various products was done by the individual dairy cooperatives. Although NZDB had an ideal product mix in mind each year, the Dairy Board was unable to mandate or otherwise assign production quotas to cooperatives. The only means by which the Dairy Board was able to influence the product mix of individual cooperatives was through the offer prices paid for various dairy products. For example, if market forecasts indicated that there would be an oversupply of skim milk powder on world markets in the coming year, then the price paid to New Zealand cooperatives for skim milk was adjusted downward to a point that the total skim milk volume from the cooperatives was close to the production target.

When additional manufacturing capacity was needed for existing or new products, interested dairy cooperatives submitted bids to NZDB prior to the construction or expansion of the new facilities. NZDB then awarded the construction right to the company that would be able to meet milk composition, product quality, and timely delivery standards at the lowest cost. The Dairy Board took into account the cost of capital employed and the interest costs associated with the new facilities. This production system was designed to be neutral. In other words, a dairy cooperative's profitability should be the same regardless of whether it produced bulk whole milk powder for the commodity markets, whey protein concentrate for the nutraceuticals markets, or cans of milk powder for the Malaysian consumer market.

The performance of all dairy companies was judged against standard cost models (one model for each of 500 products) developed by NZDB and approved by industry committees. The standard cost models were based on engineering principles and assigned costs based on the use of the latest process technology for a specified volume of milk and a given product type. When new technology became available, it was not integrated into the cost models until it had been in use for three years, at which time it was expected that cooperatives would have adopted the new technology. Dairy companies achieved profitability when they were able to produce at cost levels below those specified in the standard cost models. In early 1994, NZDB began using NZ$2.50 per kilogram as the "notional cost," or raw-materials price, of milk so that a profit-and-loss statement could be generated for manufacturing operations.

The use of standard cost models pushed the New Zealand dairy industry toward the lowest cost production possible. This was often reflected in manufacturing facilities which took full advantage of the economies of scale available. According to Dave Pilkington, group general manager of operations, "Dairy companies felt that the benefits of scale had been nearly maximized, and there were no longer any benefits to be gained by closing smaller plants in favor of larger ones. A new milk powder plant can easily cost NZ$100 million, and dairy companies were reluctant to continue investing in new facilities as they must be accountable to their individual members." For instance, Kiwi Milk Products installed the world's largest milk powder production facility in the world, a facility that was capable of processing 8 million liters of liquid milk per day. According to Pilkington, "this push for scale began to conflict with NZDB's marketing strategy, which emphasized more differentiated consumer products and a customer-oriented strategy. NZDB may need to offer financial incentives to reward dairy companies who consistently excelled in meeting quality and on-time delivery requirements."

The desired product mix prioritized products according to projected profitability and demand. Many possible combinations of products could be produced from a given volume of milk (see Exhibit 11). Standard New Zealand milk was composed of 11.5 percent cream and 88.5 percent skim milk by volume; and milk solids, including fat and protein, accounted for 8.1 percent of the total weight. The composition of standard New Zealand milk is shown in Table G. Exhibit 12 shows the production volumes of whole milk powder (WMP), skim milk powder (SMP), cheese, cream products, casein, and buttermilk powder (BMP) for the period from 1984 through 1993. From 1985 to 1990, the manufacturing cost of the New Zealand dairy industry

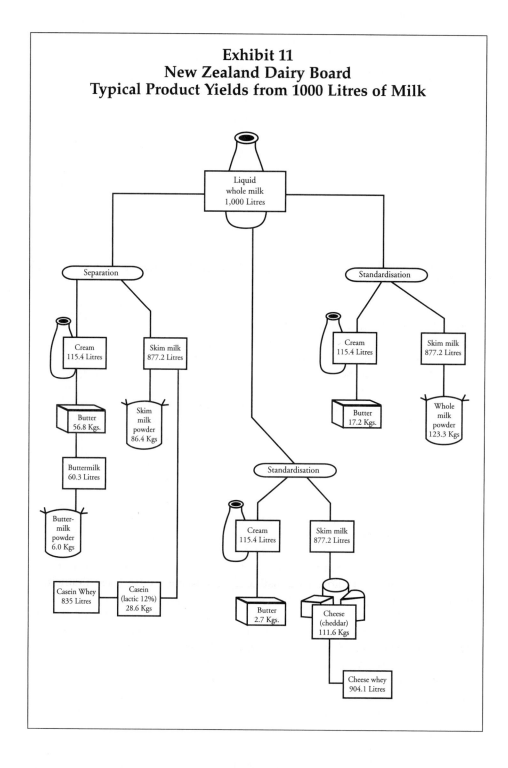

Exhibit 11
New Zealand Dairy Board
Typical Product Yields from 1000 Litres of Milk

Table G
Composition of Standard New Zealand Milk
(on a weight % basis)

Fat	4.65%
Protein	3.43
Ash	0.67
Lactose	4.64
Water	86.61
Total	100.00%

steadily declined a total of 28.57 percent. From 1990 to 1993, the manufacturing cost slowly rose a total of 7.78 percent.

The production and manufacturing area was not without controversy. NZDB had come under fire from cooperatives when decisions were made about allocating new production responsibilities as some cooperatives perceived this process to be political. Additionally, there were questions about whether the milk payment system was really neutral or whether or not it benefited some cooperatives more than others.

Finance and Treasury

Robin Golding, the group general manager of treasury, stated, "Both Standard & Poor's and Moody's gave NZDB an investment rating equivalent to that enjoyed by the New Zealand government. The Dairy Board was the first New Zealand corporation to receive a rating this high." Due to its creditworthiness, NZDB was able to secure financing at very favorable rates. The Dairy Board was also able to assist dairy companies with their financing needs—both seasonal cash flow requirements and long-term investment projects. NZDB's ability to finance dairy company investments resulted in a lower overall cost of borrowing to the industry because banks decreased interest rates in order to compete with the Dairy Board's internal rate and attract dairy company business. (See Exhibits 13, 14, and 15 for NZDB income statements and balance sheets.)

NZDB's treasury group was heavily involved in managing the foreign exchange risk associated with the offshore companies. Worldwide, dairy trade transactions were denominated primarily in U.S. dollars (80 percent), pound

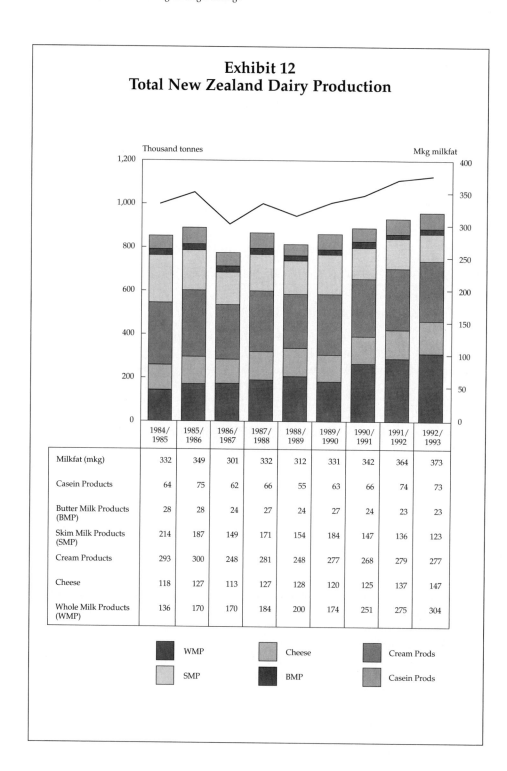

Exhibit 12
Total New Zealand Dairy Production

	1984/ 1985	1985/ 1986	1986/ 1987	1987/ 1988	1988/ 1989	1989/ 1990	1990/ 1991	1991/ 1992	1992/ 1993
Milkfat (mkg)	332	349	301	332	312	331	342	364	373
Casein Products	64	75	62	66	55	63	66	74	73
Butter Milk Products (BMP)	28	28	24	27	24	27	24	23	23
Skim Milk Products (SMP)	214	187	149	171	154	184	147	136	123
Cream Products	293	300	248	281	248	277	268	279	277
Cheese	118	127	113	127	128	120	125	137	147
Whole Milk Products (WMP)	136	170	170	184	200	174	251	275	304

Exhibit 13
New Zealand Dairy Board Consolidated Revenue
Statement for the Year Ended 31 May 1993

IN THOUSANDS OF NEW ZEALAND DOLLARS	Groupa		Board	
	1993	1992	1993	1992
Gross revenue	**$5,054,351**	$5,057,882	**$3,238,295**	$2,954,776
Earnings before taxation	**97,473**	159,722	**(91,331)**	57,449
Taxation charge	**(58,889)**	(62,845)	**(13,278)**	(23,495)
Earnings after taxation	**38,584**	96,877	**(104,609)**	33,954
Earnings attributable to minority shareholders in subsidiary companies	**(8,404)**	(8,761)	**0**	0
Share of retained earnings less losses of associate companies after taxation	**11,425**	7,580	**0**	0
Extraordinary gain arising from corporate restructuring	**0**	0	**19,576**	78,107
Earnings available for distribution transferred to the General Reserve	$ **41,605**	$ 95,696	$ **(85,033)**	$ 112,061

a"Group" includes sales by NZDB subsidiaries.
Source: NZDB Annual Report.

sterling (10 percent), and a mixture of other currencies (10 percent). Because NZDB paid its shareholders, the dairy farmers, in New Zealand dollars, this created a transaction risk. In order to attract new customers and grow market share, NZDB subsidiaries conducted business in the local currencies of the many diverse markets in which the Dairy Board operated. This, too, posed a currency risk management challenge for NZDB. In 1993, the treasury group handled more than NZ$120 billion in settlements and added more than NZ$200 million to the Board's bottom line through its foreign-exchange risk management program. Golding said, "The Dairy Board options desk is very innovative and operates on a 'best practice' level that is on a par with British Petroleum."

Exhibit 14
New Zealand Dairy Board
Consolidated Balance Sheet as of 31 May 1993
(In Thousands of New Zealand Dollars)

	Group		Board	
	1993	1992	**1993**	1992
Capital	**750,000**	0	**750,000**	0
Reserves	**708,694**	1,429,782	**685,062**	1,520,095
Total capital and reserves	**1,458,694**	1,429,782	**1,435,062**	1,520,095
Minority shareholders' interest in subsidiaries	**51,125**	47,719	**0**	0
Long-term liabilities	**150,766**	336,751	**81**	83
Deferred taxation	**9,635**	17,785	**417**	10,525
Current liabilities				
Bank overdrafts	**39,119**	37,456	**10,521**	340
Payables and accruals	**437,532**	555,080	**256,657**	297,793
Subsidiaries			**1,217,889**	758,932
Associates	**28,009**	20,235	**1,992**	17,702
Taxation	**18,752**	12,094	**22,901**	0
Short-term liabilities	**1,103,383**	851,492	**52,376**	153,330
Total current liabilities	**1,626,795**	1,476,357	**1,562,336**	1,228,097
Total capital, reserves, and liabilities	**$3,297,015**	$3,308,394	**$2,997,896**	$2,758,800
Fixed assets	**406,050**	409,394	**75,477**	84,864
Intangibles	**46,931**	37,079	**0**	0
Investments				
Subsidiaries			**659,843**	599,434
Associates	**85,471**	124,136	**13,646**	35,604
Share investments	**37,972**	40,296	**260**	242
Loans and advances	**58,287**	71,955	**54,022**	67,022
Total investments	**181,730**	236,387	**727,771**	702,302
Current assets				
Bank balances	**32,440**	69,001	**5,883**	22,060
Short-term deposits	**116,003**	50,185	**105,240**	29,162
Receivables and prepayments	**786,440**	978,303	**529,181**	615,574
Subsidiaries			**408,877**	267,500
Associates	**63,724**	63,582	**2,041**	49,708
Stocks	**1,642,931**	1,459,282	**1,143,426**	987,630
Taxation prepaid	**20,766**	5,181	**0**	0
Total current assets	**2,662,304**	2,625,534	**2,194,648**	1,971,634
Total assets	**$3,297,015**	$3,308,394	**$2,997,896**	$2,758,800

Exhibit 15
New Zealand Dairy Board Consolidated Statement
of Cash Flows for the Year Ended 31 May 1993
(In Thousands of New Zealand Dollars)

	GROUP	
	1993	1992
Opening cash balances		
Bank balances	69,001	53,076
Short-term deposits	49,948	62,544
Bank overdrafts	(37,456)	(55,136)
Short-term and overnight		
borrowings	(830,162)	(779,886)
	(748,669)	(719,402)
CASH FLOWS FROM		
OPERATING ACTIVITIES		
Cash was provided from:		
Receipts from customers	5,803,071	5,152,574
Interest received	48,866	29,653
Dividends received	4,407	7,621
Cash was disbursed to:		
Payments to suppliers		
and employees	(5,516,816)	(4,970,510)
Payment of interest	(124,322)	(122,155)
Payment of taxes	(119,118)	(54,408 }
Net cash flows		
from operating activities	96,088	42,775
CASH FLOWS FROM		
INVESTING ACTIVITIES		
Cash was provided from:		
Proceeds from sale		
of fixed assets	51,894	15,285
Proceeds from sale		
of investments	20,768	50,960
Collection of loans	17,318	0
Cash was applied to:		
Acquisition of fixed assets	(111,702)	(51,066)
Acquisition of investments	(16,170)	(16,932)
Loans made	0	(3,173)

(continued on next page)

(continued)

	GROUP	
	1993	1992
Net cash flows used in investing activities	**(37,892)**	(4,926)
CASH FLOWS FROM FINANCING ACTIVITIES		
Cash was provided from:		
Issue of shares	**1,550**	0
Cash was applied to:		
Borrowings repaid	**(137,354)**	(75,642)
Dividends paid	**(6,023)**	(2,416)
Net cash flows used in financing activities	**(141,827)**	(78,058)
EFFECT OF EXCHANGE RATE CHANGES	**15,736**	10,942
CASH OF SUBSIDIARIES ACQUIRED/SOLD	**(2,809)**	0
Net decreases in cash flows	**(70,704)**	(29,267)
Closing cash balances		
Bank balances	**32,440**	69,001
Short-term deposits	**115,925**	49,948
Bank overdrafts	**(39,119)**	(37,456)
Short-term and overnight borrowings	**(928,619)**	(830,162)
	($819,373)	($748,669)

Table H
R&D Spending in 1992 as a Percentage of Sales

Unilever	1.87%
NZDB	1.35
Nestlé	1.23
Kraft General Foods	0.81

Developing the treasury group allowed NZDB to deal with customers in any country in any currency, and customers remarked quite favorably on the lack of foreign-exchange complications when doing business with the Dairy Board. In essence, NZDB would tell customers, "Pay us in your local currency, and we'll take care of the rest."

R&D

NZDB had two primary research organizations, the Dairy Research Institute (DRI) and the Livestock Improvement Corporation (LIC). Both basic and applied research was conducted by these organizations. In 1993, DRI's budget was NZ$60 million, which was comparable on a percent-of-sales basis to the research budgets of NZDB's primary competitors (see Table H). LIC was recognized as a world leader in the development and application of breeding technology. Together, LIC and DRI combined their expertise to "engineer" milk, through breeding, to possess certain functional properties.

NZDB operated a regional research center in each of its five major markets (the United States, Southeast Asia, Europe, South Pacific, and the Middle East). This allowed the Dairy Board to tailor products to local customer needs and tastes. NZDB was successfully able to introduce dairy products in traditionally low-consumption areas like Asia and the Middle East. Previously, customer research and product development had been done at DRI in New Zealand, but NZDB discovered that its customers' needs and preferences varied significantly by region. Now, however, Dr. Kevin Marshall, NZDB's research and development manager, commented that "the independence of the individual research centers has not always allowed for synergies to be recognized in areas that are of mutual interest."

Marshall stated, "Included among NZDB's biggest research and development successes are Anlene milk powder, spreadable butter, whole milk powders, and protein hydrolysates. NZDB's future research priorities need to increase focus by spending more money on fewer products. For instance, although NZDB is comparable to competitors in R&D spending as a percent of sales, Nestlé has an entire research group focused solely on human nutrition. As the Dairy Board moves into more sophisticated products like nutraceuticals and pharmaceutical ingredients, it will eventually need to develop a capability to do clinical trials with humans."

Organization and Leadership

In early 1994, NZDB had more than 6,000 employees worldwide and was organized by function (treasury, external affairs, and so forth) and by product lines (milk powder, proteins, cheese, and cream products). The appendix that follows describes NZDB's organization and product lines. Throughout NZDB's history, the Wellington headquarters served as the nerve center of the organization. Most Dairy Board employees, including senior executives, were hired from within the New Zealand dairy industry.

In 1992, Warren Larsen became the NZDB chief executive and assumed oversight responsibilities for the Dairy Board's decentralization efforts. When Larsen took over NZDB's top job, the atmosphere at the Dairy Board seemed to Larsen to be that of a "New Zealand village, a provincial mentality. It was a real dues-paying, initiation-type atmosphere." Larsen found that "the existing power base was hard to shift because it was related to individual histories and personalities."

Larsen was preceded in his tenure by two chief executives who left their mark on the Dairy Board. Bernie Knowles served as CEO during NZDB's commodity market struggles and initial forays into value-added products during the 1970s. Marshall, NZDB's director of research and development, described Knowles as "a real seat-of-the-pants leader and a visionary who saw the need for offshore expansion. Bernie's goal was for NZDB to achieve excellence and leadership in commodity marketing because he felt it was where the future of the board lay." Murray Gough succeeded Knowles and remained as CEO for more than ten years. According to Marshall, Gough "systematized and further developed the offshore companies, and he foresaw the need for a push into consumer products. Murray still emphasized excellence in commodities, but he had worked in the United Kingdom so he recognized the value of a move into consumer products as well."

Larsen was very enthusiastic about his role as Dairy Board CEO. Larsen had set NZDB's becoming a bona-fide transnational as his primary goal. Attaining this status would require that NZDB move into consumer products to an even greater degree. Assisting Larsen in this transition was a veteran senior management team, many of whom had been with the Dairy Board since its early days, including:

- John Parker—deputy chief executive officer and a 30-year-plus veteran of the Dairy Board
- Peter Robertson—chief financial officer
- Alistair Betts—group general manager of marketing and a 25-year NZDB veteran
- Chris Kelly—a former veterinarian and a self-taught strategic planner who had recently assumed the role of manager of strategic planning
- Nigel Mitchell—director of external affairs and NZDB's "point man" on trade issues
- Chris Moller—manager of corporate development and finance who had previously headed the cheese division;
- Robin Golding—a former merchant banker and manager of the treasury group

- John Murray—company secretary who had been with NZDB since its inception
- Dr. Kevin Marshall—manager of research and development and a multi-year veteran of NZDB

The Future

Chris Kelly, manager of strategic planning, felt the primary issue facing NZDB was how to allocate the organization's resources—financial, technical, and personnel—most effectively. According to Larsen, "Capital is an increasingly scarce resource because NZDB has to retain funds from farmers to obtain it. This required a shift from NZDB's practice of just getting into business wherever possible." Many of the other senior managers concurred with that assessment. The Dairy Board was now at a point where different organizational functions were competing with one another for financing. Larsen felt that "NZDB was vulnerable in its current position. NZDB can't be all things to all people and survive in its current form. NZDB needs to move up into short-shelf-life products for security, and this will require locally sourced milk for political reasons. NZDB will focus only on the global biggies in the food service market; we will try to link it to our consumer products through our distribution systems. The ingredient markets can never escape the commodity cycles, and NZDB can't survive on commodity placements, alone. The dilemma is given that we are required to sell all the product within one year; do we sell it on the basis of volume, value, or both, and how should the performance of the marketing companies be measured?"

Larsen identified NZDB's future agenda as the following: "decentralize, which is the easy part, introduce better performance measurement systems, and then prioritize based on the results of performance measurement." Introduction of a new consumer brand required significant investment, funds that could otherwise be allocated to developing a new ingredient product. NZDB lacked internal product profitability measures, and deciding which project to fund was problematic. Compounding this problem was the Dairy Board's lack of a formal strategic planning process. Consequently, resource allocation was done on an "as available" rather than on an "as needed" basis.

As mentioned in the BCG report, NZDB was now wrestling with defining an industry vision, a process that would map out a path for the organization's future. Given the sheer volume of milk produced annually by New Zealand dairy farmers, NZDB management felt that commodities would always be one of the products marketed by the organization. Ideally, the Dairy Board would be able to control the amount of milk produced in New Zealand in order to better balance supply with product demand. However, NZDB was prohibited by statute from doing so. Individual cooperatives were considering imposing entry fees on new members in order to erect some barriers to entry and control industry capacity.

The measurement of NZDB's success had long been an issue in New Zealand, and it was an open question as to whether or not the Dairy Board was volume-driven or price-driven. There was great debate in New Zealand in early 1994 about whether or not NZDB did maximize returns to dairy farmers. Exhibit 16 shows recent trends in payouts to dairy farmers. Exhibit 17 benchmarks NZDB's performance against other leading New Zealand companies.

Although NZDB was a cooperative, it was "run just like a corporate," according to Chris Moller, the group manager of finance and corporate development. NZDB tended to hire employees from within the dairy industry and to promote from within the Dairy Board, a practice that resulted in the Board culture becoming somewhat insulated from business realities. During the Dairy Board's commodity trading period, the typical employee possessed an entrepreneurial spirit and a high degree of technical competence. As the Board assumed more of a marketing role, it became apparent that a lack of marketing, financial performance measurement, and competitive analysis skills existed at NZDB. In addition, there was a real shortage of people with work experience in multinational organizations. An entrenched entrepreneurial spirit still persisted at the Dairy Board, and this sometimes complicated efforts to standardize and formalize board policies and procedures.

The Board's structure and decision making within New Zealand emphasized internal competition for resources (including milk and product supply) among product divisions. The challenge of ensuring appropriate internal competition processes in New Zealand to match the aggressive competition in overseas markets was an ongoing issue, and the chief executive wondered whether the existing product divisions were right for the future.

On a more fundamental level, the Dairy Board's expectations of its employees had changed. As the Dairy Board became more customer focused and less focused on doing business in Wellington, demands for employees to live and work overseas increased. Traditionally, board employees worked overseas for two- to three-year periods and then moved back to Wellington. Now, there was a need for people to remain overseas indefinitely in order to maintain strong customer relationships. Implementing effective succession planning for senior managers who had been with the Dairy Board since its inception was also a key concern, especially when considering that many of the Dairy Board's senior managers had been with the board since its infancy.

As he put down the BCG report, Larsen pondered the challenges that lay ahead for both the Dairy Board and himself. He wondered which ones to tackle first.

Exhibit 16
Trend in Prices Received
for Milkfat Since 1950/1951

SEASON	DAIRY BOARD FINAL PRICE $	AVERAGE DAIRY COMPANY PAYOUT	
		TOTAL ACTUAL PAYOUT $	INFLATION ADJUSTED PAYOUT ($ DEC. 1992)*
1950/51		0.63	12.70
1955/56		0.74	11.49
1960/61		0.69	9.20
1965/66		0.80	9.35
1970/71		0.85	7.59
1971/72		1.12	9.16
1972/73		1.11	8.61
1973/74		1.32	9.29
1974/75	1.36	1.30	8.13
1975/76	1.41	1.44	7.79
1976/77	1.53	1.52	7.11
1977/78	1.67	1.71	6.93
1978/79	1.73	1.79	6.59
1979/80	2.08	2.13	6.73
1980/81	2.65	2.64	7.18
1981/82	3.33	3.39	7.97
1982/83	3.61	3.67	7.49
1983/84	3.50	3.64	7.17
1984/85	3.96	4.06	7.31
1985/86	4.00	3.98	6.21
1986/87	3.31	3.54	4.67
1987/88	3.60	4.07	4.90
1988/89	5.30	5.70	6.56
1989/90	5.80	6.30	6.76
1990/91	3.70	4.23	4.33
1991/92	5.20	5.84	5.92
1992/93	5.65	6.38	6.38

*Weighted to give real dollar values (December 1992) using the Consumers Price Index.

Exhibit 17
New Zealand Dairy Board
Relative Performance

COMPANY	CAPITALISATION MILLIONS	TOTAL SHARES SEPT. 1994 (000's)	NPAT 1994 NZ$000	EPS 1994	RETURN ON EQUITY 1994	RETURN ON ASSETS 1994
Natural Gas	588	462,000	25,300	$0.150	41.2%	10.9%
Whitcoulls Group	460	121,000	24,300	0.201	25.7	17.7
Helicopter Line	211	44,000	13,000	0.306	23.5	21.2
Telecom Corp	9,563	1,890,000	528,100	0.279	23.6	19.0
NZDB—						
1994/1995 forecast		750,000	290,000	**0.387**	**20.0**	**9.0**
Fernzcorp	791	140,000	38,300	0.301	18.9	11.8
Sanford	352	88,100	34,500	0.396	18.2	20.9
Air NZ	1,037	443,500	200,500	0.452	17.2	9.2
Skellerup	371	156,000	26,700	0.177	16.7	12.0
Independent Newspapers	642	129,000	44,200	0.383	11.2	10.7
F&P	440	104,800	27,000	0.258	10.4	11.6
Lion Nathan	1,520	547,700	185,400	0.363	9.4	9.5
Goodman Fielder	1,745	1,172,000	152,100	0.132	8.9	8.5
Carter Holt Harvey	6,338	1,690,000	325,300	0.192	8.2	7.0
Apple Fields	26	29,200	4,400	0.158	7.9	6.6
Fletcher Challenge Forests	807	757,000	58,500	0.077	7.8	6.2
DB Group	225	304,600	25,400	0.048	6.8	5.3
Fletcher Challenge Core Divisions	6,237	1,260,000	99,600	0.079	2.5	3.3

NZDB capital	750,000,000	NZDB NPAT based on SMV of $2.50/kg ms.
NZDB reserves	700,597,000	
Total Equity	1,450,597,000	

NZDB Total
   Assets (1994) 3,210,766,000

CASE APPENDIX[1]

THE NEW ZEALAND DAIRY BOARD AND ITS STRUCTURE

To undertake its chief function of purchasing all products for export and marketing them overseas, the Board has four main Product Divisions that are accountable for specific products (Cheese, Cream, Milkpowders, and Milkprotein). Two smaller divisions work with the other product divisions in carrying out their specialised activities: the Ingredients Divisions and the Consumer Products Division. (These divisions are supported by Secretariat, Services, Finance, External Policy and Planning, Group Personnel, Public Affairs, Corporate Investments, and the Computer Centre.)

PRODUCT DIVISIONS

Milkpowders

This division is responsible for coordinating the production and worldwide marketing of milk powder products.

Key Features. Many tropical countries do not have a strong local dairy industry. For them, imported milk powders from countries such as New Zealand are the most important source of dairy products. The advantage of canned milk powder in tropical countries is that it will remain fresh for up to three years, whereas liquid milk starts to deteriorate after only a few hours.

The division has four main product groups:

- **Wholemilk Powder.** This powder is ordinary full cream milk that has been dried.
- **Skimmilk Powder.** Skimmilk is milk from which cream has been separated. It has a very low fat content.
- **Nutritional Products.** This group coordinates the production and marketing of nutritional products including infant formulae, health and sports food beverages, and Stolait™ Immune Milk.
- **Special Products.** This group is responsible for the development, production, and marketing of an increasing range of specialised products including cheese powder, UHT cream, and cream powders.

---

[1]Source: NZDB brochure.

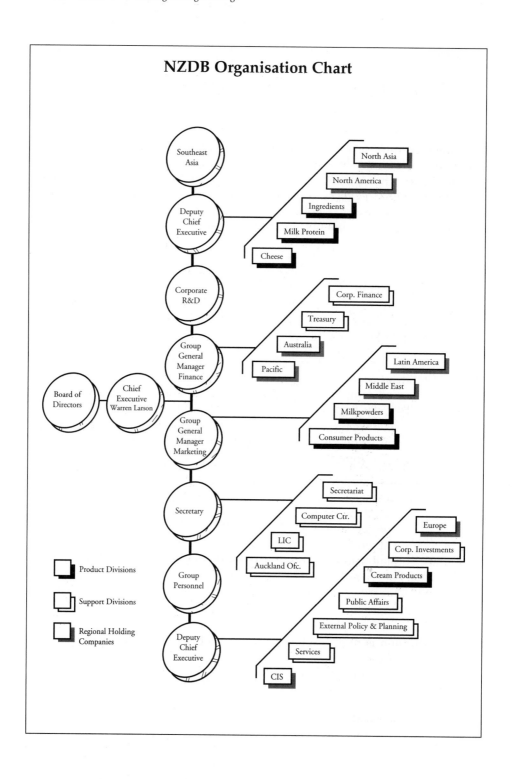

NZDB Organisation Chart

Milkproteins

This division is responsible for coordinating the production and world-wide marketing of milk protein and whey products.

Key Features. Unlike butter, cheese, and milk powders, which are largely consumed in their original form, milk proteins are sold as industrial food ingredients or technical ingredients to industrial food manufacturers and technical users throughout the world. The division therefore has a different focus to other product divisions of the Board, being involved solely in industrial marketing, with no involvement in consumer marketing.

This division has two major operating groups:

- **Casein.** This section is responsible for coordinating the global production and marketing of all New Zealand casein products.

- **Whey Products for New Zealand Limited.** This subsidiary company of the Board is responsible for the global commercial exploitation of whey produced in New Zealand. It operates as an autonomous business unit of the Board.

Cream Products

This division is responsible for coordinating the production and export marketing of products containing a high level of milkfat-butter, anhydrous milkfat (AMF), fat mixes, and other fractionated cream products.

Key Features. A substantial proportion of the division's business is the large volume of salted butter shipped to Britain each year and repacked into Anchor pats. This highly lucrative trade is under threat from a reducing EC quota. As a result, this division is working hard to foster other large alternative markets, especially in the Middle East, North Africa, and Eastern Europe.

Development work is also underway on an increased range of consumer products for retail sale and specialised butter milkfat formulations for the international bakery and food ingredients sectors.

Cheese

This division is responsible for coordinating the production and export marketing of cheese products and insuring that dairy companies generate the full potential of the local market.

Key Features. Cheese is showing an increase in consumption in most countries of the world but there is fierce competition among producing countries for a major share in this growth.

Cheese is sold in a wide range of forms, which necessitates a range of selling approaches from commodity trading, through brand management, to specialised industrial selling with a strong technical backup.

This division has three technical units:

- **Industrial Marketing.** This unit provides support for industrial export sales through stock procurement, inventory management, distribution logistics, technical service, and product development.

- **Food Service.** This unit covers the supply of cheese to organisations that perform another operation on the product before presenting it to the pubic, such as cooking, shredding, slicing, or melting.

- **Consumer.** This unit plans and supports the international consumer marketing of cheese products, the export logistics, and the procurement functions.

Ingredients

The purpose of this division is to drive the development of the Board's international dairy-based food ingredients business. The ingredients division

- provides specific functional performance attributes in its application
- is supported by a worldwide network with facilities and expertise encompassing research, development, production, product evaluation, and customer servicing

Application areas include:

- Bakery
- Confectionery
- Snack and convenience
- Cultured food products
- Ice cream

Alaco New Zealand. Alaco is a separate business unit within the Ingredients Division operating in the New Zealand market. Alaco acts as a commission agent for the four product divisions and other ingredient suppliers such as dairy companies.

Alaco was established to assist in the development of marketing specialised dairy-based ingredients on the New Zealand market as a basis for international development.

CONSUMER PRODUCTS

This division was established to further the strategic thrust into marketing its own branded consumer products. With the advent of regional holding companies, the major day-to-day marketing thrust of the Board is off-shore.

The primary functions of the Consumer Products Division are to

- provide a support function for the Board's objectives in consumer product development
- ensure commonality (where appropriate) in marketing approach, the variety of product types, and new product development
- measure overall progress in volume and returns for the consumer business
- administer the corporate brands policy
- build a corporate culture appropriate to the growth of the Board's international consumer business

Dairy Advisory Bureau. The Dairy Advisory Bureau is the advisory body of the New Zealand dairy industry that is responsible for food and health issues. The Bureau provides support for the Board's business developments offshore and has a role in nutrition promotion in the local market.

Three main areas of activity support development and marketing of consumer and ingredient products:

- **Nutrition information services.** Monitoring and advising on nutrition and health science, food regulations, media, product, and market developments.
- Coordinating of the Board's food health research programme.
- **Nutrition Programme.** In New Zealand the Bureau has a commitment to improving the knowledge and understanding of food and health issues and enhancing the value of dairy products in the diet.

CREDITS LIST

Chapter no.	Credit

Chapters

Chapter 1
Figure 1-1

Decision Flow in Product-Market Strategy Formulation, by Igor Ansoff, Corporate Strategy, Copyright © 1965, McGraw-Hill, Inc., pp. 202–203.

Chapter 2
Figure 2-1

Computer Vendors, Dealers Voice Fears About Industry Slump at Big Trade Fair, by Randall Smith, *Wall Street Journal*, November 21, 1985. Reprinted by permission of the *Wall Street Journal*, Copyright © 1985 Dow Jones & Company, Inc. All rights reserved worldwide.

Chapter 2
Figure 2-2

PC Executives Confident, by John Eckhouse, *San Francisco Chronicle*, November 21, 1985. Copyright © 1985 *San Francisco Chronicle*. Reprinted by permission.

Chapter 2
Figure 2-4

Births in the U.S., *Fortune*, November 29, 1993. Sources: Bureau of the Census, National Center for Health Statistics, *Fortune*. Copyright © 1993 Time, Inc. All rights reserved.

Chapter 4
p. 82

Reprinted by permission of Harvard Business Review. **How Competitive Forces Shape Strategy,** by Michael Porter, March–April, 1979, No. 79208. Copyright © 1979 by the President and Fellows of Harvard College. All rights reserved.

Chapter 5
Figure 5-4

Adapted with the permission of The Free Press, a Division of Simon & Schuster Inc. from "Competitive Strategy: Techniques for Analyzing Industries and Competitors" by Michael E. Porter. Copyright © 1980 by The Free Press.

Chapter 8 Article
pp. 418–435

Reprinted by permission of Harvard Business Review. **Selecting Strategies That Create Shareholder Value,** by Alfred Rappaport, May–June 1981, No. 81310. Copyright © 1981 by the President and Fellows of Harvard College. All rights reserved.

Chapter 9
Figure 9-1

Adapted from "Growth Vector Matrix," by Igor Ansoff, *Corporate Strategy,* Copyright © 1965, McGraw-Hill.

Appendix 4
pp. 718–724

Note on Strategy Implementation through Organization Design. Copyright © 1988 by the Darden School Foundation, Charlottesville, Virginia.

Case no.	Credit

Darden Cases

UVA-BP-0329

Alaskan Gold Mine—Part 1. Case authored by Jeffrey Barach, Graduate School of Business, Tulane University, New Orleans, Louisiana, 1977. Reprinted by permission. Revisions by Professor L. J. Bourgeois made with permission. Copyright © 1992 by the Darden School Foundation, Charlottesville, Virginia.

UVA-OB-0443

Astral Records, LTD., North America. This case was prepared by Lynn A. Isabella, Associate Professor of Business

Administration, and Ted Forbes. Copyright © 1993 by the Darden School Foundation, Charlottesville, Virginia.

UVA-OM-0716   **The Bacova Guild, Ltd.** This case was prepared by Eileen Filliben, MBA/J.D. 1994 under the supervision of John L. Colley, JR., Almand R. Coleman Professor of Business Administration. Copyright © 1992 by the Darden School Foundation, Charlottesville, Virginia.

UVA-OM-0743   **Southwest Airlines.** This case was prepared by Charlotte Thompson under the supervision of Professor Elliott N. Weiss. Copyright © 1996 by the Darden School Foundation, Charlottesville, Virginia.

UVA-BP-0303   **Jiffy Lube International, Inc.** This case was prepared by Kathi Breen, Darden MBA 1988, under the supervision of John L. Colley, Jr., Almand R. Coleman Professor of Business Administration, and L. J. Bourgeois, III, Associate Professor of Business Administration. Copyright © 1988 by the Darden School Foundation, Charlottesville, Virginia.

UVA-BP-0279   **Home Computers (A) Texas Instruments (August 1982).** This case was written by Paul Matteucci with the assistance of Michael Mael, Peter McAndrew, and Sunil Sanghvi, under the direction of Associate Professor L. J. Bourgeois, III. This case uses publicly available data to reconstruct the events of late 1982 and 1983 in the U.S. home-computer market. Some of the numbers have been changed, and concurrent events ordered in time for pedagogical purposes. Copyright © 1982 by the Darden School Foundation, Charlottesville, Virginia.

UVA-BP-0288   **Microcomputer Industry in 1987.** This note was prepared by Anurag Sharma, Darden MBA 1988, and revised by Jaideep Wadhwa, Darden MBA 1989, and Jeffrey Cohen, Darden MBA 1990, under the supervision of Associate Professor L. J. Bourgeois. Copyright © 1988 by the Darden School Foundation, Charlottesville, Virginia.

UVA-BP-317 **Laptops, The Machines Are Tiny, The Potential Is Huge,** by Deidre A. Depke, Larry Armstrong, and Barbara Buell, *Business Week,* March 18, 1991, pp. 118–124. Reprinted from March 18, 1991 issue of *Business Week* by special permission. Copyright © 1991 by McGraw-Hill, Inc.

UVA-BP-0317 **Microcomputers in 1991: The Notebook Wars.** This case was written by Christine Lotze under the supervision of Professor L. J. Bourgeois. Copyright © 1991 by the Darden School Foundation, Charlottesville, Virginia. Revised February 1995.

UVA-BP-0341 **Falls River Center, Inc.** This case was written by Christine Lotze, Darden '92, and Jamie Berger, Darden '92, under the supervision of Professor L. J. Bourgeois. Copyright © 1994 by the Darden School Foundation, Charlottesville, Virginia.

UVA-BP-0300 **Georgia Digital Reproductions.** This case was prepared by Ambrose S. Kalmbach, Darden 1989, under the supervision of Associate Professor L. J. Bourgeois, III and Assistant Professor Andrea Larson. Copyright © 1989 by the Darden School Foundation, Charlottesville, Virginia.

UVA-BP-0350 **International Colour Envelope Advisors A/S.** This case was prepared by Maria Holcomb, MBA 1993, under the supervision of L. J. Bourgeois. Copyright © 1993 by the Darden School Foundation, Charlottesville, Virginia.

UVA-BP-0353 **Copeland Corporation/Bain & Company: The Scroll Investment Decision.** This case was revised by Jeanne M. Liedtka, Associate Professor of Business Administration and John W. Rosenblum, Tayloe Murphy, Professor of Business Administration. Copyright © 1995 by the Darden School Foundation, Charlottesville, Virginia.

UVA-BP-0332 **Disney Productions: The Walt Years.** This case was revised by Jeanne M. Liedtka, Associate Professor of Business

Administration. The original case was written by William E. Fulmer and Robert M. Fulmer. In addition to the publications mentioned in this case, a selected bibliography is given in the teaching note. Copyright © 1993 by the Darden School Foundation, Charlottesville, Virginia.

UVA-BP-0269   **Calma Company (A) (condensed and the CAD/CAM Industry.** This case is a condensation of "Note on Computer Graphics" and CAD/CAM (S-BP-22DN) and "Calma Company (A)" (S-BP-214A), both written by Christine Blouke, Research Assistant, Stanford Graduate School of Business, and L. J. Bourgeois III, Associate Professor of Business Administration, The Colgate Darden Graduate School of Business Administration. Copyright © 1990 by the Darden School Foundation, Charlottesville, Virginia.

UVA-BP-0290   **Amer Group Ltd. (A).** This case was written by Ann Yungmeyer under the supervision of Associate Professor L. J. Bourgeois, III. Copyright © 1996 by the Darden School Foundation, Charlottesville, Virginia.

UVA-BP-0297   **Arvin Industries, Inc.** This case was written by Anurag Sharma, Darden 1988, and Associate Professor L. J. Bourgeois, III. Copyright © 1996 by the Darden School Foundation, Charlottesville, Virginia.

UVA-BP-0348   **Yamaha Corporation and the Electronic-Musical-Instruments Industry.** This case was written by Andrew W. Spreadbury, MBA/JD 1994, under the supervision of Professor L. J. Bourgeois. Copyright © 1994 by the Darden School Foundation, Charlottesville, Virginia.

UVA-BP-0291   **MacGregor Golf Company.** This case was prepared by Ann Yungmeyer and Associate Professor L. J. Bourgeois, III, with the assistance of Anurag Sharma, Darden 1988. Copyright © 1988 by the Darden School Foundation, Charlottesville, Virginia.

UVA-BP-0305   **Hewlett-Packard (Condensed).** This case, condensation of UVA-BP-268, was prepared by Professor L. J. Bourgeois, III. The original case was prepared by Professor William E. Fulmer. Copyright © 1996 by the Darden School Foundation, Charlottesville, Virginia.

UVA-BP-0254   **Marriott Corporation (A).** This case was prepared by Jim Kennedy, Research Associate, under the supervision of Professor William E. Fulmer. Copyright © 1996 by the Darden School Foundation, Charlottesville, Virginia.

UVA-BP-0253   **Dollar General Corporation (A).** This case was prepared by Jim Kennedy, Research Associate, under the supervision of Professor William E. Fulmer. Copyright © 1987 by the Darden School Foundation, Charlottesville, Virginia.

Exhibit 23   Dollar General Store Newsletter & General Story. Logo used with permission from Dollar General Corporation, Scottsville, KY.

UVA-BP-0253   **Dollar General Corporation (A).** This case was prepared by Jim Kennedy, Research Associate, under the supervision of Professor William E. Fulmer. Copyright © 1996 by the Darden School Foundation, Charlottesville, Virginia.

UVA-OB-0420   **Grupo Bacardi de Mexico, S.A.** This case was prepared by Ted Forbes under the supervision of Lynn A. Isabella, Associate Professor of Business Administration. Copyright © 1994 by the Darden School Foundation, Charlottesville, Virginia.

UVA-OB-0396   **Big Sky, Inc.: The Magasco Paper Mill (A).** Prepared by F. B. Brake, Jr., under the supervision of Alexander B. Horniman, Professor of Business Administration. Copyright © 1991 by the Darden School Foundation, Charlottesville, Virginia. All rights reserved. Revised September 1995.

Associate Professor of Business Administration. Copyright © 1993 by the Darden School Foundation, Charlottesville, Virginia.

UVA-BP-0330   **Jackie Woods (A).** This case was prepared by Catherine M. Lloyd, MBA 1993, under the supervision of James G. Clawson. Copyright © 1993 by the Darden School Foundation, Charlottesville, Virginia. Revised September 1993.

UVA-BP-0356   **New Zealand Dairy Board.** This case was prepared by Brad Webb, Darden 1995, under the supervision of Professor L. J. Bourgeois, III. Research funding was provided by Ernst & Young, New Zealand. Copyright © 1995 by the Darden School Foundation, Charlottesville, VA.

Harvard Business School Case

378-024   **Crown Cork and Seal Company, Inc.** Copyright © 1977 by the President and Fellows of Harvard College. Harvard Business School case 378-024. This case was prepared by Karen D. Gordon, John P. Reed and Richard Hammermesh as the basis for class discussion rather than to illustrate either effective or ineffective handling of an administrative situation. Reprinted by permission of the Harvard Business School.

Kenan-Flagler Case

The National Gypsum Company (A): The Gold Bond Division, by Prof. Idalene F. Kesner. Copyright © 1993 by the Kenan-Flagler Business School, University of North Carolina, Chapel Hill. Not to be reproduced without permission. All rights reserved. For multiple copies of this case, please contact the Manager of Case Services, Kenan-Flagler

Case Development Program, the Kenan-Flagler Business School, University of North Carolina, CB 3490, Carroll Hall, Chapel Hill, NC 27599-3490. Telephone: 919-962-8301. Fax: 919-933-0054.